Achieve Positive Learning Outcomes

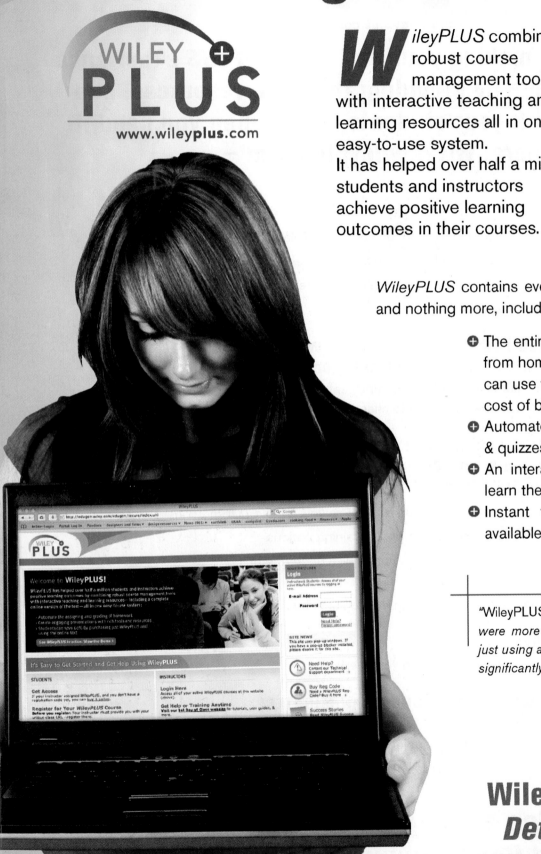

WILEY PLUS

www.wileyplus.com

WileyPLUS combines robust course management tools with interactive teaching and learning resources all in one easy-to-use system.
It has helped over half a million students and instructors achieve positive learning outcomes in their courses.

WileyPLUS contains everything you and your students need— and nothing more, including:

- ⊕ The entire textbook online—with dynamic links from homework to relevant sections. Students can use the online text and save up to half the cost of buying a new printed book.
- ⊕ Automated assigning & grading of homework & quizzes.
- ⊕ An interactive variety of ways to teach and learn the material.
- ⊕ Instant feedback and help for students… available 24/7.

"WileyPLUS *helped me become more prepared. There were more resources available using* WileyPLUS *than just using a regular [printed] textbook, which helped out significantly. Very helpful...and very easy to use."*

– Student Victoria Cazorla,
Dutchess County Community College

**See and try WileyPLUS *in action!* Details and Demo:
*www.wileyplus.com***

www.wileyplus.com

Wiley is committed to making your entire *WileyPLUS* experience productive & enjoyable by providing the help, resources, and personal support you & your students need, when you need it. It's all here: www.wileyplus.com –

TECHNICAL SUPPORT:

⊕ A fully searchable knowledge base of FAQs and help documentation, available 24/7

⊕ Live chat with a trained member of our support staff during business hours

⊕ A form to fill out and submit online to ask any question and get a quick response

⊕ **Instructor-only** phone line during business hours: 1.877.586.0192

FACULTY-LED TRAINING THROUGH THE WILEY FACULTY NETWORK:
Register online: www.wherefacultyconnect.com

Connect with your colleagues in a complimentary virtual seminar, with a personal mentor in your field, or at a live workshop to share best practices for teaching with technology.

1ST DAY OF CLASS...AND BEYOND!
Resources You & Your Students Need to Get Started & Use *WileyPLUS* from the first day forward.

⊕ 2-Minute Tutorials on how to set up & maintain your *WileyPLUS* course

⊕ User guides, links to technical support & training options

⊕ *WileyPLUS for Dummies*: Instructors' quick reference guide to using *WileyPLUS*

⊕ Student tutorials & instruction on how to register, buy, and use *WileyPLUS*

YOUR *WileyPLUS* ACCOUNT MANAGER:

Your personal *WileyPLUS* connection for any assistance you need!

SET UP YOUR *WileyPLUS* COURSE IN MINUTES!
Selected *WileyPLUS* courses with QuickStart contain pre-loaded assignments & presentations created by subject matter experts who are also experienced *WileyPLUS* users.

Interested? See and try WileyPLUS in action!
Details and Demo: www.wileyplus.com

Psychology in Action

NINTH EDITION

KAREN HUFFMAN

PALOMAR COLLEGE

John Wiley & Sons, Inc.

VICE PRESIDENT & EXECUTIVE PUBLISHER	Jay O'Callaghan
EXECUTIVE EDITOR	Christopher T. Johnson
ASSISTANT EDITOR	Eileen McKeever
MARKETING MANAGER	Danielle Torio
EDITORIAL ASSISTANT	Carrie Tupa
PRODUCTION MANAGER	Dorothy Sinclair
SENIOR PRODUCTION EDITOR	Sandra Dumas
CREATIVE DIRECTOR	Harry Nolan
SENIOR DESIGNER	Kevin Murphy
PHOTO DEPARTMENT MANAGER	Hilary Newman
SENIOR PHOTO EDITOR	Jennifer MacMillan
PHOTO RESEARCHER	Marry Ann Price
SENIOR MEDIA EDITOR	Lynn Pearlman
PRODUCTION MANAGEMENT SERVICES	Jeanine Furino/GGS Book Services PMG
INTERIOR DESIGN	Michael Jung

This book was typeset in 10/12 Janson by GGS Book Services PMG and printed and bound by R.R. Donnelley/Jefferson City. The cover was printed by Lehigh Press.

This book is printed on acid-free paper. @

To order books or for customer service please, call 1-800-CALL WILEY (225-5945).
Huffman, Karen. Psychology In Action, Ninth Edition

ISBN-13 978-0470-37911-0

Printed in the United States of America
10 9 8 7 6 5 4 3 2 1

Now Available with WebCT and Blackboard!
Now you can seamlessly integrate all of the rich content and resources available with *WileyPLUS* with the power and convenience of your WebCT or BlackBoard course. You and your students get the best of both worlds with single sign-on, an integrated gradebook, list of assignments and roster, and more. If your campus is using another course management system, contact your local Wiley Representative.

Brief Contents

Preface xiii
Prologue xli
CHAPTER 1 Introduction and Research Methods 2
CHAPTER 2 Neuroscience and Biological Foundations 50
CHAPTER 3 Stress and Health Psychology 90
CHAPTER 4 Sensation and Perception 126
CHAPTER 5 States of Consciousness 166
CHAPTER 6 Learning 202
CHAPTER 7 Memory 242
CHAPTER 8 Thinking, Language, and Intelligence 278
CHAPTER 9 Life Span Development I 314
CHAPTER 10 Life Span Development II 348
CHAPTER 11 Gender and Human Sexuality 374
CHAPTER 12 Motivation and Emotion 406
CHAPTER 13 Personality 440
CHAPTER 14 Psychological Disorders 472
CHAPTER 15 Therapy 508
CHAPTER 16 Social Psychology 544

Available separately upon request:

CHAPTER 17 Industrial / Organizational Psychology 582
CHAPTER 18 Psychology at Work in the Global Economy 610
APPENDIX A Statistics and Psychology A1
APPENDIX B Answers to Review Questions and Try It Yourself Activities B1
Glossary G1
References R1
Text and Illustration Credits T1
Name Index I1
Subject Index I11

Contents

Preface   xiii

Living Better with Huffman   xiii

What's New in the Ninth Edition?   xiii

Additional Changes   xxviii

Continuing Features   xxx

Supplements   xxxiv

Acknowledgments   xxxvii

Prologue: Critical Thinking/
Active Learning   xli

1   *Introduction to Psychology and Its*
Research Methods   2

Introducing Psychology   4
  What Is Psychology?   4
  Psychology's Goals   6
  Psychology at Work   *Careers in the Field*   7
Origins of Psychology   9
  Early Psychological Science   9
  Modern Perspectives   14
The Science of Psychology   16
  The Scientific Method   16
  Ethical Guidelines   18

Research Methods   21
  Experimental Research   21
Research Highlight   *Love at First Fright?*   27
Critical Thinking/Active Learning   *Applying Critical*
Thinking to Psychological Science   28
  Descriptive Research   28
Case Study/Personal Story   *A Life Without Fear?*   30
  Correlational Research   31
  Biological Research   33
Psychology at Work   *Becoming a Better Consumer*
of Scientific Research   37
Gender & Cultural Diversity
Are There Cultural Universals?   38
Tools for Student Success   39
  Active Reading   40
  Time Management   43
  Strategies for Grade Improvement   44
  Additional Resources   46
  A Final Word   46

2   *Neuroscience and*
Biological Foundations   50

Neural Bases of Behavior   52
  What Is a Neuron?   52
  How Do Neurons Communicate?   54
Psychology at Work   *How Neurotransmitters*
and Hormones Affect Us   54
Nervous System Organization   60
  Central Nervous System (CNS)   61
  Peripheral Nervous System (PNS)   63
A Tour Through the Brain   66
  Lower-Level Brain Structures   67
  Cerebral Cortex   71
Case Study/Personal Story   *Phineas Gage*   72
  Two Brains in One?   75
Critical Thinking/Active Learning   *Biology*
and Critical Thinking   78
Psychology at Work   *Working with*
Traumatic Brain Injuries (TBI)   79

Our Genetic Inheritance 80

    Behavioral Genetics 81

 Psychology at Work

    Overcoming Genetic Misconceptions 82

    Evolutionary Psychology 84

❋ Gender & Cultural Diversity *The Evolution of Sex Differences* 85

---

3 *Stress and Health Psychology* 90

Understanding Stress 92

    Sources of Stress 92

Research Highlight *Hurricane Katrina and Local College Students* 96

❋ Gender & Cultural Diversity *"Karoshi"—Can Job Stress Be Fatal?* 99

    Effects of Stress 100

Psychology at Work *Is My Job Too Stressful?* 104

Stress and Illness 105

    Cancer 105

    Cardiovascular Disorders 106

    Posttraumatic Stress Disorder (PTSD) 109

Research Highlight
Does Stress Cause Gastric Ulcers? 110

Health Psychology in Action 111

Psychology at Work *Would You Like to Be a Health Psychologist?* 111

    Tobacco 112

    Alcohol 113

    Chronic Pain 115

Health and Stress Management 116

    Cognitive Appraisal and Coping 116

Psychology at Work *Why You Shouldn't Procrastinate* 118

    Resources for Healthy Living 118

Psychology at Work *Coping With TechnoStress* 120

Critical Thinking/Active Learning *Reducing Stress through Critical Thinking* 122

---

4 *Sensation and Perception* 126

Understanding Sensation 129

    Processing 130

Psychology at Work *Do Subliminal Messages Improve Sales?* 132

    Adaptation 133

Case Study/Personal Story
Helen Keller's Triumph and Advice 134

How We See and Hear 135

    Vision 135

    Hearing 141

Research Highlight *Perfect (Yet Imperfect) Pitch* 144

Our Other Senses 145

    Smell and Taste 146

    The Body Senses 148

Understanding Perception 150

    Selection 150

    Organization 153

❋ Gender & Cultural Diversity *Are the Gestalt Laws Universally True?* 155

    Interpretation 158

Research Highlight *Is There Scientific Evidence for Extrasensory Perception (ESP)?* 161

Critical Thinking/Active Learning *Problems with Believing in Extrasensory Perception (ESP)* 162

Contents

5 *States of Consciousness* 166

Understanding Consciousness 168

Sleep and Dreams 170

The Power of Circadian Rhythms 171

 Psychology at Work
The Dangers of Sleeping on the Job! 171

Stages of Sleep 174

Why Do We Sleep and Dream? 178

 Gender & Cultural Diversity *Dream Variations and Similarities* 180

Critical Thinking/Active Learning *Interpreting Your Dreams* 181

Sleep Disorders 182

 Psychology at Work *Self-Help for Sleep Problems* 184

Psychoactive Drugs 185

Understanding Psychoactive Drugs 186

Research Highlight *Addictive Drugs as the Brain's "Evil Tutor"* 188

Four Major Categories of Psychoactive Drugs 189

 Psychology at Work *Club Drug Alert!* 194

Healthier Ways to Alter Consciousness 195

Getting "High" on Meditation 195

The Mystery of Hypnosis 196

6 *Learning* 202

Classical Conditioning 204

Pavlov and Watson's Contributions 205

Basic Principles 208

Operant Conditioning 212

Thorndike and Skinner's Contributions 212

Basic Principles 213

 Psychology at Work *Why Can't We Get Anything Done Around Here?* 220

Critical Thinking/Active Learning *Using Learning Principles to Succeed in College* 222

Cognitive-Social Learning 223

Insight and Latent Learning 223

Observational Learning 225

Research Highlight
"The Theory Heard Round the World" 227

Gender & Cultural Diversity *Scaffolding as a Teaching Technique in Different Cultures* 228

The Biology of Learning 229

Neuroscience and Learning 229

Using Conditioning and Learning Principles 232

 Psychology at Work *Classical Conditioning* 232

 Psychology at Work *Operant Conditioning* 235

 Psychology at Work *Cognitive-Social Learning* 237

7 *Memory* 242

The Nature of Memory 244

Memory Models 244

Sensory Memory 247

Short-Term Memory (STM) 248

Long-Term Memory (LTM) 249

Psychology at Work *Improving Long-Term Memory (LTM)* 252

Forgetting 257

How Quickly Do We Forget? 257

Why Do We Forget? 257

Psychology at Work *Key Factors in Forgetting* 260

Gender & Cultural Diversity *Cultural Differences in Memory and Forgetting* 261

Biological Bases of Memory 263

How Are Memories Formed? 263

Where Are Memories Located? 264

Biological Causes of Memory Loss 264

Research Highlight
Memory and the Criminal Justice System 268

Contents

Using Psychology to Improve Our Memory 270
  Understanding Memory Distortions 270
  Tips for Memory Improvement 271

Critical Thinking/Active Learning
Memory and Metacognition 274

8 Thinking, Language, and Intelligence 278

Thinking 280
  Cognitive Building Blocks 283
  Problem Solving 283

Psychology at Work *Heuristics and Your Career* 284

Psychology at Work
Recognizing Barriers to Problem Solving 284

Critical Thinking/Active Learning
Solving Problems in College Life 287
  Creativity 288

Language 291
  Characteristics of Language 291
  Language and Thought 291
  Language Development 293

Gender & Cultural Diversity *Unspoken Accents* 293
  Animals and Language 295

Intelligence 297
  What Is Intelligence? 297

Psychology at Work
Multiple Intelligences and Your Career 299
  How Do We Measure Intelligence? 300

The Intelligence Controversy 303
  Extremes in Intelligence 303

Research Highlight *Explaining Differences in IQ* 305

Gender & Cultural Diversity
Are IQ Tests Culturally Biased? 307

9 Life Span Development I 314

Studying Development 317
  Theoretical Issues 317
  Research Methods 318

Gender & Cultural Diversity *Cultural Psychology's Guidelines for Developmental Research* 319

Physical Development 321
  Prenatal Period and Early Childhood 321
  Adolescence and Adulthood 327

Cognitive Development 331
  Stages of Cognitive Development 333

  Assessing Piaget's Theory 336
  Information Processing 338

Social-Emotional Development 340
  Attachment 340
  Parenting Styles 340

Research Highlight *Romantic Love and Attachment* 343

Critical Thinking/Active Learning
The Development of "Suicide Bombers" 344

10 Life Span Development II 348

Moral Development 350
  Kohlberg's Research 350
  Assessing Kohlberg's Theory 351

Critical Thinking/Active Learning
Morality and Academic Cheating 353

Personality Development 354
  Thomas and Chess's Temperament Theory 354
  Erikson's Psychosocial Theory 355

Gender & Cultural Diversity
Cultural Influences on Development 357

Meeting the Challenges of Adulthood 359
  Committed Relationships 359

Psychology at Work
Are Your Marital Expectations Unrealistic? 360
  Families 361

Research Highlight
Children Who Survive Despite the Odds 363

Psychology at Work
Positive Careers and Rewarding Retirements 364

Gender & Cultural Diversity *Cultural Differences in Ageism* 365

Grief and Death 366
  Grief 367
  Attitudes Toward Death and Dying 368
  The Death Experience 368

Psychology at Work
Dealing with Your Own Death Anxiety 369

11 Gender and Human Sexuality 374

Sex and Gender 376
  What Is "Maleness" and "Femaleness"? 376
  Gender Role Development 376
  Gender Identity Formation 378

Case Study/Personal Story
The Tragic Tale of "John/Joan" 380
Sex and Gender Differences 381

Research Highlight
Video Games, Gender, and Spatial Skills 384

Critical Thinking/Active Learning
Gender Differences and Critical Thinking 385

The Study of Human Sexuality 386

Gender & Cultural Diversity
A Cross-Cultural Look at Sexual Behaviors 387

Sexual Behavior 389
Sexual Arousal and Response 389

Gender & Cultural Diversity *Are There Evolutionary Advantages to Female Nonmonogamy?* 391
Sexual Orientation 391

Sexual Problems 394
Sexual Dysfunction 394

Research Highlight *Is Cybersex Harmful?* 399
Sexually Transmitted Infections 399

Psychology at Work
Protecting Yourself and Others Against STIs 401

Critical Thinking/Active Learning
Rape Myths and Rape Prevention 402

12 *Motivation and Emotion* 406

Theories and Concepts of Motivation 408
Biological Theories 408

Research Highlight *Sensation Seeking* 410

Psychology at Work *Overcoming Test Anxiety* 411
Psychosocial Theories 412
Biopsychosocial Theory 412

Motivation and Behavior 414
Hunger and Eating 414

Research Highlight *Fuel for Thought* 416
Eating Disorders 416

Critical Thinking/Active Learning
Obesity—Weighing the Evidence 418
Achievement 419

Theories and Concepts of Emotion 421
Three Components of Emotion 421

Research Highlight *Mirron Neurons—"I Share Your Pain"* 423
Four Major Theories of Emotion 425

Critical Thinking About Motivation and Emotion 430
Intrinsic Versus Extrinsic Motivation 430
The Polygraph as a Lie Detector 432
Emotional Intelligence (EI) 432

Case Study/Personal Story
The Emotional Intelligence of Abraham Lincoln 434

Gender & Cultural Diversity
Culture, Evolution, and Emotion 435

13 *Personality* 440

Trait Theories 442
Early Trait Theorists 442
The Five-Factor Model 443
Evaluating Trait Theories 444

Psychology at Work *Personality and Your Career* 445

Research Highlight
Do Nonhuman Animals Have Personality? 446

Psychoanalytic/Psychodynamic Theories 447
Freud's Psychoanalytic Theory 448
Neo-Freudian/Psychodynamic Theories 452
Evaluating Psychoanalytic Theories 453

Humanistic Theories 455
Rogers's Theory 455

Maslow's Theory   457
Evaluating Humanistic Theories   457

Social-Cognitive Theories   458
Bandura's and Rotter's Approaches   459
Evaluating Social-Cognitive Theory   460

Biological Theories   460
Three Major Contributors   460
The Biopsychosocial Model   462

Personality Assessment   463
How Do We Measure Personality?   463
Are Personality Measurements Accurate?   466

Critical Thinking/Active Learning
Why Are Pseudo-Personality Tests So Popular?   468

14   Psychological Disorders   472

Studying Psychological Disorders   474
Identifying Abnormal Behavior   475

✳ Gender & Cultural Diversity   *Avoiding Ethnocentrism*   475
Explaining Abnormality   478
Classifying Abnormal Behavior   479

Anxiety Disorders   483
Five Major Anxiety Disorders   484
Explaining Anxiety Disorders   486

Mood Disorders   488
Understanding Mood Disorders   488

✳ Gender & Cultural Diversity
How Gender and Culture Affect Depression   489
Explaining Mood Disorders   490

Research Highlight   *Suicide and Its Prevention*   491

Critical Thinking/Active Learning   *How Your Thoughts Can Make You Depressed*   492

Schizophrenia   493
Symptoms of Schizophrenia   495
Types of Schizophrenia   496
Explaining Schizophrenia   497

✳ Gender & Cultural Diversity
Schizophrenia Around the World   498

Other Disorders   500
Substance-Related Disorders   500
Dissociative Disorders   502
Personality Disorders   503

Psychology at Work
Testing Your Knowledge of Abnormal Behavior   504

15   Therapy   508

Insight Therapies   510
Psychoanalysis/Psychodynamic Therapies   510
Evaluation   512
Cognitive Therapies   514
Humanistic Therapies   518
Group, Family, and Marital Therapies   521

Critical Thinking/Active Learning
Hunting for Good Therapy Films   523

Behavior Therapies   524
Classical Conditioning Techniques   524
Operant Conditioning Techniques   526
Observational Learning Techniques   527
Evaluating Behavior Therapies   527

Biomedical Therapies   528
Psychopharmacology   528
Electroconvulsive Therapy and Psychosurgery   530
Evaluating Biomedical Therapies   530

Therapy and Critical Thinking   532
Therapy Essentials   532

Psychology at Work   *Careers in Mental Health*   533

Research Highlight   *Mental Health and the Family— PTSD*   534

✳ Gender & Cultural Diversity   *Similarities and Differences*   535
Institutionalization   537
Evaluating and Finding Therapy   538

Psychology at Work   *Nonprofessional Therapy—Talking to the Depressed*   539

16 Social Psychology 544

Our Thoughts About Others 546

Attribution 546

Attitudes 548

Our Feelings About Others 551

Prejudice and Discrimination 551

Interpersonal Attraction 553

Gender & Cultural Diversity
Is Beauty in the Eye of the Beholder? 554

Psychology at Work *The Art and Science of Flirting* 555

Our Actions Toward Others 559

Social Influence 559

Group Processes 564

Aggression 568

Altruism 570

Critical Thinking/Active Learning
When and Why Do We Help? 572

Applying Social Psychology to Social Problems 573

Reducing Prejudice and Discrimination 573

Research Highlight *Understanding Implicit Biases* 575

Overcoming Destructive Obedience 577

Note: Chapters 17 and 18 available separately upon request.

17 Industrial/Organizational Psychology 582

The Development of I/O Psychology 585

The Beginning 585

World War II to Modern Times 587

Industrial Psychology 588

Recruitment and Selection 589

Employee Training 590

Evaluating Workers 591

Organizational Psychology 592

Leadership and Power 593

Gender and Cultural Diversity *Male/Female Differences in Leadership* 598

Critical Thinking/Active Learning *Power Versus Influence?* 599

Worker Motivation 601

Job Satisfaction 603

Psychology at Work *Job Satisfaction and Psychotherapy* 605

18 Psychology at Work in the Global Economy 610

Communication 612

Nature of Communication 612

Importance of Communication 615

Nonverbal Communication 616

Gender and Cultural Diversity *Male/Female Differences in Communication* 619

Psychology at Work *Improving Communication* 621

Persuasion 625

Powers of Persuasion 625

Routes to Persuasion 629

Conflict 631

Identifying Conflict 632

Gender and Cultural Diversity *What Hoppens to Business When Cultures Clash?* 632

Causes of Conflict 635

Psychology at Work *Five Approaches to Conflict Resolution* 637

Critical Thinking/Active Learning
Are You Assertive? 638

APPENDIX **A** *Statistics and Psychology* A1

APPENDIX **B** *Answers to Review Questions* B1

Glossary G1

References R1

Text and Illustration Credits T1

Name Index I1

Subject Index I11

Preface

Living Better With Huffman!

Why did we choose "Living better" as the theme for the Ninth Edition of *Psychology in Action*? Students too often think of psychology as primarily abnormal behavior and psychologists as therapists. And Freud is still considered by many to be psychology's most important figure. Although instructors know and appreciate the strong scientific basis and vast depth and breadth of our field, and the enormous number of important contributors, this very abundance often traps us into forgetting its overarching joy and pragmatic applications.

Psychology in Action (9e) is dedicated to capturing and celebrating all the best parts of psychology. Did you notice the happy, life-filled people pictured on the cover of this book? We chose these photos to reflect our "Living Better with Huffman" theme. In its many facets, psychology is a uniquely valuable tool for self-understanding and self-improvement. In its guiding principles are the means to live a life that is healthier, happier, less stressful, and more productive.

Psychology can definitely enlighten, entertain, and lift all of us to great heights. But can one text and one course cover all the major concepts and theories of psychology, while still presenting its exciting and practical applications? As the author of this text and a full-time teacher of psychology, I take this as an intimidating, but provocative, challenge. I must lead my readers and students step by step through the basic foundations of psychology. At the same time, I must provide time and space for life applications! Students need immediate active learning, "hands-on" exercises to master difficult concepts, and we also need to show them how psychology can be used to live a "better life."

Psychology in Action (9e) works to meet these goals by presenting concise, straightforward concepts, key terms, and theories, followed by quick activities (self-tests, check & review), examples (case studies/personal stories), and demonstrations (Try This Yourself, Visual Quizzes). Beginning with the first edition in 1987, this text has always emphasized active learning—hence the title "Psychology in *Action.*" Each edition has continued and improved upon this foundation.

What's New in the Ninth Edition?

Psychology at Work!

In response to reviewers, instructors, and students, and our "Living Better with Huffman" theme, *Psychology in Action (9e)* includes an expanded focus on applications and better living (see Table 1). Our NEW feature, *Psychology at Work*, emphasizes how psychology can be used to improve work, college, relationships, and virtually all other aspects of everyday life. These expanded applications are also closely related to chapter content, which helps students master essentials terms and concepts. For example, Chapter 1 includes a special section, "Psychology at Work: Careers in the Field," which provides job descriptions and opportunities within the field of psychology. Chapter 3's topics, "Is My Job Too Stressful" and "Coping with TechnoStress," offer valuable research information and tips for coping with stress.

TABLE 1 SAMPLE AND "BETTER LIVING WITH HUFFMAN" HIGHLIGHTS FROM *PSYCHOLOGY IN ACTION 9E* *(in addition to the shorter discussions and examples throughout the text)*

Better Living with Huffman/Psychology at Work	Better Living with Huffman/Positive Psychology
Careers in the field (pp. 7–9)	Dealing with pseudo-psychology (pp. 4–5)
Becoming a better consumer of scientific research (pp. 37–38)	Ethical research (pp. 18–20)
How neurotransmitters and hormones affect Us (pp. 53–57)	Overcoming genetic misconceptions (pp. 82–84)
Working with traumatic brain injuries (TBI) (pp. 79–80)	Better living through neuroscience (pp. 229–231)
Overcoming genetic misconceptions (pp. 82–84)	Wellness (pp. 90–122)
Is my job too stressful? (p. 104)	Hardiness (pp. 108–109)
Would you like to be a health psychologist? (pp. 111–112)	Biofeedback and behavior modification for improved health (p. 115)
Why you shouldn't procrastinate (p. 118)	Health and stress management (pp. 116–118)
Coping with technostress (pp. 120–121)	Preventing hearing loss (pp. 141–145)
Do subliminal messages improve sales? (pp. 132–133)	Understanding and overcoming sleep disorders (pp. 182–185)
The dangers of sleeping on the job (p. 171)	Healthier routes to alternate states (p. 166)
Self-help for sleep problems (pp. 184–185)	Attaining the benefits of meditation (p. 195)
Club drug alert! (pp. 194–195)	Therapeutic uses of hypnosis (p. 198)
Why can't we get anything done around here? (pp. 220–221)	Successful use of reinforcement and punishment (pp. 213–219)
Classical conditioning (pp. 232–233)	Overcoming prejudice and discrimination (pp. 235–236)
Operant conditioning (pp. 235–236)	Understanding and overcoming superstition (pp. 236–237)
Cognitive-social learning (pp. 237–238)	Improving and understanding memory (pp. 270–274)
Improving long-term memory (LTM) (pp. 252–254)	Improved problem-solving (pp. 283–286)
Key factors in forgetting (p. 260)	Creativity and multiple intelligences (pp. 288–299)
Heuristics and your career (p. 284)	Promoting secure attachment and positive parenting (pp. 340–342)
Recognizing barriers to problem solving (pp. 286–287)	Romantic love and attachment (p. 557)
Multiple intelligences and your career (p. 299)	Moral behavior (pp. 350–354)
Are your marital expectations unrealistic? (p. 360)	Marriage and family improvement (pp. 359–365)
Positive careers and rewarding retirements (p. 364)	Positive careers and retirement (pp. 364–365)
Dealing with your own death anxiety (pp. 369–370)	Resiliency (p. 363)
Protecting yourself and others against STIs (pp. 401–402)	Positive aspects of aging and dying (pp. 366–370)
Overcoming test anxiety (p. 411)	Benefits of androgyny (p. 383)
Personality and your career (pp. 445–446)	High achievers (pp. 419–421)
Testing your knowledge of abnormal behavior (p. 504)	Emotional intelligence (pp. 432–435)
Careers in mental health (p. 533)	Suicide and its prevention (pp. 491–492)
Nonprofessional therapy—talking to the depressed (pp. 539–540)	How your thoughts can make you depressed (pp. 488–491)
The art and science of flirting (pp. 555–556)	Mental health for the family (pp. 534–535)
• Optional Chapter 17 Job satisfaction and psychotherapy (p. 605)	Hunting for good therapy films (p. 523)
• Optional Chapter 18 Improving communication (pp. 621–623), improving your powers of persuasion (p. 625), and five approaches to conflict resolution (pp. 637–638)	Love and interpersonal attraction (pp. 553–559)
	Aggression—understanding and reducing (pp. 568–569)
	Altruism and helping behaviors (pp. 570–573)
	Reducing prejudice and discrimination (pp. 573–576)
	Reducing destructive obedience (pp. 559-577)

Further applications are provided with each chapter's in-depth *Critical Thinking/ Active Learning Exercises* located at the appropriate place in each chapter. These exercises are based on specific chapter content and devoted to developing various critical thinking skills. For example, the Critical Thinking/Active Learning Exercise in Chapter 16 asks readers, "Would you have obeyed Milgram's directions?" and helps develop independent thinking as a critical thinking skill.

Perhaps the most comprehensive and detailed applications are the two optional chapters. In response to increasing demand for more coverage of how psychology applies to business and work in the twenty-first century, we provide *Industrial/Organizational Psychology* (Chapter 17) and *Psychology at Work in a Global Economy* (Chapter 18). These chapters provide a general overview of industrial/organizational psychology, along with an extended discussion of communication, conflict management, leadership, and persuasion techniques. They're available as shrink-wrapped options to interested professors and their students.

APA-Linked Learning Objectives!

Given increasing calls for national and state-mandated student learning outcomes (SLOs), which are directly tied to accreditation, there is increasing pressure on professors to document how they assess their students. In 2002, the American Psychological Association (APA) task force created 10 broad-based learning goals for undergraduate psychology majors (http://www.apa.org/ed/psymajor_guideline.pdf). For each of these 10 learning goals, they also established specific learning outcomes and assessment guidelines.

Psychology in Action (9e), and its ancillaries, are all organized and directly linked to these same APA goals and outcomes. NEW, numbered learning objectives (15–25 per chapter) are found in special "Achievement" boxes located in the margin of each chapter of the text. These objectives are then repeated with summarized answers in the "Check & Review" sections found at the end of each chapter's major section. In addition to these APA-linked text objectives, the preface of the text, student study guide, test bank, and Instructor's Resource guide all contain a handy multipage table that lists the APA goals and outcomes, along with a corresponding page referenced list of the specific text objectives that meet each of these APA standards (see Table 2). The complete list of all chapter-by-chapter objectives, along with a copy of Table 2, are available electronically on our text website. This allows instructors to easily adapt our text objectives to their own course and college requirements.

Professors have responded very favorably to these new objectives, which are directly linked to the APA standards, because they can copy and print this table to quickly and easily document how this text—and their course—satisfy their campus, state, and national standards for learning outcomes and assessment.

A good friend and colleague made the following important points about assessment and the APA guidelines.

These guidelines were written by an APA task force composed of college and university faculty who have been involved in teaching and research on teaching for many years (Bill Buskist, Diane Halpern, Charles Brewer, Jane Halonen, Bill Hill, Drew Appleby, Margaret Lloyd, Jerry Rudmann and others). The intent of the task force was to outline "optimal expectations at the completion of the baccalaureate degree by students who major in psychology."

Sample text objective linked to APA outcomes

Achievement

Objective 1.4: *Contrast structuralism versus functionalism, and list the seven major perspectives that guide modern psychology.*

TABLE 2 PSYCHOLOGY IN ACTION'S (9E) DIRECT LINKS WITH APA GUIDELINES *(Note: No textbook or single course can address all these goals. These APA guidelines and Huffman objectives are intended for students who complete a baccalaureate degree with a major in psychology.)*

APA Undergraduate Learning Goals and Outcomes	Huffman Learning Objectives Psychology in Action (9e) * Optional Chapters 17 and 18
Goal 1: Knowledge Base of Psychology **Demonstrate familiarity with the major concepts, theoretical perspectives, empirical findings, and historical trends in psychology.**	
1.1 Characterize the nature of psychology as a discipline.	Ch. 1 1.1–1.5
1.2 Demonstrate knowledge and understanding representing appropriate breadth and depth in selected content areas of psychology (e.g., theory and research, history of psychology, relevant levels of analysis, overarching themes, and relevant ethical issues).	Ch. 2 2.1–2.21 Ch. 3 3.1–3.2, 3.5–3.18 Ch. 4 4.1–4.27 Ch. 5 5.1–5.2, 5.3–5.10, 5.12–5.16
1.3 Use the concepts, language, and major theories of the discipline to account for psychological phenomena.	Ch. 6 6.1–6.15, 6.17–6.19 Ch. 7 7.1–7.8, 7.10–7.13

1.4 Explain major perspectives of psychology (e.g., behavioral, biological, cognitive, evolutionary, humanistic, psychodynamic, and sociocultural).	Ch. 8 8.1–8.7, 8.9–8.20 Ch. 9 9.1–9.3, 9.5–9.15 Ch. 10 10.1–10.6, 10.8–10.12, 10.14 Ch. 11 11.1–11.6, 11.8–11.14 Ch. 12 12.1–12.3, 12.5–12.13 Ch. 13 13.1–13.2, 13.4–13.16 Ch. 14 14.2, 14.4–14.8, 14.10, 14.13–14.15, 14.17–14.19 Ch. 15 15.1–15.19, 15.24–15.25 Ch. 16 16.1–16.2, 16.4–16.8, 16.11–16.20 *Ch. 17 17.1–17.11, 17.13–17.19 *Ch. 18 18.1–18.3, 18.5–18.8, 18.10–18.13 Knowledge base also emphasized in Student Study and Review Guide, Instructor's Resource Guide, WileyPlus, Wiley web site assets www.wiley.com/college/huffman, etc.

Goal 2: Research Methods in Psychology
Understand and apply basic research methods in psychology, including research design, data analysis, and interpretation.

2.1 Describe the basic characteristics of the science of psychology.
 	
2.2 Explain different research methods used by psychologists.
 	
  a. Describe how various research designs address different types of questions and hypotheses.
 	
  b. Articulate strengths and limitations of various research designs, including distinguishing between qualitative and quantitative methods.
 	
  c. Distinguish the nature of designs that permit causal inferences from those that do not.
 	
  d. Describe how the values system of the researcher can influence research design and decisions.
 	
2.3 Evaluate the appropriateness of conclusions derived from psychological research.
 	
  a. Interpret basic statistical results.
 	
  b. Distinguish between statistical significance and practical significance.
 	
  c. Describe effect size and confidence intervals.
 	
  d. Evaluate the validity of conclusions presented in research reports.
 	
2.4 Design and conduct basic studies to address psychological questions using appropriate research methods.
 	
  a. Locate and use relevant databases, research, and theory to plan, conduct, and interpret results of research studies.
 	
  b. Formulate testable research hypotheses, based on operational definitions of variables.
 	
  c. Use reliable and valid measures of variables of interest.
	Ch. 1 1.6–1.15 (Research Highlight: Love at First Fright, Case Study: A Life Without Fear, and Psychology at Work: Becoming a Better Consumer of Scientific Research)
	
	Ch. 2 2.14, 2.18 (Case Study: Phineas Gage)
	
	Ch. 3 3.3, 3.12 (Research Highlight: Hurricane Katrina and Local College Students, and Does Stress Cause Gastric Ulcers?)
	
	Ch. 4 4.7, 4.16, 4.27 (Case Study: Helen Keller's Triumph and Advice, Research Highlight: Perfect (Yet Imperfect) Pitch, and Is There Scientific Evidence for ESP?)
	
	Ch. 5 5.12 (Research Highlight: Addictive Drugs as the Brain's "Evil Tutor")
	
	Ch. 6 6. 16 (Research Highlight: "The Theory Heard Round the World")
	
	Ch. 7 7.12–7.13 (Research Highlight: Memory and the Criminal Justice System)
	
	Ch. 8 8.20 (Research Highlight: Explaining Differences in IQ)
	
	Ch. 9 9.4 (Gender & Cultural Diversity: Cultural Guidelines for Developmental Research)
	
	Ch. 10 (Research Highlight: Children Who Survive Despite the Odds)
	
	Ch. 11 11.4, 11.6, 11.10 (Gender & Cultural Diversity: A Cross-Cultural Look at Sexual Behaviors, The Study of Human Sexuality, Research Highlight: Video Games, Gender, and Spatial Skills, Is Cybersex Harmful? Case Study: The Tragic Tale of "John/Joan," and Sexual Orientation)

d. Select and apply appropriate methods to maximize internal and external validity and reduce the plausibility of alternative explanations.

e. Collect, analyze, interpret, and report data using appropriate statistical strategies to address different types of research questions and hypotheses.

f. Recognize that the theoretical and sociocultural contexts as well as personal biases may shape research questions, design, data collection, analysis, and interpretation.

2.5 Follow the APA Code of Ethics in the treatment of human and nonhuman participants in the design, data collection, interpretation, and reporting of psychological research.

2.6 Generalize research conclusions appropriately based on the parameters of particular research methods.

a. Exercise caution in predicting behavior based on limitations of single studies.

b. Recognize the limitations of applying normative conclusions to individuals.

c. Acknowledge that research results may have unanticipated societal consequences.

d. Recognize that individual differences and sociocultural contexts may influence the applicability of research findings.

Ch. 12   12.2, 12.4, 12.14 (Research Highlight: Sensation Seeking, Fuel for Thought, and Case Study: The Emotional Intelligence of Abraham Lincoln)

Ch. 13   13.4 (Research Highlight: Do Nonhuman Animals Have Personality?)

Ch. 14   14.11 (Research Highlight: Suicide and Its Prevention)

Ch. 15   15.21 (Research Highlight: Mental Health and the Family— PTSD)

Ch. 16   (Research Highlight: Understanding Implicit Biases)

Appendix A Statistics and Psychology

Research methods also emphasized in Student Study and Review Guide, Instructor's Resource Guide, WileyPlus, Wiley web site assets www.wiley.com/college/huffman, etc.

Goal 3: Critical Thinking Skills in Psychology
Respect and use critical and creative thinking, skeptical inquiry, and, when possible, the scientific approach to solve problems related to behavior and mental processes.

3.1 Use critical thinking effectively.

3.2 Engage in creative thinking.

3.3 Use reasoning to recognize, develop, defend, and criticize arguments and other persuasive appeals.

3.4 Approach problems effectively.

Ch. 1   1.1 (Critical Thinking/Active Learning: Applying Critical Thinking to Psychological Science)

Ch. 2   2.19 (Critical Thinking/Active Learning: Biology and Critical Thinking, and Psychology at Work: Overcoming Genetic Misconceptions)

Ch. 3   3.18 (Critical Thinking/Active Learning: Reducing Stress Through Critical Thinking)

Ch. 4   4.26–4.27 (Critical Thinking/Active Learning: Problems with Believing in ESP, Research Highlight: Is There Scientific Evidence for ESP?)

Ch. 5   5.7 (Critical Thinking/Active Learning: Interpreting Your Dreams)

Ch. 6   (Critical Thinking/Active Learning: Positive Psychology, Learning, and College Success)

Ch. 7   (Critical Thinking/Active Learning: Memory and Metacognition)

Ch. 8   (Critical Thinking/Active Learning: Solving Problems in College Life)

Ch. 9   (Critical Thinking/Active Learning: The Development of "Suicide Bombers")

Ch. 10   (Critical Thinking/Active Learning: Morality and Academic Cheating)

Ch. 11 11.4, 11.10 (Critical Thinking/Active Learning: Gender Differences and Critical Thinking, Sexual Orientation, and Rape Myths and Rape Prevention)

Ch. 12 12.6, 12.11–12.14 (Critical Thinking/Active Learning: Obesity—Weighing the Evidence, and Critical Thinking About Motivation and Emotion)

Ch. 13 13.17 (Critical Thinking/Active Learning: Why Are Pseudo-Personality Tests So Popular?)

Ch. 14 14.1, 14.12 (Myths About Mental Illness, and Critical Thinking/Active Learning: How Your Thoughts Can Make You Depressed)

Ch. 15 15.1 (Myths About Therapy, and Critical Thinking/Active Learning: Hunting for Good Therapy Films)

Ch. 16 16.19–16.20 (Critical Thinking/Active Learning: When and Why Do You Help?)

*Ch. 17 17.14 (Critical Thinking/Active Learning: Power Versus Influence?)

*Ch. 18 18.13 (Critical Thinking/Active Learning: Are You Assertive?)

Critical thinking also emphasized in Student Study and Review Guide, Instructor's Resource Guide, WileyPlus, Wiley web site assets www.wiley.com/college/huffman, etc.

Goal 4: Application of Psychology
Understand and apply psychological principles to personal, social, and organizational issues.

4.1 Describe major applied areas of psychology (e.g., clinical, counseling, industrial/organizational, school, health, forensics, media, military, etc.).

4.2 Identify appropriate applications of psychology in solving problems (e.g., healthy lifestyles, origins and treatment of abnormal behavior, etc.).

4.3 Articulate how psychological principles can be used to explain social issues and inform public policy.

4.4 Apply psychological concepts, theories, and research findings as these relate to everyday life.

4.5 Recognize that ethically complex situations can develop in the application of psychological principles

Ch. 1 1.3, 1.17 (Psychology at Work: Careers in the Field, Becoming a Better Consumer of Scientific Research, and Tools for Student Success)

Ch. 2 2.3, 2.16, 2.19 (Psychology at Work: How Neurotransmitters and Hormones Affect Us, Working with Traumatic Brain Injuries (TBI), and Overcoming Genetic Misconceptions)

Ch. 3 3.4, 3.6., 3.8, 3.9–3.18 (Can Job Stress be Fatal?, Psychology at Work: Is My Job Too Stressful?, Would You Like to be a Health Psychologist?, Why You Shouldn't Procrastinate, Coping with Technostress, and Critical Thinking: Reducing Stress Through Critical Thinking)

Ch. 4 4.4, 4. 26–4.27 (Psychology at Work: Do Subliminal Messages Improve Sales?, Critical Thinking/Active Learning: Problems with Believing in ESP, Research Highlight: Is There Scientific Evidence for ESP?)

Ch. 5 5.4, 5.9, 5.12, 5.14–5.16 (Psychology at Work: Dangers of Sleeping on the Job, Self-Help for Sleep Problems, Addictive Drugs, Club Drug Alert, and Healthier Ways to Alter Consciousness,)

Ch. 6 6.6, 6.9–6.12, 6.16, 6.20–6.22 (Psychology at Work: Why Can't We Get Anything Done Around Here?, Classical Conditioning, Operant

Conditioning, Cognitive-Social Learning, Research Highlight: "The Theory Heard Round the World," and Critical Thinking/Active Learning: Using Learning Principles to Succeed in College)

Ch. 7 7.5, 7.8–7.9, 7.12–7.15 (Psychology at Work: Improving Long-Term Memory (LTM), Key Factors in Forgetting, Research Highlight: Memory and the Criminal Justice System, Using Psychology to Improve Our Memory, Critical Thinking/Active Learning: Memory and Metacognition)

Ch. 8 8.4–8.5, 8.8 (Psychology at Work: Heuristics and Your Career, Recognizing Barriers to Problem-Solving, Multiple Intelligences and Your Career, Critical Thinking/Active Learning: Solving Problems in College Life, Creativity, Gender & Cultural Diversity: Unspoken Accents,

Ch. 9 9.14–9.15 (Attachment, Parenting Styles, Critical Thinking/Active Learning: The Development of "Suicide Bombers")

Ch. 10 10.8–10.9, 10.12–10.14 (Critical Thinking/Active Learning: Morality and Academic Cheating, Meeting the Challenges of Adulthood, Psychology at Work: Are Your Marital Expectations Unrealistic? Positive Careers and Rewarding Retirements, Research Highlight: Children Who Survive Despite the Odds, Grief and Death)

Ch. 11 11.4, 11.5, 11.8, 11.11–11.14 (Case Study: Tragic Tale of "John/Joan," Research Highlight: Video Games, Gender, and Spatial Skills, Gender Differences, Androgyny, Sexual Response Cycle, Is Cybersex Harmful?, Sexual Orientation, Sexual Problems, Sexually Transmitted Infections, Rape Myths and Rape Prevention)

Ch. 12 12.3–12.7, 12.11–12.14 [Research Highlight: Sensation Seeking, Psychology at Work: Overcoming Test Anxiety, Eating Disorders, Fuel for Thought, Achievement Motivation, Intrinsic Versus Extrinsic Motivation, Polygraph Testing, and Emotional Intelligence (EI)]

Ch. 13 13.3, 13.9, 13.11 (Personality-Job-Fit Theory, Applying Humanistic and Social-Cognitive Theories)

Ch. 14 14.1, 14.11–14.12 (Myths About Mental Illness, Suicide and its Prevention, How Your Thoughts Can Make You Depressed, and Psychology at Work: Testing Your Knowledge of Abnormal Behavior)

Ch. 15 15.1, 15.20, 15.21, 15.25, 15.26 (Myths about Therapy, Psychology at Work: Careers in Mental Health, Research Highlight: Mental Health and the Family-PTSD, How to Find a Good Therapist, and Psychology at Work: Nonprofessional Therapy—Talking to the Depressed)

Ch. 16 16.5–16.8, 16.10–16.11, 16.16–16.22 (Cognitive Dissonance and Attitude Change, Prejudice and Discrimination, Psychology at Work: The Art and Science of Flirting, Romantic Versus Companionate Love, Conformity and Obedience, Aggression and Altruism)

***Ch. 17** 17.1–17.7, 17.15–17–19 (Employee Recruitment, Selection, Training, and Evaluation, Job Performance, Worker Motivation, Job Satisfaction, Personality-Job-Fit Theory, and Psychology at Work: Job Satisfaction and Psychotherapy)

***Ch. 18** 18.1–18.13 (Communication, Persuasion, Conflict, Male/Female Differences in Communication, Psychology at Work: Improving Communication, Five Approaches to Conflict Resolution, and What Happens to Business When Cultures Clash?)

Applications also emphasized in Student Study and Review Guide, Instructor's Resource Guide, WileyPlus, Wiley web site assets www.wiley.com/college/huffman, etc.

Goal 5: Values in Psychology
Weigh evidence, tolerate ambiguity, act ethically, and reflect other values that are the underpinnings of psychology as a discipline.

5.1 Recognize the necessity for ethical behavior in all aspects of the science and practice of psychology.

5.2 Demonstrate reasonable skepticism and intellectual curiosity by asking questions about causes of behavior.

5.3 Seek and evaluate scientific evidence for psychological claims.

5.4 Tolerate ambiguity and realize that psychological explanations are often complex and tentative.

5.5 Recognize and respect human diversity.

5.6 Assess and justify their engagement with respect to civic, social, and global responsibilities.

5.7 Understand the limitations of their psychological knowledge and skills.

Ch. 1 1.6–1.16 (Research Highlight: Love at First Fright, Case Study: A Life Without Fear, Psychology at Work: Becoming a Better Consumer of Scientific Research, and Gender & Cultural Diversity: Are There Cultural Universals?)

Ch. 2 2.14, 2.18, 2.21 (Case Study: Phineas Gage and Gender & Cultural Diversity: The Evolution of Sex Differences)

Ch. 3 3.3–3.4, 3.12 (Research Highlight: Hurricane Katrina and Local College Students, and Does Stress Cause Gastric Ulcers?, and Gender & Cultural Diversity: "Karoshi"—Can Job Stress be Fatal?)

Ch. 4 4.7, 4.16, 4.22 4.27 (Case Study: Helen Keller's Triumph and Advice, Research Highlight: Perfect (Yet Imperfect) Pitch, Gender & Cultural Diversity: Are the Gestalt Laws Universally True?, and Is There Scientific Evidence for ESP?)

Ch. 5 5.8, 5.12 (Gender & Cultural Diversity: Dream Variations and Similarities, Research Highlight: Addictive Drugs as the Brain's "Evil Tutor")

Ch. 6 6. 16–6.17 (Research Highlight: "The Theory Heard Round the World," and Gender &

Cultural Diversity: Scaffolding as a Teaching Technique in Different Cultures)

Ch. 7 7.9, 7.12–7.13 (Gender & Cultural Diversity: Cultural Differences in Memory and Forgetting, and Research Highlight: Memory and the Criminal Justice System)

Ch. 8 8.13, 8.20–8.21 (Gender & Cultural Diversity: Unspoken Accents, Are IQ Tests Culturally Biased?, and Research Highlight: Explaining Differences in IQ)

Ch. 9 9.4 (Gender & Cultural Diversity: Cultural Guidelines for Developmental Research)

Ch. 10 10.7, 10.13 (Gender & Cultural Diversity: Cultural Influences on Development, Cultural Differences in Ageism, and Research Highlight: Children Who Survive Despite the Odds)

Ch. 11 11.1–11.5, 11.6–11.7, 11.9–11.10 (Gender & Cultural Diversity: A Cross-Cultural Look at Sexual Behaviors, The Study of Human Sexuality, Research Highlight: Video Games, Gender, and Spatial Skills, Is Cybersex Harmful? Case Study: The Tragic Tale of "John/Joan," and Sexual Orientation)

Ch. 12 12.2, 12.4, 12.14–12.15 (Research Highlight: Sensation Seeking, Fuel for Thought, Case Study: The Emotional Intelligence of Abraham Lincoln, and Gender & Cultural Diversity: Culture, Evolution, and Emotion)

Ch. 13 13.4 (Research Highlight: Do Nonhuman Animals Have Personality?)

Ch. 14 14.3, 14.9, 14.11, 14.16 (Gender & Cultural Diversity: Avoiding Ethnocentrism, How Gender and Culture Affect Depression, Schizophrenia Around the World, and Research Highlight: Suicide and Its Prevention)

Ch. 15 15.21–15.23 (Research Highlight: Mental Health and the Family—PTSD, and Gender & Cultural Diversity: Similarities and Differences)

Ch. 16 16.3, 16.5, 16.9 (Gender & Cultural Diversity: Is Beauty in the Eye of the Beholder?, and Research Highlight: Understanding Implicit Biases)

Appendix A Statistics and Psychology

*Ch. 17 17.6, 17.12 (Gender & Cultural Diversity: Male/Female Differences in Leadership)

*Ch. 18 18.4, 18.9 (Gender & Cultural Diversity: Male/Female Differences in Communication, and Gender & Cultural Diversity: What Happens to Business When Cultures Clash?)

Values also emphasized in Student Study and Review Guide, Instructor's Resource Guide, WileyPlus, Wiley web site assets www.wiley.com/college/huffman, etc.

Goal 6: Information and Technological Literacy
Demonstrate information competence and the ability to use computers and other technology for many purposes.

6.1 Demonstrate information competence at each stage in the following process: formulate a researchable topic that can be supported by database search strategies, locate and choose relevant sources from appropriate media, use selected sources after evaluating their suitability, and read and accurately summarize the general scientific literature of psychology.

6.2 Use appropriate software to produce understandable reports of the psychological literature in APA or other appropriate style.

6.3 Use information and technology ethically and responsibly.

6.4 Demonstrate computer skills (e.g., basic word processing, search the Web for high-quality information, and use proper computer etiquette).

Ch. 1 1.6–1.15 (Research Highlight: Love at First Fright, Case Study: A Life Without Fear, and Psychology at Work: Becoming a Better Consumer of Scientific Research)

Ch. 2 2.14, 2.18 (Case Study: Phineas Gage)

Ch. 3 3.3, 3.12 (Research Highlight: Hurricane Katrina and Local College Students, and Does Stress Cause Gastric Ulcers?, and Psychology at Work: Coping with Technostress)

Ch. 4 4.7, 4.16, 4.27 (Case Study: Helen Keller's Triumph and Advice, Research Highlight: Perfect (Yet Imperfect) Pitch, and Is There Scientific Evidence for ESP?)

Ch. 5 5.12 (Research Highlight: Addictive Drugs as the Brain's "Evil Tutor")

Ch. 6 6. 16 (Research Highlight: "The Theory Heard Round the World")

Ch. 7 7.12–7.13 (Research Highlight: Memory and the Criminal Justice System)

Ch. 8 8.20 (Research Highlight: Explaining Differences in IQ)

Ch. 9 9.4 (Gender & Cultural Diversity: Cultural Guidelines for Developmental Research)

Ch. 10 (Research Highlight: Children Who Survive Despite the Odds)

Ch. 11 11.4, 11.6, 11.10 (Gender & Cultural Diversity: A Cross-Cultural Look at Sexual Behaviors, The Study of Human Sexuality, Research Highlight: Video Games, Gender, and Spatial Skills, Is Cybersex Harmful? Case Study: The Tragic Tale of "John/Joan," and Sexual Orientation)

Ch. 12 12.2, 12.4, 12.14 (Research Highlight: Sensation Seeking, Fuel for Thought, and Case Study: The Emotional Intelligence of Abraham Lincoln)

Ch. 13 13.4 (Research Highlight: Do Nonhuman Animals Have Personality?)

Ch. 14 14.11 (Research Highlight: Suicide and Its Prevention)

Ch. 15 15.21 (Research Highlight: Mental Health and the Family— PTSD)

Ch. 16 (Research Highlight: Understanding Implicit Biases)

Appendix A Statistics and Psychology

Information and technological literacy also emphasized in Student Study and Review Guide, Instructor's Resource Guide, WileyPlus, Wiley web site assets www.wiley.com/college/huffman, etc.

Preface and throughout text (SQ4R method and Huffman interactive narrative style emphasize and model communication)

Goal 7: Communication Skills
Communicate effectively in a variety of formats.

7.1 Demonstrate effective writing skills in various formats (e.g., essays, correspondence, technical papers, note taking) and for various purposes (e.g., informing, defending, explaining, persuading, arguing, teaching).	Ch. 8 8.9–8.14 (Language and Gender & Cultural Diversity: Unspoken Accents)
7.2 Demonstrate effective oral communication skills in various formats (e.g., group discussion, debate, lecture) and for various purposes (e.g., informing, defending, explaining, persuading, arguing, teaching).	Ch. 15 15.26 (Psychology at Work: Nonprofessional Therapy—Talking to the Depressed)
7.3 Exhibit quantitative literacy.	*Ch. 17 17.8–17.13 (Leadership and Power, Gender & Cultural Diversity: Male/Female Differences in Leadership)
7.4 Demonstrate effective interpersonal communication skills.	*Ch. 18 18/1–18.13 (Communication, Persuasion, Conflict, Gender & Cultural Diversity: Male/Female Differences in Communication, Psychology at Work: Improving Communication, Five Approaches to Conflict Resolution, Gender & Cultural Diversity: What Happens to Business When Cultures Clash? Critical Thinking/Active Learning: Are You Assertive?)
7.5 Exhibit the ability to collaborate effectively.	

Communication skills also emphasized in Student Study and Review Guide, Instructor's Resource Guide, WileyPlus, Wiley web site assets www.wiley.com/college/huffman, etc.

Goal 8. Sociocultural and International Awareness
Recognize, understand, and respect the complexity of sociocultural and international diversity.

8.1 Interact effectively and sensitively with people from diverse backgrounds and cultural perspectives.	Ch. 1 1.16 (Gender & Cultural Diversity: Are There Cultural Universals?)
8.2 Examine the sociocultural and international contexts that influence individual differences.	Ch. 2 2.21 (Gender & Cultural Diversity: The Evolution of Sex Differences)
8.3 Explain how individual differences influence beliefs, values, and interactions with others and vice versa.	Ch. 3 3. 4 (Gender & Cultural Diversity: "Karoshi"—Can Job Stress be Fatal?)
8.4 Understand how privilege, power, and oppression may affect prejudice, discrimination, and inequity.	Ch. 4 4. 22 (Gender & Cultural Diversity: Are the Gestalt Laws Universally True?)
8.5 Recognize prejudicial attitudes and discriminatory behaviors that might exist in themselves and others.	Ch. 5 5. 8 (Gender & Cultural Diversity: Dream Variations and Similarities)
8.6 Predict how interaction among diverse people can challenge conventional understanding of psychological processes and behavior.	Ch. 6 6. 16–6.17 (Research Highlight: "The Theory Heard Round the World," and Gender & Cultural Diversity: Scaffolding as a Teaching Technique in Different Cultures)
	Ch. 7 7.9 (Gender & Cultural Diversity: Cultural Differences in Memory and Forgetting)
	Ch. 8 8.13, 8.21 (Gender & Cultural Diversity: Unspoken Accents, and Are IQ Tests Culturally Biased?)

	Ch. 9 9.4 (Gender & Cultural Diversity: Cultural Psychology's Guidelines for Developmental Research)
	Ch. 10 10. 7, 10.13 (Gender & Cultural Diversity: Cultural Influences on Development, and Cultural Differences in Ageism)
	Ch. 11 11.1–11.5, 11.7, 11.9 (Gender & Cultural Diversity: A Cross-Cultural Look at Sexual Behaviors and Are There Evolutionary Advantages to Female Nonmonogamy?)
	Ch. 12 12.15 (Gender & Cultural Diversity: Culture, Evolution, and Emotion)
	Ch. 14 14.3, 14.9, 14.16 (Gender & Cultural Diversity: Avoiding Ethnocentrism, How Gender and Culture Affect Depression, and Schizophrenia Around the World)
	Ch. 15 15.22–15.23 (Gender & Cultural Diversity: Similarities and Differences)
	Ch. 16 16.3, 16.5, 16.9 (Gender & Cultural Diversity: Is Beauty in the Eye of the Beholder?)
	***Ch. 17** 17.6, 17.12 (Gender & Cultural Diversity: Male/Female Differences in Leadership)
	***Ch. 18** 18.4, 18.9 (Gender & Cultural Diversity: Male/Female Differences in Communication, and Gender & Cultural Diversity: What Happens to Business When Cultures Clash?)

Sociocultural and international awareness also emphasized in Student Study and Review Guide, Instructor's Resource Guide, WileyPlus, Wiley web site assets www.wiley.com/college/huffman, etc.

Goal 9: Personal Development
Develop insight into our own and other's behavior and mental processes, and apply effective strategies for self-management and self-improvement.

9.1 Reflect on their experiences and find meaning in them.	**Ch. 1** 1.12., 1.17 (Research Highlight: Love at First Fright, and Tools for Student Success)
9.2 Apply psychological principles to promote personal development.	**Ch. 2** 2.3, 2.21 (Psychology at Work: How Neurotransmitters and Hormones Affect Us, and Gender & Cultural Diversity: The Evolution of Sex Differences)
9.3 Enact self-management strategies that maximize healthy outcomes.	
9.4 Display high standards of personal integrity with others.	**Ch. 3** 3.1–3.2, 3.4–312, 3.14–3.18 (Can Job Stress be Fatal? Psychology at Work: Is My Job Too Stressful?, Why You Shouldn't Procrastinate, Coping with Technostress, Resources for Healthy Living, and Critical Thinking: Reducing Stress Through Critical Thinking)
9.5 Seek input from and experiences with diverse people to enhance the quality of solutions.	
	Ch. 5 5.4, 5.9, 5.12, 5.14–5.16 (Psychology at Work: Dangers of Sleeping on the Job, Self-Help for Sleep Problems, Addictive Drugs, Club Drug Alert, and Healthier Ways to Alter Consciousness)

Ch. 6 6.6, 6.9–6.12, 6.16, 6.20–6.22 (Psychology at Work: Why Can't We Get Anything Done Around Here?, Classical Conditioning, Operant Conditioning, Cognitive-Social Learning, and Critical Thinking/Active Learning: Using Learning Principles to Succeed in College)

Ch. 7 7.5, 7.8–7.9, 7.12–7.15 (Psychology at Work: Improving Long-Term Memory (LTM), Key Factors in Forgetting, Using Psychology to Improve Our Memory, Critical Thinking/Active Learning: Memory and Metacognition)

Ch. 8 8.4–8.5, 8.8 (Psychology at Work: Heuristics and Your Career, Recognizing Barriers to Problem-Solving, Multiple Intelligences and Your Career, Critical Thinking/Active Learning: Solving Problems in College Life, and Creativity

Ch. 9 9.14–9.15 (Attachment, Parenting Styles)

Ch. 10 10.8–10.9, 10.12–10.14 (Meeting the Challenges of Adulthood, Psychology at Work: Are Your Marital Expectations Unrealistic? Positive Careers and Rewarding Retirements, Research Highlight: Children Who Survive Despite the Odds, Grief and Death)

Ch. 11 11.4, 11.5, 11.8, 11.11–11.14 (Gender Differences, Androgyny, Sexual Response Cycle, Is Cybersex Harmful?, Sexual Orientation, Sexual Problems, Sexually Transmitted Infections, Rape Myths and Rape Prevention)

Ch. 12 12.3–12.7, 12.11–12.14 [Psychology at Work: Overcoming Test Anxiety, Eating Disorders, Fuel for Thought, Achievement Motivation, Intrinsic Versus Extrinsic Motivation, Polygraph Testing, and Emotional Intelligence (EI)]

Ch. 13 13.3, 13.9, 13.11 (Personality-Job-Fit Theory, Applying Humanistic and Social-Cognitive Theories)

Ch. 14 14.1, 14.11–14.12 (Myths About Mental Illness, Suicide and its Prevention, and How Your Thoughts Can Make You Depressed)

Ch. 15 15.1, 15.20, 15.21, 15.25, 15.26 (Research Highlight: Mental Health and the Family-PTSD, How to Find a Good Therapist, and Psychology at Work: Nonprofessional Therapy—Talking to the Depressed)

Ch. 16 16.5–16.8, 16.10–16.11, 16.16–16.22 (Cognitive Dissonance and Attitude Change, Prejudice and Discrimination, Psychology at Work: The Art and Science of Flirting, Romantic Versus Companionate Love, Conformity and Obedience, Aggression and Altruism)

*Ch. 17 17.1–17.7, 17.15–17.19 (Employee Recruitment, Selection, Training, and Evaluation, Job Performance, Worker Motivation, Job Satisfaction, Personality-Job-Fit Theory, and Psychology at Work: Job Satisfaction and Psychotherapy)

*Ch. 18 18.1–18.13 (Communication, Persuasion, Conflict, Male/Female Differences in Communication, Psychology at Work: Improving Communication, Five Approaches to Conflict Resolution, and What Happens to Business When Cultures Clash?)

Personal development also emphasized in Student Study and Review Guide, Instructor's Resource Guide, WileyPlus, Wiley web site assets www.wiley.com/college/huffman, etc.

Goal 10: Career Planning and Development
Develop realistic ideas about how to implement psychological knowledge, skills, and values in occupational pursuits in a variety of settings.

10.1 Apply knowledge of psychology (e.g., decision strategies, life span processes, psychological assessment, types of psychological careers) to formulating career choices.

10.2 Identify the types of academic experience and performance in psychology and the liberal arts that will facilitate entry into the work force, post-baccalaureate education, or both.

10.3 Describe preferred career paths based on accurate self-assessment of abilities, achievement, motivation, and work habits.

10.4 Identify and develop skills and experiences relevant to achieving selected career goals.

10.5 Articulate how changing societal needs can influence career opportunities and foster flexibility about managing changing conditions.

10.6 Demonstrate an understanding of the importance of lifelong learning and personal flexibility to sustain personal and professional development as the nature of work evolves.

Ch. 1 1.3 (Psychology at Work: Careers in the Field)

Ch. 2 2.16 [Psychology at Work: Working with Traumatic Brain Injuries (TBI)]

Ch. 3 3.4, 3.9, 3.13, 3.17–3.18 (Psychology at Work: Would You Like to be a Health Psychologist, Is My Job Too Stressful?, Coping with Technostress, and Gender & Cultural Diversity: "Karoshi"—Can Job Stress be Fatal?)

Ch. 4 4.4 (Do Subliminal Messages Improve Sales?)

Ch. 5 5.4 (Psychology at Work: The Dangers of Sleeping on the Job)

Ch. 6 6.12 (Psychology at Work: Why Can't We Get Anything Done Around Here?)

Ch. 8 (Psychology at Work: Heuristics and Your Career, Recognizing Barriers to Problem-Solving, Multiple Intelligences and Your Career)

Ch. 10 10.9 (Work and Retirement, Psychology at Work: Positive Careers and Rewarding Retirements)

Ch. 12 12.7 (Achievement Motivation)

Ch. 13 13.3 (Personality-Job-Fit Theory)

Ch. 15 15.20 (Psychology at Work: Careers in Mental Health)

*Ch. 17 17.1, 17.5–17.7, 17.15–17.19 (I/O Psychology, Employee Recruitment, Selection, Training, and Evaluation, Job Performance, Worker Motivation, Job Satisfaction, and Personality-Job-Fit)

*Ch. 18 18.9 (Gender & Cultural Diversity: What Happens to Business When Cultures Clash?)

Career planning and development also emphasized in Student Study and Review Guide, Instructor's Resource Guide, WileyPlus, Wiley web site assets www.wiley.com/college/huffman, etc.

No textbook or single course can address all these goals. The intent is that by the time students complete the major, they will be able to develop competency in all the goals. So departments should be assessing if the program attempts to meet all the goals, not any one course. Also, the framers of the guidelines included a statement to address the need for flexibility and autonomy:

"The term guidelines generally refers to pronouncements, statements, or declarations that recommend or suggest specific actions, goals or endeavors. In this spirit, they are aspirational in intent. They are not intended to be mandatory or exhaustive and may not be applicable to every situation, nor are they intended to take precedence over the judgment of college and university faculty" (p 4).

JUDY WILSON, Assistant Professor

Palomar College, San Marcos, CA

Focus on Visual Learning

As most instructors know, well-designed visuals improve the efficiency with which information is processed, and the more effectively we process information, the more likely it is that we will learn. *Psychology in Action (9e)* incorporates the best of visual learning with ongoing Try This Yourself exercises, Visual Quizzes, and two NEW features—*Process Diagrams* and *Concept Diagrams* (see Table 3).

Our text also offers a rich selection of visuals in the supplementary materials that accompany the book. For example, the Test Bank now includes numerous questions with photos, cartoons, and figures to visually capture the student's interest and aid in recall of information. The Student Study Guide, PowerPoints, Image Gallery, and other ancillaries also provide you with additional visuals and media resources.

In addition, we've added a NEW, separate ancillary composed of short, three to five minute Videos by professors across the nation. These brief, "YouTube"-like Video lectures can be used in the classroom "as is," or instructors can view them for ideas on demonstrations and activities, which they can then recreate in their own classroom.

Try This Yourself

Hypnosis or Simple Trick?

You can recreate a favorite trick that stage hypnotists promote as evidence of superhuman strength under hypnosis. Simply arrange two chairs as shown in the picture. You will see that hypnosis is not necessary—all that is needed is a highly motivated volunteer willing to stiffen his or her body.

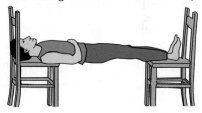

TABLE 3 VISUAL LEARNING—LIST OF NEW PROCESS AND CONCEPT DIAGRAMS

Chapters	Process Diagrams	Concept Diagrams
Chapter 1	1.1 Scientific Method (p. 17)	1.1 Understanding Correlations (p. 32)
	1.2 Key Features of an Experiment (pp. 23–24)	
	1.3 Using the SQ4R Method (p. 42)	
Chapter 2	2.1 How Neurons Communicate (pp. 55–56)	2.1 Visualizing Your Motor and Somatosensory Cortex (p. 74)
		2.2. Explaining Split-Brain Research (p. 77)
		2.3 Four Methods of Behavioral Genetics Research (p. 83)
Chapter 3	3.1 The Biology of Stress (p. 101)	
	3.2 The General Adaptation Syndrome (GAS) (p. 103)	
	3.3 Cognitive Appraisal and Coping (p. 117)	
Chapter 4	4.1 How the Eye Sees (p. 137)	4.1 Measuring the Senses (p. 131)
	4.2 How the Ear Hears (p. 142)	4.2 Four Perceptual Constancies (p. 157)
	4.3 How the Nose Smells (p. 147)	4.3 Binocular Cues (p. 159)
		4.4 Monocular Cues (p. 160)

TABLE 3 VISUAL LEARNING—LIST OF NEW PROCESS AND CONCEPT DIAGRAMS (CONTINUED)

Chapter 5	5.1 Where Does Consciousness Reside? (p. 169)	5.1 Scientific Study of Sleep and Dreaming (p. 175)
	5.2 How Drugs Work (p. 187)	5.2 Meditation and the Brain (p. 197)
Chapter 6	6.1 Pavlov's Classical Conditioning (p. 206)	6.1 Higher-Order Conditioning (p. 211)
	6.2 Prejudice and Classical Conditioning (p. 234)	6.2 Four Key Factors in Observational Learning (p. 226)
Chapter 7	7.1 Information-Processing Model (p. 245)	7.1 Brain and Memory Formation (p. 265)
	7.2 Working Memory as a Central Executive (p. 250)	7. 2 Mnemonics (p. 273)
	7.3 Why We Forget (pp. 258–259)	
Chapter 8	8.1 Building Blocks of Language (p. 292)	8.1 Stereotype Threat (p. 309)
	8.2 Language Acquisition (p. 294)	
Chapter 9	9.1 Prenatal Development (p. 323)	9.1 Scientific Research with Infants (p. 327)
	9.2 Piaget's Four Stages of Cognitive Development (p. 334)	9.2 Attachment (pp. 341–342)
Chapter 10	10.1 Kohlberg's Moral Development (p. 352)	
	10.2 Erikson's Eight Stages of Psychosocial Development (p. 356)	
Chapter 11	11.1 Sexual Response Cycle (p. 390)	
Chapter 12	12.1 Four Theories of Emotion (p. 426)	12.1 Intrinsic vs. Extrinsic Motivation (p. 431)
		12.2 Polygraph Testing (p. 433)
Chapter 13	13.1 Freud's Five Psychosexual Stages of Development (p. 451)	13.1 Projective Tests (p. 466)
Chapter 14	14.1 Criteria and Continuum for Abnormal Behavior (p. 476)	14.1 Seven Psychological Perspectives on Abnormal Behavior (p. 479)
	14.2 Biopsychosocial Model and Schizophrenia (p. 499)	
Chapter 15	15.1 Ellis's A-B-C-D Approach (p. 515)	15.1 Tracking Faulty Thoughts (p. 517)
	15.2 Overcoming Maladaptive Behaviors (p. 525)	15.2 Drug Treatments for Psychological Disorders (p. 529)
		15.3 Five Most Common Goals of Therapy (p. 532)
Chapter 16	16.1 Groupthink (p. 567)	16.1 What Influences Obedience? (p. 563)
		16.2 Helping (p. 571)

Additional Changes

In addition to the increased focus on *application (Psychology at Work)*, *assessment (APA-linked Learning Objectives,)* and *visual learning* (Process and Concept Diagrams), the new edition of *Psychology in Action* includes other important changes described below. *[Keep in mind that the following list includes only a sample of the most important new changes and additions. A full, detailed list, including material that was deleted from the previous edition, is available on our website (http://www.wiley.com/college/huffman). I also invite all instructors and their students to contact me directly if you have questions about these changes. I sincerely appreciate your choice of Psychology in Action (9e) as your text, and I want to make your teaching and learning experience as smooth and enjoyable as possible.]*

New Research Updates and Increased Focus on Psychological Science

To keep pace with the rapid progress in neuroscience, behavioral genetics, evolutionary psychology, cognitive psychology, sociocultural research, and positive psychology, I have added more than 1000 new references from 2005 to 2009 (see Table 4). We also have several new "Research Highlight" sections, such as "Hurricane Katrina and Local College students" (Chapter 3), "Fuel for Thought" (Chapter 12), "Mental Health and the Family" and "What NOT to Say to the Depressed!" (Chapter 15), and "Understanding Implicit Biases" (Chapter 16).

TABLE 4 SELECT SAMPLES OF PSYCHOLOGICAL SCIENCE
(in addition to the shorter discussions and examples found throughout the text):

Psychological Science Research Methods

Basic versus applied research (p. 16)

The scientific method (pp. 16–18)

Ethical guidelines for research with human and nonhuman animals (pp. 18–20)

Experimental, descriptive, correlational, and biological research (pp. 21–26)

Methods for studying behavioral genetics (pp. 81–84)

Split-brain research (pp. 75–80)

Does stress cause gastric ulcers? (p. 110)

Is there scientific evidence for subliminal perception and ESP? (pp. 132–133 and pp. 161–162)

How scientists study sleep (p. 175)

Discovering classical conditioning (pp. 204–211)

Studying language development in human and nonhuman animals (pp. 295–297)

Memory and the criminal justice system (pp. 268–269)

Explaining differences in IQ (p. 300)

Children who survive despite the odds (p. 363)

Scientific measures of intelligence (pp. 300–303)

Research methods for life span development (pp. 318–319)

Mirror neurons (p. 423)

Scientific measures of personality (pp. 466–468)

Is cybersex harmful? (p. 399)

Sensation seeking (p. 410)

Do nonhuman animals have personality (pp. 446–447)

Suicide and its prevention (pp. 491–492)

Mental health and the family (pp. 534–535)

Understanding implicit biases (pp. 575–576)

Neuroscience

Biological methods of research (pp. 33–36)

How neurotransmitters and hormones affect us (pp. 54–59)

Rewiring, repairing, and transplanting brains and spinal cords (pp. 61–68)

Neuroplasticity, neurogenesis, and stem cell research (p. 61)

Psychoneuroimmunology (p. 102)

Phantom pain and phantom limbs (p. 134)

Biology of stress (pp. 100–101)

Stress and the immune system (p. 102)

Biology of sleep and dreams (p. 170)

Biology and psychoactive drugs (pp. 185–194)

Neuroscience and learning (pp. 229–231)

Neuronal and synaptic changes in memory (p. 263)

Hormonal changes and memory (pp. 263–264)

Where are memories stored? (p. 244–245)

Biology and memory loss (p. 264)

Biological influences on intelligence, including brain size, speed, and efficiency (p. 461)

Brain changes during development (pp. 324–325)

Brain's role in gender differences and sexual behavior (pp. 85–86, 381–382)

Biological processes and motivation (pp. 408–411)

Brain and emotion (p. 422)

Mirror neurons (p. 423)

Biological aspects of personality (pp. 460–462)

Biological contributors to mental disorders (pp. 487–492)

Biomedical psychotherapy (pp. 528–531)

Biology of aggression (pp. 568–669)

Behavioral Genetics

Basic principles and recent research (pp. 80–86)

Methods for studying (p. 83)

Genetic influences on intelligence and the bell curve debate (pp. 306–307)

Nature versus nurture controversy (pp. 6, 293, 317)

Genetics and aging (p. 330)

Attachment and imprinting (pp. 340–341)

Genetic influences on eating disorders (pp. 417)

Genetic contributions to personality (pp. 461–462)

The role of genetics in mental disorders (p. 304)

Genetic contributors to aggression (p. 568)

Evolutionary Psychology

Genetics and evolution (pp. 84–85)

Basic principles such as natural selection (p. 84)

Evolution of sex differences (pp. 85–86)

Evolutionary/circadian theory of sleep (p. 171–172)

Evolution and learning (pp. 230)

Classical conditioning, taste aversions, and biological preparedness (pp. 524–526)

Operant conditioning and instinctive drift (pp. 212–222)

Evolution and language development (pp. 291–297)

Evolution and emotions (pp. 435–436)

Evolution and personality (pp. 444–445)

Evolution and aggression (p. 13)

Evolution and altruism (pp. 570–572)

TABLE 4 SELECT SAMPLES OF PSYCHOLOGICAL SCIENCE (CONTINUED)

Cognitive Psychology	
Bottom-up and top-down processing (p. 129)	Cognitive development over the life span (pp. 333–336)
Stress and cognitive functioning (p. 102)	Cognitive theories of motivation and emotion (p. 412)
Cognitive appraisal and coping (pp. 116–117)	Social-cognitive approaches to personality (pp. 458–460)
Cognitive view of dreams (p. 180)	Cognitive processes in mental disorders (pp. 486, 490, 491, 498, 503–504)
Cognitive-social learning (pp. 223–228)	Cognitive therapy (pp. 514–518)
Memory processes and problems (pp. 244–260, 264–269)	Cognitive processes in attribution, attitudes, prejudice, attraction, etc. (pp. 546–578)
Thinking, creativity, language, and intelligence (pp. 279–313)	

■ New Gender and Cultural Diversity and Critical Thinking/Active Learning Exercises

In addition to integrated cross-cultural examples throughout the text, we also offer extended sections in each chapter identified with this icon ✳. The ninth edition includes new topics, such as "Karoshi"—Can Job Stress Be Fatal? (Chapter 3) and "Unspoken Accents" (Chapter 8).

A great friend and colleague who specializes in critical thinking, Thomas Frangicetto at Northampton Community College, also contributed several critical thinking/ active learning exercises: "Applying Critical Thinking to Psychological Science" (Chapter 1), "The Biology of Critical Thinking" (Chapter 2), "The Development of Suicide Bombers" (Chapter 9), "Morality and Academic Cheating" (Chapter 10), "Hunting for Good Therapy Films" (Chapter 15), and "When and Why Do You Help?" (Chapter 16).

■ Expanded and Innovative Technology

Exciting new online resources can be used by the student who wants to improve skills or enrich his or her study of psychology, or by instructors who teach online courses or as a resource for their traditional lecture courses. These resources include practice quizzes, graded quizzes, demonstrations, simulations, Critical Thinking/ Active Learning exercises, and links to psychology-related topics, Internet activities, and other valuable features and activities. As a user of *Psychology in Action*, you are guaranteed access to John Wiley & Sons student and instructor resource web sites at http://www.wiley.com/college/huffman. Check us out!

Continuing Features

The latest edition of *Psychology in Action* continues its long-standing focus on active learning. As mentioned earlier, I have added several new pedagogical features, which I've integrated with the previous aids into three distinct, but overlapping A's— *Application, Achievement,* and *Assessment* (see Figure 1 on next page).

■ Application

The first A, **Application**, is essential to learning. As most instructors (and students) know, true understanding is much more than a simple memorization of terms and concepts to be retrieved during exams—and then quickly forgotten. To truly master psychology you must question, debate, experiment, and *apply* psychological principles to your everyday life. As you can see in the left-hand side of Figure 1 (on the next page), *Psychology in Action (9e)* includes numerous pedagogical aids dedicated to practical *applications* of psychology. Students often ask, "Why do I need to know this?"

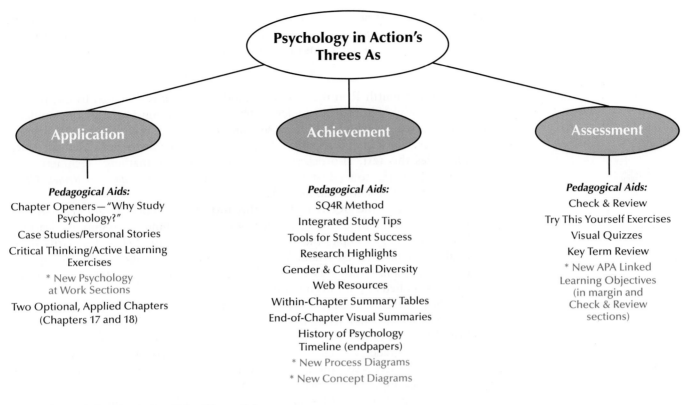

Figure 1 *Psychology in Action (9e)—Three A's!*

and "How does this help me in my everyday life?" Using specific terms and concepts found within that chapter, each of these aids clearly demonstrates the immediate relevance and application of psychology to everyday life.

Achievement

The second A is for **Achievement**. To fully master and understand information, you must employ a form of *metacognition*, which requires watching and evaluating your own thought processes. In other words, you must "think about your thinking and learning." To help insure metacognition, and this type of achievement, *Psychology in Action (9e)* helps students examine and refine their personal studying and learning style. For example, this text incorporates one of the most respected study techniques, the *SQ4R Method (Survey, Question, Read, Recite, Review, and "wRite")*:

Survey and Question
Each chapter begins with four *survey* and *question* techniques: core learning outcomes, a chapter outline, a vignette that introduces essential concepts, and an introductory paragraph that previews content and organization.

Read
Each chapter has been carefully crafted for clarity, conciseness, and student *reading* level.

Recite and Review
To encourage *recitation* and *review*, the text offers a short *Check & Review* section that summarizes the previous material and offers four or five multiple-choice, fill-in, and short

answer questions. An additional aid, the *Visual Summaries* at the end of each chapter, helps visually organize and connect essential chapter concepts. Each chapter also concludes with a review activity for the key terms that is topically organized with page references.

Write

As part of the fourth R in the SQ4R method, this book is designed to incorporate writing as a way of improving student retention. In addition to the writing students do in the survey, question, and review sections, I encourage note taking in the margin of each page, which has been kept as clear as possible. The Instructor's Manual, which accompanies this text, also describes a special "marginal marking" technique that can be easily taught to students. The accompanying *Student Study and Review Guide* discusses the SQ4R method in more detail.

In addition to the SQ4R method, this text also includes *Integrated Study Tips* (which appear throughout the text) offering specific techniques to improve learning and retention. For example, the study tip in Chapter 8 (p. 294) helps clarify overgeneralization and overextension. The study tip on positive and negative symptoms of schizophrenia in Chapter 14 (p. 497) incorporates earlier concepts of positive and negative as applied to reinforcement found in Chapter 6.

To help students become more efficient and successful, this text also includes a special feature called *Tools for Student Success*. Beginning in Chapter 1, there is a special end-of-chapter module that includes tips for active reading, time management, and improving course grades, as well as important resources for college success. In addition, several student success sections identified with a special icon are sprinkled throughout the text. For example, Chapters 6, 7, 8, 10, and 13 all include strategies for improving learning strategies, memory, test performance, and overall achievement.

To further increase metacognition and achievement, the Ninth Edition also offers the following special features:

- *Research Highlights*—Promotes understanding of the intricacies of scientific research.

- *Gender and Cultural Diversity Sections*—Encourages appreciation of similarities and differences between men and women and various cultures.

- *Web Resources*—An icon at the bottom of every right-hand page directs students to all the free resoues offered on the Wiley website. Students have found these self-tests and exercises extremely valuable in their studies.

- *Within Chapter Summary Tables*—To increase student insight and "aha" experiences, I include numerous *Summary Tables*, some containing important illustrations, such as the table on drug actions and neurotransmitters in Chapter 5. The tables that compare classical and operant conditioning in Chapter 6 and contrasting theories of memory in Chapter 7 also serve as important educational tools.

- *End-of-Chapter Visual Summaries*—Each chapter of the text ends with a unique study tool that visually summarizes and organizes the main concepts. This *Visual Summary* is a two-page spread that can be used both as an overview to get the big picture before reading the chapter and as a quick review after completing the reading. Students, faculty, and reviewers are all very excited by this feature. They report finding it "extremely helpful" and "the best study tool ever invented!"

Assessment

The third A, **Assessment**, requires students to demonstrate their learning—for themselves and others. As mentioned earlier, the Ninth Edition now has 15 to 25 specific APA-linked *Learning Objectives* that model the type of questions students should ask and answer as they read the chapter. These objectives are repeated as a reminder and guidepost in the margin next to the section where the topic is discussed.

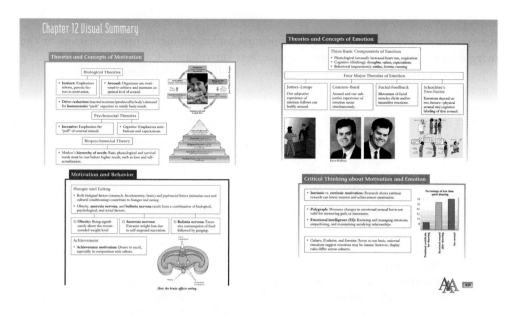

In addition to these learning objectives, numerous *Check and Review* sections are sprinkled throughout each chapter. This pedagogical aid provides a brief review of the preceding material, followed by a self-scoring quiz with four to five multiple-choice, fill-in, or short-answer questions. I've also invented and included two unique pedagogical aids—*Try This Yourself* and *Visual Quizzes*. The widely copied *Try This Yourself* feature provides an opportunity to actively apply your knowledge with brief, hands-on exercises and demonstrations, high-interest and simple-to-do experiments, and self-scoring personal inventories. For example, many people do not know that each of their eyes has a tiny "blind spot" at the center of the retina in which no visual information is received or transmitted. The *Try This Yourself* exercise on page 137 shows how you can demonstrate this for yourself.

The second unique feature is what I call *Visual Quizzes*. After watching many students open their books and turn immediately to the photos and cartoons, I wondered how I could use this natural interest to foster greater mastery and appreciation of important psychological concepts and terms. My answer? Turn these photos and cartoons into a form of assessment. Like the *Try This Yourself* exercises, the *Visual Quizzes* require active participation and provide a form of self-testing and assessment. As a reader, you are asked to answer a specific question about a photo, cartoon, or figure which requires a mastery of key terms or concepts. To assess your understanding, the correct answer is printed upside down directly below the photo or cartoon (see Figure 2).

As a further way to assess your understanding of the chapter material, we offer special end-of-chapter *Key Term Reviews*. Rather than just listing the terms and providing the page references, you are reminded: "To assess your understanding of the Key Terms in Chapter X, write a definition for each term (in your own words), and then compare your definitions with those in the text." This is an important assessment tool and a great way to review before quizzes or exams.

Additional Learning Aids

In addition to the previously mentioned pedagogical aids, *Psychology in Action (9e)* incorporates other learning aids known to increase comprehension and retention:

Key Terms
Important terms are put in **boldface type** and are immediately defined in the text.

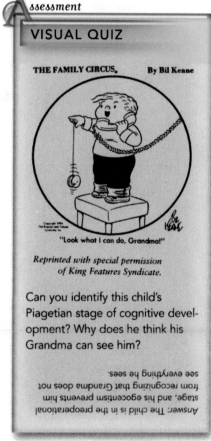

Figure 2 *Sample Visual Quiz* We all love cartoons! Psychology in Action capitalizes on this interest and highlights key concepts with a unique quizzing format to assess student understanding.

Note: Reprinted with special permission of King Features Syndicate.

* Look what I can do, Grandma.

Running Glossary

Key terms also appear with their definitions and a phonetic pronunciation in the margin of each page near where they are first introduced. Calling out and defining key terms in the margin not only increases overall comprehension, but also provides a useful review tool.

End-of-Text Glossary

All key terms are also gathered in a complete, cumulative glossary at the end of the text.

Historical Timeline

A grouping of famous contributors to psychology on the text's back endpapers provides a visual organizer and overview of the history of psychology.

Case Studies/Personal Stories

Students often enjoy and seem to learn more if they have a "personal face or story" to attach to important psychological concepts. To accommodate this need, I have included several case studies/personal stories, such as "A Life Without Fear?" (Chapter 1), "Phineas Gage" (Chapter 2), "Surviving 9/11" (Chapter 3), "Helen Keller's Personal Triumph" (Chapter 4), "The Tragic Tale of John/Joan" (Chapter 11), and "The Emotional Intelligence of Abraham Lincoln" (Chapter 12).

Supplements

Psychology in Action (9e) is accompanied by a host of ancillary materials designed to facilitate the mastery of psychology. Ordering information and policies may be obtained by contacting your local Wiley sales representative.

Instructor Supplements

Videos

In addition to the NEW "YouTube"-like Video Lecture series described earlier, created by Jim Matiya at Florida Gulf Coast University, our Instructor website contains a full assortment of short, lecture-enhancing videos designed for in-class or online courses to introduce new topics, enliven your classroom presentations, and stimulate student discussion. To help integrate these video clips into your course syllabus, we also provide a comprehensive library of teaching resources, study questions, and assignments.

Wiley also has a long-established partnership with the *Films for the Humanities*, which allows us to offer a selection of videos, such as Roger Bingham's series on the brain, to further increase your department's library of video resources. Please contact your Wiley sales representative for further information on specific titles.

PowerPoint Presentations and Image Gallery

Whether you are looking for a complete set of specific, text-related PowerPoints, or new images to enhance your current presentations, we have what you need. On the *Instructor Resource Website*, we provide a full set of dynamic and colorful PowerPoints for each chapter highlighting the major terms and concepts. We also created online electronic files for most figures and tables in the text, which allow you to easily incorporate them into your PowerPoint presentations or to create your own overhead transparencies and handouts.

Wiley Faculty Network

Are you frustrated with complicated instruction manuals and computer trained technicians who can't respond to your specific psychology-related technology needs? The *Wiley Faculty Network* is your answer. These highly trained computer specialists are also college psychology teachers who offer one-on-one, peer-to-peer technical advice and teaching support to adopters of *Psychology in Action*. They guide you through a wide array of online course management tools and discipline-specific software/ learning systems for your classroom. In addition, they help you apply innovative classroom techniques, implement specific software packages, and will tailor the technology experience to the needs of each individual class. Get connected with the *Wiley Faculty Network* at www.wherefacultyconnect.com.

Instructor Resource Web Site

Psychology in Action is accompanied by a comprehensive website with numerous resources to help you prepare for class, enhance your presentations, and assess your students' progress. All of the assets created for the Test Bank and Instructor's Resource Guide can be accessed directly from the website. Multimedia elements created for classroom presentation and student assignments are also available.

Web-Based Learning Modules

Psychology in Action offers a robust suite of multimedia learning resources, designed and developed to enrich classroom presentations and engage visual learners during study sessions. Delivered via the web, the content is organized in the following categories:

- **Animations** developed around key concepts and themes in psychology. Animations go beyond the content presented in the book, providing additional visual examples and descriptive narration.

- **Interactive Exercises** engage learners in activities that reinforce understanding of key concepts and themes. Through simple choice-making experiences, accompanied by immediate feedback, these exercises encourage learners to apply the knowledge gained by reading and viewing animations.

- **News You Can View from ScienCentral** represents a collection of 80 brief video clips, applying psychology concepts and themes to issues in the news today. All these assets are available to adopters via password-protected book companion sites, and through our eGrade Plus e-learning courses.

Test Bank (available in WileyPlus and electronic format—Microsoft Word files)

Dr. Lynda Federoff, Indiana University of Pennsylvania, prepared both the hard copy and electronic versions of the test bank. The *Computerized Test Bank*, a multi-platform CD-ROM, fully supports graphics, printed tests, student answer sheets, and answer keys. The software's advanced features allow you to create an exam to your exact specifications, within an easy-to-use interface. The test generation program has nearly 2000 test items, including approximately 10 essay questions for each chapter (with suggested answers) and a variety of multiple-choice and true/false questions. Each multiple-choice question has been linked to a specific, student learning outcome, coded as "Factual" or "Applied," and the correct answer provided with page references to its source in the text. Also included are several "humorous questions" that can be inserted in tests to reduce test anxiety. In addition, the *Computerized Test Bank* includes questions from the *Student Study and Review Guide* and the main text's *Check and Review* questions, which allows you to easily insert these questions into quizzes and exams as reinforcers for student study and preparation.

Instructor's Resource Guide (available in hard copy and electronic format—Microsoft Word files)

Prepared by Kathleen Weatherford, Trident Technical College, this comprehensive resource includes for each text chapter: an *outline, student learning outcomes, outline/ lecture organizer* (with page references to text), *lecture lead-ins, supplemental lectures* ("hot" topics), *key terms* (with page references), *a chapter summary/lecture organizer, discussion questions, suggested films and videos, activities section, three active learning/ critical thinking exercises*, and a *writing project*. This *Instructor's Resource Guide* also includes numerous *Active Learning Exercises* specifically created for use with any size class.

WebCT

In addition to the website, we also offer a WebCT course management system in the highly customizable WebCT format. Ready for use in your online or traditional class, the course includes: chapter overviews, chapter reviews for each section, assignments, Web links, discussion questions, self-tests, quiz questions and test questions, as well as all standard features of WebCT, such as bulletin board, calendar, e-mail and chat room. A brief Instructor's Manual is available (in electronic format only) to assist you in your use of this course.

Blackboard

Due to its popularity, we also offer a Web course management system in the popular Blackboard format. The course includes chapter overviews, chapter reviews for each section, homework assignments, Web links, discussion questions, self-tests, quiz questions, and test questions, as well as all standard features of Blackboard.

Assignment Questions

Numerous multiple-choice, true/false, and essay questions are available for use in content management systems, for online homework, or for use in classroom response systems.

WileyPlus

Psychology in Action is available with **WileyPlus**, a powerful online tool that provides instructors and students with an integrated suite of teaching and learning resources in one easy-to-use website.

For Instructors:

- **Prepare and Present.** WileyPlus offers a wealth of Wiley-provided resources to help you prepare dynamic class presentations, such as student interactive simulations and engaging text-specific PowerPoint slides.

- **Custom Assignments.** Professors may create, assign, and grade homework or quizzes by using the Wiley-provided question/assignment bank or by writing your own.

- **Automatic Monitoring of Student Progress.** An instructor's grade book allows you to carefully track and analyze individual and overall class results.

- **Flexible Course Administration.** WileyPlus can easily be integrated with another course management system, grade book, or other resources you are using in your class, providing flexibility to build your course, your way.

For Students:

- **Feedback and Support.** WileyPlus provides immediate feedback on student assignments and a wealth of support materials that will help students develop their conceptual understanding of the class material and increase their ability to solve problems.

- **Study and Practice.** This feature links directly to text content, allowing students to immediately review the text while studying and completing homework assignments.

- **Assignment Locator.** This area allows students to store all tasks and assignments for their psychology course in one convenient location, making it easy for them to stay "on task."

- **Student Grade Book.** Grades are automatically recorded, and students can access these results at any time.

(For more information, please view our online demo at www.wileyplus.com. You will find additional information about the features and benefits of WileyPlus, how to request a "test drive" of WileyPlus for *Psychology in Action*, and how to adopt it for class use.)

Student Supplements

WileyPlus Web-Based Modules (see previous Instructor Supplements) Student Companion website
This website provides additional resources that complement and support the textbook. Enhance your understanding of psychology and improve your grade using the following resources:

- *Interactive Key Term Flash Cards* that allow "drill and practice" in mastering key terms and concepts. You may also take self-tests on these vocabulary terms to monitor your progress.

- *Chapter Review Quizzes* provide immediate feedback for true/false, multiple-choice, and short answer questions.

- *Online Guide* offers helpful guidelines about how to use the Web for research, and how to best find your desired information.

- *Annotated Web Links* put useful electronic resources into context.

Student Study and Review Guide

Prepared by Karen Huffman and Richard Hosey, this valuable resource offers you, as a student, an easy way to review the text and ensure that you know the material before your in-class quizzes and exams. For each textbook chapter, the study guide offers numerous tools designed to save you time, while also helping you master the core information. These tools include chapter outlines, core learning outcomes, key terms, key term crossword puzzles, matching exercises, fill-in exercises, an active learning exercise, and two sample tests (20 items each) with text-referenced correct answers. Each chapter of the *Student Study and Review Guide* also includes a copy of the *Visual Summaries* that appear at the end of each chapter in the text. Students in the past have copied these summaries to use during class lecture or text reading, so we've made your studying easier by including them in this study guide.

Acknowledgments

The writing of this text has been a group effort involving the input and support of my family, friends, and colleagues. To each person I offer my sincere thanks. A special note of appreciation goes to Jay Alperson, Bill Barnard, Dan Bellack, Siri Carpenter, Haydn Davis, Katherine Dowdell, Beverly Drinnan, Tom Frangicetto, Nicholas Greco IV, Ann Haney, Peg Hanson, Sandy Harvey, Richard Hosey, Terry Humphrey, Teresa

Jacob, Jim Matiya, Kandis Mutter, Bob Miller, Roger Morrissette, Maria Pak, Judi Phillips, Harriett Prentiss, Fred Rose, Sabine Schoen, Katie Townsend-Merino, Judy Wilson, Kathy Young and Scott Wersiger.

To the reviewers, focus group, and telesession participants who gave their time and constructive criticism, I offer my sincere appreciation. I am deeply indebted to the following individuals and trust that they will recognize their contributions throughout the text.

Student Feedback

To help us verify that our book successfully addressed the needs of today's college students, we asked current introductory psychology students to provide feedback about each chapter of the text. Their reactions confirmed our belief that the book is an effective (and some even said "entertaining") learning tool. We are particularly grateful to the following students who went the extra mile in sharing their honest opinions with us: Erin Decker, *San Diego State University*; Laura Decker, *University of California at Davis*; Amanda Nichols, *Palomar College*; Idalia S. Carrillo, *University of Texas at San Antonio*; Sarah Dedford, *Delta College (Michigan)*; Laural Didham, *Cleveland State University*; Danyce French, *Northampton Community College (Pennsylvania)*; Stephanie Renae Reid, *Purdue University-Calumet*; Betsy Schoenbeck, *University of Missouri at Columbia*; and Sabrina Walkup, *Trident Technical College (South Carolina)*.

Professional Feedback

The following professionals have helped us test and refine the Critical Thinking/Active Learning pedagogy that is found in this book: Thomas Alley, *Clemson University*; David R. Barkmeier, *Northeastern University*; Steven Barnhart, *Rutgers University*; Dan Bellack, *Trident Technical College*; JoAnn Brannock, *Fullerton College*; Michael Caruso, *University of Toledo*; Nicole Judice Campbell, *University of Oklahoma*; Sandy Deabler, *North Harris College*; Diane K. Feibel, *Raymond Walters College*; Richard Griggs, *University of Florida*; Richard Harris, *Kansas State University*; John Haworth, *Florida Community College at Jacksonville*; Guadalupe King, *Milwaukee Area Technical College*; Roger Morrissette, *Palomar College*; Barbara Nash, *Bentley College*; Maureen O'Brien, *Bentley College*; Jan Pascal, *DeVry University*; John Pennachio, *Adirondack Community College*; Gary E. Rolikowki, *SUNY, Geneseo*; Ronnie Rothschild, *Broward Community College*; Ludo Scheffer, *Drexel University*; Kathy Sexton-Radek, *Elmhurst College*; Matthew Sharps, *California State University-Fresno*; Richard Topolski, *Augusta State University*; Katie Townsend-Merino, *Palomar College*; Elizabeth Young, *Bentley College*.

Focus Group and Telesession Participants

Brian Bate, *Cuyahoga Community College*; Hugh Bateman, *Jones Junior College*; Ronald Boykin, *Salisbury State University*; Jack Brennecke, *Mount San Antonio College*; Ethel Canty, *University of Texas-Brownsville*; Joseph Ferrari, *Cazenovia College*; Allan Fingaret, *Rhode Island College*; Richard Fry, *Youngstown State University*; Roger Harnish, *Rochester Institute of Technology*; Richard Harris, *Kansas State University*; Tracy B. Henley, *Mississippi State University*; Roger Hock, *New England College*; Melvyn King, *State University of New York at Cortland*; Jack Kirschenbaum, *Fullerton College*; Cynthia McDaniel, *Northern Kentucky University*; Deborah McDonald, *New Mexico State University*; Henry Morlock, *State University of New York at Plattsburgh*; Kenneth Murdoff, *Lane Community College*; William Overman, *University of North Carolina at Wilmington*; Steve Platt, *Northern Michigan University*; Janet Proctor, *Purdue University*; Dean Schroeder, *Laramie Community College*; Michael Schuller, *Fresno City College*; Alan Schultz, *Prince George Community College*; Peggy Skinner, *South Plains College*; Charles Slem, *California Polytechnic State University-San Luis Obispo*; Eugene Smith, *Western Illinois University*; David Thomas, *Oklahoma State University*; Cynthia Viera, *Phoenix College*; and Matthew Westra, *Longview Community College*.

Preface

Additional Reviewers

L. Joseph Achor, *Baylor University*; M. June Allard, *Worcester State College*; Joyce Allen, *Lakeland College*; Worthon Allen, *Utah State University*; Jeffrey S. Anastasi, *Francis Marion University*; Susan Anderson, *University of South Alabama*; Emir Andrews, *Memorial University of Newfoundland*; Marilyn Andrews, *Hartnell College*; Richard Anglin, *Oklahoma City Community College*; Susan Anzivino, *University of Maine at Farmington*; Peter Bankart, *Wabash College*; Susan Barnett, *Northwestern State University (Louisiana)*; Patricia Barker, *Schenectady County Community College*; Dan Bellack, *College of Charleston*; Daniel Bitran, *College of Holy Cross*; Terry Bluementhal, *Wake Forest University*; Theodore N. Bosack, *Providence College*; Linda Bosmajian, *Hood College*; John Bouseman, *Hillsborough Community College*; John P. Broida, *University of Southern Maine*; Lawrence Burns, *Grand Valley State University*; Bernado J. Carducci, *Indiana University Southeast*; Charles S. Carver, *University of Miami*; Marion Cheney, *Brevard Community College*; Meg Clark, *California State Polytechnic University-Pomona*; Dennis Cogan, *Texas Tech University*; David Cohen, *California State University, Bakersfield*; Anne E. Cook, *University of Massachessetts*; Kathryn Jennings Cooper, *Salt Lake Community College*; Steve S. Cooper, *Glendale Community College*; Amy Cota-McKinley, *The University of Tennessee, Knoxville*; Mark Covey, *University of Idaho*; Robert E. DeLong, *Liberty University*; Linda Scott DeRosier, *Rocky Mountain College*; Grace Dyrud, *Augsburg College*; Thomas Eckle, *Modesto Junior College*; Tami Eggleston, *McKendree College*; James A. Eison, *Southeast Missouri State University*; A. Jeanette Engles, *Southeastern Oklahoma State University*; Eric Fiazi, *Los Angeles City College*; Sandra Fiske, *Onondaga Community College*; Kathleen A. Flannery, *Saint Anselm College*; Pamela Flynn, *Community College of Philadelphia*; William F. Ford, *Bucks City Community College*; Harris Friedman, *Edison Community College*; Paul Fuller, *Muskegon Community College*; Frederick Gault, *Western Michigan University*; Russell G. Geen, *University of Missouri, Columbia*; Joseph Giacobbe, *Adirondack Community College*; Robert Glassman, *Lake Forest College*; Patricia Marks Greenfield, *University of California-Los Angeles*; David A. Griese, *SUNY Farmingdale*; Sam Hagan, *Edison County Community College*; Sylvia Haith, *Forsyth Technical College*; Frederick Halper, *Essex County Community College*; George Hampton, *University of Houston-Downtown*; Joseph Hardy, *Harrisburg Area Community College*; Algea Harrison, *Oakland University*; Mike Hawkins, *Louisiana State University*; Linda Heath, *Loyola University of Chicago*; Sidney Hochman, *Nassau Community College*; Richard D. Honey, *Transylvania University*; John J. Hummel, *Valdosta State University*; Nancy Jackson, *Johnson & Wales University*; Kathryn Jennings, *College of the Redwoods*; Charles Johnston, *William Rainey Harper College*; Dennis Jowaisis, *Oklahoma City Community College*; Seth Kalichman, *University of South Carolina*; Paul Kaplan, *Suffolk County Community College*; Bruno Kappes, *University of Alaska*; Kevin Keating, *Broward Community College*; Guadalupe Vasquez King, *Milwaukee Area Technical College*; Norman E. Kinney, *Southeast Missouri State University*; Richard A. Lambe, *Providence College*; Sherri B. Lantinga, *Dordt College*; Marsha Laswell, *California State Polytechnic University-Pomona*; Elise Lindenmuth, *York College*; Allan A. Lippert, *Manatee Community College*; Thomas Linton, *Coppin State College*; Virginia Otis Locke, *University of Idaho*; Maria Lopez-Trevino, *Mount San Jacinto College*; Tom Marsh, *Pitt Community College*; Edward McCrary III, *El Camino Community College*; David G. McDonald, *University of Missouri, Columbia*; Yancy McDougal, *University of South Carolina-Spartanburg*; Nancy Meck, *University of Kansas Medical Center*; Juan S. Mercado, *McLennan Community College*; Michelle Merwin, *University of Tennessee, Martin*; Mitchell Metzger, *Penn State University*; David Miller, *Daytona Beach Community College*; Michael Miller, *College of St. Scholastica*; Phil Mohan, *University of Idaho*; Ron Mossler, *LA Valley College*; Kathleen Navarre, *Delta College*; John Near, *Elgin Community College*; Steve Neighbors, *Santa Barbara City College*; Leslie Neumann, *Forsyth Technical Community College*; Susan Nolan, *Seton Hall University*; Sarah O'Dowd, *Community College of Rhode Island*; Joseph J. Palladino, *University of Southern Indiana*; Linda Palm, *Edison Community College*; Richard S. Perroto, *Queensborough Community College*; Larry Pervin, *Rutgers University, New Brunswick*; Valerie Pinhas, *Nassau Community College*; Leslee Pollina, *Southeast Missouri State University*; Howard R. Pollio, *University of Tennessee-Knoxville*; Christopher Potter, *Harrisburg Community College*; Derrick Proctor, *Andrews University*; Antonio Puete, *University of North Carolina-Wilmington*; Joan S. Rabin, *Towson State University*; Lillian Range, *University of Southern Mississippi*; George A. Raymond, *Providence College*; Celia Reaves, *Monroe Community College*; Michael J. Reich, *University of Wisconsin-River Falls*; Edward Rinalducci, *University of Central Florida*; Kathleen R. Rogers, *Purdue University North Central*; Leonard S. Romney, *Rockland Community College*; Thomas E. Rudy, *University of Pittsburgh*; Carol D. Ryff, *University of Wisconsin-Madison*; Neil

Salkind, *University of Kansas-Lawrence;* Richard J. Sanders, *University of North Carolina-Wilmington;* Harvey Richard Schiffman, *Rutgers University;* Steve Schneider, *Pima College;* Michael Scozzaro, *State University of New York at Buffalo;* Tizrah Schutzengel, *Bergen Community College;* Lawrence Scott, *Bunker Hill Community College;* Michael B. Sewall, *Mohawk Valley Community College;* Fred Shima, *California State Univer-sity-Dominquez Hills;* Royce Simpson, *Campbellsville University;* Art Skibbe, *Appalachian State University;* Larry Smith, *Daytona Beach Junior College;* Emily G. Soltano, *Worcester State College;* Debra Steckler, *Mary Washington College;* Michael J. Strube, *Washington University;* Kevin Sumrall, *Montgomery College;* Ronald Testa, *Plymouth State College;* Cynthia Viera, *Phoenix College;* John T. Vogel, *Baldwin Wallace College;* Benjamin Wallace, *Cleveland State University;* Mary Wellman, *Rhode Island College;* Paul J. Wellman, *Texas A & M University;* I. Eugene White, *Salisbury State College;* Delos D. Wickens, *Colorado State University-Fort Collins;* Fred Whitford, *Montana State University;* Charles Wiechert, *San Antonio College;* Jeff Walper, *Delaware Technical and Community College;* Bonnie S. Wright, *St. Olaf College;* Brian T. Yates, *American University;* Todd Zakrajsek, *Southern Oregon University;* and Mary Lou Zanich, *Indiana University of Pennsylvania.*

Special Thanks

Psychology in Action (9e) could not exist without a great ancillary author team. I gratefully acknowledge the expertise and immense talents of our Video Lecture Series author/coordinator, Jim Matiya, Test Bank author, Linda Federoff, Instructor's Resource Guide, Kathleen Weatherford, Student Study Guide co-author, Richard Hosey, Clicker Questions, Linda Fayard, Student Web Content, Kay Fernandes, Practice Tests, Rita Rodabaugh, Quick Start, Katherine Dowdell, and all the support staff who contribute to and maintain our Wiley Faculty Network, Web-Based Learning Modules, Instructor and Student website, WebCT, Blackboard, WileyPlus, and so on. Like any cooperative effort, writing a book requires an immense support team, and I am deeply grateful to this remarkable group of people.

Chris Johnson, Executive Editor for the last two editions, is one of those rare individuals who provides the perfect combination of guidance, feedback, and passionate cheerleading. I am eternally grateful for his guidance and support.

Special thanks also go to the superb editorial, sales, marketing, and production teams at John Wiley and Sons. This project benefited from the wisdom and insight of a host of superb people. A special thank-you goes to Sandra Dumas, Jennifer MacMillan, Mary Ann Price, Kevin Murphy, and many others. In addition, I am also deeply indebted to Jeffrey Rucker, Executive Marketing Manager, Danielle Torio, Marketing Manager, Lynn Pearlman, Senior Media Editor, Eileen McKeever, Assistant Editor, Carrie Tupa, Editorial Assistant, and a host of others—all of whom helped enormously in the initial launch and ongoing production. Without them, this book and its wide assortment of ancillaries would not have been possible.

Next, I would like to offer my heartfelt thanks to *GGS Book Services PMG.* Their careful and professional approach was critical to the successful production of this book. Jeanine Furino, the Senior Production Editor, deserves a special note of appreciation. She is gifted at management, while also offering a kindred "obsessive" spirit dedicated to perfection!

I also would like to express my continuing appreciation to my students. They taught me what students want to know and inspired me to write the book. In addition, these individuals deserve special recognition: John Bryant, Sandy Harvey, Michelle Hernandez, Jordan Hertzog-Merino, Richard Hosey, Christine McLean, and Kandis Mutter. They provided careful editing of this text, library research, and a unique sense of what should and should not go into an introduction to psychology text. I sincerely appreciate their contributions. If you have suggestions or comments, please contact me at my e-mail address: Karen Huffman (khuffman@palomar.edu).

Last, and definitely *not least,* I dedicate this book to my beloved husband, Bill Barnard, who has provided countless hours of careful editing, advice, and unwavering support for all nine editions of this book.

Prologue

Critical Thinking/Active Learning

(Co-authored with Thomas Frangicetto along with contributions from his students at Northampton Community College)

> A great many people think they are thinking when they are merely rearranging their prejudices.
>
> WILLIAM JAMES

Critical thinking has many meanings, and some books dedicate entire chapters to defining the term. The term *critical* comes from the Greek word *kritikos*, which means to question, make sense of, and be able to analyze. Thinking is the cognitive activity involved in making sense of the world around us (Dunn & Halonen, 2008). Critical thinking, therefore, can be defined as *thinking about and evaluating thoughts, feelings, and behavior so that we can clarify and improve them* (adapted from Chaffee, 1988, p. 29).

Unlike the common use of "critical," as a negative type of criticism and fault-finding, critical thinking is a positive, life-enhancing process. This text's focus on active learning naturally contributes to the development of critical thinking. Tom and I both believe that an active learner is by definition also a critical thinker. Critical thinking is also a process. As a process—something you do—you can do it better.

How can you develop your critical thinking skills? Each chapter of *Psychology in Action* (and corresponding chapters in the *Student Study and Review Guide* and *Instructor's Resource Guide*) includes a specific *Critical Thinking/Active Learning Exercise* devoted to improving one or more of the components of critical thinking. To learn more about each of these components, study the following ABC's: the *Affective* (emotional), *Behavioral* (action), and *Cognitive* (thinking) components of critical thinking (see Figure 3). You'll find that you already employ some of these skills, while also discovering areas you could strengthen through practice.

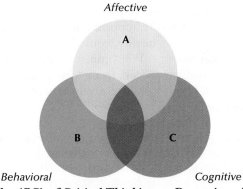

Figure 3 **The ABC's of Critical Thinking ... Dynamic and Interactive**

amana images/Getty Images

▣ Affective Components

The *emotional* foundation that either enables or limits critical thinking.

1. *Valuing truth above self-interest.* Critical thinkers hold themselves and those they agree with to the same intellectual standards to which they hold their opponents. This is one of the most difficult components to employ on a regular basis. We all have a tendency to cater to our own needs (see "self-serving bias," p. 547) and to ignore information that conflicts with our desires. Critical thinkers recognize that, even when it appears otherwise, the "truth" is always in our self-interest.

   Psychic John Edward makes a lot of money off his supposed power to communicate with people's dead relatives ... his "customers" should value the truth over self-interest. This means accepting the truth, even when it is not what they want to believe. We learned from the text that one reason people believe in psychics like Edward is because they "want to"—they willingly "suspend disbelief" and put their self-interest above the truth.

   LISA SHANK

2. *Accepting change.* Critical thinkers remain open to the need for adjustment and adaptation throughout the life cycle. Resisting change is one of the most common characteristics that human beings share. Because critical thinkers fully trust the processes of reasoned inquiry, they are willing to use these skills to examine even their most deeply held values and beliefs, and to modify these beliefs when evidence and experience contradict them.

   As one becomes a parent for the first time, that individual must face the fact that accepting change plays a very big role. A new parent can no longer drop everything and do whatever they please, such as going to a club or bar to socialize or even just going out to dinner. They now have more responsibilities and different priorities.

   JAMES CAVANAUGH

3. *Empathizing.* Critical thinkers appreciate and try to understand others' thoughts, feelings, and behaviors. Noncritical thinkers view everything and everyone in relation to themselves, which is known as "egocentrism." The ability to consider the perspective of another person—to empathize with them—is the most effective antidote to egocentric thinking.

   I think that one thing that everyone should do when they've lost a loved one is empathizing. Empathy is a great way to help each other in a time of need. Many times there is someone who just needs to talk and express his or her feelings. Being able to listen and understand what they are going through, helps make your response to them more effective and helpful.

   CHRISTOPHER FEGLEY

4. *Welcoming divergent views.* Critical thinkers value examining issues from every angle and know that it is especially important to explore and understand positions with which they disagree. This quality would be especially valuable to groups in the process of decision making. Welcoming divergent views would effectively inoculate the decision-making process from "groupthink"—faulty decision making that occurs when a highly cohesive group strives for agreement and avoids inconsistent information.

   Most Americans don't even try to understand the sociocultural influences that affect suicide bombers ... but this issue has influenced me to welcome divergent views and try to understand that people in different cultures have different beliefs. Most Americans believe that martyrs are crazy, while Palestinians believe that martyrdom is something to be idolized.

My decision to believe that martyrdom is a form of self-expression may clash with the views of many Americans but I grew up in a country where I have the right to believe what I want.

SOPHIA BLANCHET

5. ***Tolerating ambiguity.*** Formal education too often trains us to look for one single "right" answer (convergent thinking). Critical thinkers recognize that many questions and issues are frustratingly complex, with multiple and often competing opinions and answers. They recognize and value qualifiers such as "probably," "highly likely," and "not very likely." Creative artists, in particular, must be willing to deal with uncertainty and to consider many possible solutions (divergent thinking).

6. ***Recognizing personal biases.*** This involves using your highest intellectual skills to detect personal biases and self-deceptive reasoning so you can design realistic plans for self-correction. Being an effective critical thinker does not mean the total absence of bias, but rather the willingness to admit, recognize, and correct bias.

Because America is such a huge country of immigrants, many people—including me as a foreigner from Japan—become sensitive about discrimination and prejudice. I have had some difficult times. Once one of my American friends described some Asian people as "foxes," because of the way they look. She was joking, but I was not laughing. I felt very sad because she didn't even notice that I felt disrespected. She definitely needs to begin recognizing personal biases if she wants to have friends from different cultures.

SAEMI SUZUKI

📖 Behavioral Components

The *actions* necessary for critical thinking.

7. ***Delaying judgment until adequate data are available.*** A critical thinker does not make snap judgments. Impulsivity is one of the surest obstacles to good critical thinking. Rash judgments about other people, "impulse" purchases of a new car or home, uninformed choices for political candidates, or "falling in love at first sight" can all be costly mistakes that we regret for many years.

When it comes to debating the Iraqi war people are often misinformed and I believe it is my responsibility to inform them of the truth since I am in the U.S. Army Reserves. At first I did not agree with the war, but as a soldier I am supposed to do what I am told. I have worked with people who were part of the unit responsible for the Abu Ghraib prison scandal, and I have friends who are over in Iraq, some who support the war and others who do not... (but) some people judge the situation before they get all the information they need. This is why I try to convince them to delay judgment until adequate data in available.

LONGSU CHENG

8. ***Employing precise terms.*** Precise terms help critical thinkers identify issues clearly and concretely so that they can be objectively defined and empirically tested. In the everyday realm, when two people argue about an issue, they are often defining it differently without even knowing it. For example, in a romantic relationship two individuals can have very different definitions of words such as "love" and "commitment." Open communication that explores and identifies the precise shades of meaning is an important key to successful relationships.

9. ***Gathering data.*** Collecting up-to-date, relevant information on all sides of an issue is a priority before making decisions. Too often, noncritical thinkers collect only information that confirms their point of view. For example, researchers can unintentionally skew a study in the direction of a desired outcome by only collecting data that will support it.

10. ***Distinguishing fact from opinion.*** Facts are statements that can be proven true. Opinions are statements that express how a person feels about an issue or what someone thinks is true. It is easy to have an uninformed opinion about any subject, but critical thinkers seek out facts before forming their opinions.

I like that this text teaches us to distinguish fact from opinion, for example, to "recognize statements that can be proven true" versus statements that merely reveal the way we feel about something. We must learn to tell the difference between the "truth" and popular opinions we have learned from our parents and society.

WENDY MOREN

11. ***Encouraging critical dialogue.*** Critical thinkers are active questioners who challenge existing facts and opinions and welcome questions in return. Socratic questioning is an important type of critical dialogue in which the questioner deeply probes the meaning, justification, or logical strength of a claim, position, or line of reasoning. In everyday communication, it is often easier to avoid the type of dialogue that would help solve problems and strengthen relationships, but it is an essential part of living an emotionally healthy life.

My mother has been calling me for the last year and I know she is only talking to me because she is dying. It has taken me a long time to warm up to her because of the past…I currently find myself encouraging critical dialogue with her…after many years we have finally started to express our feelings with each other. This dialogue has been most gratifying because now we have learned to become friends and enjoy each other's company. My hope is that when the end comes we will know that despite our faults we really loved each other.

TIM WALKER

12. ***Listening actively.*** Critical thinkers fully engage their thinking skills when listening to another. This may sound like the easiest or most obvious of all components, but it is one of the most difficult. Test this yourself the next time you are in a conversation with someone. After you've talked for a while ask the other person to summarize what you were saying. Or monitor your own listening prowess when the other person is speaking. How often does your attention wander? Critical thinkers "actively" engage in the conversation by "encouraging critical dialogue." They ask questions, nonverbally affirm what they hear, request clarification or elaboration, and so on.

13. ***Modifying judgments in light of new information.*** Critical thinkers are willing to abandon or modify their judgments if later evidence or experience contradicts them. Noncritical thinkers stubbornly stick to their beliefs and often "value self-interest above the truth."

For much of my high school years, I procrastinated on almost every assignment. The process of change has been a slow one…however, I procrastinate less now that I am in college. In addition to prioritizing my work, and finishing the more important assignments sooner…I have "modified my judgment in light of new information." I know now that these assignments are primarily for my own benefit and that a certain level of self-motivation is required in order to succeed in life. I also realized that I am paying for my education so I may as well get as much out of it as I can."

TOM SHIMER

14. ***Applying knowledge to new situations.*** When critical thinkers master a new skill or experience an insight, they transfer this information to new contexts. Noncritical thinkers can often provide correct answers, repeat definitions, and carry out calculations, yet be unable to transfer their knowledge to new situations because of a basic lack of understanding or an inability to "synthesize" seemingly unrelated content.

Cognitive Components

The *thought* processes actually involved in critical thinking.

Thomas Barwick/Riser/Getty Images

15. ***Thinking independently.*** Critical thinking is independent thinking. Critical thinkers do not passively accept the beliefs of others and are not easily manipulated. They maintain a healthy amount of skepticism, especially about unusual or remarkable claims or reports. They are also able to differentiate being "skeptical" from just being stubborn and unyielding. They are, for example, willing to "welcome divergent views" and (1) weigh the substance of those views and (2) adjust their own thinking if warranted ("accept change").

16. ***Defining problems accurately.*** To the extent possible, a critical thinker identifies the issues in clear and concrete terms in order to prevent confusion and lay the foundation for gathering relevant information. At first glance, this component appears to contradict "tolerating ambiguity," but that is not so. Critical thinkers are able to tolerate ambiguity until it is possible to "define problems accurately."

17. ***Analyzing data for value and content.*** By carefully evaluating the nature of evidence and the credibility of the source, critical thinkers recognize illegitimate appeals to emotion, unsupported assumptions, and faulty logic. This enables them to discount sources of information that lack a record of honesty, contradict themselves on key questions, have a vested interest in selling a product or idea, or hold a viewpoint that is only partially accurate (a "half truth").

While it may be true that the majority of black people score lower than white people on IQ tests, it is important to ask: Why? To learn the answer it is indispensable to analyze data for value and content. To do so you must carefully identify the credibility of sources and evaluate all information from a multicultural perspective, for example, we must consider the daily battle against prejudice in our society and how minority students feel isolated from the rest of the white majority.... So the environment has a lot of influence and the effect can be lower self-esteem which can result in lower scores.

ARANZAZU GARCIA

18. ***Employing a variety of thinking processes in problem solving.*** Among these thinking processes are (a) *inductive logic*—reasoning that moves from the specific to the general; (b) *deductive logic*—reasoning that moves from the general to the specific; (c) *dialogical thinking*—thinking that involves an extended verbal exchange between differing points of view or frames of reference; and (d) *dialectical thinking*—thinking that tests the strengths and weaknesses of opposing points of view.

19. ***Synthesizing.*** Critical thinkers recognize that comprehension and understanding result from combining various elements into meaningful patterns. Blending the affective, cognitive, and behavioral components of critical thinking into a deeper understanding of your world involves synthesizing. For example, feeling depressed because "nobody likes you" might lead to asking other people for feedback (welcoming divergent views). Their views might help you realize that you do have good qualities that people like and that it isn't as bad as you thought (resisting overgeneralization), which could inspire you to try new behaviors (applying knowledge to new situations).

20. ***Resisting overgeneralization.*** Overgeneralization is the temptation to apply a fact or an experience to situations that are only superficially similar—for example, having a bad experience with and forming a negative judgment of a person from a particular ethnic heritage and then applying that same judgment to all members of the same ethnic group. The failure to resist overgeneralization is often at the core of prejudice.

21. ***Employing metacognition.*** Metacognition, also known as reflective or recursive thinking, involves reviewing and analyzing your own mental processes—thinking about your own thinking. Critical thinkers who are motivated to trace the origin of their beliefs put their thinking under intense scrutiny and can often be heard saying things like "What was I thinking?" or "I don't know why I believe that, I'll have to think about it."

Psychology in Action

NINTH EDITION

1

Introduction to Psychology and Its Research Methods

Welcome to the exciting world of *Psychology in Action*. As the cover of this text and its name imply, psychology is a *living*, dynamic field that affects every part of our lives—our relationships at home, college, and work, as well as politics, television, movies, newspapers, radio, and the Internet.

I did not understand or fully appreciate the personal applications and incredible range of psychology when I began my first introductory course. I thought all psychologists were therapists, and I expected to study mostly abnormal behavior. Today, as a college psychology professor, I find that most of my students share many of these same expectations—and misconceptions. Although psychologists do study and treat abnormal behavior, we also study sleep, dreaming, stress, health, drugs, personality, sexuality, motivation, emotion, learning, memory, childhood, aging, death, love, conformity, intelligence, creativity, and so much more.

My goal as your textbook author is to serve as your personal "tour guide" through all these fascinating topics. And my goal, "Dear Reader," is to take you on a fast-paced journey through all the major fields of psychology, along with exciting forays into little-known or previously uncharted territories filled with invaluable discoveries into yourself and the world around you. Be sure to pack your bags with an ample supply of curiosity, enthusiasm, and an open-minded spirit of adventure. That's all the supplies you'll need for what promises to be the most exciting and unforgettable trip of your academic lifetime!

Fondly,

Karen R. Huffman

Karen Huffman

▶ **Introducing Psychology**

What Is Psychology?
Psychology's Goals

 PSYCHOLOGY AT WORK
    Careers in the Field

▶ **Origins of Psychology**

Early Psychological Science
Modern Perspectives

▶ **The Science of Psychology**

The Scientific Method
Ethical Guidelines

▶ **Research Methods**

Experimental Research

RESEARCH HIGHLIGHT
    Love at First Fright?
CRITICAL THINKING/ACTIVE LEARNING
    Applying Critical Thinking to
    Psychological Science
Descriptive Research

CASE STUDY/PERSONAL STORY
    A Life Without Fear?
Correlational Research
Biological Research

 PSYCHOLOGY AT WORK
    Becoming a Better Consumer of
    Scientific Research

 GENDER & CULTURAL DIVERSITY
    Are There Cultural Universals?

▶ **Tools For Student Success**

Active Reading   Strategies for Grade
Time Management   Improvement
                              Additional Resources
                              A Final Word

💡 *Study Tip*

Chapter Outline
*Each chapter begins with an outline of all major topics
and subtopics. This pattern of headings is repeated
within the chapter itself. Outlines provide important
mental scaffolds to help you organize and master
information as you read.*

Application

WHY STUDY PSYCHOLOGY?

Chapter 1 (and all other chapters in this text) will:

▶ *Increase your understanding of yourself and others.* The Greek philosopher Socrates admonished long ago, "Know thyself." Psychology is about you, me, and all the peoples of the world. Studying it will greatly contribute to your understanding (and appreciation) of yourself and others.

▶ *Better your social relations.* Thanks to years of scientific research and application, psychology has developed numerous guidelines and techniques that will improve your relationships with friends, family, and coworkers.

David Hanover/Stone/Getty Images

▶ *Enhance your career.* Whether or not you decide to work directly in the field, psychology can enrich your professional life. Because all jobs require working with others, an improvement in your "people skills" can lead to direct career "profits."

▶ *Broaden your general education.* Why are you in college? Is becoming a more educated person one of your goals? Psychology is an integral part of today's political, social, and economic world, and understanding its principles and concepts is essential to becoming well informed.

▶ *Improve your critical thinking.* Would you like to become a more independent thinker and better decision maker and problem solver? These are only a few of the many critical thinking skills that are enhanced through a study of psychology.

Introducing Psychology

Achievement

Objective 1.1: *Define psychology.*

Study Tip

Learning Objectives
Each section of every chapter contains numbered learning objectives, which you should attempt to answer as you read that section. These objectives are later repeated and summarized in the "Check & Review" sections.

Psychology *Scientific study of behavior and mental processes*

Critical Thinking *Process of objectively evaluating, comparing, analyzing, and synthesizing information*

What Is Psychology? Scientific Methods and Scientific Thinking

The term *psychology* derives from the roots *psyche*, meaning "mind," and *logos*, meaning "word." Early psychologists focused primarily on the study of mind and mental life. By the 1920s, however, many psychologists believed the mind was not a suitable subject for scientific study. They initiated a movement to restrict psychology to observable behavior alone. Today we recognize the importance of both areas. Accordingly, **psychology** is now defined as the *scientific study of behavior and mental processes*. Note the three key concepts in this definition—*scientific*, *behavior*, and *mental processes* (Figure 1.1).

As part of this emphasis on science, psychologists place particular value on empirical evidence and **critical thinking**, the *process of objectively evaluating, comparing, analyzing,* and *synthesizing information*. The study of psychology will greatly improve your critical thinking abilities. If you would like to exercise your critical thinking skills and test how much you already know about psychology, complete the following "Try This Yourself" exercise.

When completing this same exercise in class, my students often miss several questions because they rely solely on common sense, personal experience, authority figures, or media reports of "pop psychology." Mistakes are also made when we confuse scientific psychology with *pseudopsychologies*, which give the appearance of science but are actually false. (*Pseudo* means "false.") Pseudopsychologies include:

*A*pplication

Testing Your Knowledge of Psychology

Answer True or False to the following:

___1. In general, we only use about 10 percent of our brain.

___2. Most brain activity stops during sleep.

___3. Advertisers and politicians often use subliminal persuasion to influence our behavior.

___4. Punishment is the most effective way to permanently change behavior.

___5. Eyewitness testimony is often unreliable.

___6. Polygraph ("lie detector") tests can accurately and reliably reveal whether or not a person is lying.

___7. People who threaten suicide seldom follow through with it.

___8. People with schizophrenia have multiple personalities.

___9. Similarity is one of the best predictors of long-term relationships.

___10. In an emergency, as the number of bystanders increases, your chance of getting help decreases.

Answers: 1. False (Chapter 2). 2. False (Chapter 5). 3. False (Chapter 4). 4. False (Chapter 6). 5. True (Chapter 7). 6. False (Chapter 12). 7. False (Chapter 14). 8. False (Chapter 14). 9. True (Chapter 16). 10. True (Chapter 16).

- *Psychics*—individuals who are supposedly sensitive to nonphysical or supernatural forces.

- *Mediums*—individuals who serve as a channel of communication between the earthly world and a world of spirits.

- *Palmistry*—reading a person's future or character from the lines on the palms.

- *Psychometry*—determining facts about an object by merely handling it.

- *Psychokinesis*—moving objects by purely mental means.

- *Astrology*—the study of how the positions of the stars and planets supposedly influence people's personalities and affairs.

For some, horoscopes or palmists are simple entertainment. Unfortunately, there are also true believers seeking guidance and comfort who waste large sums of money on charlatans purporting to know the future. Broken-hearted families have also lost valuable time and emotional energy on psychics claiming they could locate their lost children. As you can see, distinguishing scientific psychology from pseudopsychology is vitally important.

 Study Tip

Try This Yourself
These brief activities are both fun and educational. Active learning greatly increases comprehension and retention.

Gary D. Landsman/©Corbis

Scientific is a key part of the definition of psychology. Psychological science collects and evaluates information using systematic observations and measurements.

Barry Austin Photography/Getty Images

Behavior is anything we do that can be directly observed and recorded—talking, sleeping, text messaging, etc.

©AP/Wide World Photos

Mental processes are our private, internal experiences—thoughts, perceptions, feelings, memories—that cannot be observed directly.

 Study Tip

Website Icons
Note the web site icon and address at the bottom of every right-hand page. It includes free online tutorial quizzes, practice tests, active learning exercises, Internet links to psychology-related topics, and other valuable features that will be updated regularly. Visit this site often. It will help ensure success in this course.

Figure 1.1 *Defining psychology*

YOU WILL BE TOLD WHAT YOU WANT TO HEAR. IT WILL BE SO GENERALIZED THAT IT COULD FIT ANYONE. YOU WILL PAY A RIDICULOUS AMOUNT OF MONEY FOR IT...

THE MOST ACCURATE FORTUNE EVER TOLD

Cartoon by WILEY "Non Sequitur" © 1993 Distributed by Universal Press Syndicate. All rights reserved.

Henry Groskinsky/Time Life Pictures/Getty Images

"The Amazing Randi" The magician James Randi has dedicated his life to educating the public about fraudulent pseudopsychologists. Along with the prestigious MacArthur Foundation, Randi has offered $1 million to "anyone who proves a genuine psychic power under proper observing conditions" (About James Randi, 2002; Randi, 1997). After many years, the money has never been collected. If you would like more information, visit Randi's website at www.randi.org.

Nature–Nurture Controversy
Ongoing dispute over the relative contributions of nature (heredity) and nurture (environment)

 Study Tip

Key Terms and Running Glossary
All key terms and concepts are bold-faced in the text, and then defined again in the margin. This boldfacing and running glossary provide a helpful reminder of the most important terms. Key terms from all chapters also appear in a cumulative glossary at the end of this text.

Psychology's Goals: Describe, Explain, Predict, and Change

In contrast to pseudopsychologies, which rely on testimonials and opinions, psychology bases its findings on rigorous, scientific methods. When conducting their research, psychologists have four basic goals: to *describe*, *explain*, *predict*, and *change* behavior and mental processes.

1. **Description.**   Description tells "what" occurred. In some studies, psychologists attempt to *describe*, or name and classify, particular behaviors by making careful scientific observations. Description is usually the first step in understanding behavior. For example, if someone says, "Boys are more aggressive than girls," what does that mean? The speaker's definition of aggression may differ from yours. Science requires specificity.

2. **Explanation.**   An explanation tells "why" a behavior or mental process occurred. In other words, *explaining* a behavior or mental process depends on discovering and understanding its causes. One of the most enduring debates in science has been the **nature–nurture controversy**. Are we controlled by biological and genetic factors (the nature side)? Or by environment and learning (the nurture side)? As you will see throughout the text, psychology (like all sciences) generally avoids "either-or" positions and focuses instead on *interactions*. Today, almost all scientists agree that most psychological, and even physical traits, reflect an interaction between nature and nurture. For example, research indicates that there are numerous interacting causes or explanations for aggression, including culture, learning, genes, brain damage, and high levels of testosterone (e.g., Juntii, Coats, & Shah, 2008; Kelly et al., 2008; Temcheff et al., 2008).

3. **Prediction.**   Psychologists generally begin with description and explanation (answering the "whats" and "whys"). Then they move on to the higher-level goal of *prediction*, identifying the conditions under which a future behavior or mental process is likely to occur. For instance, knowing that alcohol leads to increased aggression (Tremblay, Graham, & Wells, 2008), we can predict that more fights will erupt in places where alcohol is consumed than in those where alcohol isn't consumed.

4. **Change.**   For some people, having "change" as a goal of psychology brings to mind evil politicians or cult leaders "brainwashing" unknowing victims. However, to psychologists, *change* means applying psychological knowledge to prevent unwanted outcomes or bring about desired goals. In almost all cases, change as a goal of psychology is positive. Psychologists help people improve their work environment,

Karen Huntt/©Corbis

age fotostock/SUPERSTOCK

Is this nature, nurture, or both?

stop addictive behaviors, become less depressed, improve their family relationships, and so on. Furthermore, as you know from personal experience, it is very difficult (if not impossible) to change someone against her or his will. (*Joke question:* Do you know how many psychologists it takes to change a light bulb? *Answer:* None. The light bulb has to want to change itself!)

Study Tip

Check & Review
Each major topic concludes with an interim summary and four to six self-test questions that allow you to stop and check your understanding of the important concepts just discussed. Answers appear in Appendix B at the back of the text.

Assessment

CHECK & REVIEW

Introducing Psychology

Objective 1.1: *Define psychology.*

Psychology is the scientific study of behavior and mental processes. It emphasizes the empirical approach and the value of **critical thinking**. Psychology is not the same as common sense, "pop psychology," or pseudopsychology.

Objective 1.2: *What are psychology's four main goals?*

The goals of psychology are to *describe, explain, predict,* and *change* behavior and mental processes.

Questions

1. The process of objectively evaluating, comparing, analyzing, and synthesizing information is known as _____.

   a. psychology
   b. critical thinking
   c. behaviorism
   d. the scientific method

2. _____ rely on nonscientific or deliberately fraudulent methods to explain personality.
   a. Pseudopsychologies
   b. Sociologists
   c. Astronomers
   d. Counselors

3. Psychological science often questions to what extent we are controlled by biological and genetic factors or by the environment and learning. This ongoing debate is known as the _____.
   a. nature-nurture controversy
   b. mind versus body dualism
   c. interactionist position
   d. biopsychosocial model

4. You dread going to the grocery store because you got lost there when you were

a child. This illustrates psychology's goal of _____ behavior.
   a. describing
   b. explaining
   c. predicting
   d. changing

5. The goal of _____ is to tell "what" occurred, whereas the goal of _____ is to tell "why."
   a. health psychologists; biological psychologists
   b. description; explanation
   c. psychologists; psychiatrists
   d. pseudopsychologists; clinical psychologists

Check your answers in Appendix B.

Click & Review
for additional assessment options:
wiley.com/college/huffman

PSYCHOLOGY AT WORK

Careers in the Field

Knowing what psychology is, and understanding its four major goals, would you consider a career in the field? Many students think of psychologists only as therapists. However, many psychologists work as researchers, teachers, and consultants in academic, business, industry, and government settings (Table 1.1). Many psychologists also work in a combination of settings. Your college psychology instructor may be an experimental psychologist who teaches, conducts research, and works as a paid business or government consultant—all at the same time. Similarly, a clinical psychologist might be a full-time therapist, while also teaching college courses.

   What is the difference between a psychiatrist and a clinical or counseling psychologist? The joke answer would be "about $100 an hour." The serious answer is that psychiatrists are medical doctors. They have M.D. degrees with a specialization in psychiatry and a license to prescribe medications and drugs. In contrast, most counseling and clinical psychologists have advanced degrees in human behavior and methods of therapy (e.g., Ph.D. or Psy.D.). Many clinical and counseling psychologists also work as a team with psychiatrists.

Achievement

Objective 1.3: *Summarisze psychology's major career specialties.*

Study Tip

Psychology At Work
Throughout the text, you will find many ways to use and apply your increasing knowledge of psychology. Some sections are related to work, whereas others involve relationships and everyday life.

Study Tip

Narrative Questions
These boldfaced narrative questions are part of the SQ4R method described in the Preface. They help focus your reading and increase your comprehension.

TABLE 1.1 SAMPLE CAREERS AND SPECIALTIES IN PSYCHOLOGY

©Chris Casaburi. Courtesy Candace Pert

Biopsychology/neuroscience. *Candace Pert (and others) identified the body's natural painkillers called endorphins.*

Mark Richards/Photo Edit

Clinical and counseling psychology. *For most people, this is the role they commonly associate with psychology.*

Ed Kashi

Experimental psychology. *Louis Herman's research with dolphins has provided important insight into human and nonhuman behavior and mental processes.*

Courtesy Dan Belleck

Psychologists often wear many hats. *Dan Bellack teaches full-time at Trident Technical College, serves as Department Chair, and also works with faculty on teaching improvement.*

Biopsychology/ neuroscience	Investigates the relationship between biology, behavior, and mental processes, including how physical and chemical processes affect the structure and function of the brain and nervous system.
Clinical psychology	Specializes in the evaluation, diagnosis, and treatment of mental and behavioral disorders.
Cognitive psychology	Examines "higher" mental processes, including thought, memory, intelligence, creativity, and language.
Counseling psychology	Overlaps with clinical psychology, but practitioners tend to work with less seriously disturbed individuals and conduct more career and vocational assessment.
Development psychology	Studies the course of human growth and development from conception until death.
Educational and school psychology	Studies the process of education and works to promote the intellectual, social, and emotional development of children in the school environment.
Experimental psychology	Examines processes such as learning, conditioning, motivation, emotion, sensation, and perception in humans and other animals. (The term *experimental psychologist* is somewhat misleading because psychologists working in almost all areas of specialization also conduct research.)
Forensic psychology	Applies principles of psychology to the legal system, including jury selection, psychological profiling, and so on.
Gender and/or cultural psychology	Investigates how men and women and different cultures differ from one another and how they are similar.
Health psychology	Studies how biological, psychological, and social factors affect health and illness.
Industrial/organizational psychology	Applies the principles of psychology to the workplace, including personnel selection and evaluation, leadership, job satisfaction, employee motivation, and group processes within the organization.
Social psychology	Investigates the role of social forces and interpersonal behavior, including aggression, prejudice, love, helping, conformity, and attitudes.

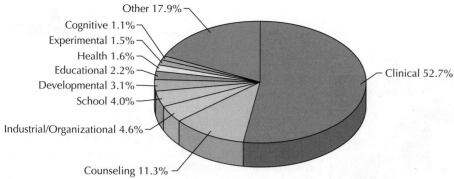

Figure 1.2 *Percentage of psychology degrees awarded by subfield*   Note that this is a small sampling of the numerous specialty areas in psychology. The percentages shown here are based on data from the American Psychological Association (APA), the largest professional psychological organization. The other major organization is the American Psychological Society (APS). Source: American Psychological Association, 2004.

To get an idea of the relative number of psychologists working in different fields of psychology, see Figure 1.2. If you are considering a career in psychology, this text will also present a rich variety of career options that may interest you. For example, Chapter 2 looks at the world of neuroscience. After studying it, you may decide you would like a career as a neuroscientist/biopsychologist. Chapter 3 explores health psychology and the work of health psychologists. And Chapters 4 and 15 examine problems in mental health and how therapists treat them. If you find a particular area of interest, ask your instructor and campus career counselors for further career guidance. It's also a good idea to check out the American Psychological Association's (APA) home page (http://www.apa.org/) and the American Psychological Society's (APS) website (http://www.psychologicalscience. org). Psychology is always looking "for a few good men"—and women.

Origins of Psychology

People have always been interested in human nature. Most of the great historical scholars, from Socrates and Aristotle to Bacon and Descartes, asked questions that we would today call psychological. What motivates people? How do we think and problem solve? Where do our emotions and reason reside? Do our emotions control us, or are they something we can control? Interest in such topics remained largely among philosophers, theologians, and writers for several thousand years. However, in the late nineteenth century, psychological science began to emerge as a separate scientific discipline.

Throughout its short history, psychologists have adopted several perspectives on the "appropriate" topics for psychological research and the "proper" research methods. As a student, you may find these multiple (and sometimes contradictory) approaches frustrating and confusing. However, diversity and debate have always been the lifeblood of science and scientific progress.

Early Psychological Science: A Brief History

Wihelm Wundt (Vill-helm Voont), generally acknowledged as the "father of psychology," established the first psychological laboratory in Leipzig, Germany in 1879. He also helped train the first scientific psychologists, and wrote one of psychology's most important books, *Principles* of *Physiological Psychology*.

Wundt and his followers were interested primarily in studying mental life and conscious experience—how we form sensations, images, and feelings. One of their earliest research methods was termed *introspection*, monitoring and reporting on the contents of consciousness (Goodwin, 2009). If you were one of Wundt's participants trained in introspection, you might be presented with the sound of a clicking metronome. You

Achievement

Objective 1.4: *Contrast structuralism versus functionalism, and list the seven major perspectives that guide modern psychology.*

How would you describe this object?

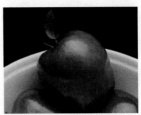

Photodisc Green/Getty

If you were a participant in Titchener's laboratory, you would describe not what it is, but your subjective experience—the intensity and clarity of color, texture, shape, and smell. Structuralists called this research method *introspection*. The fact that your reported experience might differ from others, or that Titchener had no way to check the accuracy of your report, created significant problems for the structuralists.

would be told to focus solely on the clicks and report only your immediate reactions to them—your basic sensations and feelings.

Structuralism

Edward Titchener brought Wundt's ideas to the United States and established a psychological laboratory at Cornell University. Titchener was a kind of mental chemist who sought to identify the basic building blocks, or *structures*, of the mind. Titchener's approach later came to be known as *structuralism*, which dealt with the *structure* of mental life. Just as the elements hydrogen and oxygen combine to form the compound water, Wundt believed the "elements" of conscious experience combined to form the "compounds" of the mind. Structuralists sought to identify the elements of thought through introspection and then to determine how these elements combined to form the whole of experience.

Unfortunately, it soon became clear that structuralism was doomed to failure. When different observers introspected and then disagreed on their experiences, no scientific way existed to settle the dispute. Furthermore, introspection could not be used to study nonhuman animals, children, or complex topics like mental disorders or personality. Though short-lived, structuralism established a model for studying mental processes scientifically.

Functionalism

Structuralism's intellectual successor, *functionalism*, studied how the mind *functions* to adapt human and nonhuman animals to their environment. Earlier structuralists might have studied "anger" by asking people to introspect and report on their individual experiences. In comparison, functionalists would have asked, "Why do we have the emotion of anger? What function does it serve? How does it help us adapt to our environment?" As you can see, functionalism was strongly influenced by Darwin's *theory of evolution* and his emphasis on *natural selection* (Segerstrale, 2000).

William James, an American scholar, was a leading force in the functionalist school. He also broadened psychology to include nonhuman animal behavior, various biological processes, and behaviors. In addition, his book *Principles of Psychology* (1890) became the leading psychology text—despite its length of more than 1400 pages!

Like structuralism, functionalism eventually declined. But it expanded the scope of psychology to include research on emotions and observable behaviors, initiated the psychological testing movement, and changed the course of modern education and industry.

Psychoanalytic/Psychodynamic Perspective

During the late 1800s and early 1900s, while functionalism was prominent in the United States, the **psychoanalytic/psychodynamic perspective** was forming in Europe. Its founder, Austrian physician Sigmund Freud, believed that many psychological problems are caused by conflicts between "acceptable" behavior and "unacceptable"

Bettmann/Corbis Images

William James (1842–1910). *James was a leading force in the functionalist school of psychology, which stressed the adaptive and practical functions of human behavior.*

Psychoanalytic/Psychodynamic Perspective *Focuses on unconscious processes and unresolved past conflicts*

unconscious sexual or aggressive motives (Chapter 13). To deal with these unconscious conflicts, Freud developed a form of psychotherapy, or "talk therapy," called *psychoanalysis*.

Freud's nonscientific approach and emphasis on sexual and aggressive impulses have long been controversial, and today there are few strictly Freudian psychoanalysts left. But the broad features of his theory remain in the modern *psychodynamic* approach. Although psychodynamic psychologists are making increasing use of experimental methods, their primary method is the analysis of case studies. Their primary goal is to interpret complex meanings hypothesized to underlie people's actions.

Keystone/The Image Works

Sigmund Freud (1856–1939)
Freud founded the psychoanalytic perspective, an influential theory of personality, and a type of therapy known as psychoanalysis.

Behavioral Perspective

In the early 1900s, another major school of thought appeared that dramatically shaped the course of psychology. Unlike earlier approaches, the **behavioral perspective** emphasizes objective, observable environmental influences on overt behavior.

John B. Watson (1913), the acknowledged founder of behaviorism, rejected the practice of introspection and the influence of unconscious forces. He believed these practices and topics were unscientific and too obscure to be studied empirically. Watson adopted Russian physiologist Ivan Pavlov's concept of conditioning to explain how behavior results from observable *stimuli* (in the environment) and observable *responses* (behavioral actions). In Pavlov's famous experiment teaching a dog to salivate in response to the sound of a bell, the bell is the stimulus and the salivation is the response.

Because nonhuman animals are ideal subjects for studying objective, overt behaviors, the majority of early behavior research was done with them or with techniques developed through nonhuman research. Using dogs, rats, pigeons, and other nonhuman animals, behaviorists such as John Watson in the early 1900s and, more recently B. F. Skinner, focused primarily on learning and how behaviors are acquired. They formulated a number of basic principles about learning which are explored in Chapter 6.

It sounds like behaviorists are interested only in nonhuman animals. Aren't any of them interested in humans? Yes, behaviorists are interested in people. One of the most well-known behaviorists, B. F. Skinner, was convinced that we could (and should) use behavior approaches to actually "shape" human behavior. This shaping could thereby change the present negative course (as he perceived it) of humankind. He did considerable writing and lecturing to convince others of this position. Behaviorists have been most successful in treating people with overt (observable, behavioral) problems, such as phobias (irrational fears) and alcoholism (Chapters 14 and 15) (Watson & Tharp, 2007).

Behavioral Perspective *Emphasizes objective, observable environmental influences on overt behavior*

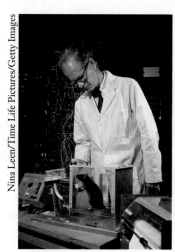

Nina Leen/Time Life Pictures/Getty Images

B. F. Skinner (1904–1990)
Skinner was a prominent figure in behaviorism and one of the most influential psychologists of the twentieth century.

Humanistic Perspective

In sharp contrast to psychoanalysts and behaviorists who saw human behavior as shaped and determined by external causes beyond personal control, humanists emphasized our unique ability to make voluntary choices about our own behavior and life. The **humanistic perspective** stresses *free will*, self-actualization, and human nature as naturally positive and growth seeking. According to Carl Rogers and Abraham Maslow, two central figures in the development of humanism, all individuals naturally strive to grow, develop, and move toward *self-actualization* (a state of self-fulfillment in which we realize our highest potential).

Many psychologists have criticized the humanistic approach for its lack of rigorous experimental methods and consider it more of a philosophy of life than a major

Humanistic Perspective
Emphasizes free will, self-actualization, and human nature as naturally positive and growth-seeking

wiley.com/
college/
huffman

Positive Psychology *Scientific study of optimal human functioning, emphasizing positive emotions, positive traits, and positive institutions*

Brand X/SUPERSTOCK

Cognitive Perspective *Focuses on thinking, perceiving, and information processing*

 Study Tip

Throughout this text, you will see citations (authors' names and publication dates) at the end of many sentences, such as (Goodwin, 2009). Most instructors rarely expect you to memorize the names and dates in parentheses. They are provided as a starting point for research projects, for additional information on a topic of interest, and to double-check the research sources. Complete publication information (title of article or chapter, author, journal name or book title, date, and page numbers) is provided in the References section at the back of this book.

Neuroscience/Biopsychology Perspective *Emphasizes genetics and other biological processes in the brain and other parts of the nervous system*

Evolutionary Perspective *Focuses on natural selection, adaptation, and evolution of behavior and mental processes*

perspective in scientific psychology. However, humanism, like psychoanalysis and behaviorism, has had an important influence on personality theories and psychotherapy (see Chapters 13 and 15).

In addition, the humanistic approach provides the foundation for a contemporary research specialty known as **positive psychology**—the scientific study of optimal human functioning (Diener, 2008; Patterson & Joseph, 2007; Seligman, 2003, 2007; Taylor & Sherman, 2008). For many years, psychology *understandably* focused on negative states, such as aggression, depression, and prejudice. In recent years, however, leaders in the positive psychology movement, such as Ed Diener, Martin Seligman, and Shelly Taylor, have pushed for a broader study of human experiences, with an emphasis on: (1) *positive emotions* (like hope, love, and happiness), (2) *positive traits* (such as altruism, courage, and compassion), and (3) *positive institutions* that help promote better lives (such as improved schools and healthier families) (Seligman, 2003). Thanks to its scientific methodology and broader focus on optimal functioning, *positive psychology* has provided a wealth of new research found throughout this text.

Cognitive Perspective

One of the most influential modern approaches, the **cognitive perspective**, recalls psychology's earliest days, in that it emphasizes thinking, perceiving, and information processing. (Sternberg, 2009).

Modern-day cognitive psychologists, however, study how we gather, encode, and store information from our environment using a vast array of mental processes. These processes include thinking, perception, memory, language, and problem solving. If you were listening to a friend describe her whitewater rafting trip, a cognitive psychologist would be interested in how you decipher the meaning of her words, how you form mental images of the turbulent water, how you incorporate your impressions of her experience into your previous concepts and experience of rafting, and so on.

Many cognitive psychologists use an *information-processing* approach, likening the mind to a computer that sequentially takes in information, processes it, and then produces a response.

Neuroscience/Biopsychology Perspective

During the last few decades, scientists have explored the role of biological factors in almost every area of psychology, including sensation, perception, learning, memory, language, sexuality, and abnormal behavior. This exploration has given rise to an increasingly important trend in psychology, known as the **neuroscience/biopsychology perspective**.

As you will see in the upcoming discussion of psychological research in this chapter, neuroscientists/biopsychologists have developed sophisticated "tools" and technologies to conduct their research. They use these tools to study the structure and function of individual nerve cells, the roles of various parts of the brain, and how genetics and other biological processes contribute to our behavior and mental processes. We will return to the neuroscience/biopsychology perspective throughout Chapter 2 and other chapters.

Evolutionary Perspective

The **evolutionary perspective** derives from a focus on natural selection, adaptation, and evolution of behavior and mental processes (Buss, 2008; Workman & Reader, 2008). Its proponents argue that natural selection favors behaviors that enhance an organism's reproductive success. That is, human and nonhuman animals exhibiting behaviors that contribute to survival will pass them on through their genes to the next generation.

Consider aggression. Behaviorists would argue that we learn aggressiveness at an early age. "Hitting another child stops him or her from taking your toys." Cognitive psychologists would emphasize how thoughts contribute to aggression. "He intended to hurt me. Therefore, I should hit him back!" Neuroscience/biopsychologists might say aggressiveness results primarily from neurotransmitters, hormones, and structures in the brain. In comparison, evolutionary psychologists would argue that human and nonhuman animals behave aggressively because aggression conveys a survival or reproductive advantage. They believe aggression evolved over many generations because it successfully met the adaptive pressures faced by our ancestors.

Sociocultural Perspective

The **sociocultural perspective** emphasizes social interactions and cultural determinants of behavior and mental processes. Sociocultural psychologists have shown how factors such as ethnicity, religion, occupation, and socio-economic class all have an enormous psychological impact (Laungani, 2007; Shiraev & Levy, 2008).

Unless someone points it out, however, few of us recognize the importance of these factors. As Segall and his colleagues (1990) suggest, when you go to school, you probably walk into a classroom at the same time on the same days, sit in the same chair, and either listen to a trained teacher or participate in an activity designed and directed by that teacher. This is because it is the schooling system of your social world and culture. In another society or culture, such as a remote region of East Africa, you and your friends might gather informally around a respected elder, some of you sitting and others standing, all of you listening to the elder tell stories of the history of the tribe.

As they say, "a fish doesn't know it is in water," and, similarly, most of us are unaware of the social and cultural forces that shape our lives. This is one of many reasons why we include such heavy coverage of sociocultural psychology throughout this text.

Women and Minorities

During the late 1800s and early 1900s, most colleges and universities provided little opportunity for women and minorities, as either students or faculty. Despite these early limitations, both women and minorities have made important contributions to psychology.

One of the first women to be recognized in the field was Mary Calkins. Calkins performed valuable research on memory and in 1905 served as the first female president of the American Psychological Association (APA). Her achievements are particularly noteworthy, considering the significant discrimination against women in those times. Even after completing all the requirements for a Ph.D. at Harvard, and being described by William James as his brightest student, the university refused to grant the degree to a woman. The first woman to receive a Ph.D. in psychology was Margaret Floy Washburn (in 1894), who wrote several influential books and served as the second female president of APA.

Francis Cecil Sumner, without benefit of a formal high school education, became the first African American to earn a Ph.D. in psychology from Clark University in 1920. He also translated over 3000 articles from German, French, and Spanish and founded one of the country's leading psychology departments at Howard University. In 1971, one of Sumner's students, Kenneth B. Clark, became the first African American to be elected APA president. Clark's research with his wife, Mamie Clark, documented the harmful effects of prejudice and directly influenced the Supreme Court's ultimate ruling against racial segregation in schools.

Sumner and Clark, Calkins and Washburn, along with other important minorities and women, made significant and lasting contributions to the developing science of psychology. In recent years, minorities and women are being actively encouraged to pursue graduate degrees in psychology. But as you can see in Figure 1.3, white (non-Hispanic) people still make up the majority of new doctorate recipients in psychology.

Psychology in a global economy Technological advances allow instant communication for people who not long ago were isolated from events in the rest of the world. How do you think these changes affect these men from the Enaotai Island in West Papua New Guinea?

Sociocultural Perspective
Emphasizes social interaction and cultural determinants of behavior and mental processes

Kenneth Clark (1914–2005) Kenneth Clark was the first African American president of the American Psychological Association. He and his wife, Mamie, also conducted research on prejudice that was cited in 1964 by the U.S. Supreme Court.

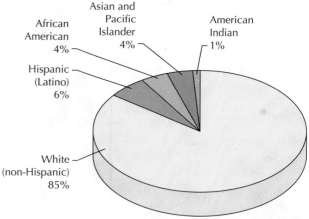

Figure 1.3 *Ethnicities of doctorate recipients in psychology*

wiley.com/ college/ huffman

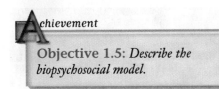

Objective 1.5: *Describe the biopsychosocial model.*

Modern Perspectives: Seven Approaches and One Unifying Theme

Early schools like structuralism and functionalism have almost entirely disappeared or have been blended into newer, broader perspectives. Contemporary psychology reflects seven major perspectives: *psychoanalytic/psychodynamic, behavioral, humanistic, cognitive, neuroscience/biopsychology, evolutionary,* and *sociocultural* (Table 1.2).

In discussing the seven modern perspectives in psychology, I have presented them separately and made distinctions between their philosophies and practices. However, most psychologists recognize the value of each orientation, and agree that no one view has all the answers.

One of the most widely accepted, and unifying, themes of modern psychology is the **biopsychosocial model**. This approach views *biological* processes (e.g., genetics, brain functions, neurotransmitters, and evolution), *psychological* factors (e.g., learning, thinking, emotion, personality, and motivation), and *social forces* (e.g., family, culture, ethnicity, social class, and politics) as interrelated influences (Figure 1.4).

Biopsychosocial Model *Unifying theme of modern psychology that incorporates biological, psychological, and social processes*

TABLE1.2 PSYCHOLOGY'S SEVEN MODERN PERSPECTIVES

Perspectives		Major Emphases
Psychoanalytic/psychody-namic		Unconscious processes and unresolved past conflicts
Behavioral		Objective, observable environmental influences on overt behavior
Humanistic		Free will, self-actualization, and human nature as naturally positive and growth-seeking
Cognitive		Thinking, perceiving, problem solving, memory, language, and information processing
Neuroscience/biopsychology		Genetics and biological processes in the brain and other parts of the nervous system
Evolutionary		Natural selection, adaptation, and evolution of behavior and mental processes
Sociocultural		Social interaction and the cultural determinants of behavior and mental processes

Why do we need multiple and competing perspectives?

What do you see in the drawing to the right? Do you see two profiles facing each other or a white vase? Your ability to see both figures is similar to a psychologist's ability to study behavior and mental processes from a number of different perspectives.

Kaiser-Porcelain Limited

This new, integrative model proposes that all three forces *affect* and *are affected by* one another. They are inseparable. For example, feelings of depression are often influenced by genetics and neurotransmitters (biology). They are also affected by our learned responses and patterns of thinking (psychology) and by our socioeconomic status and cultural views of emotion (social). In the coming chapters, I frequently refer to one or more of the seven major perspectives shown in Table 1.2. However, the common theme of modern psychology, and this text, is an integrative, *biopsychosocial* approach.

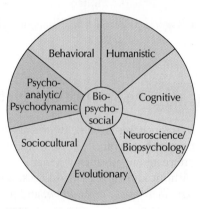

Figure 1.4 ***The biopsychosocial model combines and interacts with the seven major perspectives***

 Assessment STOP

CHECK & REVIEW

Origins of Psychology

Objective 1.3: *Summarize psychology's major career specialties.*

Many avenues exist for those who want to pursue a career in psychology. These include biopsychology/neuroscience, experimental, cognitive, developmental, clinical, counseling, industrial/organizational, educational/school, social, health, and so on.

Objective 1.4: *Contrast structuralism versus functionalism, and list the seven major perspectives that guide modern psychology.*

Among the early contributors to psychology, the *structuralists* sought to identify elements of consciousness and how those elements formed the structure of the mind. They relied primarily on the method of introspection. *Functionalists* studied how

mental processes help the individual adapt to the environment.

The **psychoanalytic/psychodynamic, behavioral, humanistic, cognitive, neuroscience/biopsychology, evolutionary,** and **sociocultural** perspectives are the key approaches in contemporary psychology.

Objective 1.5: *Describe the biopsychosocial model.*

The **biopsychosocial model** draws from all seven modern perspectives and also incorporates biological, psychological, and social processes.

Questions

1. The _____ school of psychology originated the method of introspection to examine thoughts and feelings.

2. _____ investigated the function of mental processes in adapting to the environment.
3. Why are Freud's theories so controversial?
4. Which of the following terms do not belong together? (a) structuralism, observable behavior; (b) behaviorism, stimulus-response; (c) psychoanalytic, unconscious conflict; (d) humanism, free will.
5. Define the biopsychosocial model.

Check your answers in Appendix B

 Click & Review
for additional assessment options:
wiley.com/college/huffman

Research has shown that some nonhuman animals, such as newly hatched ducks or geese, follow and become attached to (or imprinted on) the first large moving object they see or hear. Konrad Lorenz, an influential figure in early psychology, hatched these geese in an incubator. Because he was the first large moving object they saw at birth, they now closely follow him everywhere—as if he were their mother. When Lorenz was asleep on the ground with his mouth open, a goose even tried to feed him a live worm.

Using the information in Table 1.2, p. 14, can you identify which perspective of psychology would most likely study and explain these behaviors?

Nina Leen/Time Life Pictures/Getty Images

Answer: Evolutionary

The Science of Psychology

Achievement

Objective 1.6: *What is the difference between basic and applied research, and what are the six basic steps of the scientific method?*

Basic Research *Research conducted to advance scientific knowledge*

Applied Research *Research designed to solve practical problems*

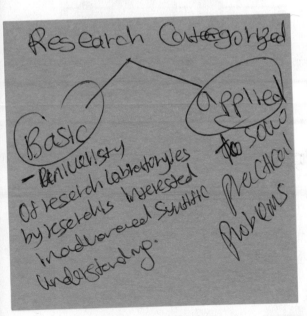

Meta-Analysis *Statistical procedure for combining and analyzing data from many studies*

In science, research strategies are generally categorized as either *basic* or *applied*. **Basic research** is typically conducted in universities or research laboratories by researchers interested in advancing general scientific understanding—knowledge for its own sake without known real-world uses. Basic research meets the first three goals of psychology (*description*, *explanation*, and *prediction*). In contrast, **applied research** is generally conducted outside the laboratory. And it meets the fourth goal of psychology—to *change* existing real-world problems. Discoveries linking aggression to testosterone, genes, learning, and other factors came primarily from basic research. In contrast, applied research has designed programs for conflict resolution and counseling for perpetrators and victims of violence. It also has generated important safety and design improvements in automobiles, airplanes, stovetop burner arrangements, and even cell phones and computer key pads (Figure 1.5).

Basic and applied research also frequently interact—one leading to or building on the other. For example, after basic research documented a strong relationship between alcohol consumption and increased aggression, applied research led some sports stadium operators to limit the sale of alcohol during the final quarter of football games and the last two innings of baseball games.

Now that you understand the distinction between basic and applied research, we can explore two core topics in psychological research: the scientific method and research ethics.

The Scientific Method: A Way of Discovering

Like scientists in any other scientific field, psychologists follow strict, standardized scientific procedures so that others can understand, interpret, and repeat or test their findings. Most scientific investigations generally involve six basic steps (Process Diagram 1.1). As you can see in this diagram, the *scientific method* is cyclical and cumulative, and scientific progress comes from repeatedly challenging and revising existing theories and building new ones. If numerous scientists, using different participants in varied settings, can repeat, or *replicate*, a study's findings, there is much greater scientific confidence in the findings. However, if the findings cannot be replicated, researchers look for explanations and conduct further studies. When different studies report contradictory findings, researchers often average or combine the results of all such studies and reach conclusions about the overall weight of the evidence. This popular statistical technique is known as **meta-analysis**.

Process Diagram 1.1
The Scientific Method

Study Tip

This ongoing, circular nature of theory building often frustrates students. In most chapters you will encounter numerous and sometimes conflicting hypotheses and theories. You will be tempted to ask, "Which theory is right?" But remember that theories are never absolute. Like most aspects of behavior, the "correct" answer is usually an interaction. In most cases, multiple theories contribute to the full understanding of complex concepts.

Cycle continues

Cycle begins

Step 1
Literature review
The scientist conducts a *literature review,* reading what has been published in major professional, scientific journals on her subject of interest.

Step 2
Testable hypothesis, operationally defined
The scientist makes a *testable* **hypothesis,** or a specific prediction about how one factor, or *variable,* is related to another. To be scientifically testable, the variables must be **operationally defined**—that is, stated precisely and in measurable terms.

Step 6
Theory
After one or more studies on a topic, researchers generally advance a **theory** to explain their results. This new theory then leads to new (possibly different) hypotheses and new methods of inquiry.

Step 3
Research design
The scientist chooses the best *research design* to test the hypothesis and collect the data. She might choose naturalistic observation, case studies, surveys, experiments, or other methods.

Step 5
Peer-reviewed scientific journal
The scientist writes up the study and its results and submits it to a *peer-reviewed scientific journal.* (Peer-reviewed journals ask other scientists to critically evaluate submitted material.) On the basis of these peer reviews, the study may then be accepted for publication.

Step 4
Statistical analysis
The scientist performs *statistical analyses* on the raw data to determine whether the findings support or reject her hypothesis. This allows her to organize, summarize, and interpret numerical data.

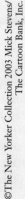

"So! How is everybody today?"

©The New Yorker Collection 2003 Mick Stevens/ The Cartoon Bank, Inc.

Study Tip

Statistics play a vital role in the scientific method. If you are interested in learning more about statistical analysis, see Appendix A at the back of this book.

Hypothesis *Specific, testable prediction about how one factor, or variable, is related to another*

Operational Definition *Precise description of how the variables in a study will be observed and measured (For example, drug abuse might be operationally defined as "the number of missed work days due to excessive use of an addictive substance.")*

Theory *Interrelated set of concepts that explain a body of data*

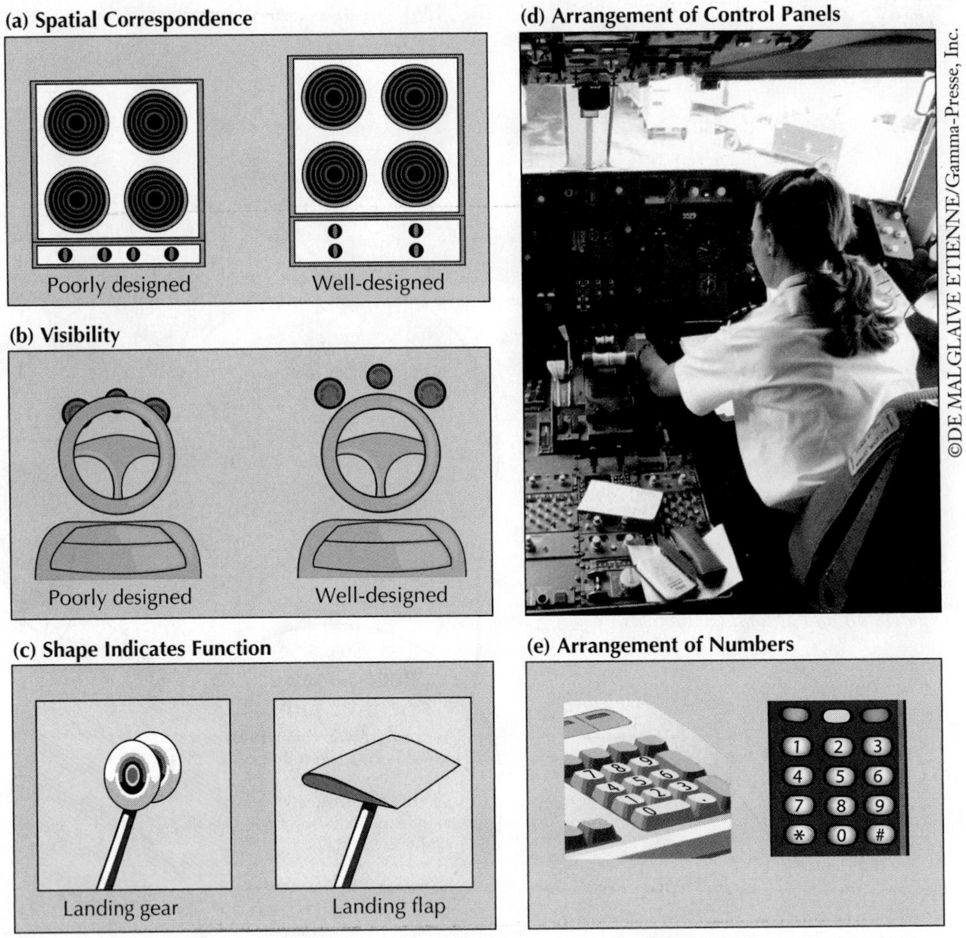

(a) Spatial Correspondence

Poorly designed   Well-designed

(b) Visibility

Poorly designed   Well-designed

(c) Shape Indicates Function

Landing gear   Landing flap

(d) Arrangement of Control Panels

©DE MALGLAIVE ETIENNE/Gamma-Presse, Inc.

(e) Arrangement of Numbers

Figure 1.5 **Applied research in psychology**   Note how psychological research has helped design safer and more reliable appliances, machinery, and instrument controls. For example: (a) Controls for stovetops should be arranged in a pattern that corresponds to the placement of the burners. (b) Automobile gauges for fuel, temperature, and speed should be easily visible to the driver. (c) Airplane controls and knobs are easier and safer to use if their shape corresponds to their function. (d) Airplane control panels should be arranged so pilots can safely operate and quickly respond to any emergency. (e) Research shows that the top-down arrangement of numbers on a cell phone are more efficient than the bottom-up arrangement on a computer's key board (*Psychology Matters*, 2006).

Ethical Guidelines: Protecting the Rights of Others

Objective 1.7: *What are the key ethical issues in psychological research and therapy?*

The two largest professional organizations of psychologists, the American Psychological Society (APS) and the American Psychological Association (APA), both recognize the importance of maintaining high ethical standards in research, therapy, and all other areas of professional psychology. The preamble to the APA's publication *Ethical Principles of Psychologists and Code of Conduct* (2002) admonishes psychologists to respect and promote civil and human rights. It also requires them to maintain their competence and to preserve the dignity and best interests of their clients, colleagues, students, research participants, and society. In this section, we will explore three important areas of ethical concern: human participants, nonhuman animal rights, and clients in therapy.

Respecting the Rights of Human Participants
The APA has developed rigorous guidelines regulating research with human participants, including:

Informed Consent *Participant's agreement to take part in a study after being told what to expect*

• *Informed consent*. One of the first research principles is obtaining an **informed consent** from all participants before initiating an experiment. Participants should be aware of the nature of the study and significant factors that might influence their willingness to participate. This includes all physical risks, discomfort, or unpleasant emotional experiences.

- *Voluntary participation.* Participants should be told they are free to decline to participate or to withdraw from the research at any time.

- *Restricted use of deception and debriefing.* If participants know the true purpose behind some studies, they will almost certainly not respond naturally. Therefore, the APA acknowledges the need for some *deception* in certain research areas. But when it is used, important guidelines and restrictions apply, including debriefing participants at the end of the experiment. **Debriefing** involves explaining the reasons for conducting the research and clearing up any misconceptions or concerns on the part of the participant.

- *Confidentiality.* All information acquired about people during a study must be kept private and not published in such a way that individual rights to privacy are compromised.

- *Alternative activities.* If research participation is a course requirement or an opportunity for extra credit for college students, all students must be given the choice of an alternative activity of equal value.

Debriefing *Informing participants after the research about the purpose of the study, the nature of the anticipated results, and any deceptions used*

Respecting the Rights of Nonhuman Animal Participants

Research in psychology usually involves human participants. Only about 7 to 8 percent of research is done on nonhuman animals, and 90 percent of that is done with rats and mice (American Psychological Association, 1984).

There are important reasons for using nonhuman animals in psychological research. For example, the field of *comparative psychology* is dedicated to the study of behavior of different species. In other cases, nonhuman animals are used because researchers need to study participants continuously over months or years (longer than people are willing to participate). Occasionally, they also want to control aspects of life that people will not let them control and that would be unethical to control (such as who mates with whom or the effects of serious food restrictions). The relative simplicity of some nonhuman animals' nervous systems also provides important advantages for research.

Most psychologists recognize the tremendous scientific contributions that laboratory nonhuman animals have made—and continue to make. Without nonhuman animals in *medical research*, how would we test new drugs, surgical procedures, and methods for relieving pain? *Psychological research* with nonhuman animals has led to significant advances in virtually every area of psychology, including the brain and nervous system, health and stress, sensation and perception, sleep, learning, memory, stress, emotion, and so on.

Nonhuman animal research also has produced significant gains for animals themselves. Effective training techniques and natural environments have been created for pets and wild animals in captivity. Also, successful breeding techniques have been developed for endangered species. Despite the advantages, using nonhuman animals in psychological research remains controversial (Guidelines for Ethical Conduct, 2008).

While debate continues over ethical questions surrounding such research, psychologists take great care in the handling of nonhuman research animals. They also actively search for new and better ways to protect them (Appiah, 2008; Guidelines for Ethical Conduct, 2008). In all institutions where nonhuman animal research is conducted, animal care committees are established to ensure proper treatment of research animals, to review projects, and to set guidelines that are in accordance with the APA standards for the care and treatment of nonhuman (and human) research animals.

Joe Raedle/Newsmakers/Getty Images

Is nonhuman animal research ethical? *Opinions are sharply divided on this question, but when research is carefully conducted within ethical guidelines, the research can yield significant benefits for both human and nonhuman animals.*

Respecting the Rights of Psychotherapy Clients

Like psychological scientists, therapists must maintain the highest of ethical standards. They also must uphold their clients' trust. All personal information and therapy records must be kept confidential, with records being available only to authorized persons and with the client's permission. However, the public's right to safety ethically outweighs the client's right to privacy. Therapists are legally required to break confidentiality if a client threatens violence to him- or herself or to others. This breaking of confidentiality also applies if a client is suspected of abusing a child or an elderly person, and in other limited situations. In general, however, a counselor's primary obligation is to protect client disclosures (Sue & Sue, 2008).

Any member of the APA who disregards the association's principles for the ethical treatment of humans or nonhuman research participants or therapy clients may be censured or expelled from the organization. Clinicians who violate the ethical guidelines for working with clients risk severe sanctions and can permanently lose their licenses to practice. In addition, both researchers and clinicians are held professionally and legally responsible by their institutions as well as by local and state agencies.

A Final Note on Ethical Issues

What about ethics and beginning psychology students? Once friends and acquaintances know you're taking a course in psychology, they may ask you to interpret their dreams, help them discipline their children, or even ask your opinion on whether they should end their relationships. Although you will learn a great deal about psychological functioning in this text and in your psychology class, take care that you do not overestimate your expertise. Remember that the theories and findings of psychological science are circular and cumulative—and continually being revised.

David L. Cole (1982), a recipient of the APA Distinguished Teaching in Psychology Award, reminds us that "Undergraduate psychology can, and I believe should, seek to liberate the student from ignorance, but also the arrogance of believing we know more about ourselves and others than we really do."

At the same time, psychological findings and ideas developed through careful research and study can make important contributions to our lives. As Albert Einstein once said, "One thing I have learned in a long life: that all our science, measured against reality, is primitive and childlike—and yet, it is the most precious thing we have."

Assessment

STOP

CHECK & REVIEW

The Science of Psychology

Objective 1.6: *What is the difference between basic and applied research, and what are the six basic steps of the scientific method?*

Basic research studies theoretical issues. **Applied research** seeks to solve specific problems. The scientific method consists of six carefully planned steps: (1) reviewing the literature, (2) formulating a testable **hypothesis**, operationally defined, (3) choosing a research design, (4) statistical analysis, (5) peer-reviewed scientific journal, and (6) building further **theory**.

Objective 1.7: *What are the key ethical issues in psychological research and therapy?*

Psychologists must maintain high standards in their relations with human and nonhuman research participants, as well as in their therapeutic relationships with clients. The APA has published specific guidelines detailing these ethical standards.

Questions

1. If you conducted a study on areas of the brain most affected by drinking alcohol, it would be called _____ research. (a) unethical; (b) experimental; (c) basic; (d) applied

2. A cardinal rule of a scientific _____ is that it must make testable predictions about observable behavior. (a) hypothesis; (b) theory; (c) meta-analysis; (d) experiment

3. A precise definition of how the variables in a study will be observed and measured is called _____. (a) a meta-analysis; (b) a theory; (c) an independent observation; (d) an operational definition

4. A participant's agreement to take part in a study after being told what to expect is known as _____. (a) participant bias; (b) placebo effect; (c) informed consent; (d) debriefing

5. Briefly explain the importance of informed consent, deception, and debriefing in scientific research.

6. Identify and label the six steps in the scientific method.

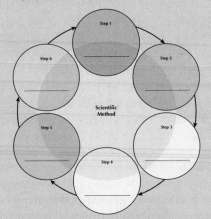

Six major methods of psychological research

Check your answers in Appendix B.

 Click & Review
for additional assessment options:
wiley.com/college/huffman

Research Methods

What is research, but a blind date with knowledge.

WILLIAM HENRY

Now that you have a good basic understanding of the scientific method, we can examine four major types of psychological research—*experimental, descriptive, correlational,* and *biological*. As Table 1.3 shows, all four types of research have advantages and disadvantages, and most psychologists use several methods to study a single problem. In fact, when multiple methods are used and lead to similar conclusions, scientists have an especially strong foundation for concluding that one variable does affect another in a particular way.

Experimental Research: A Search for Cause and Effect

The most powerful research method is the **experiment**, in which an experimenter manipulates and controls the chosen variables to determine cause and effect. Only through an experiment can researchers isolate a single factor and examine the effect of that factor alone on a particular behavior (Goodwin, 2009). For example, in studying for an upcoming test, you probably use several methods—reading lecture notes, rereading highlighted sections of your textbook, and repeating key terms with their

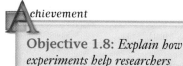

Achievement

Objective 1.8: *Explain how experiments help researchers determine cause and effect.*

Experiment *Carefully controlled scientific procedure that involves manipulation of variables to determine cause and effect*

TABLE 1.3 COMPARING THE FOUR MAJOR RESEARCH METHODS

	Method	Purpose	Advantages	Disadvantages
	Experimental (manipulation and control of variables)	Identify cause and effect (meets psychology's goal of *explanation*)	Allows researchers precise control over variables and to identify cause and effect	Ethical concerns, practical limitations, artificiality of lab conditions, uncontrolled variables may confound results, researcher and participant biases
	Descriptive (naturalistic observation, surveys, case studies)	Observe, collect, and record data (meets psychology's goal of *description*)	Minimizes artificiality, easier to collect data, allows description of behavior and mental processes as they occur	Little or no control over variables, researcher and participant biases, cannot explain cause and effect
	Correlational (statistical analyses of relationships between variables)	Identify relationships and assess how well one variable predicts another (meets psychology's goal of *prediction*)	Helps clarify relationships between variables that cannot be examined by other methods and allows prediction	Researchers cannot identify cause and effect
	Biological (studies of the brain and other parts of the nervous system)	Identify contributing biological factors (meets one or more of psychology's goals)	Shares many or all of the advantages of experimental, descriptive, and correlational research	Shares many or all of the disadvantages of experimental, description, and correlational research

Note that the four methods are not mutually exclusive. Researchers may use two or more methods to explore the same topic.

wiley.com/
college/
huffman

definitions. Using multiple methods, however, makes it impossible to determine which study methods are effective or ineffective. The only way to discover which method is most effective is to isolate each one in an *experiment*. In fact, several experiments have been conducted to determine effective learning and study techniques (Son & Metcalfe, 2000). If you are interested in the results of this research or want to develop better study habits, you can jump ahead now and read the upcoming "Tools for Student Success" at the end of this chapter. There are also additional special "Study Tips" sections throughout the text identified with this icon 🔍 *Study Tip*

Key Features of an Experiment

An experiment has several key components: *experimental* versus *control groups* and *independent* versus *dependent variables* (see Process Diagram 1.2).

Experimental Safeguards

Every experiment is designed to answer essentially the same question: Does the IV *cause* the predicted change in the DV? To answer this question, the experimenter must establish several safeguards. In addition to the previously mentioned controls within the experiment itself (e.g., operational definitions, a control group, and holding extraneous variables constant), a good scientific experiment also protects against potential sources of error from both the researcher and the participant. As we discuss these potential problems (and their possible solutions), you may want to refer several times to the summary in Figure 1.6.

Researcher Problems and Solutions Researchers must guard against two particular problems—*experimenter bias* and *ethnocentrism*.

- **Experimenter bias**. Experimenters, like everyone else, have their own personal beliefs and expectations. The danger in research, however, is that these personal biases may produce flawed results.

Consider the case of Clever Hans, the famous mathematical "wonder horse" (Rosenthal, 1965). When asked to multiply 6 times 8, minus 42, Hans would tap his hoof 6 times. Or if asked to divide 48 by 12, add 6, and take away 6, he would tap 4 times. Even when Hans's owner was out of the room and others asked the question, he was still able to answer correctly. How did he do it? Researchers eventually discovered that all questioners naturally lowered their heads to look at Hans's hoof at the end of their question. And Hans had learned that this was a signal to start tapping. When the correct answer was approaching, the questioners also naturally looked up, which in turn signaled Hans to stop.

When conducting research, this tendency of experimenters to influence the results in the expected direction is called **experimenter bias**. Just as Hans's questioners unintentionally signaled the correct answer by lowering or raising their heads, an experimenter might breathe a sigh of relief when a participant gives a response that supports the researcher's hypothesis.

You can see how experimenter bias might destroy the validity of the participant's response. But how can we prevent it? One technique is to set up objective methods for collecting and recording data, such as audiotape recordings

Achievement

Objective 1.9: *Compare and contrast experimental versus control groups and independent versus dependent variables.*

Achievement

Objective 1.10: *How do researchers guard against experimenter bias and ethnocentrism?*

Experimenter Bias *Occurs when researcher influences research results in the expected direction*

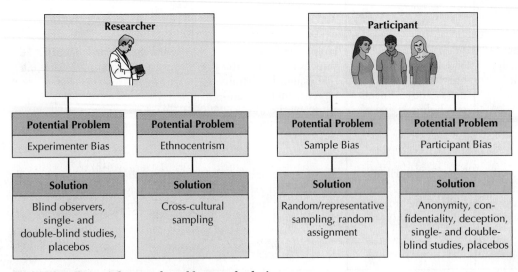

Figure 1.6 *Potential research problems and solutions*

Process Diagram 1.2
Key Features of an Experiment

Imagine yourself as a psychologist interested in determining how watching violence on television affects aggressiveness in viewers. After reviewing the literature and developing your hypothesis (Steps 1 and 2 of the scientific method), you decide to use an experiment for your research design (Step 3). (See Process Diagram 1.1 for a full review of the scientific method.)

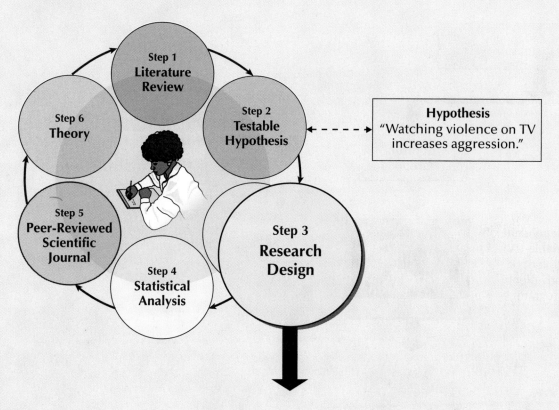

Hypothesis
"Watching violence on TV increases aggression."

Experimental Versus Control Groups

Using a very simple experiment, you begin by *randomly* assigning research participants to one of two groups: the **experimental group**, who watch a prearranged number of violent television programs, and the **control group**, who watch the same amount of television, except the programs they watch are nonviolent. (Having at least two groups allows the performance of one group to be compared with that of another.)

Independent and Dependent Variables

Now you arrange which factors, or *variables*, you will control, and those you will measure and examine for possible changes. The factor that is *manipulated*, or controlled, by the experimenter is called the **independent variable (IV)**. In contrast, the factor that is *measured* by the experimenter is called the **dependent variable (DV)**. [Note: The goal of any experiment is to learn how the dependent variable is affected by (depends on) the independent variable.]

Continuing the example of research on the effects of violence on TV and aggression, the experimenter (you) could decide to randomly assign children to watch either violent or nonviolent TV programs—the *independent variable (IV)*. More specifically, your *experimental group* would watch three violent television programs, while your *control group* would watch three nonviolent TV programs for the same amount of time. [Note: For both experimental and control groups, experimenters must ensure that all *extraneous variables* (those that are not being directly manipulated or measured) are held constant (the same). For example, time of day, heating, and lighting would need to be kept constant for all participants so that they do not affect participants' responses.]

Measuring the Dependent Variable

After all children watched either violent or nonviolent programs, you could put a large plastic, "Bobo," doll in front of each child and record for one hour the number of times the child hits, kicks, or punches the plastic doll—the *dependent variable* (DV).

[Note: Experiments can also have different *levels* of an independent variable (IV). In the TV violence example, two experimental groups could be created, with one group watching three hours of violent programming and the other watching six hours. The control group would watch only nonviolent programming. Then a researcher could relate differences in aggressive behavior (DV) to the *amount* (or level) of violent programming viewed (IV).]

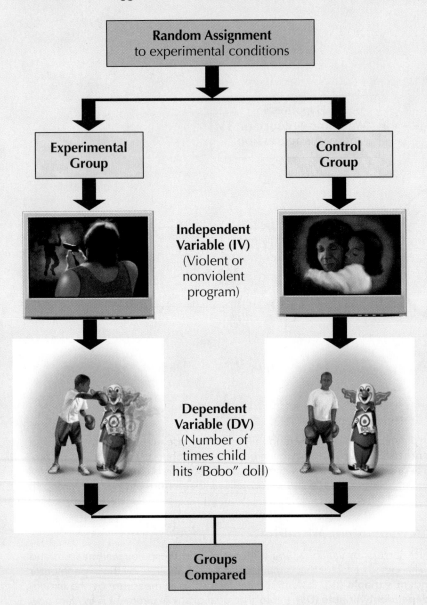

Experimental Group *Group that receives a treatment in an experiment*

Control Group *Group that receives no treatment in an experiment*

Independent Variable (IV) *Variable that is manipulated to determine its causal effect on the dependent variable*

Dependent Variable (DV) *Variable that is measured; it is affected by (or dependent on) the independent variable*

 Study Tip

Because the IV is independent *and freely selected and varied by the experimenter, it is called* independent. *The DV is called* dependent *because the behavior (or outcome) exhibited by the participants is assumed to depend, at least in part, on manipulations of the IV.*

to present the stimuli and computers to record the responses. Another option is to use "blind observers" (neutral people other than the researcher) to collect and record the data without knowing what the researcher has predicted. In addition, researchers can arrange a **double-blind study**, in which *neither* the observer nor the participant knows which group received the experimental treatment.

For example, in a typical double-blind experiment testing a new drug for pain control, both the experimenters administering the drug and the participants taking the drug are unaware (or "blind") as to who is receiving a **placebo**, a fake pill or injection, and who is receiving the drug itself. Researchers use *placebos* because they have found that the mere act of taking a pill or receiving an injection can change both the expectations and the biological experiences of participants (Dougherty et al., 2008; Price, Finniss, & Benedetti, 2008). People who are given a placebo, but believe they have been given an actual pain medication, often experience less pain! This *placebo effect* occurs when participants' expectations, rather than the experimental treatment, produce an experimental outcome.

Thus, to ensure that a particular effect is indeed due to the drug being tested, and not to the *placebo effect*, control participants must be treated exactly like the experimental participants, even if this means faking the motions of giving them drugs or medications.

• **Ethnocentrism.** When we assume that behaviors typical in our culture are typical in all cultures, we are committing a bias known as **ethnocentrism**. (*Ethno* refers to *ethnicity*, and *centrism* comes from *center*.) One way to avoid this problem is to have two researchers, one from one culture and one from another, conduct the same research study two times, once in their own culture and once in at least one other culture. When using this kind of *cross-cultural sampling*, differences due to researcher ethnocentrism can be isolated from actual differences in behavior between the two cultures.

Participant Problems and Solutions

In addition to potential problems from the researcher, several possibilities for error are associated with participants. These errors can be grouped under the larger categories of *sample bias* and *participant bias*.

• **Sample bias.** A *sample* is a group of research participants selected to represent a larger group, or *population*. When we do research, we obviously cannot measure the entire population, so we select and test a limited sample. However, using such a small group requires that the sample be reasonably similar to the composition of the population at large. If **sample bias**—systematic differences among the groups being studied—exists, experimental results may not truly reflect the influence of the independent variable.

For example, much research has been done on the increased safety of having air bags in automobiles. Unfortunately, however, the research has been conducted almost exclusively with men. When car manufacturers apply findings from this research, with no regard for the sample bias, they create air bags sized for men. Tragically, these male-sized bags may seriously damage (or even decapitate) small adults (mostly women) and kids. Because the purpose of conducting experiments is to apply, or generalize, the results to a wide population, it is extremely important that the sample represent the general population.

To safeguard against sample bias, research psychologists generally use random/representative sampling and random assignment:

• *Random/representative sampling.* Obviously, psychologists want their research findings to be applicable to more people than just those who took part in the study. For instance, critics have suggested that much psychological literature is biased because it is based primarily on white participants (see Robert Guthrie's 2004 book, *Even the Rat Was White*). One way to ensure less bias and more relevance is to select participants who constitute a representative sample of the entire population of interest. Proper *random sampling* will likely produce a representative, unbiased sample.

Martha Lazar/The Image Bank/Getty Images

Can a horse add, multiply, and divide? *Clever Hans and his owner, Mr. Von Osten, convinced many people that this was indeed the case. Can you see how this is an early example of experimenter bias? See the text for an explanation.*

Double-Blind Study *Procedure in which both the researcher and the participants are unaware (blind) of who is in the experimental or control group*

Placebo *(pluh-SEE-boh) Inactive substance or fake treatment used as a control technique, usually in drug research, or given by a medical practitioner to a patient*

Ethnocentrism *Believing that one's culture is typical of all cultures; also, viewing one's own ethnic group (or culture) as central and "correct" and judging others according to this standard*

Sample Bias *Occurs when research participants are not representative of the larger population*

Achievement

Objective 1.11: *How do researchers safeguard against sample bias and participant bias?*

Random Assignment *Using chance methods to assign participants to experimental or control conditions, thus minimizing the possibility of biases or preexisting differences in the groups*

Participant Bias *Occurs when experimental conditions influence the participant's behavior or mental processes*

- *Random assignment.* To ensure the validity of the results, participants must also be assigned to experimental groups using a chance, or random, system, such as tossing a coin or drawing numbers out of a hat. This procedure of **random assignment** ensures that each participant is equally likely to be assigned to any particular group and that differences among the participants will be spread out across all experimental conditions.

- *Participant bias.* In addition to problems with sample bias, **participant bias** can occur when experimental conditions influence participants' behavior or mental processes. For example, participants may try to present themselves in a good light (the *social desirability response*) or may deliberately attempt to mislead the researcher. They also may be less than truthful when asked embarrassing questions or placed in awkward experimental conditions.

Researchers attempt to control for this type of participant bias by offering anonymous participation and other guarantees for privacy and confidentiality. Also, as mentioned earlier, single- and double-blind studies and placebos offer additional safeguards. If participants do not know whether they are receiving the real drug or the "fake one," they will not try to overly please or deliberately mislead the experimenter.

Finally, one of the most effective, but controversial, ways to prevent participant bias is *deception.* Just like unsuspecting subjects on popular TV programs, like the old *Candid Camera* show or the newer *Jamie Kennedy's Experiment* or *Spy TV*, research participants will behave more naturally when they do not know they are part of a research project. However, many researchers consider the use of deception unethical—as we discussed in the previous section.

Assessment **STOP**

CHECK & REVIEW

Experimental Research

Objective 1.8: *Explain how experiments help researchers determine cause and effect.*

By manipulating and carefully controlling variables, an **experiment** is the only research method that can be used to identify cause-and-effect relationships.

Objective 1.9: *Compare and contrast experimental versus control groups and independent versus dependent variables.*

Experimental groups receive treatment, whereas **control groups** receive no treatment.

Independent variables (IVs) are the factors the experimenter manipulates, and **dependent variables (DVs)** are measurable behaviors of the participants. Experimental controls include having one **control group** and one or more **experimental groups**, and holding extraneous variables constant.

Objective 1.10: *How do researchers guard against experimenter bias and ethnocentrism?*

To safeguard against the researcher problem of **experimenter bias**, researchers employ blind observers, single- and **double-blind studies**, and **placebos**. To control for **ethnocentrism**, they use cross-cultural sampling.

Objective 1.11: *How do researchers safeguard against sample bias and participant bias?*

To offset participant problems with **sample bias**, researchers use random/representative sampling and **random assignment**. To control for **participant bias**, they rely on many of the same controls in place to prevent experimenter bias, such as double-blind studies. They also attempt to ensure anonymity and confidentiality and sometimes use deception.

Questions

1. Why is an experiment the only way we can determine the cause of behavior?
2. In experiments, researchers measure the _____ variables. (a) independent; (b) feature; (c) extraneous; (d) dependent
3. If researchers gave participants varying amounts of a new "memory" drug and then gave them a story to read and measured their scores on a quiz, the _____ would be the IV, and the _____ would be the DV. (a) response to the drug, amount of the drug; (b) experimental group, control group; (c) amount of the drug, quiz scores; (d) researcher variables, extraneous variables
4. What are the two primary sources of problems for both researchers and participants? What are the solutions?

Check your answers in Appendix B.

 Click & Review
for additional assessment options:
wiley.com/college/huffman

pplication

Would you like to volunteer as a participant in psychological research?

The American Psychological Society (APS) has a website with links to ongoing studies that need participants. A recent visit to this site revealed several exciting studies, including:

- What Should Be Done with Child Abusers?
- Reactions to September 11 Terrorist Attacks

- Leadership Styles and Emotional Intelligence
- Bem Sex Role Inventory
- Internet Usage, Personality, and Behavior
- Adult Attention Deficit Hyperactivity Disorder (ADHD/ADD)
- Sensation and Perception Laboratory
- Web of Loneliness

- Sexual Behavior and Alcohol Consumption
- Marriage Inventory
- Are You a Logical Thinker?
- Web Experimental Psychology Lab

If you'd like to participate, go to http://psych.hanover.edu/research/exponnet.html.

 pplication

RESEARCH HIGHLIGHT

Love at First Fright?

Objective 1.12: *Why do we sometimes mislabel our emotions?*

Suppose you are watching a scary movie with a very attractive date. You notice that your heart is pounding, your palms are sweating, and you are short of breath. Is it love? Or is it fear? As you will discover in Chapter 12, a wide variety of emotions are accompanied by the same physiological states. Because of this similarity, we frequently misidentify our emotions. How can we experimentally prove this?

To answer this question, Donald Dutton and Arthur Aron (1974) asked an attractive female or male experimenter (confederates) to approach 85 male passersby either on a fear-arousing or on a non-fear-arousing bridge. They asked all participants to fill out questionnaires, and then gave them a phone number to call if they wanted more information.

Imagine yourself as one of the participants in this experiment. You arrive at the Capilano Canyon suspension bridge in North Vancouver, British Columbia. It is a 5-foot-wide, 450-foot-long wooden bridge attached by cables spanning the Capilano Canyon. When you walk across the bridge, it tends to tilt, sway, and wobble, and you have to stoop down to hold on to the low railings. If you happen to look down, you see nothing but rapids and exposed rocks in the river 230 feet below.

While standing at the middle of this swaying bridge, the experimenter approaches

Erik Dreyer/Stone/Getty Images

and asks you to fill out a questionnaire. Would you be attracted to this person? What if this person instead approached you on a firm wooden bridge with only a 10-foot drop to a shallow rivulet? Compared to men on the low, non-fear-arousing bridge, Dutton and Aron found that a large proportion of the men on the fear-arousing bridge called the female researcher on the number she provided, and also revealed a much higher level of sexual imagery in their questionnaires.

At first glance, this may sound strange. Why would men who are in a state of fear be more attracted to a woman than men who are relaxed? According to what is now called **misattribution of arousal**, the men mistakenly attributed some of their arousal to their attraction to the female experimenter.

Although Dutton and Aron conducted this experiment in 1974, dozens of follow-up studies have generally confirmed their original findings. For example, Cindy

Meston and Penny Frohlich (2003) conducted a similar experiment with individuals at amusement parks who were either waiting to begin or had just gotten off a roller-coaster ride. Participants were shown a photograph of an average-attractive person of the opposite sex. They were then asked to rate the individual on attractiveness and dating desirability. Consistent with the earlier findings of Dutton and Aron, ratings were higher among those who were exiting than entering the ride. Interestingly, this effect was only found with participants riding with a nonromantic partner. When romantic couples were riding together, there were no significant differences in ratings of attractiveness or dating desirability.

Can you see how Meston and Frohlich's research illustrates steps 5 and 6 in the scientific method? As mentioned on page 18, experimenters often replicate or extend the work of previous researchers. And, in this case, the differing results between romantic and nonromantic partners help fine-tune the original theory, which may in turn lead to new and better future theories. Both experiments also demonstrate how *basic research* can sometimes be applied to our everyday lives. In this case, the take-home message is: Be careful of "Love at first fright!"

Misattribution of Arousal
Different emotions produce similar feelings of arousal, which leads to mistaken inferences about these emotions and the source of arousal.

Application

CRITICAL THINKING   ACTIVE LEARNING

Applying Critical Thinking to Psychological Science
(Contributed by Thomas Frangicetto)

Scientists in all fields must be good critical thinkers, and researchers (and students) in psychology are no exception. This first critical thinking exercise will help you in many ways, including:

- Insight into the interconnectivity of critical thinking and psychological science.
- Practice applying numerous critical thinking components.
- Review of important text content your professor may include on exams.

Part I. In the space beside each "Text Key Concept," enter the number of the appropriate "Suggested Critical Thinking Component." Expanded discussions of each component can be found in the Prologue of this text (pp. xxx). Although you may find several possible matches, list only your top one or two choices. For example, for the first item, "Literature Review," if you decide that "Gathering Data" is the best critical thinking component, enter the number "16" in the blank space.

Part II. On a separate sheet of paper, use specific text wording and critical thinking descriptions to fully explain your choices. Using the same example as above, you might say:

In order for researchers to do a successful review of the literature, they would have to "carefully check what has been published in major professional or scientific journals," and they would do so by employing critical thinking component #16, *Gathering Data*.

This means they would "collect up-to-date, relevant information on all sides of the issue" before proceeding with their research.

Cartoon by AUTH. 8-4-06. The Philadelphia Inquirer. Distributed by Universal Press Syndicate. All rights reserved.

Text Key Concepts	Suggested Critical Thinking Components
Scientific Method	• Valuing Truth above Self-Interest (#1)
_____ Literature Review	• Welcoming Divergent Views (#4)
_____ Testable Hypothesis,	• Tolerating Ambiguity (#5)
Operationally Defined	• Recognizing Personal Biases (#6)
_____ Research Design	• Empathizing (#7)
_____ Statistical Analysis	• Thinking Independently (#7)
_____ Peer-Reviewed	• Defining Problems Accurately (#8)
Scientific Journal	• Analyzing Data for Value and Content (#9)
_____ Theory	• Synthesizing (#11)
	• Resisting Overgeneralization (#12)
	• Delaying Judgment until Adequate Data Are Available (#14)
Research Problems	• Employing Precise Terms (#15)
_____ Experimenter Bias	• Gathering Data (#16)
_____ Ethnocentrism	• Distinguishing Fact from Opinion (#17)
_____ Sample Bias	• Modifying Judgments in Light of New Information (#20)
_____ Participant Bias	• Applying Knowledge to New Situations (#21)

Achievement

Objective 1.13: *Explain descriptive research and its three key methods—naturalistic observation, surveys, and case studies.*

Descriptive Research *Research methods that observe and record behavior and mental processes without producing causal explanations*

Descriptive Research: Naturalistic Observation, Surveys, and Case Studies

The second major type of research, **descriptive research**, observes and describes behavior and mental processes without manipulating variables. Almost everyone observes and describes other people in an attempt to understand them. But psychologists do it systematically and scientifically. In this section, we will examine three key types of descriptive research: *naturalistic observation*, *surveys*, and *case studies*. Keep in mind that most of the problems and safeguards discussed with the experimental method also apply to these nonexperimental methods.

Naturalistic Observation

When conducting **naturalistic observation**, researchers systematically measure and record the observable behavior of participants as it occurs in the real world, without interfering. The purpose of most naturalistic observation is to gather descriptive information. Because of the popularity of researchers like Jane Goodall, who studied chimpanzees in the jungle, most people picture naturalistic observation occurring in wild, remote areas. But supermarkets, libraries, subways, airports, museums, classrooms, assembly lines, and other settings also lend themselves to naturalistic observation (Figure 1.7).

The chief advantage of naturalistic observation is that researchers can obtain data about a natural behavior, rather than about behavior that is a reaction to an artificial experimental situation. On the downside, naturalistic observation can be difficult and time consuming, and the lack of control by the researcher makes it difficult to conduct observations for behavior that occurs infrequently.

Surveys

Most of us are familiar with Gallup and Harris Polls, which sample voting preferences before important state or national elections. Psychologists use similar polls (or

Naturalistic Observation
Observation and recording behavior and mental processes in the participant's natural state or habitat

Photodisc Red/Getty Images

Figure 1.7 ***Naturalistic observation*** As a researcher, how would you research questions like this one: "Do smaller classes result in greater student achievement? If so, for what type of student?" You probably wouldn't want to conduct an experiment in a controlled laboratory setting. Instead, you might choose to go to several classrooms and observe how children and teachers behave in their natural setting. In this type of *naturalistic observation*, you, the researcher, would not manipulate or control anything in the situation. You would attempt to be as unobtrusive as possible, to become, as they say, "like a fly on the wall." Like the reseacher in this photo, you might even conceal yourself behind a one-way mirror, or observe from a distance while the participants are (hopefully) unaware that they are being observed. Why would researchers try to hide? If participants know someone is watching, their behaviors become unnatural. Have you ever been driving down the street, singing along with the radio, and quickly stopped when you noticed the person in the next car was watching you? The same type of thing typically occurs when participants in scientific studies realize they are being observed.

Survey　*Research technique that questions a large sample of people to assess their behaviors and attitudes*

surveys) and interviews to measure a wide variety of psychological behaviors and attitudes (Rosnow & Rosenthal, 2008). (The psychological survey technique also includes tests, questionnaires, and interviews.)

One key advantage to surveys is that they can gather data from a much larger sample of people than is possible with other research methods. Unfortunately, most surveys rely on self-reported data, and not all participants are completely honest. In addition, survey techniques cannot, of course, be used to explain *causes* of behavior.

Case Studies

What if a researcher wants to investigate *photophobia*—fear of light? Because most people are not afraid of light, it would be difficult to find enough participants to conduct an experiment or to use surveys or naturalistic observation. In the case of such rare disorders, researchers try to find someone who has the problem and study him or her intensively. Such an in-depth study of a single research participant is called a **case study**.

Case Study　*In-depth study of a single research participant*

Throughout this text, we will present numerous expanded "Case Study/Personal Stories," which add a "human interest" touch and help you remember core concepts. In this beginning chapter, the following example helps illustrate the case study as a research method. Keep in mind, however, that case studies have their own research limits, including lack of generalizability and inaccurate or biased recall among participants.

Application

CASE STUDY / PERSONAL STORY　*A Life Without Fear?*

UpperCut Images/Getty Images

For a "first-hand" look at the case study method, imagine yourself as Dr. Antonio Damasio, distinguished professor and head of the Department of Neurology at the University of Iowa College of Medicine in Iowa City. You are introduced to a tall, slender, and extremely pleasant young female patient, referred to as "S." Tests show that she has normal, healthy sensory perceptions, language abilities, and intelligence. Shortly after being introduced, S hugs and touches you repeatedly. You discover that this same cheerful, touching behavior pervades all areas of her life. She makes friends and romantic attachments easily and is eager to interact with almost anyone. By all reports, S lives in an extremely pleasant world dominated by positive emotions.

So, what is "wrong" with S? Can you diagnose her? Damasio and his colleagues began with comprehensive evaluations of the patient's physical and mental health, intelligence, and personality. Results showed that S was in good health with normal sensory perception, language ability, and intelligence. She also had remarkable artistic and drafting skills. Her one problem was that she could not identify facial expressions of fear. She easily recognized other emotions and could mimic them with her own facial muscles. And, interestingly, she could draw finely detailed faces showing all emotions—except fear.

After extensive neurological tests and extensive interviews, Damasio and his staff discovered that S's inability to recognize fear in someone's face resulted from damage to a very small part of her brain—the *amygdala*. As a result, "she has not learned the telltale signs that announce possible danger and possible unpleasantness, especially as they show up in the face of another person" (Damasio, 1999, p. 66).

They also found that S does not experience fear in the same way as others do. She intellectually knows "what fear is supposed to be, what should cause it, and even what one may do in situations of fear, but little or none of that intellectual baggage, so to speak, is of any use to her in the real world" (Damasio, 1999, p. 66). Her inability to recognize fear in herself and others causes her to be overly trusting of strangers and romantic partners. Can you see how this might create serious problems in social interactions?

At this time, there is no "happy ending" for S and others with similar damage. But case studies like this may eventually provide valuable clues that will lead to successful treatment.

Achievement
Objective 1.14: *Compare correlational research and correlation coefficients.*

Correlational Research: Looking for Relationships

When researchers want to determine how one trait or behavior accompanies another, and the degree of relationship, or *correlation*, between these naturally occurring variables, they turn to **correlational research**. As the name implies, when any two variables are *correlated*, they are "co-related." A change in one variable is accompanied by a concurrent change in the other (Concept Diagram 1.1).

Correlational Research
Researcher observes or measures (without directly manipulating) two or more naturally occurring variables to find the relationships between them

The Value of Correlations

Correlational research is an important research method for psychologists. It also plays a critical role in your personal and everyday life. As you will see in upcoming chapters, numerous questions may be asked about how two things relate. How is stress related to susceptibility to colds? Does marijuana decrease motivation? How is intelligence related to achievement? When you read that "there is a strong correlation between…and…," you will now understand the significance. This also is true when you read news reports of the latest findings showing a strong (or weak) relationship between oatmeal and heart disease, or cellular phones and brain cancer.

In addition to providing greater knowledge of psychological data and news reports, understanding correlations also may help you live a safer and more productive life. For example, correlational studies have repeatedly found high correlation coefficients between birth defects and a pregnant mother's use of tobacco, alcohol, and other drugs (e.g., Howell, Coles, & Kable, 2008; Fryer, Crocker, & Mattson, 2008). This information enables us to reliably predict our relative risks and make informed decisions about our lives and behavior. If you would like additional information about correlations, see Appendix A at the back of the book.

The Problem with Correlations

Before we leave this topic, it is important to note that *correlation does not imply causation*. This is an error in logic commonly associated with correlational studies. Although a high correlation allows us to predict how one variable relates to another, it does not tell us whether a cause–effect relationship exists between the two variables. What if I said there was a high correlation between the size of a young child's feet and how fast he or she reads? Would this mean that having small feet *causes* a child to be a slow reader? Obviously not! Nor do increases in reading speed cause increases in foot size. Instead, both are caused by a third variable—an increase in children's age. Although we can safely *predict* that as a child's foot size increases, his or her reading speed will also increase, this *correlation does not imply causation*.

Correlation is NOT causation. Correlational, non-experimental, studies are important because they reveal associations between variables. But causality (what causes what) is much more difficult to prove. For example, ice cream consumption and drowning are highly correlated. Does this mean that eating ice cream causes people to drown? Of course not! A third factor, such as time of year, affects both ice cream consumption and swimming and other summertime activities.

Concept Diagram 1.1

Understanding Correlations

Correlational research is very important because it reveals naturally occurring relationships and assesses how well one variable predicts another. How would we study nicotine use and possible fetal damage? After randomly selecting a group of pregnant women volunteers and obtaining their *informed consent*, researchers might survey or interview the women about the amount and timing of any cigarette smoking during their pregnancies.

After the data are collected, the researchers can analyze their results using a statistical formula that results in a **correlation coefficient**, a numerical value that indicates the degree and direction of the relationship between the two variables. (Note: *Correlational research* is a methodology researchers use to identify relationships between variables, whereas *correlation coefficients* are statistical measures used in correlational research, as well as with surveys and other research designs.)

Key Features in Correlations

1. Correlation coefficients are calculated by a formula (described in Appendix A) that produces a number ranging from +1.00 to −1.00. The number indicates the strength of the relationship. Both +1.00 and −1.00 indicate the strongest possible relationship. As the number decreases and gets closer to 0.00, the relationship weakens. Note that the sign (+ or −) in front of the number indicates the direction of the correlation, positive (+) or negative (−).

2. A *positive correlation* (−) indicates that two variables move (or vary) in the same direction—they increase or decrease in a similar way. For example, when studying increases, exam scores generally increase. Conversely, when studying decreases, exam scores decrease. Both are positive correlations. The factors vary in the same direction— upward or downward.

    (a) (b)   (a) (b)

3. A *negative correlation* occurs when two variables vary in opposite directions—as one factor increases, the other factor decreases. Have you noticed that the more hours you work (or party) outside of college, the lower your exam scores? This is an example of a negative correlation—working and partying vary in opposite directions to exam scores.

    (a) (b)   (a) (b)

4. A *zero correlation* indicates no relationship between two variables. For example, there is no relation (zero correlation) between your birthday and your exam scores. And, despite popular belief, repeated scientific investigations of astrology have found no relationship between personality and the position of the stars when you were born (a zero correlation).

    (a) (b)   ?

5. Positive, negative, and zero correlations are sometimes shown on graphs (called *scatterplots*), with each dot representing an individual participant's score on the two variables. In scatterplot (a), each dot corresponds to one person's salary and years of education. Because salary and education are strongly correlated, the dots are closely aligned around the dark line, which points in an upward direction—a positive correlation. Scatterplots (b) and (c) show a negative and zero correlation.

6. In sum: A "correlation coefficient" is delineated by the letter "r," and it would be expressed something like this, r +.62. The sign in front of the number (+ or −) indicates the *direction* of the relationship, and the number (.62) indicates the *strength*. The closer the number is to 1.00, either positive or negative, the stronger the correlation between the variables. A correlation of +.92 or −.92 would represent a high (or strong) correlation, whereas a correlation of +.15 or −.15 would indicate a low (or weak) correlation.

Pregnancy and smoking *Research shows that cigarette smoking is highly correlated with serious fetal damage. The more the mother smokes the more the fetus is damaged. Is this a positive or negative correlation?*

(a) Positive Correlation — Years of Education (High/Low) vs Salary

(b) Negative Correlation — Exam Scores (High/Low) vs Class Absences

(c) Zero, or no Correlation — Intelligence (High/Low) vs Shoe Size

Sample Correlation Coefficient
$$r = \boxed{+}\boxed{.62}$$

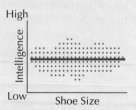

| Indicates the *direction* of the correlation (positive or negative) | Indicates the *strength* of a correlation (0 to +1.00 or 0 to −1.00) |

Correlation Coefficient *Number indicating strength and direction of the relationship between two variables*

Try This Yourself

Can you spot the positive, negative, and zero correlations?

1. Health and exercise.
2. Hours of TV viewing and student grades.
3. Level of happiness and level of helpfulness.
4. Age of driver and weight of car.
5. Resale value and age of car.

(Answers: positive, negative, positive, zero, negative)

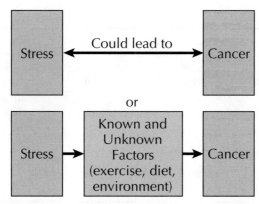

Figure 1.8 ***Correlation versus causation***   Research has found a strong correlation between stress and cancer (Chapter 3). However, this correlation does not tell us whether stress causes cancer, cancer causes stress, or whether other known and unknown factors, such as the eating, drinking, and smoking, could contribute to both stress and cancer. Can you think of a way to study the effects of stress on cancer that is not correlational?

I use this extreme example to make an important point about an all too common public reaction to research findings. People read media reports about *relationships* between stress and cancer or between family dynamics and homosexuality. They then jump to the conclusion that "stress causes cancer" or that "withdrawn fathers and overly protective mothers cause their sons' homosexuality." Unfortunately, they fail to realize that a third factor, perhaps genetics, may cause greater susceptibility to both cancer and increased rates of homosexuality.

Once again, as Figure 1.8 shows, a correlation between two variables does not mean that one variable *causes* another. Correlational studies do sometimes point to *possible* causes, like the correlation between alcohol and birth defects. However, only the experimental method manipulates the IV under controlled conditions and therefore allows one to draw conclusions about cause and effect. If you compared psychological research to a criminal investigation, finding a correlation is like finding a person at the scene of the crime. In contrast, results from an experiment are more like the "smoking gun."

Biological Research: Tools for Exploring the Nervous System

In the previous section, we explored traditional research methods in psychology—experimental, descriptive, and correlational. But how do we study the living human brain and other parts of the nervous system? This is the province of **biological research**, which has developed and employed their own remarkable scientific tools and research methods (Table 1.4).

For most of history, examination of the human brain was possible only after an individual died. The earliest explorers dissected the brains of deceased humans and conducted experiments on nonhuman animals using *lesioning techniques*. (Lesioning in brain research involves systematically destroying brain tissue to study the effects on behavior and mental processes.) By the mid-1800s, this early research had produced a basic map of the nervous system, including some areas of the brain. Early researchers also relied on clinical observations and case studies of living people who had injuries, diseases, and disorders that affected brain functioning.

Modern researchers still use *dissection, ablation/lesioning, observation/case studies* and the other methods in Table 1.4. However, they also employ other techniques, such as electrical recordings of the brain's activity. To make these electrical recordings, scientists paste *electrodes* (tiny electricity-conducting disks or wires) to the skin of the skull. These electrodes collect electrical energy from the brain (brain waves), and the equipment to which they are attached depict them as wavy lines. The recording of these brain waves is called an *electroencephalogram* (EEG). (*Electro* means "electrical,"

chievement

Objective 1.15: *Describe biological research and its major tools for discovery.*

Biological Research *Scientific studies of the brain and other parts of the nervous system*

TABLE 1.4 TOOLS FOR BIOLOGICAL RESEARCH

Method	Description	Sample Results
Brain dissection *Brain dissection. This is an actual photo of a deceased person's brain that has been vertically sliced in half to reveal inner structures.*	Careful cutting and study of a cadaver's brain to reveal structural details.	Brain dissections of Alzheimer's disease victims often show identifiable changes in various parts of the brain (Chapter 7).
Ablation/lesions	Surgically removing parts of the brain (ablation), or destroying specific areas of the brain (lesioning), is followed by observation for changes in behavior or mental processes.	Lesioning specific parts of the rat's hypothalamus greatly affects its eating behavior (Chapter 12).
Observation/case studies	Observing and recording changes in personality, behavior, or sensory capacity associated with brain disease or injuries.	Damage to one side of the brain often causes numbness or paralysis on the body's opposite side.
Electrical recordings Gary D. Landsman/©Corbis *Electroencephalogram (EEG). Electrical activity throughout the brain sweeps in regular waves across its surface, and the EEG is a readout of this activity. Unfortunately, because the electrodes only record from the surface of the scalp, they provide little precision about the location of the activity.*	Using electrodes attached to the skin or scalp, brain activity is detected and recorded on an electroencephalogram (EEG).	The EEG reveals areas of the brain most active during a particular task or changes in mental states, like sleeping and meditation (Chapter 5); it also traces abnormal brain waves caused by brain malfunctions, like epilepsy or tumors.
Electrical stimulation of the brain (ESB)  St. Jude Medical/Photo Researchers, Inc.	Using an electrode, a weak electric current stimulates specific areas or structures of the brain.	Penfield (1947) mapped the surface of the brain and found that different areas have different functions.

TABLE 1.4 (*CONTINUED*)

CT (computed tomography) scan

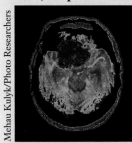

Mehau Kulyk/Photo Researchers

CT scans. *This CT scan used X-rays to locate a brain tumor, which is the deep purple mass at the top left.*

Computer-created cross sectional X-rays of the brain; least expensive type of imaging and widely used in research.

CT reveals the effects of strokes, injuries, tumors, and other brain disorders.

PET (positron emission tomography) scan

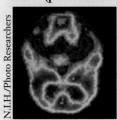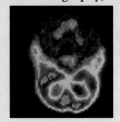

N.I.H./Photo Researchers

PET scans and brain functions. *The left scan shows brain activity when the eyes are open, whereas the one on the right is with the eyes closed. Note the increased activity, red and yellow, in the left photo when the eyes are open.*

Radioactive form of glucose is injected into the bloodstream; scanner records amount of glucose used in particularly active areas of the brain and produces computer-constructed picture of the brain.

PET scans, originally designed to detect abnormalities, are also used to identify brain areas active during ordinary activities (reading, singing, etc.).

 Study Tip

One way to remember the difference between these four scans is to keep in mind that CT and MRI scans produce static visual slices of the brain (like a photo). PET and fMRI create on-going images (like a video).

MRI (magnetic resonance imaging)

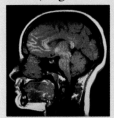

Magnetic resonance imaging (MRI). *Note the fissures and internal structures of the brain. The throat, nasal airways, and fluid surrounding the brain are dark.*

Scott Camazine/Photo Researchers

A high-frequency magnetic field is passed through the brain by means of electromagnets.

The MRI produces high-resolution three-dimensional pictures of the brain useful for identifying abnormalities and mapping brain structures and function.

fMRI (functional magnetic resonance imaging)

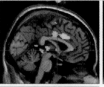

Science Photo Library/Photo Researchers, Inc.

A newer, faster version of the MRI that detects blood flow by picking up magnetic signals from blood that has given up its oxygen to activate brain cells.

The fMRI measures blood flow which indicates areas of the brain that are active or inactive during ordinary activities or responses (like reading or talking); also shows changes associated with disorders.

TMS (Transcranial magnetic stimulation)

©AP/Wide World Photos

Recent method of brain stimulation that delivers a large current through a wire coil placed on the skull.

Can be used to elicit a motor response or to temporarily inactivate an area and observe the effects; also used to treat depression (Chapter 15).

©John Chase

encephalon means "brain," and *gram* means "record.") The instrument itself, called an *electroencephalograph*, is a major research tool for studying changes in brain waves during sleep and dreaming (Chapter 5).

In addition to electrical recordings, researchers also use *electrical stimulation of the brain (ESB)*. In this case, electrodes are inserted directly into the brain to stimulate certain areas with weak electrical currents.

Other new windows into the brain include several *brain-imaging scans* (see Table 1.4). Most of these methods are relatively *noninvasive*. That is, they are performed without breaking the skin or entering the body. They can be used in clinical settings to examine suspected brain damage and disease. They are also used in laboratory settings to study brain function during ordinary activities like sleeping, eating, reading, and speaking.

A Cautionary Note—fMRI Overselling!

Like the experimental, descriptive, and correlational methods of scientific research, each of the biological methods also has its own unique advantages and disadvantages. Before moving on, one particular problem with fMRI brain scans deserves special attention.

As mentioned in Table 1.4, fMRI scans measure brain activity by monitoring blood flow to specific areas, and scientific journals turn out hundreds of brain-imaging articles each month. However, brain activity and blood flow within the brain can reflect and be altered by a large range of different biological processes. Scientist Nikos Logothetis warns us that conclusions drawn from fMRI scans "often ignore the actual limitations of the methodology" (Logothetis, 2008). Ignoring these limitations, journalists, the public, and some scientists have leapt to unwarranted (and potentially dangerous) conclusions (Weisberg et al., 2008). For example, newspapers and other media sources eagerly cover research alledgedly documenting how Democrats and Republican brains are different, how different parts of your brain "light up" when you're having religious experiences, watching Super Bowl ads, or eating chocolate, and supposedly even when you're telling a lie versus the truth (Carlat, 2008; Hutson, 2007; Vaughan, 2008). As you'll discover in Chapter 2, and throughout this text, behavior and mental processes are incredibly complex, and our scientific understanding evolves over time. While fMRI brain scans have provided unprecedented insights and invaluable aid to scientists and people around the world, they've also been oversold and over-interpreted. This is just a brief caution to not to be seduced by the "pretty pictures." Brain scans, like all scientific tools, have their limits.

STOP

CHECK & REVIEW

Descriptive, Correlational, and Biological Research

Objective 1.12: *Why do we sometimes mislabel our emotions?*

According to the **misattribution of arousal** model, different emotions produce similar feelings of arousal, which leads to mistaken inferences about these emotions and the source of their arousal.

Objective 1.13: *Explain descriptive research and its three key methods—naturalistic observation, surveys, and case studies.*

Descriptive research observes and describes, but it cannot determine the causes of behavior. **Naturalistic observation** is used to study and describe behavior in its natural habitat without altering it. **Surveys** use interviews or questionnaires to obtain information on a sample of participants. Individual **case studies** are in-depth studies of a participant.

Objective 1.14: *Compare correlational research and correlation coefficients.*

Correlational research examines how one naturally occurring trait or behavior accompanies another, and how well one variable predicts the other. **Correlation coefficients** are numerical values from correlational research that indicate the degree and direction of the relationship between two variables. (Correlation coefficients range from 0 to +1.00 or 0 to −1.00, and the plus and minus signs indicate whether the relationships are positively or negatively correlated.) Both correlational studies and correlational coefficients provide important research findings and valuable predictions. However, it is also important to remember that *correlation does not imply causation.*

Objective 1.15: *Describe biological research and its major tools for discovery.*

Biological research studies the brain and other parts of the nervous system through dissection of brains of cadavers, ablation/lesion techniques, observation or case studies, electrical recordings, and electrical stimulation of the brain (ESB). Computed tomography (CT), positron emission tomography (PET), magnetic resonance imaging (MRI), functional magnetic resonance imaging (fMRI), and transcranial magnetic stimulation (TMS) are noninvasive techniques that provide important information on intact, living brains.

Questions

1. _____ research observes and records behavior without producing causal explanations. (a) Experimental; (b) Survey; (c) Descriptive; (d) Correlational
2. Maria is thinking of running for student body president. She wonders whether her campaign should emphasize campus security, improved parking facilities, or increased health services. Which scientific method of research would you recommend? (a) a case study; (b) naturalistic observation; (c) an experiment; (d) a survey
3. Which of the following correlation coefficients indicates the strongest relationship? (a) +.43; (b) −.64; (c) −.72; (d) 0.00
4. The four major techniques used for scanning the brain are the _____, _____, _____, and _____.

Check your answers in Appendix B.

Click & Review
for additional assessment options:
wiley.com/college/huffman

PSYCHOLOGY AT WORK

Becoming a Better Consumer of Scientific Research

The news media, advertisers, politicians, teachers, close friends, and other individuals frequently use research findings in their attempts to change your attitudes and behavior. How can you tell whether their information is accurate and worthwhile?

The following exercise will improve your ability to critically evaluate sources of information. Using concepts from the previous discussion of psychological research techniques, read each "research" report and identify the primary problem or research limitation. In the space provided, use one of the following to characterize the report.

CC = Report is misleading because correlation data are used to suggest causation.

CG = Report is inconclusive because there was no control group.

EB = Results of the research were unfairly influenced by experimenter bias.

SB = Results of the research are questionable because of sample bias.

_____1. A clinical psychologist strongly believes that touching is an important adjunct to successful therapy. For two months, he touches half his patients (group A) and refrains from touching the other half (group B). He then reports a noticeable improvement in group A.

_____ 2. A newspaper reports that violent crime corresponds to phases of the moon. The reporter concludes that the gravitational pull of the moon controls human behavior.

_____ 3. A researcher interested in women's attitudes toward premarital sex sends out a lengthy survey to subscribers of *Vogue* and *Cosmopolitan* magazines.

_____ 4. An experimenter is interested in studying the effects of alcohol on driving ability. Before being tested on an experimental driving course, group A consumes 2 ounces of alcohol, group B consumes 4 ounces of alcohol, and group C consumes 6 ounces of alcohol. After the test drive, the researcher reports that alcohol consumption adversely affects driving ability.

_____ 5. After reading a scientific journal that reports higher divorce rates among couples living together before marriage, a college student decides to move out of the apartment she shares with her boyfriend.

_____ 6. A theater owner reports increased beverage sales following the brief flashing of a subliminal message to "Drink Coca-Cola" during the film showing.

Answers: 1. EB; 2. CC; 3. SB; 4. CG; 5. CC; 6. CG 7. EB

GENDER & CULTURAL DIVERSITY

Are There Cultural Universals?

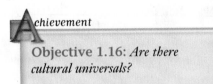

Objective 1.16: *Are there cultural universals?*

Study Tip

Gender and Cultural
These sections embedded in the narrative are identified with a separate heading and a special icon, as seen here. To succeed in today's world, it is important to be aware of other cultures and important gender issues.

Psychology is a broad field with numerous subdisciplines and professions. Until recently, most psychologists worked and conducted research primarily in Europe and North America. Given this "one-sided" research, psychology's findings may not apply equally to people in other countries—or to minorities and women in Europe and North America, for that matter (Matsumoto & Juang, 2008; Shiraev & Levy, 2007). However, modern psychology, in particular *cultural psychology*, is working to correct this imbalance. Key research from cross-cultural and multiethnic studies is integrated throughout this text. Each chapter also includes a "Gender and Cultural Diversity" section with a special icon in the margin that looks like this: ✳

In this first gender and cultural diversity discussion, we explore a central question in cultural psychology: Are there *cultural universals?* That is, are there aspects of human behavior and mental processes that are true and *pancultural* or *universal* for all people of all cultures?

For many "universalists," emotions and facial recognition of emotions provide the clearest example of a possible cultural universal. Numerous studies conducted over many years with people from very different cultures suggest that everyone can easily identify facial expressions for at least six basic emotions: happiness, surprise, anger, sadness, fear, and disgust. All humans supposedly have this capacity whether they are shown the face of a child or an adult, a Western or non-Western person (Anguas-Wong & Matsumoto, 2007; Ekman, 1980, 1993, 2003, 2004; Matsumoto & Juang, 2008). Moreover, nonhuman primates and congenitally blind infants also display similarly recognizable facial signals. In other words, across cultures (and some species), a frown is recognized as a sign of displeasure, and a smile, as a sign of pleasure (Figure 1.9). Although facial expressions of basic emotions appear to be universal, how, when, and where they are expressed varies according to cultural standards called *display rules* (Fok et al., 2008).

Critics of the universalist position emphasize problems with these studies. For example, how do you label and study the emotion described by Japanese as *hagaii* (feeling helpless anguish mixed with frustration). How can Western psychologists

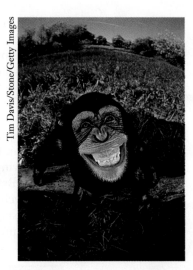

Figure 1.9 *Do you recognize these emotions?* The recognition and display of basic facial expressions may be true "cultural universals."

study a culturally specific emotion like *hagaii* if they have no experience with these emotions and no equivalent English words? Other critics argue that *if* cultural universals exist, it is because they are biological and innate—and they should be labeled as such. However, equating biology with universality has its own problem. Behaviors or mental processes that are universal may be so because of culture-constant learning rather than biological destiny (Matsumoto & Juang, 2008). For example, *if* we found that certain gender roles were expressed the same way in all cultures, it might reflect shared cultural training beginning at birth, not an "anatomy is destiny" position. As you'll discover throughout this text, psychological scientists avoid the tendency to compartmentalize behaviors into either/or categories. Like the nature–nurture controversy, the answer once again is an *interaction*. Certain behaviors, like emotions and their recognition, may be both biological and culturally universal. As a beginning student in psychology, you will encounter numerous areas of conflict, with well-respected arguments and opponents on each side. Your job is to adopt an open-minded, critically thinking approach to each of these debates.

In addition to building your critical thinking skills, hearing arguments from both sides also will develop your understanding of and appreciation for diversity, both intellectual and cultural. It might even improve your personal and business interactions. Richard Brislin (1997) told the story of a Japanese executive who gave a speech to a *Fortune* 500 company in New York. He was aware that Americans typically begin speeches by telling an amusing story or a couple of jokes. However, Japanese typically begin speeches by apologizing for the "inadequate" talk they are about to give. This savvy executive began his speech: "I realize that Americans often begin by making a joke. In Japan, we frequently begin with an apology. I'll compromise by apologizing for not having a joke" (p. 9). By appreciating cultural diversity, we can, like the Japanese executive, learn to interact successfully in other cultures.

Tools for Student Success

Achievement

Objective 1.17: *How can I use psychology to study and learn psychology?*

Congratulations! At this very moment, you are demonstrating one of the most important traits of a critical thinker and successful college student—your willingness to accept *suggestions for improvement*. Many students think that they already know how to be a student and that student success skills are only for "nerds" or "problem students." But would these same individuals assume they could become top-notch musicians, athletes, or plumbers without mastering the tools of those trades? Trying

wiley.com/
college/
huffman

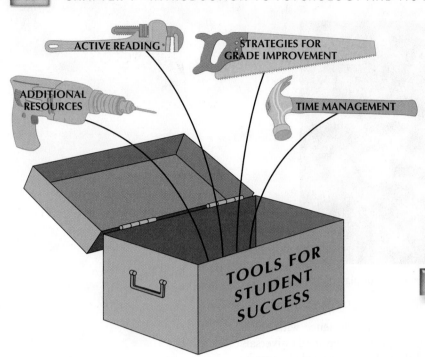

Figure 1.10 *Tools for student success*

 Study Tip

Tools for Student Success
This special feature in Chapter 1 includes tips for overall college success as well as success in this course. In addition, the Study Tip icon identifies additional sections in other chapters that address strategies for dealing with test anxiety and improving memory, performance, and overall achievement.

to compete in a college environment with minimal, or even average, study skills is like trying to ride a bicycle on a high-speed freeway. *All students* (even those who seem to get A's without much effort) can improve their "student tools."

In this section, you will find several important tools—specific, well-documented study tips and techniques—guaranteed to make you a more efficient and successful college student (Figure 1.10). Mastering these tools may require extra initial time. But they save hundreds of hours later on. Research clearly shows that good students tend to work smarter—not longer or harder (Dickinson, O'Connell, & Dunn, 1996).

ACTIVE READING

How to Study (and Master) This Text

Have you ever read several pages of a text and then found you could not recall a single detail? Or have you read the chapters (possibly many times) and still performed poorly on an exam? Do you want to know why? Try the "Visual Quiz" on the next page.

Can you see why I added this visual quiz to begin this section? I wanted to demonstrate how even a simple task of coin recognition requires *active study*. Most Americans cannot select a real penny among fake pennies even after years of using them to make purchases. Similarly, students can read and reread chapters yet still fail to recognize the correct answers on a test. To learn and remember, you must make a conscious effort. You must "intend to learn."

Admittedly, some learning (like remembering the lyrics to your favorite song) occurs somewhat automatically and effortlessly. However, most complex information (like textbook reading) requires effort and deliberate attention. There are a number of ways to *actively read*, remember, and master a college text.

STEP ONE: Familiarizing Yourself with the General Text

Your textbook is the major tool for success in any course. Most instructors rely on it to present basic course material, reserving class time for clarifying and elaborating on important topics. How can you be a more successful student (and test taker) and take full advantage of all the special features in this text? Consider the following suggestions:

- *Preface.* If you have not already read the preface, do it now. It is a road map for the rest of the text.

- *Table of contents.* Scan the table of contents for a bird's-eye view of what you will study in this course. Get the big picture from the chapter titles and the major topics within each chapter.

- *Individual chapters.* Each chapter of *Psychology in Action* contains numerous learning aids to help you master the material. There are chapter outlines, learning outcomes, running glossaries, "Check & Review" (summaries and self-test questions), "Visual Summaries," and more. These learning aids are highlighted and explained in the margin of this first chapter.

- *Appendixes.* Appendix A (Statistics) and Appendix B (Answers to Check & Review Questions and Activities) present important information. The statistics appendix

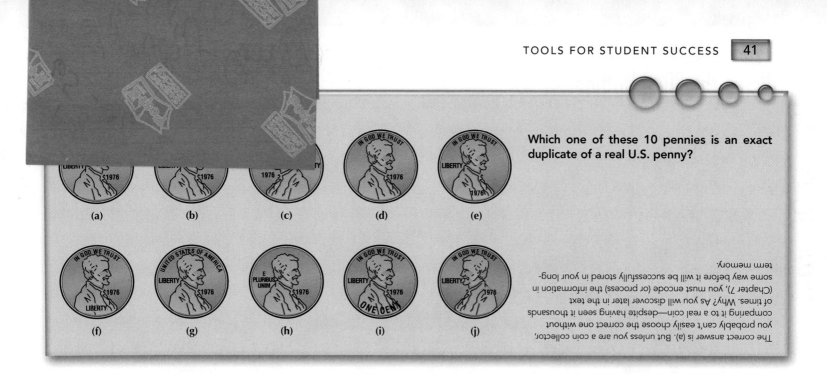

Which one of these 10 pennies is an exact duplicate of a real U.S. penny?

The correct answer is (a). But unless you are a coin collector, you probably can't easily choose the correct one without comparing it to a real coin—despite having seen it thousands of times. Why? As you will discover later in the text (Chapter 7), you must encode (or process) the information in some way before it will be successfully stored in your long-term memory.

further discusses some of the concepts introduced in Chapter 1. It also explains how to read and interpret the graphs and tables found throughout the text. Appendix B contains answers to the "Check & Review" questions, "Try This Yourself" activities, and other exercises found in the chapters.

- *Glossary.* This text presents two glossaries. A running glossary appears in the margins of each chapter alongside key terms and concepts. A cumulative glossary, which gathers all key terms from each chapter, appears at the end of this text. Use this end-of-book glossary to review terms from other chapters.

- *References.* As you read each chapter, you will see references cited in parentheses, not in footnotes, as is common in other disciplines. For example, (Ventner et al., 2001) refers to an article written by Craig Ventner and his colleagues announcing the first successful mapping of the full human genome, which was published in 2001. All the references cited in the text are listed in alphabetical order (by the author's last name) in the References section at the back of the book.

- *Name index and subject index.* If you are interested in learning more about a particular individual, look for his or her name in the Name Index. The page numbers refer you to every place in the text where the individual is mentioned. If you are interested in a specific subject (e.g., anorexia nervosa or stress), check the Subject Index for page references.

STEP TWO: How to Read a Chapter

Once you have a sense of the book as a whole, your next step to success is improving your general reading skills. The most important tool for college success is the ability to read and master the assigned class text. Many colleges offer instruction in reading efficiency, and I highly recommend that you take the course. All students can become faster and more efficient readers, and this section can offer only the highlights of a full-length course.

One of the best ways to read *actively* is to use the SQ4R method, developed by Francis Robinson (1970). The initials stand for six steps in effective reading: *Survey, Question, Read, Recite, Review, and wRite.* Robinson's technique helps you better understand and remember what you read. As you might have guessed, *Psychology in Action* was designed to incorporate each of these six steps (Process Diagram 1.3).

Process Diagram 1.3
Using the SQ4R Method

Survey
Each chapter of the text opens with an illustrated Chapter Outline, and each section includes Learning Objectives. Together they provide an overview, or survey, of the chapter. Knowing what to expect from a chapter can help you focus on the main points.

Question
To maintain your attention and increase comprehension, each chapter includes a number of Learning Objectives. Use them to form questions, then keep the questions in mind while reading each of the chapter's sections.

wRite
In addition to the writing you do in the previous steps, take your textbooks to class and write brief notes in the margins or on a separate sheet of paper. This will help keep you focused during your reading.

Read
Try to answer the questions you formed in the previous step as you read the chapter. Read carefully—in short, concentrated time periods.

Review
Review the Visual Summary at the end of each chapter. Answer the Concept Check questions that conclude each major section and the Critical and Creative Thinking Questions at the end of each chapter. Write down your responses before checking your answers. When you finish the chapter, look back over your answers, the chapter headings, and the Learning Objectives for each section. Repeat this review process before each class quiz or exam.

Recite
After you have read one small section, stop and silently recite what you've just read or make a written summary. To better retain the material, think of personal examples of major concepts and how you might apply a certain concept to real-life situations.

Pixtal/Age Fotostock

TIME MANAGEMENT *How to Succeed in College and Still Have a Life*

Time management is not only desirable; it is also essential to college success. If you answer yes to each of the following, congratulate yourself and move on to the next section.

1. I have a good balance among work, college, and social activities.

2. I set specific, written goals and deadlines for achieving them.

3. I complete my assignments and papers on time and seldom stay up late to cram the night before an exam.

4. I am generally on time for classes, appointments, and work.

5. I am good at estimating how much time it will take to complete a task.

6. I recognize that I am less productive at certain times of the day (e.g., right after lunch), and I plan activities accordingly.

7. I am good at identifying and eliminating nonessential tasks from my schedule and delegate work whenever possible.

8. I prioritize my responsibilities and assign time accordingly.

9. I arrange my life to avoid unnecessary interruptions (visitors, meetings, telephone calls during study hours).

10. I am able to say no to unnecessary or unreasonable requests for my time.

David Young-Wolff/PhotoEdit

If you cannot answer yes to each of these statements and need help with time management, here are four basic strategies:

1. *Establish a baseline.* To break any bad habit (poor time management, excessive TV watching, overeating), you must first establish a *baseline*—a characteristic level of performance for assessing changes in behavior. Before attempting any changes, simply record your day-to-day activities for one to two weeks (see the sample in Figure 1.11). Like most dieters who are shocked at their daily eating habits, most students are unpleasantly surprised when they recognize how poorly they manage their time.

2. *Set up a realistic activity schedule.* Once you realize how you typically spend your time each day, you can begin to manage it. Start by making a daily and weekly "to do" list. Be sure to include all required activities (class attendance, study time, work, etc.), as well as basic maintenance tasks like laundry, cooking, cleaning, and eating. Using this list, create a daily schedule of activities that includes time for each of these required activities and maintenance tasks. Also, be sure to schedule a reasonable amount of "downtime" for sports, movies, TV watching, and social activities with friends and family.

Try to be realistic. Some students try to replace all the hours they previously "wasted" watching TV or visiting friends with studying. Obviously, this approach inevitably fails. To make permanent time management changes, you must shape your behavior (see Chapter 6). That is, start small and build. For example, schedule 15 minutes increased study time for the first few days, then move to 30 minutes, 60 minutes, and so on.

3. *Reward yourself for good behavior.* The most efficient way to maintain good behavior is to reward it—the sooner, the better (Chapter 6). Unfortunately, the rewards of college (a degree and/or job advancement) are generally years away. To get around this problem and improve your time management skills, give yourself immediate, tangible rewards for sticking with your daily schedule. Allow yourself a guilt-free call to a friend, for example, or time for a favorite TV program after studying for your set period.

wiley.com/
college/
huffman

	Sunday	Monday	Tuesday	Wednesday	Thursday	Friday	Saturday
7:00		Breakfast		Breakfast		Breakfast	
8:00		History	Breakfast	History	Breakfast	History	
9:00		Psychology	Statistics	Psychology	Statistics	Psychology	
10:00		Review History & Psychology	Campus Job	Review History & Psychology	Statistics Lab	Review History & Psychology	
11:00		Biology		Biology		Biology	
12:00		Lunch / Study		Exercise	Lunch	Exercise	
1:00		Bio Lab	Lunch	Lunch	Study	Lunch	
2:00			Study	Study			

Figure 1.11 *Sample record of daily activities* To help manage your time, draw a grid similar to this and record your daily activities in appropriate boxes. Then fill in other necessities, such as extra study time and "downtime."

4. *Maximize your time.* Time management experts, such as Alan Lakein (1998), suggest you should "work harder, not longer." Many students report that they are studying all the time. Ironically, they may be confusing "fret time" (worrying and complaining) and useless prep time (fiddling around getting ready to study) with real, *concentrated* study time.

Time experts also point out that people generally overlook important "time opportunities." For example, if you ride the bus to class, you can use this time to review notes or read a textbook. If you drive yourself and waste time looking for parking spaces, go earlier and spend the extra time studying in your car or classroom. While waiting for doctor or dental appointments or to pick up your kids after school, take out your text and study for 10 to 20 minutes. These hidden moments count!

STRATEGIES FOR GRADE IMPROVEMENT

Note Taking, Study Habits, and General Test-Taking Tips

- **Note taking.** Effective note taking depends on *active listening*. Find a seat in the front of the class and look directly at the instructor while he or she is talking. Focus your attention on what is being said by asking yourself, "What is the main idea?" Write down key ideas and supporting details and examples, including important names, dates, and new terms. Do not try to write down everything the instructor says, word for word. This is passive, rote copying—not active listening. Also, be sure to take extra notes if your professor says, "This is an important concept," or if he or she writes notes on the board. Finally, arrive in class on time and do not leave early—you may miss important notes and assignments.
- **Distributed study time.** The single most important key to improved grades may be distributed study time. Although it does help to intensively review before a quiz or exam, if this is your major method of studying, you are not likely to do well in any college course. One of the clearest findings in psychology is that spaced practice is a much more

efficient way to study and learn than massed practice (Chapter 7). Just as you would not wait until the night before a big basketball game to begin practicing your free throws, you should not wait until the night before an exam to begin studying.

- **Complete learning.** Many students study just to the point where they can recite the immediate information. For best results, you should fully master the material, and be able to apply key terms and concepts to examples other than the ones in the text. You also should repeatedly review the material (using visualization and rehearsal) until it is firmly locked in place. This is particularly important if you suffer from test anxiety. For additional help on test anxiety and improving memory in general, see Chapter 7.

Pixtal/Age Fotostock America, Inc.

- **Understand your professor.** Pay close attention to the lecture time spent on various topics. This is generally a good indication of what your instructor considers important (and what may appear on exams). Also, try to understand the perspective (and personality) of your instructor. Recognize that most professors went into education because they love the academic life. They were probably model students who attended class regularly, submitted work on time, and seldom missed an exam. Remember that professors also have many students and hear many excuses for missing class and exams. Finally, note that most professors enjoyed lectures during college and were trained under this system. Never say, "I missed last week's classes. Did I miss anything important?" This is guaranteed to upset the most even-tempered instructor!

- **General test taking.** Here are several strategies to improve your performance on multiple-choice exams:

1. *Take your time.* Carefully read each question and each of the alternative answers. Do not choose the first answer that looks correct. There may be a better alternative farther down the list.

2. *Be test smart.* If you are unsure of an answer, make a logical guess. Begin by eliminating any answer that you know is incorrect. If two answers both seem reasonable, try to recall specific information from the text or professor's lecture. Be sure to choose "all of the above" if you know that at least two of the options are correct. Similarly, if you are confident that one of the options is incorrect, *never* choose "all of the above."

3. *Review your answers.* After you finish a test, go back and check your answers. Make sure you have responded to all the questions and recorded your answers correctly. Also, bear in mind that information relevant to one question is often found in another test question. Do not hesitate to change an answer if you get more information—or even if you simply have a hunch about a better answer. Although many students (and faculty) believe "your first hunch is your best guess," research suggests this may be bad advice (Benjamin, Cavell, & Shallenberger, 1984). Changing answers is far more likely to result in a higher score (Figure 1.12). The popular myth of not changing answers probably persists because we tend to pay more attention to failures than successes. Think about what happens when you get a test back. Most students pay attention to only the items they got wrong and fail to note the number of times they changed from an incorrect to a correct answer.

4. *Practice your test taking.* Complete the "Check & Review" sections found throughout each chapter and then check your answers in Appendix B. Make up questions from your lectures and text notes. Also, try the interactive quizzes on our website http://www.wiley.com/college/huffman. Each chapter of the text has numerous quizzes, most with individualized feedback. If you answer a question incorrectly, you get immediate feedback and further explanations that help you master the material.

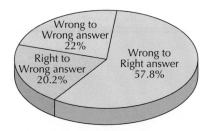

Figure 1.12 ***Should you change your answers?*** Yes! According to research, answer changes that go from a wrong to a right answer (57.8 percent) greatly outnumber those that go from a right to a wrong answer (20.2 percent). *Source:* Benjamin, L. T., Cavell, T. A., & Shallenberger, W. R. (1984). Staying with initial answers on objective tests: Is it a myth? *Teaching Psychology,* 11, 133–141.

wiley.com/ college/ huffman

ADDITIONAL RESOURCES *Frequently Overlooked Helpers*

In addition to college counselors and financial aid officers, students often overlook these resources in their search for success:

1. *Instructors.* Get to know your instructors. They can provide useful tips for succeeding in their course. However, it is up to you to discover their office hours and office location. If their office hours conflict with your schedule, ask for an alternative appointment, try to stop by right before or after class, or e-mail them.

2. *College courses.* College instructors often assign two or three books per course and numerous papers that must be typed. *All students* can improve their reading speed and comprehension, and their word-processing/typing skills, by taking additional college courses designed to develop these specific abilities.

3. *Friends and family.* Ask friends or family members to serve as your conscience/coach for improved time management and study skills. After completing your daily activity schedule (page 44), set up weekly (or biweekly) appointments with a friend or family member to check your progress and act as your "conscience." You may think it would be easy to lie to your conscience/coach. But most people find it much harder to lie to another person than to lie to themselves (about calories, study time, TV watching, etc.). Encourage your conscience/coach to ask pointed questions about your actual study time versus your *fretting* and *prepping* time.

4. *Roommates, classmates, and study groups.* Although college roommates and friendly classmates can sometimes be a distraction, you can enlist their help as your conscience/coach or study partner. Also, ask your classmates and roommates what tricks/techniques they use to maintain their attention and interest during lectures or while reading texts.

If you would like more information on student success skills, consult the *Psychology in Action* website http://www.wiley.com/college/huffman. In addition to the interactive tutorials and quizzes mentioned earlier, we also offer specific Internet links for student success and recommend books and articles on time management and the other topics discussed here.

A FINAL WORD *Your Attitude*

Imagine for a moment that the toilet in your bathroom is overflowing and creating a horrible, smelly mess. Whom should you reward? The plumber who quickly and efficiently solves the problem? Or someone who "tries very hard"?

Some students may believe they can pass college courses by simply attending class and doing the assignments. This might have worked for *some* students in *some* classes in high school. But it probably will not work in college. Most college professors seldom assign homework and may not notice if you skip class. They assume students are independent, self-motivated adult learners.

Professors also generally consider college a last stop on the way to the real world. They believe grades should reflect knowledge and performance—not effort. Points may be given in some classes for attendance, participation, and effort. However, the heaviest weight will usually come from exams, papers, and projects. Did you fix the toilet or not?

Assessment

STOP

CHECK & REVIEW

Cultural Universal and Tools for Student Success

Objective 1.16: *Are there cultural universals?*

Some cultural psychologists do believe certain aspects of human behavior and mental processes are true and universal for all cultures, and they suggest that emotions and facial recognition of emotions are prime examples. Critics of this position say that Western psychologists have no experience with culturally specific emotions, and that if cultural universals exist they are innate and biological. The answer appears to be that certain behaviors are both biological and culturally universal.

Objective 1.17: *How can I use psychology to study and learn psychology?*

There are several important psychological techniques that will help you study and learn psychology. They fall into the general categories of *active reading*, *time management*, *strategies for grade improvement*, and *additional resources*.

Questions

1. According to "universalists," _____ and _____ provide the clearest examples of possible cultural universals?

2. List the 6 steps in the SQ4R method.

3. According to the text, _____ might be the single most important key to improved grades. (a) successful time management; (b) distributed study time; (c) complete learning; (d) none of these options.

Check your answers in Appendix B.

Click & Review
for additional assessment options:
wiley.com/college/huffman

Assessment

KEY TERMS

*To assess your understanding of the **Key Terms** in Chapter 1, write a definition for each (in your own words), and then compare your definitions with those in the text.*

Introducing Psychology
critical thinking (p. 4)
nature–nurture controversy (p. 6)
psychology (p. 4)

Origins of Psychology
behavioral perspective (p. 11)
biopsychosocial model (p. 14)
cognitive perspective (p. 12)
evolutionary perspective (p. 12)
humanistic perspective (p. 11)
neuroscience/biopsychology
    perspective (p. 12)
positive psychology (p. 12)
psychoanalytic/psychodynamic
    perspective (p. 10)
sociocultural perspective (p. 13)

The Science of Psychology
applied research (p. 16)
basic research (p. 16)
debriefing (p. 19)
hypothesis (p. 17)
informed consent (p. 18)
meta-analysis (p. 16)
operational definition (p. 17)
theory (p. 17)

Research Methods
biological research (p. 33)
case study (p. 30)
control group (p. 24)
correlation coefficient (p. 32)
correlational research (p. 31)
dependent variable (DV) (p. 24)
descriptive research (p. 28)

Study Tip

Key Terms
The list of key terms at the end of each chapter is helpful to your mastery of the most important concepts. Try to recite aloud and/or write a brief definition for each term. Then, turn to the relevant pages in the chapter and check your understanding.

double-blind study (p. 25)
ethnocentrism (p. 25)
experiment (p. 21)
experimental group (p. 24)
experimenter bias (p. 22)
independent variable (IV) (p. 24)
misattribution of arousal (p. 27)
naturalistic observation (p. 29)
participant bias (p. 26)
placebo [pluh-SEE-bo] (p. 25)
random assignment (p. 26)
sample bias (p. 25)
survey (p. 30)

Achievement

WEB RESOURCES

Huffman Book Companion Site
wiley.com/college/huffman
    This site is loaded with free Interactive Self-Tests, Internet Exercises, Glossary and Flashcards for key terms, web links, Handbook for Non-Native Speakers, and other activities designed to improve your mastery of the material in this chapter.

wiley.com/
college/
huffman

Chapter 1 Visual Summary

Introducing Psychology

What Is Psychology?

Scientific study of behavior and mental processes that values empirical evidence and **critical thinking**.

Psychology's Goals

Describe, explain, predict, and change behavior and mental processes.

Careers in the Field

Occupational examples include experimental, biopsychology, cognitive, developmental, clinical, and counseling.

Gary D. Landsman/©Corbis

Origins of Psychology

- *Structuralism:* Focused on consciousness and the structure of the mind using introspection.

- *Functionalism:* Emphasized function of mental processes in adapting to the environment and practical applications of psychology.

Modern Perspectives

1. **Psychoanalytic/Psychodynamic:** Emphasizes unconscious processes and unresolved past conflicts.

2. **Behavioral:** Studies objective, observable, environmental influences on overt behavior.

3. **Humanistic:** Focuses on free will, self-actualization, and human nature as positive and growth seeking.

4. **Cognitive:** Emphasizes thinking, perception, problem solving, memory, language and information processing.

5. **Neuroscience/Biopsychology:** Studies genetics and biological processes in the brain and other parts of the nervous system.

6. **Evolutionary:** Studies natural selection, adaptation, and evolution of behavior and mental processes.

7. **Sociocultural:** Focuses on social interaction and cultural determinants of behavior and mental processes.

■ **Women and Minorities:** Sumner, Clark, Calkins, and Washburn made important contributions.

The Science of Psychology

Ethical Guidelines

Human research participants have rights, including **informed consent**, voluntary participation, limited and careful use of deception, **debriefing**, and **confidentiality**. Psychologists are expected to maintain high ethical standards in their relations with human and nonhuman animal research participants, as well as with clients in therapy. The APA has published guidelines detailing these ethical standards.

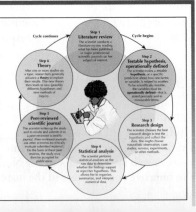

Four Major Research Methods

1. Experimental Research

Distinguishing feature: Establishes cause and effect *Components:*

- **Independent variables** (what the experimenter manipulates)
- **Dependent variables** (what the experimenter measures)
- *Experimental controls* (including **control group**, **experimental group**, extraneous variables)

2. Descriptive Research

Distinguishing feature: Unlike experiments, cannot determine causes of behavior but can describe specifics. *Types of descriptive research:*

- **Naturalistic observation** describes behavior in its natural habitat without altering it.
- **Surveys** use interviews or questionnaires on a sample of participants.
- **Case studies** are in-depth investigations.

3. Correlational Research

Distinguishing feature: Provides important research findings and predictions by examining how strongly two variables are related, and if the relationship is positively, negatively, or not at all (zero) correlated.

4. Biological Research

Methods include brain dissection, lesioning, direct observation, case studies, electrical recording (EEG), and brain imaging (such as CT, PET, MRI, fMRI).

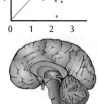
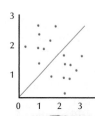

Experimental Safeguards

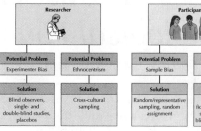

Researcher		Participant	
Potential Problem Experimenter Bias	**Potential Problem** Ethnocentrism	**Potential Problem** Sample Bias	**Potential Problem** Participant Bias
Solution Blind observers, single- and double-blind studies, placebos	**Solution** Cross-cultural sampling	**Solution** Random/representative sampling, random assignment	**Solution** Anonymity, confidentiality, deception, single- and double-blind studies, placebos

💡 *Study Tip*

Visual Summary
At the end of each chapter, the entire chapter is summarized in a unique two-page visual format that organizes all the main concepts and key terms. It also provides a quick "roadmap" to study before reading the chapter and a brief review after completing your reading.

Tools for Student Success

1. **Use Active Reading to Study this Text**
   - **Familiarize yourself with the general text**
   - **Use SQ4R to read each chapter: Survey/Question/Read/Recite/ Review/wRite**

2. **Use Time Management to Succeed in College**
   - **Establish a baseline, set up a realistic activity schedule, reward yourself for good behavior, maximize your time**

3. **Strategies for Grade Improvement**
   - **Focus on note taking, distributed study time, complete learning, understanding your instructor, and general test-taking skills**

4. **Additional Resources**
   - **Instructors, typing and speed-reading courses, friends and family, roommates, classmates, and study groups**

2

Neuroscience and Biological Foundations

W hat are you doing at this very moment? Obviously, your eyes are busily translating squiggly little black symbols called "letters" into meaningful patterns called "words." But what part of your body does the translation? If you put this book down and walk away to get a snack or talk to a friend, what moves your legs and enables you to speak? You've heard the saying, "I think; therefore I am." What if you were no longer capable of thought or feeling? Would "you" still exist?

Although ancient cultures, including the Egyptian, Indian, and Chinese, believed the heart was the center of all thoughts and emotions, we now know that the brain and the rest of the nervous system are the power behind our psychological life and much of our physical being. This chapter introduces you to the important and exciting field of **neuroscience** and *biopsychology*, the scientific study of the *biology* of behavior and mental processes. It also provides a foundation for understanding several fascinating discoveries and facts, as well as important biological processes discussed throughout the text.

The brain is the last and grandest biological frontier, the most complex thing we have yet discovered in our universe. It contains hundreds of billions of cells interlinked through trillions of connections. The brain boggles the mind.

JAMES WATSON
(Nobel Prize Winner)

We sit on the threshold of important new advances in neuroscience that will yield increased understanding of how the brain functions and of more effective treatments to heal brain disorders and diseases. How the brain behaves in health and disease may well be the most important question in our lifetime.

RICHARD D. BROADWELL
(from *Neuroscience, Memory and the Brain*, 1995)

Neuroscience *Interdisciplinary field studying how biological processes relate to behavioral and mental processes*

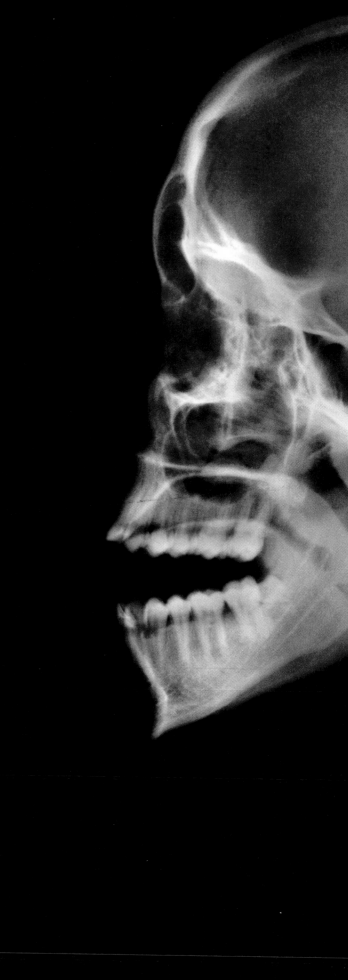

Peter Dazeley/Photographer's Choice/Getty Images

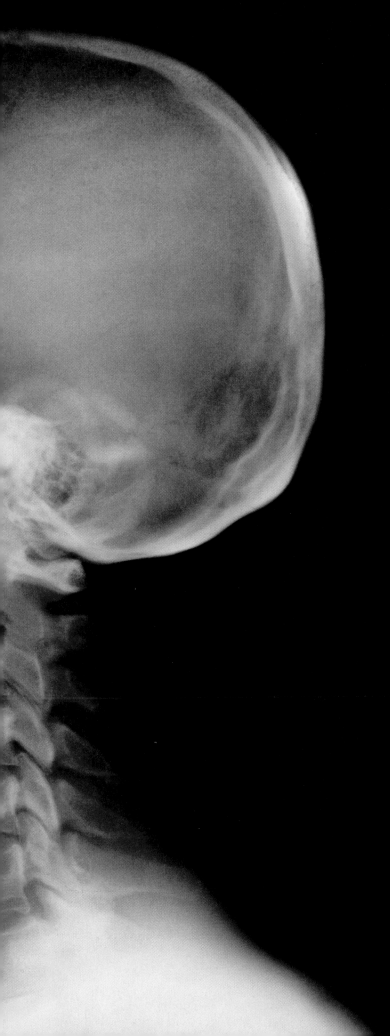

▶ **Neural Bases of Behavior**

What Is a Neuron?
How Do Neurons Communicate?

 PSYCHOLOGY AT WORK
  How Neurotransmitters and Hormones
  Affect Us

▶ **Nervous System Organization**

Central Nervous System (CNS)
Peripheral Nervous System (PNS)

▶ **A Tour Through the Brain**

Lower-Level Brain Structures
Cerebral Cortex

CASE STUDY/PERSONAL STORY
  Phineas Gage
Two Brains in One?

CRITICAL THINKING/ACTIVE LEARNING
  Biology and Critical Thinking

 PSYCHOLOGY AT WORK
  Working With Traumatic Brain Injuries (TBI)

▶ **Our Genetic Inheritance**

Behavioral Genetics

 PSYCHOLOGY AT WORK
  Overcoming Genetic Misconceptions
Evolutionary Psychology

 GENDER & CULTURAL DIVERSITY
  The Evolution of Sex Differences

Application

WHY STUDY PSYCHOLOGY?

Did you know

National Geographic/Getty Images

▶ The venom of a black widow spider is one of the most potent of all biologic toxins? Its bite releases massive amounts of a neuro-transmitter, called *acetylcholine* (ACH), which causes severe muscle pain and hypertension. Thankfully, it can only inject a small amount each time it bites.

▶ All your thoughts, feelings, and actions result from neurotransmitter messages flashing between billions of tiny nerve cells? Or that organisms from lizards to elephants all depend on much the same neurotransmitters that our own brains use?

▶ Scientists have established a link between sports-related repeated concussions and permanent and possibly fatal brain damage?

▶ The reappearance of certain infant reflexes in adults may be a sign of serious brain damage?

▶ A physician can declare you legally dead if your brain stops functioning—even though your heart and lungs are still working?

▶ Strong emotions, such as fear or anger, can stop digestion and sexual arousal?

▶ Cells in our brains die and regenerate throughout our lifetime?...They are also physically shaped and changed by learning and from experiences we have with our environment?

▶ Scientists have created human embryos through cloning? Or that extracted stem cells from embryos are also used for research and possible treatment for diseases like cancer, Parkinson's disease, and diabetes?

Sources: Abbott, 2004; Carlson, 2008; Hampton, 2007; Plomin, 1999; Romero et al., 2008; Zillmer, Spiers, & Culbertson, 2008.

Neural Bases of Behavior

Achievement

Objective 2.1: *What are the key parts and functions of the neuron?*

Neuron *Cell of the nervous system responsible for receiving and transmitting electrochemical information*

Glial Cells *Cells that provide structural, nutritional, and other support for the neurons, as well as communication within the nervous system; also called glia or neuroglia*

■ What Is a Neuron? Psychology at the Micro Level

Have you heard the expression "Information is power?" Nowhere is this truer than in the human body. Without information, we could not survive. Cells within our nervous system must take in sensory information from the outside world through our eyes, ears, and other sensory receptors, and then decide what to do with it. Just as the circulatory system handles *blood*, which conveys chemicals and oxygen, our nervous system uses chemicals and electrical processes that convey *information*.

Your brain and the rest of your nervous system essentially consist of **neurons**, cells of the nervous system that communicate electrochemical information throughout the brain and the rest of the body. Each neuron is a tiny information-processing system with thousands of connections for receiving and sending signals to other neurons. Although no one knows for sure, one well-educated guess is that each human body has as many as 100 *billion* neurons, about the same number as there are stars in the galaxy.

These neurons are held in place and supported by **glial cells** (from the Greek word for "glue"), which make up about 90 percent of the brain's cells. Glial cells surround neurons, perform cleanup tasks, and insulate one neuron from another so that their neural messages are not scrambled. Research also shows that glial cells play a direct role in nervous system communication (Arriagada et al., 2007; Wieseler-Frank, Maier, & Watkins, 2005; Zillmer, Spiers, & Culbertson, 2008). However, the "star" of the communication show is still the neuron.

Basic Parts of a Neuron

Just as no two people are alike, no two neurons are the same. However, most neurons do share three basic features: dendrites, cell body, and axon (Figure 2.1). **Dendrites** look like leafless branches of a tree. In fact, the word *dendrite* means "little tree" in Greek. Dendrites act like antennas, receiving electrochemical information from other neurons and transmitting it to the cell body. Each neuron may have hundreds or thousands of dendrites and their branches. From the many dendrites, information flows into the **cell body**, or soma (Greek for "body"), which accepts the incoming messages. If the cell body receives enough stimulation from its dendrites, it will pass the message on to the **axon** (from the Greek word for "axle"). Like a miniature cable, this long, tubelike structure then carries information away from the cell body.

The **myelin sheath**, a white, fatty coating around the axons of some neurons, is not considered one of the three key features of a neuron, but it does insulate and speed neural impulses. Its importance becomes readily apparent in certain diseases, such as multiple sclerosis, in which the myelin progressively deteriorates and the person gradually loses muscular coordination. Thankfully, the disease often goes into remission, but it can be fatal if it strikes the neurons that control basic life-support processes, such as breathing or heartbeat.

Near each axon's end, the axon branches out, and at the tip of each branch are *terminal buttons*, which release chemicals (called *neurotransmitters*). These chemicals move the message from the end of the sending neuron to the dendrites or cell body

Dendrites *Branching neuron structures that receive neural impulses from other neurons and convey impulses toward the cell body*

Cell Body *Part of the neuron containing the cell nucleus, as well as other structures that help the neuron carry out its functions; also known as the soma*

Axon *Long, tubelike structure that conveys impulses away from the neuron's cell body toward other neurons or to muscles or glands*

Myelin [My-uh-lin] Sheath
Layer of fatty insulation wrapped around the axon of some neurons, which increases the rate at which nerve impulses travel along the axon

 Study Tip

Be careful not to confuse the term neuron *with the term* nerve. *Nerves are large bundles of axons that carry impulses to and from the brain and spinal cord.*

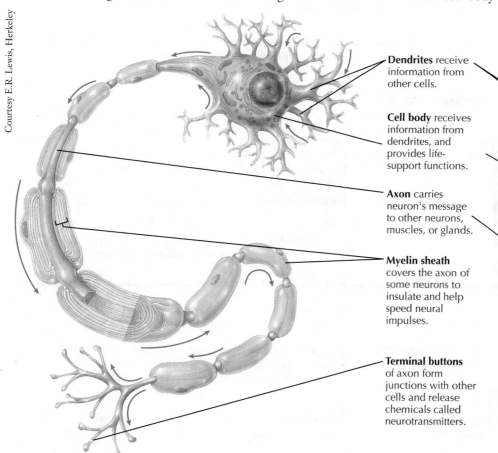

Dendrites receive information from other cells.

Cell body receives information from dendrites, and provides life-support functions.

Axon carries neuron's message to other neurons, muscles, or glands.

Myelin sheath covers the axon of some neurons to insulate and help speed neural impulses.

Terminal buttons of axon form junctions with other cells and release chemicals called neurotransmitters.

Courtesy E.R. Lewis, Herkeley

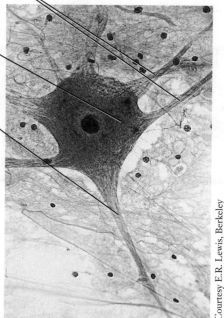

Courtesy E.R. Lewis, Berkeley

Figure 2.1 **The structure of a motor neuron** To remember how information travels through the neuron, think of the three key parts in reverse alphabetical order: Dendrite → Cell Body → Axon (D, C, B, A).

of the next receiving neuron, and the message continues. Neurotransmitters will be studied in depth in the upcoming sections.

How Do Neurons Communicate? An Electrical and Chemical Language

A neuron's basic function is to transmit information throughout the nervous system. Neurons "speak" to each other or, in some cases, to muscles or glands, in a type of electrical and chemical language (Process Diagram 2.1a,b).

PSYCHOLOGY AT WORK

How Neurotransmitters and Hormones Affect Us

After studying the admittedly complex processes of neural communication in Process Diagram 2.1, are you wondering what all of this has to do with you and your everyday life? If so, you'll be excited by the following details on *neurotransmitters* and *hormones*.

Neurotransmitters

Researchers have discovered hundreds of substances known (or suspected) to function as neurotransmitters. Some of the neurotransmitters' functions are to regulate the actions of glands and muscles, and to promote sleep, mental and physical alertness, learning and memory, motivation, and emotions. They also influence, or may cause, psychological disorders, including schizophrenia and depression. Table 2.1 lists a few of the better-understood neurotransmitters and their known or suspected effects.

SUMMARY TABLE 2.1 HOW NEUROTRANSMITTERS AFFECT US

Neurotransmitter	Known or Suspected Effects
Serotonin	Mood, sleep, appetite, sensory perception, arousal, temperature regulation, pain suppression, and impulsivity (Chapters 2, 10, 12, 16). Low levels associated with depression.
Acetylcholine (ACh)	Muscle action, learning, memory, REM (rapid-eye-movement) sleep, emotion (Chapters 2, 3, 7). Decreased ACh plays a suspected role in Alzheimer's disease.
Dopamine (DA)	Movement, attention, memory, learning, and emotion (Chapters 2, 3, 14). Excess DA associated with schizophrenia, too little with Parkinson's disease. Also plays a role in addiction and the reward system.
Norepinephrine (NE) (or noradrenaline)	Learning, memory, dreaming, emotion, waking from sleep, eating, alertness, wakefulness, reactions to stress (Chapters 2, 3, 14). Low levels of NE associated with depression, high levels with agitated, manic states.
Epinephrine (or adrenaline)	Emotional arousal, memory storage, and metabolism of glucose necessary for energy release (Chapters 2, 3, 7).
GABA (gamma aminobutyric acid)	Neural inhibition in the central nervous system (Chapters 2, 10, 15, 16). Tranquilizing drugs, like Valium, increase GABA's inhibitory effects and thereby decrease anxiety.
Endorphins	Mood, pain, memory, learning, blood pressure, appetite, and sexual activity (Chapters 2, 3, 4, 5).

Yuri Kadobnov/AFP/Getty Images

Which neurotransmitters best explain this Olympic skater's exceptional skills?

Process Diagram 2.1
How Neurons Communicate

Communication WITHIN the Neuron (Part A)

The process of neural communication begins within the neuron itself when the dendrites and cell body receive information and conduct it toward the axon. From there, the information travels down the entire length of the axon via a brief traveling electrical charge called an **action potential***, which can be described in three steps:*

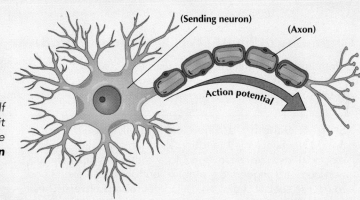

(Sending neuron)

(Axon)

Action potential

Step 1: Resting Potential When an axon is not stimulated, it is in a polarized state, called the *resting potential.* "At rest," the fluid inside the axon has more negatively charged ions than the fluid outside. This results from the selective permeability of the axon membrane and a series of mechanisms, called *sodium-potassium pumps,* which pull potassium ions in and pump sodium ions out of the axon. The inside of the axon has a charge of about -70 millivolts relative to the outside.

[Note that neurons, like a standard battery, generate electrical potential from chemical processes, and batteries have positive and negative poles that are similarly "polarized."]

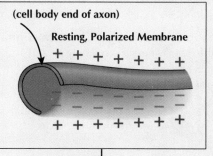

(cell body end of axon)

Resting, Polarized Membrane

Masterfile

Step 2: Action Potential Initiation When an "at rest" axon membrane is stimulated by a sufficiently strong signal, it produces an *action potential* (or depolarization). This action potential begins when the first part of the axon opens its "gates" and positively charged sodium ions rush through. The additional sodium ions change the previously negative charge inside the axon to a positive charge—thus depolarizing the axon.

[Note that an action potential is either "on" or "off"—the so-called *all-or-nothing law.* Like a standard light switch (without a dimmer), if the axon receives a stimulus above a certain threshold, the action potential "turns on." Increasing the stimulation (like flipping the switch harder) will not affect the intensity of the light or the speed or intensity of the neural message.]

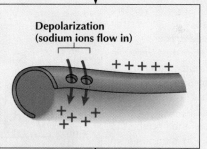

Depolarization (sodium ions flow in)

Step 3: Spreading of Action Potential and Repolarization *The initial depolarization (or action potential) of Step 2 produces a subsequent imbalance of ions in the adjacent axon membrane. This imbalance thus causes the action potential to spread to the next section. Meanwhile, "gates" in the axon membrane of the initially depolarized section open and potassium ions flow out, thus allowing the first section to repolarize and return to its resting potential.*

Overall Summary: As you can see in the figure to the right, this sequential process of depolarization, followed by repolarization, transmits the action potential along the entire length of the axon from the cell body to the terminal buttons. This is similar to an audience at an athletic event doing "the wave." One section of fans initially stands up for a brief time (action potential). This section then sits down (resting potential), and the "wave" then spreads to adjacent sections.

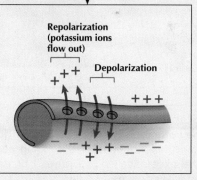

Repolarization (potassium ions flow out)

Depolarization

Lori Adamski Peet/Getty Images

[Note: This three-step description of the action potential applies to a "bare" axon. As you saw in Figure 2.1, many axons are covered with a fatty insulation, the *myelin sheath,* which blankets the axon with the exception of periodic *nodes* (points at which the myelin is very thin or absent). These nodes allow the neural message to travel about 10 times faster than in a bare axon because the action potential jumps from node to node rather than traveling along the entire axon.]

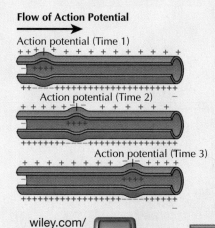

Flow of Action Potential

Action potential (Time 1)

Action potential (Time 2)

Action potential (Time 3)

Action Potential *Neural impulse, or brief electrical charge, that carries information along the axon of a neuron. The action potential is generated when positively charged ions move in and out through channels in the axon's membrane*

wiley.com/college/huffman

Communication BETWEEN Neurons (Part B)

Communication within the neuron (Part A) is not the same as communication between neurons (Part B): Within the neuron, messages travel electrically. Between neurons, messages are transmitted chemically. Steps 4, 5, and 6 summarize this chemical transmission:

Step 4: Sending a Chemical Signal When the action potential reaches the branching axon terminals, the previous *electrical impulse* is converted to a *chemical signal*. The action potential triggers the terminal buttons at the axon's end to release special chemicals, called **neurotransmitters**. These chemicals then flow across a small gap, called the **synapse**, to potentially attach to receptors in nearby neurons.

Step 5: Receiving a Chemical Signal Like a lock and key, the nearby neurons will only accept and receive the chemical message if the neurotransmitter molecules are of the appropriate shape. The successfully shaped "keys" will then either *excite or inhibit* a new action potential in the postsynaptic neuron.

It's important also to know that each receiving neuron gets multiple neurotransmitter messages. As you can see in this close-up photo to the right, the axon terminals from thousands of other nearby neurons almost completely cover the cell body of the receiving neuron.

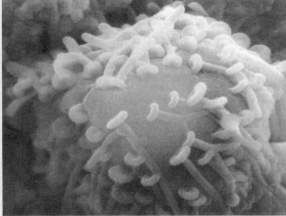

Courtesy E.R. Lewis, Berkeley

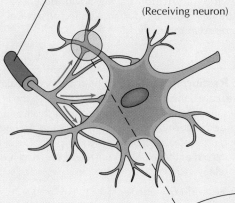

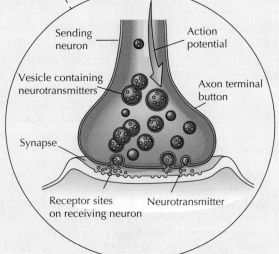

Step 6: Dealing with Left-overs What happens to excess neurotransmitters or to those that do not "fit" into the adjacent receptor sites? The sending neuron normally reabsorbs the excess (called "reuptake") or they are broken down by special enzymes.

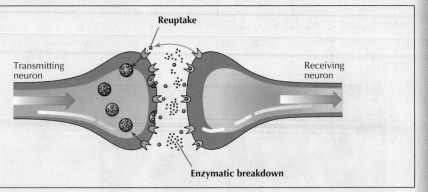

Neurotransmitters *Chemicals released by neurons that travel across the synaptic gap*

Synapse [SIN-aps] *Junction between the axon tip of the sending neuron and the dendrite or cell body of the receiving neuron. During an action potential, chemicals called neurotransmitters are released and flow across the synaptic gap*

Endorphins   Perhaps the best-known neurotransmitters are the *endogenous opioid peptides*, commonly known as **endorphins**. These chemicals mimic the effects of opium-based drugs such as morphine—they elevate mood and reduce pain.

Endorphins were discovered in the early 1970s, when Candace Pert and Solomon Snyder (1973) were doing research on morphine, a pain-relieving and mood-elevating opiate derived from opium, which is made from poppies. They found that the morphine was taken up by specialized receptors in areas of the brain linked with mood and pain sensations.

But why would the brain have special receptors for morphine—a powerfully addicting drug? Pert and Snyder reasoned that the brain must have its own internally produced, or *endogenous*, morphine-like chemicals. They later confirmed that such chemicals do exist and named them *endorphins* (a contraction of *endogenous* ["self-produced"] and *morphine*). The brain evidently produces its own naturally occurring chemical messengers that elevate mood and reduce pain, as well as affect memory, learning, blood pressure, appetite, and sexual activity (Chapters 3, 4, and 11). Endorphins also help explain why soldiers and athletes continue to fight or play the game despite horrific injuries.

Neurotransmitters and Disease   One of the many benefits of studying your brain and its neurotransmitters is an increased understanding of your own or others' medical problems and their treatment. For example, do you remember why actor Michael J. Fox retired from his popular TV sitcom, *Spin City?* It was because of muscle tremors and movement problems related to a poorly understood condition called *Parkinson's disease (PD)*. As Table 2.1 shows, the neurotransmitter *dopamine* is a suspected factor in PD, and its symptoms are reduced with L-dopa (levodopa), a drug that increases dopamine levels in the brain (Bares, Kanovsky, & Rektor, 2007; Iversen & Iversen, 2007).

Interestingly, when some Parkinson's patients are adjusting to L-dopa and higher levels of dopamine, they may experience symptoms that mimic schizophrenia, a serious psychological disorder that disrupts thought processes and produces delusions and hallucinations. As you will see in Chapter 14, excessively high levels of *dopamine* are a suspected contributor to some forms of *schizophrenia*. When patients with schizophrenia take antipsychotic drugs that suppress dopamine, their psychotic symptoms are often reduced or eliminated (Iversen & Iversen, 2007). However, the drugs may also create symptoms of Parkinson's. Why is this so? The answer is found in the levels of dopamine released in their brains—*decreased* levels of dopamine are associated with Parkinson's disease, whereas *increased* levels are related to some forms of schizophrenia.

Another neurotransmitter, *serotonin* (Table 2.1, p. 54), may also be involved in the depression that often accompanies Parkinson's disease. Although some researchers believe Parkinson's patients become depressed in reaction to the motor disabilities of the disorder, others think the depression is directly related to lower levels of serotonin. As Chapter 14 discusses, antidepressant drugs, like *Prozac* and *Zoloft*, work by boosting levels of available serotonin.

Neurotransmitters, Poisons, and Mind-Altering Drugs   An understanding of neurotransmitters explains not only the origin of certain diseases and their pharmaceutical drug treatments, but also how poisons, such as black widow spider and snake venom, and mind-altering drugs, such as nicotine, alcohol, caffeine, and cocaine, affect the brain (see also Chapter 5).

Most poisons and drugs act at the synapse by replacing, decreasing, or enhancing the amount of neurotransmitter. Given that transmission of messages *between* neurons is chemical, it is not surprising that many chemicals we ingest from food, drugs, and other sources can significantly affect neurotransmission.

Endorphins [en-DOR-fins]
Chemical substances in the nervous system that are similar in structure and action to opiates; involved in pain control, pleasure, and memory

Alex Wong/Sport Services/Getty Images

Why study neurotransmitters? *Actor Michael J. Fox has been diagnosed with Parkinson's disease, which involves a decrease in cells that produce dopamine. In this photo, he is testifying before a U.S. congressional subcommittee to urge increased funding for research on Parkinson's and other medical conditions. For more information on his foundation for Parkinson's research, see www.michaeljfox.org.*

Endocrine [EN-doh-krin] system *Collection of glands located throughout the body that manufacture and secrete hormones into the bloodstream*

Hormones *Chemicals manufactured by endocrine glands and circulated in the bloodstream to produce bodily changes or maintain normal bodily functions*

Hormones

We've just seen how the nervous system uses neurons and neurotransmitters to transmit messages throughout the body. A second type of communication system also exists, which is made up of a network of glands, called the **endocrine system** (Figure 2.2). Rather than neurotransmitters, the endocrine system uses **hormones** (from the Greek *horman*, meaning to "stimulate" or "excite") to carry its messages (Figure 2.3).

Why is the endocrine system important? Without the hypothalamus and pituitary, the testes in men would not produce *testosterone* and the ovaries in women would not produce *estrogen*. As you may know, these hormones are of critical importance to sexual behavior and reproduction. In addition, the pituitary produces its own hormone that controls body growth. Too much of this hormone results in *gigantism*; too little will make a person far smaller than average, a *hypopituitary dwarf*.

Other hormones released by the endocrine system play important roles in maintaining your body's normal functioning. For example, hormones released by the kidneys help regulate blood pressure. The pancreatic hormone (insulin) allows cells to use sugar from the blood. Stomach and intestinal hormones help control digestion and elimination.

An additional function of the endocrine system is its control of our body's response to emergencies. In times of crisis, the hypothalamus sends messages through two pathways—the neural system and endocrine system (primarily the pituitary). The pituitary sends hormonal messages to the adrenal glands (located right above the kidneys). The adrenal glands then release *cortisol*, a "stress hormone" that boosts energy and blood sugar levels, *epinephrine* (commonly called adrenaline), and *norepinephrine*. (Remember from Table 2.1 that these same chemicals also serve as neurotransmitters when released by neurons.)

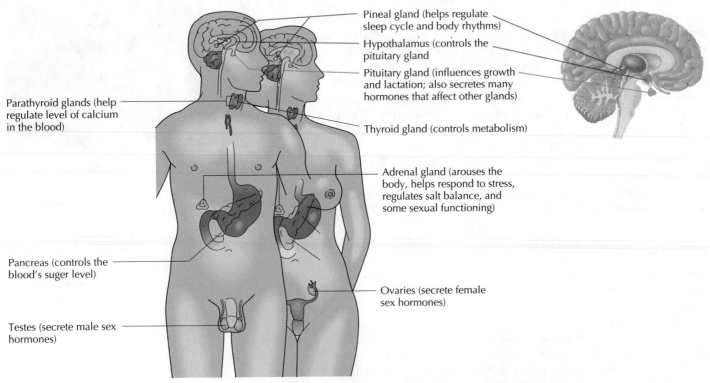

Figure 2.2 *The endocrine system* Hormones secreted by the endocrine system are as essential as neurotransmitters to the regulation of our bodily functions.

**Neurotransmitters
send individual messages**

**Hormones
send global messages**

To...	Jean Bean
CC...	
Subject:	Lunch Tomorrow?
Attach...	

Hi Jean,
Are you free for lunch tomorrow?
If so, want to meet at noon at the
Hong Kong Cafe? Hoping to see you
then.

To...	Friends; family; co-workers
CC...	
Subject:	Party!
Attach...	

Hi Everybody,
Jean Bean and I are hosting a party on
Saturday night at 9 p.m. Please come,
and tell your friends!

Figure 2.3 ***Why do we need two communication systems?*** Just as some e-mail messages are only sent to certain people, neurotransmitters only deliver messages to specific receptors, which other neurons nearby probably don't "overhear." Hormones, in contrast, are like a global e-mail message that you send to everyone in your address book. They are released from endocrine glands directly into the bloodstream, and then travel throughout the body, carrying messages to any cell that will listen. Hormones also function like your global e-mail recipients forwarding your message to yet more people. For example, a small part of the brain called the hypothalamus releases hormones that signal the pituitary (another small brain structure), which stimulates or inhibits the release of other hormones.

Assessment STOP

CHECK & REVIEW

Neural Bases of Behavior

Objective 2.1: *What are the key parts and functions of the neuron?*

Neurons are cells that transmit information throughout the body. They have three main parts: **dendrites**, which receive information from other neurons; the **cell body**, which provides nourishment and "decides" whether the axon should fire; and the **axon**, which sends along the neural information. **Glial cells** support and provide nutrients for neurons in the central nervous system (CNS).

Objective 2.2: *Describe how communication occurs within the neuron (the action potential) and between neurons.*

The process of neural communication begins *within* the neuron when the dendrites and cell body receive information and transmit it to the axon.

The axon is specialized for transmitting neural impulses, or **action potentials**. During times when no action potential is moving down the axon, the axon is at rest. The neuron is activated, and an action potential occurs when positively charged ions move in and out through channels in the axon's

membrane. Action potentials travel more quickly down myelinated axons because the **myelin sheath** serves as insulation.

Information is transferred from one neuron to another at **synapses** by chemicals called **neurotransmitters**. Neurotransmitters bind to receptor sites much as a key fits into a lock, and their effects can be excitatory or inhibitory.

Objective 2.3: *How do neurotransmitters and hormones relate to our everyday life?*

Neurotransmitters regulate glands and muscles, sleep, alertness, learning, memory, motivation, emotion, psychological disorders, etc.

Hormones are released from glands in the **endocrine system** directly into the bloodstream. They act at a distance on other glands, on muscles, and in the brain. The major functions of the endocrine system, including the hypothalamus, pituitary, thyroid, adrenals, testes, ovaries, and pancreas, are to help with regulation of long-term bodily processes (such as growth and sex characteristics), maintain ongoing bodily processes, and assist in regulating the emergency response to crises.

Questions

1. Label these five key parts of a neuron.

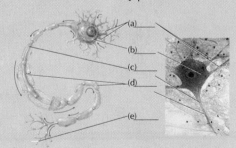

(a)
(b)
(c)
(d)
(e)

2. An impulse travels through the structures of the neuron in the following order: (a) cell body, axon, dendrites; (b) cell body, dendrites, axon; (c) dendrites, cell body, axon; (d) axon, cell body, dendrites
3. Chemical messengers that are released by axons and stimulate dendrites are called _____. (a) chemical messengers; (b) neurotransmitters; (c) synaptic transmitters; (d) neuromessengers
4. Briefly explain how neurotransmitters and hormones carry messages throughout the body.

Check your answers in Appendix B.

 Click & Review
for additional assessment options:
wiley.com/college/huffman

chievement

Objective 2.4: *Describe the nervous system's two major divisions, and explain their respective functions.*

Central Nervous System (CNS) *Brain and spinal cord*

Peripheral Nervous System (PNS) *All nerves and neurons connecting the central nervous system to the rest of the body*

Nervous System Organization

To fully comprehend the complex intricacies of the nervous system, it helps to start with an overall map or "big picture." Look at Figure 2.4. Note the organization of the nervous system as a whole, and how it is divided and subdivided into several branches. Now, look at the drawing of the body in the middle of Figure 2.4, and imagine it as your own. Visualize your entire nervous system as two separate, but interrelated, parts—the **central nervous system (CNS)** and the **peripheral nervous system (PNS)**. The first part, the CNS, consists of your brain and a bundle of nerves (your spinal cord) that runs through your spinal column. Because it is located in the *center* of your body (within your skull and spine), it is called the *central* nervous system (CNS). Your CNS is primarily responsible for processing and organizing information.

Now, picture the many nerves that lie outside your skull and spine. This is the second major part of your nervous system—the PNS. Because it carries messages (action potentials) between the central nervous system and the *periphery* of the body, it is known as the *peripheral* nervous system (PNS). Your PNS links your CNS to your body's sense receptors (skin, eyes, ears, etc.), muscles, and glands.

Having completed our quick overview of the complete nervous system, we can go inside each of these two divisions for a closer look. Let's begin with the central nervous system (CNS).

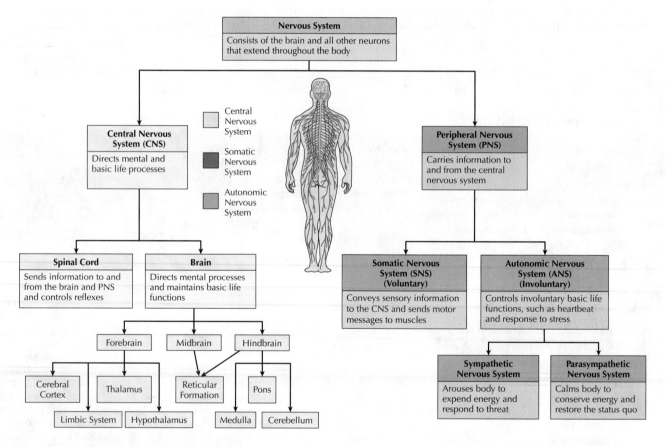

Figure 2.4 *Organizational and functional divisions of the nervous system* When attempting to learn and memorize a large set of new terms and concepts, like those in this chapter, organization is the best way to master the material and get it "permanently" stored in long-term memory (Chapter 7). A broad overview showing the "big picture" helps you organize and file specific details. Just as you need to see a globe of the world showing all the continents to easily place individual countries, you need a "map" of the entire nervous system to effectively study the individual parts. Note how the nervous system is divided and subdivided into various subsystems according to their differing functions in this figure. It will help orient you as you study upcoming sections.

■ Central Nervous System (CNS): Brain and Spinal Cord

Although we seldom think about it, our central nervous system (CNS) is what makes us unique and special. Most other animals can smell, run, see, and hear far better than we can. But thanks to our CNS, we can process information and adapt to our environment in ways that no other animal can. Unfortunately, our CNS is also incredibly fragile. Unlike neurons in the PNS, which require less protection because they can regenerate, damage to neurons in the CNS is usually serious, permanent, and sometimes fatal. However, the brain may not be as "hard wired" as we once believed.

Scientists long believed that after the first two or three years of life, humans and non-human animals are unable to repair or replace damaged neurons in the brain or spinal cord. We now know that the brain is capable of lifelong *neuroplasticity* and *neurogenesis*.

Neuroplasticity

Rather than being a fixed, solid organ, our brains are flexible and capable of changing their structure and function as a result of usage and experience (Deller et al., 2006; Romero et al., 2008; Rossignol et al., 2008). The basic brain organization (cortex, cerebellum, etc.) is irreversibly established before birth, but thanks to **neuroplasticity** some neural tissue can reorganize and change its structure and function throughout the life span. As we're learning a new sport or foreign language, for example, our brains change and "rewire." New synapses form and others disappear. Some dendrites grow longer and sprout new branches, whereas others are "pruned" away. This is what makes our brains so wonderfully adaptive.

Remarkably, this rewiring has even helped remodel the brain following strokes. For example, psychologist Edward Taub and his colleagues (2002, 2004, 2007) have had unusual success restoring function in stroke patients (Figure 2.5). Note that recovery from brain damage varies considerably, depending in large part on the age and health of the individual, as well as the extent of the damage.

Neurogenesis

In addition to the amazing process of *neuroplasticity*, our brains also continually replace lost cells with new cells, a process called **neurogenesis**. One type of neurogenesis involves the transplantation of immature, "uncommitted" **stem cells** into a patient's brain. Once inside the brain, these stem cells then develop into new healthy cells, which replace those that have died or degenerated. In addition, to transplantation into the brain, stem cells also have been used for bone marrow transplants, and clinical trials using stem cells to repopulate or replace cells devastated by injury or disease have helped patients suffering from Alzheimer's, Parkinson's, diabetes, epilepsy, stress, strokes, and depression (Chang et al., 2005; Hampton, 2006, 2007; Fleischmann & Welz, 2008; Leri, Anversa, & Frishman, 2007).

Does this mean that people paralyzed from spinal cord injuries might be able to walk again? At this point, neurogenesis in the brain and spinal cord is minimal. However, one possible bridge might be to transplant embryonic stem cells in the damaged area of the spinal cord. Researchers have successfully transplanted mouse embryonic stem cells into a damaged rat spinal cord (Jones, Anderson, & Galvin, 2003; McDonald et al., 1999). When the damaged spinal cord was viewed several weeks later, the implanted cells had survived and spread throughout the injured spinal cord area. More important, the transplant rats also showed some movement in previously paralyzed parts of their bodies. Medical researchers have also begun human trials using nerve grafts to repair damaged spinal cords (Lopez, 2002; Saltus, 2000).

Spinal Cord

Now that we have discussed the remarkable adaptability of the central nervous system (CNS), let's take an even closer look at its components—the brain and spinal cord. Because of its central importance for psychology, we'll discuss the brain in detail in

Achievement

Objective 2.5: *Discuss neuroplasticity, neurogenesis, and stem cells.*

Neuroplasticity *Brain's ability to reorganize and change its structure and function throughout the life span*

Courtesy Taub Therapy Clinic/UAB Media Relations

Figure 2.5 ***A breakthrough in neuroscience*** By immobilizing the unaffected arm or leg and requiring rigorous and repetitive exercise of the affected limb, psychologist Edward Taub and colleagues "recruit" stroke patients' intact brain cells to take over for damaged cells. The therapy has restored function in some patients as long as 21 years after their strokes.

Neurogenesis [nue-roe-JEN-uh-sis] *Process by which new neurons are generated*

Stem Cell *Immature (uncommitted) cells that have the potential to develop into almost any type of cell depending on the chemical signals they receive*

Achievement

Objective 2.6: *What are the major functions of the spinal cord?*

the next major section. But the spinal cord is also very important. It is a great highway of information into and out of the brain. But it is much more than a simple set of cables relaying messages. Your spinal cord is involved in all voluntary movements and can even initiate some automatic behaviors on its own. These involuntary, automatic behaviors are called **reflexes**, or *reflex arcs*. The response to the incoming stimuli is "reflected" back—automatically.

Think back to your most recent physical exam. Did your physician tap your knee with a special hammer to check your reflexes? Did your lower leg automatically kick out following this tap? This *knee-jerk reflex*, like the one that pulls your hand away from a painful fire, occurs within the spinal cord, without any help from the brain (Figure 2.6). Your brain later "knows" what happened a fraction of a second after the tap on the knee because neural messages are also sent along to the brain. The immediate, automatic response of the spinal cord, however, provides a faster reaction time.

We are all born with numerous reflexes (see Figure 2.7), many of which fade over time. But as adults we still blink in response to a puff of air in our eyes, gag when the back of our throat is stimulated, and urinate and defecate in response to pressure in the bladder and rectum. Even our sexual responses are somewhat controlled by reflexes. Just as a puff of air produces an automatic closing of the eyes, certain stimuli, such as the stroking of the genitals, can lead to arousal and the reflexive muscle contractions of orgasm in both men and women. However, in order to have the passion, thoughts, and emotion we normally associate with sex, the sensory information from the stroking or orgasm must be carried to the brain.

Reflex *Innate, automatic response to a stimulus (e.g., knee-jerk reflex)*

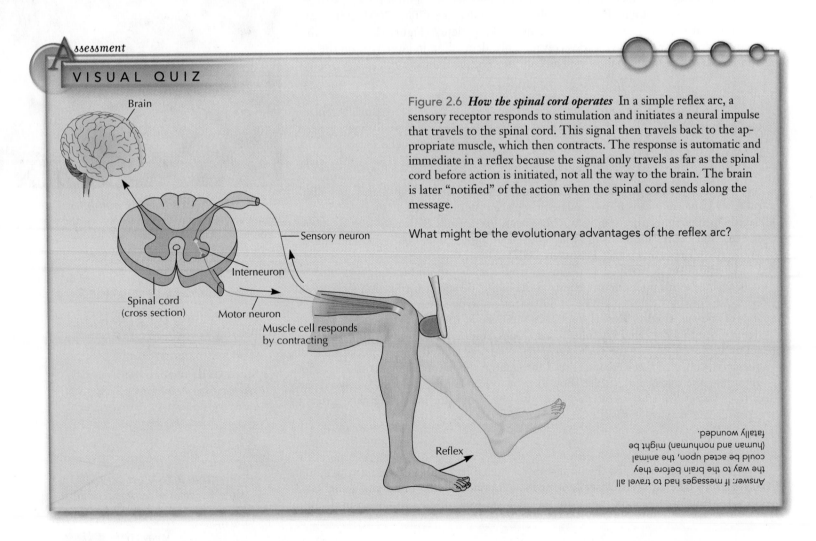

Assessment

VISUAL QUIZ

Brain

Sensory neuron

Interneuron

Spinal cord (cross section)

Motor neuron

Muscle cell responds by contracting

Reflex

Figure 2.6 *How the spinal cord operates* In a simple reflex arc, a sensory receptor responds to stimulation and initiates a neural impulse that travels to the spinal cord. This signal then travels back to the appropriate muscle, which then contracts. The response is automatic and immediate in a reflex because the signal only travels as far as the spinal cord before action is initiated, not all the way to the brain. The brain is later "notified" of the action when the spinal cord sends along the message.

What might be the evolutionary advantages of the reflex arc?

Answer: If messages had to travel all the way to the brain before they could be acted upon, the animal (human and nonhuman) might be fatally wounded.

**A**pplication

Testing for Reflexes

If you have a newborn or young infant in your home, you can easily (and safely) test for these simple reflexes. (Note: Most infant reflexes disappear within the first year of life. If they reappear in later life, it generally indicates damage to the central nervous system.)

(a) **Rooting reflex.** Lightly stroke the infant's cheek or side of the mouth, and watch how he or she will automatically (reflexively) turn toward the stimulation and attempt to suck.

(b) **Grasping reflex.** Place your finger in the infant's palm and note the automatic grasp.

(c) **Babinski reflex.** Lightly stroke the sole of the infant's foot, and the toes will fan out and the foot will twist inward.

Rooting Reflex
(a)

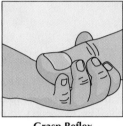

Grasp Reflex
(b)

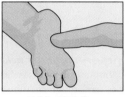

Babinski Reflex
(c)

Figure 2.7 *Infant reflexes*

■ Peripheral Nervous System (PNS): Connecting the CNS to the Rest of the Body

The *peripheral nervous system (PNS)* is just what it sounds like—the part that involves nerves *peripheral* to (or outside of) the brain and spinal cord. The chief function of the peripheral nervous system is to carry information to and from the central nervous system. It links the brain and spinal cord to the body's sense receptors, muscles, and glands.

Scientists further divide the PNS into the somatic nervous system and the autonomic nervous system. The **somatic nervous system (SNS)** (also called the *skeletal nervous system*) consists of all the nerves that connect to sensory receptors and skeletal muscles. The name comes from the term *soma*, which means "body," and the somatic nervous system plays a key role in communication throughout the entire *body*. In a kind of "two-way street," the SNS first carries sensory information to the CNS and then carries messages from the CNS to skeletal muscles (Figure 2.8).

The other subdivision of the PNS, the **autonomic nervous system (ANS)**, is responsible for *involuntary* tasks, such as heart rate, digestion, pupil dilation, and breathing. Like an automatic pilot, the ANS can sometimes be consciously overridden. But as its name implies, the autonomic system normally operates independently (*autonomic* means "autonomous").

The autonomic nervous system is itself further divided into two branches, the **sympathetic** and **parasympathetic**, to regulate the functioning of target organs like the heart, intestines, and lungs (Figure 2.9). These two subsystems tend to work in opposition to each other. A convenient, if somewhat oversimplified, distinction is that the *sympathetic branch* of the autonomic nervous system arouses the body and mobilizes it for action—the "fight-or-flight" response. In contrast, the *parasympathetic branch* calms the body and conserves energy—the relaxation response. Keep in mind that these two systems are not an "on/off" or either/or arrangement. Like two children on a playground teeter-totter, one will be up while the other is down. But they essentially balance each other out. In everyday situations, the sympathetic and parasympathetic nervous systems work together to maintain a steady, balanced, internal state.

Achievement

Objective 2.7: *What are the subdivisions of the peripheral nervous system, and what are their functions?*

Somatic Nervous System (SNS) *Subdivision of the peripheral nervous system (PNS) that connects to sensory receptors and controls skeletal muscles*

Autonomic Nervous System (ANS) *Subdivision of the peripheral nervous system (PNS) that controls involuntary functions, such as heart rate and digestion. It is further subdivided into the sympathetic nervous system, which arouses, and the parasympathetic nervous system, which calms*

Sympathetic Nervous System *Subdivision of the autonomic nervous system (ANS) responsible for arousing the body and mobilizing its energy during times of stress; also called the "fight-or-flight" system*

Parasympathetic Nervous System *Subdivision of the autonomic nervous system (ANS) responsible for calming the body and conserving energy*

wiley.com/
college/
huffman

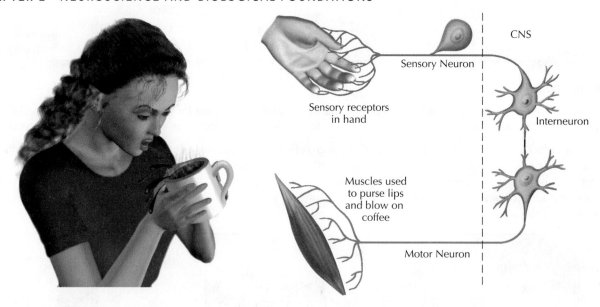

Figure 2.8 *Sensory and motor neurons* In order for you to be able to function, your brain and body must communicate with one another. This is the job of the *somatic nervous system* (SNS), which receives sensory information, sends it to the brain, and allows the brain to direct the body to act. Messages (action potentials) within the nervous system can cross the synapse in only one direction. *Sensory neurons* carry messages inward from other body areas *to* the CNS. In contrast, *motor neurons* carry messages *away* from the CNS. *Interneurons* internally communicate and intervene between the sensory inputs and the motor outputs. Most of the neurons in the brain are interneurons.

Sympathetic nervous system—"fight or flight"

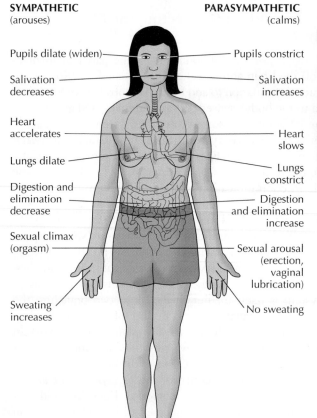

SYMPATHETIC
(arouses)

Pupils dilate (widen)

Salivation decreases

Heart accelerates

Lungs dilate

Digestion and elimination decrease

Sexual climax (orgasm)

Sweating increases

PARASYMPATHETIC
(calms)

Pupils constrict

Salivation increases

Heart slows

Lungs constrict

Digestion and elimination increase

Sexual arousal (erection, vaginal lubrication)

No sweating

Parasympathetic nervous system—"calming response"

Study Tip

One way to differentiate the two subdivisions of the ANS is to imagine skydiving out of an airplane. When you initially jump, your sympathetic nervous system has "sympathy" for your stressful situation. It alerts and prepares you for immediate action. Once your "para" chute opens, your "para" sympathetic nervous system takes over, and you can relax as you float safely to earth.

Figure 2.9 *Actions of the autonomic nervous system (ANS)* The ANS is responsible for a variety of independent (autonomous) activities, such as salivation and digestion. It exercises this control through its two divisions—the *sympathetic* and *parasympathetic* branches.

When you hear a question from your instructor and want to raise your hand, your *somatic nervous system* will report to your brain the current state of your skeletal muscles. It then carries instructions back to your muscles, allowing you to lift your arm and hand. But the somatic nervous system does not make your pupils dilate or your heartbeat quicken if a dangerous snake comes sliding into the classroom. For this, you need your *sympathetic nervous system.* It would simultaneously shut down your digestive processes and cause hormones, such as *cortisol,* to be released into the bloodstream. The net result of sympathetic activation is to get more oxygenated blood and energy to the skeletal muscles, thus allowing us to "fight or flee."

In contrast to the sympathetic nervous system, which arouses the body, the *parasympathetic nervous system* calms and returns your body to its normal functioning. It slows your heart rate, lowers your blood pressure, and increases your digestive and eliminative processes. Now, we understand why arguments during meals often cause stomachaches! Strong emotions, like anger, fear, or even joy, put the sympathetic system in dominance and prevent digestion and elimination. Strong emotions and sympathetic dominance also explain many sexual problems (Figure 2.10).

It is important to remember, however, that the sympathetic nervous system does provide adaptive, evolutionary advantages. At the beginning of human evolution, when we faced a dangerous bear or aggressive human intruder, there were only two reasonable responses—fight or flight. This automatic mobilization of bodily resources still has significant survival value in our modern life. But today our sympathetic nervous

The sympathetic nervous system in action *The fight-or-flight response of the sympathetic nervous system mobilizes the body for action in the face of perceived danger.*

Figure 2.10 ***Why study psychology?*** The complexities of sexual interaction—and in particular, the difficulties that couples sometimes have in achieving sexual arousal or orgasm—illustrate the balancing act between the sympathetic and parasympathetic nervous systems.

Parasympathetic dominance *Sexual arousal and excitement require that the body be relaxed enough to allow increased blood flow to the genitals—in other words, the nervous system must be in* parasympathetic dominance. *Parasympathetic nerves carry messages from the central nervous system directly to the sexual organs, allowing for a localized response (increased blood flow and genital arousal).*

Sympathetic dominance *When a person experiences strong emotions, such as anger, anxiety, or fear, the body shifts to* sympathetic dominance, *which can disrupt the sexual arousal that occurs under parasympathetic dominance. During sympathetic dominance, blood flow to the genitals and other organs decreases as the body readies for a "fight or flight." As a result, the person is unable (or less likely) to become sexually aroused. Any number of circumstances—for example, performance anxiety, fear of unwanted pregnancy or disease, or tensions between partners—can trigger sympathetic dominance.*

system is often activated by less life-threatening events. Instead of bears and intruders, we have chronic stressors like full-time college classes mixed with part- or full-time jobs, dual-career marriages, daily traffic jams, and rude drivers on high-speed freeways—not to mention terrorist attacks and global pollution. Unfortunately, our body responds to these sources of stress with sympathetic arousal. And, as you will see in Chapter 3, chronic arousal to stress can be very detrimental to our health.

Assessment

CHECK & REVIEW

Nervous System Organization

Objective 2.4: *Describe the nervous system's two major divisions, and explain their respective functions.*

The nervous system is divided into two major divisions: the **central nervous system (CNS)**, composed of the brain and spinal cord, and the **peripheral nervous system (PNS)**, including all nerves connecting the CNS to the rest of the body. The CNS processes and organizes information, whereas the PNS carries information to and from the CNS.

Objective 2.5: *Discuss neuroplasticity, neurogenesis, and stem cells.*

Neuroplasticity is the brain's ability to reorganize and change its structure and function throughout the life span. **Neurogenesis** is the process by which new neurons are generated. **Stem cells** are immature (uncommitted) cells that have the potential to develop into almost any type of cell depending on the chemical signals they receive.

Objective 2.6: *What are the major functions of the spinal cord?*

The spinal cord is the communications link between the brain and the rest of the body, and it is involved in all voluntary and **reflex** responses.

Objective 2.7: *What are the subdivisions of the peripheral nervous system, and what are their functions?*

The two major subdivisions of the PNS are the **somatic nervous system** and the **autonomic nervous system**.

The **somatic nervous system** includes all nerves carrying incoming sensory information and outgoing motor information to and from the sense organs and skeletal muscles. The **autonomic nervous system** includes the nerves outside the brain and spinal cord that maintain normal functioning of glands, heart muscle, and the smooth muscle of blood vessels and internal organs.

The autonomic nervous system is further divided into two branches, the *parasympathetic* and the *sympathetic*, which tend to work in opposition to one another. The **parasympathetic nervous system** normally dominates when a person is relaxed. The **sympathetic nervous system** dominates when a person is under physical or mental stress. It mobilizes the body for fight or flight by increasing heart rate and blood pressure and slowing digestive processes.

Questions

1. The nervous system is separated into two major divisions: the _____ nervous system, which consists of the brain and spinal cord, and the _____ nervous system, which consists of all the nerves going to and from the brain and spinal cord.
2. The autonomic nervous system is subdivided into two branches called the _____ and _____ systems. (a) automatic, semiautomatic; (b) somatic, peripheral; (c) afferent, efferent; (d) sympathetic, parasympathetic
3. If you are startled by the sound of a loud explosion, the _____ nervous system will become dominant. (a) peripheral; (b) somatic; (c) parasympathetic; (d) sympathetic
4. What is the major difference between the sympathetic and parasympathetic nervous systems?
5. Fill in the blank lines.

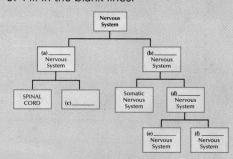

Check your answers in Appendix B.

Click & Review
for additional assessment options:
wiley.com/college/huffman

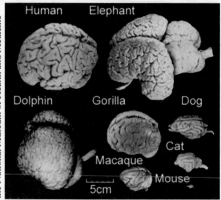

A Tour Through the Brain

As you can see in Figure 2.11, brain size and complexity vary significantly among species. We begin our exploration of the *human* brain at the lower end, where the spinal cord joins the base of the brain, and then continue upward toward the skull. Note that as we move from bottom to top, "lower," basic processes like breathing generally give way to "higher," more complex mental processes.

Figure 2.11 ***Brain Comparisons*** In general, lower species (such as fish and reptiles) have smaller, less complex brains. The most complex brains belong to dolphins, whales, and higher primates (such as gorillas, chimps, and humans).

University of Wisconsin and Michigan State Comparative Mammalian Brain Collections and the National Museum of Health and Medicine

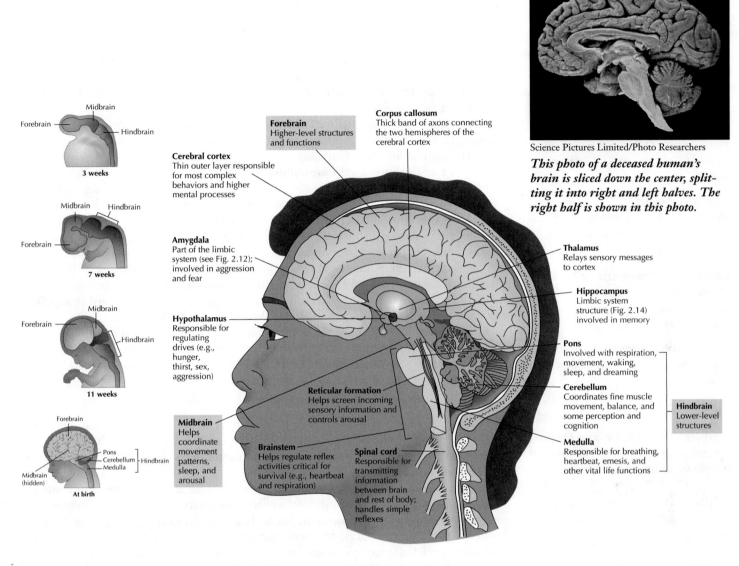

Science Pictures Limited/Photo Researchers

This photo of a deceased human's brain is sliced down the center, splitting it into right and left halves. The right half is shown in this photo.

3 weeks

Midbrain
Forebrain — Hindbrain

7 weeks

Midbrain — Hindbrain
Forebrain

11 weeks

Midbrain
Forebrain — Hindbrain

At birth

Forebrain
Pons
Cerebellum — Hindbrain
Medulla
Midbrain (hidden)

Forebrain
Higher-level structures and functions

Cerebral cortex
Thin outer layer responsible for most complex behaviors and higher mental processes

Corpus callosum
Thick band of axons connecting the two hemispheres of the cerebral cortex

Amygdala
Part of the limbic system (see Fig. 2.12); involved in aggression and fear

Hypothalamus
Responsible for regulating drives (e.g., hunger, thirst, sex, aggression)

Reticular formation
Helps screen incoming sensory information and controls arousal

Midbrain
Helps coordinate movement patterns, sleep, and arousal

Brainstem
Helps regulate reflex activities critical for survival (e.g., heartbeat and respiration)

Spinal cord
Responsible for transmitting information between brain and rest of body; handles simple reflexes

Thalamus
Relays sensory messages to cortex

Hippocampus
Limbic system structure (Fig. 2.14) involved in memory

Pons
Involved with respiration, movement, waking, sleep, and dreaming

Cerebellum
Coordinates fine muscle movement, balance, and some perception and cognition

Medulla
Responsible for breathing, heartbeat, emesis, and other vital life functions

Hindbrain
Lower-level structures

Figure 2.12 **The human brain** (a) Note how the forebrain, midbrain, and hindbrain radically change in their size and placement during prenatal development. (b) The profile drawing above highlights key structures and functions of the right half of the brain. As you read about each of these structures, keep this drawing in mind and refer back to it as necessary. (The diagram shows the brain structures as if the brain were split vertically down the center and the left hemisphere was removed.)

The brain can be divided into three major sections: the *hindbrain*, *midbrain*, and *forebrain* (Figure 2.12). Also note the large section labeled as the **brainstem**, which includes parts of all three of these sections and helps regulate reflex activities important to survival (such as heartbeat and respiration). The distinctive shape of the brainstem provides a handy geographical landmark to keep us oriented.

Lower-Level Brain Structures: Hindbrain, Midbrain, and Parts of the Forebrain

Throughout our tour of the brain, note that certain brain structures are specialized to perform certain tasks, a process known as *localization of function*. But keep in mind

Brainstem *Area of the brain that houses parts of the hindbrain, midbrain, and forebrain, and helps regulate reflex activities critical for survival (such as heartbeat and respiration)*

Achievement

Objective 2.8: *Identify the three major sections of the brain.*

that most parts of both the human and nonhuman brain are not so specialized—they perform integrating, overlapping functions.

Hindbrain *Collection of brain structures including the medulla, cerebellum, and pons*

Medulla [muh-DUL-uh] *Hindbrain structure responsible for automatic body functions such as breathing and heartbeat*

Cerebellum [sehr-uh-BELL-um] *Hindbrain structure responsible for coordinating fine muscle movement, balance, and some perception and cognition*

Pons *Hindbrain structure involved in respiration, movement, waking, sleep, and dreaming*

Midbrain *Collection of brain structures in the middle of the brain responsible for coordinating movement patterns, sleep, and arousal*

Reticular Formation (RF) *Diffuse set of neurons that screens incoming information and controls arousal*

Forebrain *Collection of upper level brain structures including the thalamus, hypothalamus, limbic system, and cerebral cortex*

Thalamus [THAL-uh-muss] *Forebrain structure at the top of the brainstem that relays sensory messages to the cerebral cortex*

Hindbrain

Have you ever wondered what allows you to automatically breathe and your heart to keep pumping despite your being sound asleep? Automatic behaviors and survival responses like these are either controlled by or influenced by parts of your **hindbrain**, which includes the *medulla*, *pons*, and *cerebellum*.

The **medulla** is essentially an extension of the spinal cord, with many nerve fibers passing through it carrying information to and from the brain. It also controls many essential automatic bodily functions, such as respiration and heartbeat.

The cauliflower-shaped **cerebellum** ("little brain" in Latin) is, evolutionarily, a very old structure. It coordinates fine muscle movement and balance. Although the actual commands for movement come from higher brain centers in the cortex, the cerebellum coordinates the muscles so that movement is smooth and precise. The cerebellum is also critical to our sense of equilibrium or physical balance. Have you noticed how people stagger and slur their speech after a few too many drinks?

Researchers using functional magnetic resonance imaging (fMRI) have also shown that parts of the cerebellum are important for some memory, sensory, perceptual, cognitive, and language tasks, as well as some learning and conditioning (Picard et al., 2008; Rönnberg et al., 2004; Thompson, 2005; Woodruff-Pak & Disterhoft, 2008).

The **pons**, located above the cerebellum and medulla, is involved in respiration, movement, sleeping, waking, and dreaming (among other things). It also contains many axons that cross from one side of the brain to the other (*pons* is Latin for "bridge").

Midbrain

The **midbrain** helps orient our eye and body movements to visual and auditory stimuli, and works with the pons to help control sleep and level of arousal. It also contains a small structure involved with the neurotransmitter dopamine, which deteriorates in Parkinson's disease.

Running through the core of the hindbrain, midbrain, and brainstem is the **reticular** (netlike) **formation (RF)**. This diffuse, finger-shaped network of neurons filters incoming sensory information and alerts the higher brain centers to important events. Without your RF, you would not be alert or perhaps even conscious. In fact, some general anesthics target the RF so pain sensations never register in the brain (Simon, 2007).

Forebrain

The **forebrain** is the largest and most prominent part of the human brain. It includes the *thalamus, hypothalamus, limbic system,* and *cerebral cortex* (Figure 2.13). The first three structures are located near the top of the brainstem. Wrapped above and around them is the cerebral cortex. (*Cerebrum* is Latin for "brain," and *cortex* is Latin for "covering" or "bark.") In this section, we will discuss only the first three structures. Because of its vital role in all complex mental activities, the cerebral cortex will have its own separate discussion following this one.

Thalamus Resembling two little footballs joined side by side, the **thalamus** serves as the major sensory relay center for the brain (Jones, 2006). Like an air traffic control center that receives information from all aircraft and then directs them to the appropriate landing or takeoff areas, the thalamus receives input from nearly all the sensory systems and then directs this information to the appropriate cortical areas. For example, while you are reading this page, your thalamus sends incoming visual signals to the visual area of your cortex. While listening to music, the information is transferred to the auditory (or hearing) area of your cortex.

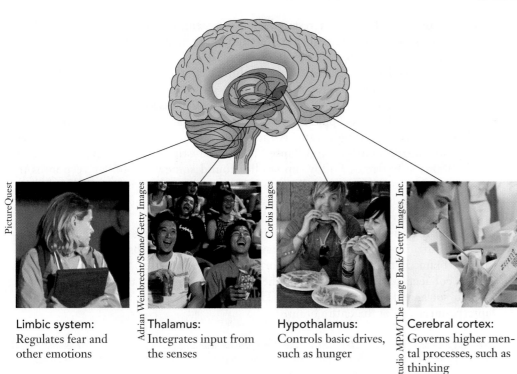

Figure 2.13 **Structures of the forebrain**

Limbic system: Regulates fear and other emotions

Thalamus: Integrates input from the senses

Hypothalamus: Controls basic drives, such as hunger

Cerebral cortex: Governs higher mental processes, such as thinking

Assessment

VISUAL QUIZ

Why do police officers ask drivers to "walk the line"?

Answer: The cerebellum is responsible for smooth and precise movement, and it is also one of the first areas of the brain affected by alcohol. Asking drivers to perform tasks like walking the white line is a quick and easy measure of potential drunk driving.

In addition to relaying sensory information to the cortex, the thalamus also integrates information from various senses and may be involved in learning and memory (Bailey & Mair, 2005; Ridley et al., 2005). Injury to the thalamus can cause deafness, blindness, or loss of any other sense (except smell). This suggests that some analysis of sensory messages may occur here. Because the thalamus is the major sensory relay area to the cerebral cortex, damage or abnormalities also might cause the cortex to misinterpret or not receive vital sensory information. Interestingly, brain-imaging research links thalamus abnormalities to *schizophrenia*, a serious psychological disorder involving problems with sensory filtering and perception (Byne et al., 2008; Clinton & Meador-Woodruff, 2004; Preuss et al., 2005).

Hypothalamus Beneath the thalamus lies the **hypothalamus** (*hypo-* means "under"). Although no larger than a kidney bean, it has been called the "master control center" for basic drives such as hunger, thirst, sex, and aggression (Hinton et al., 2004; Williams et al., 2004; Zillmer, Spiers, & Culbertson, 2008). It also helps govern hormonal processes by regulating the endocrine system. Hanging down from the hypothalamus, the pituitary gland is usually considered a key endocrine gland because it releases hormones that activate the other endocrine glands. The hypothalamus influences the pituitary through direct neural connections and by releasing its own hormones into the blood supply of the pituitary.

Limbic System An interconnected group of forebrain structures, known as the **limbic system**, is located roughly along the border between the cerebral cortex and the lower-level brain structures (hence the term *limbic*, which means "edge" or "border"). Scientists disagree about which structures should be included in the limbic system, but most include the *hippocampus, amygdala, thalamus,* and *hypothalamus* (Figure 2.14).

The limbic system is generally responsible for emotions, drives, and memory. As we'll see in chapter 7, the **hippocampus** is involved in forming and retrieving memories.

Hypothalamus [hi-poh-THAL-uh-muss] *Small brain structure beneath the thalamus that helps govern drives (hunger, thirst, sex, and aggression) and hormones*

Limbic System *Interconnected group of forebrain structures involved with emotions, drives, and memory*

Hippocampus *Part of the limbic system involved in forming and retrieving memories*

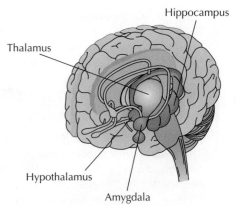

Hippocampus

Thalamus

Hypothalamus

Amygdala

Figure 2.14 **Major brain structures commonly associated with the limbic system**

wiley.com/
college/
huffman

Amygdala *Limbic system structure linked to the production and regulation of emotions (e.g., aggression and fear)*

Getty Images News and Sport Services

However, the major focus of interest in the limbic system, and particularly the **amygdala**, has been its production and regulation of emotions (e.g., aggression and fear) (Asghar et al., 2008; Carlson, 2008; LeDoux, 1998, 2002, 2007).

Another well-known function of the limbic system is its role in pleasure or reward. James Olds and Peter Milner (1954) were the first to note that electrically stimulating certain areas of the limbic system caused a "pleasure" response in rats. The feeling was apparently so rewarding that the rats would cross electrified grids, swim through water (which they normally avoid), and press a lever thousands of times until they collapsed from exhaustion—just to have this area of their brains stimulated. Follow-up studies found somewhat similar responses in other animals and even among human volunteers (e.g., Dackis & O'Brien, 2001). Modern research suggests that brain stimulation may activate neurotransmitters rather than discrete "pleasure centers."

Keep in mind that even though limbic system structures and neurotransmitters are instrumental in emotional behavior, emotion in humans is also tempered by higher brain centers in the cerebral cortex. Damage to the front part of the cortex, which connects to the amygdala and other parts of the limbic system, can permanently impair social and emotional behavior. This is yet another example of the inseparable interconnectivity of the entire brain.

Damage to the brain *The 2005 debate over Terri Schiavo was largely about whether her husband should be allowed to remove her feeding tube, even though she was still able to move and breathe on her own and showed some reflexive responses. Terri's parents and others believed that these lower-level brain functions were sufficient proof of life. Advocates on the other side felt that once the cerebral cortex ceased functioning there is no ethical or logical reason to keep the body alive. What do you think?*

A_{ssessment} CHECK & REVIEW [STOP]

Lower-Level Brain Structures

Objective 2.8: *Identify the three major sections of the brain.*

The brain is generally divided into three major sections: the hindbrain, midbrain, and forebrain.

Objective 2.9: *What are the three key components of the hindbrain and what are their functions?*

Parts of the **hindbrain,** the **pons** and **medulla,** are involved in sleeping, waking, dreaming, and control of automatic bodily functions; another part, the **cerebellum,** coordinates fine muscle movement, balance, and some perception and cognition.

Objective 2.10: *Describe the functions of the midbrain and the reticular formation.*

The **midbrain** helps coordinate movement patterns, sleep, and arousal. The **reticular formation** runs through the midbrain, hindbrain, and brainstem, and is responsible for arousal and screening incoming information.

Objective 2.11: *Identify the major structures of the forebrain, and describe their functions.*

The **forebrain** includes several structures, including the thalamus, hypothalamus, limbic system, and cerebral cortex. The **thalamus** relays sensory messages to the cerebral cortex. The **hypothalamus** helps govern basic drives and hormones. The **limbic system** is a group of forebrain structures (including the **hippocampus** and **amygdala**) involved with emotions and memory. Because the cerebral cortex controls most complex mental activities, it is discussed separately in the next section.

Questions

1. What are the three major structures within the hindbrain?
2. Roadside tests for drunk driving primarily test responses of the _____.
3. What is the major sensory relay area for the brain? (a) hypothalamus; (b) thalamus; (c) cortex; (d) hindbrain?
4. Why is the amygdala a major focus of interest for researchers?

5. Label the following structures/areas of the brain.
   a. forebrain   b. midbrain
   c. hindbrain   d. thalamus
   e. hypothalamus   f. cerebral cortex

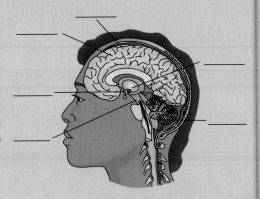

Check your answers in Appendix B.

 Click & Review for additional assessment options: wiley.com/college/huffman

Cerebral Cortex: The Center of "Higher" Processing

The gray, wrinkled **cerebral cortex** is responsible for most complex behaviors and higher mental processes (Figure 2.15). It plays such a vital role in human life that many consider it the essence of life. Without a functioning cortex, we would be almost completely unaware of ourselves and our surroundings.

Although the cerebral cortex is only about one-quarter of an inch thick, it is made up of approximately 30 billion neurons and nine times as many supporting glial cells. When spread out, the cortex would cover an area almost the size of a standard newspaper page. How does your cortex, along with all your other brain structures, fit inside your skull? Imagine crumpling and rolling the newspaper sheet into a ball. You would retain the same surface area but in a much smaller space. The cortex contains numerous "wrinkles" (called *convolutions*), allowing it to hold billions of neurons in the restricted space of the skull.

Have you watched brain surgeries in movies or on television? After the skull is opened, you'll first see a gray, wrinkled, cerebral cortex that closely resembles an over-sized walnut. Also like a walnut, the cortex has a similar division (or fissure) down the center, which marks the *left* and *right hemispheres* of the brain. The two hemispheres make up about 80 percent of the brain's weight and they are mostly filled with axon connections between the cortex and other brain structures. Each hemisphere controls the opposite side of the body (Figure 2.16).

The two cerebral hemispheres are divided into eight distinct areas, or *lobes*—four in each hemisphere (Figure 2.17). Like the lower-level brain structures, each lobe specializes in somewhat different tasks—another example of *localization of function.* However, some functions overlap between lobes.

Achievement

Objective 2.12: *What is the cerebral cortex, and what is its major function?*

Cerebral Cortex *Thin surface layer on the cerebral hemispheres that regulates most complex behavior, including sensations, motor control, and higher mental processes*

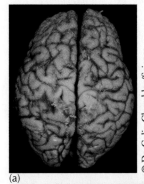

(a)

© Dr. Colin Chumbley/Science Photo Library/Photo Researchers, Inc.

(b)

© Dr. Colin Chumbley/Science Photo Library/Photo Researchers, Inc.

Figure 2.15 *The cerebral cortex*
(a) Looking at this photo of the top side of a human brain, all you can see is its outer, wrinkled surface, known as the cerebral cortex. (b) If you made a vertical cut along the center crevice of the brain, you would have this inside view of the right hemisphere. Note how the many wrinkles, or folds, allow this large mass of tissue to fit inside your skull.

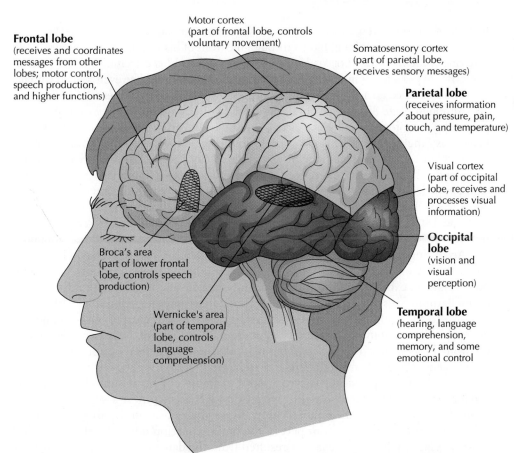

Frontal lobe
(receives and coordinates messages from other lobes; motor control, speech production, and higher functions)

Motor cortex
(part of frontal lobe, controls voluntary movement)

Somatosensory cortex
(part of parietal lobe, receives sensory messages)

Parietal lobe
(receives information about pressure, pain, touch, and temperature)

Visual cortex
(part of occipital lobe, receives and processes visual information)

Occipital lobe
(vision and visual perception)

Broca's area
(part of lower frontal lobe, controls speech production)

Wernicke's area
(part of temporal lobe, controls language comprehension)

Temporal lobe
(hearing, language comprehension, memory, and some emotional control)

Figure 2.17 ***Lobes of the brain*** This is a view of the brain's left hemisphere showing its four lobes—*frontal, parietal, temporal,* and *occipital.* The right hemisphere has the same four lobes. Divisions between the lobes are marked by visibly prominent folds. Note that Broca's and Wernicke's areas are only in the left hemisphere.

Figure 2.16 ***Information crossover*** The right hemisphere of your brain controls the left side of your body, whereas the left hemisphere controls the right side.

From Damasio H, Grabowski T, Frank R, Galaburda AM, Damasio AR: The return of Phineas Gage: Clues about the brain from a famous

Achievement

Objective 2.13: *Describe the major functions of the lobes of the cerebral cortex.*

Frontal Lobes *Two lobes at the front of the brain governing motor control, speech production, and higher functions, such as thinking, personality, emotion, and memory*

Achievement

Objective 2.14: *Why is the case study of Phineas Gage important?*

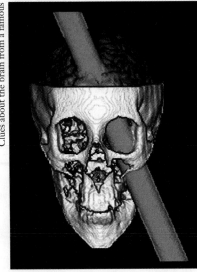

Figure 2.18 *Phineas Gage's injury*
An accidental explosion sent a 13-pound tamping iron through the brain of a young railroad supervisor, Phineas Gage. The careful record keeping and in-depth reporting of his behavior after the accident provided valuable information on the short- and long-term effects of damage to the frontal lobes.

Frontal Lobes

By far the largest of the cortical lobes, the two **frontal lobes** are located at the top front portion of the two brain hemispheres—right behind your forehead. The frontal lobes receive and coordinate messages from all other lobes of the cortex, while also being responsible for at least three additional functions:

1. *Higher functions.* Most functions that distinguish humans from other animals, such as thinking, personality, emotion, and memory, are controlled primarily by the frontal lobes. Damage to the frontal lobe affects motivation, drives, creativity, self-awareness, initiative, reasoning, and emotional behavior. Abnormalities in the frontal lobes are often observed in patients with schizophrenia (Chapter 14).

2. *Speech production.* In the *left* frontal lobe, on the surface of the cortex near the bottom of the motor control area, lies *Broca's area*, which is known to play a crucial role in speech production. In 1865, French physician Paul Broca discovered that damage to this area causes difficulty in speech, but not language comprehension. This type of impaired language ability is known as *Broca's aphasia.*

3. *Motor control.* At the very back of the frontal lobes lies the *motor cortex*, which sends messages to the various muscles that instigate voluntary movement (Figure 2.17). When you want to call your friend on your cell phone, the motor control area of your frontal lobes guides your fingers to press the desired sequence of numbers.

Assessment

CASE STUDY/PERSONAL STORY *Phineas Gage*

In 1848, a railroad foreman named Phineas Gage had a metal rod (13 pounds, 1¼ inches in diameter, and 3½ feet long) blown through the front of his face and brain (Figure 2.18). Amazingly, the blow was not fatal. Gage was stunned and his extremities shook convulsively. But in just a few minutes, he was able to talk to his men, and he even walked with little or no assistance up a flight of stairs before receiving medical treatment 1½ hours later.

Although Gage did survive physically, he did not fare well psychologically. A serious personality transformation had occurred because of the accident. Before the explosion, Gage was "the most efficient and capable foreman," "a shrewd, smart businessman," and very energetic and persistent in executing all his plans. After the accident, Gage "frequently changed what he proposed doing, and was, among other things, fitful, capricious, impatient of advice, obstinate, and lacking in deference to his fellows" (Macmillan, 2000, p. 13). In the words of his friends and acquaintances, "Gage was no longer Gage" (Harlow, 1868). Following months of recuperation, Gage attempted to return to work but was refused his old job. The damage to his brain had changed him too profoundly.

According to historical records kept by his physician, Gage never again held a job equal to that of foreman. He supported himself with odd jobs and traveled around New England, exhibiting himself and the tamping iron, and for a time he did the same at the Barnum Museum. He even lived in Chile for seven years before ill health forced a return to the United States. Near the end of his life, Gage experienced numerous epileptic seizures of increasing severity and frequency. Despite the massive damage to his frontal lobes caused by the tamping iron, Phineas Gage lived on for another 11½ years, eventually dying from the epileptic seizures.

How did Gage physically survive? What accounts for his radical change in personality? If the tamping iron had traveled through the brain at a slightly different angle, Gage would have died immediately. But as you can see in the above photo, the rod entered and exited the front part of the brain, a section unnecessary for physical survival. Gage's personality changes resulted from the damage to his frontal lobes. As this case study and other research show, the frontal lobes are intimately involved in motivation, emotion, and a host of other cognitive activities (Beer & Lombardo, 2007; Carlson, 2008; Hill, 2004; Werner et al., 2007).

Parietal Lobes

At the top of the brain, just behind the frontal lobes, are the two **parietal lobes**. They contain the *somatosensory cortex*, which interpret bodily sensations including pressure, pain, touch, temperature, and location of body parts. When you step on a sharp nail, you quickly (and reflexively) withdraw your foot because the messages travel directly to and from your spinal cord. However, you do not experience "pain" until the neural messages reach the parietal lobes of the brain. Concept Diagram 2.1 shows how different parts of the body are represented on the motor cortex and somatosensory cortex.

Temporal Lobes

The two **temporal lobes** (Latin for "pertaining to the temples") are responsible for auditory perception (hearing), language comprehension, memory, and some emotional control. The *auditory cortex* (which processes sound) is located at the top front of each temporal lobe. This area processes incoming sensory information from the ears and sends it to the parietal lobes, where it is combined with visual and other sensory information.

A section of the *left* temporal lobe, *Wernicke's area*, is involved in language comprehension. About a decade after Broca's discovery, German neurologist Carl Wernicke noted that patients with damage in this area could not understand what they read or heard, but they could speak quickly and easily. Unfortunately, their speech was often unintelligible. It contained made-up words, like *chipecke*, sound substitutions (*girl* became *curl*), and word substitutions (*bread* became *cake*). This syndrome is now referred to as *Wernicke's aphasia*.

Occipital Lobes

As the name implies, the two **occipital lobes** (Latin *ob*, "in back of," and *caput*, "head") are located at the lower back of the brain. Among other things, the occipital lobes are responsible for vision and visual perception. Damage to the occipital lobe can produce blindness, even though the eyes and their neural connection to the brain are perfectly healthy. The occipital lobes are also involved in shape, color, and motion perception.

Association Areas

Thus far, we have focused on relatively small areas of the eight lobes that have specific functions. If a surgeon electrically stimulated the parietal lobes, you would most likely report physical sensations, such as feeling touch, pressure, and so on. On the other hand, if the surgeon stimulated your occipital lobe, you would see flashes of light or color.

Surprisingly, most areas of your cortex, if stimulated, produce nothing at all. These so-called quiet sections are not dormant, however. They are clearly involved in interpreting, integrating, and acting on information processed by other parts of the brain. Thus, these collective "quiet areas" are aptly called **association areas** because they *associate* various areas and functions of the brain. The association areas in the frontal lobe, for example, help in decision making and planning. Similarly, the association area right in front of the motor cortex is involved in the planning of voluntary movement.

As you recall from Chapter 1, one of the most popular myths in psychology is that we use only 10 percent of our brain. This myth might have begun with early research on association areas of the brain. Given that approximately three-fourths of the cortex is "uncommitted" (with no precise, specific function responsive to electrical brain stimulation), researchers might have mistakenly assumed that these areas were nonfunctional.

© AP/Wide World Photos

Music and your brain *Have you ever wondered if great musicians' brains are different from yours and mine? The answer is yes! Our brains are physically shaped and changed by learning and from experiences we have with our environment (e.g., Romero et al., 2008; Rossignol et al., 2008). This musician, Carlos Santana, has trained (and shaped) the auditory cortex of his brain to detect even the smallest gradations of sound.*

 Study Tip

Remember that Broca's area in the left frontal lobes is responsible for speech production. Wernicke's area in the left temporal lobe is involved in language comprehension.

Parietal [puh-RYE-uh-tul] lobes *Two lobes at the top of the brain where bodily sensations are received and interpreted*

Temporal Lobes *Two lobes on each side of the brain above the ears involved in audition (hearing), language comprehension, memory, and some emotional control*

Occipital [ahk-SIP-ih-tul] Lobes *Two lobes at the back of the brain responsible for vision and visual perception*

Association Areas *So-called quiet areas in the cerebral cortex involved in interpreting, integrating, and acting on information processed by other parts of the brain*

Concept Diagram 2.1

Visualizing Your Motor Cortex and Somatosensory Cortex

This drawing represents a vertical cross section taken from the left hemisphere's *motor cortex* and right hemisphere's *somatosensory cortex*. If a surgeon applied electrical current to your motor cortex in your frontal lobes, you might move your arm, hand, or fingers—depending on the precise area that the surgeon stimulated.

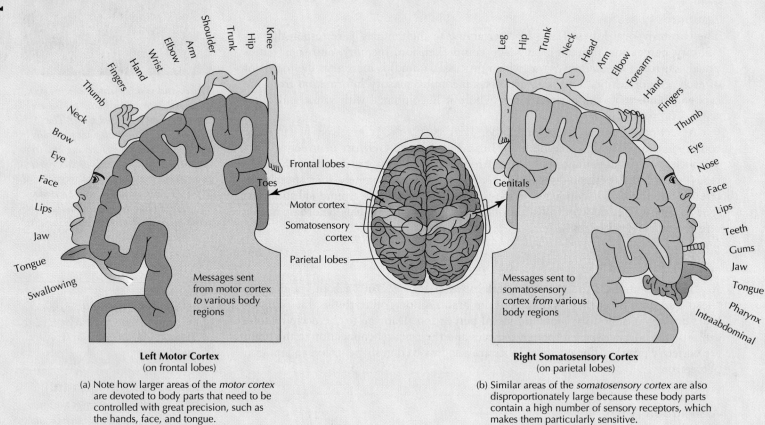

Left Motor Cortex
(on frontal lobes)

(a) Note how larger areas of the *motor cortex* are devoted to body parts that need to be controlled with great precision, such as the hands, face, and tongue.

Right Somatosensory Cortex
(on parietal lobes)

(b) Similar areas of the *somatosensory cortex* are also disproportionately large because these body parts contain a high number of sensory receptors, which makes them particularly sensitive.

Messages sent from motor cortex *to* various body regions

Messages sent to somatosensory cortex *from* various body regions

Frontal lobes
Motor cortex
Somatosensory cortex
Parietal lobes

Try This Yourself

Would you like a quick way to understand your motor cortex and somatosensory cortex?

1. **Motor cortex.** Try wiggling each of your fingers one at a time. Now try wiggling each of your toes. Note on this figure how the area of your motor cortex is much larger for your fingers than for your toes, thus explaining your greater control in your fingers.

2. **Somatosensory cortex.** Ask a friend to close his or her eyes. Using a random number of fingers (one to four), press down on the skin of your friend's back for one or two seconds. Then ask, "How many fingers am I using?"

   Repeat the same procedure on the palm or back of his or her hand. You will find much more accuracy when you are pressing on the hand than on the back. Again, note how the area of the somatosensory cortex is much larger for the hands than for the back, which explains the greater sensitivity in our hands versus our backs.

Assessment

VISUAL QUIZ

Courtesy The Natural History Museum

Can you explain why the hands and the face on this drawing are so large? Or why these same proportions may be different in nonhuman animals?

Answer: The larger size of the hands and face reflects the larger cortical area necessary for the precise motor control and greater sensitivity humans need in our hands and faces (see also Concept Diagram 2.1). Other nonhuman animals have different needs, and the proportions are different. Spider monkeys, for example, have large areas of their motor and somatosensory cortices devoted to their tails, which they use like another arm and hand.

Two Brains in One? A House Divided

We mentioned earlier that the brain's left and right hemispheres control opposite sides of the body. Each hemisphere also has separate areas of specialization. (This is another example of *localization of function*, yet it is technically referred to as *lateralization*.)

Early researchers believed that the right hemisphere was "subordinate" or "nondominant" compared to the left, and that it had few functions or abilities. In the 1960s, landmark research with **split-brain surgery** began to change this view.

Split-Brain Research

The primary connection between the left and right hemispheres is a thick, ribbonlike band of nerve fibers under the cortex called the **corpus callosum** (Figure 2.19). In some rare cases of *severe* epilepsy, when other forms of treatment have failed, surgeons cut the corpus callosum to stop the spread of epileptic seizures from one hemisphere to the other. Because this operation cuts only the direct communication link between the two hemispheres, it reveals what each half of the brain can do in isolation from the other. The resulting research has profoundly improved our understanding of how the two halves of the brain function.

Achievement

Objective 2.15: *Explain why the corpus callosum and split-brain research are important.*

CartoonStock

Split-Brain Surgery *Cutting of the corpus callosum to separate the brain's two hemispheres. When used medically to treat severe epilepsy, split-brain patients provide data on the functions of the two hemispheres*

Corpus Callosum [CORE-pus] [cah-LOH-suhm] *Bundle of nerve fibers connecting the brain's left and right hemispheres*

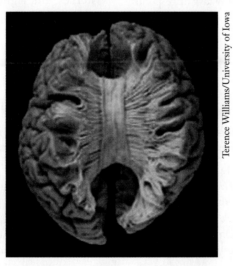

Terence Williams/University of Iowa

Figure 2.19 ***Views of the corpus callosum*** In the left photo, a human brain was sliced vertically from the top to the bottom to expose the corpus callosum, which conveys information between the two hemispheres of the cerebral cortex. In the photo on the right, a deceased person's brain was cut horizontally, which shows how fibers, or *axons*, of the corpus callosum link to both the right and left hemispheres.

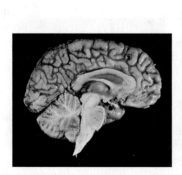

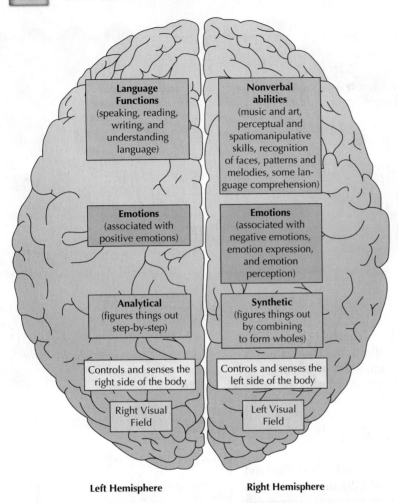

Left Hemisphere

Language Functions
(speaking, reading, writing, and understanding language)

Emotions
(associated with positive emotions)

Analytical
(figures things out step-by-step)

Controls and senses the right side of the body

Right Visual Field

Right Hemisphere

Nonverbal abilities
(music and art, perceptual and spatiomanipulative skills, recognition of faces, patterns and melodies, some language comprehension)

Emotions
(associated with negative emotions, emotion expression, and emotion perception)

Synthetic
(figures things out by combining to form wholes)

Controls and senses the left side of the body

Left Visual Field

Figure 2.20 *Functions of the left and right hemispheres* The left hemisphere specializes in verbal and analytical functions. The right hemisphere focuses on nonverbal abilities, such as spatiomanipulative skills, art and musical abilities, and visual recognition tasks. Keep in mind that both hemispheres are activated when we perform almost any task or respond to any stimuli.

How do these patients perform after the split-brain surgery? The surgery does create a few unusual responses. For example, one split-brain patient reported that when he dressed himself, he sometimes pulled his pants down with his left hand and up with his right (Gazzaniga, 2000). However, most patients generally show very few outward changes in their behavior, other than fewer epileptic seizures. The subtle changes normally appear only with specialized testing (Concept Diagram 2.2).

Hemispheric Specialization

Although most complex activities involve both hemispheres, specialization of function occurs in some areas (Figure 2.20). In general, for most adults the left hemisphere is specialized not only for language functions (speaking, reading, writing, and understanding language) but also for analytical functions, such as mathematics. In contrast, the right hemisphere is specialized primarily for nonverbal abilities. This includes art and musical abilities and perceptual and spatiomanipulative skills, such as maneuvering through space, drawing or building geometric designs, working jigsaw puzzles, building model cars, painting pictures, and recognizing faces and facial expressions (e.g., Bethmann et al., 2007; Bjornaes et al., 2005; Gazzaniga, 1970, 1995, 2000). In addition, the right hemisphere also contributes to complex word and language comprehension (Bartolomeo, 2006; Coulson & Wu, 2005; Deason & Marsolek, 2005).

In another study, a team of researchers led by Fredric Schiffer (1998) at McLean Hospital in Massachusetts reported that different aspects of personality appear in the different hemispheres. In one patient, the right hemisphere seemed more disturbed by childhood memories of being bullied than did the left. In other studies, the right hemisphere experienced more negative emotions, such as loneliness and sadness, than did the left (Foster et al., 2008; Schiffer et al., 1998).

Try This Yourself

Application

Would you like a demonstration of the specialized functions of your own two hemispheres?

Some research suggests that the eyes tend to move to the right when a mental task involves the left hemisphere and to the left when the task involves the right hemisphere (see Kinsbourne, 1972). Read the following questions to a friend and record whether his or her eyes move to the right or to the left as he or she ponders the answers. Try

to keep the monitoring of your friend's eye movements as natural as possible.

1. Define the word "heredity."
2. What is a function of punctuation marks?
3. Which arm is raised on the Statue of Liberty?
4. On a keyboard, where is the "enter" key.

The first two questions involve language skills and the left hemisphere. Answering

them should produce more eye movement to the right. Questions 3 and 4 require spatial reasoning and the right hemisphere, which should elicit more eye movement to the left.

Try the same test on at least four other friends or family members. You will note two major points: (1) Cerebral lateralization is a matter of degree—not all or nothing, and (2) individual differences do exist, especially among left-handers.

Concept Diagram 2.2
Explaining Split-Brain Research

Experiments on split-brain patients often present visual information to only the patient's left or right hemisphere, which leads to some intriguing results. For example,

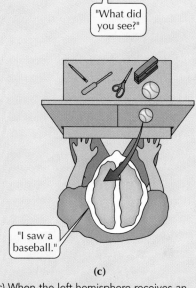

Verbal left hemisphere   Nonverbal right hemisphere

(a)

(b)

(c)

(a) When a split-brain patient is asked to stare straight ahead while a photo of a screwdriver is flashed only to the right hemisphere, he will report that he "saw nothing."

(b) However, when asked to pick up with his left hand what he saw, he can reach through and touch the items hidden behind the screen and easily pick up the screwdriver.

(c) When the left hemisphere receives an image of a baseball, the split-brain patient can easily name it.

Assuming you have an intact, nonsevered corpus callosum, if the same photos were presented to you in the same way, you could easily name both the screwdriver and the baseball. Can you explain why? The answers lie in our somewhat confusing visual wiring system:

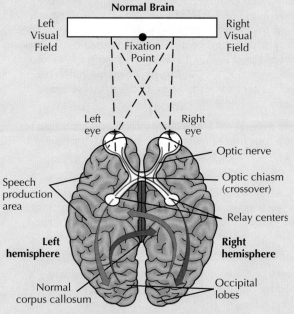

(d) Corpus callosum intact

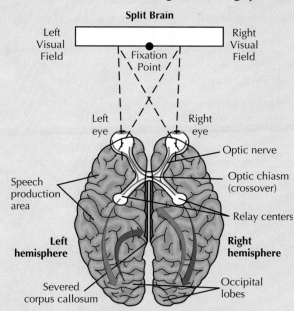

(e) Corpus callosum severed

As you can see in (d), our eyes connect to our brains in such a way that, when we look straight ahead, information from the left visual field (the blue line) travels to our right hemisphere, and information from the right visual field (the red line) travels to our left hemisphere. The messages received by either hemisphere are then quickly sent to the other across the corpus callosum. In this testing situation, you can easily name the objects because your right hemisphere sent the message to your left hemisphere, which controls speech in most adults. In contrast, when the corpus callosum is severed (e), and information is presented only to the right hemisphere, a split-brain patient cannot verbalize what he sees because the information cannot travel to the opposite (verbal) hemisphere.

Is this left- and right-brain specialization reversed in left-handed people? Not necessarily. About 68 percent of left-handers (people who use their left hands to write, hammer a nail, and throw a ball) and 97 percent of right-handers have their major language areas on the left hemisphere. This suggests that even though the right side of the brain is dominant for movement in left-handers, other types of skills are often localized in the same brain areas as for right-handers.

The Myth of the "Neglected Right Brain"

Courses and books directed at "right-brain thinking" and "drawing on the right side of the brain" often promise to increase your intuition, creativity, and artistic abilities by waking up your neglected and underused right brain. The fact is that the two hemispheres work together in a coordinated, integrated way, with each making important contributions. If you are a married student with small children, you can easily understand this principle. Just as you and your partner often "specialize" in different jobs (one giving the kids their baths, the other washing the dinner dishes), the hemispheres also divide their workload. However, both parents and both hemispheres are generally aware of what the other "half" is doing.

In our tour of the nervous system, the principles of *localization of function, lateralization,* and *specialization* are common—dendrites receive information, the occipital lobe specializes in vision, and so on. Keep in mind, however, that all parts of the brain and nervous system play *overlapping* and *synchronized* roles.

Application

CRITICAL THINKING

Biology and Critical Thinking
(Contributed by Thomas Frangicetto)

Many students find this chapter difficult because of the large number of unfamiliar terms and concepts. This exercise will help you:

- Review key biological terms that may appear on exams.
- Apply these terms to critical thinking components.
- Check your answers in Appendix B.

Part I: Match each term from Chapter 2 with the correct abbreviated description.

1. _____Amygdala	a. arousal	
2. _____Corpus Callosum	b. language/analytical	
3. _____Dopamine	c. mood, impulsivity, depression	
4. _____Frontal Lobes	d. vision/visual perception	
5. _____Hypothalamus	e. hearing/language	
6. _____Left Hemisphere	f. coordination	
7. _____Cerebellum	g. internal environment	
8. _____Occipital Lobes	h. calming	
9. _____Parasympathetic Nervous System	i. connects two hemispheres	
	j. bodily sensations	
10. _____Parietal Lobes	k. emotion	
11. _____Right Hemisphere	l. motor, speech, and higher functions	
	m. nonverbal abilities	
12. _____Serotonin	n. movement, attention, schizophrenia	
13. _____Sympathetic Nervous System		
14. _____Temporal Lobes		

ACTIVE LEARNING

Part II: As mentioned earlier, your brain and nervous system control everything you do, feel, see, or think. They also control your critical thinking. For each of situations below, first identify which critical thinking component (CTC) from the Prologue (pp. xxx) is being described. Then decide which area of the brain or nervous system listed in Part I would most likely be involved in the application of this CTC. (*Tip:* If you need help, review the related text content for each term, not just the abbreviated description above.)

1. Tamara wrote several children's storybooks and attempted to do the illustrations herself. After many failed attempts, she accepted her limitations and hired a professional artist.

   CTC: _____ Biological Area (s): _____

2. Samantha was falling behind in her college courses primarily because she was not paying close attention during class lectures. She decided to listen carefully and to take detailed notes, and her grades improved dramatically.

   CTC: _____ Biological Area (s): _____

3. After two weeks on a new job, Alex was so stressed and overwhelmed he planned to quit, but his boss persuaded him to stay on. Once Alex accepted his boss's reassurance that uncertainty and mistakes are a normal part of getting adjusted to a new job, his symptoms of stress (shortness of breath and increased blood pressure) soon disappeared.

   CTC: _____ Biological Area (s): _____

Working with Traumatic Brain Injuries (TBI)

Imagine yourself as a high school football player. If you suffered a concussion while playing a game, would you tell your coach? For Kelby Jasmon, a senior with three concussions, the answer is: "No chance." The only way I come out is on a stretcher." Would this football player answer differently if he knew about the mounting evidence linking multiple concussions with permanent (and possibly fatal) brain damage?

According to reporter Alan Schwarz (2007), "many of the 1.2 million teenagers who play high school football either don't know what a concussion is or they simply don't care. They continue to play on and get hurt much worse—sometimes fatally."

Millions of people suffer head injuries each year, and most of these injuries are minor, thanks to the bony skull's protection for the brain. This is not the case for *traumatic brain injury (TBI)*. TBI is defined as any injury to the brain caused by significant trauma, with symptoms ranging from mild to severe (headache, loss of consciousness, convulsions, coma, and death). Two of the most common types of traumatic brain injuries are *concussions* (which result from a significant blow to the head) and *contusions* (which are bruises in the brain). Either type of TBI can result in prolonged or nonreversible brain damage and serious problems, such as extreme changes in personality and significant loss of motor skills, emotional control, and mental abilities (Slobounov, 2008).

Why would a high school football player take such risks? What treatment is available for kids, teenagers, and adults who suffer traumatic brain injuries while playing games or even just riding in an automobile? Would you like a career working with these patients?

Home health-care workers, special education teachers, and life skills aides all have opportunities to work with TBI patients, but let's examine some of the specific duties and experiences of one 28-year-old occupational therapist, Jodi Levin, who has worked for six years on the brain injury unit of New Jersey's Kessler Institute for Rehabilitation. The medical care of TBI patients is generally overseen by neurologists, medical doctors, and nurses, while occupational therapists, like Ms. Levin, are responsible for planning exercises that will help patients develop or adapt skills to live as safely and independently as possible (Hoffman, 2008).

Ms. Levin, with a Master's degree in the field, has a host of professional and personal tools to help her in her work. In addition to the latest computer-generated programs, including blocks, flash cards, and cutlery adapted for stroke victims, occupational therapists like Ms. Levin use numerous psychological concepts and techniques that you will study throughout this text. For example, many TBI patients lose their most basic life functions, such as blinking and chewing, and occupational therapists establish small, measurable exercises to regain these and other higher-level functions. Chapter 6 will discuss these incremental small steps, known as "successive approximations" or *shaping* (p. 216), as well as instructor-modeled frameworks for learning, called *scaffolding* (p. 230).

In addition, Chapter 3 explores the sources and effects of stress, along with several methods and resources for coping. While the need for understanding and appreciating the stresses for TBI patients is obvious, their caregivers also experience significant job stresses and are at high risk for a unique stressor called *occupational burnout* (p. 93).

If you'd like one more example of the benefits of studying psychology think of all the information you've gained from this chapter. Knowing the general structure and function of our brains and other parts of our nervous system is important to everyone, but it's particularly valuable for health-care workers. Think back to the case of Phineas Gage (p. 72)

Todd Heisler/The New York Times/Redux Pictures

Fred R. Conrad/The New York Times/Redux Pictures

and how damage [to] [personality]. Can you see how this inform[ation] [be]come agitated and angry? Ms. Levi[n] . "The families are so embarrassed," [not] the patient."

Due to spac[e] [availa]ble career options in the field of t[he] [infor]mation, check out http://www.bia[w] patients and their therapists is goo[d] brain injury is not like the flu. It ta[kes]

Assessment
CHECK & REVIEW

STOP

The Cerebral Cortex and Two Brains in One?

Objective 2.12: *What is the cerebral cortex, and what is its major function?*

The **cerebral cortex**, the thin surface layer on the cerebral hemispheres, regulates most complex behaviors and higher mental processes.

Objective 2.13: *Describe the major functions of the lobes of the cerebral cortex.*

The two **frontal lobes** control higher functions, speech production, and motor control. The two **parietal lobes** are the receiving and interpretation area for sensory information. The two **temporal lobes** are concerned with hearing, language, memory, and some emotional control. The two **occipital lobes** are dedicated to vision and visual information processing.

Objective 2.14: *Why is the case study of Phineas Gage important?*

Phineas Gage experienced a horrific blow to his frontal lobes when a metal rod pierced his face and brain. Historical records of changes in his behavior and mental processes following the accident provide invaluable clues to the important role of the frontal lobe in motivation, emotion, and other cognitive activities.

Objective 2.1[5]: *[Explain why the] callosum and split-brain research are important.*

The two hemispheres are linked by the **corpus callosum**, through which they communicate and coordinate. **Split-brain** research shows that each hemisphere performs somewhat separate functions. In most people, the left hemisphere is dominant in verbal skills, such as speaking and writing, and analytical tasks. The right hemisphere appears to excel at nonverbal tasks, such as spatio-manipulative skills, art and music, and visual recognition.

Objective 2.16: *Describe traumatic brain injury (TBI).*

Traumatic brain injury (TBI) is any injury to the brain caused by significant trauma. Two of the most common TBIs are *concussions* (blows to the head) and *contusions* (bruises in the brain).

Questions

1. The bumpy, convoluted area making up the outside surface of the brain is the _____.
2. You are giving a speech. Name the cortical lobes involved in the following behaviors:
   a. Seeing faces in the audience
   b. Hearing questions from the audience

c. [Remembering] where your car is parked when you are ready to go home
d. Noticing that your new shoes are too tight and hurting your feet

3. The _____ lobes regulate our personality and are largely responsible for much of what makes us uniquely human. (a) frontal; (b) temporal; (c) parietal; (d) occipital
4. Label the four lobes of the brain:

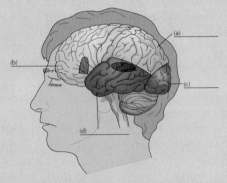

5. Although the left and right hemispheres of the brain are specialized, they are normally in close communication because of the _____. (a) reciprocating circuits; (b) thalamus; (c) corpus callosum; (d) cerebellum

Check your answers in Appendix B.

Click & Review
for additional assessment options:
wiley.com/college/huffman

Achievement

Objective 2.17: *What is behavioral genetics?*

Our Genetic Inheritance

Some of what we are today results from evolutionary forces at play thousands of years before you or I were even on this planet. During that time, our ancestors foraged for food, fought for survival, and passed on traits that were selected and transmitted down through the generations. How do these transmitted traits affect us today? For answers, psychologists often turn to **behavioral genetics**, how heredity and environ-

Behavioral Genetics *Study of the relative effects of heredity and the environment on behavior and mental processes*

Cell

Cell nucleus:
Each cell in the human body (except red blood cells) contains a nucleus.

Chromosomes:
Each cell nucleus contains 46 chromosomes arranged in 23 pairs (one chromosome of each pair is from each parent). Chromosomes are threadlike molecules of DNA (deoxyribonucleic acid).

DNA:
Each DNA molecule contains thousands of genes, which are the most basic units of heredity.

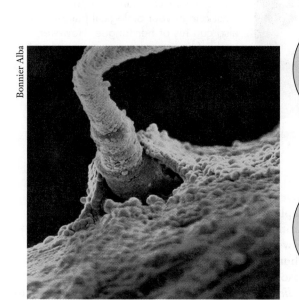

Bonnier Alba

Figure 2.21 *Hereditary codes?* (a) An actual photo of the moment of conception when sperm meets egg. (b) The nucleus of every cell in our body contains chromosomes, DNA, and genes—the essence of our heredity.

Evolutionary Psychology
Branch of psychology that studies how evolutionary processes, like natural selection and genetic mutations, affect behavior and mental processes

Chromosomes *Threadlike molecule of DNA (deoxyribonucleic acid) that carries genetic information*

Genes *Segment of DNA (deoxyribonucleic acid) that occupies a specific place on a particular chromosome and carries the code for hereditary transmission*

ment affect us, and **evolutionary psychology**, how the natural process of adapting to our environment affects us.

Behavioral Genetics: Is It Nature or Nurture?

> With a good heredity, nature deals you a fine hand at cards; and with a good environment, you learn to play the hand well.
>
> WALTER C. ALVAREZ

In earlier times, people thought inherited characteristics were passed along through the blood—"He's got his family's bad blood." We now know it's a lot more complicated than that. Let's start at the beginning.

At the moment of your conception, your mother and father each contributed 23 **chromosomes** to you, and thousands of **genes** are found on each chromosome (Figure 2.21). For some of your traits, such as blood type, a single pair of genes (one from each parent) determines what characteristics you will possess. But most traits, including aggressiveness, sociability, and even height are determined by a combination of many genes.

Dominant and Recessive Traits

When the two genes for a given trait conflict, the outcome depends on whether the gene is *dominant* or *recessive*. A dominant gene normally reveals its trait whenever the gene is present. In contrast, the gene for a recessive trait will normally be expressed only if the other gene in the pair is also recessive.

It was once assumed that characteristics such as, eye color, hair color, or height, were the result of either one dominant gene or two paired recessive genes. But modern geneticists have found that each of these characteristics is *polygenic*, meaning they are controlled by multiple genes. Many polygenic traits like height or intelligence are also affected by environmental and social factors (Figure 2.22). Fortunately, most serious genetic disorders are not transmitted through a dominant gene. Can you understand why?

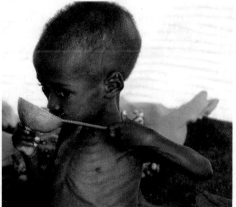

EPA/STR/Landov

Figure 2.22 *Gene–environment interaction* Children who are malnourished may not reach their full potential genetic height or maximum intelligence. Can you see how environment factors like nutrition interact with genetic factors to influence development?

Can you curl your tongue lengthwise?

Tongue curling is one of the few traits that depends on only one dominant gene. If you can curl your tongue, at least one of your biological parents can also curl his or her tongue. However, if both of your parents are "noncurlers," they both must have recessive genes for curling.

A dominant gene in action.

Methods for Studying Inheritance in Humans

Achievement

Objective 2.18: *Describe the four methods of behavioral genetics research.*

If you wanted to determine the relative influences of heredity or environment, how would you go about it? For very simple studies of inheritance in plants, you could just breed one type of plant with another to see what your desired trait would be like in the next generation. But how would you conduct research on complex traits like aggressiveness or sociability in humans? Scientists can't use selective breeding experiments—for obvious ethical reasons. Instead, they generally rely on four less direct methods: *twin studies, family studies, adoption studies,* and studies of *genetic abnormalities* (Concept Diagram 2.3).

Findings from these four methods have allowed behavioral geneticists to estimate the **heritability** of various traits. That is, to what degree are individual differences a result of genetic, inherited factors rather than differences in the environment? If genetics contributed *nothing* to the trait, it would have a heritability estimate of 0 percent. If a trait were *completely* due to genetics, we would say it had a heritability estimate of 100 percent. (Correlations of .70 and above are generally accepted as strong evidence of a genetic influence.)

Heritability *Measure of the degree to which a characteristic is related to genetic, inherited factors versus the environment*

Achievement

Objective 2.19: *Identify three key genetic misconceptions.*

 PSYCHOLOGY AT WORK

Overcoming Genetic Misconceptions

Behavioral genetics and heritability are hot topics in the general press—and in modern psychology. Each day we are bombarded with new discoveries regarding genes and the supposed heritability of intelligence, sexual orientation, and athletic abilities. But press reports are often misleading and invite misunderstanding. As you hear estimates of heritability, keep these cautions in mind:

1. *Genetic traits are not fixed or inflexible.* After listening to the latest research, some people become unreasonably discouraged. They fear they are destined for heart disease, obesity, breast cancer, depression, alcoholism, or other problems because of their particular biological inheritance. Genes do have a strong influence on diseases and behaviors. However, these genetic studies do not reflect how an environmental intervention might change the outcome. If you inherited a possible genetic predisposition for some undesirable trait, you can often improve your odds by adopting lifestyle changes, such as improved diet and frequent exercise. (Also, remember that nothing in life is 100 percent inherited—except sex. If your parents did not have it, it is 100 percent sure that you won't.)

Concept Diagram 2.3

Four Methods of Behavioral Genetics Research

1. **Twin Studies** Psychologists study twins because they have a uniquely high proportion of shared genes. *Identical (monozygotic—one egg)* twins share 100 percent of the same genes, whereas *fraternal (dizygotic—two egg)* twins share, on average, 50 percent of their genes, just like any other pair of siblings. As you can see in the figure to the right, identical twins develop from a single egg fertilized by a single sperm. They share the same placenta and have the same sex and same genetic makeup. Fraternal twins are formed when two separate sperm

Brad Wilson/Stone/Getty Images

SW Production/Age Fotostock America, Inc.

fertilize two separate eggs. They are genetically no more alike than brothers and sisters born at different times. Fraternal twins are simply nine-month "womb mates."

Because both identical and fraternal twins share the same parents and develop in relatively the same environment, they provide a valuable type of "natural experiment." If heredity influences a trait or behavior to some degree, identical twins should be more alike than fraternal twins. As you'll see in Chapter 8, pp. 306–307, scientists use an even more stringent twin study method when they compare identical and fraternal twins who were separated very early in life and raised in *different* environments. If researchers find that identical twins who were reared apart are more like their biological families than their adoptive families, can you see how this provides even stronger evidence for a genetic influence?

2. **Family Studies** Why study families? If a specific trait is inherited, blood relatives should show increased trait similarity, compared with unrelated people. Also, closer relatives, like siblings, should be more similar than distant relatives. Family studies have shown that many traits and mental disorders, such as intelligence, sociability, and depression, do indeed run in families.

3. **Adoption Studies** Another "natural experiment," adoption, also provides valuable information for researchers. If adopted children are more like their biological family in some trait, then genetic factors probably had the greater influence. Conversely, if adopted children resemble their adopted family, even though they do not share similar genes, then environmental factors may predominate.

4. **Genetic Abnormalities** Research in behavioral genetics also explores disorders and diseases that result when genes malfunction. For example, an extra twenty-first chromosome fragment almost always causes a condition called *Down syndrome.* Abnormalities in several genes or chromosomes also are suspected factors in *Alzheimer's disease,* which involves serious brain deterioration and memory loss, and *schizophrenia,* a severe mental disorder characterized by loss of contact with reality.

Identical twins

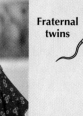

Same sex only

Fraternal twins

Same or opposite sex

Rick Rusing/Riser/Getty Images

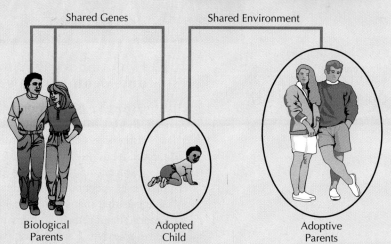

Shared Genes   Shared Environment

Biological Parents

Adopted Child

Adoptive Parents

Phanie/Photo Researchers, Inc.

Concept Diagram

Image Source/Getty Images

2. *Heritability estimates do not apply to individuals.* When you hear media reports that intelligence or athletic talents are 30 to 50 percent inherited, do you assume this applies to you as an individual? Do you believe that if intelligence is 50 percent inherited, then 50 percent is due to your parents and 50 percent to your environment? This is a common misconception. Heritability statistics are mathematical computations of the proportion of total variance in a trait that is explained by genetic variation within a group—not *individuals*. Height, for example, has one of the highest heritability estimates—around 90 percent (Plomin, 1990). However, your own personal height may be very different from that of your parents or other blood relatives. We each inherit a unique combination of genes (unless we are identical twins). Therefore, it is impossible to predict your individual height from a heritability estimate. You can only estimate for the group as a whole.

3. *Genes and the environment are inseparable.* As first discussed in Chapter 1, biological, psychological, and social forces all influence one another and are inseparable—the *biopsychosocial model.* Imagine your inherited genes as analogous to water, sugar, salt, flour, eggs, baking powder, and oil. When you mix these ingredients and pour them on a hot griddle (one environment), you get pancakes. Add more oil (a different combination of genes) and a waffle iron (a different environment), and you get waffles. With another set of ingredients and environments (different pans and an oven), you can have crepes, muffins, or cakes. How can you separate the effects of ingredients and cooking methods?

Nora Good/Masterfile

Deborah Raven/Getty Images

Rita Maas/The Image Bank/Getty Images

Evolutionary Psychology: Darwin Explains Behavior and Mental Processes

Achievement

Objective 2.20: *What is evolutionary psychology?*

As we have seen, behavioral genetics studies help explain the role of heredity (nature) and the environment (nurture) in our individual behavior. To increase our understanding of genetic predispositions, we also need to look at universal behaviors transmitted from our evolutionary past.

Evolutionary psychology is the branch of psychology that studies how evolutionary processes affect behavior and mental processes (Buss, 2008; Freeman & Herron, 2007). It suggests that many behavioral commonalities, from eating to fighting with our enemies, emerged and remain in human populations because they helped our ancestors (and ourselves) survive. This perspective is based on the writings of Charles Darwin (1859), who suggested that natural forces select traits that are adaptive to the organism's survival. This process of **natural selection** occurs when one particular genetic trait gives a person a reproductive advantage over others. Some people mistakenly believe that natural selection means "survival of the fittest." What really matters is *reproduction*—the survival of the genome. Because of natural selection, the fastest or otherwise most fit organisms will be most likely to live long enough to pass on their genes to the next generation.

Genetic mutations also help explain behavior. Everyone carries at least one gene that has *mutated*, or changed from the original. But, only very rarely, a mutated gene will be significant enough to change an individual's behavior. It might cause someone

Natural Selection *Driving mechanism behind evolution that allows individuals with genetically influenced traits that are adaptive in a particular environment to stay alive and produce offspring*

to be more social, more risk taking, or more careful. If the gene then gives the person reproductive advantage, he or she will be more likely to pass on the gene to future generations. However, this mutation does not guarantee long-term survival. A well-adapted population can perish if its environment changes.

Achievement
GENDER & CULTURAL DIVERSITY

The Evolution of Sex Differences

According to evolutionary theory, modern men and women have several sex differences that helped our ancestors adapt to their environment and hence to survive and reproduce. As you can see in Figure 2.23, some research shows a difference in lateralization of function between men and women. Figure 2.24 also illustrates how

Problem-Solving Tasks Favoring Women

Perceptual speed:
As quickly as possible identify matching items.

Displaced objects:
After looking at the middle picture, tell which item is missing from the the picture on the right.

Verbal fluency:
List words that begin with the same letter. (Women also tend to perform better in ideational fluency tests, for example, listing objects that are the same color.)

B – – –	Bat, big, bike, bang, bark, bank, bring, brand, broom, bright, brook, bug, buddy, bunk

Precision manual tasks:
Place the pegs in the holes as quickly as possible.

Mathematical calculation:
Compute the answer.

72	6 (18+4)−78+^{36}/2

Problem-Solving Tasks Favoring Men

Spatial tasks:
Mentally rotate the 3-d object to identify its match.

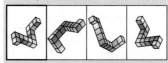

Spatial tasks:
Mentally manipulate the folded paper to tell where the holes will fall when it is unfolded.

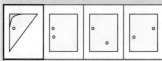

Target-directed motor skills:
Hit the bulls eye.

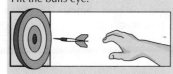

Disembedding tests:
Find the simple shape on the left in the more complex figures.

Mathematical reasoning:
What is the answer?

5 1/2	If you bicycle 24 miles a day, how many days will it take to travel 132 miles?

Figure 2.24 *Problem-solving tasks favoring women and men*

Achievement

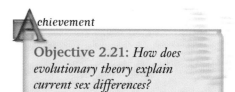

Objective 2.21: *How does evolutionary theory explain current sex differences?*

Shaywitz, et. al., 1995 NMR Research/Yale Medical School

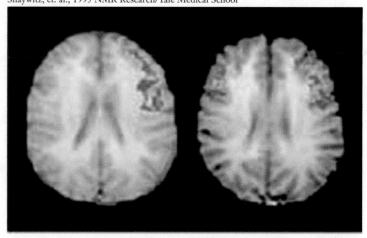

Figure 2.23 *Sex differences in lateralization* These are composite MRI scans of the brains of men (left) and women (right) during a verbal task involving rhyming. Note how activation is largely confined to only one hemisphere for men, whereas it occurs in both hemispheres for women.

wiley.com/
college/
huffman

men tend to score higher on spatial tasks, target-directed motor skills, disembedding tasks, and mathematical reasoning. In contrast, women tend to do better on tasks involving perceptual speed, displaced objects, verbal fluency, precise manual activities, and mathematical calculation. What accounts for these differences?

One possible answer from evolutionary psychologists is that gender differences are the product of gradual genetic adaptations (Freeman & Herron, 2007; Kardong, 2008). If ancient societies assigned men the task of "hunters" and women as "gatherers," the man's superiority on many spatial tasks and target-directed motor skills, for example, may have evolved from the adaptive demands of hunting. Similarly, activities such as gathering, child-rearing, and domestic tool construction and manipulation may have contributed to the woman's language superiority and fine motor coordination.

Some critics, however, suggest that evolution progresses much too slowly to account for this type of behavioral adaptation. Furthermore, there is wide cross-cultural variability in gender differences, and evolutionary explanations of sex differences are highly speculative and obviously difficult to test scientifically (Denmark, Rabinowitz, & Sechzer, 2005; Eagly & Koenig, 2006; Hyde, 2007; Matlin, 2008).

Evolutionary psychology research emphasizes heredity and early biological processes in determining gender differences in cognitive behavior. Keep in mind, however, that almost all sex differences are *correlational*. The mechanisms involved in the actual *cause* of certain human behaviors have yet to be determined. Furthermore, it is important to remember that all known variations *between* the two sexes are much smaller than differences *within* each sex. Finally, to repeat a theme discussed throughout this text, it is extremely difficult to separate the effects of biological, psychological, and social forces—the *biopsychosocial model*.

Assessment

CHECK & REVIEW

Our Genetic Inheritance

Objective 2.17: *What is behavioral genetics?*

Behavioral genetics studies the relative effects of heredity and the environment on behavior and mental processes. Two important keys to heredity are genes and chromosomes. **Genes** hold the code for certain traits that are passed on from parent to child, and they can be dominant or recessive. Each of the 46 human **chromosomes** contains many genes, which are found in DNA molecules.

Objective 2.18: *Describe the four methods of behavioral genetics research.*

Behavioral geneticists use twin studies, family studies, adoption studies, and genetic abnormalities to explore genetic contributions to behavior and make estimates of **heritability**.

Objective 2.19: *Identify three key genetic misconceptions.*

The three key misconceptions are: Genetic traits are not fixed or inflexible, heritability

estimates do not apply to individuals, and genes and the environment are inseparable.

Objective 2.20: *What is evolutionary psychology?*

Evolutionary psychology is the branch of psychology that looks at evolutionary changes related to behavior and mental processes. Several different evolutionary processes, including **natural selection** and genetic mutations can affect behavior and mental processes.

Objective 2.21: *How does evolutionary theory explain current sex differences?*

According to evolutionary theory, modern sex differences (like the male's superior spatial and motor skills and the female's superior verbal fluency and fine motor coordination) are the product of gradual genetic adaptations. They helped our ancestors adapt and survive in their environment.

Questions

1. Threadlike strands of DNA that carry genetic information are known

as _____. (a) stem cells; (b) genes; (c) neurons; (d) chromosomes
2. What are the four chief methods used to study behavioral genetics?
3. Evolutionary psychology is the branch of psychology that looks at _____. (a) how fossil discoveries affect behavior; (b) the relationship between genes and the environment; (c) how evolutionary processes affect behavior and mental processes. (d) the effect of culture change on behavior
4. From an evolutionary perspective, can you explain why people are more likely to help their family members than strangers?

Check your answers in Appendix B.

Click & Review
for additional assessment options:
wiley.com/college/huffman

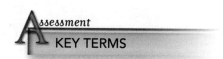

Assessment
KEY TERMS

*To assess your understanding of the **Key Terms** in Chapter 2, write a definition for each (in your own words), and then compare your definitions with those in the text.*

neuroscience (p. 50)

Neural Bases of Behavior
action potential (p. 55)
axon (p. 53)
cell body (p. 53)
dendrites (p. 53)
endocrine [EN-doh-krin] system (p. 58)
endorphins [en-DOR-fins] (p. 57)
glial cells (p. 52)
hormones (p. 58)
myelin [MY-uh-lin] sheath (p. 53)
neuron (p. 52)
neurotransmitters (p. 56)
synapse [SIN-aps] (p. 56)

Nervous System Organization
autonomic nervous system (ANS) (p. 63)
central nervous system (CNS) (p. 60)

neurogenesis [nue-roe-JEN-uh-sis] (p. 61)
neuroplasticity (p. 61)
parasympathetic nervous system (p. 63)
peripheral nervous system (PNS) (p. 60)
reflex (p. 62)
somatic nervous system (SNS) (p. 63)
stem cell (p. 61)
sympathetic nervous system (p. 63)

A Tour Through the Brain
amygdala (p. 70)
association areas (p. 73)
brainstem (p. 67)
cerebellum [sehr-uh-BELL-um] (p. 68)
cerebral cortex (p. 71)
corpus callosum [CORE-pus] [cah-LOH-suhm] (p. 75)
forebrain (p. 68)
frontal lobes (p. 72)
hindbrain (p. 68)

hippocampus (p. 69)
hypothalamus [hi-poh-THAL-uh-muss] (p. 69)
limbic system (p. 69)
medulla [muh-DUL-uh] (p. 68)
midbrain (p. 68)
occipital [ahk-SIP-ih-tul] lobes (p. 73)
parietal [puh-RYE-uh-tul] lobes (p. 73)
pons (p. 68)
reticular formation (RF) (p. 68)
split-brain surgery (p. 75)
temporal lobes (p. 73)
thalamus [THAL-uh-muss] (p. 68)

Our Genetic Inheritance
behavioral genetics (p. 80)
chromosomes (p. 81)
evolutionary psychology (p. 81)
genes (p. 81)
heritability (p. 82)
natural selection (p. 84)

Achievement
WEB RESOURCES

Huffman Book Companion Site
wiley.com/college/huffman
   This site is loaded with free Interactive Self-Tests, Internet Exercises, Glossary and Flashcards for key terms, web links, Handbook for Non-Native Speakers, and other activities designed to improve your mastery of the material in this chapter.

Chapter 2 Visual Summary

Neural Bases of Behavior

What Is a Neuron?

Neurons: Transmit information throughout the body.
Glial cells: Provide structural, nutritional, and other support for neurons, as well as some information transfer.

Key features of a neuron
- **Dendrites:** Receive information and send impulses to cell body.
- **Cell body:** Integrates incoming information.
- **Axon:** Carries information from cell body to other neurons. (**Myelin Sheath:** Fatty insulation around some axons that speeds up action potential.)

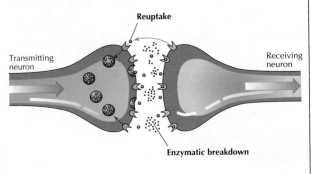

How Do Neurons Communicate?

- Communication *within the neuron* is through the **action potential**, a neural impulse that carries information along the axon.
- Communication *between neurons* occurs when an action potential reaches the axon terminal and stimulates the release of **neurotransmitters** into the **synapse**, and the chemical message is picked up by receiving neurons.

How Do Neurotransmitters and Hormones Affect Us?

Two key chemical messengers:
1. **Neurotransmitters:** Chemicals manufactured and released by neurons that alter activity in other neurons, which thereby affects behavior and mental processes.
2. **Hormones:** Chemicals released from the **endocrine system** into the bloodstream to produce bodily changes or to maintain normal bodily functions.

Reuptake

Transmitting neuron

Receiving neuron

Enzymatic breakdown

Nervous System Organization

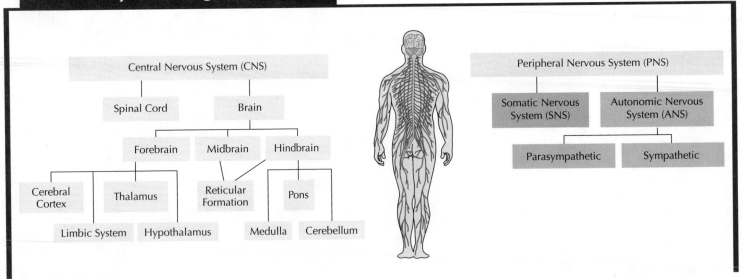

Central Nervous System (CNS)

Spinal Cord — Brain

Forebrain — Midbrain — Hindbrain

Cerebral Cortex — Thalamus

Reticular Formation — Pons

Limbic System — Hypothalamus

Medulla — Cerebellum

Peripheral Nervous System (PNS)

Somatic Nervous System (SNS) — Autonomic Nervous System (ANS)

Parasympathetic — Sympathetic

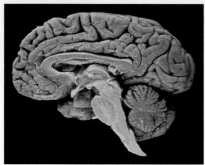

Science Pictures Limited/Photo Researchers

Three Major Sections of the Brain

- **Hindbrain:** Lower-level functions and structures (**medulla**, **cerebellum**, and **pons**)
- **Midbrain:** Middle of the brain (**reticular formation (RF)**)
- **Forebrain:** Higher-level functions and structures (**thalamus**, **hypothalamus**, **limbic system**, and **cerebral cortex**)

The Cerebral Cortex

The **cerebral cortex** is responsible for all higher mental processes and is divided into four sections

Frontal Lobes

Coordinates messages from other lobes and regulates motor control, speech production, and higher functions (thinking, personality, emotion, and memory).

Parietal Lobes

Sensory processing (pressure, pain, touch, and temperature).

Temporal Lobes

Hearing, language comprehension, memory, and some emotional control.

Occipital Lobes

Vision and visual perception.

Two Brains in One

Splitting the **corpus callosum**, which normally transfers neural impulses between the brain's left and right hemispheres, is a treatment for some forms of epilepsy. **Split-brain** research on these patients shows some specialization of functions in each hemisphere.

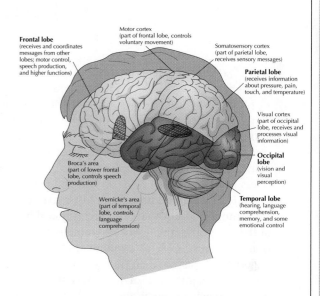

Frontal lobe (receives and coordinates messages from other lobes; motor control, speech production, and higher functions)

Motor cortex (part of frontal lobe, controls voluntary movement)

Somatosensory cortex (part of parietal lobe, receives sensory messages)

Parietal lobe (receives information about pressure, pain, touch, and temperature)

Visual cortex (part of occipital lobe, receives and processes visual information)

Occipital lobe (vision and visual perception)

Broca's area (part of lower frontal lobe, controls speech production)

Wernicke's area (part of temporal lobe, controls language comprehension)

Temporal lobe (hearing, language comprehension, memory, and some emotional control)

Our Genetic Inheritance

Behavioral Genetics

Each of the 46 human **chromosomes** contains many **genes**, which are found in DNA molecules.

Genetics studies are done with twins, adopted children, families, and genetic abnormalities. Such studies allow estimates of **heritability**.

Evolutionary Psychology

Studies evolutionary principles, like **natural selection** and genetic mutations, which affect adaptation to the environment and help explain commonalities in behavior.

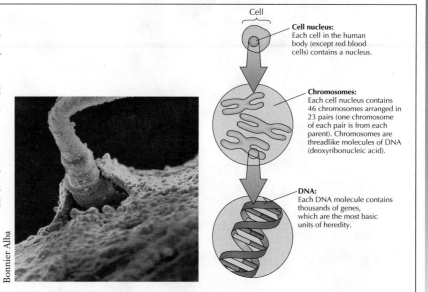

Bonnier Alba

Cell

Cell nucleus: Each cell in the human body (except red blood cells) contains a nucleus.

Chromosomes: Each cell nucleus contains 46 chromosomes arranged in 23 pairs (one chromosome of each pair is from each parent). Chromosomes are threadlike molecules of DNA (deoxyribonucleic acid).

DNA: Each DNA molecule contains thousands of genes, which are the most basic units of heredity.

3

Stress and Health Psychology

hat do you remember about the terrorist attacks of September 11, 2001? What about recent global disasters when hurricanes, tornados, and floods devastated large areas of the world? How did you feel? Have you been the victim of a disaster, robbery, rape, or wartime trauma? These are perhaps the most obvious events that come to mind when we think about being stressed. However, stress is all around us. It is an integral part of our physical and mental health. Throughout history, people have believed that emotions and thoughts affect physical health. However, in the late 1800s, the discovery of biological causes for infectious diseases, such as typhoid and syphilis, encouraged scientists to lessen their interest in psychological factors. Today, the major causes of death have shifted from contagious diseases (such as pneumonia, influenza, tuberculosis, and measles) to noncontagious chronic conditions (such as cancer, cardiovascular disease, and chronic lung disease). And the focus has returned to psychological behaviors and lifestyles (Leventhal et al., 2008; Straub, 2007). In this chapter, we will explore how biological, psychological, and social factors (the *biopsychosocial model*) affect illness as well as health and well-being.

Jan Greune/LOOK/Getty Images

Solus-Veer/©Corbis

▶ **Understanding Stress**

Sources of Stress

RESEARCH HIGHLIGHT
Hurricane Katrina and Local College Students

 GENDER & CULTURAL DIVERSITY "KAROSHI"—
CAN JOB STRESS BE FATAL?

Effects of Stress

 PSYCHOLOGY AT WORK
Is My Job Too Stressful?

▶ **Stress and Illness**

Cancer
Cardiovascular Disorders
Posttraumatic Stress Disorder (PTSD)

RESEARCH HIGHLIGHT
Does Stress Cause Gastric Ulcers?

▶ **Health Psychology in Action**

 PSYCHOLOGY AT WORK
Would You Like to Be a Health Psychologist?

Tobacco
Alcohol
Chronic Pain

▶ **Health and Stress Management**

Cognitive Appraisal and Coping

 PSYCHOLOGY AT WORK
Why You Shouldn't Procrastinate

Resources for Healthy Living

 PSYCHOLOGY AT WORK
Coping with TechnoStress

CRITICAL THINKING/ACTIVE LEARNING
Reducing Stress Through Critical Thinking

Application

WHY STUDY PSYCHOLOGY?

Did you know...

▶ Even positive events, like graduating from college and getting married, are major sources of stress?

▶ Procrastinating on homework can be harmful to your health as well as to your grades?

▶ Friends are one of your best health resources?

▶ Assembly-line jobs are a prime source of stress?

▶ Small, everyday hassles can impair your immune system functioning?

▶ Social support from family and friends can offset the damaging effects of stress?

Jose Luis Pelaez/CorbisImages

▶ Police officers, nurses, doctors, social workers, and teachers are particularly prone to "burnout"?

▶ Having few choices or little control can be dangerous to your health?

▶ Having a cynical, hostile Type A personality contributes to heart disease?

▶ Prolonged stress can lead to death?

▶ Hardy personality types may cope better with stress?

▶ You can control, or minimize, most of the negative effects of stress?

Achievement

Objective 3.1: *Define stress, eustress, and distress.*

Stress *Nonspecific response of the body to any demand made on it; the arousal, both physical and mental, to situations or events that we perceive as threatening or challenging*

Eustress *Pleasant, desirable stress*

Distress *Unpleasant, threatening stress*

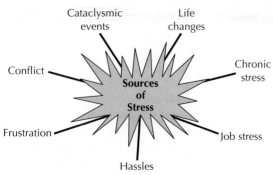

Figure 3.1 *Seven major sources of stress*

Understanding Stress

Hans Selye (SELL-yay), a physiologist renowned for his research and writing in the area of stress since the 1930s, defined **stress** as the nonspecific response of the body to any demand made on it. The trigger that prompts the stressful reaction is called a *stressor*. When you play two nonstop tennis matches in the middle of a heat wave, your body responds with a fast heartbeat, rapid breathing, and an outpouring of perspiration. When you suddenly remember that the term paper you just started is due today rather than next Friday, your body has the same physiological stress response to a very different stressor. Stress reactions can result from either internal, cognitive stimuli or external, environmental stimuli (Sarafino, 2008; Straub, 2007).

Our bodies are nearly always in some state of stress, whether pleasant or unpleasant, mild or severe. *Anything* placing a demand on the body can cause stress. A total absence of stress would mean a total absence of stimulation, which would eventually lead to death. When stress is short-lived or perceived as a challenge, it can be beneficial. As seen in athletes, business tycoons, entertainers, or great leaders, this type of pleasant stress, called **eustress**, helps arouse and motivate us toward great accomplishments. Stress that is unpleasant and threatening is called **distress** (Selye, 1974). Because health psychology has been chiefly concerned with the negative effects of stress, we will adhere to convention and use the word *stress* to refer primarily to harmful or unpleasant stress.

Sources of Stress: Seven Major Stressors

Although stress is pervasive in our lives, some things cause more stress than others. The seven major sources of stress are life changes, chronic stress, job stress, hassles, frustration, conflict, and cataclysmic events (Figure 3.1).

Life Changes

Early stress researchers Thomas Holmes and Richard Rahe (1967) believed that change of any kind that required some adjustment in behavior or lifestyle could cause some degree of stress (Figure 3.2). They also believed that exposure to numerous stressful events within a short period could have a direct detrimental effect on health.

To investigate the relationship between change and stress, Holmes and Rahe created a Social Readjustment Rating Scale (SRRS) that asked people to check off all the life events they had experienced in the last year (Table 3.1).

The SRRS scale is an easy and popular way to measure stress, and cross-cultural studies have shown that most people rank the magnitude of stressful events in similar ways (De Coteau, Hope, & Anderson, 2003; Scully, Tosi, & Banning, 2000). However, the SRRS is not foolproof. For example, it only shows a *correlation* between stress and illness. It does not prove that stress actually causes illnesses.

Chronic Stress

Not all stressful situations are single, life-changing events, like the death of a spouse or a divorce. Ongoing, unrelenting stressors, such as a bad marriage, poverty, ill health, or an intolerable political climate, also contribute to stress. Interestingly, these types of **chronic stress**, a state of ongoing physiological arousal, may be some of the most damaging of all stressors (Torpy, Lynm, & Glass, 2007). As you'll see in the upcoming section on the effects of stress, our bodies were designed to handle acute, short-acting stress, not chronic stress.

Recall from Chapter 2 that when we see a bear, our *sympathetic system* automatically kicks into "fight or flight." Once the threat passes, the *parasympathetic system* takes over and relaxes us. But our modern-day stressors are much more complex and ongoing, and our parasympathetic system rarely has the chance to activate the relaxation response. How do our soldiers in Iraq cope with the day-to-day fear of attacks, the ever-changing military demands, and the decreased time for "R and R" (rest and relaxation)? How do college students manage the ongoing threats of increasing tuition, quizzes, exams, and term papers, while also holding down part- or full-time jobs? Being in a constant state of perceived threat, without the required relaxation time, can wear down our bodies—both physically and psychologically. That's why it's so important to practice the stress management techniques discussed at the end of this chapter.

Job Stress

For many workers, the largest source of stress is a bad job. **Job stress** can come from unemployment, keeping or changing jobs, job performance, lack of control, etc. (Moore, Grunberg, & Greenberg, 2004). However, the most stressful jobs are those that make great demands on performance and concentration, but allow little control, creativity, or opportunity for advancement (Smith et al., 2008; Straub, 2007). Assembly-line work ranks very high in this category.

Job strain is a direct contributor to both initial and recurrent heart attacks, while also causing serious problems at home, not only for the worker but for other family members as well (Aboa-Éboulé, 2008; Aboa-Éboulé et al., 2007; Orth-Gomér, 2007).

Another common source of job stress comes from **role conflict**, which occurs when one is forced to take on two or more different and incompatible roles at the same time (Adebayo, 2006; Andreassi & Thompson, 2007; Huffman et al., 2008). Being a student and a worker is a prime example of a role conflict. Stress is inescapable when your professor schedules an exam on the same day that your employer requires you to work overtime.

Chronic exposure to high levels of job stress and little personal control can also lead to a state of psychological and physical exhaustion known as **burnout**. Although the term has become an overused buzzword, health psychologists use it to describe a specific syndrome that develops most commonly in idealistic people who are involved in chronically stressful and emotionally draining professions (Hätinen et al., 2004; Sarafino, 2008; Tümkaya, 2007).

Achievement

Objective 3.2: *What are the major sources of stress?*

Alan Powdrill/GettyImages

Figure 3.2 *Life changes—stressful ordeal or exciting opportunity?* Different people may perceive any given event differently, depending on how they interpret and appraise the event (Holt & Dunn, 2004). Also, some people are better able to deal with change than others, perhaps because of good coping skills, general physical health, healthier lifestyles, or even genetic predisposition.

Chronic Stress *State of ongoing arousal in which the parasympathetic system cannot activate the relaxation response*

Job Stress *Work-related stress that includes role conflict and burnout*

Role Conflict *Forced choice between two or more different and incompatible role demands*

Burnout *State of psychological and physical exhaustion resulting from chronic exposure to high levels of stress and little personal control*

TABLE 3.1 MEASURING LIFE CHANGES

Social Readjustment Rating Scale

To score yourself on this scale, add up the "life change units" for all life events you have experienced during the last year. Now compare your total score with the following standards: 0–149 = No significant problems; 150–199 = Mild life crisis (33 percent chance of illness); 200–299 = Moderate life crisis (50 percent chance of illness); 300 and above = Major life crisis (80 percent chance of illness).

Life Events	Life Change Units	Life Events	Life Change Units
Death of spouse	100	Son or daughter leaving home	29
Divorce	73	Trouble with in-laws	29
Marital separation	65	Outstanding personal achievement	28
Jail term	63	Spouse begins or stops work	26
Death of a close family member	63	Begin or end school	26
Personal injury or illness	53	Change in living conditions	25
Marriage	50	Revision of personal habits	24
Fired at work	47	Trouble with boss	23
Marital reconciliation	45	Change in work hours or conditions	20
Retirement	45	Change in residence	20
Change in health of family member	44	Change in schools	20
Pregnancy	40	Change in recreation	19
Sex difficulties	39	Change in church activities	19
Gain of a new family member	39	Change in social activities	18
Business readjustment	39	Mortgage or loan for lesser purchase (car, major appliance)	17
Change in financial state	38		
Death of a close friend	37	Change in sleeping habits	16
Change to different line of work	36	Change in number of family get-togethers	15
Change in number of arguments with spouse	35	Change in eating habits	15
Mortgage or loan for major purchase	31	Vacation	13
Foreclosure on mortgage or loan	30	Christmas	12
Change in responsibilities at work	29	Minor violations of the law	11

Source: Reprinted from *Journal of Psychosomatic Research*, Vol III; Holmes and Rahe: "The Social Readjustment Rating Scale," 213–218, 1967, with permission from Elsevier.

A cautionary note: A spokesman for the American Heart Association (AHA), Philip Greenland, is concerned that some might conclude that all one has to do to avoid heart disease is to deal with one's job stress. He warns us that the top three factors for heart disease are still "smoking, high blood pressure, and high cholesterol" (cited in "Job Stress Can Kill," 2002).

Hassles

Hassles *Small problems of daily living that accumulate and sometimes become a major source of stress*

In addition to life changes, chronic stress, and job stress, we also experience a great deal of daily stress from **hassles**—little problems of daily living that are not significant in themselves but that pile up to become a major source of stress. We all share many hassles, such as time pressures and financial concerns, but our reactions to hassles may vary. For example, compared to women, men tend to have more impairment of their immune system and an increased heart rate in response to hassles (Delahanty et al., 2000).

Some authorities believe hassles can be more significant than major life events in creating stress (Kraaij, Arensman, & Spinhoven, 2002; Kubiak et al., 2008). For example, divorce is extremely stressful, but it may be so because of the increased number of hassles— a change in finances, child-care arrangements, longer working hours, and so on.

What Are Your Major Hassles?

Write down the top 10 hassles you most commonly experience. Then compare your answers to the following list:

The 10 Most Common Hassles for College Students

	Percentage of Times Checked
1. Troubling thoughts about the future	76.6
2. Not getting enough sleep	72.5
3. Wasting time	71.1
4. Inconsiderate smokers	70.7
5. Physical appearance	69.9
6. Too many things to do	69.2
7. Misplacing or losing things	67.0
8. Not enough time to do the things you need to do	66.3
9. Concerns about meeting high standards	64.0
10. Being lonely	60.8

Source: Kanner, A. D., Coyne, J. C., Schaefer, C., & Lazarus, R. S. (1981). Comparison of two modes of stress measurement: Daily hassles and uplifts versus major life events. *Journal of Behavioral Medicine, 4,* 1–39.

Frustration

Frustration is a negative emotional state generally associated with a blocked goal, such as not being accepted for admission to your first-choice college. The more motivated we are, the more frustration we experience when our goals are blocked. After getting stuck in traffic and missing an important job interview, we may become very frustrated. However, if the same traffic jam causes us to be five minutes late getting home, we may experience little or no frustration.

Conflict

Another source of stress is **conflict**, which arises when we are forced to make a choice between at least two incompatible alternatives. There are three basic types of conflict: *approach–approach*, *avoidance–avoidance*, and *approach–avoidance*.

In an **approach–approach conflict**, we must choose between two or more *favorable alternatives*. At first, it might seem that this type of conflict should be stress free. But imagine having to choose between two great summer jobs. One job is at a resort where you will meet interesting people and have a good time. The other will provide you with valuable experience and look impressive on your résumé. Either choice will benefit you in some way. The requirement to choose is the source of stress.

An **avoidance–avoidance conflict** involves a forced choice between two or more unpleasant alternatives both of which lead to negative results. In the book (and film) *Sophie's Choice*, Sophie and her two children are sent to a German concentration camp. A soldier demands that she give up (apparently to be killed) either her daughter or her son. If she doesn't choose, they both will be killed. Obviously, neither alternative is acceptable. Although this is an extreme example, avoidance–avoidance conflicts can lead to intense stress.

Frustration *Unpleasant tension, anxiety, and heightened sympathetic activity resulting from a blocked goal*

Conflict *Forced choice between two or more incompatible goals or impulses*

Approach–Approach Conflict *Forced choice between two or more desirable alternatives*

Avoidance–Avoidance Conflict *Forced choice between two or more undesirable alternatives*

Can you explain this man's approach–avoidance conflict?

Approach–Avoidance Conflict *Forced choice between two or more alternatives both of which have desirable and undesirable results*

An **approach–avoidance conflict** occurs when we must choose between alternatives that will have both desirable and undesirable results. During the evacuation before Hurricane Katrina made landfall in 2005, residents were told they could not take their pet animals with them to the shelters. For many people, this was an approach–avoidance conflict. They wanted to avoid the dangers of the hurricane, but they couldn't leave their beloved pets in harm's way. This conflict thus led to a great deal of ambivalence. In an approach–avoidance conflict, we experience both good and bad results from any alternative we choose.

Generally, approach–approach conflicts are the easiest to resolve and produce the least stress. Avoidance–avoidance conflicts, on the other hand, are usually the most difficult because all choices lead to unpleasant results. Keep in mind that in addition to the stress of a forced choice, the longer any conflict exists, or the more important the decision, the more stress we will experience.

Cataclysmic Events

The terrorist attacks in America on September 11, 2001, the tsunami waves following the Indian Ocean earthquake on December 26, 2004, and Hurricane Katrina in August 2005 are what stress researchers call *cataclysmic events*. They occur suddenly and generally affect many people simultaneously. Politicians and the public often imagine that such catastrophes inevitably create huge numbers of seriously depressed and permanently scarred survivors. Relief agencies typically send large numbers of counselors to help with the psychological aftermath. Ironically, researchers have found that because the catastrophe is shared by so many others, there is a great deal of mutual social support from those with firsthand experience with the same disaster, which may help people cope (Collocan, Tuma, & Fleischman, 2004; Ginzburg & Bateman, 2008). On the other hand, these cataclysmic events are clearly devastating to all parts of the victims' lives (Dean-Borenstein, 2007). And some survivors may develop a prolonged and severe stress reaction, known as *posttraumatic stress disorder* (*PTSD*), which we will discuss later in this chapter.

©AP/Wide World Photos

Application

RESEARCH HIGHLIGHT

Objective 3.3: *Describe the effects of Katrina on local New Orleans college students.*

Hurricane Katrina and Local College Students: A First-Hand Report

Contributed by David W. Shwalb and Barbara J. Shwalb, formerly of Southeastern Louisiana University

Dedication ceremony for hurricane memorial fountain, Hammond, Louisiana

The last weekend of August 2005, most college students in Louisiana had just started their fall semester. Upon learning that a Category 5 hurricane was aimed directly at New Orleans, many fled their homes and dormitories, and all colleges in the region abruptly shut down. Few could imagine

that months later some universities would still be closed and lives upended by Hurricane Katrina. The devastation suffered by New Orleans and surrounding areas, caused by Katrina and the floods that followed the breach of the levees, resulted in the biggest disruption of college life in the history of the

United States. Over 80,000 students and 15,000 faculty members were displaced by Katrina and the floods, and Louisiana colleges and universities suffered huge financial and physical damage. The scale of these losses set this catastrophic event apart from previous U.S. natural disasters.

Our former university, Southeastern Louisiana University (SELU), is located in the city of Hammond, 55 miles northwest of New Orleans. We did not witness the flooding, death, chaos, and terror experienced by so many in New Orleans, but we faced winds of 70 MPH, 10 inches of rain, loss of power and other utilities, and an overnight increase in our city's population by about 30 percent. Most people in our Parish (county) of Tangipahoa were frightened and shocked, even if not in danger. Among our new residents were 1400 dislocated students from New Orleans who enrolled in September 2005 at our college.

As educators we wanted to understand how the hurricane affected our students, and as researchers we decided to document some of what our students experienced. Sociologist Duane Gill of Mississippi State University, a specialist in post-disaster research, helped us devise an online survey that we e-mailed to all displaced students and some regular students at our university. This initial questionnaire in October 2005 was followed by two additional surveys in the spring and fall of 2006. Although most displaced New Orleans students left our university after the fall of 2005 and were not available for our follow-up surveys, our research did reveal several lasting effects. The problems for both our displaced and regular students can be summarized in four major areas: (1) injuries and loss, (2) life changes, (3) physical and mental health, and (4) coping.

TABLE 3.2 KATRINA-RELATED INJURIES AND LOSSES (DISPLACED AND REGULAR STUDENTS, FALL 2005)

Item	Displaced Students	Regular Students
Personally injured by hurricane	5%	3%
Damage to their places of residence	43%	28%
Lost money	75%	65%
Lost job	53%	13%
Lost home	44%	9%
Close friends or relations missing	28%	24%
Lost automobile	23%	5%
Family members or friends died	14%	8%

Injuries and Loss

As you can see in Table 3.2, few students were personally injured, but many reported serious damage to their homes. They also suffered having either close friends or family missing following Katrina, or knew of family members or friends who had died because of the hurricane.

Loss also was the most common theme in stories written by our students. When asked to "describe an event related to Katrina that has most affected you," both regular and displaced students expressed pain and anguish. Yet many also expressed aspects of psychological resilience and health.

(Fall 2005)

...parents have decided finally to divorce.

...not having the money I need for my kids at Christmas time.

...feeling I had no power or control over what was going to happen to me.

(Fall 2006)

My fears have increased. I'm afraid of everything and nothing can stop it. I've become more aggressive and incapable of solving little problems.

My time in volunteer work helped me through the first two weeks, when it was almost impossible to concentrate on my academic work.

It made me realize how lucky my family was to not receive any damage.

Life Changes

Our students had just begun studying the Stress and Health Psychology chapter of this text the week before Katrina. When they filled out the Social Readjustment Rating Scale (Table 3.1) two weeks after Katrina, students' scores were almost all above 500 and some were over 1000. By the time students took our online survey in October, we had heard stories from our students that included *every* type of life change on the readjustment scale. But their sources of stress were not limited to life changes. Their ratings and essays included examples of all the major sources of stress mentioned in this chapter. One student described how she had evacu-

Professors David and Barbara Shwalb

ated on a couple hours' notice with few belongings (her remaining possessions were all ruined), lived in a trailer 13 months, broke up with her boyfriend, still "battled" with insurance companies and FEMA over financial problems, felt physically and mentally exhausted, was frustrated that she could not get extensions for her term papers, and was torn between desire to stay in school vs. wish to reunite with her extended family, who had now relocated to northern Louisiana.

When asked, "How have your experiences with Katrina changed *your life* or affected you *as a person*?" students described a mixture of gains and losses:

It has made me take nothing for granted and it has been a very humbling experience.

I'm not the same. I worry, fuss, and cry more than usual.

I have gained insight into how blessed I am, and I am more patient with people.

Physical and Mental Health

As we've seen in this chapter, stress is correlated with physical and psychological problems, and Table 3.3 shows that students displaced by Katrina reported more difficulties in these areas than did regular students. Note, however, that our regular students also reported significant adversity in the aftermath of the hurricane and that their problems persisted over a year later. Few displaced or regular students saw a physician specifically because of Katrina, but many reported declines in general health and eating habits.

In addition to physical problems, our research also identified several psychological problems, including sleep difficulties, nervous anxiety, and depression. On a 10-point scale (1 = no fear; 10 = uncontrollable fear), displaced students reported a mean score of 5.7 and regular students a mean fear score of 5.3 at the time of the hurricane.

Our questionnaire also measured several of the primary symptoms of *posttraumatic stress disorder* (PTSD) (Table 3.3, below), and it was clear that several of our students, especially the displaced ones, had been traumatized. We do not claim that these students had full-blown PTSD, but clearly many students were at serious risk.

On measures of positive mental health, however, the regular and displaced groups were similar. For example, on the *Optimism/Pessimism* scale, both displaced and regular students were evenly divided between optimists and pessimists. On the *Satisfaction with Life* scale, slim majorities of both groups generally were dissatisfied with

life. In response to the *Personal Growth/Initiative* scale, a majority of both regular and displaced students expressed a positive sense of control and direction.

As you also can see in Table 3.3, faith and religion were important to a majority of students for their coping. Although church attendance decreased among more students than increased after Katrina, one-third of the students reported an increase in prayerfulness (Shwalb & Shwalb, 2006).

Coping

In addition to injuries and losses, life changes, and physical and mental health, we also wanted to know how students coped in the post-Katrina environment. On pp. 92, eight resources are identified by which people manage stress: health and exercise, positive beliefs, social skills, social support, material resources, control, relaxation, and sense of humor. After Katrina, students lost some or all of these resources, making it difficult to cope with stress. Our follow-up surveys confirmed several of these as important coping resources, and surprisingly the greatest number of students rated "humor" as an important resource (see Table 3.4).

How can we be of support to students in an unstable world? Table 3.5 presented later in this chapter identifies five tips for coping with crisis, and we encourage students to have all of these experiences, first

TABLE 3.4 STUDENT COPING RESOURCES AND STRATEGIES 8 MONTHS POST-KATRINA

	Important*
Humor	77.4%
Social network	69.3%
Physical health	64.5%
Role models	56.6%
Facing up to one's fears	54.8%
Comparing own situation to that of others	50%

*Percent rating as "important" or "very important" to coping post-Katrina.

by recognizing their feelings as a normal response to an abnormal situation. Above all, we listened to our students and encouraged some to seek professional counseling. We tried to be patient with our students and sensitive to their difficulties, and we encouraged them to do enjoyable things. We did not encourage a victim mentality or learned helplessness (Chapter 6); rather, we urged students to build on their strengths. Of course, some of our students did indeed suffer from PTSD and had overwhelmingly negative experiences. But we were careful to treat each student as an individual with strengths, weaknesses, challenges, and problems. Because we knew that *hardiness* (p. 108) enables some students to cope better than others with stress, we emphasized not only the negative effect of stress, but also how some students reacted to stress as a challenge to their optimism, spirituality, and motivation.

Far too many college students in the general population experience anxiety, sleep disorders, and depression. The events that began on August 29, 2005 unexpectedly exposed vulnerabilities and resiliency, fragility and strength. In fact, a master's thesis by our student, John Travis Blaze, found the psychological impact of Katrina was still in effect during the spring of 2008. For better or worse, its effects are enduring—or not yet revealed.

Authors' Note: This article is dedicated with respect to all college professors and students affected by Katrina, in appreciation of their courage and strength. The Shwalbs now teach at Southern Utah University.

TABLE 3.3 KATRINA'S EFFECT ON PHYSICAL AND MENTAL HEALTH (PERCENTAGES EXPERIENCED BY DISPLACED AND REGULAR COLLEGE STUDENTS)

	Displaced (Fall 2005)	Regular (Fall 2005)	Regular (Spring 2006)	Regular (Fall 2006)
Poorer eating habits	33	23	21	17
General decline in health	22	15	15	11
Felt stressed out	88	68	59	83
Depressed	53	35	30	27
Sleep difficulties	51	38	22	47
Nervous/anxious	47	32	29	25
Increased worries financing education	66	37	34	26
Negative effects on academics	55	53	47	41
Decreased motivation to study/ achieve	49	51	37	26
Religion/faith important to coping	58	70	69	65
Increase in prayerfulness	32	34	36	34

Achievement
GENDER & CULTURAL DIVERSITY

"Karoshi"—Can Job Stress Be Fatal?

Have you ever dragged yourself home from work so tired you feared you couldn't make it to your bed? Do you think your job may be killing you? You may be right! Some research suggests that job stress and overwork can greatly increase your risk of dying from heart disease and stroke (Hsiu-Hui, 2007; Iwasaki, Takahashi, & Nakata, 2006). And the Japanese even have a specific word for it, "karoshi" [KAH-roe-she], which is translated literally as "death from overwork."

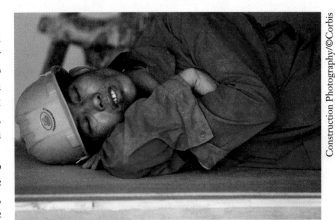

Construction Photography/©Corbis

Starting in the late 1970s, Japanese health officials began to notice serious, and potentially lethal, effects of working ten or twelve hours a day six and seven days a week, year after year) (Iwasaki, Takahasi, & Nakata, 2006; Lafayette-De Mente, 2002). Some research suggests that more than 10,000 workers die from work-related cardiovascular diseases in Japan each year, but few victims of karoshi are compensated under the Japanese workers' compensation system (Hsiu-Hui, 2007). Intense job stressors reportedly not only increase the risk for karoshi, but they also leave some workers disoriented and suffering from serious stress even when they're not working.

Ironically, while employees in Japan and several European countries have recently been working fewer hours, the average weekly work hours in the United States is now the longest in the developed world (*Working Yourself to Death*, 2003). And as we saw before, research in America shows that job strain is directly related to initial and recurrent heart attacks (Aboa-Éboulé, 2008; Orth-Gomér, 2007). Unfortunately, in our global economy, pressures to reduce costs and to increase productivity will undoubtedly continue, and job stress may prove to be a serious and growing health risk.

Achievement

Objective 3.4: *Discuss how Karoshi is related to stress.*

Assessment
CHECK & REVIEW STOP

Sources of Stress

Objective 3.1: *Define stress, eustress, and distress.*

Stress is the body's arousal, both physical and mental, to situations or events that we perceive as threatening or challenging. **Eustress** is pleasurable, desirable stress, whereas **distress** is unpleasant, threatening stress.

Objective 3.2: *What are the major sources of stress?*

The seven major sources of stress are life changes, chronic stressors, job stress, hassles, frustration, conflict, and cataclysmic events. *Life changes* require adjustment in our behaviors, which causes stress. **Chronic stress** is a state of ongoing physiological arousal, in which our para-

sympathetic cannot activate the relaxation response. **Job stress** is work-related stress that includes **role conflict** and **burnout**. **Hassles** are little everyday life problems that pile up to cause major stress. **Frustration** refers to blocked goals, whereas **conflict** involves two or more competing goals. Conflicts can be classified as **approach–approach**, **avoidance–avoidance**, or **approach–avoidance**. *Cataclysmic* events are disasters that occur suddenly and generally affect many people simultaneously.

Objective 3.3: *Describe the effects of Katrina on local New Orleans college students.*

Researchers found that the hurricane led to both temporary and lasting ill-effects, while also exposing resiliency, strengths, and various coping mechanisms.

Objective 3.4: *Discuss how Karoshi is related to stress.*

Job stress and overwork can greatly increase your risk of dying from heart disease and stroke, and the Japanese have a specific word, "Karoshi," which means "death from overwork."

Questions

1. John was planning to ask Susan to marry him. When he saw Susan kissing another man at a party, he was quite upset. In this situation, John's seeing Susan kissing another man is _____, and it illustrates _____. (a) a stressor, distress; (b) eustress, a stressor; (c) distress, a stressor; (d) a stressor, eustress

2. The Social Readjustment Rating Scale constructed by Holmes and Rahe measures the stress situation in a person's life based on _____. (a) life changes; (b) stress tolerance; (c) daily hassles; (d) the balance between eustress and distress

3. Frustration is a negative emotional state that is generally associated with _____, whereas _____ is a negative emotional state caused by difficulty in choosing between two or more incompatible goals or impulses.

4. Give a personal example for each of the three types of conflict: approach–approach, approach–avoidance, and avoidance–avoidance.

Check your answers in Appendix B.

Click & Review
for additional assessment options:
wiley.com/college/huffman

Achievement

Objective 3.5: *Describe the SAM system and the HPA axis.*

Effects of Stress: How the Body Responds

When mentally or physically stressed, our bodies undergo several physiological changes. The *SAM system* and the *HPA axis* control the most significant of these changes (Process Diagram 3.1).

Stress and cataclysmic events Hurricane Katrina in 2005 and the Southeast Asia tsunami in 2004 provided recent examples of what most people would consider extremely stressful events. But it may not be as stressful as you imagine (see text for an explanation).

The SAM System and the HPA Axis

As demonstrated in Process Diagram 3.1 (p. 101), the SAM system and the HPA axis both play an important, adaptive role in the stress response (Bao, Meynen, & Swaab, 2008; Chen & Miller, 2007; King, 2008). The SAM system provides an immediate fight-or-flight response. In contrast, the HPA axis provides a delayed, but longer-lasting, response to stress by mobilizing our immune system and energy resources. It does this through the *hypothalamus*, which alerts the *pituitary* gland to secrete hormones, which then cause the *adrenals* to secrete cortisol. Once the cortisol levels reach a certain level, parts of the brain, particularly the *hippocampus*, tell the hypothalamus to turn off the stress response. This is the proper feedback loop that "turns on and off" a healthy, appropriate response to stress. In sum, a combination of the SAM system and HPA axis allows us to effectively cope with life-threatening stressors.

So why do we hear so much about the dangers of stress? Researchers regard cortisol as the key "stress hormone" because it plays such a critical role in both adaptive and maladaptive responses to stress, and the level of circulating cortisol is the most common physiological measure of stress. Under acute, short-lived stress, cortisol helps reduce inflammation and promotes healing in case of injury. It also helps mobilize the body's energy resources.

After the stress threat has passed, the body normally regains equilibrium, or *homeostasis*. Unfortunately for some people, however, homeostasis is not restored. The stress response becomes stuck in an under- or overaroused state leading to dangerously low or high levels of cortisol. In the underaroused state, the adrenal glands become exhausted from the demands of chronic stress, which leads to chronically low levels of cortisol (*hypocortisolism*). Hypocortisolism is associated with several disorders, including asthma, rheumatoid arthritis, and fibromyalgia (Straub, 2007).

In contrast to this underarousal and low levels of cortisol, some individuals are chronically overaroused by stress, leading to a prolonged elevation of cortisol (*hypercortisolism*). Hypercortisolism not only depletes the normal supply of cortisol, but it also can permanently disrupt the feedback system that normally shuts off the stress response. Prolonged elevation of cortisol also has serious physical consequences, including hypertension, depression, post-traumatic stress disorder (PTSD), drug and alohol abuse, and even low-birth-weight infants (Ayers et al., 2007; Bremner et al., 2004; Johnson, Delahanty, & Pinna, 2008; Sarafino, 2008). As if this long list of ill-effects weren't enough, severe or prolonged stress can also produce overall physical deterioration and premature aging.

©AP/Wide World Photos

©AP/Wide World Photos

Process Diagram 3.1

The Biology of Stress

Under stress, the sympathetic nervous system prepares us for immediate action—to "fight or flee." Parts of the brain and endocrine system then kick in to maintain our arousal. How does this happen? See steps 1 and 2 to the right.

1. The **SAM system** (short for *Sympatho-Adreno-Medullary*) provides an initial, rapid-acting stress response thanks to cooperation between the sympathetic nervous system and the adrenal medulla.

2. The **HPA Axis** (short for the Hypothalamic-Pituitary Adrenocortical system) responds more slowly but lasts longer. It also helps restore the body to its baseline state, *homeostasis*.

STRESSOR

Brain

Arouses → **Hypothalamus** ← **Activates**

SAM System

Sympathetic Nervous System
↓ **Activates**
Adrenal medulla (central part of the adrenal glands)
↓ **Releases**
Norepinephrine and epinephrine
↓
Increased heart rate, blood pressure, respiration, muscle tension; decreased digestion, blood vessels constricted
↓

HPA Axis

Pituitary gland
↓ **Activates**
Adrenal cortex (outer covering of the adrenal glands)
↓ **Releases**
Corticosteroids, including cortisol, that mobolize the immune response and energy resources
↓
Cortisol raises glucose levels and increases metabolism
↓

Increased energy

Brain
↑
Cortisol sends feedback messages to the pituitary to regain homeostasis

A. Operti/American Museum of Natural History library

Deer Hunt Castellón, Spain

Stress in ancient times As shown in these ancient cave drawings, the automatic fight-or-flight response was adaptive and necessary for early human survival. However, in modern society it occurs as a response to ongoing situations where we often cannot fight or flee. This repeated arousal could be detrimental to our health.

SAM System *Body's initial, rapid-acting stress response, involving the sympathetic nervous system and the adrenal medulla; also called the Sympatho-Adreno-Medullary (SAM) system*

HPA Axis *Body's delayed stress response, involving the hypothalamus, pituitary, and adrenal cortex; also called the Hypothalamic-Pituitary-Adrenocortical (HPA) system*

Homeostasis *Body's tendency to maintain a relatively balanced and stable internal state, such as a constant internal temperature*

Cerebral cortex interprets stressor

Hypothalamus

Pituitary gland

Sympathetic nervous system

HPA Axis

Cortex
Medulla

Adrenal glands

The sympathetic nervous system stimulates the adrenal cortex, which releases corticosteroids, including cortisol.

Pituitary hormone in the bloodstream stimulates the adrenal medulla, which releases norepinephrine and epinephrine.

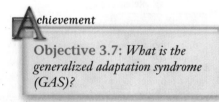

Achievement

Objective 3.6: *How does stress affect cognitive functioning?*

General Adaptation Syndrome (GAS) *Selye's three-stage (alarm, resistance, exhaustion) reaction to chronic stress*

Psychoneuroimmunology [sye-koh-NEW-roh-IM-you-NOLL-oh-gee] *Interdisciplinary field that studies the effects of psychological and other factors on the immune system*

Achievement

Objective 3.7: *What is the generalized adaptation syndrome (GAS)?*

Achievement

Objective 3.8: *How does stress affect our immune system?*

Stress and Cognitive Functioning

Now that you've discovered the overall general effects of stress on the body, are you wondering what happens to your information processing during both acute and chronic stress? Have you noticed that you sometimes forget important information during a stressful exam? What about people who "freeze" during a crisis and fail to run for cover?

As you know, cortisol helps us deal with immediate dangers by increasing our immunity and mobilizing our energy resources. However, it also can prevent the retrieval of existing memories, as well as the laying down of new memories and general information processing (Hurlemann et al., 2007; Mahoney et al., 2007). This interference with immediate cognitive functioning helps explain why people sometimes become dangerously confused and can't find the fire exit during a fire and later may not remember much of what happened during a traumatic event. The good news is that once the cortisol "washes out," memory performance generally returns to normal levels.

In addition to the problems with cognitive functioning during acute stress, Robert Sapolsky (1992, 2003) has shown that prolonged stress can permanently damage the hippocampus, a key part of the brain involved in memory (Chapter 7). Furthermore, once the hippocampus is damaged, it cannot provide proper feedback to the hypothalamus, so cortisol continues to be secreted and a vicious cycle can develop (Figure 3.3).

Selye's General Adaptation Syndrome (GAS)

Stress clearly causes destructive biological changes in our bodies. Hans Selye (1936), who was mentioned earlier in our definition of stress, provided some of the most well-respected stress research. After years of research, he noticed that most patients presented a very similar, *generalized* pattern of responses to any stress—the death of a relative, final exams, or a new job. Thus, he named it the **general adaptation syndrome (GAS)** (Process Diagram 3.2).

Stress and the Immune System

Now that you've studied the SAM system and HPA axis, stress's effect on the body and cognitive functioning, and Selye's *general adaptation syndrome*, we can explore why the discovery of the relationship between stress and the immune system is so very important. When our immune system is impaired, we are at greatly increased risk of suffering from a number of diseases, including cancer, bursitis, colitis, Alzheimer's disease, rheumatoid arthritis, periodontal disease, and even the common cold (Cohen et al., 2002; Cohen & Lemay, 2007; Dantzer et al., 2008; Gasser & Raulet, 2006; Segerstrom & Miller, 2004).

Knowledge that psychological factors have considerable control over infectious diseases has upset long-held assumptions in biology and medicine that these diseases are "strictly physical." The clinical and theoretical implications are so important that a new field of biopsychology has emerged, **psychoneuroimmunology**, which studies the interactions of psychological factors ("psycho"), the nervous and endocrine systems ("neuro"), and the immune system ("immunology") (Ayers et al., 2007; Kemeny, 2007).

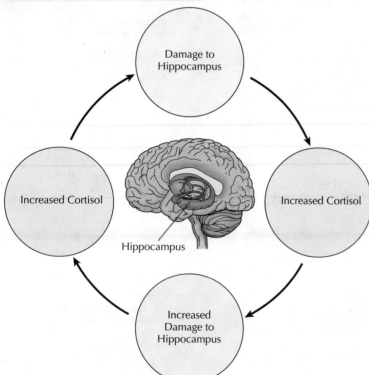

Figure 3.3 **The "Catch-22" of stress and the brain**

Process Diagram 3.2

The General Adaptation Syndrome (GAS)

Note how the three stages of this syndrome (*alarm*, *resistance*, and *exhaustion*) focus on the biological response to stress—particularly the "wear and tear" on the body with prolonged stress. As a critical thinker, can you see how the "alarm stage" corresponds to the SAM system in Process Diagram 3.1, whereas the "resistance" and "exhaustion" stages are part of the HPA axis?

(1) **Alarm Reaction**
In the initial *alarm reaction*, your body experiences a temporary state of shock and your resistance to illness and stress falls below normal limits.

(2) **Stage of Resistance**
If the stressor remains, your body attempts to endure the stressor, and enters the *resistance phase*. Physiological arousal remains higher than normal, and there is a sudden outpouring of hormones. Selye maintained that one outcome of this stage for some people is the development of *diseases of adaption*, including asthma, ulcers, and high blood pressure.

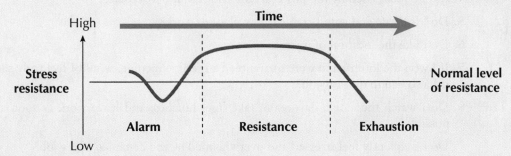

(3) **Stage of Exhaustion**
Long-term exposure to the stressor eventually depletes your body's reserves, and you enter the *exhaustion phase*. In this phase, you become more susceptible to serious illnesses, and possibly irreversible damage to your body. Unless a way of relieving stress is found, the result may be complete collapse and death.

Age Fotostock America, Inc.

Achievement

Objective 3.9: *Identify four factors important to job satisfaction.*

 PSYCHOLOGY AT WORK

Is My Job Too Stressful?

In addition to "burnout," researchers have identified several additional factors in job-related stress. Their findings suggest that one way to prevent these stresses is to gather lots of information before making a career decision.

If you would like to apply this to your own career plans, start by identifying what you like and don't like about your current (and past) jobs. With this information in hand, you'll be prepared to find jobs that will better suit your interests, needs, and abilities, which will likely reduce your stress. To start your analysis, answer yes or no to these questions:

1. Is there a sufficient amount of laughter and sociability in my workplace?

2. Does my boss notice and appreciate my work?

3. Is my boss understanding and friendly?

4. Am I embarrassed by the physical conditions of my workplace?

5. Do I feel safe and comfortable in my place of work?

6. Do I like the location of my job?

7. If I won the lottery and were guaranteed a lifetime income, would I feel truly sad if I also had to quit my job?

8. Do I watch the clock, daydream, take long lunches, and leave work as soon as possible?

9. Do I frequently feel stressed and overwhelmed by the demands of my job?

10. Compared to others with my qualifications, am I being paid what I am worth?

11. Are promotions made in a fair and just manner where I work?

12. Given the demands of my job, am I fairly compensated for my work?

Will & Deni McIntyre/PhotoResearchers

Is nursing a stressful career? *Over time, some people in chronically stressful professions who think of their job as a "calling" become emotionally drained and disillusioned—they "burn out." Burnout can cause more work absences, less productivity, and increased risk for physical problems. What other occupations might pose an especially high risk for burnout?*

Now score your answers. Give yourself one point for each answer that matches the following: 1. No; 2. No; 3. No; 4. Yes; 5. No; 6. No; 7. No; 8. Yes; 9. Yes; 10. No; 11. No; 12. No.

The questions you just answered are based on four factors that research shows are conducive to increased job satisfaction and reduced stress: supportive colleagues, supportive working conditions, mentally challenging work, and equitable rewards (Robbins, 1996). Your total score reveals your overall level of dissatisfaction. A look at specific questions can help identify which of these four factors is most important to your job satisfaction—and most lacking in your current job.

Supportive colleagues (items 1, 2, 3): For most people, work fills important social needs. Therefore, having friendly and supportive colleagues and superiors leads to increased satisfaction.

Supportive working conditions (items 4, 5, 6): Not surprisingly, most employees prefer working in safe, clean, and relatively modern facilities. They also prefer jobs close to home.

Mentally challenging work (items 7, 8, 9): Jobs with too little challenge create boredom and apathy, whereas too much challenge creates frustration and feelings of failure.

Equitable rewards (items 10, 11, 12): Employees want pay and promotions based on job demands, individual skill levels, and community pay standards.

Age Fotostock America, Inc.

Assessment STOP

CHECK & REVIEW

Effects of Stress

Objective 3.5: *Describe the SAM system and the HPA axis.*

When stressed, our bodies undergo significant biological changes due primarily to the SAM system and the HPA axis. The **SAM system** (short for *Sympatho-Adreno-Medullary*) provides an initial, rapid-acting stress response due to an interaction between the sympathetic nervous system and the adrenal medulla. The **HPA axis** (short for the *Hypothalamic-Pituitary-Adrenocortical (HPA) system*) allows for a delayed stress response, involving the hypothalamus, pituitary, and adrenal cortex. One of the main stress hormones released by the HPA axis, cortisol, helps combat inflammation and mobilize energy resources. It also sends feedback messages to the brain and pituitary to regain **homeostasis**.

Objective 3.6: *How does stress affect cognitive functioning?*

During acute stress, cortisol can prevent the retrieval of existing memories, as well as the laying down of new memories and general information processing. Under prolonged stress, cortisol can permanently damage the hippocampus, a key part of the brain involved in memory.

Objective 3.7: *What is the generalized adaptation syndrome (GAS)?*

Hans Selye described a generalized physiological reaction to severe stressors, which he called the **general adaptation syndrome (GAS)**. It has three phases: the *alarm reaction*, the *resistance phase*, and the *exhaustion phase*.

Objective 3.8: *How does stress affect the immune sysytem?*

Prolonged stress suppresses the immune system, which increases the risk for many diseases (e.g., colds, colitis, cancer). The new field of **psychoneuroimmunology** studies the effects of stress and other factors on the immune system.

Objective 3.9: *Identify four factors important to job satisfaction.*

Supportive colleagues, supportive working conditions, mentally challenging work, and *equitable rewards* are all very important to our job satisfaction.

Questions

1. How does the SAM system respond to acute stress?
2. How does the HPA axis respond to stress?

3. Label the three major structures in the HPA axis.

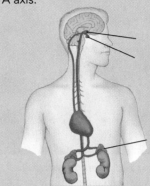

4. The GAS consists of three phases: the _____ reaction, the _____ phase, and the _____ phase.
5. As Michael watches his instructor pass out papers, he suddenly realizes this is the first major exam, and he is unprepared. Which phase of the GAS is he most likely experiencing? (a) resistance; (b) alarm; (c) exhaustion; (d) phase out.

Check your answers in Appendix B

 Click & Review
for additional assessment options:
wiley.com/college/huffman

Stress and Illness

As we have just seen, stress has dramatic effects on our bodies. This section explores how stress is related to four serious illnesses—*cancer, coronary heart disease, posttraumatic stress disorder (PTSD)*, and *gastric ulcers*.

Cancer: A Variety of Causes—Even Stress

Cancer is among the leading causes of death for adults in the United States. It occurs when a cell begins rapidly dividing and then forms a tumor that invades healthy tissue. Unless destroyed or removed, the tumor eventually damages organs and causes death. More than 100 types of cancer have been identified. They appear to be caused by an interaction between environmental factors and inherited predispositions.

In a healthy person, whenever cancer cells start to multiply, the immune system checks the uncontrolled growth by attacking the abnormal cells (Figure 3.4). Something different happens when the body is stressed. As you read earlier, stress causes the adrenal glands to release hormones that suppress the immune system. The compromised immune system is less able to resist infection and cancer development (Ben-Eliyahu, Page, & Schleifer, 2007; Kemeny, 2007).

The good news is that we can substantially reduce our risk of developing cancer by making changes that reduce our stress level and enhance our immune system.

Achievement

Objective 3.10: *How is stress related to cancer?*

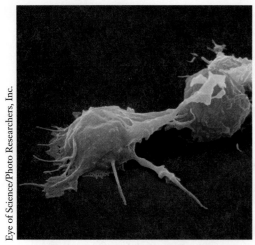

Figure 3.4 ***The immune system in action*** Stress can compromise the immune system, but the actions of a healthy immune system are shown here. The round red structures are leukemia cells. Note how the yellow killer cells are attacking and destroying the cancer cells.

Achievement

Objective 3.11: *Describe the links between stress and heart disease.*

Type A Personality *Behavior characteristics including intense ambition, competition, exaggerated time urgency, and a cynical, hostile outlook*

Type B Personality *Behavior characteristics consistent with a calm, patient, relaxed attitude*

For example, when researchers interrupted the sleep of 23 men and then measured their *natural killer cells* (a type of immune system cell), they found the number of killer cells was 28 percent below average (Irwin et al., 1994). Can you see how staying up late studying for an exam (or partying) can decrease the effectiveness of your immune system? Fortunately, these researchers also found that a normal night's sleep after the deprivation returned the killer cells to their normal levels.

Cardiovascular Disorders: The Leading Cause of Death in the United States

Cardiovascular disorders cause over half of all deaths in the United States (American Heart Association, 2008). Understandably, health psychologists are concerned because stress is a major contributor to these deaths (Aboa-Éboulé et al., 2007; Ziegelstein, 2007). *Heart disease* is a general term for all disorders that eventually affect the heart muscle and lead to heart failure. *Coronary heart disease* results from *arteriosclerosis*, a thickening of the walls of the coronary arteries that reduces or blocks the blood supply to the heart. Arteriosclerosis causes *angina* (chest pain due to insufficient blood supply to the heart) or *heart attack* (death of heart muscle tissue). Controllable factors that contribute to heart disease include stress, smoking, certain personality characteristics, obesity, a high-fat diet, and lack of exercise (Aboa-Éboulé, 2008; Ayers et al., 2007; Sarafino, 2008).

How does stress contribute to heart disease? Recall that one of the major autonomic nervous system "fight-or-flight" reactions is the release of epinephrine and cortisol into the bloodstream. These hormones increase heart rate and release fat and glucose from the body's stores to give muscles a quickly available source of energy.

If no physical "fight or flight" action is taken (as often happens in our modern lives), the fat that was released into the bloodstream is not burned as fuel. Instead, it may adhere to the walls of blood vessels (Figure 3.5). These deposits are a major cause of blood supply blockage that causes heart attacks.

Personality Types

The effects of stress on heart disease may be amplified if an individual tends to be hard-driving, competitive, ambitious, impatient, and hostile. People with such **Type A personalities** are chronically on edge, feel intense time urgency, and are preoccupied with responsibilities. The antithesis of the Type A personality is the **Type B personality**, having a laid-back, calm, relaxed attitude toward life.

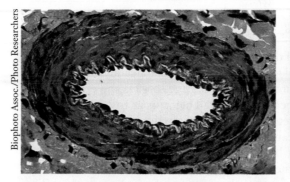
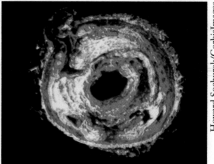

Figure 3.5 ***Fatty deposits in arteries*** One major cause of heart disease is the blockage of arteries that supply blood to the heart. The artery at the left is normal; the one on the right is almost completely blocked. Reducing stress, exercising, and eating a low-fat diet can help prevent the buildup of fatty deposits in the arteries.

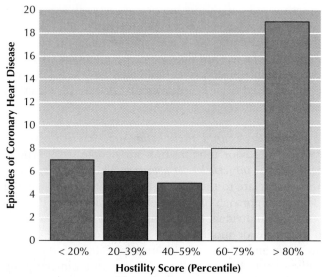

Stuart Pearce/Age Fotostock

Figure 3.6 *Type A personality, hostility and heart disease*
Source: Niaura et al., *Health Psychology*, 2002.

Two cardiologists, Meyer Friedman and Ray Rosenman (1959), were the first to identify and describe the Type A personality. The story goes that in the mid-1950s, an upholsterer who was re-covering the waiting room chairs in Friedman's office noticed an odd wear pattern. He mentioned to Friedman that the chairs looked like new except for the front edges, which were badly worn, as if all the patients sat only on the edges of the chairs. Initially, this did not seem too important to Friedman. However, he later came to believe that this chronic sense of time urgency, being literally "on the edge of your seat," was a possible contributing factor to heart disease and the hallmark of the Type A personality.

Initial research into Type A behavior suggested that Friedman and Rosenman were right. But when later researchers examined the relationship between characteristics of the Type A behavior pattern and heart disease, they found that *hostility* was the *strongest* predictor of heart disease (Bunde & Suls, 2006; Mittag & Maurischat, 2004) (Figure 3.6).

Application

Try This Yourself

Are you a Type A?

Test yourself by answering "yes" or "no" to the following:

_____ 1. Do you find it difficult to restrain yourself from hurrying others' speech (finishing their sentences for them)?

_____ 2. Do you often try to do more than one thing at a time (such as eat and read simultaneously)?

_____ 3. Do you often feel guilty if you use extra time to relax?

_____ 4. Do you tend to get involved in a great number of projects at once?

_____ 5. Do you find yourself racing through yellow lights when you drive?

_____ 6. Do you need to win in order to derive enjoyment from games and sports?

_____ 7. Do you generally move, walk, and eat rapidly?

_____ 8. Do you agree to take on too many responsibilities?

_____ 9. Do you detest waiting in lines?

_____ 10. Do you have an intense desire to better your position in life and impress others?

Source: Adapted from Friedman and Rosenman (1974). If you answer yes to most of these items, you may be a Type A, but short quizzes like these provide only a brief snapshot of your full personality.

Actually, *cynical* hostility appears to be the most important factor in the Type A relationship to heart disease. Constantly being "on watch" for problems translates physiologically into higher blood pressure and heart rate, and production of stress-related hormones. In addition, people who are hostile, suspicious, argumentative, and competitive tend to have more frequent interpersonal conflicts. This can heighten autonomic activation, leading to increased risk of cardiovascular disease (Boyle et al., 2004; Bunde & Suls, 2006; Eaker et al., 2007).

Can people with a type a personality change their behavior? Health psychologists have developed two types of behavior modification for people with Type A personality—the *shotgun approach* and the *target behavior approach*. The *shotgun approach* aims to change all the behaviors that relate to the Type A personality. Friedman and his colleagues (1986) use the shotgun approach in their Recurrent Coronary Prevention Program. The program provides individual counseling, dietary advice, exercise, drugs, and group therapy to eliminate or modify Type A behaviors. Type A's are specifically encouraged to slow down and perform tasks incompatible with their personalities. For example, they might try to listen to other people without interrupting or they could deliberately choose the longest supermarket line. The major criticism of the shotgun approach is that it may decrease *desirable* Type A traits, such as ambition, as well as *undesirable* traits, like cynicism and hostility. The alternative therapy, the *target behavior approach*, focuses on only those Type A behaviors that are likely to cause heart disease—namely, cynical hostility.

Hardiness and Positive Psychology

In addition to Type A and Type B personalities, other personality patterns may affect the way we respond to stress. Have you ever wondered how some people survive in the face of great tragedy and stress? Suzanne Kobasa was among the first to study this question (Kobasa, 1979; Maddi et al., 2006; Vogt et al., 2008). Examining male executives with high levels of stress, she found that some people are more resistant to stress than others because of a personality factor called **hardiness**, a resilient type of optimism that comes from three distinctive attitudes:

1. *Commitment.* Hardy people feel a strong sense of commitment to both their work and their personal life. They also make intentional commitments to purposeful activity and problem solving.

2. *Control.* Hardy people see themselves as being in control of their lives rather than as victims of their circumstances.

3. *Challenge.* Finally, hardy people look at change as an opportunity for growth and improvement—not as a threat. They look at setbacks as challenges (Maddi et al., 2006).

The important lesson from this research is that hardiness is a *learned behavior*—not something based on luck or genetics. If you are not one of the *hardy* souls, you can develop the trait. The next time you face a bad stressor, such as four exams in one week, try using the 3 C's: "I am fully *committed* to my college education." "I can *control* the number of tests by taking one or two of them earlier than scheduled, or I can rearrange my work schedule." "I welcome this *challenge* as a final motivation to enroll in those reading improvement and college success courses I've always planned to take."

Before we go on, it is also important to note that Type A personality and lack of hardiness are not the only controllable risk factors associated with heart disease. Smoking, obesity, diet, and lack of exercise are very important factors. Smoking restricts blood circulation, and obesity stresses the heart by causing it to pump more blood to the excess body tissue. A high-fat diet, especially one high in cholesterol, contributes to the fatty deposits that clog blood vessels. Lack of exercise contributes to weight gain. It also prevents the

Hardiness *Resilient personality with a strong commitment to personal goals, control over life, and viewing change as a challenge rather than a threat*

We cannot wait for the storm to blow over. We must learn to work in the rain

Jennifer Granholm

Stuart Hughes/©Corbis

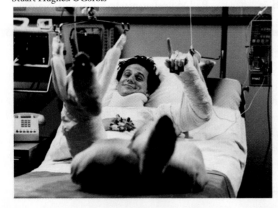

body from obtaining important exercise benefits, including strengthened heart muscle, increased heart efficiency, and the release of neurotransmitters such as serotonin that alleviate stress and promote well-being.

Posttraumatic Stress Disorder (PTSD): A Disease of Modern Times?

Achievement

Objective 3.12: *How is stress connected to PTSD and ulcers?*

One of the most powerful examples of the effects of severe stress is **posttraumatic stress disorder (PTSD)**. Children, as well as adults, can experience PTSD after exposure to a traumatic life event. Specifically, a person may have been involved in, was a witness to, or had even heard of an extreme traumatic stressor. The essential feature of PTSD is *severe anxiety* (a state of constant or recurring alarm and fearfulness). The anxiety develops after experiencing a traumatic event (such as rape, natural disaster, or war), learning about a violent or unexpected death of a family member, or even being a witness or bystander to violence (American Psychiatric Association, 2002). The individual's reaction to the trauma tends to be one of helplessness and fear, with persistent reexperiencing of the event through their dreams and daily thoughts (flashbacks), unsuccessful attempts to consciously try to avoid reminders of the event, a pattern of avoidance and emotional numbness, and fairly constant hyperarousal (easily startled, hypervilgiant of their surroundings). These symptoms may continue for months or years after the event itself. To reduce the stress, some victims of PTSD turn to alcohol and other drugs, which often compound the problem (Kaysen et al., 2008; Sullivan & Holt, 2008).

During the Industrial Revolution, workers who survived horrific railroad accidents sometimes developed a condition very similar to PTSD. It was called "railway spine" because experts thought the problem resulted from a twisting or concussion of the spine. In later times, PTSD was primarily associated with military combat. Doctors called it "shell shock" because they believed it was a response to the physical concussion caused by exploding artillery. PTSD did not become a formal category of mental disorders until 1980, and today it is officially diagnosed when the symptoms last for more than a month after the event and significantly impact occupational and social functioning (APA, 1994, 2000). In cases, where individuals' symptoms have been present for less than 1 month, a more appropriate diagnosis may be *Acute Stress Disorder* (ASD).

According to the Facts for Health website (http://www.factsforhealth.org), approximately 10 percent of Americans have had or will have PTSD at some point in their lives. The primary symptoms of PTSD are summarized in Table 3.5. The table also includes five important tips for coping with traumatic events.

Posttraumatic Stress Disorder (PTSD) *Anxiety disorder following exposure to a life-threatening or other extreme event that evoked great horror or helplessness; characterized by flashbacks, nightmares, and impaired functioning*

TABLE 3.5 IDENTIFYING PTSD AND COPING WITH CRISIS

Primary Symptoms of Posttraumatic Stress Disorder (PTSD)
• Reexperiencing the event through vivid memories or flashbacks • Feeling "emotionally numb" • Feeling overwhelmed by what would normally be considered everyday situations • Showing diminished interest in performing normal tasks or pursuing usual interests • Crying uncontrollably • Isolating oneself from family and friends and avoiding social situations • Relying increasingly on alcohol or drugs to get through the day • Feeling extremely moody, irritable, angry, suspicious, or frightened 

Bill Stormont/©Corbis

- Having difficulty falling or staying asleep, sleeping too much, and experiencing nightmares
- Feeling guilty about surviving the event or being unable to solve the problem, change the event, or prevent the disaster
- Feeling fear and sense of doom about the future

Five Important Tips for Coping with Crisis

1. Recognize your feelings about the situation and talk to others about your fears. Know that these feelings are a normal response to an abnormal situation.
2. Be willing to listen to family and friends who have been affected and encourage them to seek counseling if necessary.
3. Be patient with people. Tempers are short in times of crisis, and others may be feeling as much stress as you.
4. Recognize normal crisis reactions, such as sleep disturbances and nightmares, withdrawal, reverting to childhood behaviors, and trouble focusing on work or school.
5. Take time with your children, spouse, life partner, friends, and coworkers to do something you enjoy.

Source: American Counseling Association and adapted from Pomponio, 2002.

Application

RESEARCH HIGHLIGHT

Does Stress Cause Gastric Ulcers?

Do you have gastric ulcers or know someone who does? If so, you know that these lesions to the lining of the stomach (and duodenum—the upper section of the small intestine) can be quite painful. In extreme cases, they may even be life threatening. Have you been told ulcers are caused by bacteria and not by stress, as previously thought? Would you like to know what modern science believes?

Beginning in the 1950s, psychologists reported strong evidence that stress can lead to ulcers. Correlational studies have found that people who live in stressful situations have a higher incidence of ulcers than people who don't. And numerous experiments with laboratory animals have shown that stressors, such as shock or confinement to a very small space for a few hours, can produce ulcers in some laboratory animals (Andrade & Graeff, 2001; Bhattacharya & Muruganandam, 2003; Gabry et al., 2002; Landeira-Fernandez, 2004).

The relationship between stress and ulcers seemed well established until

researchers reported a bacterium (*Helicobacter pylori* or *H. pylori*) that appears to be associated with ulcers. Because many people prefer medical explanations, like bacteria or viruses, to psychological ones, the idea of stress as a cause of ulcers has been largely abandoned by many people.

Is this warranted? Let's take a closer look at the research. First, most ulcer patients do have the *H. pylori* bacterium in their stomachs, and it clearly damages the stomach wall. In addition, antibiotic treatment does help many patients. However, approximately 75 percent of normal control subjects' stomachs also have the bacterium. This suggests that the bacterium may cause the ulcer, but only in people who are compromised by stress. Furthermore, behavior modification and other psychological treatments, used alongside antibiotics, can help ease ulcers. Finally, studies of the hypothalamus and amygdala (parts of the brain involved in emotional response) show that they also play a role in gastric ulcer formation (Aou, 2006; Tanaka et al., 1998).

Apparently, stressful situations cause an increase in stress hormones and hydrochloric acid and a decrease in blood flow in

the stomach walls. This combination leaves the stomach more vulnerable to attack by the *H. pylori* bacteria.

In sum, it appears that *H. pylori*, increased hydrochloric acid, stress hormones, and decreased blood flow all lead to the formation of gastric ulcers. Once again, we see how biological, psychological, and social forces interact with one another (the biopsychosocial model). And, for now, the psychosomatic explanation for ulcers is back in business.

 Study Tip

Psychosomatic illness is not the same as an imagined, hypochondriacal, illness. Psychosomatic (psyche means "mind" and soma means "body") refers to symptoms or illnesses that are caused or aggravated by psychological factors, especially stress (Lipowski, 1986). Most researchers and health practitioners believe that almost all illnesses are partly psychosomatic in this sense.

Assessment

CHECK & REVIEW

Stress and Illness

Objective 3.10: *How is stress related to cancer?*

Cancer appears to result from an interaction of heredity, environmental insults (such as smoking), and immune system deficiency. Stress may be an important cause of decreased immunity. During times of stress, the body may be less able to check cancer cell multiplication because the immune system is suppressed.

Objective 3.11: *Describe the links between stress and heart disease.*

The leading cause of death in the United States is heart disease. Risk factors include smoking, stress, obesity, a high-fat diet, lack of exercise, and **Type A personality** (if it includes *cynical hostility*). The two main approaches to modifying Type A behavior are the *shotgun approach* and the *target behavior approach*. People with psychological **hardiness** are less vulnerable to stress because of three distinctive personality characteristics—*commitment, control,* and *challenge.*

Objective 3.12: *How is stress connected to PTSD and ulcers?*

Exposure to extraordinary stress (like war or rape) may lead to **posttraumatic stress disorder (PTSD)**. Contrary to current opinion that gastric ulcers are caused only by the *H. pylori* bacterium, psychological research shows that stress increases vulnerability to the bacterium.

Questions

1. Stress can contribute to heart disease by releasing the hormones _____ and _____, which increase the level of fat in the blood.
2. Which of the following is not among the characteristics associated with Type A personality? (a) time urgency; (b) patience; (c) competitiveness; (d) hostility
3. Explain how the three characteristics of the hardy personality help reduce stress.
4. What is the essential feature of PTSD?

Check your answers in Appendix B.

 Click & Review for additional assessment options: wiley.com/college/huffman

---

Health Psychology in Action

Health psychology, the study of how biological, psychological, and social factors affect health and illness, is a growing field in psychology (Figure 3.7). In this section, we will consider the psychological components of two major health risks—*tobacco* and *alcohol*. We will also explore the psychological factors that increase and decrease *chronic pain*. But first, we must learn a little about the field of health psychology and what health psychologists have learned about promoting healthy behaviors.

PSYCHOLOGY AT WORK

Would You Like to Be a Health Psychologist?

Health psychologists study how people's lifestyles and activities, emotional reactions, ways of interpreting events, and personality characteristics influence their physical health and well-being.

As researchers, health psychologists are particularly interested in how changes in behavior can improve health outcomes (Leventhal et al., 2008). They also emphasize the relationship between stress and the immune system. As we discovered earlier, a normally functioning immune system helps defend against disease. And a suppressed immune system leaves the body susceptible to a number of diseases.

As practitioners, health psychologists can work as independent clinicians or as consultants alongside physicians, physical and occupational therapists, and other health-care workers. The goal of the health psychologist is to reduce psychological distress or unhealthy behaviors. They also help patients and families make critical decisions and prepare psychologically for surgery or other treatment. Health psychologists have become so involved with health and illness that medical centers are one of their major employers (Careers in Health Psychology, 2004).

Achievement

Objective 3.13: *What is health psychology?*

Health Psychology *Studies how biological, psychological, and social factors interact in health and illness*

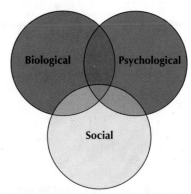

Figure 3.7 **Health psychology in action** Note how all three factors in the *biopsychosocial model* interact in health and illness.

Health psychologists also educate the public about health *maintenance*. They provide information about the effects of stress, smoking, alcohol, lack of exercise, and other health issues. In addition, health psychologists help people cope with conditions, such as chronic pain, diabetes, and high blood pressure, as well as unhealthful behaviors, such as anger expression and lack of assertiveness. Due to space limitations, only a brief overview of the wide variety of work activities and interests of health psychologists can be provided here. If you are seriously interested in pursuing a career in this field, you may want to check with the counseling or career center on your campus. Also try exploring the career website included at wiley.com/college/huffman.

Achievement

Objective 3.14: *Why do people start smoking, how do we prevent it, and what are the best ways to quit?*

Tobacco: Hazardous to Your Health

A custom loathsome to the eye, hateful to the nose, harmful to the brain, dangerous to the lungs, and in the black, stinking fume thereof, nearest resembling the horrible Stygian smoke of the pit that is bottomless.

KING JAMES I, 1604

This is what King James I wrote about smoking in 1604, shortly after Sir Walter Raleigh introduced tobacco to England from the Americas. Today, more than 400 years later, many people would agree with the king's tirade against the practice.

Most people know that smoking is bad for their health and that the more they smoke, the more at risk they are. *Tobacco* use endangers both smokers and those who breathe secondhand smoke. So it is not surprising that most health psychologists and medical professionals are concerned with preventing smoking and getting those who already smoke to stop.

Michael Newman/PhotoEdit

The first puff on a cigarette is rarely pleasant. Why, then, do people start smoking? The answer is complex. In addition to other factors, simple curiosity leads many young people to first try smoking, as well as peer pressure and imitation of role models (such as older teens and celebrities).

Unfortunately, once a person begins to smoke, there is a biological need to continue. Nicotine addiction appears to be very similar to heroin, cocaine, and alcohol addiction (Brody et al., 2004). When we inhale tobacco smoke, the nicotine quickly increases the release of acetylcholine and norepinephrine in our brain. These neurotransmitters (Chapter 2) increase alertness, concentration, memory, and feelings of pleasure. Nicotine also stimulates the release of dopamine, the neurotransmitter that is most closely related to reward centers in the brain (Fehr et al., 2008; Yang et al., 2008).

In addition to these addictive, biological rewards, smokers also learn to associate smoking with pleasant things, such as good food, friends, and sex, as well as with the "high" that nicotine gives them. To make matters worse, when smokers are deprived of cigarettes, they go through an unpleasant *physical withdrawal*. Nicotine relieves the withdrawal symptoms, so continued smoking is further rewarded.

"I told you smoking was bad for you."

CartoonStock

Smoking Prevention

Most smoking prevention programs emphasize educating the public about short- and long-term consequences of smoking, and helping nonsmokers resist social pressures to smoke. However, for all the reasons mentioned before, many health psychologists believe that the best way to reduce the number of smokers is to stop young people from ever taking that first puff. Unfortunately, smoking's long-term disadvantages often seem far off and irrelevant to teens, compared with its short-term social rewards and the addictive, reinforcing properties of nicotine. Therefore, as shown in the billboard shown in the photo, *many smoking prevention programs* focus on the more immediate problems associated with smoking. Films and discussion groups also educate teens about peer pressure and the media's influence on smoking, while also helping to improve their decision-making and coping skills. Unfortunately, these psychosocial programs can be complicated, controversial, and expensive (Hatsukami, 2008; Pierce, 2007; Vijgen et al., 2008).

One of the most successful approaches to smoking prevention involves making it less convenient and socially acceptable, while also emphasizing the financial costs. For example, many businesses, restaurants, and college campuses now ban smoking, and most states are adding heavy taxes on cigarettes. For example, in 2008 the average pack of cigarettes in New York City was over $8 ($2.75 for taxes), which was expected to stop or prevent thousands from smoking (Cigarettes Now Cost More, 2008). At this price, a pack-a-day smoker would spend about $60 a week, or $3000 per year; and a 40-year-old who quits smoking and puts the savings into a 401(k) earning 9% a year would have nearly $600,000 by age 70.

In addition to the price of cigarettes, smokers often pay higher rates for health, home, car, and other insurance programs. Employees who smoke can also be fined, fired, or not even hired in the first place. Kalamazoo Valley Community College in Michigan stopped hiring smokers for full-time positions at both its Michigan campuses, Alaska Airlines requires a nicotine test before hiring, and Union Pacific won't hire smokers (The High Cost of Smoking, 2008).

Stopping Smoking

To cease smoking is the easiest thing I ever did; I ought to know, for I have done it a thousand times.

MARK TWAIN

Unfortunately, Mark Twain was never able to quit for very long, and many ex-smokers say that stopping smoking was the most difficult thing they ever did. Although some people find the easiest way for them to cope with the physical withdrawal from nicotine is to suddenly and completely stop, the success rate for this "cold turkey" approach is extremely low. Even with medical aids, such as patches, gum, or pills, it is still difficult to quit.

As mentioned earlier, national antismoking campaigns and increasing bans on smoking in public places have helped reduce the social rewards and acceptability of smoking. However, health psychologists have noticed some unfortunate, and unforeseen, side effects of this approach. First, these strong antismoking ads unintentionally encourage some to rebel "just to show them they can't tell me what to do" (Meek, 2007). Second, the public's forced isolation of smokers may ironically create stronger social bonds and enhance their resolve to keep smoking (Figure 3.8).

To deal with the physical addiction to nicotine, smoking cessation programs have been most effective using a combination of cognitive and behavioral therapy, along with nicotine replacement techniques. Cognitively, smokers can learn to identify stimuli or situations that make them feel like smoking, they can then change or avoid them. They can also refocus their attention on something other than smoking or remind themselves of the benefits of not smoking. Behaviorally, they might cope with the urge to smoke by chewing gum, exercising, or chewing on a toothpick after a meal instead of lighting a cigarette. No program to quit smoking will work without strong personal motivation. However, the payoffs of a healthier and longer life are worth it.

Alcohol: Both a Personal and Social Health Problem

The American Medical Association considers alcohol to be the most dangerous and physically damaging of all drugs (American Medical Association, 2003). After tobacco, it is the leading cause of premature death in the United States and most European countries (Abadinsky, 2008; Cohen et al., 2004; Maisto, Galizio, & Connors, 2008). Drinking alcohol may also cause serious damage to your brain (Crews et al., 2004). The fact that alcohol seems to increase aggression also helps explain why it is a major factor in most murders, suicides, spousal assaults, child abuse, and accidental deaths (Levinthal, 2008; Sebre et al., 2004; Sher, Grekin, & Williams, 2005).

Figure 3.8 *Smokers unite?* Antismoking laws may have unwittingly made quitting smoking even more difficult for some. Being forced to gather together outside to smoke may forge stronger social bonds among smokers and strengthen their resolve to "suffer the tyranny" of antismoking laws. In addition, having to wait longer for their next nicotine dose increases the severity of withdrawal symptoms (Palfai et al., 2000). In effect, the smoker gets repeated previews of just how hard quitting would be.

Achievement
Objective 3.15: *Describe the personal and social risks associated with alcohol.*

Binge Drinking *Occurs when men consume 5 or more drinks, and women consume 4 or more drinks, in about 2 hours.*

Most people are now aware of the major risks of alcohol and driving—heavy fines, loss of driver's license, serious injuries, possible jail time, and even death. But did you know that simply *drinking* alcohol itself can be fatal? Because alcohol depresses neural activity throughout the brain, if blood levels of alcohol rise to a certain point, the brain's respiratory center stops functioning and the person dies. This is why binge drinking is so dangerous. **Binge drinking** is defined as having four or more (for women) or five or more (for men) drinks in about 2 hours (NIAAA, 2007).

Alcohol is a serious health problem for all college-age students. For those who drink, research shows that, because of alcohol use, every year:

- 1400 college students die from alcohol-related causes.

- 500,000 students suffer nonfatal injuries.

- 1.2–1.5 percent of students attempt suicide because of alcohol or other drug use.

- 400,000 students have unprotected sex, and more than 100,000 are too intoxicated to know whether they consented to sexual intercourse (Task Force of the National Advisory, 2002).

One final caution: You may know about the "21 for 21" ritual, in which the 21 birthday celebrant attempts to down 21 drinks in a row. But did you know that it could lead to serious disorientation, coma, and even death? A recent study of 2,518 college students from one university found that more than four out of five participants consumed alcohol on their 21st birthday. Based on information these students provided, study researchers estimated that 49 percent of the men and 35 percent of the women had dangerously high blood alcohol contents of 0.26 or higher, which is linked to very serious health problems and physical injuries, as well as potential driving and pedestrian accidents, risky/unwanted sexual behavior, and so on (Rutledge, Park, & Sher, 2008). As the study's lead author, Patricia Rutledge, suggests "the risks here are not limited to those with a history of problematic drinking, and there needs to be a strategy to address a custom that can lead to alcohol poisoning and, possibly, death" (cited in Study Finds 21st Birthday Binge, 2008).

Try This Yourself

pplication

Do You Have an Alcohol Problem?

In our society, drinking alcoholic beverages is generally considered a normal and appropriate way to modify mood or behavior. If you would like a quick check of your own drinking behavior, place a mark next to each of the symptoms that describes your current drinking behavior.

Seven Signs of Alcohol Dependence Syndrome

___ Drinking increases, sometimes to the point of almost continuous daily consumption.

___ Drinking is given higher priority than other activities, in spite of its negative consequences.

___ More and more alcohol is required to produce behavioral, subjective, and metabolic changes; large amounts of alcohol can be tolerated.

___ Even short periods of abstinence bring on withdrawal symptoms, such as sweatiness, trembling, and nausea.

___ Withdrawal symptoms are relieved or avoided by further drinking, especially in the morning.

___ The individual is subjectively aware of a craving for alcohol and has little control over the quantity and frequency of intake.

___ If the person begins drinking again after a period of abstinence, he or she rapidly returns to the previous high level of consumption and other behavioral patterns.

Source: World Health Organization, 2004.

Karen Moskowitz/Getty Images

College fun or a serious problem? *Binge drinking among young adults is a growing problem, and many teenage and college women are drinking as much as men.*

Chronic Pain: An Ongoing Threat to Health

Imagine having all your pain receptors removed so that you could race cars, ski, skateboard, and go to the dentist without ever worrying about pain. Does this sound too good to be true? Think again. Pain is essential to the survival and well-being of humans and all other animals. It alerts us to dangerous or harmful situations and forces us to rest and recover from injury. In contrast, **chronic pain**, the type that comes with a chronic disease or continues long past the healing of a wound, does not serve a useful function.

To treat chronic pain, medical doctors often emphasize increased activity and exercise. Health psychologists often focus their efforts on psychologically oriented treatments, such as behavior modification, biofeedback, and relaxation. Although psychological factors may not be the source of the chronic pain, they frequently encourage and intensify it and increase the related anguish and disability (Bieber et al., 2008; Keefe, Abernathy, & Campbell, 2005; McGuire, Hogan, & Morrison, 2008).

Behavior Modification

Chronic pain is a serious problem with no simple solution. For example, exercise is known to produce an increase in *endorphins*, naturally produced chemicals that attach themselves to nerve cells in the brain and block the perception of pain (Chapter 2). However, chronic pain patients tend to decrease their activity and exercise. In addition, well-meaning family members often ask chronic pain sufferers, "How are you feeling?" "Is the pain any better today?" Unfortunately, focusing our attention on pain increases its intensity (Roth et al., 2007; Sullivan, 2008). Furthermore, as the pain increases, anxiety increases. The anxiety itself then increases the pain, which further increases the anxiety, which further increases the pain!

To counteract these hidden personal and family problems and negative cycles, health psychologists may begin a *behavior modification program* for both the patient with chronic pain and his or her family. Such programs often involve establishing an individualized pain management plan that incorporates daily exercise and relaxation techniques. Health psychologists also monitor each patient's adherence to the plan and provide rewards for following through with the program.

Biofeedback

In *biofeedback*, information about physiological functions, such as heart rate or blood pressure, is monitored, and the feedback helps the individual learn to control these functions. Such feedback helps reduce some types of chronic pain.

Most biofeedback with chronic pain patients is done with the *electromyograph* (*EMG*) (Figure 3.9). This device measures muscle tension by recording electrical activity in the skin. When sufficient relaxation is achieved, the machine signals with a tone or a light. The signal serves as feedback, enabling the patient to learn how to relax. As one lifelong migraine sufferer described it, "The technique was simple. The more tense I was the louder and faster the machine beeped. As I relaxed, the sounds grew slower until they finally stopped" (Hustvedt, 2008). Research shows that biofeedback is helpful and sometimes as effective as more expensive and lengthier forms of treatment (Hammond, 2007; Monastra, 2008).

Relaxation Techniques

Because the pain always seems to be there, chronic pain sufferers tend to talk and think about their pain whenever they are not thoroughly engrossed in an activity. Watching TV shows or films, attending parties, or performing any activity that diverts attention from the pain seems to reduce discomfort. Attention might also be diverted with special *relaxation techniques* like those that are taught in some prepared childbirth classes. These techniques focus the birthing mother's attention on breathing and relaxing the muscles, which helps distract her attention from the fear and pain of the birthing process. Similar techniques also can be helpful to chronic pain sufferers (Astin, 2004). Remember, however, that these techniques do not eliminate the pain. They merely allow the person to ignore it for a time.

Objective 3.16: *What is chronic pain and how do psychologists treat it?*

Chronic Pain *Continuous or recurrent pain over a period of six months or longer*

James Schnepf

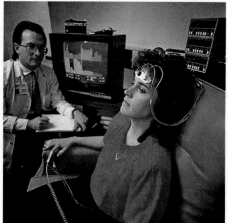

Figure 3.9 ***Pain control through biofeedback*** Using an electromyograph machine, one can record muscular tension and the patient is taught specific relaxation techniques that reduce tension and help relieve chronic pain.

Health Psychology in Action

Objective 3.13: *What is health psychology?*

Health psychology, the study of how biological, psychological, and social factors affect health and illness, is a growing field in psychology with a wide variety of career opportunites.

Objective 3.14: *Why do people start smoking, how do we prevent it, and what are the best ways to quit?*

Almost everyone knows that it's dangerous to smoke, but they first begin out of curiosity, peer pressure, imitation of role models, and other motives. Once started, the addictive nature of nicotine creates a biological need to continue. Smokers also develop pleasant associations with smoking and negative associations with withdrawal.

Smoking prevention programs focus on educating the public about short- and long-term consequences of smoking, trying to make smoking less socially acceptable, and helping nonsmokers resist social pressures to smoke. For teens, the emphasis is on immediate dangers.

Most approaches to help people quit smoking include cognitive and behavioral techniques to aid smokers in their withdrawal from nicotine, along with nicotine replacement therapy (using patches, gum, and pills).

Objective 3.15: *Describe the personal and social risks associated with alcohol.*

Alcohol is one of our most serious health problems. In addition to posing health risks to the individual, alcohol also plays a major role in social issues, such as murder, suicide, spousal abuse, and accidental death. Also a serious problem is **binge drinking**, which occurs when a man has five or more drinks and a woman has four or more in about two hours.

Objective 3.16: *What is chronic pain, and how do psychologists treat it?*

Chronic pain is continuous or recurrent pain that persists over a period of six months or more. Although psychological factors rarely are the source of chronic pain, they can encourage and intensify it. Increased activity, exercise, and dietary changes help to reduce chronic pain. Health psychologists also use behavior

modification, biofeedback, and relaxation techniques to treat chronic pain.

Questions

1. Knowing smoking is very dangerous, why is it so difficult for many people to stop?
2. If you are mounting a campaign to prevent young people from taking up smoking, you are likely to get the best results if you emphasize the_____. (a) serious, unhealthy, long-term effects of tobacco use; (b) number of adults who die from smoking; (c) value of having a relatively healthy retirement; (d) short-term detrimental effects of tobacco use
3. The American Medical Association considers _____ to be the most dangerous and physically damaging of all drugs.
4. An increase in activity and exercise levels benefits patients with pain because exercise increases the release of _____. (a) endorphins; (b) insulin; (c) acetylcholine; (d) norepinephrine

Check your answers in Appendix B.

Click & Review
for additional assessment options:
wiley.com/college/huffman

Achievement

Objective 3.17: *How do we cognitively appraise and cope with stress?*

Health and Stress Management

Simply defined, *coping* is an attempt to manage stress in some effective way. It is not one single act but a process that allows us to deal with various stressors. In this section, we will first discuss how we interpret potential stressors (*primary* and *secondary appraisal*), and then how we cope with perceived threats (*emotion-* and *problem-focused coping*). We close with eight helpful resources for stress management.

Cognitive Appraisal and Coping

It often seems like stress is an environmental thing that just happens to us and that we're helpless to control. But as we've seen before, stress is most often in the "eye of the beholder" (Figure 3.10). According to psychologist Richard Lazarus (1993, 2000), *cognitive appraisal*, or how we interpret events, is perhaps the most important determinant of how we cope with stress.

As you can see in Process Diagram 3.3, in Lazarus's view, we appraise events in two steps: **primary appraisal** (deciding if a situation is harmful, threatening, or challenging) and **secondary appraisal** (assessing our resources and choosing a coping method). Most people then tend to choose either *emotion-* or *problem-focused methods of coping*.

Primary Appraisal *Deciding if a situation is harmful, threatening, or challenging*

Secondary Appraisal *Assessing one's resources and choosing a coping method*

Process Diagram 3.3
Cognitive Appraisal and Coping

Research suggests that our emotional response to an event depends largely on how we interpret the event.

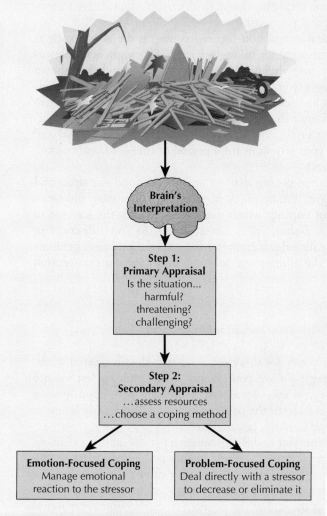

Brain's Interpretation

**Step 1:
Primary Appraisal**
Is the situation...
harmful?
threatening?
challenging?

**Step 2:
Secondary Appraisal**
...assess resources
...choose a coping method

| **Emotion-Focused Coping** | **Problem-Focused Coping** |
| Manage emotional reaction to the stressor | Deal directly with a stressor to decrease or eliminate it |

©AP/Wide World Photos

People often combine *emotion-focused* and *problem-focused* coping strategies to resolve complex stressors or to respond to a stressful situation that is in flux. In some situations, an emotion-focused strategy can allow people to step back from an especially overwhelming problem. Then they can reappraise the situation and use the problem-solving approach to look for solutions. Can you see how each form of coping is represented in these two photos?

wiley.com/
college/
huffman

©AP/Wide World Photos

Figure 3.10 *Extreme stress or exhilaration?* Traveling to India might be extremely stressful for some Americans because of overcrowding and the fact that no one lines up in the railway stations. However, as cross-cultural psychologist Pittu Luangani (2007) says: "One individual's trauma might be another individual's thrill."

Emotion-Focused Coping
Managing one's emotional reactions to a stressful situation

Problem-Solving Coping
Dealing directly with a stressor to decrease or eliminate it

In **emotion-focused coping**, we attempt to manage our emotional reactions. Suppose you are turned down for a highly desirable job or rejected by a long-term friend or partner. You could deal with your disappointment by rationalizing that you did not get the job because you didn't have the right "connections," or by telling yourself that the friend you lost wasn't really that important after all. Although this approach may make you feel better temporarily, failing to realistically evaluate the situation might block you from valuable knowledge important to future jobs and relationships.

A healthier form of emotion-focused coping is *distraction*, such as reading a book, exercising, or calling a friend. This approach helps us cope with initially overwhelming emotions, and research has shown that bereaved people who directed their attention away from their negative emotions had fewer health problems and were seen as better adjusted by their friends than bereaved individuals who did not use this approach (Coifman et al., 2007). (Keep in mind, it's also normal and okay to give in to your emotions for a period of time—to cry, feel sad, and grieve your loss.)

As you can see, emotion-focused coping may reduce or postpone our stress and help us "make it through the night." Many times, however, it is necessary and more effective to use **problem-solving coping**, which deals directly with the stressor to decrease or eliminate it (Bond & Bunce, 2000; Lever, 2008). As you'll discover in Chapter 8, good problem solving includes identifying the stressful problem, generating possible solutions, selecting the appropriate solution, and applying the solution to the problem.

PSYCHOLOGY AT WORK *Why You Shouldn't Procrastinate*

If your professor assigned a term paper for this class, have you already started working on it (problem-focused coping)? Or are you putting it off until the last minute (emotion-focused coping)? Have you ever wondered if working continuously on a term paper from the first day of class until the paper is due might ultimately be more stressful than putting off the paper until the last minute?

To answer this question, Dianne Tice and Roy Baumeister (1997) at Case Western Reserve University assigned a term paper in their health psychology class at the beginning of the semester. Throughout the semester, they carefully monitored the stress, health, and procrastination levels of 44 student volunteers from the class. After the term papers were submitted at the end of the course, Tice and Baumeister found that procrastinators suffered significantly more stress and developed more health problems than nonprocrastinators. They were also more likely to turn in their papers late and earn lower grades on those papers.

In the "Tools for Student Success" section in Chapter 1, you learned that research shows that spacing out your studying rather than cramming the night before produces higher scores on exams. Now you have additional research showing that distributed work also produces better grades on term papers—as well as less stress. The bottom line is this: *Do not procrastinate*. It can be hazardous to your health as well as to your grades (Burka & Yuen, 2004).

Achievement

Objective 3.18: *What are the best resources for stress management?*

Resources for Healthy Living: From Good Health to Money

As noted at the beginning of this chapter, stress is a normal, and necessary, part of our life. Therefore, stress *management* is the goal—not stress elimination. Although our initial, bodily responses to stress are largely controlled by nonconscious, autonomic processes, our higher brain functions can help us avoid the serious damage of chronic overarousal. The key is to consciously recognize when we are overstressed and then to choose resources that activate our parasympathetic, relaxation response. Researchers have identified at least eight important resources for healthy living and stress management.

1. *Health and exercise.* All stressors cause physiological changes. Therefore, an individual's health significantly affects his or her ability to cope. Look again at Process Diagram 3.2, p. 103, on the *general adaptation syndrome.* The resistance stage is the coping stage. The stronger and healthier you are, the better you can cope with stress. Interestingly, researchers have also found that aerobic exercise may help reduce anxiety, PTSD, and mild or moderate depression (Berk, 2007; Blumenthal et al., 2007; Diaz, 2008; Newman & Motta, 2007).

    Exercise reduces the negative effects of stress in several ways. First, it reduces the stress hormones secreted into the bloodstream, which helps speed up the immune system's return to normal functioning. Second, exercise can help reduce muscular tension. Third, exercise increases strength, flexibility, and stamina for encountering future stressors. Most important, it increases the efficiency of the cardiovascular system. The best exercise for all these purposes is aerobic exercise—brisk walking, jogging, bicycling, swimming, and dancing.

2. *Positive beliefs.* A positive self-image and a positive attitude are also significant coping resources. Even temporarily raising self-esteem reduces the amount of anxiety caused by stressful events (Greenberg et al., 1993). Also, hope can sustain a person in the face of severe odds, as is often documented in news reports of people who have triumphed over seemingly unbeatable circumstances. According to Lazarus and Folkman (1984), hope can come from a belief in oneself, which can enable us to devise our own coping strategies. It also comes from a belief in others, such as medical doctors whom we feel can effect positive outcomes, or a belief in a higher spiritual power.

3. *Social skills.* Social situations are often a source of pleasure and stress. For some people, merely meeting someone new and trying to find something to talk about can be very stressful. People who acquire social skills (such as knowing appropriate behaviors for certain situations, having conversation-starters "up their sleeves," and expressing themselves well) suffer less anxiety than people who do not. In fact, people lacking social skills are more at risk for developing illness than those who have them (Cohen & Williamson, 1991).

    Social skills help us not only to interact with others but also to communicate our needs and desires. In addition, social skills help us enlist help when we need it, and decrease hostility in tense situations. If you have weak social skills, observe others and ask people with good social skills for advice. Then practice your new skills by role-playing before applying them in real life.

4. *Social support.* Having the support of others helps offset the stressful effects of divorce, loss of a loved one, chronic illness, PTSD and other mental illnesses, job loss and other work issues (Charuvastra & Cloitre, 2008; Sarafino, 2008; Shen, McCreary, & Myers, 2004; Southwick, Vythilingam, & Charney, 2005; Tsuru et al., 2008). When we are faced with stressful circumstances, our friends and family often help us take care of our health, listen and "hold our hand," make us feel important, and provide stability to offset the changes in our lives. Professional support groups, like those for alcoholics and families of alcoholics, help people cope not only because they provide other people to lean on but also because people can learn techniques for coping from others with similar problems (see Chapter 15).

5. *Material resources.* We've all heard the saying "Money isn't everything." But when it comes to coping with stress, money, and the things money can buy, can be very important resources. Money increases the number of options available to eliminate sources of stress or reduce the effects of stress. When faced with the

Arthur Tilley//Stone/GettyImages

Coping with stress Exercise and friends are important resources for effective stress reduction. As the song says, "I get by with a little help from my friends." John Lennon and Paul McCartney, Sgt. Pepper's Lonely Hearts Club Band, 1967.

©AP/Wide World Photos

People need people An important resource for coping with stress is social support from friends, family, and support groups.

In general, *Eager Adopters* love technology. Although they make up only 10 to 15 percent of the population, eager adopters consider technology fun and are the first to upgrade their equipment. The *Hesitant* "Prove Its" account for half to two-thirds of the population. They take a wait-and-see attitude, but once they are convinced that a new technology will make their lives easier, they try to adopt it. Finally, the *Resisters* avoid—or even fear—new technology. They feel insecure around new technology and actively oppose any new purchases or upgrades.

If you are an *Eager Adopter*, you are probably not stressed by technology. But what do you do if you are one of the other types? How do you control TechnoStress? First, evaluate each new technology on its usefulness for you and your lifestyle. It isn't a black or white, "technophobe" or "technophile" choice. If something works for you, invest the energy to adopt it. Second, establish clear boundaries. Technology came into the world with an implied promise of a better and more productive life. But, for many, the servant has become the master. We've all watched harried executives frantically checking their e-mail while on vacation and families eating dinners at restaurants with their preschoolers playing video games, teenagers text messaging, and parents loudly talking on separate cell phones. We can (and must) control technology and its impact on our lives. Finally, relax and slow down. "Rethink how you react to the new wizardry," says Larry Rosen. "Just because technology works at lightning speed does not mean you should."

*A*pplication

CRITICAL THINKING

ACTIVE LEARNING

Reducing Stress Through Critical Thinking
(Contributed by Thomas Frangicetto)

According to cognitive therapist Albert Ellis, "If people look at what they are telling themselves, look at their thinking, at their irrational beliefs and self-defeating attitudes...they can then experience *healthy* stressful reactions" (Palmer & Ellis, 1995). Of all the useful coping resources described in this chapter, examining our thinking (also known as *critical thinking*) is undoubtedly one of the most important. This exercise will help you

- Understand the link between how we cognitively interpret a stressor and the amount and type of stress we actually experience.
- Review important text content your professor may include on exams.
- Practice applying numerous critical thinking components.

Part I. Fill in the letter from the list of key terms and concepts that best applies to each of the 10 stressful situations.

Text Key Terms and Concepts

a. Approach–Avoidance Conflict
b. Avoidance–Avoidance Conflict
c. Binge Drinking
d. Burnout
e. Chronic Stress
f. External Locus of Control
g. Frustration
h. Posttraumatic Stress Disorder

i. Procrastination
j. Type A Personality

Stressful Situation

___1. Wendy is *forced to choose* between the *undesirable alternative* of studying boring subjects AND the *undesirable alternative* of poor grades.

___2. John is a soldier who has returned home after serving three tours of duty in Iraq. He's now working at a stressful job, is deep in debt, and his wife is threatening divorce.

___3. Marci was fortunate to escape the terrorist attack on September 11, 2001. But ever since that *life-threatening day*, her functioning has been impaired by *flashbacks, nightmares,* and an overwhelming sense of *anxiety, helplessness, and emotional numbing.*

___4. Jason is a college freshman who is pledging a fraternity. During the "hazing": "They made me do as many beers as I could until I threw up. They had buckets nearby ready for it. I did about *10 Jell-O shots* in an hour or so. They said this was a *normal part of the Greek life.* I just wanted to fit in, that's all I ever wanted."

___5. Rodney is a high-powered executive whose *intense ambition* and *competitiveness* seem to have paid off. However, his wife complains about his *exaggerated sense of time urgency* and his *persistent cynicism and hostility.*

___6. Juanita is trapped in a traffic jam on her way to an important exam. She feels *tension and anxiety* building because she is being *blocked from achieving her goal.*

___7. Jennifer's job is *emotionally demanding* and she feels *physically, emotionally,* and *mentally exhausted.*

___8. Derek has been *putting off* working on a paper assigned three months ago. With one week to go, he is experiencing *tremendous stress and has developed a lingering cold.*

___9. Selena believes that all of the bad things that happen to her are the result of *bad luck or fate,* and she feels *powerless to change* her situation.

___10. James is a high-achieving college student, but he recently met a wonderful person and his grades are falling. He feels *forced to choose* between dating and high grades.

Part II. On a separate sheet of paper, choose FIVE of the situations above, and then identify ONE critical thinking component (CTC) from the Prologue of this text (pp. xxx–xxxiv) and describe how it could be used to help each individual "cope more effectively." Try to use a different CTC for each situation.

Check your answers in Appendix B.

Click & Review
for additional assessment options:
wiley.com/college/huffman

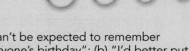

Assessment
CHECK & REVIEW

Health and Stress Management

Objective 3.17: *How do we cognitively appraise and cope with stress?*

When facing a stressor, we first evaluate it in two steps: **primary appraisal** (deciding if a situation is harmful, threatening, or challenging) and **secondary appraisal** (assessing our resources and choosing a coping method). We then tend to choose either **emotion-focused coping** (attempting to manage our emotional reactions) or **problem-solving coping** (dealing directly with the stressor to decrease or eliminate it).

Objective 3.18: *What are the best resources for stress management?*

Researchers have indentified at least eight important resources: health and exercise, positive beliefs, social skills, social support, material resources, control, relaxation, and sense of humor.

Questions

1. Describe a personal stressor and how you used both primary and secondary appraisal.
2. Imagine that you forgot your best friend's birthday. Now, identify the form of coping you would be using in each of the following reactions.

(a) "I can't be expected to remember everyone's birthday"; (b) "I'd better put Cindy's birthday on my calendar so this won't happen again."
3. People with a(n) _____ locus of control are better able to cope with stress.
4. What are the eight major resources for healthy living and stress management? Which resource is most helpful for you? Least helpful?

Check your answers in Appendix B.

Click & Review
for additional assessment options:
wiley.com/college/huffman

Assessment
KEY TERMS

*To assess your understanding of the **Key Terms** in Chapter 3, write a definition for each (in your own words), and then compare your definitions with those in the text.*

Understanding Stress
approach–approach conflict (p. 95)
approach–avoidance conflict (p. 96)
avoidance–avoidance conflict (p. 95)
burnout (p. 93)
chronic stress (p. 93)
conflict (p. 95)
distress (p. 92)
eustress (p. 92)
frustration (p. 95)
general adaptation syndrome (GAS) (p. 102)
hassles (p. 94)

homeostasis (p. 101)
HPA axis (p. 101)
job stress (p. 93)
psychoneuroimmunology (p. 102)
role conflict (p. 93)
SAM system (p. 101)
stress (p. 92)

Stress and Illness
hardiness (p. 108)
posttraumatic stress disorder (PTSD) (p. 109)
Type A personality (p. 106)
Type B personality (p. 106)

Health Psychology in Action
binge drinking (p. 114)
chronic pain (p. 115)
health psychology (p. 111)

Health and Stress Management
emotion-focused coping (p. 118)
external locus of control (p. 120)
internal locus of control (p. 120)
primary appraisal (p. 116)
problem-focused coping (p. 118)
secondary appraisal (p. 116)

Achievement
WEB RESOURCES

Huffman Book Companion Site
wiley.com/college/huffman
    This site is loaded with free Interactive Self-Tests, Internet Exercises, Glossary and Flashcards for key terms, web links, Handbook for Non-Native Speakers, and other activities designed to improve your mastery of the material in this chapter.

Understanding Stress

Sources of Stress

- *Life changes:* Holmes and Rahe Scale measures stress caused by important life events.
- **Chronic stress:** Ongoing, long-term stress related to political world, family, work, etc.
- **Job Stress:** Work-related stress, including role conflict and burnout.
- **Hassles:** Small, everyday problems that accumulate.
- **Frustration:** Negative emotional state from blocked goals.
- **Conflict:** Negative emotional state from two or more incompatible goals.
- *Cataclysmic Events:* Disasters that occur suddenly and affect many people.

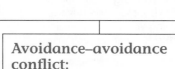

There are three types of conflict

Approach–approach conflict:

Forced choice between two or more desirable alternatives

Avoidance–avoidance conflict:

Forced choice between two or more undesirable alternatives

Approach–avoidance conflict:

Forced choice between two or more alternatives with both desirable and undesirable outcomes

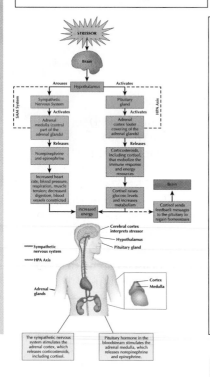

Effects of Stress

- **SAM system** (*Sympatho-Adreno-Medullary*) provides an initial, rapid-acting stress response.
- **HPA axis** (*Hypothalamic-Pituitary-Adrenocortical* allows for a delayed stress response. Cortisol (a hormone released by the HPA axis) helps combat inflammation and mobilize energy resources. It also sends feedback messages to the brain and pituitary to regain **homeostasis**.
- *Cognitive functioning* disturbed during stress.
- *Selye's general adaptation syndrome* (*GAS*) shows a 3-step response to stress.
- *Suppressed immune system* leaves body vulnerable to disease.

(1) Alarm Reaction
In the initial *alarm reaction*, your body experiences a temporary state of shock and your resistance to illness and stress falls below normal limits.

(2) Stage of Resistance
If the stressor remains, your body attempts to endure the stressor, and enters the *resistance phase*. Physiological arousal remains higher than normal, and there is a sudden outpouring of hormones. Selye maintained that one outcome of this stage for some people is the development of *diseases of adaption*, including asthma, ulcers, and high blood pressure.

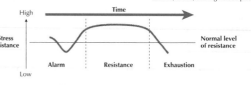

(3) Stage of Exhaustion
Long-term exposure to the stressor eventually depletes your body's reserves, and you enter the *exhaustion phase*. In this phase, you become more susceptible to serious illnesses, and possibly irreversible damage to your body. Unless a way of relieving stress is found, the result may be complete collapse and death.

Stress and Illness

Cancer

Caused by hereditary dispositions and environmental factors that lead to changes in body chemistry and the immune system.

Cardiovascular Disorders

Contributing factors:
- Behaviors such as smoking, obesity, lack of exercise
- Stress hormones
- **Type A personality**
- Lack of hardiness

Posttraumatic Stress Disorder (PTSD) and Gastric Ulcers

Exposure to extraordinary stress may lead to PTSD, and chronic stress may increase vulnerability to the *H. pylori* bacterium, which causes gastric ulcers.

Health Psychology in Action

Tobacco

- *Why do people smoke?* Curiosity, peer pressure, role models, addictive properties of nicotine, pleasant associations with smoking, and negative (withdrawal) experiences when not smoking.

- *Prevention?* Educate about short- and long-term consequences, help nonsmokers resist social pressures, and make smoking less convenient and socially acceptable, while emphasizing the financial costs.

- *Stopping?* Use cognitive and behavioral techniques to deal with withdrawal; supplement with nicotine replacement therapy (patches, gum, and pills).

Alcohol

Alcohol is one of our most serious health problems.
Binge drinking: When a man consumes 5 or more drinks, or a woman consumes 4 or more in about 2 hours.

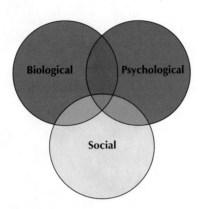

Chronic Pain

Chronic pain: Pain lasting 6 months or longer.
How to reduce?

- Increase activity and exercise.

- Use behavior modification strategies to reinforce changes.

- Employ *biofeedback* with *electromyograph (EMG)* to reduce muscle tension.

- Use relaxation techniques.

Health and Stress Management

Cognitive Appraisal and Coping

Brain's Interpretation

Step 1: Primary Appraisal
Is the situation... harmful? threatening? challenging?

Step 2: Secondary Appraisal
...assess resources ...choose a coping method

Emotion-Focused Coping
Manage emotional reaction to the stressor

Problem-Focused Coping
Deal directly with a stressor to decrease or eliminate it

Resources for Healthy Living

- Health and exercise
- Positive beliefs
- Social skills
- Social support
- Material resources
- Control
- Relaxation
- Sense of humor

4

Sensation and Perception

Imagine that your visual field is suddenly inverted and reversed. Things you normally expect to be on your right are now on your left. Things you expect to be above your head are now below your head. How would you ride a bike, read a book, or even walk through your home? Do you think you could ever adapt to this upside-down world?

To answer that question, psychologist George Stratton (1896) invented, and for eight days wore, special goggles that flipped up to down and right to left. For the first few days, Stratton had a great deal of difficulty navigating in this environment and coping with everyday tasks. But by the third day, he noted:

> Walking through the narrow spaces between pieces of furniture required much less care than hitherto. I could watch my hands as they wrote, without hesitating or becoming embarrassed thereby.

By the fifth day, Stratton had almost completely adjusted to his strange perceptual environment, and when he later removed the headgear, he quickly readapted.

What does this experiment have to do with your everyday life? At this very moment, you body is being bombarded with stimuli from the outside world—light, sound, heat, pressure, texture, and so on—while your brain is floating in complete silence and utter darkness. Stratton's experiment shows us that sensing the world is not enough. Our brains must receive, convert, and constantly adapt the information from our sense organs into useful mental representations of the world. How we get the outside world inside to our brains, and what our brains do with this information, are the key topics of this chapter.

> The senses collect the surface facts of matter
> It was sensation, when memory came
> It was knowledge, when mind acted on it
> As knowledge it was thought
>
> RALPH WALDO EMERSON

> All our knowledge has its origins in our perceptions.
>
> LEONARDO DA VINCI

▶ **Understanding Sensation**

Processing
Thresholds

 PSYCHOLOGY AT WORK
Do Subliminal Messages Improve Sales?

Adaptation

CASE STUDY/PERSONAL STORY
Helen Keller's Triumph and Advice

▶ **How We See and Hear**

Vision
Hearing

RESEARCH HIGHLIGHT
Perfect (Yet Imperfect) Pitch

▶ **Our Other Senses**

Smell and Taste
The Body Senses

▶ **Understanding Perception**

Selection
Organization

 GENDER & CULTURAL DIVERSITY
Are the Gestalt Laws Universally True?

Interpretation

RESEARCH HIGHLIGHT
Is There Scientific Evidence for Extrasensory
Perception (ESP)?

CRITICAL THINKING/ACTIVE LEARNING
Problems with Believing in Extrasensory Perception
(ESP)

Tony Hutchings/Photographer's Choice/Getty Images

127

WHY STUDY PSYCHOLOGY?

Did you know...

▶ People can experience excruciating pain in limbs that have been amputated?

▶ You can see a candle burning 30 miles away (on a clear, dark night), hear the tick of a watch at 20 feet (under quiet conditions), taste 1 teaspoon of sugar dissolved in 2 gallons of water, and smell one drop of perfume in a six-room apartment?

▶ You have a "blind spot" on the back of each eye that transmits no visual information to your brain?

▶ Loud music (or other loud noises) can lead to permanent hearing loss?

▶ Some people commonly experience *synesthesia*, which is a blending of sensory experiences. They "see" colors that feel warm or cold, "hear" sounds that are orange and purple, and "taste" foods that feel like different shapes?

▶ People born with "perfect pitch" have trouble with notes surrounding A, which may be due to our brain's neuroplasticity.

The Image Bank/Eliane Sulle/Getty Images

Achievement

Objective 4.1: *Contrast sensation and perception, and compare bottom-up processing with top-down processing.*

Sensation *Process of detecting, converting, and transmitting raw sensory information from the external and internal environments to the brain*

Perception *Process of selecting, organizing, and interpreting sensory information into meaningful patterns*

Psychologists are keenly interested in our senses—*sensation* is the mind's window to the outside world. We're equally interested in *perception*—how the brain gives meaning to sensory information. **Sensation** begins with specialized receptor cells located in our sense organs (eyes, ears, nose, tongue, skin, and internal body tissues) (Figure 4.1). When sense organs detect an appropriate stimuli (light, mechanical pressure, chemical molecules), they convert it into neural impulses (action potentials) that are transmitted to our brain. The brain then selects, organizes, and interprets the coded neural messages into meaningful patterns—a process called **perception**.

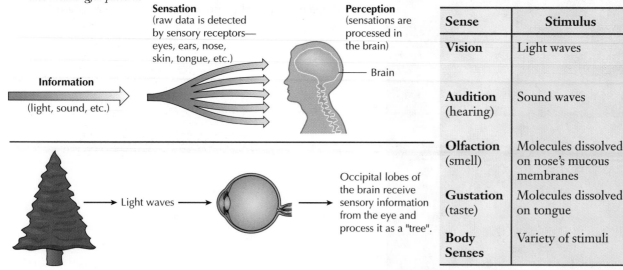

Sense	Stimulus	Receptors
Vision	Light waves	Light-sensitive rods and cones in eye's retina
Audition (hearing)	Sound waves	Pressure-sensitive hair cells in ear's cochlea
Olfaction (smell)	Molecules dissolved on nose's mucous membranes	Neurons in the nose's olfactory epithelium
Gustation (taste)	Molecules dissolved on tongue	Taste buds on tongue's surface
Body Senses	Variety of stimuli	Variety of receptors

Figure 4.1 **Sensation and perception** *Sensation* involves the detection, conversion, and transmission of raw data provided by our sensory receptors. But to make sense of these sensations, we also need our brains to select, organize, and interpret the sensory information—a process called *perception*.

In this chapter, we start with sensation, the sensory receptors (eyes, ears, and other senses), and then work up to perception. Psychologists sometimes refer to the flow of information from the sensory receptors to the brain as **bottom-up processing** (Mulckhuyse et al., 2008; Prouix, 2007). Imagine yourself as an engineer who has received an urgent package filled with wires, gauges, and an assortment of metal pieces. There are no directions or pictures in the package, and you're asked to assemble everything into a functional object. This assignment would require *bottom-up processing*.

Perception and **top-down processing** begin at the "top" with higher-level cognitive processes, such as knowledge, experience, and expectations, and then works down to the sensory level (Schuett et al., 2008; Zhaoping & Guyader, 2007). If you, the engineer, were given the same package, along with a picture and diagram, and then asked to assemble a specific object, you would be using top-down, or *conceptually driven* processing.

Bowling Green Public Library

In short, bottom-up processing is a type of *data driven* processing that moves from the parts to the whole, whereas top-down processing is *conceptually* driven and moves from the whole to the parts. Both bottom-up and top-down processing are important components of sensation and perception.

Bottom-Up Processing *Information processing beginning "at the bottom" with raw sensory data that are sent "up" to the brain for higher-level analysis; data driven processing that moves from the parts to the whole*

Top-Down Processing *Information processing starting "at the top," with higher level cognitive processes (such as, expectations and knowledge), and then working down; conceptually driven processing that moves from the whole to the parts*

Bottom-up or top-down processing? *When first learning to read, we discovered that certain arrangements of lines and "squiggles" represented specific letters—bottom-up processing. Only later did we discover that these letters joined together to make up words. Today, after years of experience and language training, we quickly perceive the words in this sentence before the individual letters—top-down processing* (Schuett et al., 2008)

Application

Sensation or Perception?

(a) When you stare at this drawing (known as the Necker cube), which area is the top, front, and back of the cube?
(b) Now look at this drawing of a woman. Do you see a young woman looking back over her shoulder, or an older woman with her chin buried in the fur of her jacket?

In the process of *sensation*, your visual sensory system receives an assortment of light waves when looking at these two drawings. This sensory data is then converted and transmitted to your brain. In contrast, during *perception* your brain learns to *interpret* sensory information into lines and patterns. Interestingly, if you stare at either the cube or the woman long enough, your perception/interpretation will inevitably change. Although basic sensory input

stays the same, your brain's attempt to interpret ambiguous stimuli creates a type of perceptual "dance," shifting from one interpretation to another (Gaetz, Rzempoluck, & Jantzen, 1998).

(a)

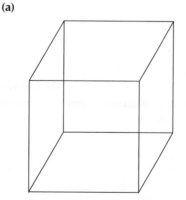

(b)

Achievement

Understanding Sensation

When presented with a high-pitched tone, a musician reported, "It looks like fireworks tinged with a pink-red hue. The strip of color feels rough and unpleasant, and it has an ugly taste—rather like that of a briny pickle" (Luria, 1968). This musician has

Objective 4.2: *Explain how transduction, coding, and sensory reduction turn raw sensory data into signals the brain can understand.*

Synesthesia *A mixing of sensory experiences (e.g., "seeing" colors when a sound is heard)*

a rare condition known as **synesthesia**, which means "mixing of the senses." People with synesthesia routinely blend their sensory experiences. They may "see" colors that feel warm or cold, "hear" sounds that are orange and purple, and "taste" foods that feel like different shapes.

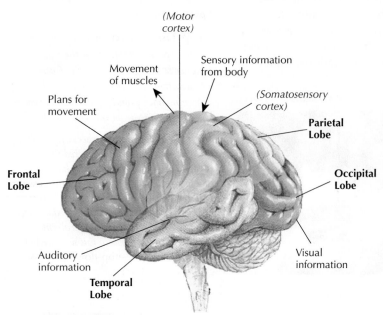

Figure 4.2 *Sensory processing within the brain* *Neural impulses travel from the sensory receptors to various parts of the brain.*

Transduction *Converting a receptor's energy into neural impulses that are sent on to the brain*

Coding *Converting sensory inputs into different sensations*

Sensory Reduction *Filtering and analyzing incoming sensations before sending a neural message to the cortex.*

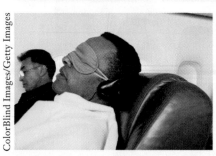

Reducing sensations *By adding a sleeping mask and special noise eliminating headphones, this traveler obtains welcome relief from unwanted sensations. The headphones work by creating opposing sound waves that cancel sounds from the environment.*

Processing: Getting the Outside Inside

To appreciate how extraordinary synesthesia is, we must first understand the basic processes of normal, *nonblended* sensations. For example, how do we turn light and sound waves from the environment into something our brain can comprehend? To do this, we first must have a means of detecting stimuli and of converting them into a language the brain can understand. We also need to filter and reduce excessive and unnecessary stimuli.

Let's start with *sensory detection*. Our eyes, ears, skin, and other sense organs all contain special cells called *receptors*, which detect and process sensory information from the environment. For each sense, these specialized cells respond to a distinct stimulus, such as light or sound waves or chemical molecules.

Next, during the process of **transduction**, the receptors convert energy from the previously detected stimuli into neural impulses, which are sent along to the brain. In hearing, for example, tiny receptor cells in the inner ear convert mechanical vibrations (from sound waves) into electrochemical signals. These messages are then carried by neurons to the brain for higher-level interpretation and analysis.

How does our brain differentiate between sensations, such as sights and sounds? Thanks to a process known as **coding**, different physical stimuli are interpreted as distinct sensations because their neural impulses travel by different routes and arrive at different parts of the brain (Figure 4.2). Interestingly, during *transduction* and *coding*, there are also processes that purposely reduce the amount of stimuli we receive.

Why would we want to reduce the sensory information? Can you imagine what would happen if you did not have some natural filtering of stimuli? You would constantly hear blood rushing through your veins and continually feel your clothes brushing against your skin. Some level of filtering is needed so that the brain is not overwhelmed with unnecessary information.

In the process of **sensory reduction**, we not only filter incoming sensations, we also analyze the sensations sent through before a neural impulse is finally sent to the cortex of the brain. For example, sudden loud noises will generally awaken sleeping animals (both human and nonhuman). This is because cells in the *reticular formation* (Chapter 2) send messages via the thalamus to alert the cortex. However, these reticular formation cells can learn to screen out certain messages, while allowing others to go on to higher brain centers. This explains why parents of a newborn can sleep through passing sirens and blaring stereos, yet still awaken to the slightest whimper of their baby.

All species have evolved selective receptors that suppress or amplify information to allow survival. For example, hawks have an acute sense of vision but a poor sense of smell. Similarly, we humans cannot sense many stimuli, such as ultraviolet light, microwaves, the ultrasonic sound of a dog whistle, or infrared heat patterns from warm-blooded animals (which rattlesnakes can). However, we can see a candle burning 30 miles away on a dark, clear night; hear the tick of a watch at 20 feet under quiet conditions; smell one drop of perfume in a six-room apartment; and taste 1 teaspoon of sugar dissolved in 2 gallons of water (Concept Diagram 4.1).

Concept Diagram 4.1
Measuring the Senses

Achievement

Objective 4.3: *Define psycho-physics, and differentiate between absolute and difference thresholds.*

How do we know that humans can hear a watch ticking at 20 feet or smell one drop of perfume in a six-room apartment? The answer comes from research in **psychophysics**, which studies the link between the physical characteristics of stimuli and our sensory experience of them. Researchers study how the strength or intensity of a stimulus affects an observer. Consider this example:

- To test for hearing loss, a hearing specialist uses a tone generator to produce sounds of differing pitches and intensities.

- You listen with earphones and indicate the earliest point at which you hear a tone. This is your **absolute threshold,** or the smallest amount of a stimulus that an observer can reliably detect.

- To test your **difference threshold**, or *just noticeable difference* (*JND*), the examiner gradually changes the volume and asks you to respond when you notice a change.

- The examiner then compares your thresholds with those of people with normal hearing to determine whether you have a hearing loss and, if so, the extent of the loss.

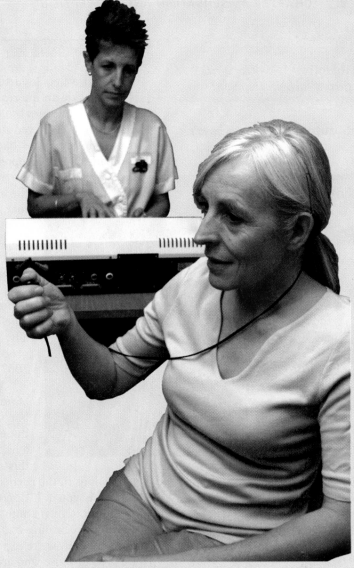

Phanie/Photo Researchers, Inc.

ABSOLUTE THRESHOLDS FOR VARIOUS SENSES

Sense	Stimulus	Absolute Threshold
Vision	Light energy	A candle flame seen from 30 miles away on a clear, dark night
Hearing	Sound waves	The tick of a watch at 20 feet
Taste	Chemical substances that contact the tongue	One teaspoon of sugar in two gallons of water
Smell	Chemical substances that enter the nose	One drop of perfume spread throughout a six-room apartment
Touch	Movement of, or pressure on, the skin	A bee's wing falling on your cheek from a height of about half an inch

Psychophysics *Studies the link between the physical characteristics of stimuli and our sensory experience of them*

Absolute Threshold *Minimum amount of a stimulus that an observer can reliably detect*

Difference Threshold *Minimal difference needed to notice a stimulus change; also called the "just noticeable difference" (JND)*

Achievement

Objective 4.4: *What are the effects of subliminal stimuli?*

Subliminal *Pertaining to stimuli presented below conscious awareness*

KAREN KASMAUSKI/NG Image Collection

Psychology at work—amazing animal senses *Many animals possess extraordinary sensory abilities. For example, a dog's sense of smell is far more sensitive than that of a human. For this reason, specially trained dogs provide invaluable help in sniffing out dangerous plants, drugs, and explosives, tracking criminals, and assisting in search-and-rescue operations. Some researchers believe dogs can even detect chemical signs of certain illnesses, such as diabetes or cancer (Akers & Denbow, 2008).*

PSYCHOLOGY AT WORK *Do Subliminal Messages Improve Sales?*

Now that we've discussed the concept of *absolute thresholds* in Concept Diagram 4.1, we can tackle an interesting and ongoing controversy. Are we affected by sensations at levels below our absolute threshold, even when we're not aware of them? Years ago many people believed movie theaters were manipulating consumers by subliminally presenting messages like "Eat popcorn" and "Drink Coca-Cola." Similarly, record companies were supposedly embedding **subliminal** messages in rock music that encouraged violence and sex. The words on the movie screen and the messages in the music were allegedly presented so quickly that they were below the threshold for awareness. Most people were both fascinated and outraged. Politicians rushed to pass laws against the "invisible sell" and the "moral corruption" of our youth. Were they right to be concerned? Is there even such a thing as subliminal messages?

Two major questions surround *subliminal perception*. First, is it possible to perceive something without conscious awareness? The answer is clearly yes. Scientific research on subliminal (literally, "below the threshold") stimuli demonstrates that information processing does occur even when we are not aware of it (Aarts, 2007; Boccato et al., 2008; Cleeremans & Sarrazin, 2007).

Experimental studies commonly use an instrument called a *tachistoscope* to flash images too quickly for conscious recognition, but slowly enough to be registered. For example, in one study the experimenter flashed one of two pictures subliminally (either a happy or an angry face) followed by a neutral face. They found this subliminal presentation evoked matching unconscious facial expressions in the participant's own facial muscles (Dimberg, Thunberg, & Elmehed, 2000). As you will discover in Chapter 12, the fact that participants were unaware of the subliminal stimuli, as well as their own matching facial response, also raises questions regarding our own emotional states. Do we unconsciously become a little happier when we're exposed to good-natured, pleasant people? And upset when we are around those who are angry?

Although this research shows that subliminal perception *does* occur, the second—and more important—question is, "Does it lead to *subliminal persuasion?*" The answer to this question is less clear. Subliminal stimuli are basically *weak* stimuli. At most, they have a modest (if any) effect on consumer behavior, and absolutely *no effect* on the minds of youth listening to rock music or citizens' voting behavior (Begg, Needham, & Bookbinder, 1993; Dijksterhuis, Aarts, & Smith, 2005; Karremans, Stroebe, & Claus, 2006). If you're wondering about buying subliminal tapes promising to help you lose weight or relieve stress, save your money. Blank "placebo" tapes appear to be just as "effective" as subliminal tapes.

Reprinted with special permission of King Features Syndicate

In sum, evidence exists that subliminal perception occurs, but the effect on subliminal persuasion is uncertain. When it comes to commercials and self-help tapes, advertisers are better off using above-threshold messages—the loudest, clearest, and most attention-getting stimuli possible. And for weight loss, the money and time are better spent on the old-fashioned methods of exercise and diet.

Adaptation: Weakening the Response

Imagine that friends have invited you to come visit their beautiful new baby. As they greet you at the door, you are overwhelmed by the odor of a wet diaper. Why don't they do something about the smell? The answer lies in the previously mentioned *sensory reduction* and **sensory adaptation**. When a constant stimulus is presented for a length of time, sensation often fades or disappears. In *sensory adaptation*, receptors higher up in the sensory system get "tired" and actually fire less frequently.

Sensory adaptation makes sense from an evolutionary perspective. To survive, we can't afford to waste attention and time on unchanging, normally unimportant stimuli. "Turning down the volume" on repetitive information helps the brain cope with an overwhelming amount of sensory stimuli and allows time to pay attention to change. Sometimes, however, adaptation can be dangerous, as when people stop paying attention to a gas leak in the kitchen.

Some senses like smell and touch adapt quickly. Interestingly, we never completely adapt to visual stimuli because our eyes are constantly moving. They quiver just enough to guarantee constantly changing sensory information. Otherwise, if we stared long enough at an object, it would vanish from sight! We also don't adapt to extremely intense stimuli, such as the heat of the desert sun or the pain of a cut hand. Again, from an evolutionary perspective, these limitations on sensory adaptation aid survival. They remind us to avoid intense heat and to do something about the damaged tissue on that cut hand.

If we don't adapt to pain, how do athletes keep playing despite painful injuries? In certain situations, the body releases natural painkillers called *endorphins* (see Chapter 2). Endorphins are neurotransmitters that act in the same way as morphine. They relieve pain by inhibiting pain perception. Pleasant stimuli, like the "runner's high," as well as unpleasant stimuli, such as injuries, can cause a release of endorphins. Pain relief through endorphins may also be the secret behind *acupuncture*, the ancient Chinese technique of gently twisting thin needles placed in the skin (Agrò et al., 2005; Cabyóglu, Ergene, & Tan, 2006).

In addition to endorphin release, another explanation for pain relief is provided by the **gate-control theory**, first proposed by Ronald Melzack and Patrick Wall (1965). According to this theory, the experience of pain depends partly on whether the neural message gets past a "gatekeeper" in the spinal cord. Normally, the gate is kept shut by impulses coming down from the brain, or by messages coming from large-diameter nerve fibers that conduct most sensory signals, such as touch and pressure. However, when body tissue is damaged, impulses from smaller pain fibers open the gate.

According to the gate-control theory, massaging an injury or scratching an itch can temporarily relieve discomfort because pressure on large-diameter neurons interferes with pain signals. Messages from the brain can also control the pain gate, explaining how athletes and soldiers can carry on despite excruciating pain. When we are soothed by endorphins or distracted by competition or fear, our experience of pain can be greatly diminished.

Achievement

Objective 4.5: *Define sensory adaptation and explain why it is helpful.*

Sensory Adaptation *Decreased sensitivity due to repeated or constant stimulation*

Lindsey Hebberd/Corbis

How does he do it? *The fact that this man willingly endures such normally excruciating pain illustrates the complex mixture of psychological and biological factors in the experience of pain.*

Achievement

Objective 4.6: *Explain the gate-control theory of pain perception.*

Gate-Control Theory *Theory that pain sensations are processed and altered by mechanisms within the spinal cord*

Ironically, when we get anxious or dwell on our pain, we can intensify it (Roth et al., 2007; Sullivan, 2008; Sullivan, Tripp, & Santor, 1998). Therefore, well-meaning friends who ask chronic pain sufferers about their pain may unintentionally reinforce and increase it (Jolliffe & Nicholas, 2004).

Research also suggests that the pain gate may be chemically opened by a neuro-transmitter called *substance P*, while endorphins close it (Bianchi et al., 2008; Cesaro & Ollat, 1997; Liu, Mantyh, & Basbaum, 1997). Other research finds that the brain not only responds to incoming signals from sensory nerves but also is capable of *generating* pain (and other sensations) entirely on its own (Melzack, 1999; Vertosick, 2000). Have you heard of *tinnitus*, the ringing-in-the-ears sensation that sometimes accompanies hearing loss? In the absence of normal sensory input, nerve cells send conflicting messages ("static") to the brain, and in this case the brain interprets the static as "ringing." A similar process happens with the strange phenomenon of *phantom pain*, in which people continue to feel pain (and itching or tickling) long after a limb is amputated. The brain interprets the static as pain because it arises in the area of the spinal cord responsible for pain signaling. Interestingly, when amputees are fitted with prosthetic limbs and begin using them, phantom pain often disappears (Crawford, 2008; Gracely, Farrell, & Grant, 2002).

Each of the sensory principles we've discussed thus far—transduction, reduction, coding, thresholds, and adaptation—applies to all the senses. Yet the way in which each sense is processed is uniquely different, as we will see in the remainder of the chapter.

Achievement

Objective 4.7: *What can Helen Keller teach us about sensation and perception?*

Application

CASE STUDY/PERSONAL STORY *Helen Keller's Triumph and Advice*

Helen Keller recognized how crucial sensation and perception are to our lives. She learned to "see" and "hear" with her sense of touch and often recognized visitors by their smell or by vibrations from their walk. Helen Keller wasn't born deaf and blind. When she was 19 months old, she suffered a fever that left her without sight or hearing and thus virtually isolated from the world. Keller's parents realized they had to find help for their daughter. After diligently searching, they found Anne Sullivan, a young teacher who was able to break through Keller's barrier of isolation by taking advantage of her sense of touch. One day, Sullivan took Keller to the pumphouse and, as Sullivan (1902) wrote:

> I made Helen hold her mug under the spout while I pumped. As the cold water gushed forth, filling the mug, I spelled "w-a-t-e-r" in Helen's free hand. The word coming so close upon the sensation of cold water rushing over her hand seemed to startle her. She dropped the mug and stood as one transfixed. A new light came into her face. (p. 257)

That one moment, brought on by the sensation of cold water on her hand, was the impetus for a lifetime of learning about, understanding, and appreciating the world through her remaining senses. In 1904, Helen Keller graduated cum laude from Radcliffe College and went on to become a famous author and lecturer, inspiring physically limited people throughout the world.

Despite her incredible accomplishments, Keller often expressed a lifelong yearning to experience a normal sensory world. She offered important advice to all whose senses are "normal":

> I who am blind can give one hint to those who see: use your eyes as if tomorrow you would be stricken blind. And the same method can be applied to the other senses. Hear the music of voices, the song of a bird, the mighty strains of an orchestra as if you would be stricken deaf tomorrow. Touch each object as if tomorrow your tactile sense would fail. Smell the perfume of flowers, taste with relish each morsel as if tomorrow you could never smell and taste again. Make the most of every sense; glory in all the facets of pleasure and beauty that the world reveals to you through the several means of contact which nature provides. (Keller, 1962, p. 23)

Helen Keller greets Eleanor Roosevelt (1955)

Bettman/CORBIS

Assessment
CHECK & REVIEW

Understanding Sensation

Objective 4.1: *Contrast sensation and perception, and compare bottom-up processing with top-down processing.*

Sensation refers to the process of detecting, converting, and transmitting raw sensory data to the brain. In contrast, **perception** is the process of selecting, organizing, and interpreting sensory information into useful mental representations of the world. **Bottom-up processing** refers to information processing that begins "at the bottom" with raw sensory data that are sent "up" to the brain for higher-level analysis. **Top-down processing** starts "at the top," with higher-level cognitive processes (such as, expectations and knowledge), and then works down.

Objective 4.2: *Explain how transduction, coding, and sensory reduction turn raw sensory data into signals the brain can understand.*

Transduction converts receptor energy into neural impulses that are sent to the brain, and **coding** converts these sensory inputs into different sensations (e.g., sight versus sound). Through **sensory reduction** we eliminate excessive and unnecessary sensory stimuli.

Objective 4.3: *Define psychophysics, and differentiate between absolute and difference thresholds.*

Psychophysics studies the link between the physical characteristics of stimuli and our sensory experience of them. The **absolute threshold** is the smallest magnitude of a stimulus we can detect, whereas the **difference threshold** is the smallest change in a stimulus that we can detect.

Objective 4.4: *What are the effects of subliminal stimuli?*

Research shows that we can perceive **subliminal** stimuli that are presented below our conscious awareness. However, they are weak stimuli that have little or no persuasive effect.

Objective 4.5: *Define sensory adaptation and explain why it is helpful.*

Sensory adaptation is a decrease in sensitivity as a result of repeated or constant stimulation. It offers important survival benefits because we can't afford to waste time paying attention to unchanging stimuli.

Objective 4.6: *Explain the gate-control theory of pain perception.*

Our experience of pain depends in part on a "gate" in the spinal cord that either blocks or allows pain signals to pass on to the brain.

Objective 4.7: *What can Helen Keller teach us about sensation and perception?*

Although blind and deaf from an early age, Helen Keller used her remaining senses to achieve greatness, and reminded everyone to fully appreciate all our senses.

Questions

1. The key functions of sensation and perception are, respectively, _____. (a) stimulation and transduction; (b) transmission and coding; (c) reduction and transduction; (d) detection and interpretation; (e) reception and transmission.
2. If a researcher were testing to determine the dimmest light a person could perceive, the researcher would be measuring the _____.
3. Experiments on subliminal perception have _____. (a) supported the existence of the phenomenon, but it has little or no effect on persuasion; (b) shown that subliminal perception occurs only among children and some adolescents; (c) shown that subliminal messages affect only people who are highly suggestible; (d) failed to support the phenomenon
4. Why can't you smell your own perfume or aftershave after a few minutes?
5. The _____ theory of pain helps explain why it sometimes helps to rub or massage an injured thumb. (a) sensory adaptation; (b) gate-control; (c) just noticeable difference; (d) Lamaze

Check your answers in Appendix B.

 Click & Review for additional assessment options: wiley.com/college/huffman

---

How We See and Hear

Many people mistakenly believe that what they see and hear is a copy of the outside world. They are not. Vision and hearing are the result of what our brains create in response to light and sound waves. Three physical properties of light and sound (*wavelength*, *frequency*, and *amplitude*) help determine our sensory experience of them (Figure 4.3).

Pictures, propagated by motion along the fibers of the optic nerves in the brain, are the cause of vision.

ISAAC NEWTON

Vision: The Eyes Have It

Did you know major league batters can hit a 90-mile-per-hour fastball four-tenths of a second after it leaves the pitcher's hand? How can the human eye receive and process information that quickly? To fully appreciate the marvels of sight, we first need to examine the properties of light waves. We will then examine the structure and function of the eye and, finally, the way in which visual input is processed.

Physical properties of vision (light waves and hearing (sound waves)

Wavelength: The distance between successive peaks.

Long wavelength/ low frequency = Reddish colors/ low-pitched sounds

Short wavelength/ high frequency = Bluish colors/ high pitched sound

Wave amplitude: The height from peak to trough.

Low amplitude/ low intensity = Dull colors/ soft sounds

High amplitude/ high intensity = Bright colors/ loud sounds

Range of wavelengths: The mixture of waves.

Small range/ low complexity = Less complex colors/ less complex sounds

Large range/ high complexity = Complex colors/ complex sounds

Figure 4.3 *The physical properties of waves* Both vision and hearing are based on wave phenomena, similar to ocean waves. Standing on a pier you see that waves have a certain distance between them (the *wavelength*), and that they pass by you at intervals. If you counted the number of passing waves in a set amount of time (e.g., 5 waves in 60 seconds), you could calculate the *frequency* (the number of complete wavelengths that pass a point in a given time). Larger wavelength means smaller frequency, and vice versa. Waves also have the characteristic of height (technically called *amplitude*)—some large (an exciting surf ride), and others small. Finally, some waves have a very simple, uniform shape, which would be good for surfing. Others are a combination of waves of different wavelengths and heights, resulting in a wave too irregular for surfing.

Waves of Light

Let's consider how the wave characteristics we discussed with regard to ocean waves (Figure 4.3) apply to light waves. The **wavelength** determines the hue (color) we see. (We could also say the **frequency** determines the color, since they are inversely related. But by convention, we use wavelength when talking about light waves.) The **amplitude** (height) of the light waves determines the intensity or brightness of the light we see. And the complexity or mix of light waves determines whether we see a pure color or one that is a mix of different colors.

Vision is based on light waves, which have the same characteristics as ocean waves, although they are very much smaller and faster moving. Technically, light is waves of electromagnetic energy in a certain range of wavelengths. As you can see in Figure 4.4, there are many different types of electromagnetic waves. Together they form what is known as the *electromagnetic spectrum*. Keep in mind that most wavelengths are invisible to the human eye. Only a small part of the spectrum, known as the *visible spectrum*, can be detected by our visual receptors.

Eye Anatomy and Function

Several structures in the eye are involved in capturing and focusing light and converting it into neural signals to be sent along to the brain. As you study Process Diagram 4.1, carefully note how light waves travel from the outside world and first enter the eye at the *cornea*, which protects the eye and bends the light to provide focus. Directly behind the cornea is the *iris*, which provides the color (usually brown or blue) of the eye. Muscles in the iris allow the *pupil* (or opening) to dilate or constrict in response to light intensity or even to inner emotions. (Recall from Chapter 2 that our pupils dilate when we're in sympathetic arousal and constrict when we're in parasympathetic dominance.) Behind the iris and pupil is the *lens*, which focuses the incoming light rays

Objective 4.8: *What is light?*

Wavelength *Distance between the crests (or peaks) of light or sound waves; the shorter the wavelength, the higher the frequency*

Frequency *How often a light or sound wave cycles (i.e., the number of complete wavelengths that pass a point in a given time)*

Amplitude *Height of a light or sound wave—pertaining to light, it refers to brightness; for sound, it refers to loudness*

Objective 4.9: *Identify the key structures and functions of the eye.*

3 Behind the iris and pupil, the muscularly controlled lens focuses incoming light into an image on the light sensitive *retina*, located on the back surface of the fluid-filled eyeball. Note how the lens reverses the image from right to left and top to bottom when it is projected on to the retina. The brain later reverses the visual input into the final image that we perceive.

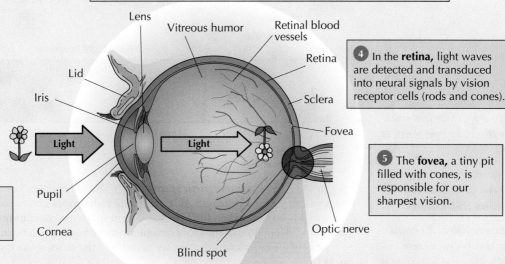

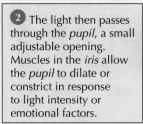

2 The light then passes through the *pupil*, a small adjustable opening. Muscles in the *iris* allow the *pupil* to dilate or constrict in response to light intensity or emotional factors.

1 Light first enters through the *cornea,* which helps focus incoming light rays.

Lens
Vitreous humor
Retinal blood vessels
Lid
Iris
Retina
Sclera
Fovea
Light
Light
Pupil
Cornea
Optic nerve
Blind spot

4 In the **retina,** light waves are detected and transduced into neural signals by vision receptor cells (rods and cones).

5 The **fovea,** a tiny pit filled with cones, is responsible for our sharpest vision.

6 **Rods** are visual receptors that detect white, black, and gray and are responsible for peripheral vision. They are most important in dim light and at night.

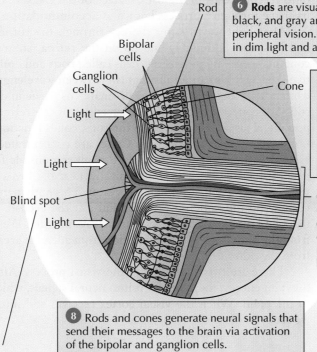

Rod
Bipolar cells
Ganglion cells
Light
Light
Blind spot
Light
Cone

10 After exiting the eye, neural messages travel along the optic nerve to the brain for further processing.

9 At the back of the retina lies an area that has no visual receptors at all and absolutely no vision. This **blind spot** is where blood vessels and nerves enter and exit the eyeball.

7 **Cones** are visual receptors adapted for color, daytime, and detailed vision. They are sensitive to many wavelengths, but each is maximally sensitive to red, green, or blue.

Optic nerve (consists of axons of the ganglion cells that carry messages to the brain)

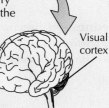

Visual cortex

8 Rods and cones generate neural signals that send their messages to the brain via activation of the bipolar and ganglion cells.

Do you have a blind spot?

Everyone with vision does. To find yours, hold this book about one foot in front of you, close your right eye, and stare at the X with your left eye. Very slowly, move the book closer to you. You should see the worm disappear and the apple become whole.

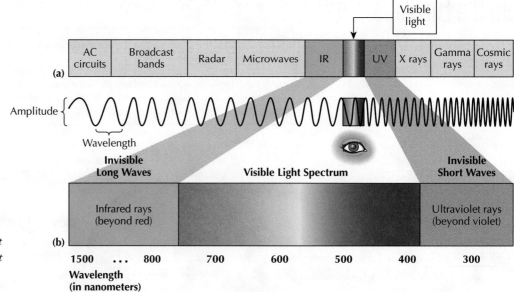

Figure 4.4 **The electromagnetic spectrum** (a) The full spectrum of electromagnetic waves contains very long wavelength AC circuits and radio waves at one end, and relatively short cosmic ray waves at the other. (b) The visible light spectrum contains only the light waves we can see, in the middle of the electromagnetic spectrum. Note how the longer visible wavelengths are the light waves that we see as red, and the shortest are those we perceive as blue. In between are the rest of the colors.

Accommodation *Automatic adjustment of the eye, which occurs when muscles change the shape of the lens so that it focuses light on the retina from objects at different distances*

Retina *Light-sensitive inner surface of the back of the eye, which contains the receptor cells for vision (rods and cones)*

Rods *Visual receptor cells in the retina that detect shades of gray and are responsible for peripheral vision; most important in dim light and at night*

Cones *Visual receptor cells, concentrated near the center of the retina, responsible for color vision and fine detail; most sensitive in brightly lit conditions*

Fovea *Tiny pit in the center of the retina filled with cones; responsible for sharp vision*

Blind Spot *Point at which the optic nerve leaves the eye; contains no receptor cells for vision—thus creating a "blind spot"*

Nearsightedness (Myopia) *Visual acuity problem resulting from the cornea and lens focusing an image in front of the retina*

Farsightedness (Hyperopia) *Visual acuity problem resulting from the cornea and lens focusing an image behind the retina.*

Achievement

Objective 4.10: *Identify common problems with vision.*

onto receptor cells in the back surface of the eyeball. The lens does this by changing its shape through a process known as **accommodation**.

After light waves enter the eye through the cornea and pass through the pupil and lens, they ultimately end up on the **retina**, an area at the back of the eye that contains special light-sensitive cells called **rods** and **cones**, so named for their distinctive shapes. Rods cannot distinguish between wavelengths of light so they only detect white, black, and gray, but they do enable us to see in dim light and at night. Because rods are concentrated at the outer edges of the retina, they're also responsible for peripheral vision. In contrast to the rods, cones function in daylight or well-lit conditions and allow us to see color. Cones are concentrated near the center of the retina around an area called the **fovea**, a tiny pit responsible for our sharpest vision because it's filled entirely with cones. Ironically, near the fovea lies an area that has no visual receptors at all and absolutely no vision. This aptly named **blind spot** is where blood vessels and the optic nerve enter and exit the eyeball. Normally, we are unaware of this blind spot because our eyes are always moving. We fill in the information missing from the blind spot with information from adjacent areas on the retina or with images from the other eye.

There are two final steps in the visual process. After the rods and cones receive the light energy, they convert it into neural signals, which travel along the optic nerve to the brain. When the visual cortex receives and interprets these neural messages, we see!

Problems with Vision

Thoroughly understanding how the eye normally sees also gives us clues for understanding common visual problems, such as **nearsightedness** (*myopia*) and **farsightedness** (*hyperopia*), which can occur at any age (Figure 4.5). Around middle age, most people also begin having trouble reading and focusing on nearby objects because the lens becomes less flexible (*presbyopia*). The good news is that these three common visual problems are generally corrected with glasses, contact lens, and, in some cases, with surgery (LASIK), which reshapes the cornea.

In addition to *myopia*, *hyperopia*, and *presbyopia*, which have to do with the shape of the eyeball or the elasticity of the *lens*, we also commonly experience visual peculiarities related to the eye's *rods* and *cones*. If you are walking outside on a sunny day and then enter a dark house, you will at first be momentarily blinded. A few minutes later, you'll see well enough to make your way around, but it takes 20 to 30 minutes to fully adjust. Why? The *cones* in your eyes, which are responsible for color, daytime, and detailed vision, adapt in the first couple of minutes after you enter the dark house. However, they never become fully functioning because the light intensity is too low. In contrast, the *rods* in your eyes, which are responsible for peripheral and nighttime vision, take longer to adapt, but they're far more sensitive to faint light than the cones.

This process of gradual adjustment is called *dark adaptation*, which involves physical and chemical changes in our eyes that allow us to see well in the dark. The fact that this adaptation is relatively slow-acting is important to keep in mind—especially when you are stepping out of a brightly lit building at night or driving a car from a brightly lit garage into a dark street. However, *light adaptation*, the adjustment that takes place when you go from darkness to a bright setting, happens relatively quickly—thanks to your faster-adapting cones.

Color Vision

Now that we understand how the eye functions we can describe the mysteries of color vision. Humans may be able to discriminate among seven million different hues, and research conducted in many cultures suggests that we all seem to see essentially the same colored world (Davies, 1998). Furthermore, studies of infants old enough to focus and move their eyes show that they are able to see color nearly as well as adults (Knoblauch, Vital-Durand, & Barbur, 2000; Werner & Wooten, 1979).

Although we know color is produced by different wavelengths of light, the actual way in which we perceive color is a matter of scientific debate. Traditionally, there have been two theories of color vision, the *trichromatic* (three-color) theory and the *opponent-process* theory. The **trichromatic theory** was first proposed by Thomas Young in the early nineteenth century. It was later refined by Hermann von Helmholtz and others. Apparently, we have three types of color receptors (cone cells in the retina) that are particularly sensitive to different, but overlapping, ranges of wavelengths. One system is maximally sensitive to blue, another maximally sensitive to green, and another maximally sensitive to red. The proponents of this theory demonstrated that mixing lights of these three colors could yield the full spectrum of colors we perceive (Figure 4.6).

Normal vision. The image is focused on the retina.

Nearsightedness (myopia). The eyeball is too long and incoming light waves focus in *front* of the retina, which blurs the images for distant objects.

Farsightedness (hyperopia). The eyeball is too short and incoming light waves focus *behind* the retina, blurring the image for nearby objects.

Figure 4.5 *Common visual problems*

Achievement

Objective 4.11: *Contrast the trichromatic, opponent-process, and dual process theories of color vision.*

Trichromatic Theory *Theory stating that color perception results from three types of cones in the retina, each most sensitive to either red, green or blue. Other colors result from a mixture of these three.*

Application

Try This Yourself

Testing the Power of Negative Afterimages

Try staring at the dot in the middle of this color-distorted United States flag for 60 seconds. Then stare at a plain sheet of white paper. You should get interesting color aftereffects—red in place of green, blue in place of yellow, and white in place of black. You perceive a "genuine" red, white, and blue U.S. flag. (If you have trouble seeing it, blink, and try again.)

What happened? This is a good example of the *opponent-process theory*. As you stared at the green, black, and yellow colors, the neural systems that process those colors became fatigued. Then when you looked at the plain white paper, which reflects all wavelengths, a reverse *opponent process* occurred. Each fatigued receptor responded with its opposing red, white, and blue colors!

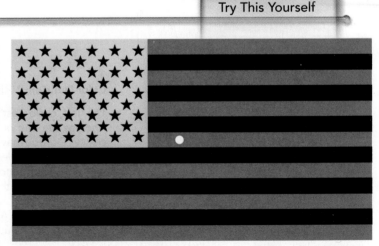

Opponent-Process Theory

Hering's theory that color perception is based on three systems of color opposites— blue–yellow, red–green, and black–white

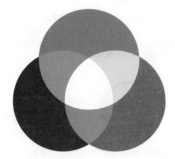

Figure 4.6 *Primary Color* Trichromatic theory found that the three primary colors (red, green, and blue) can be combined to form all colors. For example, a combination of green and red creates yellow.

The **opponent-process theory**, proposed by Ewald Hering later in the nineteenth century, also proposed three color systems. But he suggested that each system responds in an "either-or" fashion. In other words, our visual system can produce messages for either blue or yellow, red or green, and black-or-white. This theory makes a lot of sense because when different-colored lights are combined, people are unable to see reddish greens and bluish yellows. In fact, when red and green lights or blue and yellow lights are mixed in equal amounts, we see white. Further support for Hering's theory comes from the studies of *negative color afterimages*, sensations that remain after a stimulus is removed (see the Try This Yourself on p. 139).

Two Correct Theories

Judging from the discussion so far, it would seem the opponent-process theory is the correct one. Actually, however, both theories are correct (Valberg, 2006). In 1964, George Wald demonstrated that there are indeed three different types of cones in the retina, each with its own type of photopigment. One type of pigment is sensitive to blue light, one is sensitive to green light, and the third is sensitive to red light.

At nearly the same time that Wald was doing his research on cones, R. L. DeValois (1965) was studying electrophysiological recording of cells in the optic nerve and optic pathways to the brain. DeValois discovered cells that respond to color in an opponent fashion in the thalamus. Thus, it appears that both theories have been correct all along. According to the modern *dual-process theory*, color is processed in a *trichromatic* fashion at the level of the retina (in the cones) and in an *opponent* fashion at the level of the optic nerve and the thalamus (in the brain).

Color-Deficient Vision

Complete color blindness is rare. Most "color blind" people can see some colors but not others. People with normal color vision perceive three different colors—red, green, and blue—and are called *trichromats*. However, a small percentage of the population (mostly men) has a genetic deficiency in either the red–green system, the blue–yellow system, or both. Those who perceive only two colors are called *dichromats*. People who are sensitive to only the black–white system are called *monochromats*, and they are totally color blind. If you'd like to test yourself for red–green color blindness, see the Try This Yourself below.

Try This Yourself

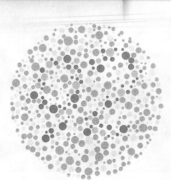

Color-Deficient Vision

The left circle tests for blue-yellow color blindness, whereas the one on the right tests for red–green deficiency. Do you have trouble perceiving the numbers within these two designs? Although we commonly use the term *color blindness*, most problems involve color confusion rather than color blindness. Furthermore, most people who have some color blindness are not even aware of it. A complete color blind assessment would involve the use of 15 stimuli like these two.

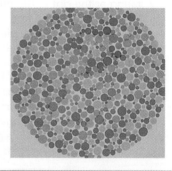

Assessment
CHECK & REVIEW   STOP

How We See

Objective 4.8: *What is light?*

Light is composed of waves of electromagnetic energy of a certain wavelength. The **wavelength** of a light determines its *hue* (color); how often a light or sound wave cycles is known as the **frequency;** and the **amplitude** (height) of a light wave determines its intensity.

Objective 4.9: *Identify the key structures and functions of the eye.*

The function of the eye is to capture light and focus it on visual receptors that convert light energy to neural impulses. Light first enters through the pupil and lens, and then travels through to the retina. Neural impulses generated by the retina are then carried by the optic nerve to the brain. Receptor cells in the **retina** called **rods** are specialized for night vision, whereas **cones** are specialized for color and fine detail.

Objective 4.10: *Identify common problems with vision.*

Nearsightedness (myopia) and *farsightedness* (hyperopia) result from problems with the lens and cornea focusing the image in front or behind the retina. *Presbyopia* occurs when the lens becomes less flexible. *Light adaptation* and *dark adaptation* result from visual peculiarities related to the rods and cones. *Dichromats* and

monochromats are terms related to problems with color perception.

Objective 4.11: *Contrast the trichromatic, opponent-process, and dual-process theories of color vision.*

The **trichromatic theory** proposes three color systems in the retina, each of which is maximally sensitive to blue, green, or red. The **opponent-process theory** also proposes three color systems but holds that each responds in an "either-or" fashion—blue or yellow, red or green, and black or white. According to the modern *dual-process theory*, both theories are correct. The trichromatic system operates at the level of the retina, whereas the opponent-process system occurs in the brain.

Questions

1. Identify the parts of the eye, placing the appropriate letter on the figure:
   - (a) cornea (d) lens   (g) cone
   - (b) iris   (e) retina (h) fovea
   - (c) pupil   (f) rod   (i) blind spot
2. Describe the normal path of light waves through the eye.
3. Explain how the modern dual-process theory explains color vision.
4. Which theory of color vision best explains the negative color afterimage?
   - (a) trichromatic theory;
   - (b) opponent-process theory;
   - (c) both of these theories;
   - (d) neither of these theories.

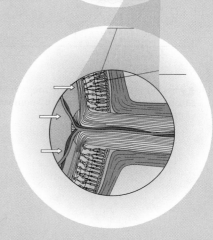

Light

Check your answers in Appendix B.

Click & Review
for additional assessment options:
wiley.com/college/huffman

🖳 Hearing: A Sound Sensation

The sense of hearing, or **audition**, has a number of important functions, ranging from alerting us to dangers to helping us communicate with others. In this section we talk first about the ear's anatomy and function, then about waves of sound, and, finally, about problems with hearing.

Ear Anatomy and Function

The ear has three major sections that function as shown in Process Diagram 4.2. Be sure to carefully study this diagram before going on.

Waves of Sound

Have you heard the philosophical question, "If a tree falls in the forest, and there is no one to hear it, does it make a sound?" The answer depends on whether you define *sound* as a sensation (which requires a receptor such as a person's ear) or as a physical stimulus. As a physical phenomenon, sound is based on pressure waves in air or other mediums. These pressure variations can result from an impact, such as a tree hitting the ground, or from a vibrating object, like a guitar string. Sound waves (like

Achievement
Objective 4.12: *Define audition and identify the three key parts of the ear.*

Audition *Sense of hearing*

Achievement
Objective 4.13: *Briefly explain the physical properties of sound waves.*

Process Diagram 4.2
How the Ear Hears

The **outer ear** (pinna, auditory canal, and eardrum) funnels sound waves to the middle ear. In turn, the three tiny bones of the **middle ear** (hammer, anvil, and stirrup) amplify and send along the eardrum's vibrations to the cochlea's oval window, which is part of the **inner ear** (cochlea, semicircular canals and vestibular sacs). Vibrations from the oval window cause ripples in the fluid-filled **cochlea**, which then cause bending of the hair cells in the cochlea's basilar membrane. The bending hair cells then trigger neural messages that are sent to the brain via the auditory nerve. Finally, when the brain's temporal lobe receives and interprets the neural messages, we hear!

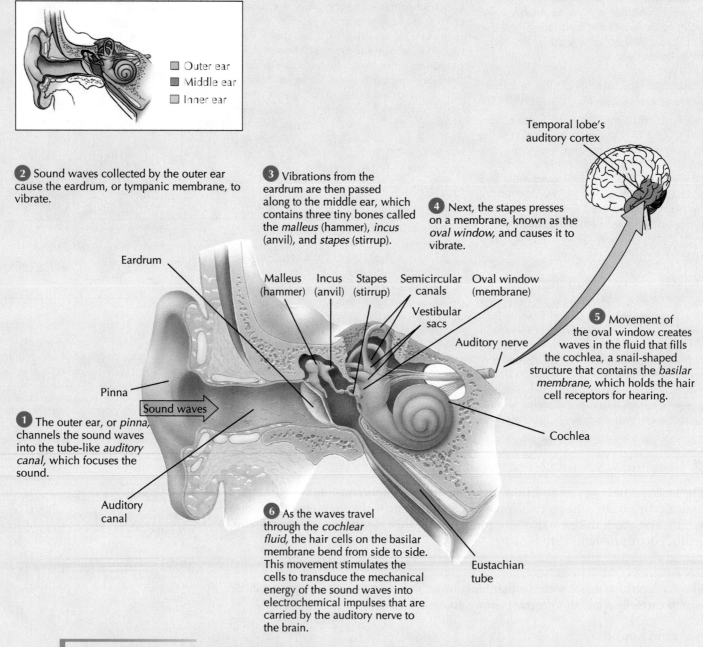

☐ Outer ear
☐ Middle ear
☐ Inner ear

2 Sound waves collected by the outer ear cause the eardrum, or tympanic membrane, to vibrate.

3 Vibrations from the eardrum are then passed along to the middle ear, which contains three tiny bones called the *malleus* (hammer), *incus* (anvil), and *stapes* (stirrup).

4 Next, the stapes presses on a membrane, known as the *oval window*, and causes it to vibrate.

Temporal lobe's auditory cortex

Eardrum

Malleus (hammer) Incus (anvil) Stapes (stirrup) Semicircular canals Oval window (membrane)

Vestibular sacs

Auditory nerve

5 Movement of the oval window creates waves in the fluid that fills the cochlea, a snail-shaped structure that contains the *basilar membrane*, which holds the hair cell receptors for hearing.

Pinna

Sound waves

1 The outer ear, or *pinna*, channels the sound waves into the tube-like *auditory canal*, which focuses the sound.

Cochlea

Auditory canal

6 As the waves travel through the *cochlear fluid*, the hair cells on the basilar membrane bend from side to side. This movement stimulates the cells to transduce the mechanical energy of the sound waves into electrochemical impulses that are carried by the auditory nerve to the brain.

Eustachian tube

Outer Ear *Pinna, auditory canal, and eardrum, which funnel sound waves to the middle ear*

Middle Ear *Hammer, anvil, and stirrup, which concentrate eardrum vibrations onto the cochlea's oval window*

Inner Ear *Cochlea, semicircular canals and vestibular sacs, which generate neural signals sent to the brain*

Cochlea [KOK-lee-uh] *Three-chambered, snail-shaped structure in the inner ear containing the receptors for hearing*

light waves) have the characteristics of *wavelength* (or frequency), *amplitude* (intensity or height), and *complexity* (mix).

When talking about sound waves, we generally use the term *frequency* rather than wavelength. The *frequency* of the sound wave determines the *pitch* of the sound we hear. High-frequency waves produce high notes, and low-frequency waves produce the bass tones. The *amplitude* determines the *loudness* of the sound we hear. And the *complexity* determines what is called *timbre*. A sound could be a pure tone of a single frequency (we seldom hear pure tones, except during a hearing test). Sound can also be a complex mix of frequencies and amplitudes. In this latter case, the timbre is what allows us to distinguish whether a C note is played on a piano or on a trumpet. Timbre is also what allows us to distinguish all the many human voices we hear.

ThinkStock/SUPERSTOCK

For whom the bell tolls Stealthy teenagers now have a biological advantage over their teachers; a cell phone ringtone that sounds at 17 kilohertz—too high for adult ears to detect. The ringtone is an ironic offshoot of another device using the same sound frequency. That invention, dubbed the Mosquito, was designed to help shopkeepers annoy and discourage loitering teens.

Why are some sounds louder than others? It depends on the intensity of the sound waves. Waves with high peaks and low valleys produce loud sounds. Those that are relatively small produce soft sounds. The relative loudness or softness of sounds is measured on a scale of decibels (Figure 4.7).

How do we hear different pitch (low to high)? According to **place theory**, pitch perception corresponds to the particular spot (or place) on the *basilar membrane* that is most stimulated. When we hear a particular sound, it causes the eardrum, the ossicles, and the oval window to vibrate. This vibration produces a "traveling wave" through the fluid in the cochlea. This wave causes some bending of hair cells all along the basilar membrane. But there is a single point where the hair cells are maximally bent for each distinct pitch.

According to **frequency theory**, pitch perception occurs when hair cells along the basilar membrane bend and fire neural messages (action potentials) at the same rate as the frequency of that sound. For example, a sound wave with a frequency of 90 hertz would produce 90 action potentials per second in the auditory nerve.

In sum, both place and frequency theories are correct, but place theory best explains how we hear high-pitched sounds, whereas frequency theory best explains how we hear low-pitched sounds.

Problems with Hearing

There are two major causes of hearing loss. **Conduction deafness**, or middle-ear deafness, results from problems with the mechanical system that conducts sound waves to the cochlea. **Nerve deafness**, or inner-ear deafness, involves damage to the inner ear or auditory nerve. Disease and biological changes associated with aging can cause nerve deafness. But the most common (and preventable) cause of nerve deafness is continuous exposure to loud noise, which can damage hair cells and lead to permanent hearing loss. Even brief exposure to really loud sounds, like a stereo or headphones at full blast, a jackhammer, or a jet airplane engine, can cause permanent nerve deafness (see again Figure 4.7).

△chievement

Objective 4.14: *Describe the place and frequency theories related to hearing.*

Place Theory *Explains that pitch perception is linked to the particular spot on the cochlea's basilar membrane that is most stimulated*

Frequency Theory *Explains that pitch perception occurs when nerve impulses sent to the brain match the frequency of the sound wave*

△chievement

Objective 4.15: *Differentiate between conduction and nerve deafness.*

Conduction Deafness *Middle-ear deafness resulting from problems with transferring sound waves to the inner ear.*

Nerve Deafness *Inner-ear deafness resulting from damage to the cochlea, hair cells, or auditory nerve*

©AP/Wide World Photos

Loud noise and nerve deafness Members of the music group Green Day (and their audience) are potential victims of noise-induced nerve deafness that is irreversible.

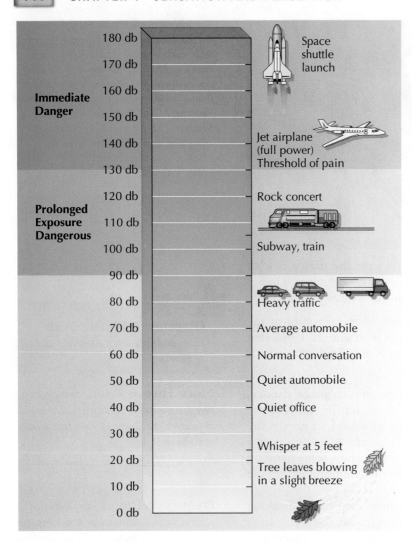

180 db	
170 db	Space shuttle launch
Immediate **Danger** 160 db	
150 db	
140 db	Jet airplane (full power)
130 db	Threshold of pain
120 db	Rock concert
Prolonged **Exposure** **Dangerous** 110 db	
100 db	Subway, train
90 db	
80 db	Heavy traffic
70 db	Average automobile
60 db	Normal conversation
50 db	Quiet automobile
40 db	Quiet office
30 db	
20 db	Whisper at 5 feet
10 db	Tree leaves blowing in a slight breeze
0 db	

Figure 4.7 *How loud is too loud?* The loudness of a sound is measured in *decibels*. The higher a sound's decibel reading, the more damaging it is to the ear. Chronic exposure to loud noise, such as loud music or heavy traffic—or brief exposure to really loud sounds, such as a stereo at full blast, a jackhammer, or a jet engine—can cause permanent nerve deafness. Disease and biological changes associated with aging can also cause nerve deafness.

Because damage to the nerve or receptor cells is almost always irreversible, the only current treatment for nerve deafness is a small electronic device called a *cochlear implant*. If the auditory nerve is intact, the implant bypasses hair cells and directly stimulates the nerve. At present, a cochlear implant produces only a crude approximation of hearing, but the technology is improving. The best bet is to protect your sense of hearing. That means avoiding exceptionally loud noises (rock concerts, jackhammers, stereo head-phones at full blast), wearing earplugs when such situations cannot be avoided, and paying attention to bodily warnings. These warnings include a change in your normal hearing threshold and *tinnitus*, a whistling or ringing sensation in your ears. These are often the first signs of hearing loss. Although normal hearing generally returns after exposure to a loud concert, keep in mind that the risk of permanent damage increases with repeated exposure.

Application

RESEARCH HIGHLIGHT

Perfect (Yet Imperfect) Pitch

By Siri Carpenter

Objective 4.16: *Define and discuss the research on "perfect pitch."*

If someone plunks a random piano key, a tiny minority of people can identify the note based on its sound alone. These people boast perfect pitch, the ability to recognize individual sound frequencies without any external reference. But even these gifted few are not truly perfect. A new study shows that their errors, though subtle, provide a previously unseen glimpse into how bio-logical and environmental factors together shape hearing (Athos et al., 2007).

Absolute pitch, commonly known as *perfect pitch*, results from the confluence of early musical training and a rare genetic endowment. Yet the neurology underly-ing absolute pitch (and its converse, con-genital tone-deafness, or *amusia*) remains obscure. In the new study, researchers identified about 1,000 people who could instantly and effortlessly label each of a series of randomly presented acoustical tones. Results revealed that people with absolute pitch formed a distinct clump of scores, far outside the normal range of ability. "There are people who have this exquisitely perfect pitch-naming ability, and the rest of us are just guessing," says the study's lead author, geneticist Jane

Michael Blann/Riser/Getty Images

Gitschier of the University of California, San Francisco. That fact, combined with previous family heritability studies, sug-gests that, unlike most complex traits, per-fect pitch may be governed by only one gene or at most very few.

The study also exposed an Achilles' heel for people with absolute pitch: the notes surrounding A. Volunteers with perfect pitch were far more likely to mistake a G-sharp for an A than to make any other error. They also perceived A-sharp frequently as A. The researchers suggest that this pattern may reflect the use of the note A as a universal tuning frequency in bands and orchestras. As a result of this disproportionate exposure, the group hypothesizes, the note may act as a "perceptual magnet," fooling the mind into lumping nearby tones into the A category.

In its ongoing research, Gitschier's group is trying to isolate a gene that governs absolute pitch, with the goal of then probing its molecular machinery. Ultimately, Gitschier says, she hopes to use absolute pitch as a platform for better understanding how the brain changes as a result of experience—a phenomenon known as neuroplasticity (see Chapter 2).

The new findings, according to Dennis Drayna, a geneticist at the *National Institute on Deafness and Other Communication Disorders* who studies pitch perception, "open the door to a powerful and precise measure of learning and neuroplasticity within the auditory system. You can look at this only in people who have absolute pitch because those are the only people for whom this learning effect is going to be stable and measurable."

(*Source*: Originally published in *Scientific American Mind*, December 2007/January 2008, p. 11. Reprinted with permission of author, Siri Carpenter.)

Assessment

STOP

CHECK & REVIEW

How We Hear

Objective 4.12: *Define audition and identify the three key parts of the ear.*

The sense of hearing is known as **audition**. The ear has three parts: The **outer ear** conducts sound waves to the **middle ear**, which in turn conducts vibrations to the **inner ear**. Hair cells in the inner ear are bent by a traveling wave in the fluid of the **cochlea** and transduced into neural impulses. The neural message is then carried along the auditory nerve to the brain.

Objective 4.13: *Briefly explain the physical properties of sound waves.*

We hear sounds via *sound waves*, which result from rapid changes in air pressure caused by vibrating objects. The *wavelength* of these sound waves is sensed as the pitch of the sound. The *amplitude* of the waves is perceived as loudness. And the range of sound waves is sensed as timbre, the purity or complexity of the tone.

Objective 4.14: *Describe the place and frequency theories related to hearing.*

Place theory proposes that pitch perception corresponds to the particular spot (or place) on the cochlea's basilar membrane that is most stimulated. **Frequency theory** suggests that pitch perception occurs when nerve impulses sent to the brain match the frequency of the sound waves. Both place and frequency theories are correct, but place theory best explains how we hear high-pitched sounds, whereas frequency theory best explains how we hear low-pitched sounds.

Objective 4.15: *Differentiate between conduction and nerve deafness.*

Conduction deafness results from problems with transferring sound waves to the cochlea, whereas **nerve deafness** involves damage to the inner ear or auditory nerve.

Objective 4.16: *Define and discuss the research on "perfect pitch"?*

Perfect pitch is the ability to recognize individual sound frequencies without any external reference, which results from a rare genetic trait and learning. The fact that these people still make a few consistent mistakes may help researchers better understand *neuroplasticity*, or how the brain changes with experience.

Questions

1. Identify the parts of the ear, placing the appropriate letter on the figure at right.

(a) pinna
(b) tympanic membrane
(c) malleus
(d) incus
(e) stapes
(f) oval window
(g) cochlea

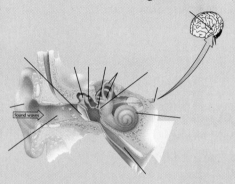

2. Describe the path of sound waves through the ear.
3. Explain how place theory differs from frequency theory.
4. Repeated exposure to loud noise may cause _____ deafness.

Check your answers in Appendix B.

Click & Review
for additional assessment options:
wiley.com/college/huffman

Our Other Senses

Vision and audition may be the most prominent of our senses, but the others—taste, smell, and the body senses—are also important for gathering information about our environment. The enjoyment of a summer's day comes not only from the visual and auditory beauty of the world but also from the taste of a fresh garden tomato, the smell of honeysuckle, and the feel of a warm gentle breeze.

Achievement

Objective 4.17: *Briefly explain the processes of olfaction and gustation.*

Olfaction *Sense of smell*

Pheromones [FARE-oh-mones]
Airborne chemicals that affect behavior, including recognition of family members, aggression, territorial marking, and sexual mating

Gustation *Sense of taste*

▢ Smell and Taste: Sensing Chemicals

Smell and taste are sometimes referred to as the *chemical senses* because they involve *chemoreceptors* that are sensitive to certain chemical molecules. Have you noticed how food seems bland when your nose is blocked by a cold and you cannot smell your food? Smell and taste receptors are located near each other and often interact so closely that we have difficulty separating the sensations.

Olfaction

Our sense of smell, or **olfaction**, is remarkably useful and sensitive. We possess about 1,000 different types of olfactory receptors (Process Diagram 4.3), and we can detect over 10,000 distinct smells (floral, musky, rotten, and so on). The nose is more sensitive to smoke than any electronic detector, and—through practice—blind people can quickly recognize others by their unique odors.

Does smell affect sexual attraction? Some research on **pheromones**—compounds found in natural body scents that may affect various behaviors—supports the idea that these chemical odors increase sexual behaviors in humans (Savic, Berglund, & Lindström, 2007; Thornhill et al., 2003). Other findings question the results, suggesting that human sexuality is far more complex than that of other animals—and more so than perfume advertisements would have us believe.

Gustation

Today, the sense of taste, **gustation**, may be the least critical of our senses. In the past, however, it probably contributed more directly to our survival. The major function of taste, aided by smell, is to help us avoid eating or drinking harmful substances. Humans have five major taste sensations—sweet, sour, salty, bitter, and *umami*. You are undoubtedly familiar with the first four. But *umami* (which means "delicious" or "savory") has only recently been added to the list. Umami is a separate taste and type of taste receptor that is sensitive to *glutamate* (the taste of protein) (Chandrashekar et al., 2006; McCabe & Rolls, 2007). Glutamate is found in meats, meat broths, and monosodium glutamate (MSG).

Like smell receptors, taste receptors respond differentially to the varying shapes of food and liquid molecules. The major taste receptors (or *taste buds*) are clustered on

Assessment

VISUAL QUIZ

AfriPics

Why Do Professional Wine Judges Sniff the Wine Instead of Just Tasting It?

Answer: Sniffing draws more smell molecules into the nose and helps speed their circulation. Professional wine judges also know that the mouth is important because smells reach the nasal cavity by wafting up the throat like smoke in a chimney. Furthermore, most of what we perceive as taste or flavor is a combination of both smell and taste, which explains why this wine tasting judge will use both his nose and his mouth.

Process Diagram 4.3

How The Nose Smells

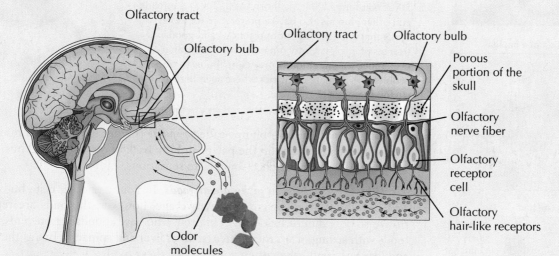

Olfactory tract

Olfactory bulb

Olfactory tract

Olfactory bulb

Porous portion of the skull

Olfactory nerve fiber

Olfactory receptor cell

Olfactory hair-like receptors

Odor molecules

1 The sensation of smell begins when we inhale airborne molecules though the nose and/or an opening in the back of the throat. These airborne odor molecules travel to the *olfactory epithelium,* a membrane lining the roof of the nasal cavity.

2 Hair-like receptor cells on the olfactory membrane make contact with the inhaled air, and the odor molecules bind to appropriately shaped receptors, like a *lock and key.*

3 After olfactory receptor cells are stimulated, a neural impulse is sent to the brain's olfactory bulb, located just under the frontal lobes.

4 In the olfactory bulb, each odorous chemical appears to create various patterns of activation, and the sense of smell is coded accordingly.

5 From the olfactory bulb, messages then travel to other areas of the brain, including the *temporal lobe* and *limbic system*. The temporal lobe is responsible for our conscious recognition of smells; the limbic system in involved in emotion and memory, which explains why smells often generate emotion-laden memories.

**Surface of the tongue
(magnified about 50 times)**

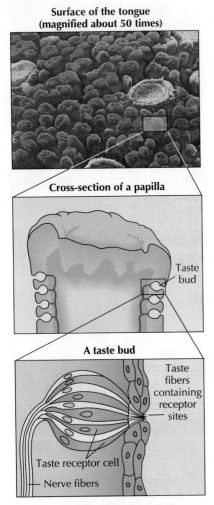

Cross-section of a papilla

Taste
bud

A taste bud

Taste
fibers
containing
receptor
sites

Taste receptor cell

Nerve fibers

Figure 4.8 *Taste sensation* When
liquids enter the mouth, or food is
chewed and dissolved, the fluid runs
over the papillae (the lavender circular
areas) and into their pores to the taste
buds, which contain the receptors for
taste.

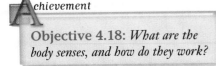chievement

Objective 4.18: *What are the
body senses, and how do they work?*

Figure 4.9 *Is this emotional response to bitterness
hard-wired?* Infants and newborn babies show the
same facial response as an adult to a bitter taste. This
shared avoidance response suggests an evolutionary
function because many plants that taste bitter contain
toxic chemicals, and animals are more likely to survive if they avoid bitter-tasting plants (Cooper et al.,
2002; Kardong, 2008; Skelhorn et al., 2008). Humans
and other animals also have a preference for sweet
foods that are generally nonpoisonous and good
sources of energy. Unfortunately, this evolutionary
preference for sweet foods now contributes to obesity
problems in affluent countries where such high-calo-
rie foods are easily available.

our tongues within little bumps called *papillae* (Figure 4.8). A small number of taste
receptors are also found in the palate and the back of our mouths. Thus, even people
without a tongue experience some taste sensations.

Why are children so picky about food? In young people, taste buds die and are
replaced about every seven days. As we age, however, the buds are replaced more
slowly, so taste diminishes. Thus, children, who have abundant taste buds, often dislike
foods with strong or unusual tastes (such as liver and spinach). But as they grow older
and lose taste buds, they often come to like these foods.

Some pickiness is also related to learning. Many food and taste preferences result
from childhood experiences and cultural influences. Many Japanese children eat raw
fish, and some Chinese children eat chicken feet as part of their normal diet. American
children might consider these foods "yucky." However, most American children love
cheese, which children in many other cultures find repulsive.

Pickiness also relates to the fact that the sense of taste normally enables human
and nonhuman animals to discriminate between foods that are safe to eat and foods
that are poisonous (Figure 4.9).

The Body Senses: More Than Just Touch

Imagine for a moment that you are an Olympic downhill skier, eagerly awaiting the
starting signal that will begin your once-in-a-lifetime race for the gold medal. What
senses will you need to manage the subtle and ever-changing balance adjustments
required for Olympic-level skiing? How will you make your skis carve the cleanest,
shortest, fastest line from start to finish? What will enable your arms, legs, and trunk
to work in perfect harmony so that you can record the shortest time and win the
gold? The senses that will allow you to do all this, and much more, are the *body senses*.
They tell the brain how the body is oriented, where and how the body is moving, the
things it touches or is touched by, and so on. These senses include the *skin senses*, the
vestibular sense, and *kinesthesia*.

The Skin Senses

The skin senses are vital. Skin not only protects the internal organs but also provides
the brain with basic survival information. With nerve endings in the various layers of
skin, our skin senses tell us when a pot is dangerously hot, when the weather is freezing
cold, and when we have been hurt. Researchers have "mapped" the skin by applying
probes to all areas of the body. Mapping shows there are three basic skin sensations:
touch (or pressure), temperature, and pain. Receptors for these sensations occur in
various concentrations and depths in the skin. For example, touch (pressure) receptors
are maximally concentrated on the face and fingers and minimally in the back and legs.

As your hands move over objects, pressure receptors register the indentations created in the skin, allowing perception of texture. For people who are blind, this is the principle underlying their ability to learn to read the raised dots that constitute Braille.

The relationship between the types of sensory receptors and the different sensations is not clear. It used to be thought that each receptor responded to only one type of stimulation. But we now know that some receptors respond to more than one. For example, because sound waves are a type of air pressure, our skin's pressure receptors also respond to certain sounds. And itching, tickling, and vibrating sensations seem to be produced by light stimulation of both pressure and pain receptors.

In conducting studies on temperature receptors, researchers have found that the average square centimeter of skin contains about six cold spots where cold can be sensed, and one or two warm spots where warmth can be felt. Interestingly, we don't seem to have separate "hot" receptors (Craig & Bushnell, 1994). See Figure 4.10.

The Vestibular Sense

The *vestibular sense* is the sense of body orientation and position with respect to gravity and three-dimensional space. In other words, it is the sense of balance. Even the most routine activities—riding a bike, walking, or even sitting up—would be impossible without this sense (Carlson, 2008; Lackner & Di Zio, 2005). The vestibular apparatus is located in the inner ear and is composed of the vestibular sacs and the semicircular canals. The *semicircular canals* provide the brain with balance information, particularly information about rotation of the head. As the head moves, liquid in the canals moves and bends hair cell receptors. At the end of the semicircular canals are the *vestibular sacs*, which contain hair cells sensitive to the specific angle of the head—straight up and down or tilted. Information from the semicircular canals and the vestibular sacs is converted to neural impulses, which are then carried to the appropriate section of the brain.

What causes motion sickness? Information from the vestibular sense is used by the eye muscles to maintain visual fixation and, sometimes, by the body to change body orientation. If the vestibular sense gets overloaded or becomes confused by boat, airplane, or automobile motion, the result is often dizziness and nausea. Random versus expected movements also are more likely to produce motion sickness. Thus, automobile drivers are better prepared than passengers for upcoming movement and are less likely to feel sick. Motion sickness also seems to vary with age. Infants are generally immune, children between ages 2 and 12 years have the highest susceptibility, and the incidence declines in adulthood.

Kinesthesia

Kinesthesia (from the Greek word for "motion") is the sense that provides the brain with information about bodily posture and orientation, as well as bodily movement. Unlike the receptors for sight, hearing, smell, taste, and balance, which are clumped together in one organ or area, kinesthetic receptors are found throughout the muscles, joints, and tendons of the body. As we sit, walk, bend, lift, turn, and so on, our kinesthetic receptors respond by sending messages to the brain. They tell which muscles are being contracted and which relaxed, how our body weight is distributed, and where our arms and legs are in relation to the rest of our body. Without these sensations, we would literally have to watch every step or movement we make.

The power of the skin senses Babies are highly responsive to touch, in part because of the density of their skin receptors.

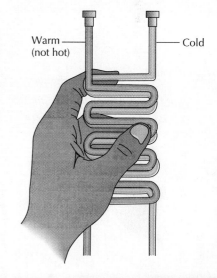

Warm (not hot) — — Cold

Figure 4.10 ***How do we experience "hot"?*** Researchers use an instrument called a "heat grill"—two pipes twisted together, one containing warm water and the other cold. If you grasp both pipes, you experience intense heat because both warm and cold receptors are activated simultaneously. We do not have separate "hot" receptors.

Kinesthesia *Sensory system for body posture, orientation, and bodily movement*

How does he do it? This surfer's finely tuned vestibular and kinesthetic senses allow him to ride his board in perfect balance, constantly compensating for the changing shape of the wave.

A*ssessment*

CHECK & REVIEW STOP

Our Other Senses

Objective 4.17: *Briefly explain the processes of olfaction and gustation.*

The sense of smell (**olfaction**) and the sense of taste (**gustation**) are called the chemical senses and are closely interrelated. The receptors for olfaction are at the top of the nasal cavity. The receptors for gustation are located primarily on the tongue and are sensitive to five basic tastes: salty, sweet, sour, bitter, and umami.

Objective 4.18: *What are the body senses and how do they work?*

The body senses include the skin senses, the vestibular sense, and **kinesthesia**. The skin senses detect touch or pressure, temperature, and pain. The vestibular

apparatus is located in the inner ear and supplies balance information. The kinesthetic sense provides the brain with information about body posture and orientation, as well as body movement. The kinesthetic receptors are spread throughout the body in muscles, joints, and tendons.

Questions

1. Human and nonhuman animals may be affected by chemical scents found in natural body odors, which are called _____.
2. The skin senses include _____.
   (a) pressure; (b) pain; (c) warmth and cold; (d) all of these
3. The weightlessness experienced by space travelers from zero gravity has its

greatest effect on the _____ senses.
   (a) visceral; (b) reticular; (c) somasthetic; (d) vestibular
4. Receptors located in the muscles, joints, and tendons of the body provide _____ information to maintain bodily posture, orientation, and movement.

Check your answers in Appendix B.

Click & Review
for additional assessment options:
wiley.com/college/huffman

A*chievement*

Objective 4.19: *What are illusions and why are they important?*

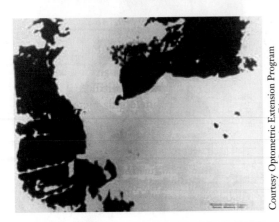

Courtesy Optometric Extension Program Foundation, Santa Ana, CA

Figure 4.11a *What is it?*

Illusion *False or misleading perception*

A*chievement*

Objective 4.20: *Describe the selection process and its three key factors—selective attention, feature detectors, and habituation.*

Understanding Perception

At this point, we are ready to move from sensation and the major senses to perception. Keep in mind, however, that the boundary between the two is ambiguous. Look, for example, at Figure 4.11a. What do you see? Most people see splotches of light and dark, but they perceive no real pattern. If you stare long enough, your brain will try to organize the picture into recognizable shapes or objects, as it does when you lie on your back outdoors and gaze at the clouds on a summer's day. Have you seen the image in the photo yet? If not, look at Figure 4.11b on page 151. Before you *perceived* the cow, you *sensed* only light and dark splotches. Only when you could select relevant splotches and organize them into a meaningful pattern were you able to interpret them as the face of a cow.

Normally, our perceptions agree with our sensations, but there are times when they do not. This results in an **illusion**. Illusions are false or misleading perceptions that can be produced by actual physical distortions, as in desert mirages, or by errors in the perceptual process, as in the illusions shown in Figures 4.12 and 4.13. Besides being amusing, illusions provide psychologists with a tool for studying the normal process of perception (e.g., Bridgeman & Hoover, 2008; Duemmler et al., 2008).

■ Selection: Extracting Important Messages

The first step in perception is *selection*—choosing where to direct our attention. Three major factors are involved in the act of paying attention to some stimuli in our environment and not to others: *selective attention*, *feature detectors*, and *habituation*.

Selective Attention

In almost every situation, there is an excess of sensory information, but the brain manages to sort out the important messages and discard the rest (Arieh & Marks, 2008;

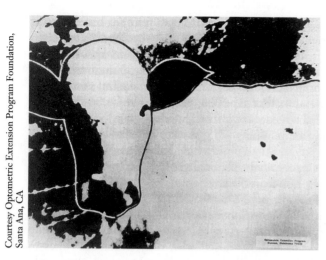

Courtesy Optometric Extension Program Foundation, Santa Ana, CA

Figure 4.11b ***It's a cow!*** Now go back to Figure 4.11a and you will easily perceive a cow.

Figure 4.12 ***The horizontal-vertical illusion*** Which is longer, the horizontal (flat) or the vertical (standing) line? People living in areas where they regularly see long straight lines, such as roads and train tracks, perceive the horizontal line as shorter because of their environmental experiences.

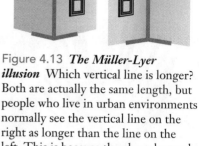

Figure 4.13 ***The Müller-Lyer illusion*** Which vertical line is longer? Both are actually the same length, but people who live in urban environments normally see the vertical line on the right as longer than the line on the left. This is because they have learned to make size and distance judgments from perspective cues created by right angles and horizontal and vertical lines of buildings and streets. They perceive the right figure as a distant corner and thus compensate for its distance by judging it as longer.

Study Tip

Be careful not to confuse illusion with hallucination or delusion [Chapters 5 and 14]. Hallucinations are imaginary sensory perceptions that occur without an external stimulus, such as hearing voices during a schizophrenic episode or seeing "pulsating flowers" after using LSD [lysergic acid diethylamide] and other hallucinogenic drugs. Delusions refer to false beliefs, often of persecution or grandeur, which also may accompany drug or psychotic experiences.

Posner & Rothbart, 2007). As you sit reading this chapter, you may be ignoring sounds from another room or the discomfort of the chair you're sitting on. This process is known as **selective attention** (Figure 4.14).

Feature Detectors

The second major factor in selection is the presence of specialized neurons in the brain called **feature detectors** (or *feature analyzers*) that respond only to certain sensory information. In 1959, researchers discovered specialized neurons in the optic nerve of a frog. They called these receptors "bug detectors" because they respond

Selective Attention *Filtering out and attending only to important sensory messages*

Feature Detectors *Specialized neurons that respond only to certain sensory information*

Ryan McVay/Photodisc Green/Getty

Figure 4.14 ***Selective attention*** When you are in a group of people, surrounded by various conversations, you can still select and attend to the voices of people you find interesting. Another example of selective attention occurs with the well-known "cocktail party phenomenon." Have you noticed how you can suddenly pick up on a nearby group's conversation if someone in that group mentions your name?

only to moving bugs (Lettvin et al., 1959). Later researchers found feature detectors in cats that respond to specific lines and angles (Hubel & Wiesel, 1965, 1979).

Similar studies with humans have found feature detectors in the temporal and occipital lobes that respond maximally to faces. Problems in these areas can produce a condition called *prosopagnosia* (*prosopon* means "face" and *agnosia* means "failure to know") (Barton, 2008; Riddoch et al., 2008; Schiltz et al., 2006). Interestingly, people with prosopagnosia can recognize that they are looking at a face. But they cannot say whose face is reflected in a mirror, even if it is their own or that of a friend or relative.

Certain basic mechanisms for perceptual selection are thus built into the brain. However, a certain amount of interaction with the environment is apparently necessary for feature detector cells to develop normally. One well-known study demonstrated that kittens raised in a cylinder with only vertically or horizontally striped walls developed severe behavioral and neurological impairments (Blakemore & Cooper, 1970) (Figure 4.15). When "horizontal cats"—those raised with only horizontal lines in their environment—were removed from the cylinder and allowed to roam, they could easily jump onto horizontal surfaces. But they had great difficulty negotiating objects with vertical lines, such as chair legs. The reverse was true for the "vertical cats." They could easily avoid table and chair legs but never attempted to jump onto horizontal structures. Examination of the visual cortex of these cats showed they had failed to develop their potential feature detectors for either vertical or horizontal lines.

Habituation

Another physiological factor important in selecting only certain sensory data is **habituation**. The brain seems "prewired" to pay more attention to changes in the environment than to stimuli that remain constant. We quickly **habituate** (or respond less) to predictable and unchanging stimuli. For example, when you buy a new CD, you initially listen carefully to all the songs. Over time, your attention declines and you can play the entire CD and not really notice it. This may not matter with CDs—we can always replace them when we become bored. But this same habituation phenomenon also applies to your friends and love life. And people aren't as easily replaced. Have you noticed how attention and compliments from a stranger are almost always more exciting and "valuable" than those from long-time friends and lovers? Unfortunately, some people misinterpret and overvalue this new attention. Some may even leave good relationships, not realizing that they will soon *habituate* to the new person. (Understanding the dangers of habituation is another payoff for studying psychology!)

How does habituation differ from sensory adaptation? Habituation is a perceptual process that occurs in the brain. Sensory adaptation occurs when sensory receptors (in the skin, eyes, ears, and so on) actually decrease the number of sensory messages they send to the brain. Sensory adaptation occurs when you first put on your shoes in the morning. Pressure/touch receptors in your feet initially send multiple messages to your brain. But with time they *adapt* and send fewer messages. You also habituate and your brain "chooses to ignore" the fact that you're wearing shoes. You only notice when something changes—when you break a buckle or shoelace, or get a blister from new shoes.

When given a wide variety of stimuli to choose from, we automatically select stimuli that are *intense, novel, moving, contrasting,* and *repetitious.* Parents and teachers often use these same attention-getting principles. But advertisers and politicians have spent millions of dollars developing them into a fine art. The next time you're watching TV, notice the commercial and political ads. Are they louder or brighter than the regular program (intensity)? Do they use talking cows to promote California cheese (novelty)? Is the promoted product or candidate set in *favorable* contrast to the competition? No need to ask about repetition. This is the foundation of almost all commercial and political ads (Figure 4.16).

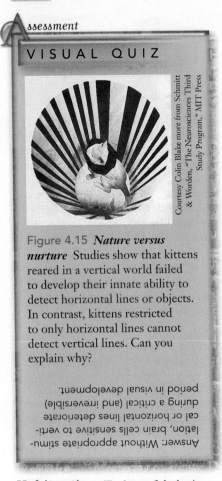
Habituation *Tendency of the brain to ignore environmental factors that remain constant*

Habituation *Thanks to habituation, these three girls may "choose to ignore" their initially painful braces. (Sensory adaptation may have also occurred. Over time pressure sensors send fewer messages to the brain.)*

VEER Stephen Simpson/Photonica/Getty Images

Erik Dreyer/Stone/Getty Images

Figure 4.16 *Psychology at work—repetition sells!* As you may have noticed from commercials on TV, obnoxious advertising doesn't seem to deter consumers. For sheer volume of sales, the question of whether or not you like the ad is irrelevant. If it gets your attention, that's all that matters!

Assessment

CHECK & REVIEW STOP

Selection

Objective 4.19: *What are illusions and why are they important?*

Illusions are false or misleading perceptions that can be produced by actual physical distortions, as in desert mirages, or by errors in perception. These errors allow psychologists insight into normal perceptual processes.

Objective 4.20: *Describe the selection process and its three key factors— selective attention, feature detectors, and habituation.*

The selection process allows us to choose which of the billions of separate sensory messages will eventually be processed.

Selective attention refers to the process of filtering out and attending only to important sensory messages. **Feature detectors** are specialized brain cells that distinguish between different sensory inputs. We **habituate** to unchanging stimuli and only pay attention when stimuli change in intensity, novelty, and location.

Questions

1. Explain how illusions differ from delusions and hallucinations.
2. Specialized cells in the brain called _____ respond only to certain types of sensory information.
3. Explain why "horizontal cats" can jump only onto horizontal surfaces.

4. You write a reminder of an appointment on a Post-it and stick it on the door, where you see it every day. A month later, you forget your appointment because of your brain's tendency to ignore constant stimuli. This is known as _____. (a) sensory adaptation; (b) selective perception; (c) habituation; (d) selective attention

Check your answers in Appendix B.

Click & Review
for additional assessment options:
wiley.com/college/huffman

Organization: Form, Constancy, and Depth

Having selected incoming information (our previous section), we must organize it into patterns and principles that will help us understand the world. Raw sensory data are like the parts of a watch. They must be assembled in a meaningful way before they are useful. We organize and perceive sensory data in terms of *form*, *constancy*, and *depth*.

Form Perception

Look at the first drawing in Figure 4.17. What do you see? Can you draw a similar object on a piece of paper? This is known as an "impossible figure." The second part

Achievement

Objective 4.21: *Describe the Gestalt laws of perceptual organization.*

wiley.com/
college/
huffman

Figure 4.17 *What is the point of "impossible figures"?*

(a)

(b)

M.C. Escher/Cordon Art b.v.

Answer: When you first glance at figure (a) and the famous painting by M. C. Escher in (b), you detect specific features of the stimuli and judge them as sensible figures. But as you try to sort and organize the different elements into a stable, well-organized whole, you realize they don't add up—they're illogical or "impossible." The point of the illustration is that there is no one-to-one correspondence between your actual sensory input and your final perception. The same stimuli looked at from another perspective can lead to very different perceptions.

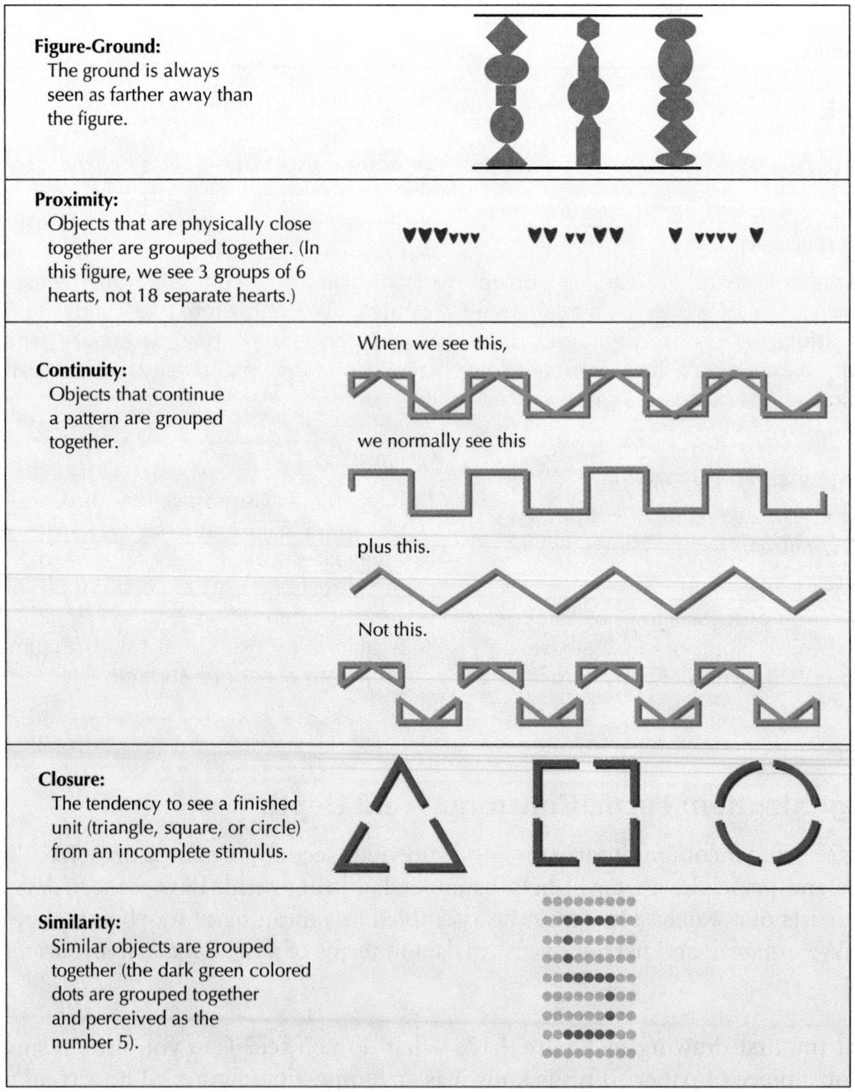

Figure 4.18 *Gestalt principles of organization* Gestalt principles are based on the notion that we all share a natural tendency to force patterns onto whatever we see. Although the examples of the Gestalt principles in this figure are all visual, each principle applies to other modes of perception as well. For example, the Gestalt principle of *contiguity* cannot be shown because it involves nearness in time, not visual nearness. You also may have experienced *aural figure and ground effects* at a movie or a concert when there was a conversation going on close by and you couldn't sort out what sounds were the background and what you wanted to be your focus.

Another good example of a Gestalt principle not shown in this figure is *visual closure*, which happens every time you watch television. The picture on the TV screen appears to be a solid image, but it's really a very fast stream of small dots being illuminated one by one, "painting" tiny horizontal lines down the screen one line at a time. Your brain closes the momentary blank gaps on the screen.

Figure-Ground:
The ground is always seen as farther away than the figure.

Proximity:
Objects that are physically close together are grouped together. (In this figure, we see 3 groups of 6 hearts, not 18 separate hearts.)

Continuity:
Objects that continue a pattern are grouped together.

When we see this,

we normally see this

plus this.

Not this.

Closure:
The tendency to see a finished unit (triangle, square, or circle) from an incomplete stimulus.

Similarity:
Similar objects are grouped together (the dark green colored dots are grouped together and perceived as the number 5).

of the figure shows a painting by M. C. Escher, a Dutch painter who created striking examples of perceptual distortion. Although drawn to represent three-dimensional objects or situations, the parts don't assemble into logical wholes. Like the illusions studied earlier, impossible figures and distorted painting help us understand perceptual principles—in this case, the principle of *form organization*.

Gestalt psychologists were among the first to study how the brain organizes sensory impressions into a whole. (The German word *gestalt* means "whole" or "pattern.") Rather than perceiving its discrete parts as separate entities, the Gestaltists emphasized the importance of organization and patterning in enabling us to perceive the whole stimulus. The Gestaltists proposed several laws of organization that specify how people perceive form (Figure 4.18). The most fundamental Gestalt principle of organization is our tendency to distinguish between *figure* and *ground*. For example, while reading this sentence, your eyes receive only sensations of black lines and white paper. Your brain then organizes these sensations into letters and words perceived against a backdrop of white pages. The letters constitute the *figure*, and the pages are the *ground*. Interestingly, the boundary between figure and ground is sometimes so vague that we have difficulty perceiving which is which. This is known as a *reversible figure* (see Figure 4.19).

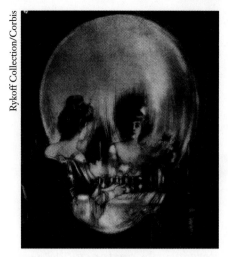

Figure 4.19 ***Reversible figure*** This so-called reversible figure demonstrates alternating figure–ground relations. It can be seen as a woman looking in a mirror or as a skull, depending on what you see as figure or ground.

Achievement
GENDER & CULTURAL DIVERSITY

Are the Gestalt Laws Universally True?

Gestalt psychologists conducted most of their work with formally educated people from urban European cultures. A.R. Luria (1976) was one of the first to question whether their laws held true for all participants, regardless of their education and cultural setting. Luria recruited a wide range of participants living in what was then the USSR. He included Ichkeri women from remote villages (with no formal education), collective farm activists (who were semiliterate), and female students in a teachers' school (with years of formal education).

Luria found that when presented with the stimuli shown in Figure 4.20, the formally trained female students were the only ones who identified the first three shapes by their categorical name of "circle." Whether circles were made of solid lines, incomplete lines, or solid colors, they called them all circles. However, participants with no formal education named the shapes according to the objects they resembled. They called a circle a watch, plate, or moon, and referred to the square as a mirror, house, or apricot-drying board. When asked if items 12 and 13 from Figure 4.20 were alike, one woman answered, "No, they're not alike. This one's not like a watch, but that one's a watch because there are dots" (p. 37).

Apparently, the Gestalt laws of perceptual organization are valid only for people who have been schooled in geometrical concepts. But an alternative explanation for

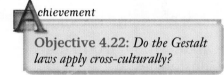

Achievement

Objective 4.22: *Do the Gestalt laws apply cross-culturally?*

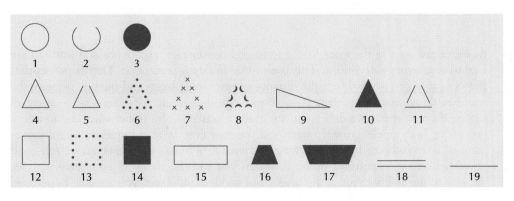

Figure 4.20 ***Luria's stimuli*** When you see these shapes, you readily identify them as circles, triangles, and other geometric forms. According to cross-cultural research, this is due to your formal educational training. If you were from a culture without formal education, you might identify them instead as familiar objects in your environment—"the circle is like the moon."

Luria's findings has also been suggested. Luria's study, as well as most research on visual perception and optical illusions, relies on two-dimensional presentations—either on a piece of paper or projected on a screen. It may be that experience with pictures and photographs (not formal education in geometrical concepts) is necessary for learning to interpret two-dimensional figures as portraying three-dimensional forms. Westerners who have had years of practice learning to interpret two-dimensional drawings of three-dimensional objects may not remember how much practice it took to learn the cultural conventions about judging the size and shape of objects drawn on paper (Matsumoto & Juang, 2008; Shiraev & Levy, 2007).

Perceptual Constancies

Now that we have seen how *form perception* contributes to organization, we will examine **perceptual constancies**. As noted earlier with sensory adaptation and habituation, we are particularly alert to change. However, we also manage to perceive a great deal of consistency in the environment. Without perceptual constancy, our world would be totally chaotic. Things would seem to grow as we got closer to them, to change shape as our viewing angle changed, and to change color as light levels changed. The four best-known constancies are size, shape, color, and brightness (Concept Diagram 4.2).

Achievement

> **Objective 4.23:** *What are perceptual constancies, and why are they important?*

Perceptual Constancy *Tendency for the environment to be perceived as remaining the same even with changes in sensory input*

Assessment

STOP

CHECK & REVIEW

Organization—Form and Constancies

Objective 4.21: *Describe the Gestalt laws of perceptual organization.*

The Gestalt psychologists set forth laws explaining how people perceive form. The most fundamental principle is the distinction between figure and ground. Other visual laws include proximity, continuity, closure, and similarity.

Objective 4.22: *Do the Gestalt laws apply cross-culturally?*

Some believe they only apply to cultures formally educated in geometrical concepts, while others say the laws reflect experience with two-dimensional figures portraying three-dimensional forms.

Objective 4.23: *What are perceptual constancies, and why are they important?*

Through the **perceptual constancies** of *size*, *shape*, *color*, and *brightness*, we are able to perceive a stable environment, even though the actual sensory information we receive may be constantly changing. These constancies develop from prior experiences and learning.

Questions

1. Name the Gestalt principle that is being described: (a) You see two adults and two children sitting on a blanket at the beach and perceive them as a family. (b) You see three people with long hair and assume they are all women. (c) You see a circle even though part of its curve is erased in three spots.

2. As a flock of Canadian geese flies overhead in its familiar V formation, the geese are seen as _____ and the sky as _____. (a) continuity, a closure; (b) a sensation, perception; (c) figure; ground; (d) ground, figure

3. The principle of _____ is at work when, as your brother walks away from you, you don't perceive him to be shrinking.

4. The principles of _____ allow us to see a white blouse as white both in sunlight and in shade.

Check your answers in Appendix B.

Click & Review
for additional assessment options:
wiley.com/college/huffman

Depth Perception

Achievement

> **Objective 4.24:** *How do we perceive depth, and why are binocular and monocular cues important?*

Depth Perception *The ability to perceive three-dimensional space and to accurately judge distance*

As we've just seen in the examples of form and constancies, experience and learning are vital to organizing perceptions. This is also true in depth perception. **Depth perception** allows us to accurately estimate the distance of perceived objects and thereby perceive the world in three dimensions. It is possible to judge the distance of objects with nearly all senses. If a person enters a dark room and walks toward you, his or her voice and footsteps get louder, body smells grow stronger, and you may even be able to feel the slight movement of air from his or her approaching movement. In most cases, however, we rely most heavily on vision to perceive distance. When you add the ability to accurately perceive distance to the ability to judge the height and width of an object, you are able to perceive

Concept Diagram 4.2
Four Perceptual Constancies

1. **Size Constancy** Our retinal image of the couple in the foreground is much larger than the trees and mountains behind them. Thanks to size constancy, however, we readily perceive them as people of normal size. Interestingly, size constancy, like all constancies, appears to develop from learning and experience. Studies of people who have been blind since birth, and then have their sight restored, find they have little or no size constancy (Sacks, 1995).

2. **Shape Constancy** As the coin is rotated, it changes shape, but we still perceive it as the same coin because of shape constancy.

An American ophthalmologist, Adelbert Ames, demonstrated the power of shape and size constancies by creating a distorted room, which is known as the *Ames room illusion*. In this photo, the young boy on the right appears to be much larger than the woman on the left. The illusion is so strong that when a person walks from the left corner to the right, the observer perceives the person to be "growing," even though that is not possible. How can this be?

The illusion is based on the unusual construction of the room, and our perceptual constancies have falsely filled in the wrong details. To the viewer, peering through the peephole, the room appears to be a normal cubic-shaped room. But the true shape is trapezoidal: the walls are slanted and the floor and ceiling are at an incline. Because our brains mistakenly assume the two people are the same distance away, we compensate for the apparent size difference by making the person on the left appear much smaller.

Several Ames room sets were used in *The Lord of the Rings* film series to make the heights of the hobbits appear correct when standing next to Gandalf.

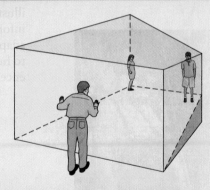

3. **Color Constancy** and 4. **Brightness Constancy** We perceive the dog's fur in this photo as having a relatively constant hue (or color) and brightness despite the fact that the wavelength of light reaching our retinas may vary as the light changes.

wiley.com/
college/
huffman

E.S.P. Institute

"What do you mean you didn't know that we were having a pop quiz today?"

knew which cards were correct, they could unknowingly give participants cues through subtle facial gestures.

The most important criticism of both experimental and casual claims of ESP is their lack of stability and replicability—a core requirement for scientific acceptance. Findings in ESP are notoriously "fragile" (Hyman, 1996). A long history of scientific research, including a meta-analysis of 30 studies using scientific controls, such as double-blind procedures and maximum security and accuracy in record keeping, has found absolutely no evidence of ESP (Milton & Wiseman, 1999, 2001; Valeo & Beyerstein, 2008). As one critic pointed out, positive ESP results usually mean "Error Some Place" (Marks, 1990).

If ESP is so unreliable, why do so many people believe in it? Our fast-paced technological world and rapid scientific progress lead many people to believe that virtually anything is possible. And *possible* is often translated as *probable*. Because ESP is by nature subjective and extraordinary, some people also tend to accept it as the best explanation for out-of-the-ordinary experiences. Moreover, as mentioned earlier in the chapter, our motivations and interests often influence our perceptions. Because research participants and researchers are strongly motivated to believe in ESP, they *selectively attend* to things they want to see or hear.

A large number of people want to believe in ESP, as evidenced by the popularity of *The Medium*, children's fairy tales, comic books, and popular movies. It seems that release from natural law is one of the most common and satisfying human fantasies. When it comes to ESP, people eagerly engage in a process known as "the willing suspension of disbelief." We seem to have a hard time accepting our finiteness, and a belief in psychic phenomena offers an increased feeling of infinite possibilities.

Extrasensory Perception (ESP)

Perceptual, or "psychic," abilities that supposedly go beyond the known senses (e.g., telepathy, clairvoyance, precognition, and psychokinesis)

Application

CRITICAL THINKING

Problems with Believing in Extrasensory Perception (ESP)

Objective 4.27: *Identify four forms of faulty reasoning behind ESP.*

The subject of extrasensory perception (ESP) often generates not only great interest but also strong emotional responses. And when individuals feel strongly about an issue, they sometimes fail to recognize the faulty reasoning underlying their beliefs. Belief in ESP is particularly associated with illogical, noncritical thinking. This exercise gives you a chance to practice your critical thinking skills as they apply to ESP. Begin by studying the following types of faulty reasoning:

1. **Fallacy of positive instances.** *Noting and remembering events that confirm personal expectations and beliefs (the "hits") and ignoring nonsupportive evidence (the "misses").* Remembering the time the palmist said you would receive a call in the middle of the night (a "hit") but ignoring that she also said that you had three children (a "miss").

2. **Innumeracy.** *Failing to recognize chance occurrences for what they are owing to a lack of training in statistics and probabilities.* Unusual events are misperceived as statistically impossible (such as predicting a president's illness).

And extraordinary explanations, such as ESP, are seen as the logical alternative.

3. **Willingness to suspend disbelief.** *Refusing to engage one's normal critical thinking skills because of a personal need for power and control.* Although few people would attribute a foreign country's acquisition of top-secret information to ESP, some of these same individuals would willingly believe that a psychic could help them find their lost child.

4. **The "vividness" problem.** *Remembering and preferring vivid information.* Human information processing and memory storage and retrieval are often based on the initial "vividness" of the information. Sincere personal testimonials, theatrical demonstrations, and detailed anecdotes easily capture our attention and tend to be remembered better than rational, scientific descriptions of events. This is the heart of most stories about extraterrestrial visitations.

Using these four types of faulty reasoning, decide which one best describes each of the following. Although more than one type may be applicable, enter only one number beside each report. Comparing your answers with your classmates' and friends' answers will further sharpen your critical thinking skills.

ACTIVE LEARNING

_____ John hadn't thought of Paula, his old high school sweetheart, for years. Yet one morning he woke up thinking about her. He was wondering what she looked like and whether she was married now, when suddenly the phone rang. For some strange reason, he felt sure the call was from Paula. He was right. John now cites this call as evidence for his personal experience with extrasensory perception.

_____ A psychic visits a class in introductory psychology. He predicts that out of this class of 23 students, two individuals will have birthdays on the same day. When a tally of birthdays is taken, his prediction is supported and many students leave class believing that the existence of ESP has been supported.

_____ A National League baseball player dreams of hitting a bases-loaded triple. Two months later, during the final game of the World Series, he gets this exact triple and wins the game. He informs the media of his earlier dream and the possibility that ESP exists.

_____ A mother sitting alone in her office at work suddenly sees a vivid image of her home on fire. She calls home and awakens the sitter. The sitter then notices smoke coming under the door and quickly extinguishes the fire. The media attribute the mother's visual images to ESP.

Depth Perception, Interpretation, and ESP

Objective 4.24: *How do we perceive depth and why are binocular and monocular cues important?*

Depth perception allows us to accurately estimate the distance of perceived objects and thereby perceive the world in three dimensions. But how do we perceive a three-dimensional world with two-dimensional receptors called eyes? There are two major types of cues: **binocular cues**, which require two eyes, and **monocular cues**, which require only one eye. Two binocular cues are **retinal disparity** and **convergence**. Monocular cues include *linear perspective, interposition, relative size, texture gradient, aerial perspective, light and shadow, accommodation,* and *motion parallax.*

Objective 4.25: *What factors influence how we interpret sensations?*

Interpretation, the final stage of perception, can be influenced by *perceptual adaptation,* **perceptual set**, and *frame of reference.*

Objective 4.26: *What is ESP and why is it so controversial?*

Extrasensory perception (ESP) is the supposed ability to perceive things that go beyond the normal senses. ESP research has produced "fragile" results, and critics condemn its lack of experimental control and replicability.

Objective 4.27: *Identify four forms of faulty reasoning behind ESP.*

Belief in ESP may reflect the *fallacy of positive instances, innumeracy, willingness to suspend disbelief,* and the "vividness" problem.

Questions

1. The visual cliff is an apparatus designed to study _____ in young children and animals. (a) color discrimination; (b) shape constancy; (c) depth perception; (d) monocular vision

2. Since Jolly Roger, the pirate, lost one eye in a fight, he can no longer use ___ as a cue for the perception of depth and distance. (a) accommodation; b) retinal disparity; (c) motion parallax; (d) aerial perspective

3. George Stratton was able to cope with an upside-down world thanks to _____.

4. The supposed ability to read other people's minds is called _____, perceiving objects or events that are inaccessible to the normal senses is known as _____, predicting the future is called _____, and moving or affecting objects without touching them is known as _____.

5. A major criticism of studies that indicate the existence of ESP is that they _____.

Check your answers in Appendix B.

Click & Review
for additional assessment options:
wiley.com/college/huffman

Assessment

KEY TERMS

*To assess your understanding of the **Key Terms** in Chapter 4, write a definition for each (in your own words), and then compare your definitions with those in the text.*

bottom-up processing (p. 129)
perception (p. 128)
sensation (p. 128)
top-down processing (p. 129)

Understanding Sensation
absolute threshold (p. 131)
coding (p. 130)
difference threshold (p. 131)
gate-control theory (p. 133)
psychophysics (p. 131)
sensory adaptation (p. 133)
sensory reduction (p. 130)
subliminal (p. 132)
synesthesia (p. 130)
transduction (p. 130)

How We See and Hear
accommodation (p. 138)
amplitude (p. 136)
audition (p. 141)
blind spot (p. 138)
cochlea (p. 142)
conduction deafness (p. 143)
cones (p. 138)

farsightedness (hyperopia) (p. 138)
fovea (p. 138)
frequency (p. 136)
frequency theory (p. 143)
inner ear (p. 142)
middle ear (p. 142)
nearsightedness (myopia) (p. 138)
nerve deafness (p. 143)
opponent-process theory (p. 140)
outer ear (p. 142)
place theory (p. 143)
retina (p. 138)
rods (p. 138)
trichromatic theory (p. 139)
wavelength (p. 136)

Our Other Senses
gustation (p. 146)
kinesthesia (p. 149)
olfaction (p. 146)
pheromones [FARE-oh-mones] (p. 146)

Understanding Perception
binocular cues (p. 158)
convergence (p. 159)

depth perception (p. 156)
extrasensory perception (ESP) (p. 162)
feature detectors (p. 151)
habituation (p. 152)
illusion (p. 150)
monocular cues (p. 158)
perceptual constancy (p. 156)
perceptual set (p. 161)
retinal disparity (p. 159)
selective attention (p. 151)

Achievement

WEB RESOURCES

Huffman Book Companion Site
wiley.com/college/huffman
This site is loaded with free Interactive Self-Tests, Internet Exercises, Glossary and Flashcards for key terms, web links, Handbook for Non-Native Speakers, and other activities designed to improve your mastery of the material in this chapter.

wiley.com/college/huffman

Understanding Sensation

General Definitions

- **Sensation:** Detecting, converting, and transmitting raw sensory data to the brain.
- **Perception:** Selecting, organizing, and interpreting sensory information.
- **Bottom-up processing:** Data driven processing moving from parts to the whole.
- **Top-down processing:** Conceptually driven processing moving from the whole to the parts.

Processing

- *Receptors:* Body cells that detect and respond to stimulus energy.
- **Transduction:** Converting receptor energy into neural impulses that are sent to the brain.
- **Coding:** Converting sensory input into specific sensations (sight, sound, touch, etc.).
- **Sensory reduction:** Filtering and analyzing of sensations before messages are sent to the cortex.

Measuring the Senses

- **Psychophysics:** Studies link between physical characteristics of stimuli and our sensory experience of them.

Thresholds

- **Absolute threshold:** Smallest *magnitude* of a stimulus we can detect.
- **Difference threshold:** Smallest *change* in a stimulus we can detect.

Adaptation

- **Sensory adaptation:** Decreased sensory response to continuous stimulation.
- **Gate-control theory:** "Gate" in spinal cord blocks or allows pain signals to pass on to brain.

How We See and Hear

Vision: Light is a form of energy and part of the *electromagnetic spectrum*.

Eye Anatomy and Function

- *Cornea:* Clear bulge at front of eye, where light enters.
- *Pupil:* Hole through which light passes into eye.
- *Iris:* Colored muscles that surround pupil.
- *Lens:* Elastic structure that bulges and flattens to focus an image on retina (a process called **accommodation**).
- **Retina:** Contains visual receptor cells, called **rods** (for night vision) and **cones** (for color vision and fine detail).
- **Fovea:** Pit in the retina responsible for sharp vision.
- **Blind Spot:** Point where optic nerve leaves the eye which has no visual receptors.

The eye's function is to capture light waves and focus them on receptors in the retina, which convert light energy to neural impulses that travel to the brain.

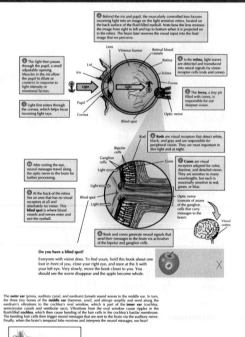

Hearing: **Audition** (or hearing) occurs via *sound waves*, which result from rapid changes in air pressure caused by vibrating objects.

Ear Anatomy and Function

- **Outer ear:** Pinna, auditory canal, and eardrum.
- **Middle ear:** Hammer, anvil, and stirrup.
- **Inner ear:** Oval window, cochlea, and basilar membrane.

The ear's function is to capture sound waves and focus them on receptors in the cochlea, which convert sound energy to neural impulses that travel to the brain.

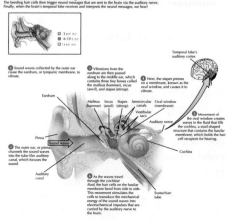

Our Other Senses

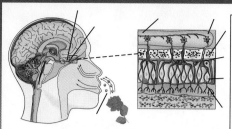

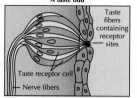

A taste bud

Smell and Taste

Olfaction (sense of smell) Receptors located at the top of the nasal cavity.

Gustation (sense of taste) Five basic tastes: salty, sweet, sour, bitter, and umami

The Body Senses

* *Skin sense*s detect touch (pressure), temperature, and pain.
* *Vestibular sense* (or sense of balance) results from receptors in inner ear.
* **Kinesthesia** (body posture, orientation, and body movement) results from receptors in muscles, joints, and tendons.

Understanding Perception

Selection

1. **Selective attention:** Filtering out and attending only to important sensory messages.

2. **Feature detectors:** Specialized brain cells that respond only to specific sensory information.

3. **Habituation:** Brain's tendency to ignore environmental factors that remain constant.

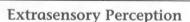

Organization

1. *Form:* Gestalt principles of *figure and ground, proximity, continuity, closure,* and *similarity.*

2. **Constancy:** *Size, shape, color,* and *brightness*

3. **Depth perception:** Binocular (2 eyes) **cues** involve **retinal disparity** and **convergence. Monocular** (one eye) **cues** include *linear perspective, interposition,* and so on.

Interpretation

1. *Perceptual adaptation:* Brain adjusts to changed environment

2. **Perceptual set:** Readiness to perceive based on expectations.

3. *Frame of Reference:* Based on context of situation.

Extrasensory Perception

Extrasensory perception (ESP) is the supposed ability to perceive things through unknown and unproven "extra" senses.

5

States of Consciousness

Did you see *The Diving Bell and the Butterfly?* This 2007 movie was based on the true story of Jean-Dominique Bauby, the highly successful and charismatic editor of French *Elle* magazine and author of the international best seller on which this movie was based. In his early 40s, Bauby suffered a massive stroke that left him almost completely paralyzed with a rare condition known as "locked-in syndrome." He regained vision and hearing, but he could not move or speak. Trapped inside this horrific isolation, Bauby's mind remained alert and aware, trying to make contact with the world outside. With the help of a speech therapist, he later learned to communicate, and eventually dictated an entire book, by "winking" one letter at a time.

What if Bauby had not been able to open or move his left eye? If he couldn't communicate, would he still be "conscious"? People commonly use the term *consciousness*, but what exactly does it mean? Is it simple awareness? What would it be like to be unaware? How can we study the contents of our consciousness when the only tool of discovery is the object itself?

In the late nineteenth century, when psychology first became a scientific discipline separate from philosophy, it defined itself as the "study of human consciousness." But the nebulousness of the area of study eventually led to great dissatisfaction within the field. One group, the behaviorists, led by John Watson, believed that *behavior*, not consciousness, was the proper focus of the new science.

More recently, psychology has renewed its original interest in consciousness, as a result of research in cognitive and cultural psychology. One current psychological definition of **consciousness** is fairly simple: *an organism's awareness of its own self and surroundings* (Damasio, 1999). And thanks to modern technological advances, scientists can now study brain activity during normal, everyday consciousness, as well as **alternate states of consciousness (ASCs)**, which include sleep, dreaming, chemically induced changes from psychoactive drugs, daydreaming, and so on.

In this chapter, we begin with a general overview of consciousness, and then go on to see how consciousness changes with circadian rhythms, sleep, and dreams. We also look at psychoactive drugs and their effects on consciousness. Finally, we explore alternative routes to altered consciousness through meditation and hypnosis.

Consciousness *Organism's awareness of its own self and surroundings (Damaslo, 1999)*

Alternate States of Consciousness (ASCs) *Mental states, other than ordinary waking consciousness, found during sleep, dreaming, psychoactive drug use, hypnosis, and so on*

The Kobal Collection, Ltd.

▶ **Understanding Consciousness**

▶ **Sleep and Dreams**

The Power of Circadian Rhythms

PSYCHOLOGY AT WORK
  Dangers of Sleeping on the Job!

Stages of Sleep
Why Do We Sleep and Dream?

GENDER & CULTURAL DIVERSITY
  Dream Variations and Similarities

CRITICAL THINKING/ACTIVE LEARNING
  Interpreting Your Dreams

Sleep Disorders

PSYCHOLOGY AT WORK
  Self-Help for Sleep Problems

▶ **Psychoactive Drugs**

  Understanding Psychoactive Drugs

RESEARCH HIGHLIGHT
  Addictive Drugs as the Brain's "Evil Tutor"
Four Major Categories of Psychoactive Drugs

PSYCHOLOGY AT WORK
  Club Drug Alert!

▶ **Healthier Ways To Alter Consciousness**

Getting "High" on Meditation
The Mystery of Hypnosis

Application

WHY STUDY PSYCHOLOGY?

Did you know...

▶ Virtually everyone dreams while they're sleeping?

▶ Approximately two-thirds of all American adults suffer from sleep problems?

▶ Sleep deprivation and shift work are key contributors to industrial and automobile accidents?

▶ People who suffer from narcolepsy may fall instantly asleep while walking, talking, or driving a car?

▶ People cannot be hypnotized against their will?

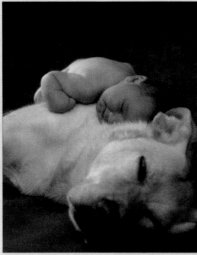

Paul Kuroda/SUPERSTOCK

▶ Addictive drugs "teach" the brain to want more and more of the destructive substances?

▶ Even small initial doses of cocaine can be fatal because they interfere with the electrical signals of the heart?

▶ An amount of LSD the size of an aspirin tablet is enough to produce psychoactive effects in over 3000 people?

▶ Since the beginning of civilization, people of all cultures have used and abused psychoactive drugs?

Achievement

Objective 5.1: *Define and describe consciousness and alternate states of consciousness (ASCs).*

The centermost processes of the brain with which consciousness is presumably associated are simply not understood. They are so far beyond our comprehension that no one I know of has been able to imagine their nature.

ROGER W. SPERRY

Understanding Consciousness

William James, the first American psychologist, likened consciousness to a stream that's constantly changing, yet always the same. It meanders and flows, sometimes where the person wills and sometimes not. However, through the process of *selective attention* (Chapter 4), we can control our consciousness by deliberate concentration and full attention. For example, at the present moment you are (I hope) fully awake and concentrating on the words on this page. At times, however, your control may weaken, and your stream of consciousness may drift to thoughts of a computer you want to buy, your job, or an attractive classmate.

In addition to meandering and flowing, your "stream of consciousness" also varies in depth. Your level of consciousness is not an all-or-nothing phenomenon—conscious or unconscious. Instead, it exists along a continuum. As you can see in Process Diagram 5.1, this continuum from high awareness and sharp, focused alertness at one extreme, to middle levels of awareness such as daydreaming, to unconsciousness and coma at the other extreme.

Achievement

Objective 5.2: *Contrast controlled versus automatic processing.*

Controlled Processes *Mental activities requiring focused attention that generally interfere with other ongoing activities*

Controlled versus Automatic Processes

Consciousness exists on a continuum, and it also involves both *controlled* and *automatic* processes. When you're working at a demanding task or learning something new, such as how to drive a car, your consciousness is at the high end of the continuum. These **controlled processes** demand focused attention and generally interfere with other ongoing activities. Have you ever been so absorbed during an exam that you completely forgot your surroundings until the instructor announced, "Time is up," and asked for your paper? This type of focused attention is the hallmark of controlled processes.

Process Diagram 5.1
Where Does Consciousness Reside?

One of the oldest philosophical debates is the *mind–body problem*. Is the "mind" (consciousness and other mental functions) fundamentally different from matter (the body)? How can a supposedly nonmaterial mind influence a physical body and vice versa? Most neuropsychologists today believe the mind *is* the brain and *consciousness* involves an activation and integration of several parts of the brain. But two aspects of consciousness, *awareness* and *arousal*, seem to rely on specific areas. Awareness generally involves the *cerebral cortex*, particularly the frontal lobes. Arousal generally results from *brain-stem activation* (Culbertson, 2008; Revonsuo, 2006; Thompson, 2007).

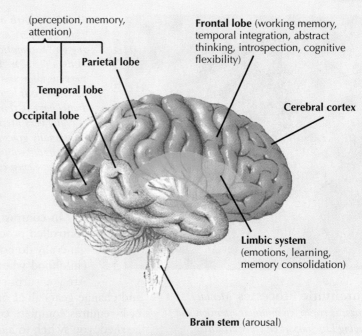

(perception, memory, attention)

Parietal lobe

Temporal lobe

Occipital lobe

Frontal lobe (working memory, temporal integration, abstract thinking, introspection, cognitive flexibility)

Cerebral cortex

Limbic system (emotions, learning, memory consolidation)

Brain stem (arousal)

Levels of Awareness

High Awareness → Middle Awareness → Low Awareness

CONTROLLED PROCESSES
Require focused, maximum attention (e.g., studying for an exam, learning to drive a car).

AUTOMATIC PROCESSES
Require minimal attention (e.g., walking to class while talking on a cell phone, listening to your boss while daydreaming).

SUBCONSCIOUS
Below conscious awareness (e.g., subliminal perception, sleeping, dreaming)

NO AWARENESS
Biologically based lowest level of awareness (e.g., head injuries, anesthesia, coma); also the *unconscious mind* (a Freudian concept discussed in Chapter 13) reportedly consisting of unacceptable thoughts and feelings too painful to be admitted to consciousness)

Photodisc/Getty Images

Stockbyte Platinum/Getty Images

MM Productions/©Corbis

Getty Images

David Madison/Duomo Photography, Inc

Alternate States of Consciousness (ASCs): Can exist on many levels of awareness, from high awareness to no awareness (e.g., drugs, sensory deprivation, sleep, dreaming, etc.)

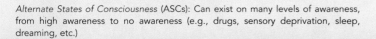

wiley.com/
college/
huffman

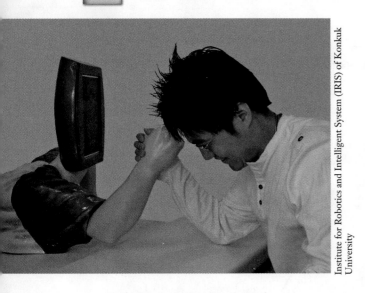

Automatic Processes *Mental activities requiring minimal attention and having little impact on other activities*

Problems with automatic processing? *Automatic processes are generally helpful. However, there are times when we are wrestling with our inner robots and operating on "automatic pilot" and don't want to be. Consider the problems of novelist Colin Wilson (1967): "When I first learned to type, I had to do it painfully and with much nervous wear and tear. But at a certain stage a miracle occurred, and this complicated operation was learned by a useful robot that I conceal in my subconscious mind. Now I only have to think about what I want to say; my robot secretary does the typing. He is really very useful. He also drives the car for me, speaks French (not very well), and occasionally gives lectures at American universities. [My robot] is most annoying when I am tired, because then he tends to take over most of my functions without even asking me. I have even caught him making love to my wife" (p. 98).*

In contrast to the high awareness and focused attention required for controlled processes, **automatic processes** require minimal attention and generally do not interfere with other ongoing activities. Think back to your childhood when you first marveled at your parents' ability to drive a car. Are you surprised that you can now effortlessly steer a car, work the brakes, and change gears all at one time with little or no focused attention? Learning a new task requires complete concentration and *controlled processing*. Once that task is well learned, you switch to *automatic processing* (Abernethy et al., 2007).

CHECK & REVIEW

Understanding Consciousness

Objective 5.1: *Define and describe consciousness and alternate states of consciousness (ASCs).*

Most of our lives are spent in normal, waking **consciousness**, an organism's awareness of its own self and surroundings. However, we also spend considerable time in various **alternate states of consciousness (ASCs)**, such as sleep and dreaming, daydreams, and states induced by psychoactive drugs, hypnosis, and meditation.

Consciousness has always been difficult to study and define. William James described it as a "flowing stream." Modern researchers emphasize that consciousness exists along a continuum.

Objective 5.2: *Contrast controlled versus automatic processing.*

Controlled processes, which require focused attention, are at the highest level of the continuum of awareness. **Automatic processes**, which require minimal attention, are found in the middle. Unconsciousness and coma are at the lowest level.

Questions

1. _____ is (are) best defined as an organism's awareness of its own self and surroundings. (a) Alternate states of consciousness (ASCs); (b) Consciousness; (c) States of consciousness; (d) Selective attention
2. Where does consciousness reside?
3. Controlled processes require _____ attention, whereas automatic processes need _____ attention.
4. As you read this text, you should _____. (a) be in an alternate state of consciousness; (b) employ automatic processing; (c) let your stream of consciousness take charge; (d) employ controlled processing

Check your answers in Appendix B.

 Click & Review
for additional assessment options:
wiley.com/college/huffman

Sleep and Dreams

Having explored the definition and description of everyday, waking consciousness, we now turn to two of our most common alternate states of consciousness (ASCs)—sleep and dreaming. These ASCs are fascinating to both scientists and the general public. Why are we born with a mechanism that forces us to sleep and dream for approximately a third of our lives? How can an ASC that requires reduced awareness and responsiveness to our environment be healthy? What are the functions and causes of sleep and dreams?

Objective 5.3: *List six common myths about sleep.*

Common Myths About Sleep and Dreams

Before reading on, test your personal knowledge of sleep and dreaming by reviewing the common myths below.

- *Myth: Everyone needs 8 hours of sleep a night to maintain sound mental and physical health.* Although most of us average 7.6 hours of sleep a night, some people get by on an incredible 15 to 30 minutes. Others may need as much as 11 hours (Doghramji, 2000; Maas, 1999).
- *Myth: It is easy to learn complicated things, like a foreign language, while asleep.* Although some learning can occur during the lighter stages (1 and 2) of sleep, the processing and retention of this material is minimal (Aarons, 1976; Ogilvie, Wilkinson, & Allison, 1989). Wakeful learning is much more effective and efficient.
- **Myth: Some people never dream.** In rare cases, adults with certain brain injuries or disorders do not dream (Solms, 1997). But otherwise, virtually all adults regularly dream. Even people who firmly believe they never dream report dreams if they are repeatedly awakened during an overnight study in a sleep laboratory. Children also dream regularly. For example, between ages 3 and 8, they dream during approximately 20 to 28 percent of their sleep time (Foulkes, 1982, 1993). Apparently, almost everyone dreams, but some people don't remember their dreams.
- Myth: Dreams last only a few seconds. Research shows that some dreams seem to occur in "real time." For example, a dream that seemed to last 20 minutes probably did last approximately 20 minutes (Dement & Wolpert, 1958).
- *Myth: When genital arousal occurs during sleep, it means the sleeper is having a sexual dream.* When sleepers are awakened during this time, they are no more likely to report sexual dreams than at other times.
- *Myth: Dreaming of dying can be fatal.* This is a good opportunity to exercise your critical thinking skills. Where did this myth come from? Has anyone ever personally experienced and recounted a fatal dream? How would we scientifically prove or disprove this belief?

The Power of Circadian Rhythms: Sleep and the 24-Hour Cycle

To understand sleep and dreaming, we need to first explore the topic of **circadian rhythms**. Most animals have adapted to our planet's cycle of days and nights by developing a pattern of bodily functions that wax and wane over each 24-hour period. Our sleep–wake cycle, alertness, moods, learning efficiency, blood pressure, metabolism, pulse rate, and other responses all follow circadian rhythms (Leglise, 2008; Sack et al., 2007; Oishi et al., 2007). Usually, these activities reach their peak during the day and their low point at night (Figure 5.1).

Objective 5.4: *What are circadian rhythms and how do they affect our lives?*

Circadian [sir-KADE-ee-un] **Rhythms** *Biological changes that occur on a 24-hour cycle (circa = "about" and dies = "day")*

PSYCHOLOGY AT WORK

Dangers of Sleeping on the Job!

Disruptions in circadian rhythms lead to increased fatigue, decreased concentration, sleep disorders, depression, and other health problems (James, Cermakian, & Boivin, 2007; Lader, 2007; Salvatore et al., 2008). As a student, you may find it comforting to know that your late-night study sessions and full- or part-time night jobs help explain your fatigue and other complaints. Less reassuring is the knowledge that 20 percent of employees in the United States (primarily in the fields of health care, data processing, and transportation) have rotating work schedules that create many of the same problems (Maas, 1999). Although many physicians, nurses, police, and others who have rotating work schedules manage to function well, studies do find that shift work and sleep deprivation lead to decreased concentration and productivity—and increased accidents (Dembe et al., 2006; Papadelis et al., 2007; Yegneswaran & Shapiro, 2007).

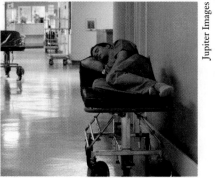

Jupiter Images

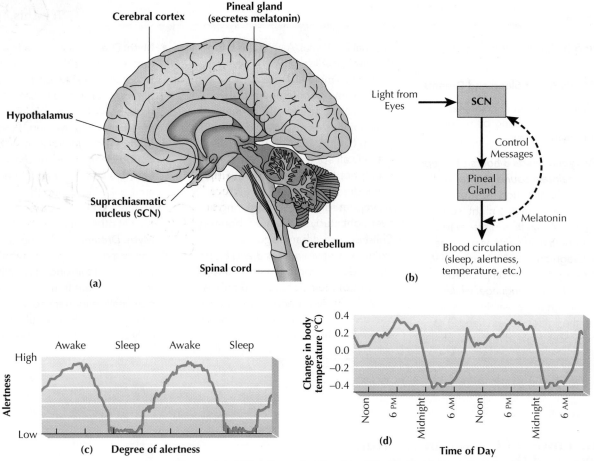

Figure 5.1 *What Controls Circadian Rhythms?* (a) Circadian rhythms are regulated by a part of the hypothalamus called the *suprachiasmatic nucleus* (SCN). (b) The SCN receives information about light and darkness from the eyes and then sends control messages to the *pineal gland*, which releases *melatonin*—a hormone thought to influence sleep, alertness, and body temperature. Like other feedback loops in the body, the level of melatonin in the blood is sensed by the SCN, which then can modify the output of the pineal to maintain the "desired" level. (c) and (d) Note how our degree of alertness and core body temperature rise and fall in similar ways.

For example, in a major review of Japanese near-collision train incidents, 82 percent took place between midnight and morning (Charland, 1992). Also, some of the worst recent disasters, including the Union Carbide chemical accident in Bhopal, India, the nuclear power plant disaster in Chernobyl, and the Alaskan oil spill from the *Exxon Valdez*, occurred during the night shift. And official investigations of airline crashes often cite pilot shift work and sleep deprivation as possible contributing factors.

While catastrophic accidents can sometimes be traced to simple, but unusual, coincidences, we need to recognize that shift workers may be fighting a dangerous battle with their own circadian rhythms. What can be done to help? Some research shows that workers find it easier to adjust when their schedules are shifted from days to evenings to nights (8–4, 4–12, 12–8). This may be because it's easier to go to sleep later than normal rather than earlier. Also, when shifts are rotated every three weeks, rather than every week, productivity increases and accidents decrease. Finally, some research suggests that brief naps for shift workers (or anyone) can help increase performance and learning potential (Purnell, Feyer, & Herbison, 2002; Tietzel & Lack, 2001).

Not only can rotating work schedules disrupt circadian cycles, but so can flying across several time zones. Have you ever taken a long airline flight and felt fatigued, sluggish, and irritable for the first few days after arriving? If so, you experienced symptoms of *jet lag*. Like rotating shift work, jet lag correlates with decreased alertness, decreased mental agility, exacerbation of psychiatric disorders, and over-all reduced efficiency (Dawson, 2004; Leglise, 2008; Morgenthaler et al., 2007; Sack et al., 2007). Jet lag also tends to be worse when we fly eastward rather than westward. This is because our bodies adjust more readily to going to sleep later, rather than earlier.

Sleep Deprivation

Disruptions in circadian cycles due to shift work and jet lag can have serious effects. But what about long-term sleep deprivation? History tells us that during Roman times and in the Middle Ages, sleep deprivation was a form of torture. Today, the armed forces of the United States and other countries sometimes use loud, blaring music and noise to disrupt their enemy's sleep.

Scientifically exploring the effects of severe sleep loss is limited by obvious ethical concerns. Research is also hampered by practical considerations. For example, after about 72 hours without sleep, research participants unwillingly slip into brief, repeated periods of "microsleep" lasting a few seconds at a time. To complicate things further, sleep deprivation increases stress, making it difficult to separate the effects of sleep deprivation from those of stress.

Despite these problems, sleep researchers have documented several hazards related to sleep deprivation that coincide with the previously mentioned effects of disrupted circadian cycles. Sleep deprivation is correlated with significant mood alterations, decreased self-esteem, reduced concentration and motivation, increased irritability, lapses in attention, reduced motor skills, and increased cortisol levels (a sign of stress) (Dembe et al., 2006; Mirescu et al., 2006; Papadelis et al., 2007;

SIGNS YOU MIGHT NOT BE GETTING ENOUGH SLEEP:

DRIVERS BEHIND YOU TEND TO HONK.

YOU WEAR FUZZY SLIPPERS TO WORK – A LOT.

YOU HAND OVER DECISIONS TO THE FAMILY PET.

Isabella Bannerman, King Features Syndicate.

$\mathbb{A}$*pplication*   **Try This Yourself**

Are You Sleep Deprived?

Part 1 Set up a small mirror next to the text and see if you can copy the star using your nondominant hand while watching your hand in the mirror. The task is difficult, and sleep-deprived people typically make more errors than the nonsleep deprived.

Part 2 Now give yourself one point each time you answer yes to the following questions:

Do you often fall asleep...

watching TV?

during boring meetings or lectures or in warm rooms?

after heavy meals or after a small amount of alcohol?

while relaxing after dinner?

within five minutes of getting into bed?

In the morning, do you generally...

need an alarm clock to wake up at the right time?

struggle to get out of bed?

hit the snooze bar several times to get more sleep?

During the day, do you...

feel tired, irritable, and stressed out?

have trouble concentrating and remembering?

feel slow when it comes to critical thinking, problem solving, and being creative?

feel drowsy while driving?

need a nap to get through the day?

have dark circles around your eyes?

If you answered yes to three or more items, you are probably sleep deprived.

Source: Quiz adapted and reprinted from Maas, 1999, with permission.

Sleep deprivation *Insufficient sleep can seriously affect your college grades, as well as your physical health, motor skills, and overall mood.*

Sack et al., 2007; Yegneswaran & Shapiro, 2007). Severe sleep deprivation in rats results in even more serious, and sometimes fatal, side effects (Rechtschaffen et al., 2002; Siegel, 2008). In addition, lapses in attention among sleep-deprived pilots, physicians, truck drivers, and other workers can also cause serious accidents and cost thousands of lives (Dembe et al., 2006; de Pinho et al., 2006; Paice et al., 2002; Yegneswaran & Shapiro, 2007).

Interestingly, however, many physiological functions are not significantly disrupted by periods of sleep deprivation. In fact, in 1965, a 17-year-old student named Randy Gardner, who wanted to earn a place in the *Guinness Book of World Records*, stayed awake for 264 consecutive hours. He did become irritable and had to remain active to stay awake. But he did not become incoherent or psychotic (Coren, 1996; Spinweber, 1993). After his marathon sleep deprivation, Randy slept a mere 14 hours and then returned to his usual 8-hour sleep cycle (Dement, 1992).

> **A**chievement
>
> Objective 5.5: *List the stages of sleep and describe a typical night's sleep.*

Stages of Sleep: How Scientists Study Sleep

Sleep is an important component of our circadian rhythms. Each night, we go through four to five cycles of distinct sleep stages. And each stage has its own rhythm and corresponding changes in brain activity and behavior. How do we know this? How can scientists study private mental events like sleep?

Surveys and interviews can provide some information about the nature of sleep. But researchers in sleep laboratories use a number of sophisticated instruments to study physiological changes during sleep.

Imagine that you are a participant in a sleep experiment. When you arrive at the sleep lab, you are assigned one of several bedrooms. The researcher hooks you up to various physiological recording devices (Concept Diagram 5.1a). You'll probably need a night or two to adapt to all this equipment before the researchers can begin to monitor your typical night's sleep.

Early Stages of Sleep

Once adapted, you are ready for the researchers to monitor your typical night's sleep. As your eyes close and you begin to relax, the researcher in the next room notices that your EEG recordings have moved from the wave pattern associated with normal wakefulness, *beta waves*, to the slower *alpha waves*, which indicate drowsy relaxation. During this relaxed "presleep" period, you may experience a *hypnagogic state*. This state is characterized by feelings of floating, weightlessness, visual images (such as flashing lights or colors), or swift, jerky movements and a corresponding feeling of slipping or falling. Hypnagogic experiences are sometimes incorporated into fragmented dreams and remembered in the morning. They also may explain reported accounts of alien abduction. These alleged encounters typically occur while the victim is falling asleep, and many abductees report "strange flashes of light" and "floating off the bed."

As you continue relaxing, your brain's electrical activity slows even further. You are now in *Stage 1* sleep. During this stage, your breathing becomes more regular, your heart rate slows, and your blood pressure decreases. But you could still be readily awakened. No one wakens you, though, so you relax more deeply and slide gently into *Stage 2* sleep. This stage is noted on your electroencephalograph by occasional short bursts of rapid, high-amplitude brain waves known as *sleep spindles*. During Stage 2 sleep, you become progressively more relaxed and less responsive to the external environment. Even deeper levels of sleep are found in *stages* 3 and 4, which are marked by the appearance of slow, high-amplitude *delta* waves. It is very hard to awaken you in stages 3 and 4, even by shouting and shaking. Stage 4 sleep also is the time when children are most likely to wet the bed and when sleepwalking occurs. (Can you see why it is difficult or impossible to learn foreign languages or other material from tapes while asleep [Wyatt & Bootzin, 1994]?)

Concept Diagram 5.1
The Scientific Study of Sleep and Dreaming

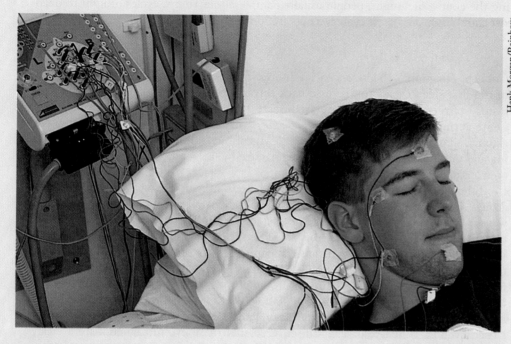

(a) Sleep research participants wear electrodes on their heads and bodies to measure brain and body responses during the sleep cycle.

Hank Morgan/Rainbow

(b) An **electroencephalograph** detects and records brain-wave changes by means of small electrodes on the scalp. Other electrodes measure muscle activity and eye movements. The stages of sleep, defined by telltale changes in brain waves, are indicated by the green stepped lines. The compact brain waves of alertness gradually lengthen as we drift into Stages 1–4. By the end of Stage 4, a change in body position generally occurs and heart rate, blood pressure, and respiratory rates all decrease. The sleeper then reverses through Stages 3 and 2 before entering the first REM period of the night. Although the brain and body are giving many signs of active arousal during REM sleep, the musculature is deeply relaxed and unresponsive. Sleepers awakened from REM sleep often report vivid, bizarre dreams, indicated in the figure by red and yellow dots. Those awakened from Stages 1–4 sleep often have more peaceful thoughts (indicated by muted dots). The heavy green line on the graph showing all four stages of sleep indicates the approximate time spent in REM sleep. Note how the length of the REM period increases as the night progresses.

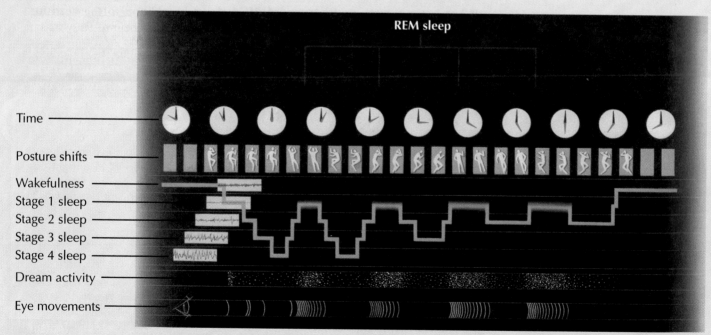

In about an hour, you have progressed through all four stages of sleep. Then the sequence begins to reverse itself (see Concept Diagram 5.1b). Keep in mind that we don't necessarily go through all four sleep stages in this exact sequence. However, during the course of a night, people usually complete four to five cycles of light to deep sleep and back. And each cycle lasts about 90 minutes.

REM and NREM Sleep

Concept Diagram 5.1b also shows an interesting phenomenon that occurs at the end of the first sleep cycle. You reverse back through Stage 3, and then to Stage 2. But instead of reentering the calm, relaxed Stage 1, something totally different happens. Quite abruptly, your scalp recordings display a pattern of small-amplitude, fast-wave activity, similar in many ways to an awake, vigilant person's brain waves. Your breathing and pulse rates become fast and irregular. And your genitals very likely show signs of arousal (an erection or vaginal lubrication).

Interestingly, although your brain and body are giving many signs of active arousal, your musculature is deeply relaxed and unresponsive. The sleeper is in some ways experiencing the deepest stage of sleep. Yet, in other ways the lightest. Because of these contradictory qualities, this stage is sometimes referred to as "paradoxical sleep." The term *paradoxical* means "apparently self-contradictory." (As a critical thinker, can you see how the muscle "paralysis" of paradoxical sleep may serve an important adaptive function? Think about the problems and dangers that would ensue if we were able to move around and act out our dreams while we were sleeping.)

During this stage of "paradoxical sleep," rapid eye movements occur under your closed eyelids. When researchers discovered that these eye movements are a clear, biological signal that the sleeper is dreaming, they labeled this stage **rapid-eye-movement sleep (REM)**. Although some people believe they do not dream, when sleepers are awakened during REM sleep they almost always report dreaming. Because of the importance of dreaming and the fact that REM sleep is so different from the other periods of sleep, Stages 1 to 4 are often collectively called **NREM** (or **non-rapid-eye-movement) sleep**. Keep in mind that dreaming does occur during NREM sleep, but less frequently. Contrary to popular misconceptions, recent research also shows that dream reports from NREM sleep are very similar to those from REM sleep (McNamara et al., 2007, Wamsley et al., 2007).

What is the purpose of REM and NREM sleep? In addition to the need for dreaming, which will be discussed in the next section, scientists believe REM sleep

Rapid-Eye-Movement (REM) Sleep *Stage of sleep marked by rapid eye movements, high-frequency brain waves, paralysis of large muscles, and dreaming*

Non-Rapid-Eye-Movement (NREM) Sleep *Stages 1 to 4 of sleep with Stage 1 as the lightest level and Stage 4 as the deepest level*

---

*A*ssessment

VISUAL QUIZ

Michael & Barbara Reed/Animals AnimalsNYC

J. P. Thomas/Jacana/PhotoResearchers, Inc.

The Sleep Cycle in Cats

During NREM (non-rapid-eye-movement) sleep, cats often sleep in an upright position. With the onset of REM sleep, cats normally lie down. Can you explain why?

Answer: During REM sleep, large muscles are temporarily paralyzed, which causes the cat to lose motor control and lie down.

may be important for learning and consolidating new memories (Marshall & Born, 2007; Massicotte-Marquez et al., 2008; Silvestri & Root, 2008). Further evidence of the importance of REM sleep for complex brain functions comes from the fact that the amount of REM sleep increases after periods of stress or intense learning. And fetuses, infants, and young children spend a large percentage of their sleep time in this stage (Figure 5.2). In addition, REM sleep occurs only in mammals of higher intelligence and is absent in nonmammals such as reptiles (Rechtschaffen & Siegel, 2000).

REM sleep also serves an important biological need. When researchers selectively deprive sleepers of REM sleep (by waking them each time they enter the state), most people experience REM *rebound*. That is, they try to "catch up" on REM sleep on subsequent occasions by spending more time than usual in this state.

NREM sleep may be even more important to our biological functioning than REM sleep. When people are deprived of *total* sleep, they spend more time in NREM sleep during their first uninterrupted night (Borbely, 1982). Apparently, it is only after our need for NREM sleep has been satisfied each night that we begin to devote more time to REM sleep. Furthermore, studies show that adults who are "short sleepers" (five or fewer hours each night) spend less time in REM sleep than do "long sleepers" (nine or more hours each night). Similarly, infants get more sleep and have a higher percentage of REM sleep than do adults (see again Figure 5.2). Apparently, the greater the total amount of sleep, the greater the percentage of REM sleep.

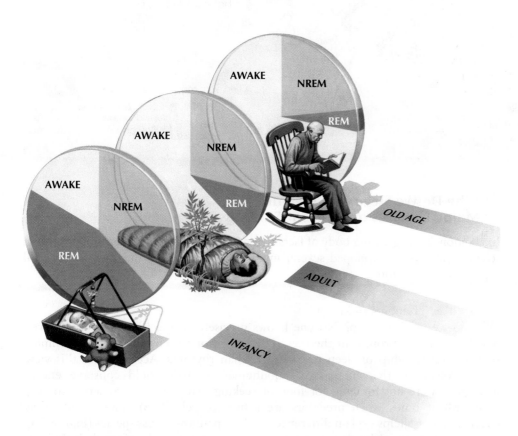

Figure 5.2 *The effect of aging on the sleep cycle* Our biological need for sleep changes throughout our life span. The pie charts in this figure show the relative amounts of REM sleep (dark blue), non-REM sleep (medium blue), and awake time (light blue) that the average person experiences as an infant, an adult, and an elderly person. An infant sleeps 14 hours and spends 40 percent of that time in REM. An adult sleeps about 7.5 hours, with 20 percent of that in REM. The average 70-year-old sleeps only about 6 hours, with 14 percent of that in REM.

Circadian Rhythms and Stages of Sleep

Objective 5.3: *List six common myths about sleep.*

Six of the most common myths include: Everyone needs 8 hours of sleep. It's easy to learn complicated things while asleep. Some people never dream. Dreams only last a few seconds. Genital arousal means the sleeper is having a sexual dream. And, dreaming of dying can be fatal.

Objective 5.4: *What are circadian rhythms and how do they affect our lives?*

Circadian rhythms are biological changes that occur on a 24-hour cycle. Our sleep–wake cycle, alertness, moods, learning, blood pressure, and the like all follow circadian rhythms. Disruptions to circadian rhythms due to shift work, jet lag, and sleep deprivation can cause accidents and other serious problems.

Objective 5.5: *List the stages of sleep and describe a typical night's sleep.*

A typical night's sleep consists of four to five 90-minute cycles. The cycle begins in Stage 1 and then moves through Stages 2,

3, and 4. After reaching the deepest level of sleep, the cycle reverses up to **REM (rapid-eye-movement) sleep**, in which the person often is dreaming. Sleep stages 1, 2, 3, 4 are called **NREM** (non-rapid-eye-movement) **sleep.**

Questions

1. Biological rhythms that occur on a daily basis are called _____ rhythms. (a) circuitous; (b) chronobiology; (c) calendrical; (d) circadian

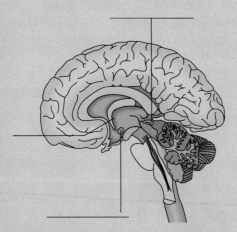

2. Identify the main areas of the brain involved in the operation of circadian rhythms in the figure to your left: (a) hypothalamus; (b) pineal gland; (c) suprachiasmatic nucleus

3. Jet lag primarily results from _____. (a) sleep deprivation; (b) disruption of the circadian rhythms; (c) the effect of light on the pineal gland; (d) disruption of brain-wave patterns that occurs at high altitudes.

4. The machine that measures the voltage (or brain waves) that the brain produces is _____.

5. Just before sleep onset, brain waves move from _____ waves, indicating normal wakefulness, to _____ waves associated with drowsy relaxation. (a) beta, alpha; (b) theta, delta; (c) alpha, beta; (d) sigma, chi

Check your answers in Appendix B

Click & Review for additional assessment options: wiley.com/college/huffman

---

Objective 5.6: *Why do we sleep?*

Why Do We Sleep and Dream? Major Theories and Recent Findings

In addition to the growing body of facts that we now know about sleep and dreaming, scientists also have developed several important, overarching theories, which we'll explore in this section.

Two Major Theories of Sleep

Why do we need to sleep? No one knows precisely all the functions sleep serves, but there are two prominent theories. The **evolutionary/circadian theory** emphasizes the relationship of sleep to basic circadian rhythms. According to this view, sleep evolved so that human and nonhuman animals could conserve energy when they were not foraging for food or seeking mates. Sleep also serves to keep them still at times when predators are active (Siegel, 2008). The evolutionary/circadian theory helps explain differences in sleep patterns across species (Figure 5.3). Opossums sleep many hours each day because they are relatively safe in their environment and are able to easily find food and shelter. In comparison, sheep and horses sleep very little because their diets require constant foraging for food. In addition, their only defense against predators is vigilance and running away.

In contrast, the **repair/restoration theory** suggests that sleep helps us recuperate from depleting daily activities. Essential factors in our brain or body are apparently repaired or replenished while we sleep. We recover not only from physical fatigue but also from emotional and intellectual demands.

Evolutionary/Circadian Theory *Sleep evolved to conserve energy and as protection from predators; also serves as part of the circadian cycle*

Repair/Restoration Theory *Sleep serves a recuperative function, allowing organisms to repair or replenish key factors*

Which theory is correct? Both theories have merit. Obviously, we need to repair and restore ourselves after a busy day. But bears don't hibernate all winter simply to recover from a busy summer. Like humans and other animals, they also need to conserve energy when the environment is hostile. It may be that sleep initially served to conserve energy and keep us out of trouble, and then later, it may have evolved to allow for repair and restoration.

Three Major Theories of Dreams

Is there special meaning and information in our dreams? Why do we have bad dreams? Why do we dream at all? These questions have long fascinated writers and poets, as well as psychologists.

The Psychoanalytic/Psychodynamic View One of the oldest and most scientifically controversial explanations for why we dream is Freud's *psychoanalytic view*. In one of his first books, *The Interpretation of Dreams*, Freud proposed that dreams are "the royal road to the unconscious." According to Freud, dreaming is a special state in which normally repressed and personally unacceptable desires rise to the surface of consciousness. Supposedly, the main purpose of dreams is to express our hidden desires and conflicts. Therefore, listening to a patient's dreams reportedly offers direct insight into his or her unconscious. When a lonely person dreams of romance or an angry child dreams of getting even with the class bully, they may be expressing wish fulfillment.

More often, though, the dream content is so threatening and anxiety producing that it must be couched in *symbols*. A journey in a dream is supposedly a symbol for death. Horseback riding and dancing are considered symbols for sexual intercourse. And a gun might represent a penis. Freud referred to these symbols (the journey, horseback riding, or the gun) as the **manifest content** (or the story line) of the dream. The underlying, true meaning (death, sex, penis) is called the **latent content**. According to Freud, by disguising the forbidden unconscious needs as symbols, the dreamer avoids anxiety and remains asleep.

Kenneth M. Highhill/Photo Researchers

Why do we sleep? *According to the evolutionary/circadian theory, a major function of sleep is to keep humans and other animals still and quiet during the time their most dangerous predators are active. In contrast, repair/restoration theory suggests we need sleep to rest and recuperate.*

Achievement

Objective 5.7: *Why do we dream?*

Manifest Content *According to Freud, the surface content of a dream, which contains dream symbols that distort and disguise the dream's true meaning*

Latent Content *According to Freud, the true, unconscious meaning of a dream*

Assessment

VISUAL QUIZ

Figure 5.3 ***Average daily hours of sleep for different mammals*** How does the fact that an opossum spends almost 20 hours a day sleeping, yet a horse spends only 2 hours support the evolutionary/circadian theory?

Answer: According to the evolutionary/circadian theory of sleep, animals that sleep the longest are least threatened by the environment and can easily find food and shelter. Note how the opossum and cat spend longer hours in sleep than the horse and sheep, presumably because of differences in diet and the number of predators.

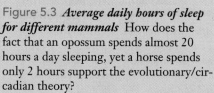

What is the scientific evidence for Freud's theory of dreams? Most modern research finds little or no scientific support for Freud's view (Domhoff, 2004; Dufresne, 2007). Critics also say that Freud's theory is highly subjective. The symbols can be interpreted according to the particular analyst's view or training. After being confronted about the symbolic nature of his beloved cigars, even Freud supposedly remarked, "Sometimes a cigar is just a cigar."

Activation–Synthesis Hypothesis *Hobson's theory that dreams are by-products of random stimulation of brain cells; the brain attempts to combine (or synthesize) this spontaneous activity into coherent patterns, known as dreams*

The Biological View In contrast to the Freudian perspective, the **activation–synthesis hypothesis** suggests dreams are a by-product of random stimulation of brain cells during REM sleep (Hobson, 1988, 2005). Alan Hobson and Robert McCarley (1977) proposed that specific neurons in the brain stem are "turned on" (*activated*) during REM sleep. The cortex then struggles to *synthesize* or make sense out of this random stimulation by manufacturing dreams.

Have you ever dreamed that you were trying to run away from a frightening situation but found that you could not move? The activation–synthesis hypothesis might explain this dream as random stimulation of the amygdala. As you recall from Chapter 2, the amygdala is a specific brain area linked to strong emotions, especially fear. If your amygdala is randomly stimulated and you feel afraid, you may try to run. But you can't move because your major muscles are temporarily paralyzed during REM sleep. To make sense of this conflict, you might create a dream about a fearful situation in which you were trapped in heavy sand or someone was holding on to your arms and legs.

This is *not* to say that Hobson believes dreams are totally meaningless. He suggests that even if dreams begin with essentially random brain activity, your individual personality, motivations, memories, and life experiences guide how your brain constructs the dream (Hobson, 1999, 2005).

The Cognitive View Finally, some researchers suport the cognitive view that dreams are simply another type of *information processing*. That is, our dreams help us sift and sort our everyday experiences and thoughts. And the brain periodically shuts out sensory input so that it can process, assimilate, and update information.

The cognitive view of dreaming is supported by the fact that REM sleep increases following stress and intense learning periods. Furthermore, other research reports strong similarities between dream content and waking thoughts, fears, and concerns (Domhoff, 2005, 2007; Erlacher & Schredl, 2004). For example, college students often report "examination-anxiety" dreams. You can't find your classroom, you're running out of time, your pen or pencil won't work, or you've completely forgotten a scheduled exam and show up totally unprepared. (Sound familiar?)

Dreams and butterflies Throughout the ages, humans have wondered about dreams. After dreaming he was a butterfly, Chuang Tzu, a Chinese Taoist (third century B.C.), spoke about the interplay of reality and dreams: "Suddenly I woke up and I was indeed Chuang Tzu. Did Chuang Tzu dream he was a butterfly? Or did the butterfly dream he was Chuang Tzu?"

In Sum The psychoanalytic/psychodynamic, biological, and cognitive views of dreaming offer three widely divergent perspectives. And numerous questions remain. How would the psychoanalytic/psychodynamic theory explain why human fetuses show REM patterns? On the other hand, how would the activation–synthesis hypothesis explain complicated, storylike dreams or recurrent dreams? Finally, according to the information-processing approach, how can we explain dreams that lie outside our everyday experiences? And how is it that the same dream can often be explained by many theories?

Objective 5.8: *How do gender and culture affect dreams?*

chievement

GENDER & CULTURAL DIVERSITY

Dream Variations and Similarities

Do men and women dream about different things? Are there differences between cultures in dream content? In reference to gender, research shows that men and women tend to share many common dream themes. But women are more likely to dream of children, family and familiar people, household objects, and indoor events. Men, on the other hand, more often dream about strangers, violence, weapons, sexual activity, achievement, and outdoor events (Domhoff, 2003, 2007; Schredl et al., 2004). Interestingly, other evidence suggests that as gender differences and stereotypes lessen, segregation of dream content by gender becomes less distinct (Hobson, 2002).

Likewise, researchers have found both similarities and differences in dream content across cultures. Dreams involving basic human needs and fears (like sex, aggression, and death) seem to be found in all cultures. And children around the world often dream about large, threatening wild ani-mals. People of all ages and cultures dream of falling, being chased, and being unable to do something they need to do. In addition, dreams around the world typically include more misfortune than good fortune, and the dreamer is more often the victim of aggression than the cause of it (Domhoff, 2003, 2007; Hall & Van de Castle, 1996).

Yet there are some cultural differences. The Yir Yoront, an Australian hunting-and-gathering group, generally prefer marriage between a man and his mother's brother's daughter (Schneider & Sharp, 1969). Therefore, it is not uncommon (or surprising) that young, single men in the group often report recurrent dreams of aggression from their mother's brother (their future father-in-law). Similarly, Americans often report embarrassing dreams of being naked in public. Such dreams are rare in cultures where few clothes are worn.

How people interpret and value their dreams also varies across cultures (Matsumoto & Juang, 2008; Laungani, 2007; Triandis, 2007). The Iroquois of North America believe that one's spirit uses dreams to communicate unconscious wishes to the conscious mind (Wallace, 1958). They often share their dreams with religious leaders, who help them interpret and cope with their underlying psychic needs to prevent illness and even death. On the other hand, the Maya of Central America share their dreams and interpretations at communal gatherings as an important means of teaching cultural folk wisdom (Tedlock, 1992). (As a critical thinker, do you notice the close similarity between Freudian theory and the Iroquois concept of dreaming? Some historians believe that Freud borrowed many concepts from the Iroquois—without giving appropriate credit.)

Application

CRITICAL THINKING

ACTIVE LEARNING

Interpreting Your Dreams

Television, movies, and other popular media often portray dreams as highly significant and easily interpreted. However, scientists are deeply divided about the meaning of dreams and their relative importance. These differences in scientific opinion provide an excellent opportunity for you to practice the critical thinking skill of tolerance for ambiguity.

To improve your tolerance for ambiguity (and learn a little more about your own dreams), begin by briefly jotting down one of your most recent and vivid dreams. It should be at least three or four paragraphs in length. Now analyze your dream using the following perspectives:

1. According to the psychoanalytic/psychodynamic view, what might be the forbidden, unconscious fears, drives, or desires represented by your dream? Can you identify the manifest content versus the latent content?

2. How would the biological view, the activation–synthesis hypothesis, explain your dream? Can you identify a specific thought that might have been stimulated and then led to this particular dream?

3. Psychologists from the cognitive perspective believe dreams provide important information, help us make needed changes in our life, and even suggest solutions to real-life problems. Do you agree or disa-

gree? Does your dream provide an insight that increases your self-understanding?

Having analyzed your dream from each perspective, can you see how difficult it is to find the one right answer? Higher-level critical thinkers recognize that competing theories are akin to the story of the four blind men who are each exploring separate parts of an elephant. By listening to their description of the trunk, tail, leg, and so on, critical thinkers can synthesize the information and develop a greater understanding. But no one part—or single theory—reveals the whole picture.

Assessment

STOP

CHECK & REVIEW

Theories of Sleep and Dreams

Objective 5.6: *Why do we sleep?*

The exact function of sleep is unknown. But according to the **evolutionary/circadian theory**, sleep evolved to conserve energy and protect us from predators. According to **repair/restoration theory**, sleep is thought to be necessary for its restorative value, both physically and psychologically.

Objective 5.7: *Why do we dream?*

Three major theories attempt to explain why we dream. According to the *psychoanalytic/ psychodynamic view*, dreams are disguised symbols of repressed desires, conflicts, and anxieties. The *biological perspective* (**activation–synthesis hypothesis**) proposes that dreams are simple by-products of random stimulation of brain cells. The *cognitive view* suggests that dreams are an important type of information processing of everyday experiences.

Objective 5.8: *How do gender and culture affect dreams?*

Researchers have found many similarities and differences in dream content between men and women and across cultures. How people interpret and value their dreams also varies across cultures.

Questions

1. How does the repair/restoration theory of sleep differ from the evolutionary/ circadian theory?

2. Freud believed that dreams were the "royal road to the _____."

(a) therapeutic alliance; (b) psyche; (c) latent content; (d) unconscious

3. _____ theory states that dreams are by-products of random stimulation of brain cells. In contrast, the _____ view suggests dreams serve an information-processing function and help us sift and sort our everyday experiences and thoughts. (a) Biological, learning; (b) Cognitive, wish-fulfillment; (c) Activation–synthesis, cognitive; (d) Psychodynamic, infodynamic

4. After periods of stress and intense learning, _____ sleep increases.

Check your answers in Appendix B

Click & Review
for additional assessment options:
wiley.com/college/huffman

Achievement

Objective 5.9: *Describe the major sleep disorders.*

Adam Gault/Digital Vision/Getty

Insomnia *Persistent problems in falling asleep, staying asleep, or awakening too early*

Sleep Disorders: When Sleep Becomes a Problem

Are you one of the lucky people who takes sleep for granted? If so, you may be surprised to discover the following facts (National Sleep Foundation, 2007; Lader, Cardinali, & Pandi-Perumal, 2006; Wilson & Nutt, 2008).

- An estimated two-thirds of American adults suffer from sleep problems, and about 25 percent of children under age 5 have a sleep disturbance.

- One in five adults is so sleepy during the day that sleepiness interferes with their daily activities. Each year Americans spend more than $98 million on over-the-counter sleep aids and another $50 million on coffee to keep them awake during the day.

- Twenty percent of all automobile drivers have fallen asleep for a few seconds (microsleep) at the wheel.

  The costs of sleep disorders are enormous, not only for the individual but also for the public. Psychologists and other mental health professionals divide sleep disorders into two major diagnostic categories: (1) *dyssomnias*, which involve problems in the amount, timing, and quality of sleep, and (2) *parasomnias*, which include abnormal disturbances occurring during sleep.

Dyssomnias

There are at least three prominent examples of dyssomnias:

1. Insomnia. The term *insomnia* literally means "lack of sleep." People with **insomnia** have persistent difficulty falling asleep or staying asleep, or they wake up too early. Many people think they have insomnia if they cannot sleep before an exciting event, which is normal. They also wrongly assume that everyone must sleep eight hours a night. Sometimes, too, people think they are not sleeping when they really are.

However, a significant percentage of the population (as much as 10 percent) genuinely suffers from insomnia, and nearly everyone occasionally experiences unwanted sleeplessness (Pearson, Johnson, & Nahin, 2006; Riemann & Volderholzer, 2003; Wilson & Nutt, 2008). A telltale complaint of insomnia is that the person feels poorly rested the next day. Most people with serious insomnia have other medical or psychological disorders as well, such as alcohol and other drug abuse, anxiety disorders, and depression.

Unfortunately, the most popular treatment for insomnia is drugs—either over-the-counter pills, such as Sominex, or prescription tranquilizers and barbiturates. The problem with nonprescription pills is that they generally don't work. Prescription pills, on the other hand, do help you sleep. But they decrease Stage 4 and REM sleep, thereby seriously affecting the quality of sleep. Frequently prescribed drugs like Ambien, Lunestra, Xanax, and Halcion may be helpful in treating sleeping problems related to anxiety and specific stressful situations, such as losing a loved one. However, chronic users run the risk of psychological and physical drug dependence. In sum, sleeping pills may be useful for occasional, short-term (two to three nights) use, but they may create more problems than they solve.

2. Sleep apnea. A second major dyssomnia, closely related to insomnia, is **sleep apnea**. (*Apnea* literally means "no breathing.") Many people have either irregular breathing or occasional periods of 10 seconds or less without breathing during their sleep. People with sleep apnea, however, may fail to breathe for a minute or longer and then wake up gasping for breath. When they do breathe during their sleep, they often snore. Repeated awakenings result in insomnia and leave the person feeling tired and sleepy during the day. Unfortunately, people are often unaware of these frequent awakenings and may fail to recognize the reason for their daytime fatigue.

Sleep apnea seems to result from blocked upper airway passages or from the brain ceasing to send signals to the diaphragm, thus causing breathing to stop. If you snore loudly or have repeated awakenings followed by gasps for breath, you may be suffering from sleep apnea and should seek medical attention. Recent research shows that sleep apnea may kill neurons in your brain that are critical for learning and memory. It also can lead to high blood pressure, stroke, heart attack, and accidents (Billiard, 2007; Hartenbaum et al., 2006; National Sleep Foundation, 2007; McNicholas & Javaheri, 2007).

Treatment for sleep apnea depends partly on its severity. If the problem occurs only when you're sleeping on your back, sewing tennis balls on the back of your pajama top may help remind you to sleep on your side. Obstruction of the breathing passages is also related to obesity and heavy alcohol use, so dieting and alcohol restriction are often recommended. For others, surgery, dental appliances that reposition the tongue, or ventilating machines may be the answer.

For many years, researchers assumed that snoring (without the accompanying stoppages of breathing in sleep apnea) was a minor problem—except for bed partners. Recent findings, however, suggest that even this "simple snoring" can also lead to heart disease and possible death (Stone & Redline, 2006). Although occasional mild snoring may be normal, chronic snoring is a possible "warning sign that should prompt people to seek help" (Christensen, 2000, p. 172).

3. Narcolepsy. A serious sleep disorder that is somewhat the opposite of insomnia is **narcolepsy**—sudden and irresistible onsets of sleep during normal waking hours. Narcolepsy afflicts about one person in 2000 and generally runs in families (Billiard, 2007; Pedrazzoli et al., 2007; Siegel, 2000). During an attack, REM-like sleep suddenly intrudes into the waking state of consciousness. Victims may experience sudden attacks of muscle weakness or paralysis (known as *cataplexy*). Such people may fall asleep while walking, talking, or driving a car. Long daily naps and stimulant or antidepressant drugs may help reduce the frequency of narcoleptic attacks. But the causes and cure of narcolepsy are still unknown (Figure 5.4).

Sleep Apnea *Repeated interruption of breathing during sleep because air passages to the lungs are physically blocked or the brain stops activating the diaphragm*

Narcolepsy [NAR-co-lep-see] *Sudden and irresistible onsets of sleep during normal waking hours. (narco = "numbness" and lepsy = "seizure")*

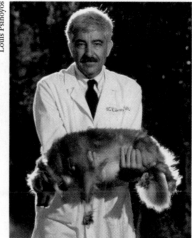

Figure 5.4 **Narcolepsy** William Dement and his colleagues at Stanford University's Sleep Disorders Center have bred a group of narcoleptic dogs, which has increased our understanding of the genetics of this disorder. Research on these specially bred dogs has found degenerated neurons in certain areas of the brain (Siegel, 2000). Whether human narcolepsy results from similar degeneration is a question for future research. (Note how the dog lapses suddenly from alert wakefulness, in the left photo, to deep sleep in the photo on the right.)

wiley.com/ college/ huffman

Figure 5.5 *Nightmare or night terrors?* Nightmares, or bad dreams, occur toward the end of the sleep cycle, during REM sleep. Less common but more frightening are night terrors, which occur early in the cycle, during Stage 3 or Stage 4 of NREM sleep. Like the child in this photo, the sleeper may sit bolt upright, screaming and sweating, walk around, and talk incoherently, and the person may be almost impossible to awaken.

Parasomnias

The second major category of sleep disorders, *parasomnias*, includes abnormal sleep disturbances such as **nightmares** and **night terrors** (Figure 5.5).

Sleepwalking, which tends to accompany night terrors, also occurs during NREM sleep. (Recall that large muscles are "paralyzed" during REM sleep, which explains why sleepwalking normally only occurs during NREM sleep.) *Sleeptalking*, on the other hand, occurs with about equal probability in REM and NREM sleep. It can include single, indistinct words or long, articulate sentences. It is even possible to engage some sleeptalkers in a limited conversation.

Nightmares, night terrors, sleepwalking, and sleeptalking are all more common among young children. But they can also occur in adults, usually during times of stress or major life events (Billiard, 2007; Hobson & Silvestri, 1999). Patience and soothing reassurance at the time of the sleep disruption are usually the only treatment recommended for both children and adults.

Nightmares *Anxiety-arousing dreams generally occurring near the end of the sleep cycle, during REM sleep*

Night Terrors *Abrupt awakenings from NREM (non-rapid-eye-movement) sleep accompanied by intense physiological arousal and feelings of panic*

 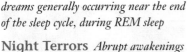 **PSYCHOLOGY AT WORK**

Self-Help for Sleep Problems

Are you wondering what is recommended for sleep problems other than drugs? Research finds consistent benefits from behavior therapy (Constantino et al., 2007; Smith et al., 2005). You can use these same techniques in your own life. For example, when you're having a hard time going to sleep, don't keep checking the clock and worrying about your loss of sleep. Instead, remove all TVs, stereos, and books, and limit the use of the bedroom to sleep (and sex). If you need additional help, try some of the relaxation techniques suggested by the Better Sleep Council, a nonprofit education organization in Burtonsville, Maryland.

During the day

Exercise. Daily physical activity works away tension. But don't exercise vigorously late in the day, or you'll get fired up instead. Keep regular hours. An erratic schedule can disrupt biological rhythms. Get up at the same time each day.

Avoid stimulants. Coffee, tea, soft drinks, chocolate, and some medications contain caffeine. Nicotine may be an even more potent sleep disrupter.

Avoid late meals and heavy drinking. Overindulgence can interfere with your normal sleep pattern.

Stop worrying. Focus on your problems at a set time earlier in the day.

Use presleep rituals. Follow the same routine every evening: listen to music, write in a diary, meditate.

In bed

Use progressive muscle relaxation. Alternately tense and relax various muscle groups.

Apply yoga. These gentle exercises help you relax.

Use fantasies. Imagine yourself in a tranquil setting. Feel yourself relax.

Use deep breathing. Take deep breaths, telling yourself you're falling asleep.

Try a warm bath. This can induce drowsiness because it sends blood away from the brain to the skin surface.

For more information, check these websites:

- www.sleepfoundation.org

- www.stanford.edu/~dement

Assessment STOP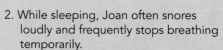

CHECK & REVIEW

Sleep Disorders

Objective 5.9: *Describe the major sleep disorders.*

Sleep disorders fall into two major diagnostic categories—*dyssomnias* (including insomnia, sleep apnea, and narcolepsy) and *parasomnias* (such as nightmares and night terrors).

People who have repeated difficulty falling or staying asleep, or awakening too early, experience **insomnia**. A person with **sleep apnea** temporarily stops breathing during sleep, causing loud snoring or poor-quality sleep. **Narcolepsy** is excessive daytime sleepiness characterized by sudden sleep attacks. **Nightmares** are bad dreams that occur during REM (rapid-eye-movement) sleep. **Night terrors** are abrupt awakenings with feelings of panic that occur during NREM sleep.

Questions

Following are four descriptions of people suffering from sleep disorders. Label each type.

1. George awakens many times each night and feels fatigued and poorly rested the next day.

2. While sleeping, Joan often snores loudly and frequently stops breathing temporarily.

3. Xavier complains to his physician about sudden and irresistible onsets of sleep during his normal work day.

4. Tyler is a young child who often wakes up terrified and cannot describe what has happened. These episodes occur primarily during NREM sleep.

Check your answers in Appendix B.

 Click & Review
for additional assessment options:
wiley.com/college/huffman

Psychoactive Drugs

Since the beginning of civilization, people of all cultures have used—and abused—psychoactive drugs (Abadinsky, 2008; Kuhn, Swartzwelder, & Wilson, 2003; Levinthal, 2008). **Psychoactive drugs** are generally defined as chemicals that change conscious awareness, mood, and/or perception. Do you (or does someone you know) use caffeine (in coffee, tea, chocolate, or cola) or nicotine (in cigarettes) as a pick-me-up? How about alcohol (in beer, wine, and cocktails) as a way to relax and lessen inhibitions? All three—caffeine, nicotine, and alcohol—are psychoactive drugs. How use

Achievement

Objective 5.10: *Define psychoactive drugs and explain how they work.*

Psychoactive Drugs *Chemicals that change conscious awareness, mood, and/or perception*

wiley.com/
college/
huffman

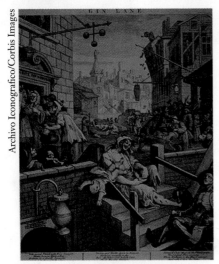

Early abuse of drugs *William Hogarth's eighteenth-century engraving shows the social chaos caused by the "gin epidemic." Infant mortality was so high that only one of four babies survived to the age of 5. In one section of London, one out of five houses was a gin shop (cited in Levinthal, 2002, p. 188).*

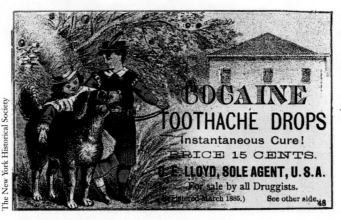

History of psychoactive drugs *Before the Food and Drug Administration (FDA) regulated the sale of such drugs as heroin, opium, and cocaine, they were commonly found in over-the-counter, nonprescription drugs.*

Objective 5.11: *Clarify the major misconceptions and confusing terminology related to psychoactive drugs.*

Drug Abuse *Drug taking that causes emotional or physical harm to the drug user or others*

Addiction *Broad term describing a compulsion to use a specific drug or engage in a certain activity*

Psychological Dependence *Desire or craving to achieve a drug's effect*

Physical Dependence *Changes in bodily processes that make a drug necessary for minimal functioning*

Withdrawal *Discomfort and distress, including physical pain and intense cravings, experienced after stopping the use of addictive drugs*

Tolerance *Bodily adjustment to higher and higher levels of a drug, which leads to decreased sensitivity*

differs from abuse, and how chemical alterations in consciousness affect a person, psychologically and physically, are important topics in psychology. In this section, we begin by clarifying how psychoactive drugs work and differences in terminology. We then go on to look at the four major categories of psychoactive drugs and "club drugs" like MDMA, or ecstasy.

Understanding Psychoactive Drugs: Clarifying the Mechanics and Terminology

How Drugs Work

Psychoactive drugs influence the nervous system (and our thoughts, feelings, and behaviors) in a variety of ways. Alcohol, for example, has a diffuse effect on neural membranes throughout the nervous system. Most psychoactive drugs, however, act in a more specific way. They either enhance a particular neurotransmitter's effect (an *agonistic drug action*) or they inhibit it (an *antagonistic drug* action) (see Process Diagram 5.2).

Misconceptions and Confusing Terminology

Is drug abuse the same as drug addiction? The term **drug abuse** generally refers to drug taking that causes emotional or physical harm to the individual or others. The drug consumption is also typically compulsive, frequent, and intense. **Addiction** is a broad term referring to a condition in which a person feels compelled to use a specific drug. In recent times, the term *addiction* has been used to describe almost any type of compulsive activity from working to surfing the Internet (Coombs, 2004).

Because of problems associated with the terms *addiction* and *drug abuse*, many drug researchers now use **psychological dependence** to refer to the mental desire or craving to achieve a drug's effects. They use the term **physical dependence** to refer to changes in bodily processes that make a drug necessary for minimum daily functioning. Physical dependence is shown most clearly when the drug is withheld and the user undergoes painful **withdrawal** reactions, including physical pain and intense cravings.

After repeated use of a drug, many of the body's physiological processes adjust to higher and higher levels of the drug, producing a decreased sensitivity called **tolerance**. Tolerance leads many users to escalate their drug use and to experiment with other drugs in an attempt to re-create the original pleasurable altered state. Sometimes, using one drug increases tolerance for another. This is known as *cross-tolerance*. Despite the benign sound of the words *tolerance* and *cross-tolerance*, it's important to remember that the brain, heart, liver, and other body organs can be seriously damaged.

Psychological dependence is often no less dangerous than physical dependence. The craving in psychological dependence can be strong enough to keep the user in a

Process Diagram 5.2
How Agonistic and Antagonistic Drugs Produce Their Psychoactive Effects

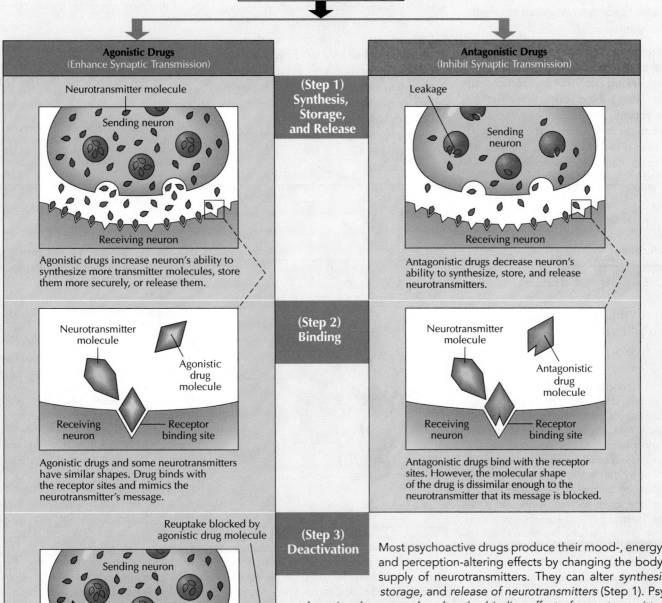

Drugs

Agonistic Drugs
(Enhance Synaptic Transmission)

Antagonistic Drugs
(Inhibit Synaptic Transmission)

**(Step 1)
Synthesis,
Storage,
and Release**

Neurotransmitter molecule

Sending neuron

Receiving neuron

Agonistic drugs increase neuron's ability to synthesize more transmitter molecules, store them more securely, or release them.

Leakage

Sending neuron

Receiving neuron

Antagonistic drugs decrease neuron's ability to synthesize, store, and release neurotransmitters.

**(Step 2)
Binding**

Neurotransmitter molecule

Agonistic drug molecule

Receiving neuron

Receptor binding site

Agonistic drugs and some neurotransmitters have similar shapes. Drug binds with the receptor sites and mimics the neurotransmitter's message.

Neurotransmitter molecule

Antagonistic drug molecule

Receiving neuron

Receptor binding site

Antagonistic drugs bind with the receptor sites. However, the molecular shape of the drug is dissimilar enough to the neurotransmitter that its message is blocked.

**(Step 3)
Deactivation**

Reuptake blocked by agonistic drug molecule

Sending neuron

Receiving neuron

Agonistic drugs block the deactivation of excess neurotransmitters by preventing reuptake or degradation. This blockage allows excess neurotransmitter molecules to remain in the synapse and thereby prolong activation of the receptor site.

Most psychoactive drugs produce their mood-, energy-, and perception-altering effects by changing the body's supply of neurotransmitters. They can alter *synthesis, storage,* and *release of neurotransmitters* (Step 1). Psychoactive drugs can also alter the *binding* effect of neurotransmitters on the receiving site of the receptor neuron (Step 2). After neurotransmitters carry their messages across the synapse, the sending neuron normally *deactivates* the excess, or leftover, neurotransmitter. However, when **agonistic** drugs block this process, excess neutrotransmitter remains in the synapse, which prolongs the psychoactive drug effect (Step 3).

Agonist Drug *Mimics a neurotransmitter's effect*

Antagonist Drug *Blocks normal neurotransmitter functioning*

wiley.com/
college/
huffman

Try This Yourself

Are You Physically or Psychologically Dependent on Alcohol or Other Drugs?

Before we go on, you may want to take the following test.

1. Have you gotten into financial difficulties due to drinking or using other drugs?
2. Has drinking alcohol or using other drugs ever been behind your losing a job?
3. Has your efficiency or ambition decreased due to drinking and using other drugs?
4. Is your drinking and drug use jeopardizing your academic performance?

5. Does drinking or using other drugs cause you to have difficulty sleeping?
6. Have you ever felt remorse after drinking and using other drugs?
7. Do you crave a drink or other drug at a definite time daily, or do you want a drink or other drug the next morning?
8. Have you ever had a complete or partial loss of memory because of drinking or using other drugs?
9. Have you ever been to a hospital or institution because of drinking or other drug use?

If you answered yes to these questions, you are more likely to be a substance abuser than someone who answered no.

Source: Bennett et al., "Identifying Young Adult Substance Abusers: The Rutgers Collegiate Substance Abuse Screening Test." *Journal of Studies on Alcohol* 54: 522–527. Copyright 1993 Alcohol Research Documentation, Inc., Piscataway, NJ. Reprinted by permission. The RCSAST is to be used only as part of a complete assessment battery because more research needs to be done with this instrument.

RESEARCH HIGHLIGHT

Addictive Drugs as the Brain's "Evil Tutor"

Objective 5.12: *Why do addicts abuse drugs?*

Why do alcoholics and other addicts continue to take drugs that are clearly destroying their lives? One explanation may be that the brain "learns" to be addicted. Scientists have long known that various neurotransmitters are key to all forms of normal learning. Now evidence suggests that addictive drugs (acting on certain neurotransmitters) "teach" the brain to want more and more of the destructive substances—whatever the cost. Drugs become the brain's "evil tutor" (Wickelgren, 1998, p. 2045).

How does this happen? The neurotransmitter dopamine has been a primary focus of drug abuse research because of its well-known effect on a part of the brain's reward system known as the nucleus accumbens (Adinoff, 2005; Balfour, 2004). Nicotine and amphetamines, for example, stimulate the release of dopamine, and cocaine blocks its reuptake. Drugs that increase dopamine activity are most likely to result in physical dependence.

Recently, however, evidence points to the importance of another neurotransmitter, glutamate. Although surges in dopamine caused by drug use appear to activate the brain's reward system, glutamate

"That is not one of the seven habits of highly effective people."

©The New Yorker Collection 1998 Leo Cullum from cartoonbank.com. All Rights

may explain compulsive drug taking. Even after the initial effects of a drug disappear, glutamate-induced learning encourages the addict to want more and more of the drug and directs the body to get it. Glutamate apparently creates lasting memories of drug use by changing the nature of "conversations" between neurons. Changes in neuronal connections result whenever we learn something and store it in memory. But in this case, glutamate "teaches" the brain to be addicted.

Glutamate's lesson is rarely forgotten. Even when users are highly motivated to end the vicious cycle of drug abuse, glutamate-related changes in the brain

keep them "hooked." In addition to the well-known intense cravings and pain of withdrawal, the addicted brain also creates cravings at the mere sight of drug-related items. When 13 cocaine addicts and 5 controls watched films of people using both neutral objects and drug-associated items (such as glass pipes and razor blades), the addicts reported significant cravings. During this same time, positron emission tomography (PET) scans of the addicts' brains showed significant neural activity in brain regions known to release glutamate (Grant et al., 1996). Apparently, activating the glutamate system—through drug use or some reminder of the drug—creates strong cravings, which helps explain the common problem of drug relapse.

As a critical thinker, are you wondering how this new research might help with drug abuse and relapse? Recalling earlier information about *agonists* and *antagonists*, what about developing and trying a glutamate antagonist? When shown drug-related objects, long-term drug addicts who received a glutamate antagonist reported a significant reduction in cravings and less drug-seeking behavior (Herman & O'Brien, 1997). Drugs that interfere with glutamate transmission are also being tested for the treatment of general drug abuse (Wickelgren, 1998).

constant drug-induced state—and to lure an "addict" back to a drug habit long after he or she has overcome physical dependence.

Four Major Categories of Psychoactive Drugs: Depressants, Stimulants, Opiates, and Hallucinogens

For convenience, psychologists divide psychoactive drugs into four broad categories: depressants, stimulants, opiates, and hallucinogens (Table 5.1). In this section, we also explore a modern concern with "club drugs" like ecstasy.

Depressants

Depressants (sometimes called *downers*) act on the central nervous system (CNS), causing relaxation, sedation, loss of consciousness, and even death. This category includes ethyl alcohol, barbiturates like Seconal, and antianxiety drugs like Valium. Because tolerance and dependence (both physical and psychological) are rapidly acquired with these drugs, there is strong potential for abuse.

It's often said that alcohol is a *stimulant* at low doses, which accounts for its reputation as a "party drug," and a *depressant* at higher doses. The truth is that alcohol is always a depressant. People become less self-conscious, less inhibited, more relaxed, and more in the mood to "party," even after just one or two drinks, because the alcohol has depressed neural activity in their brain and other parts of their nervous system. As drinking increases, so too do relaxation, disinhibition, poor judgment, and lessened emotional and behavioral control—all of which lead to serious personal and social problems. In very large doses, alcohol can be lethal (Table 5.2).

Alcohol's effects are determined primarily by the amount that reaches the brain. Because the liver breaks down alcohol at the rate of about 1 ounce per hour, the number of drinks and the speed of consumption are both very important. People can die after drinking large amounts of alcohol in a short period of time (Chapter 3). In addition, men's bodies are more efficient than women's at breaking down alcohol. Even after accounting for differences in size and muscle-to-fat ratio, women have a higher blood alcohol level than do men following equal consumption.

Finally, alcohol should not be combined with *any* other drug. But combining alcohol and barbiturates—both depressants—is particularly dangerous. Together, they can relax the diaphragm muscles to such a degree that the person literally suffocates. Actress Judy Garland is only one of many who have died from a barbiturate-and-alcohol mixture.

Stimulants

Depressants suppress central nervous system (CNS) activity, whereas **stimulants** increase its overall activity and responsiveness. Stimulant drugs (such as caffeine, nicotine, amphetamine, methamphetamine, and cocaine) produce alertness, excitement, elevated mood, decreased fatigue, and sometimes increased motor activity. They also may lead to serious problems. Let's look more closely at nicotine and cocaine.

Nicotine Like caffeine, nicotine is a widely used legal stimulant. But unlike caffeine, it kills many of its users. A sad, ironic example of the dangers of nicotine addiction is Wayne McLaren, the rugged Marlboro Man in cigarette ads, who died of lung cancer at age 51. But McLaren was only one of 400,000 who die from smoking-related illnesses each year in the United States. Tobacco kills more than AIDS, legal drugs, illegal drugs, road accidents, murder, and suicide combined (CDC, 2008).

Achievement

Objective 5.13: *List the four main categories of psychoactive drugs and explain how they work.*

Depressants *Drugs that act on the brain and other parts of the nervous system to decrease bodily processes and overall responsiveness*

Michael Newman/PhotoEdit

Drunk driving *As in this fatal car accident in Austin, Texas, drunk drivers are responsible for almost half of all highway-related deaths in America.*

Stimulants *Drugs that act on the brain and other parts of the nervous system to increase overall activity and general responsiveness*

"There's no shooting—we just make you keep smoking."

SUMMARY TABLE 5.1 EFFECTS OF THE MAJOR PSYCHOACTIVE DRUGS

	Category	Desired Effects	Undesirable effects
John E. Kelly/Stone/GettyImages	**Depressants (Sedatives)**		
	Alcohol, barbiturates, antianxiety drugs (Valium), Rohypnol (roofies), Ketamine (special K), CoHB	Tension reduction, euphoria, disinhibition, drowsiness, muscle relaxation	Anxiety, nausea, disorientation, impaired reflexes and motor functioning, amnesia, loss of consciousness, shallow respiration, convulsions, coma, death
Joe Pellegrini/Foodpix/ PictureArts Corp.	**Stimulants**		
	Cocaine, amphetamine, methamphetamine (crystal meth), MDMA (Ecstasy)	Exhilaration, euphoria, high physical and mental energy, reduced appetite, perceptions of power, sociability	Irritability, anxiety, sleeplessness, paranoia, hallucinations, psychosis, elevated blood pressure and body temperature, convulsions, death
Adam Hart-Davis/ PhotoResearchers		Caffeine	Increased alertness	Insomnia, restlessness, increased pulse rate, mild delirium, ringing in the ears, rapid heartbeat
	Nicotine	Relaxation, increased alertness, sociability	Irritability, raised blood pressure, stomach pains, vomiting, dizziness, cancer, heart disease, emphysema
Uwe Schmid/OKAPIA/ PhotoResearchers	**Opiates (Narcotics)**		
	Morphine, heroin, codeine	Euphoria, "rush" of pleasure, pain relief, prevention of withdrawal discomfort	Nausea, vomiting, constipation, painful withdrawal, shallow respiration, convulsions, coma, death
©AP/Wide World Photos	**Hallucinogens (Psychedelics)**		
	LSD (lysergic acid diethylamide)	Heightened aesthetic responses, euphoria, mild delusions, hallucinations, distorted perceptions and sensations	Panic, nausea, longer and more extreme delusions, hallucinations, perceptual distortions ("bad trips"), psychosis
	Marijuana	Relaxation, mild euphoria, increased appetite	Perceptual and sensory distortions, hallucinations fatigue, lack of motivation, paranoia, possible psychosis

TABLE 5.2 ALCOHOL'S EFFECTS ON THE BODY AND BEHAVIOR

Number of drinks in two hours[a]	Blood Alcohol Content (%)[b]	Effect
(2)	0.05	Relaxed state; increased sociability
(3)	0.08	Everyday stress lessened
(4)	0.10	Movements and speech become clumsy
(7)	0.20	Very drunk; loud and difficult to understand; emotions unstable
(12)	0.40	Difficult to wake up; incapable of voluntary action
(15)	0.50	Irregular heart beats, convulsions, coma, and/or death

[a]A drink refers to one 12-ounce beer, a 4-ounce glass of wine, or a 1.25-ounce shot of hard liquor.
[b]In America, the legal blood alcohol level for "drunk driving" varies from 0.05 to 0.12.

When smoking doesn't kill, it can result in chronic bronchitis, emphysema, and heart disease (CDC, 2008). Countless others are affected by secondhand smoke, by smoking-related fires, and by prenatal exposure to nicotine (Chapters 3 and 9). The U.S. Public Health Service considers cigarette smoking the single most preventable cause of death and disease in the United States.

As scientific evidence of the dangers of smoking accumulates, and as social pressure from nonsmokers increases, many smokers are trying to kick the habit. Although some succeed, others find it extremely difficult to quit smoking. Researchers have found that nicotine use is linked to usage of other addictive drugs, and that nicotine activates the same brain areas (nucleus accumbens) as cocaine—a drug well known for its addictive potential (Champtiaux, Kalivas, & Bardo, 2006; McQuown et al., 2007; Zanetti, Picciotto, & Zoli, 2007). The reported pleasures of smoking (relaxation, increased alertness, diminished pain and appetite) are so powerfully reinforcing that some smokers continue to smoke even after having a cancerous lung removed.

Cocaine Cocaine is a powerful central nervous system stimulant extracted from the leaves of the coca plant. It can be sniffed as a white powder, injected intravenously, or smoked in the form of crack. It produces feelings of alertness, euphoria, well-being, power, energy, and pleasure. But it also acts as an *agonist drug* to block the reuptake of our body's natural neurotransmitters that produce these same effects (Figure 5.6).

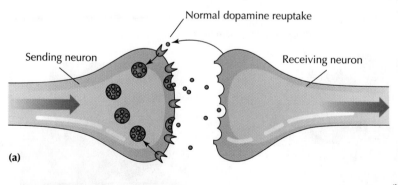

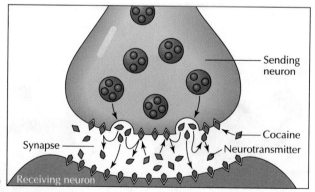

Figure 5.6 *Cocaine: an agonist drug in action* (a) After releasing neurotransmitter into the synapse, the sending neuron normally reabsorbs (or reuptakes) excess neurotransmitter back into the terminal buttons. (b) However, if cocaine is present in the synapse, it will block the reuptake of dopamine, serotonin, and norepinephrine. This blockage intensifies the normal mood-altering effect of these three mood and energy activating neurotransmitters.

Although cocaine was once considered a relatively harmless "recreational drug," its potential for physical damage and severe psychological dependence is now recognized. Sigmund Freud often is cited as a supporter of cocaine use. But few people know that in his later writings Freud called cocaine the "third scourge" of humanity, after alcohol and heroin. Even small initial doses can be fatal because cocaine interferes with the electrical system of the heart, causing irregular heartbeats and, in some cases, heart failure. It also can produce heart attacks and strokes by temporarily constricting blood vessels (Abadinsky, 2008; Westover, McBride, & Haley, 2007). The most dangerous form of cocaine is the smokeable, concentrated version known as crack or rock. Its lower price makes it affordable and attractive to a large audience. But its greater potency also makes it more quickly addictive and dangerous.

Opiates

Opiates (or narcotics), which include morphine and heroin, numb the senses and thus are used medically to relieve pain (Maisto, Galizio, & Connors, 2008). The classification term *opiates* is used because the drugs are derived from (or are similar to those derived from) the opium poppy. They are attractive to people seeking an alternate state of consciousness because they produce feelings of relaxation and euphoria. They produce their effect by mimicking the brain's own natural chemicals for pain control and mood elevation, called *endorphins* (Figure 5.7). (Recall from Chapter 2 that the word *endorphin* was derived from "endogenous morphine.")

This mimicking of the body's natural endorphins creates a dangerous pathway to drug abuse. After repeated flooding with artificial opiates, the brain eventually reduces or stops the production of its own opiates. If the user later attempts to stop, the brain lacks both the artificial and normal level of painkilling chemicals. And withdrawal becomes excruciatingly painful.

The euphoria, pain relief, and avoidance of withdrawal all contribute to make opiates, like heroin, extremely addictive. Interestingly, when opiates are used medically to relieve intense pain, they are very seldom habit-forming. However, when taken recreationally, they are strongly addictive (Field, 2007; Levinthal, 2008).

Hallucinogens

One of the most intriguing alterations of consciousness comes from **hallucinogens**. These drugs produce sensory or perceptual distortions, including visual, auditory, or kinesthetic hallucinations. According to some reports, colors are brighter and more

Opiates *Drugs derived from opium that numb the senses and relieve pain (The word* opium *comes from the Greek word meaning "juice.")*

Hallucinogens [hal-LOO-sin-oh-jenz] *Drugs that produce sensory or perceptual distortions called hallucinations*

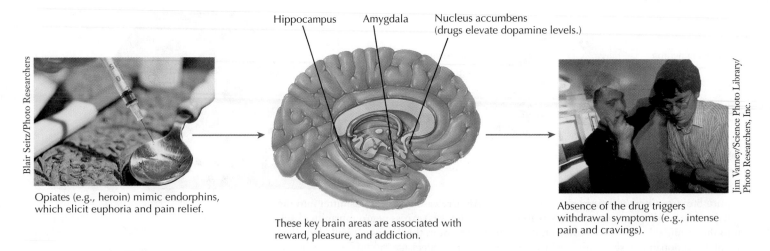

Opiates (e.g., heroin) mimic endorphins, which elicit euphoria and pain relief.

Hippocampus　Amygdala　Nucleus accumbens (drugs elevate dopamine levels.)

These key brain areas are associated with reward, pleasure, and addiction.

Absence of the drug triggers withdrawal symptoms (e.g., intense pain and cravings).

Figure 5.7 *How opiates mimic endorphins*

luminous, patterns seem to pulsate and rotate, and senses may seem to fuse—that is, colors are "heard" or sounds "tasted."

Some cultures have used hallucinogens for religious purposes, as a way to experience "other realities" or to communicate with the supernatural. In Western societies, most people use hallucinogens for their reported "mind-expanding" potential. For example, some artists highly value hallucinogens as a way of increasing creativity. But the experience is not always positive. Terror-filled "bad trips" can occur. Also, dangerous flashbacks may unpredictably recur long after the initial ingestion. The flashback experience may be brought on by stress, fatigue, marijuana use, illness, emerging from a dark room, and occasionally by the individual's intentional effort (Abadinsky, 2008).

Hallucinogens are also commonly referred to as *psychedelics* (from the Greek for "mind manifesting"). They include mescaline (derived from the peyote cactus), psilocybin (from mushrooms), phencyclidine (chemically derived), and LSD (lysergic acid diethylamide, derived from ergot, a rye mold). We will focus on LSD and marijuana in our discussion because they are the most widely used hallucinogens.

Lysergic acid diethylamide (LSD) LSD, or "acid," is a synthethic substance that produces dramatic alterations in sensation and perception. This odorless, tasteless, and colorless substance is also one of the most potent drugs known. As little as 10 micrograms of LSD can produce a measurable psychoactive effect in one individual. An amount the size of an aspirin is enough to produce effects in 3000 people. In 1943 Albert Hofman, the Swiss chemist who first synthesized LSD in a laboratory, accidentally licked some of the drug off his finger and later recorded this in his journal:

> Last Friday, April 16, 1943, I was forced to stop my work in the laboratory in the middle of the afternoon and to go home, as I was seized by a peculiar restlessness associated with a feeling of mild dizziness. Having reached home, I lay down and sank in a kind of drunkenness which was not unpleasant and which was characterized by extreme activity of imagination. As I lay in a dazed condition with my eyes closed (I experienced daylight as disagreeably bright) there surged upon me an uninterrupted stream of fantastic images of extraordinary plasticity and vividness and accompanied by an intense, kaleidoscope-like play of colors. This condition gradually passed after about two hours. (Hofman, 1968, pp. 184–185)

Vision from an LSD trip?

Perhaps because the LSD experience is so powerful, few people actually "drop acid" on a regular basis. This may account for its relatively low reported abuse rate. However, LSD can be a dangerous drug. Bad LSD trips can be terrifying and may lead to accidents, death, or suicide (Levinthal, 2008; Maisto, Galizio, & Connors, 2008).

Marijuana Marijuana is also generally classified as a hallucinogen, even though it has some properties of a depressant (including drowsiness and lethargy) and a narcotic (acting as a weak painkiller). In low doses, it also produces mild euphoria. Moderate doses lead to an intensification of sensory experiences and the illusion that time is passing very slowly. At the highest doses, marijuana may produce hallucinations, delusions, and distortions of body image (Köfalvi, 2008; Ksir, Hart, & Ray, 2008). Regardless of its classification, it is one of the most popular of all illegal consciousness-altering drugs in the Western world.

The active ingredient in marijuana (cannabis) is THC, or tetrahy-dracannabinol, which attaches to receptors that are abundant throughout the brain. The presence of these receptors implies that the brain produces some THC-like chemicals of its own. In fact, researchers have discovered a brain chemical (called anandamide) that binds to the same receptors that THC was previously found to use. In 1997, a second THC-like

©2002 Daniel Laine/Matrix International, Inc.

Culture and marijuana *These young Jamaican girls are members of the Rastafarian Church, which considers marijuana a "wisdom weed." Can you see how culture also affects attitudes toward terms like* drug abuse *and* addiction?

chemical (2-AG) was also discovered (Stella, Schweitzer, & Piomelli, 1997). At this point, no one knows the function of anandamide or 2-AG or why the brain has its own marijuana-like receptors.

With the exception of alcohol during the time of Prohibition, there has never been a drug more hotly debated than marijuana. On the positive side, some research has found marijuana therapeutic in the treatment of glaucoma (an eye disease), in alleviating the nausea and vomiting associated with chemotherapy, in increasing appetite, and in treating asthma, seizures, epilepsy, and anxiety (Darmani & Crim, 2005; Fogarty et al., 2007; Köfalvi, 2008).

But some researchers also report impaired memory, attention, and learning, and marijuana may also be related to birth defects and lower IQ in children (Carter & Wang, 2007; Goldschmidt et al., 2008; Medina et al., 2007). In addition, chronic marijuana use can lead to throat and respiratory disorders, impaired lung functioning, decreased immune response, declines in testosterone levels, reduced sperm count, and disruption of the menstrual cycle and ovulation (Levinthal, 2008; Murphy, 2006; Rossato & Pagano, 2008; Nahas et al., 2002; Roth et al., 2004). While some research supports the popular belief that marijuana serves as a "gateway" to other illegal drugs, other studies find little or no connection (Ksir, Hart, & Ray, 2008; Sabet, 2007; Tarter et al., 2006).

Marijuana also can be habit-forming, but few users experience the intense cravings associated with cocaine or opiates. Withdrawal symptoms are mild because the drug dissolves in the body's fat and leaves the body very slowly, which explains why a marijuana user can test positive for days or weeks after the last use.

PSYCHOLOGY AT WORK   *Club Drug Alert!*

Achievement

Objective 5.14: *Discuss issues and concerns related to "club drugs."*

As you may know from television or newspapers, psychoactive drugs like Rohypnol (the date rape drug) and MDMA (ecstasy) are fast becoming some of our nation's most popular drugs of abuse—especially at "raves" and other all-night dance parties. Other "club drugs," like GHB (gamma-hydroxybutyrate), ketamine (Special K), methamphetamine (crystal meth), and LSD, also are gaining in popularity (Abadinsky, 2008; Weaver & Schnoll, 2008).

Although these drugs can produce desirable effects (e.g., ecstasy's feeling of great empathy and connectedness with others), it's important to note that almost all psychoactive drugs may cause serious health problems and, in some cases, even death.

High doses of MDMA, for example, can cause dangerous increases in body temperature and blood pressure that may lead to seizures, heart attacks, and strokes (Goni-Allo et al., 2008; Weigand, Thai, & Benowitz, 2008). In addition, research shows that chronic use of MDMA may increase depression because it affects neurons that release the neurotransmitter serotonin (Frick, Wang, & Carlson, 2008; Gudelsky & Yamamoto, 2008). As you recall from Chapter 2, serotonin is critical to emotional regulation, learning, memory, and other cognitive functions.

Club drugs, like all illicit drugs, are particularly dangerous because there are no truth-in-packaging laws to protect buyers from unscrupulous practices. Sellers often substitute unknown cheaper, and possibly even more dangerous, substances for the ones they claim to be selling. Also, club drugs (like most psychoactive drugs) affect the motor coordination, perceptual skills, and reaction time necessary for safe driving.

Impaired decision making is a serious problem as well. Just as "drinking and driving don't mix," club drug use may lead to risky sexual behaviors and increased risk of AIDS (acquired immunodeficiency syndrome) and other sexually transmitted diseases. Add in the fact that some drugs, like Rohypnol, are odorless, colorless, tasteless, and can easily be added to beverages by individuals who want to intoxicate or sedate

©AP/Wide World Photos

Club drugs developed for Generation X

others, and you can see that the dangers of club drug use go far beyond the drug itself. If you would like more information on the specific dangers and effects of these club drugs, check http://www.drugabuse.gov/clubalert/clubdrugalert.html.

Assessment
STOP

CHECK & REVIEW

Psychoactive Drugs

Objective 5.10: *Define psychoactive drugs and explain how they work.*

Psychoactive drugs are chemicals that change conscious awareness, mood, and/or perception. These drugs work primarily by changing the amount and effect of neurotransmitters in the synapse. Some drugs act as *agonists* that mimic a neurotransmitter's effects, whereas other drugs act as *antagonists* and block normal neurotransmitter functioning.

Objective 5.11: *Clarify the major misconceptions and confusing terminology related to psychoactive drugs.*

Drug abuse refers to drug taking that causes emotional or physical harm to the individual or others. **Addiction** is a broad term referring to a person's feeling of compulsion to use a specific drug or to engage in certain activities.

Psychoactive drug use can lead to psychological dependence or physical dependence or both. **Psychological dependence** is a desire or craving to achieve the effects produced by a drug. **Physical dependence** is a change in bodily processes due to continued drug use that results in **withdrawal** symptoms when the drug is withheld. **Tolerance** is a decreased sensitivity to a drug brought about by its continuous use.

Objective 5.12: *Why do addicts abuse drugs?*

Research shows that their brains "learn" to be addicted. Neurotransmitters, like dopamine and glutamate, activate the brain's reward system and create lasting cravings and memories of the drug use.

Objective 5.13: *List the four main categories of psychoactive drugs and explain how they work.*

The major categories of psychoactive drugs are **depressants, stimulants, opiates**, and **hallucinogens**. Depressant drugs slow the central nervous system, whereas stimulants increase its activity. Opiates numb the senses and relieve pain. And hallucinogens produce sensory or perceptual distortions called hallucinations.

Objective 5.14: *Discuss issues and concerns related to "club drugs."*

Club drugs can produce desirable effects, but they also can cause serious health problems and impair good decision making.

Questions

1. _____ drugs that change conscious awareness, mood, and/or perception are called _____. (a) addictive; (b) hallucinogenic; (c) psychoactive; (d) mind altering
2. Drug taking that causes emotional or physical harm to the drug user or others is known as _____. (a) addiction; (b) physical dependence; (c) psychological dependence; (d) drug abuse
3. How does physical dependence differ from psychological dependence?
4. Identify the four major categories of psychoactive drugs.

Check your answers in Appendix B.

  Click & Review
for additional assessment options:
wiley.com/college/huffman

Healthier Ways to Alter Consciousness

Achievement

Objective 5.15: *Define meditation and discuss its effects.*

As we have just seen, alternate states of consciousness (ASCs) may be reached through everyday activities such as sleep and dreaming or psychoactive drugs. But there are also less common, and perhaps healthier, routes to alternate states. In this section, we will explore the fascinating world of meditation and hypnosis.

Getting "High" on Meditation: A Positive Route to Altered Consciousness?

> Suddenly, with a roar like that of a waterfall, I felt a stream of liquid light entering my brain through the spinal cord. The illumination grew brighter and brighter, the roaring louder. I experienced a rocking sensation and then felt myself slipping out of my body, entirely enveloped in a halo of light. I felt the point of consciousness that was myself growing wider, surrounded by waves of light (Khrishna, 1999, pp. 4–5).

This is how spiritual leader Gopi Khrishna describes his experience with meditation. Does it sound attractive? Most people in the beginning stages of meditation report a

simpler, mellow type of relaxation, followed by a mild euphoria. With long practice some advanced meditators experience feelings of profound rapture and joy or strong hallucinations (Aftanas & Golosheikim, 2003; Castillo, 2003; Harrison, 2005).

What is **meditation**? The term is generally used to refer to a group of techniques designed to refocus attention, block out all distractions, and produce an alternate state of consciousness. Success in meditation requires controlling the mind's natural tendency to wander (Concept Diagram 5.2).

Meditation *Group of techniques designed to refocus attention, block out all distractions, and produce an alternate state of consciousness*

The Mystery of Hypnosis: Recreational and Therapeutic Uses

Achievement

Objective 5.16: *Define hypnosis, and describe its myths and potential benefits.*

Relax…your body is so tired…your eyelids are so very heavy…your muscles are becoming more and more relaxed…your breathing is becoming deeper and deeper…relax…your eyes are closing and your whole body feels like lead…let go…relax.

These are the types of suggestions most hypnotists use to begin hypnosis. Once hypnotized, some people can be convinced they are standing at the edge of the ocean listening to the sound of waves and feeling the ocean mist on their faces. Invited to eat a delicious apple that is actually an onion, the hypnotized person may relish the flavor. Told they are watching a very funny or sad movie, they may begin to laugh or cry at their self-created visions.

What is hypnosis? Scientific research has removed much of the mystery surrounding **hypnosis**. It is defined as a trancelike state of heightened suggestibility, deep relaxation, and intense focus. It is characterized by one or more of the following:

Hypnosis *Trancelike state of heightened suggestibility, deep relaxation, and intense focus*

- narrowed, highly focused attention (the participant is able to "tune out" competing sensory stimuli)

- increased use of imagination and hallucinations (in the case of visual hallucinations, a person may see things that aren't there or not see things that are)

- a passive and receptive attitude

- decreased responsiveness to pain

- heightened suggestibility (a willingness to respond to proposed changes in perception—"this onion is an apple") (Jamieson & Hasegawa, 2007; Jensen et al., 2008; Nash & Barnier, 2008).

Try This Yourself

Application

Want the Benefits of Meditation?

Try this relaxation technique developed by Herbert Benson (1977):

1. Pick a focus word or short phrase that is calming and rooted in your personal value system (such as love, peace, one, shalom).
2. Sit quietly in a comfortable position, close your eyes, and relax your muscles.
3. Focusing on your breathing, breathe through your nose, and as you breathe out, say your focus word or phrase silently to yourself. Continue for 10 to 20 minutes. You may open your

Mischa Richter/The Cartoon Bank, Inc.

eyes to check the time, but do not use an alarm. When you have finished, sit quietly for several minutes, first with closed eyes and later with opened eyes.

4. Maintain a passive attitude throughout the exercise—permit relaxation to occur at its own pace. When distracting thoughts occur, ignore them and gently return to your repetition.
5. Practice the technique once or twice daily, but not within two hours after a meal—the digestive processes seem to interfere with a successful relaxation response.

Concept Diagram 5.2
Meditation and the Brain

Dan Dalton/PhotoDisc Red/Getty

Some meditation techniques, such as t'ai chi and hatha yoga, involve body movements and postures, while in other techniques the meditator remains motionless, chanting or focusing on a single point, like a candle flame.

Emme Lee/Photographer's Choice RF/Getty Images

Through the use of sophisticated equipment, researchers have found that a wider area of the brain responds to sensory stimuli during meditation, suggesting that meditation enhances the coordination between the brain hemispheres (see graphic, right; and Lyubimov, 1992). Researchers have also found that those who meditate use a larger portion of their brain, and that faster and more powerful gamma waves exist in individuals who meditate regularly than in those who do not (Lutz et al., 2004). Past studies have shown that the type of increased coordination associated with more powerful gamma waves correlates with improvements in focus, memory, learning, and consciousness.

Top view of head

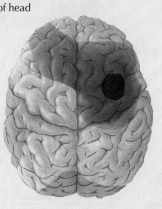

−2.6

0

2.6

Before meditation   During meditation   nV

Cerebral cortex

Attention and focus are strengthened. The cortex thickens over time.

Cerebral white matter

Research has verified that meditation can produce dramatic changes in basic physiological processes, including heart rate, oygen consumption, sweat gland activity and brain activity. Meditation has also been somewhat successful in reducing anxiety and stress, and lowering blood pressure (Carlson et al., 2007; Evans et al., 2008; Harrison, 2005). Studies have even implied that meditation can change the body's parasympathetic response (Sathyaprabha et al., 2008; Young & Taylor, 1998) and increase structural support for the sensory, decision-making, and attention processing centers of the brain (Lazar et al., 2005). It seems that during meditation, the part of the brain that is responsible for both sympathetic and parasympathetic responses, the *hypothalamus*, diminishes the sympathetic response and increases the parasympathetic response. Shutting down the so-called fight-or-flight response in this way allows for deep rest, slower respiration, and increased and more coordinated use of the brain's two hemispheres. At the same time, meditation engages the part of the brain that is responsible for decision making and reasoning, the *frontal lobe*.

Frontal lobe

Hypothalamus

Martin M. Rotker/SPL/ Photo Researchers, Inc.

During meditation, time pressures and worries decrea e, resulting in a sensation of peace and timelessness.

Hypnosis or Simple Trick?

You can recreate a favorite trick that stage hypnotists promote as evidence of superhuman strength under hypnosis. Simply arrange two chairs as shown in the picture. You will see that hypnosis is not necessary—all that is needed is a highly motivated volunteer willing to stiffen his or her body.

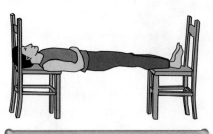

Therapeutic Uses

From the 1700s to modern times, hypnosis has been used (and abused) by entertainers and quacks (Table 5.3). At the same time, it also has been employed as a respected clinical tool by physicians, dentists, and therapists. This curious dual existence began with Franz Anton Mesmer (1734–1815). Mesmer believed that all living bodies were filled with magnetic energy, and he claimed to use this "knowledge" to cure diseases. After lulling his patients into a deep state of relaxation and making them believe completely in his curative powers, Mesmer passed magnets over their bodies and told them their problems would go away. For some people, it worked—hence the term *mesmerized*.

Mesmer's theories were eventually discredited. But James Braid, a Scottish physician, later put people in this same trancelike state for surgery. Around the same time, however, powerful and reliable anesthetic drugs were discovered, and interest in Braid's technique dwindled. It was Braid who coined the term *hypnosis* in 1843, from the Greek word for "sleep."

Today, even with available anesthetics, hypnosis is occasionally used in surgery and for the treatment of chronic pain and severe burns (Jensen et al., 2008; Nash & Barnier, 2008). Hypnosis has found its best use, however, in medical areas in which patients have a high degree of anxiety, fear, and misinformation, such as dentistry and childbirth. Because pain is strongly affected by tension and anxiety, any technique that helps the patient relax is medically useful.

In psychotherapy, hypnosis can help patients relax, remember painful memories, and reduce anxiety. It has been used with modest success in the treatment of phobias and in efforts to lose weight, stop smoking, and improve study habits (Amundson & Nuttgens, 2008; Golden, 2006; Manning, 2007).

Many athletes use self-hypnosis techniques (mental imagery and focused attention) to improve performance. Long-distance runner Steve Ortiz, for example, mentally relives all his best races before a big meet. He says that by the time the race actually begins, "I'm almost in a state of self-hypnosis. I'm just floating along" (cited in Kiester, 1984, p. 23).

TABLE 5.3 HYPNOSIS MYTHS AND FACTS

Myth	Fact
1. Forced hypnosis: People can be involuntarily hypnotized or hypnotically "brainwashed."	Hypnosis requires a willing, conscious choice to relinquish control of one's consciousness to someone else. The best potential subjects are those who are able to focus attention, are open to new experiences, and are capable of imaginative involvement or fantasy (Carvalho et al., 2008; Hutchinson-Phillips, Gow, & Jamieson, 2007; Stafford, 2002; Wickramasekera, 2008).
2. Unethical behavior: Hypnosis can make people behave immorally or take dangerous risks against their will.	Hypnotized people retain awareness and control of their behavior, and they can refuse to comply with the hypnotist's suggestions (Kirsch & Braffman, 2001; Kirsch, Mazzoni, & Montgomery, 2006).
3. Faking: Hypnosis participants are "faking it," playing along with the hypnotist.	Although most participants are not consciously faking hypnosis, some researchers believe the effects result from a blend of conformity, relaxation, obedience, suggestion, and role playing (Fassler et al., 2008; Lynn, 2007; Orne, 2006). Other theorists believe that hypnotic effects result from a special altered state of consciousness (Bob, 2008; Naisch, 2007; Bowers & Woody, 1996; Hilgard, 1978, 1992). A group of "unified" theorists suggests that hypnosis is a combination of both relaxation/role-playing and a unique alternate state of consciousness.
4. Superhuman strength: Hypnotized people can perform acts of special, superhuman strength.	When nonhypnotized people are simply asked to try their hardest on tests of physical strength, they generally can do anything that a hypnotized person can (Orne, 2006).
5. Exceptional memory: Hypnotized people can recall things they otherwise could not.	Although the heightened relaxation and focus that hypnosis engenders improves recall for some information, people also are more willing to guess (Stafford & Lynn, 2002; Wagstaff et al., 2007; Wickramasekera, 2008). Because memory is normally filled with fabrication and distortion (Chapter 7), hypnosis generally increases the potential for error.

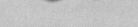

Assessment
CHECK & REVIEW

STOP

Healthier Ways to Alter Consciousness

Objective 5.15: *Define meditation and discuss its effects.*

Meditation is a group of techniques designed to focus attention, block out all distractions, and produce an alternate state of consciousness. It can produce dramatic changes in physiological processes, including brain changes, heart rate, and respiration.

Objective 5.16: *Define hypnosis, and describe its myths and potential benefits.*

Hypnosis is an alternate state of heightened suggestibility characterized by deep relaxation and intense focus. Hypnosis is the subject of many myths, such as "forced hypnosis." But it also has been used successfully to reduce pain, to increase concentration, and as an adjunct to psychotherapy.

Questions

1. _____ is a group of techniques designed to focus attention and produce an alternate state of consciousness.

(a) Hypnosis; (b) Scientology; (c) Parapsychology; (d) Meditation

2. List the five major characteristics of hypnosis.

3. Why is it almost impossible to hypnotize an unwilling participant?

Check your answers in Appendix B.

 Click & Review
for additional assessment options:
wiley.com/college/huffman

Assessment
KEY TERMS

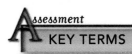

*To assess your understanding of the **Key Terms** in Chapter 5, write a definition for each (in your own words), and then compare your definitions with those in the text.*

Understanding Consciousness
alternate states of consciousness (ASCs) (p. 166)
automatic processes (p. 170)
consciousness (p. 166)
controlled processes (p. 168)

Sleep and Dreams
activation–synthesis hypothesis (p. 180)
circadian [sir-KADE-ee-un] rhythms (p. 171)
evolutionary/circadian theory (p. 178)
insomnia (p. 182)
latent content (p. 179)
manifest content (p. 179)
narcolepsy [NAR co-lep-see] (p. 183)

night terrors (p. 184)
nightmares (p. 184)
non-rapid-eye-movement (NREM) sleep (p. 176)
rapid-eye-movement (REM) sleep (p. 176)
repair/restoration theory (p. 178)
sleep apnea (p. 183)

Psychoactive Drugs
addiction (p. 186)
agonist drug (p. 187)
antagonist drug (p. 187)
depressants (p. 189)
drug abuse (p. 186)
hallucinogens [hal LOO-sin-o-jenz] (p. 192)

opiates (p. 192)
physical dependence (p. 186)
psychoactive drugs (p. 185)
psychological dependence (p. 186)
stimulants (p. 189)
tolerance (p. 186)
withdrawal (p. 186)

Healthier Ways to Alter Consciousness
hypnosis (p. 196)
meditation (p. 196)

Achievement
WEB RESOURCES

Huffman Book Companion Site
wiley.com/college/huffman
This site is loaded with free Interactive Self-Tests, Internet Exercises, Glossary and Flashcards for key terms, web links, Handbook for Non-Native Speakers, and other activities designed to improve your mastery of the material in this chapter.

Understanding Consciousness

Consciousness: Awareness of self and surroundings.
Alternate states of consciousness (ASCs): States other than ordinary waking consciousness.
Controlled processes: Require focused attention and generally interfere with other ongoing activities.
Automatic processes: Require minimal attention and have little impact on other activities.

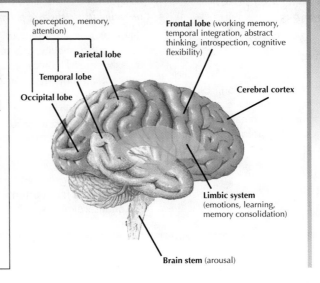

(perception, memory, attention)

Parietal lobe

Temporal lobe

Occipital lobe

Frontal lobe (working memory, temporal integration, abstract thinking, introspection, cognitive flexibility)

Cerebral cortex

Limbic system (emotions, learning, memory consolidation)

Brain stem (arousal)

Sleep and Dreams

- *Sleep as a Circadian Rhythm:* 24-hour cycles (**circadian rhythms**) affect our sleep and waking cycle. Disruptions due to shift work, jet lag, and sleep deprivation can cause serious problems.

- *Stages of Sleep:* A typical night's sleep has four to five 90-minute cycles. **NREM** cycle begins in Stage 1 and then moves through Stages 2, 3, and 4. After reaching the deepest level, the cycle reverses up to **REM** Stage.

NREM Sleep (Stages 1–4)

Function: Required for basic biological functioning.

REM Sleep (paradoxical sleep)

Function: Important for memory, learning, and basic biological functioning. Rapid eye movement often signals dreaming.

Theories of Sleep

1. **Evolutionary/Circadian:** Sleep is part of circadian cycle, and evolved to conserve energy and protect from predators.

2. **Repair/Restoration:** Sleep allows recuperation from physical, emotional. and intellectual fatigue.

REM sleep

Time
Posture shifts
Wakefulness
Stage 1 sleep
Stage 2 sleep
Stage 3 sleep
Stage 4 sleep
Dream activity

Theories of Dreaming

1. *Psychoanalytic/psychodynamic view:* Dreams are disguised symbols (**manifest** versus **latent content**) of repressed desires and anxieties.

2. *Biological view:* Random stimulation of brain cells (**activation–synthesis hypothesis**)

3. *Cognitive view:* Dreams help sift and sort everyday experiences (information processing theory).

Sleep and Dreams

Sleep Disorders

Insomnia
- Repeated difficulty falling or staying asleep or awakening too early.

Sleep Apnea
- Temporarily stopping breathing during sleep.

Narcolepsy
- Sudden and irresistible onsets of sleep during waking hours.

Nightmares
- Bad dreams generally occurring during REM sleep.

Night Terrors
- Panic, hallucinations, and abrupt awakenings during NREM sleep.

Nightmare or night terror?

Zigy Kaluzny/Stone/Getty Images

Psychoactive Drugs

Important Terminology

Drug abuse: Drug taking that causes emotional or physical harm to the individual or others.

Addiction: Broad term referring to feelings of compulsion.

Psychological dependence: Desire or craving to achieve effects produced by a drug.

Physical dependence: Change in bodily processes that make a drug necessary for minimal functioning.

Withdrawal: Discomfort and distress after stopping addictive drugs.

Tolerance: Decreased sensitivity to a drug due to its continuous use.

Four Major Categories of Drugs

1) **Depressants** or "downers" (alcohol and barbiturates) slow down CNS.
2) **Stimulants** or "uppers" (caffeine, nicotine, and cocaine) activate CNS.
3) **Opiates** (heroin or morphine) numb senses and relieve pain.
4) **Hallucinogens** or psychedelics (LSD or marijuana) produce sensory or perceptual distortions.

How cocaine works in the synapse.

Healthier Ways to Alter Consciousness

Meditation:

Group of techniques designed to refocus attention, and block out all distractions

Hypnosis:

Trancelike state of heightened suggestibility, deep relaxation, and intense focus.

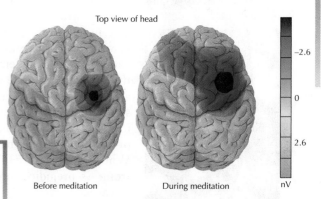

Top view of head

Before meditation   During meditation

Brain scans showing meditation's effects.

6

Learning

I n 1974, Bangladeshi economics professor Muhammad Yunus lent $27 to a group of women weavers so they could buy their own materials, rather than borrowing from a "middleman" who charged exorbitant interest. Within a year, everyone had paid him back. Yunus went on to found a bank to extend very small loans to poor people. Since 1983, his Grameen Bank has lent billions of dollars, with no collateral, to some 17 million people worldwide—97 percent of them women. Yunus's "microcredit" model has inspired many similar efforts. In 2006, Yunus and the Grameen Bank were awarded the Nobel Peace Prize for their pioneering work. In accepting the prize, Yunus said that he plans to use his share of the $1.4 million award to establish a company to sell food to the poor for a nominal price and to build an eye hospital for the poor in Bangladesh. Why? Where does such goodness come from? Is generosity innate or is it learned?

On June 7, 1998, James Byrd, a disabled 49-year-old African American, was walking home along Martin Luther King Boulevard in Jasper, Texas. Three young white men pulled up and offered him a ride. But they had no intention of taking him home. Instead, they chained Mr. Byrd by his ankles to the back of their rusted 1982 pickup and dragged him along an old logging road until his head and right arm were ripped from his body. What brought about this grisly murder? Byrd was a black man. His three murderers were "white supremacists"—two of whom were sentenced to death and the third given life imprisonment without parole. In this case, prejudice was punished, but hate crimes remain as a serious and growing problem around the world. People are ridiculed, attacked, and even murdered simply because of their ethnicity, sexual orientation, gender, or religious preference. Why? Where does such hatred come from? Is prejudice innate or is it learned?

REMEMBER HIS NAME

I'VE GOT A CURE FOR AMERICA KKK

▶ **Classical Conditioning**

Pavlov and Watson's Contributions
Basic Principles

▶ **Operant Conditioning**

Thorndike and Skinner's Contributions
Basic Principles

 PSYCHOLOGY AT WORK
Why Can't We Get Anything Done Around Here?

CRITICAL THINKING/ACTIVE LEARNING
Using Learning Principles to Succeed in College

▶ **Cognitive-Social Learning**

Insight and Latent Learning
Observational Learning

RESEARCH HIGHLIGHT
"The Theory Heard Round the World"

GENDER & CULTURAL DIVERSITY
Scaffolding as a Teaching Technique in
Different Cultures

▶ **The Biology of Learning**

Neuroscience and Learning
Evolution and Learning

▶ **Using Conditioning and
Learning Principles**

PSYCHOLOGY AT WORK
Classical Conditioning

PSYCHOLOGY AT WORK
Operant Conditioning

PSYCHOLOGY AT WORK
Cognitive-Social Learning

Application

WHY STUDY PSYCHOLOGY?

Did you know that this chapter can...

▶ *Expand your understanding and control of behavior?* A core research finding from learning theory is that people (and nonhuman animals) *do not persist in behaviors that are not reinforced.* Using this information, we can remove reinforcers of destructive or undesirable behaviors and recognize that bad habits will continue until we change the reinforcers. Keep in mind that behavior is not random! There's a reason for everything we do.

▶ *Improve the predictability of your life?* Another key finding from research in learning is that the *best predictor of future behavior is past behavior.* People can (and do) change, and all learned behavior can be unlearned. However, the statistical odds are still high that old patterns of behavior will persist in the future. If you want to predict whether the person you're dating is good marriage material, look to his or her past.

Andy Sacks/Stone/GettyImages

▶ *Enhance your enjoyment of life?* Unfortunately, many people (who haven't taken introductory psychology) choose marital partners hoping to change or "rescue" them. Or they pursue jobs they hate because they want to "make a lot of money." If you carefully study and actively apply the information in this chapter, you can avoid these mistakes and thereby greatly enrich your life.

▶ *Help you change the world?* Reinforcement also motivates greedy business practices, unethical political and environmental decisions, prejudice, and war. Knowing this, if we all work together to remove the inappropriate reinforcers, we can truly change the world. Admittedly, this sounds grandiose and simplistic. But I sincerely believe in the power of education and the usefulness of the material in this chapter. Your life and the world around you can be significantly improved with a "simple" application of learning principles.

Achievement

Objective 6.1: *Compare learning and conditioning.*

Learning *Relatively permanent change in behavior or mental processes due to experience*

Conditioning *Process of learning associations between environmental stimuli and behavioral responses*

We usually think of learning as classroom activities, such as math and reading, or as motor skills, like riding a bike or playing the piano. Psychologists define **learning** more broadly, as a relatively permanent change in behavior and mental processes due to experience. This relative permanence applies not only to useful and admirable behaviors, like using a spoon or working to help the poor, but also to bad habits and social problems, like overeating and prejudice. The good news is that what is learned can be unlearned—through retraining, counseling, and self-reflection.

In this chapter, we discuss several types of **conditioning**, the most basic form of learning. We begin with the the two most common types of conditioning, classical and operant. Then we look at cognitive-social learning and biological factors in learning. Finally, we explore how learning theories and concepts touch on everyday life.

Achievement

Objective 6.2: *Define classical conditioning, and describe Pavlov's and Watson's contributions.*

Classical Conditioning

Have you noticed that when you're hungry and see a large slice of chocolate cake or a juicy steak, your mouth starts to water? It seems natural that your mouth should water once you put food into it. But why do you salivate at just the sight of the food?

Pavlov and Watson's Contributions: The Beginnings of Classical Conditioning

The answer to this question was accidentally discovered in the laboratory of Russian physiologist Ivan Pavlov (1849–1936). Pavlov's work focused on the role of saliva in digestion, and one of his experiments involved measuring salivary responses in dogs, using a tube attached to the dog's salivary glands (Process Diagram 6.1).

Sidney Harris

"PERHAPS, DR. PAVLOV, HE COULD BE TAUGHT TO SEAL ENVELOPES."

Pavlov's (Accidental) Discovery

One of Pavlov's students noticed that many dogs began salivating at the mere sight of the food or the food dish, the smell of the food, or even the sight of the person who delivered the food long *before* receiving the actual food. This "unscheduled" salivation was intriguing. Pavlov recognized that an involuntary reflex (salivation) that occurred *before* the appropriate stimulus (food) was presented could not be inborn and biological. It had to have been acquired through experience—through *learning*.

Excited by this accidental discovery, Pavlov and his students conducted several experiments. Their most basic method involved sounding a tone on a tuning fork just before food was placed in the dog's mouth. After several pairings of tone and food, the dogs would salivate on hearing the tone alone. Pavlov and others went on to show that all sorts of things can be conditioned stimuli for salivation if they are paired with food—the ticking of a metronome, a bell, a buzzer, a light, and even the sight of a circle or triangle drawn on a card.

The type of learning that Pavlov discovered came to be known as **classical conditioning**, *learning that occurs when a neutral stimulus (NS) becomes paired (associated) with an unconditioned stimulus (UCS) to elicit a conditioned response (CR).*

To understand classical conditioning, you first need to realize that *conditioning* is just another word for learning. You also need to know that some responses are inborn and don't need conditioning or learning.

Before Pavlov's dogs *learned* to salivate at something extraneous like the sight of the experimenter, the original salivary reflex was *inborn* and biological. It consisted of an **unconditioned stimulus (UCS)**, food, and an **unconditioned response (UCR)**, salivation. Pavlov's accidental discovery (and great contribution to psychology) was that learning can occur when a **neutral stimulus (NS)** (a stimulus that does not evoke or bring out a response) is regularly paired with an unconditioned stimulus (UCS). The originally neutral stimulus (the tone or the cardboard box in Process Diagram 6.1) then becomes a **conditioned stimulus (CS)**, which elicits or produces a **conditioned response (CR)** (salivation).

Watson's Contribution to Classical Conditioning

What does a dog salivating to the sound of a tone have to do with your life? Classical conditioning is the most basic and fundamental way that all animals, including humans, learn most new responses, emotions, and attitudes. Your love for your parents (or significant other), the hatred and racism that led to the murder of James Byrd, and your drooling at the sight of chocolate cake are largely the result of classical conditioning.

In a famous (and controversial) experiment, John Watson and Rosalie Rayner (1920) demonstrated how the emotion of fear could be classically conditioned (Figure 6.1). Although this study remains a classic in psychology, the research procedures used by Watson and Rayner violated several ethical guidelines for scientific research (Chapter 1). Watson and Rayner not only deliberately created a serious fear in a child, but they also ended their experiment without *extinguishing* (removing) it. In addition, the researchers have been criticized because they did not measure Albert's fear objectively. Their subjective evaluation raises doubt about the degree of fear conditioned.

Classical Conditioning *Learning that occurs when a previously neutral stimulus (NS) is paired (associated) with an unconditioned stimulus (UCS) to elicit a conditioned response (CR)*

Unconditioned Stimulus (UCS) *Stimulus that elicits an unconditioned response (UCR) without previous conditioning*

Unconditioned Response (UCR) *Unlearned reaction to an unconditioned stimulus (UCS) that occurs without previous conditioning*

Neutral Stimulus (NS) *Stimulus that, before conditioning, does not naturally bring about the response of interest*

Conditioned Stimulus (CS) *Previously neutral stimulus that, through repeated pairings with an unconditioned stimulus (UCS), now causes a conditioned response (CR)*

Conditioned Response (CR) *Learned reaction to a conditioned stimulus (CS) that occurs because of previous repeated pairings with an unconditioned stimulus (UCS)*

wiley.com/
college/
huffman

Pavlov's Classical Conditioning

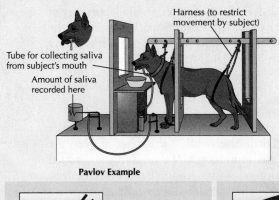

Harness (to restrict movement by subject)

Tube for collecting saliva from subject's mouth

Amount of saliva recorded here

Pavlov Example **Modern-day Example**

Step 1
Before conditioning
The neutral stimulus (NS) produces no relevant response. The unconditioned (unlearned) *stimulus* (UCS) elicits the unconditioned *response.* (UCR)

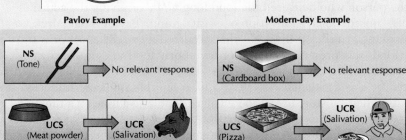

NS (Tone) → No relevant response
UCS (Meat powder) → UCR (Salivation)

NS (Cardboard box) → No relevant response
UCS (Pizza) → UCR (Salivation)

Step 2
During conditioning
The neutral stimulus (NS) is repeatedly paired with the unconditioned (unlearned) *stimulus* (UCS) to produce the unconditioned *response.* (UCR)

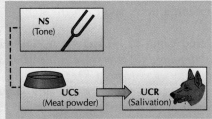

NS (Tone)
UCS (Meat powder) → UCR (Salivation)

NS (Cardboard box)
UCS (Pizza) → UCR (Salivation)

Step 3
After conditioning
The neutral stimulus (NS) has become a conditioned (learned) stimulus (CS). This CS now produces a conditioned (learned) *response* (CR), which is usually similar to the previously unconditioned (unlearned) response (UCR).

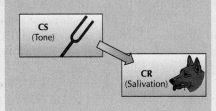
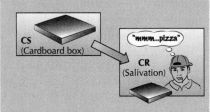

CS (Tone) → CR (Salivation)

CS (Cardboard box) → "mmm...pizza" CR (Salivation)

Summary
An originally neutral stimulus (NS) becomes a conditioned stimulus (CS), which elicits a conditioned response (CR).

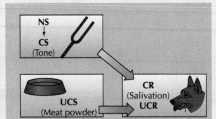
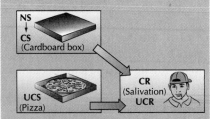

NS ↓ CS (Tone)
UCS (Meat powder) → CR (Salivation) UCR

NS ↓ CS (Cardboard box)
UCS (Pizza) → CR (Salivation) UCR

Study Tip

Use this figure to help you visualize and organize the three major stages of classical conditioning and their associated key terms. If it's confusing, first remember conditioning is essentially the same as learning. Next, when thinking of a UCS or UCR, picture how a newborn baby, with little or no previous learning, would respond. The baby's innate, unlearned response to the UCS would be the UCR.

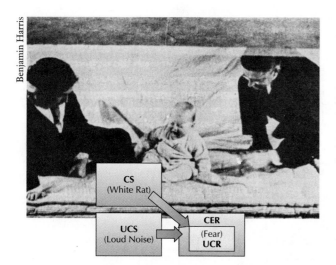

Benjamin Harris

CS
(White Rat)

UCS
(Loud Noise)

CER
(Fear)
UCR

Figure 6.1 *Conditioning and the case of Little Albert* In the famous "Little Albert" study, a healthy 11-month-old child was first allowed to play with a white laboratory rat. Like most infants, Albert was curious and reached for the rat, showing no fear. Using the fact that infants are naturally frightened (UCR) by loud noises (UCS), Watson stood behind Albert and again put the rat (NS) near him. When the infant reached for the rat, Watson banged a steel bar with a hammer. The loud noise frightened Albert and made him cry. The white rat (NS) was paired with the loud noise (UCS) only seven times before the white rat alone produced a *conditioned emotional response* (CER) in Albert, fear of the rat.

Despite such criticisms, John B. Watson made important and lasting contributions to psychology. At the time he was conducting research, psychology's early founders were defining the field as the *scientific study of the mind* (Chapter 1). Watson criticized this focus on internal mental activities, insisting that they were impossible to study objectively. Instead, he emphasized strictly *observable* behaviors. Watson is also credited with founding the new approach known as *behaviorism*, which explains behavior as a result of observable *stimuli* (in the environment) and observable *responses* (behavioral actions). In addition, Watson's study of Little Albert showed us that many of our likes, dislikes, prejudices, and fears are **conditioned emotional responses**. In Chapter 15, you will also see how Watson's research in *producing* Little Albert's fears later led to powerful clinical tools for *eliminating* extreme, irrational fears known as *phobias*.

Historical note: Shortly after the Little Albert experiment, Watson was fired from his academic position. And no other university would hire him, despite his international fame and scientific reputation. His firing resulted from his scandalous and highly publicized affair with his graduate student Rosalie Rayner and subsequent divorce. Watson later married Rayner and became an influential advertising executive. He is credited with many successful ad campaigns based on classical conditioning, including those for Johnson & Johnson baby powder, Maxwell House coffee, and Lucky Strike cigarettes (Goodwin, 2009; Hunt, 1993).

Conditioned Emotional Response (CER) *Classically conditioned emotional response to a previously neutral stimulus (NS)*

Assessment

STOP

CHECK & REVIEW

Classical Conditioning

Objective 6.1: *Compare learning and conditioning.*

Learning is a general term referring to a relatively permanent change in behavior and mental processes due to experience. **Conditioning** is a specific type of learning of associations between environmental stimuli and behavioral responses.

Objective 6.2: *Define classical conditioning, and describe Pavlov and Watson's contributions.*

In **classical conditioning**, the type of learning investigated by Pavlov and Watson, an originally **neutral stimulus (NS)** is paired with an **unconditioned stimulus (UCS)** that causes an **unconditioned response (UCR)**. After several pairings, the neutral stimulus becomes a **conditioned stimulus (CS)**, which alone will produce a **conditioned response (CR)** or **conditioned emotional response (CER)** similar to the original reflex response.

Pavlov's work laid a foundation for Watson's later insistence that psychology must be an objective science, studying only overt behavior without considering internal mental activity. Watson called this position *behaviorism*. His controversial "Little Albert" study demonstrated how simple emotions, like fear, could be classically conditioned to become a **conditioned emotional response (CER)**.

Drawing by John Chase

Questions

1. Based on the humor in this cartoon, the sound of the doorbell would be a(n) _____, and the dogs inside Pavlov's laboratory would begin salivating, which would be a(n) _____. (a) unconditioned stimulus (UCS), conditioned response (CR); (b) conditioned stimulus (CS), conditioned response (CR); (c) neutral stimulus (NS), unconditioned response (UCR); (d) none of these options

2. Eli's grandma gives him a Tootsie Roll every time she visits. When Eli sees his grandma arriving, his mouth begins to water. In this example the conditioned stimulus (CS) is _____. (a) hunger; (b) Grandma; (c) the Tootsie Roll; (d) the watering mouth

3. After conditioning, the _____ elicits the _____.
4. In John Watson's demonstration of classical conditioning with Little Albert, the unconditioned stimulus was _____. (a) symptoms of fear; (b) a rat; (c) a bath towel; (d) a loud noise
5. After pairing the rat with a loud noise, Little Albert demonstrated an intense emotional reaction to the sight of the rat. His emotional response is an example of a(n) _____. (a) CS; (b) UCS; (c) CER; (d) UCR

Check your answers in Appendix B.

 Click & Review
for additional assessment options:
wiley.com/college/huffman

Achievement

Objective 6.3: *Describe the six principles of classical conditioning.*

Acquisition *Basic classical conditioning when a neutral stimulus (NS) is consistently paired with an unconditioned stimulus (UCS) so that the NS comes to elicit a conditioned response (CR)*

Basic Principles: Fine-Tuning Classical Conditioning

Now that you understand the major key terms in classical conditioning and how they explain CERs, we can build on this foundation. In this section, we will discuss six important principles of classical conditioning: *acquisition, stimulus generalization, stimulus discrimination, extinction, spontaneous recovery,* and *higher-order conditioning* (Figure 6.2).

Acquisition

After Pavlov's original (accidental) discovery of classical conditioning, he and his associates were interested in expanding their understanding of the basic experiment we've just described. They wanted to go beyond the basic **acquisition** phase, a term describing general classical conditioning when a neutral stimulus (NS) is consistently paired

Assessment

VISUAL QUIZ

Which of the six basic principles of classical conditioning best explain(s) this cartoon?

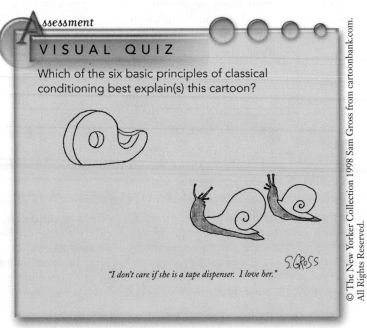

"I don't care if she is a tape dispenser. I love her."

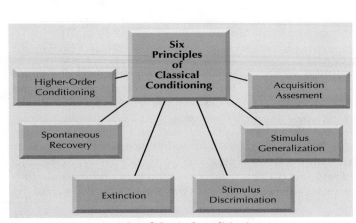

Six Principles of Classical Conditioning

- Higher-Order Conditioning
- Acquisition Assessment
- Spontaneous Recovery
- Stimulus Generalization
- Extinction
- Stimulus Discrimination

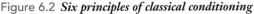

Figure 6.2 *Six principles of classical conditioning*

TABLE 6.1 ACQUISITION AND CONDITIONING SEQUENCES

Delayed conditioning (most effective)	NS presented before UCS and remains until UCR begins	Tone presented before food
Simultaneous conditioning	NS presented at the same time as UCS	Tone and food presented simultaneously
Trace conditioning	NS presented and then taken away, or ends before UCS presented	Tone sounds, but food presented only once the sound stops
Backward conditioning (least effective)	UCS presented before NS	Food presented before the tone

NS = neutral stimulus; UCR = unconditioned response; UCS = unconditioned stimulus.

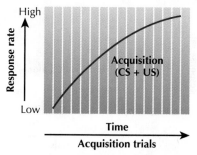

Figure 6.3 ***The process of acquisition*** During the initial, *acquisition*, phase of classical conditioning, a neutral stimulus (NS) that is consistently followed by an unconditioned stimulus (UCS) will become a conditioned stimulus (CS), which elicits a conditioned response (CR).

with an unconditioned stimulus (UCS) so that the NS comes to elicit a conditioned response (CR) (Figure 6.3).

What is the optimal amount of time for presenting the neutral stimulus (NS), and what is the best order of presentation? Should the neutral stimulus (NS) always come first? Researchers have investigated four different ways to pair stimuli (Table 6.1), and they found that both the timing and the order in which the NS is presented are very important (Chance, 2009; Chang, Stout, & Miller, 2004; Griffin & Galef, 2005). For example, *delayed conditioning*, in which the NS is presented before the UCS and remains until the UCR begins, generally yields the fastest learning. On the other hand, *backward conditioning*, in which the UCS is presented before the NS, is the least effective.

Generalization and Discrimination

In addition to the basic *acquisition phase* of classical conditioning, Pavlov and his associates also discovered that other stimuli similar to the neutral stimuli often produced a similar conditioned response (CR), a phenomenon known as **stimulus generalization**. For example, after first conditioning dogs to salivate at the sound of low-pitched tones, Pavlov later demonstrated that the dogs would also salivate in response to high-pitched tones. Similarly, after conditioning, the infant in Watson and Rayner's experiment ("Little Albert") feared not only rats, but also a rabbit, a dog, and a bearded Santa Claus mask.

Would little Albert still be afraid of a Santa Claus mask as he grew older? Probably not. As a child in the United States, he undoubtedly had numerous encounters with Santa Claus masks and would have learned to recognize differences between rats and other stimuli. This process of learning responses to a specific stimulus, but not to other similar stimuli is called **stimulus discrimination**.

Although stimulus generalization seems to follow naturally from initial classical conditioning, organisms only learn to distinguish (or *discriminate*) between an original conditioned stimulus (CS) and similar stimuli if they have enough experience with both. Just as you learn to discriminate between the sound of your cellular phone and the ringing of others, when Pavlov repeatedly presented food following a high-pitched tone, but not with a low-pitched tone, the dogs gradually learned to distinguish between the two tones. Thus, both Little Albert and Pavlov's dogs produced conditioned responses only to specific stimuli—*stimulus discrimination*.

Extinction and Spontaneous Recovery

Classical conditioning, like all learning, is only *relatively* permanent. Most responses that are learned through classical conditioning can be weakened or suppressed through **extinction**. Extinction occurs when the unconditioned stimulus (UCS) is repeatedly withheld whenever the conditioned stimulus (CS) is presented, which gradually

Stimulus Generalization *Stimuli similar to the original CS elicit a CR*

Stimulus Discrimination *Only the CS elicits the CR*

Extinction *Repeatedly presenting the CS without the UCS, which gradually weakens the CR*

wiley.com/ college/ huffman

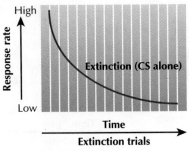

Response rate (High / Low)
Extinction (CS alone)
Time
Extinction trials

Figure 6.4 *The process of extinction* When the conditioned stimulus (CS) is repeatedly presented without the unconditioned stimulus (UCS), the response rate will decrease over time.

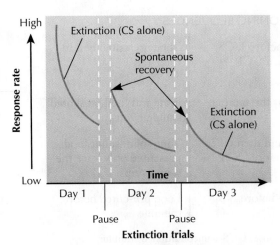

Response rate (High / Low)
Extinction (CS alone)
Spontaneous recovery
Extinction (CS alone)
Time
Day 1 | Day 2 | Day 3
Pause | Pause
Extinction trials

Figure 6.5 *Extinction and spontaneous recovery* Extinction is not the same as complete *unlearning*. Note how the previously extinguished conditioned response (CR) can *spontaneously reappear* when there is a pause in the extinction trials.

weakens the conditioned response (CR) (Figure 6.4). When Pavlov sounded the tone again and again without presenting food, the dogs' salivation gradually declined. Similarly, if you have a classically conditioned fear of the sound of a dentist's drill and later start to work as a dental assistant, your fear will gradually diminish. Can you see the usefulness of this information if you're trying to get over a destructive love relationship? Rather than thinking, "I'll always be in love with this person," remind yourself that given time and repeated contact in a nonloving situation, your feelings will gradually lessen.

Does extinction cause us to "unlearn" a classical conditioned response? No, extinction is not *unlearning* (Bouton, 1994). A behavior becomes *extinct* when the response rate decreases and the person or animal no longer responds to the stimulus. It does not mean the person or animal has "erased" the previous learned connection between the stimulus and the response. In fact, if the stimulus is reintroduced, the conditioning is much faster the second time. Furthermore, Pavlov found that if he allowed several hours to pass after the extinction procedure and then presented the tone again, the salivation would spontaneously reappear. This reappearance of a conditioned response after extinction is called **spontaneous recovery** (Figure 6.5).

Spontaneous Recovery *Sudden reappearance of a previously extinguished conditioned response (CR)*

Higher-Order Conditioning *Neutral stimulus (NS) becomes a conditioned stimulus (CS) through repeated pairings with a previously conditioned stimulus (CS)*

Higher-Order Conditioning

Children are not born salivating at the sign of McDonald's golden arches. So why do they beg their parents to stop at "Mickey D's" after simply seeing the golden arches on a passing billboard? It is because of **higher-order conditioning**, which occurs when a neutral stimulus (NS) becomes a conditioned stimulus (CS) through repeated pairings with a previously conditioned stimulus (CS) (Concept Diagram 6.1).

Concept Diagram 6.1
Higher-order Conditioning

If you wanted to demonstrate higher-order conditioning in Pavlov's dogs, you would first condition the dogs to salivate in response to the sound of the tone (a). Then you would pair a flash of light with the tone (b). Eventually, the dogs would salivate in response to the flash of light alone (c). Similarly, children first learn to pair McDonald's restaurants with food and later learn that two golden arches are a symbol for McDonald's. Their salivation and begging to eat at the restaurant upon seeing the arches are classic examples of higher-order conditioning (and successful advertising).

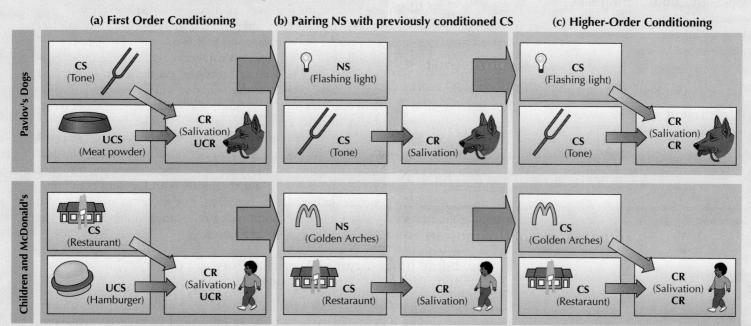

(a) First Order Conditioning   **(b) Pairing NS with previously conditioned CS**   **(c) Higher-Order Conditioning**

STOP

CHECK & REVIEW

Basic Principles of Classical Conditioning

Objective 6.3: *Describe the six principles of classical conditioning.*

Acquisition, the first of the six components, is a term describing basic classical conditioning when a neutral stimulus (NS) is consistently paired with an unconditioned stimulus (UCS) so that the NS comes to elicit a conditioned response (CR).

Stimulus generalization occurs when stimuli similar to the original conditioned stimulus (CS) elicit the conditioned response (CR). **Stimulus discrimination** takes place when only the CS elicits the CR. **Extinction** occurs when the CS is repeatedly presented without the UCS, which gradually weakens the CR. **Spontaneous recovery** occurs when a CR that had been

extinguished suddenly reappears. In **higher-order conditioning**, a NS becomes a CS through repeated pairings with a previously conditioned stimulus (CS).

Questions

1. Like most college students, your heart rate and blood pressure greatly increase when the fire alarm sounds. If the fire alarm system was malfunctioning and rang every half hour, by the end of the day, your heart rate and blood pressure would no longer increase. Using classical conditioning terms, explain this change in your response.

2. A baby is bitten by a dog and then is afraid of all small animals. This is an example of _____. (a) stimulus

discrimination; (b) extinction; (c) reinforcement; (d) stimulus generalization

3. When a conditioned stimulus is used to reinforce the learning of a second conditioned stimulus, _____ has occurred.

4. If you wanted to use higher-order conditioning to get Little Albert to fear Barbie dolls, you would present a Barbie doll with _____. (a) the loud noise; (b) the original unconditioned response; (c) the white rat; (d) the original conditioned response

Check your answers in Appendix B.

Click & Review
for additional assessment options:
wiley.com/college/huffman

Objective 6.4: *Define operant conditioning, reinforcement, and punishment.*

Operant Conditioning *Learning through the consequences of voluntary behavior; also known as instrumental or Skinnerian conditioning*

Reinforcement *Strengthens a response and makes it more likely to recur*

Punishment *Weakens a response and makes it less likely to recur*

Objective 6.5: *Describe Thorndike and Skinner's contributions.*

Law of Effect *Thorndike's rule that the probability of an action being repeated is strengthened when it is followed by a pleasant or satisfying consequence*

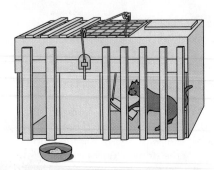

Figure 6.6 ***Thorndike box*** To investigate animal learning, Thorndike put a cat inside a specially built puzzle box. When the cat stepped on a pedal inside the box (at first, through trial and error), the door opened and the cat could get out to eat. With each additional success, the cat's actions became more purposeful, and it soon learned to open the door immediately (from Thorndike, 1898).

Operant Conditioning

Consequences are the heart of **operant conditioning**. In classical conditioning, consequences are irrelevant—Pavlov's dogs still got the meat powder whether or not they salivated. But in operant conditioning, the organism performs a voluntary behavior (an *operant*) that produces either *reinforcement* or *punishment*, which influence whether the response will occur again in the future. **Reinforcement** strengthens the response and makes it more likely to recur. **Punishment** weakens the response and makes it less likely to recur.

Classical and operant conditioning also differ in another important way. In classical conditioning, the organism's response is *passive* and *involuntary*. It "happens to" the organism when a UCS follows a NS. In operant conditioning, however, the organism's response is *active* and *voluntary*. The learner "operates" on the environment and produces consequences that influence whether the behavior will be repeated. If your friends smile and laugh when you tell a joke, your future joke telling is likely to increase. However, if they frown, groan, or ridicule you, your joke telling is likely to decrease.

It's important to note that these distinctions between classical and operant conditioning are *generally* true—but not *always* true. Technically speaking, classical conditioning does sometimes influence voluntary behavior, and operant conditioning can influence involuntary, reflexive behavior. Furthermore, both forms of conditioning often interact to produce and maintain behavior. But for most purposes, the distinction holds. In most cases, classical conditioning refers to involuntary responses and operant conditioning refers to voluntary responses.

Thorndike and Skinner's Contributions: The Beginnings of Operant Conditioning

Edward Thorndike (1874–1949), a pioneer of operant conditioning, was among the first to examine how voluntary behaviors are influenced by their consequences (Figure 6.6). According to Thorndike's **law of effect**, the probability of an action being repeated is *strengthened* if it is followed by a pleasant or satisfying consequence. In short, rewarded behavior is more likely to recur (Thorndike, 1911). Thorndike's law of effect was a first step in understanding how active *voluntary* behaviors can be modified by their consequences.

B. F. Skinner (1904–1990) extended Thorndike's law of effect to more complex behaviors. As a strict behaviorist, however, Skinner avoided terms like *pleasant, desired,* and *voluntary* because they make unfounded assumptions about what an organism feels and wants. The terms also imply that behavior is due to conscious choice or intention. Skinner believed that to understand behavior, we should consider only observable, external, or environmental stimuli and responses. We must look outside the learner, not inside.

In keeping with his focus on external, observable behavior, Skinner emphasized that reinforcement (which increases the likelihood of a response) and punishment (which decreases it) are always defined *after the fact*. This emphasis on only reinforcing or punishing *after* the behavior is important. Suppose you ask to borrow the family car on Friday night, but your parents say you have to wash the car first. If they let you put off washing the car until the weekend, what is the likelihood that you will do it? From their own "trial-and-error" experiences, most parents have learned to make sure the payoff comes *after* the car washing is completed—not before!

In addition to warning that both reinforcement and punishment must come after the response, Skinner also cautions us to check the respondent's behavior to see if it increases or decreases. Sometimes we *think* we're reinforcing or punishing when we're doing the opposite. For example, a professor may think she is encouraging shy students to talk by repeatedly praising them each time they speak up in class. But what if shy students are embarrassed by this attention? If so, they actually may decrease the number of times they talk in class. Similarly, men may buy women candy and flowers after they accept first dates with them because they *know* all women like these things. However, some women hate candy (imagine that!) or may be allergic to flowers. In this case, the man's attempt at reinforcement becomes a punishment! Skinner suggests we should watch our target's *actual* responses—not what we *think* the other person *should* like or do.

Basic Principles: Understanding Operant Conditioning

To effectively use operant conditioning in your life, you need to understand several additional principles. We'll start with factors that *strengthen* or *weaken* a response. Then we'll look at the pros and cons of punishment, and how to use operant conditioning in the workplace. We conclude with a brief overview and comparison of classical versus operant conditioning.

Achievement

Objective 6.6: *Explain how primary and secondary reinforcers and positive and negative reinforcement strengthen behavior.*

Reinforcement—Strengthening a Response

Earlier, we said that Skinner was a strict behaviorist who insisted that scientific observation be limited to that which can be observed. Therefore, instead of using words like *good, bad,* or *rewards* (which focus on feelings), Skinner talked about reinforcers and reinforcement in terms of "strengthening the response." If a toddler whines for candy and the parent gives in, the child's whining will likely increase. But what if the parent also yelled at the child for whining, yet still gave him or her the lollipop? The child might feel both happy to get the candy and sad because the parent is upset. Because we really don't know the full extent of the child's internal, mixed feelings, it's cleaner (and more scientific) to limit our focus to observable behaviors and consequences. If the child's whining for lollipops increases, we can say that whining was reinforced.

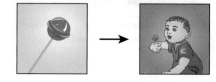

As you can see in Table 6.2, reinforcers are grouped into two types, *primary* or *secondary*, which function as either *positive* or *negative* reinforcement.

1. *Primary and secondary reinforcers.* One of the chief methods for strengthening a response is with primary and secondary reinforcers. Reinforcers such as food, water, and sex are called **primary reinforcers** because they normally satisfy an unlearned biological need. In contrast, reinforcers such as money, praise, attention, and material possessions that have no intrinsic value are called **secondary reinforcers.** Their only power to reinforce behavior results from learning. A baby, for example, would find milk much more reinforcing than a $100 bill. Needless to

Primary Reinforcers *Stimuli that increase the probability of a response because they satisfy an unlearned, biological need (e.g., food, water, and sex)*

Secondary Reinforcers *Stimuli that increase the probability of a response because of their learned value (e.g., money and material possessions)*

TABLE 6.2 HOW REINFORCEMENT STRENGTHENS AND INCREASES BEHAVIORS

	Positive reinforcement Adds to (+) and strengthens behavior	**Negative reinforcement** Takes away (−) and strengthens behavior
Primary reinforcers Meet an unlearned, biological need	You hug your baby and he smiles at you. The "addition" of his smile strengthens the likelihood that you will hug him again.	Your baby is crying, so you hug him and he stops crying. The "removal" of crying strengthens the likelihood that you will hug him again when he cries.
	You do a favor for a friend and she buys you lunch in return.	You take an aspirin for your headache, which takes away the pain.
Secondary reinforcers Meet a learned, not biological, need	You increase profits and receive $200 as a bonus.	After high sales, your boss says you won't have to work on weekends.
	You study hard and receive a good grade on your psychology exam.	You're allowed to skip the final exam because you did so well on your unit exams.

Gary Connor/Index Stock

Positive Reinforcement *Adding (or presenting) a stimulus, which strengthens a response and makes it more likely to recur*

Negative Reinforcement *Taking away (or removing) a stimulus, which strengthens a response and makes it more likely to recur*

Reinforcement in action *Is this father's attention a primary or secondary reinforcer?*

Achievement

Objective 6.7: *Explain why negative reinforcement is not punishment.*

Premack Principle *Using a naturally occurring high-frequency response to reinforce and increase low-frequency responses*

say, by the time this baby has grown to adolescence, he or she will have learned to prefer the money. Among Westerners, money may be the most widely used secondary reinforcer because of its learned association with desirable commodities.

2. *Positive and negative reinforcement.* Adding or taking away certain stimuli also strengthens behavior. Suppose you tickle your baby and he smiles at you. His smile increases (or strengthens) the likelihood that you will tickle him again in the future. The smile itself is a *positive reinforcer* for you. This is called **positive reinforcement**. On the other hand, suppose your baby is upset and crying, so you pick him up and he stops crying. The removal of crying is a *negative reinforcer* for you. The *process* is called **negative reinforcement** because picking him up takes away, or removes, the crying, which also increases (or strengthens) the likelihood that you will pick him up again in the future when he cries.

(As a critical thinker, are you worried about what's happening for the baby in these examples? While you, the parent, were being both *positively* and *negatively reinforced*, your baby was only *positively reinforced*. He learned that his smile led to more tickling, and that his crying caused you to pick him up. If you're concerned that reinforcing the crying will create lasting problems, you can relax. Your baby soon will learn to talk and develop "better" ways to communicate.)

Why Negative Reinforcement Is Not Punishment

Many people hear the term *negative reinforcement* and automatically think of punishment. But it's important to remember that these two terms are completely opposite procedures. Reinforcement (either positive or negative) *strengthens a behavior*. And, as we will see in the next section, punishment *weakens a behavior*.

My students find it easier if they think of positive and negative reinforcement in the *mathematical* sense (see again Table 6.2, p. 213) rather than as personal values of positive as "good" or negative as "bad." Think of positive reinforcement as something being added (+) that increases the likelihood that the behavior will increase. Conversely, think of negative reinforcement as something being taken away (−) that also increases the likelihood that the behavior will continue. For example, if your boss compliments you on a job well done, the compliment is added (+) as a consequence of your behavior. And, therefore, your hard work is likely to increase (*positive reinforcement*). Similarly, if your boss tells you that you no longer have to do a boring part of your job because of your excellent work, the taking away (−) of the boring task is a *negative reinforcement*. And your hard work is also likely to increase.

When I make myself study before I let myself go to the movies, Is this negative reinforcement? No, this is actually a form of *positive reinforcement*. Because you *add* "going to the movies" only *after* you study, this should increase (positively reinforce) your studying behaviors.

In this same example, you're also using the **Premack principle**. Psychologist David Premack believes any naturally occurring, high-frequency response can be used to reinforce and increase low-frequency responses. Recognizing that you love to go to movies, you intuitively tied your less desirable low-frequency activity (studying) to your high-frequency or highly desirable behavior (going to the movies). You also can use the Premack principle in other aspects of your college life, such as making yourself write 4 pages on your term paper or read 20 pages before you allow yourself to call a friend or have a snack.

Should I use the Premack principle every time I want to go to the movies or just occasionally? The answer is complex and depends on your most desired outcome. To make this decision, you need to understand various *schedules* of *reinforcement*, rules that determine when a response will be rewarded and when it will not (Kazdin, 2008).

Schedules of Reinforcement

The term *schedule of reinforcement* refers to the rate or interval at which responses are reinforced. Although there are numerous schedules of reinforcement, the most important distinction is whether they are *continuous* or *partial*. When Skinner was training his animals, he found that learning was most rapid if the response was reinforced each time it occurred—a procedure called **continuous reinforcement**. However, real life seldom provides continuous reinforcement. You do not get an A each time you write a paper or a date each time you ask. But your behavior persists because your efforts are occasionally rewarded. Most everyday behavior is similarly rewarded on a **partial** (or **intermittent**) schedule of **reinforcement**, which involves reinforcing only some responses, not all of them (Miltenberger, 2008).

For effective use of these principles in your own life, remember that continuous reinforcement leads to faster learning than does partial reinforcement. For example, if children (or adults) are rewarded every time they blast an alien starship in a video game (*continuous reinforcement*), they will learn how to play faster than if they are rewarded for every third or fourth hit (*partial reinforcement*). On the other hand, imagine having to reward your children every morning for getting up, brushing their teeth, making their beds, dressing, and so on. You simply cannot reward someone constantly for every appropriate response. Although a continuous schedule of reinforcement leads to faster initial learning, it is *not* an efficient system for maintaining long-term behaviors.

It is therefore important to move to a partial schedule of reinforcement once a task is well learned. Why? Because under partial schedules, behavior is more resistant to extinction. Have you noticed that people spend long hours pushing buttons and pulling levers on slot machines in hopes of winning the jackpot? This high response rate and the compulsion to keep gambling in spite of significant losses are evidence of the strong resistance to extinction with partial schedules of reinforcement. This type of partial, intermittent reinforcement also helps parents maintain behaviors like tooth brushing and bed making. After the child has initially learned these behaviors with continuous reinforcement, you should move on to occasional, partial reinforcement.

Four Partial (Intermittent) Schedules of Reinforcement

There are four partial schedules of reinforcement: **fixed ratio (FR)**, **variable ratio (VR)**, **fixed interval (FI)**, and **variable interval (VI)**. Table 6.3 defines these terms and provides examples.

Continuous Reinforcement
Every correct response is reinforced

Partial (Intermittent) Reinforcement *Some, but not all, correct responses are reinforced*

 Study Tip

Remember that interval is time based, whereas ratio is response based.

Fixed Ratio (FR) Schedule
Reinforcement occurs after a predetermined set of responses; the ratio (number or amount) is fixed

Variable Ratio (VR) Schedule
Reinforcement occurs unpredictably; the ratio (number or amount) varies

Fixed Interval (FI) Schedule
Reinforcement occurs after a predetermined time has elapsed; the interval (time) is fixed

Variable Interval (VI) Schedule *Reinforcement occurs unpredictably; the interval (time) varies*

TABLE 6.3 FOUR PARTIAL (INTERMITTENT) SCHEDULES OF REINFORCEMENT

		Definitions	**Response Rates**	**Examples**	
Ratio Schedules (response based)	**Fixed ratio (FR)**	Reinforcement occurs after a predetermined set of responses; the ratio (number or amount) is fixed	Produces a high rate of response, but a brief dropoff just after reinforcement	Car wash employee receives $10 for every 3 cars washed. In a laboratory, a rat receives a food pellet every time it presses the bar 7 times.	
	Variable ratio (VR)	Reinforcement occurs unpredictably; the ratio (number or amount) varies	High response rates, no pause after reinforcement, and very resistant to extinction	Slot machines are designed to pay out after an average number of responses (maybe every 10 times), but any one machine may pay out on the first response, then seventh, then the twentieth.	

(continues)

TABLE 6.3 (CONTINUED)

		Definitions	Response Rates	Examples	
Interval Schedules (time based)	**Fixed interval (FI)**	Reinforcement occurs after a predetermined time has elapsed; the interval (time) is fixed	Responses tend to increase as the time for the next reinforcer is near, but drop off after reinforcement and during interval	You get a monthly paycheck. A rat's behavior is reinforced with a food pellet when (or if) it presses a bar after 20 seconds have elapsed.	
	Variable interval (VI)	Reinforcement occurs unpredictably; the interval (time) varies	Relatively low, but steady, response rates because respondents cannot predict when reward will come	Rat's behavior is reinforced with a food pellet after a response and a variable, unpredictable interval of time has elapsed. In a class with pop quizzes, you study at a slow, but steady, rate because you can't anticipate the next quiz.	

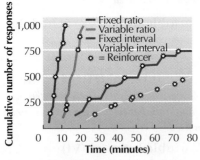

Figure 6.7 *Which schedule is best?* Each of the different schedules *of reinforcement* produces its own unique pattern of response. The best schedule depends on the specific task—see Table 6.3. (The "stars" on the lines represent the delivery of a reinforcer.) (Adapted from Skinner, 1961.)

Achievement

Objective 6.9: *Define shaping and tell why it's important.*

Shaping *Reinforcement delivered for successive approximations of the desired response*

How do I know which schedule to choose? The type of partial schedule selected depends on the type of behavior being studied and on the speed of learning desired (Kazdin, 2008; Neuringer, Deiss, & Olson, 2000; Rothstein, Jensen, & Neuringer, 2008). For example, suppose you want to teach your dog to sit. Initially, you reinforce your dog with a cookie every time he sits (continuous reinforcement). To save on your cookie bill, and to make his training more resistant to extinction, you eventually switch to one of the partial reinforcement schedules. Using the *fixed ratio* schedule, you would give your dog a cookie after he sits a certain number of times. (The dog must make a fixed number of responses before he receives the reinforcement.) As you can see in Figure 6.7, a fixed ratio leads to the highest overall response rate. But each of the four types of partial schedules has different advantages and disadvantages (see Table 6.3).

Shaping

Each of the four schedules of partial reinforcement is important for maintaining behavior. But how do you teach new or complex behaviors like playing the piano or speaking a foreign language? For new and complex behaviors such as these, which aren't likely to occur naturally, **shaping** is a particularly valuable tool. Shaping teaches a desired response by reinforcing a series of successively improving steps leading to the final goal response. Skinner believed that shaping explains a wide variety of skills and abilities that each of us possesses, from eating with a fork, to playing a musical instrument, to driving a car (Chance, 2009).

Parents, athletic coaches, teachers, and animal trainers all use shaping techniques. For example, if you want to shape a child to make his bed, you could begin by reinforcing when he first gets the sheets and pillows in the right general area on the bed—even if it's sloppily done. Over time, you would stop reinforcing that beginning level of behavior. You would only reinforce when he got the sheets, bedspread, and pillows all in the right place, with most of the wrinkles removed. Each step in shaping moves slightly beyond the previously learned behavior. This allows the person to link the new step to the behavior previously learned.

VISUAL QUIZ

Kaku Kurita

Operant Conditioning in Action

Momoko, a five-year-old female monkey, is famous in Japan for her water-skiing, deep-sea diving, and other amazing abilities. Can you explain how her trainers could use shaping to teach Momoko to water sky?

Answer: The trainers would begin by reinforcing Momoko (with a small food treat) for standing or sitting on the water ski. Then they would reinforce her each time she put her hands on the pole. Next, they would slowly drag the water ski on dry land, and reinforce her for staying upright and holding the pole. Then they would take Momoko to a shallow and calm part of the ocean and reinforce her for staying upright and holding the pole as the ski moved in the water. Finally, they would take her into the deep part of the ocean, and reinforce her for holding on and successfully water-skiing.

Punishment—Weakening a Response

Unlike reinforcement, punishment *decreases* the strength of the response-that is, the likelihood that a behavior will be repeated again is weakened. When your dog begs for food off your plate, and you loudly (and *consistently*) say "No," the begging will likely decrease.

Just as with reinforcement, there are two kinds of punishment, *positive* and *negative* (Miltenberger, 2008; Skinner, 1953). Also, as with reinforcement, remember to think in mathematical terms of adding and taking away, rather than good and bad (Table 6.4). **Positive punishment** is the addition (+) of a stimulus that decreases (or weakens) the likelihood of the response occurring again. If a parent adds new chores each time the child is late getting home, the parent is applying positive punishment. **Negative punishment** is the taking away (−) of a stimulus that decreases (or weakens) the likelihood of the response occurring again. Parents use negative punishment when they take the car keys away from a teen who doesn't come home on time. Notice that in *both* positive and negative punishment, the behavior has been punished and the behavioral tendencies have been weakened.

The Tricky Business of Punishment

First, it's important to acknowledge that punishment plays a significant and unavoidable role in our social world. In his book *Walden Two* (1948), Skinner described a utopian (ideal) world where reinforcers almost completely replaced punishment. Unfortunately, in our real world, reinforcement is not enough. Dangerous criminals

Achievement

Objective 6.10: *Explain how positive and negative punishment weaken behavior.*

Positive Punishment *Adding (or presenting) a stimulus that weakens a response and makes it less likely to recur*

Negative Punishment *Taking away (or removing) a stimulus that weakens a response and makes it less likely to recur*

Achievement

Objective 6.11: *Why is punishment "tricky," and what are its serious side effects?*

TABLE 6.4 HOW PUNISHMENT WEAKENS AND DECREASES BEHAVIORS

Positive Punishment *Adds stimulus (+) and weakens the behavior*	**Negative Punishment** *Takes stimulus away (−) and weakens the behavior*
You must run 4 extra laps in your gym class because you were late.	You're excluded from gym class because you were late.
A parent adds extra chores following a child's misbehavior.	A parent takes away a teen's cell phone following a poor report card.
Your boss complains about your performance.	Your boss reduces your expense account after a poor performance.

Is this positive or negative punishment?

must be stopped and, possibly, removed from society. Parents must stop their children from running into the street and their teenagers from drinking and driving. Teachers must stop disruptive students in the classroom and bullies on the playground. There is an obvious need for punishment. But it can be confusing and problematic (Borrego et al., 2007; Leary et al., 2008; Loxton el al., 2008).

When we hear the word *punishment*, most people think of disciplinary procedures used by parents, teachers, and other authority figures. But punishment is much more than parents giving a child a time-out for misbehaving or teachers giving demerits. Any process that adds or takes away something and causes the behavior to decrease is *punishment*. By this definition, if parents ignore all the A's on their child's report card and ask repeated questions about the B's and C's, they may unintentionally punish and weaken the likelihood of future A's. Dog owners who yell at or spank their dogs for finally coming to them after being called several times are actually punishing the desired behavior—coming when called. Similarly, college administrators who take away "leftover" money from a department's budget because it wasn't spent by the end of the year are punishing desired behavior—saving money. (Yes, I did add this last example as a subtle message to our college administrators!)

As you can see, punishment is a tricky business. We often unintentionally punish the very behaviors we're trying to encourage. Furthermore, to be effective, punishment should be immediate and consistent. However, in the real world, this is extremely hard to do. Police officers cannot immediately stop every driver every time he or she speeds.

To make matters worse, when punishment is not immediate and consistent, during the delay the undesirable behavior is likely to be reinforced. This delay and intermittent reinforcement puts the undesirable behavior on a *partial schedule of reinforcement*. And as you learned earlier, this makes the undesirable behavior even more resistant to extinction. Think about gambling. For almost everyone, it should be a *punishing* situation. On most occasions, you lose far more money than you win! However, the fact that you occasionally win keeps you "hanging in there."

Perhaps, most important, even if punishment immediately follows the misbehavior, the recipient may learn what *not* to do but not learn what he or she *should* do. Imagine trying to teach a child the word *dog* by only saying "No!" each time she said *dog* when it was inappropriate. The child (and you) would soon become very frustrated. It's much more efficient to teach someone by giving him or her clear examples of correct behavior, such as showing a child pictures of dogs and saying *dog* after each photo. Punishment has several other serious side effects, as Table 6.5 shows.

SUMMARY TABLE 6.5 SIDE EFFECTS OF PUNISHMENT

1. *Increased aggression*. Because punishment often produces a decrease in undesired behavior, at least for the moment, the punisher is in effect rewarded for applying punishment. Thus, a vicious circle may be established in which both the punisher and recipient are reinforced for inappropriate behavior—the punisher for punishing and the recipient for being fearful and submissive. This side effect partially explains the escalation of violence in family abuse and bullying (Anderson, Buckley, & Carnagey, 2008; Fang & Corso, 2007). In addition to fear and submissiveness, the recipient also might become depressed and/or respond with his or her own form of aggression.

2. *Passive aggressiveness*. For the recipient, punishment often leads to frustration, anger, and an urge to fight back. But most of us have learned from experience that retaliatory aggression toward a punisher (especially one who is bigger and more powerful) is usually followed by more punishment. We therefore tend to control our impulse toward open aggression and instead resort to more subtle techniques, such as showing up late or "forgetting" to do chores. This is a form of *passive aggressiveness* (Girardi et al., 2007; Johnson, 2008).

SUMMARY TABLE 6.5 (CONTINUED)

3. *Avoidance.* No one likes to be punished, so we naturally try to avoid the punisher. If every time you come home a parent or spouse starts yelling at you, you will delay coming home or find another place to go.

4. *Inappropriate modeling.* Have you ever seen a parent spank or hit a child for hitting another child? If so, the parent may unintentionally serve as a "model" for the same behavior he or she is attempting to stop.

5. *Temporary suppression versus elimination.* Do you notice how drivers immediately slow down when they see a nearby police car? And how quickly they later resume their previous speed once the police officer is out of sight? Punishment generally suppresses the behavior only temporarily, while the punisher is nearby.

6. *Learned helplessness.* Why do some people stay in abusive homes or marital situations? Research shows that if you repeatedly fail in your attempts to escape or control your environment, you acquire a general sense of powerlessness or *learned helplessness*, and you may become depressed and make no further attempts to escape (Bargai, Ben-Shakhar, & Shalev, 2007; Diaz-Berciano et al., 2008; Kim, 2008; Shea, 2008).

Assessment

VISUAL QUIZ

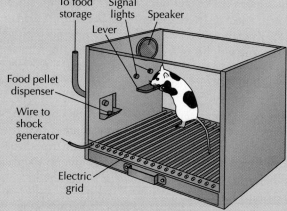

To food storage
Signal lights
Speaker
Lever
Food pellet dispenser
Wire to shock generator
Electric grid

The Skinner Box Application

To test his behavioral theories, Skinner used an animal, usually a pigeon or a rat, and an apparatus that has come to be called a **Skinner Box.** In Skinner's basic experimental design, an animal such as a rat received a food pellet each time it pushed a lever, and the number of responses was recorded. Note in this drawing that an electric grid on the cage floor could be used to deliver small electric shocks.

Test Yourself

Using the terms, *positive reinforcement, negative reinforcement, positive punishment,* or *negative punishment,* fill in the name of the appropriate learning principle in the spaces provided in each box.

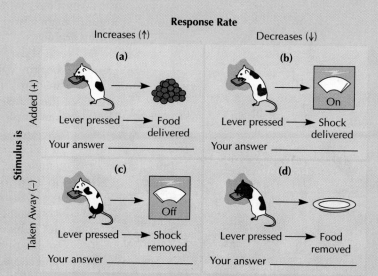

Response Rate

Increases (↑)   Decreases (↓)

Stimulus is — Added (+)

(a)
Lever pressed → Food delivered
Your answer _____

(b)
Lever pressed → Shock delivered
Your answer _____

Stimulus is — Taken Away (−)

(c)
Lever pressed → Shock removed
Your answer _____

(d)
Lever pressed → Food removed
Your answer _____

Answers: (a) positive reinforcement, (b) positive punishment, (c) negative reinforcement, (d) negative punishment.

Objective 6.12: *How can we effectively use reinforcement and punishment?*

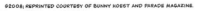

"HE'S NOT A PERFECT BOSS, BUT HE DOES GIVE YOU PLENTY OF FEEDBACK."

Have you noticed how the TV star of **The Nanny** *uses some or all of these five principles?*

PSYCHOLOGY AT WORK

Why Can't We Get Anything Done Around Here?

Imagine yourself as a midlevel manager for a big company. Your bonuses (and job) depend on your ability to motivate your employees and increase production. How could you use reinforcement and punishment to meet your goals?

1. **Provide clear directions and feedback.** Have you noticed how frustrating it is when a boss (or an instructor) asks you to do something, but doesn't give you clear directions or helpful feedback on your work? When using either reinforcement or punishment, be sure to offer specific, frequent, and clear directions and feedback to the employee whose behavior you want to encourage or change. When using punishment, it is particularly important to clearly explain and perhaps demonstrate the desired response because punishment is merely an indication that the current response is undesirable. Like all of us, employees need to know precisely what to do, as well as what NOT to do.

2. **Use appropriate timing.** Reinforcers and punishers should be presented as close in time to the response as possible. The old policy of "wait till the boss gets here" is obviously inappropriate for many reasons. In this case, it is because the delayed punishment is no longer associated with the inappropriate response. The same is true for reinforcement. If you're trying to increase production, don't tell your staff that you'll have a large party at the end of the year if they reach a significant goal. Instead, reward them with immediate compliments and small bonuses.

3. **Be consistent.** To be effective, both reinforcement and punishment must be consistent. Have you noticed how some workers get out of difficult assignments and gain special favors because they're constantly complaining or begging? A manager often responds by saying "No." But sometimes when the employee persists, gets loud, or throws an adult temper tantrum, his or her employer gives in. Although the manager is momentarily relieved (negatively reinforced) when the complaining and begging stop, can you see how this inconsistency creates larger and longer-lasting problems?

   First, the employee is being *positively reinforced* for complaining, begging, and throwing a tantrum, which almost guarantees that these inappropriate behaviors are likely to increase. To make matters worse, the manager's inconsistency (saying "No" and then giving in) places the employee's bad behavior on a *partial schedule of reinforcement*—and, therefore, highly resistant to extinction. Like a toddler screaming for a lollipop, or the gambler continuing to play despite the odds, the employee will continue the begging, screaming, and temper tantrums in hopes of the occasional payoff.

   Because effective punishment requires constant surveillance and consistent responses, it's almost impossible to be a "perfect punisher." It's best (and easiest) to use consistent reinforcement for good behavior and extinction for bad behavior. Praise the employee for productive and cooperative behavior in the workplace, and extinguish the begging, complaining, and tantrums by consistently refusing the request and ignoring the bad behavior.

4. **Follow correct order of presentation.** As a teenager, did you ever ask for an extra few dollars as an advance on your allowance and promise to mow the grass before the end of the week? Did you later conveniently "forget" your promise? As an employer, have you ever refused an employee's request to telecommute (or work from home) because you believe "all employees slough off if they're not being watched"? Can you see why advances on allowance or refusals that come

ABC Television

before the negligent behavior may create frustration and resentment? Both reinforcement and punishment should come after the behavior, never before.

5. **Combine key learning principles.** The overall best method seems to be a combination of the major principles: Reinforce appropriate behavior, extinguish inappropriate behavior, and save punishment for the most extreme cases (such as an employee caught lying or cheating).

Summarizing and Comparing Classical and Operant Conditioning

Are you feeling overwhelmed with all the important (and seemingly overlapping) terms and concepts for both classical and operant conditioning? This is a good time to stop and carefully review Table 6.6, which summarizes all the key terms and compares the two major types of conditioning. Keep in mind that while it's convenient to divide classical and operant conditioning into separate categories, almost all behaviors result from a combination of both forms of conditioning (Watson & Tharp, 2007).

As you can see, there are several areas of similarity in classical and operant conditioning. For example, in our earlier discussion of the principles of classical conditioning, you learned about *stimulus generalization*, *stimulus discrimination*, *extinction*, and *spontaneous recovery*. These same terms also are used in operant conditioning. Just as 11-month-old Albert generalized his fear of rats to rabbits and Santa Claus masks, operantly conditioned responses also generalize. After learning the word for *Daddy* (through the operant conditioning procedure of *shaping*), children often use this same word for all adult men. This would be a form of *stimulus generalization* (and potential embarrassment to the parents). After parents explain the distinction, the child learns to differentiate (stimulus discrimination) and to call only one man Daddy.

In both classical and operant conditioning, *extinction* occurs when the original source of the learning is removed. In classical conditioning, the CR (Albert's fear of the rat) is gradually extinguished if the CS (the rat) is repeatedly presented without the UCS (the loud noise). In operant conditioning, if the reinforcement (the rat's food) is removed, the response (bar pressing) will gradually decline. Following extinction in either classical or operant conditioning, you also sometimes have *spontaneous recovery*.

Objective 6.13: *Briefly summarize the similarities between classical and operant conditioning.*

Assessment

VISUAL QUIZ

Conditioning in Action

Can you explain how this is both classical and operant conditioning?

Answer: In the beginning, the dog involuntarily paired up the sound of the can opener with food (classical conditioning). Later, the dog voluntarily ran toward the sound of the can opener and was positively reinforced with food (operant conditioning).

SUMMARY TABLE 6.6 COMPARING CLASSICAL AND OPERANT CONDITIONING

	Classical Conditioning	Operant Conditioning
Pioneers	Ivan Pavlov John B. Watson	Edward Thorndike B. F. Skinner
Major Terms	Neutral stimulus (NS) Unconditioned stimulus (UCS) Conditioned stimulus (CS) Unconditioned response (UCR) Conditioned response (CR) Conditioned emotional response (CER)	Reinforcers (primary and secondary) Reinforcement (positive and negative) Punishment (positive and negative) Shaping Reinforcement schedules (continuous and partial)
Example	Cringing at the sound of a dentist's drill	A baby cries and you pick it up
Shared Terms	Generalization Discrimination Extinction Spontaneous recovery	Generalization Discrimination Extinction Spontaneous recovery
Major Differences	Learning based on paired associations Involuntary (subject is passive)	Learning based on consequences Voluntary (subject is active and "operates" on the environment)
Order of Effects	NS generally comes *before* the UCS	Reinforcement or punishment come *after* the behavior

Discriminative stimuli in everyday life.

Discriminative Stimulus *Cue signaling when a specific response will lead to the expected reinforcement*

Just as the classically conditioned fear of rats may spontaneously return, the operantly conditioned bar-pressing behaviors may recur.

One final comparison: In classical conditioning, we talked about *higher-order conditioning*. This occurs when a neutral stimulus (NS) is paired with a conditioned stimulus (CS), which is another stimulus that already produces a learned response. We said that if you wanted to demonstrate higher-order conditioning in Pavlov's dogs, you would first condition the dogs to salivate to the sound of the tone. Then you would pair the flash of light to the sound of the tone. Eventually, the dog would salivate only to the flash of light.

A similar process, with a different name, also occurs in operant conditioning. If a rat learns that bar pressing produces food *only* when a light is flashing, the rat will soon learn to respond only when the light is flashing. The light has become a **discriminative stimulus**, which signals whether or not a response will pay off. We depend on discriminative stimuli many times every day. We pick up the phone only when it rings. We look for the *Women* or *Men* signs on bathroom doors. And children quickly learn to ask grandparents for toys.

Application

CRITICAL THINKING | ACTIVE LEARNING

Using Learning Principles to Succeed in College

Psychological theory and research have taught us that an active approach to learning is rewarded by better grades. Active learning means using the SQ4R (Survey, Question, Read, Recite, Review, and Write) study techniques discussed in the "Tools for Student Success" (pages 39–46). An active learner also rises above old, easy patterns of behavior and applies new knowledge to everyday situations. When you transfer ideas or concepts you learn from class to your personal life, your insight grows.

Now that you have studied the principles of learning, use the following activity to help you apply your new knowledge to achieve your education goals and have an enjoyable college experience:

1. List three ways you can positively reinforce yourself for studying, completing assignments, and attending class.
2. Discuss with friends how participating in club and campus activities can reinforce your commitment to education.
3. Examine the time and energy you spend studying for an exam in a course you like with your study effort in a course

you don't like. How could you apply the Premack principle to your advantage in this situation?
4. When you take exams, are you anxious? How might this be a classically conditioned response? Describe how you could use the principle of extinction to weaken this response.

Assessment

CHECK & REVIEW

Operant Conditioning

Objective 6.4: *Define operant conditioning, reinforcement, and punishment.*

Operant conditioning occurs when humans and nonhuman animals learn by the consequences of their voluntary behaviors. Behavior is strengthened if followed by reinforcement and weakened if followed by punishment. **Reinforcement** is any procedure that strengthens or increases a response. **Punishment** is any procedure that weakens or decreases behavior.

Objective 6.5: *Describe Thorndike and Skinner's contributions.*

Thorndike and Skinner are the two major contributors to operant conditioning. Thorndike's **law of effect** states that rewarded behavior is more likely to recur. Skinner extended Thorndike's work to more complex behaviors, with a special emphasis on external, observable behaviors.

Objective 6.6: *Explain how primary and secondary reinforcers and positive and negative reinforcement strengthen behavior.*

Primary reinforcers, which satisfy an unlearned biological need (e.g., hunger,

thirst), and **secondary reinforcers**, which have learned value (e.g., money), both strengthen a response. **Positive reinforcement** (adds something) and **negative reinforcement** (takes something away) both strengthen a response and increase the likelihood it will occur again.

Objective 6.7: *Explain why negative reinforcement is not punishment.*

Reinforcement (either positive or negative) always strengthens a behavior, whereas punishment always weakens behavior and makes it less likely to recur.

Objective 6.8: *Contrast continuous and partial (intermittent) reinforcement, and identify the four schedules of partial reinforcement.*

Continuous reinforcement rewards each correct response. A **partial (intermittent)** schedule reinforces some, but not all correct responses. The four partial reinforcement schedules are **variable ratio (VR)**, **variable interval (VI)**, **fixed ratio (FR)**, and **fixed interval (FI)**.

Objective 6.9: *Define shaping and tell why it's important.*

Shaping is reinforcement that is delivered for successive approximations of the desired response. It is particularly important for new and complex behaviors that are unlikely to occur naturally.

Objective 6.10: *Explain how positive and negative punishment weaken behavior.*

Both **positive punishment** (adding something) and **negative punishment** (taking something away) decrease the likelihood the response will occur again.

Objective 6.11: *Why is punishment "tricky," and what are its serious side effects?*

Punishment plays an important role, but it is tricky because we often unintentionally punish the very behaviors we're trying to increase. Also, to be effective, punishment must be immediate and consistent. When it's delayed and/or inconsistent, the undesirable behavior can be unintentionally reinforced. This reinforcement then places the undesirable behavior on a *partial schedule of reinforcement*—thus making it even more resistant to extinction. Furthermore, punishment only teaches what not to do—not what should be done.

Punishment has several side effects: increased aggression, passive aggressiveness, avoidance, inappropriate modeling, temporary suppression versus elimination, and learned helplessness.

Objective 6.12: *How can we effectively use reinforcement and punishment?*

To be effective, reinforcement and punishment require *clear directions and feedback*, *appropriate timing*, *consistency*, a *correct order of presentation*, and a *combination of key learning principles*.

Objective 6.13: *Briefly summarize the similarities between classical and operant conditioning.*

Both classical and operant conditioning share terms, such as generalization, discrimination, extinction, and spontaneous recovery. Almost all behaviors also result from a combination of both classical and operant conditioning.

Questions

1. Define operant conditioning and explain how it differs from classical conditioning.
2. For both the mother and baby in this photo, touch appears to be a _____. (a) negative reinforcement; (b) secondary reinforcer; (c) continuous reinforcement; (d) positive reinforcement

Gary Connor/Index Stock

3. Negative punishment _____ and negative reinforcement _____ the likelihood the response will continue. (a) decreases, decreases; (b) increases, decreases; (c) decreases, increases; (d) increases, increases
4. Partial reinforcement schedules make responses more _____ to extinction.
5. Marshall is very disruptive in class, and his teacher uses various forms of punishment hoping to decrease his misbehavior. List five potential problems with this approach.

Check your answers in Appendix B.

Click & Review
for additional assessment options:
wiley.com/college/huffman

Cognitive-Social Learning

Achievement

Objective 6.14: *Define cognitive-social theory, and describe Köhler and Tolman's contributions.*

So far, we have examined learning processes that involve associations between a stimulus and an observable behavior. Some behaviorists believe that almost all learning can be explained in such stimulus–response terms. Other psychologists feel there is more to learning than can be explained solely by operant and classical conditioning. **Cognitive-social theory** (also called *cognitive-social learning* or *cognitive-behavioral theory*) incorporates the general concepts of conditioning. But rather than a simple S–R (stimulus and response), this theory emphasizes the interpretation or thinking that occurs within the organism—S–O–R (stimulus–organism–response). According to this view, people (as well as rats, pigeons, and other nonhuman animals) have attitudes, beliefs, expectations, motivations, and emotions that affect learning. Furthermore, both human and nonhuman animals are social creatures capable of learning new behaviors through observation and imitation of others. We begin with a look at the *cognitive* part of cognitive-social theory, followed by an examination of the *social* aspects of learning.

Cognitive-Social Theory
Emphasizes the roles of thinking and social learning in behavior

▣ Insight and Latent Learning: Where Are the Reinforcers?

As you'll discover throughout this text, cognitive factors play a large role in human behavior and mental processes. Given that these factors are covered in several other chapters (such as those on memory and thinking/language/intelligence), our discussion here is limited to the classic research of Wolfgang Köhler and Edward Tolman and their studies of *insight* and *latent learning*.

Köhler's Study of Insight

Insight *Sudden understanding of a problem that implies the solution*

Early behaviorists likened the mind to a "black box," whose workings could not be observed directly. German psychologist Wolfgang Köhler wanted to look inside the box. He believed there was more to learning—especially learning to solve a complex problem—than responding to stimuli in a trial-and-error fashion. In one series of experiments, Köhler placed a banana just outside the reach of a caged chimpanzee. To reach the banana, the chimp would have to use a stick placed near the cage to extend its reach. The chimp did not solve this problem in the random trial-and-error fashion of Thorndike's cats or Skinner's rats and pigeons. Köhler noticed that he seemed to sit and think about the situation for a while. Then, in a flash of **insight** (a sudden understanding), the chimp picked up the stick and maneuvered the banana within its grasp (Köhler, 1925).

Another one of Köhler's chimps, an intelligent fellow named Sultan, was put in a similar situation. This time two sticks were made available to him and the banana was placed even farther away, too far to reach with a single stick. Sultan seemingly lost interest in the banana, but he continued to play with the sticks. When he later discovered that the two sticks could be interlocked, he instantly used the now-longer stick to pull the banana within reach. Köhler designated this type of learning *insight learning*. Some internal mental event that we can only describe as "insight" went on between the presentation of the banana and the use of the stick to retrieve it.

American Philosophical Society

Is this insight? *Grande, one of Wolfgang Köhler's chimps, has just solved the problem of how to get the banana. (Also, the chimp in the foreground is engaged in observational learning—our next topic.)*

Cognitive Map *Mental image of a three-dimensional space that an organism has navigated*

Latent Learning *Hidden learning that exists without behavioral signs*

Tolman's Study of Latent Learning

Like Köhler, Edward C. Tolman (1898–1956) believed that previous researchers underestimated animals' cognitive processes and cognitive learning. He noted that when allowed to roam aimlessly in a maze with no food reward at the end, rats seemed to develop a **cognitive map**, or mental representation, of the maze.

To test the idea of cognitive learning, Tolman allowed one group of rats to explore a maze in an aimless fashion with no reinforcement. A second group was always reinforced with food whenever they reached the end of the maze. The third group was not rewarded during the first 10 days of the trial, but starting on day 11 they found food at the end of the maze. As expected from simple operant conditioning, the first and third groups were slow to learn the maze. The second group, which had reinforcement, showed fast, steady improvement. However, when the third group started receiving reinforcement (on the 11th day), their learning of the maze quickly caught up to the group that had been reinforced every time (Tolman & Honzik, 1930). For Tolman, this was significant. It proved that the nonreinforced rats had been thinking and building cognitive maps of the area during their aimless wandering. Their hidden **latent learning** only showed up when there was a reason to display it (the food reward).

Cognitive learning is not limited to rats. If a new log is placed in its territory, a chipmunk will explore it for a time, but will soon move on if no food is found. When a predator comes into the same territory, however, the chipmunk heads directly for and hides beneath the log. Similarly, as a child you may have casually ridden a bike around your neighborhood with no particular reason or destination in mind. You only demonstrated your hidden knowledge of the area when your dad was later searching for the closest mailbox. The fact that Tolman's nonreinforced rats quickly caught up to the reinforced ones, that the chipmunk knew about the hiding place under the log, that you knew the location of the mailbox, and recent experimental evidence (Burgdorf,

Knutson, & Panksepp, 2000) all provide clear evidence of latent learning and the existence of internal cognitive maps.

Observational Learning: What We See Is What We Do

After watching her first presidential debate, my friend's 5-year-old daughter asked, "Do we like him, Mommy?" What form of learning is this? In addition to classical and operant conditioning and cognitive processes (such as insight and latent learning), this child's question shows that we also learn many things through **observational learning**. From birth to death, observational learning is very important to our biological, psychological, and social survival (the *biopsychosocial* model). Watching others helps us avoid dangerous stimuli in our environment, teaches us how to think and feel, and shows us how to act and interact socially (Chance, 2009).

Some of the most compelling examples of observational learning come from the work of Albert Bandura and his colleagues (Bandura, 2003, 2006; Bandura, Ross, & Ross, 1961; Huesmann & Kirwil, 2007). Wanting to know whether children learn to be aggressive by watching others be aggressive, Bandura and his colleagues set up several experiments. They allowed children to watch a live or televised adult model kick, punch, and shout at a large inflated Bobo doll. Later, the children were allowed to play in the same room with the same toys (Figure 6.8). As Bandura hypothesized, children who had seen the live or televised aggressive model were much more aggressive with the Bobo doll than children who had not seen the modeled aggression. In other words, "Monkey see, monkey do."

We obviously don't copy or model everything we see, however. According to Bandura, learning by observation requires at least four separate processes: *attention*, *retention*, *reproduction*, and *reinforcement* (Concept Diagram 6.2).

Achievement

Objective 6.15: *What is observational learning, and what are the four factors needed for learning by observation?*

Observational Learning *Learning new behaviors or information by watching and imitating others (also known as social learning or modeling)*

Courtesy Albert Bandura

Figure 6.8 ***Bandura's classic Bobo doll studies*** Bandura's "Bobo doll" study is considered a classic in psychology. It demonstrated how children will imitate models they observe. Why is this new or important? Are there circumstances where observational learning (for example, gleaned from television) could have positive effects?

 1964
 1974
 1994
  1998

All GI Joe images courtesy of Dr. Harrison G. Pope, Jr.   © AP/Wide World Photos

Observational learning and modeling *Note how the bicep circumference of the G.I. Joe action figure has more than doubled since 1964. Can you see how this type of modeling might help explain why young boys and men today worry more about their chest and bicep size? Or why some may use steroids to increase their muscle development? [Source: As G.I. Joe bulks up, concern for the 98-pound weakling (May 30, 1999, New York Times, p. D2)]*

Concept Diagram 6.2

Four Key Factors in Observational Learning

1. ATTENTION

Observational learning requires attention. This is why teachers insist on having students watch their demonstrations.

2. RETENTION

To learn new behaviors, we need to carefully note and remember the model's directions and demonstrations.

3. REPRODUCTION

Observational learning cannot occur if we lack the motivation or motor skills necessary to imitate the model.

4. REINFORCEMENT

We are more likely to repeat a modeled behavior if the model is reinforced for the behavior.

Anne-Christine Poujoulat/AFP/Getty Images

Using the four factors of observational learning Does the sight of this litter upset you? Why do people help destroy their own environment? Some stores are now banning plastic bags or charging extra for their use. Is this the best way to reduce litter? Can you explain how littering (and its solution) could involve a combination of all four factors of observational learning—attention, retention, reproduction, and reinforcement?

Objective 6.16: *Describe the positive cross-cultural effects of observational learning through television.*

"The Theory Heard Round the World."

(Contributed by Thomas Frangicetto)

Bandura's "Bobo doll" study is considered a classic in psychology because it showed how children will imitate models they observe on television. Why is this new or important? Parents, educators, and politicians have long complained about all the negative things children learn from television. But what about the positive effects? Around the world, billions of people spend a large portion of their lives watching television. Could these hours of observational learning be put to good use?

Yes! In several less-developed countries, researchers working with television producers have created long-running, entertaining, serial dramas that feature attractive characters who model positive behaviors and good outcomes. Fortunately, these "soap operas" have had a dramatic effect on social problems like illiteracy, AIDS, overpopulation, and gender discrimination. Consider the following:

- In 1975, Mexican television executive Miguel Sabido produced the soap opera *Ven Conmigo* ("Come with Me") to entertain and advocate for adult literacy. The show was incredibly successful. The attendance in adult literacy classes was nine times higher than the year before.

- In the early 1990s, in the African country of Tanzania, life-threatening myths and misinformation were abundant. According to one report, Tanzanians believed that AIDS, "was transmitted through mosquitoes and having sex with a condom could cause the virus" (Smith, 2002). In 1993 an educational radio program aired in the Swahili language, *Twende na Wakati* ("Let's Go With the Time"), began broadcasting twice a week. Again, the results were spectacularly successful.

Interestingly, the social-cognitive theory of Albert Bandura played a pivotal role—not just in Mexico and Tanzania, but also in China and areas in the Caribbean (Smith, 2002). According to Smith, Bandura's theory "is the foundation of television and radio shows that have

Alan Abramowitz/Stone/Getty Images

changed the lives of millions." How do we know this?

Sabido contacted Bandura, Smith writes, and explained that he was using Bandura's work on modeling and social learning to produce *Ven Conmigo* and then showed him episodes of the drama. Bandura was duly impressed, "I thought this is a remarkably creative implementation of theory into practice," he told Smith. "I was amazed at the ingenuity." Sabido was not officially trained in psychology, but was able to apply Bandura's theories to the real world (Smith, 2002, p. 30).

But how can we be sure that the outcomes reported in Mexico and Tanzania were really the result of *cause and effect* and not *correlational*? How do we know, for example, that the changes in Tanzania—more Tanzanians knowing that multiple partners and unprotected sex could result in HIV infection—were directly caused by observational learning and the radio soap opera *Twende na Wakati*? Could other factors have been involved? Would the changes have occurred without the soap opera?

The challenge, according to researcher Peter Vaughan (2004), is to know how much of the change was caused by the program (cause and effect) and how much of the change was caused by other things that were going on in the country at the same time (correlation). Vaughan, the director of *Population Communication International* (PCI), an agency that produces educational soap operas globally, admitted the difficulty of constructing a control group in these mass media studies. However, "in Tanzania we were actually able to do that." PCI divided a map of Tanzania into two areas. One group could hear the broadcasts of *Twende na Wakati* and the other could not. Increases in positive behavioral and attitudinal changes were much higher where *Twende* was aired. A full explanation of their findings can be found at PCI's website

http://www.population.org/entsummit/transcript04_vaughan.shtm.

On this same website, PCI also explains that its methodology is based on "a theory of social learning developed by Professor Albert Bandura of Stanford University." In the spirit of Bandura's model, PCI trains their creative teams to include positive characters who are rewarded, negative characters who are punished, and transitional characters whose experiences embody the difficult choices we all face in life. And the crucial connection between art and audience that must take place if change is to occur does so here because "audience members tend to bond with the transitional characters who move to more positive behaviors, whether protecting themselves against HIV/AIDS, pursuing education, or keeping their children in school" (PCI, 2005). That is truly "psychology in action" and it is a legacy of which Albert Bandura can be justly proud.

Active Learning Questions

1. What role has observational learning played in your life? Can you think of specific examples of how role models influenced you—for better or worse? Does observational learning and role modeling violate being an *independent thinker*?

2. Using the PCI research described by Peter Vaughan, identify the following terms in his study: *hypothesis, experimental group, control group, independent variable,* and *dependent variable.* Do you have any problem with PCI doing the research on the effectiveness of their own dramatic productions? Explain.

3. A recent American Psychological Association (APA) press release highlighted the prevalence of self-destructive behaviors such as "smoking, alcohol abuse, and a sedentary lifestyle" (Winerman, 2005) in the United States. One major problem, according to psychologist James Prochaska, is that "the American healthcare system has yet to fully integrate behavior change into treatment." He encourages "psychologists to work to change that." Given what we know about the power of stories to engage the emotions of people (Giles, 2004), do you think that an American version of *Twende na Wakati* or *Ven Conmigo* would be effective? Explain.

Achievement

Objective 6.17: *What is scaffolding?*

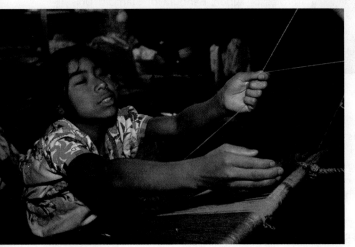

Lauren Greenfield/VII Photo Agency LLC

Achievement **A**chievement

GENDER & CULTURAL DIVERSITY

Scaffolding as a Teaching Technique in Different Cultures

Learning in the real world is often a combination of classical conditioning, operant conditioning, and cognitive-social learning. This is especially evident in informal situations in which an individual acquires new skills under the supervision of a master teacher. The ideal process used by teachers in these situations is known as *scaffolding*, or guided practice. Like the temporary platform on which construction workers stand, a cognitive *scaffold* provides temporary assistance while a learner acquires new skills. During this type of cognitive scaffolding, a more experienced person adjusts the amount of guidance to fit the student's current performance level. In most cases, scaffolding also combines *shaping* and *modeling*. The teacher selectively reinforces successes of the student and models more difficult parts of the task.

Patricia Marks Greenfield (1984, 2004) has described how scaffolding helps young girls learn to weave in Zinacantán, Mexico. Weaving is an important part of the culture of the Zinacantecos, who live in the highlands of southern Mexico. Greenfield videotaped 14 girls at different levels of learning to weave. Each girl was allowed to complete what she was able to do with ease. A more experienced weaver then created a scaffold by reinforcing correct weaving and modeling more difficult techniques. Interestingly, the teachers appear oblivious of their teaching methods or of the fact that they are teaching at all. Most of the Zinacanteco women believe that girls learn to weave by themselves. Similarly, in our Western culture, many believe that children learn to talk by themselves, ignoring how often children are reinforced (or scaffolded) by others.

Assessment **STOP**

CHECK & REVIEW

Cognitive-Social Learning

Objective 6.14: *Define cognitive-social theory, and describe Köhler and Tolman's contributions.*

Cognitive-social theory emphasizes thought processes, or cognitions, and social learning. Wolfgang Köhler showed that learning could occur with a sudden flash of **insight**. Tolman demonstrated that **latent learning** takes place in the absence of reward and remains hidden until some future time when it can be retrieved as needed. A **cognitive map** is a mental image of an area that a person or nonhuman animal has navigated.

Objective 6.15: *What is observational learning, and what are the four factors needed for learning by observation?*

According to Albert Bandura, **observational learning** is the process of learning by watching and imitating others. It requires at least four processes. We must pay attention, retain the information, be able to reproduce the behavior, and be motivated by some reinforcement.

Objective 6.16: *Describe the positive cross-cultural effects of observational learning through television.*

Specially created TV "soap operas" in less-developed countries have had a positive effect with social problems like illiteracy, HIV, overpopulation, and gender discrimination.

Objective 6.17: *What is scaffolding?*

Scaffolding is a type of guided practice used in many countries that provides a platform and guided assistance while the learner acquires new skills.

Questions

1. _____ were influential in early studies of cognitive learning. (a) William James and Ivan Pavlov; (b) B. F. Skinner and Edward Thorndike; (c) Wolfgang Köhler and Edward Tolman; (d) Albert Bandura and R. H. Walters
2. The chimpanzee in Köhler's *insight* experiment _____
   a. used trial-and-error to reach a banana placed just out of reach
   b. turned its back on the banana out of frustration
   c. sat for a while, then used a stick to bring the banana within reach
   d. didn't like bananas
3. Learning that occurs in the absence of a reward and remains hidden until some future time when it can be retrieved is called _____.
4. Mental images of an area that an organism has navigated are known as _____.
5. Bandura's observational learning studies focused on how _____. (a) rats learn cognitive maps through exploration; (b) children learn aggressive behaviors by observing aggressive models; (c) cats learn problem solving through trial and error; (d) chimpanzees learn problem solving through reasoning

Check your answers in Appendix B.

Click & Review
for additional assessment options:
wiley.com/college/huffman

The Biology of Learning

As you recall, learning is defined as a *relatively permanent change in behavior and mental processes resulting from practice or experience*. For this change in behavior to persist over time, lasting biological changes must occur within the organism. In this section, we will examine neurological and evolutionary influences on learning.

Neuroscience and Learning: The Adaptive Brain

Each time we learn something, either consciously or unconsciously, that experience changes our brains. We create new synaptic connections and alterations in a wide network of brain structures, including the cortex, cerebellum, hypothalamus, thalamus, and amygdala (Culbertson, 2008; May et al., 2007; Mohler et al., 2008; Romero, 2008).

Achievement

Objective 6.18: *How does learning affect the brain?*

Evidence that experience changes brain structure first emerged in the 1960s from studies of animals raised in *enriched* versus *deprived environments*. Research on this topic generally involves raising one group of rats in large cages with other rats and many objects to explore. This rat "Disneyland" is colorfully decorated, and each cage has ladders, platforms, and cubbyholes to investigate. In contrast, rats in the second group are raised in stimulus-poor, deprived environments. They live alone and have no objects to explore except food and water dispensers. After weeks in these environments, the brains of these two groups of rats are significantly different. The rats in the enriched environment typically develop a thicker cortex, increased nerve growth factor (NGF), more fully developed synapses, more dendritic branching, and improved performance on many tests of learning and memory (Gresack, Kerr, & Frick, 2007; Lores-Arnaiz et al., 2007; Pham et al., 2002; Rosenzweig & Bennett, 1996).

Admittedly, it is big leap from rats to humans. But research suggests that the human brain also responds to environmental conditions (Figure 6.9). For example, older adults exposed to stimulating environments generally perform better on intellectual and perceptual tasks than those who are in restricted environments (Schaie, 1994, 2008).

PhotoDisc Green/Getty Images

Courtesy Mark R. Rosenzweig

Figure 6.9 *Environmental enrichment* For human and nonhuman animals alike, environmental conditions play an important role in enabling learning. How might a classroom rich with stimulating toys, games, and books foster intellectual development in young children?

wiley.com/
college/
huffman

Objective 6.19: *What role does evolution play in learning?*

Taste Aversion *Classically conditioned negative reaction to a particular taste that has been associated with nausea or other illness*

Biological Preparedness *Built-in (innate) readiness to form associations between certain stimuli and responses*

Assessment

VISUAL QUIZ

Can You Explain This?

Raccoons can easily learn to play basketball, but they have a very difficult time learning to add coins to a small piggy bank.

Answer: Because of instinctive drift, the raccoons rub the coins together in an instinctive food-washing response rather than placing them in the piggy bank.

Instinctive Drift *Conditioned responses shift (or drift) back toward innate response patterns*

Evolution and Learning: Biological Preparedness and Biological Constraints

So far, we have emphasized the learned aspects of behavior. But humans and other non-human animals are born with other innate, biological tendencies that help ensure their survival. When your fingers touch a hot object, you immediately pull your hand away. When a foreign object approaches your eye, you automatically blink. Although these inborn, innate abilities are important to our evolutionary survival, they are inherently inflexible. Only through learning are we are able to react to important environmental cues—such as spoken words and written symbols. From an evolutionary perspective, *learning* is an adaptation that enables organisms to survive and prosper in a constantly changing world. In this section, we will explore how our biological heritage helps us learn some associations more easily than others *(biological preparedness)*, while also restricting us from learning in other situations *(biological constraints)*.

Taste Aversions—Biological Preparedness

Years ago, Rebecca (a student in my psychology class) unsuspectingly bit into a Butterfinger candy bar filled with small, wiggling bugs. Horrified, she ran gagging and screaming to the bathroom. Many years later, Rebecca still feels nauseated when she sees a Butterfinger candy bar.

Rebecca's graphic (and true!) story illustrates an important evolutionary process. When a food or drink is associated with nausea or vomiting, that particular food or drink can become a conditioned stimulus (CS) that triggers a conditioned **taste aversion**. Like other classically conditioned responses, taste aversions develop involuntarily.

Can you see why this automatic response would be adaptive? If our cave-dwelling ancestors became ill after eating a new plant, it would increase their chances for survival if they immediately developed an aversion to that plant—but not to other family members who might have been present at the time. Similarly, people tend to develop phobias to snakes, darkness, spiders, and heights more easily than to guns, knives, and electric outlets. We apparently inherit a built-in (innate) readiness to form associations between certain stimuli and responses, known as **biological preparedness**.

Laboratory experiments have provided general support for both taste aversion and biological preparedness. For example, Garcia and his colleagues (1966) produced taste aversion in lab rats by pairing flavored water (NS) and a drug (UCS) that produced gastrointestinal distress (UCR). After being conditioned and recovering from the illness, the rats refused to drink the flavored water (CS) because of the conditioned taste aversion. Remarkably, however, Garcia discovered that only certain neutral stimuli could produce the nausea. Pairings of a noise (NS) or a shock (NS) with the nausea-producing drug (UCS) produced no taste aversion. Garcia suggested that when we are sick to our stomachs, we have a natural, evolutionary tendency to attribute it to food or drink. Being *biologically prepared* to quickly associate nausea with food or drink is adaptive. It helps us avoid that or similar food or drink in the future (Domjan, 2005; Garcia, 2003; Kardong, 2008) (Figure 6.10).

Instinctive Drift—Biological Constraint

Just as Garcia couldn't produce noise–nausea associations, other researchers have found that an animal's natural behavior pattern can sometimes place limits, or *biological constraints*, on learning. For example, the Brelands (1961) tried to teach a chicken to play baseball. Through shaping and reinforcement, the chicken first learned to pull a loop that activated a swinging bat. It later learned to actually hit the ball. But instead of running to first base, it would chase the ball as though it were food. Regardless of the lack of reinforcement for chasing the ball, the chicken's natural behavior took precedence. This biological constraint is known as **instinctive drift**, when an animal's conditioned responses tend to shift (or *drift*) toward innate response patterns.

Figure 6.10 *Taste aversion in the wild* In applied research, Garcia and his colleagues used classical conditioning to teach coyotes not to eat sheep (Gustavson & Garcia, 1974). The researchers began by lacing freshly killed sheep with a chemical that caused extreme nausea and vomiting in the coyotes that ate the tainted meat. The conditioning worked so well that the coyotes would run away from the mere sight and smell of sheep. This taste aversion developed involuntarily, but the research has since been successfully applied many times and with many animals in the wild and in the laboratory (Aubert & Dantzer, 2005; Domjan, 2005; Workman & Reader, 2008).

Balog Photography

Human and nonhuman animals can be operantly conditioned to perform a variety of novel behaviors (like jumping through hoops, turning in circles, and even water skiing). However, reinforcement alone does not determine behavior. There is a biological tendency to favor natural inborn actions. In addition, learning theorists initially believed that the fundamental laws of conditioning would apply to almost all species and all behaviors. However, later researchers have identified several constraints (such as biological preparedness and instinctive drift) that limit the generality of conditioning principles. As you discovered in Chapter 1, scientific inquiry is a constantly changing and evolving process.

Assessment STOP

CHECK & REVIEW

The Biology of Learning

Objective 6.18: *How does learning affect the brain?*

Learning and conditioning produce relatively permanent changes in biochemistry and various parts of the brain.

Objective 6.19: *What role does evolution play in learning?*

At least some behavior is innate, or inborn, in the form of either reflexes or instincts. Learning and conditioning are further adaptations that have evolutionary survival benefits.

Through **biological preparedness** an organism is innately predisposed to form associations between certain stimuli and responses. **Taste aversions** are conditioned associations of food to illness that are rapidly learned, often in a single pairing. These aversions offer a protective survival mechanism for a species. Findings on **instinctive drift** show there are also biological constraints on learning.

Questions

1. From a(n)_____ perspective, learning is an adaptation that enables organisms to survive and prosper in a constantly changing world.
2. How did Garcia condition a taste aversion in coyotes?
3. What is biological preparedness?
4. _____ occurs when an animal's learned responses tend to shift backward toward innate response patterns.

Check your answers in Appendix B.

 **Click & Review**
for additional assessment options:
wiley.com/college/huffman

Objective 6.20: *How can classical conditioning be applied to everyday life?*

Using Conditioning and Learning Principles

Do you remember what I "promised" in the "Why Study Psychology" box at the start of this chapter? I claimed that studying this chapter would *expand your understanding and control of behavior, improve the predictability of your life, enhance your enjoyment of life,* and even *help you change the world!* I sincerely believe each of these claims. Unfortunately, many introductory psychology students focus only on studying all the terms and concepts. They fail to see "the forest for the trees." I don't want this to happen to you. To help you understand and appreciate the profound (and practical) benefits of this material, let's examine several applications for classical conditioning, operant conditioning, and cognitive-social learning.

PSYCHOLOGY AT WORK

Classical Conditioning—From Marketing to Medical Treatments

Advertisers, politicians, film producers, music artists, and others routinely and deliberately use classical conditioning to market their products and manipulate our purchases, votes, emotions, and motivation. In addition to marketing and manipulation classical conditioning also helps explain how (and why) we learn to be prejudiced and experience problems with phobias and certain medical procedures.

Marketing Beginning with John B. Watson's academic firing and subsequent career in advertising in the 1920s, marketers have employed numerous classical conditioning principles to promote their products. For example, TV commercials, magazine ads, and business promotions often pair their products or company logo (the neutral stimulus/NS) with pleasant images, such as attractive models and celebrities (the conditioned stimulus/CS). Through higher-order conditioning, these attractive models then trigger favorable responses (the conditioned response/CR). Advertisers know that after repeated viewings, the previously neutral stimulus (their products or logo) will become a conditioned stimulus that elicits favorable responses (CR)—purchasing their products. Psychologists caution that these ads also help produce visual stimuli that trigger conditioned responses such as urges to smoke, overeat, and drink alcohol (Kazdin, 2008; Martin et al., 2002; Tirodkar & Jain, 2003; Wakfield et al., 2003).

Classical conditioning in action *Have you every wondered why politicians kiss babies? Or why beautiful women are so often used to promote products?*

Prejudice Are children born with prejudice? Or are they the victims of classical conditioning? In a classic study in the 1930s, Kenneth Clark and Mamie P. Clark (1939) found that given a choice, both black and white children preferred white dolls to black dolls. When asked which doll was good and which was bad, both groups of children also responded that the white doll was good and nice. The black doll was seen as bad, dirty, and ugly.

The Clarks reasoned that the children had *learned* to associate inferior qualities with darker skin and positive qualities with light skin. If you're thinking this 1930 study no longer applies, follow-up research in the late 1980s found that 65 percent of the African-American children and 74 percent of the white children still preferred the white doll (Powell-Hopson & Hopson, 1988).

The Clark study not only led to important civil rights legislation (Figure 6.11), but it also provided important insights into the negative effects of prejudice on the victims—African American children. But what about the white children who also strongly preferred the white doll? Was their preference also due to classical conditioning? And did a similar type of classical conditioning contribute to the vicious murder

Figure 6.11 **Conditioned race prejudice** (a) The Clarks' research with the black and white dolls played a pivotal role in the famous *Brown v. Board of Education of Topeka* decision in 1954, which ruled that segregation of public facilities was unconstitutional. (b) Kenneth Clark (1914–2005), pictured here with his co-author, researcher, and wife, Mamie, was also elected the first African American president of the American Psychological Association.

of James Byrd? We can't be sure how the hatred and racism that took James Byrd's life originally started. However, prejudice of many types (racism, ageism, sexism, homophobia, and religious intolerance) can be classically conditioned (Process Diagram 6.2).

Medical Treatments   Examples of classical conditioning are also found in the medical field. For example, a program conducted by several hospitals in California gives an *emetic* (a nausea-producing drug) to their alcohol-addicted patients. But before the nausea begins, the patient gargles with his or her preferred alcoholic beverage to maximize the taste and odor cues paired with nausea. As a form of classical conditioning, the smell and taste of various alcoholic drinks (neutral stimulus/NS) are paired with the nausea-producing drug (the unconditioned stimulus/UCS). The drug then makes the patient vomit or feel sick (the unconditioned response/UCR). Afterward, just the smell or taste of alcohol (the conditioned stimulus/CS) makes the person sick (the conditioned response/CR). Some patients have found this treatment successful, but not all (Chapter 15).

Nausea is deliberately produced in this treatment for alcoholism. Unfortunately, it is an unintended side effect of many cancer treatments. The nausea and vomiting produced by chemotherapy increase the patient's discomfort and often generalize to other environmental cues, such as the hospital room color or odor. Using their knowledge of classical conditioning to change associations, therapists can help cancer patients control their nausea and vomiting response.

Phobias   Do you know someone who "freaks out" at the sight of a cockroach? At some time during his or her lifetime, this person probably learned to associate the NS (cockroach) with a UCS (perhaps hearing a parent scream at the sight of a cockroach) until a CR (fear at the sight of a cockroach) was conditioned. Researchers have found that most everyday fears are classically conditioned emotional responses. As you'll see in Chapter 15, classical conditioning also produces most *phobias*, exaggerated and irrational fears of a specific object or situation (Cal et al., 2006; Field, 2006; Ressler &

Process Diagram 6.2
Prejudice and Classical Conditioning

(a)
Before conditioning
The neutral stimulus produces no relevant response.
The unconditioned stimulus elicits the unconditioned response.

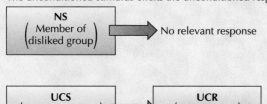

NS
(Member of disliked group) → No relevant response

UCS
(Parent's negative reaction) → **UCR** (Child is upset and fearful)

(b)
During conditioning
The neutral stimulus is repeatedly paired with the unconditioned stimulus, which produces the unconditioned response.

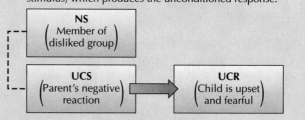

NS
(Member of disliked group)

UCS
(Parent's negative reaction) → **UCR** (Child is upset and fearful)

(c)
After conditioning
The neutral stimulus has become a conditioned stimulus (CS).
This CS now produces a conditioned response (CR) that is usually similar to the unconditioned response (UCR).)

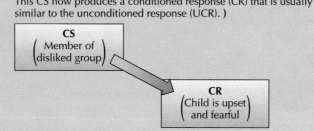

CS
(Member of disliked group) → **CR** (Child is upset and fearful)

(d)
Summary
An originally neutral stimulus comes to elicit a response that it did not previously elicit. Keep in mind that although we are calling the parents negative reaction a UCS for the child, it is also a learned response (CR) in the parent.

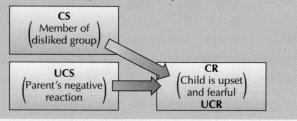

CS
(Member of disliked group)

UCS
(Parent's negative reaction) → **CR** (Child is upset and fearful) **UCR**

Randy Olsen/NG Image Collection

©AP/Wide World Photos

As described in the chapter opener, James Byrd was viciously murdered because of his skin color. How did this prejudice develop? (a) Before children are conditioned to be prejudiced, they show no response to a member of a different group. (b) Given that children are naturally upset and fearful when they see their parents upset, they can learn to be upset and fearful (UCR) if they see their parents respond negatively (UCS) to a member of a disliked group (NS). (c) After several pairings of the person from this group with their parents' negative reactions, the sight of the other person becomes a conditioned stimulus (CS). Being upset and fearful becomes the conditioned response (CR). (d) A previously unbiased child has now learned to be prejudiced.

Application

Discovering Classical Conditioning in Your Own Life

To appreciate the influences of classical conditioning on your own life, try this:

1. Look through a popular magazine and examine several advertisements. What images are used as the unconditioned stimulus (UCS) or conditioned stimulus (CS)? Note how you react to these images.

2. While watching a movie or a favorite TV show, identify what sounds and images are serving as conditioned stimuli (CS). What are your conditioned emotional responses (CERs)?

Bill Aron/PhotoEdit

(*Hint*: Differing types of music are used to set the stage for happy stories, sad events, and fearful situations.)

3. Read the words below and pay attention to your emotional response. Your reactions—positive, negative, or neutral—are a result of your own personal classical conditioning history. Can you trace back to the UCS for each of these stimuli?

father	final exams	spinach
Santa Claus	beer	mother

Davis, 2003; Stein & Matsunaga, 2006). The good news is that extreme fear of cockroaches, hypodermic needles, spiders, closets, and even snakes can be effectively treated with *behavior modification* (Chapter 15).

PSYCHOLOGY AT WORK

Achievement

Objective 6.21: *How can operant conditioning be applied to everyday life?*

Operant Conditioning—Prejudice, Biofeedback, and Superstition

Operant conditioning has numerous and important applications in everyday life. Here we talk about *prejudice*, *biofeedback*, and *superstitious behavior*.

Prejudice   Just as people can learn prejudice through classical conditioning, they also can learn prejudice through operant conditioning. Demeaning others is sadly reinforcing because it sometimes gains attention and sometimes approval from others, as well as increasing one's self-esteem (at the victim's expense) (Fein & Spencer, 1997; Kassin, Fein, & Markus, 2008). People also may have a single negative experience with a specific member of a group, which they then generalize and apply to all members of that group. Can you see how this is another example of *stimulus generalization*?

But the men who killed James Byrd were sentenced to death or life imprisonment. Why would people do something that they know could bring the death penalty? Punishment does weaken and suppress behavior. But, as mentioned earlier, to be effective it must be consistent and immediate. Unfortunately, this seldom happens. Even worse, when punishment is inconsistent and the criminal gets away with one or more crimes, that criminal behavior is put on a *partial (intermittent) schedule of reinforcement*. Thus it is more likely to be repeated and to become more resistant to *extinction*.

Biofeedback   Sit quietly for a moment and try to determine your blood pressure. Is it high or low? Is it different from what it was a few minutes ago? You can't tell, can

Biofeedback *Involuntary bodily process (such as blood pressure or heart rate) is recorded, and the information is fed back to an organism to increase voluntary control over that bodily function*

you? For most people, it is impossible to learn to control blood pressure consciously. But if you were hooked up to a monitor that recorded, amplified, and displayed this information to you by visual or auditory means, you could learn to control it (Figure 6.12). In this type of **biofeedback** (short for *biological feedback* and sometimes called *neurofeedback*), information about some biological function, such as heart rate, is conveyed to the individual through some type of signal.

Researchers have successfully used biofeedback to treat hypertension and anxiety by lowering blood pressure and muscle tension. It's also used to treat epilepsy by changing brain-wave patterns; urinary incontinence by gaining better pelvic muscle control; and cognitive functioning, chronic pain, and headache by redirecting blood flow (Andrasik, 2006; Bohm-Starke et al., 2007; Hammond, 2007; Kazdin, 2008; Moss, 2004; Stetter & Kupper, 2002; Tatrow, Blanchard, & Silverman, 2003).

Biofeedback involves several operant conditioning principles. Something is added (feedback) that increases the likelihood that the behavior will be repeated—*positive reinforcement*. The biofeedback itself is a *secondary reinforcer* because of the learned value of the relief from pain or other aversive stimuli *(primary reinforcer)*. Finally, biofeedback involves *shaping*. The person watches a monitor screen (or other instrument) that provides graphs or numbers indicating his or her blood pressure (or other bodily states). Like a mirror, the biofeedback reflects back the results of the various strategies the participant uses to gain control. Through trial and error, the participant gets progressively better at lowering heart rate (or making other desired changes). Biofeedback techniques are limited, however. They are most successful when used in conjunction with other techniques, such as behavior modification (Chapter 15).

Figure 6.12 ***Biofeedback*** In biofeedback training, internal bodily processes (like blood pressure or muscle tension) are electrically recorded. The information is then amplified, and reported back to the patient through headphones, signal lights, and other means. This information helps the person learn to control bodily processes not normally under voluntary control.

Accidental Reinforcement and Superstitious Behavior B. F. Skinner (1948, 1992) conducted a fascinating experiment to show how accidental reinforcement could lead to *superstitious behaviors*. He set the feeding mechanism in the cages of eight pigeons to release food once every 15 seconds. No matter what the birds did, they were reinforced at 15-second intervals. Interestingly, six of the pigeons acquired behaviors that they repeated over and over, even though the behaviors were not necessary to receive the food. For example, one pigeon kept turning in counterclockwise circles, and another kept making jerking movements with its head.

Why did the pigeons engage in such repetitive and unnecessary behavior? Recall that a *reinforcer* increases the probability that a response just performed will be repeated. Skinner was not using the food to reinforce any particular behavior. However, the pigeons associated the food with whatever behavior they were engaged in when the food was randomly dropped into the cage. Thus, if the bird was circling counterclockwise when the food was presented, it would repeat that motion to receive more food.

Like Skinner's pigeons, we humans also believe in many superstitions that may have developed from accidental reinforcement. In addition to the superstitions shown in Table 6.7, professional and Olympic-level athletes sometimes carry lucky charms or perform a particular ritual before every competition. Phil Esposito, a hockey player with the Boston Bruins and the New York Rangers for 18 years, always wore the same black turtleneck and drove through the same tollbooth on his way to a game. In the locker room, he put on all his clothes in the same order and laid out his equipment in exactly the same way he had for every other game. All this because once when he had behaved that way years before, he had been the team's high scorer. Alas, the power of accidental reinforcement.

TABLE 6.7 COMMON WESTERN SUPERSTITIONS

Behavior	Superstition
Wedding plans: *Why do brides wear something old and something borrowed?*	The something old is usually clothing that belongs to an older woman who is happily married. Thus, the bride will supposedly transfer that good fortune to herself. Something borrowed is often a relative's jewelry. This item should be golden, because gold represents the sun, which was once thought to be the source of life.
Spilling salt: *Why do some people throw a pinch of salt over their left shoulder?*	Years ago, people believed good spirits lived on the right side of the body and bad spirits on the left. When a man spilled salt, he believed his guardian spirit had caused the accident to warn him of evil nearby. At the time, salt was scarce and precious. Therefore, to bribe the spirits who were planning to harm him, he would quickly throw a pinch of salt over his left shoulder.
Knocking on wood: *Why do some people knock on wood when they're speaking of good fortune or making predictions?*	Down through the ages, people have believed that trees were homes of gods, who were kind and generous if approached in the right way. A person who wanted to ask a favor of the tree god would touch the bark. After the favor was granted, the person would return to knock on the tree as a sign of thanks.

 PSYCHOLOGY AT WORK

Cognitive-Social Learning—We See, We Do?

We use cognitive-social learning in many ways in our everyday lives, yet two of the most powerful examples are frequently overlooked—*prejudice* and *media influences*. As you can see in Figure 6.13, one of James Byrd's murderers, Bill King, had numerous tattoos on his body that proudly proclaimed his various prejudices. King's family and friends insist that he was pleasant and quiet until he began serving an eight-year prison sentence for burglary (Galloway, 1999). What did he learn about prejudice during his prison sentence? Did he model his killing of Byrd after his uncle's well-known killing of a gay traveling salesman a number of years earlier? Or did he learn his prejudices during his numerous years of active membership with the KKK?

The media also propagates some forms of prejudice. Experimental and correlational research clearly show that when we watch television, go to movies, and read books and magazines that portray minorities, women, and other groups in demeaning and stereotypical roles, we often learn to expect these behaviors and to accept them as "natural." Exposure of this kind initiates and reinforces the learning of prejudice (Dill & Thill, 2007; Kassin, Fein, & Markus, 2008; Neto & Furnham, 2005).

In addition to prejudice, the media also can teach us what to eat, what toys to buy, what homes and clothes are most fashionable, and what constitutes "the good life." When a TV commercial shows children enjoying a particular cereal and beaming at their Mom in gratitude (and Mom is smiling back), both children and parents in the audience are participating in a form of observational learning. They learn that they, too, will be rewarded for buying the advertised brand (with happy children) or punished (with unhappy children who won't eat) for buying a competitor's product.

 Achievement

Objective 6.22: *How can cognitive-social learning be applied to everyday life?*

©AP/Wide World Photos

Figure 6.13 *John William "Bill" King* King was sentenced to death for the murder of James Byrd. How might King and his two accomplices have learned some of their hatred and prejudice through observation and modeling?

wiley.com/
college/
huffman

Joe Raedle/Getty Images News and Sport Services

Video games and aggression Researchers suggest that violent video games and virtual reality games are more likely to increase aggression because, unlike TV and other media, they are interactive and engrossing, and require the player to identify with the aggressor. What do you think? Do video games affect your behavior or that of your friends?

©AP/Wide World Photos

Unfortunately, observational learning also encourages destructive behaviors. Correlational evidence from more than 50 studies indicates that observing violent behavior is related to later desensitization and increased aggression (Anderson, Buckley, & Carnagey, 2008; Coyne, 2004; Kronenberger et al., 2005). As a critical thinker, you may be automatically noting that correlation is not causation. However, over 100 *experimental* studies have shown a causal link between observing violence and later performing it (Primavera & Herron, 1996).

What about violent video games and virtual reality games? How do they affect behavior? Researchers are just beginning to study these questions. For example, studies have found that students who played more violent video games in junior high and high school have more aggressive attitudes and engage in more aggressive behaviors (Anderson & Bushman, 2001; Bartholow & Anderson, 2002; Brady, 2007; Wei, 2007). Craig Anderson and Karen Dill (2000) also experimentally assigned 210 students to first play either a violent or a nonviolent video game and later allowed them to punish their opponent with a loud sound blast. Those who played the violent game punished the opponent not only for a longer period of time but also with greater intensity.

A Final Note

I began this chapter with the story of Muhammad Yunus and James Byrd because generosity and prejudice are worthy (but unusual) topics for a learning chapter. And their stories deserved retelling. Yunus's great work helping the poor can serve as an inspiration and model for all of us. Similarly, the death of James Byrd can remind us of the terrible hatred and racism that still exist in our country. Sadly, his death (like others) is too quickly forgotten. The good news is that little (if anything) about prejudice is biologically driven. It is *learned*. Using the *biopsychosocial model*, you can see that the *psychological* component of prejudice (thoughts, values, and beliefs) and *sociocultural* forces (modeling, TV, and other media) are the result of experience and exposure (learning). Fortunately, *what we learn can be unlearned* through retraining, counseling, and self-reflection.

Those who won't forget Ross Byrd, left, and Renee Mullins, children of murder victim James Byrd, leaving the Jasper County Courthouse after John "Bill" King was convicted of capital murder.

Assessment

STOP

CHECK & REVIEW

Using Conditioning and Learning Principles

Objective 6.20: *How can classical conditioning be applied to everyday life?*

Classical conditioning explains how people market their products, how we sometimes learn negative attitudes toward groups of people (prejudice), and how we sometimes

have problems with certain medical treatments and phobias.

Objective 6.21: *How can operant conditioning be applied to everyday life?*

Operant conditioning helps explain how we learn prejudice through positive reinforcement and stimulus generalization. **Biofeedback**, another application, is the

feeding back of biological information, such as heart rate or blood pressure, which a person uses to control normally automatic functions of the body. Operant conditioning also helps explain many superstitions, which involve accidentally reinforced behaviors that are continually repeated because they are believed to cause desired effects.

Objective 6.22: *How can cognitive-social learning be applied to everyday life?*

Cognitive-social theory helps to further explain prejudice and media influences. People often learn their prejudices by observing and imitating what they've seen modeled by friends, family, and the media. The media affect our purchasing behaviors, as well as our aggressive tendencies. Video games may have a particularly strong influence.

Questions

1. Politicians often depict their opponent as immoral and irresponsible because they know it helps create a ___ toward their rival. (a) classically conditioned phobia; (b) negative social-learning cue; (c) conditioned aversive response; (d) negative conditioned emotional response

2. Biofeedback reinforces desired physiological changes that have beneficial results. This makes it a(n) ___. (a) operant conditioner; (b) primary reinforcer; (c) secondary reinforcer; (d) biological marker

3. You insist on wearing a red sweater each time you take an exam because you believe it helps you get higher scores. This is an example of ___.

(a) classical conditioning; (b) secondary reinforcement; (c) superstition; (d) redophilia reinforcement

4. Explain how video games increase aggression.

Check your answers in Appendix B.

Click & Review
for additional assessment options:
wiley.com/college/huffman

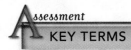

Assessment
KEY TERMS

*To assess your understanding of the **Key Terms** in Chapter 6, write a definition for each (in your own words), and then compare your definitions with those in the text.*

conditioning (p. 204)
learning (p. 204)

Classical Conditioning
acquisition (p. 208)
classical conditioning (p. 205)
conditioned emotional response (CER) (p. 207)
conditioned response (CR) (p. 205)
conditioned stimulus (CS) (p. 205)
extinction (p. 209)
higher-order conditioning (p. 210)
neutral stimulus (NS) (p. 205)
spontaneous recovery (p. 210)
stimulus discrimination (p. 209)
stimulus generalization (p. 209)
unconditioned response (UCR) (p. 205)
unconditioned stimulus (UCS) (p. 205)

Operant Conditioning
continuous reinforcement (p. 215)
discriminative stimulus (p. 222)
fixed interval (FI) schedule (p. 215)
fixed ratio (FR) schedule (p. 215)
law of effect (p. 212)
negative punishment (p. 217)
negative reinforcement (p. 214)
operant conditioning (p. 212)
partial (intermittent) reinforcement (p. 215)
positive punishment (p. 217)
positive reinforcement (p. 214)
Premack principle (p. 214)
primary reinforcers (p. 213)
punishment (p. 212)
reinforcement (p. 212)
secondary reinforcers (p. 213)

shaping (p. 216)
variable interval (VI) schedule (p. 215)
variable ratio (VR) schedule (p. 215)

Cognitive-Social Learning
cognitive map (p. 224)
cognitive-social theory (p. 223)
insight (p. 224)
latent learning (p. 224)
observational learning (p. 225)

The Biology of Learning
biological preparedness (p. 230)
instinctive drift (p. 230)
taste aversion (p. 230)

Using Conditioning and Learning Principles
biofeedback (p. 236)

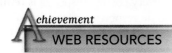

Achievement
WEB RESOURCES

Huffman Book Companion Site
wiley.com/college/huffman
This site is loaded with free Interactive Self-Tests, Internet Exercises, Glossary and Flashcards for key terms, web links, Handbook for Non-Native Speakers, and other activities designed to improve your mastery of the material in this chapter.

Classical Conditioning

Process: Involuntary
Pavlov and Watson's Contributions

1) Before **conditioning**, originally **neutral stimulus (NS)** causes no relevant response, whereas **unconditioned stimulus (UCS)** causes **unconditioned response (UCR)**.

2) During conditioning, NS is paired with UCS that elicits the UCR.

3) After conditioning, previous NS becomes **conditioned stimulus (CS)**, which now causes a **conditioned response (CR)**, or **conditioned emotional response (CER)**.

Principles of Classical Conditioning

* **Acquisition:** NS is paired with an UCS, so that the NS comes to elicit the CR.

* **Stimulus generalization:** Stimuli similar to original CS elicit CR.

* **Stimulus discrimination:** Only the CS elicits the CR.

* **Extinction:** Repeatedly presenting the CS without the UCS, which gradually weakens the CR.

* **Spontaneous recovery:** Sudden reappearance of a previously extinguished CR.

* **Higher-order conditioning:** NS becomes a CS through repeated pairings with a previously conditioned stimulus (CS).

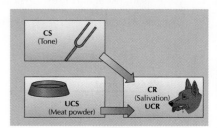

Operant Conditioning

Process: Voluntary
Organisms learn through consequences of their behavior. When responses are **reinforced**, they are strengthened and likely to increase; when **punished**, they are weakened and likely to decrease.

Thorndike and Skinner's Contributions

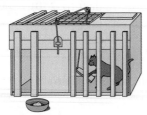

Thorndike emphasized the law of effect.

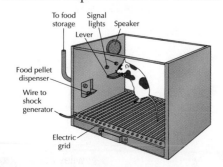

Skinner emphasized observable behaviors.

Principles of Operant Conditioning

* **Strengthening a response occurs through:**
  1) Primary and secondary reinforcers: **Primary reinforcers**, like food, satisfy a biological need. The value of **secondary reinforcers,** such as money, is learned.

  2) Positive and negative reinforcement: **Positive reinforcement** adds something that increases the likelihood of the response. **Negative reinforcement** takes away something that increases the likelihood of the response.

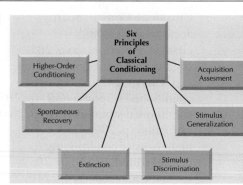

* **Schedules of reinforcement:**
  In a **continuous schedule of reinforcement**, every correct response is reinforced. In a **partial** (or **intermittent**) **schedule** only some response are reinforced. Partial schedules include **fixed ratio (FR), variable ratio (VR), fixed interval (FI),** and **variable interval (VI)**.

* **Shaping** involves reinforcement for successive approximations of the desired response.

* **Weakening a response occurs through:**
  1) **Positive punishment**—adds something that decreases the likelihood of the response.

  2) **Negative punishment**—takes away something that decreases the likelihood of the response.

Cognitive–Social Learning

Insight and Latent Learning

- *Köhler:* Learning can occur with a sudden flash of understanding (**insight**).

- *Tolman:* Learning can happen without reinforcement and remain hidden until needed (**latent learning**). After navigating their environments, people and nonhuman animals create mental images called **cognitive maps**.

Observational Learning

- *Bandura:* **Observational learning** involves watching and imitating others. It requires *attention, retention, reproduction,* and *reinforcement.*

The Biology of Learning

Learning and conditioning produce relatively permanent changes in biochemistry and various parts of the brain. Evolutionary theorists believe some behavior is unlearned (e.g., reflexes or instincts), and that learning and conditioning are further adaptations that enable organisms to survive and prosper in a constantly changing world.

© James Balog Photography

Using Conditioning Principles

Psychology at work: Classical Conditioning in Everyday Life

- *Marketing:* Products (NS) are repeatedly paired with pleasant images (UCS) until they become a (CS).

- *Prejudice:* Negative perceptions of others may be acquired through classical conditioning processes.

- *Medical treatments:* Using nausea producing drugs, alcoholics learn to pair alcohol (CS) with nausea (CR).

- *Phobias:* Irrational fears may become a CS through association of a feared object with the UCS.

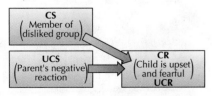

Psychology at work: Operant Conditioning in Everyday Life

- *Prejudice:* Negative perceptions of others, which may be acquired through operant conditioning.

- *Biofeedback:* "Feeding back" biological information (heart rate or blood pressure) for control of normally automatic body functions.

- *Superstitious behavior:* Develops from accidental rewarding of specific behaviors.

Psychology at work: Cognitive-Social Learning in Everyday Life

- *Prejudice:* Learned by observing, imitating, and modeling prejudices of others.

- *Media influences:* Consumerism, aggression, and other behaviors are partially learned from media models.

Joe Raedle/Getty Images News and Sport Services

7

Memory

When Elizabeth was 14 years old, her mother drowned in their backyard pool. As she grew older, the details surrounding her mother's death became increasingly vague for Elizabeth. Decades later, a relative told Elizabeth that she had been the one to find her mother's body. Despite her initial shock, memories slowly started coming back.

> I could see myself, a thin, dark-haired girl, looking into the flickering blue-and-white pool. My mother, dressed in her nightgown, is floating face down. I start screaming. I remember the police cars, their lights flashing, and the stretcher with the clean, white blanket tucked in around the edges of the body. The memory had been there all along, but I just couldn't reach it.
>
> (Loftus & Ketcham, 1994, p. 45)

This is the true story of Elizabeth Loftus, who today is a well-known psychologist specializing in the study of memory. Compare her life story with this one:

When H.M. was 27 years old, portions of his temporal lobes and limbic system were removed as treatment for severe epileptic seizures. The surgery was successful, but something was clearly wrong with H.M.'s long-term memory. Two years after the surgery, he still believed he was 27. When his uncle died, he grieved in a normal way. But soon after, he began to ask why his uncle never visited him. H.M. had to be repeatedly reminded of his uncle's death, and each reminder would begin a new mourning process. Today, more than 50 years later, H.M. cannot recognize the people who care for him daily, the scientists who have studied him for decades, or even the room where he lives. He reads the same books and magazines over and over and laughs at the same old jokes—each time as though it were the first. H.M. also thinks he is still 27, and he no longer recognizes a photograph of his own face (Corkin, 2002).

What should we make of these two stories? How could a child forget finding her mother's body? What would it be like to be H.M.—existing only in the present moment, unable to learn and form new memories? How can we remember our second-grade teacher's name, but forget the name of someone we just met? In this chapter, you'll discover answers to these and other fascinating questions about memory.

▶ **The Nature of Memory**

Memory Models
Sensory Memory
Short-Term Memory (STM)
Long-Term Memory (LTM)

 PSYCHOLOGY AT WORK
    Improving Long-Term Memory (LTM)

▶ **Forgetting**

How Quickly Do We Forget?
Why Do We Forget?

 PSYCHOLOGY AT WORK
    Key Factors in Forgetting

GENDER & CULTURAL DIVERSITY
    Cultural Differences in Memory and Forgetting

▶ **Biological Bases of Memory**

How Are Memories Formed?
Where Are Memories Located?
Biological Causes of Memory Loss

RESEARCH HIGHLIGHT
    Memory and the Criminal Justice System

▶ **Using Psychology to Improve Our Memory**

Understanding Memory Distortions
Tips for Memory Improvement

CRITICAL THINKING/ACTIVE LEARNING
    Memory and Metacognition

Application

WHY STUDY PSYCHOLOGY?

Did you know...

▶ Eyewitness testimony is common in many legal cases, but research shows it to be highly unreliable?

▶ Without long-term memory, you would be unable to recognize new friends, doctors, movie stars, or politicians regardless of how many times you saw or talked talk with them?

▶ Long-lasting "flashbulb" memories for intense emotional events, like the 9/11 terrorist attack on the United States, may be influenced by "fight-or-flight" hormones?

Digital Vision/AgeFotostock America, Inc.

▶ People can be led to create false memories they later believe to be true?

▶ Long-term memory is like a magical credit card with unlimited cash and no known expiration date?

▶ Memory tricks and techniques (called mnemonics) can help improve your memory?

The Nature of Memory

Achievement

Objective 7.1: *Define memory, and describe the information processing and parallel distributed processing (PDP) models.*

Memory *Internal record or representation of some prior event or experience*

Constructive Process *Organizing and shaping of information during processing, storage, and retrieval of memories*

Encoding *Processing information into the memory system*

Storage *Retaining information over time*

Retrieval *Recovering information from memory storage*

> The charm, one might say the genius, of memory is that it is choosy, chancy, and temperamental.
>
> ELIZABETH BOWEN (IRISH NOVELIST AND SHORT STORY AUTHOR, 1899–1973)

Among psychologists, **memory** is most often defined as "an internal record or representation of some prior event or experience" (Purdy, Markham, Schwartz, & Gordon, 2001, p. 9). Can you see how this internal record is critical to our psychological and physical survival? Without memory, we would have no past or future. We could not dress or feed ourselves, communicate, or even recognize ourselves in a mirror. Memory allows us to learn from our experiences and adapt to ever-changing environments.

However, as we've seen with the opening stories of Elizabeth Loftus and H.M., our memories are also highly fallible. Although some people think of memory as a gigantic library or an automatic tape recorder, our memories are *not* exact recordings of events. Instead, memory is a **constructive process**. We actively organize and shape information as it is processed, stored, and retrieved. This constructive process is an efficient method that allows us to cope with an abundance of information. But, as you might expect, it also lends itself to serious errors and biases discussed throughout this chapter.

Memory Models: A Brief Overview

Over the years, psychologists have developed numerous models for memory. In this section, we first briefly discuss two of the major approaches (Table 7.1), and then we'll explore the most popular model in some depth.

Information-Processing Approach

According to the *information-processing model*, the barrage of information that we encounter every day goes through three basic operations **encoding, storage**, and **retrieval** (Process Diagram 7.1). [Storage also involves *information processing* in three interacting memory systems (sensory, short-term, and long-term), which will be discussed later as a separate model.]

Process Diagram 7.1
Information-Processing Model

Memory processes have been likened to a computer's information-processing system. Data are entered on a keyboard and *encoded* in a way that the computer can understand and use. Information is then *stored* on a disk, hard drive, or memory stick, and later *retrieved* and brought to the computer screen for viewing.

 Study Tip

When you want to learn and remember a large amount of information, you must organize it into meaningful patterns or categories. Can you see how this process diagram can help you organize (and master) the upcoming discussion of the models and nature of memory? Like an atlas or a roadmap that helps you plan a car trip across the country, summary diagrams like this one provide a roadmap or "big picture" of where you are, where you're going, and what's coming up next.

 Study Tip

The boldfaced terms and concepts presented here are further defined and explored later in the chapter. They're offered now as a part of the "big picture" to help organize and direct your study.

STEP 3: RETRIEVAL

Retrieval
(recovering information from memory storage)

(a) Serial-Position Effect *(primacy, recency)*

(b) Retrieval Cues *(recognition, recall, priming)*

STEP 2: STORAGE

Storage *(retaining information over time)*

Three-Stage Memory Model *(sensory, short-term, long-term)*

STEP 1: ENCODING

Encoding *(processing information into the memory system)*

(a) Selective Attention Vs Divided Attention

(b) Automatic Processing Vs Controlled Processing

(c) Levels of Processing

Encoding--Step 1

- Clearly, we cannot—and do not—encode or process all the information available to us, and we process different information in different ways: (a) **Selective attention vs. divided attention**. *Selective attention* (Chapter 4) directs our attention to things we consider important. Note that selective attention improves encoding, *divided attention* interferes with it. Studies show that when we attend to multiple things at one time, like text-messaging during a class lecture, we do a poorer job on subsequent memory tests (Skinner & Fernandes, 2008; Naveh-Benjamin, Kilb, & Fisher, 2006; Uncapher & Rugg, 2008). (b) **Automatic processing vs. controlled** (or *effortful*) **processing**. If you've played Jeopardy or Trivial Pursuit, you know that we absorb and encode a great deal of information with little or no conscious effort—*automatic processing* (Chapter 5). In contrast, *controlled processing* requires concentrated attention and effort, which are normally required for lasting memory of difficult material. (c) **Levels of processing**. Encoding lies on a continuum from shallow to deep, and the depth of initial processing determines how well it's later remembered (Craik & Lockhart, 1972; Craik & Tulving, 1975; FitzGerald et al., 2008).

Storage--Step 2

- Memory requires retention of information for differing periods of time. (Outside the computer analogy, most information-processing models also suggest that memory storage occurs in three stages—*sensory*, *short-term*, and *long-term*, which we'll discuss in depth later as a third model.)

Retrieval--Step 3

- Retrieval involves several factors: (a) **Serial-position effect**. When study participants are given lists of words to learn and are allowed to recall them in any order they choose, they remember the words at the beginning (*primacy effect*) and the end of the list (*recency effect*) better than those in the middle (Azizian & Polich, 2007; Healey et al., 2008). (b) **Retrieval cues**. **Recognition** relies on a specific prompt (retrieval cue) to recover the information. You only have to identify (or *recognize*) the correct response, as in a multiple-choice exam. In contrast, during an essay exam, you use a general cue, called **recall**, to search and retrieve previously learned material. **Priming** is a third retrieval cue that occurs when a prior exposure to a stimulus (or *prime*) activates the recovery of related associations. You're more likely to recall your promise to call someone if you hear a phone ring.

TABLE 7.1 TWO COMMON MEMORY MODELS

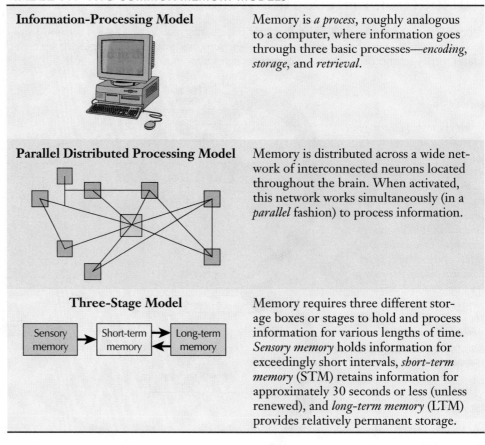

Information-Processing Model	Memory is *a process*, roughly analogous to a computer, where information goes through three basic processes—*encoding, storage,* and *retrieval.*
Parallel Distributed Processing Model	Memory is distributed across a wide network of interconnected neurons located throughout the brain. When activated, this network works simultaneously (in a *parallel* fashion) to process information.
Three-Stage Model	Memory requires three different storage boxes or stages to hold and process information for various lengths of time. *Sensory memory* holds information for exceedingly short intervals, *short-term memory* (STM) retains information for approximately 30 seconds or less (unless renewed), and *long-term memory* (LTM) provides relatively permanent storage.

The information-processing ("memory as a computer") model has its limits. Human memories are often fuzzy and fragile compared to the literal, "hard" data stored on a computer disk or hard drive. Furthermore, computers process one piece of data at a time (*sequentially*). In contrast, human memory can process a lot of information at the same time (*simultaneously*).

Parallel Distributed Processing Model

Due to the limitations of the information-processing model, some cognitive scientists prefer the **parallel distributed processing (PDP)**, or *connectionist*, model of memory (Levy & Krebs, 2006; McClelland, 1995; Passino, Seeley, & Visscher, 2008). As the name implies, instead of recognizing patterns as a sequence of information bits (like a computer), our brain and memory processes perform multiple *parallel* operations all at one time. In addition, memory is spread out, or *distributed*, throughout an entire weblike network of processing units. If you're swimming in the ocean and see a large fin nearby, your brain does not conduct a complete search of all fish with fins before urging you to begin a rush to the beach. Instead, you conduct a mental *parallel* search. You note the color of the fish, the fin, and the potential danger all at the same time. Because the processes are parallel, you can quickly process the information—and possibly avoid being eaten by the shark!

The PDP model seems consistent with neurological information of brain activity. Thanks to the richly interconnected synapses, activation of one neuron can influence many other neurons (Chapter 2). It also has been useful in explaining perception (Chapter 4), language (Chapter 8), and decision making (Chapter 8). And it allows a faster response time. As we just noted, survival in our environment requires instantaneous information processing. However, the previous information-processing model

Parallel Distributed Processing (PDP) *Memory results from weblike connections among interacting processing units operating simultaneously, rather than sequentially (also known as the connectionist model)*

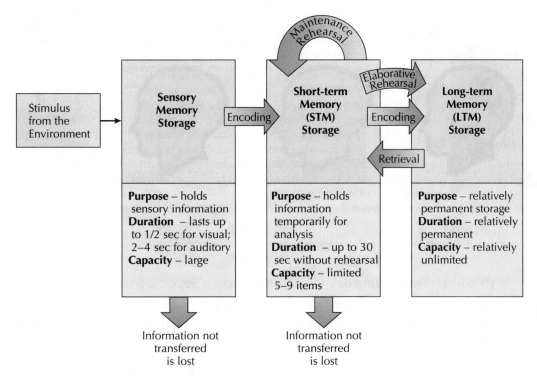

Figure 7.1 *Traditional three-stage memory model* Each "box" represents a separate memory system that differs in purpose, duration, and capacity. When information is not transferred from sensory memory or short-term memory, it is assumed to be lost. Information stored in long-term memory can be retrieved and sent back to short-term memory for use.

remains better at explaining the processing of new information and memory for single events. And the three-stage memory model remains the leading model in memory research. Let's discuss this model in more detail.

Traditional Three-Stage Memory Model

Since the late 1960s, one of the most widely used models in memory research has been the *traditional three-stage memory model* (Atkinson & Shiffrin, 1968). Modern research has added new findings and complexities to this model (Jonides et al., 2008), but it remains the leading paradigm because it offers a convenient way to organize the major findings. According to this model, three different storage "boxes," or memory stages (*sensory, short-term,* and *long-term*), hold and process information. Each stage has a somewhat different purpose, duration, and capacity (Figure 7.1). (Also, note how the three-stage model overlaps with the storage stage of the previously discussed *information-processing model*.)

Achievement

Objective 7.2: *Summarize the three-stage memory model.*

Sensory Memory *First memory stage that holds sensory information; relatively large capacity, but duration is only a few seconds*

▪ Sensory Memory: The Brief First Stage of Memory

Everything we see, hear, touch, taste, and smell first enters our **sensory memory**. Information remains in sensory memory just long enough to locate relevant bits of information and transfer them to the next stage of memory. For visual information, known as *iconic memory*, the visual icon (or image) lasts about one-half of a second (Figure 7.2). Auditory information (what we hear) is held in sensory memory about the same length of time as visual information, one-quarter to one-half of a second. However, a weaker "echo," or *echoic memory*, of this auditory information can last up to four seconds (Lu, Williamson, & Kaufman, 1992; Neisser, 1967).

Achievement

Objective 7.3: *What is sensory memory?*

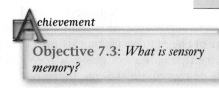

Figure 7.2 *How do researchers test iconic memory?* In an early study of iconic memory, George Sperling (1960) flashed an arrangement of letters like these for 1/20 of a second. Most people, he found, could recall only 4 or 5 letters. But when instructed to report just the top, middle, or bottom row, depending on whether they heard a high, medium, or low tone, they reported almost all the letters correctly. Apparently, all 12 letters are held in sensory memory right after they are viewed, but only those that are immediately attended to are noted and processed.

Early researchers believed sensory memory had an unlimited capacity. However, later research suggests that sensory memory does have limits and that stored images are fuzzier than once thought (Goldstein, 2008; Grondin, Ouellet, & Roussel, 2004).

Application

(a) *Iconic memory*

(b) *Echoic memory*

Demonstrating Iconic and Echoic Memory

(a) For a simple demonstration of the duration of visual, or *iconic memory*, swing a flashlight in a dark room. Because the image, or icon, lingers for a fraction of a second after the flashlight is moved, you see the light as a continuous stream, as in this photo, rather than as a succession of individual points. (b) Auditory, or *echoic memory*, works similarly. Think back to times when someone asked you a question while you were deeply absorbed in a task. Did you ask "What?" and then immediately find you could answer them without hearing their repeated response? Now you know why. A weaker "echo" (echoic memory) of auditory information can last up to four seconds. As a critical thinker, what do you think would happen if we did not possess iconic or echoic memory—or if visual or auditory sensations lingered not for seconds but for minutes?

Achievement

Objective 7.4: *Describe short-term memory (STM).*

Short-Term Memory (STM) *Second memory stage that temporarily stores sensory information and decides whether to send it on to long-term memory (LTM); capacity is limited to five to nine items and duration is about 30 seconds*

Maintenance Rehearsal *Repeating information over and over to maintain it in short-term memory (STM)*

Chunking *Grouping separate pieces of information into a single unit (or chunk)*

Short-Term Memory (STM): Memory's Second Stage

The second stage of memory processing, **short-term memory (STM)**, temporarily stores and processes information from sensory memory until the brain decides whether or not to send it along to the third stage (long-term memory). Unlike sensory memory, STM does not store exact *duplicates* of information but rather a mixture of perceptual analyses. For example, when your sensory memory registers the sound of your professor's voice, it holds the actual auditory information for a few seconds. If the information requires further processing, it moves on to STM. While being transferred from sensory memory, the sound of your professor's words is converted into a larger, more inclusive type of message capable of being analyzed and interpreted during short-term memory. If the information is important (or may be on a test), STM organizes and sends this information along to relatively permanent storage, called long-term memory (LTM).

Both the *duration* and *capacity* of STM are relatively limited. Although some researchers extend the time to a few minutes, most research shows that STM holds information for approximately 30 seconds. STM also holds a restricted *amount* of new information, five to nine items (Goldstein, 2008; Kareev, 2000). As with sensory memory, information in STM either is transferred quickly into the next stage (LTM) or it decays and is lost.

How can I increase the duration and capacity of my STM? Look back to the memory model in Figure 7.1. Note the looping arrow at the top labeled "maintenance rehearsal." You can extend the *duration* of your STM almost indefinitely if you consciously and continuously repeat the information over and over again. This is called **maintenance rehearsal**. You are using maintenance rehearsal when you look up a phone number and repeat it over and over until you dial the number.

Unfortunately, this technique requires constant vigilance. If you stop repeating the phone number it's quickly lost. Like juggling a set of plates, the plates stay in perfect shape only as long as you keep juggling them. Once you stop, the plates fall and are destroyed. (In the case of memory, the memory is lost.)

To extend the *capacity* of STM, you can use **chunking**—grouping separate pieces of information into a single unit (or *chunk*) (Boucher & Dienes, 2003; Miller, 1956; Walters & Gobet, 2008). (Figure 7.3). Have you noticed that numbers on credit cards, your Social Security identification, and telephone number are all grouped into three or four units separated by hyphens? This is because most people find it easier to remember numbers in chunks like *(760) 744–1129* rather than as a string of single digits. Similarly, in reading-improvement courses, students are taught to chunk groups of words into phrases. This allows fewer eye movements, and the brain can process the phrases as units rather than as individual words.

Figure 7.3 *Chunking in chess* To the inexpert eye, a chess game in progress looks like little more than a random assembly of black and white game pieces. Accordingly, novice chess players can remember the positions of only a few pieces when a chess game is under way. But expert players generally remember all the positions. To the experts, the scattered pieces form meaningful patterns—classic arrangements that recur often. Just as you group the letters of this sentence into meaningful words and remember them long enough to understand the meaning of the sentence, expert chess players group the chess pieces into easily recalled patterns (or chunks) (Huffman, Matthews, & Gagne, 2001; Waters & Gobet, 2008).

If I have room for five to nine units or chunks, why doesn't chunking help me remember even three or four names during introductions? The limited capacity and brief duration of STM both work against you in this situation. Instead of concentrating on the name of someone you meet for the first time, you sometimes use all your short-term memory capacity wondering how you look and thinking about what to say. You might even fill STM space worrying about your memory (Figure 7.4).

Short-Term Memory as a "Working Memory"

Does it sound as if short-term memory (STM) is just a *passive*, temporary "holding area?" Most current researchers (Baddeley, 1992, 2007; Jonides et al., 2008) emphasize that *active* processing of information also occurs in STM. Our short-term memory not only receives information from our sensory memory, it also sends and retrieves information from our long-term memory. In fact, all our conscious thought (reasoning, computing, perception) occurs in our STM. Therefore, today we think of STM as a three-part *working memory* (Process Diagram 7.2).

Long-Term Memory (LTM): The Third Stage of Memory

Think back to the opening story of H.M. If you were to meet him, you might not recognize his problem. But if you walked away and then ran into one another again 10 minutes later, H.M. would not remember ever having met you. His surgery was successful in stopping the severe epileptic seizures. Unfortunately, it also apparently destroyed the mechanism that transfers information from short-term to long-term memory.

What would it be like to live eternally in just the present—without your long-term memory? The *purpose* of the third stage, **long-term memory (LTM)**, is to serve as a storehouse for information that must be kept for long periods of time. Once information is transferred from STM, it is organized and integrated with other information in LTM. It remains there until we need to retrieve it. Then it is sent back to STM for our use.

Compared to sensory memory and short-term memory, long-term memory has relatively unlimited *capacity* and *duration*. It's like a magical credit card that lets you spend an unlimited amount of money for an unlimited time. In fact, the more you learn, or the more money you spend, the better it is!

Figure 7.4 *Problems with short-term memory?* People who are good at remembering names repeat the name of each person out loud or silently to keep it entered in STM (maintenance rehearsal). Keep in mind, however, that maintenance rehearsal saves the name only while you're actively rehearsing. If you want to really learn that name, you will need to transfer it into long-term memory.

Achievement

Objective 7.5: *Summarize long-term memory (LTM), how its divided into several subsystems, and how we can improve it.*

Long-Term Memory (LTM) *Third stage of memory that stores information for long periods of time; its capacity is virtually limitless, and its duration is relatively permanent*

Process Diagram 7.2

Working Memory as a Central Executive

The *central executive* supervises and coordinates two subsystems, the *phonological rehearsal loop* and the *visuospatial sketchpad,* while also sending and retrieving information to and from LTM. Picture yourself as a food server in a busy restaurant, and a couple has just given you a complicated food order. When you mentally rehearse the food order (the phonological loop) and combine it with a mental picture of the layout of plates on the customer's table (the visuospatial sketchpad), you're using your central executive.

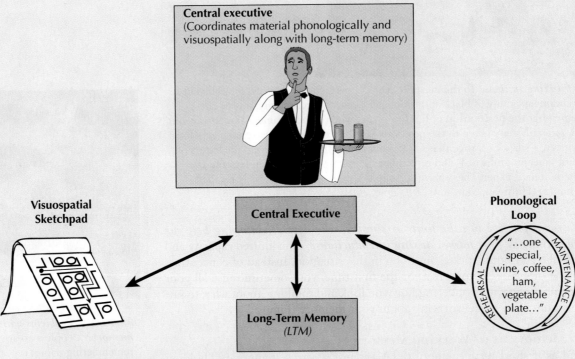

Central executive
(Coordinates material phonologically and visuospatially along with long-term memory)

Visuospatial Sketchpad

Central Executive

Phonological Loop

"...one special, wine, coffee, ham, vegetable plate..."

REHEARSAL / MAINTENANCE

Long-Term Memory
(LTM)

Visuospatial sketchpad
(Mentally imagines visual and spatial material)

Phonological loop
(Rehearses through speech, words, numbers)

The *visuospatial sketchpad* holds and manipulates visual images and spatial information (Baddeley & Jarrold, 2007; Lehnert & Zimmer, 2008). Again, imagine yourself as the food server who's delivering the food to the same customers. Using your mind's visuospatial sketchpad, you can mentally visualize where to fit all the entrees, side dishes, and dinnerware on their table.

The working memory's *phonological rehearsal loop* holds and manipulates verbal (phonological) information (Dasi et al., 2008; Jonides et al., 2008). Your phonological loop allows you to subvocally repeat all your customers' specific requests while you write a brief description on your order pad.

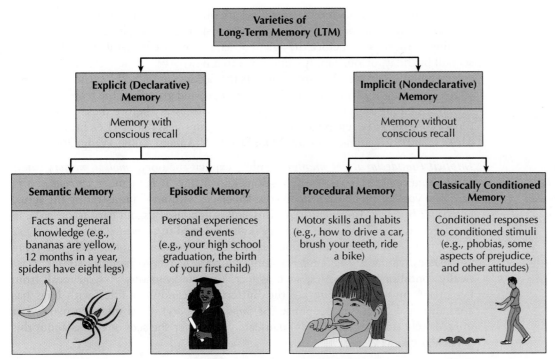

Figure 7.5 *Systems and subsystems of long-term memory (LTM)* Note how LTM is divided and subdivided into various types of memory. Taking time to study and visualize these separate systems and subsystems will improve your understanding and mastery of this material because it involves a deeper level of processing.

But why do I feel like the more I learn, the harder it is to find things? During the transfer of information from STM to LTM, incoming information is "tagged" or filed, hopefully in the appropriate place. If information is improperly stored, it creates major delays and problems during retrieval. The better we label and arrange things (whether it's our CD collection, bills, or memory), the more likely they'll be accurately stored and readily available for retrieval.

Types of Long-Term Memory

Given that LTM is believed to be generally unlimited in duration and capacity, we obviously collect a vast amount of information over a lifetime. How do we store it? As you can see in Figure 7.5, several types of LTM exist. At the top of the figure, you can see that LTM is divided into two major systems—*explicit (declarative) memory* and *implicit (nondeclarative) memory*.

1. ***Explicit (declarative) memory*** *Explicit memory* refers to intentional learning or conscious knowledge. It is *memory with awareness*. If asked to remember your phone number or the name of your first-grade teacher you can state (*declare*) the answers directly (*explicitly*). When people think of memory, they often are referring to this type of explicit (declarative) memory.

   Explicit (declarative) memory has two subsystems—*semantic memory* and *episodic memory*. **Semantic memory** is memory for facts and general knowledge (e.g., names of objects, days of the week). It is our internal mental dictionary or encyclopedia of stored knowledge. If you read and remember terms like *semantic, episodic, explicit (declarative)*, and *implicit (nondeclarative)*, it is because you have stored them in your semantic memory.

   In contrast, **episodic memory** is the explicit memory of our own past experiences—our personal mental diary. It records the major events (or *episodes*) that happen to us or take place in our presence. Some of our episodic memories are short-lived (what you ate for breakfast today). Others can last a lifetime (your first romantic kiss, your high school graduation, the birth of your first child).

Explicit (Declarative) Memory *Subsystem within long-term memory that consciously stores facts, information, and personal life experiences*

Semantic Memory *Subsystem of explicit/declarative memory that stores general knowledge; a mental encyclopedia or dictionary*

Episodic Memory *Subsystem of explicit/declarative memory that stores memories of personally experienced events; a mental diary of a person's life*

wiley.com/
college/
huffman

Have you ever wondered why toddlers are quite capable of remembering events they experienced in previous months, yet most of us as adults can recall almost nothing of those years before the age of 3? Why don't we remember our birth, our second birthday, or our family's big move to a new city? These were major events at that point in our life. Research suggests that a concept of "self," sufficient knowledge of our emotions and language development, and growth of the frontal lobes of the cortex (along with other structures) may be necessary before these early events (or episodes) can be encoded and retrieved many years later (Leichtman, 2006; Morris, 2007; Prigatano & Gray, 2008; Suzuki & Amaral, 2004; Wang, 2008).

Implicit (Nondeclarative) Memory *Subsystem within long-term memory consisting of unconscious procedural skills and simple classically conditioned responses.*

2. ***Implicit (nondeclarative) memory*** Unlike explicit memory, *implicit memory* refers to unintentional learning or unconscious knowledge. It is memory *without awareness*. Can you describe how you tie your shoelaces without demonstrating the actual behavior? Because your memory of this skill is unconscious and hard to describe in words (to "declare"), implicit memory is also referred to as *nondeclarative*.

Implicit (nondeclarative) memory consists of *procedural* motor skills like tying your shoes, riding a bike, and brushing your teeth. It also includes simple, classically conditioned responses, such as fears or taste aversions. As you recall from Chapter 6, my student who ate the Butterfinger candy bar filled with bugs has a conditioned emotional response (or *implicit memory*). This memory makes her immediately and (unconsciously) nauseated whenever she sees or thinks about this particular candy.

PSYCHOLOGY AT WORK

Improving Long-Term Memory (LTM)

After reading through all the terms and concepts associated with long-term memory, you may be wondering, "Why do I need to know this?" Understanding LTM has direct beneficial applications to your everyday life—particularly to college success. In this section, we will focus on numerous tips for improving LTM, which fall under the general categories of improved *encoding*, *storage*, and *retrieval* (Figure 7.6).

1. **Encoding and LTM** As you first discovered in Process Diagram 7.1, p. 245, encoding involves several factors, including *selective vs. divided attention*, *automatic vs. controlled processing*, and *levels of processing*. It's easy to understand how selective attention and effortful processing will improve your encoding, which in turn will enhance your LTM. However, the concept and importance of a *deeper level of processing* warrants further discussion. Fegus Craik and Robert Lockhart's (1972) **levels of processing** model suggests that successful memory relies on how *deeply* we process (or encode) initial information. During *shallow processing*, we're only aware of basic incoming sensory information. Little or no memory is formed. However, when we do something more with the information, such as adding meaning, developing organizations and associations, or relating it to things we already know, the information is *deeply processed* and can be stored for a lifetime.

Levels of Processing *Degree or depth of mental processing occurring when material is initially encountered; determines how well material is later remembered*

Rehearsal is one of the key factors in levels of processing. As we discussed earlier, if you need to hold information in STM for longer than 30 seconds, you can shallowly process it by simply repeating it over and over (*maintenance rehearsal*). However, lasting storage in LTM requires a different type of rehearsal and deeper levels of processing, called **elaborative rehearsal**. The immediate goal of elaborative rehearsal is to understand—*not* to memorize. Fortunately, this attempt to understand is one of the best ways to encode new information into long-term memory.

Elaborative Rehearsal *Linking new information to previously stored material (also known as deeper levels of processing)*

Can you see how levels of processing and elaborative rehearsal could have several practical applications for your college life? If you're casually reading this text and giving the words little thought (*shallow processing*), you will retain the information only for the briefest period of time. (And you'll remember little or nothing on exams

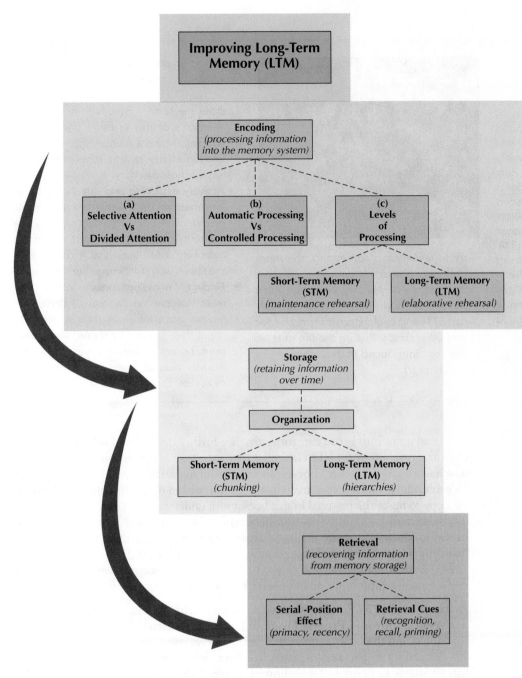

Figure 7.6 *Strategies for improving LTM* Just as the diagram of the nervous system helped organize the material in Chapter 2, a similar diagram of the current information on improving LTM memory helps you order and arrange the various terms. Encoding, storage, and retrieval in LTM are all improved through the use of hierarchies. This is why this text contains so many tables, figures, Process and Concept Diagrams, as well as end-of-chapter Visual Summaries.

 Study Tip

Don't hesitate to ask questions of your professor during exams. Most professors allow questions, and their answers often provide valuable retrieval cues.

or quizzes!) But if you stop and think deeply about the meaning of the words and relate them to your own experiences, you'll be using elaborative rehearsal and greatly increasing your mastery of the material. Similarly, rote memorization of the chapter's key terms involves only a shallow level of processing. You need to *deeply process* each key term if you want to have long-term retention.

2. **Storage and *LTM*** To successfully store information in LTM, we need to organize the material into *hierarchies*. Like Figure 7.6, this strategy involves arranging a number

wiley.com/
college/
huffman

Improving Elaborative Rehearsal

As we discovered earlier, because LTM is relatively unlimited in capacity and duration, it's like a magical credit card with an unlimited amount of money and unlimited time. Using elaborative rehearsal, you can access even more of that unlimited bounty each time you go on a spending spree! How can this be true? Think about the students in your college classes. Have you noticed that older students often tend to get better grades? This is because they've lived longer and stored more information in their LTM. Older students can tap into a greater wealth of previously stored material. If you're a younger student (or an older student just returning to college), you can learn to process information at a deeper level and build your elaborative rehearsal skills by:

- **Expanding (or elaborating on) the information.** The more you elaborate or

Teel Tamburo/NG Image Collection

try to understand something, the more likely you are to remember it. To store the term *long-term memory*, think about what it would be like if you only had STM and could store information for only 30 seconds. Picture the life of H.M. (the man introduced at the beginning of the chapter).

If you can't easily tag information to what you already know, create a new link or "tag." For instance, to encode and store the term *echoic memory*, look for examples of this in other people or in yourself. Make a mental note when you find an example and store it with the term *echoic memory*.

- **Actively exploring and questioning new information.** Think about the term *iconic memory*. Ask yourself, "Why did they use this term?" Look up the term *icon* in the dictionary. You'll learn that it comes from the Greek word for "image" or "likeness."
- **Finding meaningfulness.** When you meet people at a party, don't just maintenance-rehearse their name. Ask about their favorite TV shows, their career plans, political beliefs, or anything else that requires deeper analysis. You'll be much more likely to remember their names.

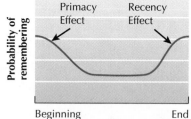

Figure 7.7 *The serial-position effect* If you try to recall a list of similar items, you'll tend to remember the first and last items best. Can you see how you can use this information to improve your chances for employment success? If a potential employer calls to set up an interview, you can increase their memory of you (and your application) by asking to be either the first or last candidate.

Serial-Position Effect *Information at the beginning and end of a list is remembered better than material in the middle.*

Retrieval Cue *Clue or prompt that helps stimulate recall or retrieval of a stored piece of information from long-term memory*

Recall *Retrieving a memory using a general cue*

Recognition *Retrieving a memory using a specific cue*

of related items into broad categories that are further divided and subdivided. (This organization strategy for LTM is similar to the strategy of *chunking* material in STM, which we discussed earlier.) For instance, by grouping small subsets of ideas together (as subheadings under larger, main headings, and within diagrams, tables, and so on), we hope to make the material in this book more understandable and memorable.

Admittedly, organization and hierarchies take time and work, so you'll be happy to know that some memory organization and other tasks are done automatically while you sleep (Mograss et al., 2008; Siccoli et al., 2008; Wagner et al., 2003). (Unfortunately, despite claims to the contrary, research shows that we can't recruit our sleeping hours to memorize new material, such as a foreign language.)

3. ***Retrieval and LTM*** Finally, effective retrieval is critical to using long-term memory. As first shown in Process Diagram 7.1, p. 245, retrieval involves several factors, including the *serial-position effect* and *retrieval cues*.

According to the **serial-position effect**, when study participants are given lists of words to learn and are allowed to recall them in any order they choose, they remember the words at the beginning (*primacy effect*) and the end of the list (*recency effect*) better than those in the middle (Azizian & Polich, 2008; Healy et al., 2008) (Figure 7.7). The reasons for this effect are complex, but it does help explain why material at the beginning and end of a chapter is better remembered than that in the middle. It also helps clarify why you remember the first and last people you meet at a party better than those you meet in-between.

Three of the most important **retrieval cues** are *recall*, *recognition*, and *priming*. **Recall** is a memory task, like an essay exam, that requires you to retrieve previously learned information with only *general*, nonspecific *cues*. In contrast, a **recognition** task offers *specific cues* and only requires you to identify (*recognize*) the correct response, as on multiple-choice tests. As you can see in Figure 7.8, recall tests have vague, general retrieval cues that require you to recover specific information by searching through all possible matches in LTM—a much more difficult task.

Antonia M. Rosario/Photographer's Choice/Getty Images

(a)

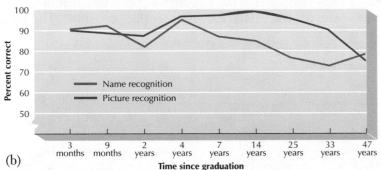

(b)

Figure 7.8 *Recall versus recognition* (a) Note how it's more difficult to *recall*, in order, the names of the planets in our solar system (general cue) than to *recognize* them when cued with the first three letters of each planet's name (specific retrieval cue): Mer-, Ven-, Ear-, Mar-, Jup-, Sat-, Ura-, Nep-, Plu-. (Note that in 2006, Pluto was officially declassified as a planet, but this finding is still being debated.) (b) Both name and picture *recognition* for high school classmates remain high even many years after graduation, whereas *recall* memory drops significantly over time.

Whether cues require recall or only recognition is not all that matters. Imagine that while house hunting, you walk into a stranger's kitchen and are greeted with the unmistakable smell of freshly baked bread. Instantly, the aroma transports you to your grandmother's kitchen, where you spent many childhood afternoons doing your homework. You find yourself suddenly thinking of the mental shortcuts your grandmother taught you to help you learn your multiplication tables. You hadn't thought about these little tricks for years, but somehow a whiff of baking bread brought them back to you. Why?

In this imagined episode, you have stumbled upon the third retrieval cue, known as **priming**. This form of memory occurs when a prior exposure to a stimulus (or *prime*) facilitates or inhibits the processing of new information (Amir et al., 2008; Becker, 2008; Woollams et al., 2008). Such priming effects may occur even when we do not consciously remember being exposed to the *prime* (Figure 7.9).

Do you want to improve your retrieval cues? According to the **encoding specificity principle** (Tulving & Thompson, 1973), memory retrieval is increased when we have *matching* context, moods, and states:

• *Context-dependent memory* In most cases, we're able to remember better when we attempt to recall information in the *same* context in which it was learned. Have you

Priming *Prior exposure to a stimulus (or prime) facilitates or inhibits the processing of new information, even when one has no conscious memory of the initial learning and storage*

Encoding Specificity Principle *Retrieval of information is improved when conditions of recovery are similar to the conditions when information was encoded*

Jupiter Images

Figure 7.9 *The power of priming* Have you noticed how your fears are heightened during and after watching a horror film? This is because your previous experiences *prime* you to more easily notice and recall related instances. (It also suggests a practical way to improve your love life—go to romantic movies!)

Nicole Duplaix/National Geographic/Getty Images

Figure 7.10 *Context-dependent memory* One important contextual cue for retrieval is location. In a clever study, Godden and Baddeley (1975) had underwater divers learn a list of 40 words either on land or underwater. The divers had better recall for lists that they had encoded underwater if they were also underwater at the time of retrieval; similarly, lists that were encoded above water were better recalled above water.

noticed that you tend to do better on exams when you take them in the same seat and classroom in which you originally studied the material? This happens because the matching location acts as a retrieval cue for the information (Figure 7.10).

- *Mood congruence* People also remember information better if their moods during learning and retrieval match (Kenealy, 1997; Nouchi & Hyodo, 2007). This phenomenon, called *mood congruence*, occurs because a given mood tends to evoke memories that are consistent with that mood. When you're sad (or happy or angry), you're more likely to remember events and circumstances from other times when you were sad (or happy or angry).

  If you suffer from test anxiety, you might try re-creating the relaxed mood you had while studying. Take deep breaths and reassure yourself during exams. To further match your study and test-taking moods, try to deliberately increase your anxiety level while studying. Consciously remind yourself of the importance of good grades and your long-range career plans. By lowering your test anxiety and upping your study anxiety, you create a better balance or match between your exam and study moods. This should improve your retrieval.

- *State-dependent memory* As generations of coffee-guzzling university students have discovered, if you learn something while under the influence of a drug, such as caffeine, you will remember it more easily when you take that drug again than at other times (Ahmadi et al., 2008; Zarrindast et al., 2005, 2007). This is called *state-dependent retrieval*.

Assessment

STOP

CHECK & REVIEW

The Nature of Memory

Objective 7.1: *Define memory, and describe the information-processing and parallel distributed processing (PDP) models of memory.*

Memory is an internal record or representation of some prior event or experience. The *information-processing model* sees analogies between human memory and a computer. Like typing on a keyboard, **encoding** translates information into neural codes that match the brain's language. **Storage** retains neural coded information over time, like saving material on the computer's hard drive or a disk. **Retrieval** gets information out of LTM storage and sends it to STM to be used, whereas the computer retrieves information and displays it on the monitor.

According to the **parallel distributed processing (PDP)**, or *connectionist*, model, the contents of our memory exist as a vast number of interconnected units distributed throughout a huge network, all operating simultaneously in parallel.

Objective 7.2: *Summarize the three-stage memory model.*

The traditional three-stage memory model proposes that information must pass through each of three stages before being stored: *sensory memory, short-term memory,* and *long-term memory.*

Objective 7.3: *What is sensory memory?*

Sensory memory preserves a brief replica of sensory information. It has a large capacity, and information lasts from a fraction of a second to four seconds. Selected information is sent to short-term memory.

Objective 7.4: *Describe short-term memory (STM).*

Short-term memory (STM), also called *working memory*, involves memory for current thoughts. Short-term memory can hold five to nine items for about 30 seconds before they are forgotten. Information can be stored longer than 30 seconds through **maintenance rehearsal**, and the capacity of STM can be increased with **chunking**.

Objective 7.5: *Summarize long-term memory (LTM), how its divided into several subsystems, and how we can improve it.*

Long-term memory (LTM) is relatively permanent memory storage with an unlimited capacity. Storage in LTM is divided into two major systems—**explicit (declarative)** and **implicit (nondeclarative) memory**. Explicit memory is further subdivided into two parts—**semantic** and **episodic memory**. Implicit memory is subdivided into procedural memory and classically conditioned memory. To improve LTM, we can use various concepts related to *encoding, storage* and *retrieval.*

Questions

1. Label the following *terms* on the figure below: In the information processing model of memory, (a) _____ would happen at the keyboard, (b) _____ on the monitor, and (c) _____ on the hard drive.

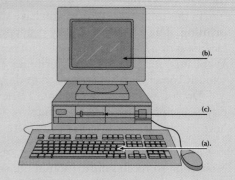

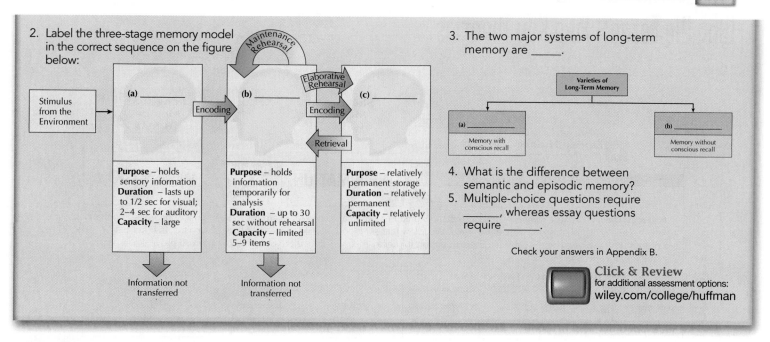

2. Label the three-stage memory model in the correct sequence on the figure below:

Stimulus from the Environment

Maintenance Rehearsal

Elaborative Rehearsal

(a) _____

Encoding

Purpose – holds sensory information
Duration – lasts up to 1/2 sec for visual; 2–4 sec for auditory
Capacity – large

Information not transferred

(b) _____

Encoding

Retrieval

Purpose – holds information temporarily for analysis
Duration – up to 30 sec without rehearsal
Capacity – limited 5–9 items

Information not transferred

(c) _____

Purpose – relatively permanent storage
Duration – relatively permanent
Capacity – relatively unlimited

3. The two major systems of long-term memory are _____.

Varieties of Long-Term Memory

(a) _____
Memory with conscious recall

(b) _____
Memory without conscious recall

4. What is the difference between semantic and episodic memory?

5. Multiple-choice questions require _____, whereas essay questions require _____.

Check your answers in Appendix B.

Click & Review
for additional assessment options:
wiley.com/college/huffman

Forgetting

Memory is what makes you wonder what you've forgotten.

ANONYMOUS

Think about what your life would be like if you couldn't forget. Your LTM would be filled with meaningless data, such as what you ate for breakfast every morning of your life. Similarly, think of the incredible pain and sorrow you would continuously endure if you couldn't distance yourself from tragedy through forgetting. The ability to forget is essential to the proper functioning of memory. But what about those times when forgetting is an inconvenience or even dangerous?

How Quickly Do We Forget? Research Findings

Hermann Ebbinghaus first introduced the experimental study of learning and forgetting in 1885. Using himself as a subject, he calculated how long it took to learn a list of three-letter nonsense syllables such as SIB and RAL. He found that one hour after he knew a list perfectly, he remembered only 44 percent of the syllables. A day later, he recalled 35 percent, and a week later, only 21 percent. Figure 7.11 shows his famous "forgetting curve."

Depressing as these findings may seem, keep in mind that meaningful material is much more memorable than nonsense syllables. Even so, we all forget some of what we have learned.

On a more cheerful note, after some time passed and he had forgotten the list, Ebbinghaus found that **relearning** a list took less time than the initial learning did. This research suggests that we often retain some memory for things that we have learned, even when we seem to have forgotten them completely. This finding should be encouraging to you if you studied a foreign language years ago. You may be unable to fully recall or recognize the vocabulary at this time. But you can expect to relearn the material more rapidly the second time.

Why Do We Forget? Five Key Theories

Five major theories have been offered to explain why forgetting occurs: *decay, interference, motivated forgetting, encoding failure,* and *retrieval failure*. Each theory focuses on a different stage of the memory process or on a particular type of problem in processing information (Process Diagram 7.3a,b).

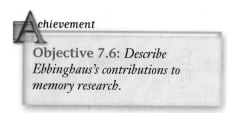

Achievement

Objective 7.6: *Describe Ebbinghaus's contributions to memory research.*

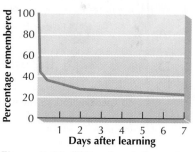

Figure 7.11 *Ebbinghaus's forgetting curve* Note how rapidly nonsense syllables are forgotten, especially in the first few hours after learning.

Relearning *Learning material a second time, which usually takes less time than original learning (also called the savings method)*

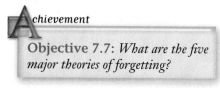

Achievement

Objective 7.7: *What are the five major theories of forgetting?*

wiley.com/ college/ huffman

Why We Forget: Five Key Theories

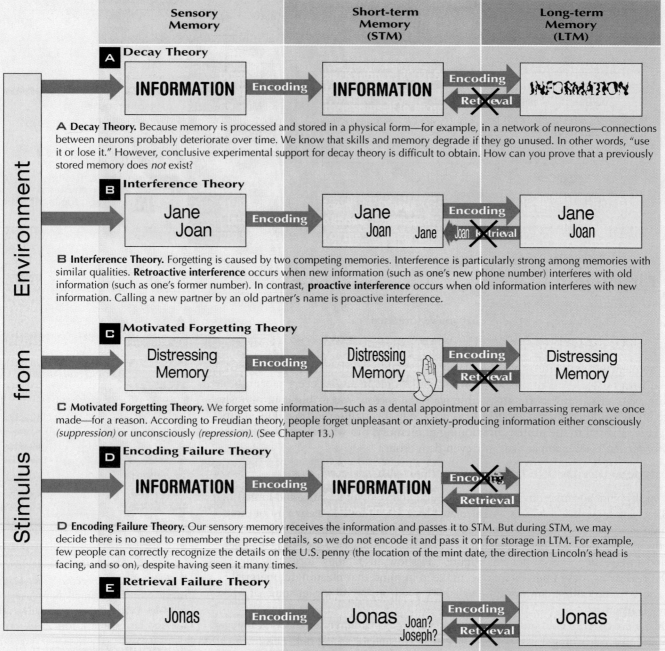

Sensory Memory	Short-term Memory (STM)	Long-term Memory (LTM)

A Decay Theory

INFORMATION → Encoding → INFORMATION → Encoding / Retrieval ✗ → INFORMATION

A Decay Theory. Because memory is processed and stored in a physical form—for example, in a network of neurons—connections between neurons probably deteriorate over time. We know that skills and memory degrade if they go unused. In other words, "use it or lose it." However, conclusive experimental support for decay theory is difficult to obtain. How can you prove that a previously stored memory does *not* exist?

B Interference Theory

Jane / Joan → Encoding → Jane / Joan / Jane → Encoding / Joan / Retrieval ✗ → Jane / Joan

B Interference Theory. Forgetting is caused by two competing memories. Interference is particularly strong among memories with similar qualities. **Retroactive interference** occurs when new information (such as one's new phone number) interferes with old information (such as one's former number). In contrast, **proactive interference** occurs when old information interferes with new information. Calling a new partner by an old partner's name is proactive interference.

C Motivated Forgetting Theory

Distressing Memory → Encoding → Distressing Memory → Encoding / Retrieval ✗ → Distressing Memory

C Motivated Forgetting Theory. We forget some information—such as a dental appointment or an embarrassing remark we once made—for a reason. According to Freudian theory, people forget unpleasant or anxiety-producing information either consciously *(suppression)* or unconsciously *(repression)*. (See Chapter 13.)

D Encoding Failure Theory

INFORMATION → Encoding → INFORMATION → Encoding ✗ / Retrieval →

D Encoding Failure Theory. Our sensory memory receives the information and passes it to STM. But during STM, we may decide there is no need to remember the precise details, so we do not encode it and pass it on for storage in LTM. For example, few people can correctly recognize the details on the U.S. penny (the location of the mint date, the direction Lincoln's head is facing, and so on), despite having seen it many times.

E Retrieval Failure Theory

Jonas → Encoding → Jonas / Joan? / Joseph? → Encoding / Retrieval ✗ → Jonas

E Retrieval Failure Theory. Memories stored in LTM aren't forgotten. They're just momentarily inaccessible—perhaps because of interference, faulty cues, or emotional states. For example, the **tip-of-the-tongue phenomenon**—the feeling that at any second, a word or event you are trying to remember and perhaps can *almost* remember—will pop out from the "tip of your tongue." Although it is difficult to distinguish retrieval failure from encoding failure, most memory failures probably stem from poor encoding, not retrieval failure.

Stimulus from Environment

Decay Theory

Istock photo

Interference Theory

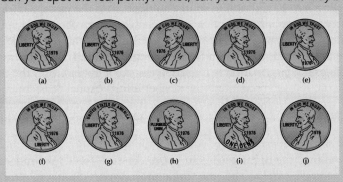

Retroactive Interference

Names of fish
Old Information

Interferes with

Names of college students
New Information

(a)

Proactive Interference

Old boyfriend or girlfriend's name — Ann / Bill
Old Information

Interferes with

New boyfriend or girlfriend's name — Sue / Bob
New Information

(b)

Two types of interference. *(a) Retroactive (backward-acting) interference occurs when new information interferes with old information. This example comes from a story about an absent-minded icthyology professor (fish specialist) who refused to learn the name of his college students. Asked why, he said, "Every time I learn a student's name, I forget the name of a fish!" (b) Proactive (forward-acting) interference occurs when old information interferes with new information. Have you ever been in trouble because you used an old partner's name to refer to your new partner? You now have a guilt-free explanation—proactive interference.*

Motivated Forgetting Theory

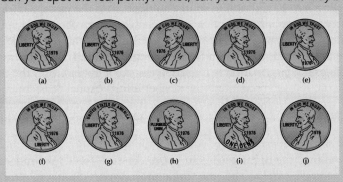

Monty Rakussen/Getty Images

Encoding Failure Theory

Assessment

VISUAL QUIZ

Can you spot the real penny? If not, can you see how this may be an example of encoding failure?

(a) (b) (c) (d) (e)

(f) (g) (h) (i) (j)

Answer: Unless we are coin collectors, we have little motivation to properly encode the details of a penny. Our sensory memory certainly received the information and passed it along (encoded it) to STM. But during STM, we probably decided there was no need to remember the precise details of the penny. Because we can easily recognize pennies by their size and color, we don't encode the fine details and pass them on for storage in LTM. The answer is "a."

Retrieval Failure Theory

DON'T YOU JUST HATE IT WHEN YOU WALK INTO A ROOM AND FORGET WHAT YOU CAME IN FOR?

SURGERY

WILEY@NON-SEQUITUR.COM   DIST. BY UNIVERSAL PRESS SYNDICATE   WWW.

Retroactive Interference *New information interferes with remembering old information; backward-acting interference*

Proactive Interference *Old information interferes with remembering new information; forward-acting interference*

Tip-of-the-Tongue (TOT) Phenomenon *Feeling that specific information is stored in long-term memory but of being temporarily unable to retrieve it*

PSYCHOLOGY AT WORK

Achievement

Objective 7.8: *Describe four key factors that contribute to forgetting.*

Misinformation Effect *Distortion of a memory by misleading post-event information*

Source Amnesia *Forgetting the true source of a memory (also called source confusion or source misattribution)*

Sleeper Effect *Information from an unreliable source, which was initially discounted, later gains credibility because the source is forgotten*

Distributed Practice *Practice (or study) sessions are interspersed with rest periods*

Massed Practice *Time spent learning is grouped (or massed) into long, unbroken intervals (also known as cramming)*

IN MCNAMEE/Reuters/Landov LLC

Key Factors in Forgetting

Scientists have discovered numerous factors that contribute to legitimate forgetting. Four of the most important are the *misinformation effect, source amnesia*, the *sleeper effect*, and *information overload*.

1. **Misinformation effect**. Many people (who haven't studied this chapter or taken a psychology class) believe that when they're recalling an event, they're remembering it as if it were an "instant replay." However, as you know, our memories are highly fallible and filled with personal "constructions" that we create during encoding and storage. Research on the **misinformation effect**, shows that information that occurs *after* an event may further alter and revise these constructions. For example, the upcoming Research Highlight on p. 000 describes a study in which subjects watched a film of a car driving through the countryside, and were then asked to estimate how fast the car was going when it passed the barn. Although there was no actual barn in the film, subjects were six times more likely to report having seen one than those who were not asked about a barn (Loftus, 1982). Other experiments have created false memories by showing subjects doctored photos of themselves taking a completely fictitious hot-air balloon ride, or by asking subjects to simply imagine an event, such as having a nurse remove a skin sample from their finger. In these and similar cases, a large number of subjects later believed that misleading information was correct and that fictitious or imagined events actually occurred (Allan & Gabbert, 2008; Garry & Gerrie, 2005; Mazzoni & Memon, 2003; Mazzoni & Vannucci, 2007; Pérez-Mata & Diges, 2007).

2. **Source amnesia**. Each day we read, hear, and process an enormous amount of information. It's easy to confuse "who said what to whom" and in what context. Forgetting the true source of a memory is known as **source amnesia** (Kleider et al., 2008; Leichtman, 2006; Mitchell et al., 2005). As a critical thinker, can you see why advertisers of shoddy services or products might benefit from "channel surfing"? If television viewers are skipping from news programs to cable talk shows to infomercials, they may give undue credit to the inferior services or products.

3. **Sleeper effect**. In addition to source amnesia, with the passage of time we also tend to confuse reliable information with unreliable. Research on this aptly named **sleeper effect** finds that when we first hear something from an unreliable source, we tend to disregard that information in favor of a more reliable source. However, over time, the source of the information is forgotten (source amnesia). And the unreliable information is no longer discounted (the sleeper effect) (Appel & Richter, 2007; Kumkale & Albarracin, 2004; Nabi, Moyer-Gusé, & Byrne, 2007). This sleeper effect can be a significant problem when reliable and unreliable information are intermixed (Figure 7.12).

4. **Information overload**. Do you attempt to memorize too much at one time by "cramming" the night before an exam? As the "Tools for Student Success" section in Chapter 1 emphasized, the single most important key to improving grades may be *distributed study*. **Distributed practice** refers to spacing your learning periods, with rest periods between sessions. Cramming is called **massed practice** because the time spent learning is *massed* into long, unbroken intervals.

Fibs or false recall? Three months after the terrorist attack on the World Trade Center on 9/11, President George Bush was asked how he heard about the first attack. He replied that he was "sitting outside the classroom waiting to go in, and I saw an airplane hit the tower—the TV was obviously on, and I used to fly myself..." However, at the exact moment of the attack on 9/11, no one saw the first plane crashing into the north tower on live TV—footage of the first crash only surfaced the next day. Furthermore, there are photos, like this one, showing that the president first learned of the attack when chief of staff, Andrew Card, whispered the news to him while he sat in front of the class. Was this a deliberate lie or the misinformation effect?

Advertisement

Stepping Out of The Shadows of Emphysema

That was daily life for Brenda Wilson. Sidelined with severe emphysema, the Bristol, Va., woman struggled with everyday tasks like dressing, bathing and walking even short distances. With conventional therapies no longer providing relief, Wilson's pulmonologist referred her to the University of Virginia Health System, a leading treatment center for Chronic Obstructive Pulmonary Disease (COPD), a group of progressive lung disorders that includes emphysema and chronic bronchitis. While her prognosis seemed poor, UVa's experts determined that Wilson could benefit from Lung Volume Reduction Surgery (LVRS), an innovative procedure that removes up to 30 percent of the lung tissue most damaged by emphysema.

The results were dramatic. Within a week of her surgery she no longer needed supplemental oxygen. Once too breathless [...] with a mile. "I can't describe how [...]

Figure 7.12 ***Capitalizing on the sleeper effect and source amnesia*** The sleeper effect and source amnesia can be significant problems when reliable and unreliable information are intermixed—for example, when advertising or PR are disguised to look like more objective reports. Can you see how, after a time, we may forget the source and no longer discount the information in the ad?

GENDER & CULTURAL DIVERSITY

Cultural Differences in Memory and Forgetting

How do you remember the dates for all your quizzes, exams, and assignments in college? What memory aids do you use if you need to buy 15 items at the supermarket? Most people from industrialized societies rely on written shopping lists, calendars, books, notepads, or computers to store information and prevent forgetting. Can you imagine living in a culture without these aids? What would it be like if you had to rely solely on your memory to store and retrieve all your learned information? Do people raised in preliterate societies with rich oral traditions develop better memory skills than do people raised in literate societies?

Ross and Millson (1970) designed a cross-cultural study to explore these questions. They compared American and Ghanaian college students' abilities to remember stories that were read aloud. Students listened to the stories without taking notes and without being told they would be tested. Two weeks later, all students were asked to write down as much as they could remember. As you might expect, the Ghanaian students had better recall than the Americans. Their superior performance was attributed to their culture's long oral tradition, which requires developing greater skill in encoding oral information (Matsumoto & Juang, 2008).

Does this mean that people from cultures with an oral tradition simply have better memories? Recall from Chapter 1 that a core requirement for scientific research is *replication* and the generation of related hypotheses and studies. In this case, when other researchers orally presented nonliterate African participants with lists of words instead of stories, they did *not* perform better (Cole et al., 1971). However, when both educated Africans and uneducated Africans were compared for memory of

Objective 7.9: *How does culture affect memory?*

Culture and memory *In many societies, tribal leaders pass down vital information through stories related orally. Because of this rich oral tradition, children living in these cultures have better memories for information related through stories than do other children.*

wiley.com/
college/
huffman

lists of words, the educated Africans performed very well (Scribner, 1977). This suggests that formal schooling helps develop memory strategies for things like lists of words. Preliterate participants may see such lists as unrelated and meaningless.

Wagner (1982) conducted a study with Moroccan and Mexican urban and rural children that helps explain the effect of formal schooling. Participants were presented with seven cards that were placed facedown in front of them, one at a time. They were then shown a card and asked to point out which of the seven cards was its duplicate. Everyone, regardless of culture or amount of schooling, was able to recall the latest cards presented (the *recency effect*). However, the amount of schooling significantly affected overall recall and the ability to recall the earliest cards presented (*primacy effect*).

Wagner suggests that the primacy effect depends on *rehearsal*—the silent repetition of things you're trying to remember—and that this strategy is strongly related to schooling. As a child in a typical classroom, you were expected to memorize letters, numbers, multiplication tables, and a host of other basic facts. This type of formal schooling provides years of practice in memorization and in applying these skills in test situations. According to Wagner, memory has a "hardware" section that does not change across culture. It also contains a "software" part that develops particular strategies for remembering, which are learned.

In summary, research indicates that the "software" part of memory is affected by culture. In cultures in which communication relies on oral tradition, people develop good strategies for remembering orally presented stories. In cultures in which formal schooling is the rule, people learn memory strategies that help them remember lists of items. From these studies, we can conclude that, across cultures, people tend to remember information that matters to them. They develop memory skills to match the demands of their environment.

Assessment

STOP

CHECK & REVIEW

Forgetting

Objective 7.6: *Describe Ebbinghaus's contribution to memory research.*

Ebbinghaus's famous "curve of forgetting" shows that it occurs most rapidly immediately after learning. However, Ebbinghaus also showed that **relearning** usually takes less time than original learning.

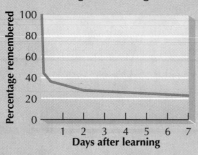

Objective 7.7: *What are the five major theories of forgetting?*

The *decay theory* of forgetting simply states that memory, like all biological processes, deteriorates as time passes. The *interference theory* of forgetting suggests that memories are forgotten because of either retroactive or proactive interference. **Retro**

active interference occurs when new information interferes with previously learned information. **Proactive interference** occurs when old information interferes with newly learned information. The *motivated forgetting theory* states that people forget things that are painful, threatening, or embarrassing. According to *encoding failure theory*, some material is forgotten because it was never encoded from short-term memory to long-term memory (LTM). *Retrieval failure theory* suggests information stored in LTM is not forgotten but may at times be inaccessible.

Objective 7.8: *Describe four key factors that contribute to forgetting.*

To prevent problems with forgetting, you should be aware of four important factors: the **misinformation effect** (distorting memory with misleading post event information); **source amnesia** (forgetting the true source of a memory); the **sleeper effect** (initially discounting information from an unreliable source but later judging it as reliable because the source is forgotten); and *information overload* (in which **distributed practice** is found to be superior to **massed practice**).

Objective 7.9: *How does culture affect memory?*

Across cultures, people remember information that matters to them, and we develop memory skills to match our differing environments.

Questions

1. Which theory of forgetting is being described in each of the following examples?
   a. You are very nervous about having to introduce all the people at a party, and you forget a good friend's name.
   b. You meet someone you haven't seen for 25 years and you cannot remember his name.
   c. You seriously mistreated a good friend in high school, and now you can't remember her name.
2. Briefly describe a personal example of source amnesia and the sleeper effect from your own life.
3. How would you study for a test using distributed practice? Using massed practice?

Check your answers in Appendix B.

Click & Review
for additional assessment options:
wiley.com/college/huffman

Biological Bases of Memory

The previous sections have emphasized the theories and models of memory and forgetting. Now we focus on the biological aspects of memory. We first explore how memories are formed and where they are located in the brain. Then we examine memory problems related to biological factors.

How Are Memories Formed? The Biological Perspective

It is obvious that something physical must happen in the brain and nervous system when we learn something new. (How else could we later recall and use this information?)

Neuronal and Synaptic Changes in Memory

We know that learning modifies the brain's neural networks (Chapters 2 and 6). As you learn to play tennis, for example, repeated practice builds neural "pathways" that make it easier and easier for you to get the ball over the net. This prolonged strengthening of neural firing, called **long-term potentiation (LTP)**, happens in at least two ways:

1. *Repeated stimulation of a synapse can strengthen the synapse by causing the dendrites to grow more spines.* As seen in Chapter 6, rats raised in "enriched" environments grew more sprouts on their dendrites compared to rats raised in "deprived" environments.

2. *The ability of a particular neuron to release or accept neurotransmitters can be increased or decreased.* This is shown in research with sea slugs (Figure 7.13) and "smart" mice (Figure 7.14). Although it is difficult to generalize from sea slugs and mice, research on long-term potentiation (LTP) in humans has been widely supportive (Berger et al., 2008; Tecchio et al., 2008; Wixted, 2004).

Hormonal Changes and Memory

When stressed or excited, we naturally produce "fight-or-flight" hormones that arouse the body, such as epinephrine and cortisol (see Chapter 3). These hormones in turn affect the amygdala (a brain structure involved in emotion), which then stimulates the hippocampus and cerebral cortex (other parts of the brain important for memory storage). Research has shown that direct injections of epinephrine or cortisol, or electrical stimulation of the amygdala, will increase the encoding and storage of new information (Hamilton & Gotlib, 2008; Jackson, 2008; van Stegeren, 2008). However, prolonged or extreme stress (and increased levels of cortisol) can interfere with memory (see Chapter 3).

Can you see why heightened (but not excessive) arousal might enhance memory? To survive, human or nonhuman animals must remember exactly how they got into a dangerous situation and how they got out of it. The naturally produced surge of hormones apparently alerts our brains to "pay attention and remember!" It also is important to note the problems with "hormonally induced memory." Have you ever become so anxious that you "blanked out" during an exam or while giving a speech? If so, you understand how extreme arousal and stress hormones can interfere with both the formation and retrieval of memories.

Flashbulb Memory

The powerful effect of hormones on memory also can be seen in what are known as *flashbulb memories*—vivid images of circumstances associated with

Achievement

Objective 7.10: *How do we form memories, and where do we store them?*

Dr. Bill Rudman/Australian Museum

Figure 7.13 *How does a sea slug learn and remember?* After repeated squirting with water, followed by a mild shock, the sea slug, *Aplysia*, releases more neurotransmitters at certain synapses. These synapses then become more efficient at transmitting signals that allow the slug to withdraw its gills when squirted. As a critical thinker, can you explain why this ability might provide an evolutionary advantage?

Long-Term Potentiation (LTP)
Long-lasting increase in neural excitability, which may be a biological mechanism for learning and memory

©AP/Wide World Photos

Figure 7.14 *Creating "smart mice" through genetic engineering* Further evidence for biological effects on learning and memory comes from studies with genetically engineered "smart mice," which have extra receptors for a neurotransmitter called NMDA (N-methyl-d-aspartate). These mice performed significantly better on memory tasks than did normal mice (Tang et al., 2001; Tsien, 2000).

September 11, 2001 The terrorist attack on the World Trade Center is a flashbulb memory for most people in the United States.

©AP/Wide World Photos

surprising or strongly emotional events (Brown & Kulik, 1977). Do you remember the moment you learned about the September 11, 2001 terrorist attacks on the World Trade Center and the Pentagon? Is this memory so clear that it seems like a flashbulb went off, capturing every detail of the event in your memory? Assassinations (John Kennedy, Robert Kennedy, Martin Luther King Jr.), important personal events (graduation, illnesses, birth of a child), and, of course, horrific terrorist attacks have lasting effects on memory. We secrete fight-or-flight hormones when we initially hear of the event. We later replay these events in our minds again and again, which further strengthens our memories.

Despite their intensity, flashbulb memories are not as accurate as you might think (Cubelli & Della Sala, 2008; Talarico & Rubin, 2007). As we learned earlier, when asked how he heard the news of the September 11 attacks, President George W. Bush's answers contained numerous inconsistencies (Greenberg, 2004). Thus, not even flashbulb memories are immune to alteration.

Where Are Memories Located? Tracking Down Memory Traces

So far, our discussion of the biological bases of memory has focused on the formation of memories as a result of neural changes or hormonal influences. But where is memory stored? What parts of the brain are involved?

Early memory researchers believed that memory was *localized*, and stored in a particular brain area. Later research suggests that, in fact, memory tends to not be localized in a single area but in many separate areas throughout the brain.

Today, research techniques are so advanced that we can experimentally induce and measure memory-related brain changes as they occur—on-the-spot reporting! For example, James Brewer and his colleagues (1998) used functional magnetic resonance imaging (fMRI) to locate areas of the brain responsible for encoding memories of pictures. They showed 96 pictures of indoor and outdoor scenes to participants while scanning their brains, and then later tested them on their ability to recall those pictures. Brewer and his colleagues identified the *right prefrontal cortex* and the *parahippocampal cortex* as the most active regions of the brain during the encoding of the pictures. As you can see in Concept Diagram 7.1, these are only two of several brain regions involved in memory storage.

Biological Causes of Memory Loss: Injury and Disease

Imagine a total loss of memory. With no memories of the past and no way to make new memories, there would be no way to use our previous skills or to learn new ones. We wouldn't know each other, nor would we know ourselves. In fact, our very survival would be in question.

Some memory problems are the result of injury and disease (organic pathology). When people are in serious accidents, suffer strokes, or encounter other events that cause trauma to the brain, memory loss or deterioration can occur. Disease also can alter the physiology of the brain and nervous system and thereby affect memory processes. This section focuses on two of the most common causes of biological memory failure: *brain injury* and *Alzheimer's disease*.

Achievement

Objective 7.11: *What are the major biological causes of memory loss?*

The Injured Brain

The leading cause of neurological disorders—including memory loss—among Americans between the ages of 15 and 25 is traumatic brain injury (TBI). These injuries most commonly result from car accidents, falls, blows, and gunshot wounds.

As we discussed in Chapter 2, *traumatic brain injury* (*TBI*) occurs when the skull has a sudden collision with another object. The compression, twisting, and distortion of the brain inside the skull all cause serious and sometimes permanent damage to the brain. The frontal and temporal lobes often take the heaviest hit because they directly impact against the bony ridges inside the skull.

Concept Diagram 7.1
Brain and Memory Formation

Damage to any one of these areas can affect *encoding*, *storage*, and *retrieval* of memories.

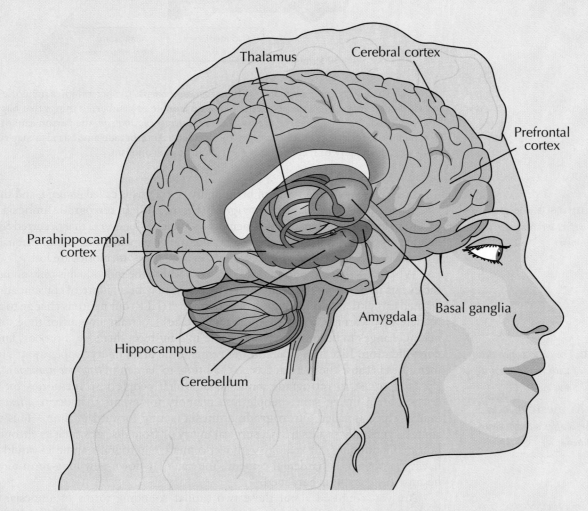

Amygdala	Emotional memory (Gerber, 2008; Hamilton & Gotlib, 2008; van Stegeren, 2008).
Basal Ganglia and Cerebellum	Creation and storage of the basic memory trace, encoding, and implicit (nondeclarative) memories (such as skills, habits, and simple classical conditioning responses) (Chiricozzi et al., 2008; Gluck, 2008; Thompson, 2005)
Cerebral Cortex	Encoding of explicit (declarative) memories; storage of episodic and semantic memories; skill learning; priming, working memory (Davidson et al., 2008; Dougal et al., 2007; Thompson, 2005)
Hippocampal Formation (hippocampus and surrounding area)	Memory recognition; implicit, explicit, spatial, episodic memory; declarative long-term memory; sequences of events (Hamilton & Gotlib, 2008; Yoo et al., 2007).
Thalamus	Formation of new memories, recognition, semantic, spatial, and working memory (Hart & Kraut, 2007; Hofer et al., 2008; Ponzi, 2008).

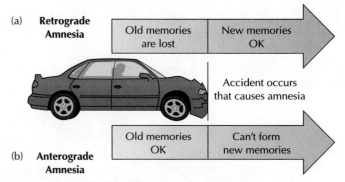

Figure 7.15 *Two types of amnesia* (a) In *retrograde amnesia*, the person loses memories of events that occurred *before* the accident yet has no trouble remembering things that happened afterward (old, "retro" memories are lost). (b) In *anterograde amnesia*, the person cannot form new memories for events that occur *after* the accident. Anterograde amnesia also may result from a surgical injury or from diseases such as chronic alcoholism.

Retrograde Amnesia *Loss of memory for events before a brain injury; backward-acting amnesia*

Consolidation *Process by which neural changes associated with recent learning become durable and stable*

Anterograde Amnesia *Inability to form new memories after a brain injury; forward-acting amnesia*

Loss of memory as a result of brain injury or trauma is called *amnesia*, and there are two major types—*retrograde* and *anterograde* (Figure 7.15). In **retrograde amnesia** (acting backward in time), the person loses memory (is amnesic) for events that occurred *before* the brain injury. However, the same person has no trouble remembering things that happened after the injury. As the name implies, only the old, "retro" memories are lost.

What causes retrograde amnesia? In cases where the individual is only amnesic for the events right before the brain injury, the cause may be a failure of consolidation. We learned earlier that during long-term potentiation (LTP) our neurons change to accommodate new learning. We also know that it takes a certain amount of time for these neural changes to become fixed and stable in long-term memory, a process known as **consolidation**. Like heavy rain on wet cement, the brain injury "wipes away" unstable memories because the cement has not had time to harden (*retrograde amnesia*).

In contrast to retrograde amnesia, in which people lose memories for events *before* a brain injury, some people lose memory for events that occur *after* a brain injury, which is called **anterograde amnesia** (acting forward in time). This type of amnesia generally results from a surgical injury or from diseases such as chronic alcoholism. Continuing our analogy with wet cement, anterograde amnesia would be like having permanently hardened cement. You can't lay down new long-term memories because the cement is hardened.

Are you confused about these two similar sounding forms of amnesia? Think back to the story of H.M. (the man introduced at the start of this chapter). H.M. suffers from both forms of amnesia. He has a mild memory loss for events in his life that happened the year or two *before* the operation (*retrograde amnesia*). Because his surgery destroyed the mechanism that transfers information from short-term memory to long-term memory, he also cannot form new lasting memories for events after the operation (*anterograde amnesia*) (Bohbot & Corkin, 2007; Corkin, 2002). In most cases, retrograde amnesia is temporary and patients generally recover slowly over time. Unfortunately, anterograde amnesia is usually permanent. But patients also show surprising abilities to learn and remember implicit/nondeclarative tasks (such as procedural motor skills).

Alzheimer's Disease

Alzheimer's [ALTS-high-merz] Disease (AD) *Progressive mental deterioration characterized by severe memory loss*

Like traumatic brain injuries, disease can alter the physiology of the brain and nervous system, affecting memory processes. For example, **Alzheimer's disease (AD)** is a progressive mental deterioration that occurs most commonly in later life (Figure 7.16). The most noticeable early symptoms are disturbances in memory, beginning with typical incidents of forgetfulness that everyone experiences from time to time. With

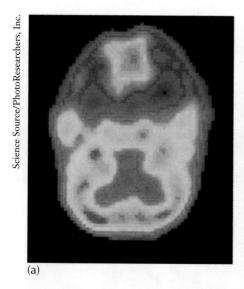
(a)

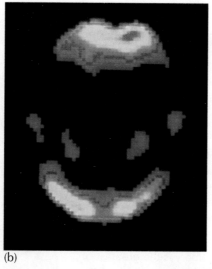
(b)

Figure 7.16 *The effect of Alzheimer's disease on the brain* Note the large amount of red and yellow color (signs of brain activity) in the positron emission tomography scans of the normal brain (a) and the reduced activity in the brain of the Alzheimer's disease patient (b) The loss is most significant in the temporal and parietal lobes, which indicates that these areas are particularly important for storing memories.

Alzheimer's, however, the forgetfulness progresses. In the final stages, the person fails to recognize loved ones, needs total nursing care, and ultimately dies.

AD does not attack all types of memory equally. A hallmark of the disease is the extreme decrease in *explicit declarative memory* (Haley, 2005; Libon et al., 2007; Satler et al., 2008). AD patients fail to recall facts, information, and personal life experiences. However, they still retain some *implicit/nondeclarative memories*, such as simple classically conditioned responses and procedural tasks, like brushing their teeth.

What causes this disease? Autopsies of the brains of people with Alzheimer's disease (AD) show unusual *tangles* (structures formed from degenerating cell bodies) and *plaques* (structures formed from degenerating axons and dendrites). Hereditary AD generally strikes its victims between the ages of 45 and 55. Some experts believe the cause of Alzheimer's is primarily genetic. But others think genetic makeup may make some people more susceptible to environmental triggers (Diamond & Amso, 2008; Ertekin-Taner, 2007; Persson et al., 2008; Vickers et al., 2000; Weiner, 2008).

Assessment

STOP

CHECK & REVIEW

Biological Bases of Memory

Objective 7.10: *How do we form memories, and where do we store them?*

Memories are formed in at least two ways: (1) through changes in neurons, called *long-term potentiation*, or (2) through elevated hormone levels. Memory storage tends to be both localized and distributed throughout the brain.

Objective 7.11: *What are the major biological causes of memory loss?*

Some memory problems are the result of injury and disease (organic pathology). Problems that result from serious brain injuries or trauma are called *amnesia*. In **retrograde amnesia**, memory for events that occurred before an accident is lost. In **anterograde amnesia**, memory for events that occur after an accident is lost.

Alzheimer's disease is a progressive mental deterioration and severe memory loss occurring most commonly in later life.

Questions

1. Describe the two processes involved in LTP.
2. Your vivid memory of what you were doing when you learned about the attack on the World Trade Center is an example of _____. (a) the encoding specificity principle; (b) long-term potentiation; (c) latent learning; (d) a flashbulb memory
3. Forgetting that results from brain damage or trauma is called _____.
4. Ralph couldn't remember anything that happened to him before he fell through the floor of his tree house. His lack of memory for events before his fall is called _____ amnesia. (a) retro-active; (b) proactive; (c) anterograde; (d) retrograde
5. Label the two types of amnesia on the figure below:

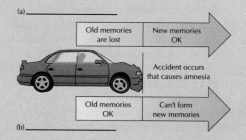
(a) _____
Old memories are lost | New memories OK
Accident occurs that causes amnesia
Old memories OK | Can't form new memories
(b) _____

Check your answers in Appendix B.

Click & Review for additional assessment options: wiley.com/college/huffman

Memory and the Criminal Justice System

When our memory errors involve the criminal justice system, they may lead to wrongful judgments of guilt or innocence and even life-or-death decisions. Let's explore two of the most well-known problems—*eyewitness testimony* and *repressed memories*.

Objective 7.12: *What's wrong with eyewitness testimony?*

Eyewitness Testimony

Misremembering the name of your new friend or forgetting where you left your car keys may be relatively harmless memory problems. But what if police mistakenly arrest and convict an innocent man because of your erroneous eyewitness testimony (Figure 7.17)?

In the past, one of the best forms of trial evidence a lawyer could have was an eyewitness. "I was there. I saw it with my own eyes." Unfortunately for lawyers, numerous research studies have identified several problems with eyewitness testimony (Loftus, 2000, 2001, 2007; Ran, 2007; Rubinstein, 2008; Sharps et al., 2007; Yarmey, 2004).

In one classic study, participants watched a film of a car driving through the countryside. Later, those who were asked to estimate how fast the car was going when it passed the barn (actually nonexistent) were six times as likely to report that they had seen a barn in the film than participants who hadn't been asked about a barn (Loftus, 1982).

Seeing nonexistent barns and other related problems are so well established and important that judges now allow expert testimony on the unreliability of eyewitness testimony. They also routinely instruct jurors on its limits (Benton et al., 2007; Rubinstein, 2008). If you serve as a member of a jury or listen to accounts of crimes in the news, remind yourself of these problems. Also, keep in mind that research participants in eyewitness studies generally report their inaccurate memories with great self-assurance and strong conviction. Eyewitnesses to actual crimes may similarly identify—with equally high confidence—an innocent person as the perpetrator (Figure 7.18).

Objective 7.13: *What do psychologists believe about repressed memories?*

False Versus Repressed Memories

> Nothing fixes a thing so intensely in the memory as the wish to forget it.
>
> MICHEL DE MONTAIGNE
> (1533–1592)

> Memory is the greatest of artists, and effaces from your mind what is unnecessary.
>
> MAURICE BARING
> (1874–1945)

Which is true? Is it impossible to forget painful memories? Or can we erase what is unnecessary? The topic of false versus repressed memories is one of the hottest debates in memory research. Do you recall the opening story of Elizabeth, who suddenly remembered finding her mother's drowned body decades after it had happened? Elizabeth's recovery of these gruesome childhood memories, though painful, initially brought great relief. "I started putting everything into place. Maybe that's why I'm such a workaholic." It also seemed to explain why she had always been fascinated by the topic of memory and had spent so many years on its research.

After all this relief and resolution, however, her brother called to say there had

Bettman/Corbis Images

Figure 7.17 *Dangers of eyewitness testimony* Seven eyewitnesses identified the man in the far left photo (Father Pagano) as the "Gentleman Bandit" accused of several armed robberies. However, the man in the right photo (Robert Clouser) later confessed and was convicted of the crimes.

been a mistake! The relative who told Elizabeth that she had been the one to discover her mother's body later remembered—and other relatives confirmed—that it had actually been Aunt Pearl, not Elizabeth Loftus. Like the eyewitnesses who erroneously recalled seeing a nonexistent barn, Loftus, an expert on memory distortions, had unknowingly created her own *false memory*.

As we've seen throughout this chapter, our memories are frequently faulty, and researchers have demonstrated that it is relatively easy to create false memories (Allan & Gabbert, 2008; Howes, 2007; Loftus & Cahill, 2007; Pérez-Mata & Diges, 2007).

So what about repressed memories? Can people recover true childhood memories? Repression, which was mentioned earlier as a potential factor in motivated forgetting, is the supposed unconscious coping mechanism by which we prevent anxiety-provoking thoughts from reaching consciousness (see Chapter 13).

This is a complex and controversial topic in psychology. No one doubts that some memories are forgotten and later recovered. What is questioned is the concept of repressed memories of painful experiences (especially childhood sexual abuse) and their storage in the unconscious mind (Goodman et al., 2003; Kihlstrom, 2004; Loftus, 2007; Loftus & Cahill, 2007).

Photo by Jean Greenwald. Courtesy Elizabeth Loftus

Elizabeth Loftus

Tom Hussey/Getty Images

Figure 7.18 *How often are eyewitnesses mistaken?* In one experiment, participants watched people committing a staged crime. Only an hour later, 20 percent of the eyewitnesses identified innocent people from mug shots, and a week later, 8 percent identified innocent people in a lineup (Brown, Deffenbacher, & Sturgill, 1977). What memory processes might have contributed to the eyewitnesses' errors?

Critics suggest that most people who have witnessed or experienced a violent crime, or are adult survivors of childhood sexual abuse, have intense, persistent memories. They have trouble forgetting, not remembering. Some critics also wonder whether therapists sometimes inadvertently create false memories in their clients during therapy. Some worry that if a clinician even suggests the possibility of abuse, the client's own constructive processes may lead him or her to create a false memory. The client might start to incorporate portrayals of abuse from movies and books into his or her own memory, forgetting their original sources and eventually coming to see them as reliable.

This is not to say that all psychotherapy clients who recover memories of sexual abuse (or other painful incidents) have invented those memories. Indeed, the repressed memory debate has grown increasingly bitter, and research on both sides is hotly contested. The stakes are high because some lawsuits and criminal prosecutions of sexual abuse are sometimes based on recovered memories of childhood sexual abuse. As researchers continue exploring the mechanisms underlying delayed remembering, we must be careful not to ridicule or condemn people who recover true memories of abuse. In the same spirit, we must protect the innocent from wrongful accusations that come from false memories. We look forward to a time when we can justly balance the interests of the victim with those of the accused.

(For more information about this continuing controversy, call or write the American Psychological Association in Washington, D.C. Ask for the pamphlet "Questions and Answers about Memories of Childhood Abuse." Also check the *Psychology in Action website*.)

Assessment **STOP**

CHECK & REVIEW

Memory and the Criminal Justice System

Objective 7.12: *What's wrong with eyewitness testimony?*

Memories are not exact duplicates. We actively shape and *construct* information as it is encoded, stored, and retrieved. Eyewitness accounts are highly persuasive in the courtroom. But they're filled with potential errors.

Objective 7.13: *What do psychologists believe about repressed memories?*

Psychologists continue to debate whether recovered memories are accurate recollections or false memories. Concern about the reliability of recovered memories has led many experts to encourage a cautious approach.

Questions

1. According to research, eyewitnesses generally report _____ confidence in the accuracy of their inaccurate memories.
(a) very little; (b) little; (c) moderate; (d) high
2. _____ memories are related to anxiety-provoking thoughts or events that are supposedly prevented from reaching consciousness.
(a) Suppressed; (b) Flashback; (c) Motivated; (d) Repressed

3. Researchers have found that it is relatively _____ to create false memories.
4. Explain the difference between false memories and repressed memories.

Check your answers in Appendix B.

 Click & Review
for additional assessment options:
wiley.com/college/huffman

Using Psychology to Improve Our Memory

One of my first memories would date, if it were true, from my second year. I can still see, most clearly, the following scene, in which I believed until I was about fifteen. I was sitting in my pram, which my nurse was pushing in the Champs-Élysées, when a man tried to kidnap me. I was held in by the strap fastened round me while my nurse bravely tried to stand between the thief and me. She received various scratches, and I can still vaguely see the scratches on her face. Then a crowd gathered, a policeman with a short cloak and a white baton came up, and the man took to his heels. I can still see the whole scene, and can even place it near the tube station. When I was about fifteen, my parents received a letter from my former nurse saying that she had been converted to the Salvation Army. She wanted to confess her past faults, and in particular to return the watch she had been given as a reward on this occasion. She had made up the whole story, faking the scratches. I, therefore, must have heard, as a child, the account of this story, which my parents believed, and projected it into the past in the form of a visual memory, which was a memory of a memory, but false. (Piaget, 1962, pp. 187–188)

This is the self-reported childhood memory of Jean Piaget, a brilliant and world-famous cognitive and developmental psychologist (Chapter 9). Why did Piaget create such a strange and elaborate memory for something that never happened?

Achievement

Objective 7.14: *Why do we distort our memories?*

■ Understanding Memory Distortions: Logic, Consistency, and Efficiency

There are several reasons why we shape, rearrange, and distort our memories. One of the most common is our need for *logic* and *consistency*. When we're initially forming new memories or sorting through old ones, we fill in missing pieces, make "corrections," and rearrange information to make it logical and consistent with our previous experiences. If Piaget's beloved nurse said someone attempted to kidnap him, it was only logical for the boy to "remember" the event.

We also shape and construct our memories for the sake of efficiency. Think about a recent, important lecture from your psychology instructor that you (hopefully)

Try This Yourself **A**pplication

A Memory Test

Carefully read through all the words in the following list.

Bed	Awake	Tired	Dream	Wake	Snooze	Snore
Rest	Blanket	Doze	Slumber	Nap	Peace	Yawn
Drowsy	Nurse	Sick	Lawyer	Medicine	Health	Hospital
Dentist	Physician	Patient	Stethoscope	Curse	Clinic	Surgeon

Now cover the list and write down all the words you remember.

Number of correctly recalled words:

21 to 28 words = excellent memory
16 to 20 words = better than most
12 to 15 words = average

8 to 11 words = below average
7 or fewer = you might need a nap

How did you do? Do you have a good or excellent memory? Did you recall seeing the words *sleep* and *doctor*? Look back over the list. These words are not there. However, over 65 percent of students commonly report seeing these words. Why? As mentioned in the introduction to this chapter, memory is not a faithful recording or duplicate of an event. It is a *constructive process*. We actively shape and build on information as it is *encoded* and *retrieved*.

encoded for storage in LTM. You obviously did not record a word-for-word copy of the lecture. You summarized, augmented, and tied it in with related memories you have in LTM. Similarly, when you need to retrieve the stored lecture from your LTM, you recover only the general ideas or facts that were said.

Despite all their problems and biases, our memories are normally quite efficient and serve us well in most situations. Our memories have evolved to encode, store, and retrieve information vital to our survival. Even while sleeping, we process and store important memories. However, when faced with tasks like remembering precise details in a college text, the faces and names of potential clients, or where we left our house keys, our brains are simply not as well equipped.

Tips for Memory Improvement: Eight Surefire Ways to Improve Your Memory

The beauty of the human brain is that we can recognize the limits and problems of memory and then develop appropriate coping mechanisms. Our ancestors domesticated wild horses and cattle to overcome the physical limits of the human body. We can develop similar approaches to improve our memory for fine detail.

The field of psychology provides numerous helpful theories and concepts for improving memory. And everyone can improve his or her memory. The harder you work at it, the better your memory will become. In this section, I have summarized key points from the chapter that you can put into practice to improve your memory. (You'll also recognize several points that were presented earlier in the "Tools for Student Success" in Chapter 1.)

- *Pay attention and reduce interference.* If you really want to remember something, you must pay attention to it. When you're in class, focus on the instructor and sit away from people who might distract you. When you study, choose a place with minimal interferences.

- *Use rehearsal techniques.* Remember that the duration of STM is about 30 seconds. To lengthen this time, use *maintenance rehearsal*. To effectively encode memory into LTM, use *elaborative* rehearsal, which involves thinking about the material and relating it to other information that has already been stored. Hopefully, you've noticed that I formally define each key term immediately in the text, in the margin, and in the glossary at the back of the book. I also give a brief explanation and one or two examples for each of these terms. While studying this text, use these tools to help your elaborative rehearsal. Also try making up your own examples. The more elaborate the encoding of information, the more memorable it will be.

- *Use the encoding specificity principle.* When we form memories, we store them with links to the way we thought about them at the time. Therefore, the closer the retrieval cues are to the original encoding situation, the better the retrieval. Because you encode a lot of material during class time, avoid "early takes" or makeup exams, which are generally scheduled in other classrooms. The *context* will be different and your retrieval may suffer. Similarly, when you take a test, try to remain calm and reinstate the same psychological and physiological state that you were in when you originally learned the material. According to the *mood congruence* effect, you will recall more if the mood of your test taking matches the mood of the original learning. Also, according to the *state-dependent memory* research, if you normally drink a cup of coffee while studying, you might want to have a cup of coffee before your exam.

- *Improve your organization.* This may be the most important key to a good memory. Although the capacity of STM is only around five to nine items, you can expand the capacity of STM by *chunking* (organizing) information into a few groups. To improve your LTM, create *hierarchies* that organize the material in

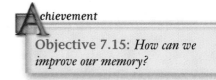

Achievement

Objective 7.15: *How can we improve our memory?*

©Callahan, Distributed by Levin Represents

"I wonder if you'd mind giving me directions. I've never been sober in this part of town before."

Can you see how this is an example of the encoding specificity principle?

meaningful patterns. The tables in this book and the "Visual Summaries" at the end of each chapter are examples of hierarchies that help you organize chapter material. Be sure to study them carefully—and make up your own whenever possible.

- **Counteract the serial-position effect**. Because we tend to remember information that occurs at the beginning or end of a sequence, spend extra time with the information in the middle. When reading or reviewing the text, start at different places—sometimes at the second section, sometimes at the fourth.

- **Manage your time**. Study on a regular basis and avoid cramming. *Distributed* (spaced) learning sessions are more efficient than *massed* practice (cramming). In other words, five separate half-hour sessions tend to produce better encoding and storage than one session of 2½ hours. When you learn something new, take the time to associate it with what you already know. By doing this, you'll be organizing the new information so that you can easily retrieve it later on. Also, get plenty of sleep, for two reasons: (1) We don't remember information acquired when we're drowsy as well as that gained when we're alert, and (2) during REM sleep we process and store most of the new information we acquired when awake.

- **Employ self-monitoring and overlearning**. When studying a text, you should periodically stop and test your understanding of the material. This is why I included numerous "Check & Review" sections throughout each chapter. Stopping to read these reviews and completing the short quiz section will provide personal feedback on your mastery of the material. Even when you are studying a single sentence, you need to monitor your understanding. Poor readers tend to read at the same speed for both easy and difficult material. Good readers tend to recognize when they are having difficulty. They slow down or repeat difficult sentences.

  When you finish reading a chapter, wait a few minutes and then do an additional monitoring of your understanding. If you evaluate your learning only while you're actively reading the material, you may overestimate your understanding (because the information is still in STM). However, if you delay making your judgment (for at least a few minutes), your evaluation will be more accurate. The best way to ensure your full understanding of material (and success on an exam) is through *overlearning*—studying information even after you think you already know it. Don't just study until you *think* you know it. Work hard until you *know* you know it!

- **Use mnemonics**. **Mnemonic devices** (derived from the Greek word for "memory") are memory aids (or tricks) based on encoding items in a special way (Concept Diagram 7.2).

Mnemonic [nih-MON-ik] Device *Memory-improvement technique based on encoding items in a special way*

"YOU SIMPLY ASSOCIATE EACH NUMBER WITH A WORD, SUCH AS 'TABLE' AND 3,467,009."

Memory problems *Unfortunately, some memories persevere even when they cause tremendous pain and suffering.*

A Final Word

As we have seen throughout this chapter, our memories are remarkable—yet highly fickle. Recognizing these limits will make us better jurors in the courtroom. It will also make us better consumers of daily news reports when we assess accounts of "eyewitness testimony" and "repressed memories." Knowing the frailties of memory might similarly improve our skills as students, teachers, and friends.

Unfortunately, sometimes our memories are better than we would like. Traumatic and extremely emotional memories can persist even when we would very much like to forget. Though painful, these memories can sometimes provide important insights. As Elizabeth Loftus suggests in a recent letter to her deceased mother:

I thought then [as a 14-year-old] that eventually I would get over your death. I know today that I won't. But I've decided to accept that truth. What does it matter if

Concept Diagram 7.2
Mnemonic Devices

As you review the key points from this chapter, think about how you might exploit basic principles of memory, using them to your own advantage. One additional "trick" for giving your memory a boost is to use *mnemonic devices* to encode items in a special way. (But be warned—you may get more "bang for your buck" using the well-researched principles discussed throughout this chapter.)

Three popular mnemonic techniques are the following.

(a) **Method of loci** Greek and Roman orators developed the *method of loci* to keep track of the many parts of their long speeches. Orators would imagine the parts of their speeches attached to places in a courtyard. For example, if an opening point in a speech was the concept of *justice*, they might visualize a courtroom placed in the first corner of their garden. As they mentally walked around their garden during their speech, they would encounter, in order, each of the points to be made.

(a) Method of loci

Grocery list

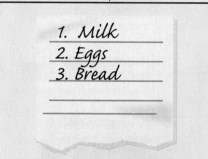

One is a bun

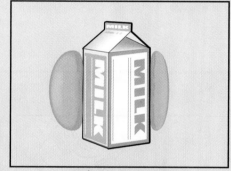

Two is a shoe

Three is a tree

(b) **Peg words** To use the *peg-word* mnemonic, you first need to memorize a set of 10 images that you can use as "pegs" on which to hang ideas. For example, if you learn 10 items that rhyme with the numbers they stand for, you can then use the images as pegs to hold the items of any list. Try it with items you might want to buy on your next trip to the grocery store: milk, eggs, and bread.

(c) **Acronyms** To use the acronym method, create a new code word from the first letters of the items you want to remember. For example, to recall the names of the Great Lakes, think of *HOMES* on a great lake (*Huron, Ontario, Michigan, Erie, Superior*). Visualizing homes on each lake also helps you remember your code word "homes."

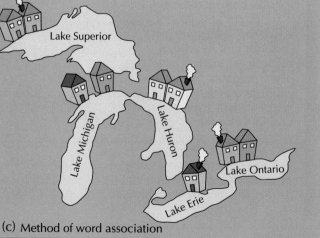

(c) Method of word association

I don't get over you? Who says I have to? David and Robert still tease me: "Don't say the M word or Beth will cry." So what if the word *mother* affects me this way? Who says I have to fix this? Besides, I'm too busy (Loftus, 2002, p. 70).

Application

CRITICAL THINKING · ACTIVE LEARNING

Memory and Metacognition

Metacognition is the ability to review and analyze your own mental processes—to "think about your thinking." It is also a vital part of critical thinking because it helps you objectively examine your thoughts and cognitive strategies and then to evaluate their appropriateness and accuracy. In the context of this chapter, you can use metacognition to examine and successfully employ the memory improvement tips we have just discussed.

Start by placing a "+" mark by those skills and strategies that you are currently using and a "−" by those that you avoid or that cause you problems. Now carefully review those items you've identified with a "−" mark. Why are you avoiding or not employing these particular skills? Are your reasons rational? Can you think of areas of your life where these skills might be useful? If so, go back and place a mark by those items you want to develop. Use these checkmarks as the starting point for your personal memory improvement plan.

_____ Pay attention and reduce interference.

_____ Use rehearsal techniques.

_____ Improve your organization.

_____ Counteract the serial position effect.

_____ Manage your time.

_____ Use the encoding specificity principle.

_____ Employ self-monitoring and overlearning.

_____ Use mnemonic devices.

Assessment

CHECK & REVIEW STOP

Using Psychology to Improve Our Memory

Objective 7.14: *Why do we distort our memories?*

Memory distortions tend to arise from the human need for logic and consistency, as well as because it's sometimes more efficient to do so.

Objective 7.15: *How can we improve our memory?*

This section offers eight concrete strategies for improving memory. These strategies include paying attention and reducing interference, using rehearsal techniques (both maintenance and elaborative rehearsal), improving your organization (by chunking and creating hierarchies), counteracting the serial position effect, managing your time, using the encoding specificity principle, employing self-monitoring and overlearning, and **mnemonic devices**.

Peg words

Questions

1. How can maintenance rehearsal and elaborative rehearsal improve your memory?

2. Explain how you can overcome the serial position effect while studying.

3. The best way to ensure your full understanding of material (and success on an exam) is through_____.

4. Which mnemonic device is being described in each of the following situations?

   a. You remember items to bring to a meeting by visualizing them in association with a previously learned sequence.

   b. You remember a speech for your communications class by forming visual images of the parts of your speech and associating them with areas in the classroom.

   c. You remember errands you need to run by making up the rhyme "First go to the store, then get books galore. Get my ring and then some gas, and the cleaners at the last."

   d. You remember the five key theories of forgetting by creating a new word "DIMER" and then visualize forgetting as your memory getting "dimmer."

Check your answers in Appendix B.

Click & Review
for additional assessment options:
wiley.com/college/huffman

Assessment
KEY TERMS

*To assess your understanding of the **Key Terms** in Chapter 7, write a definition for each (in your own words), and then compare your definitions with those in the text.*

The Nature of Memory
chunking (p. 248)
constructive process (p. 244)
elaborative rehearsal (p. 252)
encoding (p. 244)
encoding specificity principle (p. 255)
episodic memory (p. 251)
explicit (declarative) memory (p. 251)
implicit (nondeclarative) memory
    (p. 252)
levels of processing (p. 252)
long-term memory (LTM) (p. 249)
maintenance rehearsal (p. 248)
memory (p. 244)
parallel distributed processing
    (PDP) (p. 246)
priming (p. 255)

recall (p. 254)
recognition (p. 254)
retrieval (p. 244)
retrieval cue (p. 254)
serial-position effect (p. 254)
semantic memory (p. 251)
sensory memory (p. 247)
short-term memory (STM) (p. 248)
storage (p. 244)

Forgetting
distributed practice (p. 260)
massed practice (p. 260)
misinformation effect (p. 260)
proactive interference (p. 259)
relearning (p. 257)
retroactive interference (p. 259)

sleeper effect (p. 260)
source amnesia (p. 260)
tip-of-the-tongue (TOT) phenomenon
    (p. 259)

Biological Bases of Memory
Alzheimer's [ALTS-high-merz] disease
    (AD) (p. 266)
anterograde amnesia (p. 266)
consolidation (p. 266)
long-term potentiation (LTP) (p. 263)
retrograde amnesia (p. 266)

**Using Psychology to Improve Our
Memory**
mnemonic [nih-MON-ik] device
    (p. 272)

Achievement
WEB RESOURCES

Huffman Book Companion Site
wiley.com/college/huffman
    This site is loaded with free Interactive Self-Tests, Internet
    Exercises, Glossary and Flashcards for key terms, web links,
    Handbook for Non-Native Speakers, and other activities de-
    signed to improve your mastery of the material in this chapter.

The Nature of Memory

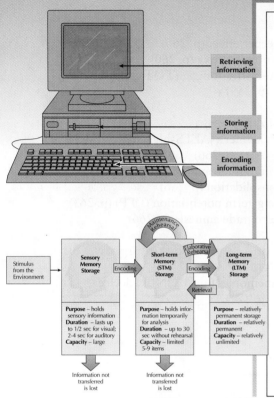

Retrieving information

Storing information

Encoding information

Memory Models

- **Information Processing:** Memory is a *process* (**encoding**, **storage**, and **retrieval**) analogous to a computer.

- **Parallel Distributed Processing:** Memory is distributed across a network of neurons working simultaneously (in a *parallel* fashion).

- **Traditional Three-Stage Memory:** Memory requires three different storage boxes or stages to hold and process information. **Sensory memory** holds information for exceedingly short intervals, **short-term memory (STM)** retains information for approximately 30 seconds or less (unless renewed), and **long-term memory (LTM)** provides relatively permanent storage.

LTM is divided and subdivided into various types of memory

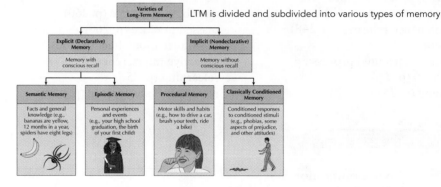

Maintenance Rehearsal

Elaborative Rehearsal

| Stimulus from the Environment | Sensory Memory Storage | Encoding | Short-term Memory (STM) Storage | Encoding | Long-term Memory (LTM) Storage |

Retrieval

Purpose – holds sensory information
Duration – lasts up to 1/2 sec for visual; 2-4 sec for auditory
Capacity – large

Purpose – holds information temporarily for analysis
Duration – up to 30 sec without rehearsal
Capacity – limited 5-9 items

Purpose – relatively permanent storage
Duration – relatively permanent
Capacity – relatively unlimited

Information not transferred is lost

Information not transferred is lost

Varieties of Long-Term Memory

Explicit (Declarative) Memory — Memory with conscious recall

Implicit (Nondeclarative) Memory — Memory without conscious recall

Semantic Memory — Facts and general knowledge (e.g., bananas are yellow, 12 months in a year, spiders have eight legs)

Episodic Memory — Personal experiences and events (e.g., your high school graduation, the birth of your first child)

Procedural Memory — Motor skills and habits (e.g., how to drive a car, brush your teeth, ride a bike)

Classically Conditioned Memory — Conditioned responses to conditioned stimuli (e.g., phobias, some aspects of prejudice, and other attitudes)

Forgetting

Why Do We Forget?

- *Decay* — Memory deteriorates over time.

- *Interference* — Memory forgotten due to **proactive interference** (old information interferes with new) or **retroactive interference** (new information interferes with old).

- *Motivated Forgetting* — Painful, threatening, or embarassing memories are forgotten.

- *Encoding Failure* — Material from STM to LTM was never successfully encoded.

- *Retrieval Failure* — Information is not forgotten, just temporarily inaccessible.

Photo by Jean Greenwald, Courtesy Elizabeth Loftus

Problems with Forgetting

- **Misinformation effect:** Distorting memory with misleading post-event information

- **Source amnesia:** Forgetting the true source of a memory

- **Sleeper effect:** Delayed effectiveness of a message from an unreliable source

- *Information overload*: **Distributed practice** is better than **massed practice**

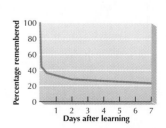

Biological Bases of Memory

Formation and Location of Memory

The biological perspective of memory focuses on changes in neurons (through **long-term potentiation**) and hormones, as well as on searching for the location of memory in the brain. Memory tends to be localized and distributed throughout the brain—not just in the cortex.

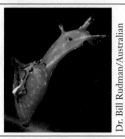

Dr. Bill Rudman/Australian Museum

Biology and Memory Loss

- *Brain* injuries or trauma: **Retrograde amnesia**, memory is lost for events that occured before the accident. **Anterograde amnesia** memory is lost for events that occur after an accident.

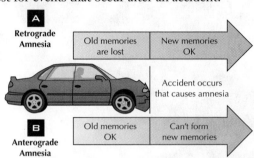

A Retrograde Amnesia

| Old memories are lost | New memories OK |

Accident occurs that causes amnesia

B Anterograde Amnesia

| Old memories OK | Can't form new memories |

- *Disease*: **Alzheimer's disease (AD)** is a progressive mental deterioration and severe memory loss occurring most commonly in old age.

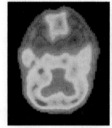 

Science Source/Photo Researchers, Inc

Using Psychology to Improve Our Memory

Specific Tips

- Pay attention and reduce interference.
- Use rehearsal techniques (maintenance for STM and elaborative for LTM).
- Use the encoding specificity principle (including context, mood congruence, and state-dependent retrieval).
- Improve organization (chunking for STM and hierarchies for LTM).
- Counteract the serial position effect.
- Use time management (distributed versus massed practice).
- Employ self-monitoring and overlearning.
- Use **mnemonic devices** (method of loci, peg-word, and acronyms).

One is bun

1. Milk
2. Eggs
3. Bread

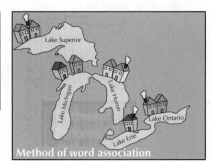

Lake Superior

Lake Michigan   Lake Huron

Lake Ontario

Lake Erie

Method of word association

8

Thinking, Language, and Intelligence

Have you heard about Koko, the gorilla who reportedly uses more than 1,000 words in American Sign Language (ASL)? According to her teacher, Penny Patterson, Koko has used ASL to converse with others, talk to herself, rhyme, joke, and even lie (Linden, 1993; Patterson, 2002). Koko also uses signs to communicate her personal preferences, including a strong attraction to cats. Do you think Koko is using true language? Do you consider Koko intelligent?

What about the famous case of the "wild child" Genie? From the age of 20 months until authorities rescued her at the age of 13, Genie lived in a tiny, windowless room in solitary confinement. By day, she sat naked and tied to a chair with nothing to do and no one to talk to. At night, she was put in a kind of straitjacket and caged in a covered crib. Genie's abusive father forbade anyone to speak to her for the entire time, and if Genie made any noise, her father would beat her, while he barked and growled like a dog. After she was discovered at age 13, linguists and psychologists worked with her intensively for many years. Sadly, Genie never progressed much beyond sentences like "Genie go" (Curtiss, 1977; LaPointe, 2005; Rymer, 1993). With her limited language skills, would you say Genie is intelligent?

What about Thomas Edison, the famous inventor of the lightbulb? Despite having attended school for only three months and suffering progressive deafness throughout his life, Edison patented over 1000 inventions—more than any other single individual in history. Yet some have labeled him a "technologist rather than a scientist, adding little to original scientific knowledge" (Baldwin, 2001). Would you consider Thomas Edison intelligent?

Being the "greatest inventor in American history" obviously requires a large repertoire of thinking processes and intellectual agility. But Genie's survival and Koko's use of sign language also require some form of intelligence. To be intelligent, you must be able to think and to learn. To express this thinking and intelligence, you need language. The three topics of this chapter—"Thinking," "Language," and "Intelligence"—are often studied together under the larger umbrella of **cognition**, *the mental activities of acquiring, storing, retrieving, and using knowledge.* In a real sense, we discuss cognition throughout the text (e.g., chapters on sensation and perception, consciousness, learning, and memory).

Achievement

Objective 8.1: *Define cognition.*

Masterfile

Cognition *Mental activities involved in acquiring, storing, retrieving, and using knowledge*

▶ **Thinking**

Cognitive Building Blocks
Problem Solving

 PSYCHOLOGY AT WORK
Heuristics and Your Career

 PSYCHOLOGY AT WORK
Recognizing Barriers to Problem Solving

CRITICAL THINKING/ACTIVE LEARNING
Solving Problems in College Life

Creativity

▶ **Language**

Characteristics of Language
Language and Thought
Language Development

 GENDER & CULTURAL DIVERSITY
Unspoken Accents

Animals and Language

▶ **Intelligence**

What Is Intelligence?

 PSYCHOLOGY AT WORK
Multiple Intelligences and Your Career

How Do We Measure Intelligence?

▶ **The Intelligence Controversy**

Extremes in Intelligence

RESEARCH HIGHLIGHT
Explaining Differences in IQ

 GENDER & CULTURAL DIVERSITY
Are IQ Tests Culturally Biased?

Application

WHY STUDY PSYCHOLOGY?

Did you know...

▶ Thomas Edison patented over 1000 inventions, yet some believe he added little to scientific knowledge?

▶ Shortly after the 9/11 terrorist attack on the World Trade Center, surveys found many Americans believed they had a 20 percent chance of being hurt in a terrorist attack within the next year?

▶ Children all over the world go through similar stages in language development at about the same age, and their babbling is the same in all languages?

National Archives/Taxi/Getty Images

▶ Chimps and dolphins can use nonvocal language to make simple sentences and communicate with human trainers?

▶ Many cultures have no language equivalent for our notion of intelligence?

▶ Overall IQ scores have increased in the last 20 years in over 20 countries?

Thinking

What is *thinking*? Every time you use information and mentally act on it by forming ideas, reasoning, solving problems, drawing conclusions, expressing thoughts, or comprehending the thoughts of others, you are thinking. We begin this section by exploring the building blocks of thoughts—*images* and *concepts*. Then, we discuss the mental processes involved in *problem solving* and *creativity*.

Achievement

Objective 8.2: *Identify the location of thinking, and describe the roles of mental images and concepts in thinking.*

Study Tip

Are your studies disrupted by images, thoughts, or linguistic statements related to your dating partner, feelings of hunger, or other distractions? Remember the Premack principle from Chapter 6—using any naturally occurring, high-frequency response to reinforce low-frequency response. In this case, don't call your sweetheart or get a snack until you've finished studying a preassigned section of your text.

Cognitive Building Blocks: Foundation of Thought

Like learning and memory, our thought processes are distributed throughout our brains in networks of neurons. However, they're also localized. For example, during problem solving or decision making, our brains are active in the *prefrontal cortex*. This region associates complex ideas; makes plans; forms, initiates, and allocates attention; and supports multitasking. The prefrontal cortex also links to other areas of the brain, such as the *limbic system* (Chapter 2), to synthesize information from several senses (Carlson, 2008; Heyder, Suchan, & Daum, 2004; Sacchetti, Sacco, & Strata, 2007).

Now that we have a general location of thinking, we need to study its three basic components—*mental images, concepts,* and *language*. We'll study the first two in this section, and then explore language in depth later in the chapter.

Mental Images

Imagine yourself lying relaxed in the warm sand on an ocean beach. Do you see tall palms swaying in the wind? Can you smell the salty ocean water and hear the laughter of the children playing in the surf? What you've just created is a

mental image, a <u>mental representation of a previously stored sensory experience</u>, which includes visual, auditory, olfactory, tactile, motor, and gustatory imagery. We all have a mental space where we visualize and manipulate our sensory images (Hamm, Johnson, & Corballis, 2004) (Figure 8.1).

Concepts

In addition to mental images, our thinking involves **concepts**—mental representations of a group or category that share similar characteristics. Our mental concept of *car* represents a large group of objects with similar characteristics (vehicles with four wheels, seating space for at least one person, and a generally predictable shape). We also form concepts for abstract ideas, such as *honesty, intelligence,* or *pornography*. These abstract ideas, however, are often our own individual constructions, which may or may not be shared by others. Therefore, it is generally harder to communicate about honesty than about a car.

Concepts are an essential part of thinking and communication because they simplify and organize information. Imagine being Genie, the "wild child" described at the beginning of the chapter. If you had been confined to a small, windowless room your entire life, how would you think and process the world around you without concepts? Normally, when you see a new object or encounter a new situation, you relate it to your existing conceptual structure and categorize it according to where it fits. If you see a metal box with four wheels driving on the highway, you know it's a car, even if you've never seen that particular model before. But if you were Genie, how would you identify a car, a telephone, or even a bathroom, having never seen them and compared them to other cars, telephones, and rooms?

How do we learn concepts? They develop through the creation and use of three major strategies:

1. ***Artificial concepts***. We create some concepts from logical rules or definitions. Consider the definition of *triangle*: "a geometric figure with three sides and three angles." Using this definition, we group together and classify all three-sided geometric forms as triangles. If any of the defining features were missing, we would not include the object in the *concept* of triangle. Concepts like *triangle* are called *artificial* (or *formal*) because the rules for inclusion are sharply defined. As you have seen in this and other college texts, artificial concepts are often a core part of the sciences and other academic disciplines.

Bill Hatcher/NG Image Collection

Figure 8.1 *Mental imagery* Some of our most creative and inspired moments come when we're forming and manipulating mental images. This mountain climber is probably visualizing her next move, and her ability to do so is critical to her success.

Mental Image *Mental representation of a previously stored sensory experience, including visual, auditory, olfactory, tactile, motor, or gustatory imagery (e.g., visualizing a train and hearing its horn)*

Concept *Mental representation of a group or category that shares similar characteristics (e.g., the concept of a river groups together the Nile, the Amazon, and the Mississippi because they share the common characteristic of being a large stream of water that empties into an ocean or lake)*

Achievement

Objective 8.3: *Explain how we learn concepts.*

Application

Try This Yourself

Manipulating Mental Images

Look at the four geometrical patterns to the right. Can you see why the two forms in (a) are the same but the two forms in (b) are different? Solving this problem requires mental manipulation of the patterns. (Those of you who are familiar with the computer game Tetris might find this puzzle rather simple. Others might want to turn to Appendix B for an explanation of the answer.)

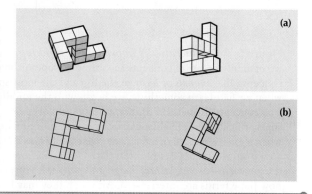

(a)

(b)

(handwritten: lately or never)

Prototype *Representation of the "best" or most typical example of a category (e.g., baseball is a prototype of the concept of sports)*

2. ***Natural concepts/prototypes***. In everyday life, we seldom use artificial definitions. When we see birds, we do not think "warm-blooded animals that fly, have wings, and lay eggs"—an *artificial concept*. Instead, we use *natural concepts*, called **prototypes**, which are based on a personal "best example" or a typical representative of that concept (Rosch, 1973) (Figure 8.2).

3. ***Hierarchies***. Some of our concepts also develop when we create *hierarchies*, and group specific concepts as subcategories within broader concepts. This mental arrangement makes mastering new material faster and easier. Note in the hierarchy depicted in Figure 8.3 how the top (superordinate) category of *animals* is very broad and includes lots of members. The midlevel categories of *bird* and *dog* are more specific but still rather general. And the lowest (subordinate) categories of *parakeet* and *poodle* are the most specific.

Stephen St. John/NG Image Collection

Gordon Wiltsie/NG Image Collection

(a)   (b)

Figure 8.2 ***Some birds are "birdier" than others*** (a) Most people have a *prototype* bird that captures the essence of "birdness" and allows us to quickly classify flying animals correctly. (b) When we encounter an example that doesn't quite fit our prototype, we need time to review our artificial concept. Because the penguin doesn't fly, it's harder to classify than a robin.

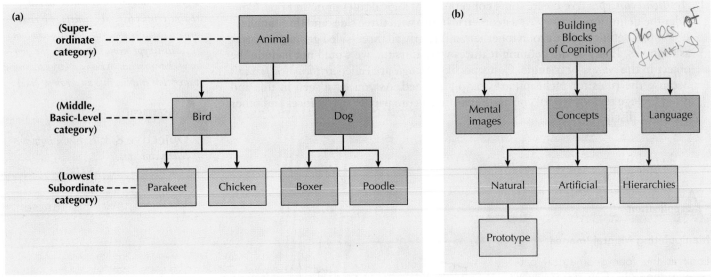

(handwritten: process of thinking)

Figure 8.3 ***Can hierarchies improve your thinking and exam scores?*** (a) When we think, we naturally organize concepts according to superordinate and subordinate classes. We place concepts, like *animals* or *birds*, at the top and the most specific at the bottom. Interestingly, when we first learn something, we begin with the middle categories, which are called *basic-level* concepts (Rosch, 1978). For example, children tend to learn *bird* before they learn higher, superordinate concepts like *animal* or lower, subordinate concepts like *parakeet*. Even as adults, when shown a picture of a parakeet, we classify it as a *bird* first. (b) Hierarchies can be generated from almost any set of interrelated facts. For example, instead of attempting to memorize the key terms *concept*, *mental image*, and *prototype*, you should begin by making a hierarchy of how these terms are interrelated. Although they may look complicated, hierarchies significantly reduce the time and effort necessary for learning. Once you have this "big picture," it speeds up your mastery of the material, which translates into better exam scores.

A*ssessment*

CHECK & REVIEW

Cognitive Building Blocks

Bill Hatcher/NG Image Collection

Objective 8.1: *Define cognition.*

Cognition, or thinking, is defined as mental activities involved in acquiring, storing, retrieving, and using knowledge.

Objective 8.2: *Identify the general location of thinking, and describe the roles of mental images and concepts in thinking.*

Thought processes are distributed throughout the brain in neural networks. However, they are also localized in the *prefrontal* *cortex*, which links to other areas of the brain, such as the *limbic system*. **Mental images** are mental representations of a sensory experience, including visual, auditory, olfactory, tactile, motor, and gustatory imagery. **Concepts** are mental representations of a group or category that that share similar characteristics.

Objective 8.3: *Explain how we learn concepts.*

We develop concepts using three key strategies: (1) *Artificial concepts* are formed by logical, specific rules or characteristics. (2) *Natural concepts* are formed by experience in everyday life. When we are confronted with a new item, we compare it with a **prototype** (most typical example) of a concept. (3) Concepts are generally organized into *hierarchies*. We most frequently use the middle, basic-level category of a hierarchy when first learning material.

Questions

1. Compare and contrast mental images and concepts.
2. All of the following are examples of concepts except _____. (a) trees; (b) tools; (c) blue; (d) umbrellas
3. How do we learn concepts?
4. When asked to describe the shape and color of an apple, you probably rely on a _____.
5. For most psychologists, consciousness is a(n) _____ concept, whereas for the layperson it is a(n) _____ concept. (a) automatic, health; (b) artificial, natural; (c) mental image, natural; (d) superordinate, basic-level

Check your answers in Appendix B.

Click & Review
for additional assessment options:
wiley.com/college/huffman

Problem Solving: Three Steps to the Goal

A*chievement*

Objective 8.4: *Describe the three stages of problem solving.*

Several years ago in Los Angeles, a 12-foot-high tractor-trailer got stuck under a bridge that was 6 inches too low. After hours of towing, tugging, and pushing, the police and transportation workers were stumped. Then a young boy happened by and asked, "Why don't you let some air out of the tires?" It was a simple, creative suggestion—and it worked.

Our lives are filled with problems, some simple, some difficult. For example, figuring out a way to make coffee without a filter is much easier than rescuing 118 Russian Navy seamen trapped inside a submarine at the bottom of the Barents Sea. In all cases, however, problem solving requires moving from a *given state* (the problem) to a *goal state* (the solution), a process that usually involves three steps (Bourne, Dominowski, & Loftus, 1979).

Step 1: Preparation

To help you appreciate the three steps for problem solving, let's look at a common problem. Are you, or is someone you know, looking for a long-term love relationship? There are at least three separate components to successful preparation:

- ***Identifying given facts.*** To find lasting love, it is important to identify your most basic, *nonnegotiable* limits and desires. For example, do you want children? Are you willing to move to another city to find love or to be with someone you love? Does your partner have to share your religion?

- ***Separating relevant from irrelevant facts.*** What are your *negotiable* items? What do you consider irrelevant and easily compromised? Would you consider a relationship with someone who is 10 years older than you? What about someone 10 years younger? Do you want someone who is college educated, or is that negotiable?

©AP/Wide World Photos

Successful problem solving? *Why hasn't this motorized scooter become a popular way to travel?*

Digital Vision/GettyImages

Looking for love in all the wrong places Are singles' bars a good place to find lasting love? Why or why not?

Algorithm *Logical, step-by-step procedure that, if followed correctly, will eventually solve the problem*

Heuristics *Simple rule or shortcut for problem solving that does not guarantee a solution but does narrow the alternatives.*

 Study Tip

Several heuristics can be particularly helpful in college, including (1) working backward, (2) means–end analysis, and (3) creating subgoals (see Table 8.1). Successful college students seem to be particularly good at breaking down a solution into subgoals. When you are faced with a heavy schedule of exams and term papers, try creating subgoals to make the immediate problems more manageable and increase the likelihood of reaching your final goal—a college degree.

• **Defining the ultimate goal.** This part of the preparation stage may seem easy, but think again. Are you interested in a long-term relationship with the ultimate goal of marriage and children? If so, dating someone who wants to travel his or her entire life and never have children is probably not a safe bet. Similarly, if your major enjoyments are camping and outdoor sports, you may not want to date a big-city museum lover.

Step 2: Production

During the *production step*, the problem solver generates possible solutions, called *hypotheses*. Two major approaches to generating hypotheses are *algorithms* and *heuristics*:

• An **algorithm** is a logical, step-by-step procedure (well suited for computers) that, if followed correctly, will always produce the solution. An algorithm for solving the math problem 2×4 is $2 + 2 + 2 + 2$. To make a soufflé, you apply an algorithm called a recipe. When driving to a new address, you carefully follow an algorithm called a map.

For complex problems, algorithms may take a long time, and you're unlikely to use them in a search for lasting love. However, they can be very useful in balancing your checkbook or calculating your grade point average.

• A **heuristic** is a simple rule or shortcut that does not guarantee a solution, but it does narrow the alternatives. Renters interested in finding an apartment couldn't visit all the possible alternatives (an algorithm), so they could shortcut their search to available rentals within 5 minutes of their job (a heuristic). Similarly, investors in the stock market often follow the heuristic of "buy low and sell high," and business owners may fire workers to reduce costs because they're applying shortcuts (heuristics) that have worked in the past.

As you can see, heuristics don't guarantee an optimal solution, but they help narrow the possible alternatives (Moons & Mackie, 2007). In your search for lasting love, psychological research has several helpful suggestions. For example, similarity is one of the best predictors of long-term relationships (Chapter 16). Therefore, a useful "dating heuristic" might be to join clubs based on what you naturally love to do—dancing, tennis, politics, movies, and so on—which will expose you to partners with similar interests.

Step 3: Evaluation

Once the hypotheses (possible solutions) are generated in Step 2, they must be evaluated to see if they meet the criteria defined in Step 1. If one or more of the hypotheses meet the criteria, the problem is solved—you know what you want in a partner and the best place to find him or her. If not, then you must return to the production stage and produce alternate solutions. Keep in mind, however, that "action must follow solution." Once the boy solved the "stuck-truck" problem, someone had to follow through and actually let some air out of the tires. Similarly, once you identify your path to the goal, you must follow through and implement the necessary solution.

PSYCHOLOGY AT WORK

Heuristics and Your Career

Are you feeling overwhelmed with the high number of possible career alternatives? Do friends and family question you about your long-term college and career plans? You obviously can't try all possible majors (an algorithm) to solve this problem, but the three heuristics presented in Table 8.1 may help you narrow your desired alternatives.

SUMMARY TABLE 8.1 PROBLEM-SOLVING HEURISTICS AND YOUR CAREER

Problem-solving Heuristics	Description	Example
Working backward	An approach that starts with the solution, a known condition, and works backward through the problem. Once the search has revealed the steps to be taken, the problem is solved.	You decide you want to major in psychology and go to graduate school to be an experimental psychologist. You ask your psychology professor and/or career counselor to recommend courses, graduate colleges and universities, and areas to emphasize. Then you contact recommended colleges or universities requesting information on their admission policies and standards. You then adapt your current college courses accordingly and work hard to meet (or exceed) the admission standards. ***Problem solving in action*** *Graduating from college requires many skills, including the successful use of several problem-solving heuristics.*
Means–end analysis	The problem solver determines what measure would reduce the difference between the given state and the goal. Once the means to reach the goal are determined, the problem is solved.	Knowing that you need a high GPA to get into a good graduate school for experimental psychology, you ask your professors for study suggestions, interview several A students to compare and contrast their study habits, assess your own study habits, and then determine the specific means (the number of hours and specific study techniques) required to meet your end goal of a high GPA.
Creating subgoals	Large, complex problems are broken down into a series of small subgoals. These subgoals then serve as a series of stepping-stones that can be taken one at a time to reach the original large goal.	Getting a good grade or passing many college courses requires specific subgoals like writing a successful term paper. To do this, you choose a topic, go to the library and Internet to locate information related to the topic. Once you have the information, you must organize it, write an outline, write the paper, review the paper, rewrite, rewrite again, and submit the final paper on or before the due date.

Gary Buss/Taxi/Getty Images

Application

Try This Yourself

Are You a Good Problem Solver?

If you want a hands-on experience with problem solving, try this classic thinking problem (Bartlett, 1958). Your task is to determine the numerals 0 through 9 that are represented by letters, with each letter representing a separate, distinct number. You get one hint before you start: $D = 5$.

$$
\begin{array}{r}
D\ O\ N\ A\ L\ D \\
+\ G\ E\ R\ A\ L\ D \\
\hline
R\ O\ B\ E\ R\ T
\end{array}
$$

Given there are 362,880 possible combinations of letters and numbers, algorithms obviously won't work. At the rate of 1 combination per minute, 8 hours per day, 5 days a week, 52 weeks a year, it would take nearly 3 years to try all the possible combinations.

If you successfully solved the problem, you probably used the "creating subgoals" heuristic in Table 8.1. You employed previous knowledge of arithmetic to set subgoals, such as determining what number T represents (if $D = 5$, then $D + D = 10$, so $T = 0$, with a carryover of 1 into the tens column). The complete answer is at the end of the next "Check & Review."

Achievement

Objective 8.5: *Identify five common barriers to problem solving.*

Study Tip

Mental sets also block some college students from using the SQ4R (Survey, Question, Read, Recite, Review, and wRite) method or other study techniques described in the "Tools for Student Success" at the end of Chapter 1. Their reliance on past study habits blocks them from considering newer and more efficient strategies. If we try to be flexible in our thinking, we can offset the natural tendency toward mental sets.

Figure 8.4 *The nine-dot problem* Can you draw no more than four lines that run through all nine dots without lifting your pencil from the paper? (See the Check & Review, page 288, for the solution.)

Mental Set *Persisting in using problem-solving strategies that have worked in the past rather than trying new ones*

Functional Fixedness *Tendency to think of an object functioning only in its usual or customary way*

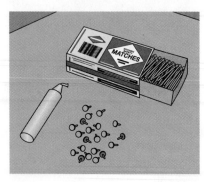

Figure 8.5 *Overcoming functional fixedness* Can you use these supplies to mount the candle on a wall so that it can be lit in a normal way—without toppling over? (See the Check & Review, page 288, for the solution.)

Confirmation Bias *Preferring information that confirms preexisting positions or beliefs, while ignoring or discounting contradictory evidence*

Recognizing Barriers to Problem Solving

Everyone frequently encounters barriers that prevent effective problem solving. The most common barriers are:

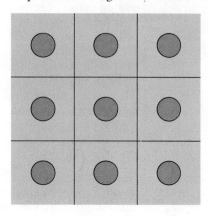

1. *Mental sets.* Like the police and transportation workers who were trying to pull or shove the truck that was stuck under the bridge, have you ever persisted in attacking problems using solutions the same as, or similar to, ones that have worked in the past? This is known as a **mental set**. Although pulling or shoving may occasionally work, in this instance the old solution created a mental barrier to new, and possibly more effective, solutions (such as deflating the tires). The habit (or *mental set*) of working arithmetic problems from the right (ones) column to the left also explains why most people fail to see the solution to the DONALD + GERALD problem. In the same way, looking for love only by going to singles' bars can be a barrier to good dating. To practice overcoming mental sets, try the nine-dot problem in Figure 8.4.

2. *Functional fixedness.* The tendency to view objects as functioning only in the usual or customary way is known as **functional fixedness**. Suppose you wanted to make coffee in your automatic coffeemaker but were out of filters. Would you dig through the trash looking for an old, dirty filter without thinking of using a paper towel? What if you were given the objects shown in Figure 8.5 and asked to mount the candle on the wall so that it could be easily lit in the normal fashion, with no danger of toppling? How would you do this?

   When a child uses sofa cushions to build a fort, or you use a table knife instead of a screwdriver to tighten a screw, you both have successfully avoided functional fixedness. Similarly, the individual who discovered a way to retrofit diesel engines to allow them to use discarded restaurant oil as fuel has overcome functional fixedness—and may become a very rich man!

3. *Confirmation bias.* We frequently complain about politicians who readily accept opinion polls that support their political views—and ignore those that conflict. But have you recognized the same bias in your own thinking? Do you pay greater attention to common sayings that support your personal biases (e.g., "opposites attract") and overlook contradictory findings (e.g., "similarity is the best predictor of long-term relationships")? This inclination to seek confirmation for our preexisting beliefs and to overlook contradictory evidence is known as **confirmation bias** (Jonas et al., 2008; Kerschreiter et al., 2008; Nickerson, 1998; Reich, 2004).

   British researcher Peter Wason (1968) first demonstrated the confirmation bias. He asked participants to generate a list of numbers that conformed to the same rule that applied to this set of numbers: 2 4 6

   Hypothesizing that the rule was "numbers increasing by two," most participants generated sets such as (4, 6, 8) or (1, 3, 5). Each time, Wason assured them that their sets of numbers conformed to the rule but that the rule "numbers increasing by two" was incorrect. The problem was that the participants were searching only for information that confirmed their hypothesis. Proposing a series such as (1, 3, 4) would have led them to reject their initial hypothesis and discover the correct rule: "numbers in increasing order of magnitude."

4. *Availability heuristic.* Cognitive psychologists Amos Tversky and Daniel Kahneman found that heuristics, as handy as they can be, can lead us to ignore relevant information (Kahneman, 2003; Tversky & Kahneman, 1974, 1993). When we use the **availability heuristic,** we judge the likelihood of an event based on how easily recalled (available) other instances of the event are (Buontempo & Brockner, 2008; Caruso, 2008; Oppenheimer, 2004). Shortly after the September 11, 2001, terrorist attacks, one study found that the average American believed that he or she had a 20.5 percent chance of being hurt in a terrorist attack within a year (Lerner et al., 2003). Can you see how intense media coverage of the attacks created this erroneously high perception of risk? Similarly, casinos use loud bells and bright flashing lights to attract attention when someone wins a slot machine jackpot. Although casino owners may not be familiar with Tversky and Kahneman's research on the availability heuristic, their business experience has taught them that calling attention to winners creates a vivid impression. This, in turn, causes nearby gamblers to overestimate the likelihood of winning (and to increase their own gambling).

©AP/Wide World Photos

5. *Representativeness heuristic.* Tversky and Kahneman also demonstrated how the **representativeness heuristic** sometimes hinders problem solving. Using this heuristic, we estimate the probability of something based on how well the circumstances match (or *represent*) our *prototype* (Fisk, Burg, & Holden, 2006; Greene & Ellis, 2008). (Remember: A prototype is a most common or representative example.) For instance, if John is 6 feet, 5 inches tall, we may guess that he is an NBA basketball player rather than, say, a bank president. But in this case, the representative heuristic ignores *base-rate information*—the probability of a characteristic occurring in the general population. In the United States, bank presidents outnumber NBA players by about 50 to 1. So despite his height, John is statistically much more likely to be a bank president.

Availability Heuristic *Judging the likelihood or probability of an event based on how readily available other instances of the event are in memory*

Psychology at work—Fast food and representative heuristics McDonald's, Dunkin' Donuts, and other fast-food franchise restaurants have found that using the same ingredients and methods at every location helps increase their sales. But do they know why? It's primarily because this repetition creates a representative heuristic for their specific restaurant. For example, after a few experiences with different McDonald's in various locations, you create a prototype that guides your expectations about how long it will take to get your food and what it will taste like. When traveling and looking for a quick "bite to eat," your "McDonald's representative heuristic" makes it easier for you to choose their restaurant over the competition.

Representativeness Heuristic *Estimating the probability of something based on how well the circumstances match (or represent) our previous prototype*

Application

CRITICAL THINKING

Solving Problems in College Life

Critical thinking requires adaptive, flexible approaches to thinking and problem solving. The following exercise offers practice in critical thinking, new insights into common college-related problems, and a quick review of terms and concepts discussed in this section.

Be sure to use the major problem-solving approaches we have discussed—algorithms (step-by-step procedures that guarantee solutions) and heuristics (shortcuts to possible solutions based on previous knowledge and experience). See Table 8.1 for three specific heuristics: working backward, means–end analysis, and creating subgoals.

Problem 1 It is the end of the semester and you have a term paper due Friday. Thursday night you try to print your previously prepared paper, and you can't find the file on your computer.

Problem 2 The financial aid office has denied your student loan until you verify your income and expenses from last year.

ACTIVE LEARNING

You need to find all your pay stubs and receipts.

For each problem, answer the following:

1. What was your first step in approaching the problem?
2. Which problem-solving approach did you select and why?
3. Did you experience mental sets, functional fixedness, confirmation bias, the availability heuristic, and the representativeness heuristic during the problem-solving process?

Assessment

STOP

CHECK & REVIEW

Problem Solving

Objective 8.4: *Describe the three stages of problem solving.*

Problem solving entails three stages: *preparation*, *production*, and *evaluation*. During the preparation stage, we identify given facts, separate relevant from irrelevant facts, and define the ultimate goal.

During the production stage, we generate possible solutions, called hypotheses. We typically generate hypotheses by using *algorithms* and *heuristics*. **Algorithms**, as problem-solving strategies, are guaranteed to lead to an eventual solution. But they are not practical in many situations. **Heuristics**, or simplified rules based on experience, are much faster but do not guarantee a solution. Three common heuristics are *working backward*, *means-end analysis*, and *creating subgoals*.

The evaluation stage in problem solving involves judging the hypotheses generated during the production stage against the criteria established in the preparation stage.

Objective 8.5: *Identity five common barriers to problem solving.*

Five major barriers to successful problem solving are **mental sets, functional fixedness, confirmation bias,** the **availability heuristic,** and the **representativeness heuristic.**

Questions

1. List and describe the three stages of problem solving.
2. Rosa is shopping in a new supermarket and wants to find a specific type of mustard. Which problem-solving strategy would be most efficient?

(a) algorithm; (b) heuristic; (c) instinct; (d) mental set

3. Which of the three stages of problem-solving is demonstrated in the figure below.

Problem = Finding a New Apartment

4. Before a new product arrives in the store, a manufacturer goes through several stages, including designing, building, testing a prototype, and setting up a production line. This approach is called _____. (a) working backward; (b) means–end analysis; (c) divergent thinking; (d) creating subgoals

5. Following the terrorist attack in 2001, many Americans overestimated the odds of another attack within the next year. This is an example of _____.

Check your answers in Appendix B.

 Click & Review
for additional assessment options:
wiley.com/college/huffman

Solution to the DONALD + GERALD = ROBERT problem:

```
    5  2  6  4  8  5
+   1  9  7  4  8  5
------------------
    7  2  3  9  7  0
```

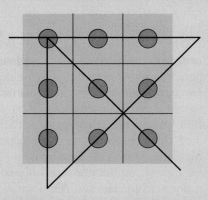

Possible solution to the nine-dot problem. People find this puzzle difficult because they see the arrangement of dots as a square, and "naturally" assume they can't go out of the boundaries of the square.

Possible solution to the candle problem. Use the tacks to mount the matchbox tray to the wall. Light the candle and use some melted wax to mount the candle to the matchbox.

Achievement

Objective 8.6: *What is creativity, and what are its three major characteristics?*

Creativity *Ability to produce valued outcomes in a novel way*

■ Creativity: Finding Unique Solutions

Are you a creative person? Like many students, you may think of painters, dancers, and composers as creative and fail to recognize examples of your own creativity. Definitions of *creativity* vary among psychologists and among cultures. But it is generally agreed that **creativity** is the *ability to produce valued outcomes in a novel way.* In general, creativity possesses three characteristics: *originality, fluency,* and *flexibility.* As you can see in Table 8.2, Thomas Edison's invention of the light bulb offers a prime example of each of these characteristics.

TABLE 8.2 THREE ELEMENTS OF CREATIVE THINKING

	Explanations	Thomas Edison Examples	
Originality	Seeing unique or different solutions to a problem	After noting that electricity passing through a conductor produces a glowing red or white heat, Edison imagined using this light for practical uses.	
Fluency	Generating a large number of possible solutions	Edison tried literally hundreds of different materials to find one that would heat to the point of glowing white heat without burning up.	
Flexibility	Shifting with ease from one type of problem-solving strategy to another	When he couldn't find a long-lasting material, Edison tried heating it in a vacuum—thereby creating the first light bulb.	

National Archives/Taxi/Getty Images

Measuring Creativity

Most tests of creativity focus on **divergent thinking**, a type of thinking in which many possibilities are developed from a single starting point.

In the divergent thinking *Unusual Uses Test*, you would be asked to think of as many uses as possible for an object (such as "How many ways can you use a brick?"). In the *Anagrams Test*, you would need to reorder the letters in a word to make as many new words as possible. Try rearranging the letters in these words to make new words. Then decide what they share in common. (Answers appear in the "Check & Review" on page 290.)

1. grevenidt _____
2. neleecitlgni _____
3. ytliibxilef _____
4. ptoyroper_____
5. yvitcearti_____

The opposite of divergent thinking is **convergent thinking**, or *conventional thinking*. In this case, lines of thinking *converge* (come together) on one correct answer. You used convergent thinking in the DONALD + GERALD problem page 285 to find the one correct number represented by each letter.

Divergent Thinking *Thinking that produces many alternatives from a single starting point; a major element of creativity (e.g., finding as many uses as possible for a paper clip)*

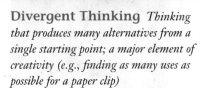

Objective 8.7: *How do we measure creativity?*

Convergent Thinking *Narrowing down alternatives to converge on a single correct answer (e.g., standard academic tests generally require convergent thinking)*

pplication

Try This Yourself

Are You Creative?

Everyone exhibits a certain amount of creativity in some aspects of life. Even when doing ordinary tasks, like planning an afternoon of errands, you are being somewhat creative. Similarly, if you've ever tightened a screw with a penny or used a telephone book on a chair as a booster seat for a child, you've found creative solutions to problems.

Would you like to test your own creativity?

- Find 10 coins and arrange them in the configuration shown here. By moving only two coins, form two rows that each contain 6 coins (see page 290 for the solution).
- In five minutes, see how many words you can make using the letters in the word *hippopotamus*.
- In five minutes, list all the things you can do with a paper clip.

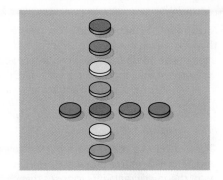

Researching Creativity

Some researchers view creativity as a special talent or ability. Therefore, they look for common personality traits among people they define as creative. Other researchers explain the distinction between creative and noncreative people in terms of cognitive

chievement

Objective 8.8: *How do creative people differ from others?*

processes. That is, creative and noncreative people differ in how they encode information, in how they store it, and in what information they generate to solve problems (Abraham & Windman, 2007; Bink & Marsh, 2000; Guilford, 1967; Ivcevic, 2006; Keller, Lavish, & Brown, 2007; Ward, 2007).

According to Sternberg and Lubart's *investment theory* (1992, 1996), creative people are willing to "buy low and sell high" in the realm of ideas, championing ideas that others dismiss. Once their creative ideas are supported and highly valued, they "sell high" and move on to another unpopular but promising idea.

Investment theory also suggests that creativity requires the coming together of six interrelated resources (Kaufman, 2002; Sternberg & Lubart, 1996). These resources are summarized in Table 8.3. One way to improve your personal creativity is to study this list and then strengthen yourself in those areas that you think need improvement.

©AP/Wide World Photos

Which resources best explain Oprah Winfrey's phenomenal success?

TABLE 8.3 RESOURCES OF CREATIVE PEOPLE

Intellectual Ability	Knowledge	Thinking Style	Personality	Motivation	Environment
Enough intelligence to see problems in a new light	Sufficient basic knowledge of the problem to effectively evaluate possible solutions	Novel ideas and ability to distinguish between the worthy and worthless	Willingness to grow and change, take risks, and work to overcome obstacles	Sufficient motivation to accomplish the task and more internal than external motivation	An environment that supports creativity

Assessment

CHECK & REVIEW

STOP

Creativity

Objective 8.6: *What is creativity, and what are its three major characteristics?*

Creativity is the ability to produce valued outcomes in a novel way. Creative thinking involves *originality, fluency,* and *flexibility.*

Objective 8.7: *How do we measure creativity?*

Most tests of creativity focus on **divergent thinking**, which involves generating as many alternatives or ideas as possible. In contrast, **convergent thinking**—or conventional thinking—works toward a single correct answer.

Objective 8.8: *How do creative people differ from others?*

Creative people may have a special talent or differing cognitive processes. The *investment theory of creativity* proposes that creative people "buy low" by pursuing promising but unpopular ideas. They then "sell high" when these ideas are widely accepted. The theory also proposes that creativity depends on six specific resources: *intellectual ability,* knowledge, thinking style, personality, motivation, and environment.

Questions

1. Which of the following items would most likely appear on a test measuring creativity? (a) How long is the Ohio River? (b) What are the primary colors? (c) List all the uses of a pot. (d) Who was the first governor of New York?

2. Identify the type of thinking for each of these examples.
   a. You create numerous excuses ("reasons") for not studying.
   b. On a test, you must select one correct answer for each question.
   c. You make a list of ways to save money.

3. Considering the six resources of creative people (Table 8.3), which resource(s) do you possess? How could you develop the resource(s) you lack?

Check your answers in Appendix B.

 Click & Review for additional assessment options: wiley.com/college/huffman

Solutions to the Anagrams Test

1. divergent
2. intelligence
3. flexibility
4. prototype
5. creativity

Note that the answers are also key terms found in this chapter

Coin Problem Solution

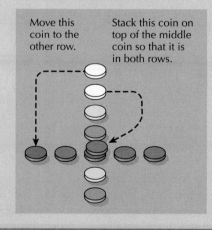

Move this coin to the other row.

Stack this coin on top of the middle coin so that it is in both rows.

Language

Any discussion of human thought processes must include a discussion of language. As mentioned earlier, language (along with mental images and concepts) is one of the three building blocks of thinking. Language enables us to mentally manipulate symbols, thereby expanding our thinking. Most importantly, whether it's spoken, written, or signed, language allows us to communicate our thoughts, ideas, and feelings.

◼ Characteristics of Language: Structure and Production

What is language? Do beavers slapping their tails, birds singing their songs, and ants laying their trails use language? Not according to a strict scientific definition. As we discussed earlier, scientists develop precise definitions and restrictions for certain *artificial concepts*. Psychologists, linguists, and other scientists define **language** as a form of communication using sounds and symbols combined according to specified rules.

Building Blocks of Language
To produce language, we first build words using *phonemes* and *morphemes*. Then we string words into sentences using rules of *grammar* (*syntax* and *semantics*) (Process Diagram 8.1).

◼ Language and Thought: A Complex Interaction

Does the fact that you speak English instead of Spanish—or Chinese instead of Swahili—determine how you reason, think, and perceive the world? Linguist Benjamin Whorf (1956) believed so. As evidence for his *linguistic relativity hypothesis*, Whorf offered a now classic example: Because Eskimos (Inuits) have many words for snow (*apikak* for "first snow falling," *pukak* for "snow for drinking water," and so on), they can perceive and think about snow differently from English speakers, who have only one word—*snow*.

Though intriguing, Whorf's hypothesis has not fared well. He apparently exaggerated the number of Inuit words for snow (Pullum, 1991), and he ignored the fact that English speakers have a number of terms to describe various forms of snow, such as *slush, sleet, hard pack*, and *powder*. Other research has directly contradicted Whorf's theory. For example, Eleanor Rosch (1973) found that although people of the Dani tribe in New Guinea possess only two color names—one indicating cool, dark colors, and the other describing warm, bright colors—they discriminate among multiple hues as well as English speakers do.

Whorf apparently was mistaken in his belief that language determines thought, but there is no doubt that language *influences* thought (Hoff, 2009). People who speak both Chinese and English report that the language they're currently using affects their sense of self (Matsumoto & Juang, 2008). When using Chinese, they tend to conform to Chinese cultural norms; when speaking English, they tend to adopt Western norms.

Our words also influence the thinking of those who hear them. That's why companies avoid *firing* employees; instead, employees are *outplaced* or *nonrenewed*. Similarly, the military uses terms like *preemptive strike* to cover the fact that they attacked first and *tactical redeployment* to refer to a retreat.

Our choice of words also has had some embarrassing and financial consequences for North American businesses. When Pepsi-Cola used its "Come alive with Pepsi" slogan in Japan, they later learned that it translated as "Pepsi brings your dead ancestors back from the grave." Similarly, Chevrolet Motor Company had great difficulty marketing its small Nova car in Mexico because it didn't understand that *No va* means "doesn't go" in Spanish. Words evoke different images and value judgments. Our words, therefore, *influence* not only our thinking but also the thinking of those who hear them.

Achievement

Objective 8.9: *What is language, and what are its basic building blocks?*

Language *Form of communication using sounds and symbols combined according to specified rules*

Achievement

Objective 8.10: *How is language related to thought?*

wiley.com/
college/
huffman

Process Diagram 8.1
Building Blocks of Language

Grammar

A system of rules (syntax and semantics) used to generate acceptable language that enables us to communicate with and understand others.

They were in my psychology class.
versus
They was in my psychology class.

Syntax
Grammatical rules for putting words in correct order

I am happy.
versus
Happy I am.

Semantics
A system of rules for using words to create meaning

I went out on a limb for you.
versus
Humans have several limbs.

Morphemes

The smallest meaningful units of language; they are created by combining phonemes. (*Function morphemes* are prefixes and suffixes. *Content morphemes* are root words.)

unthinkable = un·think·able
(prefix = *un*, root word = *think*, suffix = *able*)

Phonemes

The smallest distinctive sound units that make up every language

p in pansy; *ng* in sting

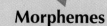

"GOT IDEA. TALK BETTER. COMBINE WORDS. MAKE SENTENCES."

Sidney Harris.

Phoneme [FOE-neem] *Smallest basic unit of speech or sound*

Morpheme [MOR-feem] *Smallest meaningful unit of language, formed from a combination of phonemes*

Grammar *System of rules (syntax and semantics) used to create language and communication*

Syntax *Grammatical rules that specify how words and phrases should be arranged in a sentence to convey meaning*

Semantics *Set of rules for using words to create meaning; or the study of meaning*

Language Development: From Crying to Talking

From birth, a child communicates through facial expressions, eye contact, and body gestures. Babies only hours old begin to "teach" their caregivers when and how they want to be held, fed, and played with. As early as the late 1800s, Charles Darwin proposed that most emotional expressions, such as smiles, frowns, and looks of disgust, are universal and innate (Figure 8.6). Darwin's contention is supported by the fact that children who are born blind and deaf exhibit the same facial expressions for emotions as sighted and hearing children.

Stages of Language Development

In addition to nonverbal communication, children also communicate verbally. Progressing through several distinct stages of language acquisition (Process Diagram 8.2). By age 5, most children have mastered basic grammar and typically use about 2000 words (a level of mastery considered adequate for getting by in any given culture). Past this point, vocabulary and grammar gradually improve throughout life (Hoff, 2009).

Theories of Language Development

What motivates children to develop language? Some theorists believe that language capability is innate, being primarily a matter of maturation. Noam Chomsky (1968, 1980) suggests that children are "prewired" with a neurological ability known as a **language acquisition device (LAD)** that enables a child to analyze language and to extract the basic rules of grammar. This mechanism needs only minimal exposure to adult speech to unlock its potential. As evidence for this nativist position, Chomsky observes that children everywhere progress through the same stages of language development at about the same ages. He also notes that babbling is the same in all languages and that deaf babies babble just like hearing babies.

"Nurturists" argue that the nativist position doesn't fully explain individual differences in language development. They hold that children learn language through a complex system of rewards, punishments, and imitation. For example, parents smile and encourage any vocalizations from a very young infant. Later, they respond even more enthusiastically when the infant babbles "mama" or "dada." In this way, parents unknowingly use *reinforcement* and *shaping* (Chapter 6) to help babies learn language (Figure 8.7).

Achievement
GENDER & CULTURAL DIVERSITY

Unspoken Accents—Nonverbal Language Reveals Your Roots

By Siri Carpenter

Just as an Irish brogue or a Minnesota lilt betrays one's background, facial expressions and body language can also reveal our cultural origins. According to new research, such "nonverbal accents" also provoke stereotyped perceptions of others' personalities. Many researchers regard nonverbal behavior to be a universal language—wherever you go, a smile looks like a smile. But a growing body of research suggests that where we hang our

---

Achievement

Objective 8.11: *Describe a child's major stages in language development.*

Myrleen Ferguson Cafe/PhotoEdit

Figure 8.6 Can you identify this emotion? Infants as young as 2.5 months can nonverbally express emotions, such as joy, surprise, or anger.

Achievement

Objective 8.12: *Contrast the "nativist" versus "nurturist" views of language development.*

Figure 8.7 Nature or nurture? Both sides of the nature-versus-nurture debate have staunch supporters. However, most psychologists believe that language acquisition is a combination of both biology (nature) and environment (nurture) (Hoff, 2009; Plomin, DeFries, & Fulker, 2007).

Language Acquisition Device (LAD) *According to Chomsky, an innate mechanism that enables a child to analyze language and extract the basic rules of grammar*

Achievement

Objective 8.13: *How does nonverbal language reveal cultural origins?*

Process Diagram 8.2
Language Acquisition

Developmental Stage	Age	Language Features	Example
Prelinguistic stage *iStockphoto*	Birth to ~12 months	Crying (reflexive in newborns; soon, crying becomes more purposeful)	hunger cry anger cry pain cry
	2 to 3 months	**Cooing** (vowel-like sounds)	"ooooh" "aaaah"
	4 to 6 months	**Babbling** (consonants added)	"bahbahbah" "dahdahdah"
Linguistic stage *iStockphoto*	~12 months	Babbling begins to resemble language of the child's home. Child seems to understand that sounds relate to meaning.	
		At first, speech is limited to one-word utterances.	"Mama" "juice" "Daddy" "up"
		Expressive ability more than doubles once child begins to join words into short phrases.	"Daddy, milk" "no night-night!"
	~2 years	Child sometimes **overextends** (using words to include objects that do not fit the word's meaning).	all men = "Daddy" all furry animals = doggy
iStockphoto	~2 years to ~5 years	Child links several words to create short but intelligible sentences. This speech is called **telegraphic speech** because (like telegrams) it omits nonessential connecting words.	"Me want cookie" "Grandma go bye-bye?"
		Vocabulary increases at a phenomenal rate.	
		Child acquires a wide variety of rules for grammar.	adding -ed for past tense adding s to form plurals
		Child sometimes **overgeneralizes** (applying the basic rules of grammar even to cases that are exceptions to the rule).	"I goed to the zoo" "Two mans"

David Young-Wolff/Photo Edit

Baby signs *Have you heard that babies and toddlers—beginning as young as 9 months of age—can learn to communicate by using a modified form of sign language, sometimes called "Baby Sign"? Advocates suggest that teaching these symbolic gestures for basic ideas such as "more," "milk," or "love" enhances parents' and caregivers' interactions with children who cannot yet talk. Many agree. They report that signing with their infant or toddler gives them a fascinating "window" into the baby's mind—and eliminates a lot of frustration for both them and baby! Some researchers also believe that teaching babies to sign helps foster better language comprehension and can speed up the process of learning to talk.*

Cooing *Vowel-like sounds infants produce beginning around 2 to 3 months of age*

Babbling *Vowel/consonant combinations that infants begin to produce at about 4 to 6 months of age*

Overextension *Overly broad use of a word to include objects that do not fit the word's meaning (e.g., calling all men "Daddy")*

Telegraphic Speech *Two- or three- word sentences of young children that contain only the most necessary words*

Overgeneralize *Applying the basic rules of grammar even to cases that are exceptions to the rule (e.g., saying "mans" instead of "men")*

 Study Tip

Are you having difficulty differentiating between overextension and overgeneralization? Remember the g in overgeneralize as a cue that this term applies to problems with grammar.

hats shapes both how we display emotion and how we perceive it in others. In a recent study, psychologists found that American volunteers could distinguish American from Australian faces when the faces were photographed smiling but not when they were photographed with neutral expressions (Marsh, Elfenbein, & Ambady, 2007). In addition, the way Americans and Australians walked or waved in greeting not only telegraphed their nationality but also triggered prevailing stereotypes about the two groups: Americans were judged more dominant (think, "Carry a big stick") and Australians more likable (think, "G'day, mate!").

A different study, led by psychologist Masaki Yuki of Hokkaido University in Japan (Yuki, Maddux, & Masuda, 2007), suggests that people from different cultures are attuned to different nonverbal cues. The study found that Americans, who tend to express emotion overtly, look to the mouth to interpret others' true feelings. Japanese, who tend to be more emotionally guarded, give greater weight to the eyes, which are less easily controlled.

"These studies show both that people can be sensitive to cultural cues that they are barely aware of, and also that their own cultural norms can lead them astray," comments Judith Hall, who studies nonverbal communication at Northeastern University. For example, "Americans who think the Japanese are unexpressive mistake subtlety for lack of expression. These Americans would misjudge facial cues that Japanese might be very successful at interpreting."

Such misjudgments can have unintended consequences, Marsh argues. "Everyone knows how spoken communication breakdowns can lead to cross-cultural misunderstandings," she says. "These studies highlight the importance of nonverbal communication as well. Improving awareness of these differences might go a long way toward improving cross-cultural interactions."

(*Source*: Originally published in *Scientific American Mind*, August/September 2007, p. 13. Reprinted with permission of author, Siri Carpenter)

Achievement

Objective 8.14: *Describe the language research conducted with nonhuman animals.*

Animals and Language: Can Humans Talk to Nonhuman Animals?

Without question, nonhuman animals communicate. They commonly send warnings, signal sexual interest, share locations of food sources, and so on. But can they master the complexity of human language? Since the 1930s, many language studies have attempted to answer this question by probing the language abilities of chimpanzees, gorillas, and other animals (e.g., Barner et al., 2008; Fields et al., 2007; Savage-Rumbaugh, 1990; Segerdahl, Fields, & Savage-Rumbaugh, 2006).

One of the most successful early studies was conducted by Beatrice and Allen Gardner (1969), who recognized chimpanzees' manual dexterity and ability to imitate gestures. The Gardners used American Sign Language (ASL) with a chimp named Washoe. By the time Washoe was 4 years old, she had learned 132 signs and was able to combine them into simple sentences such as "Hurry, gimme toothbrush" and "Please tickle more." The famous gorilla Koko, mentioned in the chapter opener, also uses ASL to communicate. In another well-known study, a chimp named Lana learned to use symbols on a computer to get things she wanted, such as food, a drink, a tickle from her trainers, and having her curtains opened (Rumbaugh et al., 1974) (Figure 8.8).

Dolphins are also the subject of interesting language research. Communication with dolphins is done by means of hand signals or audible commands transmitted through an underwater speaker system (Figure 8.9). In one typical study, trainers gave dolphins commands made up of two- to five-word sentences, such as "Big ball—square—return," which meant that they should go get the big ball, put it in

Figure 8.8 *Computer-aided communication* Apes lack the necessary anatomical structures to vocalize the way humans do. For this reason, language research with chimps and gorillas has focused on teaching the animals to use sign language, or to "speak" by pointing to symbols on a keyboard.

wiley.com/
college/
huffman

Figure 8.9 *Communicating through art?* Dolphins have learned to respond to complicated hand signals and vocal commands from their trainers. They've even learned to "express themselves" through art. But is this simple communication, operant conditioning, or true language?

the floating square, and return to the trainer (Herman, Richards, & Woltz, 1984). By varying the syntax (for example, the order of the words) and specific content of the commands, the researchers showed that dolphins are sensitive to these aspects of language.

Evaluating Animal Language Studies

Psychologists disagree about how to interpret these findings on apes and dolphins. Most psychologists believe that nonhuman animals communicate but that their ideas are severely limited. Critics claim that apes and dolphins are unable to convey subtle meanings, use language creatively, or communicate at an abstract level (Jackendoff, 2003; Siegala & Varley, 2008).

Other critics claim that these animals do not truly understand language but are simply operantly conditioned (Chapter 6) to imitate symbols to receive rewards. Finally, other critics suggest that data regarding animal language has not always been scientifically well documented (Lieberman, 1998; Willingham, 2001; Wynne, 2007). Proponents of animal language respond that apes can use language creatively and have even coined some words of their own. For example, Koko signed "finger bracelet", to describe a ring and "eye hat" to describe a mask (Patterson & Linden, 1981). Proponents also argue that, as demonstrated by the dolphin studies, animals can be taught to understand basic rules of sentence structure.

Still, the gap between human and nonhuman animals' language is considerable. Current evidence suggests that, at best, nonhuman animal language is less complex, less creative, and has fewer rules than any language used by humans. (As a critical thinker, have you ever thought about an opposite approach to this type of language research? Why don't humans learn nonhuman animal language? Could humans be taught to comprehend and use chimpanzee, whale, or elephant communication systems, for example?)

"ALTHOUGH HUMANS MAKE SOUNDS WITH THEIR MOUTHS AND OCCASIONALLY LOOK AT EACH OTHER, THERE IS NO SOLID EVIDENCE THAT THEY ACTUALLY COMMUNICATE WITH EACH OTHER."

CHECK & REVIEW

Language

Objective 8.9: *What is language, and what are its basic building blocks?*

Human **language** is a form of communication using sounds and symbols combined according to a set of specified rules. **Phonemes** are the smallest distinctive sound units. They are combined to form **morphemes**, the smallest meaningful units of language. Phonemes, morphemes, words, and phrases are put together by rules of **grammar** (syntax and semantics). **Syntax**

refers to the grammatical rules for ordering words in sentences. **Semantics** refers to rules for deriving meaning in language.

Objective 8.10: *How is language related to thought?*

According to Benjamin Whorf's *linguistic relativity hypothesis*, language shapes thought. Generally, Whorf's hypothesis is not supported. However, our choice of vocabulary can influence our mental imagery and social perceptions.

Objective 8.11: *Describe a child's major stages in language development.*

Children go through two stages in their acquisition of language: *prelinguistic* (crying, **cooing**, **babbling**) and *linguistic* (single utterances, **telegraphic speech**, and the acquisition of rules of grammar).

Objective 8.12: *Contrast the "nativist" versus and "nurturist" views of language development.*

Nativists believe that language is an inborn capacity and develops primarily by maturation. Chomsky suggests that human brains possess a **language acquisition device (LAD)** that needs only minimal environmental input. Nurturists emphasize the role of the environment and suggest that language development results from rewards, punishments, and imitation of models.

Objective 8.13: *How does nonverbal language reveal cultural origins?*

Nonverbal emotions are somewhat universal, but there are slight differences between cultures in how we display and perceive emotions. These subtle differences can also lead to problems in communication.

Objective 8.14: *Describe the language research conducted with nonhuman animals.*

The most successful nonhuman animal language studies have been done with apes using American Sign Language and written symbols. Dolphins also have been taught to comprehend sentences that vary in syntax and meaning. Some psychologists believe

that nonhuman animals can truly learn human language. Others suggest that nonhuman animals are merely responding to rewards.

Questions

1. Label the three building blocks of language on the following figure:

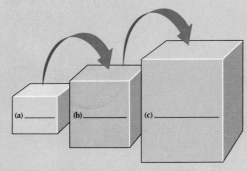

2. The basic speech sounds /ch/ and /v/ are known as _____. The smallest meaningful units of language, such as *book*, *pre-*, and *-ing*, are known as _____.

3. A child says "I hurt my foots." This is an example of _____.
4. Chomsky believes we possess an inborn ability to learn language known as a _____. (a) telegraphic understanding device (TUD); (b) language acquisition device (LAD); (c) language and grammar translator (LGT); (d) overgeneralized neural net (ONN)
5. Human language differs from the communication of nonhuman animals in that it is _____. (a) used more creatively to express thoughts and ideas; (b) the expression of an innate capability; (c) essential for thought; (d) composed of sounds

Check your answers in Appendix B.

 Click & Review
for additional assessment options:
wiley.com/college/huffman

Intelligence

Are Koko, Genie, and Thomas Edison intelligent? What exactly is intelligence? Many people equate intelligence with "book smarts," which conflicts with the common jokes and stereotypes about "absentminded professors" and geniuses with no common or practical sense. For others, what is intelligent depends on the characteristics and skills valued in a particular social group or culture (Matsumoto & Juang, 2008; Sternberg, 2008, 2009). For example, did you know that many languages have no word that corresponds to our Western notion of intelligence? The closest Mandarin word is a Chinese character meaning "good brain and talented." Interestingly, this Chinese word is commonly associated with traits like imitation, effort, and social responsibility.

What Is Intelligence? Do We Have One or Many Intelligences?

Even among Western psychologists there is debate over the definition of *intelligence*. In this discussion, we rely on a formal definition developed by psychologist David Wechsler (WEX-ler) (1944, 1977). Wechsler defined **intelligence** as *the global capacity to think rationally, act purposefully, and deal effectively with the environment*. In other words, intelligence is your ability to effectively use your thinking processes to cope with the world. An advantage of this definition is that it incorporates most modern viewpoints as well as most cultural and social influences.

For many Western psychologists, one of the prime areas of research and debate is: What are the properties of intelligence? Is it a single general ability or several distinct kinds of mental abilities (intelligences)?

In the 1920s, British psychologist Charles Spearman first observed that high scores on separate tests of mental abilities tend to correlate with each other. Spearman (1923) thus proposed that intelligence is a single factor, which he termed *general intelligence* (*g*). He believed that *g* underlies all intellectual behavior, including reasoning,

Achievement

Objective 8.15: *What is intelligence, and is it one or many abilities?*

Intelligence *Global capacity to think rationally, act purposefully, and deal effectively with the environment*

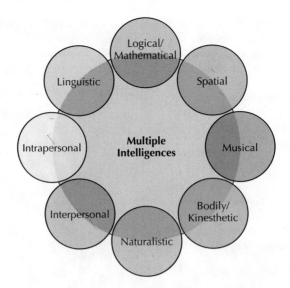

Figure 8.10 *Gardner's theory of multiple intelligences* Howard Gardner believes that there are numerous forms of intelligence and that the value of these intelligences may change according to culture. Gardner also proposed a possible ninth intelligence, spiritual/existential, shown in Table 8.5.

Fluid Intelligence *Aspects of innate intelligence, including reasoning abilities, memory, and speed of information processing, that are relatively independent of education and tend to decline as people age*

Crystallized Intelligence
Knowledge and skills gained through experience and education that tend to increase over the life span

Achievement

Objective 8.16: *Contrast Gardner's and Sternberg's theories of intelligence.*

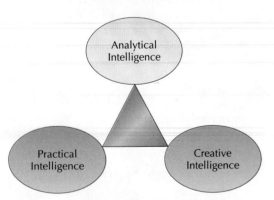

Sternberg's triarchic (three-part) theory of successful intelligence *According to Robert Sternberg's model, there are three separate and different aspects of intelligence. Each of these components is learned, not the result of genetics. Therefore, each can be strengthened or improved.*

solving problems, and performing well in all areas of cognition. Spearman's work laid the foundations for today's standardized intelligence tests (Goldstein, 2008; Johnson et al., 2004).

About a decade later, L. L. Thurstone (1938) proposed seven primary mental abilities: verbal comprehension, word fluency, numerical fluency, spatial visualization, associative memory, perceptual speed, and reasoning. J. P. Guilford (1967) later expanded this number, proposing that as many as 120 factors were involved in the structure of intelligence.

Around the same time, Raymond Cattell (1963, 1971) reanalyzed Thurstone's data and argued against the idea of multiple intelligences. He believed that two subtypes of *g* exist:

- **Fluid intelligence (*gf*)** refers to innate, inherited reasoning abilities, memory, and speed of information processing. Fluid intelligence is supposedly relatively independent of education and experience, and like other biological capacities it declines with age (Bugg et al., 2006; Daniels et al., 2006; Rozencwajg et al., 2005). However, other research has shown that cognitively stimulating activity in older adults can increase their fluid intelligence (Tranter & Koutstaal, 2008).

- **Crystallized intelligence (*gc*)** refers to the store of knowledge and skills gained through experience and education (Goldstein, 2008). Crystallized intelligence tends to increase over the life span.

Today there is considerable support for the concept of *g* as a measure of "academic smarts." However, many contemporary cognitive theorists believe that intelligence is not a single general factor but a collection of many separate specific abilities.

One of these cognitive theorists, Howard Gardner, believes that people have many kinds of intelligences. The fact that brain-damaged patients often lose some intellectual abilities while retaining others suggests to Gardner that different intelligences are located in discrete areas throughout the brain. According to Gardner's (1983, 1999, 2008) *theory of multiple intelligences*, people have different profiles of intelligence because they are stronger in some areas than in others (Figure 8.10). They also use their intelligences differently to learn new material, perform tasks, and solve problems.

Robert Sternberg's *triarchic theory of successful intelligence* also involves multiple abilities. As shown in Table 8.4, Sternberg theorized that there are three separate, learned aspects of intelligence: (1) *analytic intelligence*, (2) *creative intelligence*, and (3) *practical intelligence* (Sternberg, 1985, 2007, 2008, 2009). He also introduced the term *successful intelligence* to describe the ability to adapt to, shape, and select environments in order to accomplish personal and societal goals. In addition, Sternberg emphasizes the process underlying thinking rather than just the product, along with the importance of measuring mental abilities in real-world situations rather than testing mental abilities in isolation.

TABLE 8.4 STERNBERG'S TRIARCHIC THEORY OF SUCCESSFUL INTELLIGENCE

	Analytical Intelligence	Creative Intelligence	Practical Intelligence
Sample Skills	Good at analysis, evaluation, judgment, and comparison skills	Good at invention, coping with novelty, and imagination skills	Good at application, implementation, execution, and utilization skills
Methods of Assessment	These skills are assessed by intelligence or scholastic aptitude tests. Questions ask about meanings of words based on context and how to solve number-series problems.	These skills are assessed in many ways, including open-ended tasks, writing a short story, drawing a piece of art, or solving a scientific problem requiring insight.	Although these skills are more difficult to assess, they can be measured by asking for solutions to practical and personal problems.

PSYCHOLOGY AT WORK

Multiple Intelligences and Your Career

Have you heard from others that you're naturally good at something like writing, math, or spatial skills? Howard Gardner's research shows that most people possess one or more natural, intelligences, which are connected to success in various occupations. Carefully consider each of the multiple intelligences in Table 8.5 and how they might help guide you toward a satisfying career.

TABLE 8.5 GARDNER'S MULTIPLE INTELLIGENCES AND POSSIBLE CAREERS

Linguistic: language, such as speaking, reading a book, writing a story	**Spatial:** mental maps, such as mentally rearranging furniture or drawing blueprints	**Bodily/ Kinesthetic:** body movement, such as dancing or skate boarding	**Intrapersonal:** understanding oneself, such as setting achievable goals	**Logical/ Mathematical:** problem solving or scientific analysis, such as solving budget or research problems	**Musical:** musical skills, such as singing or playing a musical instrument	**Interpersonal:** social skills, such as managing diverse groups of people	**Naturalistic:** being attuned to nature, such as noting seasonal changes or environmental problems	**(*Possible*) Spiritual/ Existential:** attunement to meaning of life and death and other conditions of life
Careers: novelist, journalist, teacher	**Careers:** engineer, architect, pilot	**Careers:** athlete, dancer, ski instructor	**Careers:** increased success in almost all careers	**Careers:** mathematician, scientist, engineer	**Careers:** singer, musician, composer	**Careers:** salesperson manager, therapist, teacher	**Careers:** biologist, naturalist	**Careers:** philosopher, theologian

©AP/Wide World Photos

iStockphoto

Photo By Raymond Boyd/Michael Ochs Archives/Getty Images

Source: Adapted from Gardner, 1983, 1999, 2008.

What Is Intelligence?

Objective 8.15: *What is intelligence, and is it one or many abilities?*

Today, **intelligence** is commonly defined as the global capacity to think rationally, act purposefully, and deal effectively with the environment. Several theorists have debated whether intelligence is one or many abilities. Spearman viewed intelligence as one factor, called *g*, for general intelligence. Thurstone saw it as seven distinct mental abilities. Guilford believed it was composed of 120 or more separate abilities. And Cattell viewed it as two types of general intelligence (*g*), which he called **fluid intelligence** and **crystallized intelligence**.

Objective 8.16: *Contrast Gardner's and Sternberg's theories of intelligence.*

Both Gardner and Sternberg believe intelligence is a collection of multiple abilities. Gardner's theory of multiple intelligences identifies eight (and possibly nine) types of intelligence. He believes that both teaching and assessing should take into account people's learning styles and cognitive strengths. Sternberg's triarchic theory of intelligence (*analytical, creative,* and *practical*) proposed that each of these components is learned rather than the result of genetics.

Questions

1. The *g* factor, originally proposed by Spearman, is best defined as _____.

(a) skill in the use of language as a tool for thought; (b) general intelligence; (c) the ability to adapt to the environment; (d) the type of intelligence we call common sense

2. What is the difference between fluid and crystallized intelligences?

3. _____ suggested that people differ in their "profiles of intelligence" and that each person shows a unique pattern of strengths and weaknesses. (a) Spearman; (b) Binet; (c) Wechsler; (d) Gardner

4. Explain Sternberg's triarchic theory of successful intelligence.

Check your answers in Appendix B.

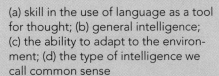

Click & Review
for additional assessment options:
wiley.com/college/huffman

Achievement

Objective 8.17: *Describe how psychologists measure intelligence.*

▨ How Do We Measure Intelligence?
IQ Tests and Scientific Standards

As you've just seen, intelligence is difficult to define. And the scientific community remains divided over whether it is one or multiple abilities. Despite this uncertainty, most college admissions officers and scholarship committees, as well as many employers, commonly use scores from intelligence tests as a significant part of their selection criteria. How well do these tests predict student and employee success? Different IQ tests approach the measurement of intelligence from different perspectives. However, most are designed to predict grades in school. Let's look at the most commonly used IQ tests.

Stanford-Binet

The *Stanford-Binet Intelligence Scale* is loosely based on the first IQ tests developed in France around the turn of the last century by Alfred Binet [bih-NAY]. In the United Stales, Lewis Terman (1916) developed the Stanford-Binet (at Stanford University) to test the intellectual ability of U.S.-born children ages 3 to 16. The test is revised periodically, and the current test measures individuals from the age of 2 through adulthood. It includes both verbal and nonverbal tasks, such as copying geometric designs, identifying similarities, and repeating number sequences.

In the original version of the Stanford-Binet, results were expressed in terms of a mental age. For example, if a 7-year-old's score equaled that of an average 8-year-old, the child was considered to have a mental age of 8. To determine the child's *intelligence quotient* (*IQ*), mental age was divided by the child's chronological age (actual age in years) and multiplied by 100 (*IQ = MA/CA* × 100). Using this example, of the 7-year-old's score, the formula would look like this:

$$IQ = \frac{MA}{CA} \times 100 = \frac{8}{7} \times 100 = 1.14 \times 100 = 114$$

Thus, a 7-year-old with a mental age of 8 would have an IQ of 114. A "normal" child would have a mental age equal to his or her chronological age. (*Normal* in this case refers to the norms or statistics used to standardize the test.)

Today, most intelligence tests, including the Stanford-Binet, no longer compute an IQ. Instead, the test scores are expressed as a comparison of a single person's score to a national sample of similar-aged people. These deviation IQs are based on how far the person's score on the test deviates from the national average (Figure 8.11). Note how this figure also shows how the distribution of IQ scores follows a bell-shaped curve. The majority of individuals (68 percent) who take the test score within the normal range—85 to 115. Even though the actual IQ is no longer calculated, the term *IQ* remains as a shorthand expression for intelligence test scores.

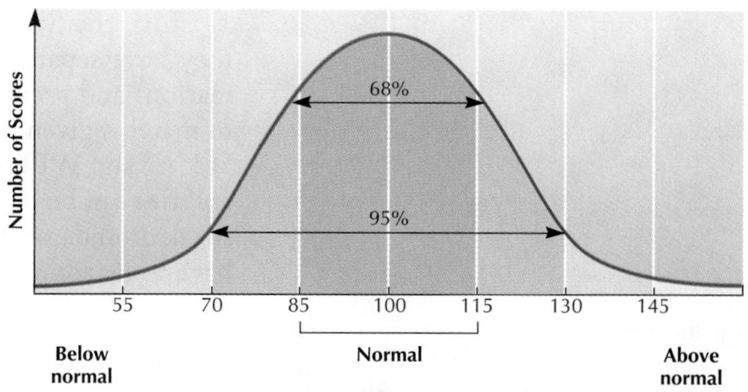

Figure 8.11 *The distribution of scores on the Stanford-Binet intelligence test* Sixty-eight percent of children score within one standard deviation (16 points) above or below the national average, which is 100 points. About 16 percent score above 116, and about 16 percent score below 84.

Wechsler Tests

David Wechsler developed the most widely used intelligence test, the *Wechsler Adult Intelligence Scale* (WAIS), now in a fourth edition (WAIS IV). He also created a similar test for school-age children, the *Wechsler Intelligence Scale for Children* (WISC-IV; Table 8.6), and one for preschool children, the *Wechsler Preschool and Primary Scale of Intelligence* (WPPSI), now revised as WPPSI-III.

TABLE 8.6 SUBTESTS OF THE WISC-IV

	Example*
Verbal Subtests	
Information	How many senators are elected from each state?
Similarities	How are computers and books alike?
Arithmetic	If one baseball card costs three cents, how much will five baseball cards cost?
Vocabulary	Define *lamp*.
Comprehension	What should you do if you accidentally break a friend's toy?
Performance Subtests	Example below:
Picture Completion What is missing from this ambulance?	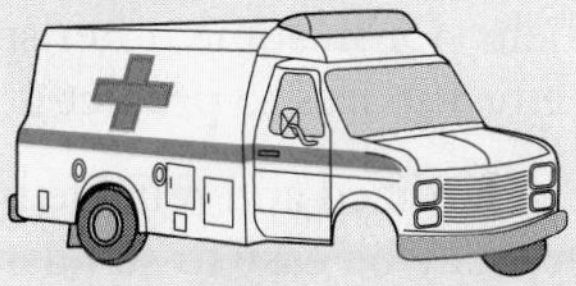
Coding Write the appropriate number above each symbol.	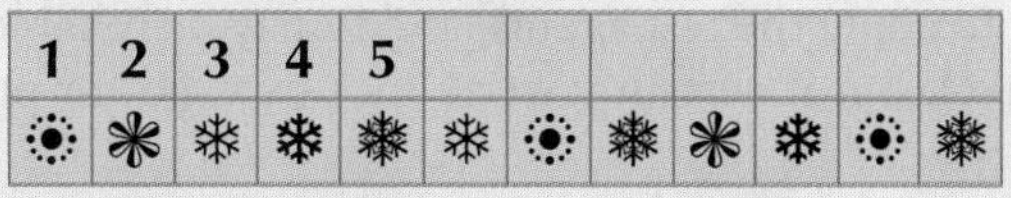
Picture Arrangement Arrange these pictures in chronological order.	
Block Design Copy this design with blocks.	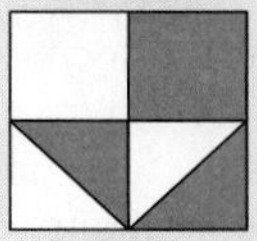
Object Assembly Assemble this small jigsaw puzzle.	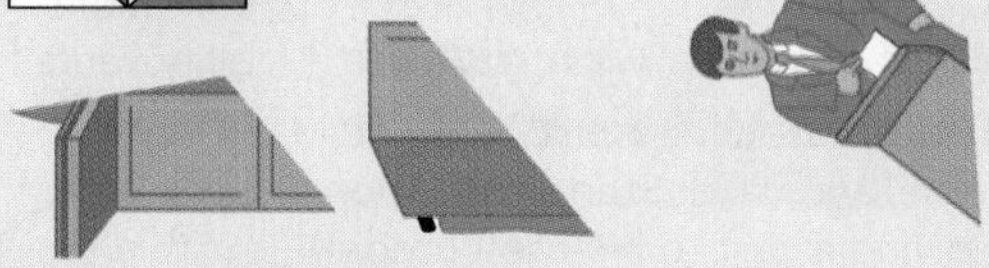

*These examples are similar to those used on the actual test.

Like the Stanford-Binet, the Wechsler tests yield a final intelligence score. But they have separate *verbal* (vocabulary, comprehension, knowledge of general information) and *performance* scores (arranging pictures to tell a story, arranging blocks to match a given pattern). Wechsler's approach has three advantages: (1) The WAIS, WISC, and WPPSI were specifically designed for different age groups. (2) Different abilities can be evaluated either separately or together. (3) People who are unable to speak or understand English can still be tested. The verbal portion of the test doesn't have to be administered because each subtest yields its own score.

Scientific Standards for Psychological Tests

What makes a good test? How are the tests developed by Binet and Wechsler any better than those published in popular magazines and presented on television? To be scientifically acceptable, all psychological tests must fulfill three basic requirements:

- **Standardization** Intelligence tests (as well as personality, aptitude, and most other tests) must exhibit **standardization** in two senses (Hogan, 2006). First, every test must have *norms*, or average scores, developed by giving the test to a representative sample of people (a diverse group of people who resemble those for whom the test is intended). Second, testing procedures must be uniform. All test takers must be given the same instructions, questions, and time limits, and all test administrators must follow the same objective score standards.

- **Reliability** To be trustworthy, test scores must be consistent and reproducible. **Reliability** is usually determined by retesting subjects to see whether their test scores change significantly (Hogan, 2006). Retesting can be done via the *test-retest method*, in which participants' scores on two separate administrations of the same test are compared, or via the *split-half method*, which involves splitting a test into two equivalent parts (e.g., odd and even questions) and determining the degree of similarity between the two halves.

- **Validity** **Validity** is the ability of a test to measure what it is designed to measure. The most important type of validity is *criterion-related validity*, or the accuracy with which test scores can be used to predict another variable of interest (known as the criterion). Criterion-related validity is expressed as the *correlation* (Chapter 1) between the test score and the criterion. If two variables are highly correlated, then one variable can be used to predict the other. Thus, if a test is valid, its scores will be useful in predicting people's behavior in some other specified situation. One example of this is using intelligence test scores to predict grades in college.

Can you see why a test that is standardized and reliable but not valid is worthless? For example, a test for skin sensitivity may be easy to standardize (the instructions specify exactly how to apply the test agent), and it may be reliable (similar results are obtained on each retest). But it certainly would not be valid for predicting college grades.

Achievement

Objective 8.18: *What are the three key requirements for a scientifically useful test?*

Standardization *Establishment of the norms and uniform procedures for giving and scoring a test*

Reliability *Measure of the consistency and reproducibility of test scores when the test is readministered*

Validity *Ability of a test to measure what it was designed to measure*

Assessment STOP

CHECK & REVIEW

How Do We Measure Intelligence?

Objective 8.17: *Describe how psychologists measure intelligence.*

Although there are many tests for intelligence, the Stanford-Binet and Wechsler are the most widely used. Both tests compute an *intelligence quotient (IQ)* by comparing a person's test score to the norm for that person's age group.

Objective 8.18: *What are the three key requirements for a scientifically useful test?*

For any test to be useful, it must be standardized, reliable, and valid. **Standardization** refers to (a) giving a test to a large number of people in order to determine norms and (b) using identical procedures in administering a test so that everyone takes the test under exactly the same testing conditions. **Reliability** refers to the stability and reproducibility of test scores over time. **Validity** refers to how well the test measures what it is intended to measure.

Questions

1. What is the major difference between the Stanford-Binet and the Wechsler Intelligence Scales?

2. If a 10-year-old's score on an original version of the Stanford-Binet test was the same as that of an average 9-year-old, the child would have an IQ of _____.

3. The IQ test sample in the figure to the right is from the _____, the most widely used intelligence test.
   a. Wechsler Intelligence Scale for Children
   b. Wechsler Adult Intelligence Scale
   c. Stanford-Binet Intelligence Scale
   d. Binet-Terman Intelligence Scale

Picture Completion
What is missing from this ambulance?

Coding
Write the appropriate number above each symbol.

1	2	3	4	5

Picture Arrangement
Arrange these pictures in chronological order.

Block Design
Copy this design with blocks.

Object Assembly
Assemble this small jigsaw puzzle.

4. Identify which testing principle—standardization, reliability, or validity—is being described in each of the following statements:
   a. _____ ensures that if a person takes the same test two weeks after taking it the first time, his or her score will not significantly change.
   b. _____ ensures that a test or other measurement instrument actually measures what it purports to measure.
   c. _____ ensures that the test has been given to large numbers of people to determine which scores are average, above average, and below average—in short, which scores are representative of the general population.

Check your answers in Appendix B.

Click & Review
for additional assessment options:
wiley.com/college/huffman

The Intelligence Controversy

As noted earlier, intelligence is extremely difficult to define. Psychologists also differ on whether it is composed of a single factor (*g*) or multiple abilities. Therefore, how valid is it to develop tests that measure intelligence? Furthermore, is intelligence inherited, or is it a result of environment? Are IQ tests culturally biased against certain ethnic groups? Intelligence testing has long been the subject of intense interest and great debate. In this section, we explore the use of intelligence tests for measuring extremes in intelligence (mental retardation and giftedness). Then we examine three possible explanations for overall differences in intelligence (the brain, genetics, and the environment). We close with a look at *supposed* ethnic differences in intelligence.

Extremes in Intelligence: Mental Retardation and Giftedness

If you want to judge the validity of any test (academic, intelligence, personality, etc.), one of the best methods is to compare people who score at the extremes. Students who get an A on a major exam should clearly know more than those who fail. As you will see, the validity of IQ tests is somewhat supported by the fact that individuals who score at the lowest level on standard IQ tests *do* have clear differences in intellectual abilities compared to those who score at the top. Intelligence tests provide one of the major criteria for diagnosing *mental retardation* and *giftedness*.

Achievement

Objective 8.19: *How do studies of extremes in intelligence help validate intelligence tests?*

Mental Retardation

According to clinical standards, the label *mentally retarded* is applied when someone is significantly below average in general intellectual functioning (IQ less than 70) and has significant deficits in adaptive functioning (such as communicating with others, living independently, social or occupational functioning, and maintaining safety and health) (American Psychiatric Association, 2000). Mental retardation (like most aspects of human behavior) is on a continuum that ranges from mildly to severely retarded.

As you can see in Table 8.7, only 1 to 3 percent of people are classified as having mental retardation. Of this group, 85 percent have only mild retardation and many

TABLE 8.7 DEGREES OF MENTAL RETARDATION

Level of Retardation	IQ Scores	Characteristics
Mild (85%)	50–70	Usually able to become self-sufficient: may marry, have families, and secure full-time jobs in unskilled occupations
Moderate (10%)	35–49	Able to perform simple unskilled tasks; may contribute to a certain extent to their livelihood
Severe (3–4%)	20–34	Able to follow daily routines, but with continual supervision; with training, may learn basic communication skills
Profound (1–2%)	below 20	Able to perform only the most rudimentary behaviors, such as walking, feeding themselves, and saying a few phrases

General Population

Mental Retardation 1–3%

85% Mild

1–2% Profound 3–4% Severe 10% Moderate

become self-supporting, integrated members of society. It should be noted that people can score low on some measures of intelligence and still be average or even gifted in others. The most dramatic examples are people with **savant syndrome** (Figure 8.12).

Some forms of retardation stem from genetic abnormalities, such as Down syndrome, fragile-X syndrome, and phenylketonuria (PKU). Other causes are environmental, including prenatal exposure to alcohol and other drugs, extreme deprivation or neglect in early life, and brain damage from accidents. However, in many cases, there is no known cause of retardation.

Savant Syndrome *Condition in which a person with mental retardation exhibits exceptional skill or brilliance in some limited field*

Mental Giftedness

At the other end of the intelligence spectrum, we have people who are "gifted" and have especially high IQs (typically defined as 135 and above or being in the top 1 or 2 percent). Have you ever wondered what happens to people with such superior intellectual abilities?

In 1921, Lewis Terman used teacher recommendations and IQ tests to identify 1500 gifted children with IQs of 140 or higher. He then tracked their progress through adulthood. His study of these gifted children—affectionately nicknamed the "Termites"—destroyed many myths and stereo-types about gifted people. As children, these Termites not only received excellent grades but were also found to be socially well adjusted. In

Timothy Fadek/©Polaris Images

Figure 8.12 *An unusual form of intelligence* Although people with *savant syndrome* score very low on IQ tests (usually between 40 and 70), they demonstrate exceptional skills or brilliance in specific areas, such as rapid calculation, art, memory, or musical ability (Bor et al., 2007; Iavarone, 2007; Miller, 2005; Pring et al., 2008). Seventeen-year-old Brittany Maier, who has autism and severe visual impairment, is a gifted composer and pianist who performs publicly and has recorded a CD. Her musical repertoire includes more than 15,000 songs.

addition, they were taller and stronger than their peers of average IQ. By the age of 40, the number of individuals who became research scientists, engineers, physicians, lawyers, or college teachers, or who were highly successful in business and other fields, was many times the number a random group would have provided (Leslie, 2000; Terman, 1954).

Although Terman's research found high intelligence to be correlated with higher academic and occupational success, as well as with better athletic ability, not every Termite was successful. There were some notable failures. The members who were the most successful tended to have extraordinary motivation and someone at home or school who was especially encouraging. However, many in this gifted group were like others their age of average intelligence. They became alcoholics, got divorced, and committed suicide at close to the national rate (Leslie, 2000). A high IQ is therefore no guarantee for success in every endeavor. It only offers more intellectual opportunities.

©The New Yorker Collection 1998 Roz Chast from cartoonbank.com. All Rights Reserved.

RESEARCH HIGHLIGHT

Explaining Differences in IQ

Objective 8.20: *Describe how research on the brain, genetics, and the environment helps explain differences in IQ.*

Some people are mentally gifted, some are mentally retarded, and most are somewhere in between. To explain these differences, we need to look at the brain, genetics, and the environment.

The Brain's Influence on Intelligence

A basic tenet of neuroscience is that all mental activity (including intelligence) results from neural activity in the brain. Three major questions have guided neuroscience research on intelligence:

1. **Does a bigger brain mean greater intelligence?** It makes logical sense. After all, humans have relatively large brains. And, as a species, we are more intelligent than dogs, which have smaller brains. Some nonhuman animals, such as whales and dolphins, do have larger brains than humans. But the brains of humans are larger in relation to the size of their bodies. Since the early 1800s, researchers have asked whether "bigger is better," and modern studies using magnetic resonance imaging (MRI) have found a significant correlation between brain size (adjusted for body size) and intelligence (Christensen et al., 2008; Deary et al., 2007; Lee,

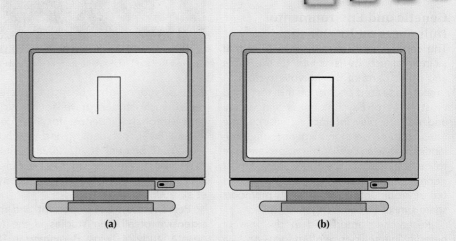

(a)   **(b)**

Figure 8.13 *A test for intelligence?* Which "leg" of the drawing in (a) is longer, the right or the left? Although the answer seems simple, researchers have found that when images like these are flashed for a few milliseconds on a computer screen, the amount of time people need to make correct judgments may reveal something about their intelligence. The second figure (b) appears immediately after figure (a) to block, or "mask," the lingering afterimage.

2007; Ivanovic et al., 2004; Stelmack, Knott, & Beauchamp, 2003).

On the other hand, anatomical studies of Einstein's brain found that it was not heavier or larger than normal (Witelson, Kigar, & Harvey, 1999). Some areas were, in fact, smaller than average. However, the area of the brain responsible for processing mathematical and spatial information (the lower region of the parietal lobe) was 15 percent larger. Also, we cannot know if Einstein was born with this difference, or if his brain changed due to his intellectual pursuits. Rather than focusing on brain size, therefore,

most of the recent research on the biology of intelligence has focused on brain functioning.

2. **Is a faster brain more intelligent?** The public seems to think so, and neuroscientists have found that a faster response time is indeed related to higher intelligence (e.g., Sheppard & Vernon, 2008). A standard experiment flashes simple images like the one in Figure 8.13, and participants must inspect them quickly and make an accurate decision. As simple as it may seem, those participants who respond most quickly also tend to score highest on intelligence tests.

3. **Does a smart brain work harder?** As you read in Chapter 1, PET scans measure brain activity by recording the amount of radioactive glucose used in different parts of the brain. (A more active area of the brain uses more glucose than a less active area.) Surprisingly, as can be seen in Figure 8.14, researchers have found that areas of the brain involved in problem solving show *less* activity in people of high intelligence than in people of lower intelligence when they are given the same problem-solving tasks (Jung & Haier, 2007; Neubauer et al., 2004; Posthuma et al., 2001). Apparently, intelligent brains work smarter, or more efficiently, than less intelligent brains.

Genetic and Environmental Influences on Intelligence

The central tenet of neuroscience is that all mental activity is linked to the brain and other parts of the nervous system. A similar, repeated theme of this text (and most areas of psychology) is that nature and nurture play interacting, *inseparable* roles. In the case of intelligence, any similarities between family members are due to *heredity* (family members share similar genetic material) combined with *inseparable environmental* factors (family members share similar living arrangements).

Researchers interested in the role of heredity in intelligence often focus on *twin studies*. Recall from Chapter 2 that one of the most popular ways to study the relative effects of genetics versus the environment

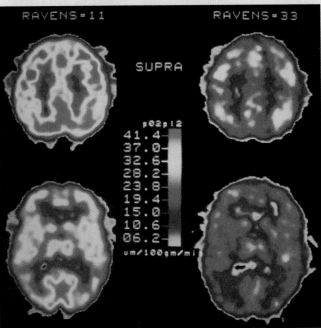

Courtesy Richard J. Haier, University of California-Irvine

Figure 8.14 *Do intelligent brains work harder?* The PET scans in the left column are from a person with a tested low IQ. The scans on the right are from someone with a high IQ. Note that when solving problems, the brain on the left is more active. (Red and yellow indicate more brain activity.) Contrary to popular opinion, this research suggests that lower-IQ brains actually work harder, but less efficiently, than higher IQ brains.

is to use monozygotic (identical, one-egg) twins. Such studies have found significant hereditary influences for intelligence (Figure 8.15), personality, and psychopathology (Blonigen et al., 2008; Johnson et al., 2007; Plomin, DeFries, & Fulkner, 2007; Sternberg, 2008, 2009; van Leeuwen et al., 2008).

Perhaps the most important and most extensive of all twin studies is the Minnesota Study of Twins. Beginning in 1979 and continuing for more than two decades, researchers from the University of Minnesota have been studying identi-

cal twins who grew up in different homes (Bouchard, 1994, 1999; Bouchard et al., 1998; Johnson et al., 2007). Each of these "reared-apart" twins was separated from his or her sibling and adopted by a different family early in life. They were reunited only as adults. Because each twin has identical genetic material but was raised in a different family, researchers have a unique natural experiment that can be used to distinguish the effects of genetics from the effects of the environment. When the IQ data were collected and the statistics computed, researchers found that

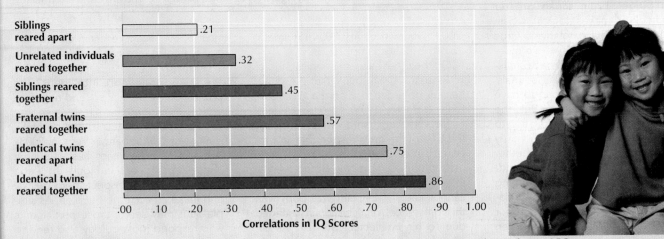

Figure 8.15 *Genetic and environmental influences* Note the higher correlations between identical twins' IQ test scores compared to correlations between all other pairs. Genes no doubt play a significant role in intelligence, but these effects are difficult to separate from environmental influences. (Based on Bouchard & McGue, 1981; Bouchard et al., 1998; McGue et al., 1993.)

genetic factors appear to play a surprisingly large role in the IQ score of monozygotic (identical) twins reared apart.

How would you critique these findings? First, adoption agencies tend to look for similar criteria in their choice of adoptive parents. Therefore, the homes of these reared-apart twins could have been quite similar. In addition, these twins also shared the same nine-month prenatal environment, which might have influenced their brain development and intelligence. Furthermore, some of the separated twins in this study had been together for many months before their adoption, and some had been reunited (for months and even years) before testing.

What about the famous reunited "Jim twins" who had the same name and almost the same personality? This is one of the most widely publicized cases of the entire Minnesota study. These two children were separated 37 days after their birth and reared with no contact until 38 years later. Despite this lifelong separation, James Lewis and James Springer both had divorced and remarried women named Betty, had undergone police training, loved carpentry, vacationed at the same beach each summer, and had named their firstborn sons James Allan and James Alan (Holden, 1980). This is only a short list of their incredible similarities.

Heredity undoubtedly plays an important role, but can you think of other explanations? One study of *unrelated* pairs of students of the same age and gender also found a striking number of similarities. People of the same age apparently share a common historical time that influences large aspects of their personality. In addition, do you recall our earlier discussion of the *confirmation bias* (the tendency to seek out and pay attention to information that confirms our existing positions or beliefs, while ignoring contradictory data)? Imagine suddenly finding your long-lost identical twin. Wouldn't you be highly excited and thrilled with all your similarities and disinclined to note the differences?

As you can see, the research is inconclusive. Although heredity equips each of us with innate intellectual capacities, the environment significantly influences whether a person will reach his or her full intellectual potential. For example, early malnutrition can cause retarded brain development, which in turn affects the child's curiosity, responsiveness to the environment, and motivation for learning—all of which can lower the child's IQ. We are reminded once again that nature and nurture are inseparable.

Identical twins reared apart Jerry Levy and Mark Newman, twins separated at birth, first met each other as adults at a firefighters' annual convention.

T.K. Wanstal/The Image Works

✳ Achievement
GENDER & CULTURAL DIVERSITY

Achievement

Objective 8.21: *How do psychologists answer the question, "Are IQ tests culturally biased"?*

Are IQ Tests Culturally Biased?

How would you answer the following questions?

1. A symphony is to a composer as a book is to a(n) _____. (a) musician; (b) editor; (c) novel; (d) author

2. If you throw dice and they land with a 7 on top, what is on the bottom? (a) snake eyes; (b) box cars; (c) little Joes; (d) eleven

Can you see how the content and answers to these questions might reflect *cultural bias*? People from some backgrounds will find the first question easier. Other groups will more easily answer the second. Which of these two questions do you think is most likely to appear on standard IQ tests?

One of the most hotly debated and controversial issues in psychology involves group differences in intelligence test scores and what they really mean. In 1969, Arthur Jensen began a heated debate when he argued that genetic factors are "strongly implicated" as the cause of ethnic differences in intelligence. A book by Richard J. Herrnstein and Charles Murray titled *The Bell Curve: Intelligence and Class Structure in American Life* reignited this debate in 1994 when the authors claimed that African Americans score below average in IQ because of their "genetic heritage."

© 2004 by Sidney Harris.

"YOU CAN'T BUILD A HUT, YOU DON'T KNOW HOW TO FIND EDIBLE ROOTS AND YOU KNOW NOTHING ABOUT PREDICTING THE WEATHER. IN OTHER WORDS, YOU DO TERRIBLY ON OUR I.Q. TEST."

Psychologists have responded to these inflammatory claims with several points:

- **IQ tests may be culturally biased, making them an inaccurate measure of true capability.** African Americans and other minorities are often unfairly disadvantaged because they are underrepresented in standardization samples and IQ test items often are loaded toward white, middle-class culture, and minorities are underrepresented in standardization samples. Minorities are also overrepresented in lower-paying jobs, which limit access to better schools and avenues for academic success. Moreover, traditional IQ tests do not measure many of our multiple intelligences (Gardner, 2002; Manly et al., 2004; Naglieri & Ronning, 2000; Rutter, 2007; Sternberg, 2007, 2009; Sternberg & Grigorenko, 2008).

- **Race, like intelligence itself, is almost impossible to define.** Depending on the definition that you use, there are between 3 and 300 races, and scientists have discovered that no single gene, trait, or characteristic distinguishes one "race" from another. Famous people of mixed race, like Senator Barack Obama, Tiger Woods, and Mariah Carey, demonstrate the limits of these outdated categories. In short, the concept of race has no meaning. It is *a social construct* (Navarro, 2008; Sternberg & Grigorenko, 2008; Yee et al., 1993).

- **Intelligence (as measured by IQ tests) is not a fixed trait.** Around the world, IQ scores have increased over the last half century, and this well-established phenomenon is known as the *Flynn effect* in honor of New Zealand researcher James Flynn. Because these increases have occurred in a relatively short period of time, the cause or causes can not be due to genetics or heredity. Other possible factors include improved nutrition, better public education, more proficient test-taking skills, and rising levels of education for a greater percentage of the world's population (Flynn, 1987, 2006, 2007; Huang & Hauser, 1998; Mingroni, 2004; Resing & Nijland, 2002). Further evidence for the lack of stability in IQ scores comes from even more recent international research. In the last decade this rise in scores has reversed itself, and several countries are now reporting a *decline* in IQ scores (Lynn & Harvey, 2008; Teasdale & Owen, 2008). Possible causes for this so-called *negative Flynn effect* are poorly understood. But whether IQ scores rise or fall, the important point is that *intelligence is not a fixed trait*.

- **Environmental factors play a significant role in IQ scores.** Minority children more often grow up in lower socioeconomic conditions with inadequate schools, fewer academic role models, lack of funds and resources, and less parental and community support. In some ethnic groups, a child who excels in school is ridiculed for trying to be different from his or her classmates. Moreover, if children's own language and dialect do not match their education system or the IQ tests they take, they are obviously at a disadvantage (Cathers-Shiffman & Thompson, 2007; Rutter, 2007; Sternberg, 2007; Sternberg & Grigorenko, 2008). No matter what the cause, the findings suggest that the environment is a significant contributor to group differences in intelligence (Figure 8.16).

- **Different groups' distribution of IQ scores overlap considerably.** IQ scores and intelligence have their greatest relevance in terms of individuals, not groups; many individual African Americans receive higher IQ scores than many individual white Americans (Garcia & Stafford, 2000; Myerson et al., 1998; Reifman, 2000).

- **Stereotype threat** can significantly reduce the test scores of people in stereotyped groups (Bates, 2007; Keller & Bless, 2008; Steele, 2003) (Concept Diagram 8.1).

The ongoing debate over the nature of intelligence and its measurement highlights the complexities of studying *cognition*. In this chapter, we've explored three cognitive processes: *thinking, language,* and *intelligence*. As you've seen, all three processes are greatly affected by numerous interacting factors.

Differences <u>within</u> groups are due almost entirely to genetics (the seed).

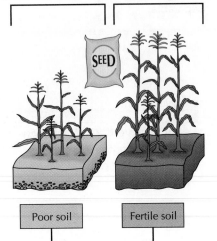

SEED

Poor soil   Fertile soil

Differences <u>between</u> groups are due almost <u>entirely</u> to environment (the soil).

Figure 8.16 *If plants could talk!* Note that even when you begin with the exact same package of seeds (genetic inheritance), the average height of corn plants in the fertile soil will be greater than those in the poor soil (environmental influences). The same may be true for intelligence. Therefore, no conclusions can be drawn about possible genetic contributions to the differences between groups.

Concept Diagram 8.1
Stereotype Threat

In the first study of **stereotype threat**, Claude Steele and Joshua Aronson (1995) recruited African American and white Stanford University students (with similar ability levels) to complete a "performance exam" that supposedly measured intellectual abilities. The exam's questions were similar to those on the Graduate Record Exam (GRE). Results showed that African American students performed far below white students. In contrast, when the researchers told students it was a "laboratory task," there was no difference between African American and white scores.

Subsequent work showed that stereotype threat occurs because members of stereotyped groups begin to doubt themselves and fear they will fulfill their group's negative stereotype. This anxiety in turn hinders their performance on tests. Some people cope with stereotype threat by *disidentifying*, telling themselves they don't care about the test scores (Major et al., 1998). Unfortunately, this attitude lessens motivation, decreasing performance.

Erick Dreyer/Stone Getty Images

Stereotype threat affects many social groups, including African Americans, women, Native Americans, Latinos, low-income people, elderly people, and white male athletes (e.g., Bates, 2007; Ford et al., 2004; Keller & Bless, 2008; Klein et al., 2007; Steele, 2003; Steele, James, & Barnett, 2002). This research helps explain some group differences in intelligence and achievement tests. As such, it underscores why relying solely on such tests to make critical decisions affecting individual lives—for example, in hiring, college admissions, or clinical application—is unwarranted and possibly even unethical.

Stereotype Threat *Negative stereotypes about minority groups cause some members to doubt their abilities*

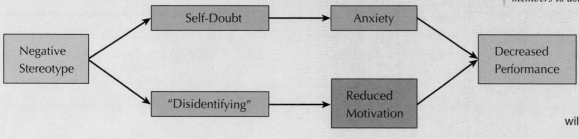

A Final Word

Think back to the questions we asked at the very beginning of our discussion of intelligence: Are Koko, Genie, and Thomas Edison intelligent? How would you answer these questions now? Hopefully, you now understand that all three cognitive processes discussed in this chapter (thinking, language, and intelligence) are complex phenomena, which are greatly affected by numerous interacting factors. As evidence, let's update our story of Genie. Her life, as you might have guessed, does not have a happy Hollywood ending. Genie's tale is a heartbreaking account of the lasting scars from a disastrous childhood. At the time of her rescue, at age 13, Genie's intellectual performance was at the level of a normal 1-year-old. Over the years, she was given thousands of hours of special training and rehabilitation, so that by the age of 19 she could use public transportation and was adapting well to her foster home and special classes at school (Rymer, 1993).

Genie was far from normal, however. Her intelligence scores were still close to the cutoff for mental retardation. And, as noted earlier, her language skills were similar to those of a 2- or 3-year-old. To make matters worse, she was also subjected to a series of foster home placements—one of which was abusive. At last report, Genie was living in a home for mentally retarded adults (Rymer, 1993; LaPointe, 2005).

Assessment

CHECK & REVIEW (STOP)

The Intelligence Controversy

Objective 8.19: *How do studies of extremes in intelligence help validate intelligence tests?*

Timothy Fadek/©Polaris Images

Intelligence testing has long been the subject of great debate. To determine whether these tests are valid, you can examine people who fall at the extremes of intelligence. People with IQs of 70 and below (classified as mentally retarded) and those with IQs of 135 and above (identified as gifted) do differ in their respective intellectual abilities.

Objective 8.20: *Describe how research on the brain, genetics, and the environment helps explain differences in IQ.*

Research on the brain's role in intelligence has focused on three major questions:

(1) Does a bigger brain mean greater intelligence? (Answer: "Not necessarily.") (2) Is a faster brain more intelligent? (Answer: "A qualified yes.") And (3) Does a smart brain work harder? (Answer: "No, the smarter brain is more efficient.")

Another topic of debate is whether intelligence is inherited or due to the environment. According to the Minnesota Study of Twins Reared Apart (1979 to present), heredity and environment are important, inseparable factors in intellectual development. Heredity equips each of us with innate capacities. The environment significantly influences whether an individual will reach full potential.

Objective 8.21: *How do psychologists answer the question, "Are IQ tests culturally biased"?*

Perhaps the most hotly debated topic is whether ethnic differences on IQ tests are primarily "genetic in origin." Research has shown IQ tests may be culturally biased. And environmental factors, including the *Flynn effect*, cultural exposure, socioeconomic differences, language, and **stereotype threat**, have all been found to be contributing factors in score differences.

Questions

1. People with _____ are often categorized as mentally retarded, but they also possess incredible abilities in specific areas, such as musical memory or math calculations. (a) IQ scores below 70; (b) phenylketonuria (PKU); (c) fragile-X syndrome; (d) savant syndrome
2. A longitudinal study of the "Termites" found that high intelligence is correlated with _____. (a) higher academic success; (b) better athletic ability; (c) higher occupational achievement; (d) all of the above
3. The more efficient brain uses fewer _____ to solve problems than a less efficient brain. (a) parts of the brain; (b) neurotransmitters; (c) synapses; (d) energy resources
4. Which is more important in determining intelligence—heredity or environment?

Check your answers in Appendix B.

Click & Review
for additional assessment options:
wiley.com/college/huffman

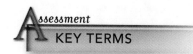

Assessment
KEY TERMS

*To assess your understanding of the **Key Terms** in Chapter 8, write a definition for each (in your own words), and then compare your definitions with those in the text.*

cognition (p. 278)

Thinking
algorithm (p. 284)
availability heuristic (p. 287)
concept (p. 281)
confirmation bias (p. 286)
convergent thinking (p. 289)
creativity (p. 288)
divergent thinking (p. 289)
functional fixedness (p. 286)
heuristics (p. 284)
mental image (p. 281)
mental set (p. 286)
prototype (p. 282)
representativeness heuristic (p. 287)

Language
babbling (p. 294)
cooing (p. 294)
grammar (p. 292)
language (p. 291)
language acquisition device
    (LAD) (p. 293)
morpheme [MOR-feem] (p. 292)
overextension (p. 294)
overgeneralize (p. 294)
phoneme [FOE-neem] (p. 292)
semantics (p. 292)
syntax (p. 292)
telegraphic speech (p. 294)

Intelligence
crystallized intelligence (p. 298)
fluid intelligence (p. 298)
intelligence (p. 297)
reliability (p. 302)
standardization (p. 302)
validity (p. 302)

The Intelligence Controversy
savant syndrome (p. 304)
stereotype threat (p. 308)

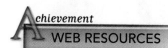

Achievement
WEB RESOURCES

Huffman Book Companion Site
wiley.com/college/huffman

> This site is loaded with free Interactive Self-Tests, Internet Exercises, Glossary and Flashcards for key terms, web links, Handbook for Non-Native Speakers, and other activities designed to improve your mastery of the material in this chapter.

Chapter 8 Visual Summary

Cognitive Building Blocks

1. **Mental image:** Mind's representation of a sensory experience.

2. **Concepts:** Mental categories that are grouped according to shared characteristics. Concepts arise out of logical rules and definitions (artificial concepts), natural concepts (**prototypes**), and when we organize them into successive ranks (hierarchies).

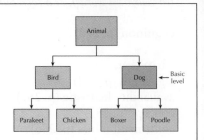

Problem Solving

| *Step: 1. Preparation*
 • Identify given facts
 • Separate relevant facts
 • Define ultimate goal | *Step 2: Production*
 Create hypotheses using **algorithms** and **heuristics** | *Step 3: Evaluation*
 Judge the hypotheses from Step 2 against criteria from Step 1 |

Barriers to problem solving: **Mental sets, functional fixedness, confirmation bias, availability heuristic,** and **representativeness heuristic**.

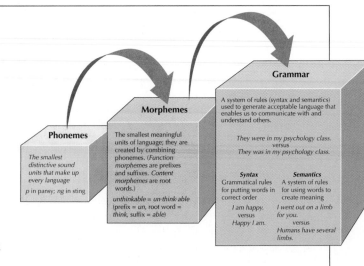

Creativity (*ability to produce valued outcomes in a novel way*)

• *Elements of creativity:* Originality, fluency, and flexibility.
• *Measuring creativity:* **Divergent thinking** versus **convergent thinking**.
• *Researching creativity:* Investment theory (buying low and selling high) says creativity is a combination of intellectual ability, knowledge, thinking style, personality, motivation, and environment.

Characteristics of Language

Language is produced from words using **phonemes** (smallest distinctive sound units) and **morphemes** (the smallest meaningful units of language). The words are strung together into sentences using rules of **grammar**, which include **syntax** (the grammatical rules for ordering words) and **semantics** (rules for deriving meaning in language).

Language Development

Stages

• *Prelinguistic:* Crying → **cooing** (vowel sounds) → **babbling** (vowel/consonant combinations).
• *Linguistic:* One-word utterances → **telegraphic** speech (omits unnecessary connecting words) → grammatical speech.
• *Problems:* **Overextension** (e.g., "bunnies" called "dogs") and **overgeneralization** (e.g., "foots," "goed").

David Young-Wolff/PhotoEdit

Theories

• *Nature:* Language results from maturation. Chomsky's innate **language acquisition device** (LAD).
• *Nurture:* Environment and rewards or punishments explain language acquisition.

Intelligence

What is Intelligence? (*Global capacity to think rationally, act purposefully, and deal effectively with the environment.*)

Competing theories and definitions.
- Spearman→Intelligence is "g," a single factor.
- Thurstone→Intelligence is seven distinct mental abilities.
- Guilford→Intelligence is composed of 120 or more separate abilities.
- Cattell→Intelligence is two types of "g" (**fluid intelligence** and **crystallized intelligence**).
- Gardner→Eight or possibly nine types of intelligence.
- Sternberg→Triarchic theory of intelligence (analytical, creative, and practical).

How Do We Measure Intelligence?

Intelligence quotient (IQ) tests are widely used in our culture.
- *Stanford-Binet* measures IQ with this formula: $IQ = (MA/CA) \times 100$.
- *Wechsler* provides an overall IQ, as well as verbal and performance IQs.

Elements of a useful test:
1. **Standardization**: Test is given to a representative sample to establish norms, and uniform administration procedures are used.
2. **Reliability:** Scores are consistent and reproducible over time.
3. **Validity:** Test measures what it is designed to measure.

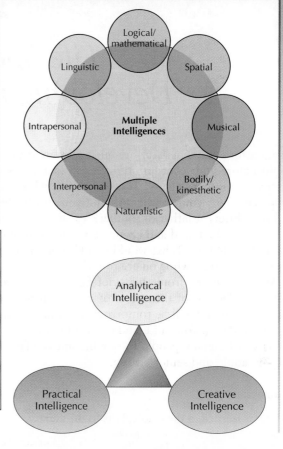

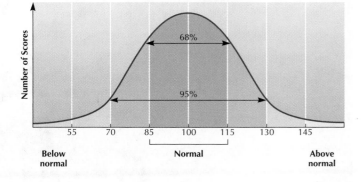

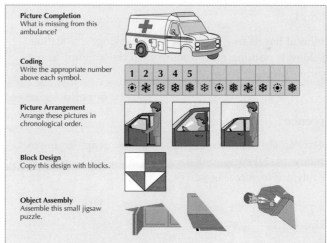

The Intelligence Controversy

Extremes and Differences in Intelligence

- Individuals with IQs of 70 and below are identified as mentally retarded. Individuals with IQs of 135 and above are identified as gifted
- Neuroscientists ask: 1) Does a bigger brain mean greater intelligence? Not necessarily. 2) Is a faster brain more intelligent? A qualified yes. 3) Does a smart brain work harder? No, the smarter brain is more efficient.
- The Minnesota Study of Twins Reared Apart found heredity and environment are important, inseparable factors in intellectual development.
- Are IQ test culturally biased? A qualified yes.

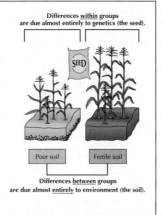

Differences **within** groups are due almost entirely to genetics (the seed).

Differences **between** groups are due almost **entirely** to environment (the soil).

9

Life Span Development I

Imagine for a moment that you could go back to the moment right before your conception—when your father's sperm met your mother's egg—and could change who would be your father or your mother. Would you still be "you" if you had a different father or mother? What if you could go back to your childhood and change your hometown or add or subtract siblings? What would you change? How might such changes affect who you are today?

As you can see from this brief fantasy, what you are now is a reflection of thousands of contributors from the past, and what you will be tomorrow is still unwritten. Life doesn't stand still. You and I (and every other human on this planet) will be many people in our lifetime—infant, child, teenager, adult, and senior citizen.

Infancy...

What is learned in the cradle, lasts to the grave.

FRENCH PROVERB

Childhood...

Childhood has its own way of seeing, thinking, and feeling. And there is nothing more foolish than the attempt to put ours in its place.

JEAN-JACQUES ROUSSEAU

Adolescence...

Adolescents are not monsters. They are just people trying to learn how to make it among the adults in the world, who are probably not so sure themselves.

VIRGINIA SATIR

Parenthood...

At last I feel the equal of my parents. Knowing you are going to have a child is like extending yourself in the world, setting up a tent and saying "Here I am, I am important." Now that I'm going to have a child it's like the balance is even. My hand is as rich as theirs, maybe for the first time. I am no longer just a child.

ANONYMOUS FATHER

There are only two lasting bequests we can hope to give our children. One of these is roots; the other wings.

HODDING CARTER

Blue Jean Images/Getty Images

▶ **Studying Development**

Theoretical Issues
Research Methods

✳ GENDER & CULTURAL DIVERSITY
   Cultural Psychology's Guidelines for
   Developmental Research

▶ **Physical Development**

Prenatal Period and Early Childhood
Adolescence and Adulthood

▶ **Cognitive Development**

Stages of Cognitive Development
Assessing Piaget's Theory
Information Processing

▶ **Social-Emotional Development**

Attachment
Parenting Styles

RESEARCH HIGHLIGHT
   Romantic Love and Attachment

CRITICAL THINKING/ACTIVE LEARNING
   The Development of "Suicide Bombers"

Application

WHY STUDY PSYCHOLOGY?

Did you know that...

▶ At the moment of conception, you were smaller than the period at the end of a sentence?

▶ During the last few months of pregnancy, you (as a fetus) could hear sounds outside your mother's womb?

▶ At birth, your head was approximately one-fourth of your total body size, but as an adult it's only one-eighth?

Davis Barber/Photoedit

▶ Within the first few days of life, breast-fed newborns can recognize and show preference for the odor and taste of their mother's milk over another mother's?

▶ Children in many cultures sleep alongside their parents for several years—not in a separate bed or room?

▶ According to Piaget, teenagers tend to believe they are alone and unique in their thoughts and feelings—"no one has ever felt like this before"?

Achievement

Objective 9.1: *Define developmental psychology.*

Developmental Psychology
Study of age-related changes in behavior and mental processes from conception to death

Would you like to know more about yourself at each of these stages? There is an entire field of knowledge, called **developmental psychology**, which *studies age-related changes in behavior and mental processes from conception to death* (Table 9.1). To emphasize that development is an ongoing, lifelong *process*, throughout this chapter we will take a *topical* approach (as opposed to a *chronological* approach, which arbitrarily divides the field into two periods—childhood–adolescence and adulthood). Thus, in this chapter, we will trace physical, cognitive, and social-emotional development—one at a time—from conception to death. Then, in Chapter 10, we will explore moral development, personality development, and special issues related to grief and death—again, one topic at a time. This topical approach will allow us to see how development affects an individual over the entire life span. Keep in mind that each of these topics is intricately interwoven (Figure 9.1).

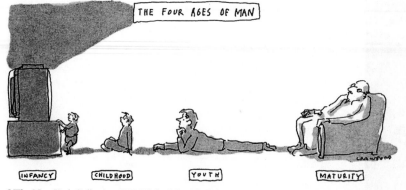

©The New York Collection 1991 Michael Crawford from cartoonbank.com. All Rights Reserved.

TABLE 9.1 LIFE SPAN DEVELOPMENT

Stage	Approximate Age
Prenatal	Conception to birth
Infancy	Birth to 18 months
Early childhood	18 months to 6 years
Middle childhood	6–12 years
Adolescence	12–20 years
Young adulthood	20–45 years
Middle adulthood	45–60 years
Later adulthood	60 years to death

Studying Development

In this section, we first explore three theoretical issues in developmental psychology, and then we'll examine how developmental psychologists conduct their research.

Theoretical Issues: Ongoing Debates

In all fields of psychology, certain theoretical issues guide the basic direction of research. The three most important debates or questions in human development are:

1. **Nature versus nurture.** The issue of *nature versus nurture* has been with us since the beginning of psychology. Even the ancient Greeks had the same debate—Plato argued that humans are born with innate knowledge and abilities, whereas Aristotle held that learning occurs through the five senses. Some early philosophers also proposed that at birth our minds are a *tabula rasa* (or blank slate) and that the environment determines what messages are written on the slate.

   According to the modern *nature position*, human behavior and development are governed by automatic, genetically predetermined signals in a process known as **maturation**. Just as a flower unfolds in accord with its genetic blueprint, we humans crawl before we walk and walk before we run. Furthermore, there is an optimal period shortly after birth, one of several **critical periods** during our lifetime, when we are particularly sensitive to certain experiences that shape the capacity for future development.

   On the other side of the debate, those who hold an extreme *nurturist position* would argue that development occurs by learning through personal experience and observation of others.

2. **Continuity versus stages.** Continuity theorists maintain that development is *continuous*, with new abilities, skills, and knowledge gradually added at a relatively uniform pace. Therefore, adult thinking and intelligence differ quantitatively from a child's. Stage theorists, on the other hand, believe development occurs at different rates, alternating between periods of little change and periods of abrupt, rapid change. In this chapter, we discuss stages in physical development and Piaget's stage theory of cognitive development. In Chapter 10, we discuss two other stage theories—Erikson's psychosocial theory of personality development and Kohlberg's theory of moral development.

3. **Stability versus change.** Have you generally maintained your personal characteristics as you matured from infant to adult (stability)? Or does your current personality bear little resemblance to the personality you displayed during infancy (change)? Psychologists who emphasize stability in development believe measurements of personality taken during childhood are important predictors of adult personality. Of course, psychologists who emphasize change disagree.

   Which of these positions in the three debates are most correct? Most psychologists do not take a hard line either way. Rather, they prefer an *interactionist perspective*. In the age-old *nature-versus-nurture* debate, for example, psychologists generally agree that development emerges both from each individual's unique genetic predisposition *and* from their experiences in the environment (Hartwell, 2008; Hudziak, 2008; Rutter, 2007). More recently, the interactionist position has evolved into the *biopsychosocial model* mentioned throughout this text. In this model, *biological* factors (genetics, brain functions, biochemistry, and evolution), *psychological* influences (learning, thinking, emotion, personality, and motivation), and *social* forces (family, school, culture, ethnicity, social class, and politics) all affect and are affected by one another.

   We will return to this biopsychosocial model several times in this chapter. Now we turn our attention to another aspect of studying development—how developmental psychologists collect their information.

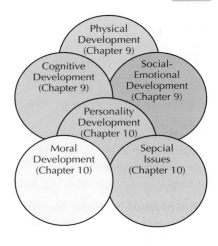

Figure 9.1 *Developmental changes result from numerous overlapping processes*

chievement

Objective 9.2: *Identify the three major issues in developmental psychology.*

Maturation *Development governed by automatic, genetically predetermined signals*

Critical Period *A period of special sensitivity to specific types of learning that shapes the capacity for future development*

Objective 9.3: *What are the two most common research methods in developmental psychology?*

Cross-Sectional Method *Measures individuals of various ages at one point in time and gives information about age differences*

Longitudinal Method *Measures a single individual or group of individuals over an extended period and gives information about age changes*

Research Methods: Two Basic Approaches

To study development, psychologists often use either a *cross-sectional* or *longitudinal* method. The **cross-sectional method** examines individuals of various ages (e.g., 20, 40, 60, and 80 years) at one point in time and gives information about *age differences*. The **longitudinal method** follows a single individual or group of same-aged individuals over an extended period and gives information about *age changes* (Figure 9.2).

Imagine you are a developmental psychologist interested in studying intelligence in adults. Which method would you choose—cross-sectional or longitudinal? Before you decide, note the different research results shown in Figure 9.3.

Why do the two methods show such different results? Researchers suggest that the different results may reflect a central problem with cross-sectional studies. These studies often confuse genuine age differences with *cohort effects*—differences that result from specific histories of the age group studied. As Figure 9.3 shows, the 81-year-olds measured by the cross-sectional method have dramatically lower scores than the 25-year-olds. But is this due to aging or possibly to broad environmental differences, such as less formal education or poorer nutrition? Because the different age groups, called *cohorts*, grew up in different historical periods, the results may not apply to people growing up at other times. With the cross-sectional method, age effects and cohort effects are hopelessly tangled.

Longitudinal studies also have their limits. They are expensive in terms of time and money, and their results are restricted in *generalizability*. Because participants often drop out or move away during the extended test period, the experimenter may end up with a self-selected sample that differs from the general population in important ways. Each method of research has its own strengths and weaknesses (Table 9.2). Keep these differences in mind when you read the findings of developmental research.

Before leaving the topic of research, let's examine the unique contributions cultural psychologists have made to the field of developmental psychology.

CROSS-SECTIONAL RESEARCH

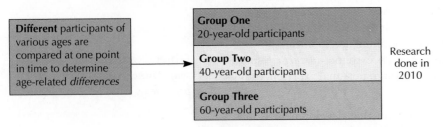

Different participants of various ages are compared at one point in time to determine age-related *differences*

Group One
20-year-old participants

Group Two
40-year-old participants

Group Three
60-year-old participants

Research done in 2010

LONGITUDINAL RESEARCH

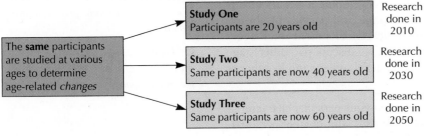

The **same** participants are studied at various ages to determine age-related *changes*

Study One
Participants are 20 years old

Research done in 2010

Study Two
Same participants are now 40 years old

Research done in 2030

Study Three
Same participants are now 60 years old

Research done in 2050

Figure 9.2 ***Cross-sectional versus longitudinal research*** Note that cross-sectional research uses different participants and is interested in age-related differences, whereas longitudinal research studies the same participants over time to find age-related changes.

TABLE 9.2 ADVANTAGES AND DISADVANTAGES OF CROSS-SECTIONAL AND LONGITUDINAL RESEARCH DESIGNS

	Cross-Sectional	**Longitudinal**
Advantages	Gives information about age differences	Gives information about age changes
	Quick	Increased reliability
	Less expensive	More in-depth information per participant
	Typically larger sample	
Disadvantages	Cohort effects are difficult to separate	More expensive
		Time consuming
	Restricted generalizability (measures behaviors at only one point in time)	Restricted generalizability (typically smaller sample and dropouts over time)

Assessment

VISUAL QUIZ

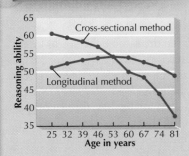

Figure 9.3 *Reasoning ability and cross-sectional versus longitudinal research*

Why do these two methods of research show such different results?

Answer: Cross-sectional studies show that reasoning and intelligence reach their peak in early adulthood and then gradually decline. But these results may reflect a problem with the research method, which is picking up on different educational experiences for the various age groups versus a true effect of aging. In contrast, longitudinal studies have found that a marked decline does not begin until about age 60 (Schaie, 1994). But these longitudinal studies have also been questioned because they generally begin with a smaller sample, and people often drop out along the way. This means that the final results may only apply to a small group of people. (Adapted from Schaie, 1994, with permission.)

Achievement

GENDER & CULTURAL DIVERSITY

Cultural Psychology's Guidelines for Developmental Research

How would you answer the following question: "If you wanted to predict how a human child anywhere in the world was going to grow up, what his or her behavior was going to be like as an adult, and you could have only one fact about that child, what fact would you choose to have?"

According to cultural psychologists like Patricia Greenfield (1994, 2004), the answer to this question should be "culture." Developmental psychology has traditionally studied people (children, adolescents, and adults) with little attention to the sociocultural context. In recent times, however, psychologists are paying increasing attention to the following points:

• ***Culture may be the most important determinant of development.*** If a child grows up in an individualistic/independent culture (such as North America or most of Western Europe), we can predict that this child will probably be competitive and question authority as an adult. Were this same child reared in a collectivist/interdependent

Achievement

Objective 9.4: *Describe cultural psychology's four guidelines for developmental research.*

Cultural influences on development *How might these two groups differ in their physical, social-emotional, cognitive, and personality development?*

culture (common in Africa, Asia, and Latin America), she or he would most likely grow up to be cooperative and respectful of elders (Delgado-Gaitan, 1994; Berry et al., 2002).

- *Human development, like most areas of psychology, cannot be studied outside its sociocultural context.* In parts of Korea, most teenagers see a strict, authoritarian style of parenting as a sign of love and concern (Kim & Choi, 1995). Korean American and Korean Canadian teenagers, however, see the same behavior as a sign of rejection. Thus, rather than studying specific behaviors, such as "authoritarian parenting styles," discussed later in this chapter, researchers in child development suggest that children should be studied only within their *developmental niche* (Singh, 2007; Sutherland & Harkness, 2007). A developmental niche has three components: the physical and social contexts in which the child lives, the culturally determined rearing and educational practices, and the psychological characteristics of the parents (Bugental & Johnston, 2000; Harkness et al., 2007).

- *Each culture's ethnotheories are important determinants of behavior.* Within every culture, people have a prevailing set of ideas and beliefs that attempt to explain the world around them (an *ethnotheory*) (Amorim & Rossetti-Ferreira, 2004; Tucker, 2007). In the area of child development, for example, cultures have specific ethnotheories about how children should be trained. As a critical thinker, you can anticipate that differing ethnotheories can lead to problems between cultures. In fact, even the very idea of "critical thinking" is part of our North American ethnotheory regarding education. And it, too, can produce culture clashes.

  Concha Delgado-Gaitan (1994) found that Mexican immigrants from a rural background have a difficult time adjusting to North American schools, which teach children to question authority and think for themselves. In their culture of origin, these children are trained to respect their elders, be good listeners, and participate in conversation only when their opinion is solicited. Children who argue with adults are reminded not to be *malcriados* (naughty or disrespectful).

- *Culture is largely invisible to its participants.* Culture consists of ideals, values, and assumptions that are widely shared among a given group and that guide specific behaviors (Matsumoto & Juang, 2008; Triandis, 2007). Precisely because these ideals and values are widely shared, they are seldom discussed or directly examined. Just as a "fish doesn't know it's in water," we take our culture for granted, operating within it, though being almost unaware of it.

Try This Yourself **Application**

Culture Invisibility

If you would like a personal demonstration of the invisibility of culture, try this simple experiment: The next time you walk into an elevator, don't turn around. Remain facing the rear wall. Watch how others respond when you don't turn around or stand right next to them rather than going to the other side of the elevator. Our North American culture has rules that prescribe the "proper" way to ride in an elevator, and people become very uncomfortable when these rules are violated.

Assessment

CHECK & REVIEW

Studying Development

Objective 9.1: *Define developmental psychology.*

Developmental psychology studies age-related changes in behavior and mental processes from conception to death.

Objective 9.2: *Identify the three major issues in developmental psychology.*

Three important research issues are *nature versus nurture*, *continuity versus stages*, and *stability versus change*.

Objective 9.3: *What are the two most common research methods in developmental psychology?*

Researchers in developmental psychology generally use **cross-sectional** (different participants of various ages at one point in time) or **longitudinal** (same participants over an extended period) **methods**. Each has advantages and disadvantages.

Objective 9.4: *Describe cultural psychology's four guidelines for developmental research.*

Cultural psychologists suggest that developmental researchers keep the following points in mind:

- Culture may be the most important determinant of development.
- Human development cannot be studied outside its sociocultural context.
- Each culture's ethnotheories are important determinants of behavior.
- Culture is largely invisible to its participants.

Questions

1. What three major questions are studied in developmental psychology?
2. Label the two basic types of research studies in the following figure:

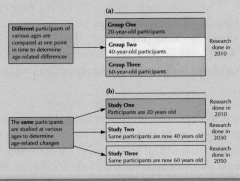

(a)_____

Different participants of various ages are compared at one point in time to determine age-related *differences*	Group One 20-year-old participants	Research done in 2010
	Group Two 40-year-old participants	
	Group Three 60-year-old participants	

(b)_____

The same participants are studied at various ages to determine age-related *changes*	Study One Participants are 20 years old	Research done in 2010
	Study Two Same participants are now 40 years old	Research done in 2030
	Study Three Same participants are now 60 years old	Research done in 2050

3. Differences in age groups that reflect factors unique to a specific age group are called _____ effects.
(a) generational; (b) social-environmental; (c) operational; (d) cohort

4. _____ studies are the most time-efficient method, whereas _____ studies provide the most in-depth information per participant.
(a) Correlational, experimental; (b) Fast-track, follow-up; (c) Cross-sectional, longitudinal; (d) Cohort-sequential, cohort-intensive

Check your answers in Appendix B.

Click & Review for additional assessment options: wiley.com/college/huffman

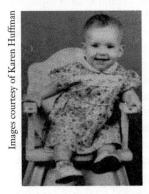

Images courtesy of Karen Huffman

Figure 9.4 *Changes in physical development* As these photos of this text's author at ages 1, 4, 10, 30, and 55 show, physical changes are the most obvious signs of aging and development. However, our cognitive, social, moral, and personality processes and traits also change across the life span.

Physical Development

After studying my photos in Figure 9.4, or looking at your own child and adult photos, you may be amused and surprised by the dramatic changes in physical appearance. But have you stopped to appreciate the incredible underlying process that transformed all of us from birth to our current adult bodies? In this section, we will explore the fascinating world of physical development. We begin with the prenatal period and early childhood, followed by adolescence and adulthood.

Prenatal Period and Early Childhood: A Time of Rapid Change

Do you remember being a young child and feeling like it would "take forever to grow up"? Contrary to a child's sense of interminable, unchanging time, the early years of development are characterized by rapid and unparalleled change. In fact, if you continued to develop at the same rapid rate that marked your first two years of life, you would weigh several tons and be over 12 feet tall as an adult! Thankfully, physical development slows, yet it is important to note that change continues until the very moment of death. Let's look at some of the major physical changes occurring throughout the life span.

Achievement

Objective 9.5: *Identify the three major stages of prenatal development.*

wiley.com/college/huffman

Francis Leroy, Biocosmos/Photo Researchers Inc.

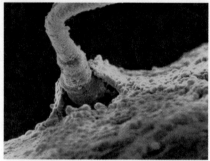

Bonnier Alba

Figure 9.5 *The moment of conception* (a) Note the large number of sperm surrounding the ovum. (b) Although a "joint effort" is required to break through the outer coating, only one sperm will actually fertilize the egg.

chievement

Objective 9.6: *What are the major hazards to prenatal development?*

Prenatal Physical Development

Your prenatal development began at *conception*, when your mother's egg, or *ovum*, united with your father's *sperm* cell (Figure 9.5). At that time, you were a single cell barely $1/175$ of an inch in diameter—smaller, as we have said, than the period at the end of this sentence. This new cell, called a *zygote*, then began a process of rapid cell division that resulted in a multimillion-celled infant (you) some nine months later.

The vast changes that occur during the nine months of a full-term pregnancy are usually divided into three stages (Process Diagram 9.1). Prenatal growth, as well as growth during the first few years after birth, is *proximodistal* (near to far), with the innermost parts of the body developing before the outermost parts. Thus, a fetus's arms develop before its hands and fingers. Development also proceeds *cephalocaudally* (head to tail). Thus, a fetus's head is disproportionately large compared to the lower part of its body.

Hazards to Prenatal Development

During pregnancy, the *placenta* (the vascular organ that unites the fetus to the mother's uterus) serves as the link for food and excretion of wastes. It also screens out some, but not all, harmful substances. Environmental hazards such as X-rays or toxic waste, drugs, and diseases such as rubella (German measles) can cross the *placental barrier* (Table 9.3). These influences generally have their most devastating effect during the first three months of pregnancy—making this a *critical period* in development.

The pregnant mother obviously plays a primary role in prenatal development because her nutrition and health directly influence the child she is carrying. Almost everything she ingests can cross the placental barrier (a better term might be *placental sieve*). However, the father also plays a role—other than just fertilization. Environmentally, the father's smoking may pollute the air the mother breathes, and genetically, he may transmit heritable diseases. In addition, research suggests that alcohol, opiates, cocaine, various gases, lead, pesticides, and industrial chemicals all can damage sperm (Baker & Nieuwenhuijsen, 2008; Bandstra et al., 2002; Ferreti, et al., 2006).

Perhaps the most important, and generally avoidable, danger to the fetus comes from drugs—both legal and illegal. Nicotine and alcohol are two of the most important **teratogens**, environmental agents that cause damage during prenatal development. Mothers who drink alcohol or use tobacco during pregnancy have significantly higher rates of spontaneous abortions, premature births, low-birth-weight infants, and fetal deaths. Their children also show increased behavioral abnormalities and cognitive problems (Abadinsky, 2008; Howell, Coles, & Kable, 2008; Fryer, Crocker, & Mattson, 2008).

Michael Newman/PhotoEdit

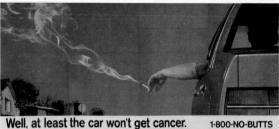

Well, at least the car won't get cancer.   1-800-NO-BUTTS

Teratogen [Tuh-RAT-uh-jen] *Environmental agent that causes damage during prenatal development; the term comes from the Greek word* teras, *meaning "malformation"*

SUMMARY TABLE 9.3 THREATS TO PRENATAL DEVELOPMENT

Maternal Factors	Possible Effects on Embryo, Fetus, Newborn, or Young Child
Malnutrition	Low birth weight, malformations, less developed brain, greater vulnerability to disease
Stress exposure	Low birth weight, hyperactivity, irritability, feeding difficulties
Exposure to X-rays	Malformations, cancer
Legal and illegal drugs	Inhibition of bone growth, hearing loss, low birth weight, fetal alcohol syndrome, mental retardation, attention deficits in childhood, and death.
Diseases German measles (rubella), herpes, AIDS, and toxoplasmosis	Blindness, deafness, mental retardation, heart and other malformations, brain infection, spontaneous abortion, premature birth, low birth weight, and death

Sources: Abadinsky, 2008; Hyde & DeLamater, 2008; Howell, Coles, & Kable, 2008; Levinthal, 2008).

Process Diagram 9.1
Prenatal Development

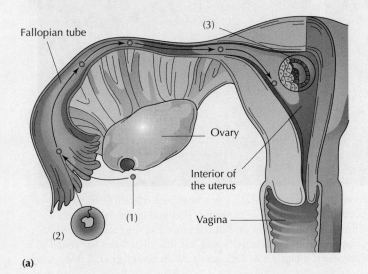

Fallopian tube

(3)

Ovary

Interior of the uterus

(1)

(2)

Vagina

(a)

Bonnier Alba

(b)

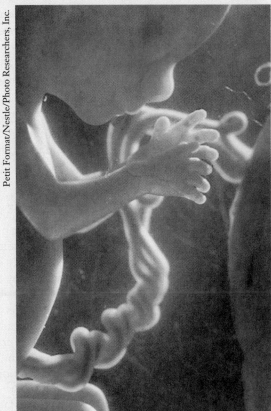

Petit Format/Nestle/Photo Researchers, Inc.

(c)

(a) Germinal period: From ovulation to implantation. After discharge from either the left or right ovary (1), the ovum travels to the opening of the fallopian tube.

If fertilization occurs (2), it normally takes place in the first third of the fallopian tube. The fertilized ovum is referred to as a zygote.

When the zygote reaches the uterus, it implants itself in the wall of the uterus (3) and begins to grow tendril-like structures that intertwine with the rich supply of blood vessels located there. After implantation, the organism is known as an embryo.

(b) Embryonic period. This stage lasts from implantation to eight weeks. At eight weeks, the major organ systems have become well differentiated. Note that at this stage, the head grows at a faster rate than other parts of the body.

(c) Fetal period. This is the period from the end of the second month to birth. At four months, all the actual body parts and organs are established. The fetal stage is primarily a time for increased growth and "fine detailing."

Germinal Period *First stage of prenatal development, which begins with conception and ends with implantation in the uterus (the first two weeks).*

Embryonic Period *Second stage of prenatal development, which begins after uterine implantation and lasts through the eighth week.*

Fetal Period *Third, and final, stage of prenatal development (eight weeks to birth), which is characterized by rapid weight gain in the fetus and the fine detailing of bodily organs and systems.*

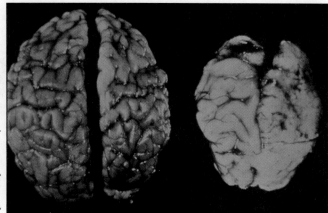

Streissguth, A.P., & Little, R.E. (1994). "Unit 5: Alcohol, Pregnancy, and the Fetal Alcohol Syndrome: Second Edition" of the Project Cork Institute Medical School Curriculum ("slide lecture series") on Biomedical Education: Alcohol Use and Its Medical Consequences, produced by Dartmouth Medical School

Figure 9.6 *Fetal alcohol syndrome* Compare the healthy newborn infant brain (left) to the brain of a newborn (right) whose mother drank while pregnant. Prenatal exposure to alcohol may also cause facial abnormalities and stunted growth. But the most disabling features of FAS are neurobehavioral problems, ranging from hyperactivity and learning disabilities to mental retardation, depression, and psychoses (Pellegrino & Pellegrino, 2008; Sowell et al., 2008; Wass, 2008).

Fetal Alcohol Syndrome (FAS)

Combination of birth defects, including organ deformities and mental, motor, and/or growth retardation, that results from maternal alcohol abuse

Achievement

Objective 9.7: *Summarize early childhood physical development.*

Alcohol also readily crosses the placenta, affects fetal development, and can result in a neurotoxic syndrome called **fetal alcohol syndrome (FAS)** (Figure 9.6). About one in a hundred babies in the United States is born with FAS or other birth defects resulting from the mother's alcohol use during pregnancy (National Organization on Fetal Alcohol Syndrome, 2008).

Early Childhood Physical Development

Although Shakespeare described newborns as capable of only "mewling and puking in the nurse's arms," they are actually capable of much more. Let's explore three key areas of change in early childhood: *brain*, *motor*, and *sensory/perceptual development*.

Brain Development. As you recall from Chapter 2, the human brain is divided into three major sections—the *hindbrain*, *midbrain*, and *forebrain*. Note in Figure 9.7 how the prenatal brain begins as a fluid-filled neural tube and then rapidly progresses. The brain and other parts of the nervous system grow faster than any other part of the body during both prenatal development and the first two years of life. At birth, a healthy newborn's brain is one-fourth its full adult size and it will grow to about 75 percent of its adult weight and size by the age of 2. At age 6, the child's brain is nine-tenths its full adult weight (Figure 9.7).

Rapid brain growth during infancy and early childhood slows down in later childhood. Further brain development and learning occur primarily because neurons grow in size and because the number of axons and dendrites, as well as the extent of their connections, increases (Figure 9.8).

Motor Development. Compared to the hidden, internal changes in brain development, the orderly emergence of active movement skills, known as *motor development*, is easily observed and measured. The newborn's first motor abilities are limited to *reflexes*—involuntary responses to stimulation. For example, the rooting reflex occurs when something touches a baby's cheek: The infant will automatically turn its head, open its mouth, and root for a nipple.

In addition to simple reflexes, the infant soon begins to show voluntary control over the movement of various body parts. As shown in Figure 9.9, a helpless newborn who cannot even lift her head is soon transformed into an active toddler capable of crawling, walking, and climbing. Keep in mind that motor development is largely due

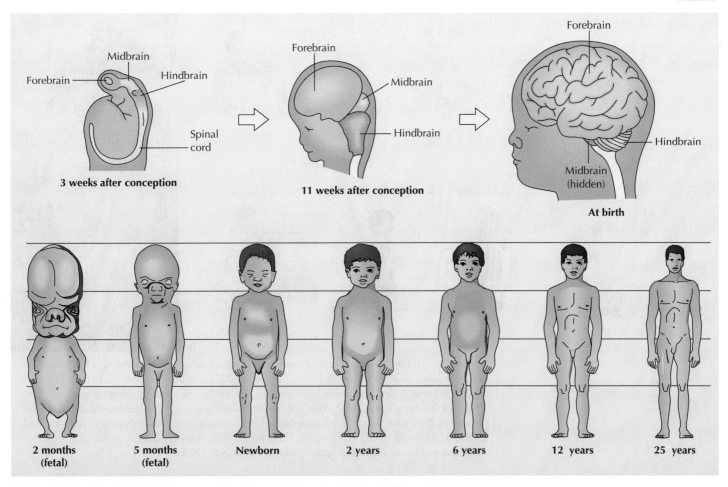

Figure 9.7 *Brain and body changes over the life span* Note the dramatic changes in our brain and body proportions as we grow older. At birth, an infant's head is one-fourth its total body's size. In adulthood, the head is one-eighth the body size.

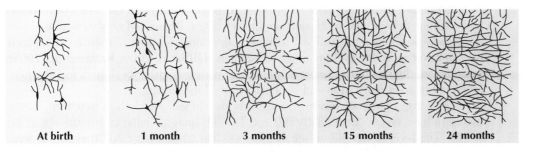

Figure 9.8 *Brain growth in the first two years* As children learn and develop, synaptic connections between active neurons strengthen, and dendritic connections become more elaborate. *Synaptic pruning* (reduction of unused synapses) helps support this process. *Myelination*, the accumulation of fatty tissue coating the axons of nerve cells, continues until early adulthood. Myelin increases the speed of neural impulses, and the speed of information processing shows a corresponding increase (Chapter 2). In addition, synaptic connections in the frontal lobes and other parts of the brain continue growing and changing throughout the entire life span (Chapters 2 and 6).

wiley.com/
college/
huffman

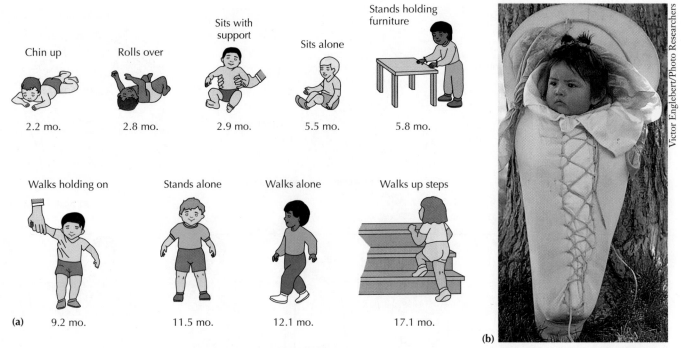

Figure 9.9 *Motor development and culture* (a) *Milestones in motor development* In the typical progression of motor abilities, "chin up" occurs at 2.2 months. However, no two children are exactly alike; all follow their own individual timetables for physical development. (Adapted from Frankenburg et al., 1992, with permission.) (b) Some Hopi Indian infants spend a great portion of their first year of life being carried in a cradleboard, rather than crawling and walking freely on the ground. Yet by age 1, their motor skills are very similar to those of infants who have not been restrained in this fashion (Dennis & Dennis, 1940).

to natural maturation, but it can also be affected by environmental influences like disease and neglect. Recent research also has shifted from describing the age at which motor skills develop to *how* they develop (Adolph & Joh, 2007).

Sensory and Perceptual Development. At birth, a newborn can smell most odors and distinguish between sweet, salty, and bitter tastes. Breast-fed newborns also recognize, show preference for, and are calmed by the odor and taste of their mother's milk over another mother's milk or other substances (DiPietro, 2000; Rattaz et al., 2005). In addition, the newborn's sense of touch and pain is highly developed, as evidenced by reactions to circumcision and heel pricks for blood testing.

The sense of vision, however, is poorly developed. At birth, a newborn is estimated to have vision between 20/200 and 20/600. Imagine what an infant's visual life is like. The level of detail you see at 200–600 feet (if you have 20/20 vision) is what they see at 20 feet! Within the first few months, vision quickly improves, and by 6 months, it is 20/100 or better. At 2 years, visual acuity reaches a near-adult level of 20/20 (Courage & Adams, 1990).

One of the most interesting findings in infant sensory and perceptual research concerns hearing. Not only can the newborn hear quite well at birth, but also, during the last few months in the womb, the fetus can hear sounds outside the mother's body. This raises the interesting possibility of fetal learning, and some have advocated special stimulation for the fetus as a way of increasing intelligence, creativity, and general alertness (e.g., Van de Carr & Lehrer, 1997).

Studies on possible fetal learning have found that newborn infants easily recognize their own mother's voice over that of a stranger (Kisilevsky et al., 2003). They also show preferences for children's stories (such as *The Cat in the Hat* or *The King*,

Scientific Research with Infants

How can psychological scientists conduct research with nonverbal infants? One of the earliest experimenters, Robert Fantz (1956, 1963), designed a "looking chamber" to measure how long infants stared at stimuli. Research using this apparatus indicates that infants prefer complex rather than simple patterns and pictures of faces rather than nonfaces.

Researchers also use newborns' heart rates and innate abilities, such as the sucking reflex, to study learning and perceptual development (Bendersky & Sullivan, 2007). To study the sense of smell, researchers measure changes in the newborns' heart rates when odors are presented. Presumably, if they can smell one odor but not another, their heart rates will change in the presence of the first but not the second. As you may recall from Chapter 4, what all of these researchers are measuring is *habituation*—a decreased responsiveness after repeated stimulation.

Brain scans, such as fMRI, MRI, and CTs, also help developmental scientists detect changes in the infant's brain.

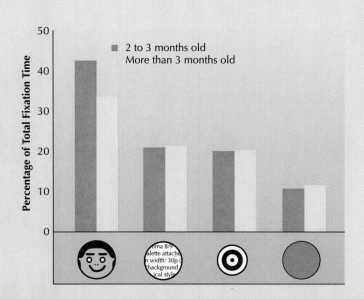

the Mice, *and the Cheese*) that were read to them while they were still in the womb (DeCasper & Fifer, 1980; Karmiloff & Karmiloff-Smith, 2002). On the other hand, some experts caution that too much or the wrong kind of stimulation before birth can be stressful for both the mother and fetus. They suggest that the fetus gets what it needs without special stimulation.

How can scientists measure perceptual abilities and preferences in such young babies? Newborns and infants obviously cannot talk or follow directions, so researchers have had to create ingenious experiments to evaluate their perceptual skill. (Concept Diagram 9.1).

Adolescence and Adulthood: A Time of Both Dramatic and Gradual Change

Whereas the adolescent years are marked by dramatic changes in appearance and physical capacity, middle age and later adulthood are times of gradual physical changes. We begin with a look at adolescence.

Adolescence

Think back for a moment to your teen years. Were you concerned about the physical changes you were going through? Did you worry about how you differed from your classmates? Changes in height and weight, breast development and menstruation for girls, and a deepening voice and beard growth for boys are important milestones for adolescents. **Puberty**, the period in adolescence when a person becomes capable of reproduction, is a major physical milestone for everyone. It is a clear biological signal of the end of childhood.

Although commonly associated with puberty, *adolescence* is the loosely defined psychological period of development between childhood and adulthood. In the United

Achievement

Objective 9.8: *Describe the major physical changes associated with adolescence and adulthood.*

Puberty *Biological changes during adolescence that lead to an adult-sized body and sexual maturity*

©AP/Wide World Photos

Figure 9.10 *Ready for responsibility?* Adolescence is not a universal concept. Unlike in the United States and other Western nations, some nonindustrialized countries have no need for a slow transition from childhood to adulthood; children simply assume adult responsibilities as soon as possible.

States, it roughly corresponds to the teenage years. The concept of adolescence and its meaning varies greatly across cultures (Figure 9.10).

The clearest and most dramatic physical sign of puberty is the *growth spurt*, characterized by rapid increases in height, weight, and skeletal growth (Figure 9.11), and by significant changes in reproductive structures and sexual characteristics. Maturation and hormone secretion cause rapid development of the ovaries, uterus, and vagina and the onset of menstruation *(menarche)* in the adolescent female. In the adolescent male, the testes, scrotum, and penis develop, and he undergoes *spermarche* (the first ejaculation). The ovaries and testes in turn produce hormones that lead to the development of *secondary sex characteristics*, such as the growth of pubic hair, deepening of the voice, growth of facial hair, growth of breasts, and so on (Figure 9.12).

Once the large and obvious pubertal changes have occurred, further age-related physical changes are less dramatic. Other than some modest increase in height and muscular development during the late teens and early twenties, most individuals experience only minor physical changes until middle age.

Middle Age

For women, *menopause*, the cessation of the menstrual cycle, which occurs somewhere between ages 45 and 55, is the second most important life milestone in physical development. The decreased production of estrogen (the dominant female hormone) produces certain physical changes. However, the popular belief that menopause (or "the change of life") causes serious psychological mood swings, loss of sexual interest, and major depression is *not* supported by current research (Matlin, 2008; Tom, 2008). In fact, most studies find that postmenopausal women report relief, increased libido, and other positive reactions to the end of their menstrual cycles (Chrisler, 2008; Leon et al., 2007).

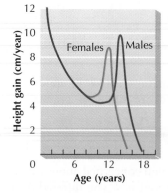

Figure 9.11 *Adolescent growth spurt* Note the gender differences in height gain during puberty. Most girls are about two years ahead of boys in their growth spurt and therefore are taller than most boys between the ages of 10 and 14.

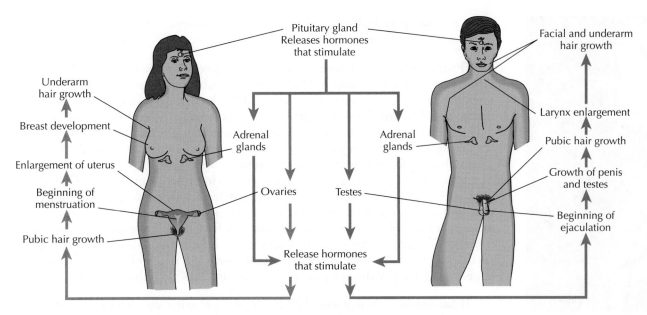

Figure 9.12 *Secondary sex characteristics* Complex physical changes in puberty primarily result from hormones secreted from the ovaries and testes, the pituitary gland in the brain, and adrenal glands near the kidneys.

When psychological problems exist, they may reflect the social devaluation of aging women, not the physiological process of menopause itself. Given our Western society in which women are highly valued for their youth and beauty, can you understand why such a biological landmark of aging may be difficult for some women?

For men, youthfulness is less important, and the physical changes of middle age are less obvious. Beginning in middle adulthood, men experience a gradual decline in the production of sperm and testosterone (the dominant male hormone), although they may remain capable of reproduction into their eighties or nineties. Physical changes such as unexpected weight gain, decline in sexual responsiveness, loss of muscle strength, and graying or loss of hair may lead some men (and women as well) to feel depressed and to question their life progress. They often see these alterations as a biological signal of aging and mortality. Such physical and psychological changes in men are known as the *male climacteric*.

Late Adulthood

After middle age, most physical changes in development are gradual and occur in the heart and arteries and sensory receptors. For example, cardiac output (the volume of blood pumped by the heart each minute) decreases, whereas blood pressure increases due to the thickening and stiffening of arterial walls. Visual acuity and depth perception decline, hearing acuity lessens, especially for high-frequency sounds, and smell and taste sensitivity decreases (Chung, 2006; Snyder & Alain, 2008; Whitbourne, 2009).

This all sounds depressing. Can anything be done about it? Television, magazines, movies, and advertisements generally have portrayed aging as a time of balding and graying hair, sagging parts, poor vision, hearing loss, and, of course, no sex life. Such negative portrayals contribute to our society's widespread **ageism**, prejudice or discrimination based on physical age. However, as advertising companies pursue revenues from the huge aging baby-boomer population, there has been a recent shift toward a

Arnie Levin© The New Yorker Collection/ The Cartoon Bank, Inc.

"As I get older, I find I rely more and more on these sticky notes to remind me."

Ageism *Prejudice or discrimination based on physical age*

Figure 9.13 *Use it or lose it?* Recent research shows that cognitive functioning in older adults can be greatly enhanced with simple aerobic training (Berchtold, 2008; Lindwall et al., 2008).

Achievement

Objective 9.9: *Identify primary aging, and compare the programmed and damage theories of aging.*

more accurate portrayal of aging also as a time of vigor, interest, and productivity (Figures 9.13 and 9.14).

What about memory problems and inherited genetic tendencies toward Alzheimer's disease and other serious diseases of old age? The public and most researchers have long thought aging is accompanied by widespread death of neurons in the brain. Although this decline does happen with degenerative disorders like Alzheimer's disease, it is no longer believed to be a part of normal aging (Chapter 2). It is also important to remember that age-related memory problems are not on a continuum with Alzheimer's disease. That is, normal forgetfulness does not reflect a predisposition for serious dementia.

Aging does seem to take its toll on the *speed* of information processing (Chapter 7). Decreased speed of processing may reflect problems with *encoding* (putting information into long-term storage) and *retrieval* (getting information out of storage). If memory is like a filing system, older people may have more filing cabinets, and it may take them longer to initially file and later retrieve information. Although mental speed declines with age, general information processing and much of memory ability are largely unaffected by the aging process (Lachman, 2004; Whitbourne, 2009).

What causes us to age and die? If we set aside aging and deaths resulting from disease, abuse, or neglect, which is known as *secondary aging*, we are left to consider *primary aging* (gradual, inevitable age-related changes in physical and mental processes). There are two main theories explaining primary aging and death—programmed theory and damage theory.

According to *programmed theory*, aging is genetically controlled. Once the ovum is fertilized, the program for aging and death is set and begins to run. Researcher Leonard Hayflick (1977, 1996) found that human cells seem to have a built-in life span. After about 50 doublings of laboratory-cultured cells, they cease to divide—they have reached the *Hayflick limit*. The other explanation of primary aging is *damage theory*, which proposes that an accumulation of damage to cells and organs over the years ultimately causes death.

Whether aging is genetically controlled or caused by accumulated damage over the years, scientists generally agree that humans appear to have a maximum life span of about 110 to 120 years. Although we can try to control secondary aging in an attempt to reach that maximum, so far we have no means to postpone primary aging.

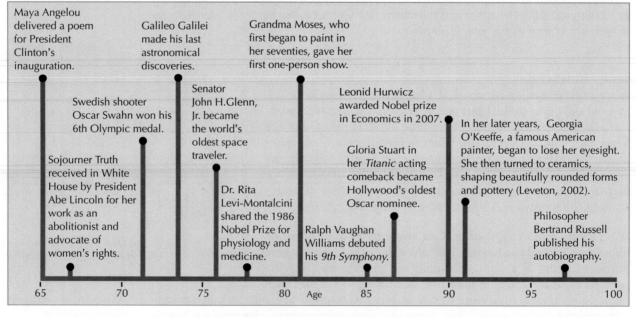

Figure 9.14 *Achievement in later years* Note the high level of productivity among some of the world's most famous figures.

Assessment

STOP

CHECK & REVIEW

Physical Development

Objective 9.5: *Identify the three major stages of prenatal development.*

The prenatal period of development consists of three major stages: the **germinal**, (ovulation to implantation), **embryonic**, (implantation to eight weeks), and **fetal** (eight weeks to birth).

Objective 9.6: *What are the major hazards to prenatal development?*

Doctors advise pregnant women to avoid all unnecessary drugs, especially nicotine and alcohol. Both legal and illegal drugs are potentially **teratogenic** (capable of producing birth defects).

Objective 9.7: *Summarize early childhood physical development.*

During the prenatal period and the first two years of life, the brain and nervous system grow faster than any other part of the body. Early motor development (crawling, standing, and walking) is largely the result of maturation, not experience. Except for vision, the sensory and perceptual abilities of newborns are relatively well developed.

Objective 9.8: *Describe the major physical changes associated with adolescence and adulthood.*

At **puberty**, the individual becomes capable of reproduction and experiences a sharp increase in height, weight, and skeletal growth, called the *pubertal growth spurt*. Both men and women experience *significant* bodily changes in middle age.

Objective 9.9: *Identify primary aging, and compare the programmed and damage theories of aging.*

Although many of the changes associated with physical aging (such as decreases in cardiac output and visual acuity) are the result of *primary aging*, others are the result of disease, abuse, or neglect. Physical aging may be genetically built in from the moment of conception (programmed theory), or it may result from the body's inability to repair damage (damage theory).

Questions

1. What are the three stages of prenatal development?
2. Teratogens are _____ that can cause birth defects. (a) DNA fragments; (b) environmental agents; (c) recessive genes; (d) dominant genes
3. At birth, an infant's head is _____ its body's size, whereas in adulthood, the head is _____ its body's size. (a) 1/3; 1/4 (b) 1/3; 1/10; (c) 1/4; 1/10 (d) 1/4; 1/8

4. The period of life when an individual first becomes capable of reproduction is known as _____. (a) the age of fertility; (b) adolescence; (c) puberty; (d) the adolescent climacteric
5. Gradual, inevitable age-related changes in physical and mental processes are called _____.

Check your answers in Appendix B.

Click & Review
for additional assessment options:
wiley.com/college/huffman

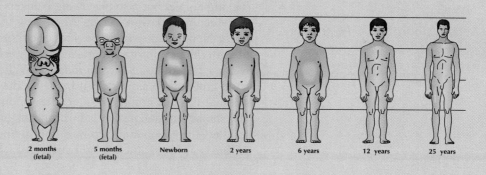

| 2 months (fetal) | 5 months (fetal) | Newborn | 2 years | 6 years | 12 years | 25 years |

Cognitive Development

The following fan letter was written to Shari Lewis (1963), a children's television performer, about her puppet Lamb Chop:

> Dear Shari:
>
> All my friends say Lamb Chop isn't really a little girl that talks. She is just a puppet you made out of a sock. I don't care even if it's true. I like the way Lamb Chop talks. If I send you one of my socks will you teach it how to talk and send it back?
>
> RANDI

Achievement

Objective 9.10: *Describe Piaget's theory of cognitive development, and compare schema, assimilation, and accommodation.*

Randi's understanding of fantasy and reality is certainly different from an adult's. Just as a child's body and physical abilities change, his or her way of knowing and perceiving the world also grows and changes. This seems intuitively obvious. But early psychologists—with one exception—focused on physical, emotional, language, and personality development. The one major exception was Jean Piaget (Pee-ah-ZHAY).

Piaget demonstrated that a child's intellect is fundamentally different from an adult's. He showed that an infant begins at a cognitively "primitive" level and that intellectual growth progresses in distinct stages, motivated by an innate need to know. Piaget's theory, developed in the 1920s and 1930s, has proven so comprehensive and insightful that it remains the major force in the cognitive area of developmental psychology today.

To appreciate Piaget's contributions, we need to consider three major concepts: schemas, assimilation, and accommodation. **Schemas** are the most basic units of intellect. They act as patterns that organize our interactions with the environment, like architect's drawings or builder's blueprints.

In the first few weeks of life, for example, the infant apparently has several schemas based on the innate reflexes of sucking, grasping, and so on. These schemas are primarily motor skills and may be little more than stimulus-and-response mechanisms—the nipple is presented and the baby sucks. Soon, however, other schemas emerge. The infant develops a more detailed schema for eating solid food, a different schema for the concepts of *mother* and *father*, and so on. It is important to recognize that schemas, our tools for learning about the world, are enlarged and changed throughout our lives. For example, older music lovers previously accustomed to LP records have had to develop different schemas for playing CDs and MP3s.

Assimilation and accommodation are the two major processes by which schemas grow and change over time. **Assimilation** is the process of absorbing new information into existing schemas. For instance, infants use their sucking schema not only in sucking nipples but also in sucking blankets or fingers.

Accommodation occurs when new information or stimuli cannot be assimilated. New schemas must be developed, or old schemas must be changed to better fit with the new information. An infant's first attempt to eat solid food with a spoon is a good example of accommodation. When the spoon first enters her mouth, the child attempts to assimilate it by using the previously successful sucking schema—shaping lips and tongue around the spoon as around a nipple. After repeated trials, she accommodates by adjusting her lips and tongue in a way that moves the food off the spoon and into her mouth. Similarly, if you meet someone through an online chat room and are later surprised when you talk face to face, it is because of

Schema *Cognitive structures or patterns consisting of a number of organized ideas that grow and differentiate with experience*

Assimilation *In Piaget's theory, absorbing new information into existing schemas*

Accommodation *In Piaget's theory, adjusting old schemas or developing new ones to better fit with new information*

Try This Yourself

Application

Study the "impossible figure" to the right.

Using a clean sheet of paper, try to draw this same figure without tracing it. Students with artistic training generally find it relatively easy to reproduce, whereas the rest of us find it "impossible." This is because we lack the necessary artistic schema and cannot assimilate what we see. With practice and training, we could accommodate the new information and easily draw the figure.

the unexamined schemas you constructed. The awkwardness and discomfort you now feel are due, in part, to the work involved in readjusting, or accommodating, your earlier schemas to match the new reality.

Stages of Cognitive Development: Birth to Adolescence

According to Piaget, all children go through approximately the same four stages of cognitive development, regardless of the culture in which they live (Process Diagram 9.2). And no stage can be skipped because skills acquired at earlier stages are essential to mastery at later stages. Let's take a closer look at these four stages: sensorimotor, preoperational, concrete operational, and formal operational.

The Sensorimotor Stage

During the **sensorimotor stage**, lasting from birth until "significant" language acquisition (about age 2), children explore the world and develop their schemas primarily through their senses and motor activities—hence the term *sensorimotor*.

One important concept acquired during this stage is **object permanence**. At birth and for the next three or four months, children lack object permanence. They seem to have no schemas for objects they cannot see, hear, or touch—out of sight is truly out of mind.

Preoperational Stage

During the **preoperational stage** (roughly age 2 to 7), language advances significantly, and the child begins to think *symbolically*—using symbols, such as words, to represent concepts. Three other qualities characterize this stage:

1. ***Concepts are not yet operational***. Piaget labeled this period "preoperational" because the child lacks *operations*, reversible mental processes. For instance, if a preoperational boy who has a brother is asked, "Do you have a brother?" he will easily respond, "Yes." However, when asked, "Does your brother have a brother?" he will answer, "No!" To understand that his brother has a brother, he must be able to *reverse* the concept of "having a brother."

2. ***Thinking is egocentric***. Children at this stage have difficulty understanding that there are points of view other than their own. **Egocentrism** refers to the preoperational child's limited ability to distinguish between his or her own perspective and someone else's. Egocentrism is not the same as "selfishness." Preschoolers who move in front of you to get a better view of the TV or repeatedly ask questions while you are talking on the telephone are not being selfish. They are demonstrating egocentric thought processes. They naively assume that others see, hear, feel, and think exactly as they do. Consider the following telephone conversation between a 3-year-old, who is at home, and her mother, who is at work:

MOTHER: Emma is that you?

EMMA: (Nods silently.)

MOTHER: Emma, is Daddy there? May I speak to him?

EMMA: (Twice nods silently.)

Egocentric preoperational children fail to understand that the phone caller cannot see their nodding head. Charming as this is, preoperational children's egocentrism also sometimes leads them to believe their "bad thoughts" caused their sibling or parent to get sick or that their misbehavior caused their parents' marital problems. Because they think the world centers on them, they often cannot separate reality from what goes on inside their own head.

Early experimentation *Piaget believed children are natural experimenters biologically driven to explore their environment.*

Erik Soh/Asia Images/Getty Images, Inc.

Sensorimotor Stage *Piaget's first stage (birth to approximately age 2 years), in which schemas are developed through sensory and motor activities*

Object Permanence *Piagetian term for an infant's understanding that objects (or people) continue to exist even when they cannot be seen, heard, or touched directly*

Preoperational Stage *Piaget's second stage (roughly age 2 to 7), characterized by the ability to employ significant language and to think symbolically, but the child lacks operations (reversible mental processes), and thinking is egocentric and animistic*

Egocentrism *The inability to consider another's point of view, which Piaget considered a hallmark of the preoperational stage*

Piaget's Four Stages of Cognitive Development

Birth to 2

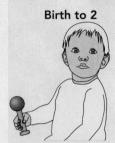

Sensorimotor
Abilities: Uses senses and motor skills to explore and develop cognitively.
Limits: Beginning of stage lacks *object permanence* (understanding things continue to exist even when not seen, heard, or felt).

Doug Goodman/PhotoResearchers, Inc.

What's happening in these photos? The child in these two photos seems to believe the toy no longer exists once it is blocked from sight. Can you explain why?

Answer: According to Piaget, young infants lack object permanence—an understanding that objects continue to exist even when they cannot be seen, heard, or touched.

Age 2–7

Preoperational
Abilities: Has significant language and thinks symbolically.
Limits:
- Cannot perform "operations."
- *Egocentric* thinking (inability to consider another's point of view).
- *Animistic* thinking (believing all things are living).

THE FAMILY CIRCUS, By Bil Keane

"Look what I can do, Grandma!"

Reprinted with special permission of King Features Syndicate.

Applying Piaget. Can you identify this child's Piagetian stage of cognitive development? Why does he think his Grandma can see him?

Answer: The child is in the preoperational stage, and his egocentrism prevents him from recognizing that Grandma does not see everything he sees.

Age 7–11

Concrete Operational
Abilities:
- Can perform "operations" on concrete objects.
- Understands *conservation* (*realizing changes in shape or appearance can be reversed*).
Limits: Cannot think abstractly and hypothetically.

(a)   (b)   (c)

Ellen B. Senisi/The Image Works

Test for conservation. (a) In the classic conservation of liquids test, the child is first shown two identical glasses with liquid at the same level. (b) The liquid is poured from one of the short, wide glasses into the tall, thin one. (c) When asked whether the two glasses have the same amount or if one has more, the preoperational child replies that the tall, thin glass has more. This demonstrates a failure to conserve volume.

Age 11 and up

SAVE THE WHALES

Formal Operational
Abilities: Can think abstractly and hypothetically.
Limits: *Adolescent egocentrism* at the beginning of this stage, with related problems of the *personal fable* and *imaginary audience*.

Roy Melnychuk/Taxi/Getty Images

Self-consciousness. What developmental phenomenon might explain why adolescents sometimes display what seem like extreme forms of self-consciousness and concern for physical appearance?

3. ***Thinking is animistic***. Children in the preoperational stage believe that objects such as the sun, trees, clouds, and bars of soap have motives, feelings, and intentions (for example, "dark clouds are angry" and "soap sinks to the bottom of the bathtub because it is tired"). *Animism* refers to the belief that all things are living (or animated). Our earlier example of Randi's letter asking puppeteer Shari Lewis to teach her sock to talk like Lamb Chop is also an example of animistic thinking.

Can preoperational children be taught how to use operations and to avoid egocentric and animistic thinking? Although some researchers have reported success in accelerating the preoperational stage, Piaget did not believe in pushing children ahead of their own developmental schedule. He believed children should be allowed to grow at their own pace, with minimal adult interference (Elkind, 1981, 2000). Piaget thought Americans were particularly guilty of pushing children, calling American childhood the "Great American Kid Race."

Michael Ventura/Image State

Can you see why this stage is called "sensorimotor"?

Concrete Operational Stage

Between the approximate ages of 7 and 11, children are in the **concrete operational stage**. During this stage many important thinking skills emerge. Unlike the preoperational stage, concrete operational children are able to perform operations on *concrete* objects. Because they understand the concept of *reversibility*, they recognize that certain physical attributes (such as volume) remain unchanged, although the outward appearance is altered, a process known as **conservation**.

Formal Operational Stage

The final period in Piaget's theory is the **formal operational stage**, which typically begins around age 11. In this stage, children begin to apply their operations to abstract concepts in addition to concrete objects. Children now find it much easier to master the abstract thinking required for geometry and algebra. For example, $(a + b)^2 = a^2 + 2ab + b^2$. They also become capable of hypothetical thinking ("What if?"), which allows systematic formulation and testing of concepts.

Adolescents considering part-time jobs, for example, may think about possible conflicts with school and friends, the number of hours they want to work, and the kind of work for which they are qualified before they start filling out applications. Formal operational thinking also allows the adolescent to construct a well-reasoned argument based on hypothetical concepts and logical processes. Consider the following argument:

1. If you hit a glass with a feather, the glass will break.

2. You hit the glass with a feather.

What is the logical conclusion? The correct answer, "The glass will break," is contrary to fact and direct experience. Therefore, the child in the concrete operational stage would have difficulty with this task, whereas the formal operational thinker understands that this problem is about abstractions that need not correspond to the real world.

Problems with Early Formal Operational Thinking

Along with the benefits of this cognitive style come several problems. Adolescents in the early stages of the formal operational period demonstrate a type of *egocentrism* different from that of the preoperational child. Although adolescents do recognize that others have unique thoughts and perspectives, they often fail to differentiate between what others are thinking and their own thoughts. This *adolescent egocentrism* has two characteristics that may affect social interactions as well as problem solving:

1. ***Personal fable***. Given their unique form of egocentrism, adolescents may conclude that they alone are having certain insights or difficulties and that no one else could

Concrete Operational Stage *Piaget's third stage (roughly age 7 to 11); the child can perform mental operations on concrete objects and understand reversibility and conservation, but abstract thinking is not yet present*

Conservation *Understanding that certain physical characteristics (such as volume) remain unchanged, even when their outward appearance changes*

Formal Operational Stage *Piaget's fourth stage (around age 11 and beyond), characterized by abstract and hypothetical thinking*

Dennis Novak/Photographer's Choice/Getty Images

Personal fable in action? *Can you see how this type of risk-taking behavior may reflect the personal fable—adolescents' tendency to believe they are unique and special and that dangers don't apply to them?*

wiley.com/
college/
huffman

understand or sympathize. David Elkind (1967, 2001, 2007) described this as the formation of a *personal fable*, an intense investment in their own thoughts and feelings, and a belief that these thoughts are unique. One student in my class remembered being very upset in junior high when her mother tried to comfort her over the loss of an important relationship. "I felt like she couldn't possibly know how it felt—no one could. I couldn't believe that anyone had ever suffered like this or that things would ever get better."

Several forms of risk taking, such as engaging in sexual intercourse without contraception, driving dangerously, and experimenting with drugs, also seem to arise from the personal fable (Alberts, Elkind, & Ginsberg, 2007; Flavell, Miller, & Miller, 2002). Although adolescents will acknowledge the risks of these activities, they don't feel personally endangered because they feel uniquely invulnerable and immortal.

Interestingly, recent scientific studies have identified important changes in the brain during adolescence that may help explain this type of risky behavior and other problems in adolescence. Thanks to advances in brain imaging, scientists now know that the prefrontal cortex of the adolescent's brain is one of the later areas to develop (Casey, Getz, & Galvan, 2008; Giedd, 2008; Steinberg, 2008). Can you see how this relatively slow development of the part of the brain responsible for higher processes, like planning ahead and controlling emotions, may provide a possible biological basis for risk taking and other cognitive limits during adolescence?

2. ***Imaginary audience.*** Adolescents also tend to believe they are the center of others' thoughts and attentions, instead of considering that everyone is equally wrapped up in his or her own concerns and plans. Elkind referred to this as the *imaginary audience*. This new form of egocentrism may explain what seems like extreme forms of self-consciousness and concern for physical appearance ("Everyone knows I don't know the answer"; or "They're noticing how fat I am and this awful haircut").

If the imaginary audience results from an inability to differentiate the self from others, the personal fable is a product of differentiating too much. Thankfully, these two forms of adolescent egocentrism tend to decrease during later stages of the formal operational period.

Assessing Piaget's Theory: Criticisms and Contributions

As influential as Piaget's account of cognitive development has been, it has received significant criticisms. Let's look briefly at two major areas of concern: *underestimated abilities* and *underestimated genetic* and *cultural influences*.

Underestimated Abilities

Research shows that Piaget may have underestimated young children's cognitive development (Figure 9.15). For example, researchers report that very young infants have a basic concept of how objects move, are aware that objects continue to exist even when screened from view, and can recognize speech sounds (Baillargeon, 2000, 2008; Charles, 2007).

Nonegocentric responses also appear in the earliest days of life. For example, newborn babies tend to cry in response to the cry of another baby (Diego & Jones, 2007; Dondi, Simion, & Caltran, 1999). And preschoolers will adapt their speech by using shorter, simpler expressions when talking to 2-year-olds rather than to adults (Figure 9.16).

Underestimated Genetic and Cultural Influences

Piaget's model, like other stage theories, has also been criticized for not sufficiently taking into account genetic and cultural differences (Cole & Gajdamaschko, 2007; Matusov & Hayes, 2000; Maynard & Greenfield, 2003). During Piaget's time, the genetic influences on cognitive abilities were poorly understood, but as you know there has been a rapid explosion

Achievement

Objective 9.12: *Identify the major criticisms and contributions of Piaget's theories.*

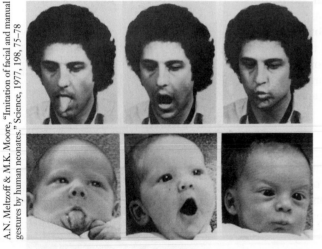

A.N. Meltzoff & M.K. Moore, "Imitation of facial and manual gestures by human neonates." Science, 1977, 198, 75–78

Figure 9.15 ***Infant imitation*** In a series of well-known studies, Andrew Meltzoff and M. Keith Moore (1977, 1985, 1994) found that newborns could imitate such facial movements as tongue protrusion, mouth opening, and lip pursing. At 9 months, infants will imitate facial actions a full day after seeing them (Heimann & Meltzoff, 1996). Can you see how this early infant facial expression raises questions about Piaget's estimates of early infant abilities? When an adult models a facial expression, even very young infants will respond with a similar expression. Is this true imitation or a simple stimulus-response reflex?

pplication

Putting Piaget to the Test

This is a sample of experiments used to test Piaget's different types of conservation. If you know children in the preoperational or concrete operational stages, you may enjoy testing their grasp of conservation by trying some of these experiments. The equipment is easily obtained, and you will find their responses fascinating. Keep in mind that this should be done as a game. Do not allow the child to feel that he or she is failing a test or making a mistake.

Type of Conservation Task (Average age at which concept is grasped)	Your task as experimenter...	Child is asked...
Length (ages 6–7)	**Step 1** Center two sticks of equal length. Child agrees that they are of equal length. **Step 2** Move one stick.	**Step 3** *"Which stick is longer?"* Preoperational child will say that one of the sticks is longer. Child in concrete stage will say that they are both the same length.
Substance amount (ages 6–7)	**Step 1** Center two identical clay balls. Child acknowledges that the two have equal amounts of clay. **Step 2** Flatten one of the balls.	**Step 3** *"Do the two pieces have the same amount of clay?"* Preoperational child will say that the flat piece has more clay. Child in concrete stage will say that the two pieces have the same amount of clay.
Area (ages 8–10)	**Step 1** Center two identical sheets of cardboard with wooden blocks placed on them in identical positions. Child acknowledges that the same amount of space is left open on each piece of cardboard. **Step 2** Scatter the blocks on one piece of the cardboard.	**Step 3** *"Do the two pieces of cardboard have the same amount of open space?"* Preoperational child will say that the cardboard with scattered blocks has less open space. Child in concrete stage will say that both pieces have the same amount of open space.

of information in this field in the last few years. In addition, formal education and specific cultural experiences can significantly affect cognitive development. In contrast to Piaget's belief that the most important source of cognition is the child itself, Lev Vygotsky, a famous Russian psychologist, proposed that our social and cultural environments play

wiley.com/
college/
huffman

Figure 9.16 *Are preoperational children always egocentric?* Contrary to Piaget's beliefs, children at this age often do take the perspective of another.

Achievement

Objective 9.13: *Describe the information-processing model of cognitive development.*

a more influential role (Fernyhough, 2008; Gredler & Shields, 2008). Consider the following example from a researcher attempting to test the formal operational skills of a farmer in Liberia (Scribner, 1977):

RESEARCHER: All Kpelle men are rice farmers. Mr. Smith is not a rice farmer. Is he a Kpelle man?

KPELLE FARMER: I don't know the man. I have not laid eyes on the man myself.

Instead of reasoning in the "logical" way of Piaget's formal operational stage, the Kpelle farmer reasoned according to his specific cultural and educational training, which apparently emphasized personal knowledge. Not knowing Mr. Smith, the Kpelle farmer did not feel qualified to comment on him. Thus, Piaget's theory may have underestimated the effect of culture on a person's cognitive functioning.

Despite criticisms, Piaget's contributions to psychology are enormous. As one scholar put it, "assessing the impact of Piaget on developmental psychology is like assessing the impact of Shakespeare on English literature or Aristotle on philosophy—impossible" (cited in Beilin, 1992, p. 191).

Information Processing: A Computer Model of Cognition

An alternative to Piaget's theory of cognitive development is the *information-processing model*, which compares the workings of the mind to a computer and studies how information is received, encoded, stored, organized, retrieved, and used by people of different ages. This model offers important insights into two major areas of cognition: attention and memory.

Attention

Attention refers to focusing awareness on a narrowed range of stimuli. Infants pay attention to their environment for only short periods of time. Even toddlers, who can pay attention for longer periods, are easily distracted. When watching television, for example, 2-year-olds talk more to other people, play more with toys, and look around the room more than 4-year-olds. As they get older, children's attention spans improve, and they learn to discriminate between what is and what is not important to concentrate on at any given time (Danis et al., 2008; Janvier & Testu, 2005; Raffaelli, Crockett & Shen, 2005).

Memory

After children attend to information and take it into their information-processing system, they must remember it. Attention determines what information enters the "computer," whereas memory determines what information is saved.

Like attention, memory skills also improve gradually throughout childhood and adolescence (Guisande et al., 2007; Hayne, Boniface, & Barr, 2000; Wang, 2008). Two-year-olds can repeat back about two digits immediately after hearing them, but 10-year-olds can repeat about six. Improvement comes as children acquire strategies during the school years for storing and retrieving information. For example, they learn to rehearse or repeat information over and over, to use mnemonics (like "*i* before *e* except after *c*"), and to organize their information in ways that facilitate retrieval (Chapter 7).

As people grow older, their use of information-processing strategies and overall memory continues to change. Recall from Chapter 8 that *fluid intelligence* (requiring speed or rapid learning) tends to decrease with age, whereas *crystallized intelligence* (knowledge and information gained over the life span) continues to increase until advanced old age.

Despite their concerns about "keeping up with 18-year-olds," older returning students often do as well or better than their younger counterparts in college classes.

This superior performance by older adult students is due in part to their generally greater academic motivation, but it also reflects the importance of prior knowledge. Cognitive psychologists have demonstrated that the more people know, the easier it is for them to lay down new memories (Goldstein, 2008; Matlin, 2008). Older students, for instance, generally find this chapter on development easier to master than younger students. Their interactions with children and greater knowledge about life changes create a framework on which to hang new information.

In summary, the more you know, the more you learn. Thus, having a college degree and stimulating occupation may help you stay mentally sharp in your later years (Schaie, 2008; Whitbourne, 2009).

Altrendo/Getty Images

Haven't studies also shown decreases in older adults' memory capabilities? As mentioned at the beginning of the chapter, this may reflect problems with cross-sectional versus longitudinal research. One ongoing, and very encouraging, longitudinal study involves almost 700 nuns in a convent in Minnesota (Mortimer, Snowdon, & Markesbery, 2007; Snowdon, 2003). This research, along with others, documents the brain's amazing ability to grow and change throughout the life span (Chapter 2).

Contrary to popular stereotypes of the frail and forgetful elderly, growing old, for most of us, will probably be better than expected—and, of course, far better than the alternative!

Assessment

STOP

CHECK & REVIEW

Cognitive Development

Objective 9.10: *Describe Piaget's theory of cognitive development, and compare schema, assimilation, and accommodation.*

Piaget believed an infant's intellectual growth progresses in distinct stages, motivated by an innate need to know. He also proposed three major concepts: **schemas**, patterns that organize our interactions with the environment; **assimilation**, absorbing new information into existing schemas; and **accommodation**, adjusting old schemas or developing new ones to fit with new information.

Objective 9.11: *Compare how children's cognitive development changes during Piaget's four stages.*

According to Piaget, cognitive development occurs in an invariant sequence of four stages: **sensorimotor** (birth to age 2), **preoperational** (between 2 and 7), **concrete operational** (between 7 and 11), and **formal operational** (age 11 and up).

In the sensorimotor stage, children acquire **object permanence**. During the preoperational stage, children are better equipped to use symbols. But their language and thinking are limited by their lack of operations, **egocentrism**, and animism.

In the concrete operational stage, children learn to perform operations (to think about concrete things while not actually doing them). They understand the principles of **conservation** and reversibility. During the formal operational stage, the adolescent is able to think abstractly and deal with hypothetical situations but again is prone to a type of adolescent egocentrism.

Objective 9.12: *Identify the major criticisms and contributions of Piaget's theories.*

Although Piaget has been criticized for underestimating abilities and genetic and cultural influences, he remains one of the most respected psychologists in modern times.

Objective 9.13: *Describe the information-processing model of cognitive development.*

Psychologists who explain cognitive development in terms of the information-processing model have found this model especially useful in explaining attention and memory changes across the life span. In contrast to pessimistic early studies, recent research is much more encouraging about age-related changes in information processing.

Questions

1. _____ was one of the first scientists to prove that a child's cognitive processes are fundamentally different from an adult's. (a) Baumrind; (b) Beck; (c) Piaget; (d) Elkind

2. Match the following list of key terms with the correct Piagetian stage:
   ___1. Egocentrism, animism
   ___2. Object permanence
   ___3. Abstract and hypothetical thinking
   ___4. Conservation, reversibility
   ___5. Personal fable, imaginary audience
   a. Sensorimotor
   b. Preoperational
   c. Concrete operational
   d. Formal operational

3. A child's belief that the moon follows him as he travels in a car is an example of _____. (a) sensory permanence; (b) perceptual constancy; (c) egocentrism; (d) object permanence

4. Briefly summarize the major contributions and criticisms of Jean Piaget.

Check your answers in Appendix B.

Click & Review
for additional assessment options:
wiley.com/college/huffman

Social-Emotional Development

chievement

Objective 9.14: *Define* attachment, *and discuss its contributions across the life span.*

Attachment *Strong affectional bond with special others that endures over time*

Imprinting *Innate form of learning within a critical period that involves attachment to the first large moving object seen*

chievement

Objective 9.15: *Discuss the three key parenting styles.*

The poet John Donne wrote, "No man is an island, entire of itself." In addition to physical and cognitive development, developmental psychologists are very interested in social-emotional development. That is, they study how our social relations and emotions grow and change over the life span. Two of the most important topics are *attachment* and *parenting styles*.

Attachment: The Importance of Bonding

An infant arrives in the world with a multitude of behaviors that encourage a strong and lasting bond of **attachment** with primary caregivers. Most research has focused on the attachment between mother and child. However, infants also form attachment bonds with fathers, grandparents, and other caregivers.

In studying attachment behavior, researchers are often divided along the lines of the now-familiar nature-versus-nurture debate. Those who advocate the nurture position suggest attachment results from a child's interactions and experiences with his or her environment. In contrast, the nativist, or innate, position cites John Bowlby's work (1969, 1989, 2000). He proposed that newborn infants are biologically equipped with verbal and nonverbal behaviors (such as crying, clinging, smiling) and with "following" behaviors (such as crawling and walking after the caregiver) that elicit instinctive nurturing responses from the caregiver. Konrad Lorenz's (1937) early studies of **imprinting** further support the biological argument for attachment (Concept Diagram 9.2).

What happens if a child does not form an attachment? Researchers have investigated this question in two ways: They have looked at children and adults who spent their early years in institutions without the stimulation and love of a regular caregiver or who lived at home but were physically isolated under abusive conditions.

Infants raised in impersonal or abusive surroundings suffer from a number of problems. They seldom cry, coo, or babble; they become rigid when picked up; and they have few language skills. As for their social-emotional development, they tend to form shallow or anxious relationships. Some appear forlorn, withdrawn, and uninterested in their caretakers, whereas others seem insatiable in their need for affection. They also tend to show intellectual, physical, and perceptual retardation, along with increased susceptibility to infection, and neurotic "rocking" and isolation behaviors. In some cases, these infants are so deprived they die from lack of attachment (Bowlby, 1973, 1982, 2000; Combrink-Graham & McKenna, 2006; Nelson, Zeanah, & Fox, 2007; Spitz & Wolf, 1946; Zeanah, 2000).

Parenting Styles: Their Effect on Development

How much of our personality comes from the way our parents treat us as we're growing up? Researchers since the 1920s have studied the effects of different methods of child-rearing on children's behavior, development, and mental health. Studies done by Diana Baumrind (1980, 1991, 1995) found that parenting styles could be reliably divided into three broad patterns, *permissive*, *authoritarian*, and *authoritative*, which could be identified by their degree of *control/demandingness* (C) and *warmth/responsiveness* (W) (Figure 9.16):

1. ***Permissive.*** Permissive parents tend to provide little discipline or control and fall into one of two styles:

   - *Permissive-neglectful* (also called *permissive-indifferent*). These parents are low on control/demandingness (C) (few demands, little structure or monitoring), and low on warmth/responsiveness (W) (little interest or emotional support, and may be actively rejecting). "I don't care about you—or what you do." Their children tend to have poor social skills and little self-control (e.g., becoming demanding and disobedient).

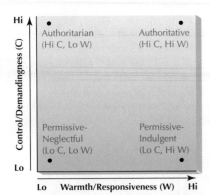

Figure 9.16 *Baumrind's parenting styles related to control/demandingness (C) and warmth/responsiveness (W).*

Concept Diagram 9.2
Attachment

According to imprinting studies, infants become attached to the first large moving object (a). But is there scientific evidence to support this claim? In a classic experiment involving infant rhesus monkeys, Harry Harlow and Robert Zimmerman (1959) investigated the variables that might affect attachment. They created two types of wire-framed surrogate (substitute) "mother" monkeys: one covered by soft terry cloth and one left uncovered (b). The infant monkeys were fed by either the cloth or the wire mother, but they otherwise had access to both mothers. The researchers found that monkeys "reared" by a cloth mother clung frequently to the soft material of their surrogate mother and developed greater emotional security and curiosity than did monkeys assigned to the wire mother.

In later research (Harlow & Harlow, 1966), monkey babies were exposed to rejection. Some of the "mothers" contained metal

Nina Leen/Getty Images/Time Life Pictures

(a) **Imprinting** *Lorenz's studies on imprinting demonstrated that baby geese attach to, and then follow, the first large moving object they see during a certain critical period in their development.*

spikes that would suddenly protrude from the cloth covering and push the babies away; others had air jets that would sometimes blow the babies away. Nevertheless, the infant monkeys waited until the rejection was over and then clung to the cloth mothers as tightly as before. From these and related findings, Harlow concluded that *contact comfort,* the pleasurable tactile sensations provided by a soft and cuddly "parent," is a powerful contributor to attachment. The satisfaction of other physical needs, such as food, is not enough.

Several studies suggest that contact comfort between human infants and mothers is similarly important (c) (d). For example, touching and massaging premature infants produce significant physical and emotional benefits (Field, 1998, 2007; Hernandez-Reif, Diego, & Field, 2007; Feldman, 2007). Mothers around the world tend to kiss, nuzzle, nurse, comfort, clean, and respond to their children with lots of physical contact.

Nina Leen/Time Life Pictures/Getty Images

(b) **Attachment** *Even when the wire "mother" provided all their food, monkeys showed strong attachment behaviors toward the cloth mother.*

James L. Stanfield/NG Image Collection

(c) **Maternal contact comfort** *Japanese mothers touch their infants to communicate with them, breast-feed, carry them around on their backs, take baths with them, and sleep in the same bed with them.*

Steve Raymer/NG Image Collection

(d) **Fathers matter too** *Although almost all research on attachment and contact comfort has focused on mothers and infants, recent research shows that the same results also apply to fathers and other caregivers (Diener et al., 2008; Grossmann et al., 2002, Lindberg, Axelsson & Öhrling, 2008; Martinelli, 2006).*

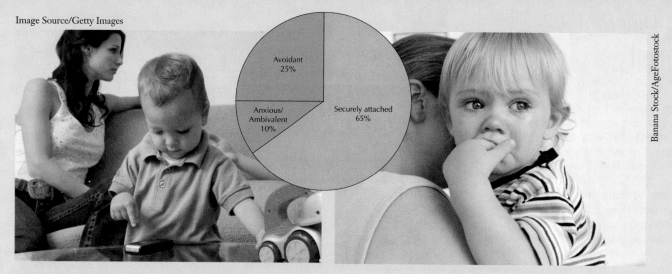

Image Source/Getty Images

Banana Stock/AgeFotostock

Concept Diagram

(e) *Mary Ainsworth and her colleagues (1967, 1978) identified three significant differences in the levels of attachment between infants and their mothers.*

- *Securely attached (65 percent).* When exposed to a stranger, the infant seeks closeness and contact with the mother, uses the mother as a safe base from which to explore, shows moderate distress on separation from the mother, and is happy when the mother returns.
- *Avoidant (25 percent).* The infant does not seek closeness or contact with the mother, treats the mother much like a stranger, and rarely cries when the mother leaves the room.
- *Anxious/Ambivalent (10 percent).* The infant becomes very upset when the mother leaves the room. When she returns, the infant seeks close contact and then squirms angrily to get away.

Ainsworth found that infants with a secure attachment style have caregivers who are sensitive and responsive to their signals of distress, happiness, and fatigue (Ainsworth et al., 1967, 1978; Gini et al., 2007; Higley, 2008; Völker, 2007). On the other hand, avoidant infants have caregivers who are aloof and distant, and anxious/ambivalent infants have inconsistent caregivers who alternate between strong affection and indifference. Follow-up studies found securely attached children were less worried and fearful, and more sociable, emotionally aware, enthusiastic, cooperative, persistent, curious, and competent (Bar-Haim et al., 2008; Brown & Whiteside, 2008; Johnson, Dweck, & Chen, 2007).

- *Permissive-indulgent* (low C, high W). Parents with this style set few limits or demands, but are highly involved and emotionally connected. "I care about you—and you're free to do what you like!" Children of these parents often fail to learn respect for others and tend to be impulsive, immature, and out of control.

2. *Authoritarian* (high C, low W). These parents are rigid and punitive, while also being low on warmth and responsiveness. "I don't care what you want. Just do it my way, or else!" Their children tend to be easily upset, moody, aggressive, and often fail to learn good communication skills.

3. *Authoritative* (high C, high W). Authoritative parents generally set and enforce firm limits, while also being highly involved, tender, and emotionally supportive. "I really care about you, but there are rules and you need to be responsible." As you might expect, children do best with authoritative parents. They become more self-reliant, self-controlled, high achieving, and emotionally well-adjusted. They also seem more content, goal oriented, friendly, and socially competent (Coplan, Arbeau, & Armer, 2008; Driscoll, Russell, & Crockett, 2008; Martin & Fabes, 2009; McKinney, Donnelly, & Renk, 2008; Shields, 2008).

 Study Tip

These last two terms are very similar. An easy way to remember is to notice the two Rs in authoRitaRian, and imagine a Rigid Ruler. Then note the last two Ts in authoriTaTive, and picture a Tender Teacher.

Evaluating Baumrind's Research

Before you conclude that the authoritative pattern is the only way to raise successful children, you should know that many children raised in the other styles also become caring, cooperative adults. Criticism of Baumrind's findings generally falls into three areas:

- *Child temperament.* Results may reflect the child's unique temperament and reactions to parental efforts rather than the parenting style per se (Bradley & Corwyn, 2008; Oldehinkel et al., 2006; Xu, 2008). That is, the parents of mature and competent children may have developed the authoritative style because of the child's behavior rather than vice versa.

- *Child expectations.* Cultural research suggests that a child's expectations of how parents should behave also play an important role in parenting styles (Laungani, 2007). As we discovered at the beginning of this chapter, adolescents in Korea expect strong parental control and interpret it as a sign of love and deep concern. Adolescents in North America, however, might interpret the same behavior as a sign of parental hostility and rejection.

- *Parental warmth.* Cross-cultural studies suggest that the most important variable in parenting styles and child development might be the degree of warmth versus rejection parents feel toward their children. Analyses of over 100 societies have shown that parental rejection adversely affects children of all cultures (Khalegue, 2007; Parmar, Ibrahim & Rohner, 2008; Rohner, 1986, 2008; Rohner & Britner, 2002). The neglect and indifference shown by rejecting parents tend to be correlated with hostile, aggressive children who have a difficult time establishing and maintaining close relationships. These children also are more likely to develop psychological problems that require professional intervention.

Kaz Mori/Photographers Choices/Getty Images

Do fathers differ from mothers in their parenting style? Until recently, the father's role in discipline and child care was largely ignored. But as more fathers have begun to take an active role in child-rearing, there has been a corresponding increase in research. From these studies, we now know that children do best with authoritative dads, and with fathers who are equally absorbed with, excited about, and responsive to their newborns. Researchers also find few differences in the way children form attachments to either parent (Diener, et al., 2002; Lopez & Hsu, 2002; Talitwala, 2007). After infancy, the father becomes increasingly involved with his children, yet he still spends less overall time in direct child care than the mother does. In general, fathers are just as responsive, nurturing, and competent as mothers when they assume child-care responsibilities.

Are fathers important? *Although overlooked in the past, the father's role in a child's development is now a topic of active research.*

Application

RESEARCH HIGHLIGHT

Romantic Love and Attachment

Objective 9.16: *Discuss how infant attachment may be related to romantic love.*

If you've been around young children, you've probably noticed how often they share toys and discoveries with a parent and how they seem much happier when a parent is nearby. You may also have thought how cute and sweet it is when infants and parents coo and share baby talk with each other. But have you noticed that these very same behaviors often occur between adults in romantic relationships?

Intrigued by these parallels, several researchers have studied the relationship between an infant's attachment to a parent figure and an adult's love for a romantic partner (Clulow, 2007; Duncan, 2007; Lele, 2008). In one study, Cindy Hazan and Phillip Shaver (1987, 1994) discovered that adults who had an avoidant pattern in infancy find it hard to trust others and to self-disclose, and they rarely report finding "true love." In short, they block intimacy by being emotionally aloof and distant.

Anxious/ambivalent infants tend to be obsessed with their romantic partners as adults,

Bill Bachmann/Index Stock

Karen Huffman

The importance of attachment *Researchers have found that the degree and quality of attachments you formed as an infant are correlated with your adult romantic relationships.*

fearing that their intense love will not be reciprocated. As a result, they tend to smother intimacy by being possessive and emotionally demanding.

In contrast, individuals who are securely attached as infants easily become close to others, expect intimate relationships to endure, and perceive others as generally trustworthy. As you may expect, the securely attached lover has intimacy patterns that foster long-term relationships and is the most desired partner by the majority of adults, regardless of their own attachment styles (Lele, 2008; Mikulincer & Goodman, 2006; Vorria et al., 2007).

As you consider these correlations between infant attachment and adult romantic love styles, remember that it is always risky to infer causation from correlation. Accordingly, the relationship between romantic love style and early infant attachment is subject to several alternative explanations. Also, be aware that early attachment experiences may predict the future, but they do not determine it. Throughout life, we can learn new social skills and different attitudes toward relationships.

Try This Yourself

What's Your Romantic Attachment Style?

Thinking of your current and past romantic relationships, place a check next to those statements that best describe your feelings.

1. *I find it relatively easy to get close to others and am comfortable depending on them and having them depend on me. I don't often worry about being abandoned or about someone getting too close.*

2. *I am somewhat uncomfortable being close. I find it difficult to trust partners completely or to allow myself to depend on them. I am nervous when anyone gets close, and love partners often want me to be more intimate than is comfortable for me.*

3. *I find that others are reluctant to get as close as I would like. I often worry that my partner doesn't really love me or won't stay with me. I want to merge completely with another person, and this desire sometimes scares people away.*

According to research, 55 percent of adults agree with item 1 (secure attachment), 25 percent choose number 2 (avoidant attachment), and 20 percent choose item 3 (anxious/ambivalent attachment) (adapted from Fraley & Shaver, 1997; Hazan & Shaver, 1987). Note that the percentages for these adult attachment styles are roughly equivalent to the percentages for infant–parent attachment.

Application

CRITICAL THINKING

ACTIVE LEARNING

Objective 9.17: *What motivates suicide bombers?*

The Development of "Suicide Bombers"
(Contributed by Thomas Frangicetto)

The war in Iraq. Suicide Bombers. The 9/11 World Trade Center terrorist attack. In varying degrees all of these horrific events are the result of culture clashes, misunderstandings, mistrust, and mistaken beliefs. They also reflect lethal hatred. A recent *60 Minutes* broadcast, "The Mind of a Suicide Bomber," examined the psychology of two "failed" suicide bombers who were captured and interviewed by Dr. Eyad Sarraj, a Palestinian psychiatrist. These individuals are obviously violent killers, right? "No, on the contrary," says Sarraj. "They usually were very timid people, introverts, the problem for them was always…communicating their feelings, so they were not violent at all." But, as so many Americans tend to believe, are these people psychotic, or out of touch with reality? According to Dr. Ariel Merari,

Q. Sakamaki/Redux Pictures

"I don't know of a single case of one of them who was really psychotic. And still, there is this absolute absence of fear…"

According to Sarraj and Merari, the decision to become a suicide bomber is positively reinforced by many sociocultural consequences that strengthen the appeal within the population. What are these sociocultural reinforcers for suicide bombers?

- They achieve the highest rank in their religion—martyrdom.
- Their families not only are rewarded monetarily, but they also attain an exalted status within their culture.
- They are revered as heroes and serve as idols worthy of emulation.
- They are promised an automatic "ticket to Paradise" where they will be immediately married to 72 beautiful virgins.

Critical Thinking Application

Using the cultural psychology guidelines for developmental research (pp. 000) and other information found throughout Chapter 9, answer the following:

1. Would suicide bombing be more likely in an individualist or a collectivist culture? Why?
2. Given that culture is largely invisible to its participants, what are the seldom discussed ideals and values in American culture that encourage young men and women to voluntarily sign up to go to war, but not to become suicide bombers?
3. Which of Piaget's four stages of cognitive development best describes the cognitive processes of suicide bombers? Why?
4. Do you think attachment theory could help explain suicide bombers? Explain why or why not.
5. Which of Baumrind's three parenting styles would be most and least likely to produce a suicide bomber?

Assessment

CHECK & REVIEW

STOP

Social-Emotional Development

Objective 9.14: *Define* attachment, *and discuss its contributions across the life span.*

Attachment is a strong affectional bond with special others that endures over time. Nativists believe it is innate. Nurturists believe it is learned. The Harlow and Zimmerman experiments with monkeys raised by cloth or wire surrogate mothers found that contact comfort might be the most important factor in attachment.

Infants who fail to form attachments may suffer serious effects. When attachments are formed, they may differ in level or degree.

Objective 9.15: *Discuss the three key parenting styles.*

Parenting styles fall into three major categories: permissive, authoritarian, and authoritative. Researchers suggest that a child's unique temperament, his or her expectations of parents, and the degree of warmth versus rejection from parents may be the three most important variables in parenting styles.

Objective 9.16: *Discuss how infant attachment may be related to romantic love.*

Research that identified *securely attached, avoidant,* and *anxious/ambivalent* infants found that their early behavioral differences may persist into romantic relationships in adulthood.

Objective 9.17: *What motivates suicide bombers?*

There are several reinforcers, including martyrdom, hero status, and a "ticket to paradise," as well as money and status for their families.

Questions

1. According to Harlow and Zimmerman's research with cloth and wire surrogate mothers, _____ is the most important variable for attachment. (a) availability of food; (b) contact comfort; (c) caregiver and infant bonding; (d) imprinting

2. List the three types of attachment reported by Ainsworth.

3. Using Hazan and Shaver's research on adult attachment styles, match the following adults with their probable type of infant attachment:

___ Mary is nervous around attractive partners and complains that lovers often want her to be more intimate than she finds comfortable.

___ Bob complains that lovers are often reluctant to get as close as he would like.

___ Rashelle finds it relatively easy to get close to others and seldom worries about being abandoned.

4. Briefly explain Baumrind's three parenting styles.

Check your answers in Appendix B.

Click & Review
for additional assessment options:
wiley.com/college/huffman

Assessment

KEY TERMS

To assess your understanding of the Key Terms in Chapter 9, write a definition for each (in your own words), and then compare your definitions with those in the text.

developmental psychology (p. 316)

Studying Development
critical period (p. 317)
cross-sectional method (p. 318)
longitudinal method (p. 318)
maturation (p. 317)

Physical Development
ageism (p. 329)
embryonic period (p. 323)

fetal alcohol syndrome (FAS) (p. 324)
fetal period (p. 323)
germinal period (p. 323)
puberty (p. 327)
teratogen [Tuh-RAT-uh-jen] (p. 322)

Cognitive Development
accommodation (p. 332)
assimilation (p. 332)
concrete operational stage (p. 335)
conservation (p. 335)

egocentrism (p. 335)
formal operational stage (p. 335)
object permanence (p. 333)
preoperational stage (p. 333)
schema (p. 332)
sensorimotor stage (p. 333)

Social-Emotional Development
attachment (p. 340)
imprinting (p. 340)

Achievement

WEB RESOURCES

Huffman Book Companion Site
wiley.com/college/huffman
This site is loaded with free Interactive Self-Tests, Internet Exercises, Glossary and Flashcards for key terms, web links, Handbook for Non-Native Speakers, and other activities designed to improve your mastery of the material in this chapter.

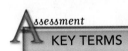

Chapter 9 Visual Summary

Studying Development

Developmental Psychology

Studies age-related changes in behavior and mental processes from conception to death.

Theoretical Issues

- nature vs. nurture
- continuity vs. stages
- stability vs. change

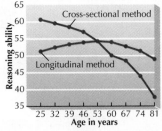

Research Methods

Cross-sectional: Different participants, various ages, one point in time. Major problem: Cohort effects (a given generation may be affected by specific cultural and historical events).
Longitudinal: Same participants, extended time period. Major problem: Expensive, time consuming.

Physical Development (Chapter 9)
Cognitive Development (Chapter 9)
Social-Emotional Development (Chapter 9)
Personality Development (Chapter 10)
Moral Development (Chapter 10)
Sepcial Issues (Chapter 10)

Physical Development

Prenatal and Early Childhood

- Three prenatal stages: **germinal**, **embryonic**, and **fetal**.
- **Teratogens:** Environmental agents capable of producing birth defects.
- Sensory and perceptual abilities are relatively well developed in newborns.
- Motor development primarily results from **maturation**.

Adolescence and Adulthood

- Adolescence: Psychological period between childhood and adulthood.
- **Puberty:** When sex organs become capable of reproduction.
- Menopause: Cessation of menstruation.
- Male climacteric: Physical and psychological changes in midlife.
- Primary aging: Inevitable, biological changes with age.
- Explanations of primary aging: *Programmed theory* (genetically built-in) and *damage theory* (body's inability to repair damage).

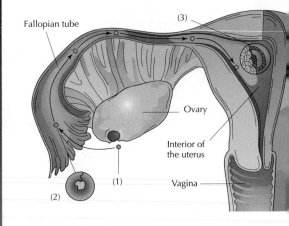

Fallopian tube
(3)
Ovary
Interior of the uterus
(1)
Vagina
(2)

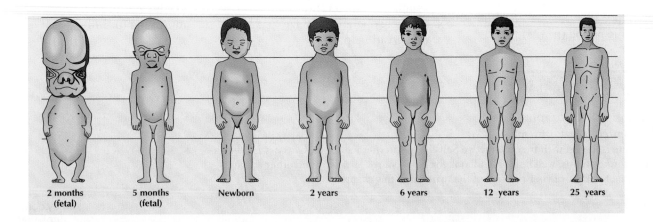

2 months (fetal)   5 months (fetal)   Newborn   2 years   6 years   12 years   25 years

Cognitive Development

Piaget's Major Concepts:

- **Schema:** Cognitive structure for organizing ideas.

- **Assimilation:** Adding new information to an existing schema.

- **Accommodation:** Revising or developing new schemas to fit with new information.

Four Stages	Abilities	Limits
Sensorimotor (Birth to 2 years)	Uses senses and motor skills to explore and develop cognitively.	At beginning of stage, infant lacks **object permanence** (understanding things continue to exist even when not seen, heard, or felt).
Preoperational (Age 2 to 7)	Has significant language and thinks symbolically.	• Cannot perform "operations." • **Egocentric** thinking (inability to consider another's point of view). • Animistic thinking (believing all things are living)
Concrete Operational (Age 7 to 11)	• Can perform "operations" on concrete objects. • Understands **conservation** (realizes changes in shape or appearance can be reversed).	Cannot think abstractly and hypothetically.
Formal Operational (11 and up)	Can think abstractly and hypothetically.	Adolescent egocentrism at the beginning of this stage, with related problems of the *personal fable* and *imaginary audience*.

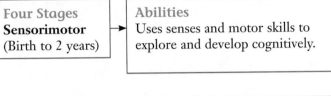

Social-Emotional Development

Attachment

- Infant attachment: **Imprinting:** Attaching to first moving object. Harlow's experiments found "contact comfort" very important to **attachment**. Infants who do not attach may suffer serious, lasting effects.

- Adult attachment: Patterns of infant attachment (secure, avoidant, and anxious/ambivalent) may carry over into adult romantic attachments.

Parenting Styles

There are three major categories (*permissive*, *authoritarian*, and *authoritative*), but critics suggest that a child's unique temperament, expectations of parents, and responsiveness degree of warmth and responsiveness from parents may be the most important determinants of parenting styles.

10

Life Span Development II

magine that you are standing on a bridge over a railroad track when you see that a runaway train is about to kill five people. Coincidentally, you are standing next to a switching mechanism, and you realize that by simply throwing a switch, you can divert the train onto a spur, allowing the five to survive. But here is the catch: diverting the train will condemn *one* person, who is standing on the spur, to death (Appiah, 2008). What would you do? Would you allow one person to die in order to save five others? Would your answer be different if that person were your mother, father, or some other much-loved person? What might lead different people to make different decisions?

It's unlikely that you will ever have to make such a gruesome choice. Yet everyone encounters moral dilemmas from time to time. (Should you remind the cable company that they forgot to disconnect the cable after you discontinued the service? Should you give spare change to a friendly panhandler in your neighborhood?) Likewise, everyone has personal relationships and particular character traits that color our decisions. How we approach moral dilemmas—as well as many other events and circumstances throughout our lives—reflects several key facets of our life span development. Chapter 9 explored life span changes in physical development, cognitive development, and social-emotional development. In this chapter, we'll look at moral development, personality development, special challenges of adulthood, and grief and death.

> Morality is the basis of things and truth is the substance of all morality.
>
> MOHANDAS GANDHI

> When morality comes up against profit, it is seldom that profit loses.
>
> SHIRLEY CHISHOLM

> Quien teme la muerte no goza la vida. (He who fears death cannot enjoy life,)
>
> SPANISH PROVERB

> Let us endeavor so to live that when we come to die even the undertaker will be sorry.
>
> SAMUEL CLEMENS (MARK TWAIN)

Taxi Japan/Getty Images

Taxi Japan/Getty Images

▶ **Moral Development**

Kohlberg's Research
Assessing Kohlberg's Theory
CRITICAL THINKING/ACTIVE LEARNING
Morality and Academic Cheating

▶ **Personality Development**

Thomas and Chess's Temperament Theory
Erikson's Psychosocial Theory

GENDER & CULTURAL DIVERSITY
Cultural Influences on Development

▶ **Meeting the Challenges of Adulthood**

Committed Relationships

PSYCHOLOGY AT WORK
Are Your Marital Expectations Unrealistic?

Families

RESEARCH HIGHLIGHT
Children Who Survive Despite the Odds

PSYCHOLOGY AT WORK
Positive Careers and Rewarding Retirements

GENDER & CULTURAL DIVERSITY
Cultural Differences in Ageism

▶ **Grief and Death**

Grief
Attitudes Toward Death and Dying
The Death Experience

PSYCHOLOGY AT WORK
Dealing with Your Own Death Anxiety

WHY STUDY PSYCHOLOGY?

Did you know...

▶ A 5-year-old typically believes that *accidentally* breaking 15 cups is "badder" and more deserving of punishment than *intentionally* breaking 1 cup?

▶ Juvenile chimpanzees will soothe a frightened or injured peer, and adult female chimps will "adopt" a motherless baby?

▶ One of the most influential factors in early personality development is goodness of fit between a child's nature and the social and environmental setting?

Left Lane Productions/Corbis Images

▶ Erikson believed that adolescents who fail to resolve their "identity crises" may later have difficulty in maintaining close personal relationships and be more prone to delinquency?

▶ Parents typically experience their highest levels of marital satisfaction before children are born and after they leave home?

▶ Kübler-Ross believed that most people go through five predictable psychological stages when facing death?

Achievement

Objective 10.1: *What is the biological perspective on morality?*

Moral Development

In Chapter 9, we noted that newborns cry when they hear another baby cry. But did you know that by age 2, most children use words like *good* or *bad* to evaluate actions that are aggressive or that might endanger their own or another's welfare? Or that juvenile chimpanzees will soothe a frightened or injured peer, and adult female chimps will "adopt" a motherless baby (Hoffman, 2007; Goodall, 1990; Malti, 2007)? How can we explain such early emergence and cross-species evidence of *morality*—the ability to take the perspective of, or empathize with, others and distinguish between right and wrong?

From a biological perspective, some researchers suggest that morality may be prewired and evolutionarily based (Krebs, 2007; Krebs & Hemingway, 2008; Workman & Reader, 2008). Behaviors like infant empathic crying and adoption of motherless chimp babies help the species survive. Therefore, evolution may have provided us with biologically based provisions for moral acts. But as with most human behaviors, biology is only one part of the *biopsychosocial model*. In this section, we will focus our attention on the psychological and social factors that explain how moral thoughts, feelings, and actions change over the life span.

Kohlberg's Research: What Is Right?

Developing a sense of right and wrong, or *morality*, is a part of psychological development. Consider the following situation in terms of what you would do.

In Europe, a woman was near death from a special kind of cancer. There was one drug that doctors thought might save her. It was a form of radium that a druggist in the same town had recently discovered. The drug was expensive to make, but the druggist was charging 10 times what the drug cost him. He paid $200 for the radium and charged $2000 for a small dose of the drug. The sick woman's husband, Heinz, went to everyone he knew to borrow the money, but he could gather together only about $1000, half of what it cost. He told the druggist that his wife was dying and asked him to sell it cheaper or let him pay later. But the druggist said, "No,

I discovered the drug, and I'm going to make money from it." So Heinz got desperate and broke into the man's store to steal the drug for his wife. (Kohlberg, 1964, pp. 18–19)

Was Heinz right to steal the drug? What do you consider moral behavior? Is morality "in the eye of the beholder," or are there universal truths and principles? Whatever your answer, your ability to think, reason, and respond to Heinz's dilemma demonstrates another type of development that is very important to psychology—*morality*.

One of the most influential researchers in moral development was Lawrence Kohlberg (1927–1987). He presented what he called "moral stories" like this Heinz dilemma to people of all ages. On the basis of his findings, he developed a highly influential model of moral development (1964, 1984).

What is the right answer to Heinz's dilemma? Kohlberg was interested not in whether participants judged Heinz right or wrong but in the reasons they gave for their decision. On the basis of participants' responses, Kohlberg proposed three broad levels in the evolution of moral reasoning, each composed of two distinct stages (Process Diagram 10.1). Individuals at each stage and level may or may not support Heinz's stealing of the drug, but their reasoning changes from level to level.

Kohlberg believed that, like Piaget's stages of cognitive development (Chapter 9), his stages of moral development are *universal* and *invariant*. That is, they supposedly exist in all cultures, and everyone goes through each of the stages in a predictable fashion.

Assessing Kohlberg's Theory: Three Major Criticisms

Kohlberg has been credited with enormous insights and contributions about how we think about moral issues (Appiah, 2008; Krebs, 2007; Lapsley, 2006). But his theories have also been the focus of three major areas of criticism.

1. ***Moral reasoning versus behavior***. Are people who achieve higher stages on Kohlberg's scale really more moral than others? Or do they just "talk a good game"? Some studies show a positive correlation between higher stages of reasoning and higher levels of moral behavior (Borba, 2001; Rest et al., 1999). But others have found that situational factors are better predictors of moral behavior (Bandura, 1986, 1991, 2008; Kaplan, 2006; Satcher, 2007; Slováčková & Slováček, 2007) (Figure 10.1). For example, research participants are more likely to steal when they are told the money comes from a large company rather than from individuals (Greenberg, 2002). And both men and women will tell more sexual lies during casual relationships than during close relationships (Williams, 2001).

2. ***Cultural differences***. Cross-cultural studies report that children from a variety of cultures generally follow Kohlberg's model and progress sequentially from his first level, the *preconventional*, to his second, the *conventional* (Rest et al., 1999; Snarey, 1995).

   Other studies find differences among cultures. For example, cross-cultural comparisons of responses to Heinz's moral dilemma show that Europeans and Americans tend to consider whether they like or identify with the victim in questions of morality. In contrast, Hindu Indians consider social responsibility and personal concerns two

Lawrence Kohlberg
(1927-1987)

Achievement

Objective 10.2: *Describe Kohlberg's three levels and six stages of moral development.*

Achievement

Objective 10.3: *What are the three major criticisms of Kohlberg's theory?*

"I swear I wasn't looking at smut—I was just stealing music."

Figure 10.1 ***Morality gap?*** What makes people who normally behave ethically willing to steal intellectual property such as music or software?

wiley.com/
college/
huffman

Process Diagram 10.1
Kohlberg's Moral Development

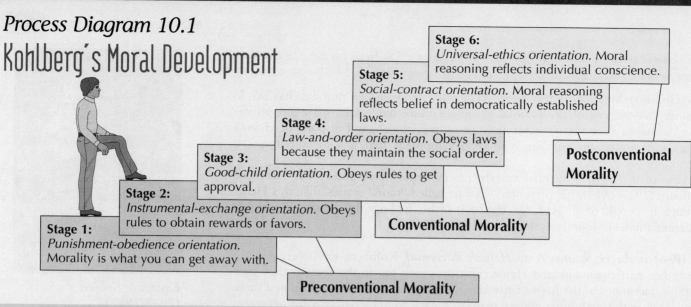

Stage 6:
Universal-ethics orientation. Moral reasoning reflects individual conscience.

Stage 5:
Social-contract orientation. Moral reasoning reflects belief in democratically established laws.

Postconventional Morality

Stage 4:
Law-and-order orientation. Obeys laws because they maintain the social order.

Stage 3:
Good-child orientation. Obeys rules to get approval.

Conventional Morality

Stage 2:
Instrumental-exchange orientation. Obeys rules to obtain rewards or favors.

Stage 1:
Punishment-obedience orientation. Morality is what you can get away with.

Preconventional Morality

Preconventional level (Stages 1 and 2—birth to adolescence). Moral judgment is *self-centered*. What is right is what one can get away with, or what is personally satisfying. Moral understanding is based on rewards, punishments, and the exchange of favors. This level is called preconventional because children have not yet accepted society's (conventional) rule-making processes.

- **Stage 1 (punishment-obedience orientation).** Focus is on self-interest—obedience to authority and avoidance of punishment. Because children at this stage have difficulty considering another's point of view, they also ignore people's intentions. A 5-year-old will often say that accidentally breaking 15 cups is "badder" and should receive more punishment than intentionally breaking 1 cup.

- **Stage 2 (instrumental-exchange orientation).** Children become aware of others' perspectives, but their morality is based on reciprocity—an equal exchange of favors. "I'll share my lunch with you because if I ever forget mine you'll share yours with me." The guiding philosophy is "You scratch my back and I'll scratch yours."

Conventional level (Stages 3 and 4—adolescence and young adulthood). Moral reasoning is *other-centered*. Conventional societal rules are accepted because they help ensure the social order. Morality is judged by degree of compliance with these societal rules.

- **Stage 3 (good-child orientation).** Primary moral concern is being nice and gaining approval, and judges others by their intentions—"His heart was in the right place."

- **Stage 4 (law-and-order orientation).** Morality based on a larger perspective—societal laws. Understanding that if everyone violated laws, even with good intentions, there would be chaos; Stage 4 individuals believe in doing one's duty and respecting law and order. According to Kohlberg, Stage 4 is the highest level attained by most adolescents and adults.

Postconventional level (Stages 5 and 6—adulthood). Moral judgments based on *personal standards for right and wrong*. Morality also defined in terms of abstract principles and values that apply to all situations and societies (e.g., judging the "discovery" and settlement of North America by Europeans as immoral because it involved the theft of land from native peoples).

- **Stage 5 (social-contract orientation).** Appreciation for the underlying purposes served by laws. Societal laws are obeyed because of the "social contract," but they can be morally disobeyed if they fail to express the will of the majority or fail to maximize social welfare.

- **Stage 6 (universal-ethics orientation).** "Right" is determined by universal ethical principles (e.g., nonviolence, human dignity, freedom) that *all* religions or moral authorities might view as compelling or fair. These principles apply whether or not they conform to existing laws. Thus, Mohandas Gandhi and Martin Luther King intentionally broke laws that violated universal principles, such as human dignity. Few individuals actually achieve Stage 6 (about 1 or 2 percent of those tested worldwide), and Kohlberg found it difficult to separate Stages 5 and 6. So, in time, he combined the stages (Kohlberg, 1981).

Associated Press

Testing your personal morality *Would you travel hundreds of miles to participate in a political demonstration, and be willing to be arrested for violating the law to express your moral convictions? If so, where would you be placed on Kohlberg's stages?*

Preconventional Level *Kohlberg's first level of moral development, in which morality is based on rewards, punishment, and exchange of favors*

Conventional Level *Kohlberg's second level of moral development, in which moral judgments are based on compliance with the rules and values of society*

Postconventional Level *Kohlberg's highest level of moral development, in which individuals develop personal standards for right and wrong and define morality in terms of abstract principles and values that apply to all situations and societies*

Process Diagram

separate issues (Miller & Bersoff, 1998). Researchers suggest that the difference reflects the Indians' broader sense of social responsibility.

In India, Papua New Guinea, and China, as well as in Israeli kibbutzim, people don't choose between the rights of the individual and the rights of society (as the top levels of Kohlberg's model require). Instead, most people seek a compromise solution that accommodates both interests (Killen & Hart, 1999; Miller & Bersoff, 1998). Thus, Kohlberg's standard for judging the highest level of morality (the postconventional) may be more applicable to cultures that value individualism over community and interpersonal relationships.

3. **Possible gender bias**. Researcher Carol Gilligan criticized Kohlberg's model because on his scale women often tend to be classified at a lower level of moral reasoning than men. Gilligan suggested that this difference occurred because Kohlberg's theory emphasizes values more often held by men, such as rationality and independence, while deemphasizing common female values, such as concern for others and belonging (Gilligan, 1977, 1990, 1993; Kracher & Marble, 2008). Most follow-up studies of Gilligan's theory, however, have found few, if any, gender differences in level or type of moral reasoning (Hoffman, 2000; Hyde, 2007; Pratt, Skoe, & Arnold, 2004; Smith, 2007).

Jonathan Nourok/Stone/Getty Images

Gilligan versus Kohlberg *According to Carol Gilligan, women score "lower" on Lawrence Kohlberg's stages of moral development because they are socialized to assume more responsibility for the care of others. What do you think?*

Application

CRITICAL THINKING

Morality and Academic Cheating
(Contributed by Thomas Frangicetto)

Photodisc/SUPERSTOCK

Recent research from *The Center for Academic Integrity* on cheating among American high school students found that: (1) cheating is widespread, (2) students have little difficulty rationalizing cheating, (3) the Internet is causing new concerns, and (4) students cheat for a variety of reasons. Do you think academic cheating is a moral issue? Consider the following moral dilemma:

It is close to final exam time in your psychology course, and you are on the border between a C or B grade. You go to your professor's office to see what you can do to make sure you get the B grade. But there's a note on the open door, "I'll be right back. Please wait." You notice the stack of exams for your upcoming final, and you could easily take one and leave without being seen.

Part I. Describe what you would do in this situation, and briefly explain your reasons.

_____

_____

_____

_____

After reviewing Kohlberg's six stages of moral development (Process Diagram 10.1), can you label your stage of moral development on this moral dilemma? Stage # _____.

Part II. To further develop your critical thinking (and help prepare you for exams on this material), read and label the following responses to the same situation.

ACTIVE LEARNING

Student A: "I wouldn't take the exam because it would be wrong. What if *everybody* cheated every chance they got? What kind of credibility would grades have? It would cheapen the value of education and the whole system would be worthless." Stage # _____.

Student B: "I would take the exam because I really need the B in this course. Psychology is not my major, and I have to keep my scholarship. Otherwise, I will not be able to stay in school and my children will suffer." Stage # _____.

Student C: "I wouldn't take it because I would be too afraid of getting caught. With my luck, the teacher would return early and catch me in the act." Stage # _____.

Student D: "I wouldn't take the exam because I wouldn't be able to live with myself. I believe that cheating is the same as stealing and is therefore a crime. My own opinion of myself as an honest person of high integrity would be permanently damaged." Stage # _____.

Student E: "I wouldn't take it because if I got caught and my parents found out they would be devastated. I care too much about what they think of me to risk that. Stage # _____.

Student F: "I wouldn't do it because it wouldn't be fair to other students who have to take the exam without any advantages.

The system is designed to work fairly for everyone and cheating definitely violates that ideal." Stage # _____.

Part III. Critical Thinking Application
Review the 21 critical thinking components (CTCs) from the Prologue (pp. 000–000). Below are a few student comments quoted in the report of The Center for Academic Integrity. Apply at least one CTC to each.
"I think that cheating has become so common that it's starting to become 'normal' in some cases." CTC: _____

"There is no way of stopping it. Only the students themselves have the power to do so. Restrictions aren't the problem, but the morals of students sure are." CTC: _____

"Cheating will always exist as long as parents place the emphasis on grades rather than learning. The parent–student relation adds greatly to the dumbing down of America." CTC: _____

"Unless someone makes teachers care about cheating, it won't be stopped. It is unfair that teachers don't take it seriously because then the honest students get the bad end of the deal." CTC: _____

Check your answers to Part II in Appendix B.

Click & Review
for additional assessment options:
wiley.com/college/huffman

Assessment

STOP

CHECK & REVIEW

Moral Development

Objective 10.1: *What is the biological perspective on morality?*

From a biological perspective, morality may be prewired and evolutionarily based (e.g., adoption of motherless chimp babies by other chimps promotes specie survival).

Objective 10.2: *Describe Kohlberg's three levels and six stages of moral development.*

According to Kohlberg, morality progresses through three levels. Each level consists of two stages. At the **preconventional level**, morality is self-centered. What is right is what one can get away with (Stage 1) or what is personally satisfying (Stage 2). **Conventional level** morality is based on a need for approval (Stage 3) and obedience to laws because they maintain the social

order (Stage 4). **Postconventional level** morality comes from adhering to the social contract (Stage 5) and the individual's own principles and universal values (Stage 6).

Objective 10.3: *What are the three major criticisms of Kohlberg's theory?*

Kohlberg's theory has been criticized for possibly measuring only moral reasoning and not moral behavior, and for possible culture and gender bias.

Questions

1. According to Kohlberg's theory of morality, self-interest and avoiding punishment are characteristic of the _____ level, personal standards or universal principles characterize the _____ level, and gaining approval or following the rules describes the _____ level.

2. Calvin would like to wear baggy, torn jeans and a nose ring, but he is concerned that others will disapprove. Calvin is at Kohlberg's _____ level of morality. (a) conformity; (b) approval seeking; (c) conventional; (d) preconventional

3. Five-year-old Tyler believes "bad things are what you get punished for." Tyler is at Kohlberg's _____ level of morality. (a) concrete; (b) preconventional; (c) postconventional; (d) punishment-oriented

4. Explain the possible cultural and gender bias in Kohlberg's theory.

Check your answers in Appendix B.

Click & Review
for additional assessment options:
wiley.com/college/huffman

Personality Development

Achievement

Objective 10.4: *Describe Thomas and Chess's temperament theory.*

Temperament *An individual's innate behavioral style and characteristic emotional response*

Thomas and Chess's Temperament Theory: Biology and Personality Development

As an infant, did you lie quietly and seem oblivious to loud noises? Or did you tend to kick and scream and respond immediately to every sound? Did you respond warmly to people, or did you fuss, fret, and withdraw? Your answers to these questions help determine what developmental psychologists call your **temperament**, an individual's innate, biological behavioral style and characteristic emotional response.

One of the earliest and most influential theories regarding temperament came from the work of psychiatrists Alexander Thomas and Stella Chess (Thomas & Chess,

1977, 1987, 1991). Thomas and Chess found that approximately 65 percent of the babies they observed could be reliably separated into three categories:

1. *Easy children*. These infants were happy most of the time, relaxed and agreeable, and adjusted easily to new situations (approximately 40 percent).

2. *Difficult children*. Infants in this group were moody, easily frustrated, tense, and overreactive to most situations (approximately 10 percent).

3. *Slow-to-warm-up children*. These infants showed mild responses, were somewhat shy and withdrawn, and needed time to adjust to new experiences or people (approximately 15 percent).

Follow-up studies have found that certain aspects of these temperament styles tend to be consistent and enduring throughout childhood and even adulthood (Caro, 2008; Kagan, 2005; McCrae, 2004). That is not to say every shy, cautious infant ends up a shy adult. Many events take place between infancy and adulthood that shape an individual's development.

One of the most influential factors in early personality development is *goodness of fit* between a child's nature, parental behaviors, and the social and environmental setting (Lindahl & Obstbaum, 2004; Realmuto, August, & Egan, 2004; Salekin & Averett, 2008). For example, a slow-to-warm-up child does best if allowed time to adjust to new situations. Similarly, a difficult child thrives in a structured, understanding environment but not in an inconsistent, intolerant home. Alexander Thomas, the pioneer of temperament research, thinks parents should work with their child's temperament rather than trying to change it. Can you see how this idea of goodness of fit is yet another example of how nature and nurture interact?

Ted Streshinsky/©Corbis

Erik Erikson (1902-1994)

Erikson's Psychosocial Theory: The Eight Stages of Life

Like Piaget and Kohlberg, Erik Erikson developed a stage theory of development. He identified eight **psychosocial stages** of social development each stage marked by a "psychosocial" crisis or conflict related to a specific developmental task (Process Diagram 10.2).

The name for each psychosocial stage reflects the specific crisis encountered at that stage and two possible outcomes. For example, the crisis or task of most young adults is *intimacy versus isolation*. This age group's developmental task is developing deep, meaningful relations with others. Those who don't meet this developmental challenge risk social isolation. Erikson believed that the more successfully we overcome each psychosocial crisis, the better chance we have to develop in a healthy manner (Erikson, 1950).

Achievement

Objective 10.5: *Describe Erikson's eight psychosocial stages.*

Psychosocial Stages *Erikson's theory that individuals pass through eight developmental stages, each involving a crisis that must be successfully resolved*

Evaluating Erikson's Theory

Many psychologists agree with Erikson's general idea that psychosocial crises, which are based on interpersonal and environmental interactions, do contribute to personality development (Berzoff, 2008; Markstrom & Marshall, 2008; Torges, Stewart, & Duncan, 2008). However, Erikson also has his critics. First, Erikson's psychosocial stages, are difficult to test scientifically. Second, the labels Erikson used to describe the eight stages may not be entirely appropriate cross-culturally. For example, in individualistic cultures, *autonomy* is highly preferable to *shame and doubt*. But in collectivist cultures, the preferred resolution might be *dependence* or *merging relations* (Matsumoto & Juang, 2008).

Despite their limits, Erikson's stages have greatly contributed to the study of North American and European psychosocial development. By suggesting that development continues past adolescence Erikson's theory has encouraged ongoing research.

Achievement

Objective 10.6: *What are the major criticisms of Erikson's stages?*

Process Diagram 10.2
Erikson's Eight Stages of Psychosocial Development

Stage 1
Trust versus mistrust
(birth–age 1)

Infants learn to trust that their needs will be met, especially by the mother; if not, mistrust develops.

Steve Raymer/NG Image Collection

Stage 2
Autonomy versus shame and doubt (ages 1–3)

Toddlers learn to exercise will, make choices, and control themselves. Caregivers' patience and encouragement help foster a sense of autonomy versus shame and doubt.

Prof. Karen Huffman

Stage 3
Initiative versus guilt (ages 3–6)

Preschoolers learn to initiate activities and enjoy their accomplishments. Supportive caregivers promote feelings of power and self-confidence versus guilt.

Dynamic Graphics, Inc./Creates

Stage 4
Industry versus inferiority (ages 6–12)

Elementary school-aged children develop a sense of industry and learn productive skills that their culture requires (such as reading, writing, and counting); if not, they feel inferior.

PhotoDisc/Getty Images, Inc.

Stage 5
Identity versus role confusion (adolescence)

During a period of serious soul-searching, adolescents develop a coherent sense of self and their role in society. Failure to resolve this *identity crisis* may lead to an unstable identity, delinquency, and difficulty in personal relationships in later life.

Randy Olson/NG Image Collection

Stage 6
Intimacy versus isolation (early adulthood)

After learning who they are and how to be independent, young adults form intimate connections with others; if not, they face isolation and consequent self-absorption.

Pablo Corral Vega/NG Image Collection

Stage 7
Generativity versus stagnation (middle adulthood)

Middle-aged adults develop concern for establishing and influencing the next generation. If this expansion and effort do not occur, an individual stagnates and is concerned solely with material possessions and personal well-being.

IT Stock

Stage 8
Ego integrity versus despair (late adulthood)

Older people enter a period of reflection; in which they feel a sense of accomplishment and satisfaction with the lives they've lived. If not, they experience regret and despair that their lives cannot be relived.

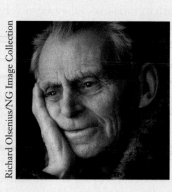

Richard Olsenius/NG Image Collection

GENDER & CULTURAL DIVERSITY

Cultural Influences on Development

As we've just seen in our discussion of Erikson and Kohlberg, and other theorists in Chapter 9, developmental psychology's theories are largely rooted in the concept of *self*—how we define and understand ourselves. Yet the very concept of self reflects our culture. In **individualistic cultures**, the needs and goals of the individual are emphasized over the needs and goals of the group. When asked to complete the statement "I am…," people from individualistic cultures tend to respond with personality traits ("I am shy"; "I am outgoing") or their occupation ("I am a teacher"; "I am a student").

In **collectivistic cultures**, however, the opposite is true. The person is defined and understood primarily by looking at his or her place in the social unit (McCrae, 2004; Laungani, 2007; Matsumoto & Juang, 2008). Relatedness, connectedness, and interdependence are valued, as opposed to separateness, independence, and individualism. When asked to complete the statement "I am…," people from collectivistic cultures tend to mention their families or nationality ("I am a daughter"; "I am Chinese").

If you are North American or Western European, you are more likely to be individualistic than collectivistic (Table 10.1). And you may find the concept of a self defined in terms of others almost contradictory. A core selfhood probably seems intuitively obvious to you. Recognizing that over 70 percent of the world's population lives in collectivistic cultures, however, may improve your cultural sensitivity and prevent misunderstandings. For example, North Americans generally define *sincerity* as behaving in accordance with one's inner feelings, whereas Japanese see it as behavior that conforms to a person's role expectations (carrying out one's duties) (Yamada, 1997). Can you see how Japanese behavior might appear insincere to a North American and vice versa?

Objective 10.7: *How do individualistic versus collectivistic cultures affect personality development?*

Individualistic Cultures *Needs and goals of the individual are emphasized over the needs and goals of the group*

Collectivistic Cultures *Needs and goals of the group are emphasized over the needs and goals of the individual*

Associated Press

TABLE 10.1 WORLDWIDE RANKING OF CULTURES

Individualistic	Intermediate	Collectivistic
United States	Israel	Hong Kong
Australia	Spain	Chile
Great Britain	India	Singapore
Canada	Argentina	Thailand
Netherlands	Japan	West Africa region
New Zealand	Iran	El Salvador
Italy	Jamaica	Taiwan
Belgium	Arab region	South Korea
Denmark	Brazil	Peru
France	Turkey	Costa Rica
Sweden	Uruguay	Indonesia
Ireland	Greece	Pakistan
Norway	Phillippines	Colombia
Switzerland	Mexico	Venezuela

Joe Carnini/The Image Works

How might these two groups differ in their physical, socioemotional, cognitive, moral, and personality development?

Try This Yourself

Cultural Effects on Personality

If asked to draw a circle with yourself in the center, and the people in your life as separate circles surrounding you, which of the two diagrams comes closest to your personal view? If you chose (a), you probably have an *individualistic* orientation, seeing yourself as an independent, separate self. However, if you chose (b), you're more closely aligned with a *collectivist* culture, seeing yourself as interdependent and interconnected with others (Kitayama & Cohen, 2007; Markus & Kitayama, 2003).

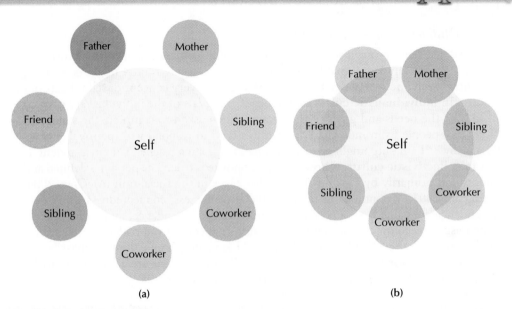

(a)　　　　　　(b)

CHECK & REVIEW

Personality Development

Steve Raymer/NG Image Collection

Objective 10.4: *Describe Thomas and Chess's temperament theory.*

Thomas and Chess emphasized the innate, biological components of traits (such as sociability) and observed that babies often exhibit differences in **temperament** shortly after birth. They found three categories of temperament (*easy*, *difficult*, and *slow-to-warm-up* children) that appear to be consistent throughout child and adulthood.

Objective 10.5: *Describe Erikson's eight psychosocial stages.*

Erikson's eight **psychosocial** stages of development cover the entire life span,

and each stage is marked by a "psychosocial" crisis or conflict related to a specific developmental task. Four stages that occur during childhood are: *trust versus mistrust, autonomy versus shame and doubt, initiative versus guilt,* and *industry versus inferiority.* The major psychosocial identity crisis of adolescence is the search for *identity versus role confusion.* During young adulthood, the individual's task is to establish *intimacy versus isolation.* During middle adulthood, the person must deal with *generativity versus stagnation.* At the end of life, the older adult must establish *ego integrity versus despair* at the realization of lost opportunities.

Objective 10.6: *What are the major criticisms of Erikson's stages?*

Erikson's eight stages are difficult to test scientifically, and they may not apply cross-culturally.

Objective 10.7: *How do individualistic versus collectivistic cultures affect personality development?*

In **individualistic cultures,** the needs and goals of the individual are emphasized over the needs and goals of the group.

However, the reverse is true in **collectivistic cultures**.

Questions

1. An infant's inborn disposition is known as _____. (a) personality; (b) reflexes; (c) temperament; (d) traits
2. Briefly describe Thomas and Chess's temperament theory.
3. Erikson suggested that problems in adulthood are sometimes related to unsuccessful resolution of one of his eight stages. For each of the following individuals, identify the most likely "problem" stage:
   a. Marcos has trouble keeping friends and jobs because he continually asks for guarantees and reassurance of his worth.
   b. Ann has attended several colleges without picking a major, has taken several vocational training programs, and has had numerous jobs over the last 10 years.
   c. Teresa is reluctant to apply for a promotion even though her coworkers have encouraged her to do so. She worries that she will be taking jobs from others and questions her worth.

d. George continually obsesses over the value of his life. He regrets that he left his wife and children for a job in another country and failed to maintain contact.

4. According to Erikson, humans progress through eight stages of psychosocial development. Label the two Eriksonian stages depicted in the photos to the right.

Prof. Karen Huffman

Richard Olsenius/ NG Image Collection

Stage 2 _____   Stage 8 _____
Check your answers in Appendix B.

Click & Review
for additional assessment options:
wiley.com/college/huffman

Meeting the Challenges of Adulthood

Achievement

Objective 10.8: *Discuss the major problems with long-term relationships.*

Having completed our whirlwind trip through the major theories and concepts explaining moral and personality development across the life span, you may be wondering how this information can be helpful in your current adult life. In this section, we will explore three of the most important developmental tasks we all face as adults: developing a long-term, committed relationship with another person, coping with the challenges of family life, and finding rewarding work and retirement.

Committed Relationships: Overcoming Unrealistic Expectations

One of the most important tasks faced during adulthood is that of establishing some kind of continuing, loving, sexual relationship with another person. Yet navigating such partnerships is often very challenging. For example, research shows that marital satisfaction is associated with greater life satisfaction, lower stress, less depression, and lower waking blood pressure (Holt-Lunstad, Birmingham, & Jones, 2008; Osler et al., 2008). Unfortunately, nearly half of all marriages in the United States end in divorce, with serious implications for both adult and child development (Amato, 2006; Gagné et al., 2006; Huurre, Junkkari, & Aro, 2006; Li, 2008; Osler et al., 2008; Siegel, 2007). For the adults, both spouses generally experience emotional as well as practical difficulties and are at high risk for depression and physical health problems. However, many problems assumed to be due to divorce are actually present before marital disruption, and, for some, divorce can be life enhancing. In a "healthy" divorce, ex-spouses must accomplish three tasks: *let go, develop new social ties*, and, when children are involved, *redefine parental roles* (Everett & Everett, 1994).

In addition to stresses on the divorcing couple, some research shows that children also suffer both short-term and long-lasting effects. Compared with children in continuously intact two-parent families, children of divorce reportedly exhibit more behavioral problems, poorer self-concepts, more psychological problems, lower academic achievement, and more substance abuse and social difficulties (D'Onofrio et al., 2007; Hetherington, 2006). On the other hand, other research finds little or no effect on children's social and behavioral problems, and that previously reported negative effects may reflect the child's level of attachment, the child's unique personality, and/or the warmth and personality traits of the parents (Amato, 2006; Brown et al., 2007; Li, 2008; Schaefer & Ginsburg-Block, 2007). Other researchers have suggested that both parents and children may also do better without the constant tension and fighting of an intact, but unhappy, home (Bernet & Ash, 2007; Rutter, 2005).

Whether children become "winners" or "losers" in a divorce depends on the (1) individual attributes of the child, (2) qualities of the custodial family, (3) continued involvement with noncustodial parents, and (4) resources and support systems available to the child and parents (Hetherington, 2006; Siegel, 2007; Torrance, 2004). If you or your parents are currently considering or going through divorce, you might want to keep these four factors in mind when making legal and other decisions about children.

PSYCHOLOGY AT WORK

Are Your Marital Expectations Unrealistic?

How can I have a good marriage and avoid divorce? One of the first steps is to examine your personal dreams and expectations for marriage. Where did they come from? Are they realistic? When you think about marriage and the roles of husband and wife, what do you imagine? Do you re-create images of television families like those on *The Cosby Show, Everybody Loves Raymond*, or even *The Sopranos*? Research shows that women are more likely than men to report trying to model their family life after what they have seen on TV situational comedies. They also tend to expect their significant other to act like the men they have seen on TV (Morrison & Westman, 2001).

When we look at men's expectations, research finds they are more likely to believe certain myths about marriage, such as "men are from Mars and women are from Venus" or "affairs are the main cause of divorce." Can you see how these expectations and myths could lead to marital problems? For both women and men, marriage therapists and researchers consistently find that realistic expectations are a key ingredient in successful marriages (Gottman & Levenson, 2002; Waller & McLanahan, 2005).

Two different kinds of families The Cosby Show and The Sopranos.

Try This Yourself

***A**pplication*

Are Your Relationship Expectations Realistic?

To evaluate your own expectations, answer the following questions about traits and factors common to happy marriages and committed long-term relationships (Amato, 2007; Gottman & Levenson, 2002; Gottman & Notarius, 2000; Marks et al., 2008; Rauer, 2007):

1. Established "love maps"

Yes __ No __
Do you believe that emotional closeness "naturally" develops when two people have the right chemistry?

In successful relationships, both partners are willing to share their feelings and life goals. This sharing leads to

detailed "love maps" of each other's inner emotional life and the creation of shared meaning in the relationship.

2. Shared power and mutual support

Yes __ No __
Have you unconsciously accepted the imbalance of power promoted by many TV sitcoms, or are you willing to fully share power and to respect your partner's point of view, even if you disagree?

The common portrayal of husbands as "head of household" and wives as the "little women" who secretly wield the true power may help create unrealistic expectations for marriage.

3. Conflict management

Yes __ No __
Do you expect to "change" your partner or to be able to resolve all your problems?

Mugshots/Corbis Stock Market

Successful couples work hard (through negotiation and accommodation) to solve their solvable conflicts, to accept their unsolvable ones, and to know the difference.

4. Similarity

Yes __ *No* __

Do you believe that "opposites attract?"

Although we all know couples who are very different but are still happy, similarity (in values, beliefs, religion, and so on) is one of the best predictors of longlasting relationships (Chapter 15).

5. Supportive social environment

Yes __ *No* __

Do you believe that "love conquers all"?

Unfortunately, several environmental factors can overpower or slowly erode even the strongest love. These include age (younger couples have higher divorce rates), money and employment (divorce is higher among the poor and unemployed), parents' marriages (divorce is higher for children of divorced parents), length of courtship (longer is better), and premarital pregnancy (no pregnancy is better, and waiting a while after marriage is even better).

6. Positive emphasis

Yes __ *No* __

Do you believe that an intimate relationship is a place where you can indulge your bad moods and openly criticize one another?

Think again. Positive emotions, positive mood, and positive behavior toward one's partner are vitally important to a lasting, happy relationship.

If you'd like a quick personal demonstration of the power of a positive emphasis, pick two or three of your most "troublesome" friends, family members, or coworkers, and try giving them four positive comments before allowing yourself to say anything even remotely negative. Note how their attitudes and behaviors quickly change. More important, pay attention to the corresponding change in your own feelings and responses toward this troublesome person when you apply this positive emphasis. Can you see how this type of positivism can dramatically improve marital satisfaction?

Families: Their Effect on Development

As we saw in the discussions of attachment and parenting styles in the last chapter, our families exert an enormous influence on our development. But it is not always for the best. Family violence as well as teen pregnancy and teen parenthood can have significant effects on development.

Family Violence

Families can be warm and loving. They also can be cruel and abusive. Maltreatment and abuse are more widely recognized than in the past. However, it is difficult to measure family violence because it usually occurs in private and victims are reluctant to report it out of shame, powerlessness, or fear of reprisal. Nevertheless, every year millions of cases of domestic violence, child abuse, and elder abuse occur, but many more are not reported to police and social service agencies (Baker, 2007; Clemants & Gross, 2007; Cooper et al., 2008; Lewin & Herron, 2007; McGuinness & Schneider, 2007).

What causes family violence? Violence occurs more often in families experiencing marital conflict, substance abuse, mental disorders, and economic stress (Abadinsky, 2008; Dixon et al., 2007; Raphel, 2008; Siever, 2008). It is important to remember that abuse and violence occur at all socioeconomic levels. However, abuse and violence do occur more frequently in families disrupted by unemployment or other financial distress.

In addition to having financial problems, many abusive parents are also socially isolated and lack good communication and parenting skills. Their anxiety and frustration may explode into spouse, child, and elder abuse. In fact, one of the clearest identifiers of abuse potential is *impulsivity*. People who abuse their children, their spouses, or their elderly parents seem to lack impulse control, especially when stressed. They also respond to stress with more intense emotions and greater arousal (Donahue & Grant, 2007; Scannapieco & Connell-Carrick, 2005). This impulsivity is related not only to psychosocial factors like economic stress and social isolation (with no one to turn to for help or feedback) but also to possible biological influences.

Biologically, three regions of the brain are closely related to the expression and control of aggression: the amygdala, the prefrontal cortex, and the hypothalamus (see Chapter 2 to review these regions). Interestingly, head injuries, strokes, dementia, schizophrenia, alcoholism, and abuse of stimulant drugs have all been linked to these three areas and to aggressive outbursts. Research also suggests that low levels of the neurotransmitters serotonin and GABA (gamma-aminobutyric acid) are associated with irritability, hypersensitivity to provocation, and impulsive rage (Haddock & Shaw, 2008; Levinthal, 2008; Siever, 2008).

Is there anything that can be done to reduce this type of aggression? Treatment with antianxiety and serotonin-enhancing drugs like fluoxetine (Prozac) may lower the risk of some forms of impulsive violence. However, given the correlation between spousal, child, sibling, and elder abuse, and because violence affects other family members who are not victims or perpetrators, treatment generally includes the entire family (Becvar & Becvar, 2006; Shlonsky & Friend, 2007).

Most professionals advocate two general approaches in dealing with family violence. *Primary programs* attempt to identify "vulnerable" families and prevent abuse by teaching parenting and marital skills, stress management, and impulse control. These programs also publicize the signs of abuse and encourage people to report suspected cases. *Secondary programs* attempt to rehabilitate families after abuse has occurred. They work to improve social services, establish self-help groups such as Parents Anonymous and AMAC (Adults Molested as Children), and provide individual and group psychotherapy for both victims and abusers.

Teen Pregnancy and Parenthood

Another factor that may affect development is becoming a parent and starting a family at too early an age. Have you heard that the United States has one of the highest rates of teen pregnancy among major industrialized nations (Wines, 2008). Regrettably, this is a sad fact. But, ironically, today's rate is somewhat lower than it was throughout much of the twentieth century.

With this decline, why is everyone so worried about teen pregnancies? Although the total rate has declined, the percentage of single parents has increased (Kimes, 2006; Hyde & DeLamater, 2008; King, 2009). The higher nonmarital rate is important because single-parent families are at greater risk of poverty. In addition, pregnancy during adolescence also carries with it considerable health risk for both the mother and child (Chapter 9) and lower educational achievement. Pregnancy, in fact, is the most common reason for girls dropping out of high school. In view of these facts, is it any wonder that teen mothers also report one of the highest levels of depression (Figure 10.2)?

What can be done to reduce the number of teen pregnancies? *Comprehensive education and health-oriented services* seem to be the most promising avenue for decreasing the rate of pregnancy among high-risk teenagers (Bennett & Assefi, 2005; Hyde & DeLamater, 2008; King, 2009). The Johns Hopkins Pregnancy Prevention Program, for example, provides complete medical care, contraceptive services, social services (such as counseling), and parenting education. This approach postponed the age of onset of sexual activity, increased contraception use, reduced the frequency of sex, and decreased the actual pregnancy rate in the experimental group by 30 percent. During the same period, pregnancy rates in a comparison school rose by 58 percent (Hardy & Zabin, 1991).

A number of other outreach programs are also working to enhance social development among adolescents through structured volunteer community service and classroom discussions of life choices, careers, and relationships. Research shows that while some teen pregnancies are planned and actually increase teenagers motivation to stay in school, many teen pregnancies are due to poverty and the perception that life options and choices are limited (Finkelhor & Jones, 2006; Levine, Emery, & Pollack, 2007; Schultz, 2008; SmithBattle & Leonard, 2006).

The Kobal Collection, Ltd.

Juno—an Oscar-nominated film
Does "Juno" glorify teen pregnancy—or show strength? What do you think?

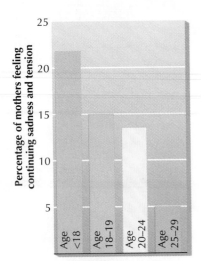

Mother's age at
birth of first offspring

Figure 10.2 ***Maternal age and satisfaction*** Note how the age of the mother relates to the percentage of reported feelings of sadness and tension.

Most research and social programs (like the two described here) focus on economics: how money (or the lack of it) affects teen pregnancies. But researchers Rebekah Coley and Lindsay Chase-Lansdale (1998) suggest we also should be exploring the *psychological* consequences of early parenting. If adolescence is a time for solidifying identity and developing autonomy from parents, what happens with teen parents? What are the effects on a teen mother if she lives with her mother? What happens to the life span development of the "early" grandparents? What about the teen father? How does early fatherhood affect his course of development? And what about the child who is being raised by a teen mother or teen father or grandparent? How does this affect his or her development? Answers to these questions rest with the next generation of researchers (perhaps some of you who are reading this text).

Application

RESEARCH HIGHLIGHT

Children Who Survive Despite the Odds

Children fortunate enough to grow up with days filled with play and discovery, nights that provide rest and security, and dedicated, loving parents usually turn out fine. But what about those who are raised in violent, impoverished, or neglectful situations? As we saw in the previous discussions of family violence, teen pregnancy and parenting, and divorce, a troubled childhood creates significantly higher risk of serious physical, emotional, and behavioral problems. There are exceptions to this rule. Some offspring of wonderful, loving parents have serious problems. And some children growing up amid major stressors are remarkably well adjusted.

What is it about children living in harsh circumstances that helps them survive and prosper—despite the odds? The answer holds great interest for both parents and society. Such resilient children can teach us

Akram Saleh/Getty Images

better ways to reduce risk, promote competence, and shift the course of development in more positive directions. **Resiliency** refers to the ability to adapt effectively in the face of threats.

Resilience has been studied throughout the world in a variety of situations, including poverty, natural disasters, war, and family violence (e.g., Kline, 2008; Johnson & Lazarus, 2008; Lewis, 2008; Schmitt-Rodermund & Silbereisen, 2008). Two researchers—Ann Masten at the University of Minnesota and Douglas Coatsworth at the University of Miami (1998)—identified several traits of the resilient child and the environmental circumstances that might account for the resilient child's success.

Most children who do well have (1) good intellectual functioning; (2) relationships with caring adults; and, as they grow older, (3) the ability to regulate their attention, emotions, and behavior. These traits

obviously overlap. Good intellectual functioning, for example, may help resilient children solve problems or protect themselves from adverse conditions. Their intelligence may also attract the interest of teachers who serve as nurturing adults. These greater intellectual skills may also help resilient children learn from their experiences and from the caring adults, so in later life they have better self-regulation skills.

In times of growing concern about homelessness, poverty, abuse, teen pregnancy, violence, and divorce, studies of successful children can be very important. On the other hand, there is no such thing as an invulnerable child. Masten and Coatsworth (1998) remind us that "if we allow the prevalence of known risk factors for development to rise while resources for children fall, we can expect the competence of individual children and the human capital of the nation to suffer" (p. 216).

Resiliency *Ability to adapt effectively in the face of threats*

Application

Try This Yourself

Are You Resilient?

Did you grow up in a "high-risk" environment? Are you a resilient child? A 30-year longitudinal study of resilience (Werner, 1989, 2006) identified several environmental factors of high-risk children. Place a check mark by each risk factor that applies to your childhood:

___ Born into chronic poverty
___ Stressful fetal or birth conditions (e.g., prenatal hazards, low birth weight)
___ Chronic discord in the family environment
___ Parents divorced
___ Mental illness in one or both parents

Two-thirds of the high-risk children who had experienced four or more of these factors by age 2 developed serious adjustment problems in later years. But one-third of the children who also experienced four or more such risk factors were resilient. They developed into competent, confident, and caring adults.

chievement

Objective 10.9: *Describe how work and retirement affect development.*

Disengagement versus activity *The disengagement theory of aging suggests that older people naturally disengage and withdraw from life. However, judging by the people in this photo, activity theory may be a better theory of aging because it suggests that everyone should remain active and involved throughout the entire life span.*

chievement

Objective 10.10: *What are the three major theories of aging?*

Activity Theory of Aging *Successful aging is fostered by a full and active commitment to life*

Disengagement Theory of Aging *Successful aging is characterized by mutual withdrawal between the elderly and society*

Socioemotional Selectivity Theory of Aging *A natural decline in social contact occurs as older adults become more selective with their time*

PSYCHOLOGY AT WORK

Positive Careers and Rewarding Retirements

Throughout most of our adult lives, work defines us in fundamental ways. It affects our health, our friendships, where we live, and even our leisure activities. Too often, however, career choices are driven by dreams of high income. Nearly 74 percent of college freshmen surveyed by the Higher Education Research Institute said that being "very well off financially" was "very important" or "essential." Seventy-one percent felt the same way about raising a family ("This Year's Freshmen," 1995).

In sharp contrast to this 1995 study, a similar survey in 2005 found that two out of three (66.3 percent) entering college freshmen believed it was "essential" or "very important" to help others, which is the highest this figure has been in the past 25 years (Engle, 2006). What explains this change? John Pryor, director of the 2005 survey, suggests that the Indian Ocean tsunami and Hurricane Katrina occurred during an "impressionable time of their lives," which might explain why this cohort will likely have a special commitment to social and civic responsibility.

Unfortunately, many college students from the original 1995 survey who dreamed of high incomes may have ended up in unsatisfying, "dead-end" jobs, or working long hours and weekends at high-paying jobs with little or no time for their families. Likewise, the idealistic 2005 students seeking to help others may have entered service professions, which are at a much higher risk for "burnout" (see Chapter 3).

How can we find personally satisfying and long-lasting careers? Choosing an occupation is one of the most important decisions in our lives, and the task is becoming ever more difficult and complex as career options rapidly change due to increasing specialization, job fluctuations, and the global economy. The *Dictionary of Occupational Titles*, a government publication, currently lists more than 200,000 job categories. One way to learn more about these job categories and potential careers is to visit your college career center. These centers typically offer an abundance of books and pamphlets as well as interesting and helpful vocational interest tests.

Enjoying Retirement

Work is a big part of adult life and self-identity. But the large majority of men and women in the United States choose to retire sometime in their sixties. Fortunately, the loss of self-esteem and depression that are commonly assumed to accompany retirement may be largely a myth. Life satisfaction after retirement appears to be most strongly related to good health, control over one's life, social support, adequate income, and participation in community services and social activities (Huguet, Kaplan, & Feeney, 2008; Reynolds, 2008). This type of active involvement is the key ingredient to a fulfilling old age, according to the **activity theory of aging**. In contrast, other theorists believe that successful aging is a natural and graceful withdrawal from life, the **disengagement theory** (Achenbaum & Bengtson, 1994; Cummings & Henry, 1961; Heckhausen, 2005; Lemus, 2008; Menec, 2003; Neugarten, Havighurst, & Tobin, 1968; Riebe et al., 2005; Sanchez, 2006).

For obvious reasons, the disengagement theory has been seriously questioned and largely abandoned. Successful aging does *not* require withdrawal from society. I mention this theory because of its historical relevance, and also because of its connection to an influential modern perspective, **socioemotional selectivity theory**. This latest model helps explain the predictable decline in social contact that almost everyone experiences as they move into their older years (Carstensen, 2006; Charles & Carstensen, 2007). According to socioemotional selectivity theory, we don't naturally withdraw from society in our later years—we just become more *selective* with our time. We deliberately choose to decrease our total number of social contacts in favor of familiar people who provide emotionally meaningful interactions (Figure 10.3).

*A*pplication

Try This Yourself

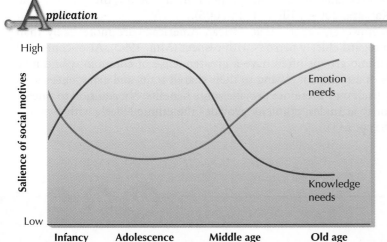

Figure 10.3 *Socioemotional selectivity* Note how our emotional needs appear to change over our life span. Can you explain why?

Answer: During infancy, emotional connection is essential to our survival. During childhood, adolescence, and early adulthood, information gathering is critical, and the need for emotional connection declines. During late adulthood, emotional satisfaction is again more important—we tend to invest our time in those who can be counted on in times of need.

Michael Newman/PhotoEdit

---

*A*chievement

GENDER & CULTURAL DIVERSITY

*A*chievement

Objective 10.11: *Discuss the major cultural differences in ageism.*

Cultural Differences in Ageism

As we've seen in this and the previous chapter, there are losses and stress associated with the aging process—although much less than most people think. Perhaps the greatest challenge for the elderly, at least in the United States, is the *ageism* they encounter. In societies that value older people as wise elders or keepers of valued traditions, the stress of aging is much less than in societies that view them as mentally slow and socially useless. In cultures like that in the United States in which youth, speed, and progress are strongly emphasized, a loss or decline in any of these qualities is deeply feared and denied.

Aren't there also cultures that honor their elderly? Yes. In Japan, China, and the United States among African Americans and most tribes of Native Americans, the elderly are more revered. Aging parents are generally respected for their wisdom and experience. They also are deferred to in family matters and often are expected to live with their children until they die (Laungani, 2007; Matsumoto & Juang, 2008; Miller et al., 2006). However, as these cultures become more urbanized and Westernized, there is often a corresponding decline in respect for the elderly. In Japan, for example, over 80 percent of the elderly lived with their adult children in 1957. This percentage declined to only 55 percent in 1994. But Japan still has one of the highest rates of adult children caring for elderly relatives (Koropeckyj-Cox & Call, 2007).

Ageism, Gender, and Ethnicity in the United States   There also is considerable difference in the status and treatment of different subgroups of the elderly. In the United States, for example, studies show that older men have more social status, income, and sexual partners than do older women. Elderly women, on the other hand, have more friends and are more involved in family relationships. But they have lower status and income. Contrary to the popular stereotype of the "rich old woman," elderly females represent one of the lowest income levels in North America.

Ethnicity also plays a role in aging in the United States. Ethnic minority elderly, especially African Americans and Latinos, face problems related to both ageism and racism. They are more likely to become ill but less likely to receive treatment. And

Elder respect *Native Americans generally revere and respect the elder members of their tribe. How would the aging experience be different if being old was an honor and blessing versus a dreaded curse?*

David W. Hamilton

they are overrepresented among the elderly poor living below the poverty line (Flores, 2008; McNamara, 2007; Miller et al., 2006).

Other research, however, reports that African Americans are more likely than Anglo Americans to regard elderly persons with respect (Mui, 1992). Also, compared with whites, other ethnic groups often have a greater sense of community and may have stronger bonds of attachment, owing to their shared traits and experiences with prejudice. Ethnicity itself may therefore provide some benefits. "In addition to shielding them from majority attitudes, ethnicity provides the ethnic elderly with a source of esteem" (Fry, 1985, p. 233).

Assessment

CHECK & REVIEW

Meeting the Challenges of Adulthood

Objective 10.8: *Discuss the major problems with long-term relationships.*

A good marriage is one of the most difficult and important tasks of adulthood. Researchers have found six major traits and factors in happy marriages: *established "love maps," shared power and mutual support, conflict management, similarity, a supportive social environment,* and a *positive emphasis.* Family violence, teenage pregnancy, and divorce all have significant effects on development. However, **resilient** children who survive abusive and stress-filled childhoods usually have good intellectual functioning, a relationship with a caring adult, and the ability to regulate their attention, emotions, and behavior.

Objective 10.9: *Describe how work and retirement affect development.*

The kind of work we do can affect our health, friendships, where we live, and even our leisure activities. Life satisfaction after retirement appears to be most strongly related to good health, control over one's life, social support, and participation in community services and social activities.

Objective 10.10: *What are the three major theories of aging?*

One theory of successful aging, **activity theory**, says people should remain active and involved throughout the entire life span. Another major theory, **disengagement theory**, says the elderly naturally and gracefully withdraw from life because they welcome the relief from roles they can no longer fulfill. Although the disengagement theory is no longer in favor, the **socioemotional selectivity theory** does find that the elderly tend to decrease their total number of social contacts as they become more selective with their time.

Objective 10.11: *Discuss the major cultural differences in ageism.*

One of the greatest challenges for the elderly, at least in the United States, is the *ageism* they encounter. However, in societies that value older people as wise elders or keepers of valued traditions, the stress of aging is much less than in societies that view them as mentally slow and socially useless. There also is considerable difference in the status and treatment of different elderly subgroups, and ethnic minority elderly, especially African Americans and Latinos, face problems of both racism and ageism.

Questions

1. Identify the three traits of resilient children.
2. The _____ theory of aging suggests that you should remain active and involved until death, whereas the _____ theory suggests that you should naturally and gracefully withdraw from life.
3. Which theory of aging is best shown in the photo in Figure 10.3? (a) activity; (b) socioemotional selectivity; (c) disengagement; (d) androgyny
4. _____ is prejudice against people based on their age. (a) Ethnocentrism; (b) Elder abuse; (c) Ageism; (d) Disengagement
5. Explain how ethnicity may help the elderly overcome some problems of aging.

Check your answers in Appendix B.

Click & Review
for additional assessment options:
wiley.com/college/huffman

Grief and Death

One unavoidable part of life is its end. How can we understand and prepare ourselves for the loss of our own life and those of loved others? In this section, we look at the four stages of grief. We then study cultural and age-related differences in attitudes toward death. We conclude with death itself as a final developmental crisis.

Grief: Lessons in Survival

> What do I do now that you're gone? Well, when there's nothing else going on, which is quite often, I sit in a corner and I cry until I am too numbed to feel. Paralyzed motionless for a while, nothing moving inside or out. Then I think how much I miss you. Then I feel fear, pain, loneliness, desolation. Then I cry until I am too numbed to feel. Interesting pastime.
>
> PETER McWILLIAMS, *HOW TO SURVIVE THE LOSS OF A LOVE*, P. 18

Have you ever felt like this? If so, you are not alone. Loss and grief are an inevitable part of all our lives. Feelings of desolation, loneliness, and heartache, accompanied by painful memories, are common reactions to loss, disaster, or misfortune. Ironically, such painful emotions may serve a useful function. Evolutionary psychologists suggest that bereavement and grief may be adaptive mechanisms for both human and nonhuman animals. The pain may motivate parents and children or mates to search for one another. Obvious signs of distress also may be adaptive because they bring the group to the aid of the bereaved individual.

What does it mean if someone seems emotionless after an important loss? Grieving is a complicated and personal process. Just as there is no right way to die, there is no right way to grieve. People who restrain their grief may be following the rules for emotional display that prevail in their cultural group. Moreover, outward signs of strong emotion may be the most obvious expression of grief. But this is only one of four stages in the "normal" grieving process (Koppel, 2000; Parkes, 1972, 1991).

In the initial phase of grief, *numbness*, bereaved individuals often seem dazed and may feel little emotion other than numbness or emptiness. They also may deny the death, insisting that a mistake has been made.

In the second stage of grief, individuals enter a stage of *yearning*, intense longing for the loved one, and pangs of guilt, anger, and resentment. The bereaved may also experience illusions. They "see" the deceased person in his or her favorite chair or in the face of a stranger, they have vivid dreams in which the deceased is still alive, or they feel the "presence" of the dead person. They also experience strong guilt feelings ("If only I had gotten her to a doctor sooner" "I should have been more loving") and anger or resentment ("Why wasn't he more careful?" "It isn't fair that I'm the one left behind").

Once the powerful feelings of yearning subside, the individual enters the third *disorganization/despair* phase. Life seems to lose its meaning. The mourner feels listless, apathetic, and submissive. As time goes by, however, the survivor gradually begins to accept the loss both intellectually (the loss makes sense) and emotionally (memories are pleasurable as well as painful). This acceptance, combined with building a new self-identity ("I am a single mother" "We are no longer a couple"), characterizes the fourth and final stage of grief—the *resolution or reorganization stage*.

Grief is obviously not the same for everyone. People vary in they way they grieve, the stages of grief that they experience, and the length of time needed for "recovery" (Balk, 2008; Corr, Nabe & Corr, 2009; Doughty, 2007; Kastembaum, 2007). You can help people who are grieving by accepting these individual differences and recognizing that there is no perfect response. Simply say, "I'm sorry." And then let the person talk if he or she wishes. Your quiet presence and caring are generally the best type of support.

When it comes to dealing with your own losses and grief, psychologists offer several techniques that you may find helpful (Balk, 2008; Corr & Corr, 2007; Kauffman, 2008).

1. *Recognize the loss and allow yourself to grieve.* Despite feelings of acute

Achievement

Objective 10.12: *Describe grief and list its four stages.*

Steven Weinberg/Stone/Getty Images

David McNew/Getty Images News and Sport Services

Grieving *Individuals vary in their emotional reactions to loss. There is no right or wrong way to grieve.*

loneliness, remember that loss is a part of everyone's life and accept comfort from others. Take care of yourself by avoiding unnecessary stress, getting plenty of rest, and giving yourself permission to enjoy life whenever possible.

2. *Set up a daily activity schedule.* One of the best ways to offset the lethargy and depression of grief is to force yourself to fill your time with useful activities (studying, washing your car, doing the laundry, and so on).

3. *Seek help.* Having the support of loving friends and family helps offset the loneliness and stress of grief. Recognize, however, that professional counseling may be necessary in cases of extreme or prolonged numbness, anger, guilt, or depression. (You will learn more about depression and its treatment in Chapters 14 and 15.)

Achievement

Objective 10.13: *Discuss cultural and age variations in attitudes toward death and dying.*

Attitudes Toward Death and Dying: Cultural and Age Variations

Cultures around the world interpret and respond to death in widely different ways: "Funerals are the occasion for avoiding people or holding parties, for fighting or having sexual orgies, for weeping or laughing, in a thousand combinations" (Metcalf & Huntington, 1991, p. 62).

Associated Press

Figure 10.4 *Culture influences our response to death* In October 2006, a dairy truck driver took over a one-room Amish schoolhouse in Pennsylvania, killed and gravely injured several young girls, then shot himself. Instead of responding in rage, his Amish neighbors attended his funeral. Amish leaders urged forgiveness for the killer and called for a fund to aid his wife and three children. Rather than creating an on-site memorial, the schoolhouse was razed, to be replaced by pasture. What do you think of this response? The fact that many Americans were offended, shocked, or simply surprised by the Amish reaction illustrates how strongly culture affects our emotion, beliefs, and values.

Similarly, subcultures within the United States also have different responses to death (Figure 10.4). Irish Americans are likely to believe the dead deserve a good send-off—a wake with food, drink, and jokes. African Americans traditionally regard funerals as a time for serious grief, demonstrated in some congregations by wailing and singing spirituals. And most Japanese Americans try to restrain their grief and smile so as not to burden others with their pain. They also want to avoid the shame associated with losing emotional control (Corr, Nabe, & Corr, 2009; Kastenbaum, 2007; Schim et al., 2007).

Attitudes toward death and dying vary among cultures and subcultures, as well as with age. As adults, we understand death in terms of three basic concepts: (1) *permanence*—once a living thing dies, it cannot be brought back to life; (2) *universality*—all living things eventually die; and (3) *nonfunctionality*—all living functions, including thought, movement, and vital signs, end at death.

Research shows that permanence, the notion that death cannot be reversed, is the first and most easily understood concept (Figure 10.5). Understanding of universality comes slightly later. By about the age of 7, most children have mastered nonfunctionality and have an adultlike understanding of death. Adults may fear that discussing death with children and adolescents will make them unduly anxious. But those who are offered open, honest discussions of death have an easier time accepting it (Corr, Nabe, & Corr, 2009; Kastenbaum, 2007).

The Death Experience: Our Final Developmental Task

Achievement

Objective 10.14: *What are Kübler-Ross's five stages of dying, and what is thanatology?*

Have you thought about your own death? Would you like to die suddenly and alone? Or would you prefer to know ahead of time so you could plan your funeral and spend time saying good-bye to your family and friends? If you find thinking about these questions uncomfortable, it may be because most people in Western societies deny death. Unfortunately, avoiding thoughts and discussion of death and associating aging with death contribute to *ageism*. Moreover, the better we understand death, and the more wisely we approach it, the more fully we can live until it comes.

During the Middle Ages (from about the fifth until the sixteenth century), people were expected to recognize when death was approaching so they could say their farewells and die with dignity, surrounded by loved ones. In recent times, Western societies have moved death out of the home and put it into the hospital and funeral parlor. Rather than personally caring for our dying family and friends, we have shifted responsibility to "experts"—physicians and morticians. We have made death a medical failure rather than a natural part of the life cycle.

This avoidance of death and dying may be changing, however. Since the late 1990s, right-to-die and death-with-dignity advocates have been working to bring death out in the open. And mental health professionals have suggested that understanding the psychological processes of death and dying may play a significant role in good adjustment.

Confronting our own death is the last major crisis we face in life. What is it like? Is there a "best" way to prepare to die? Is there such a thing as a "good death"? After spending hundreds of hours at the bedsides of the terminally ill, Elisabeth Kübler-Ross developed her stage theory of the psychological processes surrounding death (1983, 1997, 1999).

Based on extensive interviews with patients, Kübler-Ross proposed that most people go through five sequential stages when facing death:

* *denial* of the terminal condition ("This can't be true; it's a mistake!")
* *anger* ("Why me? It isn't fair!")
* *bargaining* ("God, if you let me live, I'll dedicate my life to you!")
* *depression* ("I'm losing everyone and everything I hold dear")
* *acceptance* ("I know that death is inevitable and my time is near").

Evaluating Kübler-Ross's Theory

Critics of the stage theory of dying stress that the five-stage sequence has not been scientifically validated and that each person's death is a unique experience (Kastenbaum, 2007). Emotions and reactions depend on the individual's personality, life situation, age, and so on. Others worry that popularizing such a stage theory will cause further avoidance and stereotyping of the dying ("He's just in the anger stage right now"). Kübler-Ross agreed that not all people go through the same stages in the same way and regretted that anyone would use her theory as a model for a "good death." Dying, like living, is a unique, individual experience.

Due to criticisms of Kübler-Ross's five stages, some prefer to talk about them as *potential* reactions to dying—not as stages. In spite of the potential abuses, Kübler-Ross's theory has provided valuable insights and spurred research into a long-neglected topic. **Thanatology**, the study of death and dying, has become a major topic in human development. Thanks in part to thanatology research, the dying are being helped to die with dignity by the *hospice* movement. This organization has trained staff and volunteers to provide loving support for the terminally ill and their families in special facilities, hospitals, or the patient's own home (Balk et al., 2007; DeSpelder & Strickland, 2007; Schim et al., 2007).

One of the most important contributions by Kübler-Ross (1975) may have been her suggestion that:

It is the denial of death that is partially responsible for [people] living empty, purposeless lives; for when you live as if you'll live forever, it becomes too easy to postpone the things you know you must do. In contrast, when you fully understand that each day you awaken could be the last you have, you take the time that day to grow, to become more of whom you really are, to reach out to other human beings. (p. 164)

Figure 10.5 ***How do children understand death?*** Preschoolers seem to accept the fact that the dead person cannot get up again, perhaps because of their experiences with dead butterflies and beetles found while playing outside (Furman, 1990). Later, they begin to understand all that death entails and that they, too, will someday die.

Thanatology [than-uh-TALL-uh-gee] *The study of death and dying; the term comes from thanatus, the Greek name for a mythical personification of death, and was borrowed by Freud to represent the death instinct*

PSYCHOLOGY AT WORK

Dealing with Your Own Death Anxiety

Woody Allen once said, "It's not that I'm afraid to die. I just don't want to be there when it happens." Although some people who are very old and in poor health may

welcome death, most of us have difficulty facing it. One of the most important elements of critical thinking is *self-knowledge*, which includes the ability to critically evaluate our deepest and most private fears.

Death Anxiety Questionnaire

To test your own level of death anxiety, indicate your response according to the following scale:

0	1	2
not at all	somewhat	very much

_____ 1. Do you worry about dying?

_____ 2. Does it bother you that you may die before you have done everything you wanted to do?

_____ 3. Do you worry that you may be very ill for a long time before you die?

_____ 4. Does it upset you to think that others may see you suffering before you die?

_____ 5. Do you worry that dying may be very painful?

_____ 6. Do you worry that the persons closest to you won't be with you when you are dying?

_____ 7. Do you worry that you may be alone when you are dying?

_____ 8. Does the thought bother you that you might lose control of your mind before death?

_____ 9. Do you worry that expenses connected with your death will be a burden to other people?

_____ 10. Does it worry you that your will or instructions about your belongings may not be carried out after you die?

_____ 11. Are you afraid that you may be buried before you are really dead?

_____ 12. Does the thought of leaving loved ones behind when you die disturb you?

_____ 13. Do you worry that those you care about may not remember you after your death?

_____ 14. Does the thought worry you that with death you may be gone forever?

_____ 15. Are you worried about not knowing what to expect after death?

Source: H. R. Conte, M. B. Weiner, & R. Plutchik (1982). Measuring death anxiety: Conceptual, psychometric, and factor-analytic aspects. *Journal of Personality and Social Psychology*, 43, 775–785. Reprinted with permission.

How does your total score compare to the national average of 8.5? When this same test was given to nursing-home residents, senior citizens, and college students, researchers found no significant differences, despite the fact that those tested ranged in age from 30 to 80.

Assessment **STOP**

CHECK & REVIEW

Grief and Death

Objective 10.12: *Describe grief and list its four stages.*

Grief is a natural and painful reaction to a loss. For most people, grief consists of four major stages—*numbness, yearning, disorganization/despair,* and *resolution.*

Objective 10.13: *Discuss cultural and age variations in attitudes toward death and dying.*

Attitudes toward death and dying vary greatly across cultures and among age groups. Some cultures regard death as a time for celebration, whereas others see it as a time for serious grief. Although adults understand the *permanence, universality,* and *nonfunctionality* of death, children often don't master these concepts until around age 7.

Objective 10.14: *What are Kübler-Ross's five stages of death and dying, and what is thanatology?*

Kübler-Ross's theory of the five-stage psychological process when facing death (*denial, anger, bargaining, depression,* and *acceptance*) offers important insights into the last major crisis we face in life. The study of death and dying, **thanatology**, has become an important topic in human development.

Questions

1. Explain why some people seem emotionless after an important loss.
2. Which of the following is **TRUE** about a child's understanding of death?
   a. Preschoolers understand that death is permanent.

b. Preschoolers may not understand that death is universal.

c. Children understand death is nonfunctional by the age of seven.

d. All but one of these options are true.

3. Grieving people generally begin with the _____ stage and end with the _____ stage. (a) numbness, bargaining; (b) grief, anger; (c) yearning, acceptance; (d) numbness, resolution

4. Match the following statements with Elisabeth Kübler-Ross's five-stage theory of death and dying:

____a. "I understand that I'm dying, but if I could just have a little more time . . ."

____b. "I refuse to believe the doctors. I want a fourth opinion."

____c. "I know my time is near. I'd better make plans for my spouse and children."

____d. "Why me? I've been a good person. I don't deserve this."

____e. "I'm losing everything. I'll never see my children again. Life is so hard."

5. The study of death and dying is known as _____. (a) gerontology; (b) ageism; (c) mortality; (d) thanatology

Check your answers in Appendix B.

Click & Review for additional assessment options: wiley.com/college/huffman

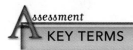

Assessment KEY TERMS

To assess your understanding of the Key Terms in Chapter 10, write a definition for each (in your own words), and then compare your definitions with those in the text.

Moral Development
conventional level (p. 352)
postconventional level (p. 352)
preconventional level (p. 352)

Personality Development
psychosocial stages (p. 355)
temperament (p. 354)

Meeting the Challenges of Adulthood
activity theory (p. 364)
collectivistic cultures (p. 357)
disengagement theory (p. 364)
individualistic cultures (p. 357)
resiliency (p. 363)
socioemotional selectivity theory (p. 364)

Grief and Death
thanatology [than-uh-TALL-uh-gee] (p. 369)

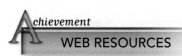

Achievement WEB RESOURCES

Huffman Book Companion Site
wiley.com/college/huffman
  This site is loaded with free Interactive Self-Tests, Internet Exercises, Glossary and Flashcards for key terms, web links, Handbook for Non-Native Speakers, and other activities designed to improve your mastery of the material in this chapter.

Moral Development

Kohlberg's Three Levels and Six Stages

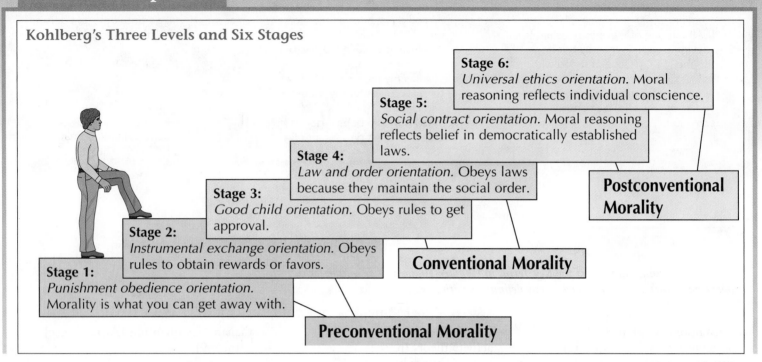

Stage 6:
Universal ethics orientation. Moral reasoning reflects individual conscience.

Stage 5:
Social contract orientation. Moral reasoning reflects belief in democratically established laws.

Stage 4:
Law and order orientation. Obeys laws because they maintain the social order.

Stage 3:
Good child orientation. Obeys rules to get approval.

Stage 2:
Instrumental exchange orientation. Obeys rules to obtain rewards or favors.

Stage 1:
Punishment obedience orientation. Morality is what you can get away with.

Postconventional Morality

Conventional Morality

Preconventional Morality

Personality Development

Thomas & Chess's Temperament Theory

Temperament: Basic, inborn disposition. Three temperament styles: *easy, difficult,* and *slow-to-warm-up*. Styles seem consistent and enduring.

Erikson's Eight Psychosocial Stages

Ted Streshinsky/©Corbis

Stage	Approximate Age
1. Trust-vs-mistrust	Birth–1
2. Autonomy-vs-shame and doubt	1–3 years
3. Initiative-vs-guilt	3–6 years
4. Industry-vs-inferiority	6–12 years
5. Identity-vs-role confusion	Adolescence
6. Intimacy-vs-isolation	Early adulthood
7. Generativity-vs-stagnation	Middle adulthood
8. Ego integrity-vs-despair	Late adulthood

Families
- Family violence, teenage pregnancies, and divorce can influence development.
- **Resilience** helps some children survive an abusive or stress-filled childhood.

The Kobal Collection, Ltd.

Occupational Choices

Occupational choice is critically important because most people channel their accomplishment needs into their work.

Aging

Three major theories of aging.

| **Activity Theory** (should remain active) | **Disengagement Theory** (should gracefully withdraw) | **Socioemotional Selectivity** (elderly reduce social contacts because they're more selective) |

Grief and Death

Grief

Grief: A natural and painful reaction to a loss, consists of four major stages:

1) numbness → 2) yearning → 3) disorganization and despair → 4) resolution

Attitudes

Attitudes toward death and dying vary greatly across cultures and among age groups. Children generally don't fully understand the *permanence*, *universality*, and *nonfunctionality* of death until around the age 7.

Death Experience

- Kübler-Ross proposes a five-stage psychological process when facing death (*denial*, *anger*, *bargaining*, *depression*, and *acceptance*).
- **Thanatology:** Study of death and dying.

11

Gender and Human Sexuality

We allow our ignorance to prevail upon us and make us think we can survive alone, alone in patches, alone in groups, alone in races, even alone in genders.

MAYA ANGELOU

I laugh, I love, I hope, I try, I hurt, I need, I fear, I cry. And I know you do the same things too, So we're really not that different, me and you.

COLLIN RAYE

Men and women, women and men, It will never work.

ERICA JONG

What do you think? Are men and women from different planets (Mars and Venus)? Or are they both from planet Earth? Is it possible that our sense of ourselves as men or women develops primarily from how our parents or others treat us? Or is biology the best predictor? You will learn more about your own gender development and sexuality in the first section of this chapter. Then we will discuss four pioneers in sex research and cultural differences in sexual practices and attitudes. The third section describes sexual arousal, response, and orientation. And the chapter concludes with discussions of sexual dysfunction and sexually transmitted infections, including AIDS (acquired immuno-deficiency syndrome).

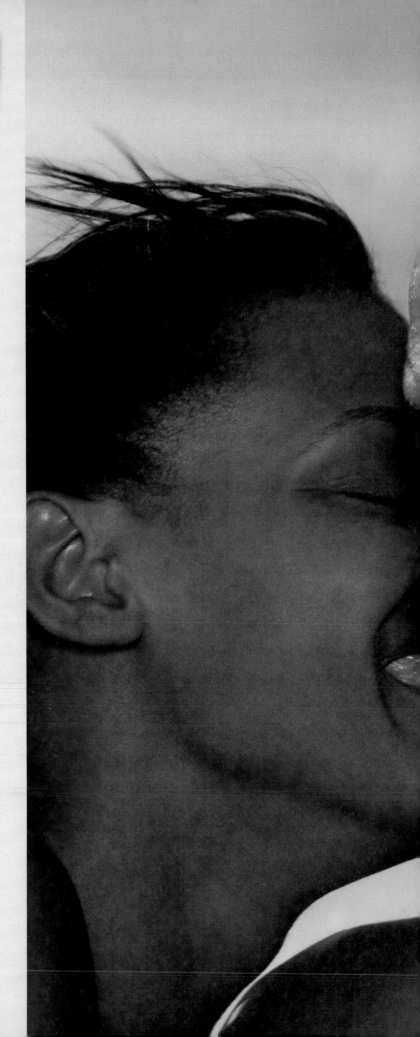

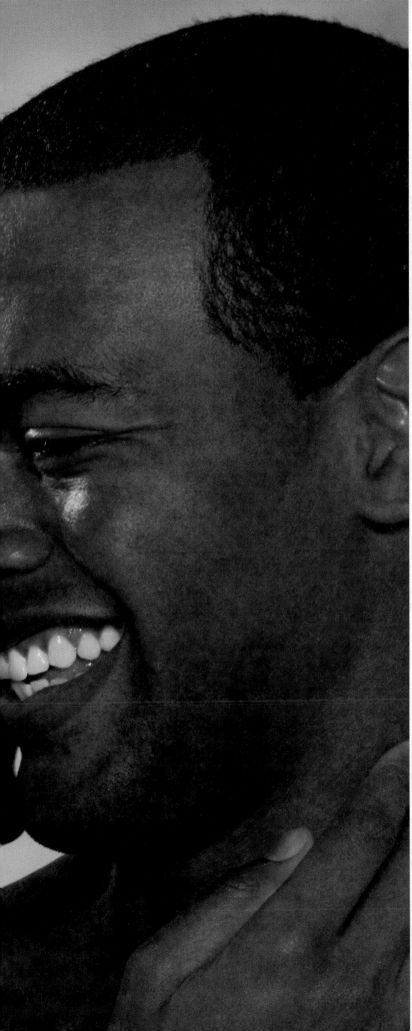

Blend Images/Getty Images

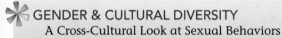 ▶ **Sex and Gender**

What Is "Maleness" and "Femaleness"?
Gender Role Development
Gender Identity Formation

CASE STUDY/PERSONAL STORY
The Tragic Tale of "John/Joan"

Sex and Gender Differences

RESEARCH HIGHLIGHT
Video Games, Gender, and Spatial Skills

CRITICAL THINKING/ACTIVE LEARNING
Gender Differences and Critical Thinking

▶ **The Study of Human Sexuality**

GENDER & CULTURAL DIVERSITY
A Cross-Cultural Look at Sexual Behaviors

▶ **Sexual Behavior**

Sexual Arousal and Response

GENDER & CULTURAL DIVERSITY
Are There Evolutionary Advantages to Female Nonmonogamy?

Sexual Orientation

▶ **Sexual Problems**

Sexual Dysfunction

RESEARCH HIGHLIGHT
Is Cybersex Harmful?

Sexually Transmitted Infections

 PSYCHOLOGY AT WORK
Protecting Yourself and Others Against STIs

CRITICAL THINKING/ACTIVE LEARNING
Rape Myths and Rape Prevention

375

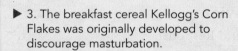

Application

WHY STUDY PSYCHOLOGY?

True or False?

Before we begin, test yourself by answering true or false to the following statements. (Answers are at the bottom and expanded explanations are found throughout this chapter.)

▶ 1. A transsexual is just another word for a transvestite.

▶ 2. Women who play action-packed video games can quickly catch up to men on their gaming skills.

▶ 3. The breakfast cereal Kellogg's Corn Flakes was originally developed to discourage masturbation.

▶ 4. Nocturnal emissions and masturbation are signs of abnormal sexual

PhotoDisc, Inc./Getty Images

adjustment.

▶ 5. The American Academy of Pediatrics (AAP) no longer recommends routine circumcision for male babies.

▶ 6. The American Psychiatric Associa-

tion and the American Psychological Association (APA) consider homosexuality a type of mental illness.

▶ 7. Men and women are more alike than different in their sexual responses.

▶ 8. Sexual skill and satisfaction are learned behaviors that can be increased through education and training.

▶ 9. If you're HIV-positive (have the human immunodeficiency virus), you cannot infect someone else. You must have AIDS (acquired immunodeficiency syndrome) to spread the disease.

▶ 10. Women cannot be raped against their will.

Answers: 1. F 2. T 3. T 4. F 5. T 6. F 7. T 8. T 9. F 10. F

Sex and Gender

chievement

Objective 11.1: *Compare and contrast sex and gender.*

Sex *Biological maleness and femaleness, including chromosomal sex; also, activities related to sexual behaviors, such as masturbation and intercourse*

Gender *Psychological and sociocultural meanings added to biological maleness or femaleness*

chievement

Objective 11.2: *Define gender role, and describe the two major theories of gender role development.*

Gender Role *Societal expectations for "appropriate" male and female behavior*

Why is it that the first question most people ask after a baby is born is "Is it a girl or a boy?" What would life be like if there were no divisions according to maleness or femaleness? Would your career plans or friendship patterns change? These questions reflect the importance of *sex* and *gender* in our lives. This section begins with a look at the various ways sex and gender can be defined, followed by a discussion of gender role development, gender identity formation, and sex and gender differences.

What Is "Maleness" and "Femaleness"? Defining Sex and Gender

In recent years, researchers have come to use the term **sex** to refer to biological elements (such as having a penis or vagina) or physical activities (such as masturbation and intercourse). **Gender**, on the other hand, encompasses the psychological and sociocultural meanings added to biology (such as "Men should be aggressive" and "Women should be nurturing"). There are at least seven dimensions or elements of *sex* and two of *gender* (Table 11.1).

Gender Role Development: Two Major Theories

Sexual orientation and gender identity also should not be confused with **gender roles**—societal expectations for "appropriate" female and male behavior. Gender roles influence our lives from the moment of birth (when we are wrapped in either a pink or blue blanket) until the moment of death (when we are buried in either a dress or a dark suit). By age 2, children are well aware of gender roles. They recognize that boys should be strong, independent, aggressive, dominant, and achieving. Conversely, girls should be soft, dependent, passive, emotional, and "naturally" interested in children (Frawley, 2008; Kimmel, 2000; Renzetti et al., 2006). The gender role expectations learned in childhood apparently influence us throughout our life.

TABLE 11.1 DIMENSIONS OF SEX AND GENDER

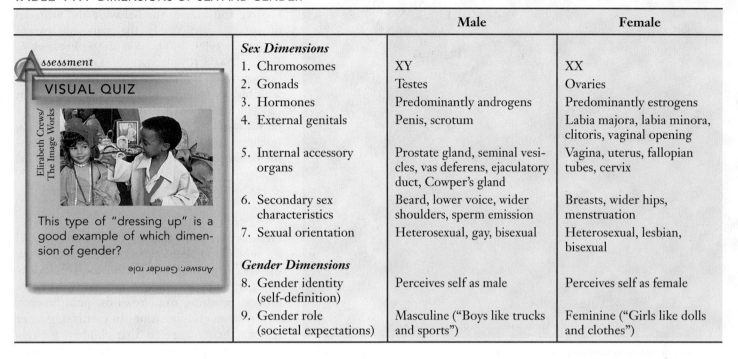

	Male	Female
Sex Dimensions		
1. Chromosomes	XY	XX
2. Gonads	Testes	Ovaries
3. Hormones	Predominantly androgens	Predominantly estrogens
4. External genitals	Penis, scrotum	Labia majora, labia minora, clitoris, vaginal opening
5. Internal accessory organs	Prostate gland, seminal vesicles, vas deferens, ejaculatory duct, Cowper's gland	Vagina, uterus, fallopian tubes, cervix
6. Secondary sex characteristics	Beard, lower voice, wider shoulders, sperm emission	Breasts, wider hips, menstruation
7. Sexual orientation	Heterosexual, gay, bisexual	Heterosexual, lesbian, bisexual
Gender Dimensions		
8. Gender identity (self-definition)	Perceives self as male	Perceives self as female
9. Gender role (societal expectations)	Masculine ("Boys like trucks and sports")	Feminine ("Girls like dolls and clothes")

Assessment

VISUAL QUIZ

Elizabeth Crews/The Image Works

This type of "dressing up" is a good example of which dimension of gender?

Answer: Gender role

How do we develop our gender roles? The existence of similar gender roles in many cultures suggests that evolution and biology may play a role. However, most research emphasizes two major theories of gender role development: *social learning* and *gender schema* (Figure 11.1).

Social Learning Theory

The **social learning theory of gender role development** emphasizes the power of the immediate situation and observable behaviors on gender role development. It suggests that girls learn how to be "feminine" and boys learn how to be "masculine" in two major ways: (1) They receive rewards or punishments

Social Learning Theory of Gender Role Development
Gender roles are acquired though rewards, punishments, observation, and imitation.

Bill Gallery/Stock, Boston

Bob Daemmrich/The Image Works

Early gender role conditioning What are the possible long-term effects of this type of gender role training on young boys and girls?

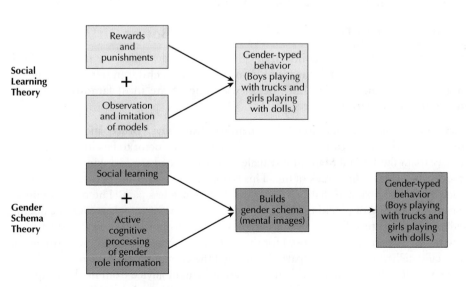

Social Learning Theory

Rewards and punishments

+

Observation and imitation of models

→ Gender-typed behavior (Boys playing with trucks and girls playing with dolls.)

Gender Schema Theory

Social learning

+

Active cognitive processing of gender role information

→ Builds gender schema (mental images) → Gender-typed behavior (Boys playing with trucks and girls playing with dolls.)

Figure 11.1 *Gender role development*

Associated Press

Modeling gendered behavior *Some computer and video games include a great deal of violence and are often criticized for modeling and encouraging violence. In a new game called Bully, shown here, the main character ultimately takes on bullies rather than become one. The game includes lots of fighting, but it also claims to show that actions have consequences. Do you think such an approach might encourage or discourage violent behavior?*

Gender Schema Theory *Gender roles are acquired through social learning and active cognitive processing*

Achievement

Objective 11.3: *Differentiate between gender identity, transsexualism, transvestitism, and sexual orientation.*

Gender Identity *Self-identification as being either a man or a woman*

for specific gender role behaviors, and (2) they observe and imitate the behavior and attitudes of others—particularly the same-sex parent (Bandura, 1989, 2000, 2006, 2008; Fredrick & Eccles, 2005; Rivadeneyra & Lebo, 2008). A boy who puts on his father's tie or baseball cap wins big, indulgent smiles from his parents. But can you imagine what would happen if he put on his mother's nightgown or lipstick? Parents, teachers, and friends generally reward or punish behaviors according to traditional boy/girl gender role expectations. Thus, a child "socially learns" what it means to be male or female.

Gender Schema Theory

Gender schema theory incorporates social learning with cognition (or thinking). Although the social learning model also involves thinking, gender development is primarily a passive process resulting from rewards, punishments, observation, and imitation. In contrast, gender schema theory suggests that children actively observe, interpret, and judge the world around them (Bem, 1981, 1993; Giles & Heyman, 2005; Ruble, Martin, & Berenbaum, 2006). As children process this information, they create internal rules governing correct gender roles for boys versus girls. Using these rules, they form *gender schemas* (mental images) of how they should act. (Recall from the discussion of Piaget in Chapter 9 that a *schema* is a cognitive structure, a network of associations, which guides perception.)

These *gender schemas* then lead to *gender-typed* behaviors. Thus, a little boy plays with fire trucks and building blocks because his parents smiled approvingly in the past. It is also because he has seen more boys than girls playing with these toys *(social learning theory)*. But his internal thought processes *(gender schema theory)* also contribute to his choice of "masculine" toys. The child realizes he is a boy, and he has learned that boys "should" prefer fire trucks to dishes and dolls.

Gender Identity Formation: "Who Am I—Boy or Girl?"

Now that we understand how children develop their gender roles, we need to examine an even more fundamental question: Why and how do children personally decide "I am a boy" or "I am a girl"? Let's begin with one of the most famous studies of **gender identity** formation.

It was an unusual circumcision. The identical twin boys, Bruce and Brian, were already 8 months old when their parents took them to the doctor to be circumcised. For many years in the United States, most male babies have had the foreskin of their penis removed during their first week of life. This is done for religious and presumed hygienic reasons. It is also assumed that newborns will experience less pain. The most common procedure is cutting or pinching off the foreskin tissue. In this case, however, the doctor used an electrocautery device, which is typically used to burn off moles or small skin growths. The electrical current used for the first twin was too high, and the entire penis was accidentally removed. (The parents canceled the circumcision of the other twin.)

In anguish over the tragic accident, the parents sought advice from medical experts. Following discussions with John Money and other specialists at Johns Hopkins University, the parents and doctors made an unusual decision—they would turn the infant with the destroyed penis into a girl. (Reconstructive surgery was too primitive at the time to restore the child's penis.)

The first step in the reassignment process occurred at age 17 months, when the child's name was changed—Bruce became "Brenda" (Colapinto, 2000). Brenda was dressed in pink pants and frilly blouses, and "her" hair was allowed to grow long. At 22 months, surgery was performed. The child's testes were removed, and external female genitals and an internal, "preliminary" vagina were created. Further surgery to complete the vagina was planned for the beginning of adolescence, when the child's physical growth would be nearly complete. At this time she would also begin to take female hormones to complete the boy-to-girl transformation.

If you apply the dimensions of sex and gender that are presented in Table 11.1 (p. 377) to the case of the reassigned twin, you can see why this is a classic in the field of human sexuality. Although born a chromosomal male, the child's genital sex was first altered by the doctor who accidentally removed the penis and later by surgeons who removed his testes and created a "preliminary" vagina. The question was whether surgery, along with female hormones and "appropriate" gender role expectations of the parents, would be enough to create a stable female gender identity. Would the child accept the sex reassignment and identify herself as a girl?

As you will discover in the upcoming case study, David ultimately rejected his assigned female gender despite strong pressure from his family and doctors. This indicates that biology may be the most important factor in gender identity formation. A recent longitudinal study offers additional evidence of a biological link. Researchers at Johns Hopkins Hospital tracked the development of 16 otherwise normal boys who had been born without a penis, a rare defect known as *cloacal exstrophy*. Fourteen of these boys had their testes removed and were raised as girls. Despite this radical treatment, researchers observed many signs of masculine behavior, including lots of "typical" male "rough-and-tumble" play. Eight of the 14 children, ranging in age from 5 to 16, later rejected their female reassignment and declared themselves to be boys (Reiner & Gearhart, 2004).

In addition to the gender difficulties involved in David's case and the cases of the boys born without a penis, other gender identity problems may develop when a person feels he or she is trapped in a body of the wrong sex. This is known as *transsexualism* (having a gender identity opposite to biological sex). Although some may see the case of Brenda/Bruce/David as a form of transsexualism, "true" transsexuals are born chromosomally and anatomically one sex. But they have a deep and lasting discomfort with their sexual anatomy. They report feeling as if they are victims of a "birth defect," and they often seek corrective reassignment surgery. At one time, the number of men seeking reassignment was much higher than the number of women who wished to be men. But the ratio has narrowed considerably in recent years.

Is a transsexual the same as a transvestite? No, *transvestism* involves individuals (almost exclusively men) who adopt the dress (cross-dressing), and often the behavior, typical of the opposite sex. Some homosexual men and women dress up as the other sex, and some entertainers cross-dress as part of their job. But for true transvestites, the cross-dressing is primarily for emotional and sexual gratification (Crooks & Bauer, 2008; King, 2009). In contrast, transsexuals feel that they are really members of the opposite sex imprisoned in the wrong body. Their gender identity does not match their gonads, genitals, or internal accessory organs. Transsexuals may also cross-dress. But their motivation is to look like the "right" sex rather than to obtain sexual arousal. Transvestites should also be distinguished from female impersonators (who cross-dress to entertain) and from gay men who occasionally "go in drag" (cross-dress).

Are transvestites and transsexuals also homosexual? When a person is described as *homosexual*, it is because of a **sexual orientation** toward the same sex. (The preferred terms today are *gay* and *lesbian* rather than *homosexual*.) Transvestites are usually

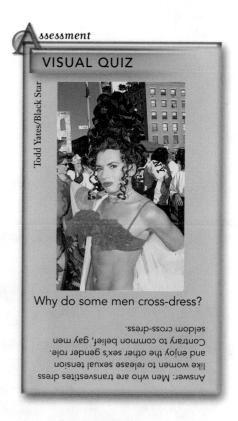

Ⓐssessment

VISUAL QUIZ

Todd Yates/Black Star

Why do some men cross-dress?

Answer: Men who are transvestites dress like women to release sexual tension and enjoy the other sex's gender role. Contrary to common belief, gay men seldom cross-dress.

Sexual Orientation *Primary erotic attraction toward members of the same sex (homosexual, gay, lesbian), both sexes (bisexual), or other sex (heterosexual)*

wiley.com/ college/ huffman

heterosexual. Transsexuality, on the other hand, has nothing to do with sexual orientation, only with gender identity. In fact, a transsexual can be heterosexual, gay, lesbian, or *bisexual* (being sexually attracted to both males and females).

"*As Nature Made Him: The Boy Who Was Raised as a Girl*", by *John Colapinto.*

Courtesy of Harper Collins Publishers

Assessment

APPLICATION CASE STUDY/PERSONAL STORY

The Tragic Tale of "John/Joan"

What do you think happened to the baby boy who suffered the botched circumcision? According to John Money (Money & Ehrhardt, 1972), after his "gender reassignment" as a girl, Bruce/Brenda easily moved into her new identity. By age 3, Brenda wore nightgowns and dresses almost exclusively and liked bracelets and hair ribbons. She also reportedly preferred playing with "girl-type" toys and asked for a doll and carriage for Christmas. In contrast, her brother, Brian, asked for a garage with cars, gas pumps, and tools. By age 6, Brian was accustomed to defending his sister if he thought someone was threatening her. The daughter copied the mother in tidying and cleaning up the kitchen, whereas the boy did not. The mother agreed that she encouraged her daughter when she helped with the housework and expected the boy to be uninterested.

During their childhood, both Brenda/Bruce and her brother Brian were brought to Johns Hopkins each year for physical and psychological evaluation. The case was heralded as a complete success. It also became the model for treating infants born with ambiguous genitalia. The story of "John/Joan," (the name used by Johns Hopkins) was heralded as proof that gender is made—not born.

What first looked like a success was, in fact, a dismal failure. Follow-up studies report that Brenda never really adjusted to her assigned gender (Colapinto, 2004). Despite being raised from infancy as a girl, she did not feel like a girl and avoided most female activities and interests. As she entered adolescence, her appearance and masculine way of walking led classmates to tease her and call her "cave woman." At this age, she also expressed thoughts of becoming a mechanic, and her fantasies reflected discomfort with her female role. She even tried urinating in a standing position and insisted she wanted to live as a boy (Diamond & Sigmundson, 1997).

By age 14, she was so unhappy that she contemplated suicide. The father tearfully explained what had happened earlier, and for Brenda, "All of a sudden everything clicked. For the first time, things made sense and I understood who and what I was" (Thompson, 1997, p. 83).

After the truth came out, "Brenda" reclaimed his male gender identity and renamed himself David. Following a double mastectomy (removal of both breasts) and construction of an artificial penis, he married a woman and adopted her children. David, his parents, and twin brother, Brian, all suffered enormously from the tragic accident and the no less tragic solution. He said, "I don't blame my parents." But they still felt extremely guilty about their participation in the reassignment. The family members later reconciled. But David remained angry with the doctors who "interfered with nature" and ruined his childhood.

Sadly, there's even more tragedy to tell. On May 4, 2004, 38-year old David committed suicide. Why? No one knows what went through his mind when he decided to end his life. But he had just lost his job, a big investment had failed, he was separated from his wife, and his twin brother had committed suicide shortly before. "Most suicides, experts say, have multiple motives, which come together in a perfect storm of misery" (Colapinto, 2004).

Corbis Images

David (aka "Brenda") as an adult

Sex and Gender Differences: Nature Versus Nurture

Now that we have looked at the different dimensions of sex and gender and examined gender role development, let's turn our attention to sex and gender differences between males and females.

Achievement

Objective 11.4: *Describe the major sex and gender differences between men and women.*

Sex Differences

Physical anatomy is the most obvious biological difference between men and women (Figure 11.2). The average man is taller, heavier, and stronger than the average woman. He is also more likely to be bald and color blind. In addition, men and women differ in their *secondary sex characteristics* (facial hair, breasts, and so on), their signs of reproductive capability (the menarche for girls and the ejaculation of sperm for boys), and their physical reactions to middle age or the end of reproduction (the female menopause and male climacteric).

There also are several functional and structural differences in the brains of men and women. These differences result, at least in part, from the influence of prenatal sex

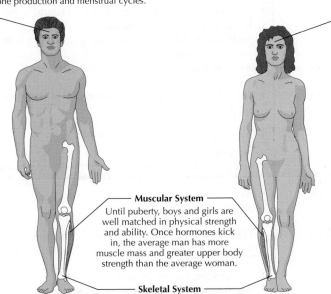

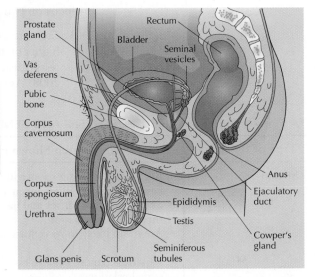

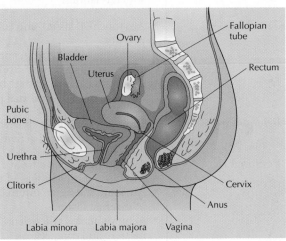

Body Size and Shape
The average man is 35 pounds heavier, has less body fat, and is 5 inches taller than the average woman. Men tend to have broader shoulders, slimmer hips and slightly longer legs in proportion to their height.

Brain
The corpus callosum, the bridge joining the two halves of the brain, is larger in women; therefore they can integrate information from the two halves of the brain and more easily perform more than one task simultaneously.

An area of the hypothalamus causes men to have a relatively constant level of sex hormones, whereas, women have cyclic sex hormone production and menstrual cycles.

Differences in the cerebral hemispheres may help explain reported sex differences in verbal and spatial skills.

Muscular System
Until puberty, boys and girls are well matched in physical strength and ability. Once hormones kick in, the average man has more muscle mass and greater upper body strength than the average woman.

Skeletal System
Men produce testosterone throughout their life span, whereas estrogen production virtually stops when a women goes through menopause. Because estrogen helps rejuvenate bones, women are more likely to have brittle bones. Women also are more prone to knee damage because a woman's wider hips may place a greater strain on the ligaments joining the thigh to the knee.

Figure 11.2 ***Major physical differences between the sexes*** *Source*: Adapted from Miracle, Tina S., Miracle, Andrew, W., and Baumeister, R. F., *Study Guide: Human sexuality: Meeting your basic needs*, 2nd edition. ©2006. Reprinted by permission of Pearson Education, Inc., Upper Saddle River, NJ.

hormones on the developing fetal brain. And the differences are most apparent in the *hypothalamus, corpus callosum, cerebral hemispheres,* and *gray* versus *white matter* (Allen et al., 2007; Cosgrove, Mazure, & Staley, 2007; Hyde, 2007; Matlin, 2008). For example, during puberty, the female's hypothalamus directs her pituitary gland to release hormones in a cyclic fashion (the menstrual cycle). In contrast, the male's hypothalamus directs a relatively steady production of sex hormones. The corpus callosum, the web of nerve fibers connecting the cerebral hemispheres, is larger in adult women and shaped differently in women than in men. Research suggests this difference may explain why men tend to rely on one hemisphere or the other in performing tasks, while women generally use both hemispheres at once. Researchers also have documented differences in the cerebral hemispheres of men and women that may account for reported differences in verbal and spatial skills, which are discussed in the next section.

Gender Differences

Do you think there are inborn psychological differences between women and men? Do you believe that women are more emotional and more concerned with aesthetics? Or that men are naturally more aggressive and competitive? Scientists have identified several gender differences, which are summarized in Table 11.2. In this section, we will focus on two of their most researched differences—cognitive abilities and aggression.

1. *Cognitive abilities.* For many years, researchers have noted that females tend to score higher on tests of verbal skills. Conversely, males score higher on math and visuospatial tests (Castelli, Corazzini, & Geminiani, 2008; Reynolds et al., 2008; van der Sluis et al., 2008). As mentioned earlier, some researchers suggest that these differences may reflect

TABLE 11.2 RESEARCH-SUPPORTED SEX AND GENDER DIFFERENCES

Type of Behavior	More Often Shown by Men	More Often Shown by Women
Sexual	• Begin masturbating sooner in life cycle and have higher overall occurrence rates. • Start sexual life earlier and have first orgasm through masturbation. • Are more likely to recognize their own sexual arousal. • Experience more orgasm consistency in their sexual relations.	• Begin masturbating later in life cycle and have lower overall occurrence rates. • Start sexual life later and have first orgasm from partner stimulation. • Are less likely to recognize their own sexual arousal. • Experience less orgasm consistency in their sexual relations.
Touching	• Are touched, kissed, and cuddled less by parents • Exchange less physical contact with other men and respond more negatively to being touched. • Are more likely to initiate both casual and intimate touch with sexual partner.	• Are touched, kissed, and cuddled more by parents. • Exchange more physical contact with other women and respond more positively to being touched. • Are less likely to initiate either casual or intimate touch with sexual partner.
Friendship	• Have larger number of friends and express friendship by shared activities.	• Have smaller number of friends and express friendship by shared communication about self.
Personality	• Are more aggressive from a very early age. • Are more self-confident of future success. • Attribute success to internal factors and failures to external factors. • Achievement is task oriented; motives are mastery and competition. • Are more self-validating. • Have higher self-esteem.	• Are less aggressive from a very early age. • Are less self-confident of future success. • Attribute success to external factors and failures to internal factors. • Achievement is socially directed with emphasis on self-improvement; have higher work motives. • Are more dependent on others for validation. • Have lower self-esteem.
Cognitive Abilities	• Are slightly superior in mathematics and visuospatial skills.	• Are slightly superior in grammar, spelling, and related verbal skills.

Sources: Crooks & Baur, 2008; Hyde & Delamater, 2008; King, 2009; Masters & Johnson, 1961, 1966, 1970; Matlin, 2008.

evolution and biology—that is, evolutionary adaptations and structural differences in the cerebral hemispheres, hormones, or the degree of hemispheric specialization.

However, some critics suggest that evolution progresses much too slowly to account for this type of behavioral adaptation. Furthermore, there are wide variations across cultures in gender differences, and biological/evolutionary explanations are difficult to test experimentally. Virtually all studies of human gender differences are *correlational* (Denmark, Rabinowitz, & Sechzer, 2005; Eagly & Koenig, 2006; Hyde, 2007; Matlin, 2008). Once again, it is extremely difficult to separate the effects of biological, psychological, and social forces—the *biopsychosocial model*.

2. *Aggression.* One of the clearest and most consistent findings in gender studies is greater physical aggressiveness in males. From an early age, boys are more likely to engage in mock fighting and rough-and-tumble play. As adolescents and adults, men are more likely to commit aggressive crimes (Campbell & Muncer, 2008; Giancola & Parrott, 2008; Ostrov & Keating, 2004). But gender differences are clearer for physical aggression (like hitting) than for other forms of aggression. Early research also suggested that females were more likely to engage in more indirect and relational forms of aggression, such as spreading rumors and ignoring or excluding someone (Bjorkqvist, 1994; Ostrov & Keating, 2004). But other studies have not found clear differences (Marsee, Weems, & Taylor 2008; Shahim, 2008).

What causes these gender differences in aggression? Those who take a nature perspective generally cite biological factors. For example, several studies have linked the male gonadal hormone testosterone to aggressive behavior (Hermans, Ramsey, & van Honk, 2008; Popma et al., 2004; Trainor, Bird, & Marler, 2004). In addition, studies on identical twins find that genetic factors account for about 50 percent of aggressive behavior (Bartels et al., 2007; Cadoret, Leve, & Devor, 1997; Segal & Bouchard, 2000).

Nurturists suggest that we should be examining gender role training and the context in which aggressive behaviors take place (Richardson & Hammock, 2007; Rowe et al., 2004). For example, children's picture books, video games, and TV programs and commercials frequently present women and men in stereotypical gender roles—with men in more aggressive roles.

Androgyny

What if we don't like the negative parts of gender roles? What can we do? One way to overcome rigid or destructive gender role stereotypes is to encourage **androgyny**, expressing both the "masculine" and "feminine" traits found in each individual. Rather than limiting themselves to rigid gender-appropriate behaviors, androgynous men and women can be assertive and aggressive when necessary, but also gentle and nurturing.

Some people think *androgyny* is a new term for asexuality or transsexualism. However, the idea of androgyny has a long history referring to positive combinations of gender roles, like the *yin* and *yang* of traditional Chinese religions. Carl Jung (1946, 1959), an early psychoanalyst, described a woman's natural masculine traits and impulses as her "animus" and feminine traits and impulses in a man as his "anima." Jung believed we must draw on both our masculine and feminine natures to become fully functioning adults.

Using personality tests and other similar measures, modern researchers have found that *masculine* and *androgynous* individuals generally have higher self-esteem, academic scores, and creativity. They are also more socially competent and motivated to achieve, and exhibit better overall mental health (Choi, 2004; Lefkowitz & Zeldow, 2006; Venkatesh et al., 2004; Wall, 2007; Woo & Oie, 2006). It seems that androgyny and masculinity, but *not* femininity, are adaptive for both sexes.

How can you explain this? It seems that traditional masculine characteristics (analytical, independent) are more highly valued than traditional feminine traits

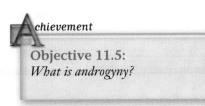

Achievement

Objective 11.5:
What is androgyny?

Androgyny [an-DRAW-juh-nee]
Exhibiting both masculine and feminine traits; from the Greek andro, meaning "male," and gyn, meaning "female"

(affectionate, cheerful). For example, in business a good manager is generally perceived as having predominantly masculine traits (Johnson et al., 2008). Also, when college students in 14 different countries were asked to describe their "current self" and their "ideal self," the ideal self-descriptions for both men and women contained more masculine than feminine qualities (Williams & Best, 1990).

This shared preference for male traits helps explain why extensive observations of children on school playgrounds have found that boys who engage in feminine activities (like skipping rope or playing jacks) lose status. The reverse of this is not true for girls (Leaper, 2000). Even as adults, it is more difficult for males to express so-called female traits like nurturance and sensitivity than for women to adopt traditionally male traits of assertiveness and independence. In short, most societies prefer "tomboys" to "sissies."

Recent studies show that gender roles in our society are becoming less rigidly defined (Kimmel, 2000; Loo & Thorpe, 1998). Asian American and Mexican American groups show some of the largest changes toward androgyny. And African Americans remain among the most androgynous of all ethnic groups (Denmark, Rabinowitz, & Sechzer, 2005; Duvall, 2006; Renzetti et al., 2006).

Try This Yourself

Application

Ranald Mackechnie/Stone/Getty Images

Androgyny in action *Combining the traits of both genders helps many couples meet the demands of modern life.*

Are You Androgynous?

Social psychologist Sandra Bem (1974, 1993) developed a personality measure that has been widely used in research. You can take this version of Bem's test by rating yourself on the following items. Give yourself a number between 1 (never or almost never true) and 7 (always or almost always true):

1. _____ Analytical
2. _____ Affectionate
3. _____ Competitive
4. _____ Compassionate
5. _____ Aggressive
6. _____ Cheerful
7. _____ Independent
8. _____ Gentle
9. _____ Athletic
10. _____ Sensitive

Now add up your points for all the odd-numbered items; then add up your points for the even-numbered items. If you have a higher total on the odd-numbered items, you are "masculine." If you scored higher on the even-numbered items, you are "feminine." If your score is fairly even, you may be androgynous.

Application

RESEARCH HIGHLIGHT

Video Games, Gender, and Spatial Skills
By Siri Carpenter

iStockphoto

Playing an action-packed video game nearly wipes out sex differences in a basic spatial thinking task, research reveals. In a study of college students, men were better than women at rapidly switching their attention among stimuli displayed on a computer screen, a common test of spatial ability (Feng, Spence, & Pratt, 2007). But after both sexes played the role of a World War II soldier in a video game for 10 hours over several weeks, women caught up to men on the spatial-attention task, as well as on an object-rotation test of more advanced spatial ability. Women's gains persisted when the volunteers were retested an average of five months later.

The study's lead author, University of Toronto psychologist Ian Spence, speculates that the video game practice may have caused "massive overexercising" of the brain's attentional system or even switched on previously inactive genes that underlie spatial cognition. Either way, he says, the results hold tantalizing potential for designing action-intensive video games that appeal to girls and women, perhaps eventually boosting women's participation in fields such as mathematics and engineering, which demand good spatial ability.

(*Source:* Originally published in *Scientific American Mind*, December 2007/January 2008, p. 10. Adapted and reprinted with permission of author, Siri Carpenter.)

*A*pplication

CRITICAL THINKING   ACTIVE LEARNING

Gender Differences and Critical Thinking
(Contributed by Thomas Frangicetto)

Part I

For each of the following:

• Fill in the blanks with terms and concepts from this chapter, including Table 11.2. This will help you review important text content that may appear on exams.

• Answer the associated critical thinking questions. They will improve your relationship skills and understanding of important gender and sexuality issues.

1. According to research, "one way to overcome rigid or destructive _____ is to encourage *androgyny*, expressing both the "masculine" and "feminine" traits found in each individual." Do you agree? Do you believe that children should be raised to be androgynous?

Which of the 21 critical thinking components (CTCs) found in the Prologue (pp. xxx–xxxiv) do you think are essential in becoming an androgynous person? Are there any CTCs that women display more than men, or vice versa?

2. "Men are encouraged to bring a certain level of sexual knowledge into the relationship. In contrast, women are expected to stop male advances and refrain from sexual activity until marriage." This _____ still exists in modern Western societies. How does this common belief affect your personal relationships or sexual behaviors? Can you identify at least two CTCs that could be useful in overcoming possible problems or negative effects associated with this belief?

3. According to research cited in Table 11.2, men have a _____ number of friends and express their friendship by

_____. Women have _____ friends and express their friendship by _____. Do you agree? Does this research help you understand differences between men and women? How might this difference create problems for married couples with few outside friendships?

4. Research cited in Table 11.2 also finds that men "have _____ self-esteem" and women "have _____ self-esteem."

Part II

Can you identify additional content from that table that might help explain this difference? For example, what role does "self-validation" play in the formation of self-esteem? What about differences in their attributions for success or failure? Choose one to three CTCs that you think could help equalize these gender differences in self-esteem.

Check your answers in Appendix B.

---

*A*ssessment **STOP**

CHECK & REVIEW

Sex and Gender

Ranald Mackechnie/Stone/Getty Images

Objective 11.1: *Compare and contrast sex and gender.*

Sex refers to biological elements (such as having a penis or vagina) or physical activities (such as masturbation and intercourse). **Gender**, on the other hand, encompasses the psychological and sociocultural meanings added to biology (such as "Men should be aggressive" and "Women should be nurturing").

Objective 11.2: *Define gender role, and describe the two major theories of gender role development.*

Gender roles are the societal expectations for normal and appropriate female and male behavior. **Social learning theory of gender role development** emphasizes rewards, punishments, observation, and imitation, whereas **gender schema theory** combines social learning theory with active cognitive processing.

Objective 11.3: *Differentiate between gender identity, transsexualism, transvestitism, and sexual orientation.*

Gender identity refers to an individual's self identification as being either a man or a woman. Transsexualism is a problem with gender identity, whereas transvestism is cross-dressing for emotional and sexual gratification. **Sexual orientation** (being gay, lesbian, bisexual, or heterosexual) is unrelated to either transsexualism or transvestism.

Objective 11.4: *Describe the major sex and gender differences between men and women.*

Studies of male and female sex differences find several obvious physical differences, such as height, body build, and reproduc-

tive organs. There are also important functional and structural sex differences in the brains of human females and males. Studies also find some gender differences (such as in aggression and verbal skills). But the cause of these differences (either nature or nurture) is controversial.

Objective 11.5: *What is androgyny?*

Androgyny is a combination of traits generally considered male (assertive, athletic) with typically female characteristics (nurturant, yielding).

Questions

1. Match the following dimensions of gender with their appropriate meaning:

___ Chromosomal sex   a. Ovaries and testes

___ Gender identity   b. XX and XY

___ Gonadal sex   c. Estrogens and androgens

___ Gender role   d. One's perception of oneself as male or female

____ Hormonal sex

____ Secondary sex characteristics

____ External genitals

____ Sexual orientation

e. Breasts, beard, menstruation

f. Uterus, vagina, prostate gland, vas deferens

g. Labia majora, clitoris, penis, scrotum

h. Homosexual, bisexual, heterosexual

____ Internal accessory organs

i. Differing societal expectations for appropriate male and female behavior

2. Briefly summarize the two major theories of gender role development.

3. Individuals who have the genitals and secondary sex characteristics of one sex but feel as if they belong to the other sex are

known as _____. (a) transvestites; (b) heterosexuals; (c) gays or lesbians; (d) transsexuals

4. A combination of both male and female personality traits is called _____. (a) heterosexuality; (b) homosexuality; (c) transsexualism; (d) androgyny

Check your answers in Appendix B.

Click & Review
for additional assessment options:
wiley.com/college/huffman

Achievement

Objective 11.6: *Describe early studies of sexuality and the contributions of Ellis, Kinsey, and Masters and Johnson.*

Assessment

VISUAL QUIZ

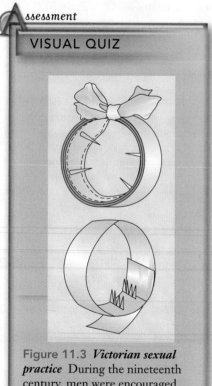

Figure 11.3 *Victorian sexual practice* During the nineteenth century, men were encouraged to wear spiked rings around their penises at night. Can you explain why?

Answer: The Victorians believed night-time erections and emissions ("wet dreams") were dangerous. If the man had an erection, the spikes would cause pain and awaken him.

The Study of Human Sexuality

Sex is used and abused in many ways. It is a major theme in literature, movies, and music, as well as a way to satisfy sexual desires. We also use and abuse sex to gain love and acceptance from partners and peer groups, to express love or commitment in a relationship, to end relationships through affairs with others, to dominate or hurt others, and, perhaps most conspicuously, to sell products.

People have probably always been interested in understanding their sexuality. But cultural forces have often suppressed and controlled this interest. During the nineteenth century, for example, polite society avoided mention of all parts of the body covered by clothing. The breast of chickens became known as "white meat," male doctors examined female patients in totally dark rooms, and some people even covered piano legs for the sake of propriety (Allen, 2000; Marcus 2008; Money, 1985a).

During this same Victorian period, medical experts warned that masturbation led to blindness, impotence, acne, and insanity (Allen, 2000; Michael et al., 1994). Believing a bland diet helped suppress sexual desire, Dr. John Harvey Kellogg and Sylvester Graham developed the original Kellogg's Corn Flakes and Graham crackers and marketed them as foods that would discourage masturbation (Money, Prakasam, & Joshi, 1991). One of the most serious concerns of many doctors was nocturnal emissions (wet dreams), which were believed to cause brain damage and death. Special devices were even marketed for men to wear at night to prevent sexual arousal (Figure 11.3).

In light of modern knowledge, it seems hard to understand these strange Victorian practices and outrageous myths about masturbation and nocturnal emissions. One of the first physicians to explore and question these beliefs was Havelock Ellis (1858–1939). When he first heard of the dangers of nocturnal emissions, Ellis was frightened—he had had personal experience with the problem. His fear led him to frantically search the medical literature. But instead of a cure, he found predictions of gruesome illness and eventual death. He was so upset he contemplated suicide.

Ellis eventually decided he could give meaning to his life by keeping a detailed diary of his deterioration. He planned to dedicate the book to science when he died. However, after several months of careful observation, he realized the books were wrong. He wasn't dying. He wasn't even sick. Angry that he had been so misinformed by the "experts," he spent the rest of his life developing reliable and accurate sex information. Today, Havelock Ellis is acknowledged as one of the most important early pioneers in the field of sex research.

Another major contribution to sex research came from Alfred Kinsey and his colleagues (1948, 1953). Kinsey and his coworkers personally interviewed over 18,000 participants, asking detailed questions about their sexual activities and preferences. Their results shocked the nation. For example, they reported that 37 percent of men and 13 percent of women had engaged in adult same-sex behavior to the point of orgasm. However, Kinsey's data were criticized because most research participants were young, single, urban, white, and middle class. Despite the criticism, Kinsey's work is still widely respected, and his data are frequently used as a *baseline* for modern research. In recent years, hundreds of similar sex surveys and interviews have been conducted on such topics as contraception, abortion, premarital sex, sexual orientation, and sexual behavior (e.g., Buss, 1989, 2007, 2008; Ellis et al., 2008). By comparing Kinsey's data to the responses found in later surveys, we can see how sexual practices have changed over the years.

In addition to surveys, interviews, and case studies, some researchers have employed direct laboratory experimentation and observational methods. To experimentally document the physiological changes involved in sexual arousal and response, William Masters and Virginia Johnson (1961, 1966, 1970) and their research colleagues enlisted several hundred male and female volunteers. Using intricate physiological measuring devices, the researchers carefully monitored participants' bodily responses as they masturbated or engaged in sexual intercourse. Masters and Johnson's research findings have been hailed as a major contribution to our knowledge of sexual physiology. Some of their results are discussed in later sections.

Havelock Ellis (1858–1939) *Ellis was one of the first sex researchers to celebrate eroticism and fully acknowledge female sexuality.*

Achievement
GENDER & CULTURAL DIVERSITY

A Cross-Cultural Look at Sexual Behaviors

Sex researchers interested in both similarities and variations in human sexual behavior conduct cross-cultural studies of sexual practices, techniques, and attitudes (Barber, 2008; Beach, 1977; Brislin, 2000; Buss, 1989, 2007, 2008). Their studies of different societies put sex in a broader perspective.

Cross-cultural studies of sex also help counteract *ethnocentrism*, judging our own cultural practices as "normal" and preferable to those of other groups. For example, do you know that kissing is unpopular in Japan and unknown among some cultures in Africa and South America? Do you find it strange that Apinaye women in Brazil often bite off pieces of their mate's eyebrows as a natural part of sexual foreplay? Does it surprise you that members of Tiwi society, off the northern coast of Australia, believe that young girls will not develop breasts or menstruate unless they first experience intercourse? Do you know that the men and women of the Amazonian Yanomamo routinely wear nothing but a thin cord around their waists? Interestingly, if you were to ask a Yanomamo woman to remove the cord, she would respond in much the same way an American woman would if you asked her to remove her blouse (Hyde & DeLamater, 2008; Frayser, 1985; Gregersen, 1996). In addition, the Sambia of New Guinea believe that young boys must swallow semen to achieve manhood (Herdt, 1981). Adolescent boys in Mangaia, a small island in the South Pacific, routinely undergo superincision, a painful initiation rite in which the foreskin of the penis is slit and folded back (Marshall, 1971). Figure 11.4 gives other examples of surprising cultural variation in sexuality.

Although other cultures' practices may seem unnatural and strange to us, we forget that our own sexual rituals may appear equally curious to others. If the description of the Mangaian practice of superincision bothered you, how do you feel about our own culture's routine circumcision of infant boys? Before you object that infant circumcision in the United States is "entirely different" and "medically safe and necessary," you might want to consider the position now taken by the American

Achievement

Objective 11.7: *Why are cross-cultural studies of sexuality important?*

M. Milner/Corbis Sygma

Circumcision and religion *Although circumcision is an important part of some religions, it is relatively rare in most parts of the world.*

wiley.com/
college/
huffman

Figure 11.4 *Cross-cultural differences in sexual behavior* Note: "Inis Beag" is a pseudonym used to protect the privacy of residents of this Irish island. *Sources:* Crooks & Baur, 2008; Hyde & DeLamater, 2008; Marshall, 1971; Money et al., 1991.

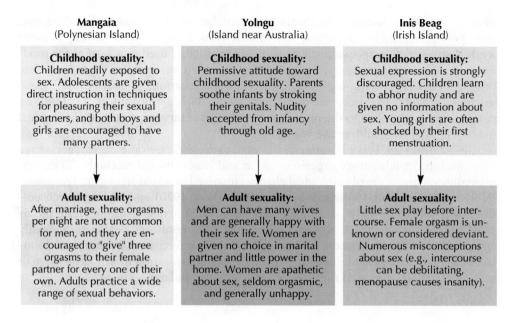

Mangaia (Polynesian Island)

Childhood sexuality: Children readily exposed to sex. Adolescents are given direct instruction in techniques for pleasuring their sexual partners, and both boys and girls are encouraged to have many partners.

Adult sexuality: After marriage, three orgasms per night are not uncommon for men, and they are encouraged to "give" three orgasms to their female partner for every one of their own. Adults practice a wide range of sexual behaviors.

Yolngu (Island near Australia)

Childhood sexuality: Permissive attitude toward childhood sexuality. Parents soothe infants by stroking their genitals. Nudity accepted from infancy through old age.

Adult sexuality: Men can have many wives and are generally happy with their sex life. Women are given no choice in marital partner and little power in the home. Women are apathetic about sex, seldom orgasmic, and generally unhappy.

Inis Beag (Irish Island)

Childhood sexuality: Sexual expression is strongly discouraged. Children learn to abhor nudity and are given no information about sex. Young girls are often shocked by their first menstruation.

Adult sexuality: Little sex play before intercourse. Female orgasm is unknown or considered deviant. Numerous misconceptions about sex (e.g., intercourse can be debilitating, menopause causes insanity).

Academy of Pediatrics (AAP). In 1999, they decided the previously reported medical benefits of circumcision were so statistically small that the procedure should *not* be routinely performed. However, the AAP does consider it legitimate for parents to take into account cultural, religious, and ethnic traditions in deciding whether to circumcise their sons.

If the controversy over infant male circumcision surprises you, so, too, may information about female genital mutilation. Throughout history and even today—in parts of Africa, the Middle East, Indonesia, and Malaysia—young girls undergo several types of *female genital mutilation* (FGM). FGM includes circumcision (removal of the clitoral hood), *clitoridectomy* (removal of the clitoris), and *genital infibulation* (removal of the clitoris and labia and stitching together of the remaining tissue to allow only a small opening for urine and menstrual flow). In most countries, the surgeries are performed on girls between ages 4 and 10 and often without anesthesia or antiseptic conditions. The young girls suffer numerous health problems because of these practices—the most serious from genital infibulation. Risks include severe pain, bleeding, chronic infection, and menstrual difficulties. As adults, these women frequently experience serious sexual problems, as well as dangerous childbirth complications or infertility.

What is the purpose of these procedures? The main objective is to ensure virginity (Orubuloye, Caldwell, & Caldwell, 1997). Without these procedures, young girls are considered unmarriageable and without status. As you might imagine, these practices create serious culture clashes. For example, physicians in Western societies are currently being asked by immigrant parents to perform these operations on their daughters. What should the doctor do? Should this practice be forbidden? Or would this be another example of ethnocentrism?

As you can see, it is a complex issue. Canada was the first nation to recognize female genital mutilation as a basis for granting refugee status (Crooks & Baur, 2008). And the United Nations has suspended its regular policy of nonintervention in the cultural practices of nations. The World Health Organization (WHO) and the United Nations International Children's Emergency Fund (UNICEF) have both issued statements opposing female genital mutilation. They also have developed programs to combat this and other harmful practices affecting the health and well-being of women and children.

Assessment

STOP

CHECK & REVIEW

The Study of Human Sexuality

Objective 11.6: *Describe early studies of sexuality and the contributions of Ellis, Kinsey, and Masters and Johnson.*

Although sex has always been an important part of human interest, motivation, and behavior, it received little scientific attention before the twentieth century. Havelock Ellis was among the first to study human sexuality despite the repression and secrecy of nineteenth-century Victorian times. Alfred Kinsey and his colleagues were the first to conduct large-scale, systematic surveys and interviews of the sexual practices and preferences of Americans during the 1940s and 1950s. In the 1960s, the research team of William Masters and Virginia Johnson pioneered the use of actual laboratory measurement and observation of human physiological response during sexual activity.

Objective 11.7: *Why are cross-cultural studies of sexuality important?*

Cross-cultural studies provide important information on the similarities and variations in human sexuality. They also help counteract *ethnocentrism*—judging one's own culture as "normal" and preferable to others.

Questions

1. During earlier times, it was believed that _____ led to blindness, impotence, acne, and insanity, whereas _____ caused brain damage and death.
   (a) female orgasms, male orgasms;
   (b) masturbation, nocturnal emissions;
   (c) menstruation, menopause;
   (d) oral sex, sodomy
2. Fill in the researchers' name that matches their contributions to the study of human sexuality:
   a. _____ based his/their groundbreaking research into human sexuality on personal diaries

   b. _____ popularized the use of the survey method in studying human sexuality
   c. _____ pioneered the use of direct observation and physiological measurement of bodily responses during sexual activities
3. What are the advantages of cultural studies in sex research?
4. Viewing one's own ethnic group (or culture) as central and "correct" and then judging the rest of the world according to this standard is known as _____.
   (a) standardization;
   (b) stereotyping;
   (c) discrimination;
   (d) ethnocentrism

Check your answers in Appendix B.

Click & Review
for additional assessment options:
wiley.com/college/huffman

Sexual Behavior

Are women and men fundamentally alike in their sexual responses? Or are they unalterably different? What causes a gay or lesbian sexual orientation? What is sexual prejudice? These are some of the questions we will explore in this section.

Sexual Arousal and Response: Gender Differences and Similarities

Males and females have obvious differences and similarities in their sexual arousal and response. But how would researchers scientifically test what happens to the human body when an individual or couple engage in sexual activities? As you can imagine, this is a highly controversial topic for research. William Masters and Virginia Johnson (1966) were the first to conduct actual laboratory studies. With the help of 694 female and male volunteers, they attached recording devices to the volunteers' bodies and monitored or filmed their physical responses as they moved from nonarousal to orgasm and back to nonarousal. They labeled the bodily changes during this series of events a **sexual response cycle** that included four stages: *excitement, plateau, orgasm,* and *resolution* (Process Diagram 11.1).

Achievement

Objective 11.8: *What are the four stages in Masters and Johnson's sexual response cycle?*

Sexual Response Cycle *Masters and Johnson's description of the four-stage bodily response to sexual arousal, which consists of excitement, plateau, orgasm, and resolution*

Process Diagram 11.1

Masters and Johnson's Sexual Response Cycle

Note that this simplified description does not account for individual variation and should not be used to judge what's "normal."

2. During the **plateau phase**, biological and sexual arousal continue at heightened levels. In the man, the penis becomes more engorged and erect while the testes swell and pull up closer to the body. In the woman, the clitoris pulls up under the clitoral hood and the entrance to the vagina contracts while the uterus rises slightly. This movement of the uterus causes the upper two-thirds of the vagina to balloon, or expand. As arousal reaches its peak, both sexes may experience a feeling that orgasm is imminent and inevitable.

3. The **orgasm phase** involves a highly intense and pleasurable release of tension. In the woman, muscles around the vagina squeeze the vaginal walls in and out and the uterus pulsates. Muscles at the base of the penis contract in the man, causing ejaculation, the discharge of semen or seminal fluid.

1. The **excitement phase** can last for minutes or hours. Arousal is initiated through touching, fantasy, or erotic stimuli. Heart rate and respiration increase and increased blood flow to the pelvic region causes penile erection in men and clitoral erection, and vaginal lubrication in women. In both men and women, the nipples may become erect, and both may experience a sex flush (reddening of the upper torso and face).

4. Biological responses gradually return to normal during the **resolution phase**. After one orgasm, most men enter a **refractory period**, during which further excitement to orgasm is considered impossible. Many women (and some men), however, are capable of multiple orgasms in fairly rapid succession.

In the diagrams to the right, note in (a) that immediately after orgasm males generally enter a refractory period, which lasts from several minutes up to a day, in which they cannot have another orgasm. Note in (b) that female sexual responses follow one or more of three basic patterns: Pattern A resembles the male pattern, except it includes the possibility of multiple orgasm (the second peak in pattern A) without falling below the plateau level. Pattern B represents nonorgasmic arousal. Pattern C portrays a rapid rise to orgasm, no definitive plateau, and a quick resolution.

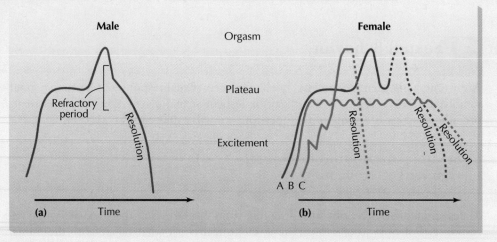

Excitement Phase *First stage of the sexual response cycle, characterized by increasing levels of arousal and increased engorgement of the genitals*

Plateau Phase *Second stage of the sexual response cycle, characterized by a leveling off in a state of high arousal*

Orgasm Phase *Third stage of the sexual response cycle, when pleasurable sensations peak and orgasm occurs*

Resolution Phase *Final stage of the sexual response cycle, when the body returns to its unaroused state*

Refractory Period *Phase following orgasm, during which further orgasm is considered physiologically impossible for men*

GENDER & CULTURAL DIVERSITY

Objective 11.9: *Describe how the evolutionary perspective and the social role approach help explain male/female differences in sexual behavior.*

Are There Evolutionary Advantages to Female Nonmonogamy?

In many ways, women and men are similar in their general sexual responses. But it is our differences that attract the most attention. For example, have you heard that men have more sexual drive, interest, and activity than women do? How do scientists investigate such a common belief? There are two major perspectives—evolutionary and social role.

The *evolutionary perspective*, emphasizing the adaptive value of behaviors, suggests that sexual differences (such as men having more sexual partners) evolved from ancient mating patterns that helped the species survive (Barber, 2008; Buss, 1989, 2007, 2008; Kardong, 2008; Manning, 2007). According to this *sexual strategies theory* (SST), men have a greater interest in sex and multiple partners. Men are also more sexually jealous and controlling because these behaviors maximize their chances for reproduction. Women, on the other hand, seek a good protector and provider to increase their chances for survival, as well as that of their offspring. These male and female sexual strategies reportedly serve to pass along their respective genes and ensure the survival of the species.

Can you see how this particular interpretation of the evolutionary perspective suggests that only men have a biological advantage in having multiple sex partners? Keep in mind, however, that in at least 18 societies around the world it is *female non-monogamy* (women having multiple sex partners) that offers survival value to women and children (Beckerman et al., 1999). People in these cultures believe in *partible paternity* (one child having more than one biological father). And pregnant women openly acknowledge their extramarital lovers as "secondary fathers."

This belief that multiple men contribute to the initial impregnation and later "building of the child" seems to benefit both the pregnant woman and her children. Among the Bari of Venezuela and Colombia, Beckerman and his colleagues found that pregnant women with lovers were less likely to miscarry, possibly because of court-ship gifts that boosted their nutrition. In addition, 80 percent of children with "extra" fathers lived to age 15, in contrast to 64 percent of children with lone dads.

The *social role approach* offers an important alternative to the evolutionary perspective and its biological emphasis. This perspective suggests that gender differences in sexual behavior result from the roles that men and women internalize from their society (Eagly & Koenig, 2006; Hyde, 2007). For instance, in traditional cultural divisions of labor, women are childbearers and homemakers. Men are providers and protectors. But as women gain more reproductive freedom and educational opportunities, they also acquire more personal resources and status through means other than mates.

This hypothesis is directly supported by a reanalysis of Buss's original data collected from 37 cultures (Buss et al., 1990). Kasser and Sharma (1999) found that women did indeed prefer resource-rich men. But this only occurred when the women lived in cultures with little reproductive freedom and educational equality. Therefore, say Kasser and Sharma, the conflict between the evolutionary and social role perspectives may be resolved by examining patriarchal cultural systems that limit women's choices.

If strong patriarchies existed during the Pleistocene epoch, enough time may have passed for psychological mechanisms to evolve in reaction to such environments. If, however, patriarchy emerged only in the past 10,000 years, with the advent of agriculture, the time span is too short for evolutionary changes, and the social role approach may be the best explanation.

Sexual Orientation: Contrasting Theories and Myths

Objective 11.10: *Discuss the latest research on sexual orientation.*

What causes homosexuality? What causes heterosexuality? Many have asked the first question, but few have asked the second. As a result, the roots of sexual orientation are poorly understood. However, research has identified several widespread myths

Fighting back against sexual prejudice *These protesters are working to increase public awareness and acceptance of different sexual orientations.*

and misconceptions about homosexuality (Bergstrom-Lynch, 2008; Boysen & Vogel, 2007; LeVay, 2003). Keep in mind that each of the following popular "theories" is *false!*

- **Seduction theory**. Gays and lesbians were seduced as children by adults of their own sex.

- **"By default" myth**. Gays and lesbians were unable to attract partners of the other sex or have experienced unhappy heterosexual experiences.

- **Poor parenting theory**. Sons become gay because of domineering mothers and weak fathers. Daughters become lesbians because of weak or absent mothers and having only fathers as their primary role model.

- **Modeling theory**. Children raised by gay and lesbian parents usually end up adopting their parents' sexual orientation.

The precise cause or causes of sexual orientation are still unknown. However, most scientists believe genetics and biology play the dominant role (Bailey, Dunne, & Martin, 2000; Byne, 2007; Ellis et al., 2008; Gooren, 2006; Zucker, 2008). Studies on identical and fraternal twins and adopted siblings found that if one identical twin was gay, about 48 to 65 percent of the time so was the second twin (Hyde, 2005; Kirk et al., 2000). (Note that if the cause were totally genetic, the percentage would be 100.) The rate for fraternal twins was 26 to 30 percent and 6 to 11 percent for adopted brothers or sisters. Estimates of homosexuality in the general population run between 2 and 10 percent.

Some researchers have also hypothesized that prenatal hormone levels affect fetal brain development and sexual orientation. Animal experiments have found that administering male hormones prenatally can cause female offspring of sheep and rats to engage in the mounting behavior associated with male sheep and rats (Bagermihl, 1999). It is obviously unethical to experiment with human fetuses. Therefore, we cannot come to any meaningful conclusions about the effect of hormones on fetal development, and no well-controlled study has ever found a difference in adult

Gay marriage *Debate, legislation, and judicial action surrounding gay marriage have brought attitudes about homosexuality into full public view.*

hormone levels between heterosexuals and gays and lesbians (Hall & Schaeff, 2008; Gooren, 2006; LeVay, 2003).

The origin of sexual orientation remains a mystery. However, we do know that gays and lesbians are often victimized by society's prejudice against them. Research shows that many suffer verbal and physical attacks; disrupted family and peer relationships; and high rates of anxiety, depression, substance use disorders, and suicide (Jellison, McConnell, & Gabriel, 2004; Espelage et al., 2008; Skinta, 2008; Talley & Bettencourt, 2008; Weber, 2008).

Some of this prejudice supposedly stems from an irrational fear of homosexuality in oneself or others, which Martin Weinberg labeled *homophobia* in the late 1960s. Today, some researchers believe this term is too limited and scientifically unacceptable. It implies that antigay attitudes are limited to individual irrationality and pathology. Therefore, psychologist Gregory Herek (2000) prefers the term **sexual prejudice**, which emphasizes multiple causes and allows scientists to draw on the rich scientific research on prejudice.

Sexual Prejudice *Negative attitudes toward an individual because of her or his sexual orientation*

In 1973 both the American Psychiatric Association and the American Psychological Association officially acknowledged that homosexuality is not a mental illness. However, it continues to be a divisive societal issue in the United States. Seeing *sexual prejudice* as a socially reinforced phenomenon rather than an individual pathology, coupled with political action by gays and lesbians, may help fight discrimination and hate crimes.

Assessment

CHECK & REVIEW STOP

Sexual Behavior

Objective 11.8: *What are the four stages in Masters and Johnson's sexual response cycle?*

William Masters and Virginia Johnson identified a four-stage **sexual response cycle** during sexual activity—the **excitement**, **plateau**, **orgasm**, and **resolution** phases.

Objective 11.9: *Describe how the evolutionary perspective and the social role approach help explain male/female differences in sexual behavior.*

Although there are numerous similarities between the sexes, differences are the focus of most research. According to the *evolutionary perspective*, men engage in more sexual behaviors with more sexual partners because it helps the species survive. The *social role* approach suggests this difference results from traditional cultural divisions of labor.

Objective 11.10: *Discuss the latest research on sexual orientation.*

Although researchers have identified several myths concerning the causes of homosexuality, the origins of sexual orientation remain a puzzle. In recent studies, the genetic and biological explanation for homosexuality has gained the strongest support. Despite increased understanding, sexual orientation remains a divisive issue in the United States.

Questions

1. Label the CORRECT sequence of events in Masters and Johnson's sexual response cycle on the figure below.

(b) _____   (c) _____

(a) _____   (d) _____

2. Briefly describe Masters and Johnson's sexual response cycle.
3. How do the evolutionary and social role perspectives explain male and female differences in sexual behavior?
4. The genetic influence on sexual orientation has been supported by research reporting that _____. (a) between identical twins, if one brother is gay, the other brother has a 48 to 65 percent chance of also being gay; (b) gay men have fewer chromosomal pairs than straight men, whereas lesbians have larger areas of the hypothalamus than straight women; (c) between adoptive pairs of brothers, if the younger brother is gay, the older brother has an increased chance of also being gay; (d) parenting style influences adult sexual orientation for men but not for women
5. A homosexual orientation appears to be the result of _____. (a) seduction during childhood or adolescence by an older homosexual; (b) a family background that includes a dominant mother and a passive, detached, father; (c) a hormonal imbalance; (d) unknown factors

Check your answers in Appendix B.

Click & Review
for additional assessment options:
wiley.com/college/huffman

Achievement

Objective 11.11: *Describe how biological, psychological, and social forces influence sexual dysfunction.*

Sexual Problems

When we are functioning well sexually, we tend to take this part of our lives for granted. But what happens when things don't go smoothly? Why does normal sexual functioning stop for some people and never begin for others? What are the major diseases that can be spread through sexual behavior? We will explore these questions in the following section.

Sexual Dysfunction: The Biopsychosocial Model

Sexual Dysfunction *Impairment of the normal physiological processes of arousal and orgasm*

There are many forms of **sexual dysfunction**, or difficulty in sexual functioning. And their causes are complex (Figure 11.5). In this section, we will discuss how biology, psychology, and social forces (the *biopsychosocial model*) all contribute to sexual difficulties.

Biological Factors

Although many people may consider it unromantic, a large part of sexual arousal and behavior is clearly the result of biological processes (Coolen et al., 2004; Hyde & DeLamater, 2008; King, 2009). *Erectile dysfunction* (the inability to get or maintain an erection firm enough for intercourse) and *orgasmic dysfunction* (the inability to respond to sexual stimulation to the point of orgasm) often reflect lifestyle factors like cigarette smoking. They also involve medical conditions such as diabetes, alcoholism, hormonal deficiencies, circulatory problems, and reactions to certain prescription and nonprescription drugs. In addition, hormones (especially testosterone) have a clear

Male ♂		Female ♀		Both Male ♂ and Female ♀	
Disorder	**Causes**	**Disorder**	**Causes**	**Disorder**	**Causes**
Erectile dysfunction (impotence) Inability to have (or maintain) an erection firm enough for intercourse *Primary erectile dysfunction* Lifetime erectile problems *Secondary erectile dysfunction* Erection problems occurring in at least 25 percent of sexual encounters	**Physical** — diabetes, circulatory conditions, heart disease, drugs, extreme fatigue, alcohol consumption, hormone deficiencies **Psychological** — performance anxiety, guilt, difficulty in expressing desires to partner, severe antisexual upbringing	**Orgasmic dysfunction** (anorgasmia, frigidity) Inability or difficulty in reaching orgasm *Primary orgasmic dysfunction* Lifetime history of no orgasm *Secondary orgasmic dysfunction* Was regularly orgasmic, but no longer is *Situational orgasmic dysfunction* Orgasms occur only under certain circumstances	**Physical** — chronic illness, diabetes, extreme fatigue, drugs, alcohol consumption, hormone deficiencies, pelvic disorders, lack of appropriate or adequate stimulation **Psychological** — fear of evaluation, poor body image, relationship problems, guilt, anxiety, severe antisexual upbringing, difficulty in expressing desires to partner, prior sexual trauma, childhood sexual abuse	**Dyspareunia** Painful intercourse **Inhibited sexual desire** (sexual apathy) Avoids sexual relations due to disinterest	**Primarily physical** — irritations, infections, or disorders of the internal or external genitals **Physical** — hormone deficiencies, alcoholism, drug use, chronic illness **Psychological** — depression, prior sexual trauma, relationship problems, anxiety
Premature ejaculation Rapid ejaculation beyond the man's control; partner is non-orgasmic in at least 50 percent of their intercourse episodes	**Almost always psychological** — because of guilt, fear of discovery while masturbating, and hurried experiences in cars or motels, man learns to ejaculate as quickly as possible	**Vaginismus** Involuntary spasms of the vagina and penile insertion is impossible or difficult and painful	**Primarily psychological** — learned association of pain or fear with intercourse, due to prior sexual trauma, severe antisexual upbringing, guilt, or lack of lubrication	**Sexual aversion** Avoids sex due to overwhelming fear or anxiety	**Psychological** — severe parental sex attitudes, prior sex trauma, partner pressure, gender identity confusion

Figure 11.5 *Major male and female sexual dysfunctions* Although sex therapists typically divide sexual dysfunctions into "male," "female," or "both," problems should never be considered "his" or "hers." Couples are almost always encouraged to work together to find solutions. For more information, check www.goaskalice.columbia.edu/Cat6.html. *Sources:* Adapted from Crooks & Baur, 2008; King, 2009.

effect on sexual desire in both men and women. But otherwise, the precise role of hormones in human sexual behavior is not well understood.

In addition to problems resulting from medical conditions and hormones, sexual responsiveness is also affected by the spinal cord and sympathetic nervous system. The human brain is certainly involved in all parts of the sexual response cycle. However, certain key sexual behaviors do not require an intact cerebral cortex to operate. In fact, some patients in comas still experience orgasms.

How is this possible? Recall from Chapter 2 that some aspects of human behavior are reflexive. They are unlearned, automatic, and occur without conscious effort or motivation. Sexual arousal for both men and women is partially reflexive and somewhat analogous to simple reflexes like the eye-blink response to a puff of air. For example, a puff of air produces an automatic closing of the eye. Similarly, certain stimuli, such as stroking of the genitals, can lead to automatic arousal in both men and women. In both situations, nerve impulses from the receptor site travel to the spinal cord. The spinal cord then responds by sending messages to target organs or glands. Normally, the blood flow into organs and tissues through the arteries is balanced by an equal outflow through the veins. During sexual arousal, however, the arteries dilate beyond the capacity of the veins to carry the blood away. This results in erection of the penis in men and an engorged clitoris and surrounding tissue in women.

If this is so automatic, why do some people have difficulty getting aroused? Unlike simple reflexes such as the eye blink, negative thoughts or high emotional states may block sexual arousal. Recall from Chapter 2 that the autonomic nervous system (ANS) is intricately involved in emotional (and sexual) responses. The ANS is composed of two subsystems: the sympathetic, which prepares the body for "fight or flight," and the parasympathetic, which maintains bodily processes at a steady, even balance. The parasympathetic branch is dominant during initial sexual excitement and throughout the plateau phase. The sympathetic branch dominates during ejaculation and orgasm. Can you see why the parasympathetic branch *must* be in control during arousal? The body needs to be relaxed enough to allow blood to flow to the genital area.

Psychological Influences

Our bodies may be biologically prepared to become aroused and respond to erotic stimulation. But psychological forces also play a role. For example, anxieties associated with many sexual experiences, such as fear of pregnancy and sexually transmitted infections, may cause sympathetic dominance, which in turn blocks sexual arousal. Many women discover that they need locked doors, committed relationships, and reliable birth control to fully enjoy sexual relations.

What about men? Most men also prefer privacy, commitment, and freedom from pregnancy concerns. But as you can see in Table 11.3, relationship status has less of an effect on male orgasms than it does on female orgasms. Apparently, women relax more under these conditions, which allows them to stay in arousal and parasympathetic dominance long enough for orgasm to occur.

Most couples also recognize that both sexes have difficulty with arousal if they drink too much alcohol or when they are stressed, ill, or fatigued. But one of the least recognized blocks of sexual arousal is **performance anxiety**, the fear of being judged in connection with sexual activity. Men commonly experience problems with erections (especially after drinking alcohol) and wonder if their "performance" will satisfy their partner. At the same time, women frequently worry about their attractiveness and their ability to orgasm. Can you see how these performance fears can lead to sexual problems? Once again, increased

TABLE 11.3 SEX AND RELATIONSHIPS

Men ♂	Women ♀	Always or Usually Have an Orgasm with Partner
94%	62%	Dating
95%	68%	Living together
95%	75%	Married

Source: Laumann, Gagnon, Michael, & Michaels, 1994.

Performance Anxiety *Fear of being judged in connection with sexual activity*

"Now, that's product placement!"

Double Standard *Beliefs, values, and norms that subtly encourage male sexuality and discourage female sexuality*

Sexual Scripts *Socially dictated descriptions of "appropriate" behaviors for sexual interactions*

anxiety causes the sympathetic nervous system to dominate, which blocks blood flow to the genitals.

Like fears of negative consequences from sex and performance anxiety, *gender roles* and the *double standard* are two additional psychological factors that contribute to both male and female sexual dysfunction.

Gender role training begins at birth and continually impacts all aspects of our life, as the story of "Brenda/David" from the beginning of this chapter shows. Can you imagine how traditional male gender roles—being dominant, aggressive, independent—could lead to different kinds of sexual thoughts and behaviors than traditional female gender roles—being submissive, passive, and dependent? Can you also imagine how this type of gender role training may lead to a **double standard**? Men are encouraged to explore their sexuality and bring a certain level of sexual knowledge into the relationship. Conversely, women are expected to stop male advances and refrain from sexual activity until marriage.

Although overt examples of this *double standard* are less evident in modern times, covert or hidden traces of this belief still exist. Examining the gender differences in Figure 11.6, can you see how items like men wanting women to "initiate sex more often" or women wanting men "to talk more lovingly" might be remnants of the double standard?

Social Factors In addition to biological and psychological influences on sexuality, we also learn explicit **sexual scripts** from society that teach us "what to do, when, where, how, and with whom" (Gagnon, 1990; Kimmel, 2007). For example, during the 1950s, societal messages said the "best" sex was at night, in a darkened room, with a man on top and a woman on the bottom. Today, the messages are more bold and varied, partly because of media portrayals. Compare, for example, the sexual scripts portrayed in Figure 11.7.

Sexual scripts, gender roles, and the double standard may all be less rigid today, but a major difficulty remains. Many people and sexual behaviors do not fit society's scripts and expectations. Furthermore, we often "unconsciously" internalize societal messages. But we seldom realize how they affect our values and behaviors. For example, modern men and women generally say they want equality. Yet both sexes may feel more comfortable if the woman is a virgin and the man has had many partners. Sex therapy encourages partners to examine and sometimes modify inappropriate sexual scripts, gender roles, and beliefs in the double standard.

Dating Couples

Men Wish Their Partners Would:	**Women Wish Their Partners Would:**
Be more experimental	Talk more lovingly
Initiate sex more often	Be more seductive
Try more oral-genital sex	Be warmer and more involved
Give more instructions	Give more instructions
Be warmer and more involved	Be more complimentary

Married Couples

Men Wish Their Partners Would:	**Women Wish Their Partners Would:**
Be more seductive	Talk more lovingly
Initiate sex more often	Be more seductive
Be more experimental	Be more complimentary
Be wilder and sexier	Give more instructions
Give more instructions	Be warmer and more involved

Figure 11.6 ***What do men and women want?*** When asked what they wish they had more of in their sexual relationships, men tended to emphasize activities, whereas women focused more on emotions and the relationship. *Source*: Based on Hatfield & Rapson, 1996, p. 142.

Figure 11.7 *Changing sexual scripts* (a) Television and movies in the 1950s and 1960s allowed only married couples to be shown in a bedroom setting (and only in long pajamas and separate twin-size beds). (b) Contrast this with modern times, where very young, unmarried couples are commonly portrayed in one bed, seemingly nude, and engaging in various stages of intercourse. (c, d) Also, note the change in body postures and clothing in these beach scenes from the 1960s and today.

How do therapists work with sex problems? Clinicians usually begin with interviews and examinations to determine whether the problem is organic, psychological, or, more likely, a combination of both (Crooks & Baur, 2008; Gambescia & Weeks, 2007; Heiman, 2007; King, 2009). Organic causes of sexual dysfunction include medical conditions (such as diabetes mellitus and heart disease), medications (such as antidepressants), and drugs (such as alcohol and tobacco—see Table 11.4). Erectile disorders are the problems most likely to have an organic component. In 1998, a medical treatment for erectile problems, *Viagra*, quickly became the fastest-selling prescription drug in U.S. history. Other medications for both men and women are currently being tested—but they are not the answer to all sexual problems.

Years ago, the major psychological treatment for sexual dysfunction was long-term psychoanalysis. This treatment was based on the assumption that sexual problems resulted from *deep-seated conflicts* that originated in childhood. During the 1950s and 1960s, behavior therapy was introduced. It was based on the idea that sexual dysfunction was *learned*. (See Chapter 15 for a more complete description of both psychoanalysis and behavior therapy.) It wasn't until the early 1970s and the publication of Masters and Johnson's *Human Sexual Inadequacy* that sex therapy gained national recognition. Because the model that Masters and Johnson developed is still popular and used by many sex therapists, we will use it as our example of how sex therapy is conducted.

Achievement

Objective 11.12: *Discuss how sex therapists treat sexual dysfunction, and list the four major principles of Masters and Johnson's approach.*

Ira Wyman/Corbis Sygma

Experiments in sex? *William Masters and Virginia Johnson were the first researchers to use direct laboratory experimentation and observation to study human sexuality.*

TABLE 11.4 SEXUAL EFFECTS OF LEGAL AND ILLEGAL DRUGS

Drugs	Effects
Alcohol	Moderate to high doses inhibit arousal. Chronic abuse causes damage to testes, ovaries, and the circulatory and nervous systems.
Tobacco	Decreases blood flow to the genitals, thereby reducing the frequency and duration of erections and vaginal lubrication.
Cocaine and amphetamines	Moderate to high doses and chronic use result in inhibition of orgasm and decrease in erection and lubrication.
Barbiturates	Moderate to high doses lead to decreased desire, erectile disorders, and delayed orgasm.

Source: Barlow, 2008; Horvath et al., 2007; Hyde & Dehamater, 2008; King, 2009.

Masters and Johnson's Sex Therapy Program

Masters and Johnson's approach is founded on four major principles:

1. *Relationship focus.* Unlike forms of therapy that focus on the individual, Masters and Johnson's sex therapy focuses on the relationship between two people. To counteract any blaming tendencies, each partner is considered fully involved and affected by sexual problems. Both partners are taught positive communication and conflict resolution skills.

2. *Investigation of both biological and psychosocial factors.* Medication and many physical disorders can cause or aggravate sexual dysfunctions. Therefore, Masters and Johnson emphasize the importance of medical histories and exams. They also explore psychosocial factors, such as how the couple first learned about sex and their current attitudes, gender role training, and sexual scripts.

3. *Emphasis on cognitive factors.* Recognizing that many problems result from fears of performance and *spectatoring* (mentally watching and evaluating responses during sexual activities), couples are discouraged from setting goals and judging sex in terms of success or failure.

4. *Specific behavioral techniques.* Couples are seen in an intensive two-week counseling program. They explore their sexual values and misconceptions and practice specific behavioral exercises. "Homework assignments" usually begin with a *sensate focus* exercise in which each partner takes turns gently caressing the other and communicating what is pleasurable. There are no goals or performance demands. Later exercises and assignments are tailored to the couple's particular sex problem.

Try This Yourself

If you would like to improve your own, or your children's, sexual attitudes and sexual functioning, sex therapists would recommend:

- *Beginning sex education as early as possible.* Children should be given positive feelings about their bodies and an opportunity to discuss sexuality in an open, honest fashion.
- *Avoiding goal- or performance-oriented approaches.* Therapists often remind clients that there really is no "right" way to have sex. When couples or individuals attempt to judge or

evaluate their sexual lives or to live up to others' expectations, they risk making sex a job rather than pleasure.

- *Communicating openly with your partner.* Mind reading belongs onstage, not in the bedroom. Partners need to tell each other what feels good and what doesn't. Sexual problems should be openly discussed without blame, anger, or defensiveness. If the problem does not improve within a reasonable time, consider professional help.

Application

RESEARCH HIGHLIGHT

Objective 11.13: *What is cybersex, and is it harmful?*

Is Cybersex Harmful?

Lisa, a 42-year-old student, says:

We bought my son a new, powerful computer, and he showed me how to go online to get into chat rooms. I started to log on just to visit and chat. But I soon found my way to chat rooms where the primary purpose was to discuss sexual fantasies. It was quite a turn-on. I was getting into these intimate discussions with all kinds of men. We talked about our sex lives and what we liked to do in bed. Then it got personal—what we'd like to do to each other. I never wanted to meet these guys face-to-face, but I started to feel like I was having sex with them.

It all came to a head when my husband saw one of the Internet bills and freaked—it was over $500 for the month. I had to explain the whole thing to him. He felt like I had cheated on him and considered separation. It took several weeks to restore his trust and convince him I still loved him. I have moved the computer into my son's room, and we've started seeing a family therapist. (Personal communication cited in Blonna & Levitan, 2000, p. 584)

The Internet is a great technological innovation. At school, work, and home, our computers help us work or study online, gather valuable information, or even rec-

David Young-Wolff/PhotoEdit

reationally "surf the Net." But, for some, *cybersex*, which includes a wide variety of online, sex-oriented conversations and exchanges, can be harmful (Barlow, 2008; Grov et al., 2008; Milner, 2008; Whitty, 2008). A survey among 18- to 64-year-old self-identified cybersex participants found several problems associated with their online sexual activities (Schneider, 2000). For example, two women with no prior history of interest in sadomasochistic sex discovered this type of behavior online and came to prefer it. Others in the survey reported increased problems with depression, social isolation, career loss or decreased job performance, financial consequences, and, in some cases, legal difficulties.

Like Lisa, some Internet users use cyberspace chat rooms and e-mail as a way to secretly communicate with an intimate other or as outlets for sexual desires they're unwilling to expose or discuss with their partners. Although these secret liaisons may be exciting, sex therapists are finding that this behavior often leads to a worsen-

ing of the participants' relationships with spouses or partners and serious harm to their marriages or primary relationships. "Cybercheating," like traditional infidelity or adultery, erodes trust and connection with the spouse or partner. The ongoing secrecy, lying, and fantasies also increase attraction to the "virtual" relationship.

What do you think? Does sex require physical contact to count as an "affair"? If you only exchange sexual fantasies with someone on the Internet, are you unfaithful? Is visiting sex sites harmful? When I ask this question in my college classes, some students consider it very harmful and eagerly talk about resulting relationship problems. In contrast, others think of it as nothing more than an X-rated movie and appear surprised that anyone would call it "cheating." I encourage all my students (and you) to openly discuss with their partners what they personally consider unacceptable in their relationships—both online and in everyday interactions.

Keep in mind that many people have developed healthy, lasting relationships through the Internet. They report that these relationships are just as intimate (or even more so) than face-to-face ones. Others suggest that cyberconnecting can be a good rehearsal for the "real" thing. Even some sex therapists see a positive use for the Internet. They find its anonymity allows open, frank, and explicit discussions about sex, which are vital components to successful therapy.

Sexually Transmitted Infections: The Special Problem of AIDS

Early sex education and open communication between partners are vitally important for full sexual functioning. They are also key to avoiding and controlling sexually transmitted infections (STIs), formerly called sexually transmitted diseases (STDs), venereal disease (VD), or social diseases. *STI* is the term used to describe the disorders caused by more than 25 infectious organisms transmitted through sexual activity.

Each year, of the millions of North Americans who contract one or more STIs, a substantial majority are under age 35. Also, as Figure 11.8 shows, women are at much greater risk than men of contracting major STIs. It is extremely important for sexually active people to get medical diagnosis and treatment for any suspicious symptoms and to inform their partners. If left untreated, many STIs can cause severe problems, including infertility, ectopic pregnancy, cancer, and even death.

Achievement

Objective 11.14: *Discuss the major issues related to STIs and the special problem of AIDS.*

Figure 11.8 *Male–female differences in susceptibility to sexually transmitted infections (STIs)* These percentages represent the chances of infection for men and women after a single act of intercourse with an infected partner. Note that women are at much greater risk than men for four of these six STIs, due in part to the internal and less visible parts of female genitalia.

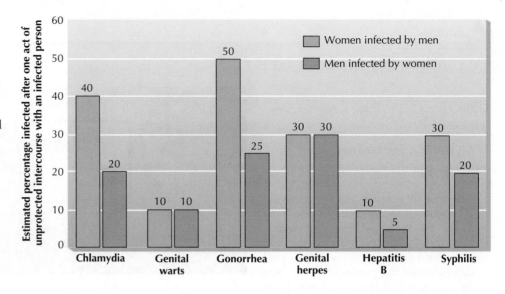

AIDS (Acquired Immunodeficiency Syndrome) *Human immunodeficiency viruses (HIVs) destroy the immune system's ability to fight disease, leaving the body vulnerable to a variety of opportunistic infections and cancers*

HIV Positive *Being infected by the human immunodeficiency virus (HIV)*

The good news is that most STIs are readily cured in their early stages. See Figure 11.9 for an overview of the signs and symptoms of the most common STIs. As you read through this table, remember that many infected people are *asymptomatic*, meaning they lack obvious symptoms. You can have one or more of the diseases without knowing it. And it is often impossible to tell if a sexual partner is infectious.

STIs such as genital warts and chlamydial infections have reached epidemic proportions. Yet, **AIDS (acquired immunodeficiency syndrome)** has received the largest share of public attention. AIDS results from infection with the *human immunodeficiency virus (HIV)*. A standard blood test can determine if someone is **HIV-positive**, which means the individual has been infected by one or more of the HIV viruses. Being

Figure 11.9 *Common sexually transmitted infections (STIs)* Note that you may have an STI without any of the danger signs listed here. If you have symptoms or concerns, see your doctor and follow all medical recommendations. This may include returning for a checkup to make sure that you are no longer infected. If you would like more information, check www.niaid.nih.gov/factsheets/stdinfo.htm. For information on protection from STIs, try www.safesex.org.
Sources: Adapted from Crooks & Baur, 2008; King 2009.

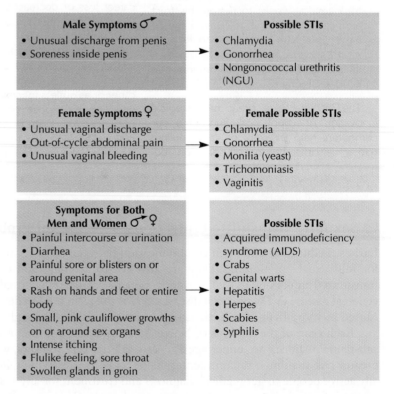

infected with the HIV virus, however, is not the same as having AIDS. AIDS is the final stage of the HIV infection process.

In the beginning of the infection process, the HIV virus multiplies rapidly. It is important to know that newly infected individuals are 100 to 1000 times more infectious than they are throughout the remainder of the disease. This is especially troubling because most infected people are likely to remain symptom free for months or even years. Unfortunately, during this time, they can spread the disease to others—primarily through sexual contact.

As the initial HIV infection advances to AIDS, the virus progressively destroys the body's natural defenses against disease and infection. The victim's body becomes increasingly vulnerable to opportunistic infections and cancers that would not be a threat if the immune system were functioning normally. The virus may also attack the brain and spinal cord, creating severe neurological and cognitive deterioration. The official term *full-blown AIDS* includes anyone infected with HIV who also has a CD4 count of 200 cells per cubic millimeter of blood or less. (The HIV virus destroys CD4 lymphocytes, also called T-cells, which coordinate the immune system's response to disease.)

AIDS is considered one of the most catastrophic diseases of our time. An estimated 34 million people worldwide are infected with HIV (CDC, 2005). Recent advances in the treatment of AIDS have increased the survival time of victims. But for almost everyone, AIDS remains an ultimately fatal disorder, and some researchers doubt that a 100 percent effective vaccine will ever be developed. Despite the severity of this disease, there are signs of public complacency due to the false notion that drugs can now cure AIDS and to a reduced emphasis on prevention and education.

Reflecting cutbacks in sex education, AIDS myths are widespread. For instance, many people still believe AIDS can be transmitted through casual contact, such as sneezing, shaking hands, sharing drinking glasses or towels, social kissing, sweat, or tears. Some also think it is dangerous to donate blood. Sadly, others are paranoid about gays, because male homosexuals were the first highly visible victims. All of these are false beliefs.

Infection by HIV spreads only by direct contact with bodily fluids—primarily blood, semen, and vaginal secretions. Blood *donors* are at *no* risk whatsoever. Furthermore, AIDS is not limited to the homosexual community. In fact, the AIDS epidemic is now spreading most quickly among heterosexuals, women, African Americans, Hispanics, and children (CDC, 2008).

PSYCHOLOGY AT WORK

Protecting Yourself and Others Against STIs

The best hope for curtailing the HIV/AIDS epidemic is through education and behavioral change. The following "safer sex" suggestions are not intended to be moralistic—but only to help reduce your chances of contracting both HIV/AIDS and other STIs.

1. *Remain abstinent or have sex with one mutually faithful, uninfected partner.* Be selective about sexual partners and postpone physical intimacy until laboratory tests verify that you are both free of STIs.

2. *Do not use intravenous illicit drugs or have sex with someone who does.* If you use intravenous drugs, do not share needles or syringes. If you must share, use bleach to clean and sterilize your needles and syringes.

3. *Avoid contact with blood, vaginal secretions, or semen.* Using latex condoms is the best way to avoid contact. (Until recently, scientists believed condoms and spermicides with nonoxynol-9 would help prevent spread of STIs. Unfortunately, recent research shows nonoxynol-9 may increase the risk, and the World Health Organization no longer recommends its use.)

4. *Avoid anal intercourse, with or without a condom.* This is the riskiest of all sexual behaviors.

5. *Do not have sex if you or your partner are impaired by alcohol or other drugs.* The same is true for your friends. "Friends don't let friends drive (or have sex) drunk."

Application

CRITICAL THINKING / ACTIVE LEARNING

Rape Myths and Rape Prevention

Sexuality can be a source of vitality and tender bonding. But it can also be traumatizing if it becomes a forcible act against the wishes of the other. Rape can be defined as oral, anal, or vaginal penetration forced on an unwilling, underage, or unconscious victim. As clear-cut as this definition seems, many people misunderstand what constitutes rape. To test your own knowledge, answer true or false to the following:

_____ 1. Women cannot be raped against their will.

_____ 2. A man cannot be raped by a woman.

_____ 3. If you are going to be raped, you might as well relax and enjoy it.

_____ 4. All women secretly want to be raped.

_____ 5. Male sexuality is biologically overpowering and beyond a man's control.

As you might have expected, all of these statements are false. Tragically, however, rape myths are believed by a large number of men and women (Carr & Van Deusen, 2004; Finch & Munro, 2005; Lee et al., 2005; Peterson & Muehlenhard, 2004). Using your critical thinking skills, can you explain how each of the following factors might contribute to rape myths?

- Gender role conditioning
- The double standard
- Media portrayals
- Lack of information

If you would like to compare your answers to ours or would like specific information regarding rape prevention, see Appendix B.

Assessment

STOP

CHECK & REVIEW

Sexual Problems

Objective 11.11: *Describe how biological, psychological, and social forces contribute to sexual dysfunction.*

Biology plays a key role in both sexual arousal and response. Ejaculation and orgasm are partially reflexive, and the parasympathetic nervous system must be dominant for sexual arousal. The sympathetic nervous system must dominate for orgasm to occur. Psychological factors like negative early sexual experiences, fears of negative consequences from sex, and **performance anxiety** contribute to **sexual dysfunction**. Sexual arousal and response are also related to social forces, such as early gender role training, the **double standard**, and **sexual scripts**, which teach us what to consider the "best" sex.

Objective 11.12: *Discuss how sex therapists treat sexual dysfunction, and list the four major principles of Masters and Johnson's approach.*

Clinicians generally begin with tests and interviews to determine the cause(s) of the **sexual dysfunction**. William Masters and Virginia Johnson emphasize the couple's relationship, biological and psychosocial factors, cognitions, and specific behavioral techniques. Professional sex therapists offer important guidelines for everyone: Sex education should be early and positive, a goal or performance orientation should be avoided, and communication should be kept open.

Objective 11.13: *What is cybersex, and is it harmful?*

Cybersex includes a wide variety of online, sex-oriented conversations and exchanges. Although some Internet connections can be healthy and satisfying, they also may contribute to serious relationship problems.

Objective 11.14: *Discuss the major issues related to STIs and the special problem of AIDS.*

Although the dangers and rate of STIs are high, and higher for women than men, most STIs can be cured in their early stages. The most publicized sexually transmitted infection (STI) is **AIDS (acquired immunodeficiency syndrome)**. Although AIDS is transmitted only through sexual contact or exposure to infected bodily fluids, many people have irrational fears of contagion. At the same time, an increasing number of North Americans are **HIV-positive** and therefore carriers.

Questions

1. Briefly explain the roles of the sympathetic and parasympathetic nervous systems in sexual response.

2. Sexual learning that includes "what to do, when, where, how, and with whom" is known as _____. (a) appropriate sexual behavior; (b) sexual norms; (c) sexual scripts; (d) sexual gender roles

3. What are the four principles of Masters and Johnson's sex therapy program?

4. What are five "safer sex" ways to reduce the chances of AIDS and other STIs?

Check your answers in Appendix B.

Click & Review
for additional assessment options:
wiley.com/college/huffman

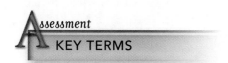

Assessment
KEY TERMS

*To assess your understanding of the **Key Terms** in Chapter 11, write a definition for each (in your own words), and then compare your definitions with those in the text.*

Sex and Gender
androgyny [an-DRAW-jah-nee] (p. 383)
gender (p. 376)
gender identity (p. 378)
gender role (p. 376)
gender schema theory (p. 378)
sex (p. 376)
sexual orientation (p. 379)
social learning theory of gender role development (p. 377)

Sexual Behavior
excitement phase (p. 390)
orgasm phase (p. 390)
plateau phase (p. 390)
refractory period (p. 390)
resolution phase (p. 390)
sexual prejudice (p. 393)
sexual response cycle (p. 389)

Sexual Problems
AIDS (acquired immunodeficiency syndrome) (p. 400)
double standard (p. 376)
HIV-positive (p. 400)
performance anxiety (p. 395)
sexual dysfunction (p. 394)
sexual scripts (p. 396)

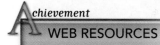

Achievement
WEB RESOURCES

Huffman Book Companion Site
wiley.com/college/huffman
  This site is loaded with free Interactive Self-Tests, Internet Exercises, Glossary and Flashcards for key terms, web links, Handbook for Non-Native Speakers, and other activities designed to improve your mastery of the material in this chapter.

Chapter 11 Visual Summary

Sex and Gender

Definitions

Sex: Biological dimensions of maleness or femaleness, and physical activities (such as intercourse).
Gender: Psychological and sociocultural meanings of maleness and femaleness.

Gender Role Development

Gender role: Social expectations for appropriate male and female behavior.
Two major theories:
Social learning (reward, punishment, observation, and imitation)
Gender schema (social learning plus active cognitive processes)

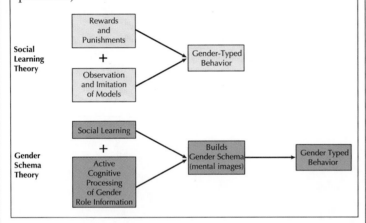

Sex and Gender Differences

Sex differences: Physical differences (like height) and brain differences (function and structure).
Gender differences: Females tend to score somewhat higher in verbal skills. Males score somewhat higher in math and are more physically aggressive.
Androgyny: Exhibiting both masculine and feminine traits.

Bob Daemmrich/The Image Works

© Romell/Masterfile

Study of Human Sexuality

Havelock Ellis	Kinsey & Colleagues	Masters & Johnson	Cultural Studies
Based his research on personal diaries.	Popularized the use of surveys and interviews.	Used direct observation and measurement of human sexual response.	Provide insight into universalities and variations in sexual behavior across cultures.

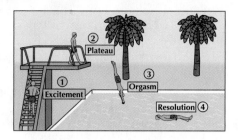

Sexual Arousal and Response

Masters and Johnson's **sexual response cycle**: **excitement**, **plateau**, **orgasm**, and **resolution**. There are numerous similarities of the sexes in this cycle, but differences are the focus of most research. According to the *evolutionary perspective*, males engage in more sexual behaviors with more sexual partners because it helps the species survive, The *social role approach* suggests this difference results from traditional cultural divisions of labor.

Sexual Orientation

False theories: Seduction, "by default," poor parenting, and modeling.

Supported theories: Genetic/biological contributors (genetic predisposition, prenatal biasing of the brain).

Associated Press

Sexual Problems

Sexual Dysfunctions

Possible causes:

Biological:
- Lifestyle factors and medical conditions
- Parasympathetic vs. sympathetic dominance

Psychological:
- Anxieties and fears
- Gender role training
- **Double standard**
- **Performance anxiety**

Social:
Sexual scripts (place restrictive boundaries)

Treatment: Masters and Johnson emphasize couple's relationship, biological and psychological factors, cognitions, and behavioral techniques.

Sexually Transmitted Infections (STIs)

Most publicized STI is **AIDS**. AIDS is transmitted only through sexual contact or exposure to infected bodily fluids, but irrational fears of contagion persist. An estimated one million in the United States are **HIV-positive** and therefore are carriers.

12

Motivation and Emotion

In 1996, when world-class bicyclist Lance Armstrong was diagnosed with testicular cancer, it seemed uncertain whether he would survive, let alone mount his bike again. By the time the cancer was discovered, it had already spread to his lungs and his brain. Armstrong's doctors told him that he had only about a 40 percent chance of survival. (Later one of his doctors revealed that the real estimate was 3 percent, but they had given him the higher figure to keep him from becoming discouraged!)

After major surgeries and intensive chemotherapy, however, Armstrong overcame the cancer, and by 1998 he was racing again—with remarkable success. He won his first Tour de France race in 1999 and then went on to win it an unprecedented six more consecutive times before retiring from professional cycling in 2005. The three-week, 2000-mile Tour de France is one of the most prestigious and physically demanding of all athletic contests.

What motivated Armstrong to fight and win his battle with cancer; to set a goal to win the Tour de France and win it seven times; and to become a famous spokesperson for cancer research and awareness? How did he cope with the fears and struggles of cancer and chemotherapy, or with the pain and exhaustion from hours, days, and years of grueling practices and races? On a personal note, what drives you to fight and overcome obstacles blocking your personal lifetime dreams? How do you cope with the chronic anxieties and frustrations that come with college life? Why are you going to college?

Research in *motivation* and *emotion* attempts to answer such "what," "how," and "why" questions. **Motivation** refers to the set of factors that activate, direct, and maintain behavior, usually toward some goal. **Emotion**, on the other hand, refers to a subjective feeling that includes arousal (heart pounding), cognitions (thoughts, values, and expectations), and expressive behaviors (smiles, frowns, and running). In other words, motivation energizes and directs behavior. Emotion is the "feeling" response. (Both *motivation* and *emotion* come from the Latin *movere*, meaning "to move.")

chievement

> **Objective 12.1:** *Define motivation and emotion, and explain why they're studied together.*

Motivation *Set of factors that activate, direct, and maintain behavior, usually toward some goal.*

Emotion *Subjective feeling that includes arousal (heart pounding), cognitions (thoughts, values, and expectations), and expressive behaviors (smiles, frowns, and running).*

▶ **Theories and Concepts of Motivation**

Biological Theories

RESEARCH HIGHLIGHT
Sensation Seeking

 PSYCHOLOGY AT WORK
Overcoming Test Anxiety

Psychosocial Theories
Biopsychosocial Theory

▶ **Motivation and Behavior**

Hunger and Eating

RESEARCH HIGHLIGHT
Fuel for Thought

Eating Disorders

CRITICAL THINKING/ACTIVE LEARNING
Obesity—Weighing the Evidence

Achievement

▶ **Theories and Concepts of Emotion**

Three Components of Emotion

RESEARCH HIGHLIGHT
Mirror Neurons—"I Share Your Pain!"

Four Major Theories of Emotion

▶ **Critical Thinking about Motivation and Emotion**

Intrinsic versus Extrinsic Motivation
The Polygraph as a Lie Detector
Emotional Intelligence (EI)

CASE STUDY/PERSONAL STORY
The Emotional Intelligence of Abraham Lincoln

 GENDER & CULTURAL DIVERSITY
Culture, Evolution, and Emotion

Friedemann Vogel/Bongarts/Getty Images

Application

WHY STUDY PSYCHOLOGY?

Did you know...

▶ Being too excited or too relaxed can interfere with test performance?

▶ Getting paid for your hobbies may reduce your overall creativity and enjoyment?

▶ After exercising self-control, we're more likely to make impulse purchases?

▶ Some controversial research finds people live longer if they're slightly overweight?

Alan Schein Photography/Corbis Images

▶ Smiling can make you feel happy and frowning can create negative feelings?

▶ Lie detector tests may be fooled by biting your tongue?

▶ Our brains have special, "mirror neurons" that help us identify with what others are feeling and to imitate their actions?

▶ People with high emotional intelligence (EI) are often more successful than people with a high intelligence quotient (IQ)?

Why cover both *motivation* and *emotion* in one chapter? Think about the joy, pride, and satisfaction that accompany your own "Lance Armstrong" type of achievements. Or the sadness, frustration, and even anger you feel when you receive a bad grade on a college exam. Motivation and emotion are inseparable.

In this chapter, we begin with the major theories and concepts of motivation, followed by three important sources of motivation—hunger, eating, and achievement. Then we turn to the basic theories and concepts related to emotion. We conclude with a look at intrinsic versus extrinsic motivation, the polygraph as a lie detector, and emotional intelligence (EI).

Theories and Concepts of Motivation

Achievement

Objective 12.2: *Describe the six major theories of motivation.*

There are six major theories of motivation that fall into three general categories—biological, psychosocial, and biopsychosocial (Table 12.1). As we discuss each theory, see if you can identify the one that best explains your reasons for going to college.

■ Biological Theories: Looking for Internal "Whys" of Behavior

Many theories of motivation are biologically based. They focus on inborn, genetically determined processes that control and direct behavior. Among these biologically oriented theories are *instinct*, *drive-reduction*, and *arousal* theories.

Instinct Theory

Instinct theory *Emphasizes inborn, genetic factors in motivation*

Instinct theory suggests that we are motivated by inborn, genetic factors. In the earliest days of psychology, researchers like William McDougall (1908) proposed that humans had numerous "instincts," such as repulsion, curiosity, and self-assertiveness. Other researchers later added their favorite "instincts." By the 1920s, the list of recognized instincts had become so long it was virtually meaningless. One early researcher found listings for over 10,000 human instincts (Bernard, 1924).

In addition, the label *instinct* led to unscientific, circular explanations—"men are aggressive because they act aggressively" or "women are maternal because they act maternally." However, in recent years, a branch of biology called *sociobiology*

TABLE 12.1 SIX MAJOR THEORIES OF MOTIVATION

Theory	View	
Biological Theories		
1. Instinct	Motivation results from behaviors that are unlearned and found in almost all members of a species.	 Mottias Klum/NG Image Collection
2. Drive-Reduction	Motivation begins with a physiological need (a lack or deficiency) that elicits a *drive* toward behavior that will satisfy the original need and restore homeostasis.	
3. Arousal	Organisms are motivated to achieve and maintain an optimal level of arousal.	
Psychosocial Theories		
4. Incentive	Motivation results from external stimuli that "pull" the organism in certain directions.	*Name that theory Curiosity is an important aspect of the human experience. Which of the six theories of motivation best explains this behavior?*
5. Cognitive	Motivation is affected by expectations and attributions, or how we interpret or think about our own or others' actions.	
Biopsychosocial Theory		
6. Maslow's Hierarchy of Needs	Lower motives (such as physiological and safety needs) must be satisfied before advancing to higher needs (such as belonging and self-actualization).	

has revived the case for **instincts** when defined as fixed response patterns that are unlearned and found in almost all members of a species (Figure 12.1).

Drive-Reduction Theory

In the 1930s, the concepts of drive and drive reduction began to replace the theory of instincts. According to **drive-reduction theory** (Hull, 1952), all living organisms have certain biological *needs* (such as food, water, and oxygen) that must be met if they are to survive. When these needs are unmet, a state of tension (known as a *drive*) is created, and the organism is motivated to reduce it.

Drive-reduction theory is based largely on the biological concept of **homeostasis**—a state of balance or stability in the body's internal environment, a term that literally means "standing still" (Figure 12.2).

Instinct *Fixed response pattern that is unlearned and found in almost all members of a species*

Drive-Reduction Theory *Motivation begins with a physiological need (a lack or deficiency) that elicits a drive toward behavior that will satisfy the original need; once the need is met, a state of balance (homeostasis) is restored and motivation decreases*

Homeostasis *Bodily tendency to maintain a relatively stable state, such as a constant internal temperature*

Joel Sartore/NG Image Collection

Associated Press

(a)

(b)

Figure 12.1 ***Instincts*** (a) Instinctual behaviors are obvious in many animals. Bears hibernate, birds build nests, and salmon swim upstream to spawn. (b) Sociobiologists such as Edward O. Wilson (1975, 1978) believe that humans also have instincts, like competition or aggression, that are genetically transmitted from one generation to the next.

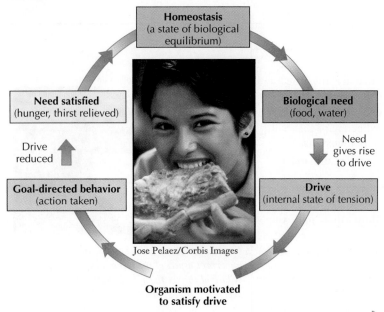

Homeostasis
(a state of biological equilibrium)

Need satisfied
(hunger, thirst relieved)

Drive reduced

Goal-directed behavior
(action taken)

Biological need
(food, water)

Need gives rise to drive

Drive
(internal state of tension)

Organism motivated to satisfy drive

Jose Pelaez/Corbis Images

Figure 12.2 *Drive-reduction theory* Homeostasis, the body's natural tendency to maintain a state of internal balance, is the foundation of drive-reduction theory. When you are hungry or thirsty, the imbalance creates a drive that motivates you to search for food or water. When the balance is restored, your motivation (to seek food or water) is also decreased.

Arousal Theory *Organisms are motivated to achieve and maintain an optimal level of arousal*

Arousal Theory—The Need for Stimulation

In addition to our obvious biological need for food and water, humans and other animals are innately curious and require a certain amount of novelty and complexity from the environment (Research Highlight below). This need for arousal and sensory stimulation begins shortly after birth and continues throughout the life span (Figure 12.3).

Is there a limit to this need for arousal? What about overstimulation? According to **arousal theory**, organisms are motivated to achieve and maintain an optimal level of arousal that maximizes their performance. Take a close look at the inverted U-shaped curve in Figure 12.4. Note how performance is diminished when arousal is either too high or too low. Also note that we tend to do our best when arousal is at its mid-range, "optimal" level.

Have you noticed this optimal level of arousal effect while taking exams? When underaroused, your mind wanders. You may make careless errors like filling in the space for option A on a multiple-choice exam when you meant to fill in B. In contrast, when overaroused, you may become

---

A pplication

RESEARCH HIGHLIGHT

Sensation Seeking

What motivates people who go bungee jumping over deep canyons or white-water rafting down dangerous rivers? According to research, these "high-sensation seekers" may be biologically "prewired" to need a higher than usual level of stimulation (Zuckerman, 1979, 1994, 2004).

To sample the kinds of questions that are asked on tests for sensation seeking, circle the choice (**A** or **B**) that BEST describes you:

1. **A** I would like a job that requires a lot of traveling.
   B I would prefer a job in one location.
2. **A** I get bored seeing the same old faces.
   B I like the comfortable familiarity of everyday friends.
3. **A** The most important goal of life is to live it to the fullest and experience as much as possible.
   B The most important goal of life is to find peace and happiness.
4. **A** I would like to try parachute jumping.

   B I would never want to try jumping out of a plane, with or without a parachute.
5. **A** I prefer people who are emotionally expressive even if they are a bit unstable.
   B I prefer people who are calm and even-tempered.

Source: Zuckerman, M. (1978, February). The search for high sensation, *Psychology Today*, pp. 38–46. Copyright © 1978 by the American Psychological Association. Reprinted by permission.

Research suggests that four distinct factors characterize sensation seeking (Legrand et al., 2007; Wallerstein, 2008; Zuckerman, 2004, 2008).

1. Thrill and adventure seeking (skydiving, driving fast, or trying to beat a train)
2. Experience seeking (travel, unusual friends, drug experimentation)
3. Disinhibition ("letting loose")
4. Susceptibility to boredom (lower tolerance for repetition and sameness)

Being very high or very low in sensation seeking might cause problems in relationships with individuals who score toward the

David Mclain/NG Image Collection

other extreme. This is true not just between partners or spouses but also between parent and child and therapist and patient. There might also be job difficulties for high-sensation seekers in routine clerical or assembly-line jobs or for low-sensation seekers in highly challenging and variable occupations.

Figure 12.3 *Arousal-seeking behavior* (a) Monkeys will work very hard at tasks like opening latches simply for the pleasure of satisfying their curiosity. (b) The arousal motive is also apparent in the innate curiosity and exploration of the human animal.

so anxious that you "freeze-up" and can't remember what you studied. This kind of forgetting results in part from anxiety and overarousal, which interfere with retrieving information from long-term memory (see Chapter 7).

PSYCHOLOGY AT WORK

Overcoming Test Anxiety

If you do become overly aroused on exam day, you may want to take a class in study skills or test anxiety. You can also try these basic study tips:

Step 1: *Prepare in advance*. The single most important cure for test anxiety is advance preparation and *hard work*. If you are well prepared, you will feel calmer and more in control.

- Read your textbook using the SQ4R (Survey, Question, Read, Recite, Review, and wRite) method (see Chapter 1).

- Practice good time management and distribute your study time; don't cram the night before.

- Actively listen during lectures and take detailed, summarizing notes.

- Follow the general strategies for test taking in the "Tools for Student Success" (Chapter 1) and the tips for memory improvement (Chapter 7).

Step 2: *Learn to cope with the anxiety*. Performance is best at a moderate level of arousal, so a few butterflies before and during exams are okay and to be expected. However, too much anxiety can interfere with concentration and cripple your performance. To achieve the right amount of arousal:

- Replace anxiety with relaxed feelings. Practice deep breathing (which activates the parasympathetic nervous system) and the relaxation response described in Chapter 3, on page 120.

- Desensitize yourself to the test situation. See Chapter 15, page 526.

- Exercise regularly. This is a great stress reliever, while also promoting deeper and more restful sleep.

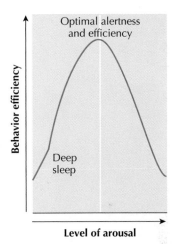

Figure 12.4 *Optimal level of arousal* Because of our need for stimulation (the *arousal motive*), our behavior efficiency increases as we move from deep sleep to increased alertness. However, once we pass the maximum level of arousal, our performance declines.

Psychosocial Theories: Incentives and Cognitions

Instinct and drive-reduction theories explain some biological motivations, but why do we continue to eat even after our biological need is completely satisfied? Or why does someone volunteer to work overtime when his or her salary is sufficient to meet all basic biological needs? And, why do some students go to parties versus studying for exams? These questions are better answered by psychosocial theories that emphasize incentives and cognition.

Incentive Theory—Environmental "Pulls"

Incentive Theory *Motivation results from external stimuli that "pull" the organism in certain directions*

Drive-reduction theory states that internal factors *push* people in certain directions. In contrast, **incentive theory** maintains that external stimuli *pull* people toward desirable goals or away from undesirable ones. Most of us initially eat because our hunger "pushes" us (drive-reduction theory). But the sight of apple pie or ice cream too often "pulls" us toward continued eating (incentive theory).

Cognitive Theories—Explaining Things to Ourselves

According to *cognitive theories*, motivation is directly affected by *attributions*, or how we interpret or think about our own and others' actions. If you receive a high grade in your psychology course, you can interpret that grade in several ways. You earned it because you really studied. You "lucked out." Or the textbook was exceptionally interesting and helpful (my preferred interpretation!). Researchers have found that people who attribute their successes to personal ability and effort tend to work harder toward their goals than people who attribute their successes to luck (Hsieh, 2005; Houtz et al., 2007; Meltzer, 2004; Weiner, 1972, 1982).

Expectancies, or what we believe will happen, are also important to cognitive theories of motivation (Haugen, Ommundsen, & Lund, 2004; Schunk, 2008). Your anticipated grade on a test affects your willingness to study—"If I can get an A in the course, then I will study very hard." Similarly, your expectancies regarding future salary increases or promotions at work affect your willingness to work overtime for no pay.

Biopsychosocial Theory: Interactionism Once Again

As we've seen throughout this text, research in psychology generally emphasizes either biological or psychosocial factors (nature or nurture). But in the final analysis, the *biopsychosocial model* (an inseparable interaction between biological, psychological, and social forces) almost always provides the best explanation. Theories of motivation are no exception. One researcher who recognized this three-way interaction was Abraham Maslow. Maslow believed that we all have numerous needs that compete for fulfillment, but that some needs are more important than others (Maslow, 1954, 1970, 1999). For example, your need for food and shelter is generally more important than your college grades. Maslow's **hierarchy of needs** *prioritizes* needs, with survival needs at the bottom and self-actualization needs at the top (Figure 12.5).

Hierarchy of Needs *Maslow's theory that lower motives (such as physiological and safety needs) must be met before advancing to higher needs (such as belonging and self-actualization)*

Maslow's hierarchy of needs seems intuitively correct. A starving person would first look for food, then seek love and friendship, then self-esteem, and finally self-actualization. This prioritizing and the concept of *self-actualization* are important contributions to the study of motivation.

On the other hand, critics argue that parts of Maslow's theory are poorly researched and biased toward Western individualism. Furthermore, people also sometimes seek to satisfy higher-level needs even when lower-level needs have not been met (Cullen & Gotell, 2002; Hanley & Abell, 2002; Neher, 1991). In some nonindustrialized societies, people may be living in a war zone, subsisting on very little food, and suffering from injury and disease. Although they have not fulfilled

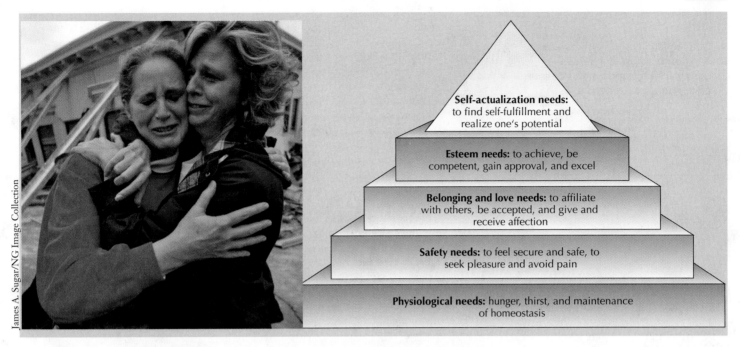

Figure 12.5 *Maslow's hierarchy of needs* As a humanistic psychologist, Maslow believed that we all have a compelling need to "move up"—to grow, improve ourselves, and ultimately become "self-actualized." What higher-level needs do these people seem to be trying to fulfill? Does it appear that their lower-level needs have been met?

Maslow's two lowest and most basic needs, they still seek the higher needs of strong social ties and self-esteem. In addition, during the famine and war in Somalia, many parents sacrificed their own lives to carry starving children hundreds of miles to food distribution centers. And parents at the centers often banded together to share the limited supplies. Because Maslow argued that each individual's own lower needs must be at least partially met before higher needs can influence behavior, these examples "stand Maslow's need hierarchy on its head" (Neher, 1991, p. 97). In sum, we're normally motivated to fulfill basic needs first. However, in certain circumstances we can bypass these lower stages and pursue higher-level needs.

Assessment STOP

CHECK & REVIEW

Theories and Concepts of Motivation

Objective 12.1: *Define motivation and emotion, and explain why they're studied together.*

Motivation refers to the set of factors that activate, direct, and maintain behavior, usually toward some goal. **Emotion**, on the other hand, refers to a subjective feeling that includes arousal (heart pounding), cognitions (thoughts, values, and expectations), and expressive behaviors (smiles, frowns, and running). We

study them together because they are inseparable.

Objective 12.2: *Describe the six major theories of motivation.*

The six theories of motivation can be grouped into three general categories: *biological*, *psychosocial*, and *biopsychosocial*. Among the biological approaches, **instinct theories** emphasize inborn, genetic components in motivation. **Drive-reduction theory** suggests that internal tensions (produced by the body's demand for **homeostasis**) "push" the organism toward

satisfying basic needs. And **arousal theory** proposes that organisms seek an optimal level of arousal that maximizes their performance.

According to the two psychosocial approaches, **incentive theory** emphasizes the "pull" of external environmental stimuli, whereas the cognitive theory focuses on the importance of attributions and expectations.

One example of the biopsychosocial approach is Maslow's **hierarchy of needs** (or motives). This theory suggests that basic survival needs must be satisfied before a person can attempt to satisfy higher needs and eventually become self-actualized.

Questions

1. Define instinct and homeostasis.
2. The figure below illustrates the _____ theory, in which motivation decreases once homeostasis occurs.

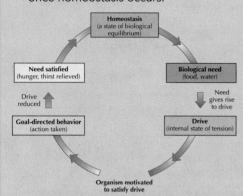

3. Match the following examples with their appropriate theory of motivation: (a) instinct; (b) drive-reduction; (c) arousal; (d) incentive; (e) cognitive; (f) Maslow's hierarchy of needs

_____ i. Joining a club because you want to be accepted by others

_____ ii. Two animals fighting because of their inherited, evolutionary desire for survival

_____ iii. Eating to reduce hunger

_____ iv. Studying hard for an exam because you expect that studying will result in a good grade

_____ v. Skydiving because you love the excitement

4. _____ theory suggests we need a certain amount of novelty and complexity from our environment. (a) Sensory; (b) Social; (c) Drive-reduction; (d) Arousal

5. _____ theories emphasize the importance of attributions and expectancies in motivating behaviors. (a) Attribution; (b) Motivational; (c) Achievement; (d) Cognitive

6. The _____ theory, illustrated in the figure below, suggests that some motives have to be satisfied before a person can advance to higher levels.

Check your answers in Appendix B.

Click & Review
for additional assessment options:
wiley.com/college/huffman

Achievement

Objective 12.3: *Discuss the major biopsychosocial factors that influence hunger and eating.*

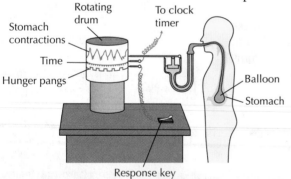

Figure 12.6 *Cannon and Washburn's technique for measuring hunger* As a participant in his own study, Washburn swallowed a special balloon designed to detect stomach movement. His stomach movements were automatically recorded on graph paper attached to a rotating drum. At the same time, whenever Washburn experienced "hunger pangs," he would press a key that made a recording on the same graph paper. The two recordings (stomach movements and hunger sensations) were then compared. Finding that Washburn's stomach contractions occurred at the same time as his feelings of hunger led these early researchers to conclude that stomach movements caused hunger. Later research altered this conclusion.

Motivation and Behavior

Why do you spend hours playing a new computer game instead of studying for a major exam? Why do salmon swim upstream to spawn? Behavior results from many motives. For example, the sleep motive was covered in Chapter 5, the sex drive was explored in Chapter 11, and aggression, altruism, and interpersonal attraction will be discussed in Chapter 16. Here, we will focus on the motives behind hunger and eating and achievement.

Hunger and Eating: Multiple Biopsychosocial Factors

What motivates hunger? Is it your growling stomach? Or is it the sight of a juicy hamburger or the smell of a freshly baked cinnamon roll? Hunger is one of our strongest motivational drives. Numerous biological factors (stomach, biochemistry, the brain) and many psychosocial forces (visual cues and cultural conditioning) affect our eating behaviors.

The Stomach

Walter B. Cannon and A. L. Washburn (1912) conducted one of the earliest experiments exploring the internal factors in hunger (Figure 12.6). In this study, Washburn swallowed a balloon and then inflated it in his stomach. His stomach contractions and subjective reports of hunger feelings were then simultaneously recorded. Because each time Washburn reported having stomach pangs (or "growling") the balloon also contracted, the researchers concluded that stomach movement *caused* the sensation of hunger.

Can you identify what's wrong with this study? As you learned in Chapter 1, correlation does not mean causation. Furthermore, researchers must always control for the possibility of *extraneous variables*, factors that contribute irrelevant data and confuse the results. In this case, it was later found that an empty stomach is relatively inactive. The stomach contractions experienced by Washburn were an experimental artifact—something resulting from the presence of the balloon. Washburn's stomach had been tricked into thinking it was full and was responding by trying to digest the balloon!

In sum, sensory input from the stomach is not essential for feeling hungry. Dieters learn this the hard way when they try to "trick" their stomachs into feeling full by eating large quantities of carrots and celery and drinking lots of water. Also, humans and nonhuman animals without stomachs continue to experience hunger.

Does this mean there is no connection between the stomach and feeling hungry? Not necessarily. Receptors in the stomach and intestines detect levels of nutrients. And specialized pressure receptors in the stomach walls signal feelings of emptiness or *satiety* (fullness or satiation). The stomach and other parts of the gastrointestinal tract also release chemicals that play a role in hunger (Donini, Savina, & Cannella, 2003; Näslund & Hellström, 2007; Nogueiras & Tschöp, 2005). These (and other) chemical signals are the topic of our next section.

Biochemistry

Like the stomach, the brain and other parts of the body produce, and are affected by, numerous neurotransmitters, hormones, enzymes, and other chemicals that affect hunger and satiety (e.g., Arumugam et al., 2008; Cummings, 2006; Wardlaw & Hampl, 2007). Research in this area is complex because of the large number of known (and unknown) bodily chemicals and the interactions among them. It's unlikely that any one chemical controls our hunger and eating. Other internal factors, such as *thermogenesis* (the heat generated in response to food ingestion), also play a role (Subramanian & Vollmer, 2002).

The Brain

In addition to its chemical signals, particular brain structures also influence hunger and eating. Let's look at the *hypothalamus*, which helps regulate eating, drinking, and body temperature.

Early research suggested that one area of the hypothalamus, the *lateral hypothalamus* (LH), stimulated eating. In contrast, the *ventromedial hypothalamus* (VMH), created feelings of satiation and signaled the animal to stop eating. When the LH area was destroyed in rats, early researchers found the animals starved to death if they were not force-fed. When the VMH area was destroyed, they overate to the point of extreme obesity (Figure 12.7).

Later research, however, showed that the LH and VMH areas are not simple on–off switches for eating. For example, lesions to the VMH make animals picky eaters—they reject food that doesn't taste good. Lesions also increase insulin secretion, which may cause overeating. Today, researchers know that the hypothalamus plays an important role in hunger and eating, but it is not the brain's "eating center." In fact, hunger and eating, like virtually all behavior, are influenced by numerous neural circuits that run throughout the brain (Berthoud & Morrison, 2008).

Psychosocial Factors

The internal motivations for hunger we've discussed (stomach, biochemistry, the brain) are powerful. But psychosocial factors—like watching a pizza commercial on TV—can be equally important *stimulus cues* for hunger and eating (Herman & Polivy, 2008). Another important environmental influence on when, what, where, and why we eat is *cultural conditioning*. North Americans, for example, tend to eat their evening meal around 6:00 P.M. People in Spain and South America tend to eat around 10:00 P.M. When it comes to *what* we eat, have you ever eaten rat, dog, or horse meat? If you are a typical North American, this might sound repulsive to you, yet most Hindus would feel a similar revulsion at the thought of eating meat from cows.

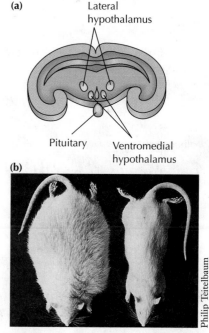

(a) Lateral hypothalamus

Pituitary   Ventromedial hypothalamus

(b)

Philip Teitelbaum

Figure 12.7 ***How the brain affects eating*** (a) This diagram shows a section of a rat's brain, including the ventromedial hypothalamus (VMH) and the lateral hypothalamus (LH). (b) The rat on the right is of normal weight. In contrast, the ventromedial area of the hypothalamus of the rat on the left was destroyed, which led to the tripling of its body weight.

Application

RESEARCH HIGHLIGHT

Objective 12.4: *How does expressing willpower affect later self-control?*

Fuel for Thought
By Siri Carpenter

iStockphoto

Day after day you fight the "battle of the bulge" and overbearing colleagues who grate on your nerves. It's a battle to keep your hunger and irritation under wraps. Suddenly, after a particularly stressful day, you snap—you grab the cookie or lose your temper and give your shocked coworker a piece of your mind.

Most of us blame ourselves for such lapses in willpower, but new research suggests that willpower may not be available in an unlimited supply. Scientists have discovered that a single, brief act of self-control expends some of the body's fuel, which undermines the brain's ability to exert further self-discipline.

Researchers at Florida State University asked volunteers to perform tasks such as ignoring a distracting stimulus while watching a video clip or suppressing racial stereotypes during a five-minute social interaction (Gailliot et al., 2007). These seemingly trivial efforts depleted glucose in the bloodstream and hindered volunteers' ability to maintain mental discipline during subsequent tasks. When the study participants were given a sugar drink to boost their blood glucose levels, their performance returned to normal. Volunteers who drank an artificially sweetened drink remained impaired.

"These findings show us that willpower is more than a metaphor," notes Matthew Gailliot, a graduate student in psychology who led the research. "It's metabolically expensive to maintain self-control."

"These are remarkably provocative results," says Kathleen Vohs, a psychologist at the University of Minnesota. Her research suggests that those who exercise self-control are more likely to make impulse purchases—a finding that fits with the glucose depletion model. Vohs observes that one tantalizing implication of the results is that self-control may be toughest for people whose bodies do not utilize blood glucose properly, such as those with type 2 diabetes. Unfortunately, such people cannot benefit from the news that a sugar drink restores mental reserves. Nor should anyone take the findings as license to go on frequent sugar benders in the name of willpower. Although glucose's precise role in self-regulation is not yet clear, Vohs says, "We can be assured that it's going to be more nuanced than that."

Source: Originally published in *Scientific American Mind*, June/July 2007, p. 11. Adapted and reprinted with permission of author, Siri Carpenter.

Achievement

Objective 12.5: *Describe the three key eating disorders—obesity, anorexia, and bulimia.*

Eating Disorders: Obesity, Anorexia, and Bulimia

As you can see, hunger and eating are complex phenomena controlled by numerous biological, psychological, and social factors. These same biopsychosocial forces also play a role in three of our most serious eating disorders—obesity, anorexia nervosa, and bulimia nervosa.

©AP/Wide World Photos

Can the environment affect body weight? *Obesity is relatively common among modern Pima Indians living in the United States. However, their close relatives living nearby in Mexico who eat traditional foods are generally slim.*

Obesity

Obesity has reached epidemic proportions in the United States and many other developed nations. Well over half of all adults in the United States meet the current criterion for clinical *obesity* (having a body weight 15 percent or more above the ideal for one's height and age). Each year, billions of dollars are spent treating serious and life-threatening medical problems related to obesity, and consumers spend billions more on largely ineffective weight-loss products and services.

Why are so many people overweight? The simple answer is our environment, overeating, and not enough exercise (Figure 12.8). However, we all know some people who can eat anything they want and still not add pounds. This may be a result of their ability to burn calories more effectively (thermogenesis), a higher metabolic rate, or other factors. Adoption and twin studies indicate that genes also play a role. Heritability for obesity is estimated to range between 30 and 70 percent (Fernández et al., 2008; Lee et al., 2008; Schmidt, 2004). Unfortunately,

Figure 12.8 *A fattening environment* For Americans, controlling weight is a particularly difficult task. We are among the most sedentary people of all nations, and we've become accustomed to "supersized" cheeseburgers, "Big Gulp" drinks, and huge servings of dessert (Carels et al., 2008; Herman & Polivy, 2008; Fisher & Kral, 2008). We've also learned that we should eat three meals a day (whether we're hungry or not); that "tasty" food requires lots of salt, sugar, and fat; and that food is an essential part of all social gatherings. To successfully lose (and maintain) weight, we must make permanent lifestyle changes regarding the amount and types of foods we eat and when we eat them. Can you see how our everyday environments, such as in the workplace scene here, might prevent a person from making healthy lifestyle changes?

identifying the genes for obesity is difficult. Researchers have isolated over 2000 genes that contribute to normal and abnormal weight.

Anorexia Nervosa and Bulimia Nervosa

Interestingly, as obesity has reached epidemic proportions, we've seen a similar rise in two other eating disorders—**anorexia nervosa** (self-starvation and extreme weight loss) and **bulimia nervosa** (intense, recurring episodes of binge eating followed by purging through vomiting or taking laxatives). Both disorders are serious and chronic conditions that require treatment. More than 50 percent of women in Western industrialized countries show some signs of an eating disorder, and approximately 2 percent meet the official criteria for anorexia nervosa or bulimia nervosa (Porzelius et al., 2001). These disorders also are found in all socioeconomic levels. A few men occasionally develop eating disorders, although the incidence is rarer among them (Raevuori et al., 2008; Jacobi et al., 2004).

Anorexia nervosa is characterized by an overwhelming fear of becoming obese, a disturbed body image, the need for control, and the use of dangerous weight-loss measures (Figure 12.9). The resulting extreme malnutrition often leads to osteoporosis and bone fractures. Menstruation in women frequently stops, and computed tomography (CT) scans of the brain show enlarged ventricles (cavities) and widened grooves. Such signs generally indicate loss of brain tissue. A significant percentage of individuals with anorexia nervosa ultimately die of the disorder (Kaye, 2008; Wentz et al., 2007; Werth et al., 2003).

Occasionally, the person suffering from anorexia nervosa succumbs to the desire to eat and gorges on food, then vomits or takes laxatives. However, this type of bingeing and purging is more characteristic of *bulimia nervosa*. Unlike anorexia, bulimia is characterized by weight fluctuations within or above the normal range, which makes the illness easier to hide. Individuals with this disorder also show impulsivity in other areas, sometimes by excessive shopping, alcohol abuse, or petty shoplifting (Kaye, 2008). The vomiting associated with both anorexia nervosa and bulimia nervosa causes eroded tooth enamel and tooth loss, severe damage to the throat and stomach, cardiac arrhythmias, metabolic deficiencies, and serious digestive disorders.

What causes anorexia nervosa and bulimia nervosa? There are almost as many suspected causes as there are victims. Some theories focus on physical causes such

Anorexia Nervosa *Eating disorder characterized by a severe loss of weight resulting from self-imposed starvation and an obsessive fear of obesity*

Bulimia Nervosa *Eating disorder involving the consumption of large quantities of food (bingeing), followed by vomiting, extreme exercise, and/or laxative use (purging)*

Figure 12.9 *Distorted body image* In anorexia nervosa, body image is so distorted that even a skeletal, emaciated body is perceived as fat. Many people with anorexia nervosa not only refuse to eat but also take up extreme exercise regimens—hours of cycling or running or constant walking.

Application

CRITICAL THINKING

Objective 12.6: *Discuss the controversial study that found people live longer if they're slightly overweight.*

Obesity—Weighing the Evidence

(Contributed by Thomas Frangicetto)

"We can't afford to be complacent about this epidemic of obesity and certainly not based on findings from an analysis that is flawed." Dr. JoAnn Manson, Brigham & Women's Hospital in Boston (*USA Today*, 2005).

"There are people who have made up their minds that obesity (and being) overweight are the biggest public health problem that we have to face. These numbers show that maybe it's not that big." Dr. Steven Blair, president, Cooper Institute (NYT, 2005).

The source of the disagreement between these two highly respected experts was a controversial study published in 2005 in the *Journal of the American Medical Association (JAMA)*. Researchers at the Centers for Disease Control and Prevention (CDC) and the National Cancer Institute combined their efforts to look at the effects of obesity. Surprisingly, their study found that people tend to live longer if they are slightly overweight (Flegal et al., 2005). Clearly contradicting numerous previous reports, this study caused an uproar in the medical community—and mass confusion in the public.

A month after its publication, critics from the Harvard School of Public Health and the American Cancer Society, reported that other studies, their own included, found that the likelihood of death from extra weight increased steadily from normal weight to being overweight to obesity. Calling the Flegal study "deeply flawed," they cited their own *Nurses' Health Study*, which followed over 120,000 women and found that as "body mass index increases,

the death rate increases dramatically" (Kolata, 2005).

Dr. Katherine Flegal, the lead author of the controversial study, countered that she and her colleagues had carefully analyzed and reanalyzed the data and the results were always the same: "There was no mortality risk from being overweight and little from being obese, except for the extremely obese" (Flegal, 2005, p. 21).

The Flegal study authors also pointed to the Harvard group's study being exclusively with nurses. In contrast, the Flegal group used volunteers, which they suggest provide data more representative of the United States population.

More confusing still, the second half of the Flegal research team, the Centers for Disease Control and Prevention (CDC), then issued a press release generally retracting their original support. They stated, "Obesity remains an important cause of death in the United States, with 75% of excess deaths from obesity occurring in people younger than 70 years." Furthermore, CDC director Dr. Julie Gerberding proposed that, "It is not OK to be overweight. People need to be fit, they need to have a healthy diet, they need to exercise. I'm very sorry for the confusion that these scientific discussions have had.... It is not healthy to be overweight" (Gerberding, 2005). Many scientists, including the CDC's former critics, expressed relief that the CDC was returning to the collective wisdom that obesity is a serious and growing health problem.

Critical Thinking Application

1. What do you think of this controversy? For more information on the health risks associated with obesity, visit the CDC website at http://www.cdc.gov/ and type "body mass index" in the CDC search

ACTIVE LEARNING

box. At this site, you'll find a chart like the one below. To calculate your own BMI (Body Mass Index), just click on the link provided or go to http://www.cdc.gov/nccdphp/dnpa/bmi/index.htm.

Weight Range	BMI	Considered
124 lbs or less	Below 18.5	Underweight
125 lbs to 168 lbs	18.5 to 24.9	Healthy weight
169 lbs to 202 lbs	25.0 to 29.9	Overweight
203 lbs or more	30 or higher	Obese

2. Based on the limited information provided here, do you think the Flegal group with its volunteers or the Harvard study of nurses made the better case? Who and what should we believe? To help you deal with the confusion, you can employ several critical thinking components such as *tolerating ambiguity, gathering data,* and *delaying judgment until adequate data is available* (see the *Prologue,* p. xxx).

You can also consider the *weight of the evidence.* Before jumping to follow the latest hot new research topic, ask yourself, "Which opposing side has the greater number of studies and a longer history of support?" As you have learned from the studies cited in this chapter, cumulative, long-term research shows that obesity is a serious health problem. To deal with the contradictory findings from the Flegal study, most scientists would advocate an open mind and a "wait and see" attitude.

as hypothalamic disorders, low levels of various neurotransmitters, and genetic or hormonal disorders. Other theories emphasize psychosocial factors, such as a need for perfection, being teased about body weight, a perceived loss of control, destructive thought patterns, depression, dysfunctional families, distorted body image, and sexual abuse (e.g., Behar, 2007; Fairburn et al., 2008; Kaye, 2008; Sachdev et al., 2008).

Culture and Eating Disorders

Cultural factors also play important roles in eating disorders (Eddy et al., 2007; Fairburn et al., 2008; Herman & Polivy, 2008). For instance, Asian and African Americans

TABLE 12.2 DSM-IV-TR[a] SYMPTOMS OF ANOREXIA NERVOSA AND BULIMIA NERVOSA

Symptoms of Anorexia Nervosa	*Symptoms of Bulimia Nervosa*
• Body weight below 85% of normal for one's height and age	• Normal or above-normal weight
• Intense fear of becoming fat or gaining weight, even though underweight	• Recurring binge eating
• Disturbance in one's body image or perceived weight	• Eating an amount of food that is much larger than most people would consume
• Self-evaluation unduly influenced by body weight	• Feeling a lack of control over eating
• Denial of seriousness of abnormally low body weight	• Purging behavior (vomiting or misuse of laxatives or diuretics)
• Absence of menstrual periods	• Excessive exercise to prevent weight gain
• Purging behavior (vomiting or misuse of laxatives or diuretics)	• Fasting to prevent weight gain
	• Self-evaluation unduly influenced by body weight

[a]DSM-IV-TR = *Diagnostic and Statistical Manual of Mental Disorders*, fourth edition, revised.

report fewer eating and dieting disorders and greater body satisfaction than do European Americans (Ruffolo et al., 2006; Taylor et al., 2007).

Although social pressures for thinness certainly contribute to the development of eating disorders Figure 12.10, anorexia nervosa also has been found in nonindustrialized areas like the Caribbean island of Curaçao (Hoek et al., 2005). On that island, being overweight is socially acceptable, and the average woman is considerably heavier than the average woman in North America. However, some women there still suffer from anorexia nervosa. This research suggests that both culture and biology help explain eating disorders. Regardless of the causes, it is important to recognize the symptoms of anorexia and bulimia (Table 12.2) and seek therapy if the symptoms apply to you.

Achievement: The Need for Success

Do you wonder what motivates Olympic athletes to work so hard for so many years for the remote possibility of a gold medal? Or what about someone like Thomas Edison, who patented over 1000 inventions? What drives some people to high achievement?

The key to understanding what motivates high-achieving individuals lies in what psychologist Henry Murray (1938) identified as a *high need for achievement* (nAch). **Achievement motivation** can be broadly defined as the desire to excel, especially in competition with others. One of the earliest tests for achievement motivation was devised by Christiana Morgan and Henry Murray (1935). Using a series of ambiguous pictures called the *Thematic Apperception Test* (TAT) (Figure 12.11), these researchers asked participants to make up a story about each picture. Their responses were scored

Figure 12.10 *Can you explain how popular movie and television stars' extreme thinness may unintentionally contribute to eating disorders?*

Achievement Motivation
Desire to excel, especially in competition with others

Achievement

Objective 12.7: *Define achievement motivation, and list the characteristics of high achievers.*

Figure 12.11 *Measuring achievement* This card is a sample from the *Thematic Apperception Test* (TAT). The strength of an individual's need for achievement is reportedly measured by stories he or she tells about the TAT drawings. If you want an informal test using this method, look closely at the two women in the photo, and then write a short story answering the following questions:

1. What is happening in this picture, and what led up to it?
2. Who are the people in this picture, and how do they feel?
3. What is going to happen in the next few moments, and in a few weeks?

Scoring Give yourself 1 point each time any of the following is mentioned: (1) defining a problem, (2) solving a problem, (3) obstructions to solving a problem, (4) techniques that can help overcome the problem, (5) anticipation of success or resolution of the problem. The higher your score on this test, the higher your overall need for achievement.

for different motivational themes, including achievement. Since that time, other researchers have developed several questionnaire measures of achievement.

Before you read on, complete the following "Try This Yourself!" activity, which provides insights into your own need for achievement.

What causes some people to be more achievement oriented than others? Achievement orientation appears to be largely learned in early childhood, primarily through interactions with parents. Highly motivated children tend to have parents who encourage independence and frequently reward success (Maehr & Urdan, 2000). The culture that we are born and raised in also affects achievement needs (Lubinski & Benbow, 2000). Events and themes in children's literature, for example, often contain subtle messages about what the culture values. In North American and Western European cultures, many children's stories are about persistence and the value of hard work (Figure 12.12).

Andy Sachs/Getty Images

Figure 12.12 *Future achiever* A study by Richard de Charms and Gerald Moeller (1962) found a significant correlation between the achievement themes in children's literature and the industrial accomplishments of various countries.

Try This Yourself

pplication

Characteristics of High Achievers
(Contributed by Thomas Frangicetto)

Do you have a high need for achievement (nAch)? People with a high achievement orientation generally have more success in life and report more satisfaction with what they've accomplished in their lives. Here is a chance for you to:

- Review the six characteristics of high achievers.
- Rate yourself on those characteristics.
- Apply critical thinking components to improve your achievement motivation scores.

Part I: Researchers have identified several personality traits that distinguish people with a high nAch from those with a low nAch (McClelland, 1958, 1987, 1993; Senko, Durik, & Harackiewicz, 2008; Quintanilla, 2007). To determine your own personal need for achievement, read the six characteristics below and rate yourself according to how accurately each one describes you.

RATING:

(Not like me at all)   0 1 2 3 4 5 6 7 8 9 10   *(Describes me accurately)*

1. *Preference for moderately difficult tasks.* I tend to avoid tasks that are too easy because they offer little challenge and avoid extremely difficult tasks because the chance of success is too low.
2. *Preference for clear goals with competent feedback.* I prefer tasks with a clear outcome and situations in which you can receive performance feedback. I also prefer criticism from a harsh but competent evaluator to one who is friendlier but less competent.

3. *Competitive.* I am more attracted to careers and tasks that involve competition and an opportunity to excel. I enjoy the challenge of having to prove myself.
4. *Responsible.* I prefer being personally responsible for a project, and when I am directly responsible I feel more satisfaction when the task is well done.
5. *Persistent.* I am highly likely to persist at a task even when it becomes difficult, and I gain satisfaction in seeing a task through to completion.
6. *More accomplished.* In comparison to others, I generally achieve more (e.g., I typically do better on exams and earn higher grades and/or receive top honors in sports, clubs, and other activities).

Add up your total need for achievement (nAch) points. 55–60 = Very high; 49–54 = High; 43–48 = Moderately high; 37–42 = Average; 31–36 = Below average; below 30 = Low.

Part II: Review your ratings and identify one critical thinking component (CTC) (Prologue, p. XXX), that you believe could help increase your score on each trait. This is an important exercise. The closer your need for achievement reflects the characteristics of high achievers, the more likely you are to accomplish your goals. Here is an example for item #1:

Preference for moderately difficult tasks. High achievers know that succeeding at an easy task results in low satisfaction. On the other hand, overly difficult tasks lead to unnecessary frustration. Therefore, the CTC "Recognizing Personal Biases" is very important. Honestly facing the facts about our knowledge and abilities helps us recognize our limitations. It can also help prevent wasteful rationalizing and blaming others for our failures. Being realistic about our abilities without being overly self-critical achieves a healthy balance.

STOP

CHECK & REVIEW

Motivation and Behavior

Reuters/Corbis Images

Objective 12.3: *Discuss the major biopsychosocial factors that influence hunger and eating.*

Several biological, internal factors, including structures in the brain, numerous chemicals, and messages from the stomach and intestines, all seem to play important roles in hunger and eating. But psychosocial factors, such as stimulus cues, cultural conditioning, and willpower also play a role.

Objective 12.4: *How does expressing willpower affect later self-control?*

Research shows that a single act of willpower expends some of our body's fuel, which undermines our brain's ability to exert further self-discipline.

Objective 12.5: *Describe the three key eating disorders—obesity, anorexia, and bulimia.*

Obesity (being 15 percent or more above the ideal for one's height and age) seems to result from biological factors, such as the individual's genetic inheritance, lifestyle factors, and numerous psychological factors.

Anorexia nervosa (extreme weight loss due to self-imposed starvation) and **bulimia nervosa** (excessive consumption of food followed by purging) are both related to an intense fear of obesity.

Objective 12.6: *Discuss the controversial study that found people live longer if they're slightly overweight.*

One group of researchers looking at the effects of obesity suggested that it might be okay to be slightly overweight, but a different team supported the conventional wisdom that obesity is a serious problem.

Objective 12.7: *Define achievement motivation, and list the characteristics of high achievers.*

Achievement motivation refers to the desire to excel, especially in competition with others. People with high achievement needs prefer moderately difficult tasks and clear goals with competent feedback. They also tend to be more competitive, responsible, persistent, and accomplished.

Questions

1. Motivation for eating is found _____. (a) in the stomach; (b) in the ventromedial section of the hypothalamus; (c) throughout the brain; (d) throughout the body
2. Severe weight loss resulting from self-imposed starvation and an obsessive fear of obesity is called _____.
3. Juan has a need for success and prefers moderately difficult tasks, especially in competition with others. Juan probably has a high _____. (a) need for approval; (b) testographic personality; (c) power drive; (d) need for achievement.
4. What are the chief identifying characteristics of high achievers?

Check your answers in Appendix B.

Click & Review
for additional assessment options:
wiley.com/college/huffman

Theories and Concepts of Emotion

We have reviewed the major theoretical explanations for motivation and specific motives such as hunger and achievement. But as we mentioned at the beginning of this chapter, motivation is inextricably linked to emotion. In this section, we begin with an exploration of the three basic components of emotion (*physiological, cognitive,* and *behavioral*). Then we examine the four major theories that help us understand emotion (*James–Lange, Cannon–Bard, facial-feedback,* and *Schachter's two-factor*).

■ Three Components of Emotion: Physiological, Cognitive, and Behavioral

Emotions play an important role in our lives. They color our dreams, memories, and perceptions. When they are disordered, they contribute significantly to psychological problems. But what do we mean by the term *emotion*? In everyday usage, we describe emotions in terms of feeling states—we feel "thrilled" when our political candidate

Achievement

Objective 12.8: *Describe the three key components of emotions.*

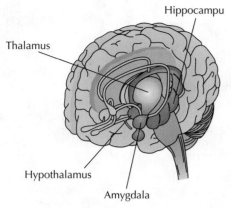

Figure 12.13 **The limbic system and emotion** In addition to drive regulation, memory, and other functions, the limbic system is very important to emotions. It consists of several subcortical structures that form a border (or limbus) around the brain stem.

Amygdala *Limbic system structure linked to the production and regulation of emotions.*

wins an election, "defeated" when our candidate loses, and "miserable" when our loved ones reject us. Obviously, what you and I mean by these terms, or what we individually experience with various emotions, can vary greatly among individuals. In an attempt to make the study of emotions more reliable and scientific, psychologists define and study emotions according to their three basic components (*physiological*, *cognitive*, and *behavioral*).

The Physiological (Arousal) Component

Internal physical changes occur in our bodies whenever we experience an emotion. Imagine walking alone on a dark street in a dangerous part of town. You suddenly see someone jump from behind a stack of boxes and start running toward you. How do you respond? Like most of us, you would undoubtedly interpret the situation as threatening and would prepare to defend yourself or run. Your predominant emotion, fear, would involve several physiological reactions, including increased heart rate and blood pressure, dilated pupils, perspiration, dry mouth, rapid or irregular breathing, increased blood sugar, trembling, decreased gastrointestinal motility, and piloerection (goose bumps). These physiological reactions are controlled by many parts of your body. But certain brain regions and the autonomic nervous system (ANS) play especially significant roles.

The Brain

Our emotional experiences appear to result from important interactions among several areas of our brain. The cerebral cortex, the outermost layer of the brain, serves as our body's ultimate control and information-processing center, including our ability to recognize and regulate our emotions. (Recall from Chapter 1 that when a 13-pound tamping iron accidentally slammed through Phineas Gage's cortex, he could no longer monitor or control his emotions.)

In addition to the cortex, the limbic system is also essential to our emotions (Figure 12.13). Electrical stimulation of specific parts of the limbic system can produce an automatic "sham rage" that turns a docile cat into a hissing, slashing animal (Morris et al., 1996). Stimulating adjacent areas can cause the same animal to purr and lick your fingers. (The rage is called "sham" because it occurs in the absence of provocation and disappears immediately when the stimulus is removed.) Several studies have also shown that one area of the limbic system, the **amygdala**, plays a key role in emotion—especially the emotional response of fear. It sends signals to other areas of the brain, causing increased heart rate and all the other physiological reactions related to fear.

Interestingly, some forms of emotional arousal can occur without conscious awareness. Have you ever been hiking and suddenly jumped back because you thought you saw a snake on the trail, only to realize a moment later that it was just a stick? How does this happen? According to psychologist Joseph LeDoux (1996, 2002, 2007), when sensory inputs capable of eliciting emotions (the sight of the stick) arrive in the thalamus (our brain's sensory switchboard), it sends messages along two independent pathways—one going up to the cortex and the other going directly to the nearby amygdala. If the amygdala senses a threat, it immediately activates the body's alarm system, long before the cortex has had a chance to really "think" about the stimulus.

Although this dual pathway occasionally leads to "false alarms," such as mistaking a stick for a snake, LeDoux believes it is a highly adaptive warning system essential to our survival. He states that "the time saved by the amygdala in acting on the thalamic interpretation, rather than waiting for the cortical input, may be the difference between life and death."

Application

RESEARCH HIGHLIGHT

Objective 12.9: *Discuss how mirror neurons contribute to emotions and observational learning.*

Mirror Neurons— "I Share Your Pain!"

As we've just discovered, our emotional response to a harmless stick or a dangerous snake can sometimes be identical—thanks to the brain's fast-acting thalamus and amygdala. But how do we explain why we also suffer and cry when we watch our loved ones in pain—or even while simply observing actors in a sad movie?

Using fMRIs and other brain-imaging techniques, researchers have identified specific **mirror neurons** believed to be responsible for human empathy and imitation (Ahlsén, E., 2008; Fogassi et al., 2005; Jacob, 2008; Hurley, 2008). These neurons are found in several key areas of the brain and they help us identify with what others are feeling and to imitate their actions. When we see another person in

pain, one reason we empathize and "share their pain" is that our mirror neurons are firing. Similarly, if we watch others smile, our mirror neurons make it harder for us to frown.

Mirror neurons were first discovered by neuroscientists who implanted wires in the brains of monkeys to monitor areas involved in planning and carrying out movement (Ferrari, Rozzi, & Fogassi, 2005; Rizzolatti et al., 2002, 2006). When these monkeys moved and grasped an object, specific neurons fired, but they also fired when the monkeys simply observed another monkey performing the same or similar tasks.

Mirror neurons in humans also fire when we perform a movement or watch someone else perform. Have you noticed how spectators at an athletic event sometimes slightly move their arms or legs in synchrony with the athletes? Also, do you recall from Chapter 9 how newborns tend to imitate adult facial expressions (p. 336)? Mirror neurons may be the underlying

biological mechanism for this imitation, as well as for the infants copying of lip and tongue movements necessary for speech. They also might help explain the emotional deficits of children and adults with autism or schizophrenia who often misunderstand the verbal and nonverbal cues of others (Arbib & Mundhenk, 2005; Dapretto et al., 2006; Martineau et al., 2008).

Although scientists are excited about the promising links between mirror neurons and human emotions, imitation, language, learning, and mental disorders, we do not yet know how they develop. Are we born with mirror neurons, or do they develop in response to our interactions with others? Stay tuned.

> **Mirror Neurons** *Brain cells that fire both when performing specific actions and when observing specific actions or emotions of another. This "mirroring" may explain empathy, imitation, language, and the emotional deficits of some mental disorders.*

The Autonomic Nervous System (ANS) The brain clearly plays a vital role in emotion. However, it is the autonomic nervous system (ANS) that produces the obvious signs of emotional arousal (increased heart rate, fast and shallow breathing, trembling, and so on). These largely automatic responses result from interconnections between the ANS and various glands and muscles (Figure 12.14).

Recall from Chapter 2 that the ANS has two major subdivisions: the *sympathetic nervous system* and the *parasympathetic nervous system*. When you are emotionally aroused, the sympathetic branch increases heart rate, respiration, and so on (the

Sympathetic		Parasympathetic
Pupils dilated	**Eyes**	Pupils constricted
Dry	**Mouth**	Salivating
Goose bumps, perspiration	**Skin**	No goose bumps
Respiration increased	**Lungs**	Respiration normal
Increased rate	**Heart**	Decreased rate
Increased epinephrine and norepinephrine	**Adrenal glands**	Decreased epinephrine and norepinephrine
Decreased motility	**Digestion**	Increased motility

Figure 12.14 *Emotion and the autonomic nervous system* During emotional arousal, the sympathetic branch of the autonomic nervous system (in connection with the brain) prepares the body for fight or flight. The hormones epinephrine and norepinephrine keep the system under sympathetic control until the emergency is over. The parasympathetic system returns the body to a more relaxed state (homeostasis).

fight-or-flight response). When you are relaxed and resting, the parasympathetic branch works to calm the body and maintain *homeostasis*. The combined action of both the sympathetic and parasympathetic systems allows you to respond to emotional arousal and then return to a more relaxed state.

The Cognitive (Thinking) Component

> There is nothing either good or bad, but thinking makes it so.
>
> SHAKESPEARE, *HAMLET*

Our thoughts, values, and expectations also help determine the type and intensity of our emotional responses. Consequently, emotional reactions are very individual. What you experience as intensely pleasurable may be boring or aversive for another.

To study the cognitive component of emotions, psychologists typically use self-report techniques such as paper-and-pencil tests, surveys, and interviews. But our cognitions (or thoughts) about our own and others' emotions are typically difficult to describe and measure scientifically. Individuals differ in their ability to monitor and report on their emotional states. In addition, some people may lie or hide their feelings because of social expectations or as an attempt to please the experimenter.

Furthermore, it is often impractical or unethical to artificially create emotions in a laboratory. How can we ethically create strong emotions like anger in a research participant just to study his or her emotional reactions? Finally, memories of emotions are not foolproof. You may remember that trip to Yellowstone as the "happiest camping trip ever." Your brother or sister may remember the same trip as the "worst." Our individual needs, experiences, and personal interpretations all affect the accuracy of our memories (Chapter 7).

The Behavioral (Expressive) Component

Emotional expression is a powerful form of communication. An infant's smile can create instant bonding, a cry of "fire" can cause crowds to panic, and a sobbing friend can elicit heartbreaking empathy. Though we can talk about our emotions, we more often express them nonverbally through facial expressions; gestures; body position; and the use of touch, eye gaze, and tone of voice.

Facial expressions may be our most important form of emotional communication, and researchers have developed very sensitive measurement techniques allowing them to detect subtleties of feeling and differentiate honest expressions from fake ones. Perhaps most interesting is the difference between the "social smile" and the "Duchenne smile." The latter is named after French anatomist Duchenne de Boulogne, who first described it in 1862 (Figure 12.15).

Assessment

VISUAL QUIZ

(a)   (b)

Karen Huffman

Figure 12.15 ***Duchenne smile*** To most people, the smile on the right looks more sincere than the one on the left. Do you know why?

Answer: (a) In a false, social smile, our voluntary cheek muscles are pulled back, but our eyes are unsmiling. (b) Smiles of real pleasure, on the other hand, use the muscles not only around the cheeks but also around the eyes. According to Duchenne de Boulogne, the eye muscle "does not obey the will" and "is put in play only by the sweet emotions of the soul" (cited in Goode, Schrof, & Burke, 1991, p. 56). Studies find that people who show a Duchenne, or real, smile and laughter elicit more positive responses from strangers and enjoy better interpersonal relationships and personal adjustment (Keltner, Kring, & Bonanno, 1999; Prkachin & Silverman, 2002).

Four Major Theories of Emotion: James–Lange, Cannon–Bard, Facial-Feedback, and Schachter's Two-Factor

Researchers generally agree on the three components of emotion (physiological, cognitive, and behavioral). There is less agreement on *how* we become emotional. The four major theories are the James–Lange, Cannon–Bard, facial-feedback, and Schachter's two-factor. Each of these theories emphasizes different sequences or aspects of the three elements (cognitions, arousal, and expression) (Process Diagram 12.1).

Achievement

Objective 12.10: *Compare and contrast the four major theories of emotion.*

James–Lange Theory

According to ideas originated by psychologist William James and later expanded by physiologist Carl Lange, emotions result from awareness of our physiological arousal of our autonomic nervous system (ANS) and our behavioral expression. Contrary to popular opinion, which says we cry because we're sad, James wrote: "We feel sorry because we cry, angry because we strike, afraid because we tremble" (James, 1890).

Why would I tremble unless I first felt afraid? According to the **James–Lange theory**, your bodily response of trembling is a reaction to a specific stimulus such as seeing a large bear in the wilderness. In other words, you perceive an event, your body reacts, and then you interpret the bodily changes as a specific emotion (Process Diagram 12.1a). It is your awareness of your ANS arousal (palpitating heart, sinking stomach, flushed cheeks), your actions (running, yelling), and changes in your facial expression (crying, smiling, frowning) that produce your subjective experience of emotion. In short, arousal and expression cause emotion. According to the James–Lange theory, if there is no arousal or expression, there is no emotion.

James–Lange Theory *Our subjective experience of emotion follows our bodily arousal ("I feel sad because I'm crying"); in this view, each emotion is physiologically distinct*

Cannon–Bard Theory

The James–Lange theory argues that arousal and expression produce emotion and each emotion has its own distinct physiological reaction. In contrast, the **Cannon–Bard theory** holds that an emotional stimulus simultaneously triggers arousal plus our subjective emotional experience. Furthermore, all emotions are physiologically similar. Walter Cannon (1927) and Philip Bard (1934) proposed that after perception of the emotion-provoking stimulus (seeing a bear), a small part of the brain, called the thalamus, sends messages to the cortex and ANS. These messages then lead to sympathetic arousal, behavioral reactions, and *simultaneous* emotions (Process Diagram 12.1b). The major point of the Cannon–Bard theory is that arousal and emotions occur at the *same* time—one does not cause the other.

Because all emotions are physiologically similar, arousal is not a necessary or even a major factor in emotion. Cannon supported this position with several experiments in which nonhuman animals were surgically prevented from experiencing physiological arousal. Yet these surgically altered animals still showed observable behaviors (like growling and defensive postures) that might be labeled emotional reactions (Cannon, Lewis, & Britton, 1927). Similarly, people with upper and lower spinal cord injuries differ in the amount of autonomic arousal they experience below the injury, yet they experience no difference in emotional intensity (Chwalisz et al., 1988).

Cannon–Bard Theory *Arousal and our subjective experience of emotion occur simultaneously ("I'm crying and feeling sad at the same time"); in this view, all emotions are physiologically similar*

Facial-Feedback Hypothesis

The third major explanation of emotion—the facial-feedback hypothesis—focuses on the *expressive* component of emotions. According to the **facial-feedback hypothesis**, sensory input (seeing a bear) is first routed to subcortical areas of the brain that activate facial movements. Subsequent facial changes then initiate and intensify emotions (Adelmann & Zajonc, 1989; Ceschi & Scherer, 2001; Prkachin, 2005; Sigall & Johnson, 2006). Contractions of the various facial muscles send specific messages to the brain, which help us identify each basic emotion. Like James, these researchers suggest that we don't smile because we are happy. We feel happy because we smile (Process Diagram 12.1c).

Facial-Feedback Hypothesis *Movements of the facial muscles produce and/or intensify our subjective experience of emotion*

Process Diagram

Process Diagram 12.1

Four Theories of Emotion

Emotional
Stimulus

iStockphoto

(a)
James-Lange
Theory

ANS Arousal
(and Behavior Responses)

Emotion/ Feelings
(Fear)

(b)
Cannon-Bard
Theory

Cognitive Arousal + **ANS Arousal**
(Thalamus/ cortex) (and Behavioral Responses)

Emotion/ Feelings
(Fear)

(c)
Facial-Feedback
Hypothesis

Subcortical Stimulation

Facial Expression

Emotion/ Feelings
(Fear)

(d)
Schachter's Two-Factor
Theory

ANS Arousal
(and Behavior Responses)

Cognitive Label
("I'm afraid")

Emotion/ Feelings
(Fear)

426

Testing the Facial-Feedback Hypothesis

Hold a pen or pencil between your teeth with your mouth closed, as shown in the left photo. Spend about 15 to 30 seconds in this position. How do you feel? Now hold the pencil between your teeth with your mouth open and your teeth showing, as in the right photo. During the next 15 to 30 seconds, pay attention to your feelings. According to research, pleasant feelings are more likely when teeth are showing. Can you explain why?

Source: Adapted from Strack, Martin, & Stepper, 1988.

The facial-feedback hypothesis also supports Darwin's (1872) evolutionary theory that freely expressing an emotion intensifies it, whereas suppressing outward expression diminishes it. Interestingly, research suggests that even watching another's facial expressions causes an automatic, *reciprocal* change in our own facial muscles (Dimberg & Thunberg, 1998). When people are exposed to pictures of angry faces, for example, the eyebrow muscles involved in frowning are activated. In contrast, the smile muscles show a significant increase in activity when participants are shown photos of a happy face. In follow-up research using the *subliminal perception* techniques discussed in Chapter 4, scientists have shown that this automatic, matching response occurs even *without* the participant's attention or conscious awareness (Dimberg, Thunberg, & Elmehed, 2000).

This automatic, innate, and generally unconscious imitation of others' facial expressions has several important applications. Have you ever felt depressed after listening to a friend's problems? Your unconscious facial mimicry of the person's sad expression may have led to similar physiological reactions and similar feelings of sadness. This theory may also provide personal insights for therapists who constantly work with depressed clients and for actors who simulate emotions for their livelihood. In addition, studies show that "happy workers are generally more productive than unhappy workers" (Hosie, Sevastos, & Cooper, 2006). Does this mean that unhappy coworkers or a constantly angry boss might affect the happiness (and productivity) of the general workforce? If Darwin was right that expressing an emotion intensifies it, and if watching others' emotions produces a matching response, should we reconsider traditional advice encouraging us to "express our anger"?

Schachter's Two-Factor Theory

According to **Schachter's two-factor theory**, our emotions depend on two factors: (1) physical arousal and (2) cognitive labeling of that arousal (Process Diagram 12.1d). If we cry at a wedding, for example, we interpret our emotion as joy or happiness. If we cry at a funeral, we label our emotion as sadness.

Schachter agrees with James–Lange that arousal causes our subjective experience of an emotion. But he also agrees with Cannon–Bard that all emotions are physiologically similar. He reconciles the two theories by proposing that we look to *external* rather than *internal* cues to differentiate and label our emotions. In Schachter and Singer's classic study (1962), participants were given shots of epinephrine and told it was a type of vitamin. Their subsequent arousal and labeling were then investigated (Figure 12.16).

Schachter's Two-Factor Theory *Physical arousal and cognitive labeling (or interpretation) of that arousal produce our subjective experience of emotion*

Figure 12.16 *Schachter's two-factor theory* In Schachter and Singer's study, after receiving an epinephrine shot, one group of participants was correctly informed about the expected effects (hand tremors, excitement, and heart palpitations). A second group was misinformed and told to expect itching, numbness, and headache. A third group was told nothing about the possible effects.

Following the injection, each participant was placed in a room with a confederate (a "stooge" who was part of the experiment but who pretended to be a fellow volunteer) who acted either happy or unhappy. The results showed that participants who lacked an appropriate cognitive label for their emotional arousal (the misinformed and uninformed groups) tended to look to the situation for an explanation. Thus, those placed with a happy confederate became happy, whereas those with an unhappy confederate became unhappy. Participants in the correctly informed group knew their physiological arousal was the result of the shot, so their emotions were generally unaffected by the confederate.

Evaluating Theories of Emotion

Which theory is correct? As you may imagine, each theory has its limits. For example, the James–Lange theory fails to acknowledge that physical arousal can occur without emotional experience (e.g., when we exercise). This theory also requires a distinctly different pattern of arousal for each emotion. Otherwise, how do we know whether we are sad, happy, or mad? Positron emission tomography (PET) scans of the brain do show subtle differences and overall physical arousal with basic emotions, such as happiness, fear, and anger (Levenson, 1992, 2007; Werner et al., 2007). But most people are not aware of these slight variations. Thus, there must be other explanations for how we experience emotion.

The Cannon–Bard theory (that arousal and emotions occur independently and simultaneously and that all emotions are physiologically similar) has received some experimental support. For instance, victims of spinal cord damage still experience emotions—often more intensely than before their injuries (Nicotra et al., 2006;

Assessment

VISUAL QUIZ

"I don't sing because I am happy. I am happy because I sing."

Can you identify which of the four major theories of emotion best explains this bird's behavior?

Answer: The James-Lange theory

Schopp et al., 2007). Instead of the thalamus, however, other research shows that it is the limbic system, hypothalamus, and prefrontal cortex that are activated in emotional experience (LeDoux, 2007; Zillmer, Spiers, & Culbertson, 2008).

As mentioned earlier, research on the facial-feedback hypothesis has found a distinctive physiological response for basic emotions such as fear, sadness, and anger—thus partially confirming James–Lange's initial position. Facial feedback does seem to contribute to the intensity of our subjective emotional experience and our overall moods. Thus, if you want to change a bad mood or intensify a particularly good emotion, adopt the appropriate facial expression. Try smiling when you're sad and expanding your smiles when you're happy.

Finally, Schachter's two-factor theory emphasizes the importance of cognitive labels in emotions. But research shows that some neural pathways involved in emotion bypass the cortex and go directly to the limbic system. Recall our earlier example of jumping at a strange sound in the dark and then a second later using the cortex to interpret what it was. This and other evidence suggest that emotions can take place without conscious cognitive processes. Thus, emotion is not simply the labeling of arousal.

In sum, certain basic emotions are associated with subtle differences in arousal. These differences can be produced by changes in facial expressions or by organs controlling the autonomic nervous system. In addition, "simple" emotions (fear and anger) do not initially require conscious cognitive processes. This allows a quick, automatic emotional response that can later be modified by cortical processes. On the other hand, "complex" emotions (jealousy, grief, depression, embarrassment, love) seem to require more extensive cognitive processes.

Assessment

STOP

CHECK & REVIEW

Theories and Concepts of Emotion

Objective 12.8: *Describe the three key components of emotions.*

All emotions have three basic components: *physiological arousal* (e.g., heart pounding), *cognitive* (thoughts, values, and expectations), and *behavioral expressions* (e.g., smiles, frowns, running). Studies of the physiological component find that most emotions involve a general, nonspecific arousal of the nervous system. The cognitive component explains how thoughts, values, and expectations help determine the type and intensity of emotional responses. The behavioral component focuses on how we express our emotions, including facial expressions.

Objective 12.9: *Discuss how mirror neurons contribute to emotions and observational learning.*

Mirror neurons fire both when performing specific actions and when simply observing the actions or emotions of others. This "mirroring" may explain our emotions, as well as imitation, language, and the emotional deficits of some mental disorders.

Objective 12.10: *Compare and contrast the four major theories of emotion.*

Four major theories explain what causes emotion. According to the **James–Lange theory**, emotions follow from physiological arousal and behavioral expression, such as smiles, increased heart rate, and trembling. The **Cannon–Bard theory** suggests that arousal and emotions occur simultaneously. According to the **facial-feedback hypothesis**, facial movements produce and/or intensify emotions. **Schachter's two-factor theory** suggests that emotions depend on two factors—physical arousal and a cognitive labeling of that arousal.

Questions

1. Identify the following examples with the appropriate emotional component: (a) cognitive; (b) physiological; (c) behavioral
   ___i. Increased heart rate
   ___ii. Crying during a sad movie
   ___iii. Believing crying is inappropriate for men
   ___iv. Shouting during a soccer match
2. When people are emotionally aroused, the _____ branch of the _____ nervous system works to increase heart rate and blood pressure and to activate other crisis responses.
3. In a _____, as shown in the photo, the cheek muscles are pulled back and the muscles around the eyes contract.
   a. Duchenne smile
   b. Madonna smile
   c. Mona Lisa smile
   d. Da vinci smile

4. We see a bear in the woods, our hearts race as we begin to run, and then we experience fear. This is best explained by _____.
   (a) the James–Lange theory;
   (b) the Cannon–Bard theory;
   (c) the facial-feedback hypothesis;
   (d) Schacter's two-factor theory
5. According to _____, physiological arousal must be labeled or interpreted for an emotional experience to occur.
   (a) the Cannon–Bard theory;
   (b) the James–Lange theory;
   (c) the facial-feedback hypothesis;
   (d) Schacter's two-factor theory

6. The Cannon–Bard theory of emotion suggests that arousal and our subjective experience of emotions occur _____.
7. According to _____, we look to external rather than internal cues to understand emotions.
   a. Cannon–Bard theory
   b. James–Lange theory
   c. the facial feedback hypothesis
   d. Schacther's two-factor theory

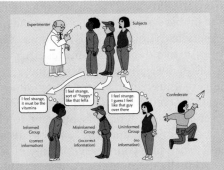

Check your answers in Appendix B.

Click & Review
for additional assessment options:
wiley.com/college/huffman

Critical Thinking about Motivation and Emotion

As you recall from Chapter 1, critical thinking is a core part of psychological science and a major goal of this text. In this section, we will use our critical thinking skills to explore four special (and sometimes controversial) topics in motivation and emotion—*intrinsic versus extrinsic motivation, the polygraph as a lie detector, emotional intelligence,* and *culture, evolution,* and *emotion.*

chievement

Objective 12.11: *Define intrinsic and extrinsic motivation, and describe how they affect motivation*

Intrinsic Motivation *Motivation resulting from personal enjoyment of a task or activity*

Extrinsic Motivation *Motivation based on obvious external rewards or threats of punishment*

Intrinsic versus Extrinsic Motivation: What's Best?

Should parents reward children for getting good grades? If someone paid you to play video games, would your enjoyment decrease? Many psychologists are concerned about the widespread practice of giving external, *extrinsic* rewards to motivate behavior (e.g., Deci & Moller, 2005; Markle, 2007; Prabhu, Sutton, & Sauser, 2008; Reeve, 2005). They're worried that providing extrinsic rewards will seriously affect the individual's personal, *intrinsic* motivation. **Intrinsic motivation** comes from within the individual. The person engages in an activity for its own sake or for internal satisfaction, with no ulterior purpose or need for an external reward. In contrast, **extrinsic motivation** stems from external rewards or avoidance of punishment and is learned through interaction with the environment (Concept Diagram 12.1).

ssessment

VISUAL QUIZ

Benelux Press B.V./Photo Researchers, Inc.

Vincent van Gogh only sold one painting during his entire lifetime, yet he was one of the most prolific nineteenth-century artists. How would you explain his motivation?

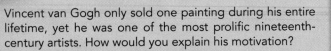
Answer: Van Gogh obviously painted for personal satisfaction or intrinsic motivation.

Concept Diagram 12.1
Extrinsic versus Intrinsic Rewards

Have you ever noticed that for all the money and glory they receive, professional athletes often don't look like they're enjoying themselves very much? What's the problem? Why don't they appreciate how lucky they are to be able to make a living by playing games?

When we perform a task for no ulterior purpose, we use internal, personal reasons ("I like it"; "It's fun"). But when extrinsic rewards are added, the explanation shifts to external, impersonal reasons ("I did it for the money"; "I did it to please my parents"). This shift generally decreases enjoyment and hampers performance. This is as true for professional athletes as it is for anyone else.

One of the earliest experiments to demonstrate this effect was conducted with preschool children who liked to draw (Lepper, Greene, & Nisbett, 1973). As shown in the figure below, the researchers found that children who were given paper and markers and promised a reward for their drawings were subsequently less interested in drawing than children who were not given a reward or who were given an unexpected reward when they were done. Likewise, for professional athletes, what is a fun diversion for most people can easily become "just a job."

William R. Salaz/Riser/Getty Images

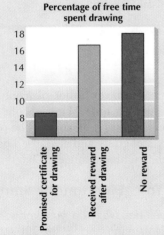

Percentage of free time spent drawing

Bar chart y-axis: 8, 10, 12, 14, 16, 18
Categories: Promised certificate for drawing; Received reward after drawing; No reward

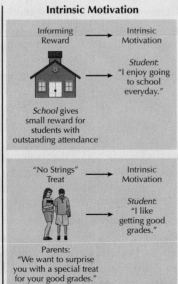

Jeffery Meyers/Corbis Images

Not all extrinsic motivation is bad, however (Banko, 2008; Konheim-Kalkstein & van den Broek, 2008; Moneta & Siu, 2002). As you can see in the figure to the left, extrinsic rewards are motivating if they are used to inform a person of superior performance or as a special "no strings attached" treat (Deci, 1995). In fact, they may intensify the desire to do well again. Thus, getting a raise or a gold medal can inform us and provide valuable feedback about our performance, which may increase enjoyment. But if rewards are used to control—for example, when parents give children money or privileges for achieving good grades—they inhibit intrinsic motivation (Eisenberger & Armeli, 1997; Eisenberger & Rhoades, 2002; Houlfort, 2006).

Extrinsic Motivation

Controlling Reward → Extrinsic Motivation

Student: "I'll attend school if I get the reward."

School pays small reward for attendance

External Pressure → Extrinsic Motivation

Student: "I'll get good grades to get their approval."

Parents: "We want you to get A's like our neighbor's boy."

Intrinsic Motivation

Informing Reward → Intrinsic Motivation

Student: "I enjoy going to school everyday."

School gives small reward for students with outstanding attendance

"No Strings" Treat → Intrinsic Motivation

Student: "I like getting good grades."

Parents: "We want to surprise you with a special treat for your good grades."

Try This Yourself

Improving Motivation

Intrinsic–extrinsic motivation has important implications for raising children, running a business, or even studying this text. Consider the following guidelines:

1. **Limit concrete extrinsic rewards**. In general, it is almost always better to use the least possible extrinsic reward and for the shortest possible time period. When children are first learning to play a musical instrument, it may help to provide small rewards until they gain a certain level of mastery. But once a child is working happily or practicing for the sheer joy of it, it is best to leave him or her alone. Similarly, if you're trying to increase your study time, begin by rewarding yourself for every significant improvement. But don't reward yourself when you're handling a difficult assignment easily. Save rewards for when you

need them. Keep in mind, that we're speaking primarily of concrete extrinsic rewards. Praise and positive feedback are generally safe to use and often increase intrinsic motivation (Carton, 1996; Henderlong & Lepper, 2002).

2. **Reward competency**. Use extrinsic rewards to provide feedback for competency or outstanding performance—not for simply engaging in the behavior. Schools can enhance intrinsic motivation by giving medals or privileges to students with no absences, rather than giving money for simple attendance. Similarly, you should reward yourself with a movie or a call to a friend after you've studied hard for your scheduled time period or done particularly well on an exam. Don't reward yourself for half-hearted attempts.

3. **Emphasize intrinsic reasons for behaviors**. Rather than thinking about all the people you'll impress with good grades or all the great jobs you'll get when you finish college, focus instead on personally satisfying, intrinsic reasons. Think about how exciting it is to learn new things or the value of becoming an educated person and a critical thinker.

Obviously, not all college classes or all aspects of our lives can be intrinsically interesting. Nor should they be. We all have to do many worthwhile things that are obviously extrinsically motivated—going to the dentist, cleaning the house, and studying for exams. It's a good idea, therefore, to save your external reinforcers for the times you're having trouble motivating yourself to do an undesirable task, and avoid "wasting" rewards on well-established intrinsic activities.

Achievement

Objective 12.12: *Discuss polygraph testing and its effectiveness in lie detection*

Polygraph *Instrument that measures sympathetic arousal (heart rate, respiration rate, blood pressure, and skin conductivity) to detect emotional arousal, which in turn supposedly reflects lying versus truthfulness*

Achievement

Objective 12.13: *What is emotional intelligence (EI), and why is it controversial?*

Emotional Intelligence (EI)

Goleman's term for the ability to know and manage one's emotions, empathize with others, and maintain satisfying relationships

The Polygraph as a Lie Detector: Does It Work?

If you suspected your friend of lying or your significant other of having an affair, would it help convince you if they took a polygraph test? Many people believe the **polygraph** can accurately detect when someone is lying. But can it? The polygraph is based on the theory that when people lie, they feel guilty and anxious. These feelings are then supposedly detected by the polygraph machine (Concept Diagram 12.2).

Emotional Intelligence (EI): Are You "Emotionally Smart"?

You've heard of IQ, the intelligence quotient, but what do you know about EI—emotional intelligence? According to Daniel Goleman (1995, 2000, 2008), **emotional intelligence (EI)** involves knowing and managing one's emotions, empathizing with others, and maintaining satisfying relationships. In other words, an emotionally intelligent person successfully combines the three components of emotions (cognitive, physiological, and behavioral).

Goleman suggests that having a high EI explains why people of modest IQ are often more successful than people with much higher IQ scores. He believes that traditional measures of human intelligence ignore a crucial range of abilities that characterize people who excel in real life: self-awareness, impulse control, persistence, zeal and self-motivation, empathy, and social deftness.

Goleman also proposes that many societal problems, such as domestic abuse and youth violence, can be attributed to a low EI. Therefore, EI should be fostered in everyone. Proponents have suggested that law schools and other professional training programs should make EI training a curriculum staple. In addition, advocates suggest parents and educators can help children develop EI by encouraging them to identify their emotions and understand how these feelings can be changed and how they are connected to their actions (Casarjian, Phillips, & Wolman, 2007; Reilly, 2005; Shriver & Weissberg, 2005; van Heck & den Oudsten, 2008). Schools that have instituted Goleman's ideas say students show not just "more positive attitudes

Polygraph Testing

(a) During a standard polygraph test, a band around the person's chest measures breathing rate, a cuff monitors blood preasure, and finger electrodes measure sweating, or galvanic skin response (GSR).

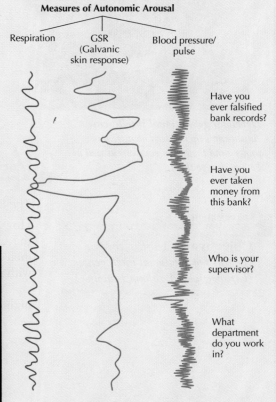

Measures of Autonomic Arousal

Respiration — GSR (Galvanic skin response) — Blood pressure/pulse

Have you ever falsified bank records?

Have you ever taken money from this bank?

Who is your supervisor?

What department do you work in?

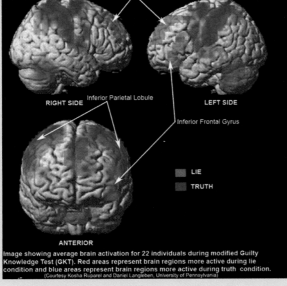

Medial Frontal Gyrus

RIGHT SIDE — Inferior Parietal Lobule — LEFT SIDE

Inferior Frontal Gyrus

LIE
TRUTH

ANTERIOR

Image showing average brain activation for 22 individuals during modified Guilty Knowledge Test (GKT). Red areas represent brain regions more active during lie condition and blue areas represent brain regions more active during truth condition.
(Courtesy Kosha Ruparel and Daniel Langleben, University of Pennsylvania)

(c) The three fMRI images appear to show several known and specific areas of the cortex most involved in lying versus truth telling.

(b) Note how the GSR rises sharply in response to the question, "Have you ever taken money from this bank?"

Some people say the innocent have nothing to fear from a polygraph test. However, research suggests otherwise (DeClue, 2003; Faigman et al., 1997; Iacono & Lykken, 1997). In fact, although proponents claim that polygraph tests are 90 percent accurate or better, actual tests show error rates ranging between 25 and 75 percent.

Traditional polygraph tests measure sympathetic and parasympathetic nervous system responses (A and B). The problem is that lying is only loosely related to anxiety and guilt. Some people become nervous even when telling the truth, whereas others remain calm when deliberately lying. A polygraph cannot tell which emotion is being felt (nervousness, excitement, sexual arousal etc.) or whether a response is due to emotional arousal or something else. One study found that people could affect the outcome of a polygraph by about 50 percent simply by pressing their toes against the floor or biting their tongues (Honts & Kircher, 1994).

For these reasons, most judges and scientists have serious reservations about using polygraphs as lie detectors (DeClue, 2003). Scientific controversy and public concern led the U.S. Congress to pass a bill that severely restricts the use of polygraphs in the courts, in government, and in private industry. In our post–9/11 world, you can see why tens of millions to hundreds of millions of dollars have been spent on new and improved lie-detection techniques (Kluger and Masters, 2006). Perhaps the most promising new technique is the use of brain scans like the function magnetic imaging (fMRI) (c). When using the fMRI, researchers often ask "guilty knowledge" questions, which include specific information only a guilty person would know (such as the time a robbery was committed). The idea is that a guilty person would recognize these specific cues and respond in a different way than an innocent person (Lykken, 1984, 1998; MacLaren, 2001; Verschuere et al., 2004). Expanding on this idea, researchers have also used computers and statistical analyses to improve polygraph reliability and validity (Saxe & Ben-Shakhar, 1999; Spence, 2003).

Unfortunately, each of these new lie-detection techniques has serious shortcomings and unique problems. Researchers have questioned their reliability and validity, while civil libertarians and judicial scholars question their ethics and legalities.

Developing emotional intelligence
Adults can help children identify and
understand their own emotions as well as
how to change them.

chievement

Objective 12.14: *List the five*
key traits of emotional intelligence
(EI) shown by Abraham Lincoln.

about ways to get along with people. They also show improvements in critical thinking skills" (Mitchell, Sachs, & Tu, 1997, p. 62).

Critics argue that the components of EI are difficult to identify and measure (Mayer, Roberts, & Barsade, 2008). Others fear that a handy term like EI invites misuse. Paul McHugh, director of psychiatry at Johns Hopkins University, suggests that Goleman is "presuming that someone has the key to the right emotions to be taught to children. We don't even know the right emotions to be taught to adults" (cited in Gibbs, 1995, p. 68).

EI is a controversial concept, but most researchers are pleased that the subject of emotion is being taken seriously. Further research will increase our understanding of emotion and perhaps even reveal the ultimate value of Goleman's theory.

Application

CASE STUDY / PERSONAL STORY

The Emotional Intelligence of Abraham Lincoln (Adapted from Goodwin, 2005)

How does a self-taught farm boy of humble origins grow up to become president of the United States? General William T. Sherman provided one answer: "Of all the men I ever met, he seemed to possess more of the elements of greatness, combined with goodness, than any other" ("Life behind the legend," 2005, p. 44).

Modern psychologists might call these same elements of greatness and goodness high emotional intelligence. Consider the following:

Empathy Known for his great ability to empathize and put himself in the place of others, Lincoln refused to criticize and castigate the Southern slaveowners like other antislavery orators did. Instead, he argued: "They are just what we would be in their situation. If slavery did not now exist amongst them, they would not introduce it. If it did now exist amongst us, we should not instantly give it up" (Goodwin, 2005, p. 49).

Magnanimity Possessing a high-minded, generous spirit, Lincoln refused to bear grudges. Opponent Edwin Stanton called him a "long-armed ape" and deliberately shunned and humiliated him. However, when Lincoln needed a new War Secretary, he noble-mindedly appointed Stanton because he was the best man for this very important position.

Generosity of Spirit Lincoln often took the blame for others, shared credit for successes, and quickly conceded his errors. After General Grant's great battle at Vicksburg, Lincoln wrote, "I now wish to make the personal acknowledgment that you were right, and I was wrong" (Goodwin, 2005, p. 53).

Self-Control Rather than lashing out at others during moments of anger, Lincoln waited until his emotions settled down. He would often write hot letters to others, but would put them aside and seldom send them.

Humor Noted for his dark, depressive moods, Lincoln also possessed a wonderful self-effacing sense of humor and a gift for storytelling. His jokes and stories not only entertained, but they also contained invaluable insights and wisdom. At the end of the Civil War, many debated the fate of the Southern Rebel leaders. Lincoln wished they could "escape the country," but could not say this publicly. Instead, he told General Sherman a story: "A man once had taken the total abstinence pledge. When visiting a friend, he was invited to take a drink, but declined, on the score of his pledge. . . . His friend suggested lemonade . . . and said the lemonade would be more palatable if he were to pour in a little brandy. . . . [The] guest said, if he could do so 'unbeknown' to him, he would not object."

Digital Vision/Getty Images

Sherman immediately grasped the point. "Mr. Lincoln wanted [Jefferson] Davis to escape, 'unbeknown' to him" (Goodwin, 2005, p. 50).

Achievement GENDER & CULTURAL DIVERSITY *Culture, Evolution, and Emotion*

Objective 12.15: *Discuss culturally universal emotions and differing display rules.*

Where do our emotions come from? Are they a product of our evolutionary past? Do they differ from one culture to the next, or are they the same? As you might suspect, researchers have found several answers.

Cultural Similarities All people of all cultures have feelings and emotions, and all must learn to deal with them. But are these emotions the same across all cultures? Given the seemingly vast array of emotions within our own culture, it may surprise you to learn that some researchers believe all our feelings can be condensed into 7 to 10 *culturally universal* emotions. Note the strong similarities among the four lists in Table 12.3.

In addition to all cultures sharing the same basic emotions, some researchers believe that each of these emotions is expressed and recognized in essentially the same way in all cultures. They point to research that finds people from very different cultures displaying remarkably similar facial expressions when experiencing particular emotions (Biehl et al., 1997; Ekman, 1993, 2004; Matsumoto & Juang, 2008). Moreover, whether respondents are from Western or non-Western societies, they can reliably identify at least six basic emotions: happiness, surprise, anger, sadness, fear, and disgust (Buck, 1984; Matsumoto, 1992, 2000). In other words, across cultures, a frown is recognized as a sign of displeasure and a smile as a sign of pleasure (Figure 12.17).

The Role of Evolution Charles Darwin first advanced the evolutionary theory of emotion in 1872. In his classic book *The Expression of the Emotions in Man and Animals*, Darwin proposed that expression of emotions evolved in different species as a part of survival and natural selection. For example, fear helps human and nonhuman animals avoid danger, and expressions of anger and aggression

Cultural differences in emotional expression Some Middle Eastern men commonly greet one another with a kiss. Can you imagine this same behavior among men in North America, who generally shake hands or pat one another's shoulders?

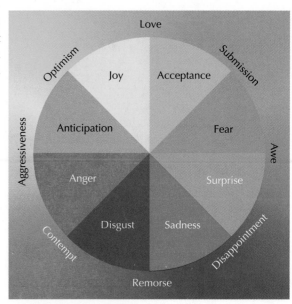

Plutchik's wheel of emotions How do we explain emotions not on this list? Robert Plutchik (1984, 1994, 2000) suggested that primary emotions (inside the circle) combine to form secondary emotions (located outside the circle). Plutchik also found that emotions that lie next to each other are more alike than those that are farther apart.

TABLE 12.3 THE BASIC HUMAN EMOTIONS

Carroll Izard	Paul Ekman and Wallace Friesen	Silvan Tomkins	Robert Plutchik
Fear	Fear	Fear	Fear
Anger	Anger	Anger	Anger
Disgust	Disgust	Disgust	Disgust
Surprise	Surprise	Surprise	Surprise
Joy	Happiness	Enjoyment	Joy
Shame	—	Shame	—
Contempt	Contempt	Contempt	—
Sadness	Sadness	—	Sadness
Interest	—	Interest	Anticipation
Guilt	—	—	—
—	—	—	Acceptance
—	—	Distress	—

Figure 12.17 *Can you identify these emotions?* Most people can reliably identify at least six basic emotions—happiness, surprise, anger, sadness, fear, and disgust. On occasion, our facial expressions don't seem to match our presumed emotions, as is the case in the photo on the right. This woman has just won an important award, yet she looks sad rather than happy.

are useful when fighting for mates and necessary resources. Modern evolutionary theory further suggests that basic emotions (such as fear and anger) originate in the limbic system. Given that higher brain areas (the cortex) developed later than the subcortical limbic system, evolutionary theory proposes that basic emotions evolved before thought.

Cross-cultural studies of emotional expression tend to support the innate, evolutionary perspective. The idea of universal facial expressions makes adaptive sense because they signal others about our current emotional state (Ekman & Keltner, 1997). Studies with infants also point to an evolutionary basis for emotions. For example, did you know that infants only a few hours old show distinct expressions of emotions that closely match adult facial expressions? Or that all infants, even those born deaf and blind, show similar facial expressions in similar situations (Field et al., 1982; Gelder et al., 2006). This collective evidence points to a strong biological, evolutionary basis for emotional expression and decoding.

Cultural Differences   How do we explain cultural *differences* in emotions? Although we all seem to share reasonably similar facial expressions for some emotions, each culture has its own *display rules* governing how, when, and where to express emotions (Ekman, 1993, 2004; Fok et al., 2008). For instance, parents pass along their culture's specific display rules by responding angrily to some emotions in their children, by being sympathetic to others, and, on occasion, by simply ignoring them. In this way, children learn which emotions they may freely express and those they are expected to control. In Japanese culture, for instance, children learn to conceal negative emotions with a stoic expression or polite smile (Dresser, 1996). Young males in the Masai culture are similarly expected to conceal their emotions in public, but by appearing stern and stony-faced (Keating, 1994).

Public physical contact is also governed by display rules. North Americans and Asians are generally not touch-oriented. Only the closest family and friends might hug in greeting or farewell. In contrast, Latin Americans and Middle Easterners often embrace and hold hands as a sign of casual friendship (Axtell, 2007).

Assessment

CHECK & REVIEW

Critical Thinking About Motivation and Emotion

Objective 12.11: *Define intrinsic and extrinsic motivation, and describe how they affect motivation.*

Intrinsic motivation comes from personal enjoyment of a task or activity. **Extrinsic motivation** stems from external rewards or threats of punishment. Research shows that extrinsic rewards can lower interest and motivation if they are not based on competency.

Objective 12.12: *Discuss polygraph testing and its effectiveness in lie detection.*

The **polygraph** machine measures changes in sympathetic arousal (increased heart rate, blood pressure, and so on). But research shows it is a poor "lie detector" because it cannot reliably identify whether a response is due to emotional arousal or something else, such as physical exercise, drugs, tense muscles, or even previous experience with polygraph tests.

Objective 12.13: *What is emotional intelligence (EI), and why is it controversial?*

Emotional intelligence (EI) involves knowing and managing one's emotions, empathizing

with others, and maintaining satisfying relationships. Critics argue that the components of EI are difficult to identify and measure, and fear that a handy term like EI invites misuse.

Objective 12.14: *List the five key traits of emotional intelligence (EI) shown by Abraham Lincoln.*

As president, Lincoln demonstrated empathy, magnanimity, generosity of spirit, self-control, and humor.

Objective 12.15: *Discuss culturally universal emotions and differing display rules.*

Studies have identified 7 to 10 basic emotions that may be universal—experienced and expressed in similar ways across almost all cultures. Display rules for emotional expression differ across cultures. Most psychologists believe that emotions result from a complex interplay between evolution and culture.

Questions

1. Which of the following would be an example of extrinsic motivation? (a) money; (b) praise; (c) threats of being fired; (d) all of these options

2. An elementary school began paying students $5 for each day they attend school. Overall rates of attendance increased in the first few weeks and then fell below the original starting point. This is because _____. (a) the students felt going to school wasn't worth $5; (b) money is a secondary versus a primary reinforcer; (c) extrinsic rewards decreased the intrinsic value of attending school; (d) the student expectancies changed to fit the situation

3. The polygraph, or lie detector, measures primarily the _____ component of emotions. (a) physiological; (b) articulatory; (c) cognitive; (d) subjective

4. Knowing and managing one's emotions, empathizing with others, and maintaining satisfying relationships are the key factors in _____. (a) self-actualization; (b) emotional intelligence; (c) emotion metacognition; (d) empathic IQ

Check your answers in Appendix B.

Click & Review
for additional assessment options:
wiley.com/college/huffman

Assessment

KEY TERMS

*To assess your understanding of the **Key Terms** in Chapter 12, write a definition for each (in your own words), and then compare your definitions with those in the text.*

emotion (p. 406)
motivation (p. 406)

Theories and Concepts of Motivation
arousal theory (p. 410)
drive-reduction theory (p. 409)
hierarchy of needs (p. 412)
homeostasis (p. 409)
incentive theory (p. 412)
instinct (p. 409)
instinct theory (p. 408)

Motivation and Behavior
achievement motivation (p. 419)
anorexia nervosa (p. 417)
bulimia nervosa (p. 417)

Theories and Concepts of Emotion
amygdala (p. 422)
Cannon–Bard theory (p. 425)
facial-feedback hypothesis (p. 425)
James–Lange theory (p. 425)
mirror neurons (p. 423)
Schachter's two-factor theory (p. 427)

Critical Thinking about Motivation and Emotion
emotional intelligence (EI) (p. 432)
extrinsic motivation (p. 430)
intrinsic motivation (p. 430)
polygraph (p. 432)

Achievement

WEB RESOURCES

Huffman Book Companion Site
wiley.com/college/huffman
This site is loaded with free Interactive Self-Tests, Internet Exercises, Glossary and Flashcards for key terms, web links, Handbook for Non-Native Speakers, and other activities designed to improve your mastery of the material in this chapter.

Chapter 12 Visual Summary

Theories and Concepts of Motivation

Biological Theories

- **Instinct:** Emphasizes inborn, genetic factors in motivation.

- **Arousal:** Organisms are motivated to achieve and maintain an *optimal level* of *arousal*.

- **Drive-reduction:** Internal tensions (produced by body's demand for **homeostasis**) "push" organism to satisfy basic needs.

Psychosocial Theories

- **Incentive:** Emphasizes the "pull" of external stimuli.

- *Cognitive:* Emphasizes attributions and expectations.

Biopsychosocial Theory

- Maslow's **hierarchy of needs:** Basic physiological and survival needs must be met before higher needs, such as love and self-actualization.

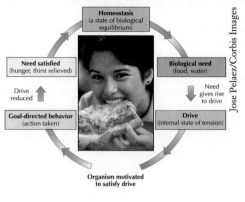

Motivation and Behavior

Hunger and Eating

- Both *biological* factors (stomach, biochemistry, brain) and *psychosocial* forces (stimulus cues and cultural conditioning) contribute to hunger and eating.

- Obesity, **anorexia nervosa**, and **bulimia nervosa** result from a combination of biological, psychological, and social factors.

1) **Obesity:** Being significantly above the recommended weight level.

2) **Anorexia nervosa:** Extreme weight loss due to self-imposed starvation.

3) **Bulimia nervosa:** Excessive consumption of food followed by purging.

Achievement

- **Achievement motivation:** Desire to excel, especially in competition with others.

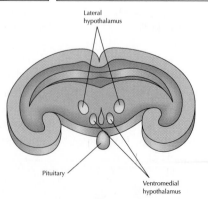

How the brain affects eating.

Theories and Concepts of Emotion

Three Basic Components of Emotion

- **Physiological (arousal):** increased heart rate, respiration
- **Cognitive (thinking):** thoughts, values, expectations
- **Behavioral (expressions):** smiles, frowns, running

Four Major Theories of Emotion

James–Lange

Our subjective experience of emotion follows our bodily arousal.

Cannon–Bard

Arousal and our subjective experience of emotion occur simultaneously.

Facial-Feedback

Movement of facial muscles elicits and/or intensifies emotions.

Schachter's Two-Factor

Emotions depend on two factors—physical arousal and cognitive labeling of that arousal.

Karen Huffman

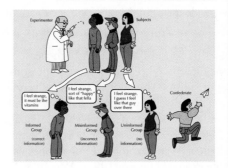

Critical Thinking about Motivation and Emotion

- **Intrinsic *vs.* extrinsic motivation:** Research shows extrinsic rewards can lower interest and achievement motivation.

- **Polygraph:** Measures changes in emotional arousal but is not valid for measuring guilt or innocence.

- **Emotional intelligence (EI):** Knowing and managing emotions, empathizing, and maintaining satisfying relationships.

- *Culture, Evolution, and Emotion:* Seven to ten basic, *universal* emotions suggest emotions may be innate; however, display rules differ across cultures.

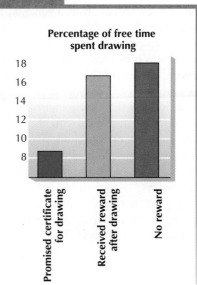

Percentage of free time spent drawing

13
Personality

Consider the following personality description. How well does it describe you?

You have a strong need for other people to like and admire you. You tend to be critical of yourself. Although you have some personality weaknesses, you are generally able to compensate for them. At times, you have serious doubts about whether you have made the right decision or done the right thing.

—Adapted from Ulrich, Stachnik, & Stainton, 1963

Does this sound like you? A high percentage of research participants who read a similar personality description reported that the description was "very accurate"—even after they were informed that it was a phony horoscope (Hyman, 1981). Other research shows that about three-quarters of adults read newspaper horoscopes and that many of them believe that astrological horoscopes were written especially for them (Halpern, 1998; Wyman & Vyse, 2008).

Why are such spurious personality assessments so popular? In part, it is because they seem to tap into our unique selves. However, the traits they supposedly reveal are characteristics that almost everyone shares. Do you know anyone who doesn't "have a strong need for other people to like and admire [them]"? The traits in horoscopes are also generally flattering, or at least neutral. Unlike the pseudopsychologies offered in supermarket tabloids, newspaper horoscopes, and Chinese fortune cookies, the descriptions presented by personality researchers are based on empirical studies. In this chapter, we examine the five most prominent theories and findings in personality research and discuss the techniques that psychologists use to assess personality.

Personality describes you as a *person:* how you are different from other people and what patterns of behavior are typical of you. You might qualify as an "extrovert," for example, if you are talkative and outgoing most of the time. Or you may be described as "conscientious" if you are responsible and self-disciplined most of the time. (Keep in mind that personality is not the same as *character*, which refers to your ethics, morals, values, and integrity.)

chievement

> **Objective 13.1:** *Differentiate personality vs. trait, and discuss early trait theories and the five-factor model.*

Personality *Unique and relatively stable pattern of thoughts, feelings, and actions*

David Trood/Stone/Getty Images

▶ **Trait Theories**   441

Early Trait Theorists
The Five-Factor Model
Evaluating Trait Theories

PSYCHOLOGY AT WORK
Personality and Your Career

RESEARCH HIGHLIGHT
Do Nonhuman Animals Have Personality?

▶ **Psychoanalytic/Psychodynamic Theories**

Freud's Psychoanalytic Theory
Neo-Freudian/Psychodynamic Theories
Evaluating Psychoanalytic Theories

▶ **Humanistic Theories**

Rogers's Theory
Maslow's Theory
Evaluating Humanistic Theories

▶ **Social-Cognitive Theories**

Bandura's and Rotter's Approaches
Evaluating Social-Cognitive Theory

▶ **Biological Theories**

Three Major Contributors
The Biopsychosocial Model

▶ **Personality Assessment**

How Do We Measure Personality?
Are Personality Measurements Accurate?

CRITICAL THINKING/ACTIVE LEARNING
Why Are Pseudo-Personality Tests So Popular?

Application

WHY STUDY PSYCHOLOGY?

Did You Know...

▶ Sigmund Freud believed that between the ages of 3 and 6, little boys develop a sexual longing for their mother and jealousy and hatred for their father?

▶ Carl Rogers believed that children raised with conditional positive regard might later have poorer mental health as adults?

▶ In the 1800s phrenologists believed personality could be measured by reading the bumps on your skull?

Cameron/Corbis Images

▶ Some measures of personality require respondents to interpret inkblots?

▶ We tend to notice and remember events that confirm our expectations and ignore those that are nonconforming?

▶ Europeans and Americans have measurable personality differences from people in Asian and African cultures?

Trait Theories

Trait *Relatively stable personal characteristic that can be used to describe someone*

The terms you use to describe other people (and yourself) are called **traits**, relatively stable personal characteristics. Trait theorists are interested in first discovering how people differ (which key traits best describe them). They then want to measure how people differ (the degree of variation in traits within the individual and among individuals).

Identifying and measuring the essential traits that distinguish individual personalities sounds much easier than it actually is. Every individual differs from others in a great number of ways.

Early Trait Theorists: Allport, Cattell, and Eysenck

> Much of our lives is spent in trying to understand others and in wishing others understood us better than they do.
>
> GORDON ALLPORT

An early study of dictionary terms found almost 18,000 words that could be used to describe personality. Of these, about 4500 were considered to fit the researchers' definition of personality *traits* (Allport & Odbert, 1936).

Faced with this enormous list of potential traits, Gordon Allport (1937) believed the best way to understand personality was to study an individual and then arrange his

Assessment

VISUAL QUIZ

1

2

3

Are you a good judge of character and personality?

Which of these three individuals is a vicious serial killer, a murderer who died by lethal injection, or the author of this text?

Answer: Photo 1: Ken Bianchi, rapist and serial killer; photo 2: Karla Faye Tucker, an executed murderer; photo 3: Karen Huffman, author of this text.

or her unique personality traits into a hierarchy. The most important and pervasive traits were listed at the top and the least important at the bottom.

Later psychologists reduced the wide array of possible personality traits with a statistical technique called **factor analysis**. Raymond Cattell (1950, 1965, 1990) condensed the list of traits to 30 to 35 basic characteristics. Hans Eysenck (1967, 1982, 1990) reduced the list even further. He described personality as a relationship among three basic types of traits—*extroversion–introversion*, *neuroticism* (tendency toward insecurity, anxiety, guilt, and moodiness), and *psychoticism* (exhibiting some qualities commonly found among psychotics). These dimensions are assessed with the *Eysenck Personality Questionnaire*.

Factor Analysis *Statistical procedure for determining the most basic units or factors in a large array of data*

The Five-Factor Model: Five Basic Personality Traits

Factor analysis was also used to develop the most talked about (and most promising) modern trait theory—the **five-factor model (FFM)** (Costa, McCrae, & Martin, 2008; McCrae & Costa, 1990, 1999; McCrae & Sutin, 2007; Wood & Bell, 2008). Combining all the previous research findings and the long list of possible personality traits, researchers discovered that several traits came up repeatedly, even when different tests were used. These five major dimensions of personality, often dubbed the "Big Five," are as follows.

Five-Factor Model (FFM) *Trait theory of personality that includes openness, conscientiousness, extroversion, agreeableness, and neuroticism*

1. *(O) Openness*. People who rate high in this factor are original, imaginative, curious, open to new ideas, artistic, and interested in cultural pursuits. Low scorers tend to be conventional, down to earth, narrower in their interests, and not artistic. [Interestingly, critical thinkers tend to score higher than others on this factor (Clifford, Boufal, & Kurtz, 2004).]

2. *(C) Conscientiousness*. This factor ranges from responsible, self-disciplined, organized, and achieving at the high end to irresponsible, careless, impulsive, lazy, and undependable at the other.

3. *(E) Extroversion*. This factor contrasts people who are sociable, outgoing, talkative, fun loving, and affectionate at the high end with introverted individuals who tend to be withdrawn, quiet, passive, and reserved.

4. *(A) Agreeableness*. Individuals who score high on this factor are good-natured, warm, gentle, cooperative, trusting, and helpful. Low scorers are irritable, argumentative, ruthless, suspicious, uncooperative, and vindictive.

5. *(N) Neuroticism (or emotional stability)*. People high on neuroticism are emotionally unstable and prone to insecurity, anxiety, guilt, worry, and moodiness. People at the other end are emotionally stable, calm, even-tempered, easygoing, and relaxed.

Study Tip

You can easily remember the five factors by noting that the first letters of each of the five-factor dimensions spell the word "ocean."

Application **Try This Yourself**

Constructing Your Own Personality Profile

Study the figure on the right, which is based on Raymond Cattell's factor analysis findings. Note how Cattell's 16 source traits exist on a continuum. There are extremes at either end, such as reserved and less intelligent at the far left and outgoing and more intelligent at the far right. Average falls somewhere in the middle.

Take a pen and make a dot on the line (from 1 to 10) that represents your own degree of reservation versus outgoingness. Then make a dot for yourself on the other 15 traits. Now connect the dots. How does your personality profile compare with the profiles of creative artists, airline pilots, and writers?

	1	10	
Reserved			Outgoing
Less intelligent			More intelligent
Affected by feelings			Emotionally stable
Submissive			Dominant
Serious			Happy-go-lucky
Expedient			Conscientious
Timid			Venturesome
Tough-minded			Sensitive
Trusting			Suspicious
Practical			Imaginative
Forthright			Shrewd
Self-assured			Apprehensive
Conservative			Experimenting
Group-dependent			Self-sufficient
Uncontrolled			Controlled
Relaxed			Tense

———— Creative artists
———— Airline pilots
———— Writers

Cattell's continuum of 16 source traits

Associated Press

Associated Press

Achievement

Objective 13.2: *What are the key research findings and criticisms of trait theories?*

Evaluating Trait Theories: The Pros and Cons

Early trait theories led to an unmanageably long list of potential personality traits, but as you will see in the "Try This Yourself" exercise, Love and the "Big Five" (p. 445), David Buss and his colleagues (1990, 1999, 2003) found strong support for the five-factor model (FFM). This may reflect an evolutionary advantage to people who are more open, conscientious, extroverted, and agreeable—and less neurotic. The evolutionary perspective also is confirmed by cross-cultural studies (Higgins, 2008; McCrae et al., 2004; Ortiz et al., 2007) and comparative studies with dogs, chimpanzees, and other species (Gosling, 2008; Gosling & John, 1999; Mehta & Gosling, 2006; Wahlgren & Lester, 2003).

Taken together, these studies suggest that the five-factor model may be a biologically based human universal. This model is the first to achieve the major goal of trait theory—to describe and organize personality characteristics using the fewest number of traits. Critics argue, however, that the great variation seen in personalities cannot be accounted for by only five traits. Furthermore, the Big Five model fails to offer *causal* explanations for these traits (Friedman & Schustack, 2006; Funder, 2000; Sollod, Monte, & Wilson, 2009). Trait theories, in general, are subject to three major criticisms:

1. **Lack of explanation**. Trait theories are good at *describing* personality. But they have difficulty *explaining* why people develop these traits or why personality traits differ across cultures. For example, cross-cultural research has found that people of almost all cultures can be reliably grouped into the FFM. However, trait theories fail to *explain* why people in cultures that are geographically close tend to have similar personalities or why Europeans and Americans tend to be higher in extroversion and openness to experience and lower in agreeableness than people in Asian and African cultures (Allik & McCrae, 2004).

2. **Stability vs. change**. Trait theorists have documented a high level of personality stability after age 30. But they haven't identified which characteristics last a lifetime and which are most likely to change (Figure 13.1).

3. **Ignoring situational effects**. Trait theorists have been criticized for ignoring the importance of situational and environmental effects. One sad example of how the environment influences personality comes from a longitudinal study of the FFM with a group of young children. Psychologists Fred Rogosch and Dante Cicchetti (2004) found that 6-year-old children who were victims of abuse and neglect scored significantly lower on the traits of openness to experience, conscientiousness, and agreeableness and higher on the trait of neuroticism than did children who were not maltreated. The children were then reassessed at ages 7, 8, and 9. Unfortunately, the traits persisted. And these maladaptive personality traits create significant liabilities that may trouble these children throughout their lifetime. More research is obviously needed to identify ways to help maltreated children—and prevent the abuse itself.

As these examples show, the situation or environment can sometimes have a powerful effect on personality. For years, a heated debate—known as "trait versus situationism" or the "person–situation controversy"—existed in psychology. After two decades of continuing debate and research, both sides seem to have won (Costa et al., 2007; Mischel, Shoda, & Ayduk, 2008). We will return to this *interactionist* position later in this and other chapters.

Figure 13.1 *Personality change over time* Have you noticed how Madonna's public image and behavior have changed over time? Cross-cultural research has found that neuroticism, extroversion, and openness to experience tend to decline from adolescence to adulthood, whereas agreeableness and conscientiousness increase (McCrae, Costa, Hrebickova, et al., 2004). How would you explain these changes? Do you think they're good or bad?

Love and the "Big Five"

Using this figure, plot your personality profile by placing a dot on each line to indicate your degree of openness, conscientiousness, and so on. Do the same for a current, previous, or prospective love partner. How do your scores compare?

Now look at the Mate Preferences chart. David Buss and his colleagues (1989, 2003a, 2003b) surveyed more than 10,000 men and women from 37 countries and found a surprising level of agreement in the characteristics that men and women value in a mate. Moreover, most of the Big Five personality traits are found at the top of the list. Both men and women prefer dependability (conscientiousness), emotional stability (low neuroticism), pleasing disposition (agreeableness), and sociability (extroversion) to the alternatives. These findings may reflect an evolutionary advantage for people who are open, conscientious, extroverted, agreeable, and free of neuroses.

Mate selection around the world

Note how the top four traits, below, are the same for both men and women, as well as how closely their desired traits match those of the five-factor model (FFM).

Source: Buss et al., "International Preferences in Selecting Mates." *Journal of Cross-Cultural Psychology*, 21, pp. 5–47, 1990. Sage Publications, Inc.

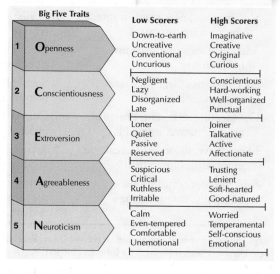

Big Five Traits	Low Scorers	High Scorers
1 **O**penness	Down-to-earth / Uncreative / Conventional / Uncurious	Imaginative / Creative / Original / Curious
2 **C**onscientiousness	Negligent / Lazy / Disorganized / Late	Conscientious / Hard-working / Well-organized / Punctual
3 **E**xtroversion	Loner / Quiet / Passive / Reserved	Joiner / Talkative / Active / Affectionate
4 **A**greeableness	Suspicious / Critical / Ruthless / Irritable	Trusting / Lenient / Soft-hearted / Good-natured
5 **N**euroticism	Calm / Even-tempered / Comfortable / Unemotional	Worried / Temperamental / Self-conscious / Emotional

♀ What Women Want in a Mate

1. Mutual attraction—love
2. Dependable character
3. Emotional stability and maturity
4. Pleasing disposition
5. Education and intelligence
6. Sociability
7. Good health
8. Desire for home and children
9. Ambition and industriousness
10. Refinement, neatness

♂ What Men Want in a Mate

1. Mutual attraction—love
2. Dependable character
3. Emotional stability and maturity
4. Pleasing disposition
5. Good health
6. Education and intelligence
7. Sociability
8. Desire for home and children
9. Refinement, neatness
10. Good looks

Purestock/Superstock

PSYCHOLOGY AT WORK

Personality and Your Career

Are some people better suited for certain jobs than others? According to psychologist John Holland's *personality–job fit theory*, a match (or "good fit") between our individual personality and our career choice is a major factor in determining job satisfaction (Holland, 1985, 1994). Holland developed a *Self-Directed Search* questionnaire that scores each person on six personality types and then matches their individual interests and abilities to the job demands of various occupations (Table 13.1). Research shows that a "good fit" between personality and occupation helps increase subjective well-being, job success, and job satisfaction. In other words, people tend to be happier and like their work when they're well matched (Borchers, 2007; Donohue, 2006; Gottfredson & Duffy, 2008; Kieffer, Schinka, & Curtiss, 2004).

Achievement

Objective 13.3: *Discuss the personality-job fit theory.*

TABLE 13.1 ARE YOU IN THE RIGHT JOB?

Personality Characteristics	Holland Personality Type	Matching/Congruent Occupation
Shy, genuine, persistent, stable, conforming, practical	1. Realistic: Prefers physical activities that require skill, strength, and coordination	Mechanic, drill press operator, assembly-line worker, farmer
Analytical, original, curious, independent	2. Investigative: Prefers activities that involve thinking, organizing, and understanding	Biologist, economist, mathematician, news reporter
Sociable, friendly, cooperative, understanding	3. Social: Prefers activities that involve helping and developing others	Social worker, counselor, teacher, clinical psychologist
Conforming, efficient, practical, unimaginative, inflexible	4. Conventional: Prefers rule-regulated, orderly, and unambiguous activities	Accountant, bank teller, file clerk, corporate manager
Imaginative, disorderly, idealistic, emotional, impractical	5. Artistic: Prefers ambiguous and unsystematic activities that allow creative expression	Painter, musician, writer, interior decorator
Self-confident, ambitious, energetic, domineering	6. Enterprising: Prefers verbal activities where there are opportunities to influence others and attain power	Lawyer, real estate agent, public relations specialist, small business manager

Reproduced by special permission of the publisher, Psychological Assessment Resources, Inc., 16204 North Florida Avenue, Lutz, Florida 33549, from the Self-Directed Search Form R by John L. Holland, Ph.D, copyright 1985. Further reproduction is prohibited without permission from PAR, Inc.

Application

RESEARCH HIGHLIGHT

Do Nonhuman Animals Have Personality?

Objective 13.4: *Summarize the research on animal personality.*

"It was exactly 33 years ago that I first met one of my oldest and dearest friends. To this day, the most outstanding aspect of her personality remains a quality I noticed the very first time I laid eyes on her: She is one of the most caring and compassionate people I know. She's also a chimpanzee" (Fouts, 2000, p. 68).

These are the words of a famous and highly respected comparative psychologist, Dr. Roger Fouts. What do you think? Do nonhuman animals have personality? Roger Fouts proposes that "like us, chimps are highly intelligent, cooperative and sometimes violent primates who nurture family bonds, adopt orphans, mourn the death of mothers, practice self-medication, struggle for power and wage war. And that only makes sense, because the chimp brain and the human brain both evolved from the same brain—that of our common ape ancestor" (Fouts, 2000, p. 68). Other scientists, however, are generally reluctant to ascribe personality traits, emotions, and cognitions to nonhuman animals, despite the often-cited statistic that humans have 98.4 percent of the same DNA as chimps.

Noting that previous studies on animal personality were scattered across multiple

Do nonhuman animals have personality?
Pet owners have long believed that their dogs and cats have unique personality traits, and recent research tends to agree with them (Fouts, 2000; Gosling, 2008). For example, when 78 dogs of all shapes and sizes were rated by both owners and strangers, a strong correlation was found on traits such as affection vs. aggression, anxiety vs. calmness, and intelligence vs. stupidity. They also found that personalities vary widely within a breed, which means that not all pit bulls are aggressive and not all labradors are affectionate (Gosling et al., 2004).

disciplines and various journals, researchers Samuel Gosling and Oliver John attempted to integrate and summarize this fragmented literature. They carefully reviewed 19 factor analytic personality studies of 12 different species: guppies, octopi,

rats, dogs, cats, pigs, donkeys, hyenas, vervet monkeys, rhesus monkeys, gorillas, and chimpanzees. To integrate the diverse, multispecies information, Gosling and John used the human five-factor model (FFM) discussed earlier. Interestingly, three human FFM dimensions—extroversion, neuroticism, and agreeableness—showed the strongest cross-species generality. How these personality traits are manifested, however, depends on the species. A human who scores low on extroversion "stays at home on Saturday night, or tries to blend into a corner at a large party. The [similarly low-scoring] octopus stays in its protective den during feedings and attempts to hide itself by changing color or releasing ink into the water" (Gosling & John, 1999, p. 70).

One nonhuman dimension was also found to be important for describing animal personality—dominance. In adult humans, dominance is part of the extroversion dimension. But dominance has a wider range of personality implications in nonhuman animals. Gosling and John explain that unlike most species, humans have multiple dominance hierarchies. The class bully may dominate on the schoolyard, the academically gifted may dominate in the classroom, and the artist may win prizes for his or her creations.

Sex differences are another area where cross-species studies provide important information. For example, research on the human FFM consistently shows that women

John Lund/Photographers Choice/Getty Images

score higher on neuroticism than men (i.e., being more emotional and prone to worry) (Chapman et al., 2007; Wu et al., 2008). However, Gosling and John found a reversal of gender differences among hyenas. It was the males that were most neurotic—being more high-strung, fearful, and nervous (Figure 13.2). They explain that, among hyenas, the female is larger and more dominant than the male. Furthermore, the hyena clan is matrilineal, with the mother recognized as the head of the family. Thus, it may be that sex differences in personality are related to the ecological niches (the place or function within the ecosystem) occupied by the two sexes in a species.

According to Gosling and John, comparative studies provide insight into the existence of nonhuman animal personality. They also offer a fresh perspective on the interplay between social and biological forces in human personality. As Roger Fouts suggested, "In the past few decades, scientific evidence on chimps and other nonhuman primates has poured in to support one basic fact: We have much more in common with apes than most people care to believe" (Fouts, 2000, p. 68)

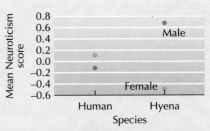

Figure 13.2 *Sex differences in standard (z) scores for neuroticism among humans and hyenas* The ratings for hyenas are from Gosling (1998). The humans were described by peers on the same rating scales used for hyenas.

Assessment

CHECK & REVIEW

Trait Theories

Objective 13.1: *Differentiate personality vs. trait, and discuss early trait theories and the five-factor model.*

Personality consists of unique and relatively stable patterns of thoughts, feelings, and actions, whereas **traits** are personal characteristics we use to describe someone. Gordon Allport described individuals by their trait hierarchy. Raymond Cattell and Hans Eysenck used **factor analysis** to identify the smallest possible number of traits. More recently, researchers identified a **five-factor model (FFM)** that can be used to describe most individuals. The five traits are *openness, conscientiousness, extroversion, agreeableness,* and *neuroticism.*

Objective 13.2: *What are the key research findings and criticisms of trait theories?*

Evolutionary research and cross-cultural studies support the five-factor model. But trait theories are subject to three major criticisms: *lack of explanation* (no explanation for why people develop certain traits and why traits sometimes change), *lack of specificity*

(no specifics provided about which early characteristics endure and which are transient), and *ignoring situational effects.*

Objective 13.3: *Discuss the personality-job fit theory.*

According John Holland, a match (or "good fit") between personality and career choice is a major factor in job satisfaction.

Objective 13.4: *Summarize the research on animal personality.*

Studies report considerable overlap between animal and human personality on three of the five factors in the FFM—extroversion, neuroticism, and agreeableness. One nonhuman dimension, dominance was important for describing animal personality. Researchers also found important cross-species sex differences.

Questions

1. A relatively stable and consistent characteristic that can be used to describe someone is known as a _____.
   (a) character; (b) trait; (c) temperament; (d) personality
2. Match the following personality descriptions with their corresponding factor from the five-factor model (FFM): (a) openness; (b) conscientiousness; (c) introversion; (d) agreeableness; (e) neuroticism
   ___i. Tending toward insecurity, anxiety, guilt, worry, and moodiness
   ___ii. Being imaginative, curious, open to new ideas, and interested in cultural pursuits
   ___iii. Being responsible, self-disciplined, organized, and high achieving
   ___iv. Tending to be withdrawn, quiet, passive, and reserved
   ___v. Being good-natured, warm, gentle, cooperative, trusting, and helpful
3. Trait theories of personality have been criticized for _____. (a) failing to explain why people develop their traits; (b) not including a large number of central traits; (c) failing to identify which traits last and which are transient; (d) not considering situational determinants of personality; (e) all but one of these options.

Check your answers in Appendix B.

Click & Review
for additional assessment options:
wiley.com/college/huffman

Psychoanalytic/Psychodynamic Theories

Achievement

Objective 13.5: *Describe Freud's psychoanalytic approach to personality.*

In contrast to trait theories that *describe* personality as it exists, *psychoanalytic* (or *psychodynamic*) theories of personality attempt to *explain* individual differences by examining how *unconscious* mental forces interplay with thoughts, feelings, and actions. The founding father of psychoanalytic theory is Sigmund Freud. We will examine Freud's theories in some detail and then briefly discuss three of his most influential followers—Alfred Adler, Carl Jung, and Karen Horney.

Freud and his famous couch Sigmund Freud (1856–1939) *was one of the most influential personality theorists. He also developed a major form of therapy (known as psychoanalysis) and treated many patients in the office pictured here.*

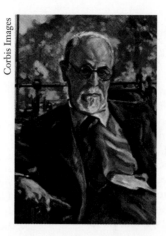

Corbis Images

AP/Wide World

Conscious *In Freudian terms, thoughts or motives that a person is currently aware of or is remembering*

Preconscious *Freud's term for thoughts, motives, or memories that can voluntarily be brought to mind*

Unconscious *Freud's term for thoughts, motives, and memories blocked from normal awareness*

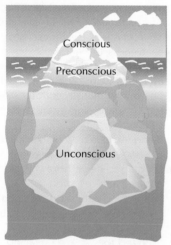

Conscious

Preconscious

Unconscious

Figure 13.3 *Freud's three levels of consciousness* Although Freud never used the analogy himself, his levels of awareness are often compared to an iceberg. The tip of the iceberg would be analogous to the *conscious* mind, which is above the water and open to easy inspection. The preconscious (the area only shallowly submerged) contains information that can be viewed with a little extra effort. The large base of the iceberg is somewhat like the *unconscious* mind, completely hidden from personal inspection. Using this Freudian idea of "levels of awareness," at this moment your conscious mind is hopefully focusing on this text. But your preconscious may include feelings of hunger and thoughts of friends you need to contact. Any repressed sexual desires, aggressive impulses, or irrational thoughts and feelings are reportedly stored in your unconscious.

▣ Freud's Psychoanalytic Theory: Four Key Concepts

Who is the best-known figure in all of psychology? Most people immediately name Sigmund Freud. Even before you studied psychology, you probably came across his name in other courses. Freud's theories have been applied in the fields of anthropology, sociology, religion, medicine, art, and literature. Working from about 1890 until he died in 1939, Freud developed a theory of personality that has been one of the most influential—and, at the same time, most controversial—in all of science (Dufresne, 2007; Heller, 2005; Sollod, Monte, & Wilson, 2009).

In discussing Freud's theory, we will focus on four of his key concepts: *levels of consciousness, personality structure, defense mechanisms,* and *psychosexual stages of development.*

Levels of Consciousness

Freud called the mind the *psyche* [sie-KEY] and believed that it functioned on three levels of awareness or consciousness—**conscious, preconscious,** and **unconscious** (Figure 13.3). According to Freud, the all-important unconscious stores our primitive, instinctual motives, plus anxiety-laden thoughts and memories blocked from normal awareness. Freud believed the unconscious is hidden from our personal awareness (Figure 13.4). But it still has an enormous impact on our behavior—and reveals

"Good morning, beheaded—uh, I mean beloved."

Figure 13.4 *Freudian slips* Freud believed that a small slip of the tongue (known as a "Freudian slip") can reflect unconscious feelings that we normally keep hidden.

itself despite our intentions. Just as the enormous mass of iceberg below the surface destroyed the ocean liner *Titanic*, the unconscious may similarly damage our psychological lives. Freud believed that most psychological disorders originate from repressed (hidden) memories and instincts (sexual and aggressive) stored in the unconscious. To treat these disorders, Freud developed *psychoanalysis* (Chapter 15).

Personality Structure

In addition to proposing that the mind functions at three levels of awareness, Freud believed personality was composed of three interacting mental structures: *id*, *ego*, and *superego*. Each of these structures resides, fully or partially, in the unconscious mind (Figure 13.5). (Keep in mind that the id, ego, and superego are mental concepts—or hypothetical constructs. They are not physical structures you could see if you dissected a human brain.)

The Id According to Freud, the **id** is made up of innate, biological instincts and urges. It is immature, impulsive, irrational, and totally unconscious. When its primitive drives build up, the id seeks immediate gratification to relieve the tension. Thus, the id operates on the **pleasure principle**, the immediate and uninhibited seeking of pleasure and the avoidance of discomfort. In other words, the ID is like a newborn baby. It wants what it wants when it wants it!

The Ego As the child grows older, the second part of the psyche, the **ego**, supposedly develops. The ego is responsible for planning, problem solving, reasoning, and controlling the id. Unlike the id, which lies entirely in the unconscious, the ego resides primarily in the conscious and preconscious. In Freud's system, the ego corresponds to the self—our conscious identity of ourselves as persons.

One of the ego's tasks is to channel and release the id's energy in ways that are compatible with the external environment. Contrary to the id's *pleasure principle*, the ego operates on the **reality principle**. This means the ego is responsible for delaying gratification until it is practical or appropriate.

The Superego The final part of the psyche to develop is the **superego**. This inner voice, sometimes known as your "conscience," is supposedly made up of a set of ethical standards or rules for behavior that resides primarily in the preconscious and unconscious. The superego develops from internalized parental and societal standards. Some Freudian followers have suggested that it operates on the **morality principle** because violating its rules results in feelings of guilt.

Defense Mechanisms

What happens when the ego fails to satisfy both the id and the superego? Anxiety slips into conscious awareness. Because anxiety is uncomfortable, people avoid it through **defense mechanisms**, which satisfy the id and superego by distorting reality. An alcoholic who uses his paycheck to buy drinks (a message from the id) may feel very guilty (a response from the superego). He may reduce this conflict by telling himself that he deserves a drink for working so hard. This is an example of the defense mechanism of *rationalization*.

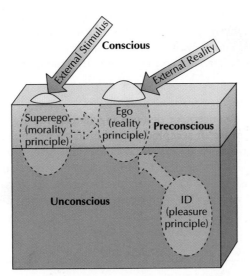

Figure 13.5 *Freud's personality structure* According to Freud, personality is composed of three structures—the *id*, *ego*, and *superego*. The id operates on the *pleasure principle*, the ego operates on the *reality principle*, and the superego is guided by the *morality principle*. Note how the ego is primarily conscious and preconscious, whereas the id is entirely unconscious.

Id *According to Freud, the source of instinctual energy, which works on the pleasure principle and is concerned with immediate gratification*

Pleasure Principle *In Freud's theory, the principle on which the id operates—seeking immediate pleasure*

Ego *In Freud's theory, the rational part of the psyche that deals with reality by controlling the id, while also satisfying the superego; from the Latin term ego, meaning "I"*

Reality Principle *According to Freud, the principle on which the conscious ego operates as it tries to meet the demands of the id and superego and the realities of the environment*

Superego *In Freud's theory, the "conscience" or part of the personality that incorporates parental and societal standards for morality*

Morality Principle *The principle on which the superego may operate, which results in feelings of guilt if its rules are violated*

Defense Mechanisms *In Freudian theory, the ego's protective method of reducing anxiety by distorting reality*

Freudian theory in action? *What might the id, ego, and superego be saying during this flirtation?*

LWA-Dann Tardiff/Corbis

wiley.com/
college/
huffman

Repression *Freud's first and most basic defense mechanism, which blocks unacceptable impulses from coming into awareness*

Although Freud described many kinds of defense mechanisms (Table 13.2), he believed repression was the most important. **Repression** is the mechanism by which the ego prevents the most anxiety-provoking or unacceptable thoughts and feelings from entering consciousness. It is the first and most basic form of anxiety reduction.

Psychosexual Stages of Development

Psychosexual Stages *In Freudian theory, five developmental periods (oral, anal, phallic, latency, and genital) during which particular kinds of pleasures must be gratified if personality development is to proceed normally*

The concept of defense mechanisms has generally withstood the test of time. And they are an accepted part of modern psychology (e.g., Chapter 3). This is not the case for Freud's theory of psychosexual stages of development.

According to Freud, strong biological urges residing within the id supposedly push all children through five universal **psychosexual stages** during the first 12 or so years of life—oral, anal, phallic, latency, and genital (Process Diagram 13.1). The

SUMMARY TABLE 13.2 SAMPLE PSYCHOLOGICAL DEFENSE MECHANISMS

Defense Mechanism	Description	Example
Repression	Preventing painful or unacceptable thoughts from entering consciousness	Forgetting the details of your parent's painful death
Sublimation	Redirecting unmet desires or unacceptable impulses into acceptable activities	Rechanneling sexual desires into school, work, art, sports, hobbies that are constructive
Denial	Protecting oneself from an unpleasant reality by refusing to perceive it	Alcoholics refusing to admit their addiction
Rationalization	Substituting socially acceptable reasons for unacceptable ones	Justifying cheating on an exam by saying "everyone else does it"
Intellectualization	Ignoring the emotional aspects of a painful experience by focusing on abstract thoughts words, or ideas	Emotionless discussion of your divorce while ignoring underlying pain
Projection	Transferring unacceptable thoughts, motives, or impulses to others	Becoming unreasonably jealous of your mate while denying your own attraction to others
Reaction formation	Refusing to acknowledge unacceptable urges, thoughts, or feelings by exaggerating the opposite state	Promoting a petition against adult bookstores even though you are secretly fascinated by pornography
Regression	Responding to a threatening situation in a way appropriate to an earlier age or level of development	Throwing a temper tantrum when a friend doesn't want to do what you'd like
Displacement	Redirecting impulses toward a less threatening person or object	Yelling at a coworker after being criticized by your boss

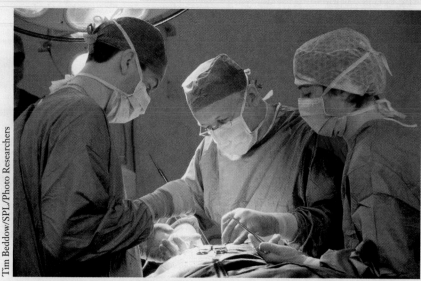

Tim Beddow/SPL/Photo Researchers

Is it bad to use defense mechanisms? *Although defense mechanisms do distort reality, some misrepresentation seems to be necessary for our psychological well being (Marshall & Brown, 2008; Wenger & Fowers, 2008). During a gruesome surgery, for example, physicians and nurses may* **intellectualize** *the procedure as an unconscious way of dealing with their personal anxieties. Can you see how focusing on highly objective technical aspects of the situation might help these people avoid becoming emotionally overwhelmed by the potentially tragic circumstances they often encounter?*

Freud's Five Psychosexual Stages of Development

Objective 13.6: *Summarize Freud's five psychosexual stages.*

Name of Stage (Approximate age)	Erogenous Zone (Key Conflict or Developmental Task)		Supposed Symptoms of Fixation and/ or Regression
Oral (0–18 months)	**Mouth** (Weaning from breast or bottle)		Overindulgence reportedly contributes to gullibility ("swallowing" anything), dependence, and passivity. Underindulgence causes aggressiveness, sadism, and a tendency to exploit others. Freud also believed orally fixated adults may orient their lives around their mouths—overeating, becoming alcoholic, smoking, or talking a great deal.
Anal (18 months–3 years)	**Anus** (Toilet training)		Fixation or regression supposedly leads to highly controlled and compulsively neat (anal-retentive) personality, or messy, disorderly, rebellious, and destructive (anal-expulsive) personality.
Phallic (3–6 years)	**Genitals** (Overcoming the Oedipus Complex by identifying with same-sex parent)		According to Freud, unresolved, sexual longing for the opposite-sex parent can lead to long-term resentment and hostility toward the same-sex parent. Freud also believed that boys develop an **Oedipus complex,** or attraction to their mothers. He thought that young girls develop an attachment to their fathers and harbor hostile feelings towards their mothers, whom they blame for their lack of a penis. According to Freud most girls never overcome *penis envy* or give up their rivalry with their mothers, which causes enduring moral inferiority.
Latency (6 years–puberty)	**None** (Interacting with same-sex peers)		The latency stage is a reported period of sexual "dormancy." Children do not have particular psychosexual conflicts that must be resolved during this period.
Genital (puberty–adult)	**Genitals** (Establishing intimate relationships with the opposite sex)		Unsuccessful outcomes at this stage, supposedly may lead to sexual relationships based only on lustful desires, not on respect and commitment.

Psychosexual Development

Oedipus [ED-uh-puss] Complex *Period of conflict during the phallic stage when children are supposedly attracted to the opposite-sex parent and hostile toward the same-sex parent*

Michael Newman/PhotoEdit

The oral stage? Is this an example of Freud's earliest stage of psychosexual development, or just a part of all infants' normal sucking behaviors?

Inferiority Complex *Adler's idea that feelings of inferiority develop from early childhood experiences of helplessness and incompetence*

Collective Unconscious *Jung's concept of a reservoir of inherited, universal experiences that all humans share*

Archetypes [AR-KEH-types] *According to Jung, the images and patterns of thoughts, feelings, and behavior that reside in the collective unconscious*

term *psychosexual* reflects Freud's emphasis on *infantile sexuality*—his belief that children experience sexual feelings from birth (although in different forms from those of adolescents or adults).

At each psychosexual stage, the id's impulses and social demands come into conflict. Therefore, if a child's needs are not met, or are overindulged, at one particular stage, the child may *fixate* and a part of the personality will remain stuck at that stage. Most individuals successfully pass through each of the five stages. But during stressful times, they may return (or *regress*) to an earlier stage in which earlier needs were badly frustrated or overgratified.

Neo-Freudian/Psychodynamic Theories: Revising Freud's Ideas

Some initial followers of Freud later rebelled and proposed theories of their own. Three of the most influential of these *neo-Freudians* were Alfred Adler, Carl Jung, and Karen Horney.

Adler's Individual Psychology

Alfred Adler (1870–1937) was the first to leave Freud's inner circle. Instead of seeing behavior as motivated by unconscious forces, he believed that it is purposeful and goal-directed. According to Adler's *individual psychology*, we are motivated by our goals in life—especially our goals of obtaining security and overcoming feelings of inferiority.

Adler believed that almost everyone suffers from an **inferiority complex**, or deep feelings of inadequacy and incompetence that arise from our feelings of helplessness as infants. According to Adler, these early feelings result in a "will-to-power" that can take one of two paths. It can either cause children to strive to develop superiority over others through dominance, aggression, or expressions of envy, or—more positively—it can cause children to develop their full potential and creativity and to gain mastery and control in their lives (Adler, 1964, 1998) (Figure 13.6).

Jung's Analytical Psychology

Associated Press

Another early Freud follower turned dissenter, Carl Jung (pronounced "YOONG"), developed *analytical psychology*. Like Freud, Jung (1875–1961) emphasized unconscious processes, but he believed that the unconscious contains positive and spiritual motives as well as sexual and aggressive forces.

Jung also thought that we have two forms of unconscious mind: the personal unconscious and the collective unconscious. The *personal unconscious* is created from our individual experiences, whereas the **collective unconscious** is identical in each person and is inherited (Jung, 1946, 1959, 1969). The collective unconscious consists of primitive images and patterns of thought, feeling, and behavior that Jung called **archetypes** (Figure 13.7).

Because of archetypal patterns in the collective unconscious, we perceive and react in certain predictable ways. One set of archetypes refers

Figure 13.6 *Adler's upside to feelings of inferiority?* Adler suggested that the will-to-power could be positively expressed through social interest—identifying with others and cooperating with them for the social good. Can you explain how these volunteers might be fulfilling their will-to-power interest?

Figure 13.7 *Jung's Archetypes in the collective unconscious* According to Jung, the collective unconscious is the ancestral memory of the human race, which explains the similarities in religion, art, symbolism, and dream imagery across cultures, such as the repeated symbol of the snake in ancient Egyptian tomb painting and early Australian aboriginal bark painting.

to gender roles (Chapter 11). Jung claimed that both males and females have patterns for feminine aspects of personality (anima) and masculine aspects of personality (animus), which allow us to express both masculine and feminine personality traits and to understand the opposite sex.

Horney's "Blended" Psychology

Like Adler and Jung, psychoanalyst Karen Horney (pronounced "HORN-eye") was an influential follower of Freud's, who later came to reject major aspects of Freudian theory. She is remembered mostly for having developed a creative blend of Freudian, Adlerian, and Jungian theory, with added concepts of her own (Horney, 1939, 1945) (Figure 13.8).

Horney is also known for her theories of personality development. She believed that adult personality was shaped by the child's relationship to the parents—not by fixation at some stage of psychosexual development, as Freud argued. Horney believed that a child whose needs were not met by nurturing parents would experience extreme feelings of helplessness and insecurity. How people respond to this **basic anxiety** greatly determines emotional health.

According to Horney, everyone searches for security in one of three ways: We can move toward people (by seeking affection and acceptance from others); we can move away from people (by striving for independence, privacy, and self-reliance); or we can move against people (by trying to gain control and power over others). Emotional health requires a balance among these three styles.

Evaluating Psychoanalytic Theories: Criticisms and Enduring Influence

In this section, we look at major criticisms of Freud's psychoanalytic theories, as well as the reasons Freud has had such an enormous influence in the field of psychology. Today there are few Freudian purists. Instead, modern psychodynamic theorists and psychoanalysts use empirical methods and research findings to reformulate and refine traditional Freudian thinking (Knekt et al., 2008; Shaver & Mikulincer, 2005; Tryon, 2008; Westen, 1998).

But wrong as he was on many counts, Freud still ranks as one of the giants of psychology (Heller, 2005; Schülein, 2007; Sollod, Monte, & Wilson, 2009). Furthermore,

Figure 13.8 *Karen Horney (1885–1952)* Horney argued that most of Freud's ideas about female personality reflected male biases and misunderstanding. She contended, for example, that Freud's concept of penis envy reflected women's feelings of cultural inferiority, not biological inferiority—*power envy*, not penis envy.

Basic Anxiety *According to Horney, the feelings of helplessness and insecurity that adults experience because as children they felt alone and isolated in a hostile environment*

Achievement

Objective 13.8: *Discuss the major criticisms of psychoanalytic theories of personality.*

PEANUTS reprinted by permission of United Features Syndicate, Inc.

Freud's impact on Western intellectual history cannot be overstated. He attempted to explain dreams, religion, social groupings, family dynamics, neurosis, psychosis, humor, the arts, and literature.

It's easy to criticize Freud if you don't remember that he began his work at the start of the twentieth century and lacked the benefit of modern research findings and technology. We can only imagine how our current theories will look 100 years from now. Right or wrong, Freud has a lasting place among the pioneers in psychology (Table 13.3).

TABLE 13.3 EVALUATING PSYCHOANALYTIC THEORIES

Criticisms	Enduring influences
• ***Difficult to test.*** From a scientific perspective, a major problem with psychoanalytic theory is that most of its concents—such as the id or unconscious conflicts—cannot be empirically tested (Domhoff, 2004; Esterson, 2002; Friedman & Schustack, 2006).	• His emphasis on the unconscious and its influence on behavior.
• ***Overemphasizes biology and unconscious forces.*** Modern psychologists believe that Freud did not give sufficient attention to learning and culture in shaping behavior.	• The conflict among the id, ego, and superego and the resulting defense mechanisms.
• ***Inadequate empirical support.*** Freud based his theories almost exclusively on the subjective case histories of his adult patients. Moreover, Freud's patients represented a small and selective sample of humanity: upper-class women in Vienna (Freud's home) who had serious adjustment problems.	• Encouraging open talk about sex in Victorian times. • The development of psychoanalysis, an influential form of therapy. • The sheer magnitude of his theory.
• ***Sexism.*** Many psychologists (beginning with Karen Horney) reject Freud's theories as derogatory toward women.	
• ***Lack of cross-cultural support.*** The Freudian concepts that ought to be most easily supported empirically—the biological determinants of personality—are generally not borne out by cross-cultural studies.	

Granger Collection

Freud and his daughter *Despite criticisms of sexism, psycho-analysis was one of the few areas where women gained prominent positions in the early twentieth century. Here Freud is walking with his daughter Anna Freud (1895–1982), who also became an influential psychoanalyst.*

Assessment

STOP CHECK & REVIEW

Psychoanalytic/Psychodynamic Theories

Objective 13.5: *Describe Freud's psycho-analytic approach to personality.*

Sigmund Freud founded the psycho-analytic approach to personality, which emphasizes the power of the unconscious. The mind (or psyche) reportedly functions on three levels of awareness (**conscious**, **preconscious**, and **unconscious**). Similarly, the personality has three distinct structures (**id**, **ego**, and **superego**). The ego struggles to meet the demands of both the id and superego. When these demands conflict, the ego may resort to **defense mechanisms** to relieve anxiety.

Objective 13.6: *Summarize Freud's five psychosexual stages.*

According to Freud, all human beings pass through five **psychosexual stages**: oral, anal, phallic, latency, and genital. How specific conflicts at each of these stages are resolved is important to personality development.

Objective 13.7: *Compare Freud's vs. the neo-Freudian approaches to personality.*

Three influential followers of Freud who later broke with him were Alfred Adler, Carl Jung, and Karen Horney. Known as neo-Freudians, they emphasized different issues. Adler emphasized the **inferiority complex** and the compensating will-to-power. Jung introduced the **collective unconscious** and **archetypes**. Horney stressed the importance of **basic anxiety** and refuted Freud's idea of penis envy, replacing it with power envy.

Objective 13.8: *Discuss the major criticisms of psychoanalytic theories of personality.*

Critics of the psychoanalytic approach, especially Freud's theories, argue that the approach is difficult to test, overemphasizes biology and unconscious forces, has inadequate empirical support, is sexist, and lacks cross-cultural support. Despite these criticisms, Freud remains a notable pioneer in psychology.

Questions

1. Using the analogy of an iceberg, explain Freud's three levels of consciousness.
2. The _____ operates on the pleasure principle, seeking immediate gratification. The _____ operates on the reality principle, and the _____ contains the conscience and operates on the morality principle. (a) psyche, ego, id; (b) id, ego, superego; (c) conscious, preconscious, unconscious; (d) oral stage; anal stage; phallic stage
3. Briefly describe Freud's five psychosexual stages.
4. Match the following concepts with the appropriate theorist: Adler, Jung, or Horney:
   a. inferiority complex: _____
   b. power envy: _____
   c. collective unconscious: _____
   d. basic anxiety: _____

Check your answers in Appendix B.

 Click & Review for additional assessment options: wiley.com/college/huffman

---

Humanistic Theories

Achievement

Objective 13.9: *Discuss humanistic theories of personality, comparing the approaches of Rogers and Maslow.*

Humanistic theories of personality emphasize internal experiences—feelings and thoughts—and the individual's own feelings of basic worth. In contrast to Freud's generally negative view of human nature, humanists believe people are naturally good (or, at worst, neutral). And that they possess a positive drive toward self-fulfillment.

According to this view, our personality and behavior depend on how we perceive and interpret the world, not on traits, unconscious impulses, or rewards and punishments. To fully understand another human being, you must know how he or she perceives the world. Humanistic psychology was developed largely by Carl Rogers and Abraham Maslow.

Self-Concept *Rogers's term for all the information and beliefs individuals have about their own nature, qualities, and behavior*

Rogers's Theory: The Importance of the Self

To psychologist Carl Rogers (1902–1987), the most important component of personality is the *self*—what a person comes to identify as "I" or "me." Today, Rogerians (followers of Rogers) use the term **self-concept** to refer to all the information and beliefs you have regarding your own nature, unique qualities, and typical behaviors. Rogers believed poor mental health and maladjustment developed from a mismatch, or incongruence, between the self-concept and actual life experiences (Figure 13.9).

Corbis Images

Carl Rogers (1902–1987) *As a founder of humanistic psychology, Rogers emphasized the importance of the self-concept. He believed our personality and individual self-esteem are heavily influenced by early childhood experiences, such as whether we received unconditional positive regard from our adult caregivers.*

 wiley.com/college/huffman

©Masterfile

Figure 13.9 *Congruence, Mental Health, and Self-Esteem* According to Carl Rogers, mental health and adjustment are related to the degree of congruence between a person's self-concept and life experiences. He argued that self-esteem—how we feel about ourselves—is particularly dependent on this congruence. Can you see how an artistic child would likely have higher self-esteem if her family valued art than if they did not?

Congruence

Experience

Self-concept

Well-adjusted individual
Considerable overlap between
self-concept and experience

Incongruence

Self-concept   Experience

Poorly adjusted individual
Little overlap between
self-concept and experience

Dear diary,
Sorry to
bother you again.

LOW SELF-ESTEEM

© The New Yorker Collection 1996 Mike Twohy
from cartoonbank.com. All Rights Reserved.

**Unconditional Positive
Regard** *Rogers's term for love and
acceptance with no contingencies attached*

PhotoDisc Green/Getty Images

Mental Health, Congruence, and Self-Esteem

According to Rogers, there is an intimate connection among mental health, congruence, and *self-esteem*—how we feel about ourselves. If our self-concept is congruent with (or matches) our life experiences, we generally have high self-esteem and better mental health. For example, an athletic child living in a family in which athletics are highly valued would have a better chance at higher self-esteem and better mental health than an artistic child in a family in which the arts aren't valued.

Mental health, congruence, and self-esteem are believed to be part of our innate biological capacities. All of us are born into the world with an innate need to survive, grow, and enhance ourselves. We naturally approach and value people and experiences that enhance our growth and fulfillment and avoid those that do not. Therefore, Rogers believed we can—and should—trust our own internal feelings to guide us toward mental health and happiness.

If everyone has an inborn, positive drive toward self-fulfillment, why do some people have low self-esteem and poor mental health? Rogers believed these outcomes generally result from early childhood experiences with parents and other adults who make their love and acceptance contingent on behaving in certain ways and expressing only certain feelings. If the child learns that his negative feelings and behaviors (which we all have) are totally unacceptable and unlovable, his self-concept and self-esteem may become distorted. He may always doubt the love and approval of others because they don't know "the real person hiding inside" (Figure 13.10).

Unconditional Positive Regard

To help children develop their fullest potential, adults need to create an atmosphere of **unconditional positive regard**. That is, a setting in which children realize that they are loved and accepted with no conditions or strings attached.

Some people mistakenly believe that, unconditional positive regard means we should allow people to do whatever they please. But humanists separate the value of the person from his or her behaviors. They accept the person's positive nature and basic worth, while discouraging destructive or hostile behaviors. Hitting a playmate or yelling at a sales clerk is contrary to the child's or adult's positive nature as well as offensive to others.

Humanistic psychologists encourage children and adults to control their behavior so that they can develop a healthy self-concept and healthy relationships with others. In the example in Figure 13.10, they would encourage the adult to say, "I know you're angry with your sister, but we don't hit. You won't be allowed to play with her for a while if you can't control your anger."

Figure 13.10 *Conditional love?* If a child is angry and hits his younger sister, some parents might punish the child or deny his anger, saying, "Nice children don't hit their sisters, they love them!" To gain parental approval, the child has to deny his true feelings of anger, but inside he secretly suspects he is not a "nice boy" because he did hit his sister and (at that moment) did not love her. How might repeated incidents of this type have a lasting effect on someone's self-esteem? What would be a more appropriate response to the child's behavior that acknowledges that it is the behavior that is unacceptable, not the child that is unacceptable?

Maslow's Theory: The Search for Self-Actualization

Like Rogers, Abraham Maslow believed there is a basic goodness to human nature and a natural tendency toward self-actualization. He saw personality as the quest to fulfill basic physiological needs and then move upward toward the highest level of self-actualization (Figure 13.11).

According to Maslow, **self-actualization** is the inborn drive to develop all one's talents and capacities. It involves understanding one's own potential, accepting oneself and others as unique individuals, and taking a problem-centered approach to life situations (Maslow, 1970). Self-actualization is an ongoing *process* of growth rather than an end *product* or accomplishment—more a road to travel than a final destination.

Maslow believed that only a few, rare individuals, such as Albert Einstein, Mohandas Gandhi, and Eleanor Roosevelt, become fully self-actualized. However, he saw self-actualization as part of every person's basic hierarchy of needs. (See Chapter 12 for more information on Maslow's theory.)

Evaluating Humanistic Theories: Three Major Criticisms

Humanistic psychology was extremely popular during the 1960s and 1970s. It was a refreshing new perspective on personality after the negative determinism of the psychoanalytic approach and the mechanical nature of learning theories. Although this early popularity has declined, many humanistic ideas have been incorporated into approaches for counseling and psychotherapy (Bozarth & Brodley, 2008; Kirschenbaum & Jourdan, 2005).

Ironically, the strength of the humanists, their focus on positivism and subjective self experiences, is also why humanistic theories have been sharply criticized (e.g., Funder, 2000). Three of the most important criticisms are:

1. *Naive assumptions*. Critics suggest that the humanists are unrealistic, romantic, and even naive about human nature (Figure 13.12).

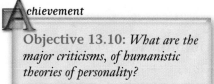

Achievement

Objective 13.10: *What are the major criticisms, of humanistic theories of personality?*

Self-Actualization *Maslow's term for the inborn drive to develop all one's talents and capabilities*

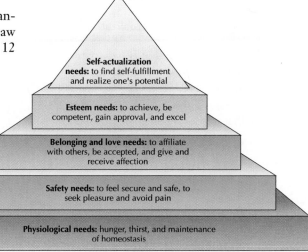

Figure 13.11 *Maslow's hierarchy of needs* According to Maslow, basic physical necessities must be satisfied before higher-growth needs can be addressed.

Dana Fradon/The Cartoon Bank.Inc.

"We do pretty well when you stop to think that people are basically good."

2. ***Poor testability and inadequate evidence.*** Like many psychoanalytic terms and concepts, humanistic concepts (such as unconditional positive regard and self-actualization) are difficult to define operationally and test scientifically.

3. ***Narrowness.*** Like trait theories, humanistic theories have been criticized for merely describing personality, rather than explaining it. For example, where does the motivation for self-actualization come from? To say that it is an "inborn drive" doesn't satisfy those who favor experimental research and hard data as the way to learn about personality.

Figure 13.12 *Are people inherently good?* Mankind's continuing history of murders, warfare, and other acts of aggression suggests otherwise.

Assessment

STOP

CHECK & REVIEW

Humanistic Theories

Objective 13.9: *Discuss humanistic theories of personality, comparing the approaches of Rogers and Maslow.*

Humanistic theories focus on internal experiences (thoughts and feelings) and the individual's **self-concept**. Carl Rogers emphasized mental health, congruence, self-esteem, and **unconditional positive regard**. Abraham Maslow emphasized the potential for **self-actualization**.

Objective 13.10: *What are the major criticisms of humanistic theories of personality?*

Critics of the humanistic approach argue that these theories are based on naive assumptions and are not scientifically testable or well supported by empirical evidence. In addition, their focus on description, rather than explanation, makes them narrow.

Questions

1. If you took the _____ approach to personality, you would emphasize internal experiences, like feelings and thoughts, and the basic worth of the individual. (a) humanistic; (b) psychodynamic; (c) personalistic; (d) motivational

2. Rogers thought that _____ is necessary for a child's uniqueness and positive self-concept to unfold naturally. (a) permissive parenting; (b) a challenging environment; (c) unconditional positive regard; (d) a friendly neighborhood

3. Abraham Maslow's belief that all people are motivated toward personal growth and development is known as _____.

4. What are three major criticisms of humanistic theories?

Check your answers in Appendix B.

Click & Review
for additional assessment options:
wiley.com/college/huffman

Achievement

Objective 13.11: *Discuss the social-cognitive perspective on personality, comparing Bandura and Rotter's approaches.*

Social-Cognitive Theories

According to the social-cognitive perspective, each of us has a unique personality because of our individual history of interactions with the environment and because we *think* about the world and interpret what happens to us (Cervone & Shoda, 1999). Two of the most influential social-cognitive theorists are Albert Bandura and Julian Rotter.

Bandura's and Rotter's Approaches: Social Learning Plus Cognitive Processes

Bandura's Self-Efficacy and Reciprocal Determinism

Although Albert Bandura is perhaps best known for his work on observational learning or social learning (Chapter 6), he has also played a major role in reintroducing thought processes into personality theory. Cognition is central to his concept of **self-efficacy**, which refers to a person's learned expectation of success (Bandura, 1997, 2000, 2006, 2008).

How do you generally perceive your ability to select, influence, and control the circumstances of your life? According to Bandura, if you have a strong sense of self-efficacy, you believe you can generally succeed, regardless of past failures and current obstacles. Your self-efficacy will in turn affect the challenges you accept and the effort you expend in reaching goals.

Doesn't such a belief also affect how others respond to you and thereby affect your chances for success? Precisely! This type of mutual interaction and influence is a core part of another major concept of Bandura's—**reciprocal determinism**. According to Bandura, our cognitions (or thoughts), behaviors, and the environment are interdependent and interactive (Figure 13.13). Thus, a cognition ("I can succeed") will affect behaviors ("I will work hard and ask for a promotion"), which in turn will affect the environment ("My employer recognized my efforts and promoted me.").

Rotter's Locus of Control

Julian Rotter's theory is similar to Bandura's. He believes that prior learning experiences create *cognitive expectancies* that guide behavior and influence the environment (Rotter, 1954, 1990). According to Rotter, your behavior or personality is determined by (1) what you *expect* to happen following a specific action and (2) the *reinforcement value* attached to specific outcomes—that is, the degree to which you prefer one reinforcer to another.

To understand your personality and behavior, for instance, Rotter would use personality tests that measure your internal versus external *locus of control* (Chapter 3). These tests ask people to respond "true" or "false" to a series of statements, such as "People get ahead in this world primarily by luck and connections rather than by hard work and perseverance" or "When someone doesn't like you, there is little you can do about it."

As you may suspect, people with an *external locus of control* think environment and external forces have primary control over their lives. Conversely, *internals* think they can control events in their lives through their own efforts (Figure 13.14).

Self-Efficacy *Bandura's term for a person's learned expectation of success*

Reciprocal Determinism *Bandura's belief that cognitions, behaviors, and the environment interact to produce personality*

William Thomas Gain/Getty Images Newsand Sport Services

Self-efficacy in action *Research shows that self-defense training has significant effects on improving women's belief that they could escape from or disable a potential assailant or rapist (Weitlauf et al., 2001). But Bandura stresses that self-efficacy is always specific to the situation. For example, women who took this course reported greater self-defense efficacy, but this increased efficacy did not transfer over to other areas of their lives.*

Figure 13.13 ***Albert Bandura's theory of reciprocal determinism*** According to Bandura, thoughts (or cognitions), behavior, and the environment all interact to produce personality.

© The New Yorker Collection 1997 Mike Twohy from cartoonbank.com. All Rights Reserved.

"We're encouraging people to become involved in their own rescue."

Figure 13.14 ***Locus of control*** Despite the sarcasm of this cartoon, research links possession of an internal locus of control with higher achievement and better mental health (Burns, 2008; Jones, 2008; Ruthig et al., 2007).

Achievement

Objective 13.12: *What are the major strengths and weaknesses of the social-cognitive theories?*

Evaluating Social-Cognitive Theory: The Pluses and Minuses

The social-cognitive perspective holds several attractions. First, it emphasizes how the environment affects, and is affected by, individuals. Second, it meets most standards for scientific research. It offers testable, objective hypotheses and operationally defined terms and relies on empirical data for its basic principles. Critics, however, believe social-cognitive theory is too narrow. It also has been criticized for ignoring unconscious, environmental, and emotional aspects of personality (Mischel, Shoda, & Ayduk, 2008; Westen, 1998). For example, certain early experiences might have prompted a person to develop an external locus of control.

Both Bandura's and Rotter's theories emphasize cognition and social learning, but they are a long way from a strict behaviorist theory, which suggests that only environmental forces control behavior. They are also a long way from the biological theories that say inborn, innate qualities determine behavior and personality. Biological theories are the topic of our next section.

Assessment

STOP

CHECK & REVIEW

Social-Cognitive Theories

Objective 13.11: *Discuss the social-cognitive perspective on personality, comparing Bandura and Rotter's approaches.*

Social-cognitive theorists emphasize the importance of our interactions with the environment and how we interpret and respond to these external events. Albert Bandura's social-cognitive approach focuses on **self-efficacy** and **reciprocal determinism**. Julian Rotter emphasizes cognitive expectancies and an internal or external locus of control.

Objective 13.12: *What are the major strengths and weaknesses of the social-cognitive theories?*

Social-cognitive theories are credited for their attention to environmental influences

and their scientific standards. However, they have been criticized for their narrow focus and lack of attention to the unconscious, environmental, and emotional components of personality.

Questions

1. The social-cognitive approach to personality emphasizes _____.

2. Bandura's theory of _____ (see figure above) suggests that cognitions,

behavior, and the environment all interact to produce personality. (a) reciprocal determinism; (b) interactionism; (c) confluence theory; (d) reverberating circuits theory

3. According to Bandura, _____ involves a person's belief about whether he or she can successfully engage in behaviors related to personal goals. (a) self-actualization; (b) self-esteem; (c) self-efficacy; (d) self-congruence

4. People with an _____ believe the environment and external forces control events, whereas those with an _____ believe in personal control.

Check your answers in Appendix B.

Click & Review
for additional assessment options:
wiley.com/college/huffman

Biological Theories

Achievement

Objective 13.13: *How does biology contribute to personality?*

As you were growing up, you probably heard comments such as "You're just like your father" or "You're so much like your mother." Does this mean that biological factors you inherited from your parents were the major contributors to your personality? This is the question we first explore in this section. We conclude with a discussion of how all theories of personality ultimately interact within the *biopsychosocial* model.

Three Major Contributors: The Brain, Neurochemistry, and Genetics

Biological theories of personality focus on the brain, neurochemistry, and genetics. We begin our study with the brain.

The Brain

> To expect a personality to survive the disintegration of the brain is like expecting a cricket club to survive when all of its members are dead.
>
> BERTRAND RUSSELL

Do you remember the case study of Phineas Gage from Chapter 2? He was the railroad supervisor who survived a horrific accident that sent a 13-pound metal rod through his frontal lobe. As shown by Gage's case, and later research, brain damage can dramatically affect personality (Blais & Boisvert, 2007; Rao et al., 2008; Singer, 2008). If you, or someone you know, has suffered brain damage from accidents, or diseases like Parkinson's or Alzheimer's, you're probably well aware of the resultant changes in behavior and personality.

Modern biological research also suggests that activity in certain brain areas may contribute to some personality traits. Tellegen (1985), for example, proposes that extroversion and introversion are associated with particular areas of the brain, and research seems to support him. For instance, fMRI brain scans of shy adults tend to show greater amygdala activation when presented with faces of strangers (Beaton et al., 2008).

A major limitation on measurements of brain damage and brain activity is the difficulty of identifying which structures are uniquely connected with particular personality traits. Damage to one structure tends to have wide-ranging effects. Neurochemistry (our next topic) seems to offer more precise data on biological bases of personality.

Neurochemistry

Do you enjoy skydiving and taking risks in general? Neurochemistry may explain why. Research has found a consistent relationship between sensation seeking and neurochemicals like monoamine oxidase (MAO), an enzyme that regulates levels of neurotransmitters such as dopamine (Ibanez, Blanco, & Saiz-Ruiz, 2002; Zuckerman, 1994, 2004). Dopamine also seems to be correlated with novelty seeking, impulsivity, and drug abuse (Dalley et al., 2007; Lang et al., 2007; Levinthal, 2008).

How can traits like sensation seeking be related to neurochemistry? Studies suggest that high sensation seekers and extroverts tend to have lower levels of physiological arousal than introverts (Lissek & Powers, 2003). Their lower arousal apparently motivates them to seek out situations that will elevate their arousal. Moreover, it is believed that a lower threshold is inherited. In other words, personality traits like sensation seeking and extroversion may be inherited. (Also see Chapter 12 on arousal and sensation seeking.)

Genetics

> Heredity is what sets the parents of a teenager wondering about each other.
>
> LAURENCE J. PETER

Psychologists have only recently recognized the importance and influence of genetic factors in personality. This relatively new area, called *behavioral genetics*, attempts to determine the extent to which behavioral differences among people are due to genetics as opposed to environment (Chapter 2).

Psychologists have long been interested in possible genetic contributions to personality, and they've utilized several methods of behavioral genetics research (see Chapter 2's Concept Diagram, p. 83). For example, they often study similarities between identical twins, fraternal twins, and twins reared apart or together. And they frequently compare the personalities of parents with their biological and/or adopted children. Findings from their twin studies generally report a relatively high correlation on certain personality traits, whereas research on parents' personalities have found moderate correlations with their biological children and very little with those of their adopted children. In sum, genetic factors contribute about 40 to 50 percent

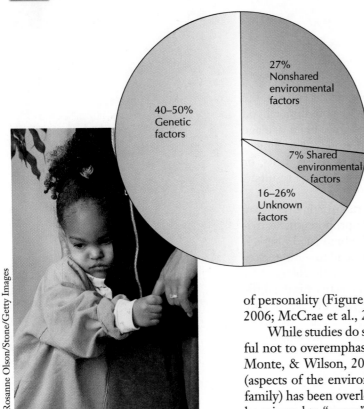

27%
Nonshared
environmental
factors

40–50%
Genetic
factors

7% Shared
environmental
factors

16–26%
Unknown
factors

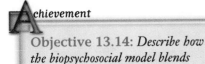

Rosanne Olson/Stone/Getty Images

Figure 13.15 *Multiple influences on personality* What gives a person certain personality characteristics, such as shyness, or conscientiousness, or aggressiveness? As shown in the figure here, research indicates that four major factors overlap to influence personality. These include *genetic* (inherited) *factors; nonshared environmenal factors,* or how each individual's genetic factors react and adjust to his or her particular environment; *shared environmental factors,* involving parental patterns and shared family experiences; and *error,* or unidentified factors or problems with testing.

For example, Hans Eysenck (1990) believed that certain traits (like introversion and extroversion) may reflect inherited patterns of cortical arousal, as well as social learning, cognitive processes, and the environment. Can you see how someone with an introverted personality (and therefore a higher level of cortical arousal) might try to avoid excessive stimulation by seeking friends and jobs with low stimulation levels? Eysenck's work exemplifies how trait, biological, and social-cognitive theories can be combined to provide better insight into personality—the *biopsychosocial model.*

of personality (Figure 13.15) (Bouchard, 1997, 2004; Eysenck, 1967, 1990; Jang et al., 2006; McCrae et al., 2004; Plomin, 1990; Weiss, Bates, & Luciano, 2008).

While studies do show a strong inherited basis for personality, researchers are careful not to overemphasize genetic contributions (Deckers, 2005, Funder, 2001; Sollod, Monte, & Wilson, 2009). Some believe the importance of the unshared environment (aspects of the environment that differ from one individual to another, even within a family) has been overlooked. Others fear that research on "genetic determinism" could be misused to "prove" that an ethnic or a racial group is inferior, that male dominance is natural, or that social progress is impossible. There is no doubt that genetics studies have produced exciting and controversial results. However, it is also clear that more research is necessary before we have a cohesive biological theory of personality.

The Biopsychosocial Model: Integrating the Perspectives

Achievement

Objective 13.14: *Describe how the biopsychosocial model blends various approaches to personality.*

With regard to personality, no one theory is more correct than another. Each provides a different perspective. And each offers different insights into how a person develops the distinctive set of characteristics we call "personality." As you can see in Figure 13.15, instead of adhering to any one theory, many psychologists believe in the *biopsychosocial* approach—the idea that several factors overlap in their contributions to personality (Mischel, Shoda, & Ayduk, 2008).

Assessment

STOP

CHECK & REVIEW

Biological Theories

Objective 13.13: *How does biology contribute to personality?*

Biological theories emphasize brain structures, neurochemistry, and inherited genetic components of personality. Research on specific traits, such as extroversion and sensation seeking, support the biological approach.

Objective 13.14: *Describe how the biopsychosocial model blends various approaches to personality.*

The biopsychosocial approach suggests that the major theories overlap and that each contributes to our understanding of personality.

Questions

1. _____ theories emphasize the importance of genetics in the development of personality. (a) Sociocultural; (b) Phenomenological; (c) Genological; (d) Biological
2. What concerns people about genetic explanations for personality?

3. What factor appears to have the greatest influence (40 to 50 percent) on personality? (a) the environment; (b) genetics; (c) learning; (d) unknown factors
4. The _____ approach represents a blending of several theories of personality. (a) unification; (b) association; (c) biopsychosocial; (d) phenomenological

Check your answers in Appendix B.

Click & Review
for additional assessment options:
wiley.com/college/huffman

Personality Assessment

Throughout history, people have sought information about their personality and that of others. Back in the 1800s, if you wanted to have your personality assessed, you would go to a *phrenologist*. This highly respected person would carefully measure your skull, examine the bumps on your head, and then give you a psychological profile of your unique qualities and characteristics. Phrenologists used a phrenology chart to determine which personality traits were associated with bumps on different areas of the skull (Figure 13.16).

Today, some people consult fortune-tellers, horoscope columns in the newspaper, tarot cards, and even fortune cookies in Chinese restaurants. But scientific research has provided much more reliable and valid methods for measuring personality. Clinical and counseling psychologists, psychiatrists, and other helping professionals use these modern methods to help with the diagnosis of patients and to assess their progress in therapy. Personality assessment is also used for educational and vocational counseling and by businesses to aid in hiring decisions.

How Do We Measure Personality: Do You See What I See?

Like a detective solving a mystery, modern psychologists typically use numerous methods and a complete *battery* (or series) of tests to fully *assess* personality. This assortment of measures can be grouped into a few broad categories: *interviews, observations, objective tests*, and *projective techniques*.

Achievement

Objective 13.15: *How do psychologists measure personality?*

Interviews

We all use informal "interviews" to get to know other people. When first meeting people, we ask about their job, college major, family, and hobbies or interests. Psychologists use a more formal type of interview—both *structured* and *unstructured*. Unstructured interviews are often used for job and college selection and for diagnosing psychological problems. In an unstructured format, interviewers get impressions and pursue hunches. They also let the interviewee expand on information that promises to disclose unique personality characteristics. In structured interviews, the interviewer asks specific questions and follows a set of preestablished procedures so that the interviewee can be evaluated more objectively. The results of a structured interview are often charted on a rating scale that makes comparisons with others easier.

Observations

In addition to structured and unstructured interviews, psychologists also use direct behavioral observation to assess personality. Most of us enjoy casual "people watching." But, as you recall from Chapter 1, scientific observation is a much more controlled and methodical process. The psychologist

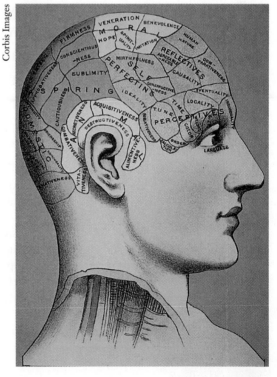

Figure 13.16 *Is personality reflected in our skulls?* Yes, at least according Franz Gall, the founder of phrenology, who believed the skull takes its shape from the brain. Therefore, by examining the shape and unevenness of a head or skull, "scientists" could discover the underlying parts of the brain responsible for different psychological traits. For example, a large bump in the area above the right ear at the position attributed to *sublimity* would indicate that the individual had a "well-developed" organ in the brain responsible for squelching natural impulses, especially sexual ones. What traits might be measured if we still believed in phrenology today? Would we find bumps and create terms like *technicity* (ability to adapt to rapidly changing technology) and *scorcesity* (enjoyment of violent and terrifying movies)?

David De Lossy/Getty Images

Figure 13.17 **Behavioral observation** Can you see how careful, scientific observation of a troubled client's real-life interactions could provide valuable insights into personality?

looks for examples of specific behaviors and follows a careful set of evaluation guidelines. For instance, a psychologist might arrange to observe a troubled client's interactions with his or her family. Does the client become agitated by the presence of certain family members and not others? Does he or she become passive and withdrawn when asked a direct question? Through careful observation, the psychologist gains valuable insights into the client's personality, as well as family dynamics (Figure 13.17).

Objective Tests

Objective self-report personality tests, or *inventories*, are standardized questionnaires that require written responses. Answers to the typically multiple-choice or true–false questions help people to describe themselves–to "self-report." The tests are considered "objective" because they have a limited number of possible responses to items. They also follow empirical standards for test construction and scoring. Another important advantage is that objective tests can be administered to a large number of people in a relatively short period of time and evaluated in a standardized fashion. These advantages help explain why objective tests are by far the most widely used method for assessing personality.

You have been introduced to several objective self-report personality tests in this textbook. We describe the sensation-seeking scale in Chapter 12, and earlier in this chapter we discussed Rotter's locus-of-control scale. The complete versions of these tests measure one specific personality trait and are used primarily in research. Often, however, psychologists in clinical, counseling, and business settings are interested in assessing a range of personality traits all at once. To do this, they generally use *multitrait* (or *multiphasic*) inventories.

The most widely studied and clinically used objective, multitrait test is the **Minnesota Multiphasic Personality Inventory (MMPI)**—or its revision, the MMPI-2 (Butcher, 2000, 2005; Butcher & Perry, 2008). The test consists of over 500 statements that participants respond to with *True, False,* or *Cannot say.* The following are examples of the kinds of statements found on the MMPI:

My stomach frequently bothers me.

I have enemies who really wish to harm me.

I sometimes hear things that other people can't hear.

I would like to be a mechanic.

I have never indulged in any unusual sex practices.

Minnesota Multiphasic Personality Inventory (MMPI) *The most widely researched and clinically used self-report personality test (MMPI-2 is the revised version)*

Why are some of these questions about really unusual, abnormal behavior? Although there are many "normal" questions on the full MMPI, the test is designed primarily for clinical and counseling psychologists to diagnose psychological disorders. Table 13.4 shows how MMPI test items are grouped into 10 *clinical scales*, each measuring a different disorder. Depressed people, for example, tend to score higher on one group of questions. People with schizophrenia score higher on a different group. Each group of items is called a *scale*. There are also four *validity scales* designed to reflect the extent to which respondents distort their answers, do not understand the items, or are being uncooperative. Research has found that the validity scales

TABLE 13.4 SUBSCALES OF THE MMPI-2

Clinical Scales	Typical Interpretations of High Scores
1. Hypochondriasis	Numerous physical complaints
2. Depression	Seriously depressed and pessimistic
3. Hysteria	Suggestible, immature, self-centered, demanding
4. Psychopathic deviate	Rebellious, nonconformist
5. Masculinity–femininity	Interests like those of other sex
6. Paranoia	Suspicious and resentful of others
7. Psychasthenia	Fearful, agitated, brooding
8. Schizophrenia	Withdrawn, reclusive, bizarre thinking
9. Hypomania	Distractible, impulsive, dramatic
10. Social introversion	Shy, introverted, self-effacing
Validity Scales	**Typical Interpretations of High Scores**
1. L (lie)	Denies common problems, projects a "saintly" or false picture
2. F (confusion)	Answers are contradictory
3. K (defensiveness)	Minimizes social and emotional complaints
4. ? (cannot say)	Many items left unanswered

Sidney Harris

"RORSCHACH! WHAT'S TO BECOME OF YOU?"

effectively detect those who may be faking psychological disturbances or trying to appear more psychologically healthy (Ben-Porath & Tellegen, 2008; Weiner, 2008).

Personality tests like the MMPI are often confused with other objective self-report tests called *career inventories* or *vocational interest tests*. For example, the *Strong Vocational Interest Inventory* asks whether you would rather write, illustrate, print, or sell a book or whether you'd prefer the work of a salesperson or teacher. Your answers to these types of questions help identify occupations that match your unique traits, values, and interests.

Given your vocational interest test profile, along with your scores on *aptitude tests* (which measure potential abilities) and *achievement tests* (which measure what you have already learned), a counselor can help you identify the types of jobs that best suit you. Most colleges have career counseling centers where you can take vocational interest tests to guide you in your career decisions.

Projective Techniques

Unlike objective tests, **projective tests** use ambiguous, unstructured stimuli, such as inkblots, which can be perceived in many ways. As the name implies, *projective* tests reportedly allow each person to *project* his or her own unconscious conflicts, psychological defenses, motives, and personality traits onto the test materials. Because respondents are unable (or unwilling) to express their true feelings if asked directly, the ambiguous stimuli are said to provide an indirect, "psychological X-ray" of their hidden, unconscious processes. Two of the most widely used projective tests are the **Rorschach Inkblot Test** and the **Thematic Apperception Test (TAT)** (Concept Diagram 13.1).

Projective Tests *Psychological tests using ambiguous stimuli, such as inkblots or drawings, which allow the test taker to project his or her unconscious onto the test material*

Rorschach [ROAR-shock] Inkblot Test *A projective test that presents a set of 10 cards with symmetrical abstract patterns, known as inkblots, and asks respondents to describe what they "see" in the image; their response is thought to be a projection of unconscious processes*

Thematic Apperception Test (TAT) *A projective test that shows a series of ambiguous black-and-white pictures and asks the test taker to create a story related to each; the responses presumably reflect a projection of unconscious processes*

Concept Diagram 13.1
Projective Tests

Responses to projective tests reportedly reflect unconscious parts of the personality that "project" onto the stimuli.

(a) A The Rorschach Inkblot Test was introduced in 1921 by Swiss psychiatrist Hermann Rorschach. With this technique, individuals are shown 10 Inkblots like this, one at a time, and are asked to report what figures or objects they see in each of them. (Reproduced with permission.)

(b) Created by personality researcher Henry Murray in 1938, the Thematic Apperception Test (TAT) consists of a series of ambiguous black-and-white pictures that are shown to the test-taker, who is asked to create a story related to each. Can you think of two different stories that a person might create for the picture of two women here? How might a psychologist interpret each story?

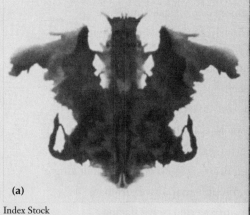

(a)

Index Stock

(b)

Harvard University Press

Achievement

Objective 13.16: *Describe the key advantages and disadvantages of personality measurement.*

■ Are Personality Measurements Accurate? Evaluating the Methods

What do you think of these widely differing methods of personality assessment? Do they accurately measure true personality? Let's evaluate each of the four major methods: *interviews, observation, objective tests,* and *projective tests.*

- *Interviews and observations.* Both interviews and observations can provide valuable insights into personality. But they are time-consuming and therefore expensive. Furthermore, just as football fans can disagree over the relative merits of the same quarterback, raters of personality tests frequently disagree in their evaluations of the same individual. Interviews and observations also involve unnatural settings. And, as we saw in Chapter 1, the very presence of an observer can alter the behavior that is being studied.

- *Objective tests.* Tests like the MMPI-2 provide specific, objective information about a broad range of personality traits in a relatively short period of time. However, they are also the subject of at least three major criticisms:

    1. *Deliberate deception and social desirability bias.* Some items on self-report inventories are easy to "see through." Thus, respondents may intentionally, or unintentionally, fake particular personality traits. In addition, some respondents want to look good and will answer questions in ways that they perceive as *socially desirable.* (The validity scales of the MMPI-2 are designed to help prevent these problems.)

2. **Diagnostic difficulties.** When self-report inventories are used for diagnosis, overlapping items sometimes make it difficult to pinpoint a diagnosis. In addition, clients with severe disorders sometimes score within the normal range, and normal clients may score within the elevated range (Gregory, 2007; Weiner, 2008).

3. **Possible cultural bias.** Some critics think that the standards for "normalcy" on objective self-report tests fail to recognize the impact of culture. For example, Latinos—such as Mexicans, Puerto Ricans, and Argentineans—generally score higher than respondents from North American and Western European cultures on the masculinity–femininity scale of the MMPI-2 (Dana, 2005; Lucio et al., 2001; Lucio-Gomez et al., 1999). The fact that these groups score higher may reflect their greater adherence to traditional gender roles and cultural training more than any individual personality traits.

- **Projective tests.** Although projective tests are widely used (Gacono et al., 2008; Gregory, 2007), they are extremely time-consuming to administer and interpret. However, their proponents suggest that because they have no right or wrong answers, respondents are less able to deliberately fake their responses. In addition, because these tests are unstructured, respondents may be more willing to talk about sensitive, anxiety-laden topics.

  Projective tests are highly controversial (Garb et al., 2005; Gacono et al., 2008). As you recall from Chapter 8's discussion of intelligence tests, the two most important measures of a good test are **reliability** (Are the results consistent?) and **validity** (Does the test measure what it's designed to measure?). One problem with the Rorschach, in particular, is that interpreting clients' responses depends in large part on the subjective judgment of the examiner. And some examiners are simply more experienced or skilled than others. Also, there are problems with *interrater reliability*: Two examiners may interpret the same response in very different ways.

In sum, each of these four methods has its limits. However, psychologists typically combine results from various methods to create a more complete understanding of an individual personality.

Reliability *Measure of the consistency and reproducibility of a test's scores when the test is readministered.*

Validity *Ability of a test to measure what it was designed to measure.*

*A*ssessment

VISUAL QUIZ

Using the information in the Critical Thinking/Active Learning exercise on page 468, can you identify the two fallacies in this cartoon?

[Cartoon: *"YOU WILL BE TOLD WHAT YOU WANT TO HEAR. IT WILL BE SO GENERALIZED THAT IT COULD FIT ANYONE. YOU WILL PAY A RIDICULOUS AMOUNT OF MONEY FOR IT..."* — "THE MOST ACCURATE FORTUNE EVER TOLD"]

Answer: The self-serving bias and the Barnum effect.

wiley.com/
college/
huffman

Application

CRITICAL THINKING | **ACTIVE LEARNING**

Why Are Pseudo-Personality Tests So Popular?

Objective 13.17: *List the three major fallacies associated with pseudo-personality tests.*

Throughout this text, we have emphasized the value of critical thinking. By carefully evaluating the evidence and credibility of the source, critical thinkers recognize faulty logic and appeals to emotion. Applying these standards to pseudo-personality evaluations like the one in our introductory incident, we can identify at least three important logical fallacies: the *Barnum effect, the fallacy of positive instances, and the self-serving bias.*

The Barnum Effect

Pseudo-personality descriptions and horoscope predictions are often accepted because we think they are accurate. We tend to believe these tests have somehow tapped into our unique selves. In fact, they are ambiguous, broad statements that fit just about anyone. Being so readily disposed to accept such generalizations is known as the *Barnum effect.* This name is based on P.T. Barnum, the legendary circus promoter who

said, "Always have a little something for everyone" (Wyman & Vyse, 2008).

Reread the bogus personality profile in the chapter opening (p. 440). Can you see how the description, "You have a strong need for other people to like and admire you," fits almost everyone? Or do you know anyone who doesn't "at times have serious doubts whether [they've] made the right decision or done the right thing"? P.T. Barnum also said, "There's a sucker born every minute."

The Fallacy of Positive Instances

Look again at the introductory personality profile and count the number of times both sides of a personality trait are given. ("You have a strong need for other people to like you" and "You pride yourself on being an independent thinker.") According to the *fallacy of positive instances,* we tend to notice and remember events that confirm our expectations and ignore those that are nonconfirming. If we see ourselves as independent thinkers, for example, we ignore the "needing to be liked by others" part. Similarly, horoscope readers easily find "Sagittarius characteristics" in a Sagittarius horoscope. However, these same readers

generally overlook Sagittarius predictions that miss or when the same traits appear for Scorpios or Leos.

The Self-Serving Bias

Now check the overall tone of the personality description. Can you see how the traits are generally positive and flattering—or at least neutral? According to the *self-serving bias,* we tend to prefer information that maintains our positive self-image (Krusemark et al., 2008; Shepperd, Malone, & Sweeny, 2008). In fact, research shows that the more favorable a personality description is, the more people believe it and the more likely they are to believe it is unique to themselves (Guastello, Guastello, & Craft, 1989). (The self-serving bias might also explain why people prefer pseudo-personality tests to bona fide tests—they're generally more flattering!)

Taken together, these three logical fallacies help explain the belief in "pop psych" personality tests and newspaper horoscopes. They offer "something for everyone" (the *Barnum effect*). We pay attention only to what confirms our expectations (the *fallacy of positive instances*). And we like flattering descriptions (the *self-serving bias*).

Assessment

STOP

CHECK & REVIEW

Personality Assessment

Objective 13.15: *How do psychologists measure personality?*

Psychologists use four basic methods to measure or assess personality: interviews, observations, objective tests, and projective techniques.

Interviews and observations can provide insights into a wide variety of behaviors and personality traits. Interviews can be either structured or unstructured. During observations, the rater looks for examples of specific behaviors and follows a careful set of evaluation guidelines.

Objective tests, such as the **Minnesota Multiphasic Personality Inventory (MMPI-2)**, use self-report questionnaires or

inventories. These tests provide objective standardized information about a large number of personality traits.

Projective tests, such as the **Rorschach Inkblot Test** and the **Thematic Apperception Test (TAT)**, ask test-takers to respond to ambiguous stimuli, which reportedly provides insight into unconscious elements of personality.

Objective 13.16: *Describe the key advantages and disadvantages of personality measurement.*

Both *interviews* and *observations* can provide valuable insights into personality, but they are time-consuming and expensive, raters frequently disagree, and they often involve

unnatural settings. *Objective tests* provide specific, objective information, but they are limited because of deliberate deception and social desirability bias, diagnostic difficulties, and possible cultural bias. *Projective tests* are time-consuming and have questionable reliability and validity. However, because they are unstructured, respondents may be more willing to talk honestly about sensitive topics, and projective tests are harder to fake.

Objective 13.17: *List the three major fallacies associated with pseudo-personality tests.*

The *Barnum effect,* the *fallacy of positive instances,* and the *self-serving bias* are the three most important fallacies of pseudo-personality tests.

Questions

1. Match each personality test with its description:

   a. a projective test using inkblots
   b. an objective, self-report personality test
   c. a projective test using ambiguous drawings of ambiguous human situations
   ___i. MMPI-2
   ___ii. Rorschach
   ___iii. TAT

2. The Rorschach *Inkblot Test* is an example of a(n) _____ test.

3. Two important criteria for evaluating the usefulness of tests used to assess personality are _____. (a) concurrence and prediction; (b) reliability and validity; (c) consistency and correlation; (d) diagnosis and prognosis

4. Describe the three logical fallacies that encourage acceptance of pseudo-personality tests and horoscopes.

Check your answers in Appendix B.

 Click & Review for additional assessment options: wiley.com/college/huffman

 **A**ssessment
KEY TERMS

*To assess your understanding of the **Key Terms** in Chapter 13, write a definition for each (in your own words), and then compare your definitions with those in the text.*

personality (p. 440)

Trait Theories
factor analysis (p. 443)
five-factor model (FFM) (p. 443)
trait (p. 442)

Psychoanalytic/Psychodynamic Theories
archetypes [AR-KEH-types] (p. 452)
basic anxiety (p. 453)
collective unconscious (p. 452)
conscious (p. 448)
defense mechanisms (p. 449)
ego (p. 449)
id (p. 449)

inferiority complex (p. 452)
morality principle (p. 449)
Oedipus [ED-uh-puss] complex (p. 451)
pleasure principle (p. 449)
preconscious (p. 448)
psychosexual stages (p. 450)
reality principle (p. 449)
repression (p. 450)
superego (p. 449)
unconscious (p. 448)

Humanistic Theories
self-actualization (p. 457)
self-concept (p. 455)
unconditional positive regard (p. 456)

Social-Cognitive Theories
reciprocal determinism (p. 459)
self-efficacy (p. 459)

Personality Assessment
Minnesota Multiphasic Personality Inventory (MMPI-2) (p. 464)
projective tests (p. 465)
reliability (p. 467)
Rorschach [ROAR-shock] Inkblot Test (p. 465)
Thematic Apperception Test (TAT) (p. 465)
validity (p. 467)

 **A**chievement
WEB RESOURCES

Huffman Book Companion Site
wiley.com/college/huffman
   This site is loaded with free Interactive Self-Tests, Internet Exercises, Glossary and Flashcards for key terms, web links, Handbook for Non-Native Speakers, and other activities designed to improve your mastery of the material in this chapter.

Major Personality Theories and Assessment Techniques

Theorists and Key Concepts

Five-Factor Model (FFM)

1 **O**penness
2 **C**onscientiousness
3 **E**xtroversion
4 **A**greeableness
5 **N**euroticism

Trait
Early theorists
- Allport: Arranged **traits** in hierarchy.
- Cattell (16PF) and Eysenck (Personality Questionnaire): Used **factor analysis** to reduce number of traits.

Modern theory
- **Five-factor model (FFM)**: Openness, conscientiousness, extroversion, agreeableness, and neuroticism.

Determinants of Personality
Heredity and environment combine to create personality traits.

Methods of Assessment
Objective (self-report) inventories (e.g., MMPI), observation.

Psychoanalytic/Psychodynamic
Freud
- Levels of Consciousness—**conscious, preconscious**, and **unconscious**.
- Personality structure—**id (pleasure principle), ego (reality principle), superego (morality principle)**.
- **Defense Mechanisms—repression** and others.
- **Psychosexual Stages**—oral, anal, phallic, latency, and genital.

Neo-Freudians
- Adler—individual psychology, **inferiority complex**, and will-to-power.
- Jung—analytical psychology, **collective unconscious**, and **archetypes**.
- Horney—power envy vs. penis envy and **basic anxiety**.

Determinants of Personality
Unconscious conflicts between id, ego, and superego lead to defense mechanisms.

Methods of Assessment
Interviews and **projective tests: Rorschach inkblot test, Thematic Apperception Test (TAT)**.

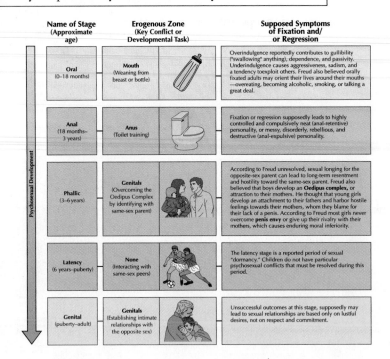

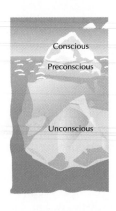

Cognitions → Personality ← Behavior

Environment →

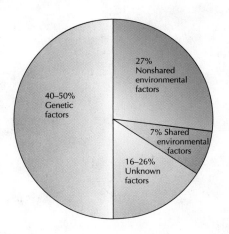

27% Nonshared environmental factors

40–50% Genetic factors

7% Shared environmental factors

16–26% Unknown factors

Humanistic
- Rogers—**self-concept**, self-esteem, and **unconditional positive regard**.
- Maslow—**self-actualization**.

Determinants of Personality
Individual's subjective experience of reality.

Methods of Assessment
Interviews, objective (self-report) inventories.

Social/Cognitive
- Bandura—**self-efficacy** and **reciprocal determinism**.
- Rotter—cognitive expectancies and locus of control.

Determinants of Personality
Interaction between cognition and environment.

Methods of Assessment
Observation, objective (self-report) inventories.

Biological
- Brain structures like the frontal lobes may play a role.
- Neurochemistry (dopamine, MAO, and others) may play a role.
- Genetic factors also contribute to personality.

Determinants of Personality
Brain, neurochemistry, genetics.

Methods of Assessment
Animal studies and biological techniques.

Personality Assessment

Psychologists use four methods to measure personality:

Interviews: Can be either structured or unstructured.

Observations: Involves direct observation with set of evaluation guidelines.

Objective Tests: Self-report paper-and-pencil questionnaires, which provide objective standardized information about a large number of personality traits.

Projective Techniques [such as the **Rorschach "inkblot"** or **Thematic Apperception Test (TAT)**]: Uses ambiguous stimuli to reportedly reveal unconscious elements of the personality.

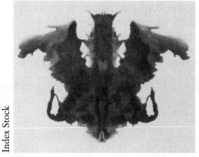

Index Stock

Reliability and **validity** are the major criteria for evaluating the accuracy of personolity tests.

14

Psychological Disorders

Steve Taylor/Stone/Getty Images

Courtesy of Erin Decker

ave you heard of the "giraffe women" of the Kayan tribe in Thailand who wear heavy copper coils around their necks to push their faces up and make their necks look longer? At the age of 5 or 6, the first coil is normally added, but some little girls are "coiled" at the age of 2. Year after year, new coils are added. Once fastened, the rings are worn for life because the neck muscles weaken and deteriorate to the point they can no longer support the weight of the head. These coils also weigh up to 12 pounds and depress the clavicle and ribs about 45 degrees from their normal position. Would you consider this behavior abnormal? What about the following cases taken from our own Western culture:

> Mary's troubles first began in adolescence. She began to miss curfew, was frequently truant, and her grades declined sharply. Mary later became promiscuous and prostituted herself several times to get drug money.... She also quickly fell in love and overly idealized new friends. But when they quickly (and inevitably) disappointed her, she would angrily cast them aside.... Mary's problems, coupled with a preoccupation with inflicting pain on herself (by cutting and burning) and persistent thoughts of suicide, eventually led to her admittance to a psychiatric hospital at age 26.

> (KRING et al., 2007, PP. 386–387)

Rain or shine, day in and day out, 43-year-old Joshua occupies his "post" on a busy street corner wearing his standard outfit—a Red Sox baseball cap, yellow T-shirt, worn-out hiking shorts, and orange sneakers. Sometimes he can be seen "conversing" with imaginary people. Without apparent cause, he also frequently explodes into shrieks of laughter or breaks down into miserable sobs. Police and social workers keep taking him to shelters for the homeless, but Joshua manages to get back on the street before he can be treated. He has repeatedly insisted that these people have no right to keep bothering him.

(HALGIN & WHITBOURNE, 2008, P. 283)

Both Mary and Joshua have severe psychological problems, and both of their stories raise interesting questions. What caused their difficulties? Was there something in their early backgrounds to explain their later behaviors? Is there something medically wrong with them? What about the "giraffe women"? What is the difference between being culturally different and being disordered?

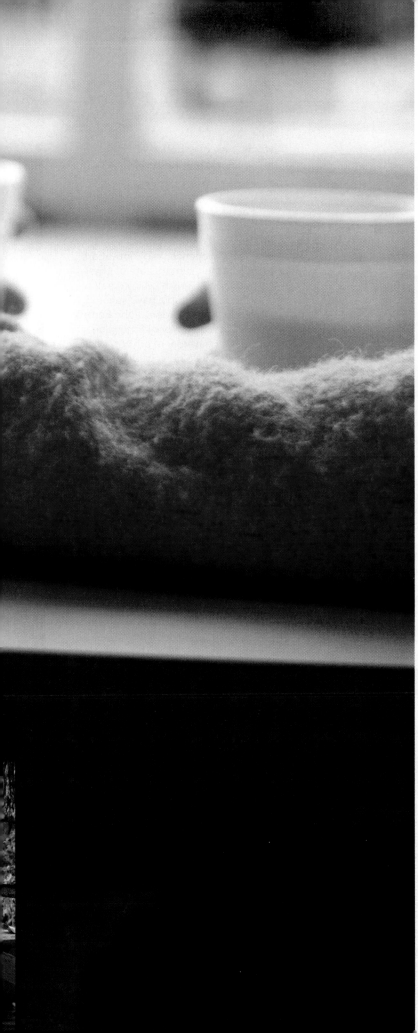

▶ **Studying Psychological Disorders**

Identifying Abnormal Behavior

✳ GENDER & CULTURAL DIVERSITY
   Avoiding Ethnocentrism

Explaining Abnormality
Classifying Abnormal Behavior

▶ **Anxiety Disorders**

Five Major Anxiety Disorders
Explaining Anxiety Disorders

▶ **Mood Disorders**

Understanding Mood Disorders

✳ GENDER & CULTURAL DIVERSITY
   How Gender and Culture Affect Depression

Explaining Mood Disorders

RESEARCH HIGHLIGHT
   Suicide and Its Prevention

CRITICAL THINKING/ACTIVE LEARNING
   How Your Thoughts Can Make You Depressed

▶ **Schizophrenia**

Symptoms of Schizophrenia
Types of Schizophrenia
Explaining Schizophrenia

✳ GENDER & CULTURAL DIVERSITY
   Schizophrenia Around the World

▶ **Other Disorders**

Substance-Related Disorders
Dissociative Disorders
Personality Disorders

PSYCHOLOGY AT WORK
   Testing Your Knowledge of Abnormal Behavior

Application

WHY STUDY PSYCHOLOGY?

Objective 14.1: *Identify five common myths about mental illness.*

Do you recognize these myths?

▶ *Myth #1: People with psychological disorders act in bizarre ways and are very different from normal people.*
Fact: This is true for only a small minority of individuals and during a relatively small portion of their lives. In fact, sometimes even mental health professionals find it difficult to distinguish normal from abnormal individuals without formal screening.

▶ *Myth #2: Mental disorders are a sign of personal weakness.*

Fact: Psychological disorders are a function of many factors, such as exposure to stress, genetic disposition, family background, and so on. Mentally disturbed individuals can't be blamed for their illness any more than we blame people who develop Alzheimer's or other physical illnesses.

▶ *Myth #3: Mentally ill people are often dangerous and unpredictable.*

Fact: Only a few disorders, such as some psychotic and antisocial

©AP/Wide World Photos

Is Scott Peterson mentally ill? Do you recall the audiotape recordings of Scott Peterson laughing and talking with his girlfriend only a few days after he brutally murdered his wife and unborn son?

personalities, are associated with violence. The stereotype that connects mental illness and violence persists because of prejudice and selective media attention.

▶ *Myth #4: A person who has been mentally ill never fully recovers.*
Fact: With therapy, the vast majority of people who are diagnosed as mentally ill eventually improve and lead normal productive lives. Moreover, mental disorders are generally only temporary. A person may have an episode that lasts for days, weeks, or months. After-

wards, they may go for years—even a lifetime—without further difficulty.

▶ *Myth #5: Most mentally ill individuals can work at only low-level jobs.*
Fact: Mentally disturbed people are individuals. As such, their career potentials depend on their particular talents, abilities, experience, and motivation, as well as their current state of physical and mental health. Many creative and successful people have suffered serious mental disorders. John Forbes Nash Jr., a recent Nobel Prize winner, has a lifetime history of schizophrenia. But he is now doing very well, as has been documented in the book and film *A Beautiful Mind* (*Famous People and Schizophrenia*, 2004).
British Prime Minister Winston Churchill, Scottish soccer player Andy Goram, writer and poet Edgar Allan Poe, Pink Floyd band member Syd Barrett, Green Bay Packers sports star Lionel Aldridge, actress Patty Duke, painter Vincent Van Gogh, and billionaire Howard Hughes are all believed to have suffered from a serious mental disorder.

(Sources: Barlow & Durand, 2009; Famous People and Schizophrenia, 2008; Famous People with Mental Illness, 2008; Hansell & Damour, 2008; Kondo, 2008.)

In this chapter, we will discover that abnormal behavior is subject to different interpretations over time and across cultures. We begin with a discussion of how psychological disorders are identified, explained, and classified. We then explore six major categories of psychological disorders: anxiety disorders, mood disorders, schizophrenia, substance-related disorders, dissociative disorders, and personality disorders. Finally, we look at gender and cultural factors related to mental disorders.

Achievement

Objective 14.2: *Define abnormal behavior, and list four standards for identifying it.*

Studying Psychological Disorders

As the introductory cases show, mental disorders vary in type and severity from person to person. Like personality, consciousness, and intelligence, *abnormal behavior* is difficult to define. In this section, we will explore how psychologists attempt to identify, explain, and classify abnormal behavior.

©AP/Wide World Photos

Would this behavior be considered abnormal?

Answer: This woman's extreme piercing does meet standards 1 and 4, but the term abnormal behavior is generally restricted to behavior that is considered pathological (diseased or disordered).

Identifying Abnormal Behavior: Four Basic Standards

The behaviors of both Mary and Joshua are clearly abnormal. But the "giraffe women's" voluntary placement of life-threatening coils around their necks shows us that many cases of **abnormal behavior** are not so clear-cut. Rather than being two discrete categories, "normal" and "abnormal," abnormal behavior, like intelligence or creativity, lies along a continuum. And at each end point, people can be unusually healthy or extremely disturbed.

Recognizing this continuum, mental health professionals generally agree on at least four criteria for identifying abnomal behavior: *statistical infrequency, disability or dysfunction, personal distress,* or *violation of norms* (Process Diagram 14.1). Keep in mind that each criterion has its merit and limits and that no single criterion is adequate for identifying all forms of abnormal behavior.

Abnormal Behavior *Patterns of emotion, thought, and action considered pathological (diseased or disordered) for one or more of four reasons: statistical infrequency, disability or dysfunction, personal distress, or violation of norms*

Achievement

GENDER & CULTURAL DIVERSITY

Avoiding Ethnocentrism

You will discover throughout this chapter that even strongly biological mental disorders, like schizophrenia, can differ greatly between cultures. Unfortunately, most research originates and is conducted primarily in Western cultures. Using your critical thinking skills, can you see how such a restricted sampling can limit our understanding of disorders in general? Or how it might lead to an ethnocentric view of mental disorders? How can you avoid this? You obviously can't randomly assign mentally ill people to different cultures and then watch how their disorders change and develop.

Fortunately, cross-cultural researchers have devised ways to overcome these difficulties, and there is a growing wealth of information (Matsumoto & Juang, 2008; Triandis, 2007). For example, Robert Nishimoto (1988) has found several *culture-general* symptoms that are useful in identifying disorders across cultures. Using the Langer (1962) index of psychiatric symptoms, Nishimoto gathered data from three diverse groups, Anglo Americans in Nebraska, Vietnamese Chinese in Hong Kong, and Mexicans living in Texas and Mexico. (The Langer index is a screening instrument widely used

Achievement

Objective 14.3: *Compare and contrast* culture-general *and* culture-bound *symptoms versus* culture-general *and* culture-bound *mental disorders.*

Process Diagram 14.1
The Four Criteria and a Continuum of Abnormal Behavior

[handwritten: 18   To identify abnormal behavior.]

Rather than being fixed categories, both "abnormal" and "normal" behaviors exist along a continuum (Hansell & Damour, 2008).

Rare ————————————————————— Common

Statistical Infrequency
(e.g., believing others are plotting against you)

Peter Cade/Iconica/Getty Images

Normal   Abnormal

Statistical Infrequency A behavior may be judged abnormal if it occurs infrequently in a given population. Statistical infrequency alone does not determine what is normal. For example, no one would classify Albert Einstein's great intelligence or Lance Armstrong's exceptional athletic ability as abnormal.

Low ————————————————————— High

Disability or Dysfunction
(e.g., being unable to go to work due to alcohol abuse)

David Young-Wolff/Getty Images

Normal   Abnormal

Disability or Dysfunction People who suffer from psychological disorders may be unable to get along with others, hold a job, eat properly, or clean themselves. Their ability to think clearly and make rational decisions also may be impaired.

Low ————————————————————— High

Personal Distress
(e.g., having thoughts of suicide)

ThinkStock, LLC/Index Stock

Normal   Abnormal

Personal Distress The personal distress criterion focuses on the individual's judgment of his or her level of functioning. Yet many people with psychological disorders deny they have a problem. Also, some serious psychological disorders (such as antisocial personality disorder) cause little or no personal emotional discomfort. The personal distress criterion by itself is not sufficient for identifying all forms of abnormal behavior.

Rare ————————————————————— Common

Violations of Norms
(e.g., shouting at strangers)

Digital Vision/Getty Images

Normal   Abnormal

Violation of Norms The fourth approach to identifying abnormal behavior is violation of social norms, or cultural rules that guide behavior in particular situations. A major problem with this criterion, however, is that cultural diversity can affect what people consider a violation of norms.

to identify psychological disorders that disrupt everyday functioning but do not require institutionalization.) When asked to think about their lives, respondents who needed professional help all named one or more of the same 12 symptoms (Table 14.1).

In addition to the culture-general symptoms (such as "nervousness" or "trouble sleeping"), Nishimoto also found several *culture-bound* symptoms. For example, the Vietnamese Chinese reported "fullness in head," the Mexican respondents had "problems with my memory," and the Anglo Americans reported "shortness of breath" and "headaches." Apparently, people *learn* to express their problems in ways acceptable to others in the same culture (Brislin, 1997, 2000; Dhikav et al., 2008; Laungani, 2007; Tolin et al., 2007). In other words, most Americans learn that headaches are a common response to stress. Conversely, many Mexicans learn that others will understand their complaints about memory.

This division between culture-general and culture-bound symptoms also helps us understand depression. Research shows that certain symptoms of depression seem to exist across all cultures: (1) frequent and intense sad affect (emotion), (2) decreased enjoyment, (3) anxiety, (4) difficulty in concentrating, and (5) lack of energy (World Health Organization, 2007, 2008). On the other hand, there is evidence of some culture-bound symptoms. For example, feelings of guilt are found more often in North America and Europe. In China, *somatization* (converting depression into bodily complaints) is more frequent than in other parts of the world (Helms & Cook, 1999).

Just as there are culture-bound and culture-general *symptoms*, researchers have found that mental disorders are themselves sometimes culturally bound and sometimes culturally general. For example, schizophrenia is widely believed to be a culturally general disorder. However, *windigo psychosis*, in which victims believe they are possessed by the spirit of a *windigo* that causes delusions and cannibalistic impulses, is an example of a culture-bound disorder. It only shows up in a small group of Canadian Indians.

Why do cultures develop such unique, culture-bound disorders? In the case of *windigo psychosis*, one explanation is that the disorder developed after fur trade competition depleted game that the Canadian tribes used for food, leading to widespread famine (Bishop, 1974). Facing starvation could have led to cannibalism and the subsequent need to create a *windigo* spirit. Belief in spirit possession is a common feature of many cultures. In this case, people may have used it to explain a socially and psychologically abhorrent behavior, cannibalism (Faddiman, 1997).

Some researchers question the famine explanation for *windigo psychosis* and even the idea of culture-bound disorders. However, there is little doubt that some mental disorders are at least somewhat *culture-bound* (Ranganathan & Bhattacharya, 2007; Sue & Sue, 2008; Tolin et al., 2007). (See Figure 14.1.)

As you can see, culture has a strong effect on mental disorders. Studying the similarities and differences across cultures can lead to better diagnosis and understanding. It also helps mental health professionals who work with culturally diverse populations understand that culturally-general and culturally-bound symptoms exist, and what these are for any population.

TABLE 14.1 TWELVE CULTURE-GENERAL SYMPTOMS OF MENTAL HEALTH DIFFICULTIES

Nervous	Trouble sleeping	Low spirits
Weak all over	Personal worries	Restless
Feel apart, alone	Can't get along	Hot all over
Worry all the time	Can't do anything worthwhile	Nothing turns out right

Source: From *Understanding Culture's Influence on Behavior*, 2nd edition by Brislin. ©2000. Reprinted with permission of Wadsworth, a division of Thompson Learning. www.thompsonrights.com. Fax 800-730-2215.

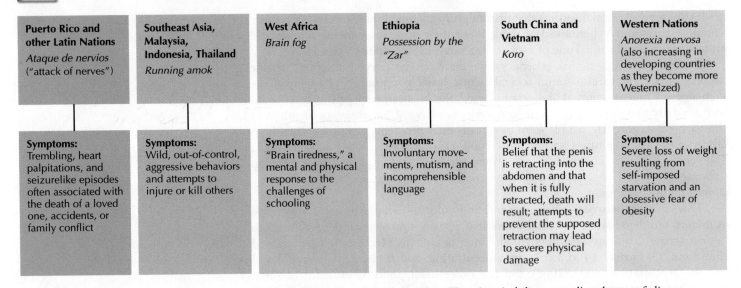

Puerto Rico and other Latin Nations *Ataque de nervios* ("attack of nerves")	Southeast Asia, Malaysia, Indonesia, Thailand *Running amok*	West Africa *Brain fog*	Ethiopia *Possession by the "Zar"*	South China and Vietnam *Koro*	Western Nations *Anorexia nervosa* (also increasing in developing countries as they become more Westernized)
Symptoms: Trembling, heart palpitations, and seizurelike episodes often associated with the death of a loved one, accidents, or family conflict	**Symptoms:** Wild, out-of-control, aggressive behaviors and attempts to injure or kill others	**Symptoms:** "Brain tiredness," a mental and physical response to the challenges of schooling	**Symptoms:** Involuntary movements, mutism, and incomprehensible language	**Symptoms:** Belief that the penis is retracting into the abdomen and that when it is fully retracted, death will result; attempts to prevent the supposed retraction may lead to severe physical damage	**Symptoms:** Severe loss of weight resulting from self-imposed starvation and an obsessive fear of obesity

Figure 14.1 ***Culture-bound disorders*** Keep in mind that some disorders are fading as remote areas become more Westernized, whereas other disorders (such as anorexia nervosa) are spreading as other countries adopt Western values. (*Source:* Barlow & Durand, 2009; Dhikav et al., 2008; Gaw, 2001; Kring et al., 2007; Laungani, 2007; Sue & Sue, 2008; Tolin et al., 2007.)

Achievement

Objective 14.4: *Briefly describe the history of abnormal behavior.*

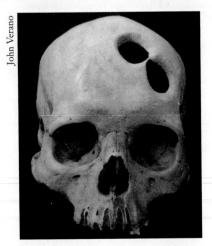

Figure 14.2 ***An early "treatment" for abnormal behavior?*** *During the Stone Age, the recommended "therapy" for mental disorders was to bore holes in the skull to allow evil spirits to escape—a process known as "trephining."*

Medical Model *Perspective that assumes diseases (including mental illness) have physical causes that can be diagnosed, treated, and possibly cured*

Psychiatry *Branch of medicine dealing with the diagnosis, treatment, and prevention of mental disorders*

Explaining Abnormality: From Superstition to Science

Having explored the criteria for defining abnormal behavior, the next logical question is, "How do we explain it?" Historically, evil spirits and witchcraft have been the primary suspects (Goodwin 2009; Millon, 2004). Stone Age people, for example, believed that abnormal behavior stemmed from demonic possession; the "therapy" was to bore a hole in the skull so that the evil spirit could escape (Figure 14.2). During the European Middle Ages, a troubled person was sometimes treated with *exorcism*, an effort to drive the Devil out through prayer, fasting, noise-making, beating, and drinking terrible-tasting brews. During the fifteenth century, many believed that some individuals chose to consort with the Devil. Many of these supposed witches were tortured, imprisoned for life, or executed.

As the Middle Ages ended, special mental hospitals called *asylums* began to appear in Europe. Initially designed to provide quiet retreats from the world and to protect society (Barlow & Durand, 2009; Millon, 2004), the asylums unfortunately became overcrowded, inhumane prisons.

Improvement came in 1792 when Philippe Pinel, a French physician in charge of a Parisian asylum, insisted that asylum inmates—whose behavior he believed to be caused by underlying physical illness—be unshackled and removed from their unlighted, unheated cells. Many inmates improved so dramatically that they could be released. Pinel's **medical model** eventually gave rise to the modern specialty of **psychiatry**.

Unfortunately, when we label people "mentally ill," we may create new problems. One of the most outspoken critics of the medical model is psychiatrist Thomas Szasz (1960, 2000, 2004). Szasz believes that the medical model encourages people to believe that they have no responsibility for their actions. He contends that mental illness is a myth used to label individuals who are peculiar or offensive to others (Cresswell, 2008). Furthermore, labels can become self-perpetuating—that is, the person can begin to behave according to the diagnosed disorder.

Despite these potential dangers, the medical model—and the concept of mental illness—remains a founding principle of psychiatry. In contrast, psychology offers a multifaceted approach to explaining abnormal behavior (Concept Diagram 14.1).

Seven Psychological Perspectives on Abnormal Behavior

Each of the seven major perspectives in psychology emphasizes different factors believed to contribute to abnormal behavior, but in practice they overlap. Consider the phenomenon of compulsive hoarding. Everyone sometimes makes an impulse purchase, and most people are reluctant to discard some possessions that are of questionable value. But when the acquisition of and inability to discard worthless items becomes extreme, it can interfere with basic aspects of living, such as cleaning, cooking, sleeping on a bed, and moving around one's home. This abnormal behavior is associated with several psychological disorders, but it is most commonly found in people who have obsessive compulsive disorder, or OCD (an anxiety disorder discussed later in this chapter). How might each of the seven major perspectives explain compulsive hoarding?

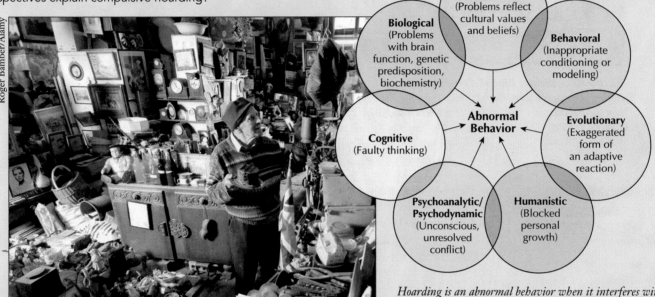

Hoarding is an abnormal behavior when it interferes with other aspects of basic living, such as job, home, and family. How might each of the seven perspectives on abnormal psychology address hoarding behavior?

▣ Classifying Abnormal Behavior: The Diagnostic and Statistical Manual IV-TR

Now that we have *identified* and *explained* abnormal behavior, we also need a clear and reliable system for *classifying* the wide range of disorders. Physicians obviously need specific terms for classifying one set of signs and symptoms as cancer and another as heart disease. Psychologists and psychiatrists also need specific terms to identify and differentiate abnormal behavior. Mary's disruptive behavior and broken relationships, as described in the opening vignette, are very different from Joshua's conversations with imaginary people. Without a uniform system for classifying and clearly describing psychological disorders, scientific research on them would be almost impossible. And communication among mental health professionals would be seriously impaired.

Fortunately, mental health specialists do share a uniform classification system, the text revision of the fourth edition of the ***Diagnostic and Statistical Manual of Mental Disorders (DSM-IV-TR)*** (American Psychiatric Association, 2000).

Each revision of the *DSM* has expanded the list of disorders and changed the descriptions and categories to reflect both the latest advances in scientific research

chievement

Objective 14.5: *Describe the purpose and criticisms of the DSM-IV-TR, and differentiate between neurosis, psychosis, and insanity.*

Diagnostic and Statistical Manual of Mental Disorders (DSM-IV-TR) *Classification system developed by the American Psychiatric Association used to describe abnormal behaviors; the "IV-TR" indicates it is the text revision (TR) of the fourth major revision (IV)*

Witchcraft or mental illness? *During the fifteenth century, some people who may have been suffering from mental disorders were accused of witchcraft and tortured or hung.*

An early catch-22. *In the Middle Ages, "dunking tests" were used to determine whether people who behaved abnormally were possessed by demons. Individuals who did not drown while being dunked were believed to be guilty of possession and then punished (usually by hanging). Those who did drown were judged to be innocent. This was the ultimate catch-22, or no-win situation.*

Neurosis *Outmoded term for disorders characterized by unrealistic anxiety and other associated problems; less severe disruptions than in psychosis*

Psychosis *Serious mental disorders characterized by extreme mental disruption and defective or lost contact with reality*

Insanity *Legal term applied when people cannot be held responsible for their actions, or are judged incompetent to manage their own affairs, because of mental illness.*

and changes in the way abnormal behaviors are viewed within our social context (First & Tasman, 2004; Smart & Smart, 1997). For example, take the terms **neurosis** and **psychosis**. In previous editions, *neurosis* reflected Freud's belief that all neurotic conditions arise from unconscious conflicts (Chapter 13). Now conditions that were previously grouped under the heading *neurosis* have been formally redistributed as anxiety disorders, somatoform disorders, and dissociative disorders.

Unlike neurosis, the term *psychosis* is still listed in the *DSM-IV-TR* because it helps distinguish the most severe mental disorders, such as schizophrenia and some mood disorders.

What about the term insanity? Where does it fit in? **Insanity** is a legal term indicating that a person cannot be held responsible for his or her actions, or is judged incompetent to manage his or her own affairs, because of mental illness. In the law, the definition of mental illness rests primarily on a person's inability to tell right from wrong. For psychologists, insanity is not the same as abnormal behavior. The case of Andrea Yates, the mother who killed her five small children, helps clarify the difference (Figure 14.3).

Understanding the *DSM*

DSM-IV-TR is organized according to five major dimensions, called *axes,* which serve as guidelines for making decisions about symptoms (Figure 14.4). Axis I describes *clinical disorders* that reflect the patient's current condition. Depression and anxiety disorders are examples of Axis I disorders. Axis II describes *trait disorders*, which are long-running personality disturbances (like antisocial personality disorder) and mental retardation.

The other three axes are used to record important supplemental information. Axis III lists general medical conditions that may be important to the person's psychopathology (such as diabetes or hypothyroidism, which can affect mood). Axis IV is reserved for psychosocial and environmental stressors that could be contributing to emotional problems (such as job or housing troubles or the death of a family member). Axis V evaluates a person's overall level of functioning, on a scale from 1 (serious attempt at suicide or complete inability to take care of oneself) to 100 (happy, productive, with many interests).

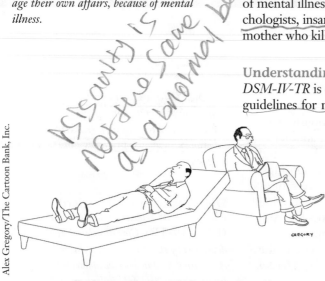

"In the mental health profession, we try to avoid negative labels, like 'a hundred and fifty bucks an hour—that's crazy!' or 'three fifty-minute sessions a week—that's insane!'"

Figure 14.3 *The insanity plea—guilty of a crime or mentally ill?* On the morning of June 20, 2001, Texas mother Andrea Yates drowned her five children in the bathtub, then calmly called her husband to tell him he should come home. At Yates's trial, both the defense and prosecution agreed that Yates was mentally ill at the time of the murders, yet the jury still found her guilty and sentenced her to life in prison. (An appellate court later overturned this conviction. In 2006, Yates was found not guilty by reason of insanity and committed to a state mental hospital in which she will be held until she is no longer deemed a threat.) How could two courts come to such opposite conclusions? *Insanity* is a complicated legal term. In most states it refers to a person who cannot be held responsible for his or her actions, or is judged incompetent to manage his or her own affairs, because of mental illness. Despite high-profile cases like that of Andrea Yates, it's important to keep in mind that the insanity plea is used in less than 1 percent of all cases that reach trial, and when used, it is rarely successful (Kirschner, Litwack, & Galperin, 2004; Slobogin, 2006; West & Lichtenstein, 2006).

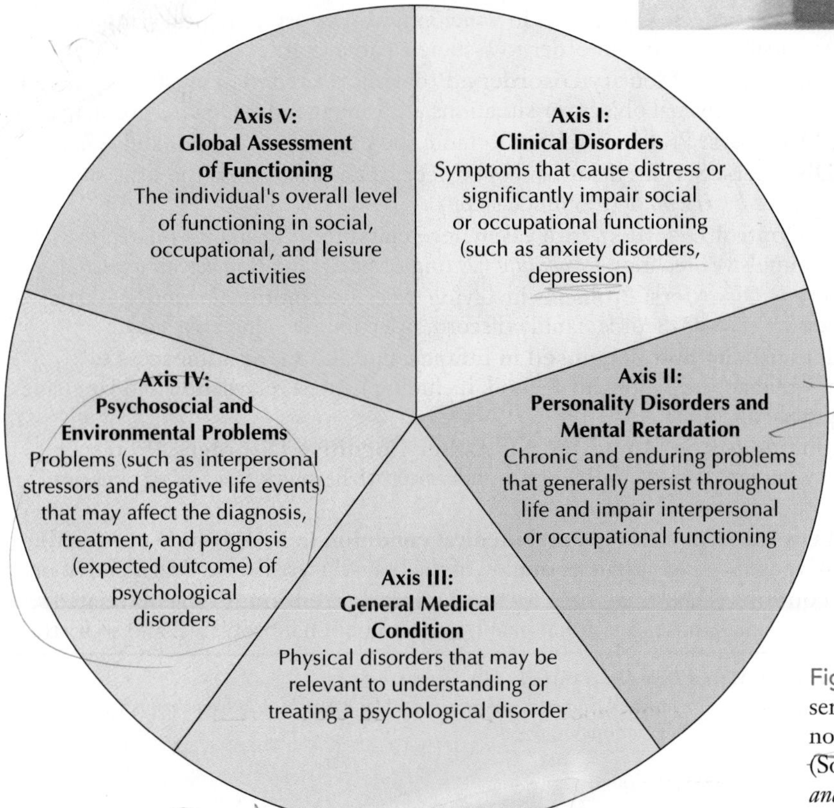

AP/Wide World

Axis V:
Global Assessment of Functioning
The individual's overall level of functioning in social, occupational, and leisure activities

Axis I:
Clinical Disorders
Symptoms that cause distress or significantly impair social or occupational functioning (such as anxiety disorders, depression)

Axis IV:
Psychosocial and Environmental Problems
Problems (such as interpersonal stressors and negative life events) that may affect the diagnosis, treatment, and prognosis (expected outcome) of psychological disorders

Axis II:
Personality Disorders and Mental Retardation
Chronic and enduring problems that generally persist throughout life and impair interpersonal or occupational functioning

Axis III:
General Medical Condition
Physical disorders that may be relevant to understanding or treating a psychological disorder

[handwritten annotations: "⊗ depression and anxiety are an example of AXIS I disorder", "→ traits disorders", "Diabetes hypothyroidism"]

Figure 14.4 *Five axes of DSM-IV-TR* Each axis serves as a broad category that helps clinicians diagnose and classify the wide variety of mental disorders. (Source: Reprinted with permission from the *Diagnostic and Statistical Manual of Mental Disorders*, copyright 2000, American Psychiatric Association.)

In sum, the *DSM* offers a comprehensive, well-defined system intended for the diagnosis and classification of psychological disorders. It does *not* suggest therapies or treatment. The current *DSM-IV-TR* contains more than 200 diagnostic categories grouped into 17 subcategories (Table 14.2). In this chapter, we focus on only the first 6 of these 17 categories. Before we go on, note that the *DSM-IV-TR* classifies disorders, *not* people. Accordingly, we use terms such as *a person with schizophrenia*, rather than describing people as *schizophrenic*.

TABLE 14.2 SUMMARY OF MAIN CATEGORIES OF MENTAL DISORDERS AND THEIR DESCRIPTIONS IN DSM-IV-TR* (THE FIRST SIX DISORDERS ARE DISCUSSED IN THIS CHAPTER)

Anxiety disorders

Mood disorders

Substance-related disorders

1. **Anxiety Disorders:** Problems associated with severe anxiety, such as *phobias, obsessive-compulsive disorder,* and *posttraumatic stress disorder.*
2. **Mood Disorders:** Problems associated with severe disturbances of mood, such as *depression, mania,* or alternating episodes of the two *(bipolar disorder).*
3. **Schizophrenia and other Psychotic Disorders:** A group of disorders characterized by major disturbances in perception, language and thought, emotion, and behavior.
4. **Dissociative Disorders:** Disorders in which the normal integration of consciousness, memory, or identity is suddenly and temporarily altered, such as *amnesia* and *dissociative identity disorder.*
5. **Personality Disorders:** Problems related to lifelong maladaptive personality traits, including *antisocial personality disorders.* (violation of others' rights with no sense of guilt) or *borderline personality disorders* (impulsivity and instability in mood and relationships).
6. **Substance-related Disorders:** Problems caused by alcohol, cocaine, tobacco, and other drugs.
7. **Somatoform Disorders:** Problems related to unusual preoccupation with physical health or physical symptoms with no physical cause.
8. **Factitious Disorders:** Conditions in which physical or psychological symptoms are intentionally produced in order to assume a patient's role.
9. **Sexual and Gender Identity Disorders:** Problems related to unsatisfactory sexual activity, finding unusual objects or situations arousing; gender identity problems.
10. **Eating Disorders:** Problems related to food, such as *anorexia nervosa* and *bulimia.*
11. **Sleep Disorders:** Serious disturbances of sleep, such as *insomnia* (too little sleep), *sleep terrors,* or *hypersomnia* (too much sleep).
12. **Impulse Control Disorders (not elsewhere classified):** Problems related to *kleptomania* (impulsive stealing), *pyromania* (setting of fires), and *pathological gambling.*
13. **Adjustment Disorders:** Problems involving excessive emotional reaction to specific stressors such as divorce, family discord, or economic concerns.
14. **Disorders usually first diagnosed in infancy, childhood, or adolescence:** Problems that appear before adulthood, including mental retardation and language development disorders.
15. **Delirium, Dementia, Amnestic, and Other Cognitive Disorders:** Problems caused by known damage to the brain, including Alzheimer's disease, strokes, and physical trauma to the brain.
16. **Mental Disorders due to a general medical condition (not elsewhere classified):** Problems caused by physical deterioration of the brain due to disease, drugs, and so on.
17. **Other conditions that may be a focus of clinical attention:** Problems related to physical or sexual abuse, relational problems, occupational problems, and so forth.

Diagnostic Manual of Mental Disorders (DSM-IV-TR).
Reprinted with permission from the *Diagnostic and Statistical Manual of Mental Disorders,* copyright 2000, American Psychiatric Association.

Evaluating the *DSM-IV-TR*

The *DSM-IV* has been praised for carefully and completely describing symptoms, standardizing diagnosis and treatment, and facilitating communication among professionals and between professionals and patients. It also is praised as a valuable educational tool. Critics, however, suggest it relies too heavily on the medical model and unfairly labels people (Cooper, 2004; Horwitz, 2007; Mitchell, 2003; Zalaguett et al., 2008). The *DSM-IV* has also been criticized for its possible cultural bias. It does provide a culture-specific section and a glossary of culture-bound syndromes. But some say the classification of most disorders still reflects a Western European and American perspective (Ancis, Chen, & Schultz, 2004; Borra, 2008; Smart & Smart, 1997). In addition, some would prefer that disorders be described not just in terms of *categories* (e.g., anxiety disorders) but also in terms of *dimensions,* or degrees, of traits or behaviors.

Studying Psychological Disorders

Objective 14.1: *Identify five common myths about mental illness.*

The five common myths are: People with psychological disorders act in bizarre ways and are very different from normal people; mental disorders are a sign of personal weakness; mentally ill people are often dangerous and unpredictable; the mentally ill never fully recover; and most can work only at low-level jobs.

Objective 14.2: *Define abnormal behavior, and list four standards for identifying it.*

Abnormal behavior refers to patterns of emotion, thought, and action considered pathological for one or more of these reasons: statistical infrequency, disability or dysfunction, personal distress, or violation of norms.

Objective 14.3: *Compare and contrast culture-general and culture-bound symptoms versus culture-general and culture-bound mental disorders.*

Culture-general symptoms (nervousness or trouble sleeping) are similarly expressed and identified in most cultures around the world, whereas *culture-bound symptoms* ("fullness in head") are unique to certain cultures. Similarly, *culture-general disorders* (schizophrenia) are similar across cultures, whereas *culture-bound disorders* (*Koro* or running amok) are unique.

Objective 14.4: *Briefly describe the history of abnormal behavior.*

In ancient times, people commonly believed that demons were the cause of abnormal behavior. The **medical model**, which emphasizes disease, later replaced this demonological model.

Objective 14.5: *Describe the purpose and criticisms of the DSM-IV-TR, and differentiate between neurosis, psychosis, and insanity.*

The **Diagnostic and Statistical Manual of Mental Disorders (DSM-IV-TR)** classification system provides detailed descriptions of symptoms. It also allows standardized diagnosis and improved communication among professionals and between professionals and patients.

The DSM has been criticized for overreliance on the medical model, unfairly labeling people, possible cultural bias, and for not providing dimensions and degrees of disorder.

Neurosis is an outmoded term for a disorder characterized by unrealistic anxiety and other associated problems, whereas **psychosis** is a current term for a disorder characterized by defective or lost contact with reality. **Insanity** is a legal term applied when people cannot be held responsible for their actions, or are judged incompetent to manage their own affairs, due to mental illness.

Questions

1. What are the four major standards for identifying abnormal behavior?

2. In early treatment of abnormal behavior, _____ was used to allow evil spirits to escape, whereas _____ was designed to make the body so uncomfortable it would be uninhabitable for the devil. (a) purging, fasting; (b) trephining, exorcism; (c) demonology, hydrotherapy; (d) the medical model, the dunking test

3. Briefly define neurosis, psychosis, and insanity.

4. Label the five axes of the *Diagnostic and Statistical Manual of Mental Disorders (DSM-IV-TR)* on the figure below.

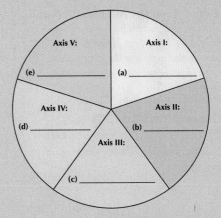

5. What are the chief advantages and disadvantages of the DSM system of classifying mental disorders?

Check your answers in Appendix B.

 Click & Review
for additional assessment options:
wiley.com/college/huffman

Anxiety Disorders

Achievement

Objective 14.6: *Define anxiety disorders and the five major subtypes.*

I was 9 years old and sitting alone in the back of a cab as it rumbled over New York City's 59th Street bridge. I noticed the driver was watching me curiously. My feet began tapping and then shaking, and slowly my chest grew tight and I couldn't get enough air in my lungs. I tried to disguise the little screams I made as throat clearings, but the noises began to rattle the driver. I knew a panic attack was coming on, but I had to hold on, get to the studio, and get through the audition. Still, if I kept riding in that car I was certain I was going to die. The black water was just a few hundred feet below. "Stop!" I screamed at the driver. "Stop right here, please! I have to get out." "Young miss, I can't stop here." "Stop!" I must have looked like I meant it, because we squealed to a halt in the middle of traffic. I got out and began to run. I ran the entire length of the bridge and kept going. Death would never catch me as long as my small legs kept propelling me forward.

ADAPTED FROM PEARCE & SCANLON, 2002, P. 69

wiley.com/college/huffman

Anxiety Disorder *Overwhelming apprehension and fear accompanied by autonomic nervous system (ANS) arousal*

A scene from **The Miracle Worker** *As a young girl, Patty Duke won an Academy Award for her role as Helen Keller. But even at this early age the young actress suffered from symptoms of a serious anxiety disorder.*

Generalized Anxiety Disorder (GAD) *Persistent, uncontrollable, and free-floating nonspecified anxiety*

Panic Disorder *Sudden and inexplicable panic attacks; symptoms include difficulty breathing, heart palpitations, dizziness, trembling, terror, and feelings of impending doom*

These are the words of actress Patty Duke describing an episode around the time she was starring as Helen Keller, the deaf and blind child in *The Miracle Worker*. Patty Duke's flight from the cab and other cases of **anxiety disorder** share one central defining characteristic—unreasonable, often paralyzing, anxiety or fear. The person feels threatened, unable to cope, unhappy, and insecure in a world that seems dangerous and hostile. Anxiety disorders—which are diagnosed twice as often in women as in men—are the most frequently occurring category of mental disorders in the general population (National Institute of Mental Health, 2008; Swartz, 2008). Fortunately, they also are among the easiest disorders to treat and have one of the best chances for recovery (see Chapter 15).

Five Major Anxiety Disorders: The Problem of Fear

Symptoms of anxiety, such as rapid breathing and increased heart rate, plague most of us during final exams and important job interviews. But some people experience unreasonable anxiety that is so intense and chronic it seriously disrupts their lives. We will consider four major types of these anxiety disorders: *generalized anxiety disorder, panic disorder, phobia,* and *obsessive-compulsive disorder* (Figure 14.5). (Note that the fifth anxiety disorder, PTSD, was discussed in Chapter 3). Although we discuss these disorders separately, it is important to remember that people with one anxiety disorder often have others (Halgin & Whitbourne, 2008).

Generalized Anxiety Disorder

This disorder affects twice as many women as it does men (Brown, O'Leary & Barlow, 2001). **Generalized anxiety disorder (GAD)** is characterized by chronic, uncontrollable, and excessive fear and worry that lasts at least six months and that is not focused on any particular object or situation. As the name implies, the anxiety is *generalized* and *nonspecific* or *free-floating*. Victims feel afraid of something, but are unable to identify and articulate the specific fear. Because of persistent muscle tension and autonomic fear reactions, people with this disorder may develop headaches, heart palpitations, dizziness, and insomnia, making it even harder to cope with normal daily activities.

Panic Disorder

As we've just seen, generalized anxiety disorder involves free-floating anxiety. In contrast, **panic disorder** is marked by sudden, but brief, *attacks* of intense apprehension that cause trembling, dizziness, and difficulty breathing. The earlier discussion

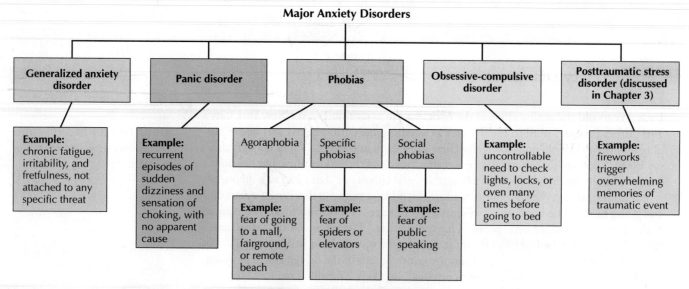

Figure 14.5 *Major anxiety disorders*

of Patty Duke's feeling of suffocation and certainty that she would die if she didn't immediately get out of the car are characteristic of panic attacks. These attacks generally happen after frightening experiences or prolonged stress (and sometimes even after exercise). Panic disorder is diagnosed when several apparently spontaneous panic attacks lead to a persistent concern about future attacks. In the DSM-IV-TR, panic disorder can be classified with or without *agoraphobia*, which is discussed below (Cully & Stanley, 2008; Roberge et al., 2008).

Phobias

Phobias involve a strong, irrational fear and avoidance of objects or situations that are usually considered harmless (fear of elevators or fear of going to the dentist, for example). Although the person recognizes that the fear is irrational, the experience is still one of overwhelming anxiety, and a full-blown panic attack may follow. The *DSM-IV-TR* divides phobic disorders into three broad categories: agoraphobia, specific phobias, and social phobias.

Agoraphobia   People with *agoraphobia* restrict their normal activities because they fear having a panic attack in crowded, enclosed, or wide-open places where they would be unable to receive help in an emergency. In severe cases, people with agoraphobia may refuse to leave the safety of their homes.

Specific Phobias   A specific phobia is a fear of a specific object or situation, such as needles, heights, rats, or spiders. Claustrophobia (fear of closed spaces) and acrophobia (fear of heights) are the specific phobias most often treated by therapists. People with specific phobias generally recognize that their fears are excessive and unreasonable, but they are unable to control their anxiety and will go to great lengths to avoid the feared stimulus (Figure 14.6).

Social Phobias   People with social phobias are irrationally fearful of embarrassing themselves in social situations. Fear of public speaking and of eating in public are the most common social phobias. The fear of public scrutiny and potential humiliation may become so pervasive that normal life is severely restricted (Acarturk et al., 2008; Swartz, 2008).

Obsessive-Compulsive Disorder (OCD)

Do you remember the movie *The Aviator* (Figure 14.7)? The main character, Howard Hughes, was endlessly counting, checking, and repeatedly washing his hands in a seemingly senseless, ritualistic pattern. What drives this behavior? The answer is **obsessive-compulsive disorder (OCD)**. This disorder involves persistent, unwanted fearful thoughts (obsessions) or irresistible urges to perform an act or repeated ritual (compulsions), which help relieve the anxiety created by the obsession. Common examples of obsessions are fear of germs, of being hurt or of hurting others, and troubling religious or sexual thoughts. Examples of compulsions are repeatedly checking, counting, cleaning, washing the body or parts of it, or putting things in

Figure 14.6 *Do you have a spider phobia?* If so, you're probably not reading this caption because you've shut your eyes or turned the page. Phobias are intense, irrational fears.

Phobia *Intense, irrational fear and avoidance of a specific object or situation*

Obsessive-Compulsive Disorder (OCD) *Intrusive, repetitive fearful thoughts (obsessions), urges to perform repetitive, ritualistic behaviors (compulsions), or both*

Figure 14.7 *The Aviator* In this film, Leonardo DiCaprio portrays the obsessive-compulsive behaviors of famous billionaire Howard Hughes.

Achievement

Objective 14.7: *Identify the major contributors to anxiety disorders.*

a certain order. While everyone worries and sometimes double-checks, people with OCD have these thoughts and do these rituals for at least an hour or more each day, often longer (NIMH, 2008).

Imagine what it would be like to worry so obsessively about germs that you compulsively washed your hands hundreds of times a day until they were raw and bleeding. Most sufferers of OCD realize that their actions are senseless. But when they try to stop the behavior, they experience mounting anxiety, which is relieved only by giving in to the urges.

Explaining Anxiety Disorders: Multiple Roots

Why people develop anxiety disorders is a matter of considerable debate. Research has focused primarily on the roles of *psychological*, *biological*, and *sociocultural* processes (the *biopsychosocial model*) (Figure 14.8).

Psychological

Two of the primary psychological contributions to anxiety disorders are faulty cognitions and maladaptive learning.

Faulty Cognitions People with anxiety disorders have certain thinking, or cognitive, habits that make them vulnerable or prone to fear. They tend to be *hypervigilant*. They constantly scan their environment for signs of danger and seem to ignore signs of safety. They also tend to magnify ordinary threats and failures. For example, most people are anxious in a public speaking situation. But those who suffer from a social phobia are excessively concerned about others' evaluation, hypersensitive to any criticism, and obsessively worried about potential mistakes. This intense self-preoccupation intensifies the social anxiety. It also leads these people to think they have failed—even when they have been successful. As you will see in Chapter 15, changing the thinking patterns of anxious people can greatly lessen their fears (Alden, Mellings, & Laposa, 2004; Craske & Waters, 2005; Swartz & Margolis, 2008).

Maladaptive Learning According to learning theorists, anxiety disorders generally result from classical conditioning and social learning (Chapter 6) (Cully & Stanley, 2008; Mineka & Oehlberg, 2008; Swartz, 2008).

During classical conditioning, for example, a stimulus that is originally neutral (e.g., a harmless spider) becomes paired with a frightening event (a sudden panic attack) so that it becomes a conditioned stimulus that elicits anxiety. The person then begins to avoid spiders in order to reduce anxiety (an operant conditioning process known as negative reinforcement).

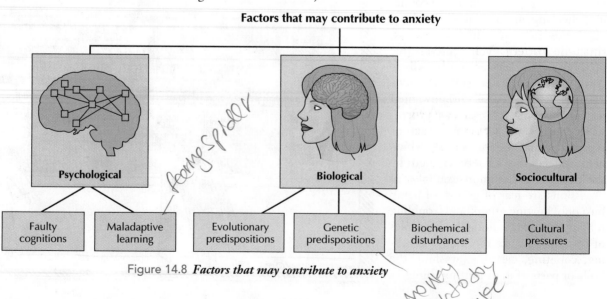

Figure 14.8 *Factors that may contribute to anxiety*

Some researchers contend that the fact that most people with phobias cannot remember a specific instance that led to their fear and that frightening experiences do not always trigger phobias suggests that conditioning may not be the only explanation. Social learning theorists propose that some phobias are the result of modeling and imitation. Phobias may also be learned vicariously (indirectly) (Figure 14.9).

Biological

The fact that the monkeys in Figure 14.9 only developed fears of the toy snake and toy crocodile, but not of the rabbit or flowers, suggests that phobias may develop from a genetic and evolutionary predisposition to fear that which was dangerous to our ancestors (Mineka & Oehlberg, 2008; Walker et al., 2008). In addition to a possible evolutionary predisposition, studies also show that anxiety disorders may be due to a disrupted biochemistry, or unusual brain activity (Anisman, Merali, & Stead, 2008; Craske & Waters, 2005; Stein & Lochner, 2008; Stein & Stein, 2008). Some people with panic disorder seem to be genetically predisposed toward an overreaction of the autonomic nervous system, further supporting the argument for a biological component. In addition, stress and arousal seem to play a role in panic attacks, and drugs such as caffeine or nicotine and even hyperventilation can trigger an attack, all suggesting a biochemical disturbance.

Sociocultural

In addition to psychological and biological components, sociocultural factors can contribute to anxiety. There has been a sharp rise in anxiety disorders in the past 50 years, particularly in Western industrialized countries. Can you see how our increasingly fast-paced lives—along with our increased mobility, decreased job security, and decreased family support—might contribute to anxiety? Unlike the dangers that humans faced in our evolutionary history, today's threats are less identifiable and immediate. This may lead some people to become hypervigilant and predisposed to anxiety disorders.

Further support for sociocultural influences on anxiety disorders is that anxiety disorders can have dramatically different forms in other cultures. For example, in a collectivist twist on anxiety, the Japanese have a type of social phobia called *taijin kyofusho (TKS)*, which involves morbid dread of doing something to embarrass others. This disorder is quite different from the Western version of social phobia, which centers on a fear of criticism.

Courtesy Susan Mineka, Northwestern University

Figure 14.9 *Vicarious phobias*
Monkeys who watch artificially created videotapes of other monkeys being afraid of a toy snake, toy rabbit, toy crocodile, or flowers will develop their own set of phobias (Cook & Mineka, 1989). The fact that the "viewing" monkeys only develop fears of snakes and crocodiles, but not of flowers or toy rabbits, demonstrates that phobias are both learned and biological.

Assessment   STOP

CHECK & REVIEW

Anxiety Disorders

Objective 14.6: *Define anxiety disorders and the five major subtypes.*

People with **anxiety disorders** experience unreasonable, often paralyzing, anxiety or fear. In **generalized anxiety disorder**, there is a persistent, uncontrollable, and free-floating anxiety. In **panic disorder**, anxiety is concentrated into sudden and inexplicable panic attacks. **Phobias** are intense, irrational fears and avoidance of specific objects or situations. **Obsessive-compulsive disorder** involves persistent anxiety-arousing thoughts (obsessions) and/or ritualistic actions (compulsions). (The fifth major anxiety disorder, PTSD, was discussed in Chapter 3.)

Objective 14.7: *Identify the major contributors to anxiety disorders.*

Anxiety disorders are influenced by psychological, biological, and sociocultural factors (the biopsychosocial model).

Psychological theories focus on faulty cognitions (hypervigilance) and maladaptive learning from classical conditioning and social learning. Biological approaches emphasize evolutionary and genetic predispositions, brain differences, and biochemistry. The sociocultural perspective focuses on environmental stressors that increase anxiety and cultural socialization that produces distinct culture-bound disorders like *taijin kyofusho* (TKS).

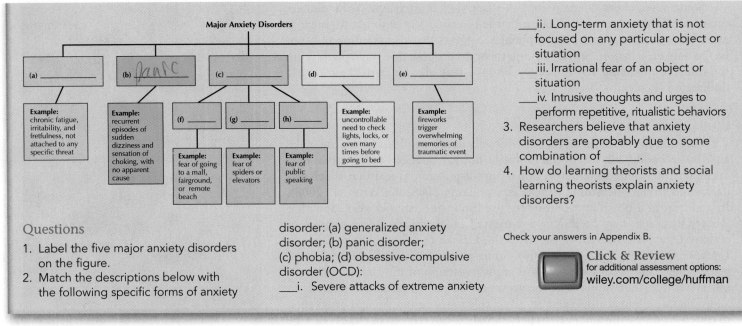

Major Anxiety Disorders

(a) _____   (b) *panic*   (c) _____   (d) _____   (e) _____

Example: chronic fatigue, irritability, and fretfulness, not attached to any specific threat

Example: recurrent episodes of sudden dizziness and sensation of choking, with no apparent cause

(f) _____   (g) _____   (h) _____

Example: fear of going to a mall, fairground, or remote beach

Example: fear of spiders or elevators

Example: fear of public speaking

Example: uncontrollable need to check lights, locks, or oven many times before going to bed

Example: fireworks trigger overwhelming memories of traumatic event

___ii. Long-term anxiety that is not focused on any particular object or situation
___iii. Irrational fear of an object or situation
___iv. Intrusive thoughts and urges to perform repetitive, ritualistic behaviors

3. Researchers believe that anxiety disorders are probably due to some combination of _____.
4. How do learning theorists and social learning theorists explain anxiety disorders?

Questions

1. Label the five major anxiety disorders on the figure.
2. Match the descriptions below with the following specific forms of anxiety disorder: (a) generalized anxiety disorder; (b) panic disorder; (c) phobia; (d) obsessive-compulsive disorder (OCD):
   ___i. Severe attacks of extreme anxiety

Check your answers in Appendix B.

Click & Review for additional assessment options: wiley.com/college/huffman

---

Non Sequiter by Wiley 7. *Distributed by Universal Press Syndicate. All Rights Reserved.*

Achievement

Objective 14.8: *Compare and contrast the two major mood disorders.*

Mood Disorder *Extreme disturbances in emotional states*

Major Depressive Disorder *Long-lasting depressed mood that interferes with the ability to function, feel pleasure, or maintain interest in life*

Mood Disorders

Ann had been divorced for eight months when she called a psychologist for an emergency appointment. Although her husband had verbally and physically abused her for years, she had had mixed feelings about staying in the marriage. She had anticipated feeling good after the divorce, but she became increasingly depressed. She had trouble sleeping, had little appetite, felt very fatigued, and showed no interest in her usual activities. She stayed home from work for two days because she "just didn't feel like going in." Late one afternoon, she went straight to bed, leaving her two small children to fend for themselves. Then, the night before calling for an emergency therapy appointment, she took five sleeping tablets and a couple of stiff drinks. As she said, "I don't think I wanted to kill myself; I just wanted to forget everything for awhile."

(MEYER & SALMON, 1988, P. 312)

Ann's case is a good example of a *mood disorder* (also known as an *affective disorder*). This category encompasses not only excessive sadness, like Ann's, but also unreasonable elation and hyperactivity.

Understanding Mood Disorders: Major Depressive Disorder and Bipolar Disorder

As the name implies, **mood disorders** are characterized by extreme disturbances in emotional states that may include psychotic distortions of reality. There are two main types of mood disorders—*major depressive disorder* and *bipolar disorder*.

Major Depressive Disorder

Depression has been recorded as far back as ancient Egypt, when the condition was called melancholia and was treated by priests. We all feel "blue" sometimes, especially following the loss of a job, end of a relationship, or death of a loved one. People suffering from **major depressive disorder**, however, may experience a lasting and continuously depressed mood without a clear trigger or precipitating event. In addition, their sadness is far more intense, interfering with their basic ability to function, feel pleasure, or maintain interest in life (Fairchild & Scogin, 2008; Swartz & Margolis, 2008).

Clinically depressed people are so deeply sad and discouraged that they often have trouble sleeping, are likely to lose (or gain) weight, and may feel so fatigued that they cannot go to work or school or even comb their hair and brush their teeth. They may sleep both day and night, have problems concentrating, and feel so profoundly sad and guilty that they consider suicide. These feelings have no apparent cause and may be so severe that the individual loses contact with reality. As in the case of Ann, depressed individuals have a hard time thinking clearly or recognizing their own problems. Family or friends are often the ones who recognize the symptoms and encourage them to seek professional help.

Bipolar Disorder

When depression is *unipolar*, the depressive episode eventually ends and people return to a "normal" emotional level. Some people, however, rebound to the opposite state, known as *mania*. In this type of **bipolar disorder**, the person experiences periods of depression as well as *mania* (an excessive and unreasonable state of overexcitement and impulsive behavior) (Figure 14.10).

During a manic episode, the person is overly excited, extremely active, and easily distracted. The person exhibits unrealistically high self-esteem and an inflated sense of importance or even delusions of grandeur. He or she often makes elaborate plans for becoming rich and famous. The individual is hyperactive and may not sleep for days at a time, yet does not become fatigued. Thinking is speeded up and can change abruptly to new topics, showing "rapid flight of ideas." Speech is also rapid ("pressured speech"), and it is difficult for others to get a word in edgewise. Poor judgment is also common: A person may give away valuable possessions or go on wild spending sprees.

Manic episodes may last a few days to a few months and generally end abruptly. The person's previous manic mood, rapid thinking and speaking style, and hyper-activity are reversed. The following depressive episode generally lasts three times as long as the manic episode. The lifetime risk for developing bipolar disorder is low—somewhere between 0.5 and 1.6 percent. Unfortunately, it can be one of the most debilitating and lethal disorders, with a high suicide rate (Carballo, et al., 2008; Kinder et al., 2008; Klimes-Dougan et al., 2008).

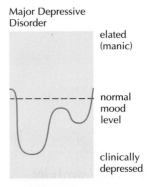

Major Depressive Disorder

elated (manic)

normal mood level

clinically depressed

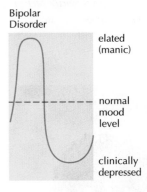

Bipolar Disorder

elated (manic)

normal mood level

clinically depressed

Figure 14.10 *Mood disorder* If major depressive disorders and bipolar disorders were depicted on a graph, they might look something like this.

Bipolar Disorder *Repeated episodes of mania (unreasonable elation, often with hyperactivity) alternating with depression*

Achievement
GENDER & CULTURAL DIVERSITY

How Gender and Culture Affect Depression

Earlier in the chapter, we discussed how certain culture-general symptoms of depression exist across all cultures, and how other symptoms are culturally specific. But how does gender affect depression? It is widely known that women are more likely than men to suffer depressive symptoms. In North America, the rate of clinical (or severe) depression for women is two to three times the rate for men. And this gender difference holds true in several other countries as well (Barry et al., 2008; Nicholson et al., 2008; Nolen-Hoeksema, Larson, & Grayson, 2000).

Why are women more depressed? Research explanations can be grouped under *biological* influences (hormones, biochemistry, and genetic predisposition), *psychological* processes (ruminative thought processes), and *social* factors (greater poverty, work–life conflicts, unhappy marriages, and sexual or physical abuse) (Cooper et al., 2008; Jackson & Williams, 2006; Shear et al., 2007).

Perhaps the best answer is the *biopsychosocial model*, which combines the biological, psychological, and social factors. According to this model, some women may inherit a genetic or hormonal predisposition toward depression. This biological predisposition then combines with our society's socialization processes to help reinforce certain

Achievement

Objective 14.9: *What are the major similarities and differences in depression across cultures and between genders?*

behaviors that increase the chances for depression. For example, gender roles for women in our culture encourage greater emotional expression, passivity, and dependence. In contrast, men are socialized toward emotional suppression, activity, and independence. So it may be that a great number of men are depressed and we just haven't recognized it (Figure 14.11). In recent years, a separate Gotland Male Depression Scale has been developed to help identify this type of *male depressive syndrome* (Walinder & Rutz, 2002).

Explaining Mood Disorders: Biological Versus Psychosocial Factors

Mood disorders differ in their *severity* (how often they occur and how much they disrupt normal functioning). They also differ in their *duration* (how long they last). In this section, we will examine the latest thinking on biological and psychosocial factors that attempts to explain mood disorders.

Biological Factors

Biological factors appear to play a significant role in both major depression and bipolar disorder. Recent research shows that some patients with bipolar and depressive disorders show decreased gray matter and decreased overall functioning in the frontal lobes. This suggests that structural brain changes may contribute to (or cause) these mood disorders. Other research, however, points to imbalances of several neurotransmitters, including serotonin, norepinephrine, and dopamine (Barton et al., 2008; Delgado, 2004; Lyoo et al., 2004; Montgomery, 2008; Wiste et al., 2008).

This makes sense because these same neurotransmitters are involved in the capacity to be aroused or energized and in the control of other functions affected by depression such as sleep cycles and hunger. Moreover, drugs that alter the activity of these neurotransmitters also decrease the symptoms of depression (and hence are called *antidepressants*). Similarly, the drug *lithium* reduces or prevents manic episodes by preventing norepinephrine- and serotonin-sensitive neurons from being overstimulated.

Evidence also suggests that major depressive disorders, as well as bipolar disorders, may be inherited. For example, when one identical twin has a mood disorder, there is about a 50 percent chance that the other twin will also develop the illness (Anisman, Merali, & Stead, 2008; Brent & Melham, 2008; Faraone, 2008; Swartz, 2008). It is important to remember, however, that relatives generally have similar environments as well as similar genes.

Finally, the evolutionary perspective suggests that moderate depression may be an adaptive response to a loss that helps us step back and reassess our goals (Nesse, 2000; Nesse & Jackson, 2006). Consistent with this theory is the observation that primates also show signs of depression when they suffer a significant loss (Spinelli et al., 2007; Suomi, 1991). Clinical, severe depression may just be an extreme version of this generally adaptive response.

Psychosocial Theories

Psychosocial theories of depression and bipolar disorder focus on environmental stressors and disturbances in the person's interpersonal relationships, thought processes, self-concept, and learning history. The psychoanalytic explanation sees depression as anger turned inward against oneself when an important relationship or attachment is lost. Anger is assumed to come from feelings of rejection or withdrawal of affection, especially when a loved one dies. The humanistic school says depression results when a person's self-concept is overly demanding or when positive growth is blocked (Belardinelli et al., 2008; Cheung, Gilbert, & Irons, 2004; Haddad et al., 2008; Hammen, 2005; O'Connell, 2008; Weinstock, 2008).

Another important contributor may be explained by the **learned helplessness** theory of depression, developed by Martin Seligman (1975, 1994, 2007). Seligman

Figure 14.11 *Depression in disguise?* In our society, men are typically socialized to suppress their emotions and to show their distress by acting out (showing aggression), acting impulsively (driving recklessly and committing petty crimes), and engaging in substance abuse. How might such cultural pressures lead us to underestimate male depression?

Learned Helplessness *Seligman's term for a state of helplessness or resignation in which human or nonhuman animals learn that escape from something painful is impossible, and depression results*

has demonstrated that when human or nonhuman animals are repeatedly subjected to pain that they cannot escape, they develop such a strong sense of helplessness or resignation that they do not attempt to escape future painful experiences. In other words, when people (or nonhuman animals) learn they are unable to change things for the better, they're more likely to give up. Can you see how this might help explain citizens who accept brutally repressive governments, or people who stay in abusive relationships? Seligman also suggests that our general societal emphasis on individualism and less involvement with others make us particularly vulnerable to depression.

The learned helplessness theory may also involve a cognitive element, known as *attribution*, or the explanations people assign to their own and others' behavior. Once someone perceives that his or her behaviors are unrelated to outcomes (learned helplessness), depression is likely to occur. This is particularly true if the person attributes failure to causes that are *internal* ("my own weakness"), *stable* ("this weakness is long-standing and unchanging"), and *global* ("this weakness is a problem in lots of settings") (Ball, McGuffin, & Farmer, 2008; Gotlieb & Abramson, 1999; Wise & Rosqvist, 2007).

*A*pplication

RESEARCH HIGHLIGHT

Objective 14.11: *What do we need to know about suicide and its prevention?*

Suicide and Its Prevention

Suicide is a serious danger associated with severe depression. Because of the shame and secrecy surrounding the suicidal person, there are many misconceptions and stereotypes. Can you correctly identify which of the following is true or false?

1. People who talk about suicide are not likely to commit suicide.
2. Suicide usually takes place with little or no warning.
3. Suicidal people are fully intent on dying.
4. Children of parents who attempt suicide are at greater risk of committing suicide.
5. Suicidal people remain so forever.
6. Men are more likely than women to actually kill themselves by suicide.
7. When a suicidal person has been severely depressed and seems to be "snapping out of it," the danger of suicide decreases substantially.
8. Only depressed people commit suicide.
9. Thinking about suicide is rare.
10. Asking a depressed person about suicide will push him or her over the edge and cause a suicidal act that would not otherwise have occurred.

Compare your responses to the experts' answers and explanations (Baldessarini & Tondo, 2008; Brent & Melhem, 2008; Dutra et al., 2008; Hansell & Damour, 2008; Kinder et al., 2008; Klimes-Dougan et al., 2008; Murray, 2009).

Brent C. Peterson/Corbis

1. and 2. **False.** About 90 percent of people who are suicidal talk about their intentions. They may say, "If something happens to me, I want you to . . ." or "Life just isn't worth living." They also provide behavioral clues, such as giving away valued possessions, withdrawing from family and friends, and losing interest in favorite activities.

3. **False.** Only about 3 to 5 percent of suicidal people truly intend to die.

Most are just unsure about how to go on living. They cannot see their problems objectively enough to realize that they have alternative courses of action. They often gamble with death, arranging it so that fate or others will save them. Moreover, once the suicidal crisis passes, they are generally grateful to be alive.

4. **True.** Children of parents who attempt or commit suicide are at much greater risk of following in their footsteps. As Schneidman (1969) puts it, "The person who commits suicide puts his psychological skeleton in the survivor's emotional closet" (p. 225).

5. **False.** People who want to kill themselves are usually suicidal only for a limited period.

6. **True.** Although women are much more likely to attempt suicide, men are more likely to actually commit suicide. Men are also more likely to use stronger methods, such as guns versus pills.

7. **False.** When people are first coming out of a depression, they are actually at greater risk! This is because they now have the energy to actually commit suicide.

8. **False.** Suicide rates are highest for people with major depressive disorders. However, suicide is also the leading cause of premature death in people who suffer from schizophrenia. In addition, suicide is a major cause of death in people with anxiety disorders and alcohol

and other substance-related disorders. Furthermore, suicide is not limited to people with depression. Poor physical health, serious illness, substance abuse (particularly alcohol), loneliness, unemployment, and even natural disasters may push many over the edge.

9. **False.** Estimates from various studies are that 40 to 80 percent of the general public have thought about committing suicide at least once in their lives.

10. **False.** Because society often considers suicide a terrible, shameful act, asking directly about it can give the person permission to talk. In fact, *not asking*

might lead to further isolation and depression.

How can you tell if someone is suicidal? If you believe someone is contemplating suicide, act on your beliefs. Stay with the person if there is any immediate danger. Encourage him or her to talk to you rather than withdraw. Show the person that you care, but do not give false reassurances that "everything will be okay." This type of response makes the suicidal person feel **more** alienated. Instead, openly ask if the person is feeling hopeless and suicidal. Do not be afraid to discuss suicide with

people who feel depressed or hopeless, fearing that you will just put ideas into their heads. The reality is that people who are left alone or who are told they can't be serious about suicide often attempt it.

If you suspect someone is suicidal, it is vitally important that you help the person obtain counseling. Most cities have suicide prevention centers with 24-hour hotlines or walk-in centers that provide emergency counseling. Also, share your suspicions with parents, friends, or others who can help in a suicidal crisis. To save a life, you may have to betray a secret when someone confides in you.

Application

CRITICAL THINKING

ACTIVE LEARNING

Objective 14.12: *Briefly explain how faulty thinking may contribute to depression.*

How Your Thoughts Can Make You Depressed

Respond to the following questions by circling the number that most closely describes how you would feel in the same situation. Answering carefully and truthfully will improve your metacognitive critical thinking skills and insight into how your thoughts may contribute to depression.

Situation 1

You are introduced to a new person at a party and are left alone to talk. After a few minutes, the person appears bored.

1. Is this outcome caused by you? Or is it something about the other person or the circumstances?

1	2	3	4	5	6	7

Other person or circumstances   Me

2. Will the cause of this outcome also be present in the future?

1	2	3	4	5	6	7

No   Yes

3. Is the cause of this outcome unique to this situation, or does it also affect other areas of your life?

1	2	3	4	5	6	7

Affects just this situation   Affects all situations in my life

Situation 2

You receive an award for a project that is highly praised.

4. Is this outcome caused by you or something about the circumstances?

1	2	3	4	5	6	7

Circumstances   Me

5. Will the cause of this outcome also be present in the future?

1	2	3	4	5	6	7

No   Yes

6. Is the cause of this outcome unique to this situation, or does it also affect other areas of your life?

1	2	3	4	5	6	7

Affects just this situation   Affects all situations in my life

This modified version of the *Attributional Style Questionnaire* measures people's explanations for the causes of good and bad events. People with a *depressive explanatory style* tend to explain *bad* events in terms of *internal* factors ("It's my fault"), a *stable* cause ("It will always be this way"), and a *global* cause ("It's this way in many situations"). Sadly, this pattern of negative thinking reverses when good things happen. They attribute good events to external factors and unstable, specific causes. ("I just got lucky, it'll never happen again, and it's only this one event.")

In sharp contrast, people with an *optimistic explanatory style* tend to explain bad events in terms of external factors ("It's just a bad economy"), and unstable, specific causes. ("It seldom happens to me, and it's only this one event."). When good things happen, they attribute them to internal factors ("I deserve this"), and stable, global causes ("I usually win out in most situations.").

	Depressive Explanatory Style	**Optimistic Explanatory Style**
Bad events	Internal, stable, global	External, unstable, specific
Good events	External, unstable, specific	Internal, stable, global

How did you score? High scores (5–7) on questions 1, 2, and 3 and low scores (1–3) on questions 4, 5, and 6 may mean you have a *depressive explanatory style*. In contrast, low scores on the first three questions and high scores on the last three suggest you have an *optimistic explanatory style*.

Unfortunately, if you have a bad experience and then blame it on your personal (internal) inadequacies, interpret it as unchangeable (stable), and draw far-reaching (global) conclusions, you are obviously more likely to feel depressed. This self-blaming, pessimistic, and overgeneralizing explanatory style results in a sense of hopelessness (Ball, McGuffin, & Farmer, 2008).

Critics have asked: Does a depressive explanatory style cause depression? Or does depression cause a depressive explanatory style? Could another variable, such as neurotransmitters or other biological factors, cause both? Evidence suggests that both thought patterns and biology interact and influence depression. Professional help is clearly needed for serious depression, while changing your explanatory style may help dispel mild or moderate depression.

Assessment

STOP CHECK & REVIEW

Mood Disorders

Objective 14.8: *Compare and contrast the two major mood disorders.*

Mood disorders are extreme disturbances of affect (emotion). In **major depressive disorder**, individuals experience a long-lasting depressed mood that interferes with their ability to function, feel pleasure or maintain interest in life. The feelings have no apparent cause, and the individual may lose contact with reality (psychosis). In **bipolar disorder**, episodes of mania and depression alternate with normal periods. During the manic episode, the person is overly excited, his or her speech and thinking are rapid, and poor judgment is common. The person also may experience delusions of grandeur and act impulsively.

Objective 14.9: *What are the major similarities and differences in depression across cultures and between genders?*

Some symptoms of depression, such as frequent and intense sad affect, seem to exist across cultures, but other symptoms, like feelings of guilt, seem to be unique to certain cultures. Although both men and

women suffer from depression, the rate for women in North America is two or three times the rate for men.

Objective 14.10: *Describe the key biological and psychosocial factors that contribute to mood disorders.*

Biological theories of mood disorders emphasize brain function abnormalities and disruptions in neurotransmitters (especially serotonin, norepinephrine, and dopamine). Genetic predisposition also plays a role in both major depression and bipolar disorder.

Psychosocial theories of mood disorders emphasize disturbed interpersonal relationships, faulty thinking, poor self-concept, and maladaptive learning. According to **learned helplessness** theory, depression results from repeatedly failing to escape from a punishing situation.

Objective 14.11: *What do we need to know about suicide and its prevention?*

Suicide is a serious problem associated with depression. If you are having suicidal thoughts, seek help immediately. You also can help others who may be contemplating suicide by becoming involved and showing concern.

Objective 14.12: *Briefly explain how faulty thinking may contribute to depression.*

People with a *depressive explanatory style* tend to attribute bad events to internal factors and stable, global causes, and good events to external factors and unstable, specific causes. This pattern of negative thinking increases the chances for depression.

Questions

1. The two main types of mood disorders are _____.
2. A major difference between major depressive disorder and bipolar disorder is that only in bipolar disorders do people have _____. (a) hallucinations or delusions; (b) depression; (c) manic episodes; (d) a biochemical imbalance
3. What is Martin Seligman's learned helplessness theory of depression?
4. According to attributional theories, depression is more likely to occur when someone attributes his or her failure to _____ cause.

Check your answers in Appendix B.

Click & Review
for additional assessment options:
wiley.com/college/huffman

Schizophrenia

Imagine for the moment that your daughter has just left for college and you hear voices inside your head shouting, "You'll never see her again! You have been a bad mother! She'll die." Or what if you saw dinosaurs on the street and live animals in your refrigerator? These are actual experiences that have plagued Mrs. T for almost three decades (Gershon & Rieder, 1993).

Mrs. T suffers from **schizophrenia**, a disorder characterized by major disturbances in perception, language, thought, emotion, and behavior. As we discussed at the beginning of this chapter, mental disorders exist on a continuum, and many people suffering

Achievement

Objective 14.13: *Define schizophrenia, and describe its five major symptoms.*

Schizophrenia [skit-so-FREE-nee-uh] Group of severe disorders involving major disturbances in perception, language, thought, emotion, and behavior

wiley.com/
college/
huffman

Stephonie Yao

Schizophrenia more severe in men than women

Figure 14.12 *Mental illness in public view* What could be more terrifying than performing at a final audition for *American Idol*? How about doing so just moments after announcing—to Simon Cowell, the show's notorious "celebrity judge"—that you have a mental illness? It's a moment that few people would relish. In fact, fear of ridicule and discrimination leads many people with psychological disorders to keep their condition secret. But singer and songwriter Tracy Moore, who was diagnosed with schizophrenia at age 21, has taken the opposite approach. Even as she combats paranoia and delusional thoughts, Moore has worked to raise public awareness and develop support networks for people with schizophrenia. And she continues to nourish her longtime dream of succeeding as a performing artist. *Source*: Roberts, M. (2006, March). "Idol dreams." *Schizophrenia Digest*, 30–33.

The Jerusalem syndrome Every year, dozens of tourists to Jerusalem are hospitalized with symptoms of *Jerusalem syndrome*, a psychological disturbance in which a person becomes obsessed with the significance of Jerusalem and engages in bizarre, deluded behavior while visiting the city. For example, the person might come to believe that he or she is Jesus Christ or some other biblical character, transform hotel linens into a long, white toga, and publicly deliver sermons or recite Bible verses. Although scholars disagree about the explanations for this "religious psychosis" and the extent to which it is a distinct psychological disorder, the symptoms themselves provide a classic example of delusional thought disturbances. Can you see how delusions of persecution, grandeur, and reference might all play out in Jerusalem syndrome?

Associated Press

from schizophrenia can still function in daily life (Figure 14.12). For some individuals, however, schizophrenia is so severe that it is considered a *psychosis*, meaning that the person is out of touch with reality. People with schizophrenia sometimes have serious problems caring for themselves, relating to others, and holding a job. In extreme cases, the individual may withdraw from others and from reality, often into a fantasy life of delusions and hallucinations. At this point, they may require institutional or custodial care.

Researchers are divided on whether schizophrenia is a distinct disorder itself or a combination of disorders (schizophrenias). However, there is general agreement that it is one of the most widespread and devastating of all mental disorders. Approximately 1 of every 100 persons will develop schizophrenia in his or her lifetime. And approximately half of all people admitted to mental hospitals are diagnosed with this disorder. Schizophrenia usually emerges between the late teens and the mid-thirties and only rarely prior to adolescence or after age 45. It also seems to be equally prevalent in men and women. For unknown reasons it is generally more severe and strikes earlier in men than in women (Combs et al., 2008; Faraone, 2008; Gottesman, 1991; Mueser & Jeste, 2008; Tsuang, Stone, & Faraone, 2001).

Is schizophrenia the same as "split or multiple personality"? No. Schizophrenia means "split mind." When Eugen Bleuler coined the term in 1911, he was referring to the fragmenting of thought processes and emotions found in schizophrenic disorders (Neale, Oltmanns, & Winters, 1983). Unfortunately, the public often confuses "split mind" with "split personality." One study of college freshmen found that 64 percent thought having multiple personalities was a common symptom of schizophrenia

(Torrey, 1998). But as you will read later, *multiple personality disorder* (now known as *dissociative identity disorder*) is the rare condition of having more than one distinct personality.

Symptoms of Schizophrenia: Five Areas of Disturbance

The two categories just discussed each have hallmark features. All people with anxiety disorders have anxiety. All people with mood disorders have depression and/or mania. People who suffer from schizophrenia are different. They can have significantly different symptoms, yet all are given the same general label. This is because schizophrenia is a group or class of disorders. Each case is identified according to some kind of basic disturbance in one or more of the following areas: *perception, language, thought, emotions* (affect), and *behavior.*

Perceptual Symptoms

The senses of people with schizophrenia may be either enhanced (as in the case of Mrs. T) or blunted. The filtering and selection processes that allow most people to concentrate on whatever they choose are impaired. Thus, sensory stimulation is jumbled and distorted. One patient reported:

> When people are talking, I just get scraps of it. If it is just one person who is speaking, that's not so bad, but if others join in then I can't pick it up at all. I just can't get in tune with the conversation. It makes me feel all open—as if things are closing in on me and I have lost control.

(McGhie & Chapman, 1961, p. 106)

These disruptions in sensation help explain why people with schizophrenia experience **hallucinations**—imaginary sensory perceptions that occur without external stimuli. Hallucinations can occur in all of the senses (visual, tactile, olfactory). But auditory hallucinations (hearing voices and sounds) are most common in schizophrenia. As with Mrs. T, people with schizophrenia often hear voices speaking their thoughts aloud, commenting on their behavior, or telling them what to do. The voices seem to come from inside their own heads or from an external source such as an animal, telephone wires, or a TV set.

On rare occasions, people with schizophrenia will hurt others in response to their distorted internal experiences or the voices they hear. Unfortunately, these cases receive undue media attention and create exaggerated fears of "mental patients." In reality, these people are more likely to be self-destructive and suicidal than violent toward others.

Hallucinations *Imaginary sensory perceptions that occur without external stimuli*

Language and Thought Disturbances

Have you heard the proverb "People who live in glass houses shouldn't throw stones?" When asked to explain its meaning, a patient with schizophrenia said,

> "People who live in glass houses shouldn't forget people who live in stone houses and shouldn't throw glass."

From this brief example, can you see how for people with schizophrenia their logic is sometimes impaired and their thoughts disorganized and bizarre? When language and thought disturbances are mild, an individual with schizophrenia jumps from topic to topic. In more severe disturbances, phrases and words are jumbled together (referred to as *word salad*). Or the person creates artificial words (*neologisms*). The person might say "splisters" for *splinters* and *blisters* or "smever" for *smart* and *clever*.

The most common thought disturbance experienced by people with schizophrenia is the lack of contact with reality (*psychosis*). Imagine yourself as Mrs. T seeing dinosaurs on the street and hearing voices saying your daughter will die. Think how frightening it would be if you lost contact with reality and could no longer separate hallucinations and delusions from reality.

"That's the doctor who is treating me for paranoia. I don't trust him."

Delusions *Mistaken beliefs based on misrepresentations of reality*

In addition to this general lack of contact with reality, another common thought disturbance of schizophrenia is that of **delusions**, mistaken beliefs based on misrepresentations of reality. We all experience mistaken thoughts from time to time, such as thinking a friend is trying to avoid us or that our parents' divorce was our fault. But the delusions of schizophrenia are much more extreme. For example, people suffering from schizophrenia sometimes believe others are stalking them or trying to kill them (a *delusion of persecution*). In *delusions of grandeur*, people believe they are someone very important, perhaps Jesus Christ or the queen of England. In *delusions of reference*, unrelated events are given special significance, as when a person believes a radio program or newspaper article is giving him or her a special message.

Emotional Disturbances

It must look queer to people when I laugh about something that has got nothing to do with what I am talking about, but they don't know what's going on inside and how much of it is running around in my head. You see, I might be talking about something quite serious to you and other things come into my head at the same time that are funny and this makes me laugh. If I could only concentrate on one thing at the same time, I wouldn't look half so silly.

(MCGHIE & CHAPMAN, 1961, P. 104)

As you can see from this quote, the emotions of people suffering from schizophrenia are sometimes exaggerated and fluctuate rapidly in inappropriate ways. In other cases, emotions may become blunted or decreased in intensity. Some people with schizophrenia have *flattened affect*—meaning almost no emotional response of any kind.

Behavior Disturbances

Disturbances in behavior may take the form of social withdrawal and/or unusual actions that have special meaning. One patient shook his head rhythmically from side to side to try to shake the excess thoughts out of his mind. Another massaged his head repeatedly "to help clear it" of unwanted thoughts. In other cases, the affected person may grimace and display unusual mannerisms. These movements, however, may also be side effects of the medication used to treat the disorder (Chapter 15).

People with schizophrenia also may become *cataleptic* and assume an uncomfortable, nearly immobile stance for an extended period. A few people with schizophrenia have a symptom called *waxy flexibility*, a tendency to maintain whatever posture is imposed on them.

These abnormal behaviors are often related to disturbances in perceptions, thoughts, and feelings. For example, experiencing a flood of sensory stimuli or overwhelming confusion, a person with schizophrenia may hallucinate, experience delusions, and/or withdraw from social contacts and refuse to communicate.

Achievement

Objective 14.14: *Describe the key methods for classifying schizophrenia.*

▢ Types of Schizophrenia: Recent Methods of Classification

For many years, researchers divided schizophrenia into *paranoid, catatonic, disorganized, undifferentiated*, and *residual* subtypes (Table 14.3). These terms are still included in the *DSM-IV-TR* and are sometimes used by the public. But critics suggest that they have little value in clinical practice and research. They contend that this classification by subtype does not differentiate in terms of prognosis (prediction for recovery), etiology (cause), or response to treatment. Furthermore, the undifferentiated type may be a catchall for cases that are difficult to diagnose (American Psychiatric Association, 2000).

For all these reasons, researchers have proposed an alternative classification system of two groups of symptoms instead of five subtypes:

1. *Positive symptoms* involve *additions* to or exaggerations of normal thought processes and behaviors, such as delusions and hallucinations. Positive symptoms are more common when schizophrenia develops rapidly (called *acute*, or *reactive*, schizophrenia),

TABLE 14.3 SUBTYPES OF SCHIZOPHRENIA

Paranoid	Dominated by delusions (persecution and grandeur) and hallucinations (hearing voices)
Catatonic	Marked by motor disturbances (immobility or wild activity) and echo speech (repeating the speech of others)
Disorganized	Characterized by incoherent speech, flat or exaggerated emotions, and social withdrawal
Undifferentiated	Varied symptoms that meet the criteria for schizophrenia but is not any of the other subtypes
Residual	No longer meets the full criteria for schizophrenia but still shows some symptoms

Study Tip

If you're having difficulty understanding the distinction between positive and negative symptoms of schizophrenia, think back to what you learned in Chapter 6 regarding positive and negative reinforcement and punishment. Positive can be seen as "the addition of," whereas negative refers to the "removal or loss of."

and positive symptoms are associated with better adjustment before the onset and a better prognosis for recovery.

Achievement

Objective 14.15: *What are the major biological and psychosocial factors that influence schizophrenia?*

2. *Negative symptoms* involve the *loss* or absence of normal thought processes and behaviors. Examples include impaired attention, limited or toneless speech, flattened affect (or emotions), and social withdrawal. Negative symptoms are more often found in slow-developing schizophrenia (*chronic,* or *process,* schizophrenia).

In addition to these two groups of positive or negative symptoms, the latest *DSM-IV-TR* suggests adding another dimension to reflect *disorganization of behavior.* Symptoms in this group would include rambling speech, erratic behavior, and inappropriate affect (or feelings). One advantage of either a two- or three-dimension model is the acknowledgment that schizophrenia is more than one disorder and that it has multiple causes.

Explaining Schizophrenia: The Biopsychosocial Model

Why do some people develop schizophrenia? Because the disorder comes in so many different forms, most researchers believe it results from multiple biological and psychosocial factors—the *biopsychosocial model.*

Biological Theories

An enormous amount of scientific research exists concerning possible biological factors in schizophrenia. Some research suggests that prenatal viral infections, birth complications, immune responses, maternal malnutrition, and advanced paternal age all contribute to the development of schizophrenia (Ellman & Cannon, 2008; Meyer et al., 2008; Tandon, Keshavan, & Nasrallah, 2008; Zuckerman & Weiner, 2005). However, most biological theories of schizophrenia focus on three main factors: *genetics, neurotransmitters,* and *brain abnormalities.*

- **Genetics** Although researchers are beginning to identify specific genes related to schizophrenia, most genetic studies have focused on twins and adoptions (Elkin, Kalidindi, & McGuffin, 2004; Faraone, 2008; Hall et al., 2007). This research indicates that the risk for schizophrenia increases with genetic similarity; that is, people who share more genes with a person who has schizophrenia are more likely to develop the disorder (Figure 14.13).

- **Neurotransmitters** Precisely how neurotransmitters contribute to schizophrenia is unclear. According to the **dopamine hypothesis**, overactivity of certain dopamine neurons in the brain may contribute to some forms of schizophrenia (Ikemoto, 2004; Paquet et al., 2004). This hypothesis is based on two important observations. First, administering amphetamines increases the amount of dopamine and can produce (or worsen) some symptoms of schizophrenia, especially in people with a genetic predisposition to the disorder. Second, drugs that reduce dopamine activity in the brain reduce or eliminate some symptoms of schizophrenia.

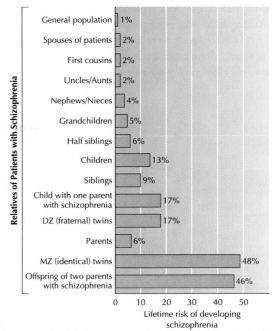

Figure 14.13 *Genetics and schizophrenia* Your lifetime risk of developing schizophrenia depends, in part, on how closely you are genetically related to someone with schizophrenia. As you evaluate the statistics, bear in mind that the risk in the general population is a little less than 1 percent (the top line on the graph). Risk increases with the degree of genetic relatedness. *Source:* Gottesman, "Schizophrenia Genesis," 1991, W. H. Freeman and Company/Worth Publishers.

Dopamine Hypothesis Theory that overactivity of dopamine neurons may contribute to some forms of schizophrenia

wiley.com/
college/
huffman

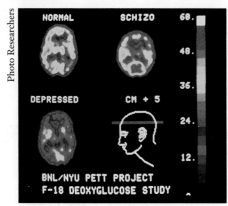

Figure 14.14 *Brain activity in schizophrenia* These positron emission tomography (PET) scans show variations in the brain activity of normal individuals, people with major depressive disorder, and individuals with schizophrenia. Warmer colors (red, yellow) indicate increased activity.

Diathesis-Stress Model *Suggests that people inherit a predisposition (or "diathesis") that increases their risk for mental disorders if exposed to certain extremely stressful life experiences*

Although researchers have found that the dopamine hypothesis is more complicated than orginally thought, it is still widely believed that dopamine plays a role in schizophrenia (Taber, Lewis, & Hurley, 2008).

- **Brain abnormalities** The third major biological theory for schizophrenia involves abnormalities in brain function and structure. Researchers have found larger cerebral ventricles (fluid-filled spaces in the brain) in some people with schizophrenia (Galderisi et al., 2008; Gascr et al., 2004).

Also, some people with chronic schizophrenia have a lower level of activity in their frontal and temporal lobes—areas that are involved in language, attention, and memory (Figure 14.14). Damage in these regions might explain the thought and language disturbances that characterize schizophrenia. This lower level of brain activity, and schizophrenia itself, may also result from an overall loss of gray matter (neurons in the cerebral cortex) (Crepo-Facorro et al., 2007; Gogtay et al., 2004).

Psychosocial Theories

Clearly, biological factors play a key role in schizophrenia. But the fact that even in identical twins—who share identical genes—the heritability of schizophrenia is only 48 percent tells us that nongenetic factors must contribute the remaining percentage. Most psychologists believe that there are at least two possible psychosocial contributors.

According to the **diathesis-stress model** of schizophrenia, stress plays an essential role in triggering schizophrenic episodes in people with an inherited predisposition (or *diathesis*) toward the disease (Jones & Fernyhough, 2007; Reulbach et al., 2007).

Some investigators suggest that communication disorders in family members may also be a predisposing factor for schizophrenia. Such disorders include unintelligible speech, fragmented communication, and parents' frequently sending severely contradictory messages to children. Several studies have also shown greater rates of relapse and worsening of symptoms among hospitalized patients who went home to families that were critical and hostile toward them or overly involved in their lives emotionally (Hooley & Hiller, 2001; McFarlane, 2006).

Evaluating the Theories

How should we evaluate the different theories about the causes of schizophrenia? Critics of the dopamine hypothesis and the brain damage theory argue that those theories fit only some cases of schizophrenia. Moreover, with both theories, it is difficult to determine cause and effect. The disturbed-communication theories are also hotly debated, and research is inconclusive. Schizophrenia is probably the result of a combination of known and unknown interacting factors—the *biopsychosocial model* (Process Diagram 14.2).

Achievement

Objective 14.16: *What are the key similarities and differences in schizophrenia across cultures?*

Achievement

GENDER & CULTURAL DIVERSITY

Schizophrenia Around the World

It is difficult to directly compare mental disorders across cultures because people tend to experience mental disorders in a wide variety of ways. However, schizophrenia seems to have a large biological component and the general symptoms tend to be shared by almost all cultures. Therefore, it may provide the best opportunity for understanding the impact of culture on abnormal behavior.

1. *Prevalence.* Schizophrenia has been found to occur in all countries and cultural groups studied so far. But there are also some interesting differences within these cultures. In Norway, men tend to develop the disease three to four years earlier than women. They also have more and longer hospitalizations and have poorer social functioning (Combs et al., 2008; Raesaenen et al., 2000). It is unclear whether these

Process Diagram 14.2

The Biopsychosocial Model and Schizophrenia

In his portrayal of the Nobel Prize-winning mathematician John Nash, actor Russell Crowe demonstrated several classic symptoms of schizophrenia, including disturbances in perception, language, thought, behavior, and emotion. For Nash, as with others with schizophrenia, no single factor led to his illness.

There is strong evidence linking schizophrenia to biological, psychological, and social factors—the biopsychosocial model.

Source: Adapted and reprinted from Meltzer, "Genetics and Etiology of Schizophrenia and Bipolar Disorder," *Biological Psychiatry*, pp. 171–178, 2000, with permission from Society of Biological Psychiatry.

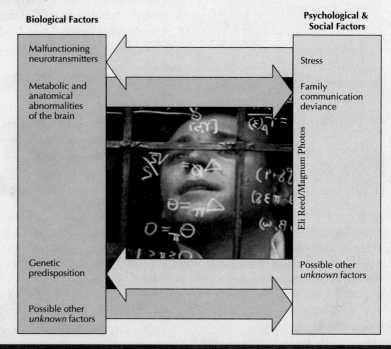

Biological Factors

Malfunctioning neurotransmitters

Metabolic and anatomical abnormalities of the brain

Genetic predisposition

Possible other *unknown* factors

Psychological & Social Factors

Stress

Family communication deviance

Possible other *unknown* factors

Eli Reed/Magnum Photos

---

differences result from an actual difference in prevalence of the disorder or from differences in definition, diagnosis, or reporting (Hoye et al., 2006).

2. ***Form***. The form and symptoms of expression of schizophrenia also vary across cultures. In Nigeria, for example, the major symptom of schizophrenia is intense suspicion of others, accompanied by bizarre thoughts of personal danger (Katz et al., 1988). In Western nations, the major symptom is auditory hallucinations. Interestingly, the "sources" of these auditory hallucinations have changed with technological advances. In the 1920s, the voices that people heard came from the radio. During the 1950s, these voices came from television. In the 1960s, patients reported voices from satellites in outer space. And in the 1970s and 1980s, the voices often came from microwave ovens (Brislin, 2000).

3. ***Onset***. As we discussed earlier, some theories suggest that stress may trigger the onset of schizophrenia. Cross-cultural research in sites such as Algeria, Asia, Europe, South America, the United States, and other cultures supports the relationship between stress and schizophrenia (Al-Issa, 2000; Browne, 2001; le Roux et al., 2007; Neria et al., 2002; Torrey & Yolken, 1998). Some stressors were shared by many cultures, such as the unexpected death of a spouse or loss of a job. But others were culturally specific, such as feeling possessed by evil forces or being the victim of witchcraft.

4. ***Prognosis***. The *prognosis* (or prediction) for recovery from schizophrenia also varies among cultures. Given the advanced treatment facilities and wider availability of trained professionals and drugs in industrialized nations, are you surprised that the prognosis for people with schizophrenia is better in nonindustrialized societies? This may be because the core symptoms of schizophrenia (poor rapport with others, incoherent speech, etc.) make it more difficult to function in highly industrialized countries. In addition, individualism is highly encouraged in most industrialized nations. Therefore, families and other support groups are less likely to feel responsible for relatives and friends with schizophrenia (Brislin, 2000; Lefley, 2000).

Peter Johnson/Corbis

Cultural effects on schizophrenia *The prevalence, form, onset, and prognosis for schizophrenia differ across cultures. Surprisingly, the prognosis, or prediction for recovery, is better for people suffering from schizophrenia in nonindustrialized countries than for those in industrialized countries. Can you explain why?*

Can you see how these four *culturally specific* factors (prevalence, form, onset, and prognosis) support a sociocultural or psychological explanation of schizophrenia? On the other hand, the large number of *culturally general* symptoms and the fact that schizophrenia is found in almost every society also support biological explanations. Once again, we have an example of the interacting factors in the *biopsychosocial model*.

Assessment

STOP

CHECK & REVIEW

Schizophrenia

Objective 14.13: *Define schizophrenia, and describe its five major symptoms.*

Schizophrenia is a serious psychotic mental disorder that afflicts approximately 1 of every 100 people. The five major symptoms are disturbances in perception (**hallucinations**), language (word salad and neologisms), thought (impaired logic and **delusions**), emotion (exaggerated, changeable, or blunted), and behavior (social withdrawal, bizarre mannerisms, catalepsy, waxy flexibility).

Objective 14.14: *Describe the key methods for classifying schizophrenia.*

There are five major subtypes of schizophrenia—*paranoid, catatonic, disorganized, undifferentiated,* and *residual.* There are also two groups of symptoms—*positive* and *negative.*

Objective 14.15: *What are the major biological and psychosocial factors that influence schizophrenia?*

Biological theories of schizophrenia emphasize the role of genetics (people inherit a predisposition), disruptions in neurotransmitters (the **dopamine hypothesis**), and abnormal brain structure and function (such as enlarged ventricles and lower levels of activity in the frontal and temporal lobes). Psychosocial theories of schizophrenia focus on the **diathesis stress model** and disturbed communication.

Objective 14.16: *What are the key similarities and differences in schizophrenia across cultures?*

Although the general symptoms of schizophrenia, like perceptual disturbance, have been found in all countries, the illness differs in *prevalence, form, onset,* and *prognosis.*

Questions

1. Schizophrenia is also a form of _____, a term describing general lack of contact with reality.

2. _____ refers to "split mind," whereas _____ refers to "split personality." (a) Psychosis, neurosis; (b) Insanity, multiple personalities; (c) Schizophrenia, dissociative identity disorder (DID); (d) Paranoia, borderline

3. Perceptions for which there are no appropriate external stimuli are called _____, and the most common type among people suffering from schizophrenia is _____. (a) hallucinations, auditory; (b) hallucinations, visual; (c) delusions, auditory; (d) delusions, visual

4. List three biological and two psychosocial factors that may contribute to schizophrenia.

Check your answers in Appendix B.

Click & Review
for additional assessment options:
wiley.com/college/huffman

Achievement

Objective 14.17: *Identify substance-related disorders and comorbidity.*

Other Disorders

We have now discussed anxiety disorders, mood disorders, and schizophrenia. In this section, we will briefly describe three additional disorders—*substance-related, dissociative,* and *personality disorders.*

Substance-Related Disorders: When Drug Use Becomes Abnormal

Substance-Related Disorders *Abuse of, or dependence on, a mood- or behavior-altering drug*

Do you consider having wine with dinner or a few beers at a party to be an acceptable way to alter mood and behavior? In the *DSM-IV-TR*, drug use becomes a disorder when the person becomes physically or psychologically dependent. As you can see in Table 14.4, **substance-related disorders** are subdivided into two general groups—*substance abuse* and *substance dependence*—each with specific symptoms. When drug use interferes with a person's social or occupational functioning, it is called *substance abuse.* Drug use becomes *substance dependence* when it also causes physical reactions, including *tolerance* (requiring more of the drug to get the desired effect) and *withdrawal* (negative physical effects when the drug is removed).

TABLE 14.4 *DSM-IV-TR* SUBSTANCE ABUSE AND SUBSTANCE DEPENDENCE

Criteria for Substance Abuse (alcohol and other drugs)	Criteria for Substance Dependence (alcohol and other drugs)	Comorbidity and Substance-related Disorders
Maladaptive use of a substance shown by one of the following: • Failure to meet obligations • Repeated use in situations where it is physically dangerous • Continued use despite problems caused by the substance • Repeated substance-related legal problems	*Three or more of the following:* • Tolerance • Withdrawal • Substance taken for a longer time or greater amount than intended • Lack of desire or efforts to reduce or control use • Social, recreational, or occupational activities given up or reduced • Much time spent in activities to obtain the substance • Use continued despite knowing that psychological or physical problems are worsened by it	Can you see how comorbidity can cause serious problems? How can the appropriate cause, course, or treatment be identified for someone dealing with a combination of disorders?

Can people use drugs and not develop a substance-related disorder? Of course. Most people drink alcohol without creating problems in their social relationships or occupations. Unfortunately, researchers have not been able to identify ahead of time those who can safely use drugs versus those who might become abusers (Abadinsky, 2008; Koob & LeMoal, 2008). Substance-related disorders also commonly coexist with other mental disorders, including anxiety disorders, mood disorders, schizophrenia, and personality disorders (Cornelius & Clark, 2008; Green et al., 2004; Munro & Edward, 2008; Thomas et al., 2008). This type of co-occurrence of disorders is known as **comorbidity**, and it creates serious problems.

Comorbidity *Co-occurrence of two or more disorders in the same person at the same time, as when a person suffers from both depression and alcoholism*

How can we identify the appropriate cause or treatment for someone if we're dealing with a combination of disorders? And what causes this type of multiple disorder? Perhaps the most influential hypothesis is that people abuse drugs to self-medicate and reduce their symptoms (Robinson, 2008). One of the most common comorbid disorders is alcohol use disorder (AUD). Research shows a high genetic correlation between alcohol use disorders and other conditions, such as depression and personality disorders (Heath et al., 2003). On the other hand, several environmental variables also predict substance abuse disorders and comorbid conditions in adolescence. These variables include reduced parental monitoring, distance from teachers, selective socialization with deviant peers, and disaffiliation with peers (Fisher & Harrison, 2005; Sher, Grekin, & Williams, 2005).

Although it may seem contradictory to have both genetic and environmental explanations, we see once again that nature and nurture interact. Researchers suggest that the interaction might result from the fact that an alcohol-abusing youth might tend to seek out deviant peers. In addition, the same genes that contribute to a parent's lax monitoring might also contribute to his or her child's early experimentation with alcohol.

The high cost of alcohol abuse *Children of alcoholic parents are at much greater risk of also abusing alcohol and developing related disorders. Is this because of a genetic predisposition, modeling by the parents, or the emotional devastation of growing up with an alcoholic parent?*

wiley.com/
college/
huffman

Regardless of the causes or correlates of alcohol abuse disorders and comorbid conditions, it is critical that patients, family members, and clinicians recognize and deal with comorbidity if treatment is to be effective. Alcohol abuse disorders often accompany serious depression, and simply stopping drinking is not a total solution (though certainly an important first step). Similarly, people suffering from schizophrenia are far more likely to relapse into psychosis, require hospitalization, neglect their medications, commit acts of violence, or kill themselves when they also suffer from AUDs (Cornelius & Clark, 2008; Goswami et al., 2004; Munro & Edward, 2008). Recognizing this pattern and potential danger, many individual and group programs that treat schizophrenia now also include methods used in drug abuse treatment.

Dissociative Disorders: When the Personality Splits Apart

Have you seen the movie *The Three Faces of Eve* or the movie *Sybil?* Both films dramatized and popularized cases of **dissociative disorders**. There are several types of dissociative disorders. But all involve a splitting apart (a *dis*-association) of significant aspects of experience from memory or consciousness. Individuals dissociate from the core of their personality by failing to recall or identify past experience (*dissociative amnesia*), by leaving home and wandering off (*dissociative fugue*), by losing the sense of reality and feeling estranged from the self (*depersonalization disorder*), or by developing completely separate personalities (*dissociative identity disorder*, previously known as *multiple personality disorder*).

The major problem underlying all dissociative disorders is the need to escape from anxiety. By developing amnesia, running away, or creating separate personalities, the individual avoids the anxiety and stress that threaten to overwhelm him or her. Unlike most psychological disorders, environmental variables are reported to be the primary cause, with little or no genetic influence (Waller & Ross, 1997).

Dissociative Identity Disorder

The most severe dissociative disorder is **dissociative identity disorder (DID)**, previously known as *multiple personality disorder* (MPD). In this disorder, two or more distinct personalities exist within the same person at different times. Each personality has unique memories, behaviors, and social relationships. Transition from one personality to another occurs suddenly and is often triggered by psychological stress. Usually, the original personality has no knowledge or awareness of the existence of the alternate subpersonalities. But all of the different personalities may be aware of lost periods of time. Often, the alternate personalities are very different from the original personality. They may be of the other sex, a different race, another age, or even another species (such as a dog or lion). The disorder is diagnosed more among women than among men. Women also tend to have more identities, averaging 15 or more, compared with men, who average 8 (American Psychiatric Association, 2000).

DID is a controversial diagnosis. Some researchers and mental health professionals suggest that many cases are faked or result from false memories and an unconscious need to please the therapist (Kihlstrom, 2005; Lawrence, 2008; Pope et al., 2007; Stafford & Lynn, 2002). These skeptics also believe that therapists may be unintentionally encouraging, and thereby overreporting, the incidence of DID.

Even the authenticity of "Sybil" is now being questioned (Miller & Kantrowitz, 1999) (Figure 14.15). The real-life patient, Shirley Ardell Mason, died in 1998, and some experts are now disputing the original diagnosis of her condition. They suggest that Shirley was highly hypnotizable and suggestible and that her therapist, Cornelia Wilbur, unintentionally "suggested" the existence of multiple personalities.

On the other side of the debate are psychologists who accept the validity of DID and believe the condition is underdiagnosed (Dalenberg et al., 2007; Lipsanen et al., 2004; Spiegel & Maldonado, 1999). Consistent with this view, DID cases have been documented in many cultures around the world. And there has been a rise in the number of reported cases (American Psychiatric Association, 2000). (Critics suggest this also may reflect a growing public awareness of the disorder.)

Dissociative Disorder *Amnesia, fugue, or multiple personalities resulting from a splitting apart of experience from memory or consciousness*

Dissociative Identity Disorder (DID) *Presence of two or more distinct personality systems in the same individual at different times; previously known as multiple personality disorder*

Figure 14.15 **Dissociative identity disorder (DID)** *Actress Sally Field won an Emmy for her sensitive portrayal of a woman suffering from dissociative identity disorder (DID) in the TV drama Sybil. Joanne Woodward portrayed the psychiatrist who guided her back to mental health. Although this drama was based on a real-life patient, experts have recently questioned the validity of the case and the diagnosis of DID. Source: Miller & Kantrowitz, 1999.*

Personality Disorders: Antisocial and Borderline

In Chapter 13, *personality* was defined as a unique and relatively stable pattern of thoughts, feelings, and actions. What would happen if these stable patterns, called personality, were so inflexible and maladaptive that they created significant impairment of someone's ability to function socially and occupationally? This is what happens with **personality disorders**. Unlike most mental disorders, which also involve maladaptive functioning, people with personality disorders generally do not feel upset or anxious about their behavior and may not be motivated to change. Several types of personality disorders are included in this category in *DSM-IV-TR*. In this section we will focus on the best-known type, *antisocial personality disorder*, and one of the most common, *borderline personality disorder*.

Antisocial Personality Disorder

The term **antisocial personality disorder** is used interchangeably with the terms *sociopath* and *psychopath*. These labels describe behavior so far outside the ethical and legal standards of society that many consider it the most serious of all mental disorders. Unlike the case with anxiety, mood disorders, and schizophrenia, people with this diagnosis feel little personal distress (and may not be motivated to change). Yet their maladaptive traits generally bring considerable harm and suffering to others. Although serial killers are often seen as classic examples of antisocial personality disorder, many sociopaths harm people in less dramatic ways—for example, as ruthless businesspeople and crooked politicians.

The four hallmarks of antisocial personality disorder are *egocentrism* (preoccupation with oneself and insensitivity to the needs of others), *lack of conscience, impulsive behavior,* and *superficial charm* (American Psychiatric Association, 2000).

Unlike most adults, individuals with antisocial personality disorder act impulsively, without giving thought to the consequences. They are usually poised when confronted with their destructive behavior and feel contempt for anyone they are able to manipulate. They also change jobs and relationships suddenly, and they often have a history of truancy from school and of being expelled for destructive behavior. People with antisocial personalities can be charming and persuasive, and they have remarkably good insight into the needs and weaknesses of other people. Twin and adoption studies suggest a possible genetic predisposition to antisocial personality disorder. Biological contributions are also suggested by studies that have found abnormally low autonomic activity during stress, right hemisphere abnormalities, reduced gray matter in the frontal lobes, and biochemical disturbances (De Oliveira-Souza et al., 2008; Huesmann & Kirwil, 2007; Kendler & Prescott, 2006; Lyons-Ruth et al., 2007; Raine & Yang, 2006).

Evidence also exists for environmental or psychological causes. Antisocial personality disorder is highly correlated with neglectful and/or abusive parenting styles and inappropriate modeling (Barnow et al., 2007; De Oliveira-Souza et al., 2008; Grover et al., 2007; Lyons-Ruth et al., 2007). People with antisocial personality disorder often come from homes characterized by emotional deprivation, harsh and inconsistent disciplinary practices, and antisocial parental behavior. Still other studies show a strong interaction between both heredity and environment (Gabbard, 2006; Hudziak, 2008).

Borderline Personality Disorder

Borderline personality disorder (BPD) is among the most commonly diagnosed personality disorders (Ansell & Grilo, 2007; Bradley, Conklin, & Westen, 2007). The core features of this disorder are impulsivity and instability in mood, relationships, and self-image. Originally, the term implied that the person was on the borderline between neurosis and schizophrenia (Kring, Davison, Neale, & Johnson, 2007). The modern conceptualization no longer has this connotation, but BPD remains one of the most complex and debilitating of all the personality disorders.

Mary's story of chronic, lifelong dysfunction, described in the chapter opener, illustrates the serious problems associated with this disorder. People with borderline personality disorder experience extreme difficulties in relationships. Subject to chronic feelings of depression, emptiness, and intense fear of abandonment, they also engage

Personality Disorders *Inflexible, maladaptive personality traits that cause significant impairment of social and occupational functioning*

Antisocial Personality Disorder *Profound disregard for, and violation of, the rights of others*

A recent example of an antisocial personality disorder Do you remember listening to audiotapes of Scott Peterson flirting and lying to his girlfriend while others frantically searched for his "missing" wife? This is a good example of the traits and behaviors of an antisocial personality disorder.

Borderline personality disorder (BPD) *Impulsivity and instability in mood, relationships, and self-image*

 wiley.com/college/huffman

in destructive, impulsive behaviors, such as sexual promiscuity, drinking, gambling, and eating sprees. In addition, they may attempt suicide and sometimes engage in self-mutilating behavior (Chapman, Leung, & Lynch, 2008; Crowell et al., 2008; Links et al., 2008; Lynch et al., 2008).

People with BPD tend to see themselves and everyone else in absolute terms—perfect or worthless (Mason & Kreger, 1998). They constantly seek reassurance from others and may quickly erupt in anger at the slightest sign of disapproval. The disorder is also typically marked by a long history of broken friendships, divorces, and lost jobs.

People with borderline personality disorder frequently have a childhood history of neglect; emotional deprivation; and physical, sexual, or emotional abuse (Christopher et al., 2007; Minzenberg, Poole, & Vinogradov, 2008). Borderline personality disorder also tends to run in families, and some data suggest it is a result of impaired functioning of the brain's frontal lobes and limbic system, areas that control impulsive behaviors (Minzenberg et al., 2008).

Although some therapists have had success treating BPD with drug therapy and behavior therapy (Johnson & Murray, 2007; Markovitz, 2004), the prognosis is generally not favorable. People with BPD appear to have a deep well of intense loneliness and a chronic fear of abandonment. Sadly, given their troublesome personality traits, friends, lovers, and even family and therapists often do "adandon" them—thus creating a tragic self-fulfilling prophecy.

PSYCHOLOGY AT WORK

Testing Your Knowledge of Abnormal Behavior

Applying abstract terminology is an important component of critical thinking. Test your understanding of the six major diagnostic categories of psychological disorders by matching the disorders with the possible diagnosis. Check your answers in Appendix B.

Description of Disorder

1. Julie mistakenly believes she has lots of money and is making plans to take all her friends on a trip around the world. She has not slept for days. Last month, she could not get out of bed and talked of suicide.

2. Steve is exceptionally charming and impulsive and apparently feels no remorse or guilt when he causes great harm to others.

3. Chris believes he is president of the United States and hears voices saying the world is ending.

4. Each day, Kelly repeatedly checks and rechecks all stove burners and locks throughout her house and washes her hands hundreds of times.

5. Lee has repeated bouts of uncontrollable drinking, frequently misses his Monday morning college classes, and was recently fired for drinking on the job.

6. Susan wandered off and was later found living under a new name, with no memory of her previous life.

Possible Diagnosis

a. Anxiety disorder

b. Schizophrenia

c. Mood disorder

d. Dissociative disorder

e. Personality disorder

f. Substance-related disorder

CHECK & REVIEW

Other Disorders

Objective 14.17: *Identify substance-related disorders and comorbidity.*

Substance-related disorders involve abuse of, or dependence on, a mood- or behavior-altering drug. People with substance-related disorders also commonly suffer from other psychological disorders, a condition known as **comorbidity**.

Objective 14.18: *Describe dissociative disorders and dissociative identity disorder (DID).*

In **dissociative disorders**, critical elements of personality split apart. This split is manifested in a disassociation of significant aspects of experience from memory or consciousness. Developing completely separate personalities [**dissociative identity disorder (DID)**] is the most severe dissociative disorder.

Objective 14.19: *Define personality disorders, and differentiate between antisocial and borderline personality disorders.*

Personality disorders involve inflexible, maladaptive personality traits. The best-known type is the **antisocial personality**, characterized by a profound disregard for, and violation of, the rights of others. Research suggests this disorder may be related to genetic inheritance, defects in brain activity, or disturbed family relationships. **Borderline personality disorder (BPD)** is the most commonly diagnosed personality disorder. It is characterized by impulsivity and instability in mood, relationships, and self-image.

Questions

1. The major underlying problem for all dissociative disorders is the psychological need to escape from _____.
2. What is DID?
3. A serial killer would likely be diagnosed as a(n) _____ personality in the Diagnostic and Statistical Manual of Mental Disorders, fourth edition, text revision.
4. One possible biological contributor to BPD is _____. (a) childhood history of neglect; (b) emotional deprivation; (c) impaired functioning of the frontal lobes; (d) all these options.

Check your answers in Appendix B.

Click & Review
for additional assessment options:
wiley.com/college/huffman

KEY TERMS

*To assess your understanding of the **Key Terms** in Chapter 14, write a definition for each (in your own words), and then compare your definitions with those in the text.*

Studying Psychological Disorders
abnormal behavior (p. 475)
Diagnostic and Statistical Manual of Mental Disorders (DSM-IV-TR) (p. 479)
insanity (p. 480)
medical model (p. 478)
neurosis (p. 480)
psychiatry (p. 478)
psychosis (p. 480)

Anxiety Disorders
anxiety disorder (p.484)
generalized anxiety disorder (GAD) (p. 484)
obsessive-compulsive disorder (OCD) (p. 485)

panic disorder (p. 484)
phobia (p. 485)

Mood Disorders
bipolar disorder (p. 489)
learned helplessness (p. 490)
major depressive disorder (p. 488)
mood disorder (p. 488)

Schizophrenia
delusions (p. 496)
diathesis-stress model (p. 498)
dopamine hypothesis (p. 497)
hallucinations (p. 495)

schizophrenia [skit-so-Free-nee-uh], (p. 493)
Other Disorders
antisocial personality disorder (p. 503)
borderline personality disorder (BPD) (p. 503)
comorbidity (p. 501)
dissociative disorder (p. 502)
dissociative identity disorder (DID) (p. 502)
personality disorders (p. 503)
substance-related disorders (p. 500)

WEB RESOURCES

Huffman Book Companion Site
wiley.com/college/huffman
This site is loaded with free Interactive Self-Tests, Internet Exercises, Glossary and Flashcards for key terms, web links, Handbook for Non-Native Speakers, and other activities designed to improve your mastery of the material in this chapter.

wiley.com/
college/
huffman

Chapter 14 Visual Summary

Studying Psychological Disorders

Identifying Abnormal Behavior

Abnormal behavior: Pattern of emotion, thought, and action considered pathological for one or more of four reasons (statistical infrequency, disability or dysfunction, personal distress, or violation of norms).

Explaining Abnormality

Stone Age—demonology model; treated with *trephining*.	*Middle Ages*—demonology model; treated with exorcism, torture, imprisonment, death.	*18th century*—Pinel reforms inhumane asylums to treat the mentally ill.	*Modern times*—**medical model** dominates (e.g., **psychiatry**).

Classifying Abnormal Behavior

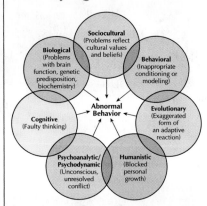

The ***Diagnostic and Statistical Manual of Mental Disorders (DSM-IV-TR)*** categorizes disorders according to major similarities and differences and provides detailed descriptions of symptoms.

* *Benefits:* Detailed descriptions, standardized diagnosis, improved communication among professionals and between professionals and patients.

* *Problems:* Overreliance on the medical model, unfairly labels people, possible cultural bias, and only offers categories—not dimensions and degrees of disorder.

Anxiety Disorders

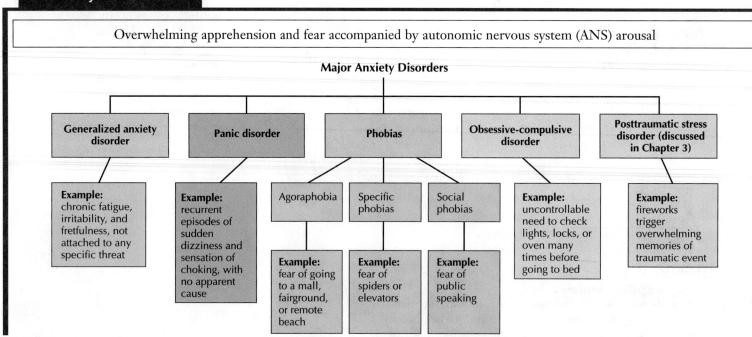

Overwhelming apprehension and fear accompanied by autonomic nervous system (ANS) arousal

Major Anxiety Disorders

Generalized anxiety disorder

Example: chronic fatigue, irritability, and fretfulness, not attached to any specific threat

Panic disorder

Example: recurrent episodes of sudden dizziness and sensation of choking, with no apparent cause

Phobias

Agoraphobia

Example: fear of going to a mall, fairground, or remote beach

Specific phobias

Example: fear of spiders or elevators

Social phobias

Example: fear of public speaking

Obsessive-compulsive disorder

Example: uncontrollable need to check lights, locks, or oven many times before going to bed

Posttraumatic stress disorder (discussed in Chapter 3)

Example: fireworks trigger overwhelming memories of traumatic event

Mood Disorders

Mood disorders are disturbances of affect (emotion) that may include psychotic distortions of reality. Two types:

- **Major depressive disorder:** Long-lasting depressed mood, feelings of worthlessness, and loss of interest in most activities. Feelings are without apparent cause and person may lose contact with reality.

- **Bipolar disorder:** Episodes of mania and depression alternate with normal periods. During manic episode, speech and thinking are rapid, and the person may experience delusions of grandeur and act impulsively.

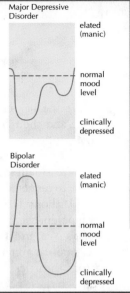

Major Depressive Disorder

elated (manic)

normal mood level

clinically depressed

Bipolar Disorder

elated (manic)

normal mood level

clinically depressed

Schizophrenia

Schizophrenia: Serious psychotic mental disorder afflicting approximately one out of every 100 people.

Five major symptoms characterized by disturbances in:

1) Perception (impaired filtering and selection, **hallucinations**)

2) Language (word salad, neologisms)

3) Thought (impaired logic, **delusions**)

4) Emotion (either exaggerated or blunted emotions)

5) Behavior (social withdrawal, bizarre mannerisms, catalepsy, waxy flexibility)

Two-type Classification System:

Positive symptoms—distorted or excessive mental activity (e.g., delusions and hallucinations).	*Negative symptoms*—behavioral deficits (e.g., toneless voice, flattened emotions).

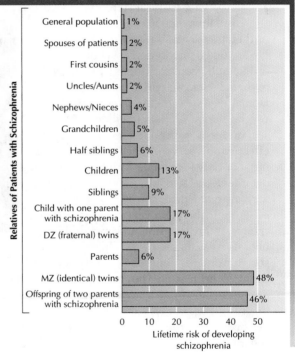

Relatives of Patients with Schizophrenia

General population	1%
Spouses of patients	2%
First cousins	2%
Uncles/Aunts	2%
Nephews/Nieces	4%
Grandchildren	5%
Half siblings	6%
Children	13%
Siblings	9%
Child with one parent with schizophrenia	17%
DZ (fraternal) twins	17%
Parents	6%
MZ (identical) twins	48%
Offspring of two parents with schizophrenia	46%

Lifetime risk of developing schizophrenia

Other Disorders

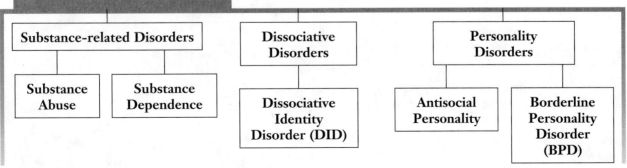

Substance-related Disorders
- **Substance Abuse**
- **Substance Dependence**

Dissociative Disorders
- **Dissociative Identity Disorder (DID)**

Personality Disorders
- **Antisocial Personality**
- **Borderline Personality Disorder (BPD)**

15

Therapy

Since the beginning of the movie age, mentally ill people and their treatment have been the subject of some of Hollywood's most popular and influential films. In addition to the false or exaggerated portrayals of mental health treatment facilities, consider how people with mental illness are depicted. They are either cruel, sociopathic criminals (Anthony Hopkins in *Silence of the Lambs*) or helpless, incompetent victims (Jack Nicholson in *One Flew Over the Cuckoo's Nest* and Winona Ryder in *Girl Interrupted*). Likewise, popular films about mental illness often feature mad doctors, heartless nurses, and brutal treatment methods. Although these portrayals may boost movie ticket sales, they also perpetuate harmful stereotypes (Kondo, 2008).

Like many people, your impressions of therapy may be unfairly guided by these Hollywood depictions of psychological disorders and their treatment. To offset this potential bias, we will present a balanced, factual overview of the latest research on psychotherapy and mental illness. As you'll see, modern psychotherapy can be very effective and prevent much needless suffering, not only for people with psychological disorders but also for those seeking help with everyday problems in living.

You'll also discover that professional therapists include not only psychologists, but also psychiatrists, psychiatric nurses, social workers, counselors, and clergy with training in pastoral counseling. There are numerous forms of psychotherapy. According to one expert (Kazdin, 1994), there may be over 400 approaches to treatment. To organize our discussion, we have grouped treatments into three categories: *insight therapies*, *behavior therapies*, and *biomedical therapies*. After exploring these approaches, we conclude with a discussion of issues that are common to all major forms of psychotherapy.

chievement

> **Objective 15.1:** *Discuss potential problems with media portrayals of therapy, four common myths about therapy, and its three general approaches.*

Paramount Pictures

ASYLUM

DAJ/Getty Images

An Overview of the Three Approaches to Therapy

Insight

Psychoanalysis (Freud) Psychodynamic

Cognitive
- Rational–emotive therapy (Ellis)
- Cognitive–behavior therapy (Beck)

Humanistic
- Client–centered therapy (Rogers)

Group, family, and marital

Behavior

Classical conditioning
- Systematic de-sensitization
- Aversion therapy

Operant conditioning
- Shaping
- Reinforcement
- Punishment
- Extinction

Observational learning
- Modeling

Biomedical

Psychopharmacology

Electroconvulsive therapy

Psychosurgery

▶ **Insight Therapies**

Psychoanalysis/Psychodynamic Therapies
Cognitive Therapies
Humanistic Therapies
Group, Family, and Marital Therapies

CRITICAL THINKING/ACTIVE LEARNING
　　Hunting for Good Therapy Films

▶ **Behavior Therapies**

Classical Conditioning Techniques
Operant Conditioning Techniques
Observational Learning Techniques
Evaluating Behavior Therapies

▶ **Biomedical Therapies**

Psychopharmacology
Electroconvulsive Therapy and Psychosurgery
Evaluating Biomedical Therapies

▶ **Therapy and Critical Thinking**

Therapy Essentials

 PSYCHOLOGY AT WORK
　　Careers in Mental Health

RESEARCH HIGHLIGHT
　　Mental Health and the Family—PTSD

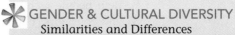 GENDER & CULTURAL DIVERSITY
　　Similarities and Differences

Institutionalization
Evaluating and Finding Therapy

 PSYCHOLOGY AT WORK
　　Non Professional Therapy—Talking to the Depressed

Application

WHY STUDY PSYCHOLOGY?

Do you recognize these myths?

▶ **Myth:** *There is one best therapy.*

Fact: Many problems can be treated equally well with many different forms of therapy.

▶ **Myth:** *Therapists can read your mind.*

Fact: Good therapists often seem to have an uncanny ability to understand how their clients are feeling and to know when someone is trying to avoid certain topics. This is not due to any special mind-reading ability. It reflects their specialized training and daily experience working with troubled people.

Michael Goldman/Masterfile

▶ **Myth:** *People who go to therapists are crazy or weak.*

Fact: Most people seek counseling because of stress in their lives or because they realize that therapy can improve their level of functioning. It is difficult to be objective about our own problems. Seeking therapy is a sign not only of wisdom but also of personal strength.

▶ **Myth:** *Only the rich can afford therapy.*

Fact: Therapy can be expensive. But many clinics and therapists charge on a sliding scale based on the client's income. Some insurance plans also cover psychological services.

Objective 15.2: *Discuss psychotherapy and insight therapy.*

Psychotherapy *Techniques employed to improve psychological functioning and promote adjustment to life*

Objective 15.3: *Define psychoanalysis, and describe its five major methods.*

Psychoanalysis *Freudian therapy designed to bring unconscious conflicts, which usually date back to early childhood experiences, into consciousness; also Freud's theoretical school of thought emphasizing unconscious processes*

Figure 15.1 ***Modern insight therapy in action*** Although each of the insight therapies is unique, they all share a common goal of increasing client/patient understanding and self-knowledge. The belief is that once people have "insight" into what motivates or troubles them, they can overcome their psychological and inter-personal difficulties and improve their adjustment (Corey, 2009).

Insight Therapies

We begin our discussion of professional **psychotherapy** with traditional *psychoanalysis* and its modern counterpart, *psychodynamic* therapy. Then we explore *cognitive, humanistic, group,* and *family therapies.* Although these therapies differ significantly, they're often grouped together as *insight therapies* because they seek to increase *insight* into clients' difficulties (Castonguay & Hill, 2007; Corey, 2009). The general goal is to help people gain greater control over and improvement in their thoughts, feelings, and behaviors (Figure 15.1).

■ Psychoanalysis/Psychodynamic Therapies: Unlocking the Secrets of the Unconscious

Zigy Kaluzny/Stone/Getty Images

As the name implies, in **psychoanalysis**, a person's *psyche* (or mind) is *analyzed.* Traditional psychoanalysis is based on Sigmund Freud's central belief that abnormal behavior is caused by unconscious conflicts among the three parts of the psyche—the *id, ego,* and *superego* (Chapter 13).

During psychoanalysis, these unconscious conflicts are brought to consciousness (Figure 15.2a). The patient discovers the underlying reasons for his or her behavior and comes to realize that the childhood conditions under which the conflicts developed no longer exist. Once this realization (or insight) occurs, the conflicts can be resolved and the patient can develop more adaptive behavior patterns.

Unfortunately, according to Freud, the ego has strong *defense mechanisms* that block unconscious thoughts from coming to light. Thus, to gain insight into the unconscious, the ego must be "tricked" into relaxing its guard. With that goal, psychoanalysts employ five major methods: *free association, dream analysis, analyzing resistance, analyzing transference, and interpretation* (Figure 15.2b).

1. *Free association*   According to Freud, when you let your mind wander and remove conscious censorship over thoughts—a process called **free association**—interesting and even bizarre connections seem to spring into awareness. Freud believed that the first thing to come to a patient's mind is often an important clue to what the person's unconscious wants to conceal.

2. *Dream analysis*   Recall from Chapter 5 that, according to Freud, defenses are lowered during sleep, and forbidden desires and unconscious conflicts can be freely expressed. Even while dreaming, however, these feelings and conflicts are recognized as being unacceptable and must be disguised as images that have deeper symbolic meaning. Thus, during Freudian **dream analysis**, a therapist might interpret a dream of riding a horse or driving a car (the *manifest content*) as a desire for, or concern about, sexual intercourse (the *latent content*).

3. *Analyzing resistance*   During free association or dream analysis, Freud believed patients often show **resistance**—for example, suddenly "forgetting" what they were saying, changing the subject, not talking, and/or arriving late or missing appointments. It is the therapist's job to confront this resistance and to help patients face their problems.

4. *Analyzing transference*   During psychoanalysis, patients supposedly disclose intimate feelings and memories, and patients often apply (or *transfer*) some of their unresolved emotions and attitudes from past relationships onto the therapist. The therapist uses this process of **transference** to help the patient "relive" painful past relationships in a safe, therapeutic setting so that he or she can move on to healthier relationships.

5. *Interpretation*   The core of all psychoanalytic therapy is **interpretation**. During free association, dream analysis, resistance, and transference, the analyst listens closely and tries to find patterns and hidden conflicts. At the right time, the therapist explains (or *interprets*) the underlying meanings to the client.

Free Association *In psychoanalysis, reporting whatever comes to mind without monitoring its contents*

Dream Analysis *In psychoanalysis, interpreting the underlying true meaning of dreams to reveal unconscious processes*

Resistance *In psychoanalysis, the person's inability or unwillingness to discuss or reveal certain memories, thoughts, motives, or experiences*

Transference *In psychoanalysis, the patient may displace (or transfer) unconscious feelings about a significant person in his or her life onto the therapist*

Interpretation *A psychoanalyst's explanation of a patient's free associations, dreams, resistance, and transference; more generally, any statement by a therapist that presents a patient's problem in a new way*

© Hulton-Deutsch Collection/© Corbis

Sigmund Freud (1856-1939) *Freud believed that during psychoanalysis the therapist's (or psychoanalyst's) major goal was to bring unconscious conflicts into consciousness.*

CartoonStock

"The way this works is that you say the first thing that comes to your mind..."

(a)

(b)   Interpretation → Unconscious ← Free Association / Dream Analysis / Analyzing Transference / Analyzing Resistance

Figure 15.2 *Freud's infamous couch* (a) The therapist's couch is a well-known fixture of traditional psychoanalysis (and cartoons). Freud believed that this arrangement—with the therapist out of the patient's view and the patient relaxed—makes the unconscious more accessible and helps patients relax their defenses. (b) Once the patient is relaxed, the psychoanalyst attempts to access the unconscious through these five methods.

Objective 15.4: *What are the two major criticisms of psychoanalysis?*

Evaluation

As you can see, most of psychoanalysis rests on the assumption that repressed memories and unconscious conflicts actually exist. But, as noted in Chapters 7 and 13, this assumption is the subject of a heated, ongoing debate. Critics also point to two other problems with psychoanalysis:

- *Limited applicability.* Freud's methods were developed in the early 1900s for a particular clientele—upper-class Viennese people (primarily women). Although psychoanalysis has been refined over the years, critics say it still seems to suit only a select group of individuals. Success appears to be best with less severe disorders, such as anxiety disorders, and with highly motivated, articulate patients. Critics jokingly proposed the acronym *YAVIS* to describe the perfect psychoanalysis patient: young, attractive, verbal, intelligent, and successful (Schofield, 1964).

  In addition, psychoanalysis is time consuming (often lasting several years with four to five sessions a week) and expensive. And it seldom works well with severe mental disorders, such as schizophrenia. This is logical because psychoanalysis is based on verbalization and rationality—the very abilities most significantly disrupted by serious disorders. Critics suggest that spending years on a couch chasing unconscious conflicts from the past allows patients to escape from the responsibilities and problems of adult life—in effect, the patient becomes "couchridden."

- *Lack of scientific credibility.* The goals of psychoanalysis are explicitly stated—to bring unconscious conflicts to conscious awareness. But how do you know when this goal has been achieved? If patients accept the analyst's interpretations of their conflicts, their "insights" may be nothing more than cooperation with the therapist's belief system.

On the other hand, if patients refuse to accept the analyst's interpretations, the analyst may say they're exhibiting resistance. Moreover, the therapist can always explain away a failure. If patients get better, it's because of their insights. If they don't, then the insight was not real—it was only intellectually accepted. Such reasoning does not meet scientific standards. The ability to prove or disprove a theory is the foundation of the scientific approach.

Psychoanalysts acknowledge that it is impossible to scientifically document certain aspects of their therapy. However, they insist that most patients benefit (Castonguay & Hill, 2007; Wachtel, 2008). Many analysands (patients) agree.

Objective 15.5: *Differentiate between psychoanalysis and psychodynamic therapy.*

Psychodynamic Therapy *A briefer, more directive, and more modern form of psychoanalysis that focuses on conscious processes and current problems*

Modern Psychodynamic Therapy

Partly in response to criticisms of traditional psychoanalysis, more streamlined forms of psychoanalysis have been developed. In modern **psychodynamic therapy**, treatment is briefer. Therapists and patients usually meet only one to two times a week, rather than several times a week, and for only a few weeks or months versus several years. The patient is also seen face to face (rather than reclining on a couch). In addition, the therapist takes a more directive approach (rather than waiting for unconscious memories and desires to slowly be uncovered).

Also, contemporary psychodynamic therapists focus less on unconscious, early childhood roots of problems, and more on conscious processes and current problems. Such refinements have helped make psychoanalysis shorter, more available, and more effective for an increasing number of people (Knekt et al., 2008; Lehto et al., 2008; Lerner, 2008).

Interpersonal therapy (IPT) is a psychodynamically based, and particularly influential, brief form of psychotherapy. As the name implies, *interpersonal* therapy focuses almost exclusively on the client's current relationships and issues that arise from those relationships. Its goal is to relieve immediate symptoms and help the client learn better ways to solve future interpersonal problems. Originally designed for acute depression, IPT is similarly effective for a variety of disorders, including marital conflict, eating disorders, parenting problems, and drug addiction (de Maat et al., 2007; Lerner, 2008; Weissman, 2007).

Assessment

VISUAL QUIZ

PT: Sometimes it doesn't seem worth the effort to continue.

TH: Have you had any thoughts of wanting to kill yourself?

PT: No, not really.

TH: What have you thought of doing?

PT: Nothing that's worth mentioning.

TH: Have you ever thought of taking an overdose of pills?

PT: No, I haven't.

TH: What about cutting yourself or jumping off a bridge?

PT: No, those options aren't very good. You might not die.

TH: Have you thought of a way you think might be more certain, perhaps like using a gun?

PT: (long pause) I have thought of shooting myself.

No small segment of therapy can truly convey an actual full-length therapy session. However, this brief excerpt of an exchange between a patient (PT) and therapist (TH) using a *psychodynamic* approach does demonstrate several psychoanalytic/psychodynamic techniques. Try to identify examples of free association, dream analysis, resistance, or transference in this discussion.

Answer: The clearest example is *resistance*. When the therapist asks her about thoughts of suicide, she initially resists and then admits she has thought of shooting herself. Keep in mind that all therapists in this situation would probe beyond this point in the discussion to follow up on the patient's suicide risk.

Assessment

🛑

CHECK & REVIEW

Psychoanalysis/Psychodynamic Therapies

Objective 15.1: *Discuss potential problems with media portrayals of therapy, four common myths about therapy, and its three general approaches.*

Films about mental illness and its treatment generally present unrealistic and negative stereotypes that bias the public. There are four common myths about therapy: There is one best therapy, therapists can read your mind, people who go to therapists are crazy or weak, and only the rich can afford therapy. There also are three general approaches to therapy—*insight*, *behavior*, and *biomedical*.

Objective 15.2: *Discuss psychotherapy and insight therapy.*

Professional **psychotherapy** refers to techniques employed to improve psychological functioning and promote adjustment to life. The general goal of *insight therapy* is to increase client/patient understanding and self-knowledge. Once people gain this "insight," they can control and improve their functioning.

Objective 15.3: *Define psychoanalysis, and describe its five major methods.*

Freudian **psychoanalysis** works to bring unconscious conflicts into consciousness. The five major techniques of psychoanalysis are **free association, dream analysis, analyzing resistance, analyzing transference,** and **interpretation.**

Objective 15.4: *What are the two major criticisms of psychoanalysis?*

It is time-consuming, expensive, and suits only a small group of people. It also has *limited availability*, and it *lacks scientific credibility*.

Objective 15.5: *Differentiate between psychoanalysis and psychodynamic therapy.*

Compared to traditional psychoanalysis, modern **psychodynamic therapy** is briefer, the patient is treated face to face (rather than reclining on a couch), the therapist takes a more directive approach (rather than waiting for unconscious memories and desires to slowly be uncovered), and the focus is on conscious processes and

current problems (rather than unconscious problems of the past).

Questions

1. The system of psychotherapy developed by Freud that seeks to bring unconscious conflicts into conscious awareness is known as _____. (a) transference; (b) cognitive restructuring; (c) psychoanalysis; (d) the "hot seat" technique

2. Which psychoanalytic concept best explains the following situations?
   a. Mary is extremely angry with her therapist, who seems unresponsive and uncaring about her personal needs.
   b. Although John is normally very punctual in his daily activities, he is frequently late for his therapy session.

3. What are the two major criticisms of psychoanalysis?

4. How does modern psychodynamic therapy differ from psychoanalysis?

Check your answers in Appendix B.

Click & Review
for additional assessment options:
wiley.com/college/huffman

chievement

Objective 15.6: *Discuss cognitive therapy, self-talk, cognitive restructuring, and cognitive-behavior therapy.*

Cognitive therapy *Therapy that treats problem behaviors and mental processes by focusing on faulty thought processes and beliefs*

Self-Talk *Internal dialogue; the things people say to themselves when they interpret events*

Cognitive Restructuring *Process in cognitive therapy to change destructive thoughts or inappropriate interpretations*

Cognitive-Behavior Therapy *Combines cognitive therapy (changing faulty thinking) with behavior therapy (changing faulty behaviors)*

chievement

Objective 15.7: *What is the general goal of Ellis's rational-emotive behavior therapy (REBT)?*

Rational-Emotive Behavior Therapy (REBT) *Ellis's cognitive therapy to eliminate emotional problems through rational examination of irrational beliefs*

Cognitive Therapies: A Focus on Faulty Thoughts and Beliefs

> The mind is its own place, and in itself can make a Heavn' of Hell, a Hell of Heav'n
>
> JOHN MILTON, *PARADISE LOST*, LINE 247

Cognitive therapy assumes that faulty thought processes—beliefs that are irrational, overly demanding, or that fail to match reality—create problem behaviors and emotions (Barlow, 2008; Corey 2009; Davies, 2008; Ellis, 1996, 2003b, 2004; Kellogg & Young, 2008).

Like psychoanalysts, cognitive therapists believe that exploring unexamined beliefs can produce insight into the reasons for disturbed behaviors. However, instead of believing that therapeutic change occurs because of insight into unconscious processes, cognitive therapists believe that insight into negative **self-talk** (the unrealistic things a person tells him- or herself) is most important. Through a process called **cognitive restructuring**, this insight allows clients to challenge their thoughts, change how they interpret events, and modify maladaptive behaviors (Figure 15.3).

This last point of changing maladaptive behavior is the central goal of a closely aligned type of cogitive therapy, called **cognitive-behavior therapy**. As you'll see in the upcoming section, the aptly named behavior therapists focus on changing behavior, and cognitive-behavior therapists work to reduce both self-destructive thoughts *and* self-destructive behaviors.

Albert Ellis and Rational-Emotive Behavior Therapy (REBT)

One of the best-known cognitive therapists, and the so-called "grandfather" of cognitive-behavior therapy, Albert Ellis (1913–2007) suggested irrational beliefs are the primary culprit in problem emotions and behaviors (David, 2007). According to Ellis, outside events do not cause us to have feelings. We feel as we do because of our irrational beliefs. Therefore, his **rational-emotive behavior therapy (REBT)** is

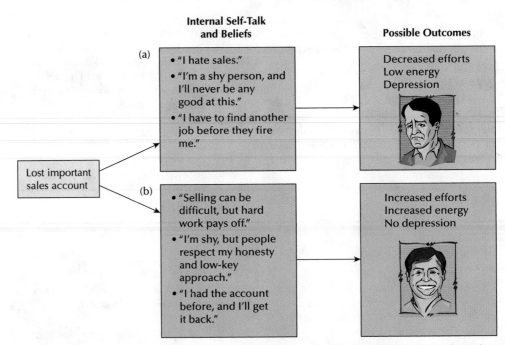

Figure 15.3 *Psychology at work—using cognitive therapy to improve sales* (a) Note how the negative interpretation and destructive self-talk leads to destructive and self-defeating outcomes. (b) Cognitive therapy teaches clients to challenge and change their negative beliefs and negative self-talk into positive ones, which, in turn, leads to more positive outcomes.

Process Diagram 15.1

Ellis's A-B-C-D Approach

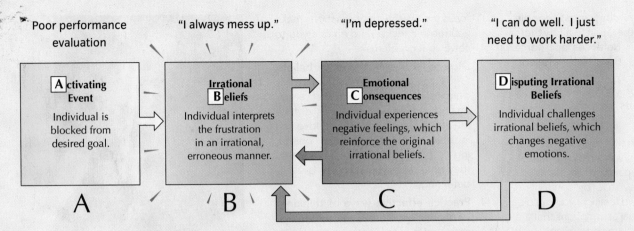

Poor performance evaluation

"I always mess up."

"I'm depressed."

"I can do well. I just need to work harder."

Activating Event	**I**rrational **B**eliefs	**E**motional **C**onsequences	**D**isputing Irrational Beliefs
Individual is blocked from desired goal.	Individual interprets the frustration in an irrational, erroneous manner.	Individual experiences negative feelings, which reinforce the original irrational beliefs.	Individual challenges irrational beliefs, which changes negative emotions.

A   B   C   D

According to Albert Ellis, our emotional reactions are produced by our interpretation of an (A) *activating* event, not by the event itself. For example, if you receive a poor performance evaluation at work, you might directly attribute your bad mood to the negative feedback. Ellis would argue that your irrational (B) belief ("I always mess up") between the event and the *emotional* (C) *consequences* is what upset you. Furthermore, ruminating on all the other bad things in your life maintains your negative emotional state. Ellis's therapy emphasizes (D) *disputing*, or challenging, these irrational beliefs, which, in turn, causes changes in maladaptive emotions—it breaks the vicious cycle.

Aaron Beck

Achievement

Objective 15.8: *Describe Beck's cognitive therapy.*

directed toward challenging and changing these irrational beliefs (Ellis, 1961, 2003a, 2003b, 2004). Ellis calls REBT an A-B-C-D approach: **A** stands for *activating event*, **B** the person's *belief system*, **C** the emotional and behavioral *consequences*, and **D** *disputing* erroneous beliefs. (See Process Diagram 15.1.)

What role does a therapist play in REBT? Ellis believes that most irrational beliefs develop when people demand certain "musts" ("I must get into graduate school") and "shoulds" ("He should love me") from themselves and others. Unfortunately, this general concept of "demandingness," as well as the person's unrealistic, irrational beliefs, generally goes unexamined unless the client is confronted directly. In therapy, Ellis actively argues with clients, cajoling and teasing them, sometimes in very blunt language. Once clients recognize their self-defeating thoughts, Ellis begins working with them on how to *behave* differently—to test out new beliefs and to learn better coping skills.

With or without professional therapy, many of us would benefit from examining and overcoming our irrational beliefs. If you'd like to apply Ellis's approach to your own life, complete the following *Try This Yourself* activity (p. 516).

Aaron Beck's Cognitive Therapy

Another well-known cognitive therapist is Aaron Beck (1976, 2000; Beck & Grant, 2008). Like Ellis, Beck believes that psychological problems result from illogical thinking and from destructive self-talk. But Beck developed a somewhat different form of *cognitive-behavior therapy* to treat psychological problems, especially depression. Beck

Try This Yourself

Overcoming Irrational Misconceptions

Albert Ellis believes that most people require the help of a therapist to allow them to see through their defenses and force them to challenge their self-defeating thoughts. However, you may be able to improve some of your own irrational beliefs and responses with the following suggestions:

1. **Identify your belief system.** Identify your irrational beliefs by asking yourself why you feel the particular emotions you do. Ellis believes that, by confronting your thoughts and feelings, you can discover the irrational assumptions that are creating the problem consequences.

2. **Evaluate the consequences.** Emotions such as anger, anxiety, and depression often seem "natural." But they don't have to happen. Rather than perpetuating negative emotions by assuming they must be experienced,

focus on whether your reactions make you more effective and enable you to solve your problems.

3. **Dispute the self-defeating beliefs.** Once you have identified an overly demanding or irrational belief, argue against it. For example, it is gratifying when people you cherish love you in return, but if they do not, continuing to pursue them or insisting that they must love you will only be self-defeating.

4. **Practice effective ways of thinking.** Continue to examine your emotional reactions to events and situations in order to create opportunities to dispute irrational beliefs and substitute realistic perceptions. Practice behaviors that are more effective by rehearsing them at home and imagining outcomes that are more successful.

Albert Ellis (1913–2007)

has identified several distorted thinking patterns that he believes are associated with depression-prone people:

1. *Selective perception.* Focusing selectively on negative events while ignoring positive events.

2. *Overgeneralization.* Over generalizing and drawing negative conclusions about one's self-worth (e.g., believing you are worthless because you lost a promotion or failed an exam).

3. *Magnification.* Magnifying or exaggerating the importance of undesirable events or personal shortcomings, and seeing them as catastrophic and unchangeable.

4. *All-or-nothing thinking.* Seeing things in black-or-white categories—everything is either totally good or bad, right or wrong, a success or a failure.

"I wish you'd stop being so negative."

In the initial phases of Beck's cognitive-behavior therapy, clients are taught to recognize and keep track of their thoughts (Concept Diagram 15.1). Examples might be: "How come I'm the only one alone at this party" (selective perception) and "If I don't get straight A's, I'll never get a good job" (all-or-nothing thinking). Next, the therapist trains the client to develop ways to test these automatic thoughts against reality. If the client believes that straight A's are necessary for a certain job, the therapist needs to find only one instance of this not being the case to refute the belief. Obviously, the therapist chooses the tests carefully so that they do not confirm the client's negative beliefs but lead instead to positive outcomes.

This approach—identifying dysfunctional thoughts followed by active testing—helps depressed people discover that negative attitudes are largely a product of unrealistic or faulty thought processes.

At this point, Beck introduces the *behavior* phase of therapy, persuading the client to actively pursue pleasurable activities. Depressed individuals often lose motivation, even for experiences they used to find enjoyable. Simultaneously taking an active rather than a passive role and reconnecting with enjoyable experiences help in recovering from depression.

Tracking Faulty Thoughts

In cognitive-behavior therapy, clients often record their thoughts in "thought journals" so that, together with the therapist, they can compare their thoughts with reality, detecting and correcting faulty thinking.

Name: Jordan Holley   Date: November 11

DYSFUNCTIONAL THOUGHT RECORD

Directions: When you notice your mood getting worse, ask yourself, **"What's going through my mind right now?"** and as soon as possible jot down the thought or mental image in the Automatic Thought Column.

DATE/ TIME	SITUATION	AUTOMATIC THOUGHT(S)	EMOTION(S)	ALTERNATIVE RESPONSE	OUTCOME
	1. What actual event or stream of thoughts, or daydreams, or re-collection led to the unpleasant emotion? 2. What (if any) distressing physical sensations did you have?	1. What thought(s) and/or image(s) went through your mind? 2. How much did you believe each one at the time?	1. What emotion(s) (sad, anxious, angry, etc.) did you feel at the time? 2. How intense (0-100%) was the emotion?	1. (optional) What cognitive distortion did you make? (e.g., all-or-nothing thinking, mind-reading, catastrophizing.) 2. Use questions at the bottom to compose a response to the automatic thought(s). 3. How much do you believe each response?	1. How much do you now believe each automatic thought? 2. What emotion(s) do you feel now? How intense (0-100%) is the emotion? 3. What will you do? (or did you do?)
Nov. 10, 9 p.m.	My mom called last night. When I saw her number on the caller I.D., I felt my jaw clench and my heart rate go up.	She's going to nag me again to spend the whole Thanks-giving weekend there to make me feel guilty. I was 90% this was it, so I didn't pick up.	I felt angry and frustrated. Intensity = about 80%	Cognitive distortion was mind-reading or maybe all-or-nothing thinking. The evidence that the automatic thoughts were true is from my past talks with my mom. Maybe she was calling for another reason, not to make me feel guilty about Thanksgiving. The worst that could happen is that she'd make me feel guilty again... If so, I could refuse to feel that way. I could also say I didn't like the repeated pressure - it makes me guilty and sad. Maybe she'd understand and we'd break this pattern, or she'd stop nagging me so much. Now, I feel angry whenever she calls and often don't pick up the phone. If I changed my thinking, maybe I'll feel better about her calls, at least sometimes. So, I should work on not expecting the worst when she calls.	1. 50% 2. Now I feel more optimistic. anger is decreased to about 20%. 3. Next time I will remind myself of the alternative response before picking up the phone.

© John Wiley & Sons

Questions to help compose an alternative response: (1) What is the evidence that the automatic thought is true? Not true? (2) Is there an alternative explanation? (3) What's the worst that could happen? If it did happen, how could I cope? What's the best that could happen? What's the most realistic outcome? (4) What's the effect of my believing the automatic thought? What could be the effect of changing my thinking? (5) What should I do about it? (6) If _____ (friend's name) was in this situation and had this thought, what would I tell him/her?

Worksheet reprinted with permission of Judith S. Beck, Ph.D., © 1993. From <u>Cognitive Therapy: Basics and Beyond</u>, (1995), Guilford Press.

Achievement

Objective 15.9: *What are the chief successes and criticisms of cognitive therapy?*

Achievement

Objective 15.10: *Define humanistic therapy and describe Rogers's client-centered therapy.*

Humanistic Therapy *Therapy that focuses on removing obstacles that block personal growth and potential*

Client-Centered Therapy *Rogers's therapy emphasizing the client's natural tendency to become healthy and productive; techniques include empathy, unconditional positive regard, genuineness, and active listening*

Empathy *In Rogerian terms, an insightful awareness and ability to share another's inner experience*

Unconditional Positive Regard *Rogers's term for love and acceptance with no contingencies attached*

"Just remember, son, it doesn't matter whether you win or lose—unless you want Daddy's love."

Evaluating Cognitive Therapies

Cognitive therapies are highly effective treatments for depression, anxiety disorders, bulimia nervosa, anger management, addiction, procrastination, and even some symptoms of schizophrenia and insomnia (Beck & Grant, 2008; Dobson, 2008; Ellis, 2003a, 2003b, 2004; Kellogg & Young, 2008; Neenan, 2008; Palmer & Gyllensten, 2008).

However, both Beck and Ellis have been criticized for ignoring or denying the client's unconscious dynamics, overemphasizing rationality, and minimizing the importance of the client's past (Hammack, 2003). Other critics suggest that cognitive therapies are successful because they employ *behavior techniques*, not because they change the underlying cognitive structure (Bandura, 1969, 1997, 2006, 2008; Laidlaw & Thompson, 2008; Wright & Beck, 1999). Imagine that you sought treatment for depression and learned to construe events more positively and to curb your *all-or-nothing* thinking. Further imagine that your therapist also helped you identify activities and behaviors that would promote greater fulfillment. If you found your depression lessening, would you attribute the improvement to your changing thought patterns or to changes in your overt behavior?

Humanistic Therapies: Blocked Personal Growth

Humanistic therapy assumes that people with problems are suffering from a disruption of their normal growth potential, and, hence, their self-concept. When obstacles are removed, the individual is free to become the self-accepting, genuine person everyone is capable of being.

Carl Rogers and Client-Centered Therapy

One of the best-known humanistic therapists, Carl Rogers, developed an approach that encourages people to actualize their potential and relate to others in genuine ways. His approach is referred to as **client-centered therapy**. Using the term *client* instead of *patient* was very significant to Rogers. He believed the label "patient" implied being sick or mentally ill rather than responsible and competent. Treating people as clients demonstrates *they* are the ones in charge of the therapy (Rogers, 1961, 1980). It also emphasizes the equality of the therapist–client relationship.

Client-centered therapy, like other insight therapies, explores thoughts and feelings to obtain insight into the causes for behaviors. For Rogerian therapists, however, the focus is on providing an accepting atmosphere and encouraging healthy emotional experiences. Clients are responsible for discovering their own maladaptive patterns.

Rogerian therapists create a therapeutic relationship by focusing on four important qualities of communication: *empathy, unconditional positive regard, genuineness,* and *active listening*.

1. **Empathy** is a sensitive understanding and sharing of another person's inner experience. When we put ourselves in other people's shoes, we enter their inner world. Therapists pay attention to body language and listen for subtle cues to help them understand the emotional experiences of clients. To help clients explore their feelings, the therapist uses open-ended statements such as "You found that upsetting" or "You haven't been able to decide what to do about this" rather than asking questions or offering explanations.

2. **Unconditional positive regard** is genuine caring for people based on their innate value as individuals. Because humanists believe human nature is positive and each person is unique, clients can be respected and cherished without their having to prove themselves worthy of the therapist's esteem. Unconditional positive regard allows the therapist to trust that clients have the best answers for their own lives.

To maintain a climate of unconditional positive regard, the therapist avoids making evaluative statements such as "That's good" and "You did the right thing." Such comments give the idea that the therapist is judging them and that clients need to receive approval. Humanists believe that when people receive unconditional caring from others, they become better able to value themselves in a similar way.

3. **Genuineness**, or *authenticity*, is being aware of one's true inner thoughts and feelings and being able to share them honestly with others. When people are genuine, they are not artificial, defensive, or playing a role. If a Rogerian therapist were pleased or displeased with a client's progress, he or she would feel free to share those feelings. When therapists are genuine with their clients, they believe their clients will, in turn, develop self-trust and honest self-expression.

4. **Active listening** involves reflecting, paraphrasing, and clarifying what the client says and means. To *reflect* is to hold a mirror in front of the person, enabling that person to see him- or herself. To *paraphrase* is to summarize in different words what the client is saying. To *clarify* is to check that both the speaker and listener are on the same wavelength. By being an *active listener*, the clinician communicates that he or she is genuinely interested in what the client is saying (Figure 15.4).

Genuineness *In Rogerian terms, authenticity or congruence; the awareness of one's true inner thoughts and feelings and being able to share them honestly with others*

Active Listening *Listening with total attention to what another is saying; involves reflecting, paraphrasing, and clarifying what the person says and means*

Evaluating Humanistic Therapies

Supporters say there is empirical evidence for the efficacy of client-centered therapy (Hardcastle et al., 2008; Kirschenbaum & Jourdan, 2005; Lein & Wills, 2007; Stiles et al., 2008). But critics argue that the basic tenets of humanistic therapy, such as self-actualization and self-awareness, are difficult to test scientifically. Most of the research on the outcomes of humanistic therapy relies on client self-reports. However, people undergoing any type of therapy are motivated to justify their time and expense. In addition, research on specific therapeutic techniques, such as Rogerian "empathy" and "active listening," has had mixed results (Clark, 2007; Hodges & Biswas-Diener, 2007; Rosenthal, 2007).

Achievement

Objective 15.11: *What are the key criticisms of humanistic therapy?*

David Young Wolff/PhotoEdit

Figure 15.4 *Active listening* Noticing a client's brow furrowing and hands clenching while he is discussing his marital problems, a clinician might respond, "It sounds like you're angry with your wife and feeling pretty miserable right now." Can you see how this statement *reflects* the client's anger, *paraphrases* his complaint, and gives *feedback* to clarify the communication?

Try This Yourself

Roger Ressmeyer/©Corbis

Carl Rogers (1902-1987)

Client-Centered Therapy in Action

Would you like to check your understanding of *empathy*, *unconditional positive regard*, *genuineness*, and *active listening*? Identify the techniques being used in the following excerpt (Shea, 1988, pp. 32–33). Check your responses with those in Appendix B.

THERAPIST (TH): What has it been like coming down to the emergency room today?

CLIENT (CL): Unsettling, to say the least. I feel very awkward here, sort of like I'm vulnerable. To be honest, I've had some horrible experiences with doctors. I don't like them.

TH: I see. Well, they scare the hell out of me, too (smiles, indicating the humor in his comment).

CL: (Chuckles) I thought you were a doctor.

TH: I am (pauses, smiles)—that's what's so scary.

CL: (Smiles and laughs)

TH: Tell me a little more about some of your unpleasant experiences with doctors, because I want to make sure I'm not doing anything that is upsetting to you. I don't want that to happen.

CL: Well, that's very nice to hear. My last doctor didn't give a hoot about what I said, and he only spoke in huge words.

In case you're wondering, this is an excerpt from an actual session—humor and informality can be an important part of the therapeutic process.

Assessment

CHECK & REVIEW

STOP

Cognitive and Humanistic Therapies

Objective 15.6: *Discuss cognitive therapy, self-talk, cognitive restructuring, and cognitive-behavior therapy.*

Cognitive therapy focuses on faulty thought processes and beliefs to treat problem behaviors. Through insight into negative **self-talk** (the unrealistic things people say to themselves), the therapist can use **cognitive restructuring** to challenge and change destructive thoughts or inappropriate behaviors. **Cognitive-behavior therapy** focuses on changing both self-destructive thoughts and self-defeating behaviors.

Objective 15.7: *What is the general goal of Ellis's rational-emotive behavior therapy (REBT)?*

The general goal of **rational-emotive behavior therapy (REBT)** is to eliminate emotional problems through rational examination of irrational and self-defeating beliefs.

Objective 15.8: *Describe Beck's cognitive therapy.*

Beck developed a form of cognitive therapy that is particularly effective for depression. He helps clients identify their distorted thinking patterns, followed by active testing of these thoughts and encouragement toward pleasurable activities.

Objective 15.9: *What are the chief successes and criticisms of cognitive therapy?*

Cognitive therapies have been successful in treating a wide variety of psychological problems (e.g., Beck's success with depression). They have been criticized for ignoring the importance of unconscious processes, overemphasizing rationality, and minimizing the client's past. Some critics also attribute any success with cognitive therapies to the use of behavioral techniques.

Objective 15.10: *Define humanistic therapy, and describe Rogers's client-centered therapy.*

Humanistic therapy assumes problems develop from blocked personal growth, and therapists work alongside clients to remove these obstacles. Rogers **client-centered therapy** emphasizes **empathy, unconditional positive regard, genuineness,** and **active listening**.

Objective 15.11: *What are the key criticisms of humanistic therapy?*

The basic tenets are difficult to evaluate scientifically, most outcome studies rely on self-reports, and research on their specific techniques has had mixed results.

Questions

1. Cognitive therapists assume that problem behaviors and emotions are caused by _____. (a) faulty thought processes and beliefs; (b) a negative self-image; (c) incongruent belief systems; (d) lack of self-discipline

2. The figure on the next page illustrates the process by which the therapist and client work to change destructive ways of thinking called _____.

3. What are the four steps (the A–B–C–D) of Ellis's REBT?

4. Beck identified four destructive thought patterns associated with depression (selective perception, overgeneralization, magnification, and all-or-nothing thinking). Using these terms, label the following thoughts:

_____ a. Mary left me, and I'll never fall in love again. I'll always be alone.

_____ b. My ex-spouse is an evil monster, and our entire marriage was a sham.

5. Label each of the following Rogerian therapy techniques:

_____ a. A sensitive understanding and sharing of another's inner experience

_____ b. The honest sharing of inner thoughts and feelings

_____ c. A nonjudgmental and caring attitude toward another that does not have to be earned

Check your answers in Appendix B.

Click & Review
for additional assessment options:
wiley.com/college/huffman

Group, Family, and Marital Therapies: Healing Interpersonal Relationships

The therapies described thus far all consider the individual as the unit of analysis and treatment. In contrast, group, family, and marital therapies treat multiple individuals simultaneously.

Group Therapy

Group therapy began as a response to the need for more therapists than were available and for a more economical form of therapy. What began as a practical and economic necessity, however, has become a preferred approach in its own right. In **group therapy**, multiple people meet together to work toward therapeutic goals. Typically, 8 to 10 people meet with a therapist on a regular basis, usually once a week for two hours. The therapist can work from any of the psychotherapeutic orientations discussed in this chapter. And, as in individual therapy, members of the group talk about problems in their own lives.

A variation on group therapy is the **self-help group**. Unlike other group therapy approaches, a professional does not guide these groups. They are simply groups of people who share a common problem (such as alcoholism, single parenthood, or breast cancer) and who meet to give and receive support. Faith-based 12-step programs such as *Alcoholics Anonymous, Narcotics Anonymous*, and *Spenders Anonymous* are examples of self-help groups.

Although group members don't get the same level of individual attention found in one-on-one therapies, group and self-help therapies provide their own unique advantages (Corey 2009; Minuchin, Lee, & Simon, 2007; Qualls, 2008):

1. *Less expense.* In a typical group of eight or more, the cost of traditional one-on-one therapy can be divided among all members of the group. Self-help groups, which typically operate without a professional therapist, are even more cost-saving.

2. *Group support.* During times of stress and emotional trouble, it is easy to imagine that we are alone and that our problems are unique. Knowing that others have similar problems can be very reassuring. In addition, seeing others improve can be a source of hope and motivation.

3. *Insight and information.* Because group members typically have comparable problems, they can learn from each other's mistakes and share insights. Furthermore, when a group member receives similar comments about his or her behavior from

Achievement

Objective 15.12: *Discuss, group, self-help, family, and marital therapies.*

Group Therapy *A number of people meet together to work toward therapeutic goals*

Self-Help Group *Leaderless or nonprofessionally guided groups in which members assist each other with a specific problem, as in Alcoholics Anonymous*

several members of the group, the message may be more convincing than if it comes from a single therapist.

4. *Behavior rehearsal.* Group members can role-play one another's employer, spouse, parents, children, or prospective dates. By role-playing and observing different roles in relationships, people gain practice with new social skills. They also gain valuable feedback and insight into their problem behaviors.

Therapists often refer their patients to group therapy and self-help groups to supplement individual therapy. Someone who has a problem with alcohol, for example, can find comfort and help with others who have "been there." They exchange useful information, share their coping strategies, and gain hope by seeing others overcome or successfully manage their shared problems. Research on self-help groups for alcoholism, obesity, and other disorders suggests they can be very effective—either alone or in addition to individual psychotherapy (McEvoy, 2007; Oei & Dingle, 2008; Silverman et al., 2008).

Family and Marital Therapies

> Mental health problems do not affect three or four out of five persons but one out of one.
>
> DR. WILLIAM MENNINGER

Mental disorders have wide ranging effects on the individual sufferer, as well as on his or her friends, family, co-workers, and society in general. Because a family or marriage is a particularly close and intimate system of interdependent parts, the problem of any one individual unavoidably affects all the others (Minuchin, Lee, & Simon, 2007; Qualls, 2008). A teen's delinquency or a spouse's drug problem affects both members of the couple and each individual within the family.

Sometimes the problems parents have with a child arise from conflicts in the marriage. Other times a child's behavior creates distress in an otherwise well-functioning couple. The line between *marital* (or *couples*) therapy and *family therapy* is often blurred. Given that most married couples have children, our discussion will focus on family therapy, in which the primary aim is to change maladaptive family interaction patterns (Figure 15.5). All members of the family attend therapy sessions. At times the therapist may also see family members individually or in twos or threes. (The therapist, incidentally, may take any orientation—cognitive, behavioral, etc.)

Many families initially come into therapy believing that one member is *the* cause of all their problems ("Johnny's delinquency" or "Mom's drinking"). However, family therapists generally find that this "identified patient" is the scapegoat (a person blamed for someone else's problems) for deeper disturbances. For example, instead of confronting their own problems with intimacy, the parents may focus all their attention and frustration on the delinquent child. It is usually necessary to change ways of interacting within the family system to promote the health of individual family members and the family as a whole.

Family therapy is also useful in treating a number of disorders and clinical problems, such as marital infidelity, anger management, etc. (Bagarozzi, 2008; Birchler et al., 2008; Greenberg et al., 2008). As we discussed in Chapter 14, patients with schizophrenia are also more likely to relapse if their family members express emotions, attitudes, and behaviors that involve criticism, hostility, or emotional overinvolvement. Family therapy can help family members modify their behavior toward the patient. It also seems to be the most favorable setting for the treatment of adolescent drug abuse (Minuchin, Lee, & Simon, 2007; Ng et al., 2008; O'Farrell et al., 2008; Sim & Wong, 2008).

Figure 15.5 *What happens in family and marital therapy?* Rather than one-on-one counseling, family therapists generally work with the entire family to improve communication and resolve conflicts.

Tony Freeman/Photoedit

Application

CRITICAL THINKING   ACTIVE LEARNING

Miramax/The Kobal Collection/ The Picture Desk

Hunting for Good Therapy Films
(Contributed by Thomas Frangicetto)

This chapter opened with Hollywood's generally negative and unrealistic portrayals of therapy. There are notable exceptions, like *Good Will Hunting*. But even this film has a few overly dramatic and unprofessional scenes. For example, during the first therapy session between Will Hunting (played by Matt Damon) and his therapist Sean (played by Robin Williams), Sean grabs Will by the throat and threatens him for insulting his deceased wife.

Despite its limits, *Good Will Hunting* provides a reasonably accurate portrayal of several therapy techniques. It also provides an opportunity to review important terms related to insight therapy and improve your critical thinking skills. If you haven't seen the film, here's a brief summary:

Will Hunting, a janitor at MIT, is an intellectual genius. But he is low in emotional intelligence (EI) (Chapter 12). Will's need for revenge gets him into a fight, and he is court-ordered to go into therapy. A number of therapists attempt to work with Will and fail. Sean proves to be up to the task because he "speaks his language"—the language of the streets.

Key Term Review
Identify which insight therapy term is being illustrated in the following:

1. From the moment Will first walks into Sean's office, he engages in a highly creative and relentless avoidance of the therapist's attempts to get him to talk about himself. This is an example of _____.
2. Despite Will's insults and verbal attacks, Sean continues working with him while expressing a nonjudgmental attitude and genuine caring for Will. Sean is displaying _____.
3. During the therapy sessions, Sean often shares his true inner thoughts and feelings with Will. This type of honest communication is called _____.
4. Will's troublesome relationships and antisocial behaviors appear to result from his hidden belief that he is unlovable,

and because he blames himself for the abuse he received as a child. How would Ellis's rational-emotive-behavior therapy explain this in terms of the A–B–C–D approach? The *activating event* (A) is _____. The *irrational belief* (B) is _____. And the *emotional consequence* (C) is _____. Can you create a *disputing irrational belief* (D) statement that Will could use to challenge this irrational belief?
5. After listening to Will focusing solely on the negative aspects of his life and ignoring all the positives, Sean says, "All you see is every negative thing 10 miles down the road." With this statement, Sean wants Will to recognize that he is using _____, one of Beck's thinking patterns associated with depression.

Check your answers in Appendix B.

Critical Thinking Application

Sean is a therapist in need of therapy himself—he is still grieving the death of his wife. A competent therapist would never behave the way Sean does in certain scenes. However, he does effectively portray several characteristics of good professional therapy. In addition, he displays several critical thinking components (CTCs) found in the Prologue (pp. 000). *Empathy* and *active listening* are two of the most obvious components that Sean—and all therapists—employ. Can you identify other CTCs that you think a good therapist might use?

Assessment

⬣STOP⬣   CHECK & REVIEW

Group, Family, and Marital Therapies

Objective 15.12: *Discuss group, self-help, family, and marital therapies.*

In **group therapy**, a number of people (usually 8 to 10) come together to work toward therapeutic goals. A variation on group therapy is the **self-help group** (like Alcoholics Anonymous), which is not guided by a professional. Although group members do not get the same level of attention as in individual therapy, group therapy has important advantages. First, it is less expensive. It also provides group support, insight and

information, and opportunities for behavior rehearsal.

The primary aim of family and marital therapy is to change maladaptive interaction patterns. Because a family is a system of interdependent parts, the problem of any one member unavoidably affects all the others.

Questions

1. In _____, multiple people meet together to work toward therapeutic goals. (a) encounter groups; (b) behavior therapy; (c) group therapy; (d) conjoint therapy

2. What are the four major advantages of group therapy?
3. Why do individual therapists often refer their patients to self-help groups?
4. _____ treats the family as a unit, and members work together to solve problems. (a) Aversion therapy; (b) An encounter group; (c) A self-help group; (d) Family therapy

Check your answers in Appendix B.

Click & Review
for additional assessment options:
wiley.com/college/huffman

Objective 15.13: *What is behavior therapy?*

Behavior Therapy *Group of techniques based on learning principles used to change maladaptive behaviors*

Sidney Harris

chievement

Objective 15.14: *Describe how classical conditioning, operant conditioning, and observational learning are used in behavior therapy.*

Systematic Desensitization
A gradual process of extinguishing a learned fear (or phobia) by working through a hierarchy of fear-evoking stimuli while staying deeply relaxed

Aversion Therapy *Pairing an aversive (unpleasant) stimulus with a maladaptive behavior*

Figure 15.6 ***Virtual reality therapy***
Rather than mental imaging or actual physical experiences of a fearful situation, modern therapy can use the latest in computer technology—virtual reality headsets and data gloves. A client with a fear of heights, for example, can have experiences ranging from climbing a stepladder all the way to standing on the edge of a tall building, while never leaving the therapist's office.

James King-Holmes/Photo Researchers

Behavior Therapies

Have you ever understood why you were doing something that you would rather not do, but continued to do it anyway? Sometimes having insight into a problem does not automatically solve it. **Behavior therapy** focuses on the problem behavior itself, rather than on any underlying causes (Cooper, Heron, & Heward, 2007; Miltenberger, 2008). That is not to say that the person's feelings and interpretations are disregarded; they are just not emphasized. The therapist diagnoses the problem by listing the maladaptive behaviors that occur and the adaptive behaviors that are absent. The therapist then attempts to shift the balance of the two, drawing on principles of classical conditioning, operant conditioning, and observational learning (Chapter 6).

Classical Conditioning Techniques: The Power of Association

Behavior therapists use the principles of classical conditioning. These principles are derived from Pavlov's model for associating two stimulus events. They work to decrease maladaptive behavior by creating new stimulus associations and behavioral responses to replace faulty ones. Two techniques based on these principles are *systematic desensitization* and *aversion therapy* (Process Diagram 15.2).

1. **Systematic desensitization** begins with relaxation training, followed by imagining or directly experiencing various versions of a feared object or situation while remaining deeply relaxed (Wolpe & Plaud, 1977).

   The goal is to replace an anxiety response with a relaxation response when confronting the feared stimulus. Recall from Chapter 2 that the parasympathetic nerves control autonomic functions when we are relaxed. Because the opposing sympathetic nerves are dominant when we are anxious, it is physiologically impossible to be both relaxed and anxious at the same time.

   Desensitization is a three-step process. First, a client is taught how to maintain a state of deep relaxation that is physiologically incompatible with an anxiety response. Next, the therapist and client construct a *hierarchy*, or ranked listing of 10 or so anxiety-arousing images (Process Diagram 15.2a). In the final step, the relaxed client mentally visualizes or physically experiences items at the bottom of the hierarchy. The client then works his or her way upward to the most anxiety-producing images at the top of the hierarchy. If at any time an image or situation begins to create anxiety, the client stops momentarily and returns to a state of complete relaxation. Eventually, the fear response is extinguished.

2. **Aversion therapy** uses principles of classical conditioning to create anxiety rather than extinguish it (Figure 15.6). People who engage in excessive drinking, for example, build up a number of pleasurable associations. These pleasurable associations cannot always be prevented. However, aversion therapy provides *negative associations* to compete with the pleasurable ones. Someone who wants to stop drinking, for example, could take a drug called Antabuse that causes vomiting whenever alcohol enters the system. When the new connection between alcohol and nausea has been classically conditioned, engaging in the once desirable habit will cause an immediate negative response (Process Diagram 15.2b).

Process Diagram 15.2

Overcoming Maladaptive Behaviors — Phobias and Alcoholism

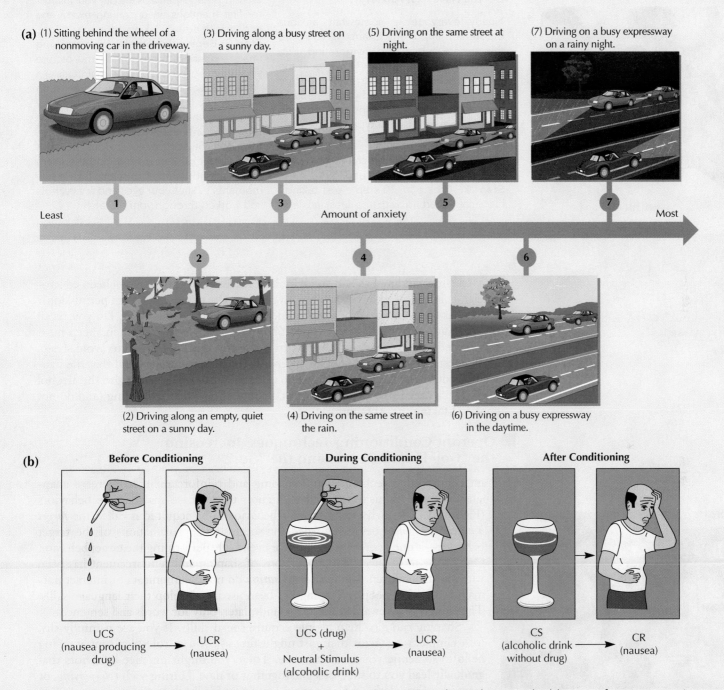

(a) (1) Sitting behind the wheel of a nonmoving car in the driveway.

(3) Driving along a busy street on a sunny day.

(5) Driving on the same street at night.

(7) Driving on a busy expressway on a rainy night.

Least — Amount of anxiety — Most

(2) Driving along an empty, quiet street on a sunny day.

(4) Driving on the same street in the rain.

(6) Driving on a busy expressway in the daytime.

(b)

Before Conditioning

UCS (nausea producing drug) → UCR (nausea)

During Conditioning

UCS (drug) + Neutral Stimulus (alcoholic drink) → UCR (nausea)

After Conditioning

CS (alcoholic drink without drug) → CR (nausea)

(a) *During systematic desensitization*, the client begins by constructing a hierarchy, or ranked listing, of anxiety-arousing images or situations starting with one that produces very little anxiety and escalating to those that arouse extreme anxiety. To extinguish a driving phobia, the patient begins with images of actually sitting behind the wheel of a nonmoving car and ends with driving on a busy expressway.

(b) *Aversion therapy for alcoholism* is based on classical conditioning. A nausea-producing drug (Antabuse) is paired with alcohol to create an aversion (dislike) for drinking.

Stockbyte/Getty Images

Do You Have Test Anxiety?

Nearly everyone is somewhat anxious before an important exam. If you find this anxiety helpful and invigorating, skip ahead to the next section. However, if the days and evenings before a major exam are ruined by your anxiety and you sometimes "freeze up" while taking the test, you can benefit from an informal type of systematic desensitization.

Step 1: Review and practice the relaxation technique taught in Chapter 3.
Step 2: Create a 10-step "test-taking" hierarchy—starting with the least anxiety-

arousing image (perhaps the day your instructor first mentions an upcoming exam) and ending with actually taking the exam.
Step 3: Beginning with the least arousing image—hearing about the exam—picture yourself at each stage. While maintaining a calm, relaxed state, work your way through all 10 steps. If you become anxious at any stage, stay there, repeating your relaxation technique until the anxiety diminishes.
Step 4: If you start to feel anxious the night before the exam, or even during the exam itself, remind yourself to relax. Take a few moments to shut your eyes and review how you worked through your hierarchy.

Aversion therapy has had some limited success, but it has always been controversial. Is it ethical to hurt someone (even when the person has given permission)? It also has been criticized because it does not provide lasting relief. Do you recall the taste aversion studies in Chapter 6? It was discovered that when sheep meat was tainted with a nausea-producing drug, coyotes quickly learned to avoid sheep. Why doesn't it work with people? Interestingly, humans understand that the nausea is produced by the Antabuse and do not generalize their learning to the alcohol itself. Once they leave treatment, most alcoholics go back to drinking (and do not continue taking the Antabuse).

Operant Conditioning Techniques: Increasing the "Good" and Decreasing the "Bad"

Operant conditioning techniques use shaping and reinforcement to increase adaptive behaviors, and punishment and extinction to decrease maladaptive behaviors (Figure 15.7). In behavior therapy, a behavior to be acquired is called the *target behavior. Shaping*—being rewarded for successive approximations of the target behavior—is one operant technique for eventually performing the target behavior. One of the most successful applications of shaping and reinforcement has been with autistic children. Children with *autism* do not communicate or interact normally with other people. Shaping has been used to develop their language skills. The child is first rewarded for any sounds; later, only for words and sentences.

Shaping can also help people acquire social skills. If you are painfully shy, for example, a behavior therapist might first ask you to role-play simply saying hello to someone you find attractive. Then, you might practice behaviors that gradually lead you to suggest a get-together or date. During such *role-playing*, or *behavior rehearsal*, the clinician would give you feedback and reinforcement.

ABC Television

Figure 15.7 *"The Nanny"—psychology at work* Like the techniques used in the popular TV program The Nanny, behavior therapists may train parents to reward children for appropriate behavior. They also train parents to withdraw attention (extinction) or to use time-out procedures (punishment) to weaken or eliminate inappropriate behavior.

Adaptive behaviors can also be taught or increased with techniques that provide immediate reinforcement in the form of tokens (Kazdin, 2008; Tarbox, Ghezzi, & Wilson, 2006). For example, patients in an inpatient treatment facility might at first be given tokens (to be exchanged for primary rewards, such as food, treats, TV time, a private room, or outings) for merely attending group therapy sessions. Later they will be rewarded only for actually participating in the sessions. Eventually, the tokens can be discontinued when the patient receives the reinforcement of being helped by participation in the therapy sessions.

■ Observational Learning Techniques: The Power of Modeling

We all learn many things by observing others. Therapists use this principle in **modeling therapy**, in which clients are asked to observe and imitate appropriate *models* as they perform desired behaviors. For example, Albert Bandura and his colleagues (1969) asked clients with snake phobias to watch other (nonphobic) people handle snakes. After only two hours of exposure, over 92 percent of the phobic observers allowed a snake to crawl over their hands, arms, and necks. When the therapy combines live modeling with direct and gradual practice, it is called *participant modeling* (Figure 15.8).

■ Evaluating Behavior Therapies: How Well Do They Work?

Behavior therapy has been effective with various problems, including phobias, obsessive-compulsive disorder, eating disorders, autism, mental retardation, and delinquency (Ekers, Richards, & Gilbody, 2008; Freeman et al., 2008; Miltenberger, 2008). Some patients have even returned to their homes and communities after years of institutionalization. However, critics of behavior therapy raise important questions that fall into two major categories:

1. *Generalizability.* Critics argue that patients are not consistently reinforced in the "real world," and their newly acquired behaviors may disappear. To deal with this possibility, behavior therapists work to gradually shape clients toward rewards that are typical of life outside the clinical setting.

2. *Ethics.* Is it ethical for one person to control another's behavior? Are there some situations in which behavior therapy should not be used? In the classic movie *A Clockwork Orange*, dangerously powerful people used behavior modification principles to control the general population. Behaviorists reply that rewards and punishments already control our behaviors. Behavior therapy actually increases a person's freedom by making these controls *overt* and by teaching people to change their own behavior.

Modeling Therapy *Watching and imitating models that demonstrate desirable behaviors*

chievement

Objective 15.15: *What are the key successes and criticisms of behavior therapies?*

Figure 15.8 *Psychology at work* Modeling is also part of social skills training and assertiveness training. Clients learn how to interview for a job by first watching the therapist role-play the part of the interviewee. The therapist models the appropriate language (assertively asking for a job), body posture, and so forth. The client then imitates the therapist's behavior and plays the same role. Over the course of several sessions, the client becomes gradually desensitized to the anxiety of interviews and learns valuable interview skills.

Assessment

CHECK & REVIEW

Behavior Therapies

Objective 15.13: *What is behavior therapy?*

Behavior therapies use learning principles to change maladaptive behaviors.

Objective 15.14: *Describe how classical conditioning, operant conditioning, and observational learning are used in behavior therapy.*

Classical conditioning principles are used to change faulty associations. In **systematic desensitization**, the client replaces anxiety with relaxation, and in **aversion therapy**, an aversive stimulus is paired with a maladaptive behavior. Shaping, reinforcement, punishment, and extinction are behavior therapy techniques based on operant con-

ditioning principles. Observational learning techniques often include **modeling therapy**, which is based on acquisition of skills or behaviors through observation.

Objective 15.15: *What are the key successes and criticisms of behavior therapies?*

Behavior therapies have been successful with a number of psychological disorders. But they are criticized for possible lack of generalizability and the questionable ethics of attempting to control behavior.

Questions

1. A group of techniques used to change maladaptive behaviors is known as _____.

2. In behavior therapy, _____ techniques use shaping and reinforcement to increase adaptive behaviors. (a) classical conditioning; (b) modeling; (c) operant conditioning; (d) social learning

3. Describe how shaping can be used to develop desired behaviors.

4. What are the two criticisms of behavior therapy?

Check your answers in Appendix B.

Click & Review
for additional assessment options:
www.wiley.com/college/huffman

Achievement

Objective 15.16: *Define biomedical therapy.*

Biomedical Therapy *Using biological interventions (drugs, electroconvulsive therapy, and psychosurgery) to treat psychological disorders*

Achievement

Objective 15.17: *Discuss psychopharmacology, electroconvulsive therapy (ECT), and psychosurgery.*

Psychopharmacology *The study of drug effects on mind and behavior*

Antianxiety Drugs *Medications used to produce relaxation, reduce anxiety, and decrease overarousal in the brain*

Antipsychotic Drugs *Medications used to diminish or eliminate hallucinations, delusions, withdrawal, and other symptoms of psychosis; also known as neuroleptics or major tranquilizers*

Mood Stabilizer Drugs *Medications used to treat the combination of manic episodes and depression characteristic of bipolar disorders*

Antidepressant Drugs *Medications used to treat depression, some anxiety disorders, and certain eating disorders (such as bulimia)*

Cordella Molloy/Photo Researchers

Biomedical Therapies

Biomedical therapies are based on the premise that mental health problems are caused, at least in part, by chemical imbalances or disturbed nervous system functioning. In most cases, a psychiatrist, rather than a psychologist, must prescribe biomedical therapies. But psychologists commonly work with patients receiving biomedical therapies. They also conduct research programs to evaluate the therapy's effectiveness. In this section, we will discuss three forms of biomedical therapies: *psychopharmacology, electroconvulsive therapy (ECT),* and *psychosurgery.*

Psychopharmacology: Treating Psychological Disorders with Drugs

Since the 1950s, drug companies have developed an amazing variety of chemicals to treat abnormal behaviors. In some cases discoveries from **psychopharmacology** (the study of drug effects on mind and behavior) have helped correct a chemical imbalance. In these instances, using a drug is similar to administering insulin to people with diabetes, whose own bodies fail to manufacture enough. In other cases, drugs are used to relieve or suppress the symptoms of psychological disturbances even when the underlying cause is not known to be biological. Psychiatric drugs are classified into four major categories: antianxiety, antipsychotic, mood stabilizer, and antidepressant (Concept Diagram 15.2).

- **Antianxiety drugs** (also known as *anxiolytics* and "minor tranquilizers") lower the sympathetic activity of the brain—the crisis mode of operation—so that anxious responses are diminished or prevented and are replaced by feelings of tranquility and calmness (Barlow, 2008; Swartz & Margolis, 2008).

- **Antipsychotic drugs**, or *neuroleptics*, are used to treat schizophrenia and other acute psychotic states. Unfortunately, these drugs are often referred to as "major tranquilizers," creating the mistaken impression that they invariably have a strong sedating effect. The main effect of antipsychotic drugs is to diminish or eliminate psychotic symptoms, including hallucinations, delusions, withdrawal, and apathy. Traditional antipsychotics work by decreasing activity at the dopamine synapses in the brain. A large majority of patients show marked improvement when treated with these drugs.

- **Mood stabilizer drugs**, such as *lithium*, can help relieve manic episodes and depression for people suffering from bipolar disorder. Because lithium acts relatively slowly—it can take three or four weeks before it takes effect—its primary use is in preventing future episodes and helping to break the manic-depressive cycle.

- **Antidepressant drugs** are used primarily to treat people with depression. There are four types of antidepressant drugs: *tricyclics, monoamine oxidase inhibitors (MAOIs), selective serotonin reuptake inhibitors (SSRIs),* and *atypical antidepressants.* Each class of drugs affects neurochemical pathways in the brain in slightly different ways, increasing or decreasing the availability of certain chemicals. SSRIs (such as *Paxil* and *Prozac*) are by far the most commonly prescribed antidepressants. The atypical antidepressants are a miscellaneous group of drugs used for patients who fail to respond to the other drugs or for people who experience side effects common to other antidepressants.

What about herbal remedies? *Some recent research suggests that the herbal supplement St. John's Wort may be an effective treatment for mild to moderate depression, with fewer side effects than traditional medications (Butterweck, 2003; Lecrubier et al., 2002; Mayers et al., 2003). However, other studies have found the drug to be ineffective for people with major depression (Hypericum Depression Trial Study, 2002). Herbal supplements, like kava, valerian, and gingko biloba, also have been used in the treatment of anxiety, insomnia, and memory problems (e.g., Connor & Davidson, 2002; Parrott et al., 2004). Although many people assume that these products are safe because they are "natural," they can produce a number of potentially serious side effects. For this reason and also because the U.S. Food and Drug Administration does not regulate herbal supplements, researchers advise caution and a wait-and-see approach (Crone & Gabriel, 2002; Swartz & Margolis, 2008).*

Concept Diagram 15.2

Drug Treatments for Psychological Disorders

"Before Prozac, she loathed company."

Type of Drug (Chemical Group)	Psychological Disorder	Generic Name	Brand Name
Antianxiety drugs (Benzodiazepines)	Anxiety disorders	Alprazolam	Xanax
		Diazepam	Valium
		Lorazepam	Ativan
Antipsychotic drugs (Phenothiazines Butyrophenones Atypical antipsychotics)	Schizophrenia and bipolar disorders	Chlorpromazine	Thorazine
		Fluphenazine	Prolixin
		Thioridazine	Mellaril
		Haloperidol	Haldol
		Clozapine	Clozaril
		Resperidone	Risperdal
		Quetiapine	Seroquel
Mood stabilizer drugs (Antimanic)	Bipolar disorder	Lithium carbonate	Eskalith CR Lithobid
		Carbamazepine	Tegretol
Antidepressant drugs (Tricyclic antidepressants Monoamine oxidase inhibitors (MAOIs) Selective serotonin re-uptake inhibitors (SSRIs) Serotonin and norepinephrine reup-take inhibitors (SNRIs) Atypical antidepressants)	Depressive disorders	Imipramine	Tofranil
		Amitriptyline	Elavil
		Phenelzine	Nardil
		Paroxetine	Paxil
		Fluoxetine	Prozac
		Venlafaxine	Effexor
		Duloxetine	Cymbalta
		Bupropion	Wellbutrin

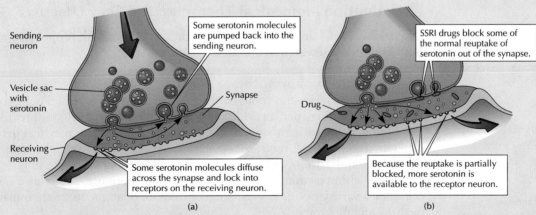

(a)   (b)

Labels (a): Sending neuron; Vesicle sac with serotonin; Receiving neuron; Synapse; Some serotonin molecules are pumped back into the sending neuron. Some serotonin molecules diffuse across the synapse and lock into receptors on the receiving neuron.

Labels (b): Drug; SSRI drugs block some of the normal reuptake of serotonin out of the synapse. Because the reuptake is partially blocked, more serotonin is available to the receptor neuron.

How Prozac and other SSRI antidepressants work (a) Under normal conditions, a nerve impulse (or action potential) travels down the axon to the terminal buttons of a sending neuron. If the vesicle sac of this particular neuron contains the neurotransmitter serotonin, the action potential will trigger its release. Some of the serotonin will travel across the synapse and lock into the receptors on the receiving neuron. Excess serotonin within the synapse will be pumped back up into the sending neuron for storage (the "serotonin reuptake"). (b) When selective serotonin reuptake inhibitors (SSRIs), like Prozac, are taken to treat depression and other disorders, they block the normal reuptake of excess serontonin that lingers in the synaptic gap after being released from the sending neuron. This leaves more serotonin molecules free to stimulate receptors on the receiving neuron, which enhances its mood lifting effects.

Electroconvulsive Therapy (ECT) *Biomedical therapy based on passing electrical current through the brain; used almost exclusively to treat serious depression when drug therapy fails*

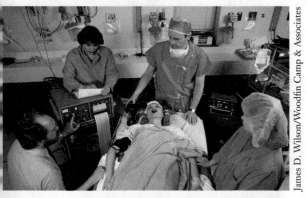

Figure 15.9 *Electroconvulsive therapy (ECT)* Electroconvulsive therapy may seem barbaric, but for some severely depressed people it is their only hope for lifting the depression. Unlike portrayals of ECT in movies like *One Flew Over the Cuckoo's Nest* and *The Snake Pit*, patients show few, if any, visible reactions to the treatment owing to modern muscle-relaxant drugs that dramatically reduce muscle contractions during the seizure. Most ECT patients are also given an anesthetic to block their memories of the treatment, but some patients still find the treatment extremely uncomfortable. However, many others find it lifesaving (Jain et al., 2008; Khalid et al., 2008).

Achievement

Objective 15.18: *What are the major contributions and criticisms of biomedical therapies?*

Psychosurgery *Operative procedures on the brain designed to relieve severe mental symptoms that have not responded to other forms of treatment*

Lobotomy *Outmoded medical procedure for mental disorders, which involved cutting nerve pathways between the frontal lobes and the thalamus and hypothalamus*

Tardive Dyskinesia *Movement disorder involving facial muscles, tongue, and limbs; a possible side effect of long-term use of antipsychotic medications*

Electroconvulsive Therapy and Psychosurgery: Promising or Perilous?

In **electroconvulsive therapy (ECT)**, also known as *electroshock therapy* (EST), a moderate electrical current is passed through the brain between two electrodes placed on the outside of the head (Figure 15.9). The current triggers a widespread firing of neurons, or convulsions. The convulsions produce many changes in the central and peripheral nervous systems, including activation of the autonomic nervous system, increased secretion of various hormones and neurotransmitters, and changes in the blood–brain barrier.

During the early years of ECT, some patients received hundreds of treatments. Today most receive 12 or fewer treatments. Sometimes the electrical current is applied only to the right hemisphere, which causes less interference with verbal memories and left-hemispheric functioning. Modern ECT is used primarily in cases of severe depression that do not respond to antidepressant drugs or psychotherapy. It also is used with suicidal patients because it works faster than antidepressant drugs (Goforth & Holsinger, 2007; Birkenhäger, Renes, & Pluijms, 2004).

Although clinical studies of ECT conclude that it is effective for very severe depression (Jain et al., 2008; Khalid et al., 2008), its use remains controversial because it creates massive functional (and perhaps structural) changes in the brain. ECT is also controversial because we simply don't know why it works. Most likely it helps reestablish levels of neurotransmitters that control moods.

The most extreme, and least used, biomedical therapy is **psychosurgery**—brain surgery to reduce serious, debilitating psychological problems. (It is important to note that psychosurgery is *not* the same as brain surgery used to remove physical problems, such as a tumor or blood clot.) Attempts to change disturbed thinking and behavior by altering the brain have a long history. In Roman times, for example, it was believed that a sword wound to the head could relieve insanity. In 1936, a Portuguese neurologist, Egaz Moniz, treated uncontrollable psychoses by cutting the nerve fibers between the frontal lobes (where association areas for monitoring and planning behavior are found) and lower brain centers (Hergenhahn 2009; Pressman, 1998; Valenstein, 1998). Thousands of patients underwent this procedure, called a **lobotomy**, before it was eliminated because of serious complications. Today lobotomies are almost never used. Psychiatric drugs offer a less risky and more effective treatment.

Evaluating Biomedical Therapies: Are They Effective?

Like all forms of therapy, the biomedical therapies have both proponents and critics. Let's explore the research in this area.

Pitfalls of Psychopharmacology

Drug therapy provides enormous benefits, but it also poses several potential problems. First, although drugs may provide relief of symptoms, they seldom provide "cures." In addition, many patients stop taking their medications once they feel better, which generally results in the return of symptoms. Also, some patients become physically dependent on the drugs, and researchers are still learning about the long-term effects and potential interactions of drug treatments. Furthermore, psychiatric medications can cause a variety of side effects, ranging from mild fatigue to severe impairments in memory and movement.

One of the most serious side effects of long-term use of antipsychotic drugs is a movement disorder called **tardive dyskinesia**, which develops in 15 to 20 percent of patients. The symptoms generally appear after the drugs have been taken for long periods of time (hence the term *tardive*, from the Latin root for "slow"). They include involuntary movements of the tongue, facial muscles, and limbs (*dyskinesia*, meaning "disorder of movement") that can be severely disabling. When my students see films depicting schizophrenia, they often confuse the patient's sucking and smacking of the lips or lateral jaw movements as signs of the disorder rather than signs of the motor disturbances of *tardive dyskinesia*.

James D. Wilson/Woodfin Camp & Associates

A final potential problem with drug treatment is that its relative inexpensiveness, and its generally faster results than traditional talk therapy, have led to its overuse in some cases. One report found that antidepressants are prescribed roughly 50 percent of the time a patient walks into a psychiatrist's office (Olfson et al., 1998).

Despite the problems associated with psychotherapeutic drugs, they have led to revolutionary changes in mental health. Before the use of drugs, some patients were destined to spend a lifetime in psychiatric institutions. Today, most patients improve enough to return to their homes and live successful lives if they continue to take their medications to prevent relapse.

Challenges to ECT and Psychosurgery

As mentioned earlier, ECT remains controversial, but it may soon become obsolete thanks to advances in treatment, such as **repetitive transcranial magnetic stimulation (rTMS)**, in which a pulsed magnetic coil is held close to a person's head. When used to treat depression, the coil is usually placed over the prefrontal cortex, a region linked to deeper parts of the brain that regulate mood. Studies have shown marked improvement in depression, and, unlike ECT, patients experience no seizures or memory loss. Currently, the cost effectiveness and long-term benefits of rTMS over ECT remain uncertain (Bloch et al., 2008; Knapp et al., 2008; Wasserman, Epstein, & Ziemann, 2008).

Like ECT, psychosurgery is highly controversial, and because of its potentially serious or fatal side effects and complications, some critics suggest it should be banned altogether.

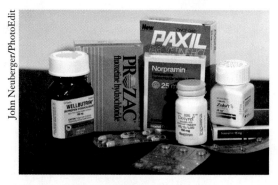

John Neuberger/PhotoEdit

The pros and cons of drug therapy *Psychotherapeutic drugs like Prozac often help relieve suffering and symptoms associated with psychological disorders. However, they also have major and minor side effects. Physicians and patients must carefully weigh both the costs and the benefits.*

Repetitive Transcranial Magnetic Stimulation (rTMS)

Biomedical treatment involving repeated pulses of magnetic energy being passed through the brain

---

Assessment

CHECK & REVIEW

Biomedical Therapies

Objective 15.16: *Define biomedical therapy.*

Biomedical therapies use biological techniques to relieve psychological disorders.

Objective 15.17: *Discuss psychopharmacology, electroconvulsive therapy (ECT) and psychosurgery.*

Psychopharmacology, or treatment with drugs, is the most common biomedical therapy. **Antianxiety drugs** (Valium, Ativan) generally are used to treat anxiety disorders, **anti-psychotic drugs** (Thorazine, Haldol) treat the symptoms of schizophrenia, **antidepressant drugs** (Prozac, Effexor) treat depression, and **mood stabilizers** (lithium) can help patients with bipolar disorder. Drug therapy has been responsible for major improvements in many disorders. However, there are also problems with dosage levels, side effects, and patient cooperation.

Electroconvulsive therapy (ECT) is used primarily to relieve serious depression when medication has not worked. But it is risky and considered a treatment of last resort. **Psychosurgeries**, such as a **lobotomy**, have been used in the past but are rarely used today.

Objective 15.18: *What are the major contributions and criticisms of biomedical therapies?*

Drug therapy is enormously beneficial, but it also has several problems. For example, it offers symptom relief, but few "cures," patients often stop medications once symptoms are relieved, patients may become dependent, and little is known about the long term effects and drug interactions. In addition, there are potentially dangerous side effects, and possible over use. ECT and psychosurgery are both controversial and are generally used as a last resort.

Questions

1. The dramatic reduction in numbers of hospitalized patients today compared to past decades is primarily attributable to _____. (a) biomedical therapy; (b) psychoanalysis; (c) psychosurgery; (d) drug therapy.
2. What are the four major categories of psychiatric drugs?
3. The effectiveness of antipsychotic drugs is thought to result primarily from blockage of _____ receptors. (a) serotonin; (b) dopamine; (c) epinephrine (d) all of these options
4. In electroconvulsive therapy (ECT), _____.

a. current is never applied to the left hemisphere
b. convulsions activate the ANS, stimulate hormone and neurotransmitter release, and change the blood-brain barrier
c. convulsions are extremely painful and long lasting
d. most patients today receive hundreds of treatments because it is safer than in the past

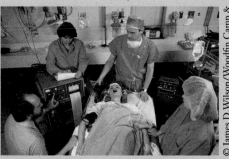

© James D. Wilson/Woodfin Camp & Associates

5. ECT is used primarily to treat _____. (a) phobias; (b) conduct disorders; (c) depression; (d) schizophrenia

Check your answers in Appendix B.

Click & Review
for additional assessment options:
wiley.com/college/huffman

Therapy and Critical Thinking

As you discovered in the Prologue to this text and throughout the individual chapters, critical thinking is one of the most important skills you'll develop while studying psychology. Nowhere is this more important than in this chapter. For example, we mentioned at the start of this chapter that there are over 400 forms of therapy. How are you going to choose one of these for yourself or someone you know?

In the first part of this section, we discuss the five goals that are common to all psychotherapies. Then we explore the key cultural similarities and differences in therapies around the world. We conclude with specific tips for finding a therapist. Can you see how these discussions help you see the overall "big picture"? Noncritical thinkers often fail to *synthesize* large bodies of information. When it comes to therapy, they may get lost "in the trees" and give up their search for therapists because they can't step outside and see "the forest."

Therapy Essentials: Five Common Goals

Achievement

> **Objective 15.19:** *Identify the five most common goals of therapy, and discuss the eclectic approach.*

All major forms of therapy are designed to help the client in five specific areas (Concept Diagram 15.3). Depending on the individual therapist's training and the client's needs, one or more of these five areas may be emphasized more than the others.

Although most therapists work with clients in several of these areas, the emphasis varies according to the therapist's training. As you learned earlier in this chapter, psychoanalysts and psychodynamic therapists generally emphasize unconscious thoughts and emotions. Cognitive therapists focus on their client's faulty thinking and belief patterns. And humanistic therapists attempt to alter the client's negative emotional

Concept Diagram

Concept Diagram 15.3
The Five Most Common Goals of Therapy

Most therapies focus on one or more of these five goals. Can you identify which would be of most interest to a psychoanalyst, a cognitive therapist, a behavior therapist, and a psychiatrist?

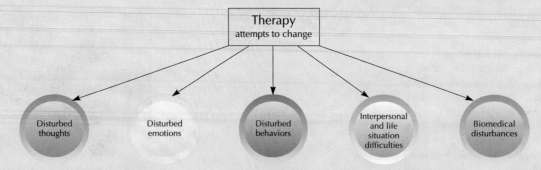

Disturbed thoughts. Therapists work to change faulty or destructive thoughts, provide new ideas or information, and guide individuals toward finding solutions to problems.

Disturbed emotions. Therapists help clients understand and control their emotions and relieve their emotional discomfort.

Disturbed behaviors. Therapists help clients eliminate troublesome behaviors and guide them toward more effective lives.

Interpersonal and life situation difficulties. Therapists help clients improve their relationships with others and avoid or minimize sources of stress in their lives.

Biomedical disturbances. Therapists work to relieve biological disruptions that directly cause or contribute to psychological difficulties (for example, chemical imbalances that lead to depression).

responses. Behavior therapists, as the name implies, focus on changing maladaptive behaviors, and therapists who use biomedical techniques attempt to change biological disorders.

Keep in mind that the terms *psychoanalyst* and *cognitive therapist* simply refer to the theoretical background and framework that guide a clinician's thinking. Just as Democrats and Republicans approach political matters in different ways, behavior and cognitive therapists approach therapy differently. And just as Democrats and Republicans borrow ideas from one another, clinicians from different perspectives also share ideas and techniques. Clinicians who regularly borrow freely from various theories are said to take an **eclectic approach**.

Eclectic Approach *Combining techniques from various theories to find the most appropriate treatment*

PSYCHOLOGY AT WORK *Careers in Mental Health*

Achievement

Objective 15.20: *Identify the six key types of mental health professionals.*

Do you enjoy helping people and think you would like a career as a therapist? Have you wondered how long you will have to go to college or the type of training that is required to be a therapist? Most colleges have counseling or career centers with numerous resources and trained staff who can help you answer these (and other) questions. To get you started, I have included a brief summary in Table 15.1 of the major types of mental health professionals, their degrees, years of required education beyond the bachelor's degree, and type of training.

TABLE 15.1 MAJOR TYPES OF MENTAL HEALTH PROFESSIONALS

Occupational Title	Degree	Nature of Training
Clinical Psychologists	Ph.D. (Doctor of Philosophy), Psy.D. (Doctor of Psychology)	Most often have a doctoral degree with training in research and clinical practice, and a supervised one-year internship in a psychiatric hospital or mental health facility. As clinicians, they work with patients suffering from mental disorders, but many also work in colleges and universities as teachers and researchers in addition to having their own private practice.
Counseling Psychologists	M.A. (Master of Arts), Ph.D. (Doctor of Philosophy), Psy.D. (Doctor of Psychology), Ed.D. (Doctor of Education)	Similar training to clinical psychologists, but counseling psychologists usually have a master's degree with more emphasis on patient care and less on research. They generally work in schools or other institutions and focus on problems of living rather than mental disorders.
Psychiatrists	M.D. (Doctor of Medicine)	After four years of medical school, an internship and residency in psychiatry are required, which involves supervised practice in psychotherapy techniques and biomedical therapies. With the exception of certain states in the U.S., M.D.s are generally the only mental health specialists who can regularly prescribe drugs.
Psychiatric Nurses	R.N. (Registered Nurse), M.A. (Master of Arts), Ph.D. (Doctor of Philosophy)	Usually have a bachelor's or master's degree in nursing, followed by advanced training in the care of mental patients in hospital settings and mental health facilities.
Psychiatric Social Workers	M.S.W. (Master in Social Work), D.S.W. (Doctorate in Social Work), Ph.D. (Doctor of Philosophy)	Normally have a master's degree in social work, followed by advanced training and experience in hospitals or outpatient settings working with people who have psychological problems.
School Psychologists	M.A. (Master of Arts), Ph.D. (Doctor of Philosophy), Psy.D. (Doctor of Psychology), Ed.D. (Doctor of Education)	Generally begin with a bachelor's degree in psychology, followed by graduate training in psychological assessment and counseling involving school-related issues and problems.

Application

RESEARCH HIGHLIGHT

Objective 15.21: *Briefly summarize the major effects of mental disorders, like PTSD, on the family.*

Mental Health and the Family—PTSD

Contributed by Nicholas Greco IV, M.S., BCETS, CATSM
COLLEGE OF LAKE COUNTY, IL

Paul Avallone/Zuma Press

Chapter 14 discussed several categories of mental disorders, while this chapter has focused on their various treatments. Unfortunately, the effects and treatment for family members, who share the suffering, are not as equally well known nor as adequately studied.

In this section, we'll focus on the growing number of military men and women returning home from the wars in Iraq and Afghanistan with serious psychological disorders, most notably posttraumatic stress disorder (PTSD). We'll also emphasize how this particular anxiety disorder affects the lives and mental health of their family members.

PTSD is a complicated, often comorbid disorder that goes beyond the symptoms of reexperiencing of the event, the avoidance of talking or thinking about the event, and the hyperarousal symptoms such as irritability, exaggerated startle response, and hypervigilance. Family members want to help but may feel alienated from their loved ones, confused about the disorder, and helpless. Many individuals with PTSD also have secondary depression or even other anxiety disorders such as panic disorder, thus straining an already taxed family life even further.

The pathology of the "typical soldier" is as varied as the soldier. By definition, the greater the trauma, the higher the likelihood of suffering from PTSD. A U.S. soldier's risk of developing PTSD is more likely when the combat is intense or they are wounded or have witnessed someone wounded or killed (Hoge, Castro, Messer, et al., 2004). Psychologists estimate that one in six soldiers deployed to Iraq or Afghanistan experience PTSD symptoms, and this number rises to one in three for those wounded, and even higher for Reserve and National Guard members (Munsey, 2008).

To put things into perspective, there have been 1.6 million soldiers deployed to Iraq or Afghanistan to date. Hypothetically, if 1 out of 6 of the 1.6 million soldiers suffer from combat-exposed PTSD, 256,000 service members may be affected (Lineberry, Bostwick, & Rundell, 2006). Each of these 256,000 soldiers has family and loved ones who may also experience the pain of PTSD. Keep in mind that while the veteran feels isolated and alone, his or her family may feel the same way. Both the veteran and their loved ones often feel no one understands what they are going through.

In many families, PTSD is not a dinner-time discussion. In fact, it is often rarely discussed at all. Family members may walk on eggshells to avoid the person's irritability and anger. Often times, the family sees the person as depressed, moody, and not someone who they want to be around—especially if the person is self-medicating with drugs or alcohol.

Ignoring the PTSD will not make it go away, but in fact, may escalate the moodiness to chronic mood instability; mood swings, verbal and physical abuse, and increased addiction to drugs and/or alcohol. Untreated PTSD may last a lifetime, and leads to various psychosocial stressors including divorce and unemployment as well as domestic violence and substance abuse. Veterans typically adopt a code of silence about the trauma, as they are fearful of being judged and criticized, and re-experiencing the event. The family shares this code of silence by failing to discuss the PTSD, ignoring or overlooking the behaviors of the person, and perpetuating the illness.

Family members also may commonly experience a number of reactions, including sympathy, depression, fear and worry, avoidance, guilt and shame, anger, and other mixed emotions (Carlson & Ruzek, 2008). Sympathy is a natural human characteristic, which is initially helpful. But it also can be detrimental, as expectations for the trauma survivor may be lowered. This, in turn, sends the wrong message to the individual—that they may not be strong enough to overcome the trauma.

Like the PTSD victim, family members may suffer from their own unique forms of anxiety and depression. Fear and worries abound when the family is unsure of what the survivor will be like on any given day. PTSD survivors often become hypervigilant and want to protect their surroundings with guard dogs, alarms, guns, and the like. They may also not want family members going too far from home or leaving home at all. Their feelings of being unsafe, coupled with this newfound reliance on safety and security, weigh heavily on the family.

Family members also may worry what the trauma survivor will do if they become angry in public, whether they can invite friends to the home, how that person's drinking will harm their health, or whether or not they will have a roof over their heads if the trauma survivor is unable to keep a job.

In addition, the family may avoid discussing the traumatic event not only with their loved one, but also with others. Here we see the code of silence wherein the family takes a protective stance against discussing something that makes them feel sad, vulnerable, and helpless. The family, also may change their lives to make the survivor feel less pain or to avoid his or her negative reactions.

Can you see how the family is assimilating many avoidance features of the family member with PTSD? They also are becoming co-dependent, and angry at the victim or the trauma itself, or its effect on their lives. They may blame the loved one for "not getting better," for "not moving on," and for ultimately changing the family life and lifestyle.

Over time, family members may also begin to mimic the victim's anger and irritability as a response to what they experience from the trauma survivor as well as their own frustrations. The drug and alcohol abuse, the sleep disruptions, and the health problems of the PTSD survivor may become a problem for the families as well.

Finally, constant worry about the trauma survivor may lead family members to neglect their own health issues and engage in bad habits such as smoking, overeating, drinking, and less physical activities. These responses are examples of secondary or vicarious traumatization. The family member is essentially living their life through the trauma survivor's life. As such, they become co-dependent, an enabler, a rescuer, and may even blame

themselves for their spouse or family member's symptoms.

How can we help? Experts agree that the key lies in support, education, and intervention for the traumatized individual as well as for family members. The Department of Defense is currently sponsoring a $25 million five-year study called the STRONG STAR Multidisciplinary Research Consortium which will include eight randomized clinical trials (Munsey, 2008). These studies will be designed to study active and recently discharged military personnel diagnosed with PTSD. There are a number of other studies underway; however, we must keep in mind that those with PTSD find it difficult to talk about the trauma, to deal with the emotions that come up in therapy, and may ultimately discontinue treatment. Family members play a key role in helping the individual with PTSD, and ultimately in helping themselves, by becoming not only an advocate for their loved one, but informing the clinician about how the family is affected.

Learning about PTSD also can be both informative and therapeutic for the family in terms of dealing with the many emotions and symptoms of PTSD. The more the family understands the condition and understands what the person is going through, the better able they will be to help the person through the difficult times.

Finally, family members must set firm boundaries for unacceptable behaviors such as verbal, physical, and substance abuse. Children of veterans with PTSD need to know that they are loved and that home is a safe place. The non-PTSD parent can play an integral role by discussing mommy or daddy's symptoms, reassuring them that it is not their fault, validating the child's emotions, calming their fears, and maintaining the family unit by having the family participate in family therapy.

PTSD may be a complicated disorder, but these steps may allow a better life for the PTSD veteran and the family who shares his or her suffering.

Achievement
GENDER & CULTURAL DIVERSITY *Similarities and Differences*

Achievement

Objective 15.22: *Describe the major similarities and differences in therapy across cultures.*

The therapies described in this chapter are based on Western European and North American culture. Does this mean they are unique? Or do our psychotherapists share some of the same techniques and approaches that, say, a native healer or shaman does? Or are there fundamental cultural differences between therapies? What about women? Do they have different issues in therapy? As mentioned earlier, looking at each of these questions requires critical thinking. Let's carefully consider these issues one at a time.

Cultural Similarities When we look at therapies in all cultures, we find that they have certain key features in common (Laungani, 2007; Lee 2002; Sue & Sue, 2008). Richard Brislin (1993, 2000) has summarized some of these features:

- *Naming the problem.* People often feel better just by knowing that others experience the same problem and that the therapist has had experience with their particular problem.

- *Qualities of the therapist.* Clients must feel that the therapist is caring, competent, approachable, and concerned with finding solutions to their problem.

- *Therapist credibility.* Among native healers, credibility may be established by having served as an apprentice to a revered healer. In Western cultures, word-of-mouth testimonials and status symbols (such as diplomas on the wall) establish the therapist's credibility.

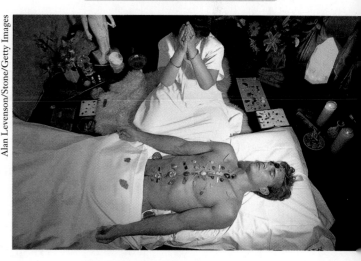

Alan Levenson/Stone/Getty Images

Alternative therapies In all cultures, therapy involves specific actions or treatments. In this photo, the therapist is using crystals, laying on of stones, and meditation.

Sky Bonillo/PhotoEdit

Figure 15.10 *Emphasizing interdependence* In Japanese *Naikan therapy*, the patient sits quietly from 5:30 A.M. to 9:00 P.M. for seven days and is visited by an interviewer every 90 minutes. During this time, the patient is instructed to reflect on his or her relationships with others, with the goals of discovering personal guilt for having been ungrateful and troublesome to others and developing gratitude toward those who have helped the patient (Nakamura, 2006; Ryback, Ikerni, & Miki, 2001; Ozawa-de Silva, 2007). The reasoning is that when these goals are attained, the patient will have a better self-image and interpersonal attitude. In what ways do the goals and methods of Naikan therapy differ from the therapies we have described in this chapter? Would this approach work with Westerners? Why or why not?

Achievement

Objective 15.23: *What are the unique concerns of women in therapy?*

- *Familiar framework*. If the client believes that evil spirits cause psychological disorders, the therapist will direct treatment toward eliminating these spirits. Similarly, if the client believes in the importance of talking through their problems, insight therapy will be the likely treatment of choice.

- *Techniques that bring relief*. In all cultures, therapy involves action. Either the client or the therapist must do something. Moreover, what they do must fit the client's expectations—whether it is performing a ceremony to expel demons or talking with the client about his or her thoughts and feelings.

- *A special time and place*. The fact that therapy occurs outside the client's everyday experiences seems to be an important feature of all therapies.

Cultural Differences Although there are basic similarities in therapies across cultures, there are also important differences. In the traditional Western European and North American model, the emphasis is on the "self" and on independence and control over one's life—qualities that are highly valued in individualistic cultures. In collectivist cultures, however, the focus of therapy is on interdependence and accepting the realities of one's life (Sue & Sue, 2008) (Figure 15.10).

Not only does culture affect the types of therapy that are developed, but it also influences the perceptions of the therapist. What one culture considers abnormal behavior may be quite common—and even healthy—in others. For this reason, recognizing cultural differences is very important for both therapists and clients and for effecting behavioral change (Laungani, 2007; Sue & Sue, 2008; Tseng, 2004).

Women and Therapy Within our individualistic Western culture, men and women present different therapy needs and problems. For example, women are generally more comfortable and familiar with their emotions, have fewer negative attitudes toward therapy, and are more likely than men to seek psychological help. However, research has identified five unique concerns related to women and psychotherapy (Halbreich & Kahn, 2007; Hall, 2007; Hyde, 2007; Matlin, 2008; Russo & Tartaro, 2008).

1. *Rates of diagnosis and treatment of mental disorders*. Women are diagnosed and treated for mental illness at a much higher rate than men. Is this because women are "sicker" than men as a group? Or are they just more willing to admit their problems? Or perhaps the categories for illness may be biased against women. More research is needed to answer this question.

2. *Stresses of poverty*. Poverty is an important contributor to many psychological disorders. Therefore, women bring special challenges to the therapy situation because of their overrepresentation in the lowest economic groups.

3. *Stresses of aging*. Aging brings special concerns for women. They live longer than men, tend to be poorer, to be less educated, and to have more serious health problems. Elderly women, primarily those with age-related dementia, account for over 70 percent of the chronically mentally ill who live in nursing homes in the United States.

4. *Violence against women*. Rape, violent assault, incest, and sexual harassment all take a harsh toll on women's mental health. With the exception of violent assault, these

WireImageStock/Masterfile

Figure 15.11 *Meeting women's unique needs* Therapists must be sensitive to possible connections between clients' problems and their gender. Rather than prescribing drugs to relieve depression in women, for example, it may be more appropriate for therapists to explore ways to relieve the stresses of multiple roles or poverty. Can you see how helping a single mother identify parenting resources such as play groups, parent support groups, and high-quality child care might be just as effective at relieving depression as prescribing drugs?

forms of violence are much more likely to happen to women than to men. These violent acts may lead to depression, insomnia, posttraumatic stress disorder, eating disorders, and other problems.

5. *Stresses of multiple roles.* Women today are mothers, wives, homemakers, wage earners, students, and so on. The conflicting demands of their multiple roles often create special stresses (Figure 15.11).

Institutionalization: Treating Chronic and Serious Mental Disorders

We all believe in the right to freedom. But what about people who threaten suicide or are potentially violent? Should some people be involuntarily committed to protect them from their own mental disorders? Despite Hollywood film portrayals, forced institutionalization of the mentally ill poses serious ethical problems, and it is generally reserved for only the most serious and life-threatening situations.

Achievement

Objective 15.24: *Discuss issues with involuntary commitment and deinstitutionalization.*

Involuntary Commitment

The legal grounds for involuntary commitment vary from state to state. But, generally, people can be sent to psychiatric hospitals if they are believed to be:

- of danger to themselves (usually suicidal) or dangerous to others (potentially violent);

- in serious need of treatment (indicated by bizarre behavior and loss of contact with reality); and/or

- there is no reasonable, less restrictive alternative.

In emergencies, psychologists and other professionals can authorize temporary commitment for 24 to 72 hours. During this observation period, laboratory tests can be performed to rule out medical illnesses that could be causing the symptoms. The patient also can receive psychological testing, medication, and short-term therapy.

James Shaffer/PhotoEdit

Figure 15.12 *Outpatient support* Community mental health (CMH) centers are a prime example of alternative treatment to institutionalization. CMH centers provide outpatient services, such as individual and group therapy and prevention programs. They also coordinate short-term inpatient care and programs for discharged mental patients, such as halfway houses and aftercare services. The downside of CMH centers and their support programs is that they are expensive. Investing in primary prevention programs (such as more intervention programs for people at high risk for mental illness) could substantially reduce these costs.

Achievement

Objective 15.25: *Is therapy effective, and how can we find a good therapist?*

Deinstitutionalization

Although the courts have established stringent requirements for involuntary commitment, abuses do occur. There are also problems with long-term chronic institutionalization. And properly housing and caring for the mentally ill is very expensive. In response to these problems, many states have a policy of *deinstitutionalization*, discharging patients from mental hospitals as soon as possible and discouraging admissions.

Deinstitutionalization has been a humane and positive step for many. But some patients are discharged without continuing provision for their protection. Many of these people end up living in rundown hotels or understaffed nursing homes, in jails, or on the street with no shelter or means of support. It is important to note that a sizable percentage of homeless people do have mental disorders. The rise in homelessness is also due to such economic factors as increased unemployment, underemployment, and a shortage of low-income housing.

What else can be done? Rather than returning patients to state hospitals, most clinicians suggest expanding and improving community care (Figure 15.12). They also recommend that general hospitals be equipped with special psychiatric units where acutely ill patients receive inpatient care. For less disturbed individuals and chronically ill patients, they recommend walk-in clinics, crisis intervention services, improved residential treatment facilities, and psychosocial and vocational rehabilitation. State hospitals can then be reserved for the most unmanageable patients.

Evaluating and Finding Therapy: Does It Work? How to Choose?

Have you ever thought about going to a therapist? If you've gone, was it helpful? In this section, we will discuss questions about the effectiveness of therapy and how to find a therapist.

Judging Effectiveness

Scientifically evaluating the effectiveness of therapy can be tricky. How can you trust the perception and self-report of clients or clinicians? Both have biases and a need to justify the time, effort, and expense of therapy.

To avoid these problems, psychologists use controlled research studies. Clients are randomly assigned to different forms of therapy or to control groups who receive no treatment. After therapy, clients are independently evaluated, and reports from friends and family members are collected. Until recently, these studies were simply compared. But with a new statistical technique called *meta-analysis*, which combines and analyzes data from many studies, years of such studies and similar research can be brought together to produce a comprehensive report.

The good news, for both consumers and therapists, is that after years of controlled research and meta-analysis we have fairly clear evidence that therapy does work! Forty to 80 percent of people who receive treatment are better off than people who do not. Furthermore, short-term treatments can be as effective as long-term treatments (Castonguay & Hill, 2007; Cleaves & Latner, 2008; Knekt et al., 2008; Loewental & Winter, 2006; Stiles et al., 2008; Wachtel, 2008). In addition, some therapies are more effective than others for specific problems. For example, phobias seem to respond best to systematic desensitization, and obsessive-compulsive disorders can be significantly relieved with cognitive-behavior therapy accompanied by medication.

Finding a Therapist

How do we find a good therapist for our specific needs? If you have the time (and the money) to explore options, take the time to "shop around" for a therapist best suited to your specific goals. Consulting your psychology instructor or college counseling system for referrals can be an important first step. However, if you are in a crisis—you have suicidal thoughts, you have failing grades, or you are the victim of abuse—get help fast. Most communities have medical hospital emergency services and telephone hotlines that provide counseling services on a 24-hour basis. And most colleges and universities have counseling centers that provide immediate, short-term therapy to students free of charge.

If you are encouraging someone else to get therapy, you might offer to help locate a therapist and go with him for his first visit. If he refuses help and the problem affects you, it is often a good idea to seek therapy yourself. You will gain insights and skills that will help you deal with the situation more effectively.

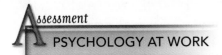

Assessment

PSYCHOLOGY AT WORK

Achievement

Objective 15.26: *Briefly summarize how to deal with someone who's seriously depressed.*

Non Professional Therapy—Talking to the Depressed

I know that everyone here knows that feeling when people say to you, "Hey, shape up! Stop thinking only about your troubles. What's to be depressed about? Go swimming or play tennis and you'll feel a lot better. Pull up your socks!" And how you, hearing this, would like nothing more than to remove one of those socks and choke them to death with it. (Laughter mixed with some minor cheering.)

(CAVETT, 2008)

These are the words of famous columnist and commentator, Dick Cavett, speaking about his personal bouts with deep depression to a large audience currently in the throes of the same disease. If you have a friend or loved one with serious depression, it may feel like you're walking through a minefield when you're attempting to comfort and help them. What do the experts suggest that you say (or NOT say)? Here are a few general tips:

1. ***Don't trivialize the disease.*** Depression, like cancer or heart disease, is a critical, life-threatening illness. Asking someone "What do you have to be depressed about?" or encouraging them to "pull up their socks" is akin to asking the cancer patient why they have cancer, why they don't just smile and exercise more, or why they can't just think positive thoughts?

2. ***Don't be a cheerleader or a Mr. or Ms. fix-it.*** You can't pep-talk someone out of deep depression, and offering cheap advice or solutions is the best way to insure that you'll be the last person they'll turn to for help. According to Dick Cavett, "When you're downed by this affliction, if there were a curative magic wand on the table eight feet away, it would be too much trouble to go over and pick it up."

© image100/Corbis

3. ***Don't equate normal, everyday "down times" with clinical depression.*** Virtually everyone has experienced down moods and times of loss and deep sadness. Unless you have shared true, clinical depression, comments like, "I know just how you feel," only makes it clear that you don't understand what clinical depression is all about. As they say, "If you don't got it, you don't get it!"

What can you do?

Educate yourself. Your psychology instructor, college library, book stores, and the Internet all provide a wealth of information. You also can check out the resources available on our text website at www.wiley.com/college/huffman.

Be Rogerian! Carl Roger's four important qualities of communication (*empathy*, *unconditional positive regard*, *genuineness*, and *active listening*) (pp. 518–519) are probably the best, and safest, approach for any situation—including talking with a depressed person.

Get help! The most dangerous problem associated with depression is the high risk of suicide (see Chapter 14, pp. 491–492). If a friend or loved one mentions suicide, or if you believe they are considering it, get professional help fast! Consider calling the police for emergency intervention, and/or the person's therapist, or the toll-free 7/24 hotline: 1-800-SUICIDE.

Assessment

CHECK & REVIEW

Therapy and Critical Thinking

Objective 15.19: *Identify the five most common goals of therapy, and discuss the eclectic approach.*

There are numerous forms of therapy. But they all focus treatment on five basic areas of disturbance—thoughts, emotions, behaviors, interpersonal and life situations, and biomedical problems. Many therapists take an **eclectic approach** and combine techniques from various theories.

Objective 15.20: *Identify the six key types of mental health professionals.*

Clinical psychologists, counseling psychologists, psychiatrists, psychiatric nurses, psychiatric social workers, and school psychologists are the six most common types of mental health professionals.

Objective 15.21: *Briefly summarize the major effects of mental disorders, like PTSD, on the family.*

Mental disorders, like PTSD, and their treatment have been studied extensively, but we often overlook the effects on the family who develop their own forms of pathology. The entire family also suffers from increased rates of divorce, substance abuse, unemployment, and other life problems. Support, education, and intervention should be provided for all family members.

Objective 15.22: *Describe the major similarities and differences in therapy across cultures.*

Therapies in all cultures share six culturally universal features: naming a problem, qualities of the therapist, therapist credibility, familiar framework, techniques that bring relief, and a special time and place. Important cultural differences in therapies also exist. For example, therapies in individualistic cultures emphasize the self and control over one's life, whereas therapies in collectivist cultures emphasize interdependence. Japan's Naikan therapy is a good example of a collectivist culture's therapy.

Objective 15.23: *What are the unique concerns of women in therapy?*

Therapists must take five considerations into account when treating women clients: higher rate of diagnosis and treatment of mental disorders, stresses of poverty, stresses of multiple roles, stresses of aging, and violence against women.

Objective 15.24: *Discuss problems with involuntary commitment and deinstitutionalization.*

People believed to be mentally ill and dangerous to themselves or others can be involuntarily committed to mental hospitals for diagnosis and treatment. Abuses of involuntary commitments and other problems associated with state mental hospitals have led many states to practice *deinstitutionalization*—discharging as many patients as possible and discouraging admissions. Community services such as community mental health (CMH) centers try to cope with the problems of deinstitutionalization.

Objective 15.25: *Is therapy effective, and how can we find a good therapist?*

Research on the effectiveness of psychotherapy has found that 40 to 80 percent of those who receive treatment are better off than those who do not receive treatment. When searching for a good therapist, it's good to "shop around," and to consult your psychology instructor or college counselors for referrals. If you're in a crisis, get immediate help through hospital emergency rooms or telephone hotlines.

Objective 15.26: *Briefly summarize how to deal with someone who's seriously depressed.*

When talking to someone who's clinically depressed, you should not trivialize the disease, be a cheerleader/"fix-it," or equate it with normal down times. Instead, you should educate yourself, be Rogerian, and get help!

Questions

1. Label the five most common goals of therapy on the figure below.

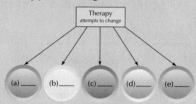

2. Match the following therapists with their primary emphasis:
   ___ psychoanalysts
   ___ humanistic therapists
   ___ biomedical therapists
   ___ cognitive therapists
   ___ behavior therapists
   (a) faulty thinking and belief patterns
   (b) unconscious thoughts
   (c) biological disorders
   (d) negative emotions
   (e) maladaptive behaviors

3. Name the six features of therapy that are culturally universal.

4. A Japanese therapy designed to help clients discover personal guilt for having been ungrateful and troublesome to others and to develop gratitude toward those who have helped them is known as _____. (a) Kyoto therapy; (b) Okado therapy; (c) Naikan therapy; (d) Nissan therapy

5. What are the five major concerns about women in therapy?

6. The policy of discharging as many people as possible from state hospitals and discouraging admissions is called _____. (a) disengagement; (b) reinstitutionalization; (c) maladaptive restructuring; (d) deinstitutionalization

Check your answers in Appendix B.

Click & Review
for additional assessment options:
wiley.com/college/huffman

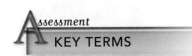

Assessment
KEY TERMS

*To assess your understanding of the **Key Terms** in Chapter 15, write a definition for each (in your own words), and then compare your definitions with those in the text.*

psychotherapy (p. 510)

Insight Therapies
active listening (p. 519)
client-centered therapy (p. 518)
cognitive-behavior therapy (p. 514)
cognitive restructuring (p. 514)
cognitive therapy (p. 514)
dream analysis (p. 511)
empathy (p. 518)
free association (p. 511)
genuineness (p. 519)
group therapy (p. 521)
humanistic therapy (p. 518)
interpretation (p. 511)
psychoanalysis (p. 510)
psychodynamic therapy (p. 512)

rational-emotive behavior therapy (REBT) (p. 514)
resistance (p. 511)
self-help group (p. 521)
self-talk (p. 514)
transference (p. 511)
unconditional positive regard (p. 518)

Behavior Therapies
aversion therapy (p. 524)
behavior therapy (p. 524)
modeling therapy (p. 527)
systematic desensitization (p. 524)

Biomedical Therapies
antianxiety drugs (p. 528)
antidepressant drugs (p. 528)

antipsychotic drugs (p. 528)
biomedical therapy (p. 528)
electroconvulsive therapy (ECT) (p. 530)
lobotomy (p. 530)
mood stabilizer drugs (p. 528)
psychopharmacology (p. 528)
psychosurgery (p. 530)
repetitive transcranial magnetic stimulation (rTMS) (p. 531)
tardive dyskinesia (p. 530)

Therapy and Critical Thinking
eclectic approach (p. 533)

Achievement
WEB RESOURCES

Huffman Book Companion Site
wiley.com/college/huffman

This site is loaded with free Interactive Self-Tests, Internet Exercises, Glossary and Flashcards for key terms, web links, Handbook for Non-Native Speakers, and other activities designed to improve your mastery of the material in this chapter.

Chapter 15 Visual Summary

Insight Therapies

Description/Major Goals

- **Psychoanalysis/psychodynamic therapies:** Bring unconscious conflicts inyo conscious awareness.

- **Cognitive therapies:** Analyze faulty thought processes, beliefs, and negative **self-talk,** and change these destructive thoughts with **cognitive restructuring. Cognitive-behavior therapy:** Focuses on changing faulty thoughts and behaviors.

- **Humanistic therapies:** Work to facilitate personal growth.

- **Group, family, and marital therapies:** Several clients meet with one or more therapists to resolve personal problems.

Techniques/Methods

Five major techniques:
- **Free association**
- **Dream analysis**
- **Resistance**
- **Transference**
- **Interpretation**

Ellis's **rational-emotive behavior therapy (REBT)** replaces irrational beliefs with rational beliefs and accurate perceptions of the world.
Beck's **cognitive therapy** emphasizes change in both thought processes and behavior.

Rogers's **client-centered therapy** offers **empathy, unconditional positive regard, genuineness,** and **active listening** to facilitate personal growth.

Provide group support, feedback, information, and opportunities for behavior-rehearsal.
- **Self-help groups** (like Alcoholics Anonymous) are sometimes considered group therapy, but professional therapists do not conduct them.

- **Family therapies:** Work to change maladaptive family interaction patterns.

David Young Wolff/PhotoEdit

Three Approaches to Therapy

Insight	Behavior	Biomedical
Psychoanalysis (Freud) Psychodynamic	Classical conditioning • Systematic de-sensitization • Aversion therapy	Psychopharmacology
Cognitive • Rational-emotive therapy (Ellis) • Cognitive-behavior therapy (Beck)	Operant conditioning • Shaping • Reinforcement • Punishment • Extinction	Electroconvulsive therapy
Humanistic • Client-centered therapy (Rogers)	Observational learning • Modeling	Psychosurgery
Group, family, and marital		

Behavior Therapies

Description/Major Goals

Behavior therapies: Use learning principles to eliminate maladaptive behaviors and substitute healthy ones.

Techniques/Methods

- Classical conditioning techniques, including **systematic desensitization** (client replaces anxiety with relaxation) and **aversion therapy** (an aversive stimulus is paired with a maladaptive behavior)

- Operant conditioning techniques, including shaping and reinforcement.

- Observational learning techniques, including **modeling therapy** (clients watch and imitate positive role models).

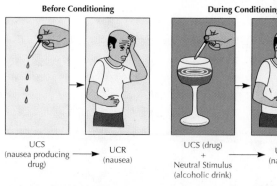

Before Conditioning

UCS (nausea producing drug) → UCR (nausea)

During Conditioning

UCS (drug) + Neutral Stimulus (alcoholic drink) → UCR (nausea)

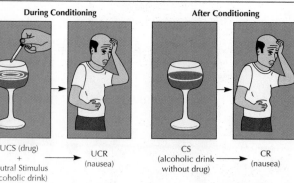

After Conditioning

CS (alcoholic drink without drug) → CR (nausea)

Description/Major Goals

- **Biomedical therapies:** Use biological techniques to relieve psychological disorders.

Techniques/Methods

Drug therapy is the most common biomedical treatment.

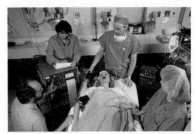

James P. Wilson/Woodfin Camp & Associates

- **Antianxiety drugs** used to treat anxiety disorders.

- **Antipsychotic drugs** relieve symptoms of psychosis.

- **Mood stabilizers** help stabilize bipolar disorder.

- **Antidepressants** used to treat depression.

Electroconvulsive therapy (ECT) used primarily to relieve serious depression, when medication fails.

Psychosurgeries, such as a **lobotomy**, are seldom used today.

Therapy and Critical Thinking

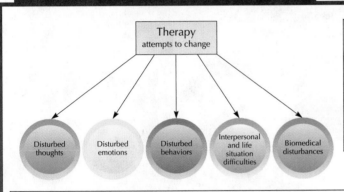

Therapy
attempts to change

Disturbed thoughts

Disturbed emotions

Disturbed behaviors

Interpersonal and life situation difficulties

Biomedical disturbances

Women in Therapy

Higher rate of diagnosis and treatment of mental disorders due to stresses of poverty, multiple roles, aging, and violence against women.

WireImageStock/Masterfill

Cultural Issues

Common features of therapy in all cultures: Naming a problem, qualities of the therapist, establishing credibility, placing the problem in a familiar framework, applying techniques to bring relief, and a special time and place.

Differences in therapy between cultures: Individualistic cultures emphasize the "self" and control over one's life. However, therapies in collectivist cultures, like Japan's Naikan therapy, emphasize interdependence.

Seeking Therapy

Forty to 80 percent of those who receive treatment are better off than those who do not.

Take time to "shop around," but a crisis requires immediate help. If others' problems affect you, get help yourself.

Institutionalization

People believed to be mentally ill and dangerous to themselves or others can be involuntarily committed to mental hospitals for diagnosis and treatment.

Abuses of involuntary commitment and other problems led to *deinstitutionalization*—discharging as many patients as possible and discouraging admissions.

Community services such as Community Mental Health (CMH) centers offset some problems of deinstitutionalization.

16

Social Psychology

Could we but draw back the curtain, That surrounds each
others lives,

See the naked heart and spirit; Know what spur the action
gives;

Often we would find it better, Purer than we think we would.

We would love each other better, If we only understood.

ANONYMOUS

What do you think? If we could "draw back the curtain,"
would we find human nature pure and loveable, or are
we at heart just "savage beasts"? Do you recall from
page one of this text when I promised to take you on
the most exciting and unforgettable trip filled with invaluable discoveries about yourself and the world around you?
After a brief introductory survey of psychology's history and
research methods (Chapter 1), our tour officially began at
the micro level of human behavior and mental processes—
the neuron, brain, and other parts of the nervous system
(Chapter 2). Now, at the end of our journey (Chapter 16),
we come to the largest macro level of study, **social psychology**, which studies how other people influence our individual thoughts, feelings, and actions.

When social psychologists scientifically draw back the
curtain that surrounds our lives, we discover theories and
principles that help explain why ordinary people around the
world commit acts of astounding bravery and kindness, as
well as acts of unspeakable evil and cruelty.

For many students and psychologists, myself included,
social psychology is the most exciting of all fields because it
is about you and me, and because almost everything we do
is *social*. Unlike earlier chapters that focused on individual
processes, like the brain and other parts of the nervous
system, memory, and personality, social psychology studies how large social forces, such as groups, social roles,
and norms, bring out the best and worst in all of us. This
chapter begins with a look at components of social psychology and concludes with a discussion of how social psychology can help reduce prejudice, discrimination, and other
destructive behaviors.

chievement

Objective 16.1: *What is social
psychology?*

Social Psychology *Study of how others influence our thoughts,
feelings, and actions*

Digital Vision/Getty Images

▶ **Our Thoughts about Others**
Attribution
Attitudes

▶ **Our Feelings about Others**
Prejudice and Discrimination
Interpersonal Attraction

GENDER & CULTURAL DIVERSITY
Is Beauty in the Eye of the Beholder?

PSYCHOLOGY AT WORK
The Art and Science of Flirting

▶ **Our Actions toward Others**
Social Influence
Group Processes
Aggression
Altruism

CRITICAL THINKING/ACTIVE LEARNING
When and Why Do We Help?

▶ **Applying Social Psychology to Social Problems**
Reducing Prejudice and Discrimination

RESEARCH HIGHLIGHT
Understanding Implicit Biases

Overcoming Destructive Obedience

Application

WHY STUDY PSYCHOLOGY?

Did You Know...

▶ Groups generally make more risky decisions than a single individual does?

▶ Most people judge others more harshly than they judge themselves?

▶ Looks are the primary factor in our initial feelings of attraction, liking, and romantic love?

▶ Opposites don't really attract?

▶ Romantic love rarely lasts longer than one or two years?

Chris Fortuna/GettyImages, Inc.

▶ Inducing cognitive dissonance is a great way to change attitudes?

▶ There are positive as well as negative forms of prejudice?

▶ Watching a violent sports match or punching a pillow is a not a good way to let off steam and reduce aggression?

▶ When people are alone, they are more likely to help another individual than when they are in a group?

Our Thoughts about Others

Why would someone run into a burning building to rescue a stranger? Why do we fall in love with some people and not others? Trying to understand the social world often means trying to understand other people's behavior. We look for reasons and explanations for others' behavior (the process of attribution). We also develop thoughts and beliefs (attitudes) about others. Let's explore both *attributions* and *attitudes*.

Attribution: Explaining Others' Behavior

Why are we all so interested in understanding and explaining why people do what they do? Social psychologists believe that developing logical explanations, or **attributions**, for behavior makes us feel safer and more in control (Chiou, 2007; Heider, 1958; Krueger, 2007). To do so, we generally begin with the basic question of whether a given action stems mainly from a person's internal disposition or from the external situation.

Achievement

Objective 16.2: *Describe the process of attribution and its two key errors.*

Attribution *An explanation for the cause of behaviors or events*

Mistaken Attributions

Making the correct choice between disposition and situation is central to accurate attributions. Unfortunately, our judgments are frequently marred by two major errors: the *fundamental attribution error* and the *self-serving bias*.

The Fundamental Attribution Error (FAE)—Judging Others   When we notice and carefully consider environmental, *situational* influences on people's behavior, we generally make accurate attributions. However, given that people have enduring personality traits (Chapter 13) and a tendency to take cognitive shortcuts (Chapter 8), we frequently ignore, and/or underestimate, situational factors, while overestimating personal, *dispositional* factors. In short, we blame people—not situations.

For example, after Hurricane Katrina hit the Gulf Coast in 2005, the public wanted to know and tried to explain why so many people were injured, killed, and/or left stranded in the evacuation centers. The media, and most television viewers, generally ignored important situational factors, like the historic unpredictability of hurricanes and a lack of transportation and financial resources, which discouraged or blocked many residents from evacuating in time. Instead, many people blamed the mayor, the governor, and other politicians, or the victims themselves for waiting so long and not evacuating ahead of time (Figure 16.1). In a like manner, students who drop out of college are often called "lazy," and battered spouses and rape survivors are criticized for somehow "provoking" their attackers. This bias is so common that it is called the **fundamental attribution error (FAE)** (Gebauer, Krempl, & Fleisch, 2008; Kimmel, 2006; Tal-Or & Papirman, 2007).

Why do we so often jump to internal, *personal* explanations? Social psychologists have suggested that one reason is that human personalities and behaviors are more *salient* (or noticeable) than situational factors, the **saliency bias**. We also tend to focus on people and "blame the victim" because of our need to believe that the world is just and fair. This **just-world phenomenon** suggests that people generally deserve what they get, while also allowing us to feel safer in an uncontrollable world.

The Self-serving Bias—Judging Ourselves   As we've just seen, when judging others we often blame people versus the situation—the FAE. However, when judging ourselves, we tend to take personal credit for our successes and externalize our failures. This **self-serving bias** is motivated by a desire to maintain positive self-esteem and a good public image (Gobbo & Raccanello, 2007; Krusemark, Campbell, & Clementz, 2008; Shepperd, Malone, & Sweeny, 2008). For example, students often credit themselves for high scores on an exam and blame the instructor, textbook, or "tricky" questions for low scores. Studies also find young children tend to blame their siblings for conflicts; and both partners in a divorce are more likely to see themselves as the victim, as less responsible for the breakup, and as being more willing to reconcile (Gray & Silver, 1990; Wilson et al., 2004). Even in the business world, professional money managers generally take credit for good investments and blame others or external forces for failures (Gebauer et al., 2008).

Fundamental Attribution Error (FAE) *Misjudging the causes of others' behavior as due to internal (dispositional) causes rather than external (situational) ones*

Saliency Bias *Focusing on the most noticeable (salient) factors when explaining the causes of behavior*

Just-World Phenomenon *Tendency to believe that people generally get what they deserve*

Self-Serving Bias *Taking credit for our successes and externalizing our failures*

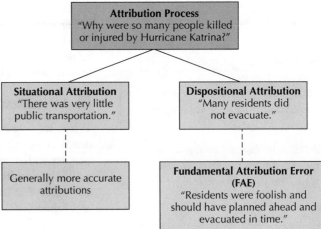

Figure 16.1 *How dispositional attributions sometimes lead to the fundamental attribution error (FAE)*

ᴀssessment

VISUAL QUIZ

Can you identify the attributional error that best explains this cartoon?

PEANUTS; drawings by Charles Schulz; 1989 United Features Syndicate, Inc. Reprinted by permission of United Features Syndicate, Inc.

Answer: Lucy's criticism of Linus may be the result of the fundamental attribution error. Her overlooking of her own faults may be the self-serving bias.

ᴀchievement

Objective 16.3: *Describe how culture affects attributional biases.*

Culture and Attributional Biases

Both the fundamental attribution error and the self-serving bias may depend in part on cultural factors. In general, *individualistic cultures*, like the United States, are more likely to make both attributional errors than *collectivistic cultures*, like China. Why? Individualistic cultures emphasize independence and personal responsibility, and people are defined and understood as individual selves—largely responsible for their own successes and failures. In contrast, collectivistic cultures, focus on interdependence and collective responsibility, and people are defined and understood as members of their social network—responsible for doing as others expect. Accordingly, they tend to be more aware of situational constraints on behavior and less susceptible to the FAE (Bozkurt & Aydin, 2004; Norenzayan, 2006).

The self-serving bias is also much less common in Eastern nations. In Japan, for instance, the ideal person is someone who is aware of his or her shortcomings and continually works to overcome them. It is not someone who thinks highly of himself or herself (Heine & Renshaw, 2002). In the East, where people do not define themselves as much in terms of their individual accomplishments, self-esteem is not related to doing better than others. Rather, fitting in and not standing out from the group is stressed. As the Japanese proverb says, "The nail that sticks up gets pounded down."

This emphasis on group relations in Asian cultures is also true of many Native Americans. For example, when the Wintun Native Americans originally described being with a close relation or intimate friend, they would not say, for example, "Linda and I," but rather, "Linda we" (Lee, 1950). This attachment to community relations instead of individual *selfhood* often seems strange to people in contemporary Western, individualist societies. But it remains common in collectivist cultures (Triandis, 2007).

ᴀchievement

Objective 16.4: *Define attitude and identify its three key components.*

Attitudes: Our Learned Predispositions Toward Others

Attitude *Learned predisposition to respond cognitively, affectively, and behaviorally to a particular object*

When we observe and respond to the world around us, we are seldom neutral. Rather, our responses toward subjects as diverse as pizza, people, AIDS, and abortion reflect our **attitudes**, which are learned predispositions to respond cognitively, affectively, and behaviorally to a particular object in a particular way. Social psychologists generally agree that most attitudes have three components (Figure 16.2): *cognitive, affective,* and *behavioral.*

ᴀchievement

Objective 16.5: *What is cognitive dissonance, how does it change attitudes, and how does culture affect it?*

Attitude Change Through Cognitive Dissonance

We are not born with our attitudes—they are learned. From earliest childhood, we form them through direct experience (we eat pizza and like the taste), and through indirect learning or observation (we listen to testimonials or watch others happily

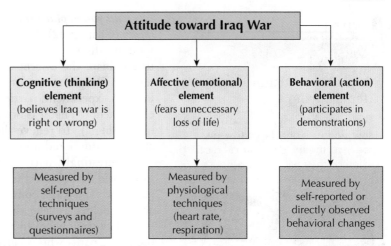

Attitude toward Iraq War		
Cognitive (thinking) element (believes Iraq war is right or wrong)	**Affective (emotional) element** (fears unneccessary loss of life)	**Behavioral (action) element** (participates in demonstrations)
Measured by self-report techniques (surveys and questionnaires)	Measured by physiological techniques (heart rate, respiration)	Measured by self-reported or directly observed behavioral changes

Figure 16.2 *Three components of attitudes* The cognitive component of our attitudes consists of thoughts and beliefs, the affective component involves feelings, and the behavioral component consists of a predisposition to act in certain ways. When social psychologists study attitudes, they measure each of the three components.

eating pizza). Although attitudes begin in early childhood, they are not permanent. Advertisers and politicians spend millions of dollars on campaigns because they know attitudes can be shaped and changed throughout the entire life span.

Attitude change often results from persuasive appeals (such as TV ads like "Friends Don't Let Friends Drive Drunk"). An even more efficient method is by creating **cognitive dissonance**, a feeling of discomfort caused by a discrepancy between an attitude and a behavior or between two competing attitudes (Cooper & Hogg, 2007; Gringart, Helmes, & Speelman, 2008). *Dissonance* comes from disagreement or conflict. According to Leon Festinger (1957), when we notice a conflict between our attitudes and behaviors, or between two conflicting attitudes, the contradiction makes us uncomfortable. This discomfort (cognitive dissonance) makes us want to change our attitude to agree with our behaviors or to match our other attitudes (Figure 16.3).

Cognitive Dissonance *A feeling of discomfort resulting from a mismatch between an attitude and a behavior or between two competing attitudes*

The theory of cognitive dissonance has been widely tested in a large number of experiments. One of the best-known studies was conducted by Leon Festinger and J. Merrill Carlsmith (1959). Students selected as participants were given excruciatingly boring tasks for an hour. After finishing the task, participants were approached by the experimenter and asked for a favor. The experimenter asked if they would serve as research assistants and tell the next "participant" (who was really a confederate of the experimenter) that the task was "very enjoyable" and "fun." In one experimental condition, the person was offered $1 for helping. In the second condition, the person was offered $20. If the person lied to the incoming participant and was paid, he or she was then led to another room and asked about his or her true feelings toward the experimental tasks.

The participants were obviously coaxed into doing something (lying) that was inconsistent with their actual experiences and attitudes. What do you think happened? Most people expect that those who were paid $20 for lying would feel more positive toward the task than would those paid $1. Ironically, the reverse occurred.

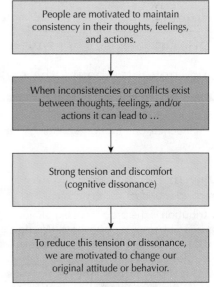

Cognitive Dissonance Theory

People are motivated to maintain consistency in their thoughts, feelings, and actions.
When inconsistencies or conflicts exist between thoughts, feelings, and/or actions it can lead to ...
Strong tension and discomfort (cognitive dissonance)
To reduce this tension or dissonance, we are motivated to change our original attitude or behavior.

Figure 16.3 *Cognitive dissonance theory* How would health professionals, who obviously know the dangers of smoking, deal with their cognitive dissonance? They could quit smoking, but, like most people, they probably take the easier route. They change their attitudes about the dangers of smoking by reassuring themselves with examples of people who smoke and live to be 100, or they simply ignore or discount contradictory information.

Can you explain this? Cognitive dissonance theory is essentially a *drive-reduction theory* (Chapter 12). Just as the discomfort of being hungry motivates us to search for food, the discomfort or tension of cognitive dissonance motivates us to search for ways to eliminate the discrepancy between our behavior and attitudes and the resulting tension. People strive for consistency in their cognitions and behaviors. In the boring task experiment, participants faced a mismatch between their attitude toward the experiment ("That was boring!") and their behavior ("I told another participant it was interesting!"). To relieve the resulting tension, all participants changed their original attitude from boredom to "I enjoyed the task."

Interestingly, participants who were paid $20 changed their attitudes less than those paid $1 because they could readily explain their behavior in terms of the larger payment. ($20 was a considerable amount in the late 1950s.) Being paid well for their actions helped relieve the logical inconsistency (the cognitive dissonance) between what they truly believed about the boring task and what they told others. In contrast, the participants who received $1 had *insufficient justification* for lying to another participant. Thus, they had more cognitive dissonance and stronger motivation to change their attitudes.

Culture and Dissonance

The experience of cognitive dissonance may depend on a distinctly Western way of thinking about and evaluating the self. As noted earlier, North Americans are highly individualistic and independent. Therefore, making a bad choice or decision has strong, negative effects on self-esteem and results in more cognitive dissonance and greater motivation for attitude change because we believe this bad choice reflects somehow on our worth as individuals.

Collectivistic cultures, on the other hand, tend to be much more interdependent. Consequently, they experience less individual cognitive dissonance because they are more concerned over a potential loss of connection with others than with a threat to their individual self-esteem. Research comparing Japanese and other Asian participants with Canadian and U.S. participants supports this position (Hoshino Browne, 2005; Markus & Kitayama, 1998, 2003).

Assessment   STOP

CHECK & REVIEW

Our Thoughts About Others

Objective 16.1: *What is social psychology?*

Social psychology is the study of how others influence our thoughts, feelings, and actions.

Objective 16.2: *Describe the process of attribution and its two key errors.*

Attribution is the process of explaining the causes of behaviors or events. We do this by determining whether actions resulted from internal, *dispositional* factors or external, *situational* factors. The two key errors are: (1) the **fundamental attribution error (FAE)**, which overestimates dispositional factors and underestimates situational factors when judging others; and (2) the **self-serving bias**, which involves taking credit for successes and externalizing failures when judging ourselves.

Objective 16.3: *Describe how culture affects attributional biases.*

Collectivistic cultures, like China, are less likely to make the fundamental attribution error and the self-serving bias because they focus on interdependence and collective responsibility, whereas individualistic cultures, like the United States, emphasize independence and personal responsibility.

Objective 16.4: *Define attitude and identify its three key components.*

An **attitude** is a learned predisposition to respond cognitively, affectively, and behaviorally toward a particular object. Its three components are: (1) cognitive (thoughts and beliefs), (2) affective (feelings), and (3) behavioral (predispositions to actions).

Objective 16.5: *What is cognitive dissonance, how does it change attitudes, and how does culture affect it?*

Cognitive dissonance is a feeling of discomfort caused by a discrepancy between an attitude and a behavior or between two competing attitudes. This mismatch and resulting tension motivate us to change our attitude or behavior to reduce the tension and restore balance. Individualistic cultures experience more cognitive dissonance than collectivistic cultures because our emphasis on independence and personal responsibility creates more tension when our attitudes are in conflict.

Questions

1. The principles people follow in making judgments about the causes of events, others' behavior, and their own behavior are known as ___. (a) impression management; (b) stereotaxic determination; (c) attributions; (d) person perception
2. What is the fundamental attribution error?
3. Label the three components of attitudes on the following figure.

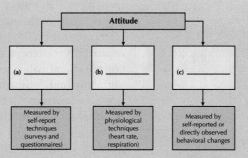

Attitude

(a) _____   (b) _____   (c) _____

Measured by self-report techniques (surveys and questionnaires)   Measured by physiological techniques (heart rate, respiration)   Measured by self-reported or directly observed behavioral changes

4. According to _____ theory, people are motivated to change their attitudes because of tension created by a mismatch between two or more competing attitudes or between their attitudes and behavior.

Check your answers in Appendix B.

Click & Review
for additional assessment options:
wiley.com/college/huffman

Our Feelings about Others

Having explored our thoughts about others (attribution and attitudes), we now turn our attention to our feelings about others. We begin by examining the negative feelings (and thoughts and actions) associated with *prejudice* and *discrimination*. We will then explore the generally positive feelings of *interpersonal attraction*.

Prejudice and Discrimination: It's the Feeling That Counts

Prejudice, which literally means "prejudgment," is a learned, generally *negative* attitude directed toward specific people solely because of their membership in an identified group. Prejudice is not innate. It is learned. It also creates enormous problems for its victims and limits the perpetrator's ability to accurately judge others and process information.

Positive forms of prejudice do exist, such as "all women love babies" or "African Americans are natural athletes." However, most research and definitions of prejudice focus on the negative forms. (It is also interesting to note that even positive forms of prejudice can be harmful. For example, women might think there must be something wrong with them if they don't like being around babies. Similarly, African Americans might see athletics or entertainment as their only routes to success.)

Like all attitudes, prejudice is composed of three elements: (1) a *cognitive component* or **stereotype**, thoughts and beliefs held about people strictly because of their membership in a group; (2) an *affective component*, consisting of feelings and emotions associated with objects of prejudice; and (3) a *behavioral component*, consisting of predispositions to act in certain ways toward members of the group (**discrimination**).

Although the terms *prejudice* and *discrimination* are often used interchangeably, there is an important difference between them. *Prejudice* refers to an *attitude*. **Discrimination** refers to *action*. For example, many African Americans experience extra surveillance (discrimination) in a variety of settings, such as driving or shopping. Discrimination often results from prejudice, but not always (Figure 16.4).

Major Sources of Prejudice and Discrimination

How do prejudice and discrimination originate? Why do they persist? Five commonly cited sources of prejudice and discrimination are: *learning, personal experience, mental shortcuts, economic* and *political competition*, and *displaced aggression* (Figure 16.5).

Achievement

Objective 16.6: *Define prejudice, identify its three key components, and differentiate between prejudice and discrimination.*

Prejudice *A learned, generally negative, attitude toward members of a group; it includes thoughts (stereotypes), feelings, and behavioral tendencies (possible discrimination)*

Stereotype *A set of beliefs about the characteristics of people in a group that is generalized to all group members; also, the cognitive component of prejudice*

Discrimination *Negative behaviors directed at members of a group*

Achievement

Objective 16.7: *Discuss the five major sources of prejudice and discrimination.*

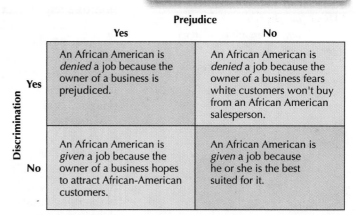

		Prejudice	
		Yes	No
Discrimination	**Yes**	An African American is *denied* a job because the owner of a business is prejudiced.	An African American is *denied* a job because the owner of a business fears white customers won't buy from an African American salesperson.
	No	An African American is *given* a job because the owner of a business hopes to attract African-American customers.	An African American is *given* a job because he or she is the best suited for it.

Figure 16.4 **Prejudice and discrimination** Note how prejudice and discrimination are closely related, but either condition can exist without the other. The only situation in this example without prejudice or discrimination is when someone is given a job simply because he or she is the best candidate.

wiley.com/college/huffman

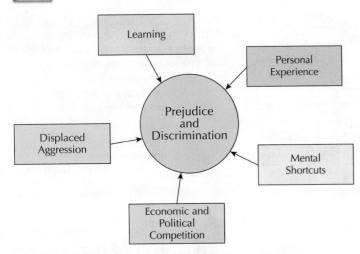

Figure 16.5 *Common sources of prejudice and discrimination*

THE FAMILY CIRCUS By Bil Keane

"That's the DOLL aisle, Daddy. Somebody might see us!"

©Bill Keane, Inc. Reprinted with special permission of King Features Syndicate.

Ingroup Favoritism *Viewing members of the ingroup more positively than members of an outgroup*

Outgroup Homogeneity Effect *Judging members of an outgroup as more alike and less diverse than members of the ingroup*

Learning People learn prejudice the same way they learn all attitudes—through *classical* and *operant conditioning* and *social learning* (Chapter 6). For example, when the media repeatedly portrays minorities and women in demeaning or stereotypical roles, viewers accept these portrayals as correct and "normal." Similarly, when parents, friends, and teachers demonstrate and express their prejudices, they serve as reinforcers and models for all who observe them (Anderson & Hamilton, 2005; Bennett et al., 2004; Kassin, Fein, & Markus, 2008; Levitan, 2008; Livingston & Drwecki, 2007; Neto & Furnham, 2005). *Ethnocentrism*, believing one's own culture represents the norm or is superior to all others, is also a form of learned prejudice.

Personal Experience People also develop prejudice through direct experience. For example, when people make prejudicial remarks or "jokes," they often gain attention and even approval from others. Sadly, derogating others also seems to boost one's self-esteem (Fein & Spencer, 1997; Plummer, 2001). Also, once someone has one or more negative interactions and experience with members of a specific group, they often generalize their bad feelings and prejudice to all members of that group.

Mental Shortcuts Prejudice may stem from normal attempts to simplify a complex social world (Kulik, 2005; Sternberg, 2007, 2009). Stereotypes allow people to make quick judgments about others, thereby freeing up their mental resources for other activities. In fact, stereotypes and prejudice can occur even without a person's conscious awareness or control. This process is known as "automatic" or "implicit" bias (see our Research Highlight, p. 575).

People use stereotypes to classify others in terms of their membership in a group. Given that people generally classify themselves as part of the preferred group, they also create ingroups and outgroups. An *ingroup* is any category that people see themselves as belonging to; an *outgroup* is any other category.

In sharp contrast to how they judge members of the outgroup, people generally tend to judge ingroup members as being more attractive, having better personalities, and so on—a phenomenon known as **ingroup favoritism** (Ahmed, 2007; Dunham, 2007; Harth, Kessler, & Colin, 2008). People also tend to recognize greater diversity among members of their ingroup than they do among members of outgroups (Cehajic, Brown, & Castano, 2008; Wegener, Clark, & Petty, 2006). A danger of this **outgroup homogeneity effect** is that when members of minority groups are not recognized as varied and complex individuals, it is easier to treat them in discriminatory ways.

During the Vietnam and Iraq wars, for example, labeling Asians "gooks" and Iraqis "towel heads" made it easier to accept the "civilian casualties." As in most wars, facelessness makes it easier to dehumanize our enemies, and facelessness also helps perpetuate our current high levels of fear and anxiety associated with terrorism (Haslam et al., 2007; Hodson & Costello, 2007; Zimbardo, 2004, 2007).

Economic and Political Competition Most people understand that prejudice and discrimination exact a high price on their victims, but few acknowledge the significant economic and political advantages they offer to the dominant group (Esses et al., 2001; Mays, Cochran, & Barnes, 2007; Schaefer, 2008). For example, the stereotype that blacks and Mexicans are inferior to whites helps justify and perpetuate a social order in the United States, in which whites hold disproportionate power and resources.

Displaced Aggression As we discuss in the next section, frustration sometimes leads people to attack the source of frustration. But, as history has shown, when the

(a) ©AP/Wide World Photos

(b) Granger Collection

(c) Anthony Njuguna/Reuters/Corbis

The price of prejudice *If pictures truly are "worth a thousand words," these photos speak volumes about the atrocities associated with prejudice: (a) the Holocaust, when millions of Jews, and other minorities, were exterminated by the Nazis, (b) slavery in the United States, where Africans were bought and sold as slaves, and (c) recent acts of genocide in Sudan, where thousands have been slaughtered.*

cause of frustration is ambiguous, or too powerful and capable of retaliation, people often redirect their aggression toward an alternative, innocent target, known as a *scapegoat*. There is strong historical evidence for the dangers of scapegoating. Jewish people were blamed for economic troubles in Germany prior to World War II. In America, beginning in the 1980s, gay men were blamed for the AIDs epidemic, and since the 9/11 terrorist attacks, recent immigrants are being blamed for our current economic troubles.

Understanding the many causes of prejudice is just a first step toward overcoming it, and later in this chapter, we consider several methods psychologists recommend to reduce prejudice.

Getty Images

Prejudice and war *This group is supporting Osama Bin Laden and demonstrating against the United States. How would you explain their loyalty to Bin Laden and prejudice against Americans?*

Interpersonal Attraction: Why We Like and Love Others

Stop for a moment and think about someone you like very much. Now picture someone you really dislike. Can you explain your feelings? Social psychologists use the term **interpersonal attraction** to refer to the degree of positive feelings toward another. Attraction accounts for a variety of social experiences—admiration, liking, friendship, intimacy, lust, and love. In this section, we will discuss several factors that explain interpersonal attraction.

Three Key Factors in Attraction—Physical Attractiveness, Proximity, and Similarity

Social psychologists have identified three compelling factors in interpersonal attraction—*physical attractiveness*, *proximity*, and *similarity*. Physical attractiveness and proximity are most influential in the beginning stages of relationships. However, similarity is more important in maintaining long-term relationships.

Physical Attractiveness
Can you remember what first attracted you to your best friend or romantic partner? Was it his or her warm personality, sharp intelligence, or great sense of humor? Or was it looks? Research consistently shows that *physical attractiveness* (size, shape, facial characteristics, and manner of dress) is one of the most important

Interpersonal Attraction
Positive feelings toward another

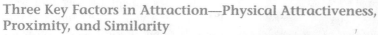

Achievement

Objective 16.8: *What are the three key factors in attraction?*

wiley.com/
college/
huffman

factors in our initial liking or loving of others (Andreoni & Petric, 2008; Buss, 2003, 2005, 2007, 2008; Cunningham, Fink, & Kenix, 2008; Lippa, 2007; Maner et al., 2008).

Like it or not, attractive individuals are seen by both men and women as more poised, interesting, cooperative, achieving, sociable, independent, intelligent, healthy, and sexually warm (Fink & Penton-Voak, 2002; Swami & Furnham, 2008; Willis, Esqueda, & Schacht, 2008). Human infants, just a few days old prefer attractive human faces, and three-to-four-month olds prefer attractive over unattractive domestic and wild cat faces (Quinn et al., 2008). Perhaps even more distressing, premature infants who are rated as physically more attractive by nurses caring for them thrive better during their hospital stay. They gain more weight and are released earlier than infants perceived as less attractive, presumably because they receive more nurturing (Badr & Abdallah, 2001). Attractive defendents in a simulated vehicular homicide case were also given shorter sentences than unattractive defendants (Staley, 2008).

GENDER & CULTURAL DIVERSITY

Objective 16.9: *Describe cultural and historical similarities and differences in judgments of attractiveness.*

Is Beauty in the Eye of the Beholder?

If you found the previous list of advantages for attractiveness unnerving, you'll be even more surprised to know that some research also shows that judgments of attractiveness appear consistent across cultures. For example, in numerous cultures around the world, women are valued more for looks and youth, whereas men are valued more on maturity, ambitiousness, and financial resources (Buss, 1989, 1999, 2005, 2007, 2008; Evans & Brase, 2007; Lippa, 2007; Swami & Furnham, 2008).

How can this be so universally true? Evolutionary psychologists would suggest that both men and women prefer attractive people because good looks generally indicate good health, sound genes, and high fertility. For example, facial and body symmetry appear to be key elements in attractiveness (Fink et al., 2004; Jones, DeBruine, & Little, 2007), and symmetry seems to be correlated with genetic health. The fact that across cultures men prefer youthful appearing women is reportedly because this is a sign of their future fertility. Similarly, women prefer men with maturity and financial resources because the responsibility of rearing and nurturing children more often falls on women's shoulders. Therefore, they prefer mature men "who will stick around" and men with greater resources to invest in children.

In contrast to this seeming universal agreement on standards of attractiveness, evidence also exists that beauty is in "the eye of the beholder." What we judge as beautiful varies somewhat from era to era and culture to culture (Figure 16.6). For example, the Chinese once practiced foot binding because small feet were considered beautiful in women. All the toes except the big one were bent under a young girl's foot and into the sole. The physical distortion made it almost impossible for her to walk. And she suffered excruciating pain, chronic bleeding, and frequent infections throughout her life (Dworkin, 1974). Even in modern times, cultural demands for attractiveness encourage an increasing number of women (and men) to undergo expensive and often

Figure 16.6 *Culture and attraction* Which of these women do you find most attractive? Can you see how your cultural background might train you to prefer one look to the others?

painful surgery to *increase* the size of their eyes, breasts, lips, chest, and penis. They also undergo surgery to *decrease* the size of their nose, ears, chin, stomach, hips, and thighs.

How do those of us who are not "superstar beautiful" manage to find mates? The good news is that perceived attractiveness for *known* people, in contrast to *unknown* people, is strongly influenced by nonphysical traits. This means that traits like respect and familiarity increase our judgments of beauty in friends and family (Kniffin & Wilson, 2004; Lewandowski, Aron, & Gee, 2007). Also, what people judge as "ideally attractive" may be quite different from what they eventually choose for a mate. According to the *matching hypothesis*, men and women of approximately equal physical attractiveness tend to select each other as partners (Regan, 1998; Sprecher & Regan, 2002). Further good news, as you will see in the following application section, is that *flirting* offers a "simple" way to increase attractiveness.

PSYCHOLOGY AT WORK

Achievement

Objective 16.10: *Discuss scientific research on flirting.*

The Art and Science of Flirting

Picture yourself watching a man (Tom) and woman (Kaleesha) at a singles' bar.

> As Tom approaches the table, Kaleesha sits up straighter, smiles, and touches her hair. Tom asks her to dance. Kaleesha quickly nods and stands up while smoothing her skirt. During the dance, she smiles and sometimes glances at him from under her lashes. When the dance finishes, Kaleesha waits for Tom to escort her back to her chair. She motions him to sit in the adjacent chair, and they engage in a lively conversation. Kaleesha allows her leg to briefly graze his. When Tom reaches for popcorn from the basket in front of Kaleesha, she playfully pulls it away. This surprises Tom, and he frowns at Kaleesha. She quickly turns away and starts talking to her friends. Despite his repeated attempts to talk to her, Kaleesha ignores him.

What happened? Did you recognize Kaleesha's sexual signals? Did you understand why she turned away at the end? If so, you are skilled in the art and science of flirting. If not, you may be very interested in the work of Monica Moore at the University of Missouri (1998). Moore is a scientist interested in describing and understanding flirting and the role it plays in human courtship. She has observed and recorded many scenes—in singles' bars and shopping malls—like the one with Tom and Kaleesha. Although she prefers the term *nonverbal courtship signaling*, what Moore and her colleagues have spent thousands of hours secretly observing is *flirting*.

From these naturalistic observations, we know a great deal more about what works, and doesn't work, in courtship. First of all, both men and women flirt. But women generally initiate a courtship. The woman signals her interest with glances that may be brief and darting, or direct and sustained. Interested women often smile at the same time they gesture with their hands—often with an open or extended palm. Primping (adjusting clothing or patting hair) is also common. A flirting woman will also make herself more noticeable by sitting straighter, with stomach pulled in and breasts pushed out.

Once contact is made and the couple is dancing or sitting at a table, Moore noticed the woman increases the level of flirting. She orients her body toward his, whispers in his ear, and frequently nods and smiles in response to his conversation. Most significant, she touches the man or allows the man to touch her. Like Kaleesha with Tom, allowing her leg to graze his is a powerful indication of her interest.

Charles Gupton/Stock, Boston

wiley.com/
college/
huffman

Women also use play behaviors to flirt. They tease, mock-hit, and tell jokes. They do this to inject humor, while also testing the man's receptivity to humor. As in the case of Tom's reaction to the popcorn tease, when a man doesn't appreciate the playfulness, a woman often uses rejection signals to cool or end the relationship. Other studies confirm Moore's description of women's nonverbal sexual signaling (Lott, 2000).

Now that you know what to look for, watch for flirting behavior in others—or perhaps in your own life. According to Moore and other researchers, flirting may be the single most important thing a woman can do to increase her attractiveness. Because the burden of making the first approach is usually the man's, men are understandably cautious and uncomfortable. They generally welcome a woman clearly signaling her interest.

Two cautions are in order. First, signaling interest does not mean that the woman is ready to have sex with the man. She flirts because she wants to get to know the man better. She'll later decide whether she wants to develop a relationship. Second, Moore reminds women to "use their enhanced flirting skills only when genuinely interested" (1997, p. 69). Flirting should be reserved for times when you genuinely want to attract and keep the attention of a particular partner.

Proximity *Attraction based on geographic closeness*

Proximity   Attraction also depends on people being in the same place at the same time. Thus, **proximity**, or geographic nearness, is another major factor in attraction. A study of friendship in college dormitories found that the person next door was more often liked than the person two doors away, the person two doors away was liked more than someone three doors away, and so on (Priest & Sawyer, 1967).

Why is proximity so important? It's largely because of *mere exposure*. Just as familiar people become more physically attractive over time, repeated exposure also increases overall liking (Monin, 2003; Rhodes, Halberstadt, & Brajkovich, 2001). This makes sense from an evolutionary point of view. Things we have seen before are less likely to pose a threat than novel stimuli. It also explains why modern advertisers tend to run highly redundant ad campaigns with familiar faces and jingles. Repeated exposure increases our liking—and purchases. We even like *ourselves* better when we see ourselves in a familiar way (Figure 16.7).

One caution: Repeated exposure to a *negative* stimulus can *decrease* attraction, as evidenced by the high number of negative political ads. Politicians have learned that repeatedly running an attack ad associating an opposing candidate with negative cues (like increased taxes) decreases the viewers' liking of the opponent. On the other hand, running ads showing themselves in a positive light (kissing babies, helping flood victims) helps build positive associations and increased liking.

Bernhard Kuhmsted/Retna   Bernhard Kuhmsted/Retna

Figure 16.7 *The face in the mirror* According to the "mere exposure effect," this model would prefer the reversed photo on the left because this is the familiar version she sees in the mirror. Similarly, people presented with pictures of themselves and reversed images of themselves strongly prefer the reversed images. Close friends prefer the nonreversed images (Mita, Dermer, & Knight, 1977).

Similarity   Once we've had repeated opportunity to get to know someone through simple physical proximity, and assuming we find him or her attractive, we then need something to hold the relationship together over time. The major cementing factor for long-term relationships, whether liking or loving, is *similarity*. We tend to prefer, and stay with, people (and organizations) who are most like us, those who share our ethnic background, social class, interests, and attitudes (Caprara et al., 2007; Morry, 2005; Smithson & Baker, 2008). In other words, "Birds of a feather flock together."

Assessment

VISUAL QUIZ

Based on your reading of this section, can you explain what is wrong with Kvack's love for the wooden dummy?

Reprinted with special permission of King Features Syndicate.

Answer: Research shows that similarity is the best predictor of long-term relationships. As shown here, however, many people ignore dissimilarities and hope that their chosen partner will change over time.

What about the old saying "opposites attract"? It does seem that this bit of common folklore is contradictory. But the term *opposites* here probably refers to personality traits rather than to social background or values. An attraction to a seemingly opposite person is more often based on the recognition that in one or two important areas that person offers something we lack. If you are a talkative and outgoing person, for example, your friendship with a quiet and reserved individual may endure because each of you provides important resources for the other. Psychologists refer to this as **need complementarity**, as compared with the **need compatibility** represented by similarity. In sum, lovers can enjoy some differences, but the more alike people are, the more their liking endures.

Loving Others

We can think of interpersonal attraction as a fundamental building block of how we feel about others. But how do we make sense of love? Many people find the subject to be alternately mysterious, exhilarating, comforting—and even maddening. In this section, we explore two perspectives on love—*romantic love* and *companionate love*.

Romantic Love   When you think of romantic love, do you think of falling in love, a magical experience that puts you on cloud nine? **Romantic love**, also called *passionate love* or *limerence*, has been defined as "any intense attraction that involves the idealization of the other, within an erotic context, with the expectation of enduring for some time in the future" (Jankowiak, 1997, p. 8).

Romantic love has intrigued people throughout history. Its intense joys and sorrows have also inspired countless poems, novels, movies, and songs around the world. A cross-cultural study by anthropologists William Jankowiak and Edward Fischer found romantic love in 147 of the 166 societies they studied. The researchers concluded that "romantic love constitutes a human universal or, at the least, a near universal" (1992, p. 154).

Problems with Romantic Love   Romantic love may be almost universal, but it's not problem free. First, romantic love is typically short lived. Even in the most devoted couples, the intense attraction and excitement generally

Need Complementarity *Attraction toward those with qualities we admire but personally lack*

Need Compatibility *Attraction based on sharing similar needs*

Achievement

Objective 16.11: *Differentiate between romantic and companionate love, and discuss problems associated with romantic love.*

Romantic Love *Intense feeling of attraction to another within an erotic context and with future expectations*

Robin Davies/Taxi/Getty Images

Symbols of romantic love? *Do you consider this a romantic gesture? How might other cultures signal their attraction and love for one another?*

wiley.com/
college/
huffman

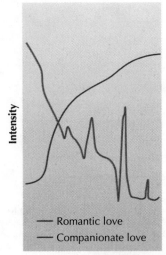

Figure 16.8 *Love over the life span* Romantic love is high in the beginning of a relationship but tends to diminish over time, with periodic resurgences or "spikes." Companionate love usually increases over time.

Companionate Love *Strong and lasting attraction characterized by trust, caring, tolerance, and friendship*

Figure 16.9 *The benefits of companionate love* ***This couple just celebrated their 60th wedding anniversary.*** Unlike romantic love, which rarely lasts longer than 6 to 30 months, companionate love can last a lifetime.

begin to fade after 6 to 30 months (Hatfield & Rapson, 1996; Livingston, 1999). Although this research finding may disappoint you, as a critical thinker, do you really think any emotion of this intensity could last forever? What would happen if other intense emotions, such as anger or joy, were eternal? Moreover, given the time-consuming nature of romantic love, what would happen to other parts of our lives, such as school, career, and family?

Another major problem with romantic love is that it is largely based on mystery and fantasy. People fall in love with others not necessarily as they are but as they want them to be (Fletcher & Simpson, 2000; Levine, 2001). What happens to these illusions when we are faced with everyday interactions and long-term exposure? Our "beautiful princess" isn't supposed to snore. And our "knight in shining armor" doesn't look very knightly flossing his teeth. And, of course, no princess or knight would ever notice our shortcomings, let alone comment on them.

Is there any way to keep love alive? If you mean romantic love, one of the best ways to fan the flames is through some form of frustration that keeps you from fulfilling your desire for the presence of your love. Researchers have found that this type of interference (for example, the parents in Shakespeare's *Romeo and Juliet*) often increases the feelings of love (Driscoll, Davis, & Lipetz, 1972).

Because romantic love depends on uncertainty and fantasy, it can also be kept alive by situations in which we never really get to know the other person. This may explain why computer chat room romances or old high school sweethearts have such a tug on our emotions. Because we never really get to test these relationships, we can always fantasize about what might have been.

One of the most constructive ways of keeping romantic love alive is to recognize its fragile nature and nurture it with carefully planned surprises, flirting, flattery, and special dinners and celebrations. In the long run, however, romantic love's most important function might be to keep us attached long enough to move on to companionate love.

Companionate Love   **Companionate love** is based on admiration and respect, combined with deep feelings of caring for the person and commitment to the relationship. Studies of close friendships show that satisfaction grows with time as we come to recognize the value of companionship and of having an intimate confidante (Kim & Hatfield, 2004). Unlike romantic love, which is very short lived, companionate love seems to grow stronger with time and often lasts a lifetime (Figure 16.8).

Companionate love is what we feel for our best friends. It also is the best bet for a strong and lasting marriage (Figure 16.9). But finding and keeping a long-term companionate love is no easy task. Many of our expectations for love are based on romantic fantasies and unconscious programming from fairy tales and TV shows in which everyone lives happily ever after. Therefore, we are often ill equipped to deal with the hassles and boredom that come with any long-term relationship.

One tip for maintaining companionate love is to *overlook each other's faults*. Studies of both dating and married couples find that people report greater satisfaction with—and stay longer in—relationships where they have a somewhat idealized or unrealistically positive perception of their partner (Campbell et al., 2001; Fletcher & Simpson, 2000). This makes sense in light of research on cognitive dissonance (discussed earlier). Idealizing our mates allows us to believe we have a good deal—and hence avoids the cognitive dissonance that might naturally arise every time we saw an attractive alternative. As Benjamin Franklin wisely put it, "Keep your eyes wide open before marriage, half shut afterwards."

Assessment   **STOP**

CHECK & REVIEW

Our Feelings About Others

Objective 16.6: *Define prejudice, identify its three key components, and differentiate between prejudice and discrimination.*

Prejudice is a learned, generally negative, attitude directed toward members of a group. It contains all three components of attitudes—*cognitive, affective,* and *behavioral.* (The cognitive component involves **stereotypes**, and the behavioral component is called **discrimination**.)

Objective 16.7: *Discuss the five major sources of prejudice and discrimination.*

The five major sources of prejudice are *learning* (classical and operant conditioning and social learning), *personal experience, mental shortcuts* (categorization), *economic* and *political competition,* and *displaced aggression* (scapegoating). Mental shortcuts involve viewing members of the ingroup more positively than members of the outgroup (**ingroup favoritism**) and seeing less diversity in the outgroup (**outgroup homogeneity effect**).

Objective 16.8: *What are the three key factors in attraction?*

Physical attractiveness, **proximity**, and similarity are the three major factors in **interpersonal attraction**. Although people commonly believe that "opposites attract" (**need complementarity**), research shows that similarity (**need compatibility**) is more important in long-term relationships.

Objective 16.9: *Describe cultural and historical similarities and differences in judgments of attractiveness.*

Many cultures share similar standards of attractiveness (e.g., youthful appearance and facial and body symmetry are important for women, whereas maturity and financial resources are more important for men). Historically, what is judged as beautiful varies from era to era.

Objective 16.10: *Discuss scientific research on flirting.*

People use nonverbal flirting behaviors to increase their attractiveness and signal interest. In heterosexual couples, women are more likely to use flirting to initiate courtship.

Objective 16.11: *Differentiate between romantic and companionate love, and discuss problems with romantic love.*

Romantic love is intense, passionate, and highly valued in our society. However, because it is based on mystery and fantasy, it is hard to sustain. **Companionate love** relies on mutual trust, respect, and friendship and seems to grow stronger with time.

Questions

1. Explain how prejudice differs from discrimination.
2. Saying that members of another ethnic group "all look alike to me" may be an example of _____. (a) ingroup favoritism; (b) the outgroup homogeneity (c) outgroup negativism; (d) ingroup bias
3. Cross-cultural research on physical attractiveness has found all but one of the following.
   (a) The Chinese once practiced foot binding because small feet were considered attractive in women.
   (b) Across most cultures, men prefer youthful appearing women.
   (c) In most Eastern cultures, men prefer women with power and financial status over beauty.
   (d) For men, maturity and financial resources are more important than appearance in their ability to attract a mate.
4. Compare the dangers associated with romantic love with the benefits of companionate love.

Check your answers in Appendix B.

 Click & Review
for additional assessment options:
wiley.com/college/huffman

Our Actions toward Others

Having just completed our whirlwind examination of how our thoughts and emotions influence others—and vice versa—we turn to topics associated with actions toward others. We begin with a look at social influence (conformity and obedience) and then continue with group processes (membership and decision making). We conclude by exploring two opposite kinds of behavior—aggression and altruism.

Social Influence: Conformity and Obedience

The society and culture into which we are born influence us from the moment of birth until the moment of death. Our culture teaches us to believe certain things, feel certain ways, and act in accordance with these beliefs and feelings. These influences are so strong and so much a part of who we are that we rarely recognize them. Just as a fish doesn't know it's in water, we are largely unaware of the strong impact cultural and social factors have on all our behaviors. In this section, we will discuss two kinds of *social influence*: conformity and obedience.

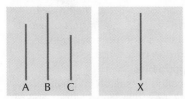

Achievement

Objective 16.12: *Define conformity, and explain the three factors that contribute to this behavior.*

Figure 16.10 *Solomon Asch's study of conformity* Participants were shown four lines such as these and then asked which line (A, B, or C) was most similar to the one on the right (X).

Conformity *Changing behavior because of real or imagined group pressure*

Normative Social Influence *Conforming to group pressure out of a need for approval and acceptance*

Norm *Cultural rule of behavior prescribing what is acceptable in a given situation*

Informational Social Influence *Conforming because of a need for information and direction*

Reference Groups *People we conform to, or go along with, because we like and admire them and want to be like them*

Conformity—Going Along with Others

Imagine that you have volunteered for a psychology experiment on perception. You are seated around a table with six other students. You are all shown a card with three lines labeled A, B, and C, as in Figure 16.10. You are then asked to select the line that is closest in length to a fourth line, X.

At first, everyone agrees on the correct line. On the third trial, however, the first participant selects line A, obviously a wrong answer. When the second, third, fourth, and fifth participants also say line A, you really start to wonder: "What's going on here? Are they blind? Or am I?"

What do you think you would do at this point in the experiment? Would you stick with your convictions and say line B, regardless of what the others have answered? Or would you go along with the group?

In the original version of this experiment, conducted by Solomon Asch (1951), six of the seven participants were actually confederates of the experimenter (that is, they were working with the experimenter and purposely gave wrong answers). Their incorrect responses were actually designed to test the participant's degree of **conformity**.

More than one-third of Asch's participants conformed—they agreed with the group's obviously incorrect choice. In contrast, participants in a control group experienced no group pressure and almost always chose correctly. Surprisingly, Asch's study has been conducted dozens of times, in at least 17 countries, and always with similar results (Bond & Smith, 1996; Jung, 2006; Takano & Sogon, 2008).

Why would so many people conform? To the onlooker, conformity is often difficult to understand. Even the conformer sometimes has a hard time explaining his or her behavior. Let's look at three factors that drive conformity:

- *Normative social influence.* Have you ever asked what others are wearing to a party, or watched your dining companion to decide what fork to use at an expensive dinner party? Such inquiries reflect our shared need for approval and acceptance by the group, a process called **normative social influence**. **Norms** are unwritten rules for behavior that are adhered to by members of a group. Most norms are quite subtle and implicit, like the one for personal space (Figure 16.11).

- *Informational social influence.* Like most of us, you've probably asked for advice and even bought a specific product simply because of friends' recommendations. We conform in this case not to gain their approval (the previous *normative social influence*). We conform because we assume they have more information than we do, **informational social influence**. Participants in Asch's experiment observed all the other participants giving unanimous decisions on the length of the lines, so they logically may have conformed because they believed the others had more information.

- *Reference groups.* The third major factor in conformity is the power of **reference groups**—people we most admire, like, and want to resemble. Attractive actors and popular sports stars are paid millions of dollars to endorse products because advertisers know that we want to be as cool as Wesley Snipes or as beautiful as Jennifer Lopez. Of course, we also have more important reference groups in our lives—parents, friends, family members, teachers, religious leaders, and so on.

Figure 16.11 *Norms for personal space* Culture and socialization have a lot to do with shaping norms for personal space. If someone invades the invisible "personal bubble" around our bodies, we generally feel very uncomfortable. People from Mediterranean, Muslim, and Latin American countries tend to maintain smaller interpersonal distances than do North Americans and Northern Europeans (Axtell, 2007; Steinhart, 1986). Children also tend to stand very close to others until they are socialized to recognize and maintain a greater personal distance. Furthermore, friends stand closer than strangers, women tend to stand closer than men, and violent prisoners prefer approximately three times the personal space of nonviolent prisoners (Axtell, 2007; Gilmour & Walkey, 1981; Lawrence & Andrews, 2004).

Conformity in action? *What's "in" during the latest fashion trends changes dramatically over the years. But note how both groups from different eras generally conform to their group's overall "dress code."*

Application

Testing Personal Space

If you want to personally experience the power of social norms, approach a fellow student on campus and ask for directions to the bookstore, library, or some other landmark. As you are talking, move toward the person until you invade his or her personal space. You should be close enough to almost touch toes. How does the person respond? How do you feel? Now repeat the process with another student. This time try standing 5 to 6 feet away while asking directions. Which procedure was most difficult for you? Most people think this will be a fun assignment. However, they often find it extremely difficult to willingly break our culture's unwritten norms for personal space.

Obedience—Going Along with a Command

As we've seen, conformity involves going along with the group. A second form of social influence, **obedience,** involves going along with a direct command, usually from someone in a position of authority.

Conformity and obedience aren't always bad (Figure 16.12). In fact, most people conform and obey most of the time because it is in their own best interest (and everyone else's) to do so. Like most North Americans, you stand in line at the movie theater instead of pushing ahead of others. This allows an orderly purchasing of tickets. Conformity and obedience allow social life to proceed with safety, order, and predictability.

On some occasions, however, it is important not to conform or obey. We don't want teenagers (or adults) engaging in risky sex or drug use just to be part of the crowd. And we don't want soldiers (or anyone else) mindlessly following orders just because they were told to do so by an authority figure. Because recognizing and resisting destructive forms of obedience are particularly important to our society, we'll explore this material in greater depth at the end of this chapter. For the moment, imagine yourself as a volunteer in the following situation:

You have responded to a newspaper ad seeking participants for a study at Yale University. When you show up at the laboratory, an experimenter explains to you and another participant that he is studying the effects of punishment on learning and memory. You are selected to play the role of the "teacher." The experimenter leads you into a room where he straps the other

Achievement

Objective 16.13: *Define obedience and describe Milgram's classic study.*

Obedience *Following direct commands, usually from an authority figure*

Figure 16.12 ***The advantages of conformity and obedience*** These people willingly obey the firefighters who order them to evacuate a building, and many lives are saved. What would happen to our everyday functioning if people did not go along with the crowd or generally did not obey orders?

wiley.com/ college/ huffman

participant—the "learner"—into a chair. He applies electrode paste to the learner's wrist "to avoid blisters and burns" and attaches an electrode that is connected to a shock generator.

You are led into an adjacent room and told to sit in front of this same shock generator, which is wired through the wall to the chair of the learner. The shock machine consists of 30 switches representing successively higher levels of shock, from 15 volts to 450 volts. Written labels appear below each group of switches, ranging from "Slight Shock" to "Danger: Severe Shock," all the way to "XXX." The experimenter explains that it is your job to teach the learner a list of word pairs and to punish any errors by administering a shock. With each wrong answer, you are to increase the shock by one level.

You begin teaching the word pairs, but the learner's responses are often wrong. Before long, you are inflicting shocks that you can only assume must be extremely painful because the learner is moaning and protesting. In fact, after you administer 150 volts, the learner begins to shout; "Get me out of here.... I refuse to go on."

You hesitate, but the experimenter tells you to continue. He insists that even if the learner refuses to answer, you must keep increasing the shock levels. But the other person is obviously in pain. What should you do?

Actual participants in this research—the "teachers"—suffered real conflict and distress when confronted with this problem. They sweated, trembled, stuttered, laughed nervously, and repeatedly protested that they did not want to hurt the learner. But still they obeyed.

The psychologist who designed this study, Stanley Milgram, was actually investigating not punishment and learning but obedience to authority. What do you think happened? Would participants obey the experimenter's prompts and commands to shock another human being?

In Milgram's public survey, fewer than 25 percent thought they would go beyond 150 volts. And no respondents predicted they would go past the 300-volt level. Yet 65 percent of the teacher-participants in this series of studies obeyed completely—going all the way to the end of the scale. They even went beyond the point when the "learner" (Milgram's confederate, who actually received no shocks at all) stopped responding altogether.

Even Milgram was surprised by his results. Before the study began, he polled a group of psychiatrists, and they predicted that most people would refuse to go beyond 150 volts and that less than 1 percent of those tested would "go all the way." The psychiatrists generally agreed that only someone who was "disturbed and sadistic" would obey to the fullest extent. But, as Milgram discovered, most of his participants—men and women, of all ages, and from all walks of life—administered the highest voltage. The study was replicated many times and in many other countries, with similarly high levels of obedience.

Being the psychological scientist that he was, Milgram wanted to follow up on his original experiment to find out exactly what conditions would increase or decrease obedience. As you can see in Concept Diagram 16.1, he identified four major factors: (1) *legitimacy and closeness of the authority figure*, (2) *remoteness of the victim*, (3) *assignment of responsibility*, and (4) *modeling or imitating others* (Blass, 1991, 2000; Meeus & Raaijmakers, 1989; Snyder, 2003).

Achievement
Objective 16.14: *Identify the four key factors in obedience.*

Important Reminders   Many people are upset both by Milgram's findings and by the treatment of the participants in his research. Although deception is a necessary part of some research, the degree of deception and discomfort of participants in Milgram's research is now viewed as highly unethical. His study would never be undertaken today. On the other hand, Milgram carefully debriefed every subject after the study and followed up with the participants for several months. Most of his "teachers" reported the experience as being personally informative and valuable.

Concept Diagram 16.1
What Influences Obedience?

Milgram conducted a series of studies to discover the specific conditions that either increased or decreased obedience to authority.

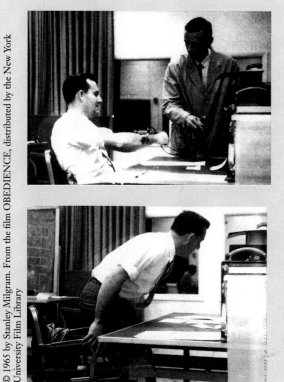

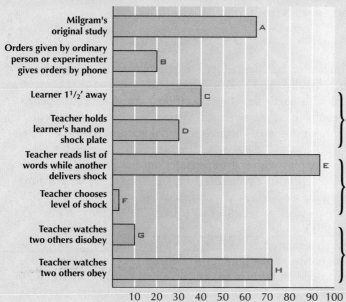

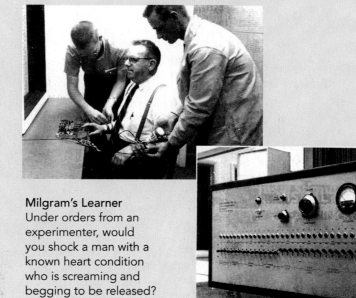

Milgram's Learner
Under orders from an experimenter, would you shock a man with a known heart condition who is screaming and begging to be released? Few people believe they would. But research shows otherwise.

Milgram's Shock Generator

Percent of participants who gave 450-volt shocks

- Milgram's original study — **A**
- Orders given by ordinary person or experimenter gives orders by phone — **B**
- Learner 1¹/₂' away — **C**
- Teacher holds learner's hand on shock plate — **D**
- Teacher reads list of words while another delivers shock — **E**
- Teacher chooses level of shock — **F**
- Teacher watches two others disobey — **G**
- Teacher watches two others obey — **H**

(scale: 10 20 30 40 50 60 70 80 90 100)

As you can see in the first bar on the graph (**A**), 65 percent of the participants in Milgram's original study gave the learner the full 450-volt level of shocks.

Four Factors in Obedience

1) Legitimacy and closeness of the authority figure

In the second bar (**B**), note that when orders came from an ordinary person, and when the experimenter left the room and gave orders by phone, the participants' obedience dropped to 20 percent.

2) Remoteness of the victim

Now look at the third and fourth bars (**C** and **D**), and note that the remoteness of the victim had an important impact. When the "learner" was only 1 1/2 feet away from the teacher, obedience dropped to 40 percent. And when the teacher had to actually hold the learner's hand on the shock plate, obedience was only 30 percent.

3) Assignment of responsibility

Looking at bars (**E**) and (**F**), note the dramatic importance of the teacher's degree of responsibility When the teacher was responsible for choosing the level of shock, only 3 percent obeyed.

4) Modeling or imitating others

Finally, looking at bars (**G**) and (**H**), recognize the incredible power of modeling and imitation. When the teachers watched two others disobey, their own obedience was only 10 percent, but when they watched others follow orders, their obedience jumped to over 70 percent (Milgram, 1963, 1974).

There's another very important reminder: *The "learner" was an accomplice of the experimenter and only pretended to be shocked.* Milgram provided specific scripts that they followed at every stage of the experiment. In contrast, the "teachers" were true volunteers who believed they were administering real shocks. Although they suffered and protested, in the final analysis, they still obeyed.

Assessment

STOP

CHECK & REVIEW

Social Influence

Objective 16.12: *Define conformity, and explain the three factors that contribute to this behavior.*

Conformity involves changes in behavior in response to real or imagined group pressure. People conform for approval and acceptance (**normative social influence**), out of a need for more information and direction (**informational social influence**), and to match the behavior of those they admire and want to be like (**reference group**).

Objective 16.13: *Define obedience and describe Milgram's classic study.*

Obedience refers to following direct commands, usually from an authority figure. Milgram's study showed that a surprisingly large number of people obey orders even when they believe another human being is physically threatened.

Objective 16.14: *Identify the four key factors in obedience.*

Legitimacy and closeness of the authority figure, remoteness of the victim, assignment of responsibility, and modeling or imitation of others are the four major factors in obedience.

Questions

1. Explain how conformity differs from obedience.
2. The classic study showing the power of comformity on people's behavior was conducted by _____.
   (a) Zimbardo;
   (b) Bandura;
   (c) Asch;
   (d) Milgram
3. Milgram's participants thought they were participating in an experiment designed to study the effect of _____.
4. What percentage of people in Milgram's study were willing to give the highest level of shock (450 volts)?
   (a) 45 percent;
   (b) 90 percent;
   (c) 65 percent;
   (d) 10 percent

Check your answers in Appendix B.

Click & Review
for additional assessment options:
wiley.com/college/huffman

Group Processes: Membership and Decision Making

Although we seldom recognize the power of group membership, social psychologists have identified several important ways that groups affect us.

Achievement

Objective 16.15: *Discuss the importance of roles and deindividuation in Zimbardo's Stanford prison study.*

Group Membership

In simple groups, such as couples or families, as well as complex groups, like classes or sports teams, each person generally plays one or more roles. These *roles* (or sets of behavioral patterns connected with particular social positions) are specifically spelled out and regulated in some groups (e.g., the different roles of teachers and students). Other roles, like being a parent, are assumed through informal learning and inference.

Roles   How do the roles that we play within groups affect our behavior? This question fascinated social psychologist Philip Zimbardo. In his famous study at Stanford University, 24 carefully screened, well-adjusted young college men were paid $15 a day for participating in a two-week simulation of prison life (Haney, Banks, & Zimbardo, 1978; Zimbardo, 1993).

The students were randomly assigned to the role of either prisoner or guard. Prisoners were "arrested," frisked, photographed, fingerprinted, and booked at the police station. They were then blindfolded and driven to the "Stanford Prison." There, they were given ID numbers, deloused, issued prison clothing (tight nylon caps, shapeless gowns, and no underwear), and locked in cells. Participants assigned to be guards were outfitted with official-looking uniforms, billy clubs, and whistles, and they were given complete control.

Not even Zimbardo foresaw how his study would turn out. Although some guards were nicer to the prisoners than others, they all engaged in some abuse of power. The slightest disobedience was often punished with degrading tasks or the loss of "privileges" (such as eating, sleeping, and washing).

As demands increased and abuses began, the prisoners became passive and depressed. Only one prisoner fought back with a hunger strike, which ended with a forced feeding by the guards. Four prisoners had to be released within the first four days because of severe psychological reactions. And the entire study was stopped after only six days because of the alarming psychological changes in all participants. (It was originally planned to last two weeks.)

Although this was not a true experiment in that it lacked control groups and clear measurements of the dependent variable (Chapter 1), it offers insights into the potential effects of roles on individual behavior (Figure 16.13). According to interviews conducted after the study, the students became so absorbed in their roles that they forgot they were *volunteers* in a university study (Zimbardo, Ebbeson, & Maslach, 1977). For them the simulated *roles* of prisoner or guard became real—too real.

Many have criticized the ethics of Zimbardo's study. It does, however, alert us to potentially serious dangers inherent in roles and group membership. Consider the following: If this type of personality disintegration and abuse of power could be generated in a mere six days in a mock prison with fully informed volunteers, what happens during life imprisonment, six-year sentences, or even overnight jail stays? Similarly, what might happen when military personnel, who are under tremendous pressure, are put in charge of guarding deadly enemies (Figure 16.14)?

Deindividuation   Zimbardo's prison study also demonstrates an interesting phenomenon called **deindividuation**. To be deindividuated means that you feel less self-conscious, less inhibited, and less personally responsible as a member of a group than when you're alone. This is particularly likely under conditions of anonymity. To increase allegiance and conformity, groups sometimes actively encourage deindividuation, such as by requiring uniforms or masks. Unfortunately, deindividuation sometimes leads to abuses of power, angry mobs, rioters, and tragic consequences like gang rapes, lynchings, and hate crimes (Rodriques, Assmar, & Jablonski, 2005; Zimbardo, 2007) (Figure 16.15).

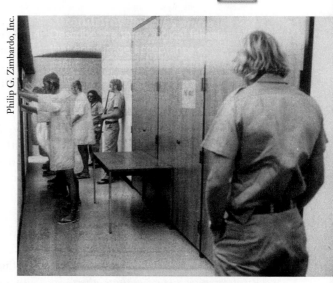
Philip G. Zimbardo, Inc.

Figure 16.13 *Power corrupts* Zimbardo's prison study showed how the demands of roles and situations could produce dramatic changes in behavior in just a few days. Can you imagine what happens to prisoners during life imprisonment, six-year sentences, or even a few nights in jail?

Deindividuation *Reduced self-consciousness, inhibition, and personal responsibility that sometimes occurs in a group, particularly when the members feel anonymous*

©AP/Wide World Photos

Figure 16.14 *Psychology at work in Abu Ghraib?* Do you remember the prisoner abuse scandal at the Iraqi Abu Ghraib prison in 2004? When these degrading photos surfaced of U.S. military guards smiling as they posed next to naked prisoners at Abu Ghraib, people around the world were shocked and outraged. Politicians and military officials claimed that the abuses were the "vile acts of a few bad soldiers" and a "gross aberration for U.S. soldiers" (Ripley, 2004; Warner, 2004; Zimbardo, 2007). Can you use information from Zimbardo's Stanford prison study to offer other explanations for the guards' behaviors?

The Kobal Collection/The Picture Desk

Figure 16.15 *Deindividuation* In the classic movie *To Kill a Mockingbird*, a young girl (named Scout) asked one of the angry lynch mob members about his son. Her simple question destroyed the mob's feeling of anonymity and deindividuation. Once this happened, their anger subsided and they slowly (and harmlessly) dispersed.

wiley.com/
college/
huffman

© AP/Wide World Photos

Figure 16.16 *Lost in the crowd* One of the most compelling explanations for deindividuation is the fact that the presence of others tends to increase arousal and feelings of anonymity. Anonymity is a powerful disinhibitor, helping to explain why vandalism seems to increase on Halloween (when people commonly wear masks) and why most crimes and riots occur at night—under the cover of darkness.

There are also positive forms of deindividuation. We all enjoy being swept along with a crowd's joyous celebration on New Year's Eve and the raucous cheering and shouting during an exciting sports competition. Deindividuation also encourages increased helping behaviors and even heroism, as we will see later in this chapter. What causes deindividuation? See Figure 16.16.

Group Decision Making

We have seen that the groups we belong to and the roles that we play within them influence how we think about ourselves. But how do groups affect our decisions? Are two heads truly better than one?

Group Polarization People generally assume that group decisions are better because they're more conservative, cautious, and middle-of-the-road than individual decisions. Is this true? Initial investigations indicated that after discussing an issue, groups actually support *riskier* decisions than ones they made as individuals before the discussion (Stoner, 1961).

Subsequent research on this so-called *risky-shift phenomenon* found mixed results. Some groups did support riskier decisions, but others actually became more conservative (Liu & Latané, 1998). Interestingly, researchers discovered that the final decision (risky or conservative) depends primarily on the dominant *preexisting tendencies* of the group. If the dominant initial position is risky, the final decision will be even riskier, and the reverse is true if the initial position is conservative—a process called **group polarization**. Why? It appears that as individuals interact and share their opinions, they pick up new and more persuasive information that supports their original opinions.

How is this important to your everyday life? Most of our daily interactions are with family, friends, and work buddies who share our basic values and beliefs. The danger is that when most of our information comes only from these like-minded people, we're more likely to make extreme, polarized decisions. Thus, when making important decisions, like what career to pursue, or when to buy or sell a home or stocks, we need to seek out more objective information outside our likeminded groups.

Groupthink A related phenomenon is **groupthink** (Process Diagram 16.1). When a group is highly cohesive (a family, a panel of military advisers, an athletic team), the members' desire for agreement may lead them to ignore important information or points of view held by outsiders—especially when it is contradictory.

Many presidential errors—from Franklin Roosevelt's failure to anticipate the attack on Pearl Harbor to Ronald Reagan's Iran-Contra scandal—have been blamed on groupthink. Groupthink also may have contributed to the losses of the space shuttles *Challenger* and *Columbia*, the terrorist attack of September 11, and the war in Iraq (Barlow, 2008; Ehrenreich, 2004; Janis, 1972, 1989; Landay & Kuhnehenn, 2004; Rodriques, Assmar, & Jablonski, 2005). Because most informal, political, or business groups consist of like-minded individuals, discussion generally only reinforces the group's original opinion. Thus, the group's preexisting tendencies are strengthened by the group discussion (Figure 16.17).

Achievement

Objective 16.16: *How do group polarization and groupthink affect group decision making?*

Group Polarization *Group's movement toward either riskier or more conservative behavior, depending on the members' initial dominant tendency*

Groupthink *Faulty decision making that occurs when a highly cohesive group strives for agreement and avoids inconsistent information*

John Neubauer/Photoedit

Figure 16.17 *Juries and group polarization* Is group polarization a desirable part of jury deliberation? Yes and no. In an ideal world, attorneys from both sides present the facts of the case. Then, after careful deliberation, the jury moves from its initially neutral position toward the defendant to a more extreme position—either conviction or acquittal. In a not-so-ideal world, the quality of legal arguments from opposing sides may not be equal, the individual members of the jury may not be neutral at the start, and some jurors may unduly influence other jurors.

Process Diagram 16.1

Groupthink

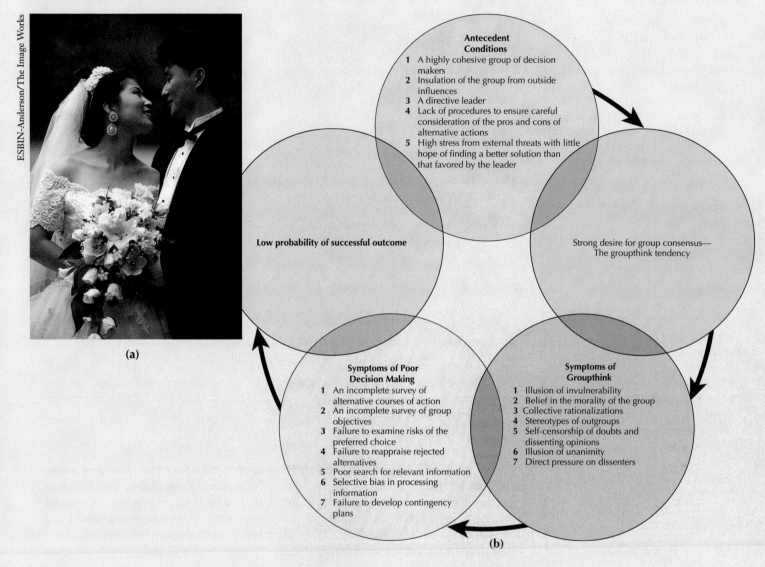

(a)

Antecedent Conditions
1 A highly cohesive group of decision makers
2 Insulation of the group from outside influences
3 A directive leader
4 Lack of procedures to ensure careful consideration of the pros and cons of alternative actions
5 High stress from external threats with little hope of finding a better solution than that favored by the leader

Strong desire for group consensus— The groupthink tendency

Low probability of successful outcome

Symptoms of Groupthink
1 Illusion of invulnerability
2 Belief in the morality of the group
3 Collective rationalizations
4 Stereotypes of outgroups
5 Self-censorship of doubts and dissenting opinions
6 Illusion of unanimity
7 Direct pressure on dissenters

Symptoms of Poor Decision Making
1 An incomplete survey of alternative courses of action
2 An incomplete survey of group objectives
3 Failure to examine risks of the preferred choice
4 Failure to reappraise rejected alternatives
5 Poor search for relevant information
6 Selective bias in processing information
7 Failure to develop contingency plans

(b)

(a) *An example of groupthink?* Few people realize that the decision to marry can be a form of groupthink. (Remember that a "group" can have as few as two members.) While dating, the couple may show several of the antecedent conditions (top box). This includes a strong need for cohesiveness ("We agree on almost everything"), insulation from outside influences ("We do almost everything as a couple"), and failure to carefully consider the pros and cons of alternative actions. When planning for marriage, they also sometimes show symptoms of groupthink. These symptoms include an illusion of invulnerability ("We're different—we won't ever get divorced"), collective rationalizations ("Two can live more cheaply than one"), shared stereotypes of the outgroup ("Couples with problems just don't know how to communicate"), and pressure on dissenters ("If you don't support our decision to marry, we don't want you at the wedding!")

(b) *What happens in groupthink?* The process of groupthink begins when group members feel a strong sense of cohesiveness and isolation from the judgments of qualified outsiders. Add a directive leader and little chance for debate, and you have the recipe for a potentially dangerous decision.

Group Processes

Objective 16.15: *Discuss the importance of roles and deindividuation in Zimbardo's Stanford prison study.*

Zimbardo conducted a simulated prison study assigning college students to be either prisoners or guards. The study showed that both the roles we play in groups and **deindividuation** (reduced self-consciousness, inhibition, and personal responsibility) dramatically affect behavior.

Objective 16.16: *How do group polarization and groupthink affect group decision making?*

Group polarization is the process of most group members initially tending toward an extreme idea, followed by the rest of the

group moving (polarizing) in that extreme direction. This phenomenon occurs because discussions with likeminded members reinforce the preexisting tendencies. **Group-think** is a faulty type of decision making that occurs when a highly cohesive group strives for agreement and avoids inconsistent information.

Questions

1. Zimbardo stopped his prison study before the end of the scheduled two weeks because _____.
2. During _____, a person who feels anonymous within a group or crowd experiences an increase in arousal and a decrease in self-consciousness, inhibitions, and personal responsibility.

3. The critical factor in deindividuation is _____. (a) loss of self-esteem; (b) anonymity; (c) identity diffusion; (d) group cohesiveness
4. What are the major symptoms of groupthink?
5. Overlooking serious problems in their relationship, a couple decides to marry because they believe they're very different from couples who divorce. This may be an example of _____. (a) mind guarding; (b) stereotypes of the out group; (c) illusion of invulnerability; (d) none of these options

Check your answers in Appendix B.

Click & Review
for additional assessment options:
wiley.com/college/huffman

Achievement

Objective 16.17: *Define aggression, and identify the biological and psychosocial factors that contribute to its expression.*

Aggression *Any behavior intended to harm someone*

Aggression: Explaining and Controlling It

Aggression is any form of behavior intended to harm or injure another living being. Why do people act aggressively? We will explore a number of possible explanations for aggression—both *biological* and *psychosocial*. Then we will look at how aggression can be controlled or reduced.

Biological Factors

Instincts Because aggression has such a long history and is found in all cultures, many theorists believe that humans are instinctively aggressive. Evolutionary psychologists and ethologists (scientists who study animal behavior) believe that aggression evolved because it prevents overcrowding and allows the strongest animals to win mates and reproduce (Buss, 2008; Kardong, 2008). Most social psychologists, however, reject the view that instincts drive aggression.

Genes Twin studies suggest that some individuals are genetically predisposed to have hostile, irritable temperaments and to engage in aggressive acts (Haberstick et al., 2006; Hartwell, 2008; van Lier et al., 2007). Remember, though, that biology interacts with social experience to shape behavior.

The Brain and Nervous System Electrical stimulation and the severing of specific parts of an animal's brain have direct effects on aggression. Research with brain injuries and organic disorders has also identified possible aggression circuits in the brain (Anderson & Silver, 2008; Delgado, 1960; Kotulak, 2008; Siever, 2008).

Substance Abuse and Other Mental Disorders Substance abuse (particularly alcohol) is a major factor in most forms of aggression (Tremblay, Graham, & Wells, 2008; Levinthal, 2008). Homicide rates are also higher among people with schizophrenia and antisocial disorders, particularly if they abuse alcohol (Carballo et al., 2008, Fresán et al., 2007; Garno, Gunawardane, & Goldberg, 2008; Haddock, 2008).

Hormones and Neurotransmitters   Studies have linked the male hormone testosterone with aggressive behavior (Hermans, Ramsey, & van Honk, 2008; Juntii, Coats, & Shah, 2008; Popma et al., 2007; Sato et al., 2008). Violent behavior has also been correlated with lowered levels of the neurotransmitters serotonin and GABA (gamma-aminobutyric acid) (Kovacic et al., 2008; Siever, 2008).

Psychosocial Factors

Aversive Stimuli   Noise, heat, pain, bullying, insults, and foul odors all can increase aggression (Anderson, 2001; Anderson et al., 2008; Monks et al., 2008; Twenge et al., 2001). According to the **frustration–aggression hypothesis**, developed by John Dollard and colleagues (1939), another aversive stimulus—frustration—creates anger, which for some leads to aggression.

Culture and Learning   Social learning theory (Chapter 6) suggests that people raised in a culture with aggressive models will learn aggressive responses (Matsumoto & Juang, 2008). For example, the United States has a high rate of violent crimes, and American children grow up with numerous models for aggression, which they tend to imitate.

Violent Media and Violent Video Games   The media can contribute to aggression in both children and adults (Figure 16.18). However, the link between violent media and aggression appears to be a two-way street. Laboratory studies, correlational research, and cross-cultural studies have found that exposure to TV violence increases aggressiveness and that aggressive children tend to seek out violent programs (Barlett, Harris, & Bruey, 2008; Carnagey, Anderson, & Bartholow, 2007; Giumetti & Markey, 2007).

Reducing Aggression

Some therapists advise people to release aggressive impulses by engaging in harmless forms of aggression, such as exercising vigorously, punching a pillow, or watching competitive sports. But studies suggest that this type of *catharsis*, or "draining the aggression reservoir," doesn't really help (Bushman, 2002; Kuperstok, 2008). In fact, as we pointed out in Chapter 12, expressing an emotion, anger or otherwise, tends to intensify the feeling rather than reduce it.

A second approach, which does seem to effectively reduce or control aggression and stress, is to introduce *incompatible responses*. Certain emotional responses, such as empathy and humor, are incompatible with aggression. Thus, purposely making a joke or showing some sympathy for the other person's point of view can reduce anger and frustration (Garrick, 2006; Kassin, Fein & Markus, 2008; Kaukiainen et al., 1999; Oshima, 2000; Weiner, 2006).

A third approach to controlling aggression is to improve social and communication skills. Studies show that poor communication accounts for a disproportionate share of the violence in society (Gordis, Margolin, & Vickerman, 2005; Hettrich & O'Leary, 2007; Kassinove, 2007). Unfortunately, little effort is made in our schools or families to teach basic communication skills or techniques for conflict resolution.

Najah Feanny Hicks/Corbis

Nature or nurture? *From a very early age, Andrew Golden was taught to fire hunting rifles. At the age of 11, he and his friend Mitchell Johnson killed four classmates and a teacher at an elementary school in Jonesboro, Arkansas. Was this tragedy the result of nature or nurture?*

Frustration–Aggression Hypothesis *Blocking of a desired goal (frustration) creates anger that may lead to aggression*

Achievement

Objective 16.18: *Describe three approaches to reducing aggression.*

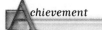

Jodi Cobb/NG Image Collection

Figure 16.18 ***Video violence*** Video games such as *Doom, Mortal Kombat, Resident Evil,* and *Half-Life* all feature realistic sound effects and gory depictions of "lifelike" violence. Should parents restrict children from playing these games? Why or Why not?

Objective 16.19: *Define altruism, and describe the three models that attempt to explain it.*

Altruism: Why We Help (and Don't Help) Others

After reading about prejudice, discrimination, and aggression, you will no doubt be relieved to discover that human beings also behave in positive ways. People help and support one another by donating blood, giving time and money to charities, helping stranded motorists, and so on. There are also times when people do not help. Consider the following:

> In 1964, a woman named Kitty Genovese was raped and stabbed repeatedly by a knife-wielding assailant as she returned from work to her apartment in Queens, New York. It was about 3:00 A.M., but 38 of her neighbors watched as she struggled to fight off her attacker and heard her screams and pleas for help: "Oh my God, he stabbed me! Please help me! Please help me!" The attack lasted for over half an hour; yet no one came to help her. By the time one neighbor finally called the police, it was too late. Kitty Genovese had died.

How could such a thing have happened? Why didn't her neighbors help? More generally, under what conditions do people sometimes help and sometimes ignore others' pleas for help?

Why Do We Help?

Altruism *Actions designed to help others with no obvious benefit to the helper*

Altruism (or prosocial behavior) refers to actions designed to help others with no obvious benefit to the helper. There are three key approaches to explaining why we help—*evolutionary*, *egoistic*, and *empathy–altruism* (Concept Diagram 16.2a).

Evolutionary theory suggests that altruism is an instinctual behavior that has evolved because it favors survival of one's genes (de Waal, Kardong, 2008; McNamara et al., 2008). As evidence, these theorists cite altruistic acts among lower species (e.g., worker bees cooperatively working and living only for their mother, the queen). They also point out that altruism in humans is strongest toward one's own children and other relatives. Altruism protects not the individual but the individual's genes. By helping, or even dying for, your child or sibling, you increase the odds that the genes you share will be passed on to future generations.

Other research suggests that helping may actually be a form of egoism or disguised self-interest. According to this **egoistic model**, helping is always motivated by some degree of anticipated gain. We help others because we hope for later reciprocation, because it makes us feel good about ourselves, or because it helps us avoid feelings of distress and guilt that loom if we don't help (Cialdini, 2009; Williams et al., 1998).

Egoistic Model *Helping that's motivated by anticipated gain—later reciprocation, increased self-esteem, or avoidance of distress and guilt*

Empathy–Altruism Hypothesis *Helping because of empathy for someone in need*

Opposing the egoistic model is the **empathy–altruism hypothesis** proposed by C. D. Batson and his colleagues (Batson, 1991, 1998, 2006; Batson & Ahmad, 2001). Batson thinks some altruism is motivated by simple, selfish concerns (the top part of the diagram). In other situations, however, helping is truly selfless and motivated by concern for others (the bottom part of the diagram).

According to the empathy–altruism hypothesis, simply seeing another person's suffering or hearing of his or her need can create *empathy*, a subjective grasp of that person's feelings or experiences. When we feel empathic toward another, we focus on that person's distress, not our own. We're also more likely to help the person for his or her own sake. In concert with the evolutionary model, the ability to empathize may even be innate. Perceiving the emotional state of others appears to automatically activate a matching state of our own, which, in turn, increases our helping of others and our own long-term survival (de Waal, 2008).

Why Don't We Help?

Objective 16.20: *Describe Latané and Darley's decision-making model, and other factors that help explain why we don't help.*

Many theories have been proposed to explain why people help, but few explain why we do not. How do we explain why Kitty Genovese's neighbors did not help her? One of the most comprehensive explanations for helping or not helping comes from the research of Bibb Latané and John Darley (1970) (Concept Diagram 16.2b). They found that whether or not someone helps depends on a series of interconnected events and decisions. The potential helper must first *notice* what is happening, must clarify

Concept Diagram 16.2

Helping

Concept Diagram

(a) Three Models for Helping

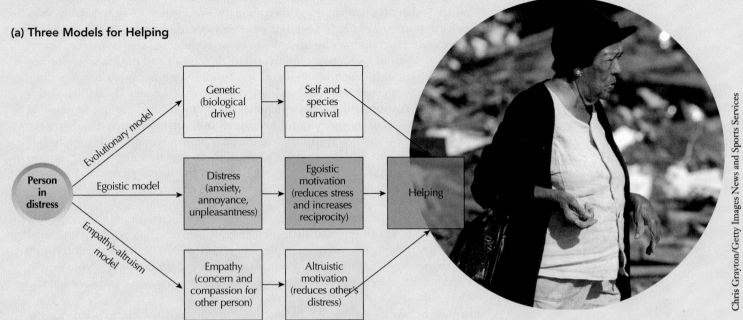

Person in distress

Evolutionary model → Genetic (biological drive) → Self and species survival

Egoistic model → Distress (anxiety, annoyance, unpleasantness) → Egoistic motivation (reduces stress and increases reciprocity) → Helping

Empathy–altruism model → Empathy (concern and compassion for other person) → Altruistic motivation (reduces other's distress)

Chris Grayton/Getty Images News and Sports Services

(b) When and Why Do We Help?

Photodisc Green/Getty Images

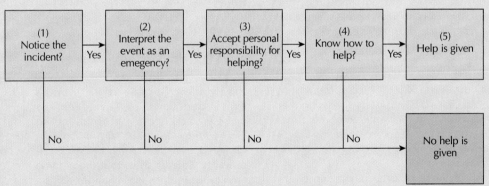

(1) Notice the incident? —Yes→ (2) Interpret the event as an emegency? —Yes→ (3) Accept personal responsibility for helping? —Yes→ (4) Know how to help? —Yes→ (5) Help is given

No ↓   No ↓   No ↓   No → No help is given

According to Latané and Darley's five-step decision process, if the answer at each step is yes, help is given. If the answer is no at any point, the helping process ends.

and *interpret* the event as an emergency, must accept *personal responsibility* for helping, and then must *decide how to help* and actually initiate the helping behavior.

Diffusion of Responsibility *The dilution (or diffusion) of personal responsibility for acting by spreading it among all other group members*

Where did the sequence break down for Kitty Genovese? Kitty's neighbors obviously noticed what was happening. Although many emergency situations are ambiguous, and it's unclear if help is required or even desired, Kitty's attack was clearly interpreted as an emergency. The breakdown came at the third stage—*taking personal responsibility for helping*. Newspaper interviews with each of the neighbors described a great deal of anguish. Each individual failed to intervene because they were certain that someone must already have called the police. Latané and Darley called this the **diffusion of responsibility** phenomenon—the dilution (or diffusion) of personal responsibility for acting by spreading it among all other group members. If you see someone drowning at the beach and you are the only person around, then responsibility falls squarely on you. But if others are present, there may be a diffusion of responsibility. It is ironic that if only one neighbor had seen the brutal attack, and thought that there were no other witnesses, Kitty might still be alive today.

How Can We Promote Helping?

The most obvious way to increase altruistic behavior is to clarify when help is needed and then assign responsibility. For example, if you notice a situation in which it seems unclear whether someone needs help, simply ask. On the other hand, if you are the one in need of help, look directly at anyone who may be watching and give specific directions, such as "Call the police. I am being attacked!"

Helping behaviors could also be encouraged through societal rewards. Some researchers suggest that states need to enact more laws that protect the helper from potential suits. Certain existing police programs, such as Crime Stoppers, actively recruit public compliance in reporting crime, give monetary rewards, and ensure anonymity. Such programs have apparently been highly effective in reducing crime.

---

*A*pplication

CRITICAL THINKING   ACTIVE LEARNING

When and Why Do We Help?
(Contributed by Thomas Frangicetto)

A 12-year-old girl sells lemonade in front of her house to raise $82 for the survivors of Hurricane Katrina . . . A 9-year-old boy and his 6-year-old sister tell their parents they want to give all their toys to the children of the earthquake in China . . . A local radio station raises $54,000. A USA Today story reports that "U.S. businesses showing their altruism likely will have pledged more than $100 million . . ." A Zogby poll finds that 68 percent of Americans had donated money to hurricane relief . . .

All of these reports reflect one of the most uplifting aspects of human behavior—the desire to help those who are less fortunate. Of course there is a darker, flip side to altruistic behavior. For example, if 68 percent of Americans donate money to hurricane relief—what prevents the other 32% from doing so? And for every corporation that donates $1 million to the relief effort, there is a corporation or business that gives nothing.

Critical Thinking Questions

1. Think back to personal situations in which you did (and did not) help others. Which model of helping (egoistic, empathy-altruism, or Latané and Darley's decision-making) best explains when and why you helped? Which CTC is most necessary for being altruistic?

2. Have you ever experienced a "helper's high"? Consider this: People who exercise vigorously often describe feeling high during a workout, and a sense of calmness and freedom from stress afterwards. Studies show that these same emotional and physical changes can be produced with activity requiring much less exertion – helping others" (Luks, 1988). What do you think about the article at: http://findarticles.com/p/articles/mi_m1175/is_n10_v22/ai_6652854/. Should helping agencies "sell this benefit" to recruit volunteers and increase donations? When you've helped others, did you experience anything like this so-called "feel-good sensation"?

3. Review the Psychology and Altruism section at: http://www.altruists.org/ideas/psychology. Do you think applying Abraham Maslow's "hierarchy of needs" model to altruism makes sense? What about treating people as "human resources," as tools for making money? Is it resulting in widespread stress, depression, and meaninglessness amongst both rich and poor in the so-called developed countries?

4. Why did Kitty Genovese die? Check out: http://www.objectivistcenter.org/articles/csilk_why-kitty-genovese-die.asp. What do you think about the author's defense of individualism and her claim that it does not "breed callousness and apathy toward others"? Do you agree that collectivism or community responsibility fosters "exactly the kind of group inaction whereby Kitty Genovese was murdered"? Can you make an effective counter-argument? Would you prefer to live in a predominantly individualistic or collectivistic society? Why?

Assessment

STOP

CHECK & REVIEW

Aggression and Altruism

Objective 16.17: *Define aggression, and identify the biological and psychosocial factors that contribute to its expression.*

Aggression is any behavior intended to harm someone. Some researchers believe it is caused by biological factors, such as instincts, genes, the brain and nervous system, substance abuse and other mental disorders, and hormones and neurotransmitters. Other researchers emphasize psychosocial factors, such as aversive stimuli, culture and learning, and violent media.

Objective 16.18: *Describe three approaches to reducing aggression.*

Releasing aggressive feelings through violent acts or watching violence (catharsis) is not an effective way to reduce aggression. Introducing incompatible responses (such as humor) and teaching social and communication skills are more efficient.

Objective 16.19: *Define altruism, and describe the three models that attempt to explain it.*

Altruism refers to actions designed to help others with no obvious benefit to the helper. The *evolutionary model* suggests altruism is innate and has survival value, the **egoistic model** proposes that helping is motivated by anticipated gain, and the **empathy–altruism hypothesis** suggests helping increases when the helper feels empathy for the victim.

Objective 16.20: *Describe Latané and Darley's decision-making model, and other factors that help explain why we don't help.*

According to Latané and Darley, whether or not someone helps depends on a series of interconnected events, starting with noticing the problem and ending with a decision to help. Some people don't help because of the ambiguity of many emergencies or because of **diffusion of responsibility** (assuming someone else will respond).

Questions

1. What are the five major biological and three chief psychosocial factors that contribute to aggression?
2. According to research, what are the best ways to reduce aggression?
3. How do evolutionary theorists, the egoistic model, and the empathy–altruism hypothesis explain altruism?
4. Kitty Genovese's neighbors failed to respond to her cries for help because of the _____ phenomenon.
   (a) empathy–altruism;
   (b) egoistic model;
   (c) inhumanity of large cities;
   (d) diffusion of responsibility

Check your answers in Appendix B.

Click & Review
for additional assessment options:
wiley.com/college/huffman

Applying Social Psychology to Social Problems

Each and every day of your life you're confronted with social problems. Driving or riding to work, you note how the freeways get busier each year. Camping in the wilderness, you find your favorite remote site occupied by other campers and cluttered with trash. Watching television, you check to see if the terror level is elevated and wonder if and when terrorists will attack. Reading the newspaper, you ask yourself what makes someone a suicide bomber.

Unfortunately, social psychology has been more successful in describing, explaining, and predicting social problems than in solving them. However, researchers have found several helpful techniques. In this section, we'll first explore what scientists have discovered about reducing prejudice. We'll then discuss effective ways to cope with destructive forms of obedience.

Reducing Prejudice and Discrimination

> Let's go hand in hand, not one before another.
>
> WILLIAM SHAKESPEARE

What can be done to combat prejudice? Four major approaches can be used: *cooperation and common goals, intergroup contact, cognitive retraining,* and *cognitive dissonance.*

1. *Cooperation and common goals.* Research shows that one of the best ways to combat prejudice is to encourage *cooperation* rather than *competition* (Cunningham, 2002; Sassenberg et al., 2007). Muzafer Sherif and his colleagues (1966, 1998) conducted an

Achievement

Objective 16.21: *List four major approaches useful for reducing prejudice and discrimination.*

© AP/Wide World Photos

Figure 16.19 *Reducing prejudice and discrimination* Tension and conflict between groups often decrease when groups cooperate and work together for a common goal. Here people of mixed ages and ethnicities work with Habitat for Humanity to build new homes for needy families.

Only equals can be friends.
ETHIOPIAN PROVERB

ingenious study to show the role of competition in promoting prejudice. The researchers artificially created strong feelings of ingroup and outgroup identification in a group of 11- and 12-year-old boys at a summer camp. They did this by physically separating the boys in different cabins and assigning different projects to each group, such as building a diving board or cooking out in the woods.

Once each group developed strong feelings of group identity and allegiance, the researchers set up a series of competitive games, including tug-of-war and touch football. They awarded desirable prizes to the winning teams. Because of this treatment, the groups began to pick fights, call each other names, and raid each other's camps. Researchers pointed to these behaviors as evidence of the experimentally produced prejudice.

After using competition to create prejudice between the two groups, the researchers demonstrated how cooperation could be successfully used to eliminate it. They created "minicrises" and tasks that required expertise, labor, and cooperation from both groups. And once again prizes were awarded to all. The hostilities and prejudice between the groups slowly began to dissipate. At the end of the camp experience, the boys voted to return home in the same bus. And the self-chosen seating did not reflect the earlier camp divisions. Sherif's study showed not only the importance of cooperation as opposed to competition but also the importance of *common goals* (resolving the minicrises) (Figure 16.19).

2. *Intergroup contact.* A third approach to reducing prejudice is increasing contact between groups (Cameron, Rutland, & Brown, 2007; Gómez & Huici, 2008; Wagner, Christ, & Pettigrew, 2008). But as you just discovered with Sherif's study of the boys at the summer camp, contact can sometimes increase prejudice. Increasing contact only works under certain conditions: (1) *close interaction* (if minority students are "tracked" into vocational education courses and white students are primarily in college prep courses, they seldom interact and prejudice is increased), (2) *interdependence* (both groups must be involved in superordinate goals that require cooperation), and (3) *equal status* (everyone must be at the same level). Once people have positive experiences with a group, they tend to generalize to other groups.

3. *Cognitive retraining.* One of the most recent strategies in prejudice reduction requires taking another's perspective or undoing associations of negative stereotypical traits (Buswell, 2006; Galinsky & Ku, 2004; Galinsky & Moskowitz, 2000). For example, in a computer training session, North American participants were asked to *try not* to think of cultural associations when they saw a photograph of an elderly person. They were also asked to press a *no* button when they saw a photograph of an elderly person with a trait stereotypically associated with elderly people (e.g., slow, weak). Conversely, they were instructed to press a *yes* button when they saw a photograph of an elderly person with a trait not normally associated with the elderly. After a number of trials, their response times became faster and faster, indicating they were undoing negative associations and learning positive ones. Following the training, participants were less likely to activate any negative stereotype of elderly people in another activity than were others who did not participate in the training exercise (Kawakami et al., 2000).

People can also learn to be nonprejudiced if they are taught to selectively pay attention to *similarities* rather than *differences* (Phillips & Ziller, 1997). When we focus on how "black voters feel about affirmative action" or how Jewish people feel about "a Jewish candidate for vice president of the United States," we are indirectly encouraging stereotypes and ingroups versus outgroups. Can you see how this might also apply to gender? By emphasizing gender differences (*Men Are from Mars, Women Are from Venus*), we may be perpetuating gender stereotypes.

4. *Cognitive dissonance*. As mentioned earlier, prejudice is a type of attitude that has three basic components—affective (feelings), behavioral tendencies, and cognitive (thoughts). And one of the most efficient methods to change an attitude uses the principle of *cognitive dissonance*, a perceived discrepancy between an attitude and a behavior or between an attitude and a new piece of information. Each time we meet someone who does not conform to our prejudiced views, we experience dissonance—"I thought all gay men were effeminate. This guy is a deep-voiced professional athlete. I'm confused." To resolve the dissonance, we can maintain our stereotypes by saying, "This gay man is an exception to the rule." However, if we continue our contact with a large variety of gay men, this "exception to the rule" defense eventually breaks down and attitude change occurs.

> *You cannot judge another person until you have walked a mile in his moccasins.*
> AMERICAN INDIAN PROVERB

As a critical thinker, can you see how social changes, such as school busing, integrated housing, and increased civil rights legislation, might initially create cognitive dissonance that would lead to an eventual reduction in prejudice? Moreover, do you recognize how the five methods of reducing prejudice we just described also involve cognitive dissonance? Cooperation, superordinate goals, increased contact, and cognitive retraining all create cognitive dissonance for the prejudiced person. And this uncomfortable dissonance motivates the individual to eventually change his or her attitudes, thereby reducing their prejudice.

Application

RESEARCH HIGHLIGHT

Objective 16.22: *Describe recent research on implicit biases.*

Understanding Implicit Biases

BY SIRI CARPENTER

Implicit Bias *Hidden attitude activated by the mere encounter of an attitude object; may serve as a guide to behaviors independent of a person's awareness and control*

For making anti-Semitic remarks during a drunk-driving arrest, actor Mel Gibson pleaded with the public: "Please know from my heart that I am not an anti-Semite. I am not a bigot. Hatred of any kind goes against my faith."

After shouting a series of racist slurs during a performance, comedian Michael Richards of Seinfeld fame apologized to a late-night television audience: "I went into a rage. . . . I'm deeply, deeply sorry . . . I'm not a racist."

And backing away from intimations that black people are not as intelligent as whites, biologist and Nobel laureate James Watson expressed bewilderment and contrition: "I cannot understand how I could have said what I am quoted as having said. There is no scientific basis for such a belief."

Because most people have no conception of the hidden, **implicit bias** in all of us, they react with shock and alarm when prejudiced remarks surface from those they admire. The offenders are sometimes similarly perplexed. The unsettling truth is that just about any of us

could have made them. Using a variety of sophisticated methods, psychologists have established that people unwittingly hold an astounding assortment of stereotypical beliefs and attitudes about social groups: black and white, female and male, elderly and young, gay and straight, fat and thin, and so on (Greenwald et al., 2008; Hofman, Gschwendner, Castelli, & Schmitt, 2008; von Hippel, Brener, & von Hippel, 2008).

Where do such hidden biases come from? To make sense of the world around us, we naturally put things into groups and remember relations between objects and actions or adjectives. For instance, people automatically note that cars move fast, cookies taste sweet and mosquitoes bite. Without such deductions, we would have a lot more trouble navigating our environment and surviving in it. Unfortunately, many of our implicit associations about social groups form before we are old enough to consider them rationally. In a 2006 study, researchers showed that full-fledged implicit racial bias emerges by age six—and never retreats (Baron & Banaji, 2006).

Some implicit biases also appear to be rooted in strong emotions. For example, scientists have measured white people's brain activity as they viewed a series of white and black faces and found that black faces triggered greater activity in the amygdala (a brain area associated with vigilance and sometimes fear). The effect was most pronounced among participants who demonstrated strong implicit racial bias. Provocatively, the same study revealed that when faces were shown for half a second—enough time for participants to consciously process them—black faces instead elicited heightened activity in prefrontal brain areas associated with detecting internal conflicts and controlling responses, hinting that individuals were consciously trying to suppress their implicit associations (Cunningham et al., 2004).

© Bettmann/Corbis

Overt versus covert racism *When you think of racism, do you imagine scenes like this—with separate drinking facilities? Can you see how today's covert racism and implicit bias may be even more damaging than the overt forms of prejudice and discrimination in America's past?*

Detecting Implicit Bias

How do we measure these hidden, implicit attitudes? Psychologists rely on indirect tests that do not depend on people's ability or willingness to reflect on their feelings and thoughts. The most prominent method for measuring implicit bias, the *Implicit Association Test* (IAT), measures how quickly people sort stimuli into particular categories. For example, on an IAT examining implicit attitudes toward young versus old people, a test taker uses one key to respond to young faces and positive words such as "joy" and "peace" and another to respond to old

faces and negative words such as "agony" and "terrible." Then the test taker does the reverse, pairing young faces with negative words and old faces with positive words. (Researchers vary the order of the pairings for different test takers.) The difference in response times for the two conditions suggests how strongly that person associates these social groups with positive versus negative concepts (Greenwald, McGhee, & Schwartz, 1998). To take the IAT, visit http://implicit.harvard.edu/implicit.

Dangerous Games

Studies using the IAT and related methods of measuring covert prejudice have led most scientists to agree that almost everyone, even well-meaning people, harbors unconscious prejudices. But, as we know, it's what we do with our feelings that matters most, and a growing body of work indicates that implicit attitudes can contaminate our behavior in important ways. Reflexive actions and snap judgments may be especially vulnerable to implicit associations. A number of studies have shown, for instance, that both blacks and whites tend to mistake a harmless object such as a cell phone or hand tool for a gun if a black face accompanies the object. This "weapon bias" is especially strong when people have to judge the situation very quickly.

Implicit biases can infect more deliberate decisions, too. In a 2007 study, researchers found that white people who exhibited greater implicit bias toward black people also reported a stronger tendency to engage in a variety of discriminatory acts in their everyday lives. These included avoiding or excluding blacks socially, uttering racial slurs and jokes, and insulting, threatening or physically harming black people (Rudman & Ashmore, 2007).

Hidden prejudices can even affect the quality of health care. One study presented 287 physicians with a photograph and brief clinical vignette describing a middle-aged patient—in some cases black and in others white—who came to the hospital complaining of chest pain. Most physicians did not acknowledge racial bias, but on average they showed a moderate to large implicit anti-black bias. And the greater a physician's racial bias, the less likely he or she was to give a black patient clot-busting, thrombolytic drugs (Green et al., 2007).

Beating Back Prejudice

Researchers long believed that because implicit associations develop early in our lives, and because we are often unaware of their influence, they may be virtually impervious to change. But recent work suggests that we can reshape our implicit attitudes and beliefs—or at least curb their effects on our behavior.

Seeing targeted groups in more favorable social contexts can help thwart biased attitudes. In laboratory studies, seeing a black face with a church as a background, instead of a dilapidated street corner, considering familiar examples of admired blacks such as actor Denzel Washington and athlete Michael Jordan, and reading about Arab-Muslims' positive contributions to society all weaken people's implicit racial and ethnic biases. In real college classrooms, students taking a course on prejudice reduction who had a black professor showed greater reductions in both implicit and explicit prejudice at the end of the semester than did those who had a white professor. "These altitudes can form quickly, and they can change quickly" if we restructure our environments to crowd out stereotypical associations and replace them with egalitarian ones," concludes psychologist Nilanjana Dasgupta, of the University of Massachusetts Amherst.

Some evidence suggests that confronting implicit biases head-on with conscious effort can also work. People who report a strong personal motivation to be nonprejudiced tend to harbor less implicit bias. And some studies indicate that people who are good at using logic and willpower to control their more primitive urges, such as trained mediators, exhibit less implicit bias.

If we accept that implicit bias is an inescapable part of the human condition, then we have a choice about how to respond. We can respond with sadness or, worse, with apathy. Or we can react with a determination to overcome bias, "The capacity for change is deep and great in us," says Harvard University psychologist Mahzarin Banaji. "But do we want the change? That's the question for each of us as individuals—individual scientists, and teachers, and judges, and businesspeople, and the communities to which we belong."

(*Source*: Originally published in *Scientific American* Mind, April/May, 2008, pp. 32–39. Adapted and reprinted with permission of author, Siri Carpenter.)

Overcoming Destructive Obedience: When Is It Okay to Say No?

Obedience to authority is an important part of our lives. If people routinely refused to obey police officers, firefighters, and other official personnel, our individual safety and social order would collapse. However, there are also many times when obedience may be unnecessary and destructive—and should be reduced.

Achievement

Objective 16.23: *Identify six ways to reduce destructive obedience.*

For example, do you remember the story of Jim Jones? In 1978, over 900 members of the People's Temple in Guyana committed mass suicide because he ordered them to do so. People who resisted were murdered. But the vast majority took their lives willingly by drinking cyanide-laced Kool-Aid. A less depressing example of mass obedience occurred in 1983 when 2075 identically dressed couples were married by the Reverend Sun Myung Moon in Madison Square Garden. Although most partners were complete strangers to one another, they married because the Reverend Moon ordered them to do so.

How do we explain (and hopefully reduce) destructive obedience? In addition to all the factors associated with Milgram's study discussed earlier, social psychologists have developed other helpful theories and concepts on the general topic of obedience.

Overcoming destructive obedience *New military recruits understand that effective military action requires quick and immediate obedience. However, social psychological principles, such as socialization, the power of the situation, and groupthink also encourage these individuals to willingly do push-ups in response to their officer's orders. Can you explain why?*

- ***Socialization.*** As mentioned before, our society and culture have a tremendous influence on all our thoughts, feelings, and actions. Obedience is no exception. From very early childhood, we're taught to respect and obey our parents, teachers, and other authority figures. Without this obedience we would have social chaos. Unfortunately, this early (and lifelong) socialization often becomes so deeply ingrained that we no longer consciously recognize it. This helps explain many instances of mindless obedience to immoral requests from people in positions of authority. For example, participants in Milgram's study came into the research lab with a lifetime of socialization toward the value of scientific research and respect for the experimenter's authority. They couldn't suddenly step outside themselves and question the morality of this particular experimenter and his orders. American soldiers accused of atrocities in Iraq or in the Abu Ghraib prison shared this general socialization toward respect for authority combined with military training requiring immediate, unquestioning obedience. Unfortunately, history is replete with instances of atrocities committed because people were "just following orders."

- ***Power of the situation.*** Situational influences also have a strong impact on obedience. For example, the roles of police officer or public citizen, teacher or student, and parent or child all have built-in guidelines for appropriate behavior. One person is ultimately "in charge." The other person is supposed to follow along. Because these roles are so well socialized, we mindlessly play them and find it difficult to recognize the point where they become maladaptive. As we discovered earlier with the Zimbardo prison study, well-adjusted and well-screened college students became so absorbed in their roles of prisoners and guards that their behaviors clearly passed the point of moral behaviors. The "simple" role of being a research participant in Milgram's study—or a soldier in Vietnam, Iraq, or Afghanistan—helps explain many instances of destructive obedience.

- ***Groupthink.*** When discussing Milgram's study and other instances of destructive obedience, most people believe that they and their friends would never do such a thing. Can you see how this might be a form of *groupthink*, a type of faulty thinking that occurs when group members strive for agreement and avoid inconsistent information? When we smugly proclaim that Americans would never follow orders like some German people did during World War II, we're demonstrating several

Figure 16.20 **Foot-in-the-door technique** *If this homeowner allows the salesperson to give him a small gift (a "foot-in-the-door" technique), he's more likely to agree to buy something.* Can you explain why?

symptoms of groupthink—stereotypes of the outgroup, the illusion of unanimity, belief in the morality of the group, and so on.

- *Foot-in-the-door.* The gradual nature of many obedience situations may also help explain why so many people were willing to give the maximum shocks in Milgram's study. The initial mild level of shocks may have worked as a **foot-in-the-door technique**, in which a first, small request is used as a setup for later, larger requests (Figure 16.20). Once Milgram's participants complied with the initial request, they might have felt obligated to continue.

Foot-in-the-Door Technique
A first, small request is used as a setup for later, larger request

- *Relaxed moral guard.* One common intellectual illusion that hinders critical thinking about obedience is the belief that only evil people do evil things or that evil announces itself. For example, the experimenter in Milgram's study looked and acted like a reasonable person who was simply carrying out a research project. Because he was not seen as personally corrupt and evil, the participants' normal moral guard was down and obedience was maximized. This relaxed moral guard might similarly explain why so many people followed Hitler's commands to torture and kill millions of Jews during World War II. Although most believe only "monsters" would obey such an order, Milgram's research suggests otherwise. He revealed the conditions that breed obedience as well as the extent to which ordinary, everyday people will mindlessly obey an authority. As philosopher Hannah Arendt has suggested, the horrifying thing about the Nazis was not that they were so deviant but that they were so "terrifyingly normal."

- *Disobedient models.* In addition to recognizing and understanding the power of these forces, it's equally important to remember that each of us must be personally alert to immoral forms of obedience. On occasion, we also need the courage to stand up and say "No!" One of the most beautiful and historically important examples of just this type of bravery occurred in Alabama in 1955. Rosa Parks boarded a bus and, as expected in those times, she obediently sat in the back section marked "Negroes." When the bus became crowded, the driver told her to give up her seat to a white man. Surprisingly for those days, Parks refused and was eventually forced off the bus by police and arrested. This single act of disobedience was an important catalyst for the small, but growing, civil rights movement and the later repeal of Jim Crow laws in the South. Her courageous stand also inspires the rest of us to think about when it is good to obey authorities and when to disobey unethical demands from authorities.

The power of one! *In late October 2005, Americans mourned the passing of Rosa Parks—the "mother of the civil rights movement." History books typically emphasize her 1955 arrest and jailing for refusing to give up her bus seat to a white man. They fail to mention that this "simple" refusal threatened her job and possibly her life. (Both her mother and husband warned her that she might be lynched for her actions.) They also overlook that long before this one defiant bus ride, Parks fought hard and courageously against segregated seating on buses and for voting rights for blacks.*

Assessment

CHECK & REVIEW

STOP

Applying Psychology to Social Problems

Objective 16.21: *List four major approaches useful for reducing prejudice and discrimination.*

The four key approaches are *cooperation and common goals, intergroup contact, cognitive retraining,* and *cognitive dissonance.*

Objective 16.22: *Describe recent research on implicit biases.*

Research shows that people have hidden, **implicit biases** that are activated by a mere encounter with an attitude object, and that these biases can be used as a quick guide to behaviors that they are not aware of and do not control. Although these biases were previously thought to be impervious to change, newer studies show that we can reshape them (or at least curb) their effects on our behavior.

Objective 16.23: *Identify six ways to reduce destructive obedience.*

To decrease destructive obedience, we need to reexamine *socialization,* the *power of the situation, groupthink,* the *foot-in-the-door* technique, a *relaxed moral guard,* and *disobedient models.*

Questions

1. If your college or hometown were suddenly threatened by a raging wildfire, prejudice might decrease because groups would come together to fight the fire and help rebuild the community. This is an example of how _____ is (are) important in reducing prejudice and discrimination.
   (a) outgroup homogeneity;
   (b) scapegoating;
   (c) displaced competition;
   (d) cooperation and common goals.

2. Cooperation and common goals, superordinate goals, increased contact, and cognitive retraining all create _____ for a prejudiced person.

3. A social influence technique in which a first, small request is used as a setup for later requests is known as _____.
   (a) the lowball technique;
   (b) the foot-in-the-door technique;
   (c) the infiltration technique;
   (d) ingratiation

4. Explain why Rosa Parks is a good example of the power of disobedient models in reducing obedience.

Check your answers in Appendix B.

Click & Review
for additional assessment options:
wiley.com/college/huffman

Assessment

*To assess your understanding of the **Key Terms** in Chapter 16, write a definition for each (in your own words), and then compare your definitions with those in the text.*

social psychology (p. 544)

Our Thoughts about Others
attitude (p. 548)
attribution (p. 546)
cognitive dissonance (p. 549)
fundamental attribution error (FAE) (p. 547)
just-world phenomenon (p. 547)
saliency bias (p. 547)
self-serving bias (p. 547)

Our Feelings about Others
companionate love (p. 558)
discrimination (p. 551)
ingroup favoritism (p. 552)
interpersonal attraction (p. 553)

need compatibility (p. 557)
need complementarity (p. 557)
outgroup homogeneity effect (p. 552)
prejudice (p. 551)
proximity (p. 556)
romantic love (p. 557)
stereotype (p. 551)

Our Actions toward Others
aggression (p. 568)
altruism (p. 570)
conformity (p. 560)
deindividuation (p. 565)
diffusion of responsibility (p. 572)
egoistic model (p. 570)
empathy–altruism hypothesis (p. 570)

frustration–aggression hypothesis (p. 569)
group polarization (p. 566)
groupthink (p. 566)
informational social influence (p. 560)
norm (p. 560)
normative social influence (p. 560)
obedience (p. 561)
reference groups (p. 560)

Applying Social Psychology to Social Problems
foot-in-the-door technique (p. 578)
implicit bias (p. 575)

Achievement

WEB RESOURCES

Huffman Book Companion Site
wiley.com/college/huffman
This site is loaded with free Interactive Self-Tests, Internet Exercises, Glossary and Flashcards for key terms, web links, Handbook for Non-Native Speakers, and other activities designed to improve your mastery of the material in this chapter.

Our Thoughts About Others

Attribution

Attribution: Explaining others' behavior by deciding that their actions resulted from internal (dispositional) factors (their own traits and motives) or external (situational) factors. Problems: **fundamental attribution error** and **self-serving bias**.

Attitude

Attitude: Learned predisposition toward a particular object. Three components of all attitudes: cognitive, affective, and behavioral tendencies.

Cognitive Dissonance Theory

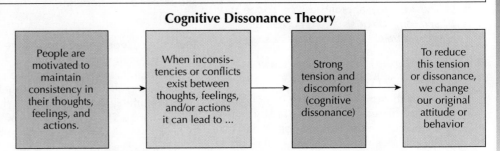

People are motivated to maintain consistency in their thoughts, feelings, and actions. → When inconsistencies or conflicts exist between thoughts, feelings, and/or actions it can lead to ... → Strong tension and discomfort (cognitive dissonance) → To reduce this tension or dissonance, we change our original attitude or behavior

Our Feelings About Others

Prejudice and Discrimination

Prejudice: Learned, generally negative attitude toward members of a group. Contains all three components of attitudes—cognitive (**stereotype**), affective, and behavioral (discrimination).

Discrimination: Refers to the actual negative behavior directed at members of a group.

Learning: Classical and operant conditioning and social learning

Personal experience

Mental shortcuts: **Ingroup favoritism, outgroup homogeneity effect**

Economic and political competition

Displaced aggression: Scapegoating

Interpersonal attraction

Three key factors:

Physical attractiveness is important to initial attraction and more important to men than women.

Physical **proximity** increases attraction largely due to the *mere exposure effect.*

Although many believe "opposites attract" (**need complementarity**), research shows *similarity* (**need compatibility**) is more important.

Karen Huffman

- **Romantic love** highly valued in our society, but it's based on mystery and fantasy; thus, hard to sustain.
- **Companionate love** relies on mutual trust, and friendship and grows stronger with time.

Our Actions Toward Others

Social Influence

Conformity: Changing behavior in response to real or imagined pressure from others.

Three reasons we conform:

A _____
B _____
C _____
X _____

For approval and acceptance (**normative social influence**).

Need for more information (**informational social influence**).

To match behavior of those we admire and feel similar to (**reference group**).

Obedience: Going along with a direct command. Milgram's study showed a high degree of obedience. Why?

| Legitimacy and closeness of the authority figure | Remoteness of victim | Assignment of responsibility | Modeling/ imitation |

Aggression

Aggression: Any behavior intended to harm someone.

- *Biological factors:* Instincts, genes, brain and nervous system, substance abuse and other mental disorders, hormones, and neurotransmitters.
- *Psychosocial factors:* Aversive stimuli, culture and learning, violent media, and video games
- *Treatment:* Incompatible responses (like humor) and improved social and communication skills help reduce aggression, but expressing it doesn't.

Group Processes

- *Group membership* affects us through the roles we play and **deindividuation**
- *Group decision making* is affected by two key factors:

Group polarization: When most group members initially tend toward an extreme idea, the entire group will move toward that extreme.

Groupthink: Faulty type of decision making where group's desire for agreement overrules critical evaluation.

Altruism

Altruism: Actions designed to help others with no obvious benefit to the helper.

Why do we help?
- Evolutionary theorists believe altruism is innate and has survival value.
- Psychological explanations suggest helping is motivated by anticipated gain (**egoistic model**) or when helper feels empathy for the victim (**empathy–altruism hypothesis**).

Why don't we help?
- It depends on a series of interconnected events, starting with noticing the problem and ending with a decision to help.
- Many emergency situations are ambiguous.
- We assume others will respond (**diffusion of responsibility**).

How do we increase altruism?
- Reduce ambiguity by giving clear directions to observers.
- Increase rewards, while decreasing costs.

Applying Social Psychology to Social Problems

Social psychological research applied to social problems:

- Cooperation and common goals, intergroup contact, cognitive retraining, and reducing cognitive dissonance may help decrease prejudice and discrimination.
- Understanding socialization, the power of the situation, groupthink, the foot-in-the-door, a relaxed moral guard, and disobedient models may help reduce destructive obedience.

Statistics and Psychology

e are constantly bombarded by numbers: "On sale for 30 percent off," "70 percent chance of rain," "9 out of 10 doctors recommend . . ." The president uses numbers to try to convince us that the economy is healthy. Advertisers use numbers to convince us of the effectiveness of their products. Psychologists use statistics to support or refute psychological theories and demonstrate that certain behaviors are indeed results of specific causal factors.

When people use numbers in these ways, they are using statistics. **Statistics** is a branch of applied mathematics that uses numbers to describe and analyze information on a subject.

Statistics make it possible for psychologists to quantify the information they obtain in their studies. They can then critically analyze and evaluate this information. Statistical analysis is imperative for researchers to describe, predict, or explain behavior. For instance, Albert Bandura (1973) proposed that watching violence on television causes aggressive behavior in children. In carefully controlled experiments, he gathered numerical information and analyzed it according to specific statistical methods. The statistical analysis helped him substantiate that the aggression of his subjects and the aggressive acts they had seen on television were related, and that the relationship was not mere coincidence.

Although statistics is a branch of applied mathematics, you don't have to be a math whiz to use statistics. Simple arithmetic is all you need to do most of the calculations. For more complex statistics involving more complicated mathematics, computer programs are available for virtually every type of computer. What is more important than learning the mathematical computations, however, is developing an understanding of when and why each type of statistic is used. The purpose of this appendix is to help you understand the significance of the statistics most commonly used.

EIGHTY-TWO PER CENT OF THE POPULATION DOESN'T GET ENOUGH FIBRE IN ITS DIET!

TWO OUT OF THREE KIDS IN AMERICA CAN'T SPELL "CHOLESTEROL"!

NINETY-NINE PER CENT OF THOSE INTERVIEWED SAID THEY HATED CARROTS!

STATISTICS ARE TOTALLY WRONG FIFTY-SIX PER CENT OF THE TIME!

THE STAT FAMILY

Drawing by M. Stevens; © 1989 the New Yorker Magazine, Inc.

Gathering and Organizing Data

Psychologists design their studies to facilitate gathering information about the factors they want to study. The information they obtain is known as **data** (**data** is plural; its singular is **datum**). When the data are gathered, they are generally in the form of numbers; if they aren't, they are converted to numbers. After they are gathered, the data must be organized in such a way that statistical analysis is possible. In the following section, we will examine the methods used to gather and organize information.

Variables

When studying a behavior, psychologists normally focus on one particular factor to determine whether it has an effect on the behavior. This factor is known as a **variable**, which is in effect anything that can assume more than one value (see Chapter 1). Height, weight, sex, eye color, and scores on an IQ test or a video game are all factors that can assume more than one value and are therefore variables. Some will vary between people, such as sex (you are either male *or* female but not both at the same time). Some may even vary within one person, such as scores on a video game (the same person might get 10,000 points on one try and only 800 on another). Opposed to a variable, anything that remains the same and does not vary is called a **constant**. If researchers use only females in their research, then sex is a constant, not a variable.

In nonexperimental studies, variables can be factors that are merely observed through naturalistic observation or case studies, or they can be factors about which people are questioned in a test or survey. In experimental studies, the two major types of variables are independent and dependent variables.

Independent variables are those that are manipulated by the experimenter. For example, suppose we were to conduct a study to determine whether the sex of the debater influences the outcome of a debate. In this study, one group of subjects watches a videotape of a debate between a male arguing the "pro" side and a female arguing the "con"; another group watches the same debate, but with the pro and con roles reversed. In such a study, the form of the presentation viewed by each group (whether "pro" is argued by a male or a female) is the independent variable because the experimenter manipulates the form of presentation seen by each group. Another example might be a study to determine whether a particular drug has any effect on a manual dexterity task. To study this question, we would administer the drug to one group and no drug to another. The independent variable would be the amount of drug given (some or none). The independent variable is particularly important when using **inferential statistics**, which we will discuss later.

The **dependent variable** is a factor that results from, or depends on, the independent variable. It is a measure of some outcome or, most commonly, a measure of the subjects' behavior. In the debate example, each subject's choice of the winner of the debate would be the dependent variable. In the drug experiment, the dependent variable would be each subject's score on the manual dexterity task.

Frequency Distributions

After conducting a study and obtaining measures of the variable(s) being studied, psychologists need to organize the data in a meaningful way. Table A.1 presents test scores from a statistics aptitude test collected from 50 college students. This information is called **raw data** because there is no order to the numbers. They are presented as they were collected and are therefore "raw."

The lack of order in raw data makes them difficult to study. Thus, the first step in understanding the results of an experiment is to impose some order on the raw data. There are several ways to do this. One of the simplest is to create a **frequency distribution**, which shows the number of times a score or event occurs. Although frequency distributions are helpful in several ways, the major advantages are that they allow us to see the data in an organized manner and they make it easier to represent the data on a graph.

The simplest way to make a frequency distribution is to list all the possible test scores, then tally the number of people (*N*) who received those scores. Table A.2 presents a frequency distribution using the raw data from Table A.1. As you can see, the data are now easier to read. From looking at the frequency distribution, you can see that most of the test scores lie in the middle with only a few at the very high or very low end. This was not at all evident from looking at the raw data.

This type of frequency distribution is practical when the number of possible scores is 20 or fewer. However, when there are more than 20 possible scores it can be even harder to make sense out of the frequency distribution than the raw data. This can be seen in Table A.3, which presents the Scholastic Aptitude Test scores for 50 students. Even though there are only 50 actual scores in this table, the number of possible scores

TABLE A.2 FREQUENCY DISTRIBUTION OF 50 STUDENTS ON STATISTICS APTITUDE TEST

Score	Frequency
73	2
72	3
71	0
70	1
69	0
68	5
67	1
66	2
65	3
64	2
63	5
62	5
61	2
60	2
59	5
58	1
57	3
56	1
55	0
54	1
53	0
52	2
51	1
50	3
Total	50

ranges from a high of 1390 to a low of 400. If we included zero frequencies there would be 100 entries in a frequency distribution of this data, making the frequency distribution much more difficult to understand than the raw data. If there are more than 20 possible scores, therefore, a **group** frequency distribution is normally used.

In a **group frequency distribution**, individual scores are represented as members of a group of scores or as a range of scores (see Table A.4). These groups are called **class intervals**. Grouping these scores makes it much easier to make sense out of the distribution, as you can see from the relative ease in understanding Table A.4 as compared to Table A.3. Group frequency distributions are easier to represent on a graph.

When graphing data from frequency distributions, the class intervals are represented along the **abscissa** (the horizontal or *x* axis). The frequency is represented along the **ordinate** (the vertical or *y* axis). Information can be graphed in the form of a bar graph, called a **histogram**, or in the form of a point or line graph, called a **polygon**. Figure A.1 shows a histogram presenting the

TABLE A.1 STATISTICS APTITUDE TEST SCORES FOR 50 COLLEGE STUDENTS

73	57	63	59	50
72	66	50	67	51
63	59	65	62	65
62	72	64	73	66
61	68	62	68	63
59	61	72	63	52
59	58	57	68	57
64	56	65	59	60
50	62	68	54	63
52	62	70	60	68

TABLE A.3 SCHOLASTIC APTITUDE TEST SCORES FOR 50 COLLEGE STUDENTS

1350	750	530	540	750
1120	410	780	1020	430
720	1080	1110	770	610
1130	620	510	1160	630
640	1220	920	650	870
930	660	480	940	670
1070	950	680	450	990
690	1010	800	660	500
860	520	540	880	1090
580	730	570	560	740

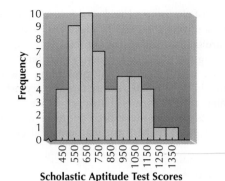

Figure A.1 A histogram illustrating the information found in Table A.4.

data from Table A.4. Note that the class intervals are represented along the bottom line of the graph (the *x* axis) and the height of the bars indicates the frequency in each class interval. Now look at Figure A.2. The information presented here is exactly the same as that in Figure A.1 but is represented in the form of a polygon rather than a histogram. Can you see how both graphs illustrate the same information? Even though reading information from a graph is simple, we have found that many students have never learned to read graphs. In the next section we will explain how to read a graph.

How to Read a Graph

Every graph has several major parts. The most important are the labels, the axes (the vertical and horizontal lines), and the points, lines, or bars. Find these parts in Figure A.1.

The first thing you should notice when reading a graph are the labels because they tell what data are portrayed. Usually the data consist of the descriptive statistics, or the numbers used to measure the dependent variables. For example, in Figure A.1

the horizontal axis is labeled "Scholastic Aptitude Test Scores," which is the dependent variable measure; the vertical axis is labeled "Frequency," which means the number of occurrences. If a graph is not labeled, as we sometimes see in TV commercials or magazine ads, it is useless and should be ignored. Even when a graph *is* labeled, the labels can be misleading. For example, if graph designers want to distort the information, they can elongate one of the axes. Thus, it is important to pay careful attention to the numbers as well as the words in graph labels.

Next, you should focus your attention on the bars, points, or lines on the graph. In the case of histograms like the one in Figure A.1, each bar represents the class interval. The width of the bar stands for the width of the class interval, whereas the height of the bar stands for the frequency in that interval. Look at the third bar from the left in Figure A.1. This bar represents the interval "600 to 690 SAT Scores," which has a frequency of 10. You can see that this directly corresponds to the same class interval in Table A.4, since graphs and tables are both merely alternate ways of illustrating information.

Reading point or line graphs is the same as reading a histogram. In a point graph, each point represents two numbers, one found along the horizontal axis and the other found along the vertical axis. A polygon is identical to a point graph except that it has lines connecting the points. Figure A.2 is an example of a polygon, where each point represents a class interval and is placed

TABLE A.4 GROUP FREQUENCY DISTRIBUTION OF SCHOLASTIC APTITUDE TEST SCORES FOR 50 COLLEGE STUDENTS

Class Interval	Frequency
1300–1390	1
1200–1290	1
1100–1190	4
1000–1090	5
900–990	5
800–890	4
700–790	7
600–690	10
500–590	9
400–490	4
Total	50

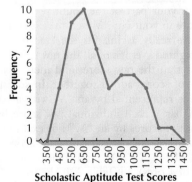

Figure A.2 A polygon illustrating the information found in Table A.4.

at the center of the interval and at the height corresponding to the frequency of that interval. To make the graph easier to read, the points are connected by straight lines.

Displaying the data in a frequency distribution or in a graph is much more useful than merely presenting raw data and can be especially helpful when researchers are trying to find relations between certain factors. However, as we explained earlier, if psychologists want to make predictions or explanations about behavior, they need to perform mathematical computations on the data.

Uses of the Various Statistics

The statistics psychologists use in a study depend on whether they are trying to describe and predict behavior or explain it. When they use statistics to describe behavior, as in reporting the average score on the Scholastic Aptitude Test, they are using **descriptive statistics**. When they use them to explain behavior, as Bandura did in his study of children modeling aggressive behavior seen on TV, they are using **inferential statistics**.

Descriptive Statistics

Descriptive statistics are the numbers used to describe the dependent variable. They can be used to describe characteristics of a **population** (an entire group, such as all people living in the United States) or a **sample** (a part of a group, such as a randomly selected group of 25 students from Cornell University). The major descriptive statistics include measures of central tendency (mean, median, and mode), measures of variation (variance and standard deviation), and correlation.

Measures of Central Tendency

Statistics indicating the center of the distribution are called **measures of central tendency** and include the mean, median, and mode. They are all scores that are typical of the center of the distribution. The **mean** is what most of us think of when we hear the word "average." The **median** is the middle score. The **mode** is the score that occurs most often.

Mean What is your average golf score? What is the average yearly rainfall in your part of the country? What is the average reading test score in your city? When these questions ask for the average, they are really asking for the "mean." The arithmetic **mean** is the weighted average of all the raw scores, which is computed by totaling all the raw scores and then dividing that total by the number of scores added together. In statistical computation, the mean is represented by an "X" with a bar above it ($\overline{X}$, pronounced "X bar"), each individual raw score by an "**X**," and the total number of scores by an "**N**." For example, if we wanted to compute the $\overline{X}$ of the raw statistics test scores in Table A.1, we would sum all the X's (?X, with ? meaning sum) and divide by N (number of scores). In Table A.1, the sum of all the scores is equal to 3100 and there are 50 scores. Therefore, the mean of these scores is

$$\overline{X} = \frac{3100}{50} = 62$$

Table A.5 illustrates how to calculate the mean for 10 IQ scores.

TABLE A.5 COMPUTATION OF THE MEAN FOR 10 IQ SCORES

IQ Scores X
143
127
116
98
85
107
106
98
104
116
$\Sigma X = 1100$

$$\text{Mean} = \overline{X} = \frac{\Sigma X}{N} = \frac{1,100}{10} = 110$$

Median The **median** is the middle score in the distribution once all the scores have been arranged in rank order. If N (the number of scores) is odd, then there actually is a middle score and that middle score is the median. When N is even, there are two middle scores and the median is the mean of those two scores. Table A.6 shows the computation of the median for two different sets of scores, one set with 15 scores and one with 10.

TABLE A.6 COMPUTATION OF MEDIAN FOR ODD AND EVEN NUMBERS OF IQ SCORES

IQ	IQ
139	137
130	135
121	121
116	116
107	108 ← middle score
101	106 ← middle score
98	105
96 ← middle score	101
84	98
83	97
82	N = 10
75	N is even
75	
68	
65	Median = $\frac{106 + 108}{2} = 107$
N = 15	
N is odd	

TABLE A.7 FINDING THE MODE FOR TWO DIFFERENT DISTRIBUTIONS

IQ	IQ
139	139
138	138
125	125
116 ←	116 ←
116 ←	116 ←
116 ←	116 ←
107	107
100	98 ←
98	98 ←
98	98 ←
Mode = most frequent score	Mode = 116 and 98
Mode = 116	

TABLE A.8 COMPUTATION OF THE STANDARD DEVIATION FOR 10 IQ SCORES

IQ Scores X	$X - \overline{X}$	$(X - \overline{X})^2$
143	33	1089
127	17	289
116	6	36
98	−12	144
85	−25	625
107	−3	9
106	−4	16
98	−12	144
104	−6	36
116	6	36
$\Sigma X = 1100$		$\Sigma(X - \overline{X})^2 = 2424$

Standard Deviation = s

$$= \sqrt{\frac{\Sigma(X - \overline{X})^2}{N}} = \sqrt{\frac{2424}{10}}$$

Mode   Of all the measures of central tendency, the easiest to compute is the **mode**, which is merely the most frequent score. It is computed by finding the score that occurs most often. Whereas there is always only one mean and only one median for each distribution, there can be more than one mode. Table A.7 shows how to find the mode in a distribution with one mode (unimodal) and in a distribution with two modes (bimodal).

There are several advantages to each of these measures of central tendency, but in psychological research the mean is used most often. A book solely covering psychological statistics will provide a more thorough discussion of the relative values of these measures.

Measures of Variation

When describing a distribution, it is not sufficient merely to give the central tendency; it is also necessary to give a **measure of variation**, which is a measure of the spread of the scores. By examining the spread, we can determine whether the scores are bunched around the middle or tend to extend away from the middle. Figure A.3 shows three different distributions, all with the same mean but with different spreads of scores. You can see from this figure that, in order to describe these different distributions accurately, there must be some measures of the variation in their spread. The most widely used measure of variation is the standard deviation, which is represented by a lowercase s. The standard deviation is

a standard measurement of how much the scores in a distribution deviate from the mean. The formula for the standard deviation is

$$s = \sqrt{\frac{\Sigma(X - \overline{X})^2}{N}}$$

Table A.8 illustrates how to compute the standard deviation.

Most distributions of psychological data are bell-shaped. That is, most of the scores are grouped around the mean, and the farther the scores are from the mean in either direction, the fewer the scores. Notice the bell shape of the distribution in Figure A.4. Distributions such as this are called **normal** distributions. In normal distributions, as shown in Figure A.4, approximately two-thirds of the scores fall within a range that is one standard deviation below the mean to one standard deviation above the mean. For example, the Wechsler IQ tests (see Chapter 7) have a mean of 100 and a standard deviation of 15. This means that approximately two-thirds of the people taking these tests will have scores between 85 and 115.

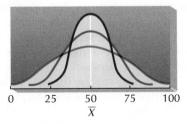

Figure A.3 Three distributions having the same mean but a different variability.

Percent of cases under portions of the normal curve

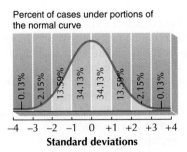

Figure A.4 The normal distribution forms a bell-shaped curve. In a normal distribution, two-thirds of the scores lie between one standard deviation above and one standard deviation below the mean.

Correlation

Suppose for a moment that you are sitting in the student union with a friend. To pass the time, you and your friend decide to play a game in which you try to guess the height of the next male who enters the union. The winner, the one whose guess is closest to the person's actual height, gets a piece of pie paid for by the loser. When it is your turn, what do you guess? If you are like most people, you will probably try to estimate the mean of all the males in the union and use that as your guess. The mean is always your best guess if you have no other information.

Now let's change the game a little and add a friend who stands outside the union and weighs the next male to enter the union. Before the male enters the union, your friend says "125 pounds." Given this new information, will you still guess the mean height? Probably not—you will probably predict *below* the mean. Why? Because you intuitively understand that there is a **correlation**, a relationship, between height and weight, with tall people usually weighing more than short people. Given that 125 pounds is less than the average weight for males, you will probably guess a less-than-average height. The statistic used to measure this type of relationship between two variables is called a correlation coefficient.

Correlation Coefficient   A **correlation coefficient** measures the relationship between two variables, such as height and weight or IQ and SAT scores. Given any two variables, there are three possible relationships between them: **positive**, **negative**, and **zero** (no relationship). A positive relationship exists when the two variables vary in the same direction (e.g., as height increases, weight normally also increases). A negative relationship occurs when the two variables vary in opposite directions (e.g., as temperatures go up, hot chocolate sales go down). There is no relationship when the two variables vary totally independently of one another (e.g., there is no relationship between peoples' height and the color of their toothbrushes). Figure A.5 illustrates these three types of correlations.

The computation and the formula for a correlation coefficient (correlation coefficient is delineated by the letter "r") are shown in Table A.9. The correlation coefficient (r) always has a value between +1 and −1 (it is never greater than +1 and it is never smaller than −1). When r is close to +1, it signifies a high positive relationship between the two variables (as one variable goes up, the other variable also goes up). When r is close to −1, it signifies a high negative relationship between the two variables (as one variable goes up, the other variable goes down). When r is 0, there is no linear relationship between the two variables being measured.

Correlation coefficients can be quite helpful in making predictions. Bear in mind, however, that predictions are just that: *predictions*. They will have some error as long as the correlation coefficients on which they are based are not perfect (+1 or −1). Also, correlations cannot reveal any information regarding causation. Merely because two factors are correlated, it does not mean that one factor causes the other. Consider, for example, ice cream consumption and swimming pool use. These two variables are positively correlated with one another, in that as ice cream consumption increases, so does swimming pool use. But nobody

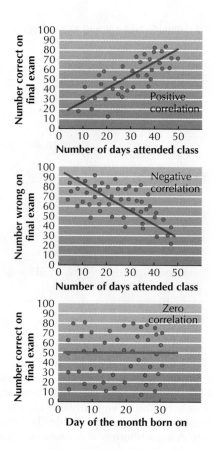

Figure A.5 Three types of correlation. Positive correlation (top): As the number of days of class attendance increases, so does the number of correct exam items. Negative correlation (middle): As the number of days of class attendance increases, the number of incorrect exam items decreases. Zero correlation (bottom): The day of the month on which one is born has no relationship to the number of exam items correct.

would suggest that eating ice cream *causes* swimming, or vice versa. Similarly, just because Michael Jordan eats Wheaties and can do a slam dunk it does not mean that you will be able to do one if you eat the same breakfast. The only way to determine the cause of behavior is to conduct an experiment and analyze the results by using inferential statistics.

Inferential Statistics

Knowing the descriptive statistics associated with different distributions, such as the mean and standard deviation, can enable us to make comparisons between various distributions. By making these comparisons, we may be able to observe whether one variable is related to another or whether one variable has a causal effect on another. When we design an experiment specifically to measure causal effects between two or more variables, we use **inferential** statistics to analyze the data collected. Although there are many inferential statistics, the one we will discuss is the t-test, since it is the simplest.

TABLE A.9 COMPUTATION OF CORRELATION COEFFICIENT BETWEEN HEIGHT AND WEIGHT FOR 10 MALES

Height (inches) X	X^2	Weight (pounds) Y	Y^2	XY
73	5,329	210	44,100	15,330
64	4,096	133	17,689	8,512
65	4,225	128	16,384	8,320
70	4,900	156	24,336	10,920
74	5,476	189	35,721	13,986
68	4,624	145	21,025	9,860
67	4,489	145	21,025	9,715
72	5,184	166	27,556	11,952
76	5,776	199	37,601	15,124
71	5,041	159	25,281	11,289
700	49,140	1,630	272,718	115,008

$$r = \frac{N \cdot \Sigma XY - \Sigma X \cdot \Sigma Y}{\sqrt{[N \cdot \Sigma X^2 - (\Sigma X)^2}\sqrt{[N \cdot \Sigma Y^2 - (\Sigma Y)^2]}}$$

$$r = \frac{10 \cdot 115,008 - 700 \cdot 1,630}{\sqrt{[10 \cdot 49,140 - 700^2]}\sqrt{[10 \cdot 272,718 - 1,630^2]}}$$

$$r = 0.92$$

TABLE A.10 REACTION TIMES IN MILLISECONDS (MSEC) FOR SUBJECTS IN ALCOHOL AND NO ALCOHOL CONDITIONS AND COMPUTATION OF t

RT (msec) Alcohol X_1	RT (msec) No Alcohol X_2
200	143
210	137
140	179
160	184
180	156
187	132
196	176
198	148
140	125
159	120
$SX_1 = 1,770$	$SX_2 = 1,500$
$N_1 = 10$	$N_2 = 10$
$\overline{X}_1 = 177$	$\overline{X}_2 = 150$
$s_1 = 24.25$	$s_2 = 21.86$

$$\Sigma_{\overline{X}1} = \frac{s}{\sqrt{N_1 - 1}} = 8.08 \qquad \Sigma_{\overline{X}2} = \frac{s}{\sqrt{N_2 - 1}} = 7.29$$

$$S_{\overline{X}_1 - \overline{X}_2} = \sqrt{S_{\overline{X}_1}^2 + S_{\overline{X}_2}^2} = \sqrt{8.08^2 + 7.29^2} = 10.88$$

$$t = \frac{\overline{X}_1 - \overline{X}_2}{S_{\overline{X}1 - \overline{X}2}} = \frac{177 - 150}{10.88} = 2.48$$

$$t = 2.48, p < .05$$

t-Test Suppose we believe that drinking alcohol causes a person's reaction time to slow down. To test this hypothesis, we recruit 20 participants and separate them into two groups. We ask the participants in one group to drink a large glass of orange juice with one ounce of alcohol for every 100 pounds of body weight (e.g., a person weighing 150 pounds would get 1.5 ounces of alcohol). We ask the control group to drink an equivalent amount of orange juice with no alcohol added. Fifteen minutes after the drinks, we have each participant perform a reaction time test that consists of pushing a button as soon as a light is flashed. (The reaction time is the time between the onset of the light and the pressing of the button.) Table A.10 shows the data from this hypothetical experiment. It is clear from the data that there is definitely a difference in the reaction times of the two groups: There is an obvious difference between the means. However, it is possible that this difference is due merely to chance. To determine whether the difference is real or due to chance, we can conduct a t-test. We have run a sample t-test in Table A.10.

The logic behind a t-test is relatively simple. In our experiment we have two samples. If each of these samples is from the *same* population (e.g., the population of all people, whether drunk or sober), then any difference between the samples will be due to chance. On the other hand, if the two samples are from *different* populations (e.g., the population of drunk people *and* the population of sober people), then the difference is a significant difference and not due to chance.

If there is a significant difference between the two samples, then the independent variable must have caused that difference. In our example, there is a significant difference between the alcohol and the no alcohol groups. We can tell this because p (the probability that this t value will occur by chance) is less than .05. To obtain the p, we need only look up the t value in a statistical table, which is found in any statistics book. In our example, because there is a significant difference between the groups, we can reasonably conclude that the alcohol did cause a slower reaction time.

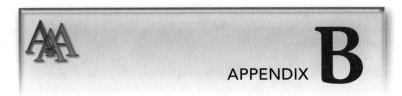
Answers to Review Questions and Try This Yourself Activities

CHAPTER 1 Introducing Psychology (p. 7) 1. b. 2. a. 3. a. 4. b. 5. b. **Origins of Psychology (p. 15)** 1. structuralist. 2. Functionalists. 3. Freud's theories are controversial because of his nonscientific approach and emphasis on sexual and aggressive impulses. 4. c. 5. The biopsychosocial model is a unifying theme of modern psychology that incorporates the biological, psychological, and social processes. **The Science of Psychology (p. 20)** 1. c. 2. a. 3. d. 4. c. 5. Obtaining informed consent from research participants and debriefing them after the research is conducted helps ensure the well-being of the participant and helps maintain high ethical standards. Deception is sometimes necessary in psychological research because if participants know the true purpose of the study, their response will be unnatural. 6. Compare your answers with Process Diagram 1.1. **Experimental Research (p. 26)** 1. In an experiment, the experimenter manipulates and controls the variables, which allows them to isolate a single factor and examine the effect of that factor alone on a particular behavior. 2. d. 3. c. 4. The two primary problems for researchers are experimenter bias and ethnocentrism. The two problems for participants are sample bias and participant bias. To guard against experimenter bias, researchers employ blind observers, single-blind and double-blind studies, and placebos. To control for ethnocentrism, they use cross-cultural sampling. To offset participant problems with sample bias, researchers use random/representative sampling and random assignment. To control for participant bias, they rely on many of the same controls in place to prevent experimenter bias, such as double-blind studies. They also attempt to assure anonymity, confidentiality, and sometimes use deception. **Descriptive, Correlational, and Biological Research (p. 37)** 1. c. 2. d. 3. c. 4. CT, PET, MRI, fMRI. **Cultural Universals and Tools for Student Success (p. 47)** 1. emotions, facial recognition of emotions. 2. Compare your answers with Process Diagram 1.3. 3. b.

CHAPTER 2 Neural Bases of Behavior (p. 59) 1. Check your answers with Figure 2.1. 2. c. 3. b. 4. Neurotransmitters are manufactured and released at the synapse, where the messages are picked up and relayed by neighboring neurons. Hormones are released from glands in the endocrine system directly into the bloodstream. **Nervous System Organization (p. 66)** 1. central; peripheral. 2. d. 3. d. 4. The sympathetic nervous system arouses the body and mobilizes energy stores to deal with emergencies. The parasympathetic nervous system calms the body and conserves the energy stores. 5. Compare your answers with Figure 2.4. **Lower-Level Brain Structures (p. 70)** 1. medulla, pons, and cerebellum. 2. cerebellum. 3. b. 4. The amygdala is important

because of its role in the production and regulation of emotions, particularly aggression and fear. 5. Compare your answers with Figure 2.12. **Critical Thinking/Active Learning (p. 78–The Biology of Critical Thinking)** Part I 1-K, 2-I, 3-N, 4-L, 5-G, 6-B, 7-F, 8-D, 9-H, 10-J, 11-M, 12-C, 13-A, 14-E. Part II 1. Modifying judgment in light of new information/Left Hemisphere; 2. Listening actively/Temporal Lobes; 3. Tolerating ambiguity/ Sympathetic and Parasympathetic Nervous Systems. **The Cerebral Cortex and Two Brains in One? (p. 80)** 1. cerebral cortex. 2. occipital; temporal; frontal; parietal. 3. a. 4. Compare your answers with Figure 2.17. 5. c. **Our Genetic Inheritance (p. 86)** 1. d. 2. Behavioral geneticists use twin studies, family studies, adoption studies, and genetic abnormalities. 3. c. 4. Because natural selection favors animals whose concern for kin is proportional to their degree of biological relatedness, most people will devote more resources, protection, love, and concern to close relatives, which helps ensure their genetic survival.

CHAPTER 3 Sources of Stress (p. 99) 1. a. 2. a. 3. a blocked goal; conflict. 4. Your personal answers will vary, but here are some examples: A forced choice between apple or pumpkin pie is an example of an approach–approach conflict. Having to choose between attending a desirable college versus not going to that college because you know your ex is also going there is an example of an approach–avoidance conflict. Taking an exam when you're underprepared or not taking the exam and receiving an automatic "F" is an example of an avoidance-avoidance conflict. **Effects of Stress (p. 105)** 1. The SAM system provides an initial, rapid-acting response to stress. 2. The HPA axis provides a delayed stress response. 3. Compare your answers to Process Diagram 3.1. 4. alarm; resistance; exhaustion. 5. b. **Stress and Illness (p. 111)** 1. epinephrine; cortisol. 2. b. 3. A hardy personality is based on three qualities: a commitment to personal goals, control over life, and viewing change as a challenge rather than a threat. People with these qualities are more successful at dealing with stress because they take a more active, positive approach and assume responsibility for their stress. 4. Severe anxiety. **Health Psychology in Action (p. 116)** 1. In addition to social pressures that encourage smoking, nicotine is a powerfully addictive drug and smokers learn to associate positive things with smoking. 2. d. 3. alcohol. 4. a. **Critical Thinking/Active Learning (p. 122—Reducing Stress Through Critical Thinking)** 1-B, 2-E, 3-H, 4-C, 5-J, 6-G, 7-D, 8-I, 9-F, 10-A. **Health and Stress Management (p. 123)** 1. Personal answers will vary. 2. emotion-focused; b. problem-focused. 3. internal. 4. The eight resources are health and exercise, positive beliefs, social skills, social support, material resources, control, relaxation, and sense of humor. Individual responses to the most and least helpful resources will vary depending on personality and individual life style.

CHAPTER 4 **Understanding Sensation (p. 135)** 1. d. 2. absolute threshold. 3. a. 4. Your sensory receptors for smell adapt and send fewer messages to your brain. 5. b. **How We See (p. 141)** 1. Compare your answers with Process Diagram 4.1. 2. After light waves enter the eye through the cornea and pass through pupil, the lens focuses the incoming light into an image onto the retina, the eye's light-sensitive back surface. Special receptor cells in the retina, called rods and cones, then convert light energy into neural signals that send messages to the brain via the bipolar cells and ganglion cells. After exiting the blind spot, neural messages travel along the optic nerve to the brain for further processing. 3. Color is processed in a trichromatic fashion in the retina, and in an opponent-process fashion in the brain. 4. b. **How We Hear (p. 145)** 1. Compare your answers to Process Diagram 4.2. 2. The outer ear (pinna, auditory canal, and eardrum) funnels sound waves to the middle ear. Bones in the middle ear (hammer, anvil, and stirrup) amplify and send along the eardrum's vibrations to the cochlea's oval window, which is part of the inner ear. Vibrations from the oval window cause ripples in the fluid, which, in turn, cause bending of the hair cells in the cochlea's basilar membrane. This bending generates neural signals that travel along the auditory nerve to the brain for further processing. 3. Place theory explains pitch perception according to the place where the cochlea's basilar membrane is most stimulated. Frequency theory says pitch perception occurs when nerve impulses sent to the brain match the frequency of the sound wave. 4. nerve. **Our Other Senses (p. 150)** 1. pheromones. 2. d. 3. d. 4. kinesthetic. **Selection (p. 153)** 1. Illusions are false or misleading perceptions of the physical world produced by actual physical distortions. Hallucinations are imaginary sensory perceptions that occur without an external stimulus. Delusions are false beliefs. 2. feature detectors. 3. "Horizontal cats" reared in a horizontal world fail to develop potential feature detectors for vertical lines or objects. 4. c. **Organization—Form and Constancies (p. 156)** 1. proximity, similarity, closure. 2. c. 3. size constancy. 4. color and brightness constancy. **Depth Perception, Interpretation, and ESP (p. 163)** 1. c. 2. b. 3. perceptual adaptation. 4. telepathy, clairvoyance, precognition, psychokinesis. 5. generally cannot be replicated.

CHAPTER 5 **Understanding Consciousness (p. 170)** 1. b. 2. General consciousness involves activation and integration of several parts of the brain. Awareness involves the cerebral cortex, particularly the frontal lobes, whereas arousal generally results from activation of the brain stem. 3. focused, minimal. 4. d. **Circadian Rhythms and Stages of Sleep (p. 178)** 1. d. 2. Compare your answers with Process Diagram 5.1. 3. b. 4. an electroencephalograph (EEG). 5. a. **Theories of Sleep and Dreams (p. 182)** 1. Repair/restoration theory suggests we sleep to physically restore our mind and body. Evolutionary/circadian theory says that sleep evolved because it helped conserve energy and provided protection from predators. 2. d. 3. c. 4. REM. **Sleep Disorders (p. 185)** 1. insomnia. 2. sleep apnea. 3. narcolepsy. 4. night terrors. **Psychoactive Drugs (p. 195)** 1. c. 2. d. 3. Physical dependence refers to changes in the bodily processes that make a drug necessary for minimal functioning. Psychological dependence refers to the mental desire or craving to achieve the effects produced by the drug. 4. depressants, stimulants, opiates, and hallucinogens. **Healthier**

Ways to Alter Consciousness (p. 199) 1. d. 2. narrowed, highly focused attention; increased use of imagination and hallucinations; a passive and receptive attitude; decreased responsiveness to pain; and heightened suggestibility. 3. Hypnosis requires the subject to make a conscious decision to relinquish some personal control of his or her consciousness. fact that organisms are innately predisposed to form associations between certain stimuli and responses.

CHAPTER 6 **Classical Conditioning (p. 208)** 1. b. 2. b. 3. conditioned stimulus, conditioned response. 4. d. 5. c. **Basic Principles of Classical Conditioning (p. 211)** 1. You no longer respond to the sound of the fire alarm because your response has been extinquished, which occurs when the UCS is repeatedly withheld, and the association between the CS and the UCS is broken. 2. d. 3. higher-order conditioning. 4. c. **Operant Conditioning (p. 223)** 1. Operant conditioning occurs when organisms learn by the consequences of their responses, whereas in classical conditioning organisms learn by pairing up associations. Also, operant conditioning is voluntary, whereas classical conditioning is involuntary. 2. d. 3. c. 4. resistant. 5. Possible answers: Punishment is often not immediate or consistent, the recipient of the punishment only learns what not to do, increased aggression, passive aggressiveness, avoidance behavior, modeling, temporary suppression, and learned helplessness. **Cognitive-Social Learning (p. 228)** 1. c. 2. a. 3. latent learning. 4. cognitive maps. 5. b. **The Biology of Learning (p. 231)** 1. evolutionary. 2. Garcia and his colleagues laced freshly killed sheep meat with a chemical that caused nausea and vomiting in coyotes. After the coyotes ate the tainted meat and became ill, they avoided all sheep. 3. Biological preparedness refers to the built-in readiness to form associations between certain stimuli and responses. 4. Instinctive drift. **Using Conditioning and Learning Principles (p. 239)** 1. d. 2. c. 3. c. 4. Video games may increase aggressive tendencies because they are interactive, engrossing, and require the player to identify with the aggressor.

CHAPTER 7 **The Nature of Memory (p. 256)** (a) encoding; (b) retrieval; (c) storage. 2. (a) sensory; (b) short-term memory (STM); (c) long-term memory (LTM). 3. (a) explicit; (b) implicit. 4. Semantic memory stores general knowledge and facts, whereas episodic memory stores memories of events. 5. recognition, recall. **Forgetting (p. 262)** 1. (a) retrieval failure theory; (b) decay theory; (c) motivated forgetting theory. 2. Answers will vary. 3. Using distributed practice, you would space your study time into many learning periods with rest periods in between; using massed practice, you would "cram" all your learning into long, unbroken periods. **Biological Bases of Memory (p. 267)** 1. Repeated stimulation of a synapse can strengthen the synapse by stimulating the dendrites to grow more spines, and the ability of a particular neuron to release its neurotransmitters can be increased or decreased. 2. d. 3. amnesia. 4. d. 5. (a) retrograde amnesia; (b) anterograde amnesia. **Research Highlight—Memory and the Criminal Justice System (p. 269)** 1. d. 2. d. 3. easy. 4. False memories are imagined events constructed in the mind, whereas repressed memories are painful memories that are reportedly forgotten in an effort to avoid the pain of their retrieval. **Using Psychology to Improve Our Memory (p. 274)** 1. Given that the duration of short-term memory is about 30 seconds, to lengthen this time use maintenance rehearsal, which involves continuously repeating the material. To effectively encode memory into long-term memory, use elaborative rehearsal, which involves thinking about the material and relating it to other information that has already been stored. 2. Because we tend to remember information that falls at the beginning or end of a sequence, we should spend extra time studying information in the middle of the chapter. 3. organization. 4. (a) peg-word system; (b) method of loci; (c) peg-word system; (d) acronyms.

CHAPTER 8 **Try This Yourself (p. 281)** The figures in b are not the same. To solve this problem, mentally rotate one of the objects and then compare the rotated image with the other object to see whether they matched or not. The figures in b were more difficult to solve because they required a greater degree of mental rotation. This is also true of real objects in physical space. It takes more time and energy to turn a cup 20 degrees to the right, than to turn it 150 degrees. **Cognitive Building Blocks (p. 283)** 1. Mental images and concepts are both mental representations. However, mental images are of a sensory experience (e.g., remembering a smell), whereas concepts are representations of a group or category that share similar characteristics (e.g., the concept of a bird). 2. c. 3. To learn concepts we create artificial concepts, natural concepts, and hierarchies. 4. natural concept/ prototype. 5. b. **Problem Solving (p. 288)** 1. Preparation, in which we identify the facts, determine which ones are relevant, and define the goal; production, in which we propose possible solutions, or hypotheses; and evaluation, in which we determine whether the solutions meet the goal. 2. b. 3. preparation; 4. d. 5. improperly using the availability heuristic. **Creativity (p. 290)** 1. c. 2. divergent, convergent, divergent. 3. Answers will vary. **Language (p. 297)** 1. (a) phonemes; (b) morphemes; (c) grammar. 2. phonemes; morphemes. 3. overgeneralization. 4. b. 5. a. **What Is Intelligence? (p. 300)** 1. b. 2. Fluid intelligence refers innate abilities, such as reasoning abilities, memory, and speed of information processing. Crystallized intelligence refers to knowledge and skills gained through experience and education. 3. d. 4. Sternberg proposed that intelligence is composed of three aspects, analytic, creative, and practical, and each component is learned versus being innate. He also introduced the term successful intelligence and emphasized the importance of the underlying thought processes versus the end product and the need to test mental abilities in the real world versus in isolation. **How Do We Measure Intelligence (p. 303)** 1. Both tests compute an overall intelligence score, but the Wechsler has a separate verbal and performance score. 2. 90. 3. a. 4. reliability, validity, standardization. **The Intelligence Controversy (p. 310)** 1. d. 2. d. 3. d. 4. Heredity and environment are both important, interacting influences. You cannot separate out which one is more important.

CHAPTER 9 **Studying Development (p. 321)** 1. nature or nurture; continuity or stages; stability or change. 2. (a) cross-sectional; (b) longitudinal. 3. d. 4. c. **Physical Development (p. 331)** 1. The three major stages are the germinal period, the embryonic period, and the fetal period. 2. b. 3. d. 4. c. 5. primary aging. **Cognitive development (p. 339)** 1. c. 2. 1b, 2a, 3d, 4c, 5d. 3. c. 4. Piaget has been criticized for underestimating abilities, genetic, and cultural influences, but his contributions to the understanding of a child's cognitive development offset these criticisms. **Social-Emotional Development (p. 345)** 1. b. 2. Securely attached, avoidant, and anxious-ambivalent; 3. 1a, 2c, 3. Mary shows an avoidant style. Bob demonstrates an anxious/ambivalent style. Rashelle shows a secure attachment style. 4. Permissive parents are either low on control/demandingness and low

on warmth/responsiveness (the permissive-neglectful), or they're low on control/demandingness and high on warmth/responsiveness (the permissive-indulgent). Authoritarian parents are high on control/demandingness, but low on warmth/responsiveness. They value unquestioning obedience and mature responsibility from their children. Authoritative parents are high on control/demandingness, and high on warmth/responsiveness. They're caring and sensitive, but also set firm limits and enforce them.

CHAPTER 10 **Critical Thinking/Active Learning (p. 353—Morality and Academic Cheating) Part II.** Student A—Stage 4: Law and Order Orientation ("Obey laws because they maintain the social order.") Student B—No Stage: This student is disobeying the rules and invoking "the greater good" rationalization to justify her "any means to an end" behavior. Student C—Stage 1: Punishment-obedience Orientation ("Morality is what you get away with.") Student D—Stage 6: Universal Ethics Orientation ("Moral reasoning reflects individual conscience.") Student E—Stage 3: Good Child Orientation ("Obey rules to get approval.") Student F—Stage 5: Social Contract Orientation ("Moral reasoning reflects belief in democratically accepted laws.") NOTE: Here's an example of Stage 2, Instrumental-exchange Orientation ("Obey laws to obtain rewards or favors"): A student doesn't take the exam but waits for the teacher to return and tells her that he has been guarding her office because the final exam was left out for anyone to take. He does so hoping the teacher might give him extra credit for his honesty and diligence. **Moral Development (p. 354)** 1. Preconventional; postconventional; conventional. 2. c. 3. b. 4. Kohlberg's theory may be culturally biased toward individualism versus community and toward interpersonal relationships. His theory may be gender biased because it supposedly favors the male perspective. **Personality Development (p. 358)** 1. c. 2. Thomas and Chess describe three categories of temperament—easy, difficult, and slow-to-warm-up—that seem to correlate with stable personality differences. 3. (a) trust versus mistrust, (b) identity versus role confusion, (c) initiative versus guilt, (d) ego integrity versus despair. 4. initiative versus guilt; ego integrity versus despair. **Meeting the Challenges of Adulthood (p. 366)** 1. Resilient children tend to have good intellectual functioning, relationships with caring adults, and the ability to regulate their attention, emotions, and behavior. 2. activity; disengagement. 3. b. 4. c. 5. Ethnic elderly tend to have greater social support, which may help reduce the losses that accompany aging. **Grief and Death (p. 370)** 1. Grieving is a complicated and personal process, and there is no right or wrong way to grieve. 2. d. 3. d. 4. (a) bargaining, (b) denial, (c) acceptance, (d) anger, (e) depression. 4. d.

CHAPTER 11 **Critical Thinking/Active Learning (p. 385—Gender Differences and Critical Thinking) Part I.** 1. gender role stereotypes; 2. double standard; 3. ". . . men have a *larger* number of friends and express their friendship by shared activities, whereas women have a smaller number of friends and express their friendship by shared communication about self." 4. "men have higher self-esteem, whereas women have lower self-esteem." **Sex and Gender (p. 385)** 1. b) Chromosomal sex, d) gender identity a) gonadal sex, i) gender role c) hormonal sex e) secondary sex characteristics g) external genitals, h) sexual orientation, f) internal accessory organs. 2. Social learning theory emphasizes learning through rewards, punishments, and imitation. Gender-schema theory focuses on the active, thinking processes of the

individual. 3. d. 4. d. **The Study of Human Sexuality (p. 389)** 1. b. 2. Ellis based his research on personal diaries. Kinsey popularized the use of the survey method. Masters and Johnson pioneered the use of direct observation and measurement of bodily responses during sexual activities. 3. Cultural comparisons put sex in a broader perspective and help counteract ethnocentrism. 4. d. **Sexual Behavior (p. 393)** 1. (a) excitement; (b) plateau; (c) orgasm; (d) resolution. 2. Masters and Johnson identified a four-stage sexual response cycle (excitement, plateau, orgasm, and resolution) that acknowledged both similarities and differences between the sexes. However differences are the focus of most research. 3. According to the evolutionary perspective, males engage in more sexual behaviors with more sexual partners because it helps the species survive. The social role perspective suggests this difference reflects a double standard, which subtly encourages male sexuality while discouraging female sexuality. 4. a. 5. d. **Sexual Problems (p. 402)** 1. The parasympathetic branch of the autonomic nervous system dominates during sexual arousal, whereas the sympathetic branch dominates during ejaculation and orgasm. 2. c. 3. Relationship focus, investigation of both biological and psychosocial factors, emphasis on cognitive factors, emphasis on specific behavioral techniques. 4. Remain abstinent or have sex with one mutually faithful, uninfected partner. Do not use IV drugs or have sex with someone who does. If you do use IV drugs, sterilize or don't share equipment. Avoid contact with blood, vaginal secretions, and semen. Avoid anal intercourse. Don't have sex if either you or your partner is impaired by drugs. **Critical Thinking/Active Learning Exercise (p. 402)** Gender role conditioning—A main part of traditional gender conditioning is the belief that women should be the "gatekeepers" for sexuality and men should be the "pursuers." This belief contributes to the myth that male sexuality is overpowering and women are responsible for controlling the situation. Double standard—Female gender role also encourages passivity, and women are not taught how to aggressively defend themselves. People who believe the myth that women cannot be raped against their will generally overlook the fact that the female gender role encourages passivity and women are not taught how to aggressively defend themselves. Media portrayals—Novels and films typically portray a woman resisting her attacker and then melting into passionate responsiveness. This helps perpetuate the myth that women secretly want to be raped and the myth that she might as well "relax and enjoy it." Lack of information—The myth that women cannot be raped against their will overlooks the fact that most men are much stronger and much faster than most women, and a woman's clothing and shoes further hinder her ability to escape. The myth that women cannot rape men ignores the fact that men can have erections despite negative emotions while being raped. Furthermore, an erection is unnecessary, since many rapists (either male or female) often use foreign objects to rape their victims. The myth that all women secretly want to be raped overlooks the fact that if a woman fantasizes about being raped she remains in complete control, whereas in an actual rape she is completely powerless. Also, fantasies contain no threat of physical harm, while rape does. **Tips for Rape Prevention** Sex educators and researchers suggest the following techniques for reducing stranger rape (the rape of a person by an unknown assailant) and acquaintance (or date) rape (committed by someone who is known to the victim) (Crooks & Baur, 2008; King, 2009). To avoid stranger rape: 1. Follow commonsense advice for avoiding all forms of crime: lock your car, park in lighted areas, install dead-bolt locks on your doors, don't open your door to strangers, don't hitchhike, etc. 2. Make yourself as strong as possible. Take a self-defense course, carry a loud whistle with you, and demonstrate self-confidence with your body language. Research shows that rapists tend to select women who appear passive and weak (Richards et al., 1991). 3. During an attack, run away if you can, talk to the rapist as a way to stall, and/or attempt to alert others by screaming ("Help, rape, call the police"). When all else fails, women should actively resist an attack, according to research. Loud shouting, fighting back, and causing a scene may deter an attack. To prevent acquaintance rape: 1. Be careful on first dates—date in groups and in public places; avoid alcohol and other drugs. 2. Be assertive and clear in your communication—say what you want and what you don't want. Accept a partner's refusal. If sexual coercion escalates, match the assailant's behavior with your own form of escalation—begin with firm refusals, get louder, threaten to call the police, begin shouting and use strong physical resistance. Don't be afraid to make a scene!

CHAPTER 12 **Theories and Concepts of Motivation (p. 414)** 1. An instinct is a fixed response pattern that is unlearned and found in almost all members of a species. Homeostasis is the body's tendency to maintain a relatively stable state, such as a constant internal temperature. 2. drive-reduction. 3. (a)ii, (b)iii, (c)v, (e)iv, (f)i. 4. d. 5. d. 6. hierarchy of needs. **Motivation and Behavior (p. 421)** 1. d. 2. anorexia nervosa. 3. d. 4. preference for moderately difficult tasks, preference for clear goals with competent feedback, competitiveness, responsibility, persistence, more accomplishments. **Theories and Concepts of Emotion (p. 429)** 1. (a)iii, (b)i, (c)ii and iv. 2. sympathetic, autonomic. 3. a. 4. a. 5. d. 6. simultaneously. 7. d. **Critical Thinking About Motivation and Behavior (p. 437)** 1. d. 2. c. 3. a. 4. b.

CHAPTER 13 **Trait Theories (p. 447)** 1. b. 2. (a)ii, (b)iii, (c)iv, (d)v, (e)i. 3. e. **Psychoanalytic/Psychodynamic Theories (p. 455)** 1. The conscious is the tip of the iceberg and the highest level of awareness; the preconscious is just below the surface but can readily be brought to awareness; the unconscious is the large base of the iceberg and operates below the level of awareness. 2. b. 3. Freud believed an individual's adult personality reflected his or her resolution of the specific crisis presented in each psychosexual stage (oral, anal, phallic, latency, and genital). 4. (a) Adler, (b) Horney, (c) Jung, (d) Horney. **Humanistic Theories (p. 458)** 1. a. 2. c. 3. self-actualization. 4. Humanistic theories are criticized for their naive assumptions, poor testability and inadequate evidence, and narrowness in merely describing, not explaining, behavior. **Social-Cognitive Theories (p. 460)** 1. how each individual thinks about the world and interprets experiences. 2. a. 3. c. 4. external locus of control, internal locus of control. **Biological Theories (p. 462)** 1. d. 2. Some researchers emphasize the importance of the unshared environment, while others fear that genetic determinism could be misused to "prove" certain ethnic groups are inferior, male dominance is natural, or that social progress is impossible. 3. b. 4. c. **Personality Assessment (p. 469)** 1. (a)ii, (b)i, (c)iii. 2. projective; 3. b. 4. People accept pseudo-personality tests because they offer generalized statements that apply to almost everyone (Barnum effect), they notice and remember events that confirm predictions and ignore the misses (fallacy of positive instances), and they prefer information that maintains a positive self-image (self-serving bias).

CHAPTER 14   Studying Psychological Disorders (p. 483) 1. Statistical infrequency, disability or dysfunction, personal distress, and violation of norms. 2. b. 3. Early versions of the DSM used neurosis to refer to mental disorders related to anxiety. In contrast, psychosis is currently used to describe disorders characterized by loss of contact with reality and extreme mental disruption. Insanity is a legal term for people with a mental disorder that implies a lack of responsibility for behavior and an inability to manage their own affairs. 4. Axis I Clinical Disorders; Axis II Personality Disorders and Mental Retardation; Axis III General Medical Condition; IV Psychosocial and Environmental Problems; V Global Assessment of Functioning. 5. The chief advantages of the DSM include detailed descriptions of symptoms, which in turn allow standardized diagnosis and improved communication among professionals and between professionals and patients. The major disadvantages are possible overreliance on the medical model, unfair labeling, insufficient attention to cultural factors, and for only describing disorders versus offering dimensions or degrees. **Anxiety Disorders (p. 488)** 1. (a) generalized anxiety disorder; (b) panic disorder; (c) phobias; (d) obsessive-compulsive disorder; (e) posttraumatic stress disorder; (f) agoraphobia; (g) specific phobias; (h) social phobias. 2. (a)ii, (b)i, (c)iii, (d)iv. 3. psychological, biological, and sociocultural factors. 4. Learning theorists most often believe anxiety disorders result from classical conditioning. Social learning theorists propose that imitation and modeling are the cause. **Mood Disorders (p. 493)** 1. major depressive disorder and bipolar disorder 2. c. 3. Seligman believes the individual becomes resigned to pain and sadness and feels unable to change, which leads to depression. 4. internal factors and stable, global causes. **Schizophrenia (p. 500)** 1. psychosis. 2. c. 3. a. 4. Three biological causes include a genetic predisposition, malfunctioning neurotransmitters, and brain abnormalities. Two possible psychosocial causes of schizophrenia may be the diathesis-stress model and family and communication problems. **Psychology at Work (p. 504)** 1. c. 2. e. 3. b. 4. a. 5. f. 6. d. **Other Disorders (p. 505)** 1. anxiety. 2. Dissociative identity disorder (DID) refers to a dissociative disorder characterized by the presence of two or more distinct personality systems within the same individual. 3. antisocial personality. 4. d.

CHAPTER 15   Psychoanalysis/Psychodynamic Therapies (p. 513) 1. c. 2. Mary is exhibiting transference, reacting to her therapist as she apparently did to someone earlier in her life. John is exhibiting resistance, arriving late because he fears what his unconscious might reveal. 3. Limited availability, lack of scientific credibility. 4. Modern psychodynamic therapy is briefer, face-to-face, more directive, and emphasizes current problems and conscious processes. **Try This Yourself (p. 520)** All four techniques are shown in this example: empathy ("they scare the hell out of me too"), unconditional positive regard (therapist's acceptance and nonjudgmental attitude and caring about not wanting to do "anything that is upsetting" to the client), genuineness (the therapist's ability to laugh and make a joke at his or her own expense); and active listening (therapist demonstrated genuine interest in what the client was saying). **Cognitive and Humanistic Therapies (p. 520)** 1. a. 2. cognitive restructuring. 3. A = activating event, B = belief system, C = emotional consequence, and D = disputing irrational thoughts. 4. (a) magnification, (b) all-or-nothing thinking. 5. (a) empathy, (b) genuineness, (c) unconditional positive regard. **Critical Thinking/Active Learning (p. 520—Hunting for Good Therapy Films)** 1—resistance; 2—unconditional positive regard; 3—genuineness; 4—A = Will's abuse as a child (**A**ctivating event), B = Will's belief that he is unlovable or to blame for the abuse (irrational **B**elief), C = Will's depression, low EI, and antisocial behavior (**C**onsequences), D = He could **D**ispute B above by echoing Sean's affirming refrain: "It's NOT my fault."; 5—selective perception. **Group, Family, and Marital Therapies (p. 523)** 1. c. 2. Less expense, group support, insight and information, behavior rehearsal. 3. Self-help groups are recommended as a supplement to individual therapy. 4. d. **Behavior Therapies (p. 527)** 1. behavior therapy. 2. c. 3. By rewarding successive approximations of a target behavior, the patient is "shaped" toward more adaptive behaviors. 4. Behavior therapy is criticized for possible lack of generalizability and questionable ethics. **Biomedical Therapies (p. 531)** 1. d. 2. antianxiety, antipsychotic, mood stabilizer, and antidepressant. 3. b. 4. b. 5. c. **Therapy and Critical Thinking (p. 540)** 1. (a) disturbed thoughts; (b) disturbed emotions; (c) disturbed behaviors; (d) interpersonal and life situation difficulties; (e) biomedical disturbances. 2. (a) cognitive therapists, (b) psychoanalysts, (c) biomedical therapists, (d) humanistic therapists, (e) behavior therapists. 3. Naming the problem, qualities of the therapist, establishment of credibility, placing the problem in a familiar framework, applying techniques to bring relief, a special time and place. 4. c. 5. Rates of diagnosis and treatment of mental disorders, stresses of poverty, stresses of aging, violence against women, stresses of multiple roles. 6. d.

CHAPTER 16   Our Thoughts about Others (p. 551) 1. c. 2. When judging the causes of others' behaviors, we tend to overestimate internal personality factors and underestimate external situational factors. 3. (a) cognitive; (b) affective; (c) behavioral. 4. cognitive dissonance. **Our Feelings about Others Pages (p. 559)** 1. Prejudice is an attitude with behavioral tendencies that may or may not be activated. Discrimination is actual negative behavior directed at members of an outgroup. 2. b. 3. c. 4. Romantic love is short lived (6 to 30 months) and largely based on mystery and fantasy, which leads to inevitable disappointment. Companionate love is long lasting and grows stronger with time. **Social Influence (p. 564)** 1. Conformity involves changing behavior in response to real or imagined pressure from others. Obedience involves giving in to a command from others. 2. c. 3. punishment on learning. 4. c. **Group Processes (p. 568)** 1. Guards were abusing their power and prisoners were becoming dehumanized and depressed. 2. deindividuation; 3. b. 4. illusion of invulnerability, belief in the morality of the group, collective rationalizations, stereotypes of the outgroup, self-censorship of doubts and dissenting opinions, illusion of unanimity, and direct pressure on dissenters. 5. b. **Aggression and Altruism (p. 573)** 1. The five major biological factors are instincts, genes, brain and nervous system, substance use and other mental disorders, hormones and neurotransmitters. The three key psychosocial factors are aversive stimuli, culture and learning, and violent media and video games. 2. Introduce incompatible responses, show sympathy, and improve social and communication skills. 3. According to evolutionary theorists, altruism evolved because it favored overall genetic survival. The egoistic model says helping is motivated by anticipated gain for the helper. The empathy–altruism hypothesis suggests helping is activated when the helper feels empathy for the victim. 4. d. **Applying Social Psychology to Social Problems (p. 579)** 1. d. 2. cognitive dissonance. 3. b. 4. Rosa Parks' act of disobedience was an important catalyst for the small but growing civil rights movement and the later repeal of Jim Crow laws in the South.

Abnormal Behavior Patterns of emotion, thought, and action considered pathological (diseased or disordered) for one or more of these reasons: statistical infrequency, disability or dysfunction, personal distress, or violation of norms *Page 475*

Absolute Threshold Minimum amount of a stimulus that an observer can reliably detect *Page 131*

Accommodation Automatic adjustment of the eye, which occurs when muscles change the shape of the lens so that it focuses light on the retina from objects at different distances *Page 138*

Accommodation In Piaget's theory, adjusting old schemas or developing new ones to better fit with new information *Page 332*

Achievement Motivation Desire to excel, especially in competition with others *Page 419*

Acquisition Basic classical conditioning when a neutral stimulus (NS) is consistently paired with an unconditioned stimulus (UCS) so that the NS comes to elicit a conditioned response (CR) *Page 208*

Action Potential Neural impulse, or brief electrical charge that carries information along the axon of a neuron. The action potential is generated when positively charged ions move in and out through channels in the axon's membrane *Page 55*

Activation–Synthesis Hypothesis Hobson's theory that dreams are by-products of random stimulation of brain cells; the brain attempts to combine (or synthesize) this spontaneous activity into coherent patterns, known as dreams *Page 180*

Active Listening Listening with total attention to what another is saying; involves reflecting, paraphrasing, and clarifying what the person says and means *Page 519*

Activity Theory of Aging Successful aging is fostered by a full and active commitment to life *Page 364*

Addiction Broad term describing a compulsion to use a specific drug or engage in a certain activity *Page 186*

Ageism Prejudice or discrimination based on physical age *Page 329*

Agonist Drug Mimics a neurotransmitter's effect *Page 187*

Aggression Any behavior intended to harm someone *Page 568*

AIDS (Acquired Immunodeficiency Syndrome) Human immunodeficiency viruses (HIVs) destroy the immune system's ability to fight disease, leaving the body vulnerable to a variety of opportunistic infections and cancers *Page 400*

Algorithm Logical, step-by-step procedure that, if followed correctly, will eventually solve the problem *Page 284*

Alternate States of Consciousness (ASCs) Mental states other than ordinary waking consciousness, found during sleep, dreaming, psychoactive drug use, hypnosis, and so on *Page 166*

Altruism Actions designed to help others with no obvious benefit to the helper *Page 570*

Alzheimer's [ALTS-high-merz] Disease Progressive mental deterioration characterized by severe memory loss *Page 266*

Amplitude Height of a light or sound wave—pertaining to light, it refers to brightness; for sound, it refers to loudness *Page 136*

Amygdala Limbic system structure linked to the production and regulation of emotions (e.g., aggression and fear) *Page 70, 422*

Androgyny [an-DRAW-juh-nee] Exhibiting both masculine and feminine traits; from the Greek andro, meaning "male," and gyn, meaning "female" *Page 383*

Anorexia Nervosa Eating disorder characterized by a severe loss of weight resulting from self-imposed starvation and an obsessive fear of obesity *Page 417*

Antagonist Drug Blocks normal neurotransmitter functioning *Page 187*

Anterograde Amnesia Inability to form new memories after a brain injury; forward-acting amnesia *Page 266*

Antianxiety Drugs Medications used to produce relaxation, reduce anxiety, and decrease overarousal in the brain *Page 528*

Antidepressant Drugs Medications used to treat depression, some anxiety disorders, and certain eating disorders (such as bulimia) *Page 528*

Antipsychotic Drugs Medications used to diminish or eliminate hallucinations, delusions, withdrawal, and other symptoms of psychosis; also known as neuroleptics or major tranquilizers *Page 528*

Antisocial Personality Disorder Profound disregard for, and violation of, the rights of others *Page 503*

Anxiety Disorder Overwhelming apprehension and fear accompanied by autonomic nervous system (ANS) arousal *Page 484*

Applied Research Research designed to solve practical problems *Page 16*

Approach–Approach Conflict Forced choice between two or more desirable alternatives *Page 95*

Approach–Avoidance Conflict Forced choice between two or more alternatives of which have both desirable and undesirable results *Page 96*

Archetypes [AR-KEH-types] According to Jung, the images and patterns of thoughts, feelings, and behavior that reside in the collective unconscious *Page 452*

Arousal Theory Organisms are motivated to achieve and maintain an optimal level of arousal *Page 410*

Assimilation In Piaget's theory, absorbing new information into existing schemas *Page 332*

Association Areas So-called quiet areas in the cerebral cortex involved in interpreting, integrating, and acting on information processed by other parts of the brain *Page 73*

Attachment Strong affectional bond with special others that endures over time *Page 340*

Attitude Learned predisposition to respond cognitively, affectively, and behaviorally to a particular object *Page 548*

Attribution An explanation for the cause of behaviors or events *Page 546*

Audition Sense of hearing *Page 141*

Automatic Processes Mental activities requiring minimal attention and having little impact on other activities *Page 170*

Autonomic Nervous System (ANS) Subdivision of the peripheral nervous system (PNS) that controls involuntary functions, such as heart rate and digestion. It is further subdivided into the sympathetic nervous system, which arouses, and the parasympathetic nervous system, which calms *Page 63*

Availability Heuristic Judging the likelihood or probability of an event based on how readily available other instances of the event are in memory *Page 287*

Aversion Therapy Pairing an aversive (unpleasant) stimulus with a maladaptive behavior *Page 524*

Avoidance–Avoidance Conflict Forced choice between two or more undesirable alternatives *Page 95*

Axon Long, tubelike structure that conveys impulses away from the neuron's cell body toward other neurons or to muscles or glands *Page 53*

Babbling Vowel/consonant combinations that infants begin to produce at about 4 to 6 months of age *Page 294*

Basic Anxiety According to Horney, the feelings of helplessness and insecurity that adults experience because as children they felt alone and isolated in a hostile environment *Page 453*

Basic Research Research conducted to advance scientific knowledge *Page 16*

Behavior Therapy Group of techniques based on learning principles used to change maladaptive behaviors *Page 524*

Behavioral Genetics Study of the relative effects of heredity and environment on behavior and mental processes *Page 80*

Behaviorial Perspective Emphasizes objective, observable environmental influences on overt behavior *Page 11*

Binge Drinking Occurs when men consume five or more drinks and women consume four or more drinks in about 2 hours *Page 114*

Binocular Cues Visual input from two eyes that allows perception of depth or distance *Page 158*

Biofeedback Involuntary bodily process (such as blood pressure or heart rate) is recorded, and the information is fed back to an organism to increase voluntary control over that bodily function *Page 236*

Biological Preparedness Built-in (innate) readiness to form associations between certain stimuli and responses *Page 230*

Biological Research Scientific studies of the brain and other parts of the nervous system *Page 33*

Biomedical Therapy Using biological interventions (drugs, electroconvulsive therapy, and psychosurgery) to treat psychological disorders *Page 528*

Biopsychosocial Model Unifying theme of modern psychology that incorporates biological, psychological, and social processes *Page 14*

Bipolar Disorder Repeated episodes of mania (unreasonable elation, often with hyperactivity) alternating with depression *Page 489*

Blind Spot Point at which the optic nerve leaves the eye; contains no receptor cells for vision—thus creating a "blind spot" *Page 138*

Borderline Personality Disorder (BPD) Impulsivity and instability in mood, relationships, and self-image *Page 503*

Bottom-Up Processing Information processing beginning "at the bottom" with raw sensory data that are sent "up" to the brain for higher-level analysis; data driven processing that moves from the parts to the whole *Page 129*

Brainstem Area of the brain that houses parts of the hindbrain, midbrain, and forebrain, and helps regulate reflex activities critical for survival (such as heartbeat and respiration) *Page 67*

Bulimia Nervosa Eating disorder involving the consumption of large quantities of food (bingeing), followed by vomiting, extreme exercise, and/or laxative use (purging) *Page 417*

Burnout State of psychological and physical exhaustion resulting from chronic exposure to high levels of stress and little personal control *Page 93*

Cannon–Bard Theory Arousal and our subjective experience of emotion occur simultaneously ("I'm crying and feeling sad at the same time"); in this view, all emotions are physiologically similar *Page 425*

Case Study In-depth study of a single research participant *Page 30*

Cell Body Part of the neuron containing the cell nucleus, as well as other structures that help the neuron carry out its functions; also known as the soma *Page 53*

Central Nervous System (CNS) Brain and spinal cord *Page 60*

Cerebellum [sehr-uh-BELL-um] Hindbrain structure responsible for coordinating fine muscle movement, balance, and some perception and cognition *Page 68*

Cerebral Cortex Thin surface layer on the cerebral hemispheres that regulates most complex behavior, including sensations, motor control, and higher mental processes *Page 71*

Chromosome Threadlike molecule of DNA (deoxyribonucleic acid) that carries genetic information *Page 81*

Chronic Pain Continuous or recurrent pain over a period of six months or longer *Page 115*

Chronic Stress State of ongoing arousal in which the parasympathetic system cannot activate the relaxation response *Page 93*

Chunking Grouping separate pieces of information into a single unit (or chunk) *Page 248*

Circadian [ser-KAY-dee-un] Rhythms Biological changes that occur on a 24-hour cycle (*circa* = "about" and *dies* = "day") *Page 171*

Classical Conditioning Learning that occurs when a previously neutral stimulus (NS) is paired (associated) with an unconditioned stimulus (UCS) to elicit a conditioned response (CR) *Page 205*

Client-Centered Therapy Rogers's therapy emphasizing the client's natural tendency to become healthy and productive; techniques include empathy, unconditional positive regard, genuineness, and active listening *Page 518*

Cochlea [KOK-lee-uh] Three-chambered, snail-shaped structure in the inner ear containing the receptors for hearing *Page 142*

Coding Converting sensory inputs into different sensations *Page 130*

Cognition Mental activities involved in acquiring, storing, retrieving, and using knowledge *Page 278*

Cognitive Behavior Therapy Combines cognitive therapy (changing faulty thinking) with behavior therapy (changing faulty behaviors) *Page 514*

Cognitive Dissonance A feeling of discomfort resulting from a mismatch between an attitude and a behavior or between two competing attitudes *Page 549*

Cognitive Map Mental image of a three-dimensional space that an organism has navigated *Page 224*

Cognitive Perspective Focuses on thinking, perceiving, and information processing *Page 12*

Cognitive Restructuring Process in cognitive therapy to change destructive thoughts or inappropriate interpretations *Page 514*

Cognitive-Social Theory Emphasizes the roles of thinking and social learning in behavior *Page 223*

Cognitive Therapy Therapy that treats problem behaviors and mental processes by focusing on faulty thought processes and beliefs *Page 512*

Collective Unconscious Jung's concept of a reservoir of inherited, universal experiences that all humans share *Page 452*

Collectivistic Cultures Needs and goals of the group are emphasized over the needs and goals of the individual *Page 357*

Comorbidity Co-occurrence of two or more disorders in the same person at the same time, as when a person suffers from both depression and alcoholism *Page 501*

Companionate Love Strong and lasting attraction characterized by trust, caring, tolerance, and friendship *Page 558*

Concept Mental representation of a group or category that shares similar characteristics (e.g., the concept of a river groups together the Nile, the Amazon, and the Mississippi because they share the common characteristic of being a large stream of water that empties into an ocean or lake) *Page 281*

Concrete Operational Stage Piaget's third stage (roughly age 7 to 11); the child can perform mental operations on concrete objects and understand reversibility and conservation, but abstract thinking is not yet present *Page 335*

Conditioned Emotional Response (CER) Classically conditioned emotional response to a previously neutral stimulus (NS) *Page 207*

Conditioned Response (CR) Learned reaction to a conditioned stimulus (CS) that occurs because of previous repeated pairings with an unconditioned stimulus (UCS) *Page 205*

Conditioned Stimulus (CS) Previously neutral stimulus that, through repeated pairings with an unconditioned stimulus (UCS), now causes a conditioned response (CR) *Page 205*

Conditioning Process of learning associations between environmental stimuli and behavioral responses *Page 204*

Conduction Deafness Middle-ear deafness resulting from problems with transferring sound waves to the inner ear *Page 143*

Cones Visual receptor cells, concentrated near the center of the retina, responsible for color vision and fine detail; most sensitive in brightly lit conditions *Page 138*

Confirmation Bias Preferring information that confirms preexisting positions or beliefs, while ignoring or discounting contradictory evidence *Page 286*

Conflict Forced choice between two or more incompatible goals or impulses *Page 95*

Conformity Changing behavior because of real or imagined group pressure *Page 590*

Conscious In Freudian terms, thoughts or motives that a person is currently aware of or is remembering *Page 448*

Consciousness An organism's awareness of its own self and surroundings (Damaslo, 1999) *Page 166*

Conservation Understanding that certain physical characteristics (such as volume) remain unchanged, even when their outward appearance changes *Page 335*

Consolidation Process by which neural changes associated with recent learning become durable and stable *Page 266*

Constructive Process Organizing and shaping of information during processing, storage, and retrieval of memories *Page 244*

Continuous Reinforcement Every correct response is reinforced *Page 215*

Control Group Group that receives no treatment in an experiment *Page 24*

Controlled Processes Mental activities requiring focused attention that generally interfere with other ongoing activities *Page 168*

Conventional Level Kohlberg's second level of moral development, in which moral judgments are based on compliance with the rules and values of society *Page 352*

Convergence Binocular depth cue in which the closer the object, the more the eyes converge, or turn inward *Page 159*

Convergent Thinking Narrowing down a list of alternatives to converge on a single correct answer (e.g., standard academic tests generally require convergent thinking) *Page 289*

Cooing Vowel-like sounds infants produce beginning around 2 to 3 months of age *Page 294*

Corpus Callosum [CORE-pus] [cah-LOH-suhm] Bundle of nerve fibers connecting the brain's left and right hemispheres *Page 75*

Correlation Coefficient Number indicating the strength and direction of the relationship between two variables *Page 32*

Correlational Research Researcher observes or measures (without directly manipulating) two or more naturally occurring variables to find the relationships between them *Page 31*

Creativity Ability to produce valued outcomes in a novel way *Page 288*

Critical Period A period of special sensitivity to specific types of learning that shapes the capacity for future development *Page 317*

Critical Thinking Process of objectively evaluating, comparing, analyzing, and synthesizing information *Page 4*

Cross-Sectional Method Measures individuals of various ages at one point in time and gives information about age differences *Page 318*

Crystallized Intelligence Knowledge and skills gained through experience and education that tend to increase over the life span *Page 298*

Debriefing Informing participants after the research about the purpose of the study, the nature of the anticipated results, and any deceptions used *Page 19*

Defense Mechanisms In Freudian theory, the ego's protective method of reducing anxiety by distorting reality *Page 449*

Deindividuation Reduced self-consciousness, inhibition, and personal responsibility that sometimes occurs in a group, particularly when the members feel anonymous *Page 565*

Delusions Mistaken beliefs based on a misrepresentations of reality *Page 496*

Dendrites Branching neuron structures that receive neural impulses from other neurons and convey impulses toward the cell body *Page 53*

Dependent Variable (DV) Variable that is measured; it is affected by (or dependent on) the independent variable *Page 24*

Depressants Drugs that act on the brain and other parts of the nervous system to decrease bodily processes and overall responsiveness *Page 189*

Depth Perception The ability to perceive three-dimensional space and to accurately judge distance *Page 156*

Descriptive Research Research methods that observe and record behavior and mental processes without producing causal explanations *Page 28*

Developmental Psychology Study of age-related changes in behavior and mental processes from conception to death *Page 316*

Diagnostic and Statistical Manual of Mental Disorders (DSM-IV-TR) Classification system developed by the American Psychiatric Association used to describe abnormal behaviors; the "IV-TR" indicates it is the text revision (TR) of the fourth major revision (IV) *Page 479*

Diathesis-Stress Model Suggests that people inherit a predisposition (or "diathesis") that increases their risk for mental disorders if exposed to certain extremely stressful life experiences *Page 498*

Difference Threshold Minimal difference needed to notice a stimulus change; also called the "just noticeable difference" (JND) *Page 131*

Diffusion of Responsibility The dilution (or diffusion) of personal responsibility for acting by spreading it among all other group members *Page 572*

Discrimination Negative behaviors directed at members of a group *Page 551*

Discriminative Stimulus Cue signals when a specific response will lead to the expected reinforcement *Page 222*

Disengagement Theory of Aging Successful aging is characterized by mutual withdrawal between the elderly and society *Page 364*

Dissociative Disorder Amnesia, fugue, or multiple personalities resulting from a splitting apart of experience from memory or consciousness *Page 502*

Dissociative Identity Disorder (DID) Presence of two or more distinct personality systems in the same individual at different times; previously known as multiple personality disorder *Page 502*

Distress Unpleasant, objectionable stress *Page 92*

Distributed Practice Practice (or study) sessions are interspersed with rest periods *Page 260*

Divergent Thinking Thinking that produces many alternatives from a single starting point; a major element of creativity (e.g., finding as many uses as possible for a paper clip) *Page 289*

Dopamine Hypothesis Theory that overactivity of dopamine neurons may contribute to some forms of schizophrenia *Page 497*

Double-Blind Study Procedure in which both the researcher and the participants are unaware (blind) of who is in the experimental or control group *Page 25*

Double Standard Beliefs, values, and norms that subtly encourage male sexuality and discourage female sexuality *Page 396*

Dream Analysis In psychoanalysis, interpreting the underlying true meaning of dreams to reveal unconscious processes *Page 511*

Drive-Reduction Theory Motivation begins with a physiological need (a lack or deficiency) that elicits a drive toward behavior that will satisfy the original need; once the need is met, a state of balance (homeostasis) is restored and motivation decreases *Page 409*

Drug Abuse Drug taking that causes emotional or physical harm to the drug user or others *Page 186*

Eclectic Approach Combining techniques from various theories to find the most appropriate treatment *Page 533*

Ego In Freud's theory, the rational part of the psyche that deals with reality by controlling the id, while also satisfying the superego; from the Latin term *ego*, meaning "I" *Page 449*

Egocentrism The inability to consider another's point of view, which Piaget considered a hallmark of the preoperational stage *Page 333*

Egoistic Model Helping that's motivated by anticipated gain—later reciprocation, increased self-esteem, or avoidance of distress and guilt *Page 570*

Elaborative Rehearsal Linking new information to previously stored material (also known as deeper levels of processing) *Page 252*

Electroconvulsive Therapy (ECT) Biomedical therapy based on passing electrical current through the brain; used almost exclusively to treat serious depression when drug therapy does not work *Page 530*

Embryonic Period Second stage of prenatal development, which begins after uterine implantation and lasts through the eighth week *Page 323*

Emotion Subjective feeling that includes arousal (heart pounding), cognitions (thoughts, values, and expectations), and expressions (frowns, smiles, and running) *Page 406*

Emotion-Focused Coping Managing one's emotional reactions to a stressful situation *Page 118*

Emotional Intelligence Goleman's term for the ability to know and manage one's emotions, empathize with others, and maintain satisfying relationships *Page 432*

Empathy In Rogerian terms, an insightful awareness and ability to share another's inner experience *Page 518*

Empathy–Altruism Hypothesis Helping because of empathy for someone in need *Page 570*

Encoding Processing information into memory system *Page 244*

Encoding Specificity Principle Retrieval of information is improved when conditions of recovery are similar to the conditions when information was encoded *Page 255*

Endocrine [EN-doh-krin] System Collection of glands located throughout the body that manufacture and secrete hormones into the bloodstream *Page 58*

Endorphins [en-DOR-fins] Chemical substances in the nervous system that are similar in structure and action to opiates, involved in pain control, pleasure, and memory *Page 57*

Episodic Memory Subsystem of explicit/declarative memory that stores memories of personally experienced events; a mental diary of a person's life *Page 251*

Ethnocentrism Believing that one's culture is typical of all cultures; also, viewing one's own ethnic group (or culture) as central and "correct," and judging others according to this standard *Page 25*

Eustress Pleasant, desirable stress *Page 92*

Evolutionary/Circadian Theory Sleep evolved to conserve energy and as protection from predators; also serves as part of the circadian cycle *Page 178*

Evolutionary Perspective Focuses on natural selection, adaptation, and evolution of behavior and mental processes *Page 12*

Evolutionary Psychology Branch of psychology that studies how evolutionary processes, like natural selection and genetic mutations, affect behavior and mental processes *Page 81*

Excitement Phase First stage of the sexual response cycle, characterized by increasing levels of arousal and increased engorgement of the genitals *Page 390*

Experiment Carefully controlled scientific procedure that involves manipulation of variables to determine cause and effect *Page 21*

Experimental Group Group that receives a treatment in an experiment *Page 24*

Experimenter Bias Occurs when researcher influences research results in the expected direction *Page 22*

Explicit (Declarative) Memory Subsystem within long-term memory that consciously stores facts, information, and personal life experiences *Page 251*

External Locus of Control Believing that chance or outside forces beyond one's control determine one's fate *Page 120*

Extinction Repeatedly presenting the CS without the UCS, which gradually weakens the CR *Page 209*

Extrasensory Perception (ESP) Perceptual, or "psychic," abilities that supposedly go beyond the known senses (e.g., telepathy, clairvoyance, precognition, and psychokinesis) *Page 162*

Extrinsic Motivation Motivation based on obvious external rewards or threats of punishment *Page 430*

Facial-Feedback Hypothesis Movements of the facial muscles produce and/or intensify our subjective experience of emotions *Page 444*

Factor Analysis Statistical procedure for determining the most basic units or factors in a large array of data *Page 443*

Family Therapy Treatment to change maladaptive interaction patterns within a family *Page 522*

Farsightedness (Hyperopia) Visual acuity problem resulting from the cornea and lens focusing an image behind the retina *Page 138*

Feature Detectors Specialized neurons that respond only to certain sensory information *Page 151*

Fetal Alcohol Syndrome (FAS) Combination of birth defects, including organ deformities and mental, motor, and/or growth retardation, that results from maternal alcohol abuse *Page 324*

Fetal Period Third, and final, stage of prenatal development (eight weeks to birth), which is characterized by rapid weight gain in the fetus and the fine detailing of body organs and systems *Page 323*

Five-Factor Model (FFM) Trait theory of personality that includes openness, conscientiousness, extroversion, agreeableness, and neuroticism *Page 443*

Fixed Interval (FI) Schedule Reinforcement occurs after a predetermined time has elapsed; the interval (time) is fixed *Page 215*

Fixed Ratio (FR) Schedule Reinforcement occurs after a predetermined set of responses; the ratio (number or amount) is fixed *Page 215*

Fluid Intelligence Aspects of innate intelligence, including reasoning abilities, memory, and speed of information processing, that are relatively independent of education and tend to decline as people age *Page 298*

Foot-in-the-Door Technique A first, small request is used as a setup for later, larger requests *Page 578*

Forebrain Collection of upper-level brain structures including the thalamus, hypothalamus, limbic system, and cerebral cortex *Page 68*

Formal Operational Stage Piaget's fourth stage (around age 11 and beyond), characterized by abstract and hypothetical thinking *Page 335*

Fovea Tiny pit in the center of the retina filled with cones and responsible for sharp vision *Page 138*

Free Association In psychoanalysis, reporting whatever comes to mind without monitoring its contents *Page 511*

Frequency How often a light or sound wave cycles (i.e., the number of complete wavelengths that pass a point in a given time) *Page 136*

Frequency Theory Explains that pitch perception occurs when nerve impulses sent to the brain match the frequency of the sound wave *Page 143*

Frontal Lobes Two lobes at the front of the brain governing motor control, speech production, and higher functions, such as thinking, personality, emotion, and memory *Page 72*

Frustration Unpleasant tension, anxiety, and heightened sympathetic activity resulting from a blocked goal *Page 95*

Frustration–Aggression Hypothesis Blocking of a desired goal (frustration) creates anger that may lead to aggression *Page 569*

Functional Fixedness Tendency to think of an object functioning only in its usual or customary way *Page 286*

Fundamental Attribution Error (FAE) Misjudging the causes of others' behavior as due to internal (dispositional) causes rather than external (situational) ones *Page 547*

Gate-Control Theory Theory that pain sensations are processed and altered by mechanisms within the spinal cord *Page 133*

Gender Psychological and sociocultural meanings added to biological maleness or femaleness *Page 376*

Gender Identity Self-identification as either a man or a woman *Page 378*

Gender Role Societal expectations for "appropriate" male and female behavior *Page 376*

Gender Schema Theory Gender roles are acquired through social learning and active cognitive processing *Page 378*

Gene Segment of DNA (deoxyribonucleic acid) that occupies a specific place on a particular chromosome and carries the code for hereditary transmission *Page 81*

General Adaptation Syndrome (GAS) Selye's three-stage (alarm, resistance, exhaustion) reaction to chronic stress *Page 102*

Generalized Anxiety Disorder Persistent, uncontrollable, and free-floating nonspecified anxiety *Page 484*

Genuineness In Rogerian terms, authenticity or congruence; the awareness of one's true inner thoughts and feelings and being able to share them honestly with others *Page 519*

Germinal Period First stage of prenatal development, which begins with conception and ends with implantation in the uterus (the first two weeks) *Page 323*

Glial Cells Cells that provide structural, nutritional, and other support for the neurons, as well as communication within the nervous system; also called glia or neuroglia *Page 52*

Grammar System of rules (syntax and semantics) used to create language and communication *Page 292*

Group Polarization Group's movement toward either riskier or more conservative behavior, depending on the members' initial dominant tendency *Page 566*

Group Therapy A number of people meet together to work toward therapeutic goals *Page 521*

Groupthink Faulty decision making that occurs when a highly cohesive group strives for agreement and avoids inconsistent information *Page 566*

Gustation Sense of taste *Page 146*

Habituation Tendency of the brain to ignore environmental factors that remain constant *Page 152*

Hallucinations Imaginary sensory perceptions that occur without external stimuli *Page 495*

Hallucinogens [hal-LOO-sin-oh-jenz] Drugs that produce sensory or perceptual distortions called hallucinations *Page 192*

Hardiness Resilient personality with a strong commitment to personal goals, control over life, and viewing change as a challenge rather than a threat *Page 108*

Hassles Small problems of daily living that accumulate and sometimes become a major source of stress *Page 94*

Health Psychology Studies how biological, psychological, and social factors affect health and illness *Page 111*

Heritability Measure of the degree to which a characteristic is related to genetic, inherited factors versus the environment *Page 82*

Heuristics Simple rule or shortcut for problem solving that does not guarantee a solution but does narrow the alternatives *Page 284*

Hierarchy of Needs Maslow's theory that lower motives (such as physiological and safety needs) must be met before advancing to higher needs (such as belonging and selfactualization) *Page 412*

Higher-Order Conditioning Neutral stimulus (NS) becomes a conditioned stimulus (CS) through repeated pairings with a previously conditioned stimulus (CS) *Page 210*

Hindbrain Collection of brain structures including the medulla, cerebellum, and pons *Page 68*

Hippocampus Part of the limbic system involved in forming and retrieving memories *Page 69*

HIV Positive Being infected by the human immunodeficiency virus (HIV) *Page 400*

Homeostasis Body's tendency to maintain a relatively stable state, such as a constant internal temperature *Page 101, 409*

Hormones Chemicals manufactured by endocrine glands and circulated in the bloodstream to produce bodily changes or maintain normal bodily functions *Page 58*

Glossary

HPA Axis Body's delayed stress response, involving the hypothalamus, pituitary, and adrenal cortex; also called the Hypothalamic-Pituitary-Adrenocortical (HPA) system *Page 101*

Humanist Perspective Emphasizes free will, self-actualization, and human nature as naturally positive and growth-seeking *Page 11*

Humanistic Therapy Therapy that focuses on removing obstacles that block personal growth and potential *Page 518*

Hypnosis Trancelike state of heightened suggestibility, deep relaxation, and intense focus *Page 196*

Hypothalamus [hi-poh-THAL-uh-muss] Small brain structure beneath the thalamus that helps govern drives (hunger, thirst, sex, and aggression), and hormones *Page 69*

Hypothesis Specific testable prediction about how one factor or variable is related to another *Page 17*

Id According to Freud, the source of instinctual energy, which works on the pleasure principle and is concerned with immediate gratification *Page 449*

Illusion False or misleading perceptions *Page 150*

Implicit Bias Hidden attitude activated by the mere encounter of an attitude object; may serve as a guide to behaviors independent of a person's awareness and control *Page 575*

Implicit (Nondeclarative) Memory Subsystem within long-term memory consisting of unconscious procedural skills and simple classically conditioned responses *Page 252*

Imprinting Innate form of learning within a critical period that involves attachment to the first large moving object seen *Page 340*

Incentive Theory Motivation results from external stimuli that "pull" the organism in certain directions *Page 412*

Independent Variable (IV) Variable that is manipulated to determine its causal effect on the dependent variable *Page 24*

Individualistic Cultures Needs and goals of the individual are emphasized over the needs and goals of the group *Page 357*

Inferiority Complex Adler's idea that feelings of inferiority develop from early childhood experiences of helplessness and incompetence *Page 452*

Informational Social Influence Conforming because of a need for information and direction *Page 560*

Informed Consent Participant's agreement to take part in a study after being told what to expect *Page 18*

Ingroup Favoritism Viewing members of the ingroup more positively than members of an outgroup *Page 552*

Inner Ear Cochlea, semicircular canals and vestibular sacs, which generate neural signals sent to the brain *Page 142*

Insanity Legal term applied when people cannot be held responsible for their actions, or are judged incompetent to manage their own affairs, because of mental illness *Page 480*

Insight Sudden understanding of a problem that implies the solution *Page 224*

Insomnia Persistent problems in falling asleep, staying asleep, or awakening too early *Page 112*

Instinct Fixed response pattern that is unlearned and found in almost all members of a species *Page 409*

Instinct theory Emphasizes inborn, genetic factors in motivation *Page 408*

Instinctive Drift Conditioned responses shift (or drift) back toward innate response patterns *Page 230*

Instinct Fixed response pattern that unlearned and found in almost all members of a species *Page 409*

Intelligence Global capacity to think rationally, act purposefully, and deal effectively with the environment *Page 297*

Internal Locus of Control Believing that one controls one's own fate *Page 120*

Interpersonal Attraction Positive feelings toward another *Page 553*

Interpretation A psychoanalyst's explanation of a patient's free associations, dreams, resistance, and transference; more generally, any statement by a therapist that presents a patient's problem in a new way *Page 511*

Intrinsic Motivation Motivation resulting from personal enjoyment of a task or activity *Page 430*

James–Lange Theory Our subjective experience of emotion follows our bodily arousal ("I feel sad because I'm crying"); in this view, each emotion is physiologically distinct *Page 425*

Job Stress Work-related stress that includes role conflict and burnout *Page 93*

Just-World Phenomenon Tendency to believe that people generally get what they deserve *Page 547*

Kinesthesia Sensory system for body posture, orientation, and bodily movement *Page 149*

Language Form of communication using sounds and symbols combined according to specified rules *Page 291*

Language Acquisition Device (LAD) According to Chomsky, an innate mechanism that enables a child to analyze language and extract the basic rules of grammar *Page 293*

Latent Content According to Freud, the true, unconscious meaning of a dream *Page 179*

Latent Learning Hidden learning that exists without behavioral signs *Page 224*

Law of Effect Thorndike's rule that the probability of an action being repeated is strengthened when it is followed by a pleasant or satisfying consequence *Page 212*

Learned Helplessness Seligman's term for a state of helplessness or resignation in which human or nonhuman animals learn that escape from something painful is impossible and depression results *Page 490*

Learning Relatively permanent change in behavior or mental processes due to experience *Page 208*

Levels of Processing Degree or depth of mental processing occurring when material is initially encountered; determines how well material is later remembered *Page 252*

Limbic System Interconnected group of forebrain structures involved with emotions, drives, and memory *Page 69*

Lobotomy Outmoded medical procedure for mental disorders, which involved cutting nerve pathways between the frontal lobes and the thalamus and hypothalamus *Page 530*

Longitudinal Method Measures a single individual or group of individuals over an extended period and gives information about age changes *Page 318*

Long-Term Memory (LTM) Third stage of memory that stores information for long periods of time; its capacity is virtually limitless, and its duration is relatively permanent *Page 249*

Long-Term Potentiation (LTP) Longlasting increase in neural excitability, which may be a biological mechanism for learning and memory *Page 263*

Maintenance Rehearsal Repeating information over and over to maintain it in shortterm memory (STM) *Page 248*

Major Depressive Disorder Longlasting depressed mood that interferes with the ability to function, feel pleasure, or maintain interest in life *Page 512*

Manifest Content According to Freud, the surface content of a dream, which contains dream symbols that distort and disguise the dream's true meaning *Page 179*

Massed Practice Time spent learning is grouped (or massed) into long, unbroken intervals (also known as cramming) *Page 260*

Maturation Development governed by automatic, genetically predetermined signals *Page 317*

Medical Model Perspective that assumes diseases (including mental illness) have physical causes that can be diagnosed, treated, and possibly cured *Page 478*

Meditation Group of techniques designed to refocus attention, block out all distractions, and produce an alternate state of consciousness *Page 196*

Medulla [muh-DUL-uh] Hindbrain structure responsible for automatic body functions such as breathing and heartbeat *Page 68*

Memory Internal record or representation of some prior event or experience *Page 244*

Mental Image Mental representation of a previously stored sensory experience, including visual, auditory, olfactory, tactile, motor, or gustatory imagery (e.g., visualizing a train and hearing its horn) *Page 281*

Mental Set Persisting in using problem solving strategies that have worked in the past rather than trying new ones *Page 286*

Meta-Analysis Statistical procedure for combining and analyzing data from many studies *Page 16*

Midbrain Collection of brain structures in the middle of the brain responsible for coordinating movement patterns, sleep, and arousal *Page 68*

Middle Ear Hammer, anvil, and stirrup, which concentrate eardrum vibrations onto the cochlea's oval window *Page 142*

Minnesota Multiphasic Personality Inventory (MMPI) The most widely researched and clinically used self-report personality test (MMPI-2 is the revised version) *Page 464*

Mirror Neurons Brain cells that fire both when performing specific actions and when observing specific actions or emotions of another. This "mirroring" may explain empathy, imitation, language, and the emotional deficits of some mental disorders *Page 423*

Misattribution of Arousal Different emotions produce similar feelings of arousal, which leads to mistaken inferences about these emotions and the source of arousal *Page 27*

Misinformation Effect Distortion of a memory by misleading post-event information *Page 260*

Mnemonic [nih-MON-ik] Device Memory- improvement technique based on encoding items in a special way *Page 272*

Modeling Therapy Watching and imitating models that demonstrate desirable behaviors *Page 527*

Monocular Cues Visual input from a single eye alone that contributes to perception of depth or distance *Page 158*

Mood Disorder Extreme disturbances in emotional states *Page 488*

Mood Stabilizer Drugs Medications used to treat the combination of manic episodes and depression characteristic of bipolar disorders *Page 528*

Morality Principle The principle on which the superego may operate, which results in feelings of guilt if its rules are violated *Page 449*

Morpheme [MOR-feem] Smallest meaningful unit of language, formed from a combination of phonemes *Page 292*

Motivation Set of factors that activate, direct, and maintain behavior, usually toward a goal *Page 406*

Myelin [MY-uh-lin] Sheath Layer of fatty insulation wrapped around the axon of some neurons, which increases the rate at which nerve impulses travel along the axon *Page 53*

Narcolepsy [NAR-co-lep-see] Sudden and irresistible onsets of sleep during normal waking hours. (*narco* = "numbness" and *lepsy* = "seizure") *Page 183*

Natural Selection Driving mechanism behind evolution, that allows individuals with genetically influenced traits that are adaptive in a particular environment to stay alive and produce offspring *Page 84*

Naturalistic Observation Observation and recording behavior and mental processes in the participant's natural state or habitat *Page 29*

Nature–Nurture Controversy Ongoing dispute over the relative contributions of nature (heredity) and nurture (environment) *Page 6*

Nearsightedness (Myopia) Visual acuity problem resulting from cornea and lens focusing an image in front of the retina *Page 138*

Need Compatibility Attraction based on sharing similar needs *Page 557*

Need Complementarity Attraction toward those with qualities we admire but personally lack *Page 557*

Negative Punishment Taking away (or removing) a stimulus that weakens a response and makes it less likely to recur *Page 217*

Negative Reinforcement Taking away (or removing) a stimulus, which strengthens a response and makes it more likely to recur *Page 214*

Nerve Deafness Inner-ear deafness resulting from damage to the cochlea, hair cells, or auditory nerve *Page 143*

Neurogenesis [nue-roe-JEN-uh-sis] Process by which new neurons are generated *Page 61*

Neuron Cell of the nervous system responsible for receiving and transmitting electrochemical information *Page 52*

Neuroplasticity Brain's ability to reorganize and change its structure and function throughout the life span *Page 61*

Neuroscience Interdisciplinary field studying how biological processes relate to behavioral and mental processes *Page 50*

Neuroscience/Biopsychology Perspective Emphasizes genetics and other biological processes in the brain and other parts of the nervous system *Page 12*

Neurosis Outmoded term for disorders characterized by unrealistic anxiety and other associated problems; less severe disruptions than in psychosis *Page 480*

Neurotransmitters Chemicals released by neurons that travel across the synaptic gap *Page 56*

Neutral Stimulus (NS) A stimulus that, before conditioning, does not naturally bring about the response of interest *Page 205*

Night Terrors Abrupt awakenings from NREM (non-rapid-eye-movement) sleep accompanied by intense physiological arousal and feelings of panic *Page 184*

Nightmares Anxiety-arousing dreams generally occurring near the end of the sleep cycle, during REM sleep *Page 184*

Non-Rapid-Eye-Movement (NREM) Sleep Stages 1 to 4 of sleep with Stage 1 as the lightest level and Stage 4 as the deepest level *Page 176*

Norm Cultural rule of behavior prescribing what is acceptable in a given situation *Page 591*

Normative Social Influence Conforming to group pressure out of a need for approval and acceptance *Page 560*

Obedience Following direct commands, usually from an authority figure *Page 561*

Object Permanence Piagetian term for an infant's understanding that objects (or people) continue to exist even when they cannot be seen, heard, or touched directly *Page 333*

Observational Learning Learning new behavior or information by watching and imitating others (also known as social learning or modeling) *Page 225*

Obsessive-Compulsive Disorder (OCD) Intrusive, repetitive fearful thoughts (obsessions), urges to perform repetitive, ritualistic behaviors (compulsions), or both *Page 485*

Occipital [ahk-SIP-ih-tal] Lobes Two lobes at the back of the brain responsible for vision and visual perception *Page 73*

Oedipus [ED-uh-puss] Complex Period of conflict during the phallic stage when children are supposedly attracted to the opposite-sex parent and hostile toward the same-sex parent *Page 451*

Olfaction Sense of smell *Page 146*

Operant Conditioning Learning through the consequences of voluntary behavior; also known as instrumental or Skinnerian conditioning *Page 212*

Operational Definition Precise description of how the variables in a study will be observed and measured (For example, drug abuse might be operationally defined as "the number of missed work days due to excessive use of an addictive substance.") *Page 17*

Opiates Drugs derived from opium that numb the senses and relieve pain (The word *opium* comes from the Greek word meaning "juice.") *Page 192*

Opponent-Process Theory Hering's theory that color perception is based on three systems of color opposites—blue–yellow, red–green, and black–white *Page 140*

Orgasm Phase Third stage of the sexual response cycle, when pleasurable sensations peak and orgasm occurs *Page 390*

Outer Ear Pinna, auditory canal, and eardrum, which funnel sound waves to the middle ear *Page 142*

Outgroup Homogeneity Effect Judging members of an outgroup as more alike and less diverse than members of the ingroup *Page 552*

Overextension Overly broad use of a word to include objects that do not fit the word's meaning (e.g., calling all men "Daddy") *Page 294*

Overgeneralize Applying the basic rules of grammar even to cases that are exceptions to the rule (e.g., saying "mans" instead of "men") *Page 294*

Panic Disorder Sudden and inexplicable panic attacks; symptoms include difficulty breathing, heart palpitations, dizziness, trembling, terror, and feelings of impending doom *Page 484*

Parallel Distributed Processing (PDP) Memory results from weblike connections among interacting processing units operating simultaneously, rather than sequentially (also known as the connectionist model) *Page 246*

Parasympathetic Nervous System Subdivision of the autonomic nervous system (ANS) responsible for calming the body and conserving energy *Page 63*

Parietal [puh-RYE-uh-tul] Lobes Two lobes at the top of the brain where bodily sensations are received and interpreted *Page 73*

Partial (Intermittent) Reinforcement Some, but not all, correct responses are reinforced *Page 215*

Participant Bias Occurs when experimental conditions influence the participant's behavior or mental proccesses *Page 26*

Perception Process of selecting, organizing, and interpreting sensory information into meaningful patterns *Page 128*

Perceptual Constancy Tendency for the environment to be perceived as remaining the same even with changes in sensory input *Page 156*

Perceptual Set Readiness to perceive in a particular manner based on expectations *Page 161*

Performance Anxiety Fear of being judged in connection with sexual activity *Page 395*

Peripheral Nervous System (PNS) All nerves and neurons connecting the central nervous system to the rest of the body *Page 60*

Personality Unique and relatively stable pattern of thoughts, feelings, and actions *Page 440*

Personality Disorders Inflexible, maladaptive personality traits that cause significant impairment of social and occupational functioning *Page 503*

Pheromones   [FARE-oh-mones] Airborne chemicals that affect behavior, including recognition of family members, aggression, territorial marking, and sexual mating *Page 146*

Phobia Intense, irrational fear and avoidance of a specific object or situation *Page 485*

Phoneme [FOE-neem] Smallest basic unit of speech or sound *Page 292*

Physical Dependence Changes in bodily processes that make a drug necessary for minimal functioning *Page 186*

Place Theory Explains that pitch perception is linked to the particular spot on the cochlea's basilar membrane that is most stimulated *Page 143*

Placebo (pluh-SEE-boh) Inactive substance or fake treatment used as a control technique, usually in drug research, or given by a medical practitioner to a patient *Page 25*

Plateau Phase Second stage of the sexual response cycle, characterized by a leveling off in a state of high arousal *Page 390*

Pleasure Principle In Freud's theory, the principle on which the id operates—seeking immediate pleasure *Page 449*

Polygraph Instrument that measures sympathetic arousal (heart rate, respiration rate, blood pressure, and skin conductivity) to detect emotional arousal, which in turn supposedly reflects lying versus truthfulness *Page 432*

Pons Hindbrain structure involved in respiration, movement, waking, sleep, and dreaming *Page 68*

Positive Psychology Scientific study of optimal human functioning, emphasizing positive emotions, positive traits, and positive institutions *Page 12*

Positive Punishment Adding (or presenting) a stimulus that weakens a response and makes it less likely to recur *Page 217*

Positive Reinforcement Adding (or presenting) a stimulus, which strengthens a response and makes it more likely to recur *Page 214*

Postconventional Level Kohlberg's highest level of moral development, in which individuals develop personal standards for right and wrong, and define morality in terms of abstract principles and values that apply to all situations and societies *Page 352*

Posttraumatic Stress Disorder (PTSD) Anxiety disorder following exposure to a life-threatening or other extreme event that evoked great horror or helplessness; characterized by flashbacks, nightmares, and impaired functioning *Page 109*

Preconscious Freud's term for thoughts, motives, or memories that can voluntarily be brought to mind *Page 448*

Preconventional Level Kohlberg's first level of moral development, in which morality is based on rewards, punishment, and exchange of favors *Page 352*

Prejudice A learned, generally negative, attitude toward members of a group; it includes thoughts (stereotypes), feelings, and behavioral tendencies (possible discrimination) *Page 551*

Premack Principle Using a naturally occurring high-frequency response to reinforce and increase low-frequency responses *Page 214*

Preoperational Stage Piaget's second stage (roughly age 2 to 7), characterized by the ability to employ significant language and to think symbolically, but the child lacks operations (reversible mental processes), and thinking is egocentric and animistic *Page 333*

Primary Appraisal Deciding if a situation is harmful, threatening, or challenging *Page 116*

Primary Reinforcers Stimuli that increase the probability of a response because they satisfy an unlearned biological need (e.g., food, water, and sex) *Page 218*

Priming Prior exposure to a stimulus (or prime) facilitates or inhibits the processing of new information, even when one has no conscious memory of the initial learning and storage *Page 255*

Proactive Interference Old information interferes with remembering new information; forward-acting interference *Page 259*

Problem-Solving Coping Dealing directly with a stressor to decrease or eliminate it *Page 118*

Projective Tests Psychological tests using ambiguous stimuli, such as inkblots or drawings, which allow the test taker to project his or her unconscious onto the test material *Page 465*

Prototype A representation of the "best" or most typical example of a category (e.g., baseball is a prototype of the concept of sports) *Page 282*

Proximity Attraction based on geographic closeness *Page 556*

Psychiatry Branch of medicine dealing with the diagnosis, treatment, and prevention of mental disorders *Page 478*

Psychoactive Drugs Chemicals that change conscious awareness, mood, and/or perception *Page 185*

Psychoanalysis Freudian therapy designed to bring unconscious conflicts, which usually date back to early childhood experiences, into consciousness; also Freud's theoretical school of thought emphasizing *Page 510*

Psychoanalytic/Psychodynamic Perspective Focuses on unconscious processes and unresolved past conflicts *Page 10*

Psychodynamic Therapy A briefer, more directive, and more modern form of psychoanalysis that focuses on conscious processes and current problems *Page 512*

Psychological Dependence Desire or craving to achieve a drug's effect *Page 186*

Psychology Scientific study of behavior and mental processes *Page 4*

Psychoneuroimmunology [sye-koh-NEW-roh-IM-you-NOLL-oh-gee] Interdisciplinary field that studies the effects of psychological and other factors on the immune system *Page 102*

Psychopharmacology The study of drug effects on mind and behavior *Page 528*

Psychophysics Studies the link between the physical characteristics of stimuli and our sensory experience of them *Page 131*

Psychosexual Stages In Freudian theory, five developmental periods (oral, anal, phallic, latency, and genital) during which particular kinds of pleasures must be gratified if personality development is to proceed normally *Page 450*

Psychosis Serious mental disorders characterized by extreme mental disruption and loss of contact with reality *Page 480*

Psychosocial Stages Erikson's theory that individuals pass through eight developmental stages, each involving a crisis that must be successfully resolved *Page 355*

Psychosurgery Operative procedures on the brain designed to relieve severe mental symptoms that have not responded to other forms of treatment *Page 530*

Psychotherapy Techniques employed to improve psychological functioning and promote adjustment to life *Page 510*

Puberty Biological changes during adolescence that lead to an adult-sized body and sexual maturity *Page 327*

Punishment Weakens a response and makes it less likely to recur *Page 212*

Random Assignment Using chance methods to assign participants to experimental or control conditions, thus minimizing the possibility of biases or preexisting differences in the groups *Page 26*

Rapid-Eye-Movement (REM) Sleep Stage of sleep marked by rapid eye movements, high-frequency brain waves, paralysis of large muscles, and dreaming *Page 176*

Rational-Emotive Behavior Therapy (REBT) Ellis's cognitive therapy to eliminate emotional problems through rational examination of irrational beliefs *Page 514*

Reality Principle According to Freud, the principle on which the conscious ego operates as it tries to meet the demands of the id and superego and the realities of the environment *Page 449*

Recall Retrieving a memory using a general cue *Page 254*

Reciprocal Determinism Bandura's belief that cognitions, behaviors, and the environment interact to produce personality *Page 459*

Recognition Retrieving a memory using a specific cue *Page 254*

Reference Groups People we conform to, or go along with, because we like and admire them and want to be like them *Page 560*

Reflex Innate, automatic response to a stimulus (e.g., knee-jerk reflex) *Page 62*

Refractory Period Phase following orgasm, during which further orgasm is considered physiologically impossible for men *Page 390*

Reinforcement Strengthens a response and makes it more likely to recur *Page 212*

Relearning Learning material a second time, which usually takes less time than original learning (also called the savings method) *Page 257*

Reliability Measure of the consistency and reproducibility of test scores when the test is readministered *Page 302, 467*

Repair/Restoration Theory Sleep serves a recuperative function, allowing organisms to repair or replenish key factors *Page 178*

Repetitive Transcranial Magnetic Stimulation (rTMS) Biomedical treatment involving repeated pulses of magnetic energy being passed through the brain *Page 531*

Representativeness Heuristic Estimating the probability of something based on how well the circumstances match (or represent) our previous prototype *Page 287*

Repression Freud's first and most basic defense mechanism, which blocks unacceptable impulses from coming into awareness *Page 450*

Resiliency The ability to adapt effectively in the face of threats *Page 363*

Resistance In psychoanalysis, the person's inability or unwillingness to discuss or reveal certain memories, thoughts, motives, or experiences *Page 511*

Resolution Phase Final stage of the sexual response cycle, when the body returns to its unaroused state *Page 390*

Reticular Formation (RF) Diffuse set of neurons that screens incoming information and controls arousal *Page 68*

Retina Light-sensitive inner surface of the back of the eye, which contains the receptor cells for vision (rods and cones) *Page 138*

Retinal Disparity Binocular cue to distance in which the separation of the eyes causes different images to fall on each retina *Page 159*

Retrieval Recovering information from memory storage *Page 244*

Retrieval Cue A clue or prompt that helps stimulate recall or retrieval of a stored piece of information from long-term memory *Page 254*

Retroactive Interference New information interferes with remembering old information; backward-acting interference *Page 259*

Retrograde Amnesia Loss of memory for events before a brain injury; backward-acting amnesia *Page 266*

Rods Visual receptor cells in the retina that detect shades of gray and are responsible for peripheral vision; most important in dim light and night *Page 139*

Role Conflict Forced choice between two or more different and incompatible role demands *Page 93*

Romantic Love Intense feeling of attraction to another within an erotic context and with future expectations *Page 557*

Rorschach [ROAR-shock] Inkblot Test A projective test that presents a set of 10 cards with symmetrical abstract patterns, known as inkblots, and asks respondents to describe what they "see" in the image; their response is thought to be a projection of unconscious processes *Page 465*

Saliency Bias Focusing on the most noticeable (salient) factors when explaining the causes of behavior *Page 547*

SAM System Body's initial, rapid-acting stress response, involving the sympathetic nervous system and the adrenal medulla; also called the Sympatho-Adreno-Medullary (SAM) system *Page 101*

Sample Bias Occurs when research participants are not representative of the larger population *Page 25*

Savant Syndrome Condition in which a person with mental retardation exhibits exceptional skill or brilliance in some limited field *Page 304*

Schachter's Two-Factor Theory Physical arousal and cognitive labeling (or interpretation) of that arousal produce our subjective experience of emotion *Page 427*

Schema Cognitive structures or patterns consisting of a number of organized ideas that grow and differentiate with experience *Page 332*

Schizophrenia [skit-so-FREE-nee-uh] Group of severe disorders involving major disturbances in perception, language, thought, emotion, and behavior *Page 493*

Secondary Appraisal Assessing one's resources and choosing a coping method *Page 116*

Secondary Reinforcers Stimuli that increase the probability of a response because of their learned value (e.g., money and material possessions) *Page 213*

Selective Attention Filtering out and attending only to important sensory messages *Page 151*

Self-Actualization Maslow's term for the inborn drive to develop all one's talents and capabilities *Page 457*

Self-Concept Rogers's term for all the information and beliefs individuals have about their own nature, qualities, and behavior *Page 455*

Self-Efficacy Bandura's term for a person's learned expectation of success *Page 459*

Self-Help Group Leaderless or non-professionally guided groups in which members assist each other with a specific problem, as in Alcoholics Anonymous *Page 521*

Self-Serving Bias Taking credit for our successes and externalizing our failures *Page 547*

Self-Talk Internal dialogue; the things people say to themselves when they interpret events *Page 514*

Semantic Memory Subsystem of explicit/declarative memory that stores general knowledge; a mental encyclopedia or dictionary *Page 251*

Semantics Set of rules for using words to create meaning; or the study of meaning *Page 292*

Sensation Process of detecting, converting, and transmitting raw sensory information from the external and internal environments to the brain *Page 128*

Sensorimotor Stage Piaget's first stage (birth to approximately age 2 years), in which schemas are developed through sensory and motor activities *Page 333*

Sensory Adaptation Decreased sensitivity due to repeated or constant stimulation *Page 132*

Sensory Memory First memory stage that holds sensory information; relatively large capacity, but duration is only a few seconds *Page 247*

Sensory Reduction Filtering and analyzing incoming sensations before sending a neural message to the cortex *Page 130*

Serial-Position Effect Information at the beginning and end of a list is remembered better than material in the middle *Page 254*

Sex Biological maleness and femaleness, including chromosomal sex; also, activities related to sexual behaviors, such as masturbation and intercourse *Page 376*

Sexual Dysfunction Impairment of the normal physiological processes of arousal and orgasm *Page 394*

Sexual Orientation Primary erotic attraction toward members of the same sex (homosexual, gay, lesbian), both sexes (bisexual), or other sex (heterosexual) *Page 379*

Sexual Prejudice Negative attitudes toward an individual because of her or his sexual orientation *Page 393*

Sexual Response Cycle Masters and Johnson's description of the four-stage bodily response to sexual arousal, which consists of excitement, plateau, orgasm, and resolution *Page 389*

Sexual Scripts Socially dictated descriptions of "appropriate" behaviors for sexual interactions *Page 396*

Shaping Reinforcement delivered for successive approximations of the desired response *Page 216*

Short-Term Memory (STM) Second memory stage that temporarily stores sensory information and decides whether to send it on to long-term memory (LTM); capacity is limited to five to nine items and duration is about 30 seconds *Page 248*

Sleep Apnea Repeated interruption of breathing during sleep because air passages to the lungs are physically blocked or the brain stops activating the diaphragm *Page 183*

Sleeper Effect Information from an unreliable source, which was initially discounted, later gains credibility because the source is forgotten *Page 260*

Social Learning Theory of Gender Role Development Gender roles are acquired though rewards, punishments, observation, and imitation *Page 377*

Social Psychology Study of how others influence our thoughts, feelings, and actions *Page 544*

Sociocultural Perspective Emphasizes social interaction and cultural determinants of behavior and mental processes *Page 13*

Socioemotional Selectivity Theory of Aging A natural decline in social contact occurs as older adults become more selective with their time *Page 364*

Somatic Nervous System (SNS) Subdivision of the peripheral nervous system (PNS) that connects to sensory receptors and controls skeletal muscles *Page 63*

Source Amnesia Forgetting the true source of a memory (also called source confusion or source misattribution) *Page 260*

Split Brain Cutting of the corpus callosum to separate the brain's two hemispheres. When used medically to treat severe epilepsy, split-brain patients provide data on the functions of the two hemispheres *Page 75*

Spontaneous Recovery Sudden reappearance of a previously extinguished conditioned response (CR) *Page 210*

Standardization Establishment of the norms and uniform procedures for giving and scoring a test *Page 302*

Stem Cell Immature (uncommitted) cells that have the potential to develop into almost any type of cell depending on the chemical signals they receive *Page 61*

Stereotype A set of beliefs about the characteristics of people in a group that is generalized to all group members; also, the cognitive component of prejudice *Page 551*

Stereotype Threat Negative stereotypes about minority groups cause some members to doubt their abilities *Page 309*

Stimulants Drugs that act on the brain and other parts of the nervous system to increase their overall activity and general responsiveness *Page 189*

Stimulus Discrimination Only the CS elicits the CR *Page 209*

Stimulus Generalization Stimuli similar to the original CS elicit a CR *Page 209*

Storage Retaining neurally coded information over time *Page 244*

Stress Nonspecific response of the body to any demand made on it; the arousal, both physical and mental, to situations or events that we perceive as threatening or challenging *Page 92*

Subliminal Pertaining to any stimulus presented below the threshold of conscious awareness *Page 132*

Substance-Related Disorders Abuse of, or dependence on, a mood- or behavior-altering drug *Page 500*

Superego In Freud's theory, the conscious or the part of the personality that incorporates parental and societal standards for morality *Page 449*

Survey Research technique that questions a large sample of people to assess their behaviors and attitudes *Page 30*

Sympathetic Nervous System Subdivision of the autonomic nervous system (ANS) responsible for arousing the body and mobilizing its energy during times of stress; also called the "fight-or-flight" system *Page 63*

Synapse [SIN-aps] Junction between the axon tip of the sending neuron and the dendrite or cell body of the receiving neuron. During an action potential, chemicals called neurotransmitters are released and flow across the synaptic gap *Page 56*

Synesthesia A mixing of sensory experiences (e.g., "seeing" colors when a sound is heard) *Page 130*

Syntax Grammatical rules that specify how words and phrases should be arranged in a sentence to convey meaning *Page 292*

Systematic Desensitization A gradual process of extinguishing a learned fear (or phobia) by working through a hierarchy of fear-evoking stimuli while staying deeply relaxed *Page 524*

Tardive Dyskinesia Movement disorder involving facial muscles, tongue, and limbs; a possible side effect of long-term use of antipsychotic medications *Page 530*

Taste Aversion Classically conditioned negative reaction to a particular taste that has been associated with nausea or other illness *Page 230*

Telegraphic Speech Two- or three-word sentences of young children that contain only the most necessary words *Page 294*

Temperament An individual's innate behavioral style and characteristic emotional response *Page 354*

Temporal Lobes Two lobes on each side of the brain above the ears involved in audition (hearing), language comprehension, memory, and some emotional control *Page 73*

Teratogen [Tuh-RAT-uh-jen] Environmental agent that causes damage during prenatal development; the term comes from the Greek word *teras*, meaning "malformation" *Page 322*

Thalamus [THAL-uh-muss] Forebrain structure at the top of the brainstem that relays sensory messages to the cerebral cortex *Page 68*

Thanatology [than-uh-TALL-uh-gee] The study of death and dying; the term comes from *thanatos*, the Greek name for a mythical personification of death, and was borrowed by Freud to represent the death instinct *Page 369*

Thematic Apperception Test (TAT) A projective test that shows a series of ambiguous black-and-white pictures and asks the test taker to create a story related to each; the responses presumably reflect a projection of unconscious processes *Page 465*

Theory Interrelated set of concepts that explain a body of data *Page 17*

Tip-of-the-Tongue (TOT) Phenomenon Feeling that specific information is stored in long-term memory but of being temporarily unable to retrieve it *Page 259*

Tolerance Bodily adjustment to higher and higher levels of a drug, which leads to decreased sensitivity *Page 186*

Top-Down Processing Information processing starting "at the top," with higher level cognitive processes (such as, expectations and knowledge), and then working down; conceptually driven processing that moves from the whole to the parts *Page 129*

Trait Relatively stable personal characteristic that can be used to describe someone *Page 442*

Transduction Converting a receptor's energy into neural impulses that are sent on to the brain *Page 130*

Transference In psychoanalysis, the patient may displace (or transfer) unconscious feelings about a significant person in his or her life onto the therapist *Page 511*

Trichromatic Theory Theory stating that color perception results from three types of cones in the retina, each most sensitive to either red, green or blue. Other colors result from a mixture of these three *Page 139*

Type A Personality Behavior characteristics including intense ambition, competition, exaggerated time urgency, and a cynical, hostile outlook *Page 106*

Type B Personality Behavior characteristics consistent with a calm, patient, relaxed attitude *Page 106*

Unconditional Positive Regard Rogers's term for love and acceptance with no contingencies attached *Page 456, 518*

Unconditioned Response (UCR) Unlearned reaction to an unconditioned stimulus (UCS) that occurs without previous conditioning *Page 205*

Unconditioned Stimulus (UCS) Stimulus that elicits an unconditioned response (UCR) without previous conditioning *Page 205*

Unconscious Freud's term for thoughts, motives, and memories blocked from normal awareness *Page 448*

Validity Ability of a test to measure what it was designed to measure *Page 302, 467*

Variable Interval (VI) Schedule Reinforcement occurs unpredictably; the interval (time) varies *Page 215*

Variable Ratio (VR) Schedule Reinforcement occurs unpredictably; the ratio (number or amount) varies *Page 215*

Wavelength Distance between the crests (or peaks) of light or sound waves; the shorter the wavelength, the higher the frequency *Page 136*

Withdrawal Discomfort and distress, including physical pain and intense cravings, experienced after stopping the use of addictive drugs *Page 186*

Aarts, H. (2007). Unconscious authorship ascription: The effects of success and effect-specific information priming on experienced authorship. *Journal of Experimental Social Psychology, 43,* 119–126.

Abadinsky, H. (2008). *Drug use and abuse: A comprehensive introduction* (6th ed.). Belmont, CA: Cengage.

Abbey, C., & Dallos, R. (2004). The experience of the impact of divorce on sibling relationships: A qualitative study. *Clinical Child Psychology and Psychiatry, 9*(2), 241–259.

Abbott, A. (2004). Striking back. *Nature, 429* (6990), 338–339.

Abernethy, B., Maxwell, J. P., Masters, R. S. W., van der Kamp, J., & Jackson, R. C. (2007). Attentional processes in skill learning and expert performance. In G. Tenenbaum & R. C. Eklund (Eds.), *Handbook of sport psychology* (3rd ed.) (pp. 245–263). Hoboken, NJ: Wiley.

Aboa-Éboulé, C. (2008). Job strain and recurrent coronary heart disease events—Reply. *Journal of the American Medical Association, 299,* 520–521.

Aboa-Éboulé, C., Brisson, C., Maunsell, E., Benoît, M., Bourbonnais, R., Vézina, M., Milot, A., Théroux, P., & Dagenais, G. R. (2008). Job strain and risk of acute recurrent coronary heart disease events. *Journal of the American Medical Association, 298,* 1652–1660.

Aboud, F. E. (2003). The formation of in-group favoritism and out-group prejudice in young children: Are they distinct attitudes? *Developmental Psychology, 39*(1), 48–60.

About James Randi. (2002). *Detail biography.* [On-line]. Available: http://www.randi.org/jr/bio.html.

Abraham, A., & Windmann, S. (2007). Creative cognition: The diverse operations and the prospect of applying a cognitive neuroscience perspective. *Methods, 42,* 38–48.

Acarturk, C., de Graaf, R., van Straten, A., ten Have, M., & Cuijpers, P. (2008). Social phobia and number of social fears, and their association with comorbidity, health-related quality of life and help seeking: A population-based study. *Social Psychiatry and Psychiatric Epidemiology, 43,* 273–279.

Achenbaum, W. A., & Bengtson, V. L. (1994). Re-engaging the disengagement theory of aging: On the history and assessment of theory development in gerontology. *Gerontologist, 34,* 756–763.

Adebayo, D. O. (2006). Workload, social support, and work-school conflict among Nigerian nontraditional students. *Journal of Career Development, 33*(2), 125–14.

Adelmann, P. K., & Zajonc, R. B. (1989). Facial efference and the experience of emotion. *Annual Review of Psychology, 40,* 249–280.

Adinoff, B. (2004). Neurobiologic processes in drug reward and addiction. *Harvard Review of Psychiatry, 12*(6), 305–320.

Adler, A. (1964). The individual psychology of Alfred Adler. In H. L. Ansbacher & R. R. Ansbacher (Eds.), *The individual psychology of Alfred Adler.* New York: Harper & Row.

Adler, A. (1998). *Understanding human nature.* Center City: MN: Hazelden Information Education.

Adolph, K. E., & Joh, A. S. (2007). Motor development: How infants get into the act. In A. Slater & M. Lewis (Eds.), *Infant Development* (2nd ed.). New York: Oxford University Press.

Aftanas, L. I., & Golosheikin, S. A. (2003). Changes in cortical activity in altered states of consciousness: The study of meditation by high-resolution EEG. *Human Physiology, 29,* 143–151.

Agar, M., & Reisinger, H. S. (2004). Ecstasy: Commodity or disease? *Journal of Psychoactive Drugs. 36*(2), 253–264.

Agrò, F., Liguori, A., Petti, F., Bangrazi, F., Cataldo, R., & Totonelli, A. (2005). Does acupuncture analgesia have a bihumoral mechanism? *The Pain Clinic, 17,* 243–244.

Ahijevych, K., Yerardi, R., & Nedilsky, N. (2000). Descriptive outcomes of the American Lung Association of Ohio hypnotherapy smoking cessation program. *International Journal of Clinical and Experimental Hypnosis, 48*(4), 374–387.

Ahlsén, E. (2008). Embodiment in communication – Aphasia, apraxia, and the possible role of mirroring and imitation. *Clinical Linguistics & Phonetics, 22,* 311–315.

Ahmadi, S., Zarrindast, M. R., Nouri, M., Haeri-Rohani, A. & Rezayof, A. (2007). N-Methyl-D-aspartate receptors in the ventral tegmental area are involved in retrieval of inhibitory avoidance memory by nicotine. *Neurobiology of Learning and Memory, 88,* 352–358.

Ahmed, A. M. (2007). Group identity, social distance, and intergroup bias. *Journal of Economic Psychology, 28,* 324–337.

Ainsworth, M. D. S. (1967). *Infancy in Uganda: Infant care and the growth of love.* Baltimore: Johns Hopkins University Press.

Ainsworth, M. D. S., Blehar, M., Waters, E., & Wall, S. (1978). *Patterns of attachment: Observations in the strange situation and at home.* Hillsdale, NJ: Erlbaum.

Akan, G. E., & Grilo, C. M. (1995). Sociocultural influences on eating attitudes and behaviors, body image, and psychological functioning: A comparison of African American, Asian American, and Caucasian college women. *International Journal of Eating Disorders, 18,* 181–187.

Akers, R. M., & Denbow, D. (2008). *Anatomy and physiology of domestic animals.* Hoboken, NJ: Wiley.

Akirav, I., & Richter-Levin, G. (1999). Biphasic modulation of hippocampal plasticity by behavioral stress and basolateral amygdala stimulation in the rat. *Journal of Neuroscience, 19,* 10530–10535.

Al'absi, M., Hugdahl, K., & Lovallo, W. R. (2002). Adrenocortical stress responses and altered working memory performance. *Psychophysiology, 39*(1), 95–99.

Alden, L. E., Mellings, T. M. B., & Laposa, J. M. (2004). Framing social information and generalized social phobia. *Behaviour Research & Therapy, 42*(5), 585–600.

Alberts, A., Elkind, D., & Ginsberg, S. (2007). The personal fable and risk-taking in early adolescence. *Journal of Youth and Adolescence, 36,* 71–76.

Al-Issa, I. (2000). Culture and mental illness in Algeria. In I. Al-Issa (Ed.), Al-Junun: *Mental illness in the Islamic world* (pp. 101–119). Madison, CT: International Universities Press.

Allan, K., & Gabbert, F. (2008). I still think it was a banana: Memorable "lies" and forgettable "truths." *Acta Psychologica, 127,* 299–308.

Allen, B. (2006). *Personality theories: Development, growth, and diversity* (5th ed.). Boston: Allyn & Bacon/Longman.

Allen, L. S., Hines, M., Shryne, J. E., & Gorski, R. A. (2007). Two sexually dimorphic cell groups in the human brain. In G. Einstein (Ed.), *Sex and the brain* (pp. 327–337). Cambridge, MA: MIT Press.

Allen, P. L. (2000). *The wages of sin: Sex and disease, past and present.* Chicago: University of Chicago Press.

Allik, J., & McCrae, R. R. (2004). Toward a geography of personality traits: Patterns of profiles across 36 cultures. *Journal of Cross-Cultural Psychology, 35*(1), 13–28.

Alloy, L. B., & Clements, C. M. (1998). Hopelessness theory of depression. *Cognitive Therapy and Research, 22,* 303–335.

Alloy, L. B., Abramson, L. Y., Whitehouse, W. G., Hogan, M. E., Tashman, N. A., Steinberg, D. L., Rose, D. T., & Donovan, P. (1999). Depressogenic cognitive styles: Predictive validity, information processing and personality characteristics, and developmental origins. *Behavior Research and Therapy, 37,* 503–531.

Allport, G. W. (1937). *Personality: A psychological interpretation.* New York: Holt, Rinehart and Winston.

Allport, G. W., & Odbert, H. S. (1936). Trait-names: A psycho-lexical study. *Psychological Monographs: General and Applied, 47,* 1–21.

Almeida, O. P., Burton, E. J., Ferrier, N., McKeith, I. G., & O'Brien, J. T. (2003). Depression with late onset is associated with right frontal lobe atrophy. *Psychological Medicine, 33*(4), 675–681.

Aluja-Fabregat, A., & Torrubia-Beltri, R. (1998). Viewing of mass media violence, perception of violence, personality and academic achievement. *Personality and Individual Differences, 25,* 973–989.

Amato, P. R. (2006). Marital discord, divorce, and children's well-being: Results from a 20-year longitudinal study of two generations. In A. Clarke-Stewart & J. Dunn (Eds.), *Families count: Effects on child and adolescent development* (pp. 179–202). *The Jacobs Foundation series on adolescence.* New York: Cambridge University Press.

Amato, P. R. (2007). Transformative processes in marriage: Some thoughts from a sociologist. *Journal of Marriage and Family, 69,* 305–309.

American Cancer Society (2004). *Women and smoking.* [On-line]. Available: http://cancer.org/docroot/PED/content/PED_10_2X_Women_and_Smoking.asp?sitearea=PED.

American Heart Association. (2008). *Heart disease and stroke statistics—2008 update.* [Online]. Available: http://www.americanheart.org/presenter.jhtml?identifier=3054076

American Medical Association. (2008). *Alcohol and other drug abuse.* [On-line]. Available: http://www.ama-assn.org/ama/pub/category/3337.html.

American Psychiatric Association. (2000). *Diagnostic and statistical manual of mental disorders* (4th ed. TR). Washington, DC: American Psychiatric Press.

American Psychiatric Association. (2002). *APA Let's talk facts about posttraumatic stress disorder.* [On-line]. Available: http://www.psych.org/disasterpsych/fs/ptsd.cfm.

American Psychological Association. (1984). *Behavioral research with animals.* Washington, DC: Author.

American Psychological Association. (1992). Ethical principles of psychologists and code of conduct. *American Psychologist, 47,* 1597–1611.

Amidzic, O., Rieble, H. J., Fehr, T., Wienbruch, C., & Elbert, T. (2001). Pattern of focal outbursts in chess players. *Nature, 412*(6847), 603.

Amiot, C. E., Terry, D. J., Jimmieson, N. L., & Callan, V. J. (2006). A longitudinal investigation of coping processes during a merger: Implications for job satisfaction and organizational identification. *Journal of Management, 32,* 552–574.

Amir, N., Cobb, M., & Morrison, A. S. (2008). Threat processing in obsessive-compulsive disorder: Evidence from a modified negative priming task. *Behaviour Research and Therapy, 46,* 728–736.

Amorim, K. S., & Rossetti-Ferreira, M. C. (2004). Ethnotheories and childrearing practices: Some constraints on their investigation. *Culture & Psychology, 10,* 337–351.

Amundson, J. K., & Nuttgens, S. A. (2008). Strategic eclecticism in hypnotherapy: Effectiveness research considerations. *American Journal of Clinical Hypnosis, 50,* 233–245.

Ancis, J. R., Chen, Y., & Schultz, D. (2004). Diagnostic challenges and the so-called culture bound syndromes. In J. R. Ancis (Ed.), *Culturally responsive interventions: Innovative approaches to working with diverse populations* (pp. 197–209). New York: Brunner-Routledge.

Anderson, C. A. (2001). Heat and violence. *Current Directions in Psychological Science, 10*(1), 33–38.

Anderson, C. A. (2004). An update on the effects of playing violent video games. *Journal of Adolescence, 27*(1), 113–122.

Anderson, C. A., Anderson, K. B., Dorr, N., DeNeve, K. M., & Flanagan, M. (2000). Temperature and aggression. *Advances in Experimental Social Psychology, 32,* 63–133.

Anderson, C. A., Buckley, K. E., & Carnegey, N. L. (2008). Creating your own hostile environment: A laboratory examination of trait aggressiveness and the violence escalation cycle. *Personality and Social Psychology Bulletin, 34,* 462–473.

Anderson, C. A., & Bushman, B. J. (2001). Effects of violent video games on aggressive behavior, aggressive cognition, aggressive affect, physiological arousal, and prosocial behavior: A meta-analytic review of the scientific literature. *Psychological Science, 12*(5), 353–359.

Anderson, C. A., & Dill, K. E. (2000). Video games and aggressive thoughts, feelings, and behavior in the laboratory and in life. *Journal of Personality and Social Psychology, 78*(4), 772–790.

Anderson, C. A., & Hamilton, M. (2005). Gender role stereotyping of parents in children's picture books: The invisible father. *Sex Roles, 52,* 145–151.

Anderson, L. E., & Silver, J. M. (2008). Neurological and medical disorders. In R. I. Simon & K. Tardiff (Eds.), *Textbook of violence assessment and management* (pp. 185–209). Arlington, VA: American Psychiatric Publishing.

Anderson, M. C., Bjork, R. A. & Bjork, E. L. (1994). Remembering can cause forgetting: Retrieval dynamics in long-term memory. *Journal of Experimental Psychology: Learning, Memory, and Cognition, 20,* 1063–1087.

Anderson, M. C., Ochsner, K. N., Kuhl, B., Cooper, J., Robertson, E., Gabrieli, S. W., Glover, G. H., & Gabrieli, J. D. E. (2004). Neural systems underlying the suppression of unwanted memories. *Science, 303*(5655), 232–235.

Andrade, T. G. C. S., & Graeff, F. G. (2001). Effect of electrolytic and neurotoxic lesions of the median raphe nucleus on anxiety and stress. *Pharmacology, Biochemistry & Behavior, 70*(1), 1–14.

Andrasik, F. (2006). Psychophysiological disorders: Headache as a case in point. In F. Andrasik (Ed.), *Comprehensive handbook of personality and psychopathology: Vol. 2: Adult Psychopathology* (pp. 409–422). Hoboken, NJ: Wiley.

Andreassi, J. K., & Thompson, C. A. (2007). Dispositional and situational sources of control: Relative impact on work-family conflict and positive spillover. *Journal of Managerial Psychology, 22*(8), 722–740.

Andreoni, J., & Petrie, R. (2008). Beauty, gender and stereotypes: Evidence from laboratory experiments. *Journal of Economic Psychology, 29,* 73–93.

Angenendt, A. (2003). Safety and security from the air traffic control services' point of view. *Human Factors & Aerospace Safety, 3*(3), 207–209.

Angst, J., Gamma, A., Gastpar, M., Lepine, J. P., Mendlewicz, J., & Tylee, A. (2002). Gender differences in depression: Epidemiological findings from the European DEPRES I and II studies. *European Archives of Psychiatry & Clinical Neuroscience, 252*(5), 201–209.

Anguas-Wong, A. M., & Matsumoto, D. (2007). Reconocimiento de la expresión facial de la emoción en mexicanos universitarios. [Acknowledgement of emotional facial expression in Mexican college students.] *Revista de Psicología, 25,* 277–293.

Anisman, H., Merali, Z., & Stead, J. D. H. (2008). Experiential and genetic contributions to depressive- and anxiety-like disorders: Clinical and experimental studies. *Neuroscience & Biobehavioral Reviews, 32,* 1185–1206.

Ansell, E. B., & Grilo, C. M. (2007). Personality disorders. In M. Hersen, S. M. Turner, & D. C. Beidel (Eds.), *Adult psychopathology and diagnosis* (5th ed.) (pp. 633–678). Hoboken, NJ: Wiley.

Aou, S., (2006). Role of medial hypothalamus on peptic ulcer and depression. In C. Kubo & T. Kuboki (Eds), *Psychosomatic medicine: Proceedings of the 18th World Congress on Psychosomatic Medicine.* New York: Elsevier Science.

Appel, M., & Richter, T. (2007). Persuasive effects of fictional narratives increase over time. *Media Psychology, 10,* 113–134.

Appiah, K. A. (2008). *Experiments in ethics.* Cambridge, MA: Harvard University Press.

Arbib, M. A., & Mundhenk, T. N. (2005). Schizophrenia and the mirror system: An essay. *Neuropsychologia, 43,* 268–280.

Arcuri, L., Castelli, L., Galdi, S., Zogmaister, C., & Amadori, A. (2008). Predicting the vote: Implicit attitudes as predictions of the future behavior of decided and undecided voters. *Political Psychology, 29,* 369–387.

Arieh, Y., & Marks, L. E. (2008). Cross-modal interaction between vision and hearing: A speed-accuracy analysis. *Perception & Psychophysics, 70,* 412–421.

Ariznavarreta, C., Cardinali, D. P., Villanua, M. A., Granados, B., Martin, M., Chiesa, J. J., Golombek, D. A., & Tresguerres, J. A. F. (2002). Circadian rhythms in airline pilots submitted to long-haul transmeridian flights. *Aviation, Space, & Environmental Medicine, 73*(5), 445–455.

Arriagada, O., Constandil, L., Hernández, A., Barra, R., Soto-Moyano, R., & Laurido, C. (2007). Brief communication: Effects of interleukin-1B on spinal cord nociceptive transmission in intact and propentofylline-treated rats. *International Journal of Neuroscience, 117,* 617–625.

Arumugam, V., Lee, J-S., Nowak, J. K., Pohle, R. J., Nyrop, J. E., Leddy, J. J., & Pelkman, C. L. (2008). A high-glycemic meal pattern elicited increased subjective appetite sensations in overweight and obese women. *Appetite, 50,* 215–222.

Asch, S. E. (1951). Effects of group pressure upon the modification and distortion of judgment. In H. Guetzkow (Ed.), *Groups, leadership, and men.* Pittsburgh: Carnegie Press.

Asghar, A. U. R., Chiu, Y-C., Hallam, G., Liu, S., Mole, H., Wright, H., & Young, A. W. (2008). An amygdala response to fearful faces with covered eyes. *Neuropsychologia, 46,* 2364–2370.

Astin, J. A. (2004). Mind-body therapies for the management of pain. *Clinical Journal of Pain, 20*(1), 27–32.

Atchley, P., & Kramer, A. F. (2000). Age related changes in the control of attention in depth. *Psychology & Aging, 15*(1), 78–87.

Atchley, R. C. (1997). *Social forces and aging* (8th ed.). Belmont, CA: Wadsworth.

Athos, E. A., Levinson, B., Kistler, A., Zemansky, J., Bostrom, A., Freimer, N., & Gitschier, J. (2007). Dichotomy and perceptual distortions in absolute pitch ability. *Proceedings of the National Academy of Sciences, 104,* 14795–14800.

Atkins, C. K., Panicker, S., & Cunningham, C. L. (2005). *Laboratory animals in research and teaching: Ethics, care, and methods.* Washington, DC: American Psychological Association.

Atkinson, R. C., & Shiffrin, R. M. (1968). Human memory: A proposed system and its control processes. In K. W. Spence & J. T. Spence (Eds.), *The psychology of learning and motivation* (Vol. 2). New York: Academic Press.

Aubert, A., & Dantzer, R. (2005). The taste of sickness: Lipopolysaccharide-induced finickiness in rats. *Physiology & Behavior, 84*(3), 437–444.

Axtell, R. E. (1998). *Gestures: The do's and taboos of body language around the world,* revised and expanded ed. New York: Wiley.

Axtell, R. E. (2007). *Essential do's and taboos: The complete guide to international business and leisure travel.* Hoboken, NJ: Wiley.

Ayers, S., Baum, A., McManus, C., Newman, S., Wallston, K., Weinman, J., & West, R. (Eds.). (2007). *Cambridge handbook of psychology, health, and medicine.* New York: Cambridge University Press.

Azizian, A., & Polich, J. (2007). Evidence for attentional gradient in the serial position memory curve from event-related potentials. *Journal of Cognitive Neuroscience, 19,* 2071–2081.

Bachevalier, J., & Vargha-Khadem, F. (2005). The primate hippocampus: Ontogeny, early insult and memory. *Current Opinion in Neurobiology, 15*(2), 168–174.

Bachman, G., & Zakahi, W. R. (2000). Adult attachment and strategic relational communication: Love schemas and affinity-seeking. *Communication Reports, 13*(1), 11–19.

Badawy, A. B. (2003). Alcohol and violence and the possible role of serotonin. *Criminal Behaviour & Mental Health, 13*(1), 31–44.

Baddeley, A. D. (1992). Working memory. *Science, 255,* 556–559.

Baddeley, A. D. (1998). Recent developments in working memory. *Current Opinion in Neurobiology, 8,* 234–238.

Baddeley, A. D. (2000). Short-term and working memory. In E. Tulving & F. I. M. Craik (Eds.), *The Oxford handbook of memory* (pp. 77–92). New York: Oxford University Press.

Baddeley, A. D. (2007). Working memory, thought, and action. *Oxford psychology series.* New York: Oxford University Press.

Baddeley, A., & Jarrold, C. (2007). Working memory and Down syndrome. *Journal of Intellectual Disability Research, 51,* 925–931.

Badr, L. K., & Abdallah, B. (2001). Physical attractiveness of premature infants affects outcome at discharge from the NICU. *Infant Behavior & Development, 24,* 129–133.

Baer, J. (1994). Divergent thinking is not a general trait: A multi-domain training experiment. *Creativity Research Journal, 7,* 35–36.

Bagarozzi Sr., D. A. (2008). Understanding and treating marital infidelity: A multidimensional model. *American Journal of Family Therapy, 36,* 1–17.

Bagermihl, B. (1999). *Biological exuberance: Animal homosexuality and natural diversity.* New York: St Martins Press.

Bailer, U., de Zwaan, M., Leisch, F., Strnad, A., Lennkh-Wolfsberg, C., El-Giamal, N., Hornik, K., & Kasper, S. (2004). Guided self-help versus cognitive-behavioral group therapy in the treatment of bulimia nervosa. *International Journal of Eating Disorders, 35*(4), 522–537.

Bailey, J. M., Dunne, M. P., & Martin, N. G. (2000). Genetic and environmental influences on sexual orientation and its correlates in an Australian twin sample. *Journal of Personality and Social Psychology,* 78(3), 524–536.

Bailey, K. R., & Mair, R. G. (2005). Lesions of specific and nonspecific thalamic nuclei affect prefrontal cortex-dependent spects of spatial working memory. *Behavioral Neuroscience,* 119(2), 410–419.

Baillargeon, R. (2000). Reply to Bogartz, Shinskey, and Schilling; Schilling; and Cashon and Cohen. *Infancy,* 1, 447–462.

Baillargeon, R. (2008). Innate ideas revisited: For a principle of persistence in infants' physical reasoning. *Perspectives on Psychological Science,* 3, 2–13.

Baker, D., & Nieuwenhuijsen, M. J. (Eds.) (2008). *Environmental epidemiology: Study methods and application.* New York: Oxford University Press.

Baker, M. W. (2007). Elder mistreatment: Risk, vulnerability, and early mortality. *Journal of the American Psychiatric Nurses Association,* 12, 313–321.

Baker, R. A. (1996). *Hidden memories.* New York: Prometheus Books.

Baker, R. A. (1998). A view of hypnosis. *Harvard Mental Health Letter,* 14, 5–6.

Baldessarini, R. J., & Hennen, J. (2004). Genetics of suicide: An overview. *Harvard Review of Psychiatry,* 12(1), 1–13.

Baldessarini, R. J., & Tondo, L. (2008). Lithium and suicidal risk. *Bipolar Disorders,* 10, 114–115.

Baldwin, N. (2001). *Edison: Inventing the century.* Chicago: University of Chicago Press.

Baldwin, S., & Oxlad, M. (2000). *Electroshock and minors: A fifty year review.* New York: Greenwood Publishing Group.

Balfour, D. J. K. (2004). The neurobiology of tobacco dependence: A preclinical perspective on the role of the dopamine projections to the nucleus. *Nicotine & Tobacco Research,* 6(6), 899–912.

Balk, D. E. (2008). A modest proposal about bereavement and recovery. *Death Studies,* 32, 84–93.

Balk, D., Wogrin, C., Thornton, G., & Meagher, D. (Eds.) (2007). *Handbook of thanatology: The essential body of knowledge for the study of death, dying, and bereavement.* New York: Routledge/Taylor & Francis Group.

Ballesteros, S., & Manuel Reales, J. (2004). Intact haptic priming in normal aging and Alzheimer's disease: Evidence for dissociable memory systems. *Neuropsychologia,* 42(8), 1063–1070.

Balu, M. (2007). An investigation of subjective bias/halo in 360-degree multi-source assessment through differential item function and structural equation model. *Dissertation Abstracts International: Section B: The Sciences and Engineering,* 67(9-B), 5461.

Bandstra, E. S., Morrow, C. E., Vogel, A. L., Fifer, R. C., Ofir, A. Y., Dausa, A. T., Xue, L., & Anthony, J. C. (2002). Longitudinal influence of prenatal cocaine exposure on child language functioning. *Neurotoxicology & Teratology,* 24(3), 297–308.

Bandura, A. (1969). *Principles of behavior modification.* New York: Holt, Rinehart and Winston.

Bandura, A. (1986). *Social foundations of thought and action: A social cognitive theory.* Englewood Cliffs, NJ: Prentice Hall.

Bandura, A. (1989). Social cognitive theory. In R. Vasta (Ed.), *Annals of child development* (Vol. 6). Greenwich, CT: JAI Press.

Bandura, A. (1991). Social cognitive theory of moral thought and action. In W. M. Kurtines & J. L. Gewirtz (Eds.), *Handbook of moral behavior and development: Vol. 1. Theory.* Hillsdale, NJ: Erlbaum.

Bandura, A. (1997). *Self-efficacy: The exercise of control.* New York: Freeman.

Bandura, A. (2000). Exercise of human agency through collective efficacy. *Current Directions in Psychological Science,* 9(3), 75–83.

Bandura, A. (2003). On the psychosocial impact and mechanisms of spiritual modeling: Comment. *International Journal for the Psychology of Religion,* 13(3), 167–173.

Bandura, A. (2006). Going global with social cognitive theory: From prospect to paydirt. In D. E. Berger & K. Pezdek (Eds.), *The rise of applied psychology: New frontiers and rewarding careers.* Mahwah, NJ: Erlbaum.

Bandura A. (2008). Reconstrual of "free will" from the agentic perspective of social cognitive theory. In J. Baer, J. C. Kaufman, & R. F. Baumeister (Eds.), *Are we free? Psychology and free will.* New York: Oxford University Press.

Bandura, A., Ross, D., & Ross, S. (1961). Transmission of aggression through imitation of aggressive models. *Journal of Abnormal & Social Psychology,* 63, 575–582.

Bandura, A., & Walters, R. H. (1963). *Social learning and personality development.* New York: Holt, Rinehart and Winston.

Banko, K. M. (2008). Increasing intrinsic motivation using rewards: The role of the social context. *Dissertation Abstracts International: Section B: The Sciences and Engineering,* 68(10-B), 7005.

Banks, A., & Gartrell, N. K. (1995). Hormones and sexual orientation: A questionable link. *Journal of Homosexuality,* 28(3–4), 247–268.

Banks, M. S., & Salapatek, P. (1983). Infant visual perception. In M. M. Haith & J. J. Campos (Eds.), *Handbook of child psychology.* New York: Wiley.

Bao, A. M., Meynen, G., & Swaab, D. F. (2008). The stress system in depression and neurodegeneration: Focus on the human hypothalamus. *Brain Research Reviews,* 57, 531–553.

Bar-Haim, Y., Dan, O., Eshel, Y., & Sagi-Schwartz, A. (2007). Predicting childrens' anxiety from early attachment relationships. *Journal of Anxiety Disorders,* 21, 1061–1068.

Barber, N. (2008). Explaining cross-national differences in polygyny intensity: Resource-defense, sex ratio, and infectious diseases. *Cross-Cultural Research: The Journal of Comparative Social Science,* 42, 103–117.

Barber, T. X. (2000). A deeper understanding of hypnosis: Its secrets, its nature, its essence. *American Journal of Clinical Hypnosis,* 42(3–4), 208–272.

Bard, C. (1934). On emotional expression after decortication with some remarks on certain theoretical views. *Psychological Review,* 41, 309–329.

Barefoot, J. C. (2004). Hostility as a predictor of survival in patients with coronary artery disease. *Psychosomatic Medicine,* 66(5), 629–632.

Bareš, M., Kanovský, P., & Rektor, I. (2007). Disturbed intracortical excitability in early Parkinson's disease is L-DOPA dose related: A prospective 12-month paired TMS study. *Parkinsonism & Related Disorders,* 13, 489–494.

Bargai, N., Ben-Shakar, G., & Shalev, A. Y. (2007). Posttraumatic stress disorder and depression in battered women: The mediating role of learned helplessness. *Journal of Family Violence,* 22(5), 267–275.

Barinaga, M. (1999). Learning visualized, on the double. *Science,* 286, 1661.

Barlett, C. P., Harris, R. J., & Bruey, C. (2008). The effect of the amount of blood in a violent video game on aggression, hostility, and arousal. *Journal of Experimental Social Psychology,* 44, 539–546.

Barlow, D. H. (Ed.). (2008). *Clinical handbook of psychological disorders: A step-by-step treatment manual (4th ed.).* New York: Guilford Press.

Barlow, D. H., & Durand, V. M. (2009). *Abnormal psychology: An integrative approach* (5th ed.). Belmont, CA: Cengage.

Barlow, D. H., Esler, J. L., & Vitali, A. E. (1998). Psychosocial treatments for panic disorders, phobias, and generalized anxiety disorder. In P. E. Nathan & J. M. Gorman (Eds.), *A guide to treatments that work* (pp. 288–318). New York: Oxford University Press.

Barner, D, Wood, J., Hauser, M., & Carey, S. (2008). Evidence for a non-linguistic distinction between singular and plural sets in rhesus monkeys. *Cognition, 107,* 603–622.

Barnouw, V. (1985). *Culture and personality* (4th ed.). Homewood, IL: Dorsey Press.

Barnow, S., Ulrich, I., Grabe, H-J., Freyberger, H. J., & Spitzer, C. (2007). The influence of parental drinking behaviour and antisocial personality disorder on adolescent behavioural problems: Results of the Greifswalder family study. *Alcohol and Alcoholism, 42,* 623–628.

Baron, A. S., & Banaji, M. R. (2006). The development of implicit attitudes. *Psychological Science, 17,* 53–58.

Barrett, L. F., Mesquita, B., Ochsner, K. N., & Gross, J. J. (2007). The experience of emotion. *Annual Review of Psychology, 58,* 373–403.

Barry, D. T., Grilo, C. M., & Masheb, R. M. (2002). Gender differences in patients with binge eating disorder. *International Journal of Eating Disorders, 31*(1), 63–70.

Barry, L. C., Allore, H. G., Guo, Z., Bruce, M. L., & Gill, T. M. (2008). Higher burden of depression among older women: The effect of onset, persistence, and mortality over time. *Archives of General Psychiatry, 65,* 172–178.

Bartels, M., van Beijsterveldt, C. E. M., Derks, E. M., Stroet, T. M., Polderman, T. J. C., Hudziak, J. J., & Boomsma, D. I. (2007). Young Netherlands Twin Register (Y-NTR): A longitudinal multiple informant study of problem behavior. *Twin Research and Human Genetics, 10,* 3–11.

Bartholow, B. D., & Anderson, C. A. (2002). Effects of violent video games on aggressive behavior: Potential sex differences. *Journal of Experimental Social Psychology, 38*(3), 283–290.

Bartlett, F. C. (1958). *Thinking.* London: Allen & Unwin.

Bartolomeo, P. (2006). A parietofrontal network for spatial awareness in the right hemisphere of the human brain. *Archives of Neurology, 63,* 1238–1241.

Barton, J. J. S. (2008). Prosopagnosia associated with a left occipitotemporal lesion. *Neuropsychologia, 46,* 2214–2224.

Batel, P. (2000). Addiction and schizophrenia. *European Psychiatry, 15,* 115–122.

Bateman, T. S., & Snell, S. A. (2007). *Management* (7th ed.). New York: McGraw-Hill.

Bates, A. L. (2007). How did you get in? Attributions of preferential selection in college admissions. *Dissertation Abstracts International: Section B: The Sciences and Engineering, 68*(4-B), 2694.

Bates, P., & Rutherford, J. (2003). Problem substance use and schizophrenia. *British Journal of Psychiatry, 182*(5), 455.

Batson, C. D. (1991). *The altruism question: Toward a social-psychological answer.* Hillsdale, NJ: Erlbaum.

Batson, C. D. (1998). Altruism and prosocial behavior. In D.T. Gilbert, S.T. Fiske, & G. Lindzey (Eds.). *The handbook of social psychology, Vol. 2* (4th ed.) (pp. 282–316). Boston, MA: McGraw-Hill.

Batson, C. D. (2006). "Not all self-interest after all": Economics of empathy-induced altruism. In D. De Cremer, M. Zeelenberg, & J. K. Murnighan (Eds.), *Social psychology and economics* (pp. 281–299). Mahwah, NJ: Erlbaum.

Batson, C. D., & Ahmad, N. (2001). Empathy-induced altruism in a prisoner's dilemma II: What if the target of empathy has defected? *European Journal of Social Psychology, 31*(1), 25–36.

Baumrind, D. (1980). New directions in socialization research. *American Psychologist, 35,* 639–652.

Baumrind, D. (1991). Effective parenting during the early adolescent transition. In P. A. Cowan & E. M. Hetherington (Eds.), *Family transition* (pp. 111–163). Hillsdale, NJ: Erlbaum.

Baumrind, D. (1995). *Child maltreatment and optimal caregiving in social contexts.* New York: Garland.

Beach, F. A. (1977). *Human sexuality in four perspectives.* Baltimore: The Johns Hopkins University Press.

Bearer, C. F., Stoler, J. M., Cook, J. D., & Carpenter, S. J. (2004–2005). Biomarkers of alcohol use in pregnancy. *Alcohol Research & Health, 28*(1), 38–43.

Beaton, E. A., Schmidt, L. A., Schulkin, J., Antony, M. M., Swinson, R. P., & Hall, G. B. (2008). Different neural responses to stranger and personally familiar faces in shy and bold adults. *Behavioral Neuroscience, 122,* 704–709.

Beck, A. T. (1976). *Cognitive therapy and the emotional disorders.* New York: International Universities Press.

Beck, A. T. (2000). *Prisoners of hate.* New York: Harper Perennial.

Beck, A., & Rector, N. A. (2005). Cognitive approaches to schizophrenia: Theory and therapy. *Annual Review of Clinical Psychology, 1,* 577–606.

Beck, A. T., & Grant, P. M. (2008). Negative self-defeating attitudes: Factors that influence everyday impairment in individuals with schizophrenia. *American Journal of Psychiatry, 165,* 772.

Becker, S. I. (2008). The mechanism of priming: Episodic retrieval or priming of pop-out? *Acta Psychologica, 127,* 324–339.

Beckerman, S., Hardy, S. B., Baker, R. R., Crocker, W. H., Valentine, P., & Hawkes, K. (1999). Partible paternity: Matings with multiple men leading to multiple fathers per child. *Meeting of the American Association for the Advancement of Science.* Anaheim, CA.

Becvar, D., & Becvar, R. (2006). *Family therapy: A systemic integration* (6th ed.). Boston: Allyn & Bacon/Longman.

Beer, J. S., & Lombardo, M. V. (2007). Insights into emotion regulation from neuropsychology. In J. J. Gross (Ed.), *Handbook of emotion regulation.* New York: Guilford Press.

Begg, I. M., Needham, D. R., & Bookbinder, M. (1993). Do backward messages unconsciously affect listeners? No. *Canadian Journal of Experimental Psychology, 47,* 1–14.

Begic, D., & Jokic-Begic, N. (2002). Violent behaviour and post-traumatic stress disorder. *Current Opinion in Psychiatry, 15*(6), 623–626.

Behar, R. (2007). Gender related aspects of eating disorders: A psychosocial view. In J. S. Rubin (Ed.), *Eating disorders and weight loss research* (pp. 39–65). Hauppauge, NY: Nova Science Publishers.

Beilin, H. (1992). Piaget's enduring contribution to developmental psychology. *Developmental Psychology, 28,* 191–204.

Belardinelli, C., Hatch, J. P., Olvera, R. L., Fonseca, M., Caetano, S. C., Nicoletti, M., Pliszka, S., & Soares, J. C. (2008). Family environment patterns in families with bipolar children. *Journal of Affective Disorders, 107,* 299–305.

Bellis, S. J. (2008). The development and field test of an employment interview system to identify successful middle school principals. *Dissertation Abstracts International: Section A: Humanities and Social Sciences, 68*(7-A), 2734.

Belsky, J., & Cassidy, J. (1994). Attachment: Theory and evidence. In M. Rutter & D. Hay (Eds.), *Development through life: A* *handbook for clinicians* (pp. 373–402). Oxford, England: Blackwell.

Bem, S. L. (1981). Gender schema theory: A cognitive account of sex typing. *Psychological Review, 88,* 354–364.

Bem, S. L. (1993). *The lenses of gender: Transforming the debate on sexual inequality.* New Haven, CT: Yale University Press.

Ben-Eliyahu, S., Page, G. G., & Schleifer, S. J. (2007). Stress, NK cells, and cancer: Still a promissory note. *Brain, Behavior, & Immunity, 21,* 881–887.

Ben-Porath, Y. S., & Tellegen, A. (2008). Empirical correlates of the MMPI-2 Restructured Clinical (RC) scales in mental health, forensic, and nonclinical settings: An introduction. *Journal of Personality Assessment, 90,* 119–121.

Benazzi, F. (2004). Testing early-onset chronic atypical depression subtype. *Neuropsychopharmacology, 29*(2), 440–441.

Bendersky, M., & Sullivan, M. W. (2007). Basic methods in infant research. In A. Slater & M. Lewis (Eds.), *Introduction to infant development* (2nd ed.). New York: Oxford University Press.

Benjamin, L. T., Cavell, T. A., & Shallenberger, W. R. (1984). Staying with initial answers on objective tests: Is it a myth? *Teaching of Psychology, 11,* 133–141.

Benloucif, S., Orbeta, L., Ortiz, R., Janssen, I., Finkel, S., Bleiberg, J., & Zee, P. C. (2004). Morning or evening activity improves neuropsychological performance and subjective sleep quality in older adults. *Sleep, 27*(8), 1542–1551.

Bennett, M., Barrett, M., Karakozov, R., Kipiani, G., Lyons, E., Pavlenko, V., & Riazanova, T. (2004). Young children's evaluations of the ingroup and of outgroups: A multi-national study. *Social Development, 13*(1), 124–141.

Bennett, S., & Assefi, N. P. (2005). School-based teenage pregnancy prevention programs: A systematic review of randomized controlled trials. *Journal of Adolescent Health, 36,* 72–81.

Benton, D. A., Esler, M. D., Dawood, T., Lambert, E. A., Haikerwal, D., Brenchley, C., Socratous, F., Hastings, J., Guo, L., Wiesner, G., Kaye, D. M., Bayles, R., Schlaich, M. P., & Lambert, G. W. (2008). Elevated brain serotonin turnover in patients with depression: Effect of genotype and therapy. *Archives of General Psychiatry, 65,* 38–46.

Benton, T. R., McDonnell, S., Ross, D. F., Thomas III, W. N., & Bradshaw, E. (2007). Has eyewitness research penetrated the American legal system? A synthesis of case history, juror knowledge, and expert testimony. In R. C. L. Lindsay, D. F. Ross, J. D. Read, & M. P. Toglia (Eds.), *The handbook of eyewitness psychology, Vol II: Memory for people* (pp. 453–500). Mahwah, NJ: Erlbaum.

Beraki, S., Aronsson, F., Karlsson, H., Ögren, S. O., & Kristensson, K. (2005). Influenza A virus infection causes alterations in expression of synaptic regulatory genes combined with changes in cognitive and emotional behaviors in mice. *Molecular Psychiatry, 10*(3), 299–308.

Berchtold, N. C. (2008). Exercise, stress mechanisms, and cognition. In W. W. Spirduso, L. W. Poon, & W. Chodzko-Zajko (Eds), *Exercise and its mediating effects on cognition* (pp. 47–67). *Aging, exercise, and cognition series.* Champaign, IL: Human Kinetics.

Berger, M., Speckmann, E.-J., Pape, H. C., & Gorji, A. (2008). Spreading depression enhances human neocortical excitability in vitro. *Cephalalgia, 28,* 558–562.

Bergstrom-Lynch, C. A. (2008). Becoming parents, remaining childfree: How same-sex couples are creating families and confronting social inequalities. *Dissertation Abstracts International Section A: Humanities and Social Sciences, 68*(8-A), 3608.

Berk, M. (2007). Should we be targeting exercise as a routine mental health intervention? *Acta Neuropsychiatrica, 19,* 217–218.

Berman, M. E., Tracy, J. I., & Coccaro, E. F. (1997). The serotonin hypothesis of aggression revisited. *Clinical Psychology Review, 17*(6), 651–665.

Bermond, B., Fasotti, L., Nieuwenhuyse, B., & Schuerman, J. (1991). Spinal cord lesions, peripheral feedback, and intensities of emotional feelings. *Cognition and Emotion, 5,* 201–220.

Bernard, L. L. (1924). *Instinct.* New York: Holt.

Bernhardt, T., Seidler, A., & Froelich, L. (2002). Der Einfluss von psychosozialen Faktoren auf das Demenzerkrankungsrisiko [The effect of psychosocial factors on risk of dementia]. *Fortschritte der Neurologie, Psychiatrie, 70*(6), 283–288.

Bernet, W., & Ash, D. R. (2007). *Children of divorce: A practical guide for parents, therapists, attorneys, and judges* (2nd ed.). Malabar, FL: Krieger.

Bernheim, K. F., & Lewine, R. R. J. (1979). *Schizophrenia: Symptoms, causes, and treatments.* New York: Norton.

Berreman, G. (1971). *Anthropology today.* Del Mar, CA: CRM Books.

Berry, J. W., Poortinga, Y. H., Segall, M. H., & Dasen, P. R. (2002). *Cross-cultural psychology: Research and applications* (2nd ed.). New York: Cambridge University Press.

Berthoud, H. (2002). Multiple neural systems controlling food intake and body weight. *Neuroscience & Biobehavioral Reviews, 26*(4), 393–428.

Berthoud, H-R., & Morrison, C. (2008). The brain, appetite, and obesity. *Annual Review of Psychology, 59,* 55–92.

Berzoff, J. (2008). Psychosocial ego development: The theory of Erik Erikson. In J. Berzoff, L. M. Flanagan, & P. Hertz (Eds.), *Inside out and outside in: Psychodynamic clinical theory and psychopathology in contemporary multicultural contexts* (2nd ed.) (pp. 99–120). Lanham, MD: Jason Aronson.

Besançon, F. (2004). Warning signs for suicide: Everyone's business. *Suicide & Life-Threatening Behavior, 34,* 197–198.

Best, J. B. (1999). *Cognitive psychology* (5th ed.). Belmont, CA: Wadsworth.

Bethmann, A., Tempelmann, C., De Bleser, R., Scheich, H., & Brechmann, A. (2007). Determining language laterality by fMRI and dichotic listening. *Brain Research, 1133,* 145–157.

Beutler, L. E., Brown, M. T., Crothers, L., Booker, K., & Seabrook, M. K. (1996). The dilemma of factitious demographic distinctions in psychological research. *Journal of Consulting and Clinical Psychology, 64,* 892–902.

Bhattacharya, S. K., & Muruganandam, A. V. (2003). Adaptogenic activity of Withania somnifera: An experimental study using a rat model of chronic stress. *Pharmacology, Biochemistry & Behavior, 75*(3), 547–555.

Bianchi, M., Franchi, S., Ferrario, P., Sotgiu, M. L., & Sacerdote, P. (2008). Effects of the bisphosphonate ibandronate on hyperalgesia, substance P, and cytokine levels in a rat model of persistent inflammatory pain. *European Journal of Pain, 12,* 284–292.

Bieber, C., Müller, K. G., Blumenstiel, K., Hochlehnert, A., Wilke, S., Hartmann, M., & Eich, W. (2008). A shared decision-making communication training program for physicians treating fibromyalgia patients: Effects of a randomized controlled trial. *Journal of Psychosomatic Research, 64,* 13–20.

Biehl, M., Matsumoto, D., Ekman, P., Hearn, V., Heider, K., Kudoh, T., & Ton, V. (1997). Matsumoto and Ekman's Japanese and Caucasian facial expressions of emotion (JACFEE): Reliability data and cross-national differences. *Journal of Nonverbal Behavior, 21,* 3–21.

Billiard, M. (2007). Sleep disorders. In L. Candelise, R. Hughes, A. Liberati, B. M. J. Uitdehaag, & C. Warlow (Eds.), *Evidence-based neurology: Management of neurological* disorders (pp. 70–78). *Evidence-based medicine.* Malden, MA: Blackwell Publishing.

Bink, M. L., & Marsh, R. L. (2000). Cognitive regularities in creative activity. *Review of General Psychology, 4*(1), 59–78.

Birchler, G. R., Simpson, L. E., & Fals-Stewart, W. (2008). Marital therapy. In M. Hersen & A. M. Gross (Eds.), *Handbook of clinical psychology, vol 1: Adults* (pp. 617–646). Hoboken, NJ: Wiley.

Birkenhäger, T. K., Renes, J., & Pluijms, E. M. (2004). One-year follow-up after successful ECT: A naturalistic study in depressed inpatients. *Journal of Clinical Psychiatry, 65*(1), 87–91.

Bishop, C. A. (1974). *The northern Objibwa and the fur trade.* Toronto: Holt, Rinehart, and Winston.

Bjorkqvist, K. (1994). Sex differences in physical, verbal, and indirect aggression: A review of recent research. *Sex Roles, 30,* 177–188.

Blackburn, J. L. (2006). Motivated reasoning: A framework for understanding hiring managers' intentions to use personnel selection instruments. *Dissertation Abstracts International: Section B: The Sciences and Engineering, 67*(6-B), 3493.

Blaine, B., & McElroy, J. (2002). Selling stereotypes: Weight loss infomercials, sexism, and weightism. *Sex Roles, 46*(9–10), 351–357.

Blair, H. T., Huynh, V. K., Vaz, V. T., Van, J., Patel, R. R., Hiteshi, A. K., Lee, J. E., & Tarpley, J. W. (2005). Unilateral storage of fear memories by the amygdala. *Journal of Neuroscience, 25*(16), 4198–4205.

Blair, R. J. R. (2004). The roles of orbital frontal cortex in the modulation of antisocial behavior. *Brain & Cognition, 55*(1), 198–208.

Blais, M. C., & Boisvert, J-M. (2007). Psychological adjustment and marital satisfaction following head injury: Which critical personal characteristics should both partners develop? *Brain injury, 21,* 357–372.

Blakemore, C., & Cooper, G. F. (1970). Development of the brain depends on the visual environment. *Nature, 228,* 477–478.

Blanco, C., Schneier, F. R., Schmidt, A., Blanco-Jerez, C. R., Marshall, R. D., Sanchez-Lacay, A., & Liebowitz, M. R. (2003). Pharmacological treatment of social anxiety disorder: A metaanalysis. *Depression & Anxiety, 18*(1), 29–40.

Blass, T. (1991). Understanding behavior in the Milgram obedience experiment: The role of personality, situations, and their interactions. *Journal of Personality and Social Psychology, 60*(3), 398–413.

Blass, T. (2000). Stanley Milgram. In A. E. Kazdin (Ed.), *Encyclopedia of psychology* (Vol. 5) (pp. 248–250). Washington, DC: American Psychological Association.

Bleckley, M. K., Durso, F. T., Crutchfield, J. M., Engle, R. W., & Khanna, M. M. (2003). Individual differences in working memory capacity predict visual attention allocation. *Psychonomic Bulletin & Review, 10*(4), 884–889.

Bloch, Y., Grisaru, N., Hard, E. V., Beitler, G., Faivel, N., Ratzoni, G., Stein, D., & Levkovitz, Y. (2008). Repetitive transcranial magnetic stimulation in the treatment of depression in adolescents: An open-label study. *Journal of ECT, 24,* 153–159.

Blonigen, D. M., Carlson, M. D., Hicks, B. M., Krueger, R. F., & Iacono, W. G. (2008). Stability and change in personality traits from late adolescence to early adulthood: A longitudinal twin study. *Journal of Personality, 76,* 229–266.

Blonna, R., & Levitan, J. (2000). *Healthy sexuality.* Englewood, CO: Morton.

Bloom, P. N., McBride, C. M., Pollack, K. I., Schwartz-Bloom, R. D., & Lipkus, I. M. (2006). Recruiting teen smokers in shopping malls to a smoking-cessation program using the foot-in-the-door technique. *Journal of Applied Social Psychology, 36,* 1129–1144.

Blum, K., Braverman, E. R., Holder, J. M., Lubar, J. F., Monastra, V. J., Miller, D., Lubar, J. O., Chen, T. J. H., & Comings, D. E. (2000). Reward deficiency syndrome: A biogenetic model for the diagnosis and treatment of impulsive, addictive, and compulsive behaviors. *Journal of Psychoactive Drugs, 32*(Suppl), 1–68.

Blumenthal, J. A., Babyak, M. A., Doraiswamy, P. M., Watkins, L., Hoffman, B. M., Barbour, K. A., Herman, S., Craighead, W. E., Brosse, A. L., Waugh, R., Hinderliter, A., & Sherwood, A. (2007). Exercise and pharmacotherapy in the treatment of major depressive disorder. *Psychosomatic Medicine, 69,* 587–596.

Bob, P. (2008). Pain, dissociation and subliminal self-representations. *Consciousness and Cognition: An International Journal, 17,* 355–369.

Boccato, G., Capozza, D., Falvo, R., & Durante, F. (2008). Capture of the eyes by relevant and irrelevant onsets. *Social Cognition, 26,* 224–234.

Bock, G. R., & Goode, J. A. Eds. (1996). *Genetics of criminal and antisocial behavior.* Chichester, England: Wiley.

Bohbot, V. D., & Corkin, S. (2007). Posterior parahippocampal place learning in H. M. *Hippocampus, 17,* 863–872.

Bohm-Starke, N., Brodda-Jansen, G., Linder, J., & Danielson, I. (2007). The result of treatment on vestibular and general pain thresholds in women with provoked vestibulodynia. *Clinical Journal of Pain, 23*(7), 598–604.

Bohus, M., Haaf, B., Simms, T., Limberger, M. F., Schmahl, C., Unckel, C., Lieb, K., & Linehan, M. M. (2004). Effectiveness of inpatient dialectical behavioral therapy for borderline personality disorder: A controlled trial. *Behaviour Research & Therapy, 42*(5), 487–499.

Bolino, M. C., & Turnley, W. H. (2008). Old faces, new places: Equity theory in cross-cultural contexts. *Journal of Organizational Behavior, 29,* 29–50.

Bond, F. W., & Bunce, D. (2000). Mediators of change in emotion-focused and problemfocused worksite stress management intervention. *Journal of Occupational Health Psychology, 5,* 153–163.

Bond, M. H., & Smith, P. B. (1996). Cross-cultural social and organizational psychology. *Annual Review of Psychology, 47,* 205–235.

Bonnel, A., Mottron, L., Peretz, I., Trudel, M., Gallun, E., & Bonnel, A-M. (2003). Enhanced pitch sensitivity in individuals with autism: A signal detection analysis. *Cognitive Neuroscience, 5*(2), 226–235.

Bonner, C. D. (2007). From coercive to spiritual: What style of leadership is prevalent in K-12 public schools? *Dissertation Abstracts International: Section A: Humanities and Social Sciences, 68*(3-A), 802.

Bonness, B. M. (2008). Using structured employment interviews to predict task and contextual performance. *Dissertation Abstracts International: Section B: The Sciences and Engineering, 68*(10-B), 7009.

Book, A. S., Starzyk, K. B., & Qunisey, V. L. (2002). The relationship between testosterone and aggression: A meta-analysis. *Aggression & Violent Behavior, 6*(6), 579–599.

Bor, D., Billington, J., & Baron-Cohen, S. (2007). Savant memory for digits in a case of synaesthesia and Asberger Syndrome is related to hyperactivity in the lateral prefrontal cortex. *Neurocase, 13,* 311–319.

Borba, M. (2001). *Building moral intelligence: The seven essential virtues that teach kids to do the right thing.* San Francisco: Jossey-Bass.

Borbely, A. A. (1982). Circadian and sleep dependent processes in sleep regulation. In J. Aschoff, S. Daan, & G. A. Groos (Eds.),

Vertebrate circadian rhythms (pp. 237–242). Berlin: Springer/Verlag.

Borchers, B. J. (2007). Workplace environment fit, commitment, and job satisfaction in a nonprofit association. *Dissertation Abstracts International: Section B: The Sciences and Engineering, 67*(7-B), 4139.

Borra, R. (2008). Working with the cultural formulation in therapy. *European Psychiatry, 23*, S43-S48.

Borrego, J., Ibanez, E. S., Spendlove, S. J., & Pemberton, J. R. (2007). Treatment acceptability among Mexican American parents. *Behavior Therapy, 38*(3), 218–227.

Bouchard, T. J., Jr. (1994). Genes, environment, and personality. *Science, 264*, 1700–1701.

Bouchard, T. J., Jr. (1997). The genetics of personality. In K. Blum & E. P. Noble (Eds.), *Handbook of psychiatric genetics.* Boca Raton, FL: CRC Press.

Bouchard, T. J., Jr. (1999). The search for intelligence. *Science, 284*, 922–923.

Bouchard, T. J., Jr. (2004). Genetic influence on human psychological traits: A survey. *Current Directions in Psychological Science, 13*(4), 148–151.

Bouchard, T. J., Jr. & McGue, M. (1981). Familial studies of intelligence: A review. *Science, 212*(4498), 1055–1059.

Bouchard, T. J., Jr., McGue, M., Hur, Y., & Horn, J. M. (1998). A genetic and environmental analysis of the California Psychological Inventory using adult twins reared apart and together. *European Journal of Personality, 12*, 307–320.

Boucher, L., & Dienes, Z. (2003). Two ways of learning associations. *Cognitive Science, 27*(6), 807–842.

Bourgeois-Bougrine, S., Carbon, P., Gounelle, C., Mollard, R., & Coblentz, A. (2003). Perceived fatigue for short-and long-haul flights: A survey of 739 airline pilots. *Aviation, Space, and Environmental Medicine, 74*(10), 1072–1077.

Bourne, L. E., Dominowski, R. L., & Loftus, E. F. (1979). *Cognitive processes.* Englewood Cliffs, NJ: Prentice Hall.

Bouton, M. E. (1994). Context, ambiguity, and classical conditioning. *Current Directions in Psychological Science, 2*, 49–53.

Bouton, M. E., Mineka, S., & Barlow, D. H. (2001). A modern learning theory perspective on the etiology of panic disorder. *Psychological Review, 108*(1), 4–32.

Bovbjerg, D. H. (2003). Circadian disruption and cancer: Sleep and immune regulation. *Brain, Behavior & Immunity, 17*(Suppl1), 48-S50.

Bower, B. (2000). Cooperative strangers turn a mutual profit. *Science News, 157*, 231.

Bower, G. H. (2008). The evolution of a cognitive psychologist: A journey from simple behaviors to complex mental acts. *Annual Review of Psychology, 59*, 1–27.

Bowers, K. S., & Woody, E. Z. (1996). Hypnotic amnesia and the paradox of intentional forgetting. *Journal of Abnormal Psychology, 105*, 381–390.

Bowlby, J. (1969). *Attachment and loss: Vol. 1. Attachment.* New York: Basic Books.

Bowlby, J. (1973). *Attachment and loss: Vol. 2. Separation and anxiety.* New York: Basic Books.

Bowlby, J. (1982). Attachment and loss: Retrospect and prospect. *American Journal of Orthopsychiatry, 52*, 664–678.

Bowlby, J. (1989). *Secure attachment.* New York: Basic Books.

Bowlby, J. (2000). *Attachment.* New York: Basic Books.

Bowling, A. C., & Mackenzie, B. D. (1996). The relationship between speed of information processing and cognitive ability. *Personality & Individual Differences, 20*(6), 775–800.

Boyle, S. H., Williams, R. B., Mark, D. B., Brummett, B. H., Siegler, I. C., Helms, M. J., & Brady, S. S. (2007). Young adults' media use and attitudes toward interpersonal and institutional forms of aggression. *Aggressive Behavior, 33*(6), 519–525.

Boysen, G. A., & Vogel, D. L. (2007). Biased assimilation and attitude polarization in response to learning about biological explanations of homosexuality. *Sex Roles, 56*, 755–762.

Bozarth, J. D., & Brodley, B. T. (2008). Actualization: A functional concept in client-centered therapy. In B. E. Levitt (Ed.), *Reflections on human potential: Bridging the person-centered approach and positive psychology* (pp. 33–45). Ross-on-Wye, England: PCCS Books.

Bozkurt, A. S., & Aydin, O. (2004). Temel yükleme hatasinin degisik yas ve iki alt kültürde incelenmesi. [A developmental investigation of fundamental attribution error in two subcultures.] *Türk Psikoloji Dergisi, 19*, 91–104.

Bradley, R., Conklin, C. Z., & Westen, D. (2007). Borderline personality disorder. In W. O'Donohue, K. A. Fowler, S. O. Lilienfeld (Eds.), *Personality disorders: Toward the DSM-V* (pp. 167–201). Thousand Oaks, CA: Sage.

Bradley, R. H., & Corwyn, R. F. (2008). Infant temperament, parenting, and externalizing behavior in first grade: A test of the differential susceptibility hypothesis. *Journal of Child Psychology and Psychiatry, 49*, 124–131.

Braeger, D. (2007). Developing charisma with caution. In D. Crandell (Ed.), *Leadership lessons from West Point.* Hoboken, NJ: Wiley.

Bragdon, A. D., & Gamon, D. (1999). *Building left-brain power: Left-brain conditioning exercises and tips to strengthen language, math, and uniquely human skills.* Thousand Oaks, CA: Brainwaves Books.

Brandon, T. H., Collins, B. N., Juliano, L. M., & Lazev, A. B. (2000). Preventing relapse among former smokers: A comparison of minimal interventions through telephone and mail. *Journal of Consulting and Clinical Psychology, 68*(1), 103–113.

Brawman-Mintzer, O., & Lydiard, R. B. (1996). Generalized anxiety disorder: Issues in epidemiology. *Journal of Clinical Psychiatry, 57*, 3–8.

Brawman-Mintzer, O., & Lydiard, R. B. (1997). Biological basis of generalized anxiety disorder. *Journal of Clinical Psychiatry, 58*, 16–25.

Breland, K., & Breland, M. (1961). The misbehavior of organisms. *American Psychologist, 16*, 681–684.

Bremner, J. D., Vythilingam, M., Vermetten, E., Anderson, G., Newcomer, J. W. & Charney, D. S. (2004). Effects of glucocorticoids on declarative memory function in major depression. *Biological Psychiatry, 55*(8), 811–815.

Brendgen, M., Vitaro, F., & Bukowski, W. M. (2000). Deviant friends and early adolescents' emotional and behavioral adjustment. *Journal of Research on Adolescence, 10*(2), 173–189.

Brenner, S. (2005). *Vietnam war crimes.* Farmington Hills, MI: Greenhaven Press.

Brent, D. A., Melhem, N. (2008). Familial transmission of suicidal behavior. *Psychiatric Clinics of North America, 31*, 157–177.

Brewer, J. B., Zhao, Z., Desmond, J. E., Glover, G. H., & Gabrieli, J. D. (1998). Making memories: Brain activity that predicts how well visual experience will be remembered. *Science, 281*, 1185–1187.

Brewer, M. B. (1996). When contact is not enough: Social identity and intergroup cooperation. *International Journal of Intercultural Relations, 20*(3–4), 291–303.

Brewer, W. F., & Pani, J. R. (1996). Reports of mental imagery in retrieval from long-term memory. *Consciousness & Cognition: An International Journal, 5*, 265–287.

Bridgeman, B., & Hoover, M. (2008). Processing spatial layout by perception and sensimotor interaction. *The Quarterly Journal of Experimental Psychology, 61,* 851–859.

Brim, O. (1999). *The MacArthur Foundation study of midlife development.* Vero Beach, FL: MacArthur Foundation.

Brislin, R. W. (1997). *Understanding culture's influence on behavior* (2nd ed.). San Diego: Harcourt Brace.

Brislin, R. W. (2000). *Understanding culture's influence on behavior.* Ft. Worth, TX: Harcourt.

Brkich, M., Jeffs, D., & Carless, S. A. (2002). A global self-report measure of person-job fit. *European Journal of Psychological Assessment, 18*(1), 43–51.

Brody, A., Olmstead, R. E., London, E. D., Farahi, J., Meyer, J. H., Grossman, P., Lee, G. S., Huang, J., Hahn, E. L., & Mandelkern, M. A. (2004). Smoking-induced ventral striatum dopamine release. *American Journal of Psychiatry, 161*(7), 1211–1218.

Broman-Fulks, J. J., Berman, M. E., Rabian, B. A., & Webster, M. J. (2004). Effects of aerobic exercise on anxiety sensitivity. *Behaviour Research & Therapy, 42*(2), 125–136.

Brown, A., & Whiteside, S. P. (2008). Relations among perceived parental rearing behaviors, attachment style, and worry in anxious children. *Journal of Anxiety Disorders, 22,* 263–272.

Brown, A. C., Wolchik, S. A., Tein, J-Y., & Sandler, I. N. (2007). Maternal acceptance as a moderator of the relation between threat to self appraisals and mental health problems in adolescents from divorced families. *Journal of Youth and Adolescence, 36,* 927–938.

Brown, D. (2001). (Mis)representations of the long-term effects of childhood sexual abuse in the courts. *Journal of Child Sexual Abuse, 9*(3–4), 79–108.

Brown, E., Deffenbacher, K., & Sturgill, K. (1977). Memory for faces and the circumstances of encounter. *Journal of Applied Psychology, 62,* 311–318.

Brown, J. C. (2008). Full and part-time employee stress and job satisfaction at two upstate New York colleges. *Dissertation Abstracts International: Section A: Humanities and Social Sciences, 68*(8-A), 3303.

Brown, K. T., Brown, T. N., Jackson, J., Sellers, R. M., & Manuel, W. J. (2003). Teammates on and off the field? White student athletes. *Journal of Applied Social Psychology, 33*(7), 1379–1403.

Brown, P. K., & Wald, G. (1964). Visual pigments in single rods and cones of the human retina. Direct measurements reveal mechanisms of human night and color vision. *Science, 144,* 45–52.

Brown, R., & Kulik, J. (1977). Flashbulb memories. *Cognition, 5,* 73–99.

Brown, R. P., & Josephs, R. A. (1999). A burden of proof: Stereotype relevance and gender differences in math performance. *Journal of Personality and Social Psychology, 76*(2), 246–257.

Brown, T. A., O'Leary, T. A., & Barlow, D. H. (2001). Generalized anxiety disorder. In D. H. Barlow (Ed.), *Clinical handbook of psychological disorders: A step-by-step treatment manual* (3rd ed.) (pp. 154–208). New York: Guilford Press.

Browne, K. O. (2001). Cultural formulation of psychiatric diagnoses. *Culture, Medicine & Psychiatry, 25*(4), 411–425.

Bruck, C. S., & Allen, T. D. (2003). The relationship between big five personality traits, negative affectivity, type A behavior, and workfamily conflict. *Journal of Vocational Behavior, 63*(3), 457–472.

Bruggeman, E. L., & Hart, K. J. (1996). Cheating, lying, and moral reasoning by religious and secular high school students. *Journal of Educational Research, 89,* 340–344.

Brummett, B. H., Babyak, M. A., Mark, D. B., Clapp-Channing, N. E., Siegler, I. C., & Barefoot, J. C. (2004). Prospective study of perceived stress in cardiac patients. *Annals of Behavioral Medicine, 27*(1), 22–30.

Brunsma, D., Overfelt, D., & Picou, S., (Eds.) (2007). *Sociology of Katrina.* Lanham, MD: Rowman & Littlefield.

Buchanan, T. W., & Lovallo, W. R. (2001). Enhanced memory for emotional material following stress-level cortisol treatment in humans. *Psychoneuroendocrinology, 26*(3), 307–317.

Buck, R. (1984). *The communication of emotion.* New York: Guilford Press.

Buddie, A. M, & Parks, K. A. (2003). The role of the bar context and social behaviors on women's risk for aggression. *Journal of Interpersonal Violence, 18*(12), 1378–1393.

Bugental, D. B., & Goodnow, J. J. (1998). Socialization process. In W. Damon & N. Eisenberg (Eds.), *Handbook of child psychology* (5th ed.). New York: Wiley.

Bugental, D. B., & Johnston, C. (2000). Parental and child cognitions in the context of the family. *Annual Review of Psychology, 51,* 315–344.

Bugg, J. M., Zook, N. A., DeLosh, E. L., Davalos, D. B., & Davis, H. P. (2006). Age differences in fluid intelligence: Contributions of general slowing and frontal decline. *Brain and Cognition, 62,* 9–16.

Bulik, C. M., Sullivan, P. F., & Kendler, K. S. (2002). Medical and psychiatric morbidity in obese women with and without binge eating. *International Journal of Eating Disorders, 32*(1), 72–78.

Bull, L. (2003). What can be done to prevent smoking in pregnancy? A literature review. *Early Child Development & Care, 173*(6), 661–667.

Bunde, J., & Suls, J. (2006). A quantitative analysis of the relationship between the cook-medley hostility scale and traditional coronary artery disease risk factors. *Health Psychology, 25,* 493–500.

Buontempo, G., & Brockner, J. (2008). Emotional intelligence and the ease of recall judgment bias: The mediating effect of private self-focused attention. *Journal of Applied Social Psychology, 38,* 159–172.

Burgdorf, J., Knutson, B., & Panksepp, J. (2000). Anticipation of rewarding electrical brain stimulation evokes ultrasonic vocalization in rats. *Behavioural Neuroscience, 114*(2), 320–327.

Burns, N. R., Nettelbeck, T., & Cooper, C. J. (2000). Event-related potential correlates of some human cognitive ability constructs. *Personality & Individual Differences, 29*(1), 157–168.

Burns, R. A., Johnson, K. S., Harris, B. A., Kinney, B. A., & Wright, S. E. (2004). Functional cues for position learning effects in animals. *Psychological Record, 54*(2), 233–254.

Burns, R. G., & Katovich, M. A. (2003). Examining road rage/aggressive driving: Media depiction and prevention suggestions. *Environment & Behavior, 35*(5), 621–636.

Burns, S. M. (2008). Unique and interactive predictors of mental health quality of life among men living with prostate cancer. *Dissertation Abstracts International: Section B: The Sciences and Engineering, 68*(10-B), 6953.

Burton, L. A., Rabin, L., Vardy, S. B., Frohlich, J., Wyatt, G., Dimitri, D., Constante, S., & Guterman, E. (2004). Gender differences in implicit and explicit memory for affective passages. *Brain & Cognition, 54*(3), 218–224.

Bushman, B. J. (2002). Does venting anger feed or extinguish the flame? Catharsis, rumination, distraction, anger and aggressive responding. *Personality & Social Psychology Bulletin, 28*(6), 724–731.

Bushman, B. J., Baumeister, R. F., & Stack, A. D. (1999). Catharsis, aggression, and persuasive influence: Self-fulfilling or self-defeating prophecies? *Journal of Personality and Social Psychology, 76,* 367–376.

Buss, D. M. (1989). Sex differences in human mate preferences: Evolutionary hypotheses tested in 37 cultures. *Behavioral and Brain Sciences, 12,* 1–49.

Buss, D. M. (2003). *The evolution of desire: Strategies of human mating.* New York: Basic Books.

Buss, D. M. (2005). *The handbook of evolutionary psychology.* Hoboken, NJ: Wiley.

Buss, D. M. (2007). The evolution of human mating. *Acta Psychologica Sinica. 39,* 502–512.

Buss, D. M. (2008). *Evolutionary psychology: The new science of the mind* (3rd ed.). Boston: Allyn & Bacon.

Buss, D. M. and 40 colleagues. (1990). International preferences in selecting mates: A study of 37 cultures. *Journal of Cross-Cultural Psychology, 21,* 5–47.

Buswell, B. N. (2006). The role of empathy, responsibility, and motivations to respond without prejudice in reducing prejudice. *Dissertation Abstracts International: Section B: The Sciences and Engineering, 66,* 6968.

Butcher, J. N. (2000). Revising psychological tests: Lessons learned from the revision of the MMPI. *Psychological Assessment, 12*(3), 263–271.

Butcher, J. N. (2005). *A beginner's guide to the MMPI-2* (2nd ed.). Washington, DC: American Psychological Association.

Butcher, J. N., & Perry, J. N. (2008). *Personality assessment in treatment planning: Use of the MMPI-2 and BTPI.* New York: Oxford University Press.

Butcher, J. N., & Rouse, S. V. (1996). Personality: Individual differences and clinical assessment. *Annual Review of Psychology, 47,* 87–111.

Butler, K. Joel, J. C., & Jeffries, M. (2000). *Clinical handbook of psychotropic drugs.* New York: Wiley.

Butler, R. A. (1954, February). Curiosity in monkeys. *Scientific American, 190,* 70–75.

Butterweck, V. (2003). Mechanism of action of St John's Wort in depression: What is known? *CNS Drugs, 17*(8), 539–562.

Buunk, B. P., Dijkstra, P., Fetchenhauer, D., & Kenrick, D. (2002). Age and gender differences in mate selection criteria for various involvement levels. *Personal Relationships, 9*(3), 271–278.

Byne, W. (2007). Biology and sexual minority status. In I. H. Meyer & M. E. Northridge (Eds.), *The health of sexual minorities: Public health perspectives on lesbian, gay, bisexual, and transgender populations* (pp. 65–90). New York: Springer Science + Business Media.

Byne, W., Dracheva, S., Chin, B., Schmeidler, J. M., Davis, K. L., & Haroutunian, V. (2008). Schizophrenia and sex associated differences in the neuronal and oligodendrocyte-specific genes in individual thalamic nuclei. *Schizophrenia Research, 98,* 118–128.

Cabýoglu, M. T., Ergene, N., & Tan, U. (2006). The mechanism of acupuncture and clinical applications. *International Journal of Neuroscience, 116,* 115–125.

Cadoret, R. J., Leve, L. D., & Devor, E. (1997). Genetics of aggressive and violent behavior. *Psychiatric Clinics of North America, 20,* 301–322.

Cai, W-H., Blundell, J., Han, J., Greene, R. W., & Powell, C. M. (2006). Postreactivation glucocorticoids impair recall of established fear memory. *Journal of Neuroscience, 26*(37), 9560–9566.

Callahan, C. M., & Berrios, G. E. (2005). *Reinventing depression: A history of the treatment of depression in primary care, 1940–2004.* New York: Oxford University Press.

Camarena, B., Santiago, H., Aguilar, A., Ruvinskis, E., González-Barranco, J., & Nicolini, H. (2004). Family-based association study between the monoamine oxidase A gene and obesity: Implications for psychopharmacogenetic studies. *Neuropsychobiology, 49*(3), 126–129.

Cameron, L., Rutland, A. & Brown, R. (2007). Promoting children's positive intergroup attitudes towards stigmatized groups: Extended contact and multiple classification skills training. *International Journal of Behavioral Development, 31,* 454–466.

Camodeca, M., Goossens, F. A., Meerum T. M., & Schuengel, C. (2002). Bullying and victimization among school-age children: Stability and links to proactive and reactive aggression. *Social Development, 11*(3), 332–345.

Campbell, A., & Muncer, S. (2008). Intent to harm or injure? Gender and the expression of anger. *Aggressive Behavior, 34,* 282–293.

Campbell, L., Simpson, J. A., Kashy, D. A., & Fletcher, G. J. O. (2001). Ideal standards, the self, and flexibility of ideals in close relationships. *Personality & Social Psychology Bulletin, 27*(4), 447–462.

Cannon, T. D., van Erp, T. G. M., Rosso, I. M., Huttunen, M., Loenqvist, J., Pirkola, T., Salonen, O., Valanne, L., Poutanen, V., & Standertskjoeld-Nordenstam, C. (2002). Fetal hypoxia and structural brain abnormalities in schizophrenic patients, their siblings, and controls. *Archives of General Psychiatry, 59*(1), 35–41.

Cannon, W. B. (1927). The James-Lange theory of emotions: A critical examination and an alternative theory. *American Journal of Psychology, 39,* 106–124.

Cannon, W. B., Lewis, J. T., & Britton, S. W. (1927). The dispensability of the sympathetic division of the autonomic nervous system. *Boston Medical Surgery Journal, 197,* 514.

Cannon, W. B., & Washburn, A. (1912). An explanation of hunger. *American Journal of Physiology, 29,* 441–454.

Cantor, J. M., Blanchard, R., Paterson, A. D., & Bogaert, A. F. (2002). How many gay men owe their sexual orientation to fraternal birth order? *Archives of Sexual Behavior, 31*(1), 63–71.

Caprara, G. V., Vecchione, M., Barbaranelli, C., & Fraley, R. C. (2007). When likeness goes with liking: The case of political preference. *Political Psychology, 28,* 609–632.

Carballo, J. J., Harkavy-Friedman, J., Burke, A. K., Sher, L., Baca-Garcia, E., Sullivan, G. M., Gruneman, M. F., Parsey, R. V., Mann, J. J., & Oquendo, M. A. (2008). Family history of suicidal behavior and early traumatic experiences: Addictive effect on suicidality and course of bipolar illness? *Journal of Affective Disorders, 109,* 57–63.

Carducci, B. J. (1998). *The psychology of personality: Viewpoints, research, and applications.* Pacific Grove, CA: Brooks/Cole.

Carels, R. A., Konrad, K., Young, K. M., Darby, L. A., Coit, C., Clayton, A. M., & Oemig, C. K. (2008). Taking control of your personal eating and exercise environment: A weight maintenance program. *Eating Behaviors, 9,* 228–237.

Carlat, D. (2008). *Brain scans as mind readers? Don't believe the hype.* [On-line]. Available: http://www.wired.com/print/medtech/health/magazine/16–06/mf_neurohacks.

Carlo, G. (2006). Care-based and altruistically-based morality. In M. Killen & J. Smetana (Eds.), *Handbook of moral development.* Mahwah, NJ: Erlbaum.

Carlson, E., & Ruzek, J. (2008). *PTSD and the Family.* [On-line]. Available: http://www.ncptsd.va.gov/ncmain/ncdocs/fact_shts/fs_family.html.

Carlson, L. E., Speca, M., Faris, P., & Patel, K. D. (2007). One year pre-post intervention follow-up of psychological, immune, endocrine and blood pressure outcomes of mindfulness-based stress reduction (MBSR) in breast and prostate cancer outpatient. *Brain, Behavior, and Immunity, 21,* 1038–1049.

Carlson, N. R. (2008). *Foundations of physiological psychology: International edition.* Boston: Allyn & Bacon.

Carmaciu, C. D., Anderson, C. S., & Markar, H. R. (2001). Secondary koro with unusual features in a Briton. *Transcultural Psychiatry, 38*(4), 528–533.

Carnagey, N. L., & Anderson, C. A. (2004). Violent video game exposure and aggression: A literature review. *Minerva Psichiatrica, 45*(1), 1–18.

Carnagey, N. L., Anderson, C. A., & Bartholow, B. D. (2007). Media violence and social neuroscience: New questions and new opportunities. *Current Directions in Psychological Science, 16*, 178–182.

Carney, S., Cowen, P., Geddes, J., Goodwin, G., Rogers, R., Dearness, K., Tomlin, A., Eastaugh, J., Freemantle, N., Lester, H., Harvey, A., & Scott, A. (2003). Efficacy and safety of electroconvulsive therapy in depressive disorders: A systematic review and meta-analysis. *Lancet, 361*(9360), 799–808.

Caro, D. M. (2008). The relationship between temperament and personality over time and across the generations. *Dissertation Abstracts International: Section B: The Sciences and Engineering, 68*(7-B), 4863.

Carpenter, S., & Radhakrishnan, P. (2002). The relation between allocentrism and perceptions of ingroups. *Personality & Social Psychology Bulletin, 28*(11), 1528–1537.

Carr, J. L., & VanDeusen, K. M. (2004). Risk factors for male sexual aggression on college campuses. *Journal of Family Violence, 19*(5), 279–289.

Carskadon, M. A., & Dement, W. C. (2002). *Adolescent sleep patterns.* New York: Cambridge University Press.

Carstensen, L. L. (2006). The influence of a sense of time on human development. *Science, 312*, 1913–1915.

Carstensen, L. L., Fung, H. H., & Charles, S. (2003). Socioemotional selectivity theory and the regulation of emotion in the second half of life. *Motivation & Emotion, 27*(2), 103–123.

Carter, E., & Wang, X-J. (2007). Cannabinoid-mediated disinhibition and working memory: Dynamical interplay of multiple feedback mechanisms in a continuous attractor model of prefrontal cortex. *Cerebral Cortex, 17*(Suppl 1), 16–26.

Carton, J. S. (1996). The differential effects of tangible rewards and praise on intrinsic motivation: A comparison of cognitive evaluation theory and operant theory. *Behavior Analyst, 19*, 237–255.

Caruso, E. M. (2008). Use of experienced retrieval ease in self and social judgments. *Journal of Experimental Social Psychology, 44*, 148–155.

Carvalho, C., Mazzoni, G., Kirsch, I., Meo, M., & Santandrea, M. (2008). The effect of posthypnotic suggestion, hypnotic suggestibility, and goal intentions on adherence to medical instructions. *International Journal of Clinical and Experimental Hypnosis, 56*, 143–155.

Casarjian, R., Phillips, J., & Wolman, R. (2007). An emotional literacy intervention with incarcerated individuals. *American Journal of Forensic Psychology, 25*, 43–63.

Casey, B. J., Getz, S., & Galvan, A. (2008). The adolescent brain. *Developmental Review, 28*, 62–77.

Caspi, A., Chajut, E., & Saporta, K. (2008). Participation in class and in online discussions: Gender differences. *Computers & Education, 50*, 718–724.

Castelli, L., Corazzini, L. L., & Geminiani, G. C. (2008). Spatial navigation in large-scale virtual environments: Gender differences in survey tasks. *Computers in Human Behavior, 24*, 1643–1667.

Casti, J. L. (2000). *Paradigms regained: A further exploration of the mysteries of modern science.* New York: Morrow.

Castillo, R. J. (2003). Trance, functional psychosis, and culture. *Psychiatry: Interpersonal & Biological Processes, 66*(1), 9–21.

Castonguay, L. G., & Hill, C. (Eds.) (2007). *Insight in psychotherapy.* Washington, DC: American Psychological Association.

Cathers-Schiffman, T. A., & Thompson, M. S. (2007). Assessment of English-and Spanish-speaking students with the WISC-III and Leiter-R. *Journal of Psychoeducational Assessment, 25*, 41–52.

Cattell, R. B. (1950). *Personality: A systematic, theoretical, and factual study.* New York: McGraw-Hill.

Cattell, R. B. (1963). Theory of fluid and crystallized intelligence: A critical experiment. *Journal of Educational Psychology, 54*, 1–22.

Cattell, R. B. (1965). *The scientific analysis of personality.* Baltimore: Penguin.

Cattell, R. B. (1971). *Abilities: Their structure, growth, and action.* Boston: Houghton Mifflin.

Cattell, R. B. (1990). Advances in Cattellian personality theory. In L. A. Pervin (Ed.), *Handbook of personality: Theory and research.* New York: Guilford Press.

Cavacuiti, C. A. (2004). You, me, and drugs—A love triangle: Important considerations when both members of a couple are abusing substances. *Substance Use & Misuse, 39*(4), 645–656.

Cavett, D. (2008). Smiling through. New York Times. [On-Line]. Available: http://cavett.blogs.nytimes.com/2008/06/27/smiling-through/?scp=6&sq=dick%20cavett&st=cse

Cehajic, S., Brown, R., & Castano, E. (2008). Forgive and forget? Antecedents and consequences of intergroup forgiveness in Bosnia and Herzegovina. *Political Psychology, 29*, 351–367.

Centers for Disease Control and Prevention (CDC). (2008). Fact sheets. [On-line]. Available: http://www.cdc.gov/hiv/resources/factsheets/ index.htm#Surveillance.

Centers for Disease Control and Prevention (CDC). (2008). Quick stats. [On-line]. Available: http://www.cdc.gov/alcohol/quickstats/general_info.htm.

Centers for Disease Control and Prevention (CDC). (2008). *Tobacco use.* [On-line]. Available: http://www.cdc.gov/HealthyYouth/tobacco/index.htm.

Cervone, D., & Shoda, Y. (1999). Beyond traits in the study of personality coherence. *Current Directons in Psychological Science, 8*(a), 27–32.

Cesario, J. F. (2006). Regulatory fit from nonverbal behaviors: How source delivery style influences message effectiveness. *Dissertation Abstracts International: Section B: The Sciences and Engineering, 67*(4-B), 2276.

Cesaro, P., & Ollat, H. (1997). Pain and its treatments. *European Neurology, 38*, 209–215.

Ceschi, G., & Scherer, K. R. (2001). Contrôler l'expression faciale et changer l'émotion: Une approche développementale. The role of facial expression in emotion: A developmental perspective. *Enfance, 53*(3), 257–269.

Chabrol, H., Montovany, A., Ducongé, E., Kallmeyer, A., Mullet, E., & Leichsenring, F. (2004). Factor structure of the borderline personality inventory in adolescents. *European Journal of Psychological Assessment, 20*(1), 59–65.

Chaikin, N. D., & Prout, M. F. (2004). Treating complex trauma in women within community mental health. *American Journal of Orthopsychiatry, 74*(2), 160–173.

Challem, J., Berkson, B., Smith, M. D., & Berkson, B. (2000). *Syndrome X: The complete program to prevent and reverse insulin resistance.* New York: Wiley.

Champtiaux, N., Kalivas, P. W., & Bardo, M. T. (2006). Contribution of dihydro-beta-erythroidine sensitive nicotinic acetylcholine receptors in the ventral tegmental area to cocaine-induced behavioral sensitization in rats. *Behavioural Brain Research, 168,* 120–126.

Chance, P. (2009). *Learning and behavior: Active learning edition* (6th ed.). Belmont, CA: Cengage.

Chandrashekar, J., Hoon, M. A., Ryba, N. J. P., & Zuker, C. S. (2006). The receptors and cells for mammalian taste. *Nature, 444,* 288–294.

Chaney, J. M., Mullins, L. L., Wagner, J. L., Hommel, K. A., Page, M. C., Doppler, & Matthew J. (2004). A longitudinal examination of causal attributions and depression symptomatology in rheumatoid arthritis. *Rehabilitation Psychology, 49*(2), 126–133.

Chang, G., Orav, J., McNamara, T. K., Tong, MY., & Antin, J. H. (2005). Psychosocial function after hematopoietic stem cell transplantation. *Psychosomatics: Journal of Consultation Liaison Psychiatry, 46*(1), 34–40.

Chang, R. C., Stout, S., & Miller, R. R. (2004). Comparing excitatory backward and forward conditioning. *Quarterly Journal of Experimental Psychology: Comparative & Physiological Psychology, 57B*(1), 1–23.

Chapelot, D., Marmonier, C., Aubert, R., Gausseres, N., & Louis-Sylvestre, J. (2004). A role for glucose and insulin preprandial profiles to differentiate meals and snacks. *Physiology & Behavior, 80*(5), 721–731.

Chapman, A. L., Leung, D. W., & Lynch, T. R. (2008). Impulsivity and emotion dysregulation in borderline personality disorder. *Journal of Personality Disorders, 22,* 148–164.

Chapman, B. P., Duberstein, P. R., Sörensen, S., & Lyness, J. M. (2007). Gender differences in Five Factor Model personality traits in an elderly cohort. *Personality and Individual Differences, 43,* 1594–1603.

Charland, W. A. (1992, January). Nightshift narcosis. *The Rotarion, 160,* 16–19.

Charles, E. P. (2007). Object permanence, an ecological approach. *Dissertation Abstracts International: Section B: The Sciences and Engineering, 67*(8-B), 4737.

Charles, S. T., & Carstensen, L. L. (2007). Emotion regulation and aging. In J. J. Gross (Ed.), *Handbook of emotion regulation.* New York: Guilford Press.

Chartrand, T., Pinckert, S., & Burger, J. M. (1999). When manipulation backfires: The effects of time delay and requester on the foot-in-the-door technique. *Journal of Applied Social Psychology, 29,* 211–221.

Charuvastra, M. C. (2008). Social bonds and posttraumatic stress disorder. *Annual Review of Psychology, 59,* 301–328.

Chavez, C. I., & Weisinger, J. Y. (2008). Beyond diversity training: A social infusion for cultural inclusion. *Human Resource Management, 47,* 331–350.

Chebat, J., El Hedhli, K., Gélinas-Chebat, C., & Boivin, R. (2007). Voice and persuasion in a banking telemarketing context. *Perceptual and Motor Skills, 104,* 419–437.

Chen, A. C. C., Keith, V. M., Leong, K. J., Airriess, C., Li, W., Chung, K.-Y., & Lee, C-C. (2007). Hurricane Katrina: Prior trauma, poverty and health among Vietnamese-American survivors. *International Nursing Review, 54,* 324–331.

Chen, E., & Miller, G. E. (2007). Stress and inflammation in exacerbations of asthma. *Brain, Behavior, and Immunity, 21,* 993–999.

Chen, F., & Kenrick, D. T. (2002). Repulsion or attraction? Group membership and assumed attitude similarity. *Journal of Personality and Social Psychology, 83*(1), 111–125.

Cherney, I. D. (2005). Children's and adults' recall of sex-stereotyped toy pictures: Effects of presentation and memory task. *Infant & Child Development, 14*(1), 11–27.

Cheung, C., & Rudowicz, E. (2003). Underachievement and attributions among students attending schools stratified by student ability. *Social Psychology of Education, 6*(4), 303–323.

Cheung, M. S., Gilbert, P., & Irons, C. (2004). An exploration of shame, social rank, and rumination in relation to depression. *Personality & Individual Differences, 36*(5), 1143–1153.

Chi, I., & Chou, K. (1999). Financial strain and depressive symptoms among Hong Kong Chinese elderly: A longitudinal study. *Journal of Gerontological Social Work, 32,* 41–60.

Chiesa, M., & Hobbs, S. (2008). Making sense of social research: How useful is the Hawthorne Effect? *European Journal of Social Psychology, 38,* 67–74.

Chiou, W-B. (2007). Customers' attributional judgments towards complaint handling in airline service: A confirmatory study based on attribution theory. *Psychological Reports, 100,* 1141–1150.

Chiricozzi, F. R., Clausi, S., Molinari, M., & Leggio, M. G. (2008). Phonological short-term store impairment after cerebellar lesion: A single case study. *Neuropsychologia, 46,* 1940–1953.

Chislett, L. (2008). Congruence, consistency and differentiation of career interests: A study of construct validity and relationships with achievement, satisfaction and personality adjustment. *Dissertation Abstracts International Section A: Humanities and Social Sciences, 68*(7-A), 2807.

Cho, K. (2001). Chronic "jet lag" produces temporal lobe atrophy and spatial cognitive deficits. *Nature Neuroscience, 4*(6), 567–568.

Choi, I., & Nisbett, R. E. (2000). Cultural psychology of surprise: Holistic theories and recognition of contradiction. *Journal of Personality and Social Psychology, 79*(6), 890–905.

Choi, N. (2004). Sex role group differences in specific, academic, and general self-efficacy. *Journal of Psychology: Interdisciplinary & Applied, 138*(2), 149–159.

Chomsky, N. (1968). *Language and mind.* New York: Harcourt, Brace, World.

Chomsky, N. (1980). *Rules and representations.* New York: Columbia University Press.

Chrisler, J. C. (2008). The menstrual cycle in a biopsychosocial context. In F. Denmark & M. A. Paludi (Eds.), *Psychology of women: A handbook of issues and theories* (2nd ed.) (pp. 400–439). *Women's psychology.* Westport, CT: Praeger/Greenwood.

Christ, G. H., Siegel, K., & Christ, A. E. (2002). Adolescent grief: "It never really hit me…until it actually happened." *Journal of the American Medical Association, 288*(10), 1269–1278.

Christensen, D. (2000). Is snoring a diZZZease? Nighttime noises may serve as a wake-up call for future illness. *Science News, 157,* 172–173.

Christensen, H., Anstey, K. J., Leach, L. S., & Mackinnon, A. J. (2008). Intelligence, education, and the brain reserve hypothesis. In F. I. M. Craik & T. A. Salthouse (Eds.), *The handbook of aging and cognition* (3rd ed.) (pp. 133–188). New York: Psychology Press.

Christian, K. M., & Thompson, R. F. (2005). Long-term storage of an associative memory trace in the cerebellum. *Behavioral Neuroscience, 119*(2), 526–537.

Christopher, K., Lutz-Zois, C. J., & Reinhardt, A. R. (2007). Female sexual-offenders: Personality pathology as a mediator of the relationship between childhood sexual abuse history and sexual abuse. *Child Abuse & Neglect, 31,* 871–883.

Chuang, D. (1998). Cited in J. Travis, Stimulating clue hints how lithium works. *Science News, 153,* 165.

Chung, J. C. C. (2006). Measuring sensory processing patterns of older Chinese people: Psychometric validation of the adult sensory profile. *Aging & Mental Health, 10,* 648–655.

Chwalisz, K., Diener, E., & Gallagher, D. (1988). Autonomic arousal feedback and emotional experience: Evidence from the spinal cord injured. *Journal of Personality and Social Psychology, 54,* 820–828.

Cialdini, R. B. (2001). *Influence: Science and practice* (4th ed.). Boston: Allyn & Bacon.

Cialdini, R. B. (2009). *Influence: Science and practice* (5th ed.). Boston: Allyn & Bacon.

Cicchetti, D., & Toth, S. L. (2005). Child maltreatment. *Annual Review of Clinical Psychology, 1,* 409–438.

Cigarettes Now Cost More. (2008). [Online]. Available: http://www.wstm.com/news/news_story.aspx?id5141948.

Cillessen A. H. N., & Mayeux L. (2004). From censure to reinforcement: Developmental changes in the association between aggression and social status. *Child Development, 75,* 147–163.

Clark, A. J. (2007). *Empathy in counseling and psychotherapy: Perspectives and practices.* Mahwah, NJ: Erlbaum.

Clark, K. B., & Clark, M. P. (1939). The development of consciousness of self and the emergence of racial identification in Negro preschool children. *Journal of Social Psychology, 10,* 591–599.

Cleaves, D. H., & Latner, J. D. (2008). Evidence-based therapies for children and adolescents with eating disorders. In R. G. Steele, D. T. Elkin, & M. C. Roberts (Eds.), *Handbook of evidence-based therapies for children and adolescents: Bridging science and practice (pp. 335–353). Issues in clinical child psychology.* New York: Springer Science + Business Media.

Cleeremans, A., & Sarrazin, J. C. (2007). Time, action, and consciousness. *Human Movement Science, 26,* 180–202.

Clemants, E., & Gross, A. (2007). "Why aren't we screening?" A survey examining domestic violence screening procedures and training protocol in community mediation centers. *Conflict Resolution Quarterly, 24,* 413–431.

Clifford, J. S., Boufal, M. M., & Kurtz, J. E. (2004). Personality traits and critical thinking: Skills in college students empirical tests of a two-factor theory. *Assessment, 11*(2), 169–176.

Clinton, S. M., & Meador-Woodruff, J H. (2004). Thalamic dysfunction in schizophrenia: Neurochemical, neuropathological, and in vivo imaging abnormalities. *Schizophrenia Research, 69*(2–3), 237–253.

Cloud, J. (2001, February 26). New sparks over electroshock. *Time,* 60–62.

Clulow, C. (2007). John Bowlby and couple psychotherapy. *Attachment & Human Development, 9,* 343–353.

Cohen, D., Mason, K., & Farley, T. A. (2004). Beer consumption and premature mortality in Louisiana: An ecologic analysis. *Journal of Studies on Alcohol, 65*(3), 398–403.

Cohen, R. A., Brumm, V., Zawacki, T. M., Paul, R., Sweet, L., & Rosenbaum, A. (2003). Impulsivity and verbal deficits associated with domestic violence. *Journal of the International Neuropsychological Society, 9,* 760–770.

Cohen, R. A., Paul, R., Zawacki, T. M., Moser, D. J., Sweet, L., & Wilkinson, H. (2001). Emotional and personality changes following cingulotomy. *Emotion, 1*(1), 38–50.

Cohen, S., Hamrick, N., Rodriguez, M. S., Feldman, P. J., Rabin, B. S., & Manuck, S. B. (2002). Reactivity and vulnerability to stress associated risk for upper respiratory illness. *Psychosomatic Medicine, 64*(2), 302–310.

Cohen, S., & Lemay, E. P. (2007). Why would social networks be linked to affect and health practices? *Health Psychology, 26,* 410–417.

Cohen, S., & Williamson, G. M. (1991). Stress and infectious disease in humans. *Psychological Bulletin, 109,* 5–24.

Coifman, K. G., Bonanno, G. A., Ray, R. D., & Gross, J. J. (2007). Does repressing coping promote resilience? Affective-autonomic response discrepancy during bereavement. *Journal of Personality and Social Psychology, 92,* 745–758.

Colapinto, J. (2000). *As nature made him: The boy that was raised as a girl.* New York: HarperCollins.

Colapinto, J. (2004, June 3). *What were the real reasons behind David Reimer's suicide?* [On-line]. Available: http://slate.msn.com/id/2101678/.

Cole, D. L. (1982). Psychology as a liberating art. *Teaching of Psychology, 9,* 23–26.

Cole, M., & Gajdamaschko, N. (2007). Vygotsky and culture. In H. Daniels, J. Wertsch, & M. Cole (Eds.), *The Cambridge companion to Vygotsky.* New York: Cambridge University Press.

Cole, M., Gray, J., Glick, J. A., & Sharp, D. W. (1971). *The cultural context of learning and thinking.* New York: Basic Books.

Coley, R. L., & Chase-Lansdale, P. L. (1998). Adolescent pregnancy and parenthood: Recent evidence and future directions. *American Psychologist, 53*(2), 152–166.

Collins, J., & Singh, V. (2006). Exploring gendered leadership. In D. McTavish & K. Miller (Eds.), *Women in leadership and management.* Northampton, MA: Edward Elgar Publishing.

Collocan, L. K., Tuma, F. K., & Fleischman, A. R. (2004). Research with victims of disaster: Institutional review board considerations. *IRB: Ethics and Human Research, 26,* 9–11.

Combrink-Graham, L., & McKenna, S. B. (2006). Families with children with disrupted attachments. In L. Combrinck-Graham (Ed.), *Children in family contexts: Perspectives on treatment* (pp. 242–264). New York: Guilford Press.

Combs, D. R., Basso, M. R., Wanner, J. L., & Ledet, S. N. (2008). Schizophrenia. In M. Hersen & J. Rosqvist (Eds.), *Handbook of psychological assessment, case conceptualization, and treatment, Vol 1: Adults* (pp. 352–402). Hoboken, NJ: Wiley.

Conger, R. D., & Donnellan, M. B. (2007). An interactionist perspective on the socioeconomic context of human development. *Annual Review of Psychology, 58,* 175–199.

Connolly, S. (2000). *LSD (just the facts).* Baltimore: Heinemann Library.

Connor, J., Norton, R., Ameratunga, S., Robinson, E., Civil, I., Dunn, R., Bailey, J., & Jackson, R. (2002). Driver sleepiness and risk of serious injury to car occupants: Population based case control study. *BMJ: British Medical Journal, 324*(7346), 1125–1128.

Connor, K. M., & Davidson, J. R. T. (2002). A placebo-controlled study of Kava kava in generalized anxiety disorder. *International Clinical Psychopharmacology, 17*(4), 185–188.

Constantino, M. J., Manber, R., Ong, J., Kuo, T. F., Huang, J. S., & Arnow, B. A. (2007). Patient expectations and therapeutic alliance as predictors of outcome in group cognitive-behavioral therapy for insomnia. *Behavioral Sleep Medicine, 5,* 210–228.

Conway, M. A., & Pleydell-Pearce, C. W. (2000). The construction of autobiographical memories in the self-memory system. *Psychological Review, 107,* 261–288.

Cook, M., & Mineka, S. (1989). Observational conditioning of fear to fear-relevant versus fear-irrelevant stimuli in rhesus monkeys. *Journal of Abnormal Psychology, 98,* 448–459.

Cook, P. F. (2000). Effects of counselors' etiology attributions on college students' procrastination. *Journal of Counseling Psychology, 47*(3), 352–361.

Coolen, L. M., Allard, J., Truitt, W. A., & McKenna, K. E. (2004). Central regulation of ejaculation. *Physiology & Behavior, 83,* 203–215.

Coombs, R. H. (2004). *Handbook of addictive disorders.* Hoboken, NJ: Wiley.

Coombs, W. T., & Holladay, S. J. (2006). Unpacking the halo effect: Reputation and crisis management. *Journal of Communication Management, 10,* 123–137.

Cooper, C., Bebbington, P. E., Meltzer, H., Bhugra, D., Brugha, T., Jenkins, R., Farrell, M., & King, M. (2008). Depression and common mental disorders in lone parents: Results of the 2000 National Psychiatric Morbidity Survey. *Psychological Medicine, 38,* 335–342.

Cooper, C., Manela, M., Katona, C., & Livingston, G. (2008). Screening for elder abuse in dementia in the LASER-AD study: Prevalence, correlates, and validation of instruments. *International Journal of Geriatric Psychiatry, 23,* 283–288.

Cooper, J., & Hogg, M. A. (2007). Feeling the anguish of others: A theory of vicarious dissonance. In M. P. Zanna (Ed.), *Advances in experimental social psychology.* San Diego, CA: Elsevier.

Cooper, J., Heron, T. E., & Heward, W. L. (2007). *Applied behavior analysis* (2nd ed.). Upper Saddle River, NJ: Prentice-Hall.

Cooper, M. L., Shaver, P. R., & Collins, N. L. (1998). Attachment styles, emotion regulation, and adjustment in adolescence. *Journal of Personality and Social Psychology, 74*(5), 1380–1397.

Cooper, R. (2004). What is wrong with the DSM? *History of Psychiatry, 15*(1), 5–25.

Cooper, W. E. Jr., Pérez-Mellado, V., Vitt, L. J., & Budzinsky, B. (2002). Behavioral responses to plant toxins in two omnivorous lizard species. *Physiology & Behavior, 76*(2), 297–303.

Coplan, R. J., Arbeau, K. A., & Armer, M. (2008). Don't fret, be supportive! Maternal characteristics linking child shyness to psychosocial and school adjustment in kindergarten. *Journal of Abnormal Child Psychology, 36,* 359–371.

Corcoran, C., Walker, E., Huot, R., Mittal, V., Tessner, K., Kestler, L., & Malaspina, D. (2003). The stress cascade and schizophrenia: Etiology and onset. *Schizophrenia Bulletin, 29*(4), 671–692.

Coren, S. (1996). *Sleep thieves: An eye-opening exploration into the science and mysteries of sleep.* New York: Freeman.

Corey, G. (2001). *The art of integrative counseling.* Belmont, CA: Wadsworth.

Corey, G. (2005). *Theory and practice of counseling and psychotherapy* (7th ed.). Belmont, CA: Wadsworth.

Corey, G. (2008). *Theory and practice of group counseling* (7th ed.). Belmont, CA: Cengage.

Corey, G. (2009). *Theory and practice of counseling and psychotherapy* (8th ed.). Belmont, CA: Cengage.

Corkin, S. (2002). What's new with the amnesic patient H.M.? *Nature Reviews Neuroscience, 3,* 153–160.

Cornelius, J. R., & Clark, D. B. (2008). Depressive disorders and adolescent substance use disorders. In Y. Kaminer & O. G. bukstein (Eds.), *Adolescent substance abuse: Psychiatric comorbidity and high-risk behaviors* (pp. 221–242). New York: Routledge/Taylor & Francis Group.

Corr, C. A., & Corr, D. M. (2007). Historical and contemporary perspectives on loss, grief, and mourning. In D. Balk, C. Wogrin, G. Thornton, & D. Meagher (Eds.), *Handbook of thanatology: The essential body of knowledge for the study of death, dying, and bereavement* (pp. 131–142). New York: Routledge/Taylor & Francis Group.

Corr, C. A., Nabe, C. M., & Corr, D. M. (2009). *Death and dying: Life and living* (6th ed.). Belmont, CA: Wadsworth.

Corydon, H. D. (2007). What is neurofeedback? *Journal of Neurotherapy, 10,* 25–36.

Cosgrove, K. P., Mazure, C. M., & Staley, J. K. (2007). Evolving knowledge of sex differences in brain structure, function, and chemistry. *Biological Psychiatry, 62,* 847–855.

Costa, J. L., Brennen, M. B., & Hochgeschwender, U. (2002). The human genetics of eating disorders: Lessons from the leptin/melanocortin system. *Child & Adolescent Psychiatric Clinics of North America, 11*(2), 387–397.

Costa Jr., P.T., McCrae, R. R., & Martin, T. A. (2008). Incipient adult personality: The NEO-PI-3 in middle-school-aged children. *British Journal of Developmental Psychology, 26,* 71–89.

Costa Jr., P. T., Terracciano, A., Uda, M., Vacca, L., Mameli, C., Pilia, G., Zonderman, A. B., Lakatta, E., Schlessinger, D., & McCrae, R. R. (2007). Personality traits in Sardinia: Testing founder population effects on trait means and variances. *Behavior Genetics, 37,* 376–387.

Courage, M. L., & Adams, R. J. (1990). Visual acuity assessment from birth to three years using the acuity card procedures: Cross-sectional and longitudinal samples. *Optometry and Vision Science, 67,* 713–718.

Covington, M. V., & Mueller, K. J. (2001). Intrinsic versus extrinsic motivation: An approach/avoidance reformulation. *Educational Psychology Review, 13*(2), 157–176.

Cowen, P. J. (2002). Cortisol, serotonin and depression: All stressed out? *British Journal of Psychiatry, 180*(2), 99–100.

Coyne, S. M., Archer, J., & Eslea, M. (2004). Cruel intentions on television and in real life: Can viewing indirect aggression increase viewers' subsequent indirect aggression? *Journal of Experimental Child Psychology, 88*(3), 234–253.

Craig, A. D., & Bushnell, M. C. (1994). The thermal grill illusion: Unmasking the burn of cold pain. *Science, 265,* 252–255.

Craik, F. I. M., & Lockhart, R. S. (1972). Levels of processing: A framework for memory research. *Journal of Verbal Learning and Verbal Behavior, 11,* 671–684.

Craik, F. I. M., & Tulving, E. (1975). Depth of processing and the retention of words in episodic memory. *Journal of Experimental Psychology. 104,* 68–294.

Crair, M. C., Gillespie, D. C., & Stryker, M. P. (1998). The role of visual experience in the development of columns in cat visual cortex. *Science, 279,* 566–570.

Crandall, C. S., & Martinez, R. (1996). Culture, ideology, and antifat attitudes. *Personality and Social Psychology Bulletin, 22,* 1165–1176.

Crano, W. D., & Prislin, R. (2006). Attitudes and persuasion. In S. T. Fiske, A. E. Kazdin, & D. L. Schacter (Eds.), *Annual Review of Psychology, 51,* 345–374.

Craske, M. C., & Waters, A. M. (2005). Panic disorder, phobias, and generalized anxiety disorder. *Annual Review of Clinical Psychology, 1,* 197–225.

Craske, M. G. (2000). *Mastery of your anxiety and panic: Therapist guide* (3rd ed.). New York: Academic Press.

Crawford, C. S. (2008). Ghost in the machine: A genealogy of phantom-prosthetic relations (amputation, dismemberment, prosthetic). *Dissertation Abstracts International Section A: Humanities and Social Sciences, 68*(7-A), 3173.

Creed, P. A., & Bartrum, D.A. (2008). Personal control as a mediator and moderator between life strains and psychological well-being in the unemployed. *Journal of Applied Social Psychology, 38,* 460–481.

Crespo, M. R. (2007). Intelligence and personality as antecedents to leadership effectiveness and extrinsic career success: The predictive power of individual differences. *Dissertation Abstracts International: Section B: The Sciences and Engineering, 68*(1-B), 658.

Crespo-Facorro, B., Barbadillo, L., Pelayo-Terán, J., Rodríguez-Sánchez, J. M., & *Teran, J. M.* (2007). Neuropsychological functioning and brain structure in schizophrenia. *International Review of Psychiatry, 19*, 325–336.

Cresswell, M. (2008). Szasz and his interlocutors: Reconsidering Thomas Szasz's "Myth of Mental Illness" thesis. *Journal for the Theory of Social Behaviour, 38*, 23–44.

Crews, F. (1997). The verdict on Freud. *Psychological Science, 7*(2), 63–68.

Crews, F. T., Collins, M. A., Dlugos, C., Littleton, J., Wilkins, L., Neafsey, E. J., Pentney, R., Snell, L. D., Tabakoff, B., Zou, J., & Noronha, A. (2004). Alcohol-induced neurodegeneration: When, where and why? *Alcoholism: Clinical & Experimental Research, 28*(2), 350–364.

Cristofalo, V. J. (1996). Ten years later: What have we learned about human aging from studies of cell cultures? *Gerontologist, 36*, 737–741.

Cronbach, L. (1990). *Essentials of psychological testing.* New York: Harper & Row.

Crone, C. C., & Gabriel, G. (2002). Herbal and nonherbal supplements in medical-psychiatric patient populations. *Psychiatric Clinics of North America, 25*(1), 211–230.

Crooks, R. & Bauer, K. (2008). *Our sexuality* (10th ed.). Belmont, CA: Cengage.

Crosby, B. (2003). Case studies in rational emotive behavior therapy with children and adolescents. *Journal of Cognitive Psychotherapy, 17*(3), 289–291.

Crow, T. J. (2004). Cerebral asymmetry and the lateralization of language: Core deficits in schizophrenia as pointers to the gene. *Current Opinion in Psychiatry, 17*(2), 97–106.

Crowell, S. E., Beauchaine, T. P., & Lenzenweger, M. F. (2008). The development of borderline personality disorder and self-injurious behavior. In T. P. Beauchaine & S. P. Hinshaw (Eds.), *Child and adolescent psychopathology* (pp. 510–539). Hoboken, NJ: Wiley.

Csíkszentmihályi, M., & Csíkszentmihályi, I. S. (Eds.. (2006). *A life worth living: Contributions to positive psychology.* New York: Oxford University Press.

Cuadrado, I., Morales, J. F., Recio, P., & Howard, V. N. (2008). Women's access to managerial positions: An experimental study of leadership styles and gender. *The Spanish Journal of Psychology, 11*, 55–65.

Cubelli, R., & Della Sala, S. (2008). Flashbulb memories: Special but not iconic. *Cortex, 44*, 908–909.

Cullen, D., & Gotell, L. (2002). From orgasms to organizations: Maslow, women's sexuality and the gendered foundations of the needs hierarchy. *Gender, Work & Organization, 9*(5), 537–555.

Cully, J. A., & Stanley, M. A. (2008). Assessment and treatment of anxiety in later life. In K. Laidlaw & B. Knight (Eds.), *Handbook of emotional disorders in later life: Assessment and treatment.* New York: Oxford University Press.

Cummings, D. E. (2006). Ghrelin and the short-and long-term regulation of appetite and body weight. *Physiology & Behavior, 89*, 71–84.

Cummings, E., & Henry, W. E. (1961). *Growing old: The process of disengagement.* New York: Basic Books.

Cunningham, G. B. (2002). Diversity and recategorization: Examining the effects of cooperation on bias and work outcomes. *Dissertation Abstracts International Section A: Humanities and Social Sciences, 63*, 1288.

Cunningham, G. B., Fink, J. S., & Kenix, L. J. (2008). Choosing an endorser for a women's sporting event: The interaction of attractiveness and expertise. *Sex Roles, 58*, 371–378.

Cunningham, W. A., Johnson, M. K., Raye, C. L., Gatenby, J. C., Gore, J. C., & Banaji, M. R. (2004). Separable neural components in the processing of black and white faces. *Psychological Science, 15*, 806–813.

Currie, S., & Wang, J. (2004). Chronic back pain and major depression in the general Canadian population. *Pain, 107*(1–2), 54–60.

Curtiss, S. (1977). *Genie: A psycholinguistic study of a modern-day "wild child."* New York: Academic Press.

Dabbs, J. M., & Dabbs, M. G. (2000). *Heroes, rogues, and lovers: Testosterone and behavior.* New York: McGraw-Hill.

Dackis, C. A., & O'Brien, C. P. (2001). Cocaine dependence: A disease of the brain's reward centers. *Journal of Substance Abuse Treatment, 21*(3), 111–117.

Dalenberg, C., Loewenstein, R., Spiegel, D., Brewin, C., Lanius, R., Frankel, S., Gold, S., Van der Kolk, B., Simeon, D., Vermetten, E., Butler, L., Koopman, C., Courtois, C., Dell, P., Nijenhuis, E., Chu, J., Sar, V., Palesh, O., Cuevas, C., & Paulson, K. (2007). Scientific study of the dissociative disorders. *Psychotherapy and Psychosomatics, 76*, 400–401.

D'Alessio, D., & Allen, M. (2002). Selective exposure and dissonance after decisions. *Psychological Reports, 91*(2), 527–532.

Dalley, J. W., Fryer, T. D., Brichard, L., Robinson, E. S. J, Theobald, D. E. H., Lääne, K., Peña, Y., Murphy, E. R., Shah, Y., Probst, K., Abakumova, I., Aigbirhio, F. I., Richards, H. K., Hong, Y., Baron, J-C., Everitt, B. J., & Robbins, T. W. (2007). Nucleus accumbens D2/3 receptors predict trait impulsivity and cocaine reinforcement. *Science, 315*, 1267–1270.

Dalman, C., & Allebeck, P. (2002). Paternal age and schizophrenia: further support for an association. *American Journal of Psychiatry, 159*(9), 1591–1592.

Damak, S., Rong, M., Yasumatsu, K., Kokrashvili, Z., Varadarajan, V., Zou, S., Jiang, P., Ninomiya, Y., & Margolskee, R.F. (2003). Direction of sweet and umami taste in the absence of taste receptor Tlr3. *Science, 301*(5634), 850–851.

Damasio, A. R. (1999). *The feeling of what happens: Body and emotion in the making of consciousness.* New York: Harcourt Brace.

Dana, R. H. (1998). Cultural identity assessment of culturally diverse groups. *Journal of Personality Assessment, 70*(1), 1–16.

Dana, R. H. (2005). *Multicultural assessment: Principles, applications, and examples.* Mahwah, NJ: Erlbaum.

Daniels, K., Toth, J., & Jacoby, J. (2006). The aging of executive functions. In E. Bialystok & F. I. M. Craik (Eds.) *Lifespan cognition: Mechanisms of change.* New York: Oxford University Press.

Danis, A., Pêcheux, M-G., Lefèvre, C., Bourdais, C., & Serres-Ruel, J. (2008). A continuous performance task in preschool children: Relations between attention and performance. *European Journal of Developmental Psychology, 5*, 401–418.

Dantzer, R., O'Connor, J. C., Freund, G. C., Johnson, R. W., & Kelley, K. W. (2008). From inflammation to sickness and depression: When the immune system subjugates the brain. *Nature Reviews Neuroscience, 9*, 46–57.

Dapretto, M., Davies, M. S., Pfeifer, J. H., Scott, A. A., Sigman, M., Bookheimer, S. Y., & Iacoboni, M. (2006). Understanding emotions in others: Mirror neuron dysfunction in children with autism spectrum disorders. *Nature Neuroscience, 9.* 28–30.

Darmani, N. A., & Crim, J. L. (2005) Delta-9- tetrahydrocannabinol prevents emesis more potently than enhanced locomotor activity produced by chemically diverse dopamine D2/D3 receptor agonists in the least shrew (Cryptotis parva). *Pharmacology Biochemistry and Behavior, 80*, 35–44.

Darwin, C. (1859). *On the origin of species.* London: Murray.

Darwin, C. (1872). *The expression of the emotions in man and animals.* London: Murray.

Dasí, C., Soler, M. J., Cervera, T., & Ruiz, J. C. (2008). Influence of articulation rate on two memory tasks in young and older adults. *Perceptual and Motor Skills, 106,* 579–589.

Davalos, D. B., Compagnon, N., Heinlein, S., & Ross, R. G. (2004). Neuropsychological deficits in children associated with increased familial risk for schizophrenia. *Schizophrenia Research, 67*(2–3), 123–130.

David, D. (2007). In memorian Albert Ellis. *Journal of Cognitive and Behavioral Psychotherapies, 7,* 125–126.

David, D., & Brown, R. J. (2002). Suggestibility and negative priming: Two replication studies. *International Journal of Clinical & Experimental Hypnosis, 50*(3), 215–228.

David, D., Schnur, J. E., & Belloiu, A. (2002). Another search for the "hot" cognitions: Appraisal, irrational beliefs, attributions, and their relation to emotion. *Journal of Rational-Emotive & Cognitive Behavior Therapy, 20*(2), 93–132.

David, D., Woodward, C., Esquenazi, J., & Mellman, T. A. (2004). Comparison of comorbid physical illnesses among veterans with PTSD and veterans with alcohol dependence. *Psychiatric Services, 55*(1), 82–85.

Davidson, J. R., Waisberg, J. L., Brundage, M. D., & MacLean, A. W. (2001). Non-pharmacologic group treatment of insomnia: A preliminary study with cancer survivors. *Psycho-Oncology, 10*(5), 389–397.

Davidson, P. S. R., Anaki, D., Ciaramelli, E., Cohn, M., Kim, A. S. N., Murphy, K. J., Troyer, A. K., Moscovitch, M., & Levine, B. (2008). Does lateral parietal cortex support episodic memory? Evidence from focal lesion patients. *Neuropsychologia, 46,* 1743–1755.

Davies, I. (1998). A study of colour grouping in three languages: A test of the linguistic relativity hypothesis. *British Journal of Psychology, 89,* 433–452.

Davies, J. M. (1996). Dissociation, repression and reality testing in the countertransference: the controversey over memory and false memory in the psychoanalytic treatment of adult survivors of childhood sexual abuse. *Psychoanalytic Dialogues, 6,* 189–218.

Davies, M. F. (2008). Irrational beliefs and unconditional self-acceptance. III. The relative importance of different types of irrational belief. *Journal of Rational-Emotive & Cognitive Behavior Therapy, 26,* 102–118.

Davis, C., Dionne, M., & Shuster, B. (2001). Physical and psychological correlates of appearance orientation. *Personality & Individual Differences, 30*(1), 21–30.

Davison, G.C., Neale, J.M., & Kring, A.M. (2004). *Abnormal psychology* (9th. ed.). Hoboken, NJ: Wiley.

Dawson, K. A. (2004). Temporal organization of the brain: Neurocognitive mechanisms and clinical implications. *Brain & Cognition, 54*(1), 75–94.

De Charms, R., & Moeller, G. H. (1962). Values expressed in American children's readers: 1800–1950. *Journal of Abnormal and Social Psychology, 64*(2), 136–142.

De Coteau, T. J., Hope, D. A., & Anderson, J. (2003). Anxiety, stress, and health in northern plains Native Americans. *Behavior Therapy, 34*(3), 365–380.

De Houwer, J., Beckers, T., & Moors, A. (2007). Novel attitudes can be faked on the Implicit Association Test. *Journal of Experimental Social Psychology, 43,* 972–978.

De Maat, S., Philipszoon, F., Schoevers, R., Dekker, J., & De Jonghe, F. (2007). Costs and benefits of long-term psychoanalytic therapy: Changes in health care use and work impairment. *Harvard Review of Psychiatry, 15,* 289–300.

De Oliveira-Souza, R., Moll, J., Ignácio, F.A., & Hare, R. D. (2008). Psychopathy in a civil psychiatric outpatient sample. *Criminal Justice and Behavior, 35,* 427–437.

De Pinho, R. S. N., da Silva-Júnior, F. P., Bastos, J. P. C., Maia, W. S., de Mello, M. T., de Bruin, V. M. S., & de Bruin, P. F. C. (2006). Hypersomnolence and accidents in truck drivers: A cross-sectional study. *Chronobiology International, 23,* 963–971.

De Rosnay, M., & Harris, P. L. (2002). Individual differences in children's understanding of emotion: The roles of attachment and language. *Attachment & Human Development, 4*(1), 39–54.

De Waal, F. B. M. (2008). Putting the altruism back into altruism: The evolution of empathy. *Annual Review of Psychology, 59,* 279–300.

Dean-Borenstein, M. T. (2007). The long-term psychosocial effects of trauma on survivors of human-caused extreme stress situations. *Dissertation Abstracts International: Section B: The Sciences and Engineering, 67*(11-B), 6733.

Deary, I. J., Bell, P. J., Bell, A. J., Campbell, M. L., & Fazal, N. D. (2004). Sensory discrimination and intelligence: Testing Spearman's other hypothesis. *American Journal of Psychology, 117*(1), 1–18.

Deary, I. J., Ferguson, K. J., Bastin, M. E., Barrow, G. W. S., Reid, L. M., Seckl, J. R., Wardlaw, J. M., & MacLullich, A. M. J. (2007). Skull size and intelligence, and King Robert Bruce's IQ. *Intelligence, 35,* 519–528.

Deary, I. J., & Stough, C. (1996). Intelligence and inspection time: Achievements, prospects, and problems. *American Psychologist, 51,* 599–608.

Deary, I. J., & Stough, C. (1997). Looking down on human intelligence. *American Psychologist, 52,* 1148–1149.

Debaere, F., Wenderoth, N., Sunaert, S., Van Hecke, P., & Swinnen, S. P. (2004). Changes in brain activation during the acquisition of a new bimanual coordination task. *Neuropsychologia, 42*(7), 855–867.

DeCasper, A. J., & Fifer, W. D. (1980). Of human bonding: Newborns prefer their mother's voices. *Science, 208,* 1174–1176.

Deci, E. L. (1995). *Why we do what we do: The dynamics of personal autonomy.* New York: Putnam's Sons.

Deci, E. L., Koestner, R., & Ryan, R. M. (1999). A meta-analytic review of experiments examining the effects of extrinsic rewards on intrinsic motivation. *Psychological Bulletin, 125*(6), 627–668.

Deci, E. L., & Moller, A. C. (2005). The concept of competence: A starting place for understanding intrinsic motivation and self-determined extrinsic motivation. In A. J. Elliot & C. S. Dweck (Eds.), *Handbook of competence and motivation* (pp. 579–597). New York: Guilford.

Deckers, L. (2005). *Motivation: Biological, psychological, and environmental* (2nd ed.). Boston: Allyn & Bacon/Longman.

DeClue, G. (2003). The polygraph and lie detection. *Journal of Psychiatry & Law, 31*(3), 361–368.

Delahanty, D. L., Liegey, D. A., Hayward, M., Forlenza, M., Hawk, L. W., & Baum, A. (2000). Gender differences in cardiovascular and natural killer cells reactivity to acute stress following a hassling task. *International Journal of Behavioral Medicine, 7,* 19–27.

Delgado, J. M. R. (1960). Emotional behavior in animals and humans. *Psychiatric Research Report, 12,* 259–271.

Delgado, P. L. (2004). How antidepressants help depression: Mechanisms of action and clinical response. *Journal of Clinical Psychiatry, 65,* 25–30.

Delgado-Gaitan, C. (1994). Socializing young children in Mexican-American families: An intergenerational perspective. In P.M. Greenfield & R.R. Cocking (Eds.), *Cross-cultural* *roots of minority child development* (pp. 55–86). Hillsdale, NJ: Erlbaum.

DeLisi, L. E., Sakuma, M., Maurizio, A. M., Relja, M., & Hoff, A. L. (2004). Cerebral ventricular change over the first 10 years after the onset of schizophrenia. *Psychiatry Research: Neuroimaging, 130*(1), 57–70.

Deller, T., Haas, C. A., Freiman, T. M., Phinney, A., Jucker, M., & Frotscher, M. (2006). Lesion-induced axonal sprouting in the central nervous system. *Advances in Experimental Medicine and Biology, 557,* 101–121.

Dellve, L., Eriksson, J., & Vilhelmsson, R. (2007). Assessment of long-term attendance within human service organizations. *Journal of Prevention, Assessment & Rehabilitation, 29,* 71–80.

Delville, Y., Mansour, K. M., & Ferris. C. F. (1996). Testosterone facilitates aggression by modulating vasopressin receptors in the hypothalamus. *Physiology and Behavior, 60,* 25–29.

DeMarree, K. G., & Petty, R. E. (2007). The elaboration likelihood model of persuasion. In R. F. Baumeister & K. D. Vohs (Eds.), *Encyclopedia of social psychology.* Thousand Oaks, CA: Sage.

Dembe, A. E., Erickson, J. B., Delbos, R. G., & Banks, S. M. (2006). Nonstandard shift schedules and the risk of job-related injuries. *Scandinavian Journal of Work, Environment, & Health, 32,* 232–240.

Dement, W. C. (1992, March). The sleepwatchers. *Stanford,* pp. 55–59.

Dement, W. C., & Vaughan, C. (1999). *The promise of sleep.* New York: Delacorte Press. den Boer, J. A. (2000). Social anxiety disorder/social phobia: Epidemiology, diagnosis, neurobiology, and treatment. *Comprehensive Psychiatry, 41*(6), 405–415.

Dement, W. C., & Wolpert, E. (1958). The relation of eye movements, bodily motility, and external stimuli to dream content. *Journal of Experimental Psychology, 53,* 543–553.

Denmark, F. L., Rabinowitz, V. C., & Sechzer, J. A. (2005). *Engendering psychology: Women and gender revisited* (2nd ed.). Boston: Allyn and Bacon.

Dennis, W., & Dennis, M. G. (1940). Cradles and cradling customs of the Pueblo Indians. *American Anthropologist, 42,* 107–115.

Depue, R. A., & Collins, P. F. (1999). Neurobiology of the structure of personality: Dopamine, facilitation of incentive motivation, and extraversion. *Behavioral & Brain Sciences, 22*(3), 491–569.

Der-Karabetian, A., Stephenson, K., & Poggi, T. (1996). Environmental risk perception, activism and world-mindedness among samples of British and U. S. college students. *Perceptual and Motor Skills, 83*(2), 451–462.

DeSpelder, L. A., & Strickland, A. (2007). Culture, socialization, and death education. In D. Balk, C. Wogrin, G. Thornton, & D. Meagher (Eds.), *Handbook of thanatology: The essential body of knowledge for the study of death, dying, and bereavement* (pp. 303–314). New York: Routledge/Taylor & Francis Group.

DeStefano, D., & LeFevre, J. (2004). The role of working memory in mental arithmetic. *European Journal of Cognitive Psychology, 16*(3), 353–386.

DeValois, R. L. (1965). Behavioral and electrophysiological studies of primate vision. In W. D. Neff (Ed). *Contributions to sensory physiology* (Vol. 1). New York: Academic Press.

Devine, P. G., Plant, E. A., Amodio, D. M., Harmon-Jones, E., & Vance, S. L. (2002). The regulation of explicit and implicit race bias: The role of motivations to respond without prejudice. *Journal of Personality and Social Psychology, 82,* 835–848.

Devlin, M. J., Yanovski, S. Z., & Wilson, G. T. (2000). Obesity: What mental health professionals need to know. *American Journal of Psychiatry, 157*(6), 854–866.

Dhikav, V., Aggarwal, N., Gupta, S., Jadhavi, R., & Singh, K. (2008). Depression in Dhat syndrome. *Journal of Sexual Medicine, 5,* 841–844.

Di Blasio, P., & Milani, L. (2008). Computer-mediated communication and persuasion: Peripheral vs. central route to opinion shift. *Computers in Human Behavior, 24,* 798–815.

Diamond, A., & Amso, D. (2008). Contributions of neuroscience to our understanding of cognitive development. *Current Directions in Psychological Science, 17,* 136–141.

Diamond, L. M. (2004). Emerging perspectives on distinctions between romantic love and sexual desire. *Current Directions in Psychological Science, 13*(3), 116–119.

Diamond, M., & Sigmundson, H. K. (1997). Sex reassignment at birth: Long-term review and clinical implications. *Archives of Pediatrics and Adolescent Medicine, 151,* 298–304.

Diaz, A. B., & Motta, R. (2008). The effects of an aerobic exercise program on posttraumatic stress disorder symptom severity in adolescents. *International Journal of Emergency Mental Health, 10,* 49–60.

Diaz-Berciano, C., de Vicente, F., & Fontecha, E. (2008). *Modulating effects in learned helplessness of dyadic dominance-submission relations. Aggressive Behavior, 34*(3), 273–281.

Dickens, W. T., & Flynn, J. R. (2001). Heritability estimates versus large environmental effects: The IQ paradox resolved. *Psychological Review, 108*(2), 346–369.

Dickinson, D. J., O'Connell, D. Q., & Dunn, J. S. (1996). Distributed study, cognitive study strategies and aptitude on student learning. *Psychology: A Journal of Human Behavior, 33*(3), 31–39.

Diego, M. A., & Jones, N. A. (2007). Neonatal antecedents for empathy. In T. Farrow & P. Woodruff (Eds.), *Empathy in mental illness* (pp. 145–167). New York: Cambridge University Press.

Diehm, R., & Armatas, C. (2004). Surfing: An avenue for socially acceptable risk-taking, satisfying needs for sensation seeking and experience seeking. *Personality & Individual Differences, 36*(3), 663–677.

Diener, E. (2008). Myths in the science of happiness, and directions for future research. In M. Eid & R. J. Larsen (Eds.), *The science of subjective well-being.* New York: Guilford Press.

Diener, E., & Biswas-Diener, R. (2008). *Happiness: Unlocking the mysteries of psychological wealth.* Hoboken, NJ: Wiley-Blackwell.

Diener, M. L., Isabella, R. A., Behunin, M. G., & Wong, M. S. (2008). Attachment to mothers and fathers during middle childhood: Associations with child gender, grade, and competence. *Social Development, 7,* 84–101.

Diener, M. L., Mengelsdorf, S. C., McHale, J. L., & Frosch, C. A. (2002). Infants' behavioral strategies for emotion regulation with fathers and mothers: Associations with emotional expressions and attachment quality. *Infancy, 3*(2), 153–174.

Dieter, J. N. I., Field, T., Hernandez-Reif, M., Emory, E. K., & Redzepi, M. (2003). Stable preterm infants gain more weight and sleep less after five days of massage therapy. *Journal of Pediatric Psychology, 28*(6), 403–411.

Dietrich, A. (2003). Functional neuroanatomy of altered states of consciousness: The transient hypofrontality hypothesis. *Conciousness and Cognition, 12,* 231–256.

Dietz, T. L. (1998). An examination of violence and gender role portrayals in video games. *Sex Roles, 38,* 425–442.

Dijksterhuis, A., Aarts, H., & Smith, P. K. (2005). The power of the subliminal: On subliminal persuasion and other potential applications. In R. R. Hassin, J. S. Uleman, & J. A. Bargh (Eds.), The new unconscious (pp. 77–106). *Oxford series in social cognition* *and social neuroscience.* New York: Oxford University Press.

DiLauro, M. D. (2004). Psychosocial factors associated with types of child maltreatment. *Child Welfare, 83*(1), 69–99.

Dill, K. E., & Thill, K. P. (2007). Video game characters and the socialization of gender roles: Young people's perceptions mirror sexist media depictions. *Sex Roles, 57,* 851–864.

Dillard, A. J. (2007). Humor, laughter, and recovery from stressful experiences. *Dissertation Abstracts International: Section B: The Sciences and Engineering, 68,* 3432.

Dimberg, U., & Thunberg, M. (1998). Rapid facial reactions to emotion facial expressions. *Scandinavian Journal of Psychology, 39*(1), 39–46.

Dimberg, U., Thunberg, M., & Elmehed, K. (2000). Unconscious facial reactions to emotional facial expressions. *Psychological Science, 11*(1), 86–89.

DiPietro, J. A. (2000). Baby and the brain: Advances in child development. *Annual Review of Public Health, 21,* 455–71.

Dixon, L., Hamilton-Giachritsis, C., Browne, K., & Ostapuik, E. (2007). The co-occurrence of child and intimate partner maltreatment in the family: Characteristics of the violent perpetrators. *Journal of Family Violence, 22,* 675–689.

Dobbin, A., Faulkner, S., Heaney, D., Selvaraj. S., & Gruzelier, J. (2004). Impact on health status of a hypnosis clinic in general practice. *Contemporary Hypnosis, 21*(4), 153–160.

Dobson, K. S. (2008). Cognitive therapy for depression. In M. A. Whisman (Ed.), *Adapting cognitive therapy for depression: Managing complexity and comorbidity* (pp. 3–35). New York: Guilford.

Dodd, M. D., & MacLeod, C. M. (2004). False recognition without intentional learning. *Psychonomic Bulletin & Review, 11*(1), 137–142.

Doghramji, K. (2000, December). *Sleepless in America: Diagnosing and treating insomnia.* [On-line serial]. Available: http://psychiatry.medscape.com/Medscape/psychiatry/ClinicalMgmt/CM.v02/public/indexCM.v02.html.

Dollard, J., Doob, L., Miller, N., Mowrer, O. H., & Sears, R. R. (1939). *Frustration and aggression.* New Haven, CT: Yale University Press.

Dols, M., Willems, B., van den Hout, M., & Bittoun, R. (2000). Smokers can learn to influence their urge to smoke. *Addictive Behaviors, 25*(1), 103–108.

Domhoff, G. W. (1999). New directions in the study of dream content using the Hall and Van de Castle coding system. *Dreaming, 9,* 115–137.

Domhoff, G. W. (2003). *The scientific study of dreams: Neural networks, cognitive development, and content analysis.* Washington, DC: American Psychological Association.

Domhoff, G. W. (2004). Why did empirical dream researchers reject Freud? A critique of historical claims by Mark Solms. *Dreaming, 14*(1), 3–17.

Domhoff, G. W. (2005). A reply to Hobson. (2005). *Dreaming, 15*(1), 30–32.

Domhoff, G. W. (2007). Realistic simulation and bizarreness in dream content: Past findings and suggestions for future research. In D. Barrett & P. McNamara (Eds.), *The new science of dreaming: Volume 2. Content, recall, and personality correlates* (pp. 1–27). Praeger perspectives. Westport, CT: Praeger.

Domjan, M. (2005). Pavlovian conditioning: A functional perspective. *Annual Review of Psychology, 56,* 179–206.

Dompnier, B., Pansu, P., & Bressoux, P. (2006). An integrative model of scholastic judgments: Pupils' characteristics, class context, halo effect and internal attributions. *European Journal of Psychology of Education, 21,* 119–133.

Donahue, C. B., & Grant, J. E. (2007). Stress and impulsive behaviors. In M. Al'Absi (Ed.), *Stress and addiction: Biological and psychological mechanisms* (pp. 191–210). San Diego, CA: Elsevier Academic Press.

Dondi, M., Simion, F., & Caltran, G. (1999). Can newborns discriminate between their own cry and the cry of another newborn infant? *Developmental Psychology, 35,* 418–426.

Donini, L. M., Savina, C., & Cannella, C. (2003). Eating habits and appetite control in the elderly: The anorexia of aging. *International Psychogeriatrics, 15*(1), 73–87.

D'Onofrio, B. M., Turkheimer, E., Emery, R. E., Maes, H. H., Silberg, J., & Eaves, L. J. (2007). A children of twins study of parental divorce and offspring psychopathology. *Journal of Child Psychology and Psychiatry, 48,* 667–675.

Donohue, R. (2006). Person-environment congruence in relation to career change and career persistence. *Journal of Vocational Behavior, 68,* 504–515.

Donovan, J. J., & Radosevich, D. J. (1999). A meta-analytic review of the distribution of practice effect: Now you see it, now you don't. *Journal of Applied Psychology, 84,* 795–805.

Dorian, L., & Garfinkel, P. E. (2002). Culture and body image in western culture. *Eating & Weight Disorders, 7*(1), 1–19.

Dougal, S., Phelps, E. A., & Davachi, L. (2007). The role of medial temporal lobe in item recognition and source recollection of emotional stimuli. *Cognitive, Affective & Behavioral Neuroscience, 7,* 233–242.

Dougherty, D. D., Baer, L., Cosgrove, G. R., Cassem, E. H., Price, B. H., Nierenberg, A. A., Jenike, M. A., & Rauch, S. L. (2002). Prospective long-term follow-up of 44 patients who received cingulotomy for treatment-refractory obsessive-compulsive disorder. *American Journal of Psychiatry, 159*(2), 269–275.

Dougherty, D. M., Marsh-Richard, D. M., Hatzis, E. S., Nouvion, S. O., & Mathias, C. W. (2008). A test of alcohol dose effects on multiple behavioral measures of impulsivity. *Drug and Alcohol Dependence, 96,* 111–120.

Doughty, E. A. (2007). Investigating a model of adult bereavement grief: A delphi study. *Dissertation Abstracts International Section A: Humanities and Social Sciences, 67*(11-A), 4103.

Dowd, E. T. (2004). Cognition and the cognitive revolution in psychotherapy: Promises and advances. *Journal of Clinical Psychology, 60*(4), 415–428.

Doyle, A., & Pollack, M. H. (2004). Long-term management of panic disorder. *Journal of Clinical Psychiatry. 65*(Suppl5), 24–28.

Draguns, J., & Tanaka-Matsumi, J. (2003). Assessment of psychopathology across and within cultures: Issues and findings. *Behaviour Research & Therapy, 41*(7), 755–776.

Drescher, J. (2003). Gold or lead? Introductory remarks on conversions. *Journal of Gay & Lesbian Psychotherapy, 7*(3), 1–13.

Dresser, N. (1996). *Multicultural manners: New rules of etiquette for a changing society.* New York: Wiley.

Driscoll, A. K., Russell, S. T., & Crockett, L. J. (2008). Parenting styles and youth well-being across immigrant generations. *Journal of Family Issues, 29,* 185–209.

Driscoll, R., Davis, K. E., & Lipetz, M. E. (1972). Parental interference and romantic love: The Romeo and Juliet effect. *Journal of Personality and Social Psychology, 24,* 1–10.

Druckman, D., & Bjork, R. A. (Eds.) (1994). *Learning, remembering, believing: Enhancing human performance.* Washington, DC: National Academies Press.

Drummey, A. B., & Newcombe, N. S. (2002). Developmental changes in source memory. *Developmental Science, 5*(4), 502–513.

Dryer, D. C., & Horowitz, L. M. (1997). When do opposites attract? Interpersonal complementarity versus similarity. *Journal of Personality and Social Psychology, 72,* 592–603.

Duckworth, K., & Borus, J. F. (1999). Population-based psychiatry in the public sector and managed care. In A. M. Nicholi (Ed.), *The Harvard guide to psychiatry.* Cambridge, MA: Harvard University Press.

Duehr, E. E., & Bono, J. E. (2006). Men, women, and managers: Are stereotypes finally changing? *Personnel Psychology, 59,* 815–846.

Duemmler, T., Franz, V. H., Jovanovic, B., & Schwarzer, G. (2008). Effects of the Ebbinghaus illusion on children's perception and grasping. *Experimental Brain Research, 186,* 249–260.

Dufresne, T. (2007). *Against Freud: Critics talk back.* Palo Alto, CA: Stanford University Press.

Duncan, T. B. (2007). Adult attachment and value orientation in marriage. *Dissertation Abstracts International: Section B: The Sciences and Engineering, 68,* 3447.

Dunham, Y. C. (2007). Assessing the automaticity of intergroup bias. *Dissertation Abstracts International: Section B: The Sciences and Engineering, 68(6-B),* 4153.

Dunn, D., & Halonen, J. S. (2008). *Teaching critical thinking in psychology.* Hoboken, NJ: Wiley/Blackwell.

Dunn, M. (2000). *Good death guide: Everything you wanted to know but were afraid to ask.* New York: How to Books.

Durham, M. D., & Dane, F. C. (1999). Juror knowledge of eyewitness behavior: Evidence for the necessity of expert testimony. *Journal of Social Behavior & Personality, 14,* 299–308.

Dutra, L., Callahan, K., Forman, E., Mendelsohn, M., & Herman, J. (2008). Core schemas and suicidality in a chronically traumatized population. *Journal of Nervous and Mental Disease, 196,* 71–74.

Dutton, D. G., & Aron, A. P. (1974). Some evidence for heightened sexual attraction under conditions of high anxiety. *Journal of Personality & Social Psychology, 30,* 510–517.

Duval, D. C. (2006). The relationship between African centeredness and psychological androgyny among African American women in middle adulthood. *Dissertation Abstracts International: Section B: The Sciences and Engineering. 67(2-B),* 1146.

Dworkin, A. (1974). *Woman hating.* New York: E. P. Dutton.

Eagly, A. H., & Koenig, A. M. (2006). Social role theory of sex differences and similarities: Implication for prosocial behavior. In K. Dindia & D. J. Canary (Eds.), *Sex differences and similarities in communication* (2nd ed.) (pp. 161–177). Mahwah, NJ: Erlbaum.

Eaker, E. D., Sullivan, L. M., Kelly-Hayes, M., D'Agostino, R. B., & Benajmin, E. J. (2007). Marital status, marital strain, and risk of coronary heart disease or total mortality: The Framingham offspring study. *Psychosomatic Medicine, 69,* 509–513.

Eddy, K. T., Hennessey, M., & Thompson-Brenner, H. (2007). Eating pathology in East African women: The role of media exposure and globalization. *Journal of Nervous and Mental Disease, 195,* 196–202.

Edery-Halpern, G., & Nachson, I. (2004). Distinctiveness in flashbulb memory: Comparative analysis of five terrorist attacks. *Memory, 12(2),* 147–157.

Edwards, B. (1999). *The new drawing on the right side of the brain.* Baltimore: J P Tarcher.

Edwards, S. (2007). *50 plus one ways to improve your study habits,* Chicago, IL: New Eductaion Encouragement Press.

Ehrenreich, B. (2004, July 15). *All together now.* [On-line]. Available: http://select.nytimes.com/gst/abstract.html?res=F00E16FA3C5E0C768DDDAE0894DC404482.

Eibl-Eibesfeldt, I. (1980). Strategies of social interaction. In R. Plutchik & H. Kelerman (Eds.), *Emotion: Theory, research, and experience.* New York: Academic Press.

Eisen, S. A., Chantarujikapong, Sta, Xian, H., Lyons, M. J., Toomey, R., True, W. R., Scherrer, J. F., Goldberg, J., & Tsuang, M. T. (2002). Does marijuana use have residual adverse effects on self-reported health measures, sociodemographics and quality of life? A monozygotic co-twin control study in men. *Addiction, 97(9),* 1137–1144.

Eisenberger, R., & Armeli, S. (1997). Can salient reward increase creative performance without reducing intrinsic creative interest? *Journal of Personality and Social Psychology, 72,* 652–663.

Eisenberger, R., & Rhoades, L. (2002). Incremental effects of reward on creativity. *Journal of Personality and Social Psychology, 81(4),* 728–741.

Eisend, M. (2007). Understanding two-sided persuasion: An empirical assessment of theoretical approaches. *Psychology & Marketing, 24,* 615–640.

Ekers, D., Richards, D., & Gilbody, S. (2008). A meta-analysis of randomized trials of behavioural treatment of depression. *Psychological Medicine, 38,* 611–623.

Ekman, P. (1980). *The face of man.* New York: Garland.

Ekman, P. (1993). Facial expression and emotion. *American Psychologist, 48,* 384–392.

Ekman, P. (2003). Emotions inside out: 130 years after Darwin's "The expression of emotions in man and animal." *Annals of the New York Academy of Science, 1000,* 1–6.

Ekman, P. (2004). *Emotions revealed: Recognizing faces and feelings to improve communication and emotional life.* Thousand Oaks, CA: Owl Books.

Ekman, P., & Keltner, D. (1997). Universal facial expressions of emotion: An old controversy and new findings. In U. C. Segerstrale & P. Molnar (Eds.), *Nonverbal communication: Where nature meets culture.* Mahwah, NJ: Erlbaum.

Elder, G. (1998). The life course as developmental theory. *Current Directions in Psychological Science, 69,* 1–12.

Elkin, A., Kalidindi, S., & McGuffin, P. (2004). Have schizophrenia genes been found? *Current Opinion in Psychiatry, 17(2),* 107–113.

Elkind, D. (1967). Egocentrism in adolescence. *Child Development, 38,* 1025–1034.

Elkind, D. (1981). *The hurried child.* Reading, MA: Addison-Wesley.

Elkind, D. (2000). A quixotic approach to issues in early childhood education. *Human Development, 43(4–5),* 279–283.

Elkind, D. (2007). *The hurried child: Growing up too fast too soon* (25th anniversary ed.). Cambridge, ME: Da Capo Press.

Ellis, A. (1961). *A guide to rational living.* Englewood Cliffs, NJ: Prentice-Hall.

Ellis, A. (1996). *Better, deeper, and more enduring brief therapy.* New York: Institute for Rational Emotive Therapy.

Ellis, A. (1997). Using rational emotive behavior therapy techniques to cope with disability. *Professional Psychology: Research and Practice, 28,* 17–22.

Ellis, A. (2003a). Early theories and practices of rational emotive behavior therapy and how they have been augmented and revised during the last three decades. *Journal of Rational- Emotive & Cognitive Behavior Therapy, 21(3–4),* 219–243.

Ellis, A. (2003b). Similarities and differences between rational emotive behavior therapy and cognitive therapy. *Journal of Cognitive Psychotherapy, 17(3),* 225–240.

Ellis, A. (2004). Why rational emotive behavior therapy is the most comprehensive and effective form of behavior therapy. *Journal of Rational Emotive & Cognitive Behavior Therapy, 22(2),* 85–92.

Ellis, L., Ficek, C., Burke, D., & Das, S. (2008). Eye color, hair color, blood type, and the rhesus factor: Exploring possible genetic links to sexual orientation. *Archives of Sexual Behavior, 37,* 145–149.

Ellman, L. M., & Cannon, T. D. (2008). Environmental pre-and perinatal influences in etiology. In K. T. Mueser & D. V. Jeste (Eds.), *Clinical handbook of schizophrenia* (pp. 65–73). New York: Guilford.

Engel, J. M., Jensen, M. P., & Schwartz, L. (2004). Outcome of biofeedback-assisted relaxation for pain in adults with cerebral palsy: Preliminary findings. *Applied Psychophysiology & Biofeedback, 29*(2), 135–140.

Engle, S. (2006). *More college freshmen commit to social and civic responsibility, UCLA survey reveals.* [On-line]. Available: http://www.gseis.ucla.edu/heri/PDFs/CIRPPressRelease05.PDF.

Ennis, N. E., Hobfoll, S. E., & Schroeder, K. E. E. (2000). Money doesn't talk, it swears: How economic stress and resistance resources impact inner-city women's depressive mood. *American Journal of Community Psychology, 28,* 149–173.

Epel, E. S., Lin, J., Wilhelm, F. H., Wolkowitz, O. M., Cawthon, R., Adler, N. E., Dolbier, C., Mendes, W. B., & Blackburn, E. H. (2006). Cell aging in relation to stress arousal and cardiovascular disease risk factors. *Psychoneuroendocrinology, 31,* 277–287.

Erdelyi, M. H., & Applebaum, A. G. (1973). Cognitive masking: The disruptive effect of an emotional stimulus upon the perception of contiguous neutral items. *Bulletin of the Psychonomic Society, 1,* 59–61.

Eriksen, J., Jensen, M. K., Sjogren, P., Ekholm, O., & Rasmussen, N. K. (2003). Epidemiology of chronic non-malignant pain in Denmark. *Pain, 106*(3), 221–228.

Erikson, E. (1950). *Childhood and society.* New York: Norton.

Erlacher, D., & Schredl, M. (2004). Dreams reflecting waking sport activities: A comparison of sport and psychology students. *International Journal of Sport Psychology, 35*(4), 301–308.

Ertekin-Taner, N. (2007). Genetics of Alzheimer's disease: A centennial review. *Neurologic Clinics, 25,* 611–667.

Espelage, D. L., Aragon, S. R., Birkett, M., & Koenig, B. W. (2008). Homophobic teasing, psychological outcomes, and sexual orientation among high school students: What influence do parents and schools have? *School Psychology Review, 37,* 202–216.

Esses, V. M., Dovidio, J. F., Jackson, L. M., & Armstrong, T. L. (2001). The immigration dilemma: The role of perceived group competition, ethnic prejudice, and national identity. *Journal of Social Issues, 57*(3), 389–412.

Esterson, A. (2002). The myth of Freud's ostracism by the medical community in 1896–1905: Jeffrey Masson's assault on truth. *History of Psychology, 5*(2), 115–134.

Ethical Principles of Psychologists and Code of Conduct. (2002). [On-line]. Available: http://www.apa.org/ethics/code2002.html.

Evans, G. W., Boxhill, L., & Pinkava, M. (2008). Poverty and maternal responsiveness: The role of maternal stress and social resources. *International Journal of Behavioral Development, 32,* 232–237.

Evans, J. S. B. T. (2003). In two minds: Dualprocess accounts of reasoning. *Trends in Cognitive Sciences, 7*(10), 454–459.

Evans, K., & Brase, G. L. (2007). Assessing sex differences and similarities in mate preferences: Above and beyond demand characteristics. *Journal of Social and Personal Relationships, 24,* 781–791.

Evans, S., Ferrando, S., Findler, M., Stowell, C., Smart, C., & Haglin, D. (2008). Mindfulness-based cognitive therapy for generalized anxiety disorder. *Journal of Anxiety Disorders, 22,* 716–721.

Everett, C., & Everett, S. V. (1994). *Healthy divorce.* San Francisco: Jossey-Bass.

Ewart, C. K., & Fitzgerald, S. T. (1994). Changing behaviour and promoting well-being after heart attack: A social action theory approach. *Irish Journal of Psychology, 15*(1), 219–241.

Eysenck, H. J. (1967). *The biological basis of personality.* Springfield, IL: Charles C Thomas.

Eysenck, H. J. (1982). *Personality, genetics, and behavior: Selected papers.* New York: Prager.

Eysenck, H. J. (1990). Biological dimensions of personality. In L. A. Pervin (Ed.), *Handbook of personality: Theory and research.* New York: Guilford Press.

Eysenck, H. J. (1991). *Smoking, personality, and stress: Psychosocial factors in the prevention of cancer and coronary heart disease.* New York: Springer-Verlag.

Facon, B., & Facon-Bollengier, T. (1999). Chronological age and crystallized intelligence of people with intellectual disability. *Journal of Intellectual Disability Research, 43*(6), 489–496.

Faddiman, A. (1997). *The spirit catches you and you fall down.* New York: Straus & Giroux.

Faigman, D. L., Kaye, D., Saks, M. J., & Sanders, J. (1997). *Modern scientific evidence: The law and science of expert testimony.* St. Paul, MN: West.

Fairburn, C. G., Cooper, Z., Shafran, R., & Wilson, G. T. (2008). Eating disorders: A transdiagnostic protocol. In D. H. Barlow (Ed.), *Clinical handbook of psychological disorders: A step-by-step treatment manual* (4th ed.) (pp. 578–614). New York: Guilford Press.

Fairchild, K., & Scogin, F. (2008). Assessment and treatment of depression. In K. Laidlaw & B. Knight (Eds.), *Handbook of emotional disorders in later life: Assessment and treatment.* New York: Oxford University Press.

Famous people with mental illness. (2008). [On-line]. Available: http://www.naminh.org/action-famous-people.php

Famous people with schizophrenia. (2008). [On-line]. Available: http://www.signsofschizophrenia.net/famous-people-with-schizophrenia.html

Fang, X., & Corso, P. S. (2007). Child maltreatment, youth violence, and intimate partner violence: Developmental relationships. *American Journal of Preventive Medicine, 33,* 281–290.

Fanselow, M. S., & Poulos, A. M. (2005). The neuroscience of mammalian associative learning. *Annual Review of Psychology, 56,* 207–234.

Fantz, R. L. (1956). A method for studying early visual development. *Perceptual and Motor Skills, 6,* 13–15.

Fantz, R. L. (1963). Pattern vision in newborn infants. *Science, 140,* 296–297.

Faraone, S. V. (2008). Statistical and molecular genetic approaches to developmental psychopathology: The pathway forward. In J. J. Hudziak (Ed.), *Developmental psychopathology and wellness: Genetic and environmental influences* (pp. 245–265). Arlington, VA: American Psychiatric Publishing.

Farrington, D. P. (2000). Psychosocial predictors of adult antisocial personality and adult convictions. *Behavioral Sciences & the Law, 18*(5), 605–622.

Farris, C., Treat, T. A., Viken, R. J., & McFall, R. M. (2008). Perceptual mechanisms that characterize gender differences in decoding women's sexual intent. *Psychological Science, 19,* 348–354.

Fassler, O., Lynn, S. J., & Knox, J. (2006). Is hypnotic suggestibility a stable trait? *Consciousness and Cognition: An International Journal, 17,* 240–253.

Fazio, R. H., & Olson, M. A. (2003). Implicit measures in social cognition research: Their meaning and use. *Annual Review of Psychology, 54,* 297–327.

Fehr, C., Yakushev, I., Hohmann, N., Buchholz, H-G., Landvogt, C., Deckers, H., Eberhardt, A., Kläger, M., Smolka, M. N., Scheurich, A., Dielentheis, T., Schmidt, L. G., Rösch, F., Bartehstein, P., Gründer, G., & Schreckenberger, M. (2008). Association of low striatal dopamine D-sub-2 receptor availability with nicotine dependence similar to that seen with other drugs of abuse. *American Journal of Psychiatry, 165,* 507–514.

Fein, S. & Spencer, S. J. (1997). Prejudice as selfimage maintenance: Affirming the self through derogating others. *Journal of Personality and Social Psychology, 73*(1), 31–44.

Feiring, C., Deblinger, E., Hoch-Espada, A., & Haworht T. (2002). Romantic relationship aggression and attitudes in high school students: The role of gender, grade, and attachment and emotional styles. *Journal of Youth & Adolescence, 31*(5), 373–385.

Feldman, R. (2007). Maternal-infant contact and child development: Insights from the kangaroo intervention. In L. L'Abate (Ed.), *Low-cost approaches to promote physical and mental health: Theory, research, and practice* (pp. 323–351). New York: Springer.

Feldman, R. S. (1982). *Development of nonverbal behavior in children.* Seacaucus, NJ: Springer-Verlag.

Feng, J., Spence, I., & Pratt, J. (2007). Playing an action video game reduces gender differences in spatial cognition. *Psychological Science, 18,* 850–855.

Fernández, J. R., Casazza, K., Divers, J., & López-Alarcón, M. (2008). Disruptions in energy balance: Does nature overcome nurture? *Physiology & Behavior, 94,* 105–112.

Fernández, M. I., Bowen, G. S., Varga, L. M., Collazo, J. B., Hernandez, N., Perrino, T., & Rehbein, A. (2005). High rates of club drug use and risky sexual practices among Hispanic men who have sex with men in Miami, Florida. *Substance Use & Misuse, 40*(9–10), 1347–1362.

Fernández-Dols, J-M., Carrera, P., & Russell, J. A. (2002). Are facial displays social? Situational influences in the attribution of emotion to facial expressions. *Spanish Journal of Psychology, 5*(2), 119–124.

Fernyhough, C. (2008). Getting Vygotskian theory of mind: Mediation, dialogue, and the development of social understanding. *Developmental Review, 28,* 225–262.

Ferrari, P. F., Rozzi, S., & Fogassi, L. (2005). Mirror neurons responding to observation of actions made with tools in monkey ventral premotor cortex. *Journal of Cognitive Neuroscience, 17,* 212–226.

Ferretti, P., Copp, A., Tickle, C., & Moore, G. (Eds.) (2006). *Embryos, genes, and birth defects* (2nd ed.). Hoboken, NJ: Wiley.

Festinger, L. A. (1957). *A theory of cognitive dissonance.* Palo Alto, CA: Stanford University Press.

Festinger, L. A., & Carlsmith, L. M. (1959). Cognitive consequences of forced compliance. *Journal of Abnormal and Social Psychology, 58,* 203–210.

Field, A. P. (2006). Is conditioning a useful framework for understanding the development and treatment of phobias? *Clinical Psychology Review, 26,* 857–875.

Field, K. M., Woodson, R., Greenberg, R., & Cohen, D. (1982). Discrimination and imitation of facial expressions by neonates. *Science, 218,* 179–181.

Field, T. (2007). *The amazing infant.* Malden, MA: Blackwell.

Field, T., Diego, M., & Hernandez-Reif, M. (2007). Massage therapy research. *Developmental Review, 27,* 75–89.

Field, T., & Hernandez-Reif, M. (2001). Sleep problems in infants decrease following massage therapy. *Early Child Development & Care, 168,* 95–104.

Fields, R. (2007). *Drugs in perspective* (6th ed.). New York: McGraw-Hill.

Fields, W. M., Segerdahl, P., & Savage-Rumbaugh, S. (2007). The material practices of ape language research. In J. Valsiner & A. Rosa (Eds.), *The Cambridge handbook of sociocultural psychology* (pp. 164–186). New York: Cambridge University Press.

Finch, E., & Munro, V. E. (2005). Juror stereotypes and blame attribution in rape cases involving intoxicants: The findings of a pilot study. *British Journal of Criminology, 45,* 25–38.

Fink, B., Manning, J. T., Neave, N., & Grammer, K. (2004). Second to fourth digit ratio and facial asymmetry. *Evolution and Human Behavior, 25*(2), 125–132.

Fink, B., & Penton-Voak, I. (2002). Evolutionary psychology of facial attractiveness. *Current Directions in Psychological Science, 11*(5), 154–158.

Fink, M. (1999). *Electroshock: Restoring the mind.* London: Oxford University Press.

Finklehor, D., & Jones, L. (2006). Why have child maltreatment and child victimization declined? *Journal of Social Issues, 62,* 685–716.

First, M., & Tasman, A. (2004). *DSM-IV-TR mental disorders: Diagnosis, etiology, and treatment.* Hoboken, NJ: Wiley.

Fisher, C. B., & Fried, A. L. (2008). Internet-mediated psychological services and the American Psychological Association Ethics Code. In D. N. Bersoff (Ed.), *Ethical conflicts in psychology* (4th ed.) (pp. 376–383). Washington, DC: American Psychological Association.

Fisher, G., & Harrison, T. (2005). *Substance abuse: Information for school counselors, social workers, therapists, and counselors* (3rd ed.). Boston, MA: Allyn & Bacon/Longman.

Fisher, J. O. & Kral, T. V. E. (2008). Super-size me: Portion size effects on young children's eating. *Physiology & Behavior, 94,* 39–47.

Fisher, S., & Greenberg, R. P. (1996). *Freud scientifically reappraised: Testing the theories and therapy.* New York: Wiley.

Fisk, J. E., Bury, A. S., & Holden, R. (2006). Reasoning about complex probabilistic concepts in childhood. *Scandinavian Journal of Psychology, 47,* 497–504.

Fiske, S. T. (1998). Stereotyping, prejudice, and discrimination. In D. T. Gilbert, S. T. Fiske, and G. Lindzey (Eds.), *The handbook of social psychology* (4th ed., Vol. 2, pp. 357–411). Boston: McGraw-Hill.

FitzGerald, D. B., Crucian, G. P., Mielke, J. B., Shenal, B. V., Burks, D., Womack, K. B., Ghacibeh, G., Drago, V., Foster, P. S., Valenstein, E., & Heilman, K. M. (2008). Effects of donepezil on verbal memory after semantic processing in healthy older adults. *Cognitive and Behavioral Neurology, 21,* 57–64.

Flavell, J. H., Miller, P. H., & Miller, S. A. (2002). *Cognitive development* (4th ed.). Upper Saddle River, NJ: Prentice-Hall. Fletcher, G. J. O., & Simpson, J. A. (2000). Ideal standards in close relationships: Their structure and functions. *Current Directions in Psychological Science, 9*(3), 102–105.

Fleischmann, B. K., & Welz, A. (2008). Cardiovascular regeneration and stem cell therapy. *Journal of the American Medical Association, 299*(6), 700–701.

Fletcher, G. J. O., & Simpson, J. A. (2000). Ideal standards in close relationships: Their structure and functions. *Current Directions in Psychological Science, 9,* 102–105.

Flores, Y. G. (2008). Race related stress of Latino elders: Implications for quality of life. *Dissertation Abstracts International: Section B: The Sciences and Engineering, 68*(8-B), 5567.

Flynn, J. R. (1987). Massive IQ gains in 14 nations: What IQ tests really measure. *Psychological Bulletin, 101,* 171–191.

Flynn, J. R. (2000). IQ gains and fluid g. *American Psychologist, 55*(5), 543.

Flynn, J. R. (2003). Movies about intelligence: The limitations of g. *Current Directions in Psychological Science, 12*(3), 95–99.

Flynn, J. R. (2006). The history of the American mind in the 20th century: A scenario to explain gains over time and a case for the irrelevance of g. In P. C. Kyllonen, R. D. Roberts, & L. Stankov (Eds.), *Extending intelligence.* Mahwah, NJ: Erlbaum.

Flynn, J. R. (2007). *What is intelligence?: Beyond the Flynn Effect.* New York: Cambridge University Press. (2007).

Fogarty, A., Rawstorne, P., Prestage, G., Crawford, J., Grierson, J., & Kippax, S. (2007). Marijuana as therapy for people living with HIV/AIDS: Social and health aspects. *AIDS Care, 19,* 295–301.

Fogassi, L., Ferrari, P. F., Gesierich, B., Rozzi, S., Chersi, F., & Rizzolatti, G. (2005). Parietal lobe: From action understanding to intention understanding. *Science, 308,* 662–667.

Fok, H. K., Hui, C. M., Bond, M. H., Matsumoto, D., & Yoo, S. H. (2008). Integrating personality, context, relationship, and emotion type into a model of display rules. *Journal of Research in Personality, 42,* 133–150.

Folk, C. L., & Remington, R. W. (1998). Selectivity in distraction by irrelevant featural singletons: Evidence for two forms of attentional capture. *Journal of Experimental Psychology: Human Perception and Performance, 24,* 1–12.

Fone, B. R. S. (2000). *Homophobia: A history.* New York: Metropolitan Books.

Ford, T. E., Ferguson, M. A., Brooks, J. L., & Hagadone, K. M. (2004). Coping sense of humor reduces effects of stereotype threat on women's math performance. *Personality & Social Psychology Bulletin, 30*(5), 643–653.

Foster, P. S., Drago, V., Webster, D. G., Harrison, D. W., Crucian, G. P., & Heilman, K. M. (2008). Emotion influences on spatial attention. *Neuropsychology, 22,* 127–135.

Fouad, N. A. (2007). Work and vocational psychology: Theory, research, and applications. *Annual Review of Psychology, 58,* 515–541.

Foulkes, D. (1993). Children's dreaming. In D. Foulkes & C. Cavallero (Eds.), *Dreaming as cognition* (pp. 114–132). New York: Harvester Wheatsheaf.

Fouts, R. (2000, July). One-on-one with our closest cousins: "My best friend is a chimp." *Psychology Today, 33,* 34–36.

Fraley, R. C., & Shaver, P. R. (1997). Adult attachment and the suppression of unwanted thoughts. *Journal of Personality and Social Psychology, 73,* 1080–1091.

Frank, M. J. (2005). Dynamic dopamine modulation in the basal ganglia: A neurocomputational account of cognitive deficits in medicated and nonmedicated Parkinsonism. *Journal of Cognitive Neuroscience, 17*(1), 51–72.

Frankenburg, W., Dodds, J., Archer, P., Shapiro, H., & Bresnick, B. (1992). The Denver II: A major revision and restandardization of the Denver Developmental Screening Test. *Pediatrics, 89,* 91–97.

Frawley, T. J. (2008). Gender schema and prejudicial recall: How children misremember, fabricate, and distort gendered picture book information. *Journal of Research in Childhood Education, 22,* 291–303.

Frayser, S. (1985). *Varieties of sexual experience: An anthropological perspective on human sexuality.* New Haven, CT: Human Relations Area Files Press.

Fredricks, J. A., & Eccles, J. S. (2005). Family socialization, gender, and sport motivation and involvement. *Journal of Sport & Exercise Psychology, 27*(1), 3–31.

Freeman, S., & Herron, J. C. (2007). *Evolutionary analysis* (4th ed.). Upper Saddle River, NJ: Prentice-Hall.

Freeman, W. J. (2007). Indirect biological measures of consciousness from field studies of brains as dynamical systems. *Neural Networks, 20,* 1021–1031.

Fresán, A., Apiquian, R., García-Anaya, M., de la Fuente-Sandoval, C., Nicolini, H., & Graff-Guerrero, A. (2007). The P50 auditory evoked potential in violent and non-violent patients with schizophrenia. *Schizophrenia Research, 97,* 128–136.

Frick, R. S., Wang, J., & Carlson, R. G. (2008). Depressive symptomatology in young adults with a history of MDMA use: a longitudinal analysis. *Journal of Psychopharmacology, 22*(1), 47–54.

Frick, W. B. (2000). Remembering Maslow: Reflections on a 1968 interview. *Journal of Humanistic Psychology, 40*(2), 128–147.

Friedman, H., & Schustack, M. (2006). *Personality: Classic theories and modern research* (3rd ed.). Boston: Allyn & Bacon/Longman.

Friedman, M., & Rosenman, R. H. (1959). Association of specific overt behavior patterns with blood and cardiovascular findings: Blood cholesterol level, blood clotting time, incidence of arcus senilis and clinical coronary artery disease. *Journal of the American Medical Association, 169,* 1286–1296.

Frisby, C. J. (1995). When facts and orthodoxy collide: The bell curve and the robustness criterion. *School Psychology Review, 24,* 12–19.

Fry, C. L. (1985). Culture, behavior, and aging in the comparative perspective. In J. E. Birren, K. W. Schaie, et al. (Eds.), *Handbook of the psychology of aging* (2nd ed.) (pp, 216–244). New York: Van Nostrand Reinhold Co.

Fryer, S. L., Crocker, N. A., & Mattson, S. N. (2008). Exposure to teratogenic agents as a risk factor for psychopathology. In T. P. Beauchaine & S. P. Hinshaw (Eds.), *Child and adolescent psychopathology* (pp. 180–207). Hoboken, NJ: Wiley.

Funder, D. C. (2000). Personality. *Annual Review of Psychology, 52,* 197–221.

Funder, D. C. (2001). The really, really fundamental attribution error. *Psychological Inquiry, 12*(1), 21–23.

Furman, E. (1990, November). Plant a potato, learn about life (and death). *Young Children, 46*(1), 15–20.

Gaab, J., Rohleder, N., Nater, U. M., & Ehlert, U. (2005). Psychological determinants of the cortisol stress response: The role of anticipatory cognitive appraisal. *Psychoneuroendocrinology, 30*(6), Jul 2005, 599–610.

Gabbard, G. O. (2006). Mente, cervello e disturbi di personalita. / Mind, brain, and personality disorders. *Psicoterapia e scienze umane, 40,* 9–26.

Gabry, K. E., Chrousos, G. P., Rice, K. C., Mostafa, R. M., Sternberg, E., Negrao, A. B., Webster, E. L., McCann, S. M., & Gold, P. W. (2002). Marked suppression of gastric ulcerogenesis and intestinal responses to stress by a novel class of drugs. *Molecular Psychiatry, 7*(5), 474–483.

Gacono, C. B., Evans, F. B., & Viglione, D. J. (2008). Essential issues in the forensic use of the Rorschach. In C. B. Gacono (Ed.), F. B. Evans (Ed.), N. Kaser-Boyd (Col.), & L. A. Gacono (Col.), *The handbook of forensic Rorschach assessment* (pp. 3–20). *The LEA series in personality and clinical psychology.* New York: Routledge/Taylor & Francis Group.

Gaetz, M., Weinberg, H., Rzempoluck, E., & Jantzen, K. J. (1998). Neural network classifications and correlational analysis of EEG and MEG activity accompanying spontaneous reversals of the Necker Cube. *Cognitive Brain Research, 6,* 335–346.

Gagné, M-H., Drapeau, S., Melançon, C., Saint-Jacques, M-C., & Lépine, R. (2007). Links between parental psychological violence, other family disturbances, and children's adjustment. *Family Process, 46,* 523–542.

Gagnon, J. H. (1990). The explicit and implicit use of the scripting perspective in sex research. *Annual Review of Sex Research, 1,* 1–43.

Gailliot, M. T., Baumeister, R. F., DeWall, C. N., Maner, J. K., Plant, E. A., Tice, D. M., Brewer, L. E., & Schmeichel, B. J. (2007). Self-control relies on glucose as a limited energy source: Willpower is more than a metaphor. *Journal of Personality and Social Psychology, 92,* 325–336.

Galderisi, S., Quarantelli, M., Volpe, U., Mucci, A., Cassano, G. B., Invernizzi, G., Rossi, A., Vita, A., Pini, S., Cassano, P., Daneluzzo, E., De Peri, L., Stratta, P., Brunetti, A., & Maj, M. (2008). Patterns of structural MRI abnormalities in deficit and nondeficit schizophrenia. *Schizophrenia Bulletin, 34,* 393–401.

Galea, S., Brewin, C. R., Gruber, M., Jones, R. T., King, D. W., King, L. A., McNally, R. J., Ursano, R. J., Petukhova, M., & Kessler, R. C. (2007). Exposure to hurricane-related stressors and mental illness after Hurricane Katrina. *Archives of General Psychiatry, 64(12),* 1427–1434.

Galinsky, A., D., & Ku, G. (2004). The effects of perspective-taking on prejudice: The moderating role of self-evaluation. *Personality & Social Psychology Bulletin, 30(5),* 594–604.

Galinsky, A. D., & Moskowitz, G. B. (2000). Perspective-taking: Decreasing stereotype expression, stereotype accessibility, and ingroup favoritism. *Journal of Personality and Social Psychology, 78(4),* 708–724.

Gallagher, A. M., De Lisi, R., Holst, P. C., McGillicuddy-De Lisi, A. V., Morely, M., & Cahalan, C. (2000). Gender differences in advanced mathematical problem solving. *Journal of Experimental Child Psychology, 75(3),* 165–190.

Galloway, J. L. (1999, March 8). Into the heart of darkness. *U. S. News and World Report,* pp. 25–32.

Gambescia, N., & Weeks, G. (2007). Sexual dysfunction. In N. Kazantzis & L. L'Abate (Eds.), *Handbook of homework assignments in psychotherapy: Research, practice, prevention* (pp. 351–368). New York: Springer Science + Business Media.

Gamian-Wilk, M., & Lachowicz-Tabaczek, K. (2007). Implicit theories and compliance with the foot-in-the-door technique. *Polish Psychological Bulletin, 38,* 50–63.

Gangestad, S. W., & Thornhill, R. (2003). Facial masculinity and fluctuating asymmetry. *Evolution and Human Behavior, 24(4),* 231–241.

Garb, H. N., Wood, J. M., Lilienfeld, S. O., & Nezworski, M. T. (2005). Roots of the Rorschach controversy. *Clinical Psychology Review, 25,* 97–118.

Garbarino, S., Beelke, M., Costa, G., Violani, C., Lucidi, F., & Ferrillo, F. (2002). Brain function and effects of shift work: Implications for clinical neuropharmacology. *Neuropsychobiology, 45(1),* 50–56.

Garcia, G. M., & Stafford, M. E. (2000). Prediction of reading by Ga and Gc specific cognitive abilities for low-SES White and Hispanic English-speaking children. *Psychology in the Schools, 37(3),* 227–235.

Garcia, J. (2003). Psychology is not an enclave. In R. Sternberg (Ed.), *Psychologists defying the crowd: Stories of those who battled the establishment and won* (pp. 67–77). Washington, DC: American Psychological Association.

Garcia, J., & Koelling, R. S. (1966). Relation of cue to consequence in avoidance learning. *Psychonomic Science, 4,* 123–124.

Gardiner, H., & Kosmitzki, G. (2005). *Lives across cultures: Cross-cultural human development* (3rd ed.). Boston: Allyn & Bacon/Longman.

Gardner, H. (1983). *Frames of mind.* New York: Basic Books.

Gardner, H. (1998). A multiplicity of intelligences. *Scientific American Presents Exploring Intelligence, 9,* 18–23.

Gardner, H. (1999, February). Who owns intelligence? *Atlantic Monthly,* pp. 67–76.

Gardner, H. (2002). The pursuit of excellence through education. In M. Ferrari (Ed.), *Learning from extraordinary minds.* Mahwah, NJ: Erlbaum.

Gardner, H. (2008). Who owns intelligence? In M. H. Immordino-Yang (Ed.), *Jossey-Bass Education Team. The Jossey-Bass reader on the brain and learning* (pp. 120–132). San Francisco: Jossey-Bass.

Gardner, R. A., & Gardner, B. T. (1969). Teaching sign language to a chimpanzee. *Science, 165,* 664–672.

Garnefski, N., Teerds, J., Kraaij, V., Legerstee, J., & van den Kommer, T. (2004). Cognitive emotion regulation strategies and Depressive symptoms: differences between males and females. *Personality & Individual Differences, 36(2),* 267–276.

Garner, H. (2002). The pursuit of excellence through education. In M. Ferrari (Ed.), *Learning from extraordinary minds.* Mahwah, NJ: Erlbaum.

Garno, J. L., Gunawardane, N., & Goldberg, J. F. (2008). Predictors of trait aggression in bipolar disorder. *Bipolar Disorders, 10,* 285–292.

Garrick, J. (2006). The humor of trauma survivors: Its application in a therapeutic milieu. *Journal of Aggression, Maltreatment & Trauma, 12,* 169–182.

Garry, M., & Gerrie, M. P. (2005). When photographs create false memories. *Current Directions in Psychological Science, 14,* 321–324.

Gaser, C., Nenadic, I., Buchsbaum, B. R., Hazeltt, E. A., & Buchsbaum, M. S. (2004). Ventricular enlargement in schizophrenia related to volume reduction of the thalamus, striatum, and superior temporal cortex. *American Journal of Psychiatry, 161(1),* 154–156.

Gasser, S., & Raulet, D. H. (2006). Activation and self-tolerance of natural killer cells. *Immunology Review, 214,* 130–142.

Gaw, A. C. (2001). *Concise guide to cross-cultural psychiatry. Concise guides.* Washington, DC: American Psychiatric Association.

Gawronski, B. (2003). On difficult questions and evident answers: Dispositional inference from role-constrained behavior. *Personality & Social Psychology Bulletin, 29(11),* 1459–1475.

Gay, M-C., Philippot, P., & Luminet, O. (2002). Differential effectiveness of psychological interventions for reducing osteoarthritis pain: A comparison of Erickson hypnosis and Jacobson relaxation. *European Journal of Pain, 6,* 1–16.

Gay, P. (1999, March 29). Psychoanalyst Sigmund Freud. *Time,* 65–69.

Gay, P. (2000). *Freud for historians.* Boston: Replica Books.

Geary, D. C. (2005). The motivation to control and the origin of mind: Exploring the lifemind joint point in the tree of knowledge system. *Journal of Clinical Psychology, 61(1),* 21–46.

Gebauer, H., Krempl, R., & Fleisch, E. (2008). Exploring the effect of cognitive biases on customer support services. *Creativity and Innovation Management, 17,* 58–70.

Gelder, B. D., Meeren, H. K., Righart, R. Stock, J. V., van de Riet, W. A., & Tamietto, M. (2006). Beyond the face: Exploring rapid influences of context on face processing. *Progress in Brain Research, 155,* 37–48.

Gemignani, A., Santarcangelo, E., Sebastiani, L., Marchese, C., Mammoliti, R., Simoni, A., & Ghelarducci, B. (2000). Changes in autonomic and EEG patterns induced by hypnotic imagination of aversive stimuli in man. *Brain Research Bulletin, 53(1),* 105–111.

Gerber, A. J., Posner, J., Gorman, D., Colibazzi, T., Yu, S., Wang, Z., Kangarlu, A., Zhu, H., Russell, J., & Peterson, B. S. (2008). An affective circumplex model of neural systems subserving valence, arousal, and cognitive overlay during the appraisal of emotional faces. *Neuropsychologia, 46,* 2129–2139.

Gerra, G., Angioni, L., Zaimovic, A., Moi, G., Bussandri, M., Bertacca, S., Santoro, G., Gardini, S., Caccavari, R., & Nicoli, M. A. (2004). Substance use among high-school students: Relationships with temperament, personality traits, and parental care perception. *Substance Use & Misuse, 39*(2), 345–367.

Gershon, E. S., & Rieder, R. O. (1993). Major disorders of mind and brain. *Mind and brain: Readings from Scientific American Magazine* (pp. 91–100). New York: Freeman.

Giacobbi, P. Jr., Foore, B., & Weinberg, R. S. (2004). Broken clubs and expletives: The sources of stress and coping responses of skilled and moderately skilled golfers. *Journal of Applied Sport Psychology, 16*(2), 166–182.

Giancola, P. R., & Parrott, D. J. (2008). Further evidence for the validity of the Taylor aggression paradigm. *Aggressive Behavior, 34,* 214–229.

Gibbs, N. (1995, October 2). The EQ factor. *Time,* pp. 60–68.

Gibson, E. J., & Walk, R. D. (1960). The visual cliff. *Scientific American, 202*(2), 67–71.

Giedd, J. N. (2008). The teen brain: Insights from neuroimaging. *Journal of Adolescent Health, 42,* 335–343.

Gielin, U. P. (2007). Foreword: Understanding cross-cultural psychology. In P. D. Laungani (Ed.), *Understanding cross-cultural psychology.* Thousand Oaks, CA: Sage Publications.

Gilbert, T. (2003). Managing passive-aggressive behavior of children and youth at school and home: The angry smile. *Education & Treatment of Children, 26*(3), 305–306.

Gilboa, S., Shirom, A., Fried, Y., & Cooper, C. (2008). A meta-analysis of work demand stressors and job performance: Examining main and moderating effects. *Personnel Psychology, 61*(2), 227–271.

Giles, B. (2004). Thinking about storytelling and narrative journalism. *Neiman Reports,* p. 3. [On-line]. Available: http://www.nieman.harvard.edu/reports/04–1NRSpring/3 V58N1.pdf.

Giles, J. W., & Heyman, G. D. (2005). Young children's beliefs about the relationship between gender and aggressive behavior. *Child Development, 76*(1), 107–121.

Gill, D., et al. (2006). Responding to disaster: Mississippi State University student experiences, impacts, and needs in the aftermath of Hurricane Katrina. *Unpublished report.*

Gilligan, C. (1977). In a different voice: Women's conception of morality. *Harvard Educational Review, 47*(4), 481–517.

Gilligan, C. (1990). Teaching Shakespeare's sister. In C. Gilligan, N. Lyons, & T. Hanmer (Eds.), *Mapping the moral domain* (pp. 73–86). Cambridge, MA: Harvard University Press.

Gilligan, C. (1993). Adolescent development reconsidered. In A. Garrod (Ed.), *Approaches to moral development: New research and emerging themes.* New York: Teachers College Press.

Gillispie, J. F. (2007). Cyber shrinks: Expanding the paradigm. In J. Gackenbach (Ed.), *Psychology and the Internet: Intrapersonal, interpersonal, and transpersonal implications* (2nd ed.) (pp. 245–273). San Diego, CA: Academic Press.

Gilmour, D. R., & Walkey, F. H. (1981). Identifying violent offenders using a video measure of interpersonal distance. *Journal of Consulting and Clinical Psychology, 49,* 287–291.

Gilovich, T., Griffin, D., & Kahneman, D. (2002). *Heuristics and biases: The psychology of intuitive judgment.* Cambridge, UK: Cambridge University Press.

Gini, M., Oppenheim, D., & Sagi-Schwartz, A. (2007). Negotiation styles in mother-child narrative co-construction in middle childhood: Associations with early attachment. *International Journal of Behavioral Development, 31,* 149–160.

Ginzburg, H. M., & Bateman, D. J. (2008). New Orleans medical students post-Katrina—An assessment of psychopathology and anticipatory transference of resilience. *Psychiatric Annals, 38,* 145–156.

Girardi, P., Monaco, E., Prestigiacomo, C., Talamo, A., Ruberto, A., & Tatarelli, R. (2007). Personality and psychopathological profiles in individuals exposed to mobbing. *Violence & Victims, 22,* 172–188.

Gitau, R., Modi, N., Gianakoulopoulos, X., Bond, C., Glover, V., & Stevenson, J. (2002). Acute effects of maternal skin-to-skin contact and massage on saliva cortisol in preterm babies. *Journal of Reproductive & Infant Psychology, 20*(2), 83–88.

Giumetti, G. W., & Markey, P. M. (2007). Violent video games and anger as predictors of aggression. *Journal of Research in Personality, 41,* 1234–1243.

Gluck, M. A. (2008). Behavioral and neural correlates of error correction in classical conditioning and human category learning. In M. A. Gluck, J. R. Anderson, & S. M. Kosslyn (Eds.), *Memory and mind: A festschrift for Gordon H. Bower* (pp. 281–305). Mahwah, NJ: Lawrence Erlbaum.

Gobbo, C., & Raccanello, D. (2007). How children narrate happy and sad events: Does affective state count? *Applied Cognitive Psychology, 21,* 1173–1190.

Godden, D. R., & Baddeley, A. D. (1975). Context-dependent memory in two natural environments: On land and underwater. *British Journal of Psychology, 66,* 325–331.

Goebel, M. U., & Mills, P. J. (2000). Acute psychological stress and exercise and changes in peripheral leukocyte adhesion molecule expression and density. *Psychosomatic Medicine, 62*(5), 664–670.

Goerke, M., Möller, J., Schulz-Hardt, S., Napiersky, U., & Frey, D. (2004). "It's not my fault but only I can change it": Counterfactual and prefactual thoughts of managers. *Journal of Applied Psychology, 89*(2), 279–292.

Goforth, H. W., & Holsinger, T. (2007). Response to effect of the first ECT in a series by C. Kellner, MD. *Journal of ECT, 23,* 209.

Gogtay, N., Sporn, A., Clasen, L. S., Nugent, T. F. III, Greenstein, D., Nicolson, R., Giedd, J. N., Lenane, M., Gochman, P., Evans, A., & Rapoport, J. L. (2004). Comparison of progressive cortical gray matter loss in childhood-onset schizophrenia with that in childhood-onset atypical psychoses. *Archives of General Psychiatry, 61*(1), 17–22.

Goldberg, D. P. (1972). *The detection of psychiatric illness by questionnaire.* London: Oxford University Press.

Goldberg, S. (2000). *Attachment and development.* New York: Edward Arnold.

Goleman, D. (1980, February). 1,528 little geniuses and how they grew. *Psychology Today,* pp. 28–53.

Golden, W. L. (2006). Hypnotherapy for anxiety, phobias and psychophysiological disorders. In R. A. Chapman (Ed.), *The clinical use of hypnosis in cognitive behavior therapy: A practitioner's casebook* (pp. 101–137). New York: Springer.

Goldschmidt, L., Richardson, G. A., Willford, J., & Day, N. L. (2008). Prenatal marijuana exposure and intelligence test performance at age 6. *Journal of the American*

Academy of Child & Adolescent Psychiatry, 47, 254–263.

Goldstein, E. G. (2008). Cognitive psychology: Connecting mind, research, and everyday experience (2nd ed.). Belmont, CA: Cengage.

Goleman, D. (1995). Emotional intelligence: Why it can matter more than IQ. New York: Bantam.

Goleman, D. (2000). Working with emotional intelligence. New York: Bantam Doubleday.

Goleman, D. (2008). Leading resonant teams. In F. Hesselbein & A. Shrader (Eds.), Leader to leader 2: Enduring insights on leadership from the Leader to Leader Institute's award-winning journal (pp. 186–195). Leader to Leader Institute. San Francisco, CA: Jossey-Bass.

Golob, E. J., & Starr, A. (2004). Serial position effects in auditory event-related potentials during working memory retrieval. Journal of Cognitive Neuroscience, 16(1), 40–52.

Gómez, Á., & Huici, C. (2008). Vicarious intergroup contact and role of authorities in prejudice reduction. The Spanish Journal of Psychology, 11, 103–114.

Goni-Allo, B., Mathúna, B., Segura, M., Puerta, E., Lasheras, B., de la Torre, R., & Aguirre, N. (2008). The relationship between core body temperature and 3,4-methylenedioxymethamphetamine metabolism in rats: Implications for neurotoxicity. Psychopharmacology, 197, 263–278.

Gonzales, P. M., Blanton, H., & Williams, K. J. (2002). The effects of stereotype threat and double-minority status on the test performance of Latino women. Personality & Social Psychology Bulletin, 28(5), 659–670.

Goodall, J. (1990). Through a window: My thirty years with the chimpanzees of Gombe. Boston: Houghton-Mifflin.

Goode, E. E., Schrof, J. M., & Burke, S. (1991, June 24). Where emotions come from. U. S. News and World Report, pp. 54–60.

Goodman, G. S., Ghetti, S., Quas, J. A., Edelstein, R. S., Alexander, K. W., Redlich, A. D., Cordon, I. M., & Jones, D. P. H. (2003). A prospective study of memory for child sexual abuse: New findings relevant to the repressed memory controversy. Psychological Science, 14(2), 113–118.

Goodman, M., & Yehuda, R. (2002). The relationship between psychological trauma and borderline personality disorder. Psychiatric Annals, 32(6), 337–345.

Goodwin, C. J. (2005). A history of modern psychology (2nd ed.). Hoboken, NJ: Wiley.

Goodwin, C. J. (2009). A history of modern psychology (3rd ed.). Hoboken, NJ: Wiley.

Goodwin, F. K., Simon, G., Revicki, D., Hunkeler, E., Fireman, B., & Lee, E. (2004). "Pharmacotherapy and risk of suicidal behaviors among patients with bipolar disorder": Reply. JAMA: Journal of the American Medical Association, 291(8), 940.

Gooren, L. (2006). The biology of human psychosexual differentiation. Hormones and Behavior, 50, 589–601.

Gordis, E. B., Margolin, G., & Vickerman, K. (2005). Communication and frightening behavior among couples with past and recent histories of physical marital aggression. American Journal of Community Psychology, 36, 177–191.

Gordon, R. A. (2000). Eating disorders: Anatomy of a social epidemic (2nd ed.). Malden, MA: Blackwell Publishers.

Gordon, W. C. (1989). Learning and memory. Belmont, CA: Brooks/Cole.

Gorman, J. (2000). Neuroanatomical hypothesis of panic disorder revised. American Journal of Psychiatry, 57, 493–505.

Gosling, S. D. (2008). Personality in non-human animals. Social and Personality Compass, 2, 985–1001.

Gosling, S. D., & John, O. P. (1999). Personality dimensions in nonhuman animals: A cross-species review. Current Directions in Psychological Science, 8, 69–75.

Gosling, S. D., Kwan, V. S. Y., & John, O. P. (2004). A dog's got personality: A cross-species comparative approach to personality judgments in dogs and humans. Journal of Personality and Social Psychology, 85, 1161–1169.

Goswami, S., Mattoo, S. K., Basu, D., & Singh, G. (2004). Substance-abusing schizophrenics: Do they self-medicate? American Journal on Addictions, 13(2), 139–150.

Gotlieb, I. H., & Abramson, L. Y. (1999). Attributional theories of emotion. In T. Dalgleish & M. Power (Eds.), Handbook of cognition and emotion. New York: Wiley.

Gottesman, I. I. (1991). Schizophrenia genesis: The origins of madness. New York: Freeman.

Gottesman, I. I., & Hanson, D. R. (2005). Human development: Biological and genetic processes. Annual Review of Psychology, 56, 263–286.

Gottfredson, G. D., & Duffy, R. D. (2008). Using a theory of vocational personalities and work environments to explore subjective well-being. Journal of Career Assessment, 16, 44–59.

Gottman, J. M., Coan, J., Carrere, S., & Swanson, C. (1998). Predicting happiness and stability from newlywed interactions. Journal of Marriage and the Family, 60, 42–48.

Gottman, J. M., & Levenson, R. W. (2002). A two-factor model for predicting when a couple will divorce: Exploratory analyses using 14-year longitudinal data. Family Process, 41(1), 83–96.

Gottman, J. M., & Notarius, C. I. (2000). Decade review: Observing marital interaction. Journal of Marriage & the Family, 62(4), 927–947.

Goveas, J. S., Csernansky, J. G., & Coccaro, E. F. (2004). Platelet serotonin content correlates inversely with life history of aggression in personality-disordered subjects. Psychiatry Research, 126(1), 23–32.

Gracely, R. H., Farrell, M. J., & Grant, M. A. (2002). Temperature and pain perception. In H. Pashler & S. Yantis (Eds.), Steven's handbook of experimental psychology: Vol. 1. Sensation and perception (3rd ed.). Hoboken, NJ: Wiley.

Graham, J. R. (1991). Comments on Duckworth's review of the Minnesota Multiphasic Personality Inventory-2. Journal of Counseling and Development, 69, 570–571.

Grant, S., et al. (1996). Activation of memory circuits during the cue-elicited cocaine craving. Proceedings of the National Academy of Sciences, 93, 12–40.

Gravetter, F. J., & Forzano, L.-A. B. (2009). Research methods for the behavioral sciences (3rd ed.). Belmont, CA: Cengage.

Graw, P., Krauchi, K., Knoblauch, V., Wirz-Justice, A., & Cajochen, C. (2004). Circadian and wake-dependent modulation of fastest and slowest reaction times during the psychomotor vigilance task. Physiology & Behavior, 80(5), 695–701.

Gray, J. D., & Silver, R. C. (1990). Opposite sides of the same coin: Former spouses' divergent perspectives in coping with their divorce. Journal of Personality & Social Psychology, 59, 1180–1191.

Gredler, M. E., & Shields, C. C. (2008). Vygotsky's legacy: A foundation for research and practice. New York: Guilford Press.

Greeff, A. P., & Malherbe, H. L. (2001). Intimacy and marital satisfaction in spouses. Journal of Sex & Marital Therapy, 27(3), 247–257.

Greeff, A. P., & Van Der Merwe, S. (2004). Variables associated with resilience in divorced families. Social Indicators Research, 68(1), 59–75.

Green, A. I. (2000). What is the relationship between schizophrenia and substance abuse? Harvard Mental Health Letter, 17(4), 8.

Green, A. I., Tohen, M. F., Hamer, R. M., Strakowski, S. M., Lieberman, J. A., Glick, I., Clark, W. S., & HGDH Research Group. (2004). First episode schizophrenia-related psychosis and substance use disorders: Acute response to olanzapine and haloperidol. *Schizophrenia Research, 66*(2–3), 125–135.

Green, A. R., Carney, D. R., Pallin, D. J., Ngo, L. H., Raymond, K. L., Iezzoni, L., & Banaji, M. R. (2007). Implicit bias among physicians and its prediction of thrombolysis decisions for black and white patients. *Journal of General Internal Medicine, 22,* 1231–1238.

Green, J. W. (1999). *Cultural awareness in the human services: A multi-ethnic approach.* Needham Heights, MA: Allyn & Bacon.

Greenberg, D. L. (2004). President Bush's false "flashbulb" memory of 9/11/01. *Applied Cognitive Psychology, 18*(3), 363–370.

Greenberg, J. (2002). Who stole the money, and when? Individual and situational determinants of employee theft. *Organizational Behavior and Human Decision Processes, 89*(1), 985–1003.

Greenberg, J., Pyszczynski, T., Solomon, S., Pinel, E., Simon, L., & Jordon, K. (1993). Effects of self-esteem on vulnerability-denying defensive distortions: Further evidence of an anxiety-buffering function of self-esteem. *Journal of Experimental Social Psychology, 29*(3), 229–251.

Greenberg, L. S., & Goldman, R. N. (2008). Anger in couples therapy. In L. S. Greenberg & R. N. Goldman (Eds.), *Emotion-focused couples therapy: The dynamics of emotion, love, and power* (pp. 227–257). Washington, DC: American Psychological Association.

Greene, E., & Ellis, L. (2008). Decision making in criminal justice. In D. Carson, R. Milne, F. Pakes, K. Shalev, & A. Shawyer (Eds.), *Applying psychology to criminal justice* (pp. 183–200). New York: Wiley.

Greene, K., Kremar, M., Walters, L. H., Rubin, D. L., Hale, J., & Hale, L. (2000). Targeting adolescent risk-taking behaviors: The contributions of egocentrism and sensation-seeking. *Journal of Adolescence, 23,* 439–461.

Greenfield, P. M. (1984). A theory of the teacher in the learning activities of everyday life. In B. Rogoff & J. Lave (Eds.), *Everyday cognition* (pp. 117–138). Cambridge, MA: Harvard University Press.

Greenfield, P. M. (1994). *Cross-cultural roots of minority child development.* Hillsdale, NJ: Erlbaum.

Greenfield, P. M. (1997). You can't take it with you: Why ability assessments don't cross cultures. *American Psychologist, 52,* 1115–1124.

Greenfield, P. M. (2004). *Weaving generations together: Evolving creativity in the Maya of Chiapas.* Santa Fe, NM: School of American Research Press.

Greenwald, A. G., Banaji, M. R., Rudman, L. A., Farnham, S. D., Nosek, B. A., & Mellott, D. S. (2002). A unified theory of implicit attitudes, stereotypes, self-esteem, and self-concept. *Psychological Review, 109,* 3–25.

Greenwald, A. G., McGhee, D. E., & Schwartz, J. L. K. (1998). Measuring individual differences in implicit cognition: The implicit association test. *Journal of Personality and Social Psychology, 74,* 1464–1480.

Greenwald, A.G., Poehlman, A., Uhlmann, E., Banaji, M. R. (2008). Understanding and interpreting the Implicit Association Test III: Meta-analysis of predictive validity. *Journal of Personality and Social Psychology* (in press).

Gregersen, E. (1996). *The world of human sexuality: Behaviors, customs, and beliefs.* New York: Irvington.

Gregory, R. J. (2007). *Psychological testing: History, principles, and applications (5th ed.).* Needham Heights, MA: Allyn and Bacon.

Gresack, J. E., Kerr, K. M., & Frick, K. M. (2007). Life-long environmental enrichment differentially affects the mnemonic response to estrogen in young, middle-aged, and aged female mice. *Neurobiology of Learning & Memory, 88,* 393–408.

Griffin, A. S., & Galef, Jr., B. G. (2005). Social learning about predators: Does timing matter? *Animal Behavior, 69,* 669–678.

Grigorenko, E. L., Jarvin, L., & Sternberg, R. J. (2002). School-based tests of the triarchic theory of intelligence: Three settings, three samples, three syllabi. *Contemporary Educational Psychology, 27*(2), 167–208.

Gringart, E., Helmes, E., & Speelman, C. (2008). Harnessing cognitive dissonance to promote positive attitudes toward older workers in Australia. *Journal of Applied Social Psychology, 38,* 751–778.

Grondin, S., Ouellet, B., & Roussel, M. (2004). Benefits and limits of explicit counting for discriminating temporal intervals. *Canadian Journal of Experimental Psychology, 58*(1), 1–12.

Grossmann, K., Grossmann, K.E., Fremmer-Bombik, E., Kindler, H., Scheuerer-Englisch, H., & Zimmermann, P. (2002). The uniqueness of the child-father attachment relationship: Fathers' sensitive and challenging play as a pivotal variable in a 16-year longitudinal study. *Social Development, 11*(3), 307–331.

Grov, C., Bamonte, A., Fuentes, A., Parsons, J. T., Bimbi, D. S., & Morgenstern, J. (2008). Exploring the internet's role in sexual compulsivity and out of control sexual thoughts/behaviour: A qualitative study of gay and bisexual men in New York City. *Culture, Health, and Sexuality, 10,* 107–124.

Grove, W. M., Barden, R. C., Garb, H. N., & Lilienfeld, S. O. (2002). Failure of Rorschach-Comprehensive-System-based testimony to be admissible under the Daubert-Joiner-Kumho standard. *Psychology, Public Policy, & Law, 8*(2), 216–234.

Grover, K. E., Carpenter, L. L., Price, L. H., Gagne, G. G., Mello, A. F., Mello, M. F., & Tyra, A. R. (2007). The relationship between childhood abuse and adult personality disorder symptoms. *Journal of Personality Disorders, 21,* 442–447.

Gruber, U., Fegg, M., Buchmann, M., Kolb, H-J., & Hiddemann, W. (2003). The long-term psychosocial effects of haematopoetic stem cell transplantation. *European Journal of Cancer Care, 12*(3), 249–256.

Guarnaccia, P. J. (Ed.). (2003). Editorial. *Culture, Medicine, and Psychiatry, 27,* 249–257.

Guarnaccia, P. J., & Rogler, L. H. (1999). Research on culture-bound syndromes: New directions. *American Journal of Psychiatry, 156*(9), 1322–1327.

Gudelsky, G. A., & Yamamoto, B. K. (2008). Actions of 3,4-methylenedioxymethamphetamine (MDMA) on cerebral dopaminergic, serotonergic and cholinergic neurons. *Pharmacology, Biochemistry and Behavior, 90,* 198–207.

Guidelines for Ethical Conduct in the Care and Use of Animals. (2008). [On-line]. Available: http://www.apa.org/science/anguide.html. Guidelines for the treatment of animals in behavioural research and teaching. (2005). *Animal Behaviour, 69*(1), i–vi.

Guilarte, T. R., Toscano, C. D., McGlothan, J. L., & Weaver, S. A. (2003). Environmental enrichment reverses cognitive and molecular deficits induced developmental lead exposure. *Annals of Neurology, 53*(1), 50–56.

Guilford, J. P. (1967). *The nature of human intelligence.* New York: McGraw-Hill.

Guinard, J. X., Zoumas-Morse, C., Dietz, J., Goldberg, S., Holz, M., Heck, E., & Amoros, A. (1996). Does consumption of beer, alcohol, and bitter substances affect bitterness perception? *Physiology and Behavior, 49,* 625–631.

Guinote, A., & Fiske, S. T. (2003). Being in the outgroup territory increases stereotypic perceptions of outgroups: Situational sources of category activation. *Group Processes & Intergroup Relations, 6*(4), 323–331.

Guisande, M. A., Páramo, M. F., Tinajero, C., & Almeida, L. S. (2007). Field dependence-independence (FDI) cognitive style: An analysis of attentional functioning. *Psicothema, 19*, 572–577.

Gunnar, M., & Quevedo, K. (2007). The neurobiology of stress and development. *Annual Review of Psychology, 58*, 145–173.

Gunzerath, L., Faden, V., Zakhari, S., & Warren, K. (2004). National Institute on Alcohol Abuse and Alcoholism report on moderate drinking. *Alcoholism: Clinical & Experimental Research, 28*(6), 829–847.

Gustavson, C. R., & Garcia, J. (1974, August). Pulling a gag on the wily coyote. *Psychology Today*, pp. 68–72.

Guthrie, E., Margison, F., Mackay, H., Chew-Graham, C., Moorey, J., & Sibbald, B. (2004). Effectiveness of psychodynamic interpersonal therapy training for primary care counselors. *Psychotherapy Research, 14*(2), 161–175.

Gutierrez, F. J. (2008). Counseling queer youth: Preventing another Matthew Shepard and Gwen Araujo story. In D. Capuzzi & D. R. Gross (Eds.), *Youth at risk: A prevention resource for counselors, teachers, and parents* (pp. 347–381). Alexandria, VA: American Counseling Association.

Haberstick, B. C., Schmitz, S. Young, S. E., & Hewitt, J. K. (2006). Genes and developmental stability of aggressive behavior problems at home and school in a community sample of twins aged 7–12. *Behavior Genetics, 36*, 809–819.

Haddad, S. K., Reiss, D., Spotts, E. L., Ganiban, J., Lichtenstein, P., & Neiderhiser, J. M. (2008). Depression and internally directed aggression: Genetic and environmental contributions. *Journal of the American Psychoanalytic Association. 56*, 515–550.

Haddock, G., & Shaw, J. J. (2008). Understanding and working with aggression, violence, and psychosis. In K. T. Mueser & D. V. Jeste (Eds.), *Clinical handbook of schizophrenia* (pp. 398–410). New York: Guilford Press.

Haier, R. J., Chueh, D., Touchette, P., Lott, I., Buchsbaum, M. S., MacMillan, D., Sandman, C., LaCasse, L., & Sosa, E. (1995). Brain size and cerebral glucose metabolic rate in nonspecific mental retardation and Down Syndrome. *Intelligence, 20*, 191–210.

Haith, M. M., & Benson, J. B. (1998). Infant cognition. In W. Damon & R. M. Lerner (Eds.), *Handbook of child psychology* (Vol. 1). New York: Wiley.

Halbreich, U., & Kahn, L. S. (2007). Atypical depression, somatic depression and anxious depression in women: Are they gender-preferred phenotypes? *Journal of Affective Disorders, 102*, 245–258.

Haley, A. P. (2005). Effects of orally administered glucose on hippocampal metabolites and cognition in Alzheimer's disease. *Dissertation Abstracts International: Section B: The Sciences and Engineering, 66*(3-B), 1719.

Halgin, R. P., & Whitbourne, S. K. (2008). *Abnormal psychology: Clinical perspectives on psychological disorders.* New York: McGraw-Hill.

Hall, C. S., & Van de Castle, R. L. (1996). *The content analysis of dreams.* New York: Appleton-Century-Crofts.

Hall, K. (2007). Sexual dysfunction and childhood sexual abuse: Gender differences and treatment implications. In S. R. Leiblum (Ed.), *Principles and practice of sex therapy* (4th ed.) (pp. 350–378). New York: Guilford.

Hall, M-H., Rijsdijk, F., Picchioni, M., Schulze, K., Ettinger, U., Toulopoulou, T., Bramon, E., Murray, R. M., & Sham, P. (2007). Substantial shared genetic influences on schizophrenia and event-related potentials. *American Journal of Psychiatry, 164*, 804–812.

Hall, P. A., Schaeff, C. M. (2008). Sexual orientation and fluctuating asymmetry in men and women. *Archives of Sexual Behavior, 37*, 158–165.

Haller, S., Radue, E. W., Erb, M., Grodd, W., & Kircher, T. (2005). Overt sentence production in event-related fMRI. *Neuropsychologia, 43*(5), 807–814.

Halperin, J. M., Schulz, K. P., McKay, K. E., Sharma, V., & Newcorn, J. H. (2003). Familial correlates of central serotonin function in children with disruptive behavior disorders. *Psychiatry Research, 119*(3), 205–216.

Halpern, D. F. (1997). Sex differences in intelligence: Implications for education. *American Psychologist, 52*, 1091–1102.

Halpern, D. F. (1998). Teaching critical thinking for transfer across domains. *American Psychologist, 53*, 449–455.

Halpern, D. F. (2000). *Sex differences in cognitive abilities.* Hillsdale, NJ: Erlbaum.

Hamer, D. H., & Copeland, P. (1999). *Living with our genes: Why they matter more than you think.* New York: Anchor Books.

Hamid, P. N., & Chan, W. T. (1998). Locus of control and occupational stress in Chinese professionals. *Psychological Reports, 82*, 75–79.

Hamilton, J. P., & Gotlib, I. H. (2008). Neural substrates of increased memory sensitivity for negative stimui in major depression. *Biological Psychiatry, 63*, 1155–1162.

Hamm, J. P., Johnson, B. W., & Corballis, M. C. (2004). One good turn deserves another: An event-related brain potential study of rotated mirror-normal letter discriminations. *Neuropsychologia, 42*(6), 810–820.

Hammack, P. L. (2003). The question of cognitive therapy in a postmodern world. *Ethical Human Sciences & Services, 5*(3), 209–224.

Hammen, C. (2005). Stress and depression. *Annual Review of Clinical Psychology, 1*, 293–319.

Hammond, D. C. (2005). Neurofeedback with anxiety and affective disorders. *Child & Adolescent Psychiatric Clinics of North America, 14*(1), 105–123.

Hampton, T. (2006). Stem cells probed as diabetes treatment. *Journal of American Medical Association, 296*, 2785–2786.

Hampton, T. (2007). Stem cells ease Parkinson symptoms in monkeys. *Journal of American Medical Association, 298*, 165.

Haney, C., Banks, C., & Zimbardo, P. (1978). Interpersonal dynamics in a simulated prison. *International Journal of Criminology and Penology, 1*, 69–97.

Hanley, S. J., & Abell, S. C. (2002). Maslow and relatedness: Creating an interpersonal model of self-actualization. *Journal of Humanistic Psychology, 42*(4), 37–56.

Hanna, S. M., & Brown, J. H. (1999). *The practice of family therapy: Key elements across models* (2nd ed.). Belmont, CA: Brooks/Cole.

Hansell, J. H., & Damour, L. K. (2008). *Abnormal psychology* (2nd ed.). Hoboken, NJ: Wiley.

Harandi, A. A., Esfandani, A., & Shakibaei, F. (2004). The effect of hypnotherapy on procedural pain and state anxiety related to physiotherapy in women hospitalized in a burn unit. *Contemporary Hypnosis, 21*(1), 28–34.

Hardcastle, S., Taylor, A., Bailey, M., & Castle, R. (2008). A randomized controlled trial on the effectiveness of a primary health care based counseling intervention on physical activity, diet and CHD risk. *Patient Education and Counseling, 70*, 31–39.

Hardy, J. B., & Zabin, L. S. (1991). *Adolescent pregnancy in an urban environment: Issues, programs, and evaluation.* Baltimore: Urban and Schwarzenberg.

Harker, L., & Keltner, D. (2001). Expressions of positive emotion in women's college yearbook pictures and their relationship to personality and life outcomes across adulthood. *Journal of Personality and Social Psychology. Jan80*(1), 112–124.

Harkness, S., Super, C. M., Sutherland, M. A., Blom, M. J. M., Moscardino, U., Mavbdis, C. J., & Axia, G. (2007). Culture and the construction of habits in daily life: Implications for the successful development of children with disabilities. *OTJR: Occupation, Participation and Health, 27*, 33S–40S.

Harlow, H. F., & Harlow, M. K. (1966). Learning to love. *American Scientist, 54*, 244–272.

Harlow, H. F., Harlow, M. K., & Meyer, D. R. (1950). Learning motivated by a manipulation drive. *Journal of Experimental Psychology, 40*, 228–234.

Harlow, H. F., & Zimmerman, R. R. (1959). Affectional responses in the infant monkey. *Science, 130*, 421–432.

Harlow, J. (1868). Recovery from the passage of an iron bar through the head. *Publications of the Massachusetts Medical Society, 2*, 237–246.

Harper, F. D., Harper, J. A., & Stills, A. B. (2003). Counseling children in crisis based on Maslow's hierarchy of basic needs. *International Journal for the Advancement of Counselling, 25*(1), 10–25.

Harris, A. C. (1996). African American and Anglo American gender identities: An empirical study. *Journal of Black Psychology, 22*, 182–194.

Harris, L. C., Ogbonna, E., & Goode, M. M. H. (2008). Intra-functional conflict: An investigation of antecedent factors in marketing functions. *European Journal of Marketing, 42*, 453–476.

Harrison, E. (2005). *How meditation heals: Scientific evidence and practical applications* (2nd ed.). Berkeley, CA: Ulysses Press.

Hart Jr., J., & Kraut, M. A. (2007). Neural hybrid model of semantic object memory (version 1.1). In J. Hart Jr. & M. A. Kraut (Eds.), *Neural basis of semantic memory* (pp. 331–359). New York: Cambridge University Press.

Hartenbaum, N., Collop, N., Rosen, I. M., Phillips, B., George, C. F. P., Rowley, J. A., Freedman, N., Weaver, T. E., Gurubbagavatula, I., Strohl, K., Leaman, H. M., Moffitt, G. L., & Rosekind, M. R. (2006). Sleep apnea and commercial motor vehicle operators: Statement from the Joint Task Force of the American College of Chest Physicians, American College of Occupational and Environmental Medicine, and the National Sleep Foundation. *Journal of Occupational & Environmental Medicine, 48*, S4–S37.

Harth, N. S., Kessler, T., & Leach, C. W. (2008). Advantaged group's emotional reactions to intergroup inequality: The dynamics of pride, guilt, and sympathy. *Personality and Social Psychology Bulletin, 34*, 115–129.

Hartwell, L. (2008). *Genetics* (3ed ed.). New York: McGraw-Hill.

Harvey, M. G., & Miceli, N. (1999). Antisocial behavior and the continuing tragedy of the commons. *Journal of Applied Social Psychology, 29*, 109–138.

Harwood, R., Miller, S. A., & Vasta, R. (2008). *Child psychology: Development in a changing society* (5th ed.). Hoboken, NJ: Wiley.

Haslam, N., Loughnan, S., Reynolds, C., & Wilson, S. (2007). Dehumanization: A new perspective. *Social and Personality Psychology Compass, 1*, 409–422.

Hatfield, E., & Rapson, R. L. (1996). *Love and Sex: Cross-cultural perspectives*. Needham Heights, MA: Allyn & Bacon.

Hatinen, M., Kinnunen, U., Pekkonen, M., & Aro, A. (2004). Burnout patterns in rehabilitation: Short-term changes in job conditions, personal resources, and health. *Journal of Occupational Health Psychology, 9*, 220–237.

Hatsukami, D. K. (2008). Nicotine addiction: Past, present and future. *Drug and Alcohol Dependence, 92*, 312–316.

Haugen, R., Ommundsen, Y., & Lund, T. (2004). The concept of expectancy: A central factor in various personality dispositions. *Educational Psychology, 24*(1), 43–55.

Hawkins, R. S., & Hart, A. D. (2003). The use of thermal biofeedback in the treatment of pain associated with endometriosis: Preliminary findings. *Applied Psychophysiology & Biofeedback, 28*(4), 279–289.

Hawkley, L. C., & Cacioppo, J. T. (2004). Stress and the aging immune system. *Brain, Behavior & Immunity, 18*(2), 114–119.

Hay, D. F. (1994). Prosocial development. *Journal of Child Psychology and Psychiatry, 35*, 29–71.

Hayflick, L. (1977). The cellular basis for biological aging. In C. E. Finch & L. Hayflick (Eds.), *Handbook of the biology of aging* (pp. 159–186). New York: Van Nostrand Reinhold.

Hayflick, L. (1996). *How and why we age*. New York: Ballantine Books.

Hayne, H., Boniface, J., & Barr, R. (2000). The development of declarative memory in human infants: Age-related changes in deferred imitation. *Behavioral Neuroscience, 114*, 77–83.

Hays, W. S. T. (2003). Human pheromones: Have they been demonstrated? *Behavioral Ecology & Sociobiology, 54*(2), 89–97.

Hazan, C., & Shaver, P. (1987). Romantic love conceptualized as an attachment process. *Journal of Personality and Social Psychology, 52*, 511–524.

Hazan, C., & Shaver, P. R. (1994). Attachment as an organizational framework for research on close relationships. *Psychological Inquiry, 5*, 1–22.

Healy, A. F., & McNamara, D. S. (1996). Verbal learning and memory: Does the modal model still work? *Annual Review of Psychology, 47*, 143–172.

Healy, A. F., Shea, K. M., Kole, J. A., & Cunningham, T. F. (2008). Position distinctiveness, item familiarity, and presentation frequency affect reconstruction of order in immediate episodic memory. *Journal of Memory and Language, 58*, 746–764.

Heath, A. C., Madden, P. A. F., Bucholz, K. K., Nelson, E. C., Todorov, A., Price, R. K., Whitfield, J. B., Martin, N. G., Plomin, R. (Ed.), DeFries, J. C. (Ed.), et al. (2003). *Genetic and environmental risks of dependence on alcohol, tobacco, and other drugs. Behavioral genetics in the postgenomic era* (pp. 309–334). Washington, DC, US: American Psychological Association.

Heaton, T. B. (2002). Factors contributing to increasing marital stability in the US. *Journal of Family Issues, 23*(3), 392–409.

Heckhausen, J. (2005). Competence and motivation in adulthood and old age: Making the most of changing capacities and resources. In A. J. Elliot & C. S. Dweck (Eds.), *Handbook of competence and motivation* (pp. 240–256). New York: Guilford.

Hedges, D., & Burchfield, C. (2006). *Mind, brain, and drug: An introduction to psychopharmacology*. Boston: Allyn & Bacon/Longman.

Heffelfinger, A. K., & Newcomer, J. W. (2001). Glucocorticoid effects on memory function over the human life span. *Development & Psychopathology, 13*(3), 491–513.

Heider, F. (1958). *The psychology of interpersonal relations*. New York: Wiley.

Heiman, J. R. (2007). Orgasmic disorders in women. In S. R. Leiblum (Ed.), *Principles and practice of sex therapy* (4th ed.) (pp. 84–123). New York: Guilford Press.

Heimann, M., & Meltzoff, A. N. (1996). Deferred imitation in 9-and 14-month-old infants. *British Journal of Developmental Psychology, 14*, 55–64.

Heine, S. J., & Renshaw, K. (2002). Inter-judge agreement, self-enhancement, and liking: Cross-cultural divergences. *Personality & Social Psychology Bulletin, 28*(5), 578–587.

Helgeland, M. I., & Torgersen, S. (2004). Developmental antecedents of borderline personality disorder. *Comprehensive Psychiatry, 45*(2), 138–147.

Heller, S. (2005). *Freud A to Z.* Hoboken, NJ: Wiley.

Helms, J. E., & Cook, D. A. (1999). *Using race and culture in counseling and psychotherapy: Theory and process.* Boston: Allyn & Bacon.

Henderlong, J., & Lepper, M. R. (2002). The effects of praise on children's intrinsic motivation: A review and synthesis. *Psychological Bulletin, 128,* 774–795.

Henke, P. G. (1992). Stomach pathology and the amygdala. In J. P. Aggleton (Ed.), *The amygdala: Neurobiological aspects of emotion, memory, and mental dysfunction* (pp. 323–338). New York: Wiley.

Hennessey, B. A., & Amabile, T. M. (1998). Reward, intrinsic motivation, and creativity. *American Psychologist, 53,* 674–675.

Henning, K., & Feder, L. (2004). A comparison of men and women arrested for domestic violence: Who presents the greater threat? *Journal of Family Violence, 19*(2), 69–80.

Herdt, G. H. (1981). *Guardians of the flutes: Idioms of masculinity.* New York: McGraw-Hill.

Herek, G. (2000). The psychology of prejudice. *Current Directions in Psychological Science, 9,* 19–22.

Hergenhahn, B. R. (2009). *An introduction to the history of psychology* (6th ed.). Belmont, CA: Cengage.

Hergovich, A., & Olbrich, A. (2003). The impact of the Northern Ireland conflict on social identity, groupthink and integrative complexity in Great Britain. *Review of Psychology, 10*(2), 95–106.

Heriot, S. A., & Pritchard, M. (2004). Test of time: Reciprocal inhibition as the main basis of psychotherapeutic effects' by Joseph Wolpe (1954) [Book review]. *Clinical Child Psychology and Psychiatry, 9*(2), 297–307.

Herman, B. H., & O'Brien, C. P. (1997). Clinical medications development for opiate addiction: Focus on nonopiods and opiod antagonists for the amelioration of opiate withdrawal symptoms and relapse prevention. *Seminars in Neuroscience, 9,* 158.

Herman, C. P., & Polivy, J. (2008). External cues in the control of food intake in humans: The sensory-normative distinction. *Physiology & Behavior, 94,* 722–728.

Herman, L. M., Richards, D. G., & Woltz, J. P. (1984). Comprehension of sentences by bottlenosed dolphins. *Cognition, 16,* 129–139.

Hermans, E. J., Ramsey, N. F., & van Honk, J. (2008). Exogenous testosterone enhances responsiveness to social threat in the neural circuitry of social aggression in humans. *Biological Psychiatry, 63*(3), 263–270.

Hernandez-Reif, M., Diego, M., & Field, T. (2007). Preterm infants show reduced stress behaviors and activity after 5 days of massage therapy. *Infant Behavior & Development, 30,* 557–561.

Herrera, E. A., Johnston, C. A., & Steele, R. G. (2004). A comparison of cognitive and behavioral treatments for pediatric obesity. *Children's Health Care, 33*(2), 151–167.

Herrnstein, R. J., & Murray, C. (1994). *The bell curve: Intelligence and class structure in American life.* New York: Free Press.

Hervé, H., Mitchell, D., Cooper, B. S., Spidel, A., & Hare, R. D. (2004). Psychopathy and unlawful confinement: An examination of perpetrator and event characteristics. *Canadian Journal of Behavioural Science, 36*(2), 137–145.

Hetherington, E. M. (2006). The influence of conflict, marital problem solving, and parenting on children's adjustment in nondivorced, divorced, and remarried families. In A. Clarke-Stewart & J. Dunn (Eds), *Families count.* New York: Cambridge University Press.

Hettich, E. L., & O'Leary, K. D. (2007). Females' reasons for their physical aggression in dating relationships. *Journal of Interpersonal Violence, 22,* 1131–1143.

Hewitt, J. K. (1997). The genetics of obesity: What have genetic studies told us about the environment? *Behavior Genetics, 27,* 353–358.

Heyder, K. Suchan, B., & Daum, I. (2004). Cortico-subcortical contributions to executive control. *Acta Psychologica, 115*(2–3), 271–289.

Higgins, E. T. (2008). Culture and personality: Variability across universal motives as the missing link. *Social and Personality Psychology Compass, 2,* 608–634.

Higgins, N. C., & Bhatt, G. (2001). Culture moderates the self-serving bias: Etic and emic features of causal attributions in India and in Canada. *Social Behavior & Personality, 29*(1), 49–61.

Higley, E. R. (2008). Nighttime interactions and mother-infant attachment at one year. *Dissertation Abstracts International: Section B: The Sciences and Engineering,. 68,* 2008, 5575.

Hilgard, E. R. (1978). Hypnosis and consciousness. *Human Nature, 1,* 42–51.

Hilgard, E. R. (1986). *Divided consciousness: Multiple controls in human thought and action* (expanded ed.). New York: Wiley-Interscience.

Hilgard, E. R. (1992). Divided consciousness and dissociation. *Consciousness and Cognition, 1,* 16–31.

Hill, E. L. (2004). Evaluating the theory of executive dysfunction in autism. *Developmental Review, 24*(2), 189–233.

Hilsenroth, K. J., Ackerman, S. J., Blagys, M. D., Baity, M. R., & Mooney, M. A. (2003). Short-term psychodynamic psychotherapy for depression: An examination of statistical, clinically significant, and technique-specific change. *Journal of Nervous & Mental Disease, 191*(6), 2003, 349–357.

Hinton, E. C., Parkinson, J. A., Holland, A. J., Arana, F. S., Roberts, A. C., & Owen, A. M. (2004). Neural contributions to the motivational control of appetite in humans. *European Journal of Neuroscience, 20*(5), 1411–1418.

Hirao-Try, Y. (2003). Hypertension and women: Gender specific differences. *Clinical Excellence for Nurse Practitioners, 7*(1–2), 4–8.

Hirosumi, J., Tuncman, G., Chang, L., Gorgun, C. Z., Uysal, K. T., Maeda, K., Karin, M., & Hotamisligil, G. S. (2002). Obesity is closely associated with insulin resistance and establishes the leading risk factor for type 2 diabetes mellitus, yet the molecular mechanisms. *Nature, 420,* 333–336.

Hirshkowitz, M., Moore, C. A., & Minhoto, G. (1997). The basics of sleep. In M. R. Pressman & W. C. Orr (Eds.), *Understanding sleep: The evaluation and treatment of sleep disorders.* Washington, DC: American Psychological Association.

Hittner, J. B., & Daniels, J. R. (2002). Gender-role orientation, creative accomplishments and cognitive styles. *Journal of Creative Behavior, 36*(1), 62–75.

Hobson, J. A. (1988). *The dreaming brain.* New York: Basic Books.

Hobson, J. A. (1999). *Dreaming as delirium: How the brain goes out of its mind.* Cambridge, MA: MIT Press.

Hobson, J. A. (2002). *Dreaming: An introduction to the science of sleep.* New York: Oxford University Press.

Hobson, J. A. (2005). In bed with Mark Solms? What a nightmare! A reply to Domhoff. *Dreaming, 15*(1), 21–29.

Hobson, J. A., & McCarley, R. W. (1977). The brain as a dream state generator: An activation-synthesis hypothesis of the dream process. *American Journal of Psychiatry, 134,* 1335–1348.

Hobson, J. A., & Silvestri, L. (1999). Parasomnias. *The Harvard Mental Health Letter, 15*(8), 3–5.

Hodges, S. D., & Biswas-Diener, R. (2007). Balancing the empathy expense account: Strategies for regulating empathic response. In T. Farrow & P. Woodruff (Eds.), *Empathy in mental illness* (pp. 389–407). New York: Cambridge University Press.

Hodson, G., & Costello, K. (2007). Interpersonal disgust, ideological orientations, and dehumanization as predictors of intergroup attitudes. *Psychological Science, 18,* 691–698.

Hoek, H. W., van Harten, P. N., Hermans, K. M. E., Katzman, M. A., Matroos, G. E., & Susser, E. S. (2005). The incidence of anorexia nervosa on Curacao. *American Journal of Psychiatry, 162,* 748–752.

Hofer, A., Siedentopf, C. M., Ischebeck, A., Rettenbacher, M. A., Verius, M., Golaszewski, S. M., Felber, S., & Fleischhacker, W. W. (2007). Neural substrates for episodic encoding and recognition of unfamiliar faces. *Brain and Cognition, 63,* 174–181.

Hoff, E. (2009). *Language development* (4th ed.). Belmont, CA: Wadsworth.

Hoffman, J. (2008, January 15). Coaching the comeback. *New York Times.* [On-line]. Available: http://www.nytimes.com/2008/01/15/health/15tren.html.

Hoffman, M. L. (1993). Empathy, social cognition, and moral education. In A. Garrod (Ed.), *Approaches to moral development: New research and emerging themes.* New York: Teachers College Press.

Hoffman, M. L. (2000). *Empathy and moral development: Implications for caring and justice.* New York: Cambridge University Press.

Hoffman, M. L. (2007). The origins of empathic morality in toddlerhood. In C. A. Brownell & C. B. Kopp (Eds.), *Socioemotional development in the toddler years: Transitions and transformations* (pp. 132–145). New York: Guilford Press.

Hofman, A. (1968). Psychotomimetic agents. In A. Burger (Ed.), *Drugs affecting the central nervous system* (Vol. 2). New York: Dekker.

Hofmann, W., Gschwendner, T., Castelli, L., & Schmitt, M. (2008). Implicit and explicit attitudes and interracial interaction: The moderating role of situationally available control resources. *Group Processes & Intergroup Relations, 11,* 69–87.

Hogan, T. P. (2006). *Psychological testing: A practical Introduction (2nd ed.).* Hoboken, NJ: Wiley.

Hoge, C. W., Castro, C. A., Messer, S. C. et al. (2004). Combat duty in Iraq and Afghanistan, mental health problems, and barriers to care. *New England Journal of Medicine, 351,* 13–22.

Holden, C. (1980). Identical twins reared apart. *Science, 207,* 1323–1325.

Holland, J. L. (1985). *Making vocational choices: A theory of vocational personalites and work environments* (2nd ed). Englewood Cliffs, NJ: Prentice Hall.

Holland, J. L. (1994). *Self-directed search form R.* Lutz, Fl: Psychological Assessment Resources.

Holmes, T. H., & Rahe, R. H. (1967). The social readjustment rating scale. *Journal of Psychosomatic Research, 11,* 213–218.

Holt, N. L., & Dunn, J. G. H. (2004). Longitudinal idiographic analyses of appraisal and coping responses in sport. *Psychology of Sport & Exercise, 5*(2), 213–222.

Holt-Lunstad, Birmingham, W., & Jones, B. Q. (2008). Is there something unique about marriage? The relative impact of marital status, relationship quality, and network social support on ambulatory blood pressure and mental health. *Annals of Behavioral Medicine, 35.* [On-line]. Available: http://www.springer.com/psychology/health+and+behavior/journal/12160.

Holtzworth-Munroe, A. (2000). A typology of men who are violent toward their female partners: Making sense of the heterogeneity in husband violence. *Current Directions in Psychological Science, 9*(4), 140–143.

Hong, S. (2000). Exercise and psychoneuroimmunology. *International Journal of Sport Psychology, 31*(2), 204–227.

Honts, C. R., & Kircher, J. C. (1994). Mental and physical countermeasures reduce the accuracy of polygraph tests. *Journal of Applied Psychology, 79*(2), 252–259.

Hooley, J. M., & Hiller, J. B. (2001). Family relationships and major mental disorder: Risk factors and preventive strategies. In B. R. Sarason & S. Duck (Eds.), *Personal relationships: implications for clinical and community psychology.* New York: Wiley.

Horiuchi, Y., Nakayama, K., Ishiguro, H., Ohtsuki, T., Detera-Wadleigh, S. D., Toyota, T., Yamada, K., Nankai, M., Shibuya, H., Yoshikawa, T., & Arinami, T. (2004). Possible association between a haplotype of the GABA-A receptor alpha 1 subunit gene (GABRA1) and mood disorders. *Biological Psychiatry, 55*(1), 40–45.

Horney, K. (1939). *New ways in psychoanalysis.* New York: International Universities Press.

Horney, K. (1945). *Our inner conflicts: A constructive theory of neurosis.* New York: Norton.

Horowitz, A. V. (2007). Transforming normality into pathology: The DSM and the outcomes of stressful social arrangements. *Journal of Health and Social Behavior, 48,* 211–222.

Horowitz, M., Wilner, N., & Alvarez, W. (1979). Impact of event scale: A measure of subjective stress. *Psychosomatic Medicine, 41,* 209–218.

Horvath, K. J., Calsyn, D. A., Terry, C., & Cotton, A. (2007). Erectile dysfunction medication use among men seeking substance abuse treatment. *Journal of Addictive Diseases, 26,* 7–13.

Hoshino Browne, E. (2005). On the cultural guises of cognitive dissonance: The case of Asian-Canadians and European-Canadians. *Dissertation Abstracts International: Section B: The Sciences and Engineering, 65*(10-B), 5460.

Hosie, P. J., Sevastos, P. P., & Cooper, Cary L. (2006). Happy-performing managers: The impact of affective wellbeing and intrinsic job satisfaction in the workplace. *New horizons in management.* Northampton, MA: Edward Elgar Publishing.

Houlfort, N. (2006). The impact of performance-contingent rewards on perceived autonomy and intrinsic motivation. *Dissertation Abstracts International Section A: Humanities and Social Sciences, 67*(2-A), 460.

Houtz, J. C., Matos, H., Park, M-K. S., Scheinholtz, J., & Selby, E. (2007). Problem-solving style and motivational attributions. *Psychological Reports, 101,* 823–830.

Hovland, C. I. (1937). The generalization of conditioned responses: II. The sensory generalization of conditioned responses with varying intensities of tone. *Journal of Genetic Psychology, 51,* 279–291.

Howe, M. L., & O'Sullivan, J. T. (1997). What children's memories tell us about recalling our childhoods: A review of storage and retrieval processes in the development of longterm retention. *Developmental Review, 17,* 148–204.

Howell, K. K., Coles, C. D., & Kable, J. A. (2008). The medical and developmental consequences of prenatal drug exposure. In J. Brick (Ed.), *Handbook of the medical consequences of alcohol and drug abuse* (2nd ed.) (pp. 219–249). *The Haworth Press series in neuropharmacology.* New York: Haworth Press/Taylor and Francis Group.

Howes, M. B. (2007). *Human memory: Structures and images*. Thousand Oaks, CA: Sage Publications.

Hoye, A., Rezvy, G., Hansen, V., & Olstad, R. (2006). The effect of gender in diagnosing early schizophrenia: An experimental case simulation study. *Social Psychiatry and Psychiatric Epidemiology, 41*, 549–555.

Hsieh, P.-H. (2005). How college students explain their grades in a foreign language course: The interrelationship of attributions, self-efficacy, language learning beliefs, and achievement. *Dissertation Abstracts International Section A: Humanities and Social Sciences, 65*(10-A), 3691.

Hsiu-Hui, C. (2007). *Work stress and death from overwork*. [On-line]. Available: http://www.ceps.com.tw/ec/ecjnlarticleView.aspx.

Huang, L. N., & Ying, Y. (1989). Japanese children and adolescents. In J. T. Gibbs & Ln N. Huang (Eds.), *Children of color*. San Francisco: Jossey-Bass.

Huang, M., & Hauser, R. M. (1998). Trends in Black–White test-score differentials: II. The WORDSUM Vocabulary Test. In U. Neisser (Ed.), *The rising curve: Long-term gains in IQ and related measures* (pp. 303–334). Washington, DC: American Psychological Association.

Hubel, D. H., & Wiesel, T. N. (1965). Receptive fields and the functional architecture in two nonstriate visual areas (18 and 19) of the cat. *Journal of Neurophysiology, 28*, 229–289.

Hubel, D. H., & Wiesel, T. N. (1979). Brain mechanisms of vision. *Scientific American, 241*, 150–162.

Hudziak, J. J. (Ed). (2008). *Developmental psychopathology and wellness: Genetic and environmental influences*. Arlington, VA: American Psychiatric Publishing.

Huesmann, L. R., & Kirwil, L. (2007). Why observing violence increases the risk of violent behavior by the observer. In D. J. Flannery, A. T. Vazsonyi, & I. D. Waldman (Eds.), *The Cambridge handbook of violent behavior and aggression* (pp. 545–570), New York: Cambridge University Press.

Huffcutt, A. I., & Youngcourt, S. S. (2007). Employment interviews. In D. L. Whetzel & G.R. Wheaton (Eds.), *Applied measurement*. Mahwah, NJ: Erlbaum.

Huffman, A. H., Youngcourt, S. S., Payne, S. C., & Castro, C. A. (2008). The importance of construct breadth when examining interrole conflict. *Educational and Psychological Measurement, 68*(3), 515–530.

Huffman, C. J., Matthews, T. D., & Gagne, P. E. (2001). The role of part-set cuing in the recall of chess positions: Influence of chunk- ing in memory. *North American Journal of Psychology, 3*(3), 535–542.

Huguet, N., Kaplan, M. S., & Feeny, D. (2008). Socioeconomic status and health-related quality of life among elderly people: Results from the Joint Canada/United States Survey of Health. *Social Science & Medicine, 66*, 803–810.

Hull, C. (1952). *A behavior system*. New Haven, CT: Yale University Press.

Hulshoff Pol, H. E., Brans, R. G. H., van Haren, N. E. M., Schnack, H. G., Langen, M., Baare, W. F. C., van Oel, C. J., & Kahn, R. S. (2004). Gray and white matter volume abnormalities in monozygotic and same-gender dizygotic twins discordant for schizophrenia. *Biological Psychiatry, 55*(2), 126–130.

Hunt, M. (1993). *The story of psychology*. New York: Doubleday.

Hurlemann, R., Matusch, A., Hawellek, B., Klingmuller, D., Kolsch, H., Maier, W., & Dolan, R. J. (2007). Emotion-induced retrograde amnesia varies as a function of noradrenergic-glucocorticord activity. *Psychopharmacology, 194*, 261–269.

Hurley, S. (2008). The shared circuits model (SCM): How control, mirroring, and simulation can enable imitation, and deliberation, and mindreading. *Behavioral and Brain Sciences, 31*, 1–22.

Hurt, H. (2008, February 9). Sending an SOS for a PC exorcist. *New York Times*. [On-line]. Available: http://www.nytimes.com/2008/02/09/business/smallbusiness/09pursuits.html

Hustvedt, S. (2008, February 7). Arms at rest. *New York Times*. [On-line]. Available: http://migraine.blogs.nytimes.com/2008/02/07/arms-at-rest/

Hutchinson-Phillips, S., Gow, K., & Jamieson, G. A. (2007). Hypnotizability, eating behaviors, attitudes, and concerns: A literature survey. *International Journal of Clinical and Experimental Hypnosis, 55*, 84–113.

Hutson, M. (2007). Neurorealism. *New York Times*. [On-line]. Available: http://www.nytimes.com/2007/12/09/magazine/09neurorealism.html?_r=1&scp=1&sq=neurorealism%20hutson&st=cse&oref=slogin

Huurre, T., Junkkari, H., & Aro, H. (2006). Long-term psychosocial effects of parental divorce: A follow-up study from adolescence to adulthood. *European Archives of Psychiatry and Clinical Neuroscience, 256*, 256–263.

Hvas, L. (2001). Positive aspects of menopause: A qualitative study. *Maturitas, 39*(1), 11–17.

Hyde, J. S. (2005). The genetics of sexual orientation. In J. S. Hyde (Ed.), *Biological substrates of human sexuality*. Washington, DC: American Psychological Association.

Hyde, J. S. (2007). *Half the human experience: The psychology of women* (7th ed.). Boston: Houghton Mifflin.

Hyde, J. S., & DeLamater, J. D. (2006). *Understanding human sexuality* (9th ed.). New York: McGraw-Hill.

Hyde, J. S., & DeLamater, J. D. (2008). *Understanding human sexuality* (10th ed.). New York: McGraw-Hill.

Hyman, R. (1981). Cold reading: How to convince strangers that you know all about them. In K. Fraizer (Ed.), *Paranormal borderlands of science* (pp. 232–244). Buffalo, NY: Prometheus.

Hyman, R. (1996). The evidence for psychic functioning: Claims vs. reality. *Skeptical Inquirer, 20*, 24–26.

Hypericum Depression Trial Study Group. (2002). Effect of Hypericum performatum (St John's wort) in major depressive disorder: A randomized controlled trial. *JAMA: Journal of the American Medical Association, 287*(14), 1807–1814.

Iacono, W. G., & Lykken, D. T. (1997). The validity of the lie detector: Two surveys of scientific opinion. *Journal of Applied Psychology, 82*(3), 426–433.

Iavarone, A., Patruno, M., Galeone, F., Chieffi, S., & Carlomagno, S. (2007). Brief report: Error pattern in an autistic savant calendar calculator. *Journal of Autism and Developmental Disorders, 37*, 775–779.

Ibáñez, A., Blanco, C., & Sáiz-Ruiz, J. (2002). Neurobiology and genetics of pathological gambling. *Psychiatric Annals, 32*(3), 181–185.

Ice, G. H., Katz-Stein, A., Himes, J., & Kane, R. L. (2004). Diurnal cycles of salivary cortisol in older adults. *Psychoneuroendocrinology, 29*(3), 355–370.

Ikemoto, K. (2004). Significance of human striatal D-neurons: Implications in neuropsychiatric functions. *Neuropsychopharmacology, 29*(4), 429–434.

Irwin, M., Mascovich, A., Gillin, J. C., Willoughby, R., Pike, J., & Smith, T. L. (1994). Partial sleep deprivation reduced natural killer cell activity in humans. *Psychosomatic Medicine, 56*(6), 493–498.

Israel, P. (1998). *Edison: A life of invention*. New York: Wiley.

Itakura, S. (1992). Symbolic association between individuals and objects by a

References

chimpanzee as an initiation of ownership. *Psychological Reports, 70,* 539–544.

Ivanovic, D. M., Leiva, B. P., Pérez, H. T., Olivares, M. G., Díaz, N. S., Urrutia, M. S. C., Almagià, A. F., Toro, T. D., Miller, P. T., Bosch, E. O., & Larraín, C. G. (2004). Head size and intelligence, learning, nutritional status and brain development: Head, IQ, learning, nutrition and brain. *Neuropsychologia, 42*(8), 1118–1131.

Ivcevic, Z. (2006). Creativity or creativities: A study of domain generality and specificity. *Dissertation Abstracts International: Section B: The Sciences and Engineering, 66,* 3998.

Iversen, L. (2003). Cannabis and the brain. *Brain, 126*(6), 1252–1270.

Iversen, S. D., & Iversen, L. L. (2007). Dopamine: 50 years in perspective. *Trends in Neurosciences, 30,* 188–193.

Iwasaki, K., Takahashi, M., & Nakata, A. (2006). Health problems due to long working hours in Japan: Working hours, workers' compensation (Karoshi), and preventive measures. *Industrial Health, 44*(2006), 537–540.

Iyer, P. (2001). *The global soul: Jet lag, shopping malls, and the search for home.* London: Vintage Books.

Jackendoff, R. (2003). Foundations of language, brain, meaning, grammar, evolution. *Applied Cognitive Psychology, 17*(1), 121–122.

Jackson, E. D. (2008). Cortisol effects on emotional memory: Independent of stress effects. *Dissertation Abstracts International: Section B: The Sciences and Engineering, 68* (11-B), 7666.

Jackson, P. B., & Williams, D. R. (2006). Culture, race/ethnicity, and depression. In C. L. M. Keyes & S. H. Goodman (Eds), *Women and depression: A handbook for the social, behavioral, and biomedical sciences* (pp. 328–359). New York: Cambridge University Press.

Jacob, P. (2008). What do mirror neurons contribute to human social cognition? *Mind & Language, 23,* 190–223.

Jacob, S., McClintock, M. K., Zelano, B., & Ober, C. (2002). Peternally inherited HLA alleles are associated with women's choice of male odor. *Nature Genetics, DOI: 10.1038/ng830.*

Jacobi, C., Hayward, C., de Zwaan, M., Kraemer, H. C., & Agras, W. S. (2004). Coming to terms with risk factors for eating disorders: Application of risk terminology and suggestions for a general taxonomy. *Psychological Bulletin, 130*(1), 19–65.

Jacobsen, T., & Hofmann, V. (1997). Children's attachment representations: Longitudinal relations to school behavior and academic competency in middle childhood and adolescence. *Developmental Psychology, 33,* 703–710.

Jaffee, S., & Hyde, J. S. (2000). Gender differences in moral orientation: A meta-analysis. *Psychological Bulletin, 126*(5), 703–726.

Jain, G., Kumar, V., Chakrabarti, S., & Grover, S. (2008). The use of electroconvulsive therapy in the elderly: A study from the psychiatric unit of a North Indian teaching hospital. *Journal of ECT, 24,* 122–127.

James, F. O., Cermakian, N., & Boivin, D. B. (2007). Circadian rhythms of melatonin, cortisol, and clock gene expression during simulated night shift work. *Sleep: Journal of Sleep and Sleep Disorders Research, 30*(11), 1427–1436.

James, W. (1890). *The principles of psychology* (Vol. 2). New York: Holt.

James, W. H. (2005). Biological and psychosocial determinants of male and female human sexual orientation. *Journal of Biosocial Science, 37,* 555–567.

Jamieson, G. A., & Hasegawa, H. (2007). *New paradigms of hypnosis research.* In G. A. Jamieson (Ed.), *Hypnosis and conscious states: The cognitive neuroscience perspective* (pp. 133–144). New York: Oxford University Press.

Jang, K. L., Stein, M. B., Taylor, S., Asmundson, G. J. G., & Livesley, W. J. (2003). Exposure to traumatic events and experiences: Aetiological relationships with personality function. *Psychiatry Research, 120*(1), 61–69.

Jang, K. L., Livesley, W. J., Anso, J., Yamagata, S., Suzuki, A., Angleitner, A., Ostendort, F., Riemann, R., & Spinath, F. (2006). Behavioral genetics of the higher-order factors of the Big Five. *Personality and Individual Differences, 41,* 261–272.

Janis, I. L. (1972). *Victims of groupthink: A psychological study of foreign-policy decisions and fiascoes.* Boston: Houghton Mifflin.

Janis, I. L. (1989). *Crucial decisions: Leadership in policymaking and crisis management.* New York: Free Press.

Jankowiak, W. (1997). *Romantic passion: A universal experience.* New York: Columbia University Press.

Jankowiak, W., & Fischer, E. (1992). Cross-cultural perspective on romantic love. *Ethnology, 31,* 149–155.

Janvier, B., & Testu, F. (2005). Développement des fluctuations journalières de l'attention chez des élèves de 4 à 11 ans. / Development of the daily fluctuations of attention from 4 to 11 year old pupils. *Enfance, 57,* 155–170.

Javo, C., Ronning, J. A., Heyerdahl, S., & Rudmin, F. W. (2004). Parenting correlates of child behavior problems in a multiethnic community sample of preschool children in northern Norway. *European Child & Adolescent Psychiatry, 13*(1), 8–18.

Jellison, W. A., McConnell, A. R., & Gabriel, S. (2004). Implicit and explicit measures of sexual orientation attitudes: Ingroup preferences and related behaviors and beliefs among gay and straight men. *Personality & Social Psychology Bulletin, 30*(5), 629–642.

Jennings, L., & Skovholt, T. M. (1999). The cognitive, emotional, and relational characteristics of master therapists. *Journal of Counseling Psychology, 46*(1), 3–11.

Jensen, M. P., Hakimian, S., Sherlin, L. H., & Fregni, F. (2008). New insights into neuromodulatory approaches for the treatment of pain. *The Journal of Pain, 9,* 193–199.

Jiang, Y., Olson, I. R., & Chun, M. M. (2000). Organization of visual short-term memory. *Journal of Experimental Psychology: Learning, memory, and cognition, 26,* 683–702.

Job stress can kill your heart. (2002, October 17). *WebMD.* [On-line]. Available: http://www.webmd.com/balance/news/20021017/job-stress-can-kill-your-heart.

John, U., & Hanke, M. (2003). Tobacco- and alcohol-attributable mortality and years of potential life lost in Germany. *European Journal of Public Health, 13*(3), 275–277.

Johnson, B., & Lazarus, S. (2008). The role of schools in building the resilience of youth faced with adversity. *Journal of Psychology in Africa, 18,* 19–30.

Johnson, D. M., Delahanty, D. L., & Pinna, K. (2008). The cortisol awakening response as a function of PTSD severity and abuse chronicity in sheltered battered women. *Journal of Anxiety Disorders, 22,* 793–800.

Johnson, N. J. (2008). Leadership styles and passive-aggressive behavior in organizations. *Dissertation Abstracts International: Section B: The Sciences and Engineering, 68*(7-B), 4828.

Johnson, S. C., Dweck, C. S., & Chen, F. S. (2007). Evidence for infants' internal working methods of attachment. *Psychological Science, 18,* 501–502.

Johnson, S. K., Murphy, S. E., Zewdie, S., & Reichard, R. J. (2008). The strong, sensitive type: Effects of gender stereotypes and leadership prototypes on the evaluation of male and female leaders. *Organizational Behavior and Human Decision Processes, 106,* 39–60.

Johnson, T. J., & Cropsey, K. L. (2000). Sensation seeking and drinking game participation in heavy-drinking college students. *Addictive Behaviors, 25*(1), 109–116.

Johnson, T. M. (2008). Dallas region 10 school instructional technologists' perceptions of the evaluation process used to assess their job performance. *Dissertation Abstracts International: Section A: Humanities and Social Sciences, 68*(9-A), 3684.

Johnson, W., & Bouchard Jr., T. J. (2007). Sex differences in mental ability: A proposed means to link them to brain structure and function. *Intelligence, 35,* 197–209.

Johnson, W., Bouchard Jr., T. J., McGue, M., Segal, N. L., Tellegen, A., Keyes, M., & Gottesman, I. I. (2007). Genetic and environmental influences on the Verbal-Perceptual-Image Rotation (VPR) model of the structure of mental abilities in the Minnesota study of twins reared apart. *Intelligence, 35,* 542–562.

Johnson, W., Bouchard, T. J. Jr., Krueger, R. F., McGue, M., & Gottesman, I. I. (2004). Just one g: Consistent results from three test batteries. *Intelligence, 32*(1), 95–107.

Johnson, W., McGue, M., Krueger, R. F., & Bouchard, T. J. Jr. (2004). Marriage and personality: A genetic analysis. *Journal of Personality and Social Psychology. 86*(2), 285–294.

Johnson, W. B., & Murray, K. (2007). *Crazy love: Dealing with your partner's problem personality.* Atascadero, CA: Impact Publishers.

Johnstone, L. (1999). Adverse psychological effects of ECT. *Journal of Mental Health, 8*(1), 69–85.

Jolliffe, C. D., & Nicholas, M. K. (2004). Verbally reinforcing pain reports: An experimental test of the operant conditioning of chronic pain. *Pain, 107,* 167–175.

Jonas, E., Traut-Mattausch, E., Frey, D., & Greenberg, J. (2008). The path or the goal? Decision vs. information focus in biased information seeking after preliminary decisions. *Journal of Experimental Social Psychology, 44,* 1180–1186.

Jones, B. C., DeBruine, L. M., & Little, A. C. (2007). The role of symmetry in attraction to average faces. *Perception & Psychophysics, 69,* 1273–1277.

Jones, D. G., Anderson, E. R., & Galvin, K. A. (2003). Spinal cord regeneration: Moving tentatively towards new perspectives. *NeuroRehabilitation, 18*(4), 339–351.

Jones, E. (2008). Predicting performance in first-semester college basic writers: Revisiting the role of self-beliefs. *Contemporary Educational Psychology, 33,* 209–238.

Jones, E. G. (2006). *The thalamus.* New York: Cambridge University Press.

Jones, M., Luce, K. H., Osborne, M. I., Taylor, K., Cunning, D., Doyle, A. C., Wilfley, D. E., & Taylor, C. B. (2008). Randomized, controlled trial of an Internet-facilitated intervention for reducing binge eating and overweight in adolescents. *Pediatrics, 121,* 453–462.

Jones, S. R., & Fernyhough, C. (2007). A new look at the neural diathesis-stress model of schizophrenia: The primacy of social-evaluative and uncontrollable situations. *Schizophrenia Bulletin, 33,* 1171–1177.

Jonides, J., Lewis, R. L., Nee, D. E., Lustig, C. A., Berman, M. G., & Moore, K. S. (2008). The mind and brain of short-term memory. *Annual Review of Psychology, 59,* 193–224.

Josephs, R. A., Newman, M. L., Brown, R. P., & Beer, J. M. (2003). Status, testosterone, and human intellectual performance: Stereotype threat as status concern. *Psychological Science, 14*(2),158–163.

Joung, H-M., & Miller, N. J. (2007). Examining the effects of fashion activities on life satisfaction of older females: Activity theory revisited. *Family & Consumer Sciences Research Journal, 35,* 338–356.

Jung, C. (1969). The concept of collective unconscious. In *Collected Works* (Vol. 9, Part 1). Princeton, NJ: Princeton University Press (Original work published 1936).

Jung, C. G. (1946). *Psychological types.* New York: Harcourt Brace.

Jung, C. G. (1959). The archetypes and the collective unconscious. In H. Read, M. Fordham, & G. Adler (Eds.), *The collected works of C. G. Jung, Vol. 9.* New York: Pantheon.

Jung, H. (2006). Assessing the influence of cultural values on consumer susceptibility to social pressure for conformity: Self-image enhancing motivations vs. information searching motivation. In L. R. Kahle & C-H. Kim (Eds.), *Creating images and the psychology of marketing communication (pp. 309–329). Advertising and Consumer Psychology.* Mahwah, NJ: Erlbaum.

Jung, R. E., & Haier, R. J. (2007). The Parieto-Frontal Integration Theory (P-FIT) of intelligence: Converging neuroimaging evidence. *Behavioral and Brain Sciences, 30,* 135–154.

Juntii, S. A., Coats, J. K., & Shah, N. M. (2008). A genetic approach to dissect sexually dimorphic behaviors. *Hormones and Behavior, 53,* 627–637.

Kagan, J. (1998). Biology and the child. In W. Damon & R. M. Lerner (Eds.), *Handbook of child psychology (Vol. 1).* New York: Wiley.

Kagan, J. (2005). Personality and temperament: Historical perspectives. In M. Rosenbluth, S. H. Kennedy, & R. M. Bagby (Eds), *Depression and personality: Conceptual and clinical challenges* (pp. 3–18). Washington, DC: American Psychiatric Publishing.

Kahneman, D. (2003). Experiences of collaborative research. *American Psychologist, 58*(9), 723–730.

Kane, T. A., Loxton, N. J., Staiger, P. K., & Dawe, S. (2004). Does the tendency to act impulsively underlie binge eating and alcohol use problems? An empirical investigation. *Personality & Individual Differences, 36*(1), 83–94.

Kaplan, L. E. (2006). Moral reasoning of MSW social workers and the influence of education. *Journal of Social Work Education, 42,* 507–522.

Kapner, D. A. (2004). *Infofacts resources: Alcohol and other drugs on campus.* [On-line]. Available: http://www.edc.org/hec//hec/pubs/factsheets/scope.html.

Kardong, K. (2008). *Introduction to biological evolution* (2nd ed.). New York: McGraw-Hill.

Kareev, Y. (2000). Seven (indeed, plus or minus two) and the detection of correlations. *Psychological Review, 107*(2):397–402.

Karmiloff, K, & Karmiloff-Smith, A. (2002). *Pathways to language: From fetus to adolescent.* Cambridge, MA: Harvard University Press.

Karon, B. P., & Widener, A. J. (1998). Repressed memories: The real story. *Professional Psychology: Research & Practice, 29,* 482–487.

Karremans, J. C., Stroebe, W., & Claus, J. (2006). Beyond Vicary's fantasies: The impact of subliminal priming and brand choice. *Journal of Experimental Social Psychology, 42,* 792–798.

Kasser, T., & Sharma, Y. S. (1999). Reproductive freedom, educational equality, and females' preference for resource-acquisition characteristics in mates. *Psychological Science, 10,* 374–377.

Kassin, S., Fein, S., & Markus, H. R. (2008). *Social psychology* (7th ed.). Belmont, CA: Cengage.

Kassinove, H. (2007). Finding a useful model for the treatment of aggression. In T. A. Cavell & K. T. Malcolm (Eds.), *Anger, aggression and interventions for interpersonal violence* (pp. 77–96). Mahwah, NJ: Erlbaum.

Kastenbaum, R. (1999). Dying and bereavement. In J. C. Cavanaugh & S. K. Whitbourne

References

(Eds.), *Gerontology: An interdisciplinary perspective*. New York: Oxford University Press.

Kastenbaum, R. J. (2007). *Death, society, and human experience* (9th ed.). Upper Saddle River, NJ: Prentice Hall.

Katz, G., Knobler, H. Y., Laibel, Z., Strauss, Z., & Durst, R. (2002). Time zone change and major psychiatric morbidity: The results of a 6-year study in Jerusalem. *Comprehensive Psychiatry, 43*(1), 37–40.

Katz, M., Marsella, A., Dube, K., Olatawura, M., et al. (1988). On the expression of psychosis in different cultures: Schizophrenia in an Indian and in a Nigerian community. *Culture, Medicine, and Psychiatry, 12*, 331–355.

Kauffman, J. (2008). What is "no recovery?" *Death Studies, 32*, 74–83.

Kaufman, J. C. (2002). Dissecting the golden goose: Components of studying creative writers. *Creativity Research Journal, 14*(1), 27–40.

Kaukiainen, A., Björkqvist, K., Lagerspetz, K., Österman, K., Salmivalli, C., Rothberg, S., et al. (1999). The relationships between social intelligence, empathy, and three types of aggression. *Aggressive Behavior, 25*(2), 81–89.

Kavanau, J. L. (2000). Sleep, memory maintenance, and mental disorders. *Journal of Neuropsychiatry & Clinical Neurosciences, 12*(2), 199–208.

Kawakami, K., Dovidio, J. F., & Dijksterhuis, A. (2003). Effect of social category priming on personal attitudes. *Psychological Science, 14*, 315–319.

Kawakami, K., Dovidio, J. F., Moll, J., Hermsen, S., & Russin, A. (2000). Just say no (to stereotyping): Effects of training in the negation of stereotypic associations on stereotype activation. *Journal of Personality & Social Psychology, 78*, 871–888.

Kaye, W. (2008). Neurobiology of anorexia and bulimia nervosa. *Physiology & Behavior, 94*, 121–135.

Kaysen, D., Pantalone, D. W., Chawla, N., Lindgrren, K. P., Clum, G. A., Lee, C., & Resick, P. A. (2008). Posttraumatic stress disorder, alcohol use, and physical health concerns. *Journal of Behavioral Medicine, 31*, 115–125.

Kazdin, A. E. (1994). Methodology, design, and evaluation in psychotherapy research. In A.E. Bergin & S.L. Garfield (Eds.), *Handbook of psycho and behavior change* (4th ed.). New York: Wiley.

Kazdin, A. E. (2008). *Behavior modification in applied settings*. Long Grove, IL: Waveland Press.

Keating, C. R. (1994). World without words: Messages from face and body. In W. J. Lonner & R. Malpass (Eds.), *Psychology and culture* (pp. 175–182). Boston: Allyn & Bacon.

Keats, D. M. (1982). Cultural bases of concepts of intelligence: A Chinese versus Australian comparison. In P. Sukontasarp, N. Yongsiri, P. Intasuwan, N. Jotiban, & C. Suvannathat (Eds.), *Proceedings of the Second Asian Workshop on Child and Adolescent Development* (pp. 67–75). Bangkok: Burapasilpa Press.

Keefe, F. J., Abernethy, A. P., & Campbell, L. C. (2005). Psychological approaches to understanding and treating disease-related pain. *Annual Review of Psychology, 56*, 601–630.

Keen, S. (1991). *Faces of the enemy: Reflections of the hostile imagination*. New York: HarperCollins.

Keillor, J. M., Barrett, A. M., Crucian, G. P., Kortenkamp, S., & Heilman, K. M. (2002). Emotional experience and perception in the absence of facial feedback. *Journal of the International Neuropsychological Society, 8*, 130–135.

Keller, C. J., Lavish, L. A., & Brown, C. (2007). Creative styles and gender roles in undergraduate students. *Creativity Research Journal, 19*, 273–280.

Keller, J., & Bless, H. (2008). *The interplay of stereotype threat and regulatory focus*. In Y. Kashima, K. Fiedler, & P. Freytag (Eds.), *Stereotype dynamics: Language-based approaches to the formation, maintenance, and transformation of stereotypes* (pp. 367–389). Mahwah, NJ: Erlbaum.

Kellogg, S. H., & Young, J. E. (2008). Cognitive therapy. In J. L. Lebow (Ed.), *Twenty-first century psychotherapies: Contemporary approaches to theory and practice* (pp. 43–79). Hoboken, NJ: Wiley.

Kelly, G., Brown, S., Todd, J., & Kremer, P. (2008). Challenging behaviour profiles of people with acquired brain injury living in community settings. *Brain Injury, 22*, 457–470.

Keltner, D., Kring, A. M., & Bonanno, G. A. (1999). Fleeting signs of the course of life: Facial expression and personal adjustment. *Current Directions in Psychological Science, 8*(1), 18–22.

Kemeny, M. E. (2007). Psychoneuroimmunology. In H. S. Friedman & R. C. Silver (Eds.), *Foundations of health psychology*. New York: Oxford University Press.

Kemps, E., Tiggemann, M., Woods, D., & Soekov, B. (2004). Reduction of food cravings through concurrent visuospatial processing. *International Journal of Eating Disorders, 36*(1), 31–40.

Kendler, K. S., Gallagher, T. J., Abelson, J. M., & Kessler, R. C. (1996). Lifetime prevalence, demographic risk factors, and diagnostic validity of nonaffective psychosis as assessed in a U. S. community sample. *Archives of General Psychiatry, 53*, 1022–1031.

Kendler, K. S., & Prescott, C. A. (2006). *Genes, environment, and psychopathology: Understanding the causes of psychiatric and substance use disorders*. New York: Guilford Press.

Kenealy, P. M. (1997). Mood-state-dependent retrieval: The effects of induced mood on memory reconsidered. *Quarterly Journal of Experimental Psychology: Human Experimental Psychology, 50A*, 290–317.

Kerschreiter, R., Schulz-Hardt, S., Mojzisch, A., & Frey, D. (2008). Biased information search in homogeneous groups: Confidence as a moderator for the effect of anticipated task requirements. *Personality & Social Psychology Bulletin, 34*, 679–691.

Kessler, R. C., McGonagle, K. A., Zhao, S., Nelson, C. B., Hughes, M., Eshleman, S., Wittchen, H., & Kendler, K. S. (1994). Lifetime and 12-month prevalence of DSM-III-R psychiatric disorders in the United States. *Archives of General Psychiatry, 51*, 8–19.

Khachaturian, A. S., Corcoran, C. D., Mayer, L. S., Zandi, P. P., Breitner, J. C. S., & Cache County Study Investigators, UT, US. (2004). Apolipoprotein E e4 count affects age at onset of Alzheimer disease, but not lifetime susceptibility: The Cache County Study. *Archives of General Psychiatry, 61*(5), 518–524.

Khaleque, A., Rohner, R. P., Riaz, M., Laukkala, H., & Sadeque, S. (2007). Perceived parental acceptance-rejection and psychological adjustment of children: A cross-cultural study in Finland, Pakistan, and the United States. *Psychological Studies, 52*, 114–119.

Khalid, N., Atkins, M., Tredget, J., Giles, M., Champney-Smith, K., & Kirov, G. (2008). The effectiveness of electroconvulsive therapy in treatment-resistant depression. *Journal of ECT, 24*, 141–145.

Khandai, P. (2004). Managing stress. *Social Science International, 20*(1), 100–106.

Kieffer, K. M., Schinka, J. A., & Curtiss, G. (2004). Person-environment congruence and personality domains in the prediction of job performance and work quality. *Journal of Counseling.Psychology, 51*(2), 168–177.

Kiehl, K. A., Smith, A. M., Mendrek, A., Forster, B. B., Hare, R.D., & Liddle, P. F. (2004). Temporal lobe abnormalities in semantic processing of criminal psychopaths as revealed by functional magnetic resonance imaging. *Psychiatry Research: Neuroimaging*, *130*(1), 27–42.

Kiessling, J., Pichora-Fuller, M. K., Gatehouse, S., Stephen, D., Arlinger, S., Chisolm, T., Davis, A. C., Erber, N. P., Hickson, L., Holmes, A., Rosenhall, U., & von Wedel, H. (2003). Candidature for and delivery of audiological services: Special needs of older people. *International Journal of Audiology*, *42*(Suppl2), 2S92–2S101.

Kiester, E. (1984, July). The playing fields of the mind. *Psychology Today*, pp. 18–24.

Kihlstrom, J. F. (2004). An unbalanced balancing act: Blocked, recovered, and false memories in the laboratory and clinic. *Clinical Psychology: Science & Practice*, *11*(1), 34–41.

Kihlstrom, J. F. (2005). Dissociative disorders. *Annual Review of Clinical Psychology*, *1*, 227–253.

Kikusui, T., Aoyagi, A., & Kaneko, T. (2000). Spatial working memory is independent of hippocampal CA1 long-term potentiation in rats. *Behavioral Neuroscience*, *114*, 700–706.

Kilicarslan, A., Isildak, M., Guven, G. S., Oz, S. G., Tannover, M. D., Duman, A. E., Sarabasi, O., & Sozen, T. (2006). Demographic, socioeconomic, and educational aspects of obesity in an adult population. *Journal of the National Medical Association*, *98*, 1313–1317.

Killen, M., & Hart, D. (1999). *Morality in everyday life: Developmental perspectives*. New York: Cambridge University Press.

Kim, D-H., Moon, Y-S., Kim, H-S., Jung, J-S, Park, H-M., Suh, H-W., Kim, Y-H., & Song, DK. (2005). Effect of Zen meditation on serum nitric oxide activity and lipid peroxidation. *Progress in Neuropsychopharmacology & Biological Psychiatry*, *29*(2), 327–331.

Kim, J., & Hatfield, E. (2004). Love types and subjective well-being: A cross cultural study. *Social Behavior & Personality*, *32*(2), 173–182.

Kim, J-H., Auerbach, J. M., Rodriquez-Gomez, J. A., Velasco, I., Gavin, D., Lumelsky, N., Lee, SH., Nguyen, J., Sanchez-Pernaute, R., Bankiewicz, K., & McKay, R. (2002). Dopamine neurons derived from embryonic stem cells function in an animal model of Parkinson's disease. *Nature*, *418*, 50–56.

Kim, S. U. (2004). Human neural stem cells genetically modified for brain repair in neurological disorders. *Neuropathology*, *24*(3), 159–171.

Kim, U., & Choi, S. (1995). Individualism, collectivism, and child development:

A Korean perspective. In P. M. Greenfield & R. R. Cocking (Eds.), *Cross-cultural roots of minority child development* (pp. 227–257). Hillsdale, NJ: Erlbaum.

Kim, Y. H. (2008). Rebounding from learned helplessness: A measure of academic resilience using anagrams. *Dissertation Abstracts International: Section B: The Sciences and Engineering.* *68*(10-B), 6947.

Kimes, L. M. (2006). Adolescent parents' understanding of the social and emotional development of their very young children. *Dissertation Abstracts International: Section B: The Sciences and Engineering*, *67*(6-B), 3483.

Kimmel, M. (Ed). (2007). *The sexual self: The construction of sexual scripts*. Nashville, TN: Vanderbilt University Press.

Kimmel, M. S. (2000). *The gendered society*. London: Oxford University Press.

Kimmel, P. R. (2006). Culture and conflict. In M. Deutsch, P. T. Coleman, & E. C. Marcus (Eds.), *The handbook of conflict resolution: Theory and practice* (2nd ed.) (pp. 625–648). Hoboken, NJ: Wiley.

Kinder, L. S., Bradley, K. A., Katon, W. J., Ludman, E., McDonnell, M. B., & Bryson, C. L. (2008). Depression, posttraumatic stress disorder, and mortality. *Psychosomatic Medicine*, *70*, 20–26.

King, B. M. (2009). *Human sexuality today* (6th ed.). Boston: Allyn & Bacon.

King, N. J., Clowes-Hollins, V., & Ollendick, T. H. (1997). The etiology of childhood dog phobia. *Behaviour Research and Therapy*, *35*, 77.

King, S. A., & Moreggi, D. (2007). Internet self-help and support groups: The pros and cons of text-based mutual aid. In J. Gackenbach (Ed.), *Psychology and the Internet: Intrapersonal, interpersonal, and transpersonal implications* (2nd ed.) (pp. 221–244). San Diego, CA: Academic Press.

King, S. L. (2008). A prospective study of physiological hyperarousal and coping as correlates of symptoms of acute stress disorder and posttraumatic stress disorder in motor vehicle crash survivors. *Dissertation Abstracts International: Section B: The Sciences and Engineering*, *68*(10-B), 6587.

Kinoshita, S., & Peek-O'Leary, M. (2005). Does the compatibility effect in the race Implicit Association Test reflect familiarity or affect? *Psychonomic Bulletin & Review*, *12*, 442–452.

Kirk, K. M., Bailey, J. M., Dunne, M. P., & Martin, N. G. (2000). Measurement models for sexual orientation in a community twin sample. *Behavior Genetics*, *30*(4), 345–356.

Kirkman, C. A. (2002). Non-incarcerated psychopaths: Why we need to know more about the psychopaths who live amongst us. *Journal of Psychiatric & Mental Health Nursing*, *9*(2), 155–160.

Kirmayer, L. J., & Jarvis, G. E. (2006) Depression across cultures. In D. J. Stein, D. J. Kupfer, & A. F. Schatzberg (Eds.), *The American Psychiatric Publishing textbook of mood disorders* (pp. 699–715). Washington, DC: American Psychiatric Publishing.

Kirsch, I., & Braffman, W. (2001). Imaginative suggestibility and hypnotizability. *Current Directions in Psychological Science*, *10*(2), 57–61.

Kirsch, I., & Lynn, S. J. (1995). The altered state of hypnosis. *American Psychologist*, *50*, 846–858.

Kirsch, I., Mazzoni, G., & Montgomery, G. H. (2006). Remembrance of hypnosis past. *American Journal of Clinical Hypnosis*, *49*, 171–178.

Kirschenbaum, H. & Jourdan, A. (2005). The current status of Carl Rogers and the personcentered approach. *Psychotherapy: Theory, Research Practice, Training*, *42*(1), 37–51.

Kirschner, S. M., Litwack, T. R., & Galperin, G. J. (2004). The defense of extreme emotional disturbance: A qualitative analysis of cases in New York county. *Psychology, Public Policy, & Law*, *10*(1–2), 102–133.

Kisilevsky, B. S., Hains, S. M. J., Lee, K., Xie, X., Huang, H., Ye, H., Zhang, K., & Wang, Z. (2003). Effects of experience on fetal voice recognition. *Psychological Science*, *14*(3), 220–224.

Kitayama, S., & Cohen, D. (Eds.). (2007). *Handbook of cultural psychology*. New York: Guilford Press.

Klatzky, R. L. (1984). *Memory and awareness*. New York: Freeman.

Kleider, H. M., Pezdek, K., Goldinger, S. D., & Kirk, A. (2008). Schema-driven source misattribution errors: Remembering the expected from a witnessed event. *Applied Cognitive Psychology*, *22*, 1–20.

Klein, O., Pohl, S., & Ndagijimana, C. (2007). The influence of intergroup comparisons on Africans' intelligence test performance in a job selection context. *Journal of Psychology: Interdisciplinary and Applied*, *141*, 453–467.

Kleinman, A., & Cohen, A. (1997, March). Psychiatry's global challenge. *Scientific American*, 86–89.

Klimes-Dougan, B., Lee, C-Y. S., Ronsaville, D., & Martinez, P. (2008). Suicidal risk in young adult offspring of mothers with bipolar or major depressive disorder: A longitudinal family risk study. *Journal of Clinical Psychology, 64,* 531–540.

Kline, K. K. (Ed.. (2008). *Authoritative communities: The scientific case for nurturing the whole child. The Search Institute series on developmentally attentive community and society.* New York: Springer Science + Business Media.

Klohnen, E. C., & Bera, S. (1998). Behavioral and experiential patterns of avoidantly and securely attached women across adulthood: A 31-year longitudinal perspective. *Journal of Personality and Social Psychology, 74*(1), 211–223.

Kluger, J., & Masters, C. (2006, August 28). How to spot a liar. *Time,* 46–48.

Knapp, M., Romeo, R., Mogg, A., Eranti, S., Pluck, G., Purvis, R., Brown, R. G., Howard, R., Philpot, M., Rothwell, J., Edwards, D., & McLoughlin, D. M. (2008). Cost-effectiveness of transcranial magnetic stimulation vs. electroconvulsive therapy for severe depression: A multi-centre randomized controlled trial. *Journal of Affective Disorders, 109,* 273–285.

Knekt, P., Lindfors, O., Laaksonen, M. A., Raitasalo, R., Haaramo, P., Järvikoski, A., & The Helsinki Psychotherapy Study Group, Helsinki, Finlan. (2008). Effectiveness of short-term and long-term psychotherapy on work ability and functional capacity—A randomized clinical trial on depressive and anxiety disorders. *Journal of Affective Disorders, 107,* 95–106.

Kniffin, K. M., & Wilson, D. S. (2004). The effect of nonphysical traits on the perception of physical attractiveness: Three naturalistic studies. *Evolution & Human Behavior, 25,* 88–101.

Knoblauch, K., Vital-Durand, F., & Barbur, J. L. (2000). Variation of chromatic sensitivity across the life span. *Vision Research, 41*(1), 23–36.

Knutson, K. M., Mah, L., Manly, C. F., & Grafman, J. (2007). Neural correlates of automatic beliefs about gender and race. *Human Brain Mapping, 28,* 915–930.

Kobasa, S. (1979). Stressful life events, personality, and health: An inquiry into hardiness. *Journal of Personality and Social Psychology, 37,* 1–11.

Köfalvi, A. (Ed). (2008). *Cannabinoids and the brain.* New York: Springer Science + Business Media.

Kohlberg, L. (1964). Development of moral character and moral behavior. In L. W. Hoffman & M. L. Hoffman (Eds.), *Review of child development research (Vol. 1).* New York: Sage.

Kohlberg, L. (1969). Stage and sequence: The cognitive-developmental approach to socialization. In D. A. Goslin (Ed.), *Handbook of socialization theory and research.* Chicago: Rand McNally.

Kohlberg, L. (1981). *The meaning and measurement of moral development.* Worcester, MA: Clark University Press.

Kohlberg, L. (1984). *The psychology of moral development: Essays on moral development (Vol. 2).* San Francisco: Harper & Row.

Köhler, W. (1925). *The mentality of apes.* New York: Harcourt, Brace.

Kohn, A. (2000). *Punished by rewards: The trouble with gold stars, incentive plans, A's, and other bribes.* New York: Houghton Mifflin.

Komiya, N., Good, G. E., & Sherrod, N. B. (2000). Emotional openness as a predictor of college students' attitudes toward seeking psychological help. *Journal of Counseling Psychology, 47*(1), 138–143.

Kondo, N. (2008). Mental illness in film. *Psychiatric Rehabilitation Journal, 31,* 250–252.

Konheim-Kalkstein, Y. L., & van den Broek, P. (2008). The effect of incentives on cognitive processing of text. *Discourse Processes, 45,* 180–194.

Koob, G. F., & Le Moal, M. L. (2008). Addiction and the brain antireward system. *Annual Review of Psychology, 59,* 29–53.

Koop, C. E., Richmond, J., & Steinfeld, J. (2004). America's choice: Reducing tobacco addiction and disease. *American Journal of Public Health, 94*(2), 174–176.

Koppel, J. (2000). *Good/Grief.* New York: Harperperennial.

Koppes, L. L., & Pickren, W. (2007). Industrial and organizational psychology: An evolving science. In L. L. Koppes (Ed.), *Historical perspectives in industrial and organizational psychology.* Mahwah, NJ: Erlbaum.

Korkman, M., Kettunen, S., & Autti-Rämö, I. (2003). Neurocognitive impairment in early adolescence following prenatal alcohol exposure of varying duration. *Child Neuropsychology, 9*(2), 117–128.

Kornstein, S. G. (2002). Chronic depression in women. *Journal of Clinical Psychiatry, 63*(7), 602–609.

Koropeckyj-Cox, T., & Call, V. R. A. (2007). Characteristics of older childless persons and parents: Cross-national comparisons. *Journal of Family Issues, 28,* 1362–1414.

Kotulak, R. (2008). The effect of violence and stress in kids' brains. In M. H. Immordino-Yang (Ed.), *Jossey-Bass Education Team. The Jossey-Bass reader on the brain and learning* (pp. 216–225). San Francisco, CA: Jossey-Bass.

Kovacic, Z., Henigsberg, N., Pivac, N., Nedic, G., & Borovecki, A. (2008). Platelet serotonin concentration and suicidal behavior in combat related posttraumatic stress disorder. *Progress in Neuro-Psychopharmacology & Biological Psychiatry, 32,* 544–551.

Kraaij, V., Arensman, E., & Spinhoven, P. (2002). Negative life events and depression in elderly persons: A meta-analysis. *Journals of Gerontology: Series B: Psychological Sciences & Social Sciences, 57B*(1), 87–94.

Kracher, B., & Marble, R. P. (2008). The significance of gender in predicting the cognitive moral development of business practitioners using the Socioemotional Reflection Objective Measure. *Journal of Business Ethics, 78,* 503–526.

Kramer, A. F., Hahn, S., Irwin, D. E., & Theeuwes, J. (2000). Age differences in the control of looking behavior. *Psychological Science, 11*(3), 210–217.

Krantz, D. S., & McCeney, M. K. (2002). Effects of psychological and social factors on organic disease: A critical assessment of research on coronary heart disease. *Annual Review of Psychology, (1),* 341–369.

Krebs, D. (2007). Understanding evolutionary approaches to human behavior. *Human Development, 50,* 286–291.

Krebs, D. L. (2007). Deciphering the structure of the moral sense: A review of moral minds: How nature designed our universal sense of right and wrong. *Evolution and Human Behavior, 28,* 294–296.

Krebs, D. L., & Hemingway, A. (2008). The explanatory power of evolutionary approaches to human behavior: The case of morality. *Psychological Inquiry, 19,* 35–38.

Kring, A. M., Davison, G. C., Neale, J. M., & Johnson, S. L. (2007). *Abnormal psychology (10th ed.).* Hoboken, NJ: Wiley.

Krishma, G. (1999). *The dawn of a new science.* Los Angeles: Institute for Consciousness Research.

Kronenberger, W. G., Mathews, V. P., Dunn, D. W., Wang, Y., Wood, E. A., Larsen, J. J., Rembusch, M. E., Lowe, M. J., Giauque, A. L., & Lurito, J. T. (2005). Media violence exposure in aggressive and control adolescents: Differences in self- and parent-reported exposure to violence on television and in video games. *Aggressive Behavior, 31*(3), 201–216.

Krueger, J. I. (2007). From social projection to social behaviour. *European Review of Social Psychology, 18,* 1–35.

Krusemark, E. A., Campbell, W. K., & Clementz, B. A. (2008). Attributions, deception, and event related potentials: An investigation of the self-serving bias. *Psychophysiology, 45,* 511–515.

Kryger, M. H., Walld, R., & Manfreda, J. (2002). Diagnoses received by narcolepsy patients in the year prior to diagnosis by a sleep specialist. *Sleep: Journal of Sleep & Sleep Disorders Research, 25*(1), 36–41.

Ksir, C. J., Hart, C. I., & Ray, O. S. (2008). *Drugs, society, and human behavior.* New York: McGraw-Hill.

Kubiak, T., Vögele, C., Siering, M., Schiel, R., & Weber, H. (2008). Daily hassles and emotional eating in obese adolescents under restricted dietary conditions—The role of ruminative thinking. *Appetite, 51,* 206–209.

Kübler-Ross, E. (1975). *Questions and answers on death and dying.* Oxford, England: Macmillan.

Kübler-Ross, E. (1983). *On children and death.* New York: Macmillan.

Kübler-Ross, E. (1997). *Death: The final stage of growth.* New York: Simon & Schuster.

Kübler-Ross, E. (1999). *On death and dying.* New York: Simon & Schuster.

Kudo, E., & Numazaki, M. (2003). Explicit and direct self-serving bias in Japan. Reexamination of self-serving bias for success and failure. *Journal of Cross-Cultural Psychology, 34*(5), 511–521.

Kuhn, C., Swartzwelder, S., & Wilson, W. (2003). *Buzzed: The straight facts about the most used and abused drugs from alcohol to ecstasy* (2nd ed.). New York: Norton.

Kulich, C., Ryan, M. K., & Haslam, S. A. (2007). Where is the romance for women leaders? The effects of gender on leadership attributions and performance-based pay. *Applied Psychology: An International Review, 56,* 582–601.

Kulik, L. (2005). Intrafamiliar congruence in gender role attitudes and ethnic stereotypes: The Israeli case. *Journal of Comparative Family Studies, 36*(2), 289–303.

Kumkale, G. T., & Albarracín, D. (2004). The sleeper effect in persuasion: A meta-analytic review. *Psychological Bulletin, 130*(1), 143–172.

Kumpfer, K. L., Alvarado, R., Whiteside, H. O. (2003). Family-based interventions for substance use and misuse prevention. *Substance Use & Misuse, 38*(11–13), 1759–1787.

Kunz, D., & Hermann, W. M. (2000). Sleepwake cycle, sleep-related disturbances, and sleep disorders: A chronobiological approach. *Comparative Psychology, 41,* 104–105.

Kuperstok, N. (2008). Effects of exposure to differentiated aggressive films, equated for levels of interest and excitation, and the vicarious hostility catharsis hypothesis. *Dissertation Abstracts International: Section B: The Sciences and Engineering 68*(7-B), 4806.

Labiano, L. M., & Brusasca, C. (2002). Tratamientos psicológicos en la hipertensión arterial [Psychological treatments in arterial hypertension]. *Interdisciplinaria, 19*(1), 85–97.

Lachman, M. E. (2004). Development in midlife. *Annual Review of Psychology, 55,* 305–331.

Lackner, J. R., & DiZio, P. (2005). Vestibular, proprioceptive, and haptic contributions to spatial orientation. *Annual Review of Psychology, 56,* 115–147.

Lader, M. (2007). Limitations of current medical treatments for depression: Disturbed circadian rhythms as a possible therapeutic target. *European Neuropsychopharacology, 17,* 743–755.

Lader, M., Cardinali, D. P., & Pandi-Perumal, S. R. (Eds.). (2006). *Sleep and sleep disorders: A neuropsychopharmacological approach.* New York: Springer-Verlag.

Lafayette-De Mente (2002, May). *Karoshi: Death from Overwork.* [On-line]. Available: http://www.apmforum.com/columns/boye51.htm.

Laidlaw, K., & Thompson, L. W. (2008). Cognitive behavior therapy with depressed older people. In K. Laidlaw & B. Knight (Eds.), *Handbook of emotional disorders in later life: Assessment and treatment.* New York: Oxford University Press.

Laine, T., Pekka, J., Ahonen, A., Raesaenen, P., & Tiihonen, J. (2001). Dopamine transporter density and novelty seeking among alcoholics. *Journal of Addictive Diseases, 20*(4), 91–96.

Lakein, A. (1998). *Give me a moment and I'll change your life: Tools for moment management.* New York: Andrews McMeel Publishing.

Lamb, H. R. (2000). Deinstitutionalization and public policy. In R. W. Menninger & J.C. Nemiah (Eds.), *American psychiatry after World War II.* Washington, DC: American Psychiatric Press.

Lamberg, L. (1998). Gay is okay with APA—Forum honors landmark 1973 events. *Journal of the American Medical Association, 280,* 497–499.

Landay, J. S., & Kuhnehenn, J. (2004, July 10). Probe blasts CIA on Iraq data. *The Philadelphia Inquirer,* p. AO1.

Landeira-Fernandez, J. (2004). Analysis of the cold-water restraint procedure in gastric ulceration and body temperature. *Physiology & Behavior, 82*(5), 827–833.

Lane, R. D., Reiman, E. M., Ahern, G. L., & Schwartz, G. E. (1997). Neuroanatomical correlates of happiness, sadness, and disgust. *American Journal of Psychiatry, 154,* 926–933.

Lang, F. R., & Carstensen, L. L. (2002). Time counts: Future time perspective, goals, and social relationships. *Psychology & Aging, 17*(1), 125–139.

Lang, U. E., Bajbouj, M., Sander, T., & Gallinat, J. (2007). Gender-dependent association of the functional catechol-O-methyltransferase Val158Met genotype with sensation seeking personality trait. *Neuropsychopharmacology, 32,* 1950–1955.

Langenecker, S. A., Bieliauskas, L. A., Rapport, L. J., Zubieta, J-K., Wilde, E. A., & Berent, S. (2005). Face emotion perception and executive functioning deficits in depression. *Journal of Clinical & Experimental Neuropsychology, 27*(3), 320–333.

Langlois, J. H., Kalakanis, L., Rubenstein, A. J., Larson, A., Hallam, M., & Smoot, M. (2000). Maxims or myths of beauty? A meta-analytic and theoretical review. *Psychological Bulletin, 126*(3), 390–423.

LaPointe, L. L. (Ed.. (2005). Feral children. *Journal of Medical Speech-Language Pathology, 13,* vii–ix.

Lapsley, D. K. (2006). Moral stage theory. In M. Killen & J. Smetana (Eds.), *Handbook of moral development.* Mahwah, NJ: Erlbaum.

Larzelere, R. E., & Johnson, B. (1999). Evaluations of the effects of Sweden's spanking ban on physical child abuse rates: A literature review. *Psychological Reports, 85*(2), 381–392.

Latane, B., & Darley, J. M. (1970). *The unresponsive bystander: Why doesn't he help?* New York: Appleton-Century-Crofts.

Lauc, G., Zvonar, K., Vuksic-Mihaljevic, Z., & Flögel, M. (2004). Post-awakening changes in salivary cortisol in veterans with and without PTSD. *Stress & Health: Journal of the International Society for the Investigation of Stress, 20*(2), 99–102.

Laumann, E., Gagnon, J., Michael, R., & Michaels, S. (1994). *The social organization of sexuality: Sexual practices in the United States.* Chicago: University of Chicago Press.

Laungani, P. D. (2007). *Understanding cross-cultural psychology.* Thousand Oaks, CA: Sage.

Lawrence, C., & Andrews, K. (2004). The influence of perceived prison crowding on male inmates' perception of aggressive events. *Aggressive Behavior, 30*, 273–283.

Lawrence, M. (2008). Review of the bifurcation of the self: The history and theory of dissociation and its disorders. *American Journal of Clinical Hypnosis, 50*, 281–282.

Lawrence, S. A. (2002). Behavioral interventions to increase physical activity. *Journal of Human Behavior in the Social Environment, 6*(1), 25–44.

Lazar, S. W., Kerr, C. E., Wasserman, R. H., Gray, J. R., Greve, D. N., Treadway, M. T., McGarvey, M., Quinn, B. T., Dusek, J. A., Benson, H., Rauch, S. L., Moore, C. I., Fischl, B. (2005). Meditation experience is associated with increased cortical thickness. *Neuroreport, 16*(17), 1893–1897.

Lazarus, R. S. (1993). Coping theory and research: Past, present, and future. *Psychosomatic Medicine, 55*, 234–247.

Lazarus, R. S. (1999). *Stress and emotion: A new synthesis.* New York: Springer.

Lazarus, R. S. (2000). Toward better research on stress and coping. *American Psychologist, 55*, 665–673.

Le Roux, R., Niehaus, D. J. H., Koen, L., Seller, C., Lochner, C., & Emsley, R. A. (2007). Initiation rites as a perceived stressor for Isixhosa males with schizophrenia. *Transcultural Psychiatry, 44*, 292–299.

Leaper, C. (2000). Gender, affiliation, assertion, and the interactive context of parent-child play. *Developmental Psychology, 36*(3), 381–393.

Leary, C. E., Kelley, M. L., Morrow, J., & Mikulka, P. J. (2008). Parental use of physical punishment as related to family environment, psychological well-being, and personality in undergraduates. *Journal of Family Violence, 23*(1), 1–7.

Lecrubier, Y., Clerc, G., Didi, R., & Kieser, M. (2002). Efficacy of St. John's wort extract WS 5570 in major depression: A double-blind, placebo-controlled trial. *American Journal of Psychiatry, 159*(8), 1361–1366.

LeDoux, J. (1996a). *The emotional brain: The mysterious underpinnings of emotional life.* New York: Simon & Schuster.

LeDoux, J. E. (1996b). Sensory systems and emotion: A model of affective processing. *Integrative Psychiatry, 4*, 237–243.

LeDoux, J. E. (1998). *The emotional brain.* New York: Simon & Schuster.

LeDoux, J. E. (2002). *Synaptic self: How our brains become who we are.* New York: Viking.

LeDoux, J. E. (2007). Emotional memory. *Scholarpedia, 2*, 180.

Lee, D. (1950). The conception of the self among the Wintu Indians. *In D. Lee (Ed.), Freedom and culture.* Englewood Cliffs, NJ: Prentice-Hall.

Lee, W-Y. (2002). One therapist, four cultures: Working with families in Greater China. *Journal of Family Therapy, 24*, 258-275.

Lee, J-H., Kwon, Y-D., Hong, S-H., Jeong, H-J., Kim, H-M., & Um, J-Y. (2008). Interleukin-1 beta gene polymorphism and traditional constitution in obese women. *International Journal of Neuroscience, 118*, 793–805.

Lee, J. J. (2007). A g beyond Homo sapiens? Some hints and suggestions. *Intelligence, 35*, 253–265.

Lee, K. T., Mattson, S. N., & Riley, E. P. (2004). Classifying children with heavy prenatal alcohol exposure using measures of attention. *Journal of the International Neuropsychological Society, 10*(2), 271–277.

Lefkowitz, E. S., & Zeldow, P. B. (2006). Masculinity and femininity predict optimal mental health: A belated test of the androgyny hypothesis. *Journal of Personality Assessment, 87*, 95–101.

Lefley, H. P. (2000). Cultural perspectives on families, mental illness, and the law. *International Journal of Law and Psychiatry, 23*, 229–243.

Leglise, A. (2008). *Progress in circadian rhythm research.* Hauppauge, NY: Nova Science.

Legrand, F. D., Gomà-i-freixanet, M., Kaltenbach, M. L., & Joly, P. M. (2007). Association between sensation seeking and alcohol consumption in French college students: Some ecological data collected in "open bar" parties. *Personality and Individual Differences, 43*, 1950–1959.

Lehnert, G., & Zimmer, H. D. (2008). Modality and domain specific components in auditory and visual working memory tasks. *Cognitive Processing, 9*, 53–61.

Lehto, S. M., Tolmunen, T., Joensuu, M., Saarinen, P. I., Valkonen-Korhonen, M., Vanninen, R., Ahola, P., Tiihonen, J., Kuikka, J., & Lehtonen, J. (2008). Changes in midbrain serotonin transporter availability in atypically depressed subjects after one year of psychotherapy. Progress in Neuro-*Psychopharmacology & Biological Psychiatry, 32*, 229–237.

Leichtman, M. D. (2006). Cultural and maturational influences on long-term event memory. In L. Balter & C. S. Tamis-LeMonda (Eds.), *Child psychology: A handbook of contemporary issues* (2nd ed.) (pp. 565–589). New York: Psychology Press.

Leichtman, M. D., & Ceci, S. J. (1995). The effects of stereotypes and suggestions on preschoolers' reports. *Developmental Psychology, 31*, 568–578.

Lein, C., & Wills, C. E. (2007). Using patient-centered interviewing skills to manage complex patient encounters in primary care. *Journal of the American Academy of Nurse Practitioners, 19*, 215–220.

Lele, D. U. (2008). The influence of individual personality and attachment styles on romantic relationships (partner choice and couples' satisfaction). *Dissertation Abstracts International: Section B: The Sciences and Engineering, 68*, 6316.

Lemus, D. R. (2008). Communication during retirement planning: An information-seeking process. *Dissertation Abstracts International Section A: Humanities and Social Sciences, 68*(10-A), 4139.

Lengua, L. J., Wolchik, S. A., Sandler, I. N., & West, S. G. (2000). The additive and interactive effects of parenting and temperament in predicting problems of children of divorce. *Journal of Clinical Child Psychology, 29*(2), 232–244.

Lensvelt-Mulders, G., & Hettema, J. (2001). Analysis of genetic influences on the consistency and variability of the Big Five across different stressful situations. *European Journal of Personality, 15*(5), 355–371.

Leon, P., Chedraui, P., Hidalgo, L., & Ortiz, F. (2007). Perceptions and attitudes toward the menopause among middle-aged women from Guayaquil, Ecuador. *Maturitas, 57*, 233–238.

Leonard, B. E. (2003). *Fundamentals of psychopharmacology* (3rd ed.). Hoboken, NJ: Wiley.

Lepper, M. R., Greene, D., & Nisbett, R. E. (1973). Undermining children's intrinsic interest with extrinsic rewards: A test of the overjustification hypothesis. *Journal of Personality and Social Psychology, 28*, 129–137.

Leri, A., Anversa, P., & Frishman, W. H. (Eds.) (2007). *Cardiovascular regeneration and stem cell therapy.* Hoboken, NJ: Wiley-Blackwell.

Lerner, H. D. (2008). Psychodynamic perspectives. In M. Hersen & A. M. Gross (Eds.), *Handbook of clinical psychology, vol 1: Adults* (pp. 127–160). Hoboken, NJ: Wiley.

Lerner, J. S., Gonzalez, R. M., Small, D. A., & Fischhoff, B. (2003). Effects of fear and anger on perceived risks of terrorism: A national field experiment. *Psychological Science, 14*, 144–150.

Leslie, M. (2000, July/August). The Vexing Legacy of Lewis Terman. *Stanford Magazine.*

[On-line]. Available: http://www.stanforda-lumni.org/news/magazine/2000/julaug/articles/terman.html.

Lettvin, J. Y., Maturana, H. R., McCul-loch, W. S., & Pitts, W. H. (1959). What the frog's eye tells the frog's brain. *Proceedings of the Institute of Radio Engineers, 47,* 1940–1951.

LeVay, S. (2003). Queer science: The use and abuse of research into homosexuality. *Archives of Sexual Behavior, 32*(2),187–189.

Levenson, R. W. (1992). Autonomic nervous system differences among emotions. *Psychological Science, 3,* 23–27.

Levenson, R. W. (2007). Emotion elicitation with neurological patients. In J. A. Coan & J. J. B. Allen (Eds.), *Handbook of emotion elicitation and assessment.* (pp. 158–168). *Series in affective science.* New York: Oxford University Press.

Leventhal, H., Weinman, J., Leventhal, E. A., & Phillips, L. A. (2008). Health psychology: The search for pathways between behavior and health. *Annual Review of Psychology, 59,* 477–505.

Lever, J. P. (2008). Poverty, stressful life events, and coping strategies. *The Spanish Journal of Psychology, 11,* 228–249.

Levine, J. R. (2001). *Why do fools fall in love: Experiencing the magic, mystery, and meaning of successful relationships.* New York: Jossey-Bass.

Levine, J. A., Emery, C. R., & Pollack, H. (2007). The well-being of children born to teen mothers. *Journal of Marriage and Family, 69,* 105–122.

Levinthal, C. (2006). *Drugs, society, and criminal justice.* Boston, MA: Allyn & Bacon/Longman.

Levinthal, C. (2008). *Drugs, behavior, and modern society (5th ed.).* Boston: Allyn & Bacon.

Levitan, L. C. (2008). Giving prejudice an attitude adjustment: The implications of attitude strength and social network attitudinal composition for prejudice and prejudice reduction. *Dissertation Abstracts International: Section B: The Sciences and Engineering, 68* (8-B), 5634.

Levy, F., & Krebs, P. R. (2006). Cortical-subcortical re-entrant circuits and recurrent behavior. *Australian and New Zealand Journal of Psychiatry, 40,* 752–758.

Lewandowski Jr., G. W., Aron, A., & Gee, J. (2007). Personality goes a long way: The malleability of opposite-sex physical attractiveness. *Personal Relationships, 14,* 571–585.

Lewig, K. A., & Dollard, M. F. (2003). Emotional dissonance, emotional exhaustion and job satisfaction in call centre workers. *European Journal of Work & Organizational Psychology, 12*(4), 366–392.

Lewin, D., & Herron, H. (2007). Signs, symptoms, and risk factors: Health visitors' perspectives of child neglect. *Child Abuse Review, 16,* 93–107.

Lewis, R. E. (2008). Resilience: Individual, family, school, and community perspectives. In D. Capuzzi & D. R. Gross (Eds.), *Youth at risk: A prevention resource for counselors, teachers, and parents* (pp. 39–68). Alexandria, VA: American Counseling Association.

Lewis, S. (1963). *Dear Shari.* New York: Stein & Day.

Li, J-C. A. (2008). Rethinking the case against divorce. *Dissertation Abstracts International Section A: Humanities and Social Sciences, 68,* 4093.

Li, N. P., Bailey, J. M., Kenrick, D. T., & Linsenmeier, J. A. W. (2002). The necessities and luxuries of mate preferences: Testing the tradeoffs. *Journal of Personality and Social Psychology, 82*(6), 947–955.

Li, S., Lindenberger, U., Hommel, B., Aschersleben, G., Prinz, W., & Baltes, P. B. (2004). Transformations in the couplings among intellectual abilities and constituent cognitive processes across the life span. *Psychological Science, 15*(3), 155–163.

Libon, D. J., Xie, S. X., Moore, P., Farmer, J., Antani, S., McCawley, G., Cross, K., & Grossman, M. (2007). Patterns of neuropsychological impairment in frontotemporal dementia. *Neurology, 68,* 369–375.

Liebenberg, L., & Ungar, M. (2008). *Resilience in action: Working with youth across cultures and contexts.* Toronto, Ontario: University of Toronto Press.

Lieberman, P. (1998). *Eve spoke: Human language and human evolution.* New York: Norton.

Liggett, D. R. (2000). Enhancing imagery through hypnosis: A performance aid for athletes. *American Journal of Clinical Hypnosis, 43*(2), 149–157.

Lillard, A. (1998). Ethnopsychologies: Cultural variations in theories of mind. *Psychological Bulletin, 123,* 3–32.

Lindahl, K., & Obstbaum, K. (2004). Entering the canon: A tribute to Chess and Thomas. PsycCRITIQUES. [np].

Lindberg, B., Axelsson, K., & Öhrling, K. (2008). Adjusting to being a father to an infant born prematurely: Experiences from Swedish fathers. *Scandinavian Journal of Caring Sciences, 22,* 79–85.

Linden, E. (1993). Can animals think? *Time,* pp. 54–61.

Lindholm, E., Aberg, K., Ekholm, B., Pettersson, U., Adolfsson, R., & Jazin, E. E. (2004). Reconstruction of ancestral haplotypes in a 12-generation schizophrenia pedigree. *Psychiatric Genetics, 14*(1), 1–8.

Lindsay, D. S., Allen, B. P., Chan, J. C. K., & Dahl, L. C. (2004). Eyewitness suggestibility and source similarity: Intrusions of details from one event into memory reports of another event. *Journal of Memory & Language, 50*(1), 96–111.

Lindwall, M., Rennemark, M., & Berggren, T. (2008). Movement in mind: The relationship of exercise with cognitive status for older adults in the Swedish National Study on Aging and Care (SNAC). *Aging & Mental Health, 12,* 212–220.

Lineberry, T. W., Bostwick, J. M., & Rundell J. R. (2006). U.S. troops returning home: Are you prepared? *Current Psychiatry, 5,* 13–22.

Links, P. S., Eynan, R., Heisel, M. J., & Nisenbaum, R. (2008). Elements of affective instability associated with suicidal behaviour in patients with borderline personality disorder. *The Canadian Journal of Psychiatry 53,* 112–116.

Links, P. S., Heslegrave, R., & van Reekum, R. (1998). Prospective follow-up of borderline personality disorder: Prognosis, prediction outcome, and Axis II comorbidity. *Canadian Journal of Psychiatry, 43,* 265–270.

Linzer, M., Gerrity, M., Douglas, J. A., McMurray, J. E., Williams, E. S., Konrad, T. R., & Society of General Medicine Career Satisfaction Study Grou. (2002). Physician stress: Results from the physician worklife study. *Stress & Health: Journal of the International Society for the Investigation of Stress, 18*(1), 37–42.

Lipowski, Z. J. (1986). Psychosomatic medicine: Past and present: I. Historical background. *Canadian Journal of Psychiatry, 31,* 2–7.

Lippa, R. A. (2007). The preferred traits of mates in a cross-national study of heterosexual and homosexual men and women: An examination of biological and cultural influences. *Archives of Sexual Behavior, 36,* 193–208.

Lipsanen, T., Korkeila, J., Peltola, P., Järvinen, J., Langen, K., & Lauerma, H. (2004). Dissociative disorders among psychiatric patients: Comparison with a nonclinical sample. *European Psychiatry, 19*(1), 53–55.

Lissek, S., & Powers, A. S. (2003). Sensation seeking and startle modulation by physically threatening images. *Biological Psychology, 63*(2), 179–197.

Liu, H., Mantyh, P., & Basbaum, A. I. (1997). NMDA-receptor regulation of substance P release from primary afferent nociceptors. *Nature, 386,* 721–724.

Liu, J. H., & Latané, B. (1998). Extremitization of attitudes: Does thought- and discussion-induced polarization cumulate? *Basic and Applied Social Psychology, 20,* 103–110.

Livi, S., Kenny, D. A., Albright, L., & Pierro, A. (2008). A social relations analysis of leadership. *Leadership Quarterly, 19,* 235–248.

Livingston, J. A. (1999). Something old and something new: Love, creativity, and the enduring relationship. *Bulletin of the Menninger Clinic, 63,* 40–52.

Livingston, R. W., & Drwecki, B. B. (2007). Why are some individuals not racially biased? Susceptibility to affective conditioning predicts nonprejudice toward Blacks. *Psychological Science, 18,* 816–823.

Lizarraga, M. L. S., & Ganuza, J. M. G. (2003). Improvement of mental rotation in girls and boys. *Sex Roles, 49*(5–6), 277–286.

Locke, E. A. (2007). The case for inductive theory building. *Journal of Management, 33,* 867–890.

Locke, E. A., & Latham, G. P. (2006). New directions in goal-setting theory. *Current Directions in Psychological Science, 15,* 265–268.

Loewenthal, D., & Winter, D. (Eds.. (2006). *What is psychotherapeutic research?* London, England: Karnac Books.

Loftus, E. (1982). Memory and its distortions. In A. G. Kraut (Ed.), *The G. Stanley Hall Lecture Series Vol. 2,* (pp. 123–154). Washington, DC: American Psychological Association.

Loftus, E., & Ketcham, K. (1994). *The myth of repressed memories: False memories and allegations of sexual abuse.* New York: St. Martin's Press.

Loftus, E., & Polage, D. C. (1999). Repressed memories: When are they real? When are they false? *Psychiatric Clinics of North America, 22,* 61–70.

Loftus, E. (2002, May/June). My story: Dear Mother. *Psychology Today,* pp. 67–70.

Loftus, E. F. (1993). Psychologists in the eyewitness world. *American Psychologist, 48,* 550–552.

Loftus, E. F. (1997). Memory for a past that never was. *Current Directions in Psychological Science, 6*(3), 60–65.

Loftus, E. F. (2000). Remembering what never happened. In E. Tulving, et al. (Eds.), *Memory, consciousness, and the brain: The Tallinn Conference,* pp. 106–118. Philadelphia: Psychology Press/Taylor & Francis.

Loftus, E. F. (2001). Imagining the past. *Psychologist, 14*(11), 584–587.

Loftus, E. F. (2007). Memory distortions: Problems solved and unsolved. In M. Garry, & H. Hayne (Eds.), *Do justice and let the skies fall.* Mahwah, NJ: Erlbaum.

Loftus, E. F., & Cahill, L. (2007). Memory distortion from misattribution to rich false memory. In J. S. Nairne (Ed.), *The foundations of remembering: Essays in honor of Henry L. Roediger, III* (pp. 413–425). New York: Psychology Press.

Loftus, G. R. (2007). Elizabeth F. Loftus: The early years. In M. Garry & H. Hayne (Eds.), *Do justice and let the sky fall: Elizabeth Loftus and her contributions to science, law, and academic freedom* (pp. 27–31). Mahwah, NJ: Erlbaum.

Logothetis, N. K. (2008). What we can do and what we cannot do with fMRI. *Nature, 453,* 869–878. [On-line]. Available: http://www.nature.com/nature/journal/v453/n7197/abs/nature06976.html

London, L. H., Tierney, G., Buhin, L., Greco, D. M., & Cooper, C. J. (2002). Kids' college: Enhancing children's appreciation and acceptance of cultural diversity. *Journal of Prevention & Intervention in the Community, 24*(2), 63–78.

Loo, R., & Thorpe, K. (1998). Attitudes toward women's roles in society. *Sex Roles, 39,* 903–912.

Lopez, F., & Hsu, P-C. (2002). Further validation of a measure of parent-adult attachment style. *Measurement & Evaluation in Counseling & Development, 34,* 223–237.

Lopez, J. C. (2002). Brain repair: A spinal scaffold. *Nature Reviews Neuroscience, 3,* 256.

Lopez, S. R., & Guarnaccia, P. J. J. (2000). Cultural psychopathology: Uncovering the social world of mental illness. *Annual Review of Psychology, 51,* 571–598.

Lorenz, K. Z. (1937). The companion in the bird's world. *Auk, 54,* 245–273.

Lorenz, K. Z. (1981). *The foundations of ethology.* New York: Springer-Verlag.

Lores-Arnaiz, S., Bustamante, J., Czernizyniec, A., Galeano, P., Gervasoni, M. G., Martinez, A. R., Paglia, N., Cores, V., & Lores-Arnaiz, M. R. (2007). Exposure to enriched environments increases brain nitric oxide synthase and improves cognitive performance in prepubertal but not in young rats. *Behavioural Brain Research, 184,* 117–123.

Lott, D. A. (2000). *The new flirting game.* London: Sage.

Loxton, N. J., Nguyen, D., Casey, L., & Dawe, S. (2008). Reward drive, rash impulsivity and punishment sensitivity in problem gamblers. *Personality & Individual Differences, 45,* 167–173.

Lu, L., Kao, S-F., Cooper, C. L., & Spector, P. E. (2000). Managerial stress, locus of control, and job strain in Taiwan and UK: A comparative study. *International Journal of Stress Management, 7*(3), 209–226.

Lu, Z. L., Williamson, S. J., & Kaufman, L. (1992). Behavioral lifetime of human auditory sensory memory predicted by physiological measures. *Science, 258,* 1668–1670.

Lubinski, D., & Benbow, C. P. (2000). States of excellence. *American Psychologist, 55*(1), 137–150.

Lubinski, D., & Dawis, R. V. (1992). Aptitudes, skills, and proficiencies. In M. D. Dunnette & L. M. Hough (Eds.), *The handbook of industrial/organizational psychology* (pp. 1–59). Palo Alto, CA: Consulting Psychologists Press.

Lucio, E., Ampudia, A., Durán, C., León, I., & Butcher, J. N. (2001). Comparison of the Mexican and American norms of the MMPI-2. *Journal of Clinical Psychology, 57,* 1459–1468.

Lucio-Gómez, E., Ampudia-Rueda, A., Durán Patiño, C., Gallegos-Mejía, L., & León Guzmán, I. (1999). La nueva versión del inventario multifásico de la personalidad de Minnesota para adolescentes mexicanos. [The new version of the Minnesota Multiphasic Personality Inventory for Mexican adolescents]. *Revista Mexicana de Psicología, 16*(2), 217–226.

Luecken, L. J., & Lemery, K. S. (2004). Early caregiving and physiological stress responses. *Clinical Psychology Review, 24*(2), 171–191.

Luecken, L. J., Tartaro, J., & Appelhans, B. (2004). Strategic coping responses and attentional biases. *Cognitive Therapy & Research, 28*(1), 23–37.

Luria, A. R. (1968). *The mind of a mnemonist: A little book about a vast memory.* New York: Basic Books.

Luria, A. R. (1976). *Cognitive development: Its cultural and social foundations.* Cambridge, MA: Harvard University Press.

Lutz, A., Greischar, L. L., Rawlings, N. B., Ricard, M., & Davidson, R. J. (2004). Long-term mediators self-induce high-amplitude gamma synchrony during mental practice. *Proceedings of the National Academy of Sciences, 101*(46) 16369–16373.

Lynch, L., & Happell, B. (2008). Implementing clinical supervision: Part 1: Laying the ground work. *International Journal of Mental Health Nursing, 17*, 57–64.

Lynch, P. E. (2003). An interview with Richard C. Pillard, MD. *Journal of Gay & Lesbian Psychotherapy, 7*(4), 63–70.

Lynn, R., & Harvey, J. (2008). The decline of the world's IQ. *Intelligence, 36*, 112–120.

Lynn, S. J. (2007). Hypnosis reconsidered. *American Journal of Clinical Hypnosis, 49*, 195–197.

Lynn, S. J., Vanderhoff, H., Shindler, K., & Stafford, J. (2002). Defining hypnosis as a trance vs. cooperation: Hypnotic inductions, suggestibility, and performance standards. *American Journal of Clinical Hypnosis, 44*(3–4), 231–240.

Lyons-Ruth, K., Holmes, B. M., Sasvari-Szekely, M., Ronai, Z., Nemoda, Z., & Pauls, D. (2007). Serotonin transporter polymorphism and borderline or antisocial traits among low-income young adults. *Psychiatric Genetics, 17*, 339–343.

Lyoo, I. K., Kim, M. J., Stoll, A. L., Demopulos, C. M., Parow, A. M., Dager, S. R., Friedman, S. D., Dunner, D. L., & Renshaw, P. F. (2004). Frontal lobe gray matter density decreases in Bipolar I Disorder. *Biological Psychiatry, 55*(6), 648–651.

Lytle, M. E., Bilt, J. V., Pandav, R. S., Dodge, H. H., & Ganguli, M. (2004). Exercise level and cognitive decline: The MoVIES project. *Alzheimer Disease & Associated Disorders, 18*(2), 57–64.

Lyubimov, N.N. (1992). *Electrophysiological characteristics of sensory processing and mobilization of hidden brain reserves. 2nd Russian-Swedish Symposium New Research in Neurobiology,* Moscow: Russian Academy of Science Institute of Human Brain.

Maas, J. B. (1999). *Power sleep.* New York: HarperPerennial.

Maccoby, E. E. (2000). Parenting and its effects on children: On reading and misreading behavior genetics. *Annual Review of Psychology, 51*, 1–27.

Mackey, R. A., & O'Brien, B. A. (1998). Marital conflict management: Gender and ethnic differences. *Social Work, 43*(2), 128–141.

MacKinnon, D. F., Jamison, K. R., & DePaulo, J. R. (1997). Genetics of manic-depressive illness. *Annual Review of Neuroscience, 10*, 355–373.

MacLaren, V. V. (2001). A qualitative review of the Guilty Knowledge Test. *Journal of Applied Psychology, 86*(4), 674–683.

Macmillan, M. B. (2000). *An odd kind of fame: Stories of Phineas Gage.* Cambridge, MA: MIT Press.

Maddi, S. R. (2004). Hardiness: An operationalization of existential courage. *Journal of Humanistic Psychology, 44*(3), 279–298.

Maddi, S. R., Harvey, R. H., Khoshaba, D. M., Lu, J. L., Persico, M., & Brow, M. (2006). The personality construct of hardiness, III: Relationships with repression, innovativeness, authoritarianism, and performance. *Journal of Personality, 74*, 575–597.

Maehr, M. L., & Urdan, T. C. (2000). *Advances in motivation and achievement: The role of context.* Greewich, CT: JAI Press.

Magura, S., Laudet, A. B., Mahmood, D., Rosenblum, A., Vogel, H. S., & Knight, E. L. (2003). Role of self-help processes in achieving abstinence among dually diagnosed persons. *Addictive Behaviors, 28*(3), 399–413.

Mahoney, C. R., Castellani, J., Kramer, F. M., Young, A., & Lieberman, H. R. (2007). Tyrosine supplementation mitigates working memory decrements during cold exposure. *Physiology & Behavior, 92*, 575–582.

Maisto, S. A., Galizio, M., & Connors, G. J. (2008). *Drug use and abuse* (5th ed.). Belmont: Cengage.

Major, B., & O'Brien, L. T. (2005). The social psychology of stigma. *Annual Review of Psychology, 56*, 393–421.

Major, B., Spencer, S., Schmader, T., Wolfe, C., & Crocker, J. (1998). Coping with negative stereotypes about intellectual performance: The role of psychological disengagement. *Personality & Social Psychology Bulletin, 24*(1), 34–50.

Malti, T. (2007). Moral emotions and aggressive behavior in childhood. In G. Steffgen & M. Gollwitzer (Eds.), *Emotions and aggressive behavior* (pp. 185–200). Ashland, OH: Hogrefe & Huber.

Maner, J. K., DeWall, C. N., & Gailliot, M. T. (2008). Selective attention to signs of success: Social dominance and early stage interpersonal perception. *Personality and Social Psychology Bulletin, 34*, 488–501.

Manly, J. J., Byrd, D., Touradji, P., Sanchez, D., & Stern, Y. (2004). Literacy and cognitive change among ethnically diverse elders. *International Journal of Psychology, 39*(1), 47–60.

Manning, B. (2007). Sex and perceptions of mate value in women: An evolutionary perspective. *Dissertation Abstracts International: Section B: The Sciences and Engineering, 68*(6-B), 4177.

Manning, J. (2007). The use of meridian-based therapy for anxiety and phobias. *Australian Journal of Clinical Hypnotherapy and Hypnosis, 28*, 45–50.

Maquet, P., Peigneux, P., Laureys, S., Boly, M., Dang-Vu, T., Desseilles, M., & Cleeremans, A. (2003). Memory processing during human sleep as assessed functional neuroimaging. *Revue Neurologique, 159*(11), 6S27–6S29.

Marcia, J. E. (2002). Identity and psychosocial development in adulthood. *Identity, 2*(1), 7–28.

Marcus, S.. (2008). *The other Victorians: A study of sexuality and pornography in mid-nineteenth-century England.* Piscataway, NJ: Transaction Publishers.

Mark, L. (2008). Review of the bifurcation of the self: The history and theory of dissociation and its disorders. *American Journal of Clinical Hypnosis, 50*, 281–282.

Markle, A. (2007). Asymmetric disconfirmation in managerial beliefs about employee motivation. *Dissertation Abstracts International Section A: Humanities and Social Sciences, 68*(5-A), 2051.

Markon, K. E., Krueger, R. F., Bouchard, T. J., & Gottesman, I. I. (2002). Normal and abnormal personality traits: Evidence for genetic and environmental relationships in the Minnesota Study of Twins Reared Apart. *Journal of Personality, 70*(5), 661–693.

Markovitz, P. J. (2004). Recent trends in the pharmacotherapy of personality disorders. *Journal of Personality Disorders, 18*(1), 99–101.

Marks, D. F. (1990). Comprehensive commentary, insightful criticism. *Skeptical Inquirer, 14*, 413–418.

Marks, L. D., Hopkins, K. C., Monroe, P. A., Nesteruk, O., & Sasser, D. D. (2008). "Together, we are strong": A qualitative study of happy, enduring African American marriages. *Family Relations, 57*, 172–185.

Markstrom, C. A., & Marshall, S. K. (2007). The psychosocial inventory of ego strengths: Examination of theory and psychometric properties. *Journal of Adolescence, 30*, 63–79.

Markus, H. R., & Kitayama, S. (1998). The cultural psychology of personality. *Journal of Cross-Cultural Psychology, 29*, 63–87.

Markus, H. R., & Kitayama, S. (2003). Culture, self, and the reality of the social. *Psychological Inquiry, 14*(3–4), 277–283.

Marsee, M. A., Weems, C. F., Taylor, L. K. (2008). Exploring the association between aggression and anxiety in youth: A look at aggressive subtypes, gender, and social cognition. *Journal of Child and Family Studies, 17,* 154–168.

Marsh, A.A., Elfenbein, H.A., Ambady, N. (2007). Separated by a common language: Nonverbal accents and cultural stereotypes about Americans and Australians. *Journal of Cross-Cultural Psychology, 38,* 284–301.

Marshall, D. S. (1971). Sexual behavior in Mangaia. In D. S. Marshall & R. C. Suggs (Eds.), *Human sexual behavior* (pp. 103–162). Englewood Cliffs, NJ: Prentice Hall.

Marshall, L., & Born, J. (2007). The contribution of sleep to hippocampus-dependent memory consolidation. *Trends in Cognitive Sciences, 11,* 442–450.

Marshall, M., & Brown, J. D. (2008). On the psychological benefits of self-enhancement. In E. C. Chang (Ed.). *Self-criticism and self-enhancement: Theory, research, and clinical implications* (pp. 19–35). Washington, DC: American Psychological Association.

Martin, C. L., & Fabes, R. (2009). *Discovering child development* (2nd ed.). Belmont, CA: Cengage.

Martin, S. E., Snyder, L. B., Hamilton, M., Fleming- Milici, F., Slater, M. D., Stacy, A., Chen, M., & Grube, J. W. (2002). Alcohol advertising and youth. *Alcoholism: Clinical & Experimental Research, 26*(6), 900–906.

Martineau, J., Cochin, S., Magne, R., & Barthelemy, C. (2008). Impaired cortical activation in autistic children: Is the mirror neuron system involved? *International Journal of Psychophysiology, 68,* 35–40.

Martinelli, E. A. (2006). Paternal role development and acquisition in fathers of pre-term infants: A qualitative study. *Dissertation Abstracts International: Section B: The Sciences and Engineering, 66*(9-B), 5125.

Martins, S. S., Mazzotti, G., & Chilcoat, H. D. (2005). Trends in ecstasy use in the United States from 1995 to 2001: Comparison with marijuana users and association with other drug use. *Experimental and Clinical Psychopharmacology, 13*(3), 244–252.

Maslow, A. H. (1954). *Motivation and personality.* New York: Harper & Row.

Maslow, A. H. (1970). *Motivation and personality (2nd ed.).* New York: Harper & Row.

Maslow, A. H. (1999). *Toward a psychology of being* (3rd ed.). New York: Wiley.

Mason, P. T., & Kreger, R. (1998). *Stop walking on eggshells: Taking your life back when someone you care about has borderline personality disorder.* New York: New Harbinger Publishers.

Massicotte-Marquez, J., Décary, A., Gagnon, J. F., Vendette, M., Mathieu, A., Postuma, R. B., Carrier, J., & Montplaisir, J. (2008).

Executive dysfunction and memory impairment in idiopathic REM sleep behavior disorder. *Neurology, 70,* 1250–1257.

Masten A. S., & Coatsworth, J. D. (1998). The development of competence in favorable and unfavorable environments. *American Psychologist, 53,* 205–220.

Masters, W. H., & Johnson, V. E. (1966). *Human sexual response.* Boston: Little, Brown.

Masters, W. H., & Johnson, V. E. (1961). Orgasm, anatomy of the female. In A. Ellis & A. Abarbonel (Eds.), *Encyclopedia of Sexual Behavior,* Vol. 2. New York: Hawthorn.

Masters, W. H., & Johnson, V. E. (1970). *Human sexual inadequacy.* Boston: Little, Brown.

Mathews, A., & MacLeod, C. (2005). Cognitive vulnerability to emotional disorders. *Annual Review of Clinical Psychology, 1,* 167–195.

Matlin, M. W. (2003). From menarche to menopause: Misconceptions about women's reproductive lives. *Psychology Science, 45*(Suppl2), 106–122.

Matlin, M. W. (2008). *The psychology of women* (6th ed.). Belmont, CA: Cengage.

Matlin, M. W., & Foley, H. J. (1997). *Sensation and perception* (4th ed.). Boston: Allyn and Bacon.

Matsumoto, D. (1992). More evidence for the universality of a contempt expression. *Motivation and Emotion, 16,* 363–368.

Matsumoto, D. (2000). *Culture and psychology: People around the world.* Belmont, CA: Wadsworth.

Matsumoto, D., & Juang, L. (2008). *Culture and psychology* (4th ed.). Belmont, CA: Cengage.

Matsumoto, D., & Kupperbusch, C. (2001). Idiocentric and allocentric differences in emotional expression, experience, and the coherence between expression and experience. *Asian Journal of Social Psychology, 4*(2), 113–131.

Matusov, E., & Hayes, R. (2000). Sociocultural critique of Piaget and Vygotsky. *New Ideas in Psychology, 18*(2–3), 215–239.

Maurer, T. J., Solamon, J. M., & Lippstreu, M. (2008). How does coaching interviewees affect the validity of a structured interview? *Journal of Organizational Behavior, 29,* 355–371.

May, A., Hajak, G., Gänßbauer, S., Steffens, T., Langguth, B., Kleinjung, T., & Eichhammer, P. (2007). Structural brain alterations following 5 days of intervention: Dynamic aspects of neuroplasticity. *Cerebral Cortex,17,* 205–210.

Mayer, J. D., Roberts, R. D., & Barsade, S. G. (2008). Human abilities: Emotional

intelligence. *Annual Review of Psychology, 59,* 507–536.

Mayers, A. G., Baldwin, D. S., Dyson, R., Middleton, R. W., & Mustapha, A. (2003). Use of St John's wort (Hypericum perforatum L) in members of a depression self-help organization: A 12-week open prospective pilot study using the HADS scale. *Primary Care Psychiatry, 9*(1), 15–20.

Maynard, A. E., & Greenfield, P. M. (2003). Implicit cognitive development in cultural tools and children: Lessons from Maya Mexico. *Cognitive Development, 18*(4), 489–510.

Mays, V. M., Cochran, S. D., & Namdi, W. B. (2007). Race, race-based discrimination, and health outcomes among African-Americans. *Annual Review of Psychology, 58,* 201–225.

Mazzoni, G., & Memon, A. (2003). Imagination can create false autobiographical memories. *Psychological Science, 14,* 186–188.

Mazzoni, G., & Vannucci, M. (2007). Hindsight bias, the misinformation effect, and false autobiographical memories. *Social Cognition, 25,* 203–220.

McAllister-Williams, R. H., & Rugg, M. D. (2002). Effects of repeated cortisol administration on brain potential correlates of episodic memory retrieval. *Psychopharmacology, 160*(1), 74–83.

McCabe, C., & Rolls, E. T. (2007). Umami: A delicious flavor formed by convergence of taste and olfactory pathways in the human brain. *European Journal of Neuroscience, 25,* 1855–1864.

McCabe, M. P., & Ricciardelli, L. A. (2003). Body image and strategies to lose weight and increase muscle among boys and girls. *Health Psychology, 22*(1), 39–46.

McCarley, J. S., Kramer, A. F., Colcombe, A. M., & Scialfa, C. T. (2004). Priming of pop-out in visual search: A comparison of young and old adults. *Aging, Neuropsychology, & Cognition, 11*(1), 80–88.

McCartt, A. T., Rohrbaugh, J. W., Hammer, M. C., & Fuller, S. Z. (2000). Factors associated with falling asleep at the wheel among long-distance truck drivers. *Accident Analysis and Prevention, 32*(4), 493–504.

McClelland, D. C. (1958). Risk-taking in children with high and low need for achievement. In J. W. Atkinson (Ed.), *Motives in fantasy, action, and society.* Princeton, NJ: Van Nostrand.

McClelland, D. C. (1987). Characteristics of successful entrepreneurs. *Journal of Creative Behavior, 3,* 219–233.

McClelland, D. C. (1993). Intelligence is not the best predictor of job performance. *Current Directions in Psychological Science, 2*, 5–6.

McClelland, J. L. (1995). Constructive memory and memory distortions: A parallel-distributed processing approach. In D. L. Schachter (Ed.), *Memory distortions: How minds, brains, and societies reconstruct the past* (pp. 69–90). Cambridge: Harvard University Press.

McCrae, R. R. (2004). Human nature and culture: A trait perspective. *Journal of Research in Personality, 38*(1), 3–14.

McCrae, R. R., & Costa, P. T. Jr. (1990). *Personality in adulthood.* New York: Guilford Press.

McCrae, R. R., & Costa, P. T. Jr. (1999). A fivefactor theory of personality. In L. A. Pervin, & O. P. John (Eds.), *Handbook of personality: Theory and research.* New York: Guilford Press.

McCrae, R. R., Costa, P. T. Jr., Hrebícková, M., Urbánek, T., Martin, T. A., Oryol, V. E., Rukavishnikov, A. A., & Senin, I. G. (2004). Age differences in personality traits across cultures: Self-report and observer perspectives. *European Journal of Personality, 18*(2), 143–157.

McCrae, R. R., Costa, P. T. Jr., Martin, T. A., Oryol, V. E., Rukavishnikov, A. A., Senin, I. G., Hrebícková, M., & Urbánek, T. (2004). Consensual validation of personality traits across cultures. *Journal of Research in Personality, 38*(2), 179–201.

McCrae, R. R., Costa, P. T., Jr., Ostendorf, F., Angleitner, A., Hrebickova, M., Avia, M. D., Sanz, J., Sanchez-Bernardos, M. L., Kusdil, M. E., Woodfield, R., Saunders, P. R., & Smith, P. B. (2000). Nature over nurture: Temperament, personality, and life span development. *Journal of Personality and Social Psychology, 78*(1), 173–186.

McCrae, R. R., & Sutin, A. R. (2007). New frontiers for the Five-Factor Model: A preview of the literature. *Social and Personality Psychology Compass, 1*, 423–440.

McDonald, J. W., Liu, X. Z., Qu, Y., Liu, S., Mickey, S. K., Turetsky, D., Gottlieb, D. I., & Choi, D. W. (1999). Transplanted embryonic stem cells survive, differentiate, and promote recovery in injured rat spinal cord. *Nature & Medicine, 5*, 1410–1412.

McDougall, W. (1908). *Social psychology.* New York: Putnam's Sons.

McEvoy, P. M. (2007). Effectiveness of cognitive behavioural group therapy for social phobia in a community clinic: A benchmarking study. *Behaviour Research and Therapy, 45*, 3030–3040.

McFarlane, W. R. (2006). Family expressed emotion prior to onset of psychosis. In S. R. H. Beach, M. Z. Wamboldt, N. J. Kaslow, R. E. Heyman, M. B. First, et al., (Eds), *Relational processes and DSM-V: Neuroscience, assessment, prevention, and treatment* (pp. 77–87). Washington, DC: American Psychiatric Association.

McGaugh, J. L., & Roozendaal, B. (2002). Role of adrenal stress hormones in forming lasting memories in the brain. *Current Opinion in Neurobiology, 12*(2), 205–210.

McGhie, A., & Chapman, H. (1961). Disorders of attention and perception in early schizophrenia. *British Journal of Medical Psychology, 34*, 103–116.

McGrath, P. (2002). Qualitative findings on the experience of end-of-life care for hematological malignancies. *American Journal of Hospice & Palliative Care, 19*(2), 103–111.

McGue, M., Bouchard, T. J., Iacono, W. G., & Lykken, D. T. (1993). Behavioral genetics of cognitive ability: A life-span perspective. In R. Plomin & G. McClearn (Eds.), *Nature, nurture, and psychology.* Washington, DC: American Psychological Association.

McGuinness, T. M., & Schneider, K. (2007). Poverty, child mistreatment, and foster care. *Journal of the American Psychiatric Nurses Association,13*, 296–303.

McGuire, B. E., Hogan, M. J., & Morrison, T. G. (2008). Dimensionality and reliability assessment of the Pain Patient Profile Questionnaire. *European Journal of Psychological Assessment, 24*, 22–26.

McKay, D., Gavigan, C. A., & Kulchycky, S. (2004). Social skills and sex-role functioning in borderline personality disorder: Relationship to self-mutilating behavior. *Cognitive Behaviour Therapy, 33*(1), 27–35.

McKee, P., & Barber, C. E. (2001). Plato's theory of aging. *Journal of Aging & Identity, 6*(2), 93–104.

McKellar, P. (1972). Imagery from the standpoint of introspection. In P. W. Sheehan (Ed.), *The function and nature of imagery.* New York: Academic Press.

McKelvie, S. J., & Drumheller, A. (2001). The availability heuristic with famous names: A replication. *Perceptual & Motor Skills, 92*(2), 507–516.

McKim, W. A. (2002). *Drugs and behavior: An introduction to behavioral pharmacology* (5th ed). Englewood Cliffs, NJ: Prentice Hall.

McKinney, C., Donnelly, R., & Renk, K. (2008). Perceived parenting, positive and negative perceptions of parents, and late adolescent emotional adjustment. *Child and Adolescent Mental Health, 13*, 66–73.

McMahon, J. A. (2002). An explanation for normal and anomalous drawing ability and some implications for research on perception and imagery. *Visual Arts Research, 28*(1,Issue55), 38–52.

McNally, R. J. (2004). The science and folklore of traumatic amnesia. *Clinical Psychology: Science & Practice, 11*(1), 29–33.

McNamara, J. M. (2007). Long-term disadvantage among elderly women: The effects of work history. *Social Service Review, 81*, 423–452.

McNamara, J. M., Barta, Z., Fromhage, L., & Houston, A. I. (2008). The coevolution of choosiness and cooperation. *Nature, 451*, 189–201.

McNamara, P., McLaren, D., & Durso, K. (2007). Representation of the self in REM and NREM dreams. *Dreaming, 17*, 113–126.

McNicholas, W. T., & Javaheri, S. (2007). Pathophysiologic mechanisms of cardiovascular disease in obstructive sleep apnea. *Sleep Medicine Clinics, 2*, 539–547.

McQuown, S. C., Belluzzi, J. D., & Leslie, F. M. (2007). Low dose nicotine treatment during early adolescence increases subsequent cocaine reward. *Neurotoxicology and Teratology, 29*, 66–73.

Medina, J. J. (1996). *The clock of ages: Why we age.* Cambridge, MA: Cambridge University Press.

Medina, K. L., Hanson, K. L., Schweinsburg, A. D., Cohen-Zion, M., Nagel, B. J., & Tapert, S. F. (2007). Neuropsychological functioning in adolescent marijuana users: Subtle deficits detectable after a month of abstinence. *Journal of the International Neuropsychological Society, 13*, 807–820.

Meek, W. (2007, July 26). Side-effect of anti-smoking ads. *PsychCentral.* [On-line]. Available: http://psychcentral.com/blog/archives/2007/07/26/side-effect-of-anti-smoking-ads/.

Meeus, W., & Raaijmakers, Q. (1989). Autoritätsgehorsam in Experimenten des Milgram-Typs: Eine Forschungsübersicht [Obedience to authority in Milgram-type studies: A research review]. *Zeitschrift für Sozialpsychologie, 20*(2), 70–85.

Mehta, P. H., Gosling, S. D. (2006). How can animal studies contribute to research on the biological bases of personality? In T. Canli (Ed.), *Biology of personality and individual differences* (pp. 427–448). NY: Guilford.

Meltzer, G. (2000). Genetics and etiology of schizophrenia and bipolar disorder. *Biological Psychiatry, 47*(3), 171–178.

References

Meltzer, L. (2004). Resilience and learning disabilities: Research on internal and external protective dynamics. *Learning Disabilities Research & Practice,* 19(1), 1–2.

Meltzoff, A. N., & Moore, M. K. (1977). Imitation of facial and manual gestures by human neonates. *Science, 198,* 75–78.

Meltzoff, A. N., & Moore, M. K. (1985). Cognitive foundations and social functions of imitation and intermodal representation in infancy. In J. Mehler & R. Fox (Eds.), *Neonate cognition: Beyond the blooming buzzing confusion.* Hillsdale, NJ: Erlbaum.

Meltzoff, A. N., & Moore, M. K. (1994). Imitation, memory, and the representation of persons. *Infant Behavior and Development, 17,* 83–99.

Melzack, R. (1999). Pain and stress: A new perspective. In R. J. Gatchel & D. C. Turk (Eds.), *Psychosocial factors in pain: Critical perspectives.* New York: Guilford Press.

Melzack, R., & Wall, P. D. (1965). Pain mechanisms: A new theory. *Science, 150,* 971–979.

Mendrek, A., Kiehl, K. A., Smith, A. M., Irwin, D., Forster, B. B., & Liddle, P. F. (2005). Dysfunction of a distributed neural circuitry in schizophrenia patients during a working memory performance. *Psychological Medicine, 35*(2), 187–196.

Menec, V. H. (2003). The relation between everyday activities and successful aging: A 6-year longitudinal study. *Journals of Gerontology B: Psychological Sciences and Social Sciences, 58,* 574–582.

Messinger, L.M. (2001). *Georgia O'Keeffe.* London: Thames & Hudson.

Meston, C. M., & Frohlich, P. F. (2003). Love at first fright: Partner salience moderates roller-coaster-induced excitation transfer. *Archives of Sexual Behavior, 32*(6), 537–544.

Metcalf, P., & Huntington, R. (1991). *Celebrations of death: The anthropology of mortuary ritual* (2nd ed.). Cambridge, England: Cambridge University Press.

Meyer, I. H. (2003). Prejudice, social stress, and mental health in lesbian, gay, and bisexual populations: Conceptual issues and research evidence. *Psychological Bulletin, 129*(5), 674–697.

Meyer, R. G., & Salmon, P. (1988). *Abnormal psychology* (2nd ed.). Boston: Allyn & Bacon.

Meyer, U., Nyffleler, M., Schwendener, S., Knuesel, I., Yee, B. K., & Feldon, J. (2008). Relative prenatal and postnatal maternal contributions to schizophrenia-related neurochemical dysfunction after in utero immune challenge. *Neuropsychopharmacology, 33,* 441–456.

Michael, R., Gagnon, J., Laumann, E., & Kolata, G. (1994). *Sex in America.* Boston: Little, Brown.

Migueles, M, & Garcia-Bajos, E. (1999). Recall, recognition, and confidence patterns in eyewitness testimony. *Applied Cognitive Psychology, 13,* 257–268.

Mikulincer, M., & Goodman, G. S. (Eds.). (2006). *Dynamics of romantic love: Attachment, caregiving, and sex.* New York: Guilford Press.

Miles, D. R., & Carey, G. (1997). Genetic and environmental architecture on human aggression. *Journal of Personality and Social Psychology, 72,* 207–217.

Milgram, S. (1963). Behavioral study of obedience. *Journal of Abnormal and Social Psychology, 67,* 371–378.

Milgram, S. (1974). *Obedience to authority: An experimental view.* New York: Harper & Row.

Miller, B., Wood, B., Balkansky, A., Mercader, J., & Panger, M. (2006). *Anthropology.* Boston, MA: Allyn & Bacon/Longman.

Miller, G. (2004). Brain cells may pay the price for a bad night's sleep. *Science, 306*(5699), 1126.

Miller, G. A. (1956). The magical number seven, plus or minus two: Some limits on our capacity for processing information. *Psychological Review, 63,* 81–97.

Miller, J. G., & Bersoff, D. M. (1998). The role of liking in perceptions of the moral responsibility to help: A cultural perspective. *Journal of Experimental Social Psychology, 34,* 443–469.

Miller, L. (2008). *From difficult to disturbed: Understanding and managing dysfuntional employees.* New York: AMACOM.

Miller, L. K. (2005). What the savant syndrome can tell us about the nature and nurture of talent. *Journal for the Education of the Gifted, 28,* 361–373.

Miller, M., & Kantrowitz, B. (1999, January 25). Unmasking Sybil: A reexamination of the most famous psychiatric patient in history. *Newsweek,* pp. 11–16.

Millner, V. S. (2008). Internet infidelity: A case of intimacy with detachment. *The Family Journal, 16,* 78–82.

Millon, T. (2004). *Masters of the mind: Exploring the story of mental illness from ancient times to the new millennium.* Hoboken, NJ: Wiley.

Mills, G. E. (2008). Transformational leadership and employee retention: An exploratory investigation of the four characteristics. *Dissertation Abstracts International: Section A: Humanities and Social Sciences, 68*(9-A), 3953.

Mills, T. C., Paul, J., Stall, R., Pollack, L., Canchola, J., Chang, Y. J., Moskowitz, J. T., & Catania, J. A. (2004). Distress and depression in men who have sex with men: The urban men's health study. *American Journal of Psychiatry, 161*(2), 278–285.

Miltenberger, R. G. (2008). *Behavior modification: Principles and procedures* (4th ed.). Belmont, CA: Cengage.

Milton, J., & Wiseman, R. (1999). Does psi exist? Lack of replication of an anomalous process of information transfer. *Psychological Bulletin, 125,* 387–391.

Milton, J., & Wiseman, R. (2001). Does psi exist? Reply to Storm and Ertel 2000. *Psychological Bulletin, 127* (3), 434–438.

Mineka, S., & Oehlberg, K. (2008). The relevance of recent developments in classical conditioning to understanding the etiology and maintenance of anxiety disorders. *Acta Psychologica, 127,* 567–580.

Mineka, S., & Oehman, A. (2002). Phobias and preparedness: The selective, automatic, and encapsulated nature of fear. *Biological Psychiatry, 51*(9), 927–937.

Mingo, C., Herman, C. J., & Jasperse, M. (2000). Women's stories: Ethnic variations in women's attitudes and experiences of menopause, hysterectomy, and hormone replacement therapy. *Journal of Women's Health and Gender Based Medicine, 9,* S27-S38.

Mingroni, M. A. (2004). The secular rise in IQ. *Intelligence, 32,* 65–83.

Minuchin, S., Lee, W-Y., & Simon, G. M. (2007). *Mastering family therapy: Journeys of growth and transformation* (2nd ed.). Hoboken, NJ: Wiley.

Minzenberg, M. J., Fan, J., New, A. S., Tang, C. Y., & Siever, L. J. (2008). Frontolimbic structural changes in borderline personality disorder. *Journal of Psychiatric Research, 42,* 727–733.

Minzenberg, M. J., Poole, J. H., & Vinogradov, S. (2008). A neurocognitive model of borderline personality disorder: Effects of childhood sexual abuse and relationship to adult social attachment disturbance. *Development and Psychopathology, 20,* 341–368.

Miracle, T. S., Miracle, A. W., & Baumeister, R. F. (2006). *Human sexuality: Meeting your basic needs* (2nd ed.). Upper Saddle River, NJ: Pearson Education.

Mirescu, C., Peters, J. D., Noiman, L., & Gould, E. (2006). Sleep deprivation inhibits adult neurogenesis in the hippocampus by elevating glucocorticoids. *PNAS Proceedings of the National Academy of Sciences of the United States of America, 103*(50), 19170–19175.

Mischel, W., Shoda, Y., & Ayduk, O. (2008). Introduction to personality: Toward an integrative science of the person (8th ed.). Hoboken, NJ: Wiley.

Mita, T. H., Dermer, M., & Knight, J. (1977). Reversed facial images and the mere-exposure hypothesis. Journal of Personality and Social Psychology, 35(8), 597–601.

Mitchell, E., Sachs, A., & Tu, J. I-Chin (1997, September 29). Teaching feelings 101. Time, p. 62.

Mitchell, J. P., Dodson, C. S., & Schacter, D. L. (2005). fMRI evidence for the role of recollection in suppressing misattribution errors: The illusory truth effect. Journal of Cognitive Neuroscience, 17, 800–810.

Mitchell, R. (2003). Ideological reflections on the DSM-IV-R (or pay no attention to that man behind the curtain, Dorothy!). Child & Youth Care Forum, 32(5), 281–298.

Mitchell, S. A. (2002). Psychodynamics, homosexuality, and the question of pathology. Studies in Gender & Sexuality, 3(1), 3–21.

Mitchell, T. W., Mufson, E. J., Schneider, J. A., Cochran, E. J., Nissanov, J., Han, L., et al. (2002). Parahippocampal tau pathology in healthy aging, mild cognitive impairment, and early Alzhiemer's disease. Annals of Neurology, 51(2), 182–189.

Mittag, O., & Maurischat, C. (2004). Die Cook-Medley Hostility Scale (Ho-Skala) im Vergleich zu den Inhaltsskalen "Zynismus", "Ärger" sowie "Typ A" aus dem MMPI-2: Zur zukünftigen Operationalisierung von Feindseligkeit [A comparison of the Cook-Medley Hostility Scale (Ho-scale) and the content scales "cynicism," "anger," and "type A" out of the MMPI-2: On the future assessment of hostility]. Zeitschrift für Medizinische Psychologie, 13(1), 7–12.

Moffitt, T. E., Caspi, A., Harrington, H., & Milne, B. J. (2002). Males on the life-course-persistent and adolescence-limited antisocial pathways: Follow-up at age 26 years. Development & Psychopathology, 14(1), 179–207.

Moghaddam, F. M. (2008). Subjective justice: From equity theory to relative deprivation theory. In F. M. Moghaddam (Ed.), Multiculturalism and intergroup relations: Psychological implications for democracy in global context (pp. 107–124). Washington, DC: American Psychological Association.

Möbler, H., Rudolph, U., Boison, D., Singer, P., Feldon, J., & Yee, B. K. (2008). Regulation of cognition and symptoms of psychosis: Focus on GABA-sub(A) receptors and glycine transporter 1. Pharmacology, Biochemistry & Behavior, 90, 58–64.

Mohr, G., & Wolfram, H-J. (2008). Leadership and leadership effectiveness in the context of gender: The role of leaders' verbal behavior. British Journal of Management, 19, 4–16.

Monastra, V. J. (2008). Electroencephalographic biofeedback in the treatment of ADHD. In V. J. Monastra (Ed.), Unlocking the potential of patients with ADHD: A model for clinical practice. Washington, DC: APA.

Moneta, G. B., & Siu, C. M. Y. (2002). Trait intrinsic and extrinsic motivations, academic performance, and creativity in Hong Kong college students. Journal of College Student Development, 43(5), 664–683.

Money, J. (1985). Sexual reformation and counter-reformation in law and medicine. Medicine and Law, 4, 479–488.

Money, J., & Ehrhardt, A. A. (1972). Man and woman, boy and girl. Baltimore: The Johns Hopkins University Press.

Money, J., Prakasam, K. S., & Joshi, V. N. (1991). Semen-conservation doctrine from ancient Ayurvedic to modern sexological theory. American Journal of Psychotherapy, 45, 9–13.

Mong, J. A., & Pfaff, D. W. (2003). Hormonal and genetic influences underlying arousal as it drives sex and aggression in animal and human brains. Neurobiology of Aging, 24(Suppl1), S83-S88.

Monin, B. (2003). The warm glow heuristic: When liking leads to familiarity. Journal of Personality and Social Psychology, 85(6), 1035–1048.

Monks, C. P., Ortega-Ruiz, R., & Rodríguez-Hidalgo, A. J. (2008). Peer victimization in multicultural schools in Spain and England. European Journal of Developmental Psychology, 5, 507–535.

Monteleone, P., Martiadis, V., Fabrazzo, M., Serritella, C., & Maj, M. (2003). Ghrelin and leptin responses to food ingestion in bulimia nervosa: Implications for binge-eating and compensatory behaviours. Psychological Medicine, 33(8), 1387–1394.

Montgomery, S. A. (2008). The under-recognized role of dopamine in the treatment of major depressive disorder. International Clinical Psychopharmacology, 23, 63–69.

Montgomery, G. H., Weltz, C. R., Seltz, M., & Bovbjerg, D. H. (2002). Brief presurgery hypnosis reduces distress and pain in excisional breast biopsy patients. International Journal of Clinical & Experimental Hypnosis, 50(1), 17–32.

Montpetit, M. A., & Bergeman, C. S. (2007). Dimensions of control: Mediational analyses of the stress-health relationship. Personality and Individual Differences, 43, 2237–2248.

Montuori, A., & Fahim, U. (2004). Cross-cultural encounter as an opportunity for personal growth. Journal of Humanistic Psychology. 44(2), 243–265.

Moons, W. G., & Mackie, D. M. (2007). Thinking straight while seeing red: The influence of anger on information processing. Personality and Social Psychology Bulletin, 33, 706–720.

Moore, E. M. (2008). The impact of leadership style on organizational effectiveness: Leadership in action within United Way of America. Dissertation Abstracts International Section A: Humanities and Social Sciences, 68(9-A), 3953.

Moore, M. M. (1998). The science of sexual signaling. In G. C. Brannigan, E. R. Allgeier, & A. R. Allgeier (Eds.), The sex scientists (pp. 61–75). New York: Longman.

Moore, S., Grunberg, L., & Greenberg, E. (2004). Repeated downsizing contact: The effects of similar and dissimilar layoff experiences on work and well-being outcomes. Journal of Occupational Health Psychology, 9(3), 247–257.

Morgan, C. D., & Murray, H. A. (1935). A method of investigating fantasies. The Thematic Apperception Test. Archives of Neurology and Psychiatry, 34, 289–306.

Morgan, M. J., McFie, L., Fleetwood, L. H., & Robinson, J. A. (2002). Ecstasy (MDMA): Are the psychological problems associated with its use reversed by prolonged abstinence? Psychopharmacology, 159(3), 294–303.

Morgenthaler, T. I., Lee-Chiong, T., Alessi, C., Friedman, L., Aurora, R. N., Boehlecke, B., Brown, T., Chesson Jr., A. L., Kapur, V., Maganti, R., Owens, J., Pancer, J., Swick, T. J., Zak, R., & Standards of Practice Committee of the AASM. (2007). Practice parameters for the clinical evaluation and treatment of circadian rhythm sleep disorders: An American academy of sleep medicine report. Sleep: Journal of Sleep and Sleep Disorders Research, 30, 1445–1459.

Morris, J. S., Frith, C. D., Perrett, D. L., Rowland, D., Young, A. W., Calder, A. J., & Dolan, R. J. (1996). A differential neural response in the human amygdala to fearful and happy expressions. Nature, 383, 812–815.

Morris, S. G. (2007). Influences on childrens' narrative coherence: Age, memory breadth, and verbal comprehension. Dissertation Abstracts International: Section B: The Sciences and Engineering, 68(6-B), 4157.

References

Morrison, C., & Westman, A. S. (2001). Women report being more likely than men to model their relationships after what they have seen on TV. *Psychological Reports, 89*(2), 252–254.

Morrison, M. F., & Tweedy, K. (2000). Effects of estrogen on mood and cognition in aging women. *Psychiatric Annals, 30*(2), 113–119.

Morry, M. M. (2005). Relationship satisfaction as a predictor of similarity ratings: A test of the attraction-similarity hypothesis. *Journal of Social and Personal Relationships, 22,* 561–584.

Mortimer, J. A., Snowdon, D. A., & Markesbery, W. R. (2007). Brain reserve and risk of dementia: Findings from the nun study. In Y. Stern (Ed.), *Cognitive reserve: Theory and applications* (pp. 237–249). Philadelphia, PA: Taylor & Francis.

Moss, D. (2004). Biofeedback. *Applied Psychophysiology & Biofeedback, 29*(1), 75–78.

Mueller, C. M., & Dweck, C. S. (1998). Praise for intelligence can undermine children's motivation and performance. *Journal of Personality and Social Psychology, 75,* 33–52.

Mueser, K. T., & Jeste, D. V. (Eds.). (2008). *Clinical handbook of schizophrenia.* New York: Guildford Press.

Mui, A. C. (1992). Caregiver strain among Black and White daughter caregivers: A role theory perspective. *The Gerontologist, 32,* 203–212.

Mulckhuyse, M., van Zoest, W., & Theeuwes, J. (2008). Capture of the eyes by relevant and irrelevant onsets. *Experimental Brain Research, 186,* 225–235.

Munro, I., & Edward, K-L. (2008). Mental illness and substance use: An Australian perspective. *International Journal of Mental Health Nursing, 17,* 255–260.

Munsey, C. (2008). DOD allocates $25 million to study PTSD: A randomized, controlled trial will test two behavioral treatments. *Monitor on Psychology,* pp. 16–17.

Murakami, K., & Hayashi, T. (2002). Interaction between mind-heart and gene. *Journal of International Society of Life Information Science, 20*(1), 122–126.

Muris, P., Merckelbach, H., Gadet, B., & Moulaert, V. (2000). Fears, worries, and scary dreams in 4- to 12-year-old children: Their content, developmental pattern, and origins. *Journal of Clinical Child Psychology, 29*(1), 43–52.

Murphy, L. L. (2006). Endocannabinoids and endocrine function. In E. S. Onaivi, T. Sugiura, & V. Di Marzo (Eds.), *Endocannabinoids:* *The brain and body's marijuana and beyond* (pp. 467–474). Boca Raton, FL: CRC Press.

Murray, A. (2009). *Suicide in the Middle Ages: The violent against themselves* (Vol. 1). New York: Oxford University Press.

Murray, H. A. (1938). *Explorations in personality.* New York: Oxford University Press.

Myers, L. B., & Vetere, A. (2002). Adult romantic attachment styles and health-related measures. *Psychology, Health & Medicine, 7*(2), 175–180.

Myerson, J., Rank, M. R., Raines, F. Q., & Schnitzler, M. A. (1998). Race and general cognitive ability: The myth of diminishing returns to education. *Psychological Science, 9,* 139–142.

Nabi, R.L., Moyer-Gusé, E., & Byrne, S. (2007). All joking aside: A serious investigation into the persuasive effect of funny social issue messages. *Communication Monographs, 74,* 29–54.

Naglieri, J. A., & Ronning, M. E. (2000). Comparison of White, African American, Hispanic, and Asian children on the Naglieri Nonverbal Ability Test. *Psychological Assessment, 12*(3), 328–334.

Nahas, G. G., Frick, H. C., Lattimer, J. K., Latour, C., & Harvey, D. (2002). Pharmacokinetics of THC in brain and testis, male gametotoxicity and premature apoptosis of spermatozoa. *Human Psychopharmacology: Clinical & Experimental., 17*(2), 103–113.

Naish, P. L. N. (2006). Time to explain the nature of hypnosis? *Contemporary Hypnosis, 23,* 33–46.

Nakajima, S., & Masaki, T. (2004). Taste aversion learning induced forced swimming in rats. *Physiology & Behavior, 80*(5), 623–628.

Nakamura, K. (2006). The history of psychotherapy in Japan. *International Medical Journal, 13,* 13–18.

Nash, M., & Barnier, A. (Eds.). (2008). *The Oxford handbook of hypnosis.* New York: Oxford University Press.

Näslund, E., & Hellström, P. M. (2007). Appetite signaling: From gut peptides and enteric nerves to brain. *Physiology & Behavior, 92,* 256–262.

Nathan, R., Rollinson, L., Harvey, K., & Hill, J. (2003). The Liverpool violence assessment: An investigator-based measure of serious violence. *Criminal Behaviour & Mental Health, 13*(2), 106–120.

National Center for Health Statistics. (2004). *New report examines Americans' health behaviors.* [On-line]. Available: http://gov/nchs/pressroom/04facts/healthbehaviors.htm.

National Institute of Mental Health (NIMH). (2001). *Facts about anxiety disorders.* [On-line]. Available: http://www.nimh.nih.gov/publicat/adfacts.cfm.

National Institute of Mental Health (NIMH). (2008). *Anxiety disorders.* [On-Line]. Available: http://www.nimh.nih.gov/health/publications/anxiety-disorders/summary.shtml

National Institute of Mental Health (NIMH). (2008). *When unwanted thoughts take over: Obsessive-compulsive disorder.* [On-Line]. Available: http://www.nimh.nih.gov/health/publications/when-unwanted-thoughts-take-over-obsessive-compulsive-disorder/complete-publication.shtml

National Institute on Drug Abuse (NIDA). (2005). *NIDA infofacts: Club drugs.* [On-line]. Available: http://www.nida.nih.gov/infofacts/clubdrugs.html.

National Organization on Fetal Alcohol Syndrome. (2006). *What are the statistics and facts about FAS and FASD?* (November 3, 2006). [On-line]. Available: http://www.nofas.org/faqs.aspx?id512.

National Organization on Fetal Alcohol Syndrome. (2008). *Facts about FAS and FASD.* [On-line]. Available: http://www.nofas.org/family/facts.aspx

National Research Council. (2003). *The polygraph and lie detection.* [On-line]. Available: http://fermat.nap.edu/catalog/10420.html.

National Sleep Foundation. (2007). *Myths and facts about sleep.* [On-line]. Available: http://www.sleepfoundation.org/site/c.huIXKjM0IxF/b.2419251/k.2773/Myths__and_Facts__About_Sleep.

Nauta, M. M. (2007). Career interests, self-efficacy, and personality as antecedents of career exploration. *Journal of Career Assessment, 15,* 162–180.

Navarro, M. (2008). Who are we? New dialogue on mixed race. *New York Times.* [On-line]. Available: http://www.nytimes.com/2008/03/31/us/politics/31race.html.

Naveh-Benjamin, M., Kilb, A., & Fisher, T. (2006). Concurrent task effects on memory encoding and retrieval: Further support for an asymmetry. *Memory & Cognition, 34,* 90–101.

Navickas, T. (2006). A study of Chief Learning Officer's (CLO) role and best practices for the optimal leveraging of human capital in creating fundamental organizational change during times of constant and continuous change. *Dissertation Abstracts International Section A: Humanities and Social Sciences, 66*(7-A), 2640.

Nayda, R. (2002). Influences on registered nurses' decision-making in cases of suspected child abuse. *Child Abuse Review, 11*(3), 168–178.

Neale, J. M., Oltmanns, T. F., & Winters, K. C. (1983). Recent developments in the assessment and conceptualization of schizophrenia. *Behavioral Assessment, 5,* 33–54.

Neenan, M. (2008). Tackling procrastination: An REBT perspective for coaches. *Journal of Rational-Emotive & Cognitive Behavior Therapy, 26,* 53–62.

Neher, A. (1991). Maslow's theory of motivation: A critique. *Journal of Humanistic Psychology, 31,* 89–112.

Neisser, U. (1967). *Cognitive psychology.* New York: Appleton-Century-Crofts.

Neisser, U. (1998). Introduction: Rising test scores and what they mean. In U. Neisser (Ed.), *The rising curve: Long-term gains in IQ and related measures.* Washington, DC: American Psychological Association.

Nelson III, C. A., Zeanah, C. H., & Fox, N. A. (2007). The effects of early deprivation on brain-behavioral development: The Bucharest Early Intervention Project. In D. Romer & E. F. Walker (Eds.), *Adolescent psychopathology and the developing brain: Integrating brain and prevention science* (pp. 197–215). New York: Oxford University Press.

Nelson, G., Chandrashekar, J., Hoon, M. A., Feng, L., Zhao, G., Ryba, N.J.P., & Zuker, C.S. (2002). An amino-acid taste receptor. *Nature, 416,* 199–202.

Nelson, R. J., & Chiavegatto, S. (2001). Molecular basis of aggression. *Trends in Neurosciences, 24*(12), 713–719.

Neria, Y., Bromet, E. J., Sievers, S., Lavelle, J., & Fochtmann, L. J. (2002). Trauma exposure and posttraumatic stress disorder in psychosis: Findings from a first-admission cohort. *Journal of Consulting & Clinical Psychology, 70*(1), 246–251.

Nesse, R. M. (2000). Is depression an adaptation? *Archives of General Psychiatry, 57,* 14–20.

Nesse, R. M., & Jackson, E. D. (2006). Evolution: Psychiatric nosology's missing biological foundation. *Clinical Neuropsychiatry: Journal of Treatment Evaluation, 3,* 121–131.

Neto, F., & Furnham, A. (2005). Gender-role portrayals in children's television advertisements. *International Journal of Adolescence & Youth, 12*(1–2), 69–90.

Neubauer, A. C., Grabner, R. H., Freudenthaler, H. H., Beckmann, J. F., & Guthke, J. (2004). Intelligence and individual differences in becoming neurally efficient. *Acta Psychologica, 116*(1), 55–74.

Neugarten, B. L., Havighurst, R. J., & Tobin, S. S. (1968). The measurement of life satisfaction. *Journal of Gerontology,16,* 134–143.

Neumann, K., Preibisch, C., Euler, H. A., von Gudenberg, A. W., Lanfermann, H., Gall, V., & Giraud, A-L. (2005). Cortical plasticity associated with stuttering therapy. *Journal of Fluency Disorders, 30*(1), 23–39.

Neumark-Sztainer, D., Wall, M. M., Story, M., & Perry, C. L. (2003). Correlates of unhealthy weight-control behaviors among adolescents: Implications for prevention programs. *Health Psychology, 22*(1), 88–98.

Neuringer, A., Deiss, C., & Olson, G. (2000). Reinforced variability and operant learning. *Journal of Experimental Psychology: Animal Behavior Processes, 26*(1), 98–111.

Newman, C. L., & Motto, R. L. (2007). The effects of aerobic exercise on childhood PTSD, anxiety, and depression. *International Journal of Emergency Mental Health, 9,* 133–158.

Newman, L. S., Duff, K., & Baumeister, R. (1997). A new look at defensive projection: Thought suppression, accessibility, and biased person perception. *Journal of Personality and Social Psychology, 72,* 980–1001.

Ng, S. M., Li, A. M., Lou, V. W. Q., Tso, I. F., Wan, P. Y. P., & Chan, D. F. Y. (2008). Incorporating family therapy into asthma group intervention: A randomized waitlist-controlled trial. *Family Process, 47,* 115–130.

Ngo, H-Y., Lau, C-M, & Foley, S. (2008). Strategic human resource management, firm performance, and employee relations climate in China. *Human Resource Management, 47,* 73–90.

NIAAA (National Institute on Alcohol Abuse and Alcoholism). (2007). Binge drinking. [On-line]. Available: http://pubs.niaaa.nih.gov/publications/AA73/AA73.htm

Niaura, R., Todaro, J.F., Stroud, L., Spiro, A., Ward, K.D., & Weiss, S. (2002). Hostility, the metabolic syndrome, and incident cornary heart disease. *Health Psychology, 21* (6), 598–593.

Nicholson, A., Pikhart, H., Pajak, A., Malyutina, S., Kubinova, R., Peasey, A., Topor-Madry, R., Nikitin, Y., Capkova, N., Marmot, M., & Bobak, M. Socioeconomic status over the life-course and depressive symptoms in men and women in Eastern Europe. *Journal of Affective Disorders, 105,* 125–136.

Nickerson, R. (1998). Confirmation bias: A ubiquitous phenomenon in many guises. *Review of General Psychology, 2,* 175–220.

Nickerson, R. S., & Adams, M. J. (1979). Longterm memory for a common object. *Cognitive Psychology, 11,* 287–307.

Nicotra, A., Critchley, H. D., Mathias, C. J., & Dolan, R. J. (2006). Emotional and autonomic consequences of spinal cord injury explored using functional brain imaging. *Brain: A Journal of Neurology, 129,* 718–728.

Nishimoto, R. (1988). A cross-cultural analysis of psychiatric symptom expression using Langer's twenty-two item index. *Journal of Sociology and Social Welfare, 15,* 45–62.

Noble, E. P. (2000). Addiction and its reward process through polymorphisms of the D_2 dopamine receptor gene: A review. *European Psychiatry, 15*(2), 79–89.

Noël, M., Désert, M., Aubrun, A., & Seron, X. (2001). Involvement of short-term memory in complex mental calculation. *Memory & Cognition, 29*(1), 34–42.

Nogueiras, R., & Tschöp, M. (2005). Separation of conjoined hormones yields appetite rivals. *Science, 310,* 985–986.

Nolen-Hoeksema, S., Larson, J., & Grayson, C. (2000). Explaining the gender difference in depressive symptoms. *Journal of Personality and Social Psychology, 77,* 1061–1072.

Nordhus, I. H., & Pallesen, S. (2003). Psychological treatment of late-life anxiety: An empirical review. *Journal of Consulting & Clinical Psychology, 71*(4), 643–651.

Norenzayan, A., & Nisbett, R. E. (2000). Culture and causal cognition. *Current Directions in Psychological Science, 9*(4), 132–135.

Norenzayan, A. (2006). Cultural variation in reasoning. In R. Viale, D. Andler, & L. Hirschfeld (Eds.), *Biological and cultural bases of human inference.* Mahwah, NJ: Erlbaum.

Norris, F. (2008, April, 25). Where the fingers are pointing. *New York Times.* [On-line]. Available: http://www.nytimes.com/2008/04/25/business/25norris.html.

Nouchi, R., & Hyodo, M. (2007). The congruence between the emotional valences of recalled episodes and mood states influences the mood congruence effect. *Japanese Journal of Psychology, 78,* 25–32.

Núñez, J. P., & de Vicente, F. (2004). Unconscious learning. Conditioning to subliminal visual stimuli. *Spanish Journal of Psychology, 7*(1), 13–28.

Oakes, M. A., & Hyman, I. E., Jr. (2001). The role of the self in false memory creation. *Journal of Aggression, Maltreatment & Trauma, 4*(2), 87–103.

O'Connell, K. L. (2008). What can we learn? Adult outcomes in children of seriously mentally ill mothers. *Journal of Child and Adolescent Psychiatric Nursing, 21,* 89–104.

O'Connor, D. B., Archer, J., Hair, W. M., Wu, F. C. W. (2002). Exogenous testosterone, aggression, and mood in eugonadal and hypogonadal men. *Physiology & Behavior, 75*(4), 557–566.

Oei, T. P. S., & Dingle, G. (2008). The effectiveness of group cognitive behaviour therapy for unipolar depressive disorders. *Journal of Affective Disorders, 107,* 5–21.

Oeztuerk, L., Tufan, Y., & Gueler, F. (2002). Self-reported traffic accidents and sleepiness in a professional group of Turkish drivers. *Sleep & Hypnosis, 4*(3), 106–110.

O'Farrell, T. J., Murphy, M., Alter, J., & Fals-Stewart, W. (2008). Brief family treatment intervention to promote continuing care among alcohol-dependent patients in inpatient detoxification: A randomized pilot study. *Journal of Substance Abuse Treatment, 34,* 363–369.

Ogilvie, R. D., Wilkinson, R. T., & Allison, S. (1989). The detection of sleep onset: Behavioral, physiological, and subjective convergence. *Sleep, 12*(5), 458–474.

O'Hara, S. (2005). *Real people. Real jobs. Real rewards, What can you do with a major in psychology?* Hoboken, NJ: Wiley.

Ohayon, M. M., & Schatzberg, A. F. (2002). Prevalence of depressive episodes with psychotic features in the general population. *American Journal of Psychiatry, 159*(11), 1855–1861.

Oishi, K., Ohkura, N., Sei, H., Matsuda, J., & Ishida, N. (2007). CLOCK regulates the circadian rhythm of kaolin-induced writhing behavior in mice. *Neuroreport: For Rapid Communication of Neuroscience Research, 18,* 1925–1928.

Oken, B. S. (2008). Placebo effects: Clinical aspects and neurobiology. *Brain: A Journal of Neuroscience.* [On-line]. Available: http://brain.oxfordjournals.org/cgi/content/abstract/awn116v1

Oldehinkel, A., J., Veenstra, R., Ormel, J., de Winter, A. F., & Verhulst, F. C. (2006). Temperament, parenting, and depressive symptoms in a population sample of preadolescents. *Journal of Child Psychology and Psychiatry, 47,* 684–695.

Olds, J., & Milner, P. M. (1954). Positive reinforcement produced by electrical stimulation of septal area and other regions of rat brains. *Journal of Comparative and Physiological Psychology, 47,* 419–427.

Olfson, M., Marcus, S., Pincus, H. A., Zito, J. M., Thompson, J. W., & Zarin, D. A. (1998). Antidepressant prescribing practices of outpatient psychiatrists. *Archives of General Psychiatry, 55,* 310, 316.

Oliver, R. J. (2002). Tobacco abuse in pregnancy. *Journal of Prenatal Psychology & Health, 17*(2), 153–166.

Olson, R. K. (2004). SSSR, environment, and genes. *Scientific Studies of Reading, 8*(2), 111–124.

O'Neil, D. P. (2007). Predicting leader effectiveness: Personality traits and character strengths. *Dissertation Abstracts International: Section B: The Sciences and Engineering, 68*(6-B), 4178.

Oppenheimer, D. M. (2004). Spontaneous discounting of availability in frequency judgment tasks. *Psychological Science, 15*(2), 100–105.

Orne, M. T. (2006). The nature of hypnosis. artifact and essence: An experimental study. *Dissertation Abstracts International: Section B: The Sciences and Engineering, 67*(2-B), 1207.

Orth-Gomér, K. (2007). Job strain and risk of recurrent coronary events. *Journal of the American Medical Association, 298,* 1693–1694.

Ortiz, F. A., Church, A. T., Vargas-Flores, J. D. J., Ibáñez-Reyes, J., Flores-Galaz, M., Luit-Briceño, J. I., &Escamilla, J. M. (2007). Are indigenous personality dimensions culture-specific? Mexican inventories and the Five-Factor Model. *Journal of Research in Personality, 41,* 618–649.

Orubuloye, I., Caldwell, J., & Caldwell, P. (1997). Perceived male sexual needs and male sexual behavior in southwest Nigeria. *Social Science and Medicine, 44,* 1195–1207.

Oshima, K. (2000). Ethnic jokes and social function in Hawaii. *Humor: International Journal of Humor Research, 13*(1), 41–57.

Osler, M., McGue, M., Lund, R., & Christensen, K. (2008). Marital status and twins' health and behavior: An analysis of middle-aged Danish twins. *Psychosomatic Medicine, 70,* 482–487.

Ostrov, J. M., & Keating, C. F. (2004). Gender differences in preschool aggression during free play and structured interactions: An observational study. *Social Development, 13*(2), 255–277.

O'Sullivan, M. (2003). The fundamental attribution error in detecting deception: The boy-who-cried-wolf effect. *Personality & Social Psychology Bulletin, 29*(10), 1316–1327.

Overmier, J. B., & Murison, R. (2000). Anxiety and helplessness in the face of stress predisposes, precipitates, and sustains gastric ulceration. *Behavioural Brain Research, 110*(1–2), 161–174.

Owens, M. J. (2004). Selectivity of antidepressants: From the monoamine hypothesis of depression to the SSRI revolution and beyond. *Journal of Clinical Psychiatry, 65,* 5–10.

Ozawa-de Silva, C. (2007). Demystifying Japanese therapy: An analysis of Naikan and the Ajase complex through Buddhist thought. *Ethos, 35,* 411–446.

Ozinga, J. A. (2000). *Altruism.* New York: Praeger.

Paice, E., Rutter, H., Wetherell, M., Winder, B., & McManus, I. C. (2002). Stressful incidents, stress and coping strategies in the pre-registration house officer year. *Medical Education, 36*(1), 56–65.

Palfai, T. P., Monti, P. M., Ostafin, B., & Hutchinson, K. (2000). Effects of nicotine deprivation on alcohol-related information processing and drinking behavior. *Journal of Abnormal Psychology, 109,* 96–105.

Palma, A. C. (2008). An analysis of leadership styles of school principals of end-of-grade test scores in the third and fifth grades in rural and urban elementary schools in North Carolina. *Dissertation Abstracts International: Section A: Humanities and Social Sciences, 68*(10-A), 4207.

Palmer, J. K., & Loveland, J. M. (2008). The influence of group discussion on performance judgments: Rating accuracy, contrast effects, and halo. *Journal of Psychology: Interdisciplinary and Applied, 142,* 117–130.

Palmer, S., & Ellis, A. (1995). Stress counseling and stress management: The rational emotive behavior approach. Dr. Stephen Palmer interviews Dr. Albert Ellis. *The Rational Emotive Behaviour Therapist, 3,* 82–86.

Palmer, S., & Gyllensten, K. (2008). How cognitive behavioural, rational emotive behavioural or multimodal coaching could prevent mental health problems, enhance performance, and reduce work related stress. *Journal of Rational-Emotive & Cognitive Behavior Therapy, 26,* 38–52.

Panksepp, J. (2005). Affective consciousness: Core emotional feelings in animals and humans. *Consciousness & Cognition: An International Journal, 14*(1), 30–80.

Papadelis, C, Chen, Z., Kourtidou-Papadeli, C., Bamidis, P. D, Chouvarda, I., Bekiaris, E., & Maglaveras, N. (2007). Monitoring sleepiness with on-board electrophysiological recordings for preventing sleep-deprived traffic accidents. *Clinical Neurophysiology, 118,* 1906–1922.

Pappas, N. T., McKenry, P. C., & Catlett, B. S. (2004). Athlete aggression on the rink and off the ice: Athlete violence and aggression in hockey and interpersonal relationships. *Men & Masculinities, 6*(3), 291–312.

Paquet, F., Soucy, J. P., Stip, E., Lévesque, M., Elie, A., & Bédard, M. A. (2004). Comparison between olanzapine and haloperidol on procedural learning and the relationship with striatal D-sub-2 receptor occupancy in schizophrenia. *Journal of Neuropsychiatry & Clinical Neurosciences, 16*(1), 47–56.

Paquier, P. F., & Mariën, P. (2005). A synthesis of the role of the cerebellum in cognition. *Aphasiology, 19*(1), 3–19.

Paris, J. (2000). Childhood precursors of personality disorder. *Psychiatric Clinics of North America, 23,* 77–88.

Paris, J. (2004). Half in love with easeful death: The meaning of chronic suicidality in borderline personality disorder. *Harvard Review of Psychiatry, 12*(1), 42–48.

Parker, G. B., & Brotchie, H. L. (2004). From diathesis to dimorphism: The biology of gender differences in depression. *Journal of Nervous & Mental Disease, 192*(3), 210–216.

Parker-Oliver, D. (2002). Redefining hope for the terminally ill. *American Journal of Hospice & Palliative Care, 19*(2), 115–120.

Parkes, C. M. (1972). *Bereavement: Studies of grief in adult life.* New York: International Universities Press.

Parkes, C. M. (1991). Attachment, bonding, and psychiatric problems after bereavement in adult life. In C. M. Parkes, J. Stevenson-Hinde, & P. Marris (Eds.), *Attachment across the life cycle.* London: Tavistock/Routledge.

Parmar, P., Ibrahim, M., & Rohner, R. P. (2008). Relations among perceived spouse acceptance, remembered parental acceptance in childhood, and psychological adjustment among married adults in Kuwait. *Cross-Cultural Research: The Journal of Comparative Social Science, 42,* 67–76.

Parrott, A., Morinan, A., Moss, M., & Scholey, A. (2004). *Understanding drugs and behavior.* Hoboken, NJ: Wiley.

Pascual, A., & Guéguen, N. (2005). Foot-in-the-door and door-in-the-face: A comparative meta-analytic study. *Psychological Reports, 96,* 122–128.

Passino, K. M., Seeley, T. D., & Visscher, P. K. (2008). Swarm recognition in honey bees. *Behavioral Ecology and Sociobiology, 62,* 401–414.

Pasternak, T., & Greenlee, M. W. (2005). Working memory in primate sensory systems. *Nature Reviews Neuroscience, 6*(2), 97–107.

Patterson, F., & Linden, E. (1981). *The education of Koko.* New York: Holt, Rinehart and Winston.

Patterson, J. M., Holm, K. E., & Gurney, J. G. (2004). The impact of childhood cancer on the family: A qualitative analysis of strains, resources, and coping behaviors. *Psycho-Oncology, 13*(6), 390–407.

Patterson, P. (2002). *Penny's journal: Koko wants to have a baby.* [On-line]. Available: http://www.koko.org/world/journal.phtml?offset58.

Patterson, T. G., & Joseph, S. (2007). Person-centered personality theory: Support from self determination theory and positive psychology. *Journal of Humanistic Psychology, 47,* 117–139.

Paul, D. B., & Blumenthal, A. L. (1989). On the trail of little Albert. *The Psychological Record, 39,* 547–553.

Pearce, A., & Scanlon, M. (2002, July/August). Through a lens darkly. *Psychology Today,* p. 69.

Pearlman, C. (2002). Electroconvulsive therapy in clinical psychopharmacology. *Journal of Clinical Psychopharmacology, 22*(4), 345–346.

Pearson, N. J., Johnson, I. M., & Nahin, R. L. (2006). Insomnia, trouble sleeping, and complementary and alternative medicine: Analysis of the 2002 National Health Interview Survey data. *Archives of Internal Medicine, 166,* 1775–1782.

Pedrazzoli, M., Pontes, J. C., Peirano, P., & Tufik, S. (2007). HLA-DQB1 genotyping in a family with narcolepsy-cataplexy. *Brain Research, 1165,* 1–4.

Peleg, G., Katzir, G., Peleg, O., Kamara, M., Brodsky, L., Hel-Or, H., et al. (2006). Hereditary family signature of facial expression. *Proceedings of the National Academy of Sciences, 103,* 15921–15926.

Pellegrino, J. E., & Pellegrino, L. (2008). Fetal alcohol syndrome and related disorders. In P. J. Accardo (Ed.), *Capute and Accardo's neurodevelopmental disabilities in infancy and childhood: Vol 1: Neurodevelopmental diagnosis and treatment* (3rd ed.) (pp. 269–284). Baltimore, MD: Paul H Brookes.

Pelletier, J. G., & Paré, D. (2004). Role of amygdale oscillations in the consolidation of emotional memories. *Biological Psychiatry, 55*(6), 559–562.

Penfield, W. (1947). Some observations in the cerebral cortex of man. *Proceedings of the Royal Society, 134,* 349.

Penzien, D. B., Rains, J., C., & Andrasik, F. (2002). Behavioral management of recurrent headache: Three decades of experience and empiricism. *Applied Psychophysiology & Biofeedback, 27*(2), 163–181.

Peppard, P. E., Young, T., Palta, M., & Skatrud, J. (2000). Prospective study of the association between sleep-disordered breathing and hypertension. *New England Journal of Medicine, 342*(19), 1378–1384.

Peretti, P. O., & Abplanalp, R. R. Jr. (2004). Chemistry in the college dating process: Structure and function. *Social Behavior & Personality, 32*(2), 147–154.

Pérez-Mata, N., & Diges, M. (2007). False recollections and the congruence of suggested information. *Memory, 15,* 701–717.

Perry, C., Orne, M. T., London, R. W., & Orne, E. C. (1996). Rethinking per se exclusions of hypnotically elicited recall as legal testimony. *International Journal of Clinical & Experimental Hypnosis, 44*(1), 66–81.

Persson, J., Lind, J., Larsson, A., Ingvar, M., Sleegers, K., Van Broeckhoven, C., Adolfsson, R., Nilsson, L-G., & Nyberg, L. (2008). Altered deactivation in individuals with genetic risk for Alzheimer's disease. *Neuropsychologia, 46,* 1679–1687.

Peterson, C., & Vaidya, R. S. (2001). Explanatory style, expectations, and depressive symptoms. *Personality & Individual Differences, 31*(7), 1217–1223.

Peterson, N. G., & Jeanneret, P. R. (2007). Job analysis: An overview and description of deductive methods. In D. L. Whetzel & G. R. Wheaton (Eds.), *Applied Measurement.* Mahwah, NJ: Erlbaum.

Peterson, Z. D., & Muehlenhard, C. L. (2004). Was it rape? The Function of women's rape myth acceptance and definitions of sex in labeling their own experiences. *Sex Roles, 51,* 129–144.

Petronis, A. (2000). The genes for major psychosis: Aberrant sequence or regulation? *Neuropsychopharmacology, 23,* 1–12.

Pettigrew, T. F. (1998). Reactions towards the new minorities of Western Europe. *Annual Review of Sociology, 24,* 77–103.

Petty, R. E., & Briñol, P. (2008). Persuasion: From single to multiple to metacognitive processes. *Perspectives on Psychological Science, 3,* 137–147.

Pfeffer, C. R., Jiang, H., Kakuma, T., Hwang, J., & Metsch, M. (2002). Group intervention for children bereaved the suicide of a relative. *Journal of the American Academy of Child & Adolescent Psychiatry, 41*(5), 505–513.

Pham, T.M., Winblad, B., Granholm, A-C., & Mohammed, A. H. (2002). Environmental influences on brain neurotrophins in rats.

Pharmacology, Biochemistry & Behavior, 73(1), 167–175.

Philipsen, M. I. (2003). Race, the college classroom, and service learning: A practitioner's tale. *Journal of Negro Education, 72*(2), 230–240.

Phillips, S. T., & Ziller, R. C. (1997). Toward a theory and measure of the nature of non-prejudice. *Journal of Personality and Social Psychology, 72*, 420–434.

Piaget, J. (1962). *Play, dreams and imitation in Childhood.* New York: Norton.

Picard, H., Amado, I., Mouchet-Mages, S., Olié, J-P., & Krebs, M-O. (2008). The role of the cerebellum in schizophrenia: An update of clinical, cognitive, and functional evidences. *Schizophrenia Bulletin, 34*, 155–172.

Pich, E. M., Pagliusi, S. R., Tessari, M., Talabot-Ayer, D., Van Huijsduijnen, R. H., & Chiamulera, C. (1997). Common neural substrates for the addictive properties of nicotine and cocaine. *Science, 275*, 83–86.

Pickering, A., Farmer, A., & McGuffin, P. (2004). The role of personality in childhood sexual abuse. *Personality & Individual Differences, 36*(6), 1295–1303.

Pierce, J. D. Jr., Cohen, A. B., & Ulrich, P. M. (2004). Responsivity to two odorants, androstenone and amyl acetate, and the affective impact of odors on interpersonal relationships. *Journal of Comparative Psychology, 118*(1), 14–19.

Pierce, J. P. (2007). Tobacco industry marketing, population-based tobacco control, and smoking behavior. *American Journal of Preventive Medicine, 33*, 327–334.

Pietromonaco, P. R., & Carnelley, K. B. (1994). Gender and working models of attachment: Consequences for perception of self and romantic relationships. *Personal Relationships, 1*, 3–26.

Plomin, R. (1990). The role of inheritance in behavior. *Science, 248*, 183–188.

Plomin, R. (1997, May). Cited in B. Azar, Nature, nurture: Not mutually exclusive. *APA Monitor*, p. 32.

Plomin, R. (1999). Genetics and general cognitive ability. *Nature, 402*, C25-C29.

Plomin, R., & Crabbe, J. (2000). DNA. *Psychological Bulletin, 126*, 806–828.

Plomin, R., DeFries, J. C., & Fulker, D. W. (2007). *Nature and nurture during infancy and early childhood.* New York: Cambridge University Press.

Plummer, D. C. (2001). The quest for modern manhood: Masculine stereotypes, peer culture and the social significance of homophobia. *Journal of Adolescence, 24*(1), 15–23.

Plutchik, R. (1984). Emotions: A general psychoevolutionary theory. In K. R. Scherer, & P. Ekman (Eds.), *Approaches to emotion.* Hillsdale, NJ: Erlbaum.

Plutchik, R. (1994). *The psychology and biology of emotion.* New York: HarperCollins.

Plutchik, R. (2000). *Emotions in the practice of psychotherapy: Clinical implications of affect theories.* Washington, DC: American Psychological Association.

Pomponio, A. T. (2001). *Psychological consequences of terror.* New York: Wiley.

Pontius, A. A. (2005). Fastest fight/flight reaction via amygdalar visual pathway implicates simple face drawing as its marker: Neuroscientific data consistent with neuropsychological findings. *Aggression & Violent Behavior, 10*(3), 363–373.

Ponzi, A. (2008). Dynamical model of salience gated working memory, action selection and reinforcement based on basal ganglia and dopamine feedback. *Neural Networks, 21*, 322–330.

Pope Jr., H. G., Barry, S., Bodkin, J. A., & Hudson, J. (2007). "Scientific study of the dissociative disorders": Reply. *Psychotherapy and Psychosomatics, 76*, 401–403.

Popma, A., Vermeiren, R., Geluk, C. A. M. L., Rinne, T., van den Brink, W., Knol, D. L., Jansen, L. M. C., van Engeland, H., & Doreleijers, T. A. H. (2007). Cortisol moderates the relationship between testosterone and aggression in delinquent male adolescents. *Biological Psychiatry, 61*, 405–411.

Porter, J. F., Spates, C. R., & Smitham, S. (2004). Behavioral activation group therapy in public mental health settings: A pilot investigation. *Professional Psychology: Research & Practice, 35*(3), 297–301.

Porzelius, L. K., Dinsmore, B. D., & Staffelbach, D. (2001). Eating disorders. In M. Hersen & V. B. Van Hasselt (Eds.), *Advanced abnormal psychology* (2nd ed.). Netherlands: Klewer Academic Publishers.

Posner, M. I., & Rothbart, M. K. (2007). Research on attention networks as a model for integration of psychological science. *Annual Review of Psychology, 58.* Palo Alto, CA: Annual Reviews.

Posthuma, D., de Geus, E. J. C., Baare, W. E. C., Hulshoff Pol, H. E., Kahn, R. S., & Boomsma, D. I. (2002). The association between brain volume and intelligence is of genetic origin. *Nature Neuroscience, 5*(2), 83–84.

Posthuma, D., de Geus, E. J. C., & Boomsma, D. I. (2001). Perceptual speed and IQ are associated through common genetic factors. *Behavior Genetics, 31*(6), 593–602.

Posthuma, D., Neale, M. C., Boomsma, D. I., & de Geus, E. J. C. (2001). Are smarter brains running faster? Heritability of alpha peak frequency, IQ, and their interrelation. *Behavior Genetics, 31*(6), 567–579.

Powell, D. H. (1998), *The nine myths of aging: Maximizing the quality of later life.* San Francisco: Freeman.

Powell, D. R. (2006). Families and early childhood interventions. In W. Damon & R. Lerner (Eds.), *Handbook of child psychology* (6th ed.). New York: Wiley.

Powell-Hopson, D., & Hopson, D. S. (1988). Implications of doll color preferences among Black preschool children and White preschool children. *Journal of Black Psychology, 14*, 57–63.

Prabhu, V., Sutton, C., & Sauser, W. (2008). Creativity and certain personality traits: Understanding the mediating effect of intrinsic motivation. *Creativity Research Journal, 20*, 53–66.

Pratt, M. W., Skoe, E. E., & Arnold, M. (2004). Care reasoning development and family socialisation patterns in later adolescence: A longitudinal analysis. *International Journal of Behavioral Development, 28*(2), 139–147.

Pressman, J. D. (1998). *Last resort psychosurgery and the limits of medicine.* Cambridge, MA: Cambridge University Press.

Preuss, U. W., Zetzsche, T., Jäger, M., Groll, C., Frodl, T., Bottlender, R., Leisinger, G., Hegerl, U., Hahn, K., Möller, H. J., & Meisenzahl, E. M. (2005). Thalamic volume in first-episode and chronic schizophrenic subjects: A volumetric MRI study. *Schizophrenia Research, 73*(1), 91–101.

Price, D. D., Finniss, D. G., & Benedetti, F. (2008). A comprehensive review of the placebo effect: Recent advances and current thought. *Annual Review of Psychology, 59*, 565–590.

Priest, R. F., & Sawyer, J. (1967). Proximity and peership: Bases of balance in interpersonal attraction. *American Journal of Sociology, 72*, 633–649.

Prigatano, G. P., & Gray, J. A. (2008). Predictors of performance on three developmentally sensitive neuropsychological tests in children with and without traumatic brain injury. *Brain Injury, 22*, 491–500.

Primavera, L. H., & Herron, W. G. (1996). The effect of viewing television violence on aggression. *International Journal of Instructional Media, 23*, 91–104.

Pring, L., & Hermelin, B. (2002). Numbers and letters: Exploring an autistic savant's unpractised ability. *Neurocase, 8*(4), 330–337.

Pring, L., Woolf, K., & Tadic, V. (2008). Melody and pitch processing in five musical savants with congenital blindness. *Perception, 37,* 290–307.

Prinstein, M. J., & Aikins, J. W. (2004). Cognitive moderators of the longitudinal association between peer rejection and adolescent depressive symptoms. *Journal of Abnormal Child Psychology, 32*(2), 147–158.

Prkachin, K. M. (2005). Effects of deliberate control on verbal and facial expressions of pain. *Pain, 114,* 328–338.

Prkachin, K. M., & Silverman, B. E. (2002). Hostility and facial expression in young men and women: Is social regulation more important than negative affect? *Health Psychology, 21*(1), 33–39.

Prouix, M. J. (2007). Bottom-up guidance in visual search for conjunctions. *Journal of Experimental Psychology, 33,* 48–56.

Prudic, J., Olfson, M., Marcus, S. C., Fuller, R. B., & Sackeim, H. A. (2004). Effectiveness of electroconvulsive therapy in community settings. *Biological Psychiatry, 55*(3), 301–312.

Psychology Matters. (2006, June 30). *Pushing buttons.* [On-line]. Available: http://www.psychologymatters.org/pushbutton.

Pullum, G. K. (1991). *The great Eskimo vocabulary hoax and other irreverent essays on the study of language.* Chicago: University of Chicago Press.

Purdy, J. E., Markham, M. R., Schwartz, B. L., & Gordon, W. C. (2001). *Learning and memory* (2nd ed.). Belmont, CA: Wadsworth.

Purnell, M. T., Feyer, A. M., & Herbison, G. P. (2002). The impact of a nap opportunity during the night shift on the performance and alertness of 12-hour shift workers. *Journal of Sleep Research, 11*(3), 219–227.

Quaiser-Pohl, C., & Lehmann, W. (2002). Girls' spatial abilities: Charting the contributions of experiences and attitudes in different academic groups. *British Journal of Educational Psychology, 72*(2), 245–260.

Qualls, S. H. (2008). Caregiver family therapy. In K. Laidlaw & B. Knight (Eds.), *Handbook of emotional disorders in later life: Assessment and treatment.* New York: Oxford University Press.

Quinn, J., Barrowclough, C., & Tarrier, N. (2003). The Family Questionnaire (FQ): A scale for measuring symptom appraisal in relatives of schizophrenic patients. *Acta Psychiatrica Scandinavica, 108*(4), 290–296.

Quinn, P. C., Kelly, D. J., Lee, K., Pascalis, O., & Slater, A. M. (2008). Preference for attractive faces in human infants extends beyond conspecifics. *Developmental Science, 11,* 76–83.

Quintanilla, Y. T. (2007). Achievement motivation strategies: An integrative achievement motivation program with first year seminar students. *Dissertation Abstracts International Section A: Humanities and Social Sciences, 68* (6-A), 2339.

Raesaenen, P. M., Tiihonen, J., Isohanni, M., Rantakallio, P., Lehtonen, J., & Moring, J. (1998). Schizophrenia, alcohol abuse, and violent behavior: A 26-year follow up study of an unselected birth cohort. *Schizophrenia Bulletin, 24,* 437–441.

Raesaenen, S., Pakaslahti, A., Syvaelahti, E., Jones, P. B., & Isohanni, M. (2000). Sex differences in schizophrenia: A review. *Nordic Journal of Psychiatry, 54,* 37–45.

Raevuori, A., Keski-Rahkonen, A., Hoek, H. W., Sihvola, E., Rissanen, A., & Kaprio, J. (2008). Lifetime anorexia nervosa in young men in the community: Five cases and their co-twins. *International Journal of Eating Disorders, 41,* 458–463.

Raffaelli, M., Crockett, L. J., & Shen, Y-L. (2005). Developmental stability and change in self-regulation from childhood to adolescence. *Journal of Genetic Psychology, 166,* 54–75.

Rahman, Q. (2006). Biobehavioural science research on human sexual orientation. In K. Yip (Ed.), *Psychology of gender identity: An International Perspective.* Hauppauge: Nova Science Publishers.

Rahman, Q., & Wilson, G. D. (2003). Born gay? The psychobiology of human sexual orientation. *Personality & Individual Differences. 34*(8), 1337–1382.

Raine, A., Lencz, T., Bihrle, S., LaCasse, L., & Colletti, P. (2000). Reduced prefrontal gray matter volume and reduced autonomic activity in antisocial personality disorder. *Archives of General Psychiatry, 57,* 119–127.

Raine, A., Meloy, J. R., Bihrle, S., Stoddard, J., LaCasse, L., & Buchsbaum, M. S. (1998). Reduced prefrontal and increased subcortical brain functioning assessed using positron emission tomography in predatory and effective murderers. *Behavioral Sciences & the Law, 16*(3), 319–332.

Raine, A., & Yang, Y. (2006). The neuroanatomical bases of psychopathy: A review of brain imaging findings. In C. J. Patrick (Ed.), *Handbook of the psychopathy* (pp. 278–295). New York: Guilford Press.

Ramirez, G., Zemba, D., & Geiselman, R. E. (1996). Judges' cautionary instructions on eyewitness testimony. *American Journal of Forensic Psychology, 14,* 31–66.

Ramirez, J. M. (2003). Hormones and aggression in childhood and adolescence. *Aggression & Violent Behavior, 8*(6), 621–644.

Ran, M. (2007). Experimental research on the reliability of the testimony from eyewitnesses. *Psychological Science (China), 30,* 727–730.

Randi, J. (1997). *An encyclopedia of claims, frauds, and hoaxes of the occult and supernatural: James Randi's decidedly skeptical definitions of alternate realities.* New York: St Martin's Press.

Ranganath, K. A., Smith, C. T., & Nosek, B. A. (2008). Distinguishing automatic and controlled components of attitudes from direct and indirect measurement methods. *Journal of Experimental Social Psychology, 44,* 386–396.

Ranganathan, S., & Bhattacharya, T. (2007). Culture-bound syndromes: A problematic category. *Psychological Studies, 52,* 153–157.

Rao, V., Spiro, J. R., Handel, S., & Onyike, C. U. (2008). Clinical correlates of personality changes associated with traumatic brain injury. *Journal of Neuropsychiatry & Clinical Neurosciences, 20,* 118–119.

Raphel, S. (2008). Kinship care and the situation for grandparents. *Journal of Child and Adolescent Psychiatric Nursing, 21,* 118–120.

Rattaz, C., Goubet, N., & Bullinger, A. (2005). The calming effect of a familiar odor on full-term newborns. *Journal of Developmental & Behavioral Pediatrics, 26,* 86–92.

Rauer, A. J. (2007). Identifying happy, healthy marriages for men, women, and children. *Dissertation Abstracts International: Section B: The Sciences and Engineering, 67*(10-B), 6098.

Rauhut, A. S., Thomas, B. L., & Ayres, J. J. B. (2001). Treatments that weaken Pavlovian conditioned fear and thwart its renewal in rats: Implications for treating human phobias. *Journal of Experimental Psychology: Animal Behavior Processes, 27*(2), 99–114.

Ray, W. J. (2003). *Methods: Toward a science of behavior and experience.* (7th ed.). Wadsworth: Belmont, CA.

Raz, A. (2007). Suggestibility and hypnotizability: Mind the gap. *American Journal of Clinical Hypnosis, 49,* 205–210.

Realmuto, G. M., August, G. J., & Egan, E. A. (2004). Testing the goodness-of-fit of a multifaceted preventive intervention for children at risk for conduct disorder. *Canadian Journal of Psychiatry, 49,* 743–752.

Rechtschaffen, A., & Siegel, J.M. (2000). Sleep and Dreaming. In E. R. Kandel, J. H. Schwartz, & T. M. Jessel (Eds.), *Principles of Neuroscience* (4th ed., pp. 936–947). New York: McGraw-Hill.

Reed, L. J., Lasserson, D., Marsden, P., Bright, P., Stanhope, N., & Kopelman, M. D. (2005). Correlations of regional cerebral metabolism with memory performance and executive function in patients with herpes encephalitis or frontal lobe lesions. *Neuropsychology, 19*(5), 555–565.

Reeder, C., Newton, E., Frangou, S., & Wykes, T. (2004). Which executive skills should we target to affect social functioning and symptom change? A study of a cognitive remediation therapy program. *Schizophrenia Bulletin, 30*(1), 87–100.

Reeve, J. (2005). *Understanding motivation and emotion* (4th ed.). Hoboken, NJ: Wiley.

Regan, P. (1998). What if you can't get what you want? Willingness to compromise ideal mate selection standards as a function of sex, mate value, and relationship context. *Personality and Social Psychology Bulletin, 24,* 1294–1303.

Regier, D. A., Narrow, W. E., Rae, D. S., Manderscheid, R. W., Locke, B. Z., & Goodwin, F. K. (1993). The de facto US mental and addictive disorders service system. *Archives of General Psychiatry, 50,* 85–93.

Reich, D. A. (2004). What you expect is not always what you get: The roles of extremity, optimism, and pessimism in the behavioral confirmation process. *Journal of Experimental Social Psychology, 40*(2), 199–215.

Reifman, A. (2000). Revisiting the Bell Curve. *Psychology, 11,* 21–29.

Reilly, P. (2005). Teaching law students how to feel: Using negotiations training to increase motional intelligence. *Negotiation Journal, 21*(2), 301–314.

Reineke, A. (2008). The effects of heart rate variability biofeedback in reducing blood pressure for the treatment of essential hypertension. *Dissertation Abstracts International: Section B: The Sciences and Engineering, 67*(7-B), 4880.

Reiner, W. G., & Gearhart, J. P. (2004). Discordant sexual identity in some genetic males with cloacal exstrophy assigned to female sex at birth. *New England Journal of Medicine, 350,* 333–341.

Reinhard, M-A., Messner, M., & Sporer, S. L. (2006). Explicit persuasive intent and its impact on success at persuasion: The determining roles of attractiveness and likeableness. *Journal of Consumer Psychology, 16,* 249–259.

Reis, C., Ahmed, A. T., Amowitz, L. L., Kushner, A. L., Elahi, M., & Iacopino, V. (2004). Physician participation in human rights abuses in southern Iraq. *JAMA: Journal of the American Medical Association, 291*(12), 1480–1486.

Renzetti, C., Curran, D., & Kennedy-Bergen, R. (2006). *Understanding diversity.* Boston: Allyn & Bacon/Longman.

Resing, W. C., & Nijland, M. I. (2002). Worden kinderen intelligenter? Een kwart eeuw onderzoek met de Leidse Diagnostische Test [Are children becoming more intelligent? Twenty-five years' research using the Leiden Diagnostic Test.] *Kind en Adolescent, 23*(1), 42–49.

Ressler, K., & Davis, M. (2003). Genetics of childhood disorders: L. Learning and memory, part 3: Fear conditioning. *Journal of the American Academy of Child & Adolescent Psychiatry, 42*(5), 612–615.

Rest, J., Narvaez, D., Bebeau, M., & Thoma, S. (1999). A neo-Kohlbergian approach: The DIT and schema theory. *Educational Psychology Review, 11*(4), 291–324.

Reulbach, U., Bleich, S., Biermann, T., Pfahlberg, A., & Sperling, W. (2007). Late-onset schizophrenia in child survivors of the Holocaust. *Journal of Nervous and Mental Disease, 195,* 315–319.

Revonsuo, A., (2006). *Inner presence: Consciousness as a biological phenomenon.* Cambridge, MA: MIT Press.

Reynolds, L. R. (2008). Predictors of productive aging among older persons in the United States. *Dissertation Abstracts International Section A: Humanities and Social Sciences, 68*(9-A), 4072.

Reynolds, M. R., Keith, T. Z., Ridley, K. P., & Patel, P. G. (2008). Sex differences in latent general and broad cognitive abilities for children and youth: Evidence from higher-order MG-MACS and MIMIC models. *Intelligence, 36,* 236–260.

Rhodes, G., Halberstadt, J., & Brajkovich, G. (2001). Generalization of mere exposure effects to averaged composite faces. *Social Cognition, 19*(1), 57–70.

Richardson, D. S., & Hammock, G. S. (2007). Social context of human aggression: Are we paying too much attention to gender? *Aggression and Violent Behavior, 12,* 417–426.

Richardson, G. A., Ryan, C., Willford, J., Day, N. L., & Goldschmidt, L. (2002). Prenatal alcohol and marijuana exposure: Effects on neuropsychological outcomes at 10 years. *Neurotoxicology & Teratology, 24*(3), 311–320.

Riddoch, M. J., Johnston, R. A., Bracewell, R. M., Boutsen, L., & Humphreys, G. W. (2008). Are faces special? A case of pure prosopagnosia. *Cognitive Neuropsychology, 25,* 3–26.

Ridley, R. M., Baker, H. F., Cummings, R. M., Green, M. E., & Leow-Dyke, A. (2005). Mild topographical memory impairment following crossed unilateral lesions of the mediodorsal thalamic nucleus and the inferotemporal cortex. *Behavioral Neuroscience, 119*(2), 518–525.

Riebe, D., Garber, C. E., Rossi, J. S., Greaney, M. L., Nigg, C. R., Lees, F. D., Burbank, P. M., & Clark, P. G. (2005). Physical activity, physical function, and stages of change in older adults. *American Journal of Health Behavior, 29,* 70–80.

Riemann, D., & Voderholzer, U. (2003). Primary insomnia: a risk factor to develop depression? *Journal of Affective Disorders, 76*(1–3), 255–259.

Riggio, H. R. (2004). Parental marital conflict and divorce, parent-child relationships, social support, and relationship anxiety in young adulthood. *Personal Relationships, 11*(1), 99–114.

Ripley, A. (2004, June 31). Redefining torture. *Time, 163,* p. 29.

Rivadeneyra, R., & Lebo, M. J. (2008). The association between television-viewing behaviors and adolescent dating role attitudes and behaviors. *Journal of Adolescence, 31,* 291–305.

Rizolatti, G., Fadiga, L., Fogassi, L. & Gallese, V. (2002). From mirror neurons to imitation: Facts and speculations. In A. N. Meltzoff & W. Prinz (Eds.), *The imitative mind: Development, evolution, and brain bases.* Cambridge, MA: Cambridge University Press.

Rizolatti, G., Fogassi, L. & Gallese, V. (2006, November). In the mind. *Scientific American,* 54–61.

Roberge, P., Marchand, A., Reinharz, D., & Savard, P. (2008). Cognitive-behavioral treatment for panic disorder with agoraphobia: A randomized, controlled trial and cost-effectiveness analysis. *Behavior Modification, 32,* 333–351.

Roberts, M. (2006, March). Idol dreams. *Schizophrenia Digest,* 30–33.

Roberts, W. W., & Nagel, J. (1996). First-order projections activated by stimulation of hypothalamic sites eliciting attack and flight in rats. *Behavioral Neuroscience, 110,* 509–527.

Robinson, A. J. (2008). McGregor's Theory X-Theory Y model. In J. Gordon (Ed.), *The*

Pfeiffer book of successful leadership development tools: The most enduring, effective, and valuable training activities for developing leaders. San Francisco: Pfeiffer/John Wiley.

Robinson, F. P. (1946). *Effective study.* New York: Harper & Row.

Robinson, F. P. (1970). *Effective study* (4th ed.). New York: Harper & Row.

Robinson, R. J. (2008). Comorbidity of alcohol abuse and depression: Exploring the self-medication hypothesis. *Dissertation Abstracts International: Section B: The Sciences and Engineering, 68*(9-B), 6332.

Rodafinos, A., Vucevic, A., & Sideridis, G. D. (2005). The effectiveness of compliance techniques: Foot-in-the-door versus door-in-the-face. *Journal of Social Psychology, 145,* 237–239.

Rodrigues, A., Assmar, E. M., & Jablonski, B. (2005). Social-psychology and the invasion of Iraq. *Revista de Psicología Social, 20,* 387–398.

Roediger, H. L. & Gallo, D. A. (2002). Levels of processing: Some unanswered questions. In Naveh-Benjamin, M., Moscovitch, M. & Roediger, H.L. (Eds.), *Perspectives on human memory and cognitive aging: Essays in honour of Fergus I.M. Craik* (pp. 28–47). Philadelphia: Psychology Press.

Roelcke, V. (1997). Biologizing social facts: An early 20th century debate on Kraepelin's concepts of culture, neurasthenia, and degeneration. *Culture, Medicine, and Psychiatry, 21,* 383–403.

Rogers, C. R. (1961). *On becoming a person.* Boston: Houghton Mifflin.

Rogers, C. R. (1980). *A way of being.* Boston: Houghton Mifflin.

Rogers, T. T., Lambon Ralph, M. A., Garrard, P., Bozeat, S., McClelland, J. L., Hodges, J. R., & Patterson, K. (2004). Structure and deterioration of semantic memory: A neuropsychological and computational investigation. *Psychological Review, 111*(1), 205–235.

Rogosch, F. A., & Cicchetti, D. (2004). Child maltreatment and emergent personality organization: Perspectives from the five-factor model. *Journal of Abnormal Child Psychology, 32*(2), 123–145.

Rohner, R. (1986). *The warmth dimension.* Newbury Park, CA: Sage.

Rohner, R. P. (2008). Parental acceptance-rejection theory studies of intimate adult relationships. (2008). *Cross-Cultural Research: The Journal of Comparative Social Science, 42,* 5–12.

Rohner, R. P., & Britner, P. A. (2002). World-wide mental health correlates of parental acceptance-rejection: Review of cross-cultural and intracultural evidence. *Cross-Cultural Research: The Journal of Comparative Social Science, 36,* 15–47.

Romero, S. G., McFarland, D. J., Faust, R., Farrell, L., & Cacace, A. T. (2008). Electrophysiological markers of skill-related neuroplasticity. *Biological Psychology, 78,* 221–230.

Rönnberg, J., Rudner, M., & Ingvar, M. (2004). Neural correlates of working memory for sign language. *Cognitive Brain Research, 20*(2), 165–182.

Rook, K. S. (2000). The evolution of social relationships in later adulthood. In S. H. Qualls & N. Abeles (Eds.), *Psychology and the aging revolution.* Washington, DC: American Psychological Association.

Roques, P. Lambin, M., Jeunier, B., Strayer, F. (1997). Multivariate analysis of personal space in a primary school classroom. *Enfance, 4,* 451–468.

Rosch, E. (1978). Principles of organization. In E. Rosch & H. L. Lloyd (Eds.), *Cognition and categorization.* Hillsdale, NJ: Erlbaum.

Rosch, E. H. (1973). Natural categories. *Cognitive Psychology, 4,* 328–350.

Rose, C. R., & Konnerth, A. (2002). Exciting glial oscillations. *Nature Neuroscience, 4,* 773–774.

Rosen-Grandon, J. R., Myers, J. E., & Hattie, J. A. (2004). The relationship between marital characteristics, marital interaction processes, and marital satisfaction. *Journal of Counseling & Development, 82*(1), 58–68.

Rosenberg, M. (2003). Recognizing gay, lesbian, and transgender teens in a child and adolescent psychiatry practice. *Journal of the American Academy of Child & Adolescent Psychiatry, 42*(12), 1517–1521.

Rosenthal, H. G. (2007). The Tiger Woods analogy: The seven-minute active listening solution. In L. L. Hecker & C. F Sori (Eds.), *The therapist's notebook: More homework, handouts, and activities for use in psychotherapy (Vol. 2)* (pp. 277–280). *Haworth practical practice in mental health.* New York: Haworth Press.

Rosenthal, R. (1965). *Clever Hans: A case study of scientific method, Introduction to Clever Hans.* New York: Holt, Rinehart & Winston.

Rosenzweig, E. S., Barnes, C. A., & McNaughton, B. L. (2002). Making room for new memories. *Nature Neuroscience, 5*(1), 6–8.

Rosenzweig, M. R., & Bennett, E. L. (1996). Psychobiology of plasticity: Effects of training and experience on brain and behavior. *Behavioural Brain Research, 78*(1), 57–65.

Rosenzweig, M. R., Bennett, E. L., & Diamond, M. C. (1972). Brain changes in response to experience. *Scientific American, 226,* 22–29.

Rosnow, R. L., & Rosenthal, R. (2008). *Beginning behavioral research* (6th ed.). Upper Saddle River, NJ: Prentice-Hall.

Ross, B. M., & Millson, C. (1970). Repeated memory of oral prose in Ghana and New York. *International Journal of Psychology, 5,* 173–181.

Ross, H., Smith, J., Spielmacher, C., & Recchia, H. (2004). Shading the truth: Self-serving biases in children's reports of sibling conflicts. *Merrill-Palmer Quarterly, 50*(1), 61–85.

Rossano, M. J. (2003). *Evolutionary psychology: The science of human behavior and evolution.* Hoboken, NJ: Wiley.

Rossato, M., Pagano, C., & Vettor, R. (2008). The cannabinoid system and male reproductive functions. *Journal of Neuroendocrinology, 20,* 90–93.

Rossignol, S., Barrière, G., Frigon, A., Barthélemy, D., Bouyer, L., Provencher, J., Leblond, H., & Bernard, G. (2008). Plasticity of locomotor sensorimotor interactions after peripheral and/or spinal lesions. *Brain Research Reviews, 57,* 228–240.

Roth, M. D., Whittaker, K., Salehi, K., Tashkin, D. P., & Baldwin, G. C. (2004). Mechanisms for impaired effector function in alveolar macrophages from marijuana and cocaine smokers. *Journal of Neuroimmunology, 147*(1–2), 82–86.

Roth, M. L., Tripp, D. A. Harrison, M. H., Sullivan, M., & Carson, P. (2007). Demographic and psychosocial predictors of acute perioperative pain for total knee arthroplasty. *Pain Research & Management, 12,* 185–194.

Rothermund, K., & Wentura, D. (2004). Underlying processes in the Implicit Association Test: Dissociating salience from associations. *Journal of Experimental Psychology: General, 133,* 139–165.

Rothstein, J. B., Jensen, G., & Neuringer, A. (2008). Human choice among five alternatives when reinforcers decay. *Behavioural Processes, 78,* 231–239.

Rotter, J. B. (1954). *Social learning and clinical psychology.* Englewood Cliffs, NJ: Prentice Hall.

Rotter, J. B. (1990). Internal versus external control of reinforcement: A case history of a variable. *American Psychologist, 45,* 489–493.

Rowe, R., Maughan, B., Worthman, C. M., Costello, E. J., & Angold, A. (2004). Testosterone, antisocial behavior, and social dominance in boys: Pubertal development and biosocial interaction. *Biological Psychiatry, 55*(5), 546–552.

Roy, T. S., Seidler, F. J., & Slotkin, T. A. (2002). Prenatal nicotine exposure evokes alterations of cell structure in hippocampus and somatosensory cortex. *Journal of Pharmacology & Experimental Therapeutics, 300*(1), 124–133.

Rozencwajg, P., Cherfi, M., Ferrandez, A. M., Lautrey, J., Lemoine, C., & Loarer, E. (2005). Age related differences in the strategies used by middle aged adults to solve a block design task. *International Journal of Aging & Human Development, 60*(2), 159–182.

Rubin, Z. (1970). Measurement of romantic love. *Journal of Personality and Social Psychology, 16,* 265–273.

Rubinstein, E. (2008). Judicial perceptions of eyewitness testimony. *Dissertation Abstracts International: Section B: The Sciences and Engineering, 68*(8-B), 5592.

Ruble, D. N., Martin, C. L., & Berenbaum, S. A. (2006). Gender development. In N. Eisenberg, W. Damon, & R. M. Lerner (Eds.), *Handbook of Child Psychology* (6th ed). Hoboken, NJ: Wiley.

Rudman, L. A., & Ashmore, R. D. (2007). Discrimination and the Implicit Association Test. *Group Processes & Intergroup Relations, 10,* 359–372.

Rudman, L. A., & Fairchild, K. (2004). Reactions to counterstereotypic behavior: The role of backlash in cultural stereotype maintenance. *Journal of Personality and Social Psychology, 87*(2), 157–176.

Ruffolo, J. S., Phillips, K. A., Menard, W., Fay, C., & Weisberg, R. B. (2006). Comorbidity of body dysmorphic disorder and eating disorders: Severity of psychopathology and body image disturbance. *International Journal of Eating Disorders, 39,* 11–19.

Rumbaugh, D. M., von Glasersfeld, E. C., Warner, H., Pisani, P., & Gill, T. V. (1974). Lana (chimpanzee) learning language: A progress report. *Brain & Language, 1*(2), 205–212.

Rumpel, S., LeDoux, J., Zador, A., & Malinow, R. (2005). Postsynaptic receptor trafficking underlying a form of associative learning. *Science, 308*(5718), 83–88.

Russo, N. F., & Tartaro, J. (2008). Women and mental health. In F. L. Denmark & M. A. Paludi (Eds.), *Psychology of women: A handbook of issues and theories* (2nd ed.) (pp. 440–483). *Women's psychology.* Westport, CT: Praeger/Greenwood.

Ruthig, J. C., Chipperfield, J. G., Perry, R. P. Newall, N. E., & Swift, A. (2007). Comparative risk and perceived control: Implications for psychological and physical well-being

among older adults. *Journal of Social Psychology, 147,* 345–369.

Rutledge, P. C., Park, A., & Sher, K. J. (2008). 21st birthday drinking: Extremely extreme. *Journal of Consulting and Clinical Psychology, 76*(3), 511–516.

Rutler, M. L. (1997). Nature–nurture integration: The example of antisocial behavior. *American Psychologist, 52,* 390–398.

Rutter, M. (2007). Gene-environment interdependence. *Developmental Science, 10,* 12–18.

Rutter, V. E. (2005). The case for divorce: Under what conditions is divorce beneficial and for whom? *Dissertation Abstracts International Section A: Humanities and Social Sciences, 65*(7-A), 2784.

Ryback, D., Ikemi, A., & Miki, Y. (2001). Japanese psychology in crisis: Thinking inside the (empty) box. *Journal of Humanistic Psychology, 41*(4), 124–136.

Rybacki, J.J., & Long, J.W. (1999). *The essential guide to prescription drugs 1999.* New York: Harper Perennial.

Rymer, R. (1993). *Genie: An abused child's first flight from silence.* New York: HarperCollins.

Saab, C. Y., & Willis, W. D. (2003). The cerebellum: Organization, functions and its role in nociception. *Brain Research Reviews, 42*(1), 85–95.

Saadeh, W., Rizzo, C. P., & Roberts, D. G. (2002). Spanking. *Clinical Pediatrics, 41*(2), 87–88.

Sabet, K. A. (2007). The (often unheard) case against marijuana leniency. In M. Earleywine (Ed), *Pot politics: Marijuana and the costs of prohibition* (pp. 325–352). New York: Oxford University Press.

Sabini, J., & Silver, M. (1993). Critical thinking and obedience to authority. In J. Chaffee (Ed.), *Critical thinking* (2nd ed., pp. 367–376). Palo Alto, CA: Houghton Mifflin.

Sacchetti, B., Sacco, T., & Strata, P. (2007). Reversible inactivation of amygdala and cerebellum but not perirhinal cortex impairs reactivated fear memories. *European Journal of Neuroscience, 25*(9), 2875–2884.

Sachdev, P., Mondraty, N., Wen, W., & Gulliford, K. (2008). Brains of anorexia nervosa patients process self-images differently from non-self-images: An fMRI study. *Neuropsychologia, 46,* 2161–2168.

Sack, R. L., Auckley, D., Auger, R. R., Carskadon, M. A., Wright, Jr., K. P., Vitiello, M. V., & Zhdanova, I. V. (2007). Circadian rhythm sleep disorders: Part I, basic principles, shift work and jet lag disorders:

An American academy of sleep medicine review. *Sleep: Journal of Sleep and Sleep Disorders Research, 30,* 1460–1483.

Sacks, O. (1995) *An anthropologist on Mars.* New York: Vintage books.

Sacks, O. (2006, June 19). Stereo Sue. *New Yorker,* 64–73.

Salas, E., DeRouin, & Gade, P.A. (2007). The military's contribution to our science and practice: People, places, and findings. In L. L. Koppes (Ed.), *Historical perspectives in industrial and organizational psychology,* pp. 169–189. Mahwah, NJ: Erlbaum.

Salekin, R. T., & Averett, C. A. (2008). Personality in childhood and adolescence. In M. Hersen & A. M. Gross (Eds.), *Handbook of clinical psychology, vol 2: Children and adolescents* (pp. 351–385). Hoboken, NJ: Wiley.

Salmivalli, C., & Kaukiainen, A. (2004). "Female aggression" revisited: Variable-and personcentered approaches to studying gender differences in different types of aggression. *Aggressive Behavior, 30*(2),158–163.

Salovey, P., Bedell, B. T., Detweiler, J. B., & Mayer, J. D. (2000). Current directions in emotional intelligence research. In M. Lewis & J.M. Haviland (Eds.), *Handbook of emotions* (2nd ed., pp. 504–520). New York: Guilford Press.

Salovey, P., & Mayer, J. D. (1990). Emotional intelligence. *Imagination, Cognition, and Personality, 9,* 185–211.

Saltus, R. (2000, June 22). Brain cells are coaxed into repair duty. *Boston Globe,* A18.

Salvatore, P., Ghidini, S., Zita, G., De Panfilis, C., Lambertino, S., Maggini, C., & Baldessarini, R. J. (2008). Circadian activity rhythm abnormalities in ill and recovered bipolar I disorder patients. *Bipolar Disorders, 10,* 256–265.

Salyers, M.P., & Mueser, K.T. (2001). Schizophrenia. In M. Hersen & V.B. Van Hasselt (Eds.), *Advanced abnormal psychology* (2nd ed.). New York: Klewer Academic/Plenum.

Sampselle, C. M., Harris, V. Harlow, S. D., & Sowers, M. F. (2002). Midlife development and menopause in African American and Caucasian women. *Health Care for Women International, 23*(4), 351–363.

Sanchez Jr., J. (2006). Life satisfaction factors impacting the older Cuban-American population. *Dissertation Abstracts International Section A: Humanities and Social Sciences, 67*(5-A), 1864.

Sanderson, C. A. (2004). *Health psychology.* Hoboken, NJ: Wiley.

Sangha, S., McComb, C., Scheibenstock, A., Johannes, C., & Lukowiak, K. (2002).

The effects of continuous versus partial reinforcement schedules on associative learning, memory, and extinction in Lymnaea stagnalis. *Journal of Experimental Biology, 205*, 1171–1178.

Sangwan, S. (2001). Ecological factors as related to I.Q. of children. *Psycho-Lingua, 31*(2), 89–92.

Sansone, R. A., Levengood, J. V., & Sellbom, M. (2004). Psychological aspects of fibromyalgia research vs. clinician impressions. *Journal of Psychosomatic Research, 56*(2), 185–188.

Sapolsky, R. (2003). Taming stress. *Scientific American*, pp. 87–95.

Sapolsky, R. M. (1992). *Stress, the aging brain, and the mechanisms of neuron death*. Cambridge, MA: MIT Press.

Sarafino, E. P. (2000). *Behavior modification: Understanding principles of behavior change*. Springfield, MA: Mayfield.

Sarafino, E. P. (2008). *Health psychology: Biopsychosocial interactions* (6th ed.). Hoboken, NJ: Wiley.

Sarnthein, J., Morel, A., von Stein, A., & Jeanmonod, D. (2005). Thalamocortical theta coherence in neurological patients at rest and during a working memory task. *International Journal of Psychophysiology, 57*(2), 87–96.

Sassenberg, K., Moskowitz, G. B., Jacoby, J., & Hansen, N. (2007). The carry-over effect of competition: The impact of competition on prejudice towards uninvolved outgroups. *Journal of Experimental Social Psychology, 43*, 529–538.

Satcher, N. D. (2007). Social and moral reasoning of high school athletes and non-athletes. *Dissertation Abstracts International Section A: Humanities and Social Sciences, 68*(3-A), 928.

Sathyaprabha, T. N., Satishchandra, P., Pradhan, C., Sinha, S., Kaveri, B., Thennarasu, K., Murthy, B. T. C., & Raju, T. R. (2008). Modulation of cardiac autonomic balance with adjuvant yoga therapy in patients with refractory epilepsy. *Epilepsy & Behavior, 12*, 245–252.

Satler, C., Garrido, L. M., Sarmiento, E. P., Leme, S., Conde, C., & Tomaz, C. (2007). Emotional arousal enhances declarative memory in patients with Alzheimer's disease. *Acta Neurologica Scandinavica, 116*, 355–360.

Sato, S. M., Schulz, K. M., Sisk, C. L., & Wood, R. I. (2008). Adolescents and androgens, receptors and rewards. *Hormones and Behavior, 53*, 647–658.

Saudino, K. J. (1997). Moving beyond the heritability question: New directions in behavioral genetic studies of personality. *Current Directions in Psychological Science, 6*, 86–90.

Savage-Rumbaugh, E. S. (1990). Language acquisition in a nonhuman species: Implications for the innateness debate. *Developmental Psychobiology, 23*, 599–620.

Savic, I., Berglund, H., & Lindström, P. (2007). Brain response to putative pheromones in homosexual men. In G. Einstein (Ed.), *Sex and the brain* (pp. 731–738). Cambridge, MA: MIT Press.

Sawa, A., & Kamiya, A. (2003). Elucidating the pathogenesis of schizophrenia: DISC-1 gene may predispose to neurodevelopmental changes underlying schizophrenia. *BMJ: British Medical Journal, 327*(7416), 632–633.

Sawaya, A. L., Fuss, P. J., Dallal, G. E., Tsay, R., McCrory, M. A., Young, V., & Roberts, S. B. (2001). Meal palatability, substrate oxidation and blood glucose in young and older men. *Physiology & Behavior, 72*(1–2), 5–12.

Saxe, L., & Ben-Shakhar, G. (1999). Admissibility of polygraph tests: The application of scientific standards post-Daubert. *Psychology, Public Policy, & Law, 5*(1), 203–223.

Scannapieco, M., & Connell-Carrick, K. (2005). Focus on the first years: Correlates of substantiation of child maltreatment for families with children 0 to 4. *Children and Youth Services Review, 27*, 1307–1323.

Schachter, S., & Singer, J. E. (1962). Cognitive, social, and physiological determinants of emotional state. *Psychological Review, 69*, 379–399.

Schaefer, B. A., & Ginsburg-Block, M. (2007). Helping children and adolescents dealing with divorce. In R. W. Christner, J. L. Stewart, & A Freeman (Eds.), *Handbook of cognitive-behavior group therapy with children and adolescents: Specific settings and presenting problems* (pp. 241–252). New York: Routledge/Taylor & Francis Group.

Schaefer, R. T. (2008). Power and power elite. In V. Parillo (Ed.), *Encyclopedia of social problems*. Thousand Oaks, CA: Sage.

Schaie, K. W. (1994). The life course of adult intellectual development. *American Psychologist, 49*, 304–313.

Schaie, K. W. (2008). A lifespan developmental perspective of psychological ageing. In K. Laidlaw & B. Knight (Eds.), *Handbook of emotional disorders in later life: Assessment and treatment*. New York: Oxford University Press.

Scherer, K. R., & Wallbott, H. G. (1994). Evidence for universal and cultural variation of differential emotion response patterning. *Journal of Personality and Social Psychology, 66*(2), 310–328.

Schiffer, F., Zaidel, E., Bogen, J., & Chasan-Taber, S. (1998). Different psychological status in the two hemispheres of two split-brain patients. *Neuropsychiatry, Neuropsychology, & Behavioral Neurology, 11*, 151–156.

Schiltz, C., Sorger, B., Caldara, R., Ahmed, F., Mayer, E., Goebel, R & Rossion, B. (2006), Impaired face discrimination in acquired prosogagnosia is associated with abnormal response to individual faces in the right middle fusiform gyrus. *Cerebral Cortex, 16*, 574–586.

Schim, S. M., Briller, S. H., Thurston, C. S., & Meert, K. L. (2007). Life as death scholars: Passion, personality, and professional perspectives. *Death Studies, 31*, 165–172.

Schmahl, C. G., Vermetten, E., Elzinga, B. M., & Bremner, J. D. (2004). A positron emission tomography study of memories of childhood abuse in borderline personality disorder. *Biological Psychiatry, 55*(7), 759–765.

Schmidt, L.A. (1999). Frontal brain electrical activity in shyness and sociability. *Psychological Science, 10* (4), 316–320.

Schmidt, U. (2004). Undue influence of weight on self-evaluation: A population-based twin study of gender differences. *International Journal of Eating Disorders, 35*(2), 133–135.

Schmitt-Rodermund, E., & Silbereisen, R. K. (2008). Well-adapted adolescent ethnic German immigrants in spite of adversity: The protective effects of human, social, and financial capital. *European Journal of Developmental Psychology, 5*, 186–209.

Schneider, D. M., & Sharp, L. (1969). *The dream life of a primitive people: The dreams of the Yir Yoront of Australia*. Ann Arbor, MI: University of Michigan.

Schneider, J. P. (2000). A qualitative study of cybersex participants: Gender differences, recovery issues, and implications for therapists. *Sexual Addiction & Compulsivity, 7*, 249–278.

Schneidman, E. S. (1969). Suicide, lethality and the psychological autopsy. *International Psychiatry Clinics, 6*, 225–250

Schnider, A. (2008). *The confabulating mind: How the brain creates reality*. New York: Oxford University Press.

Schnurr, P.P, & Green, B. L. (2004). *Trauma and health: Physical health consequences of exposure to extreme stress*. Washington, DC: American Psychological Association.

Schofield, W. (1964). *Psychotherapy: The purchase of friendship*. Englewood Cliffs, NJ: Prentice Hall.

Schopp, L. H., Good, G. E., Mazurek, M. O., Barker, K. B., & Stucky, R. C. (2007). Masculine role variables and outcomes among men with spinal cord injury. *Disability and Rehabilitation: An International, Multidisciplinary Journal, 29,* 625–633.

Schredl, M., Ciric, P., Gotz, S., & Wittmann, L. (2004). Typical dreams: Stability and gender differences. *Journal of Psychology: Interdisciplinary & Applied, 138*(6),485–494.

Schuett, S., Heywood, C. A., Kentridge, R. W., & Zihl, J. (2008). The significance of visual information processing in reading: Insights from hemianopic dyslexia. *Neuropsychologia, 46,* 2445–2462.

Schülein, J. A. (2007). Science and psychoanalysis. *Scandinavian Psychoanalytic Review, 30,* 13–21.

Schultz, K. (2008). Constructing failure, narrating success: Rethinking the "problem" of teen pregnancy. In D. L. Browning (Ed.), Adolescent identities: A collection of readings (pp. 113–137). *Relational perspectives book series.* New York: The Analytic Press/Taylor & Francis Group.

Schunk, D. H. (2008). Attributions as motivators of self-regulated learning. In D. H. Schunk & B. J. Zimmerman (Eds.), *Motivation and self-regulated learning: Theory, research, and applications* (pp. 245–266). Mahwah, NJ: Lawrence Erlbaum.

Schwartz, B., & Flowers, J. V. (2008). *Thoughts for therapists: Reflections on the art of healing.* Atascadero, CA: Impact Publishers.

Schwartz, J. & Broder, J.M. (2003, February 13). Loss of the shuttle: The overview; Engineer warned about dire impact of liftoff damage. *New York Times,* p. A1.

Schwartz, M. W., & Morton, G. J. (2002). Obesity: Keeping hunger at bay. *Nature, 418,* 595–597.

Schwartz, R. C., & Smith, S. D. (2004). Suicidality and psychosis: The predictive potential of symptomatology and insight into illness. *Journal of Psychiatric Research, 38*(2), 185–191.

Schwarz, A. (2007, September 15) Silence on concussions raises risks of injury. *New York Times.* [On-line]. Available: http://www.nytimes.com/2007/09/15/sports/football/15concussions.html.

Scribner, S. (1977). Modes of thinking and ways of speaking: Culture and logic reconsidered. In P. N. Johnson-Laird & P. C. Wason (Eds.), *Thinking: Readings in cognitive science* (pp. 324–339). New York: Cambridge University Press.

Scully, J. A., Tosi, H., & Banning, K. (2000). Life event checklists: Revisiting the Social Readjustment Rating Scale after 30 years. *Educational & Psychological Measurement, 60*(6), 864–876.

Sebre, S., Sprugevica, I., Novotni, A., Bonevski, D., Pakalniskiene, V., Popescu, D., Turchina, T., Friedrich, W., & Lewis, O. (2004). Crosscultural comparisons of child-reported emotional and physical abuse: Rates, risk factors and psychosocial symptoms. *Child Abuse & Neglect, 28*(1), 113–127.

Secker, D. L., Kazantzis, N., Pachana, N. A., & Kazantzis, N. (2004). Cognitive behavior therapy for older adults: Practical guidelines for adapting therapy structure. *Journal of Rational-Emotive & Cognitive Behavior Therapy, 22*(2), 93–109.

Segal, N. L., & Bouchard, T. J. (2000). *Entwined lives: Twins and what they tell us about human behavior.* New York: Plumsock.

Segall, M. H., Dasen, P. R., Berry, J. W., & Portinga, Y. H. (1990). *Human behavior in global perspective: An introduction to cross-cultural psychology.* Elmsford, NY: Pergamon Press.

Segerdahl, P., Fields, W., & Savage-Rumbaugh, S. (2006). Kanzi's primal language: *The cultural initiation of primates into language.* New York: Palgrave Macmillan.

Segerstrale, U. (2000). *Defenders of the truth: The battle for science in the sociobiology debate and beyond.* London: Oxford University Press.

Segerstrom, S., C., & Miller, G. E. (2004). Psychological stress and the human immune system: A meta-analytic study of 30 years of inquiry. *Psychological Bulletin, 130*(4), 601–630.

Seligman, M. E. P. (1975) *Helplessness: On depression, development, and death.* San Francisco: Freeman.

Seligman, M. E. P. (1994). *What you can change and what you can't.* New York: Alfred A. Knopf.

Seligman, M. E. P. (2003). The past and future of positive psychology. In C. L. M. Keyes & J. Daidt (Eds.), *Flourishing: Positive psychology and the life well-lived.* Washington, DC: American Psychological Association.

Seligman, M. E. P. (2007). Coaching and positive psychology. *Australian Psychologist, 42,* 266–267.

Selye, H. (1936). A syndrome produced by diverse nocuous agents. *Nature, 138,* 32.

Selye, H. (1974). *Stress without distress.* New York: Harper & Row.

Senko, C., Durik, A. M., & Harackiewicz, J. M. (2008). Historical perspectives and new directions in achievement goal theory: Understanding the effects of mastery and performance-approach goals. In J. Y. Shah & W. L. Gardner (Eds.), *Handbook of motivation science* (pp. 100–113). New York: Guilford Press.

Sequeira, A., Mamdani, F., Lalovic, A., Anguelova, M., Lesage, A., Seguin, M., Chawky, N., Desautels, A., & Turecki, G. (2004). Alpha 2A adrenergic receptor gene and suicide. *Psychiatry Research, 125*(2), 87–93.

Sergerdahl, P., Fields, W., & Savage-Rumbaugh, E. S. (2006). *Kanzi's primal language: The cultural initiation of primates into language.* New York: Palgrave Macmillan.

Seyranian, V., & Bligh, M. C. (2008). Presidential charismatic leadership: Exploring the rhetoric of social change. *Leadership Quarterly, 19,* 54–76.

Shadish, W. R., & Baldwin, S. A. (2003). Metaanalysis of MFT interventions. *Journal of Marital & Family Therapy, 29*(4), 547–570.

Shahim, S. (2008). Sex differences in relational aggression in preschool children in Iran. *Psychological Reports, 102,* 235–238.

Shao, L., & Webber, S. (2006). A cross-cultural test of the five-factor model of personality and transformational leadership. *Journal of Business Research, 59,* 936–944.

Sharps, M. J., Hess, A. B., Casner, H., Ranes, B., & Jones, J. (2007). Eyewitness memory in context: Toward a systematic understanding of eyewitness evidence. *The Forensic Examiner, 16,* 20–27.

Shaver, P. R., & Mikulincer, M. (2005). Attachment theory and research: Resurrection of the psychodynamic approach to personality. *Journal of Research in Personality, 39*(1), 22–45.

Shea, D. J. (2007). Effects of sexual abuse by Catholic priests on adults victimized as children. *Dissertation Abstracts International: Section B: The Sciences and Engineering, 67*(10-B), 6078.

Shea, S.C. (1988). *Psychiatric interviewing: The art of understanding.* Philadelphia, PA: Saunders.

Shear, K., Halmi, K. A., Widiger, T. A., & Boyce, C. (2007). Sociocultural factors and gender. In W. E. Narrow, M. B. First, P. J. Sirovatka, & D. A. Regier (Eds.), *Age and gender considerations in psychiatric diagnosis: A research agenda for DSM-V* (pp. 65–79). Arlington, VA: American Psychiatric Publishing.

Shen, B-J., McCreary, C. P., & Myers, H. F. (2004). Independent and mediated contributions of personality, coping, social support, and depressive symptoms to physical functioning outcome among patients in cardiac rehabilitation. *Journal of Behavioral Medicine, 27*(1), 39–62.

Sheppard, L. D., & Vernon, P. A. (2008). Intelligence and speed of information-processing: A review of 50 years of research. *Personality & Individual Differences, 44,* 535–551.

Shepperd, J., Malone, W., & Sweeny, K. (2008). Exploring causes of the self-serving bias. *Social and Personality Psychology Compass, 2,* 895–908.

Sher, K. J., Grekin, E. R., & Williams, N. A. (2005). The development of alcohol use disorders. *Annual Review of Clinical Psychology, 1,* 493–523.

Sherif, M. (1966). *In common predicament: Social psychology of intergroup conflict and cooperation.* Boston: Houghton Mifflin.

Sherif, M. (1998). Experiments in group conflict. In J. M. Jenkins, K. Oatley, & N. L. Stein (Eds.), *Human emotions: A reader* (pp. 245–252). Malden, MA: Blackwell.

Sherwin, C. M., Christiansen, S. B., Duncan, I. J., Erhard, H. W., Lay, D. C., Jr., Mench, J. A., O'Connor, C. E., & Petherick, J. C. (2003). Guidelines for the ethical use of animals in applied ethology studies. *Applied Animal Behaviour Science, 81*(3), 291–305.

Shi, Y., Devadas, S., Greeneltch, K. M., Yin, D., Mufson, R. A., & Zhou, J. (2003). Stressed to death: Implication of lymphocyte apoptosis for psychoneuroimmunology. *Brain, Behavior & Immunity.* 7(Suppl1), S18-S26.

Shields, C. D. (2008). The relationship between goal orientation, parenting style, and self-handicapping in adolescents. *Dissertation Abstracts International Section A: Humanities and Social Sciences, 68*(10-A), 4200.

Shimizu-Albergine, M., Ippolito, D. L., & Beavo, J. A. (2001). Downregulation of fastinginduced cAMP response element-mediated gene induction by leptin in neuropeptide Y neurons of the arcuate nucleus. *Journal of Neuroscience, 21*(4), 1238–1246.

Shiraev, E., & Levy, D. (2007). *Cross-cultural psychology* (3rd ed.). Boston: Allyn & Bacon.

Shlomof-Cohen, S. (2007). Attribution of organizational success and failure to leaders: The role of charismatic leadership and organizational crisis. *Dissertation Abstracts International: Section B: The Sciences and Engineering, 68*(6-B), 4120

Shlonsky, A., & Friend, C. (2007). Child maltreatment and domestic violence editorial: Current state of knowledge and emerging strategies for policy and practice. *Brief Treatment and Crisis Intervention,* 7, 249–252.

Shors, T. J. (2004). Learning during stressful times. *Learning and Memory, 11,* 137–144.

Shriver, T. P., & Weissberg, R. P. *(2005, August 16).* No emotion left behind. *New York Times.* [On-line]. Available: http://www .casel.org/downloads/NYToped.doc.

Shwalb, B. J., & Shwalb, D. W. (2006). The psychological effects of Hurricane Katrina on college students from New Orleans and Southeastern Louisiana. *Invited presentation at the annual Depression on College Campuses Conference* (Ann Arbor, MI).

Shwalb, D. W., & Shwalb, B. J. (2006). The effects of Hurricane Katrina on displaced vs. regular college students in New Orleans and Southeast Louisiana. *Paper presented at the annual convention of the American Psychological Association (APA)* (New Orleans).

Sias, P. M., Heath, R. G., Perry, T., Silva, D., & Fix, B. (2004). Narratives of workplace friendship deterioration. *Journal of Social & Personal Relationships, 21*(3), 321–340.

Sibley, C. G., & Liu, J. H. (2007). New Zealand = bicultural? Implicit and explicit associations between ethnicity and nationhood in the New Zealand context. *European Journal of Social Psychology, 37,* 1222–1243.

Siccoli, M. M., Rölli-Baumeler, N., Achermann, P., & Bassetti, C. L. (2008). Correlation between sleep and cognitive functions after hemispheric ischaemic stroke. *European Journal of Neurology, 15,* 565–572.

Siegala, M., & Varley, R. (2008). If we could talk to the animals. *Behavioral & Brain Sciences, 31,* 146–147.

Siegel, D. J. (2001). Toward an interpersonal neurobiology of the developing mind: Attachment relationships, "mindsight," and neural integration. *Infant Mental Health Journal, 22,* 67–94.

Siegel, J. M. (2000, January). Narcolepsy. *Scientific American,* pp. 76–81.

Siegel, J. M. (2008). Do all animals sleep? *Trends in Neurosciences, 31,* 208–213.

Siegel, J. P. (2007). The enduring crisis of divorce for children and their parents. In N. B. Boyd (Ed.), *Play therapy with children in crisis: Individual, group, and family treatment* (3rd ed.) (pp. 133–151). New York: Guilford Press.

Siegel, P. H., Schraeder, M., & Morrison, R. (2008). A taxonomy of equity factors. *Journal of Applied Social Psychology, 38,* 61–75.

Siever, L. J. (2008). Neurobiology of aggression and violence. *American Journal of Psychiatry, 165,* 429–442.

Sigall, H., & Johnson, M. (2006). The relationship between facial contact with a pillow

and mood. *Journal of Applied Social Psychology, 36,* 505–526.

Sigelman, C. K., & Rider, E. A. (2009). *Lifespan human development* (6th ed.). Belmont, CA: Cengage.

Silke, A. (2003). Deindividuation, anonymity, and violence: Findings from Northern Ireland. *Journal of Social Psychology, 143*(4), 493–499.

Silverman, W. K., Pina, A. A., & Viswesvaran, C. (2008). Evidence-based psychosocial treatments for phobic and anxiety disorders in children and adolescents. *Journal of Clinical Child and Adolescent Psychology, 37,* 105–130.

Silvester, J., Anderson-Gough, F. M., Anderson, N. R., & Mohamed, A. R. (2002). Locus of control, attributions and impression management in the selection interview. *Journal of Occupational & Organizational Psychology, 75*(1), 59–76.

Silvestri, A. J., & Root, D. H. (2008). Effects of REM deprivation and an NMDA agonist on the extinction of conditioned fear. *Physiology & Behavior, 93,* 274–281.

Sim, T., & Wong, D. (2008). Working with Chinese families in adolescent drug treatment. *Journal of Social Work Practice, 22,* 103–118.

Simcock, G., & Hayne, H. (2002). Breaking the barrier? Children fail to translate their preverbal memories into language. *Psychological Science, 13*(3), 225–231.

Simon, C. (2007). *Neurology.* New York: Oxford University Press.

Singelis, T. M., Triandis, H. C., Bhawuk, D. S., & Gelfand, M. (1995). Horizontal and vertical dimensions of individualism and collectivism: A theoretical and measurement refinement. *Cross-Cultural Research, 29,* 240–275.

Singer, M. I., Slovak, K., Frierson, T., & York, P. (1998). Viewing preferences, symptoms of psychological trauma, and violent behaviors among children who watch television. *Journal of the American Academy of Child and Adolescent Psychiatry, 37,* 1041–1048.

Singer, R. (2008). Neuropsychological assessment of toxic exposures. In A. M. Horton Jr. & D. Wedding (Eds.), *The neuropsychology handbook* (3rd ed.) (pp. 753–770). New York: Springer.

Singh, A. (2007). Culture, gender, identity, and adolescents' niche-building behavior: A cross-cultural comparison (India, United States). *Dissertation Abstracts International: Section B: The Sciences and Engineering, 67*(12-B), 7408.

Sinha, R., Talih, M., Malison, R., Cooney, N., Anderson, G. M., & Kreek, M. J. (2003).

Hypothalamic-pituitary-adrenal axis and sympatho-adreno-medullary responses during stress-induced and drug cue-induced cocaine craving states. *Psychopharmacology, 170*(1), 62–72.

Siqueland, L., Crits-Christoph, P., Gallop, R., Barber, J. P., Griffin, M. L., Thase, M. E., Daley, D., Frank, A., Gastfriend, D. R., Blaine, J., Connolly, M. B., & Gladis, M. (2002). Retention in psychosocial treatment of cocaine dependence: Predictors and impact on outcome. *American Journal on Addictions, 11*(1), 24–40.

Sirin, S. R., & Rogers-Sirin, L. (2004). Exploring school engagement of middle-class African American adolescents. *Youth & Society, 35*(3), 323–340.

Skelhorn, J., Griksaitis, D., Rowe, C. (2008). Colour biases are more than a question of taste. *Animal Behaviour, 75,* 827–835.

Skinner, B. F. (1948). Superstition in the pigeon. *Journal of Experimental Psychology, 38,* 168–172.

Skinner, B. F. (1953). *Science and human behavior.* New York: Macmillan.

Skinner, B. F. (1961). Diagramming schedules of reinforcement. *Journal of the Experimental Analysis of Behavior, 1,* 67–68.

Skinner, B. F. (1992). "Superstition" in the pigeon. *Journal of Experimental Psychology: General, 121*(3), 273–274.

Skinner, E. I., & Fernandes, M. A. (2008). Interfering with remembering and knowing: Effects of divided attention at retrieval. *Acta Psychologica, 127,* 211–221.

Skinta, M. D. (2008). The effects of bullying and internalized homophobia on psychopathological symptom severity in a community sample of gay men. *Dissertation Abstracts International: Section B: The Sciences and Engineering, 68*(7-B), 4847.

Slobogin, C. (2006). *Minding justice: Laws that deprive people with mental disability of life and liberty.* Cambridge, MA: Harvard University Press.

Slobounov, S. M. (2008). *Injuries in athletics: Causes and consequences.* New York: Springer.

Slováčková, B., & Slováček, L. (2007). Moral judgement competence and moral attitudes of medical students. *Nursing Ethics, 14,* 320–328.

Sluzenski, J., Newcombe, N., & Ottinger, W. (2004). Changes in reality monitoring and episodic memory in early childhood. *Developmental Science, 7*(2), 225–245.

Smart, D. W., & Smart, J. F. (1997). DSM-IV and culturally sensitive diagnosis: Some observations for counselors. *Journal of Counseling and Development, 75,* 392–398.

Smith, C., & Smith, D. (2003). Ingestion of ethanol just prior to sleep onset impairs memory for procedural but not declarative tasks. *Sleep, 26*(2), 185–191.

Smith, D. (2002). The theory heard 'round the world. *Monitor on Psychology,* p. 30–32.

Smith, E. E. (1995). Concepts and categorization. In E. E. Smith & D. N. Osherson (Eds.), *Thinking: An invitation to cognitive science* (2nd ed., Vol. 3, pp. 3–33). Cambridge: MIT Press.

Smith, K. D. (2007). Spinning straw into gold: Dynamics of Rumpelstiltskin style of leadership. *Dissertation Abstracts International Section A: Humanities and Social Sciences, 68*(5-A), 1760.

Smith, L. J., Nowakowski, S., Soeffing, J. P., Orff, H. J., & Perlis, M. L. (2003). The measurement of sleep. In L. Michael & K. L. Lichstein (Eds.), *Treating sleep disorders: Principles and practice of behavioral sleep medicine.* Hoboken, NJ: Wiley.

Smith, M. T., Huang, M. I., & Manber, R. (2005). Cognitive behavior therapy for chronic insomnia occurring within the context of medical and psychiatric disorders. *Clinical Psychology Review, 25,* 559–592.

Smith, P., Frank, J., Bondy, S., & Mustard, C. (2008). Do changes in job control predict differences in health status? Results from a longitudinal national survey of Canadians. *Psychosomatic Medicine, 70,* 85–91.

Smith, T. W., Orleans, C. T., & Jenkins, C. D. (2004). Prevention and health promotion: Decades of progress, new challenges, and an emerging agenda. *Health Psychology, 23*(2), 126–131.

Smith, V. W. (2006). The development and field testing of a school psychology employment interview instrument. *Dissertation Abstracts International Section A: Humanities and Social Sciences, 67*(2-A), 418.

SmithBattle, L., & Leonard, V. W. (2006). Teen mothers and their teenaged children: The reciprocity of developmental trajectories. *Advances in Nursing Science, 29,* 351–365.

Smithson, M., & Baker, C. (2008). Risk orientation, loving, and liking in long-term romantic relationships. *Journal of Social and Personal Relationships, 25,* 87–103.

Snarey, J. R. (1985). Cross-cultural universality of social-moral development: A critical review of Kohlbergian research. *Psychological Bulletin, 97,* 202–233.

Snarey, J. R. (1995). In communitarian voice: The sociological expansion of Kohlbergian theory, research, and practice. In W. M. Kurtines & J. L. Gerwirtz (Eds.), *Moral development: An introduction* (pp. 109–134). Boston: Allyn & Bacon.

Snowden, L. R., & Yamada, A-M. (2005). Cultural differences in access to care. *Annual Review of Clinical Psychology, 1,* 143–166.

Snowdon, D. A. (2003). Healthy aging and dementia: Findings from the nun study. *Annals of Internal Medicine, 139,* 450–454.

Snyder, C. R. (2003). "Me conform? No way": Classroom demonstrations for sensitizing students to their conformity. *Teaching of Psychology, 30*(1), 59–61.

Snyder, J. S., & Alain, C. (2007). Sequential auditory sense analysis is preserved in normal aging adults. *Cerebral Cortex, 17,* 501–512.

Sokol, R. J. Jr., Delaney-Black, V., & Nordstrom, B. (2003). Fetal alcohol spectrum disorder. JAMA: *Journal of the American Medical Association, 290*(22), 2996–2999.

Solan, H. A., & Mozlin, R. (2001). Children in poverty: Impact on health, visual development, and school failure. *Issues in Interdisciplinary Care, 3*(4), 271–288.

Sollod, R. N., Monte, C. F., & Wilson, J. P. (2009). *Beneath the mask: An introduction to theories of personality* (8th ed.). Hoboken, NJ: Wiley.

Solms, M. (1997). *The neuropsychology of dreams.* Mahwah, NJ: Lawrence Erlbaum.

Son, L. K., & Metcalfe, J. (2000). Metacognitive and control strategies in study-time allocation. *Journal of Experimental Psychology: Learning, Memory, & Cognition, 26,* 204–221.

Sotres-Bayón, F., & Pellicer, F. (2000). The role of the dopaminergic mesolimbic system in the affective component of chronic pain. *Salud Mental, 23*(1), 23–29.

Soussignan, R. (2002). Duchenne smile, emotional experience, and autonomic reactivity: A test of the facial feedback hypothesis. *Emotion, 2*(1), 52–74.

Southwick, S. M., Vythilingam, M., & Charney, D. S. (2005). The psychobiology of depression and resilience to stress: Implications for prevention and treatment. *Annual Review of Clinical Psychology, 1,* 255–291.

Sowell, E. R., Mattson, S. N., Kan, E., Thompson, P. M., Riley, E. P., Edward, P., & Toga, A. W. (2008). Abnormal cortical thickness and brain-behavior correlation patterns in individuals with heavy prenatal alcohol exposure. *Cerebral Cortex, 18,* 136–144.

Spearman, C. (1923). *The nature of "intelligence" and the principles of cognition.* London: Macmillan.

Spector, P. E. (2009). *Industrial organizational psychology: Research and practice* (5th ed.). Hoboken, NJ: Wiley.

Spek, V., Cuijpers, P., Nyklícek, I., Smits, N., Riper, H., Keyzer, J., & Pop, V. (2008). One-year follow-up results of a randomized controlled clinical trial on Internet-based cognitive behavioural therapy for subthreshold depression in people over 50 years. *Psychological Medicine, 38,* 635–639.

Spence, S. A. (2003). Detecting lies and deceit: The psychology of lying and the implications for professional practice. *Cognitive Neuropsychiatry, 8*(1), 76–77.

Sperling, G. (1960). The information available in brief visual presentations. *Psychological Monographs, 74* (Whole No. 498).

Spiegel, D. (1999). An altered state. *Mind/ Body Health Newsletter, 8*(1), 3–5.

Spiegel, D., & Maldonado, J. R. (1999). Dissociative disorders. In R. E. Hales, S. C. Yudofsky, & J. C. Talbott (Eds.), *American psychiatric press textbook of psychiatry.* Washington, DC: American Psychiatric Press.

Spinelli, S., Schwandt, M. L., Lindell, S. G., Newman, T. K., Heilig, M., Suomi, S. J., Higley, J. D., Goldman, D., & Barr, C. S. (2007). Association between the recombinant human serotonin transporter linked promoter region polymorphism and behavior in rhesus macaques during a separation paradigm. *Development and Psychopathology, 19,* 977–987.

Spinweber, C. L. (1993). Randy Gardner. In M. A. Carskadon (Ed.), *Encyclopedia of sleep and dreaming.* New York: Macmillan.

Spitz, R. A., & Wolf, K. M. (1946). The smiling response: A contribution to the ontogenesis of social relations. *Genetic Psychology Monographs, 34,* 57–123.

Spokane, A. R., Meir, E. I., & Catalano, M. (2000). Person-environment congruence and Holland's theory: A review and reconsideration. *Journal of Vocational Behavior, 57*(2), 137–187.

Sprecher, S., & Regan, P. C. (2002). Liking some things (in some people) more than others: Partner preferences in romantic relationships and friendships. *Journal of Social & Personal Relationships, 19*(4), 463–481.

Squier, L. H., & Domhoff, G. W. (1998). The presentation of dreaming and dreams in introductory psychology textbooks: A critical examination. *Dreaming, 10,* 21–26.

Squire, L. R., Schmolck, H., & Buffalo, E. A. (2001). Memory distortions develop over time: A reply to Horn. *Psychological Science, 121*(2), 182.

Stafford, J., & Lynn, S. J. (2002). Cultural scripts, memories of childhood abuse, and multiple identities: A study of role-played enactments. *International Journal of Clinical & Experimental Hypnosis, 50*(1), 67–85.

Staley, C. (2008). Facial attractiveness and the sentencing of male defendants. *Dissertation Abstracts International: Section B: The Sciences and Engineering, 68*(8-B), 5639.

Stanton, M. D. (2004). Getting reluctant substance abusers to engage in treatment/selfhelp: A review of outcomes and clinical options. *Journal of Marital & Family Therapy, 30*(2), 165–182.

Steadman, H. J. (1993). *Reforming the insanity defense: An evaluation of pre-and post-Hinckley reforms.* New York: Guilford Press.

Steele, C. M. (2003). Through the back door to theory. *Psychological Inquiry, 14*(3–4), 314–317.

Steele, C. M., & Aronson, J. (1995). Stereotype threat and the intellectual test performance of African Americans. *Journal of Personality and Social Psychology, 69,* 797–811.

Steele, J., James, J. B., & Barnett, R. C. (2002). Learning in a man's world: Examining the perceptions of undergraduate women in male-dominated academic areas. *Psychology of Women Quarterly, 26*(1), 46–50.

Steffens, D. C., McQuoid, D. R., Welsh-Bohmer, K. A., & Krishnan, K. R. R. (2003). Left orbital frontal cortex volume and performance on the Benton Visual Retention Test in older depressives and controls. *Neuropsychopharmacology, 28*(12), 2179–2183.

Steiger, H., Israël, M., Gauvin, L., Kin, N. M. K. N. Y., & Young, S. N. (2003). Implications of compulsive and impulsive traits for serotonin status in women with bulimia nervosa. *Psychiatry Research, 120*(3), 219–229.

Stein, D. J., & Lochner, C. (2008). The empirical basis of the obsessive-compulsive spectrum. In J. S. Abramowitz, D. McKay, & S. Taylor (Eds.), *Clinical handbook of obsessive-compulsive disorder and related problems* (pp. 177–187). Baltimore, MD: Johns Hopkins University Press.

Stein, D. J., & Matsunaga, H. (2006). Specific phobia: A disorder of fear conditioning and extinction. *CNS Spectrums, 11*(4), 248–251.

Stein, M. B., & Stein, D. J. (2008). Social anxiety disorder. *Lancet, 371,* 1115–1125.

Steinberg, L. (2008). A social neuroscience perspective on adolescent risk-taking. *Developmental Review, 28,* 78–106.

Steinhart, P. (1986, March). Personal boundaries. *Audubon,* pp. 8–11.

Stella, N., Schweitzer, P., & Piomelli, D. (1997). A second endogenous cannabinoid that modulates long-term potentiation. *Nature, 382,* 677–678.

Stelmack, R. M., Knott, V., & Beauchamp, C. M. (2003). Intelligence and neural transmission time: A brain stem auditory evoked potential analysis. *Personality & Individual Differences, 34*(1), 97–107.

Sternberg, R. J. (1985). *Beyond IQ: A triarchic theory of human intelligence.* New York: Cambridge University Press.

Sternberg, R. J. (1998). Principles of teaching for successful intelligence. *Educational Psychologist, 33,* 65–72.

Sternberg, R. J. (1999). The theory of successful intelligence. *Review of General Psychology, 3,* 292–316.

Sternberg, R. J. (2005). The importance of converging operations in the study of human intelligence. *Cortex. 41*(2), 243–244.

Sternberg, R. J. (2007). Developing successful intelligence in all children: A potential solution to underachievement in ethnic minority children. In M. C. Wang & R. D. Taylor (Eds.), *Closing the achievement gap.* Philadelphia: Laboratory for Student Success at Temple University.

Sternberg, R. J. (2008). The triarchic theory of human intelligence. In N. Salkind (Ed.), *Handbook of multicultural assessment* (3rd ed.). New York: Jossey-Bass.

Sternberg, R. J. (2009). *Cognitive psychology* (5th ed.). Belmont, CA: Wadsworth.

Sternberg, R. J. (Ed.). (2004). *Definitions and conceptions of giftedness.* Thousand Oaks, CA: Corwin Press.

Sternberg, R. J., & Grigorenko, E. L. (2008). Ability testing across cultures. In L. Suzuki (Ed.), *Handbook of multicultural assessment* (3rd ed.). New York: Jossey-Bass.

Sternberg, R. J., & Hedlund, J. (2002). Practical intelligence, g, and work psychology. *Human Performance, 15*(1–2), 143–160.

Sternberg, R. J., & Lubart, T. I. (1992). Buy low and sell high: An investment approach to creativity. *Current Directions in Psychological Science, 1*(1), 1–5.

Sternberg, R. J., & Lubart, T. I. (1996). Investing in creativity. *American Psychologist, 51*(7), 677–688.

Stetter, F., & Kupper, S. (2002). Autogenic training: A meta-analysis of clinical outcome studies. *Applied Psychophysiology & Biofeedback, 27*(1), 45–98.

Stiles, W. B., Barkham, M., Mellor-Clark, J., & Connell, J. (2008). Effectiveness of cognitive-behavioural, person-centered, and psychodynamic therapies in UK primary-care routine practice: Replication in a larger sample. *Psychological Medicine, 39,* 677–688.

Stompe, T. G., Ortwein-Swoboda, K., Ritter, K., & Schanda, H. (2003). Old wine in new bottles? Stability and plasticity of the contents of schizophrenic delusions. *Psychopathology, 36*(1), 6–12.

Stone, K. L., & Redline, S. (2006). Sleep-related breathing disorders in the elderly. *Sleep Medicine Clinics, 1*(2), 247–262.

Stoner, J. A. (1961). *A comparison of individual and group decisions involving risk.* Unpublished master's thesis, School of Industrial Management, MIT, Cambridge, MA.

Stormshak, E. A., Bierman, K. L., McMahon, R. J., & Lengua, L. J., Conduct Problems Prevention Research Group. (2000). Parenting practices and child disruptive behavior problems in early elementary school. *Journal of Clinical Child Psychology, 29*(1), 17–29.

Storosum, J. G., Elferink, A. J. A., van Zwieten, B. J., van den Brink, W., & Huyser, J. (2004). Natural course and placebo response in short-term, placebo-controlled studies in major depression: A meta-analysis of published and non-published studies. *Pharmacopsychiatry, 37*(1), 32–36.

Strack, F., Martin, L. L., & Stepper, S. (1988). Inhibiting and facilitating conditions of the human smile: A nonobstrusive test of the facial feedback hypothesis. *Journal of Personality and Social Psychology, 54,* 768–777.

Stratton, G. M. (1896). Some preliminary experiments on vision without inversion of the retinal image. *Psychological Review 3,* 611–617.

Straub, R. O. (2007). *Health psychology: A biopsychosocial approach* (2nd ed.). New York: Worth.

Streri, A., Gentaz, E., Spelke, E., & Van de Walle, G. (2004). Infants' haptic perception of object unity in rotating displays. *Quarterly Journal of Experimental Psychology: Human Experimental Psychology, 57A*(3), 523–538.

Study finds 21st birthday binge. (2008, May 19). *APA Press Release.* [On-line]. Available: http://www.apa.org/releases/21birthday0508.html.

Subramanian, S., & Vollmer, R. R. (2002). Sympathetic activation fenfluramine depletes brown adipose tissue norepinephrine content in rats. *Pharmacology, Biochemistry & Behavior, 73*(3), 639–646.

Sue, D.W., & Sue, D. (2008). *Counseling the culturally diverse: Theory and practice* (5th ed.). Hoboken, NJ: Wiley.

Suhr, J. A. (2002). Malingering, coaching, and the serial position effect. *Archives of Clinical Neuropsychology, 17*(1), 69–77.

Sullivan, M. J. L. (2008). Toward a biopsychomotor conceptualization of pain: Implications for research and intervention. *Clinical Journal of Pain, 24,* 281–290.

Sullivan, M. J. L., Tripp, D. A., & Santor, D. (1998). *Gender differences in pain and pain behavior: The role of catastrophizing.* Paper presented at the annual meeting of the American Psychological Association, San Francisco.

Sullivan, P. F., Kendler, K. S., & Neale, M. C. (2003). Schizophrenia as a complex trait: Evidence from a meta-analysis of twin studies. *Archives of General Psychiatry, 60*(12), 1187–1192.

Sullivan, T. P., & Holt, L. J. (2008). PTSD symptom clusters are differentially related to substance use among community women exposed to intimate partner violence. *Journal of Traumatic Stress, 21,* 173–180.

Sun, L-Y., & Pan, W. (2008). HR practices perceptions, emotional exhaustion, and work outcomes: A conservation-of-resources theory in the Chinese context. *Human Resource Development Quarterly, 19,* 55–74.

Suomi, S. J. (1991). Adolescent depression and depressive symptoms: Insights from longitudinal studies with rhesus monkeys. *Journal of Youth & Adolescence, 20,* 273–287.

Surawy, C., Roberts, J., & Silver, A. (2005). The effect of mindfulness training on mood and measures of fatigue, activity, and quality of life in patients with chronic fatigue syndrome on a hospital waiting list: A series of exploratory studies. *Behavioural & Cognitive Psychotherapy. 33*(1), 103–109.

Sutherland, M. A., & Harkness, S. (2007). At home in an institution: Daily life on a pediatric inpatient psychiatric unit as viewed through the developmental niche framework. *OTJR: Occupation, Participation and Health, 27,* 93S–95S.

Suzuki, L., & Aronson, J. (2005). The cultural malleability of intelligence and its impact on the racial/ethnic hierarchy. *Psychology, Public Policy, and Law, 11*(2), 320–327.

Suzuki, W. A., & Amaral, D. G. (2004). Functional neuroanatomy of the medial temporal lobe memory system. *Cortex, 40*(1), 220–222.

Swami, V., & Furnham, A. (2008). *The psychology of physical attraction.* New York: Routledge/Taylor & Francis Group.

Swanson, J. W., Swartz, M. S., & Elbogen, E. B. (2004). Effectiveness of atypical antipsychotic medications in reducing violent behavior among persons with schizophrenia in community-based treatment. *Schizophrenia Bulletin, 30*(1), 3–20.

Swartz, K. L. (2004). Depression and anxiety. *Johns Hopkins White Papers.* Baltimore: Johns Hopkins Medical Institutions.

Sylvester, A. P., Mulsant, B. H., Chengappa, K. N. R., Sandman, A. R., & Haskett, R. F. (2000). Use of electroconvulsive therapy in a state hospital: A 10-year review. *Journal of Clinical Psychiatry, 61,* 534–544.

Szabo, A. (2003). The acute effects of humor and exercise on mood and anxiety. *Journal of Leisure Research, 35,* 152–162.

Szasz, T. (1960). The myth of mental illness. *American Psychologist, 15,* 113–118.

Szasz, T. (2000). Second commentary on "Aristotle's function argument." *Philosophy, Psychiatry, & Psychology, 7,* 3–16.

Szasz, T. (2004). The psychiatric protection order for the "battered mental patient." *British Medical Journal, 327*(7429), 1449–1451.

Taber, K. H., Lewis, D. A., & Hurley, R. A. (2008). Schizophrenia: What's under the microscope? In R. A. Hurley & K. H. Taber (Eds.), *Windows to the brain: Insights from neuroimaging* (pp. 221–225). Arlington, VA: American Psychiatric Publishing.

Tait, R. J., & Hulse, G. K. (2003). A systematic review of the effectiveness of brief interventions with substance using adolescents by type of drug. *Drug & Alcohol Review, 22*(3), 337–346.

Takano, Y., & Sogon, S. (2008). Are Japanese more collectivistic than Americans? Examining conformity in in-groups and the reference-group effect. *Journal of Cross-Cultural Psychology, 39,* 237–250.

Tal-Or, N., & Papirman, Y. (2007). The fundamental attribution error in attributing fictional figures' characteristics to the actors. *Media Psychology, 9,* 331–345.

Talarico, J. M., & Rubin, D. C. (2007). Flashbulb memories are special after all; in phenomenology, not accuracy. *Applied Cognitive Psychology, 21,* 557–578.

Talbot, N. L., Duberstein, P. R., King, D. A., Cox, C., & Giles, D. E. (2000). Personality traits of women with a history of childhood sexual abuse. *Comprehensive Psychiatry, 41,* 130–136.

Talitwala, E. M. (2007). Fathers' parenting strategies: Their influence on young people's social relationships. *Dissertation Abstracts International Section A: Humanities and Social Sciences, 68*(5-A), 2191.

Talley, A. E., & Bettencourt, B. A. (2008). Evaluations and aggression directed at a gay male target: The role of threat and antigay prejudice. *Journal of Applied Social Psychology, 38,* 647–683.

Tanaka, T., Yoshida, M., Yokoo, H., Tomita, M., & Tanaka, M. (1998). Expression of aggression attenuates both stress-induced gastric ulcer formation and increases in noradrenaline release in the rat amygdala assessed intracerebral microdialysis. *Pharmacology, Biochemistry & Behavior, 59*(1), 27–31.

Tanda, G., & Goldberg, S. R. (2003). Cannabinoids: Reward, dependence, and underlying neurochemical mechanisms—a review of recent preclinical data. *Psychopharmacology, 169*(2), 115–134.

Tandon, R., Keshavan, M. S., & Nasrallah, H. A. (2008). Schizophrenia, "just the facts" what we know in 2008. 2. Epidemiology and etiology. *Schizophrenia Research, 102,* 1–18.

Tang, Y.-P., Wang, H., Feng, R., Kyin, M., & Tsien, J. Z. (2001). Differential effects of enrichment on learning and memory function in NR2B transgenic mice. *Neuropharmacology, 41*(6), 779–790.

Tangney, J. P., Stuewig, J., & Mashek, D. J. (2007). Moral emotions and moral behavior. *Annual Review of Psychology, 58,* 345–372.

Tannen, D. (2007). Talking voices: Repetition, dialogue, and imagery in conversational discourse (2nd ed). *In studies in interactional sociolinguistics.* New York: Cambridge University Press.

Tanner-Halverson, P., Burden, T., & Sabers, D. (1993). WISC-III normative data for Tohono O'odham Native-American children. In B. A. Bracken & R. S. McCallum (Eds.), *Journal of Psychoeducational Assessment Monograph Series, Advances in Psychoeducational Assessment: Wechsler Intelligence Scale for Children–Third Edition* (pp. 125–133). Germantown, TN: Psychoeducational Corporation.

Tarbox, R. S. F., Ghezzi, P. M., & Wilson, G. (2006). The effects of token reinforcement on attending in a young child with autism. *Behavioral Interventions, 21,* 155–164.

Tarter, R. E., Vanyukov, M., Kirisci, L., Reynolds, M., & Clark, D. B. (2006). Predictors of marijuana use in adolescents before and after licit drug use: Examination of the gateway hypothesis. *American Journal of Psychiatry, 163,* 2134–2140.

Task Force of the National Advisory Council on Alcohol Abuse and Alcoholism, National Institute on Alcohol Abuse and Alcoholism (2002). *A call to action: Changing the culture of drinking at U.S. colleges.* Washington, DC: National Institutes of Health. [On-line]. Available: http://www.collegedrinkingprevention.gov/.NIAAACollegeMaterials/TaskForce/TaskForce_TOC.aspx.

Tatrow, K., Blanchard, E. B., & Silverman, D. J. (2003). Posttraumatic headache: An exploratory treatment study. *Applied Psychophysiology & Biofeedback, 28*(4), 267–279.

Taub, E. (2004). Harnessing brain plasticity through behavioral techniques to produce new treatments in neurorehabilitation. *American Psychologist, 59*(8), 692–704.

Taub, E., Gitendra, U., & Thomas, E. (2002). New treatments in neurorehabilitation founded on basic research. *Nature Reviews Neuroscience, 3,* 228–236.

Taub, E., Griffin, A., Nick, J., Gammons, K., Uswatte, G., & Law, C. R. (2007). Pediatric CI therapy for stroke-induced hemiparesis in young children. *Developmental Neurorehabilitation, 10,* 3–18.

Taub, E., & Morris, D. (2002). Constraint-induced movement therapy to enhance recovery after stroke. *Current Artherosclerosis Reports, 3,* 279–86.

Taub, E., Ramey, S. L., DeLuca, S., & Echols, K. (2004). Efficacy of constraint-induced movement therapy for children with cerebral palsy with asymmetric motor impairment. *Pediatrics, 113,* 305–312.

Taylor, D. J., Lichstein, K. L., & Durrence, H. H. (2003). Insomnia as a health risk factor. *Behavioral Sleep Medicine, 1*(4), 227–247.

Taylor, J. Y., Caldwell, C. H., Baser, R. E., Faison, N., & Jackson, J. S. (2007). Prevalence of eating disorders among Blacks in the national survey of American life. *International Journal of Eating Disorders, 40*(Supl), S10-S14.

Taylor, R. C., Harris, N. A., Singleton, E. G., Moolchan, E. T., & Heishman, S. J. (2000). Tobacco craving: Intensity-related effects of imagery scripts in drug abusers. *Experimental and Clinical Psychopharmacology, 8*(1), 75–87.

Taylor, S. E., & Armor, D. A. (1996). Positive illusions and coping with adversity. *Journal of Personality, 64,* 873–898.

Taylor, S. E., & Sherman, D. K. (2008). Self-enhancement and self-affirmation: The consequences of positive self-thoughts for motivation and health. In J. Y. Shah & W. L. Gardner (Eds.), *Handbook of motivation science* (pp. 57–70). New York: Guilford Press.

Taylor, S. E., & Stanton, A. L. (2007). Coping resources, coping processes, and mental health. *Annual Review of Clinical Psychology, 3,* 377–401.

Teasdale, T. W., & Owen, D. R. (2008). Secular declines in cognitive test scores: A reversal of the Flynn Effect. *Intelligence, 36,* 121–126.

Tebartz van Elst, L, Hesslinger, B., Thiel, T., Geiger, E., Haegele, K., Lemieux, L., Lieb, K., Bohus, M., Hennig, J., & Ebert, D. (2003). Frontolimbic brain abnormalities in patients with borderline personality disorder: A volumetric magnetic resonance imaging study. *Biological Psychiatry, 54*(2), 163–171.

Tecchio, F., Zappasodi, F., Pasqualetti, P., De Gennaro, L., Pellicciari, M. C., Ercolani, M., Squitti, R., & Rossini, P. M. (2008). Age dependence of primary motor cortex plasticity induced by paired associative stimulation. *Clinical Neurophysiology, 119,* 675–682.

Tedlock, B. (1992). Zuni and Quiche dream sharing and interpreting. In B. Tedlock (Ed.), *Dreaming: Anthropological and psychological interpretations.* Santa Fe, NM: School of American Research Press.

Teesson, M., Hodder, T., & Buhrich, N. (2004). Psychiatric disorders in homeless men and women in inner Sydney. *Australian & New Zealand Journal of Psychiatry, 38*(3),162–168.

Tellegen, A. (1985). Structures of mood and personality and their relevance to assessing anxiety with an emphasis on self-report. In A. H. Tuma & J. D. Maser (Eds.), *Anxiety and the anxiety disorders* (pp. 681–706). Hillsdale, NJ: Erlbaum.

Temcheff, C. E., Serbin, L. A., Martin-Storey, A., Stack, D. M., Hodgins, S., Ledingham, J., & Schwartzman, A. E. (2008). Continuity and pathways from aggression in childhood to family violence in adulthood: A 30-year longitudinal study. *Journal of Family Violence, 23,* 231–242.

Terman, L. M. (1916). *The measurement of intelligence.* Boston: Houghton Mifflin.

Terman, L. M. (1954). Scientists and nonscientists in a group of 800 gifted men. *Psychological Monographs, 68*(7), 1–44.

Terrace, H. S. (1979, November). How Nim Chimpsky changed my mind. *Psychology Today,* pp. 65–76.

Terry, S. W. (2003). *Learning and memory: Basic principles, processes, and procedures* (2nd ed.). Boston: Allyn & Bacon.

Tett, R. P., & Murphy, P. J. (2002). Personality and situations in co-worker preference: Similarity and complementarity in worker compatibility. *Journal of Business & Psychology, 17*(2), 223–243.

Teusch, L., Boehme, H., Finke, J., & Gastpar, K. (2001). Effects of client-centered psychotherapy for personality disorders alone and in combination with psychopharmacological treatment. *Psychotherapy & Psychosomatics, 70*(6), 328–336.

Thapar, A., Fowler, T., Rice, F., Scourfield, J., van den Bree, M., Thomas, H., Harold, G., & Hay, D. (2003). Maternal smoking during pregnancy and attention deficit hyperactivity disorder symptoms in offspring. *American Journal of Psychiatry, 160*(11), 1985–1989.

The High Cost of Smoking. (2008). [On-line]. Available: http://articles.moneycentral.msn.com/Insurance/InsureYourHealth/HighCostOfSmoking.aspx

Theobarides, T. C., & Cochrane, D. E. (2004). Critical role of mast cells in inflammatory diseases and the effect of acute stress. *Journal of Neuroimmunology, 146*(1–2), 1–12.

Thøgersen, J. (2004). A cognitive dissonance interpretation of consistencies and inconsistencies in environmentally responsible behavior. *Journal of Environmental Psychology, 24*(1), 93–103.

Thomas, A., & Chess, S. (1977). *Temperament and development.* New York: Brunner/Mazel.

Thomas, A., & Chess, S. (1987). Round-table: What is temperament: Four approaches. *Child Development, 58,* 505–529.

Thomas, A., & Chess, S. (1991). Temperament in adolescence and its functional significance. In R. M. Lerner, A. C. Petersen, & J. Brooks-Gunn (Eds.), *Encyclopedia of adolescence* (Vol. 2). New York: Garland.

Thomas, B. L., & Ayres, J. J. B. (2004). Use of the ABA fear renewal paradigm to assess the effects of extinction with co-present fear inhibitors or excitors: Implications for theories of extinction and for treating human fears and phobias. *Learning & Motivation, 35*(1), 22–52.

Thomas, S. E., Randall, P. K., Book, S. W., & Randall, C. L. (2008). The complex relationship between co-occurring social anxiety and alcohol use disorders: What effect does treating social anxiety have on drinking? *Alcoholism: Clinical and Experimental Research, 32,* 77–84.

Thompson, D. (1997, March 24). A boy without a penis. *Time,* p. 83.

Thompson, R. F. (2005). In search of memory traces. *Annual Review of Clinical Psychology, 56,* 1–23.

Thomson, E. (2007). *Mind in life: Biology, phenomenology, and the sciences of mind.* Cambridge, MA: Belknap Press.

Thomson, W. M., Poulton, R., Broadbent, J. M., Moffitt, T. E., Caspi, A., Beck, J. D., Welch, D., & Hancox, R. J. (2008). Cannabis smoking and periodontal disease among young adults. *Journal of the American Medical Assocation, 299,* 525–531.

Thorndike, E. L. (1898). Animal intelligence. *Psychological Review Monograph, 2*(8).

Thorndike, E. L. (1911). *Animal intelligence.* New York: Macmillan.

Thornhill, R., Gangestad, S. W., Miller, R., Scheyd, G., McCollough, J. K., & Franklin, M. (2003). Major histocompatibility complex genes, symmetry, and body scent attractiveness in men and women. *Behavioral Ecology, 14*(5), 668–678.

Thurstone, L. L. (1938). *Primary mental abilities.* Chicago: University of Chicago Press.

Tice, D. M., & Baumeister, R. F. (1997). Longitudinal study of procrastination, performance, stress, and health: The costs and benefits of dawdling. *Psychological Science, 8,* 454–458.

Tietzel, A. J., & Lack, L. C. (2001). The short-term benefits of brief and long naps following nocturnal sleep restriction. *Sleep: Journal of Sleep Research & Sleep Medicine, 24*(3), 293–300.

Tiihonen, J., Isohanni, M., Rasanen, P., Koiranen, M., & Moring, J. (1997). Specific major mental disorders and criminality: A 26-year prospective study of the 1966 northern Finland birth cohort. *American Journal of Psychiatry, 154,* 840–845.

Timmers, R., & van der Wijst, P. (2007). Images as anti-smoking fear appeals: The effects of emotion on the persuasion process. *Information Design Journal, 15,* 21–36.

Tirodkar, M. A., & Jain, A. (2003). Food messages on African American television shows. *American Journal of Public Health, 93*(3), 439–441.

Todorov, A., & Bargh, J. A. (2002). Automatic sources of aggression. *Aggression & Violent Behavior, 7*(1), 53–68.

Tolin, D. F., Robison, J. T., Gaztambide, S., Horowitz, S., & Blank, K. (2007). Ataques de nervios and psychiatric disorders in older Puerto Rican primary care patients. *Journal of Cross-Cultural Psychology, 38,* 659–669.

Tolman, E. C., & Honzik, C. H. (1930). Introduction and removal of reward and maze performance in rats. *University of California Publications in Psychology, 4,* 257–275.

Tom, S. E. (2008). Menopause and women's health transitions through mid-life. *Dissertation Abstracts International Section A: Humanities and Social Sciences, 68*(8-A), 3605.

Torges, C. M., Stewart, A. J., & Duncan, L. E. (2008). Achieving ego-integrity: Personality development in late midlife. *Journal of Research in Personality, 42,* 1004–1019.

Tormala, Z. L., & Clarkson, J. L. (2007). Assimilation and contrast in persuasion: The effects of source credibility in multiple message situations. *Personality and Social Psychology Bulletin, 33,* 559–571.

Torpy, J. M., Lynm, C., & Glass, R. M. (2007). Chronic stress and the heart. *Journal of the American Medical Association, 298,* 1722.

Torrance, E. P. (2004). Great expectations: Creative achievements of the sociometric stars in a 30-year study. *Journal of Secondary Gifted Education, 16*(1), 5–13.

Torrey, E. F. (1998). *Out of the shadows: Confronting America's mental illness crisis.* New York: Wiley.

Torrey, E. F., & Yolken, R. H. (1998). Is household crowding a risk factor for schizophrenia and bipolar disorder? *Schizophrenia Bulletin, 24,* 321–324.

Trainor, B. C., Bird, I. M., & Marler, C. A. (2004). Opposing hormonal mechanisms of aggression revealed through short-lived testosterone manipulations and multiple winning experiences. *Hormones & Behavior, 45*(2), 115–121.

Tranter, L. J., & Koutstaal, W. (2008). Age and flexible thinking: An experimental demonstration of the beneficial effects of increased cognitively stimulating activity on fluid intelligence in healthy older adults. *Aging, Neuropsychology, & Cognition, 15,* 184–207.

Trappey, C. (1996). A meta-analysis of consumer choice and subliminal advertising. *Psychology and Marketing, 13,* 517–530.

Tremblay, P. F., Graham, K., & Wells, S. (2008). Severity of physical aggression reported by university students: A test of the interaction between trait aggression and alcohol consumption. *Personality and Individual Differences, 45,* 3–9.

Triandis, H. C. (2001). Individualism-collectivism and personality. *Journal of Personality, 69*(6), 907–924.

Triandis, H. C. (2007). Culture and psychology: A history of the study of their relationship. In S. Kitayama & D. Cohen (Eds), *Handbook of cultural psychology.* New York: Guilford.

Trull, T., Sher, K. J., Minks-Brown, C., Durbin, J., & Burr, R. (2000). Borderline personality disorder and substance use disorders: A review and integration. *Clinical Psychology Review, 20,* 235–253.

Tryon, W. W. (2008). Whatever happened to symptom substitution? *Clinical Psychology Review, 28,* 963–968.

Tseng, W. (2004). Culture and psychotherapy: Asian perspectives. *Journal of Mental Health, 13*(2), 151–161.

Tsien, J. Z. (2000, April). Building a brainier mouse. *Scientific American,* pp. 62–68.

Tsuang, M. T., Stone, W. S., & Faraone, S. V. (2001). Genes, environment and schizophrenia. *British Journal of Psychiatry, Suppl 40,* s18–24.

Tsuru, J., Akiyoshi, J., Tanaka, Y., Matsushita, H., Hanada, H., Kodama, K., Hikichi, T., Ohgami, H., Tsutsumi, T., Isogawa, K., & Nagayama, H. (2008). Social support and enhanced suppression of adrenocorticotropic hormone and cortisol responses to hypothalamic-pituitary-adrenal function and thyrotropin-releasing hormone tests in patients with major depressive disorder. *Biological Psychology, 78,* 159–163.

Tucker, B. (2007). Perception of interannual covariation and strategies for risk reduction among Mikea of Madagascar: Individual and social learning. *Human Nature, 18,* 162–180.

Tulving, E. (2000). Concepts of memory. In E. Tulving & F. I. M. Craik (Eds.), *The Oxford handbook of memory* (pp. 33–44). New York: Oxford University Press.

Tulving, E., & Thompson, D. M. (1973). Encoding specificity and retrieval processes in episodic memory. *Psychological Review, 80,* 352–373.

Tümkaya, S. (2007). Burnout and humor relationship among university lecturers. *Humor: International Journal of Humor Research, 20,* 73–92.

Turkington, D., Dudley, R., Warman, D. M., & Beck, A. T. (2004). Cognitive-behavioral therapy for schizophrenia: A review. *Journal of Psychiatric Practice, 10*(1), 5–16.

Turnipseed, D. L. (2003). Hardy personality: A potential link with organizational citizenship behavior. *Psychological Reports, 93*(2), 529–543.

Tversky, A., & Kahneman, D. (1974). Judgment under uncertainty: Heuristics and biases. *Science, 185,* 1124–1131.

Tversky, A., & Kahneman, D. (1993). Probabilistic reasoning. In A. I. Goldman (Ed.), *Readings in philosophy and cognitive science.* Cambridge, MA: The MIT Press.

Twenge, J. M., Baumeister, R. F., Tice, D. M., & Stucke, T. S. (2001). If you can't join them, beat them: Effects of social exclusion on aggressive behavior. *Journal of Personality and Social Psychology, 81*(6), 1058–1069.

Uehara, I. (2000). Differences in episodic memory between four- and five-year-olds: False information versus real experiences. *Psychological Reports, 86*(3,Pt1), 745–755.

Uhlmann, E., & Swanson, J. (2004). Exposure to violent video games increases automatic aggressiveness. *Journal of Adolescence, 27*(1), 41–52.

Ulrich, R. E., Stachnik, T. J., & Stainton, N. R. (1963). Student acceptance of generalized personality interpretations. *Psychological Reports, 13,* 831–834.

Uncapher, M. R., & Rugg, M. D. (2008). Fractionation of the component processes underlying successful episodic encoding: A combined fMRI and divided-attention study. *Journal of Cognitive Neuroscience, 20,* 240–254.

Underwood, J., & Pezdek, K. (1998). Memory suggestibility as an example of the sleeper effect. *Psychonomic Bulletin & Review, 5,* 449–453.

Unger, J. B., Chou, C-P., Palmer, P. H., Ritt-Olson, A., Gallaher, P., Cen, S., Lichtman, K., Azen, S., & Johnson, C. A. (2004). Project FLAVOR: 1-Year outcomes of a multicultural, school-based smoking prevention curriculum for adolescents. *American Journal of Public Health, 94*(2), 263–265.

Valberg, A. (2006). *Light vision color.* Hoboken, NJ: Wiley.

Valdez, P., Ramírez, C., & García, A. (2003). Adjustment of the sleep-wake cycle to small (1–2 h) changes in schedule. *Biological Rhythm Research, 34*(2), 145–155.

Valenstein, E. S. (1998). *Blaming the brain: The truth about drugs and mental health.* New York: Free Press.

Valeo, T. & Beyerstein, L. (2008). Curses! In D. Gordon (Ed.), *Your brain on Cubs: Inside the players and fans* (pp. 59–74, 139–140). Washington, DC: Dana Press.

Van de Carr, F. R., & Lehrer, M. (1997). *While you are expecting: Your own prenatal classroom.* New York: Humanics Publishing.

van der Sluis, S., Derom, C., Thiery, E., Bartels, M., Polderman, T. J. C., Verhulst, F. C., Jacobs, N., van Gestel, S., de Geus, E. J. C., Dolan, C. V., Boomsma, D. I., & Posthuma, D. (2008). Sex differences on the WISC-R in Belgium and the Netherlands. *Intelligence, 36,* 48–67.

van Heck, G. L., & den Oudsten, B. L. (2008). Emotional intelligence: Relationships to stress, health, and well-being. In A. Vingerhoets & I. Nyklíček (Eds.), *Emotion regulation: Conceptual and clinical issues* (pp. 97–121). New York: Springer Science + Business Media.

Van Hulle, C. A., Goldsmith, H. H., & Lemery, K. S. (2004). Genetic, environmental, and gender effects on individual differences in toddler expressive language. *Journal of Speech, Language, & Hearing Research, 47*(4), 904–912.

van IJzendoorn, M. H., & De Wolff, M. S. (1997). In search of the absent father: Metaanalyses of infant-father attachment: A rejoinder to our discussants. *Child Development, 68,* 604–609.

van Leeuwen, M., van den Berg, S. M., & Boomsma, D. I. (2008). A twin-family study of general IQ. *Learning and Individual Differences, 18,* 76–88.

van Lier, P., Boivin, M., Dionne, G., Vitaro, F., Brendgen, M., Koot, H., Tremblay, R. E., & Pérusse, D. (2007). Kindergarten children's genetic variabilities interact with friends' aggression to promote children's own aggression. *Journal of the American Academy of Child & Adolescent Psychiatry, 46,* 1080–1087.

Van Overwalle, F., & Jordens, K. (2002). An adaptive connectionist model of cognitive dissonance. *Personality and Social Psychology Review, 6,* 204–231.

Van Scotter, J. R., Moustafa, K., Burnett, J. R., & Michael, P. G. (2007). Influence of prior acquaintance with the rate on rater accuracy and halo. *Journal of Management Development, 26,* 790–803.

van Stegeren, A. H. (2008). The role of the noradrenergic system in emotional memory. *Acta Psychologica, 127,* 532–541.

Van Vugt, M., Chang, K., & Hart, C. (2005). The impact of leadership style on group stability. *Chinese Journal of Psychology, 47,* 380–394.

Vanderwerker, L. C., & Prigerson, H. G. (2004). Social support and technological connectedness as protective factors in bereavement. *Journal of Loss & Trauma, 9*(1), 45–57.

Vasyura, S. A. (2008). Psychology of male and female communicative activity. *The Spanish Journal of Psychology, 11,* 289–300.

Vaughan, A. (2007). *The fMRI smackdown cometh.* [On-line]. Available: http://www.mindhacks.com/blog/2008/06/the_fmri_smackdown_c.html

Vaughan, P. (2004). Telling stories, saving lives. *Population Communications International (PCI).* [On-line]. Available: http://population.org/entsummit/transcript04_vaughan.shtm

Vaughn, D. (1996). *The Challenger launch decision: Risky technology, culture, and deviance at NASA.* Chicago: University of Chicago Press.

Venkatesh, V., Morris, M. G., Sykes, T. A., & Ackerman, P. L. (2004). Individual reactions to new technologies in the workplace: The role of gender as a psychological construct. *Journal of Applied Social Psychology, 34*(3), 445–467.

Verschuere, B., Crombez, G., & Koster, E. H. W. (2004). Orienting to guilty knowledge. *Cognition & Emotion, 18*(2), 265–279.

Vertosick, F. T. (2000). *Why we hurt: The natural history of pain.* New York: Harcourt.

Vickers, J. C., Dickson, T. C., Adlard, P. A., Saunders, H. L., King, C. E., & McCormack, G. (2000). The cause of neuronal degeneration in Alzheimer's disease. *Progress in Neurobiology, 60*(2), 139–165.

Vidmar, N. (1997). Generic prejudice and the presumption of guilt in sex abuse trials. *Law and Human Behavior, 21*(1), 5–25.

Vijgen, S. M. C., van Baal, P. H. M., Hoogenveen, R. T., de Wit, G. A., & Feenstra, T. L. (2008). Cost-effectiveness analyses of health promotion programs: A case study of smoking prevention and cessation among Dutch students. *Health Education Research, 23,* 310–318.

Villarreal, D. M., Do, V., Haddad, E., & Derrick, B. E. (2002). MDA receptor antagonists sustain LTP and spatial memory: Active processes mediate LTP decay. *Nature Neuroscience, 5*(1), 48–52.

Visser, P. S., & Cooper, J. (2007). Attitude change. In M. A. Hogg & J. Cooper (Eds.), *The Sage handbook of social psychology* (2nd ed.). Thousand Oaks, CA: Sage.

Vocks, S., Ockenfels, M., Jürgensen, R., Mussgay, L., & Rüddel, H. (2004). Blood pressure reactivity can be reduced by a cognitive behavioral stress management program. *International Journal of Behavioral Medicine, 11*(2), 63–70.

Vogt, D. S., Rizvi, S. L., Shipherd, J. C., & Resick, P. A. (2008). Longitudinal investigation of reciprocal relationship between stress reactions and hardiness. *Personality and Social Psychology Bulletin, 34,* 61–73.

Völker, S. (2007). Infants' vocal engagement oriented towards mother versus stranger at 3 months and avoidant attachment behavior at 12 months. *International Journal of Behavioral Development, 31,* 88–95.

von Hippel, W., Brener, L., & von Hippel, C. (2008). Implicit prejudice toward injecting drug users predicts intentions to change jobs among drug and alcohol nurses. *Psychological Science, 19,* 7–11.

Vorria, P., Vairami, M., Gialaouzidis, M., Kotroni, E., Koutra, G., Markou, N., Marti, E., & Pantoleon, I. (2007). Romantic relationships, attachment syles, and experiences of childhood. *Hellenic Journal of Psychology, 4,* 281–309.

Wachtel, P. L. (2008). *Relational theory and the practice of psychotherapy.* New York: Guilford.

Wagner, D. A. (1982). Ontogeny in the study of culture and cognition. In D. A. Wagner & H. W. Stevenson (Eds.), *Cultural perspectives on child development* (pp. 105–123). San Francisco, Freeman.

Wagner, U., Christ, O., & Pettigrew, T. F. (2008). Prejudice and group-related behaviors in Germany. *Journal of Social Issues, 64,* 403–416.

Wagner, U., Hallschmid, M., Verleger, R., & Born, J. (2003). Signs of REM sleep dependent enhancement of implicit face memory: A repetition priming study. *Biological Psychology, 62*(3), 197–210.

Wagstaff, G. G., Cole, J., Wheatcroft, J., Marshall, M., & Barsby, I. (2007). A componential approach to hypnotic memory facilitation: Focused meditation, context reinstatement and eye movements. *Contemporary Hypnosis, 24,* 97–108.

Wahl, H., Becker, S., Burmedi, D., & Schilling, O. (2004). The role of primary and secondary control in adaptation to age-related vision loss: A study of older adults with macular degeneration. *Psychology & Aging, 19*(1), 235–239.

Wahlgren, K., & Lester, D. (2003). The big four: Personality in dogs. *Psychological Reports, 92,* 828.

Wakfield, M., Flay, B., Nichter, M., & Giovino, G. (2003). Role of the media in influencing trajectories of youth smoking. *Addiction, 98*(Suppl 1), 79–103.

Wakimoto, S., & Fujihara, T. (2004). The correlation between intimacy and objective similarity in interpersonal relationships. *Social Behavior & Personality, 32*(1), 95–102.

Walinder, J., & Rutz, W. (2002). Male depression and suicide. *International Clinical Psychopharmacology, 16*(Suppl 2), S21–S24.

Walker, E., Kestler, L., Bollini, A., & Hochman, K. M. Schizophrenia: Etiology and course. (2004). *Annual Review of Psychology, 55,* 401–430.

Walker, F. R., Hinwood, M., Masters, L., Deilenberg, R. A., & Trevor, A. (2008). Individual differences predict susceptibility to conditioned fear arising from psychosocial trauma. *Journal of Psychiatric Research, 42,* 371–383.

Walker, I., & Crogan, M. (1998). Academic performance, prejudice, and the jigsaw classroom: New pieces to the puzzle. *Journal of Community and Applied Social Psychology, 8,* 381–393.

Wall, A. (2007). Review of integrating gender and culture in parenting. *The Family Journal, 15,* 196–197.

Wallace, A. F. C. (1958). Dreams and wishes of the soul: A type of psychoanalytic theory among the seventeenth century Iroquois. *American Anthropologist, 60,* 234–248.

Wallace, D. C. (1997, August). Mitochondrial DNA in aging and disease. *Scientific American,* 40–47.

Waller, M. R., & McLanahan, S. S. (2005). "His" and "her" marriage expectations: Determinants and consequences. *Journal of Marriage & Family, 67*(1), 53–67.

Waller, N. G., & Ross, C. A. (1997). The prevalence and biometric structure of pathological dissociation in the general population: Taxometric and behavior genetics findings. *Journal of Abnormal Psychology, 106,* 499–510.

Wallerstein, G. (2008). *The pleasure instinct: Why we crave adventure, chocolate, pheromones, and music.* New York: Wiley.

Walter, T. & Siebert, A. (1990). *Student success* (5th ed.). Fort Worth, TX: Holt, Rinehart & Winston.

Wamsley, E. J., Hirota, Y., Tucker, M. A., Smith, M. R., Doan, T., & Antrobus, J. S. (2007). Circadian and ultradian influences on dreaming: A dual rhythm model. *Brain Research Bulletin, 71,* 347–354.

Wang, Q. (2008). Emotion knowledge and autobiographical memory across the preschool years: A cross-cultural longitudinal investigation. *Cognition, 108,* 117–135.

Ward, T. B. (2007). Creative cognition as a window on creativity. *Methods, 42,* 28–37.

Wardlaw, G. M., & Hampl, J. (2007). *Perspectives in nutrition* (7th ed.). New York: McGraw-Hill.

Warner, M. (2004, May 11). *Heart of darkness.* PBS Online NewsHour. [On-line]. Available: http://www.pbs.org/newshour/bb/middle_east/jan-june04/prisoners_5–11.html.

Warr, P., Butcher, V., & Robertson, I. (2004). Activity and psychological well-being in older people. *Aging & Mental Health, 8*(2), 172–183.

Wason, P. C. (1968). Reasoning about a rule. *Quarterly Journal of Experimental Psychology, 20*(3), 273–281.

Wass, T. S. (2008). Neuroanatomical and neurobehavioral effects of heavy prenatal alcohol exposure. In J. Brick (Ed.), *Handbook of the medical consequences of alcohol and drug abuse* (2nd ed.) (pp. 177–217). *The Haworth Press series in neuropharmacology.* New York: Haworth Press/Taylor and Francis Group.

Wasserman, D., & Wachbroit, R. S. (2000). *Genetics and criminal behavior.* Cambridge, MA: Cambridge University Press.

Wasserman, E., Epstein, C., & Ziemann, U. (Eds.). (2008). *Oxford handbook of transcranial stimulation.* New York: Oxford University Press.

Waters, A. J., & Gobet, F. (2008). Mental imagery and chunks: Empirical and conventional findings. *Memory & Cognition, 36,* 505–517.

Watkins, L. M., & Johnston, L. (2000). Screening job applicants: The impact of physical attractiveness and application quality. *International Journal of Selection & Assessment, 8*(2), 76–84.

Watkins, L. R., & Maier, S. F. (2000). The pain of being sick: Implications of immune-to-brain communication for understanding pain. *Annual Review of Psychology, 51,* 29–57.

Watson, D. L., & Tharp, R. G. (2007). *Self-directed behavior* (9th ed.). Belmont, CA: Wadsworth.

Watson, J. (1913). Psychology as the behaviorist views it. *Psychological Review, 20,* 158–177.

Watson, J. B., Mednick, S. A., Huttunen, M. & Wang, X. (1999). Prenatal teratogens and the development of adult mental illness. *Development & Psychopathology, 11*(3), 457–466.

Watson, J. B., & Rayner, R. (1920). Conditioned emotional reactions. *Journal of Experimental Psychology, 3,* 1–14.

Watson, J. B., & Rayner, R. (2000). Conditioned emotional reactions. *American Psychologist, 55*(3), 313–317.

Watson, K. K., Matthews, B. J., & Allman, J. M. (2007). Brain activation during sight gags and language-dependent humor. *Cerebral Cortex, 17,* 314–324.

Waye, K. P., Bengtsson, J., Rylander, R., Hucklebridge, F., Evans, P., & Clow, A. (2002). Low frequency noise enhances cortisol among noise sensitive subjects during work performance. *Life Sciences, 70*(7), 745–758.

Waynforth, D. (2001). Mate choice trade-offs and women's preference for physically attractive men. *Human Nature, 12*(3), 207–219.

Weaver, M. F., & Schnoll, S. H. (2008). Hallucinogens and club drugs. In M. Galanter & H. D. Kleber (Eds.), *The American Psychiatric Publishing textbook of substance abuse treatment* (4th ed.) (pp. 191–200). Arlington, VA: American Psychiatric Publishing.

Weber, G. N. (2008). Using to numb the pain: Substance use and abuse among lesbian, gay and bisexual individuals. *Journal of Mental Health Counseling, 30,* 31–48.

Wechsler, D. (1944). *The measurement of adult intelligence* (3rd ed.). Baltimore: Williams & Wilkins.

Wechsler, D. (1977). *Manual for the Wechsler Intelligence Scale for Children* (Rev.). New York: Psychological Corporation.

Wechsler, H., Lee, J. E., Kuo, M., Seibring, M., Nelson, T. F., & Lee, H. (2002). Trends in college binge drinking during a period of increased prevention efforts: Findings from 4 Harvard School of Public Health College Alcohol Study Surveys, 1993–2001. *Journal of American College Health, 50,* 203–217.

Wegener, D. T., Clarl, J. K., & Petty, R. E. (2006). Not all stereotyping is created equal: Differential consequences of thoughtful versus nonthoughtful stereotyping. *Journal of Personality and Social Psychology, 90,* 42–59.

Wei, R. (2007). Effects of playing violent videogames on Chinese adolescents' pro-violence attitudes, attitudes toward others, and aggressive behavior. *CyberPsychology & Behavior, 10,* 371–380.

Weil, M. M., & Rosen, L. D. (1997). *Coping with technology @ work @ home @ play.* New York: Wiley.

Weinberger, J., & Westen, D. (2001). Science and psychodynamics: From arguments about Freud to data. *Psychological Inquiry, 12*(3), 129–132.

Weiner, A. (2005). Perceptions of leadership style as affected by gender and culture: A cross-national study. *Dissertation Abstracts International: SectionB: the Sciences and Engineering, 66*(3-B), 1773.

Weiner, B. (1972). *Theories of motivation.* Chicago: Rand-McNally. REFERENCES 479 767964_References 2nd.qxd 12/21/06 4:38 PM Page 479.

Weiner, B. (1982). The emotional consequences of causal attributions. In M. S. Clark & S. T. Fiske (Eds.), *Affect and cognition.* Hillsdale, NJ: Erlbaum.

Weiner, B. (2006). *Social motivation, justice, and the moral emotions: An attributional approach.* Mahwah, NJ: Erlbaum.

Weiner, G. (2008). *Handbook of personality assessment.* Hoboken, NJ: Wiley.

Weiner, M. F. (2008). Perspective on race and ethnicity in Alzheimer's disease research. *Alzheimer's & Dementia, 4,* 233–238.

Weinstock, M. (2008). The long-term behavioural consequences of prenatal stress. *Neuroscience & Biobehavioral Reviews, 32,* 1073–1086.

Weisberg, D.S., Keil, F.C., Goodstein, J., Rawson E. & Gray, J.R. (2008). The seductive allure of neuroscience explanations. *Journal of Cognitive Neuroscience, 20,* 470–477.

Weiss, A., Bates, T. C., & Luciano, M. (2008). Happiness is a personal(ity) thing: The genetics of personality and well-being in a representative sample. *Psychological Science, 19,* 205–210.

Weissman, M. M. (2007). Recent non-medication trials of interpersonal psychotherapy for depression. *International Journal of Neuropsychopharmacology, 10,* 117–122.

Weitlauf, J. C., Cervone, D., Smith, R. E., & Wright, P. M. (2001). Assessing generalization in perceived self-efficacy: Multidomain and global assessments of the effects of self-defense training for women. *Personality & Social Psychology Bulletin, 27*(12), 1683–1691.

Wenger, A., & Fowers, B. J. (2008). Positive illusions in parenting: Every child is above average. *Journal of Applied Social Psychology, 38,* 611–634.

Wentura, D., & Rothermund, K. (2007). Paradigms we live by: A plea for more basic research on the Implicit Association Test. In B. Wittenbrink & N. Schwarz (Eds.), *Implicit measures of attitudes.* New York: Guilford Press.

Wentz, E., Mellström, D., Gillberg, I. C., Gillberg, C., & Råstam, M. (2007). Brief report: Decreased bone mineral density as a long-term complication of teenage-onset anorexia nervosa. *European Eating Disorders Review, 15,* 290–295.

Werner, E. E. (1989). Children of the garden island. *Scientific American, 260,* 106–111.

Werner, E. E. (2006). What can we learn about resilience from large-scale longitudinal studies? In S. Goldstein & R. Brooks (Eds.), *Handbook of resilience in children* (pp. 91–106). New York: Springer.

Werner, J. S., & Wooten, B. R. (1979). Human infant color vision and color perception. *Infant Behavior and Development, 2*(3), 241–273.

Werner, K. H., Roberts, N. A., Rosen, H. J., Dean, D. L., Kramer, J. H., Weiner, M. W., Miller, B. L., & Levenson, R. W. (2007). Emotional reactivity and emotion recognition in frontotemporal lobar degeneration. *Neurology, 69,* 148–155.

Werth, J. L. Jr., Wright, K. S., Archambault, R. J., & Bardash, R. (2003). When does the "duty to protect" apply with a client who has anorexia nervosa? *Counseling Psychologist. 31*(4), 427–450.

West, D. A., & Lichtenstein B. (2006). Andrea Yates and the criminalization of the filicidal maternal body. *Feminist Criminology, 1,* 173–187.

Westen, D. (1998). Unconscious thought, feeling, and motivation: The end of a centurylong debate. In R. F. Bornstein & J. M. Masling (Eds.), *Empirical perspectives on the psychoanalytic unconscious.* Washington, DC: American Psychological Association.

Westover, A. N., McBride, S., & Haley, R. W. (2007). Stroke in young adults who abuse amphetamines or cocaine: A population-based study of hospitalized patients. *Archives of General Psychiatry, 64*, 495–502.

Whitbourne, S. K. (2009). *Adult development and aging: Biopsychosocial perspectives* (3rd ed.). Hoboken, NJ: Wiley.

White, J. R., & Freeman, A. S. (2000). *Cognitivebehavioral group therapy for specific problems and populations.* Washington, DC: American Psychological Association.

White, L. K., & Rogers, S. J. (1997). Strong support but uneasy relationships: Coresidence and adult children's relationships with their parents. *Journal of Marriage and the Family, 59*, 62–76.

White, T., Andreasen, N. C., & Nopoulos, P. (2002). Brain volumes and surface morphology in monozygotic twins. *Cerebral Cortex, 12*(5), 486–493.

Whitney, D. K., Kusznir, A., & Dixie, A. (2002). Women with depression: The importance of social, psychological and occupational factors in illness and recovery. *Journal of Occupational Science, 9*(1), 20–27.

Whitty, M. T., & Fisher, W. A. (2008). The sexy side of the Internet: An examination of sexual activities and materials in cyberspace. In A. Barak (Ed.), *Psychological aspects of cyberspace: Theory, research, applications* (pp. 185–208). New York: Cambridge University Press.

Whorf, B. L. (1956). Science and linguistics. In J. B. Carroll (Ed.), *Language, thought and reality.* Cambridge, MA: MIT Press.

Whyte, M. K., (1992, March-April). Choosing mates—the American way. *Society*, 71–77.

Wickelgren, I. (1998). Teaching the brain to take drugs. *Science, 280*, 2045–2047.

Wickelgren, I. (2002). *Animal studies raise hopes for spinal cord repair.* [On-line]. Available: http://www.sciencemag.org/cgi/content/full/297/5579/178.

Wickramasekera II, I. (2008a). Review of how can we help witnesses to remember more? It's an eyes open and shut case. *American Journal of Clinical Hypnosis, 50*, 290–291.

Wickramasekera II, I. (2008b). Review of hypnotizability, absorption and negative cognitions as predictors of dental anxiety: Two pilot studies. *American Journal of Clinical Hypnosis, 50*, 285–286.

Widiger, T. A., & Sankis, L. M. (2000). Adult psychopathology. *Annual Review of Psychology, 51*, 377–404.

Wiegand, T., Thai, D., & Benowitz, N. (2008). Medical consequences of the use of hallucinogens: LSD, mescaline, PCP, and MDMA ("ecstasy"). In J. Brick (Ed.), *Handbook of the medical consequences of alcohol and drug abuse* (2nd ed.) (pp. 461–490). *The Haworth Press series in neuropharmacology.* New York: Haworth Press/Taylor and Francis Group.

Wieseler-Frank, J., Maier, S. F., & Watkins, L. R. (2005). Immune-to-brain communication dynamically modulates pain: Physiological and pathological consequences. *Brain, Behavior, & Immunity, 19*(2), 104–111.

Wigfield, A., & Eccles, J. S. (2000). Expectancyvalue of achievement motivation. *Contemporary Educational Psychology, 25*(1), 68–81.

Wild, B., Rodden, F. A., Grodd, W., & Ruch, W. (2003). Neural correlates of laughter and humour. *Brain, 126*(10), 2121–2138.

Williams, A. L., Haber, D., Weaver, G. D., & Freeman, J. L. (1998). Altruistic activity: Does it make a difference in the senior center? *Activities, Adaptation and Aging, 22*(4), 31–39.

Williams, G., Cai, X. J., Elliott, J. C., & Harrold, J. A. (2004). Anabolic neuropeptides. *Physiology & Behavior, 81*(2), 211–222.

Williams, J. E., & Best, D. L. (1990). *Sex and psyche: Gender and self viewed cross-culturally.* Newbury Park, CA: Sage.

Williams, S. S. (2001). Sexual lying among college students in close and casual relationships. *Journal of Applied Social Psychology, 31*(11), 2322–2338.

Williamson, M. (1997). Circumcision anesthesia: A study of nursing implication for dorsal penile nerve block. *Pediatric Nursing, 23*, 59–63.

Willingham, D.B. (2001). *Cognition: The thinking animal.* Upper Saddle River, NJ: Prentice Hall.

Willis, M. S., Esqueda, C. W., & Schacht, R. N. (2008). Social perceptions of individuals missing upper front teeth. *Perceptual and Motor Skills, 106*, 423–435.

Wilson, A. E., Smith, M. D., Ross, H. S., & Ross, M. (2004). Young children's personal accounts of their sibling disputes. *Merrill-Palmer Quarterly, 50*(1), 39–60.

Wilson, C. (1967). Existential psychology: A novelist's approach. In J. F. T. Bugental (Ed.), *Challenges of humanistic psychology.* New York: McGraw-Hill.

Wilson, E. O. (1975). *Sociobiology: The new synthesis.* Cambridge, MA: Harvard University Press.

Wilson, E. O. (1978). *On human nature.* Cambridge, MA: Harvard University Press.

Wilson, R. S., Gilley, D. W., Bennett, D. A., Beckett L. A., & Evans, D. A. (2000). Person-specific paths of cognitive decline in Alzheimer's disease and their relation to age. *Psychology & Aging, 15*(1), 18–28.

Wilson, S., & Nutt, D. (2008). *Sleep disorders.* Oxford: Oxford University Press.

Wilson, T. G. (2005). Psychological treatment of eating disorders. *Annual Review of Clinical Psychology, 1*, 439–465.

Windsor, T. D., Anstey, K. J., Butterworth, P., & Rodgers, B. (2008). Behavioral approach and behavioral inhibition as moderators of the association between negative life events and perceived control in midlife. *Personality and Individual Differences, 44*, 1080–1092.

Winerman, L. (2005). A joint call for increased attention to behavior change in health care. *Monitor on Psychology, 36*(5). [On-line]. Available: http://www.apa.org/monitor/may05/ attention.html

Wines, M. (2008). Decision making skills and general self-efficacy in pregnant and non-pregnant adolescents. *Dissertation Abstracts International: Section B: The Sciences and Engineering, 68*(9-B), 5865.

Winterich, J. A. (2003). Sex, menopause, and culture: Sexual orientation and the meaning of menopause for women's sex lives. *Gender & Society, 17*(4), 627–642.

Wise, P. M. (2006). Aging of the female reproductive system. In E. J. Masor & S. N. Austed (Eds.), *Handbook of the biology of aging* (6th ed.). San Diego: Academic.

Wise, D., & Rosqvist, J. (2006). Explanatory style and well-being. In J. C. Thomas, D. L. Segal, & M. Hersen (Eds.), *Comprehensive Handbook of Personality and Psychopathology, Vol. 1: Personality and Everyday Functioning* (pp. 285–305). Hoboken, NJ: Wiley.

Wiste, A. K., Arango, V., Ellis, S. P., Mann, J. J., & Underwood, M. D. (2008). Norepinephrine and serotonin imbalance in the locus coeruleus in bipolar disorder. *Bipolar Disorders, 10*, 349–359.

Witelson, S. F., Kigar, D. L., & Harvey, T. (1999). The exceptional brain of Albert Einstein. *The Lancet, 353*, 2149–2153.

Witherington, D. C., Campos, J. J., Anderson, D. I., Lejeune, L., & Seah, E. (2005). Avoidance of heights on the visual cliff in newly walking infants. *Infancy, 7*, 285–298.

Wixted, J. T. (2004). The psychology and neuroscience of forgetting. *Annual Review of Psychology, 55*, 235–269.

Wixted, J. T. (2005). A theory about why we forget what we once knew. *Current Directions in Psychological Science, 14*(1), 6–9.

Wolpe, J. & Plaud, J.J. (1997). Pavlov's contributions to behavior therapy. *American Psychologist, 52*(9), 966–972.

Wong, S. (2008). Diversity—Making space for everyone at NASA/Goddard Space Flight Center using dialogue to break through barriers. *Human Resource Management, 47,* 389–399.

Woo, M., & Oei, T. P. S. (2006). The MMPI-2 Gender-Masculine and Gender-Feminine scales: Gender roles as predictors of psychological health in clinical patients. *International Journal of Psychology, 41,* 413–422.

Wood, J. M., Lilienfeld, S. O., Nezworski, M. T., & Garb, H. N. (2001). Coming to grips with negative evidence for the comprehensive system for the Rorschach: A comment on Gacono, Loving, and Bodholdt, Ganellen, and Bornstein. *Journal of Personality Assessment, 77*(1), 48–70.

Wood, V. F., & Bell, P. A. (2008). Predicting interpersonal conflict resolution styles from personality characteristics. *Personality and Individual Differences, 45,* 126–131.

Wood, W., Christensen, P. N., Hebl, M. R., & Rothgerber, H. (1997). Conformity to sextyped norms, affect, and the self-concept. *Journal of Personality and Social Psychology, 73*(3), 523–535.

Woodruff-Pak, D. S., & Disterhoft, J. F. (2008). Where is the trace in trace conditioning? *Trends in Neurosciences, 31,* 105–112.

Woods, S. C., Schwartz, M. W., Baskin, D. G., & Seeley, R. J. (2000). Food intake and the regulation of body weight. *Annual Review of Psychology, 51,* 255–277.

Woollams, A. M., Taylor, J. R., Karayanidis, F., & Henson, R. N. (2008). Event-related potentials associated with masked priming of test cues reveal multiple potential contributions to recognition memory. *Journal of Cognitive Neuroscience, 20,* 1114–1129.

Working Yourself to Death. (2003). *Facts of Life: Issue Briefings for Health Reporters, 8*(9). [On-line]. Available: http://www.cfah.org/factsoflife/vol8no9.cfm#1.

Workman, L., & Reader, W. (2008). *Evolutionary psychology: An introduction.* New York: Cambridge University Press.

World Health Organization. (1992). *ICD-10: International statistical classification of diseases and related health problems* (10th rev. ed.). Arlington, VA: American Psychiatric Publishing.

World Health Organization (WHO). (2007). *Cultural diversity presents special challenges for mental health.* [On-line]. Available: http://www.paho.org/English/DD/PIN/pr071010.htm

World Health Organization (WHO). (2008). *Mental health and substance abuse.* [On-line]. Available: http://www.searo.who.int/en/section1174/section1199/section1567_6741.htm

Wright, J. H., & Beck, A. T. (1999). Cognitive therapies. In R. E. Hales, S. C. Yudofsky, & J. A. Talbott (Eds.), *American Psychiatric Press textbook of psychiatry.* Washington, DC: American Psychiatric Press.

Wright, K. (2003). Relationships with death: The terminally ill talk about dying. *Journal of Marital & Family Therapy, 29*(4), 439–454.

Wright, W. (1998). *Born that way: Genes, behavior, personality.* New York: Knopf.

Wu, K., Lindsted, K. D., Tsai, S-Y., & Lee, J. W. (2008). Chinese NEO-PI-R in Taiwanese adolescents. *Personality and Individual Differences, 44,* 656–667.

Wüst, S., Entringer, S., Federenko, I. S., Schlotz, W., & Hellhammer, D. H. (2005). Birth weight is associated with salivary cortisol responses to psychosocial stress in adult life. *Psychoneuroendocrinology. 30*(6), 591–598.

Wyatt, J. K., & Bootzin, R. R. (1994). Cognitive processing and sleep: Implications for enhancing job performance. *Human Performance, 7,* 119–139.

Wyatt, R. C. (2004). Thomas Szasz: Liberty and the practice of psychotherapy. *Journal of Humanistic Psychology, 44*(1), 71–85.

Wyman, A. J., & Vyse, S. (2008). Science versus the stars: A double-blind test of the validity of the NEO Five Factor Inventory and computer-generated astrological natal charts. *Journal of General Psychology, 135,* 287–300.

Wynne, C. D. L. (2007). What the ape said. *Ethology, 113,* 411–413.

Xu, C. (2008). Direct and indirect effects of parenting style with child temperament, parent-child relationship, and family functioning on child social competence in the Chinese culture: Testing the latent models. *Dissertation Abstracts International Section A: Humanities and Social Sciences, 68,* 3274.

Yacoubian, G. S. Jr., Green, M. K., & Peters, R. J. (2003). Identifying the prevalence and correlates of ecstasy and other club drug (EOCD) use among high school seniors. *Journal of Ethnicity in Substance Abuse, 2*(2), 53–66.

Yamada, H. (1997). *Different games, different rules: Why Americans and Japanese misunderstand each other.* London: Oxford University Press.

Yang, Y. K., Yao, W. J., Yeh, T. L., Lee, I. H., Chen, P. S., Lu, R. B, & Chiu, N. T. (2008). Decreased dopamine transporter availability in male smokers—A dual isotope SPECT study. *Progress in Neuro-Psychopharmacology & Biological Psychiatry, 32,* 274–279.

Yarmey, A. D. (2004). Eyewitness recall and photo identification: A field experiment. *Psychology, Crime & Law, 10*(1), 53–68.

Yee, A. H., Fairchild, H. H., Weizmann, F., & Wyatt, G. E. (1993). Addressing psychology's problem with race. *American Psychologist, 48,* 1132–1140.

Yegneswaran, B., & Shapiro, C. (2007). Do sleep deprivation and alcohol have the same effects on psychomotor performance? *Journal of Psychosomatic Research, 63,* 569–572.

Yeh, S. J., & Lo, S. K. (2004). Living alone, social support, and feeling lonely among the elderly. *Social Behavior & Personality, 32*(2), 129–138.

Yesavage, J. A., Friedman, L., Kraemer, H., Tinklenberg, J. R., Salehi, A., Noda, A., Taylor, J. L., O'Hara, R., & Murphy, G. (2004). Sleep/wake disruption in Alzheimer's disease: APOE status and longitudinal course. *Journal of Geriatric Psychiatry & Neurology, 17*(1), 20–24.

Yoo, S-S., Hu, P. T., Gujar, N., Jolesz, F. A., & Walker, M. P. (2007). A deficit in the ability to form new human memories without sleep. *Nature Neuroscience, 10,* 385–392.

Young, J. D., & Taylor, E. (1998). Meditation as a voluntary hypometabolic state of biological estivation. *News in Physiological Science, 13,* 149–153.

Young, T. (1802). *Color vision.* Philosophical Transactions of the Royal Society, p. 12.

Young, T., Skatrud, J., & Peppard, P. E. (2004). Risk factors for obstructive sleep apnea in adults. *JAMA: Journal of the American Medical Association, 291*(16), 2013–2016.

Yuki, M., Maddux, W.W. & Masuda, T. (2007). Are the windows to the soul the same in the East and West? Cultural differences in using the eyes and mouth as cues to recognize emotions in Japan and the United States. *Journal of Experimental Social Psychology, 43,* 303–311.

Zagnoni, P. G., & Albano, C. (2002). Psychostimulants and epilepsy. *Epilepsia, 43,* 28–31.

Zalaquett, C. P., Fuerth, K. M., Stein, C., Ivey, A. E., & Ivey, M. B. (2008). Reframing the DSM-IV-TR from a multicultural/social justice perspective. *Journal of Counseling & Development, 86,* 364–371.

Zanetti, L., Picciotto, M. R., & Zoli, M. (2007). Differential effects of nicotinic antagonists perfused into the nucleus accumbens or the ventral tegmental area on cocaine-induced dopamine release in the nucleus accumbens of mice. *Psychopharmacology, 190,* 189–199.

Zarrindast, M-R., Fazli-Tabaei, S., Khalilzadeh, A., Farahmanfar, M., & Yahyavi, S-Y. (2005). Cross state-dependent retrieval between histamine and lithium. *Physiology & Behavior, 86,* 154–163.

Zarrindast, M-R., Shendy, M. M., & Ahmadi, S. (2007). Nitric oxide modulates states dependency induced by lithium in an inhibitory avoidance task in mice. *Behavioural Pharmacology, 18,* 289–295.

Zeanah, C. H. (2000). Disturbances of attachment in young children adopted from institutions. *Journal of Developmental & Behavioral Pediatrics, 21*(3), 230–236.

Zebrowitz, L. A., Hall, J. A., Murphy, N. A., & Rhodes, G. (2002). Looking smart and looking good: Facial cues to intelligence and their origins. *Personality & Social Psychology Bulletin, 28*(2), 238–249.

Zhaoping, L., & Guyader, N. (2007). Interference with bottom-up feature detection by higher-level object recognition. *Current biology, 17,* 26–31.

Zhukov, D. A., & Vinogradova, K. P. (2002). Learned helplessness or learned inactivity after inescapable stress? Interpretation depends on coping styles. *Integrative Physiological & Behavioral Science, 37*(1), 35–43.

Ziegelstein, R. C. (2007). Acute emotional stress and cardiac arrhythmias. *Journal of the American Medical Association, 298,* 324–329.

Ziegert, Jonathan C., & Hanges, Paul J. (2005). Employment Discrimination: The Role of Implicit Attitudes, Motivation, and a Climate for Racial Bias. *Journal of Applied Psychology, 90*(3), 553–562.

Zillmer, E. A., Spiers, M. V., & Culbertson, W. (2008). *Principles of neuropsychology* (2nd ed.). Belmont, CA: Cengage.

Zimbardo, P. G. (1993). Stanford prison experiment: A 20-year retrospective. *Invited presentation at the meeting of the Western Psychological Association,* Phoenix, AZ.

Zimbardo, P. G. (2004). A situationist perspective on the psychology of evil: Understanding how good people are transformed into perpetrators. In A. G. Miller (Ed.), *The social psychology of good and evil* (pp. 21–50). New York: Guilford Press.

Zimbardo, P. (2007). *The Lucifer effect: Understanding how good people turn evil.* New York: Random House.

Zimbardo, P. G., Ebbeson, E. B., & Maslach, C. (1977). *Influencing attitudes and changing behavior.* Reading, MA: Addison-Wesley.

Zucker, K. J. (2008). Special issue: Biological research on sex-dimorphic behavior and sexual orientation. *Archives of Sexual Behavior, 37,* 1.

Zuckerman, L., &, Weiner, I. (2005). Maternal immune activation leads to behavioral and pharmacological changes in the adult offspring. *Journal of Psychiatric Research, 39*(3), 311–323.

Zuckerman, M. (1978, February). The search for high sensation. *Psychology Today,* 38–46.

Zuckerman, M. (1979). *Sensation seeking: Beyond the optimal level of arousal.* Hillsdale, NJ: Erlbaum.

Zuckerman, M. (1994). *Behavioral expressions and biosocial bases of sensation seeking.* New York: Cambridge University Press.

Zuckerman, M. (2004). The shaping of personality: Genes, environments, and chance encounters. *Journal of Personality Assessment, 82*(1), 11–22.

Zuckerman, M. (2008). Rose is a rose is a rose: Content and construct validity. *Personality and Individual Differences, 45,* 110–112.

Text and Illustration Credits

Chapter 1 *Figure 1.2:* From Caccioppo, Petty, and Jarvis; *Dispositional Differences in Cognitive Motivation*, Psychological Bulletin, 119(2), pg. 197–253, © 1996 American Psychological Association. Table 1.4: From Plous, S., *An attitude survey of animal rights activists*, American Psychological Society. Reprinted by permission of the American Psychological Society and S. Plous.

Chapter 2 *Figure 2.21 and Concept Diagram 2.3:* From Kimura, D.; *Sex Differences in the Brain*, Scientific American, Sept. 1002, pg. 120 © 1992 Jared Schneidman Designs.

Chapter 3 *Process Diagram 3.1:* From Selye; *Stress Without Distress*, © 1974 Harper & Row Publishers. Critical Thinking/Active Learning Exercise (pg. 104); Robbins, S.P., *Organizational behavior: Concepts, controversies, and applications* © 1996 Prentice-Hall, Englewood Cliffs, NJ reprinted with permission. Table 3.1: From Holmes & Rahe, *The social readjustment rating scale*, © 1967 Journal of Psychosomatic Research, 11, pg. 213–218. Table 3.5: From Pomponio, © 2002 John Wiley & Sons, Inc. Figure 3.6: From *"Hostility, the metabolic syndrome, and incident coronary heart disease,"* R. Niaura, Ph.D., published in *Health Psychology*, 2002.

Chapter 4 *Figure 4.20:* From Luria, A.R., *Cognitive development: Its cultural and social foundations*, Harvard University Press (1976). Reprinted with permission of Harvard University Press. Copyright © 1976 by the President and Fellows of Harvard College. Figure 4.22: From Erdelyi, M.H. & Applebaum, A.G., *Cognitive Masking*, © 1973 Bulletin of the Psychonomic Society I, pg. 59–61.

Chapter 5 *Prose (pg. 196):* From Benson, Herbert, "Systematic hypertension and the relaxation response". *New England Journal of Medicine*, 296, 1997. Reprinted with permission.

Chapter 7 *Figure 7.7:* From Murdock, Jr.; *The Serial Effect of Free Recall*, the Journal of Experimental Psychology, 64(5) pg. 482–488, Figure 1 pg. 483, © 1962 American Psychological Association. Figure 7.11: From Bahrick, Bahrick, and Wittlinger; *Those Unforgettable High School Days*. Reprinted with permission from Psychology Today Magazine, © 1978 Sussex Publishers, Inc.

Chapter 8 *Try This Yourself pg. 281:* From Shepard and Metzler; *Mental Rotation of Three-Dimensional Objects*, © 1971 American Association for the Advancement of Science. Figure 8.10: From Gardner; *The Atlantic Monthly*, Feb. 1999 pp. 67–76, © 1999 Howard Gardner. Table 8.4: From Sternberg; *Beyond IQ*, © 1985 Cambridge University Press. Objective 8.16: From Sternberg; *The Theory of Successful Intelligence*, Review of General Psychology, 3, pg. 292–316, © 1999 American Psychological Association.

Chapter 9 *Figure 9.3:* From Schaie; *The life course of Adult Intellectual Abilities*, American Psychologist, 49, pg. 304–313. © 1994 The American Psychological Association. Reprinted with Permission. Figure 9.7: From Frankenburg & Dodds, Denver II Training Manual © 1991 *Denver Developmental Materials*. Figure 9.9: "Milestones in motor development." Source: WK Frankenburg, J Dobbs, P Archer, H Shapiro and B Bresnick, *The Denver II: a major revision and restandardization of the Denver Developmental Screening Test*. Pediatrics, Jan 1992; 89: 91–97. Figure 9.11: From Tanner, J.M., Whitehouse, R.N., and Takaislu, M., "Male/female growth sport." *Archives of Diseases in Childhood*, 41, 454–471, 1966. Reprinted with permission. Application: From Schaie, K.W., The life course of adult intellectual abilities. American Psychologist, 49, 304–313, 1994. Copyright © 1994 by the American Psychological Association. Reprinted with permission. Figure 9.14: From Chart of elderly achievers. In *The brain: A user's manual*. Copyright © 1982 by Diagram Visual Information.

Chapter 10 *Process Diagram 10.1:* Kohlberg's Stages of Moral Development. Source: Adapted from Kohlberg, L. "Stage and Sequence: The Cognitive Development Approach to Socialization." In D.A. Goslin, *The Handbook of Socialization Theory and Research*. Chicago: Rand McNally, 1969, p. 376 (Table 6.2). Process Diagram 10.2: From Papalia, Olds & Feldman; *Human Development 8e*, © 2001 McGraw-Hill. Reprinted with permission. Figure 10.3: From Cartensen et al.; The Social Context of Emotion, Annual Review of Geriatrics & Gerontology, 17, pg. 331, © 1997 Springer Publishing Company Inc., New York 10012. Used by permission.

Chapter 11 *Figure 11.2:* From Miracle, Miracle, & Baumeister; *Human Sexuality: Meeting Your Basic Needs*, Study Guide Figure 10.4, pg. 302, Reprinted by permission of Pearson Education, Inc. © 2003 Pearson Education. Figure 11.6: From Hat-field, Elaine and Rapson, Richard L, Love, sex, and intimacy. Copyright © 1993 by Elaine Hat-field and Richard L. Rapson. Reprinted by permission of Addison-Wesley Educational Publishers Inc. Figure 11.8: From Strong, DeVault, and Sayad, Core Concepts in human sexuality. Mountain View, California: Mayfield. Reprinted by permission. Try This Yourself: From Hyde, Janis S., Half the human experience: The psychology of women (fifth edition). Copyright © 1995 by D.C. Heath & Company, Lexington, Mass. Reprinted by permission of Houghton-Mifflin Co. Table 11.4: From Laumann et al.; The Social Organization of Sexuality, © 1994 University of Chicago Press. Process Diagram 11.1: From Hebb, D.O., Organization of Behavior, John Wiley and Sons, Inc. Copyright (1949). Reprinted by permission of D.O. Hebb and J. Nichols Hebb Paul, sole executor and daughter.

Chapter 12 *Table 12.1:* From Diagnostic and Statistical Manual of Mental Disorders; fourth edition text revision, Washington DC, © 2000 American Psychiatric Association. Figure 12.11: From Murray, H.H. Thematic Apperception Test (TAT) card. Harvard University Press. Printed with permission. Concept Diagram 12.1: From Lepper, Greene, and Nisbett; *Undermining Children's Intrinsic Interest in Extrinsic Rewards*, Journal of Personality and Social Psychology, 8e, pg. 129–137, © 1973 American Psychological Association. Figure 12.4: From Maslow; *"A Theory of Motivation,"* in Motivation and Personality, 3e © 1997. Reprinted by permission of Pearson Education, Inc., Upper Saddle River, NJ. Figure on pg. 495: From Plutchik; *Emotion: A Psychoevolutionary Synthesis*, © 1980 Published by Allyn and Bacon, Boston, MA. Copyright © 1980 by Pearson Education. Adapted by permission of the publisher. Research Highlight, pg. 410: From Zuckerman; *"The Search for High Sensation,"* Psychology Today, pp. 38–46, Reprinted with Permission from Psychology Today Magazine, © 1978 Sussex Publishers, Inc.

Chapter 13 *Try This Yourself pg. 443:* From Cattell; "Personality Pinned Down," Psychology Today, pg. 44, Reprinted with Permission from Psychology Today Magazine, © 1974 Sussex Publishers, Inc. Try This Yourself pg. 445: From Buss et al., *"International Preferences in Selecting Mates,"* Journal of Cross-Cultural Psychology, 21, pp. 5–47, © 1990 Sage Publications, Inc. Figure 13.2: From Gosling, "Personality Dimensions in Spotted Hyenas," Journal of Comparative Psychology, 112, pp. 107–118, © 1974 American Psychological Association.

Chapter 14 *Figure 14.4:* From Diagnostic and Statistical Manual of Mental Disorders; fourth edition text revision, Washington DC, © 2000 American Psychiatric Association. Figure 14.13: From Gottesman, *Schizophrenia Genesis*, © 1991 W.H. Freeman. Process Diagram 14.2: From Meltzer; "Genetics and Etiology of Schizophrenia and Bipolar Disorder" Biological Psychiatry, 47, pg. 171–173, © 2000 Biological Psychiatry. Table 14.3: From Diagnostic and Statistical Manual of Mental Disorders; fourth edition text revision, Washington DC, © 2000 American Psychiatric Association.

Chapter 16 *Figure 16.9:* From Janis, Irving L. *Groupthink: Psychological Studies of Policy Decisions and Fiascoes, 2e,* © 1982 Houghton Mifflin. Adapted with permission. Table 16.1: From Rubin, *"Measurement of Romantic Love,"* Journal of Personality and Social Psychology, 16, pp. 265–273, © 1970 Z. Rubin.

A

Aarons, L., 171
Aarts, H., 132
Abadinsky, H., 113, 185, 192, 193, 194, 322, 361, 501
Abbott, A., 52
Abdallah, B., 554
Abell, S. C., 412
Abernathy, A. P., 115
Abernathy, B., 170
Aboa-Éboulé, C., 92, 99, 106
Abraham, A., 290
Abramson, L. Y., 491
Abreau, K. A., 342
Acarturk, C., 485
Achenbaum, W. A., 364
Adams, R. J., 326
Adebayo, D. O., 93
Adelmann, P. K., 425
Adinoff, B., 188
Adler, A., 447, 452
Adolph, K. E., 326
Aftanas, L. I., 196
Agró, F., 133
Ahlsén, E., 423
Ahmad, N., 570
Ahmadi, S., 256
Ahmed, A. M., 552
Ainsworth, M., 342
Akers, R. M., 132
Alain, C., 329
Albarracin, D., 260
Alberts, A., 336
Alden, L. E., 486
Aldridge, L., 474
Al-Issa, I., 499
Allan, K., 260, 268
Allen, L. S., 382
Allen, P. L., 386
Allen, W., 369
Allik, J., 444
Allison, S., 171
Allport, G., 442
Alvarez, W. C., 81
Amaral, D. G., 252
Amato, P. R., 359, 360
Ambady, N., 295
American Academy of Pediatrics, 387–388
American Cancer Society, 418
American Counseling Association, 110
American Heart Association, 94, 106
American Medical Association, 113
American Psychiatric Association, 303, 393, 478, 481, 482, 496, 502, 503

American Psychological Association, 9, 13, 18, 19, 109, 227, 269, 393
American Psychological Society, 9, 18
Ames, A., 157
Amir, N., 255
Amorim, K. S., 320
Amso, D., 267
Amundson, J. K., 198
Ancis, J. R., 482
Anderson, C. A., 218, 238, 552, 568, 569
Anderson, E. R., 61
Anderson, J., 93
Andrade, T. G. C. S., 110
Andrasik, F., 236
Andreassi, J. K., 93
Andreoni, J., 554
Andrew, W., 381
Andrews, K., 560
Angelou, M., 374
Anguas-Wong, A. M., 38
Anisman, H., 487, 490
Ansell, E. B., 503
Anversa, P., 61
Aou, S., 110
Appel, M., 260
Appiah, K. A., 19, 348, 351
Applebaum, A. G., 161
Arbib, M. A., 423
Arendt, H., 578
Arensman, E., 94
Arieh, Y., 150
Aristotle, 9
Armeli, S., 431
Armer, M., 3422
Armstrong, L., 406
Arnold, M., 353
Aro, H., 359
Aron, A., 27, 555
Aronson, J., 309
Arriagada, O., 52
Arumugam, V., 415
Asch, S., 560
Asghar, A. U. R., 70
Ash, D. R., 359
Ashmore, R. D., 576
Assefi, N. P., 362
Assmar, E. M., 565, 566
Astin, J. A., 115
Athos, E. A., 144
Atkinson, R. C., 247
Aubert, A., 231
August, G. J., 355
Averett, C. A., 355
Axelsson, K., 341
Axtell, R. E., 436, 560

Aydin, O., 548
Ayduk, O., 444, 460, 462
Ayers, S., 100, 102, 106
Azizian, A., 245, 254

B

Bacon, R., 9
Baddeley, A., 250
Baddeley, A. D., 249, 256
Badr, L. K., 554
Bagarozzi, D. A., Sr., 522
Bagermihl, B., 392
Bailey, J. M., 392
Bailey, K. R., 69
Baillargeon, R., 336
Baker, C., 556
Baker, D., 198, 322
Baker, M. W., 361
Baldessarini, R. J., 491
Baldwin, N., 278
Balfour, D. J. K., 188
Balk, D., 369
Balk, D. E., 367
Ball, H. A., 491, 493
Banaji, M., 576
Bandstra, E. S., 322
Bandura, A., 225, 227, 351, 378, 459, 460, 518, 527
Banko, K. M., 431
Banks, C., 564
Banks, M. S., 158
Banning, K., 93
Bao, A. M., 100
Barber, N., 387, 391
Barbur, J. L., 139
Bard, P., 425, 427
Bardo, M. T., 191
Bares, M., 57
Bargai, N., 219
Bar-Haim, Y., 342
Baring, M., 268
Barlett, C. P., 569
Barlow, D. H., 398, 399, 478, 484, 514, 528, 566
Barner, D., 295
Barnes, C. A., 258
Barnett, R.C., 392
Barnier, A., 196, 198
Barnow, S., 503
Baron, A. S., 576
Barr, R., 338
Barrett, S., 474
Barry, L. C., 489
Barsade, S. G., 434
Bartels, M., 383
Bartholow, B. D., 238, 569
Bartlett, F. C., 285

Bartolomeo, P., 76
Barton, J. J. S., 152, 490
Bartrum, D. A., 120
Basbaum, A. I., 134
Bateman, D. J., 96
Bates, A. L., 308, 309
Bates, T. C., 462
Batson, C. D., 570
Bauby, J.-D., 166
Bauer, K., 379, 382, 388
Baumeister, R., 118
Baumeister, R. F., 381
Baumrind, D., 340, 343
Baur, K., 394, 397, 400
Beach, F. A., 387
Beaton, E .A., 461
Beauchamp, C. M., 305
Beck, A., 515–516, 518, 520
Beck, A. T., 518
Beck, J. S., 517
Becker, S. I., 255
Beckerman, S., 391
Becvar, D., 362
Becvar, R., 362
Beer, J. S., 72
Begg, I. M., 132
Behar, R., 418
Beilin, H., 338
Belardinelli, C, 490
Bell, P. A., 443
Bellack, D., 8
Bem, S. L., 378, 384
Benazzi, F., 36
Benbow, C. P., 420
Benderksy, M., 327
Benedetti, F., 25
Ben-Eliyahu, S., 105
Bengtson, V. L., 364
Benjamin, L. T., 45
Bennett, E. L., 228
Bennett, M., 552
Bennett, S., 362
Benowitz, N., 194
Ben-Porath, Y. S., 465
Ben-Shakhar, G., 219, 433
Benson, H ., 196
Benton, D. A., 268
Berchtold, N. C., 330
Berenbaum, S. A., 378
Bergeman, C. S., 120
Berger, M., 263
Berglund, H., 146
Bergstrom-Lynch, C. A., 392
Berk, M., 119
Bernard, L. L., 408
Bernet, W., 350
Berry, J. W., 320

Bersoff, D. M., 353
Berthoud, H.-R., 415
Berzoff, J., 355
Best, D. L., 384
Bethmann, A., 76
Bettencourt, B. .A, 393
Better Sleep Council, 184
Beyerstein, L., 162
Bhattacharya, S. K., 110
Bhattacharya, T., 477
Bianchi, K., 442
Bianchi, M., 134
Bieber, C., 115
Biehl, M., 435
Billiard, M., 183, 184
Bind, K. M. L., 290
Binet, A., 300
Bink, M. L., 290
Bin Ladin, O., 553
Birchler, G. R., 522
Bird, I. M., 383
Birmingham, W., 359
Bishop, C. A., 477
Biswas-Diener, R., 519
Bjorkqvist, K., 383
Bjornaes, H., 76
Blair, S., 418
Blais, M. C., 461
Blakemore, C., 152
Blanchard, E. B., 236
Blanco, C., 461
Blass, T., 562
Bless, H., 308, 309
Bloch, Y., 531
Blonigen, D. M., 306
Blonna, R., 399
Blumenthal, J. A., 119
Bob, P., 198
Boccato, G., 132
Bohbot, V. D., 266
Bohm-Starke, N., 236
Boisvert, J.-M., 461
Boivin, D. B., 171
Bonanno, G. A., 424
Bond, F. W., 118
Bond, M. H., 560
Boniface, J., 338
Bookbinder, M., 132
Bootzin, R., 174
Bor, D., 304
Borba, M., 351
Borbely, A. A., 177
Borchers, B. J., 445
Born, J., 177
Borra, R., 482
Borrego, J., 218
Bostwick, J. M., 534
Bouchard, T. J., 383
Bouchard, T. J., Jr., 306, 462
Boucher, L., 248
Boufal, M. M., 443
Bourne, L. E., 283
Bouton, M. E., 210
Bowen, E., 244
Bowers, K. S., 198
Bowlby, J., 340

Boxhill, L., 120
Boyle, S. H., 108
Boysen, G. A., 392
Bozarth, J. D., 457
Bozkurt, A. S., 548
Bradley, R., 503
Bradley, R. H., 343
Brady, S. S., 238
Braffman, W., 198
Braid, J., 198
Brajkovich, G., 556
Brase, G. L., 554
Breland, K., 230
Bremner, J. D., 100
Brener, L., 575
Brent, D. A., 490, 491
Brewer, J., 264
Brislin, R., 39, 535
Brislin, R. B., 387, 477, 499
Brislin, R. W., 477
Britner, P. A., 343
Britton, S. W., 425
Broadwell, R. D., 50
Broca, P., 72
Brockner, J., 287
Brodley, B. T., 457
Brody, A., 112
Brown, A., 342
Brown, A. C., 359
Brown, C., 290
Brown, D., 484
Brown, E., 264, 269
Brown, J. D., 450
Brown, R., 552, 574
Browne, K. O., 499
Bruey, C., 569
Buck, R., 435
Buckley, K. E., 218, 238
Bugental, D. B., 320
Bugg, J. M., 298
Bunce, D., 118
Bunde, J., 107, 108
Buontempo, G., 287
Burg, A. S., 287
Burgdorf, J., 224–225
Burka, J. B., 118
Burke, S., 424
Burns, S. M., 459
Bush, G. W., 260, 264
Bushman, B. J., 238, 569
Bushnell, M. C., 149
Buss, D. M, 84
Buss, D. M., 12, 387, 391, 444, 445,
    554, 568
Buswell, B. N., 574
Butcher, J. N., 464
Butterweck, V., 528
Byne, W., 69, 392
Byrd, J., 202, 232, 234, 237, 238
Byrne, R. L., 260

C

Cabýóglu, M. T., 133
Cadoret, R. J., 383
Cahill, L., 268
CaI, W.-H., 233

Caldwell, J., 388
Caldwell, P., 388
Calkins, M., 13
Call, V. R. A., 365
Caltran, G., 336
Cameron, L., 574
Campbell, A., 383
Campbell, L., 558
Campbell, L. C., 115
Campbell, W. K., 547
Cannella, C., 415
Cannon, T. D., 497
Cannon, W., 425, 427
Cannon, W. B., 414
Caprara, G. V., 556
Carballo, J. J., 489, 568
Cardinali, D. P., 182
Careers in Health Psychology, 111
Carels, R. A., 417
Carey, M., 308
Carlsmith, J. M., 549
Carlson, E., 534
Carlson, L. E., 197
Carlson, N. R., 52, 70, 72, 149, 280
Carlson, R. G., 194
Carnagey, N. L., 218, 238, 569
Caro, D. M., 355
Carpenter, S., 144–145, 293, 295,
    384, 416, 575
Carr, J. L., 402
Carstensen, L. L., 354, 364
Carter, E., 194
Carter, H., 314
Carton, J. S., 432
Caruso, E. M., 287
Carvalho, C., 198
Casarjian, R., 432
Casey, B. H., 336
Castano, E., 552
Castelli, L., 382, 575
Castillo, R. J., 196
Castonguay, L. G., 510, 512, 538
Castro, C. A., 534
Cathers-Shiffman, T. A., 308
Cattell, R., 298, 443, 447
Cavell, T. A., 45
Cavett, D., 539
Cehajic, S., 552
Centers for Disease Control and
    Prevention (CDC), 189, 191,
    401, 418
Cermakian, N., 171
Cervone, D., 458
Cesaro, P., 134
Ceschi, G., 425
Champtiaux, N., 191
Chance, P., 209, 216, 225
Chandrashekar, J., 146
Chang, G., 61
Chang, R. C., 209
Chapman, A. L., 504
Chapman, B. P., 447
Chapman, H., 495, 496
Charland, W. A., 172
Charles, S. T., 336, 364
Charney, D. S., 119

Charuvastra, M. C., 119
Chase-Lansdale, L., 363
Chen, A. C. C., 100
Chen, E., 120
Chen, F. S., 342
Chen, Y., 482
Chess, S., 354–355
Cheung, M. S., 490
Chilcoat, H. D., 195
Chiou, W.-B., 546
Chiricozzi, F. R., 265
Chisolm, S., 348
Choi, N., 383
Choi, S., 320
Chomsky, N., 293
Chrisler, J. C., 328
Christ, O., 574
Christensen, D., 183, 305
Christopher, K., 504
Chruchill, W., 474
Chung, J. C. C., 329
Chwalisz, K., 425
Cialdini, R. B., 570
Cichetti, D., 444
Clark, A. J., 519
Clark, D. B., 501, 502
Clark, J. K., 552
Clark, K., 232, 233
Clark, K. B., 13
Clark, M., 13
Clark, M. P., 232, 233
Claus, J., 132
Cleaves, D. H., 538
Cleeremans, A., 132
Clemants, E., 361
Clemens, S. (Mark Twain), 348
Clementz, B. A., 547
Clifford, J. S., 443
Clinton, S. M., 69
Clouser, R., 268
Clulow, C., 343
Coats, J. K., 6
Coats, J.K., 569
Coatsworth, D., 363
Cochran, S.D., 552
Cohen, D., 113, 358
Cohen, S., 102, 119
Coifman, K. G., 118
Colapinto, J., 379, 380
Cole, D. L., 20
Cole, M., 261, 336
Coles, C. D., 31, 322
Coley, R., 363
Collocan, L. K., 96
Combrink-Graham, L., 340
Combs, D. R., 494, 498
Conklin, C. Z., 503
Connell-Carrick, K., 361
Connor, K. M., 528
Connors, G. J., 113, 192, 193
Constantino, M. J., 184
Conte, H. R., 370
Cook, D. A., 477
Cook, M., 487
Coolen, L. M., 394
Coombs, R. H., 186

Cooper, C., 361, 489
Cooper, C. L., 427
Cooper, G. F., 152
Cooper, J., 524, 549
Cooper, R., 482
Cooper, W. E., Jr., 148
Coplan, R. J., 342
Corazzini, L. L., 382
Corballis, J.P., 281
Coren, S., 174
Corey, G., 510, 514, 521
Corkin, S., 242, 266
Cornelius, J. R., 501, 502
Corr, C. A., 367, 368
Corr, D. M., 367, 368
Corso, P. S., 218
Corwyn, R., 343
Cosgrove, K. P., 382
Costa, P. T., Jr., 443, 444
Costello, K., 552
Coulson, S., 76
Courage, M. L., 326
Cowell, S., 494
Coyne, J. C., 95
Coyne, S. M., 238
Craft, L. L., 468
Craig, A. A., 149
Craik, F., 252
Craik, F. I. M., 245
Craske, M. C., 486, 487
Crawford, C. S., 134
Creed, P. A., 120
Crespo-Facorro, B., 498
Cresswell, M., 478
Crim, J., 194
Crocker, N. A., 31, 322
Crockett, L. J., 338, 342
Crone, C. C., 528
Crooks, R., 379, 382, 388, 394,
    397, 400
Crowe, R., 499
Crowell, S. E., 504
Cubelli, R., 264
Culbertson, W., 52, 69, 169,
    229, 429
Cullen, D., 412
Cully, J. A., 485, 486
Cummings, D. E., 415
Cummings, E., 364
Cunningham, G. B., 554, 573, 576
Curtiss, G., 445
Curtiss, S., 278

D

Dackis, C. A., 70
Dalenberg, C., 502
Dalley, J. W., 461
Damani, A., 30, 31
Damasio, A. R., 166
Damon, M., 523
Damour, L. K., 476, 491
Dana, R. H., 467
Daniels, K., 298
Danis, A., 338
Dantzer, R., 102, 231
Dapretto, M., 423

Darley, J., 570–572
Darmani, N. A., 194
Darwin, C., 10, 84, 293, 427, 435
Dasgupta, N., 576
Dasi, C., 250
Daum, I., 280
David, D., 514
Davidson, J. R. T., 528
Davidson, P. S. R., 265
Davies, I., 139
Davies, M. F., 514
Da Vinci, L., 126
Davis, K. E., 558
Davis, M., 234–235
Davison, G. C., 478, 503
Dawson, K. A., 173
Dean-Borenstein, M. T., 96
Deary, I. J., 305
Deason, R. G., 76
de Boulogne, D., 424
DeBruine, L. M., 554
DeCasper, A. J., 327
de Charms, R., 420
Deci, E. L., 430
Deckers, L., 462
DeClue, G., 433
De Coteau, T. J., 93
Deffenbacher, K., 269
DeFries, J. C., 293, 306
Deiss, C., 216
Delahanty, D. L., 94, 100
DeLamater, J. D., 322, 362, 382,
    387, 388, 394, 398
Delgado, J. M. R., 568
Delgado, P. L., 490
Delgado-Gaitan, C., 320
Dell, M., 121
Deller, T., 61
Dell Sala, S., 264
de Maat, S., 512
Dembe, A. E., 171, 173, 174
Dement, W., 183
Dement, W. C., 171, 174
De Montaigne, M., 268
Denbow, D., 132
Denmark, F. L., 86, 383, 384
Dennis, M. G., 326
Dennis, W., 326
den Oudsten, B. L., 432
De Oliveira-Souza, R., 503
de Pinho, R. S. N., 174
Dermer, M., 556
Descartes, R., 9
DeSpelder, L. A., 369
DeValois, R. L., 140
Devor, E., 383
de Waal, F. B. M., 570
Dhikav, V., 477, 478
Diamond, A., 267
Diamond, M., 380
Diaz, A. B., 119
Diaz-Berclano, C., 219
DiCaprio, L., 486
Dickinson, D. J., 40
Diego, M., 341
Diego, M. A., 336

Diener, E., 12, 341, 343
Dienes, Z., 248
Diges, M., 260, 268
Dijksterhuis, A., 132
Dill, K., 238
Dill, K. E., 237
Dillard, A. J., 120
Dimberg, U., 132, 427
Dingle, G., 522
DiPietro, J. A., 326
Disterhoft, J. F., 68
Dixon, L., 361
Di Zio, P., 149
Dobson, K. S., 518
Doghraji, K., 171
Dollard, J., 569
Domhoff, G. W., 180, 181, 454
Dominowski, R. L., 283
Domjan, M., 230, 231
Donahue, C. B., 361
Dondi, M., 336
Donini, L. M., 415
Donne, J., 340
Donnelly, R., 342
D'Onofrio, B. M., 359
Donohue, R., 445
Dougal, S., 265
Dougherty, D. M., 25
Dougherty, K., 269
Doughty, E. A., 367
Dresser, N., 436
Driscoll, A. K., 342
Driscoll, R., 558
Drwecki, B. B., 552
Duffy, R. D., 445
Dufresne, T., 180, 448
Duke, P., 474, 484
Duncan, L. E., 355
Duncan, T. B., 343
Dunham, Y. C., 552
Dunn, J. G. H., 93
Dunn, J. S., 40
Dunne, M. P., 392
Durand, V. M., 478
Durik, A. M., 420
Dutra, L., 491
Dutton, D., 27
Duval, D. C., 384
Dweck, C. S., 342
Dworkin, A., 554

E

Eagly, A. H., 86, 383, 391
Eaker, E. D., 108
Ebbeson, E. B., 565
Ebbinghaus, H., 257
Eccles, J. A., 378
Eddy, K. T., 418
Edison, T., 280, 289, 297, 310, 419
Edward, K.-L., 501, 502
Egan, E. A., 355
Ehrenreich, B., 566
Ehrhardt, A. A., 380
Einstein, A., 305, 457, 476
Eisenberger, R., 431
Ekers, D., 527
Ekman, P., 38, 435, 436

Elfenbein, H. A., 295
Elkin, A., 497
Elkind, D., 335, 336
Ellis, A., 122, 514, 515, 516,
    518, 520
Ellis, H., 386, 387, 389
Ellis, L., 287, 392
Ellman, L. M., 497
Elmehed, K., 132, 427
Emerson, R. W., 126
Emery, C. R., 362
Engle, S., 364
Epstein, C., 531
Erdelyi, M. H., 161
Ergene, N., 133
Erikson, E., 355–357
Erlacher, D., 180
Escher, M. C., 155
Eslinger, P. J., 36
Espelage, D. L., 393
Esposito, P., 236
Esqueda, C. W., 554
Esses, V. M., 552
Esterson, A., 454
Evans, G. W., 120, 197
Evans, K., 554
Everett, C., 359
Everett, S. V., 359
Eysenck, H., 443, 447, 462

F

Fabes, R., 342
Faddiman, A., 477
Faigman, D. L., 433
Fairburn, C. G., 418
Fairchild, K., 489
Fang, X., 218
Fantz, R., 327
Faraone, S. V., 490, 494, 497
Farmer, A. E., 491, 493
Farrell, M. J., 134
Fassler, O., 198
Feeney, D., 364
Fehr, C., 112
Fein, S., 235, 237, 552, 569
Feldman, R., 341
Feng, J., 384
Fernandes, M. A., 245
Fernández, J. R., 416
Fernandez, M. I., 195
Fernyhough, C., 338, 498
Ferrari, P. F., 423
Ferreti, P., 322
Festinger, L., 549
Feyer, A. M., 172
Field, A. P., 233
Field, K. M., 436
Field, T., 192, 336, 341
Fields, W., 295
Fifer, W. D., 327
Finch, E., 402
Fink, B., 554
Fink, J. S., 554
Finklehor, D., 362
Finniss, D. G., 25
First, M., 480

Fischer, E., 557
Fisher, G., 501
Fisher, J. O., 417
Fisher, T., 245
Fisk, J. E., 287
Fitzgerald, D. B., 245
Flavell, J. H., 336
Flegal, D., 418
Fleisch, E., 547
Fleischman, A. R., 96
Fleischmann, B., 61
Fletcher, G. J. O., 558
Flores, Y. G., 366
Flynn, J., 308
Fogarty, A., 194
Fogassi, I., 423
Fogassi, L., 423
Fok, H. K., 38, 436
Folkman, S., 119
Food and Drug Administration
    (FDA), 186
Ford, T. E., 309
Foster, P. S., 76
Foulkes, D., 171
Fouts, R., 446, 447
Fowers, B. J., 450
Fox, M. J., 57
Fox, N. A., 340
Fraley, R. C., 344
Frangicetto, T., 227, 353, 418, 420,
    523, 572
Frankenberg, W., 326
Franklin, B., 558
Frawley, T. J., 376
Frayser, S., 387
Fredrick, T. A., 378
Freeman, S., 84, 86
Freeman, W. J., 527
Fresán, A., 568
Freud, A., 454
Freud, S., 10–11, 179, 181, 192, 442,
    448, 449, 450, 451, 452, 453,
    454, 480, 510–511
Frick, K. M., 228
Frick, R. S., 194
Friedman, H., 444, 454
Friedman, M., 107, 108
Friend, C., 362
Frishman, W. H., 61
Friston, K. J., 36
Frohlich, P., 27
Fry, C. L., 366
Fryer, S. L., 31, 322
Fulker, D. W., 293, 306
Funder, D. C., 444, 457, 462
Furman, E., 369
Furnham, A., 237, 552, 554

G

Gabbard, G. O., 503
Gabbert, F., 260, 268
Gabriel, G., 528
Gabriel, S., 393
Gabry, K. E., 110
Gacono, C. B., 467

Gaetz, M., 129
Gage, P., 72, 79, 422, 461
Gagné, M.-H., 359
Gagne, P. E., 249
Gagnon, J., 395
Gagnon, J. H., 396
Gailiot, M. T., 416
Gajdamaschko, N., 336
Galderisi, S., 498
Galef, B. G., Jr., 209
Galinsky, A. D., 574
Galizio, M., 113, 192, 193
Gall, F., 463
Galloway, J. L., 237
Galperin, G. J., 481
Galvan, S., 336
Galvin, K. A., 61
Gambescia, N., 397
Gandhi, M., 457
Gandi, M., 348
Garb, H. N., 467
Garcia, G. M., 308
Garcia, J., 230, 231
Gardner, A., 295
Gardner, B., 295
Gardner, H., 298, 299, 308
Gardner, R., 174
Garland, J., 189
Garno, J. L., 568
Garrick, J., 569
Garry, M., 260
Gaser, C., 498
Gasser, S., 102
Gates, B., 121
Gaw, A. C., 478
Gazzaniga, M. S., 76
Gearhart, J. P., 379
Gebauer, H., 547
Gee, J., 555
Gelder, B. D., 436
Geminiani, G. C., 382
Genie, 278, 281, 297, 310
Genovese, K., 570
Gerber, A. J., 265
Gerberding, J., 418
Gerrie, M. P., 260
Gershon, E. S., 493
Getz, S., 336
Ghezzi, P. M., 526
Giancola, P. R., 383
Gibbs, N., 434
Gibson, E. J., 158
Gibson, M., 575
Giedd, J. N., 336
Gil, D., 97
Gilbert, P., 490
Gilbody, S., 527
Giles, B., 227
Giles, J. W., 378
Gilligan, C., 353
Gilmour, D. R., 560
Gini, M., 342
Ginsberg, S., 336
Ginsburg-Block, M., 359
Ginzburg, H. M., 96

Girardi, P., 218
Gitschier, D., 145
Giumetti, G. W., 569
Glass, R. M., 93
Gluck, M. A., 265
Gobbo, C., 547
Gobet, F., 248, 249
Godden, D. R., 256
Goforth, H. W., 530
Gogtay, N., 498
Goldberg, J. F., 568
Golden, A., 569, 572
Golden, W. L., 198
Goldschmidt, L., 194
Goldstein, E. G., 247, 248, 298, 339
Goleman, D., 432, 434
Golosheikim, S. A., 196
Gómez, A., 574
Goni-Allo, B., 194
Goodall, J., 29, 350
Goode, E. E., 424
Goodman, G. S., 268, 344
Goodwin, C. J., 9, 12, 21, 207, 434,
    435, 478
Gooren, L., 392, 393
Goram, A., 474
Gordis, E. B., 569
Gordon, W. C., 244
Gosling, S., 446–447
Gosling, S. D., 444
Goswami, S., 502
Gotell, L., 412
Gotlieb, I. H., 263, 265, 491
Gottesman, I. I., 494, 497
Gottfredson, G. D., 445
Gottman, J. M., 360
Gow, K., 198
Gracely, R. H., 134
Graeff, F. G., 110
Graham, K., 6, 568
Graham, S., 386
Grant, J. E., 361
Grant, M. A., 134
Grant, P. M., 515, 518
Grant, S., 188
Grant, U. S., 434
Gray, J. A., 252
Gray, J. D., 547
Grayson, C., 489
Greco, N., 534
Gredler, M. E., 338
Green, A. I., 501
Green, A. R., 576
Greenberg, D. L., 264
Greenberg, E., 93
Greenberg, J., 119, 351
Greenberg, L. S., 522
Greene, D., 431
Greene, K., 287
Greenfield, P., 319
Greenfield, P. M., 228, 336
Greenwald, A. G., 575, 576
Gregersen, E., 387
Gregory, R. J., 467
Grekin, E. R., 113, 501

Gresack, J. E., 228
Griffin, A. S., 209
Grigorenko, E. L., 308
Grilo, C. M., 503
Gringart, E., 549
Grondin, S., 247
Gross, A., 361
Grossmann, K., 341
Grov, C., 399
Grover, 503
Grunberg, L., 93
Gschwendner, T., 575
Guanawardane, N., 568
Guastello, D. D., 468
Guastello, S. J., 468
Gudelsky, G. A., 194
Guidelines for Ethical Conduct, 19
Guilford, J. P., 290, 298
Guisande, M. A., 338
Gunzerath, L., 31
Gustavson, C. R., 231
Guthrie, R., 25
Guyader, N., 129
Gyllensten, K., 518

H

Haberstick, B. C., 568
Haddad, S. K., 490
Haddock, G., 362, 568
Haier, R. J., 306
Halberstade, J., 556
Halbreich, U., 536
Haley, A. P., 267
Haley, R. W., 192
Halgin, R. P., 472, 484
Hall, C. S., 181
Hall, J., 295
Hall, K., 497, 536
Hall, P. A., 393
Haller, S., 36
Halpern, D. F., 440
Hamilton, J. P., 263, 265
Hamilton, M., 552
Hamm, J. P., 281
Hammack, P. L., 518
Hammen, C., 490
Hammock, G. S., 383
Hammond, D. C., 115, 236
Hampl, J., 415
Hampton, T., 52, 61
Haney, C., 564
Hanley, S. J., 412
Hansell, J. H., 476, 491
Harackiewicz, J. M., 420
Hardcastle, S., 519
Hardy, J. B., 362
Harkness, S., 320
Harlow, H. F., 341
Harlow, J., 72
Harlow, M. K., 341
Harris, R. J., 569
Harrison, E., 196
Harrison, T., 501
Hart, C. I., 193, 194
Hart, D., 353

Hart, J., Jr., 265
Hartenbaum, N., 183
Harth, N. S., 552
Hartwell, L., 317, 568
Harvard School of Public Health, 418
Harvey, J., 30
Harvey, T., 305
Hasegawa, H., 196
Haslam, N., 552
Hatfield, E., 396, 558
Hätinen, M., 93
Hatsukami, D. K., 113
Haugen, R., 412
Hauser, R. M., 308
Havighurst, R. J., 364
Hayes, R., 336
Hayflick, L., 330
Hayne, H., 338
Hazan, C., 343, 344
Healey, A. F., 245
Healy, A. F., 254
Heath, A. C., 501
Heckhausen, J., 364
Heider, F., 546
Heiman, J. R., 397
Heimann, M., 336
Heine, S. J., 548
Heller, S., 448, 453
Hellström, P. M., 415
Helmes, E., 549
Helms, J. E., 477
Hemingway, A., 350
Henderlong, J., 432
Henry, W. E., 364
Herbison, G. P., 172
Herdt, G. H., 386
Herek, G., 393
Hergenhahn, B. R., 530
Hering, E., 140
Herman, B. H., 188
Herman, C. P., 415, 417, 418
Herman, L., 8
Herman, L. M., 295
Hermans, E. J., 383, 569
Hernandez-Reif, M., 341
Herrnstein, R. J., 307
Herron, H., 361
Herron, J. C., 84, 86
Herron, W. G., 238
Hetherington, E. M., 359, 360
Hettrich, E. L., 569
Heward, W. L., 524
Heyder, K., 280
Heyman, G. D., 378
Higgins, E. T., 444
Higher Education Research
    Institute, 364
Higley, E. R., 342
Hilgard, E. R., 198
Hill, C., 510, 512, 538
Hill, E. L., 72
Hiller, J. B., 498
Hinton, E. C., 69
Hitler, A., 578
Hobson, A., 180, 181
Hobson, J. A., 184

Hodges, S. D., 519
Hodson, G., 552
Hoek, H. W., 419
Hofer, A., 265
Hoff, E., 291, 293
Hoffman, M. L., 350, 353
Hoffman, W., 79, 80, 575
Hofman, A., 193
Hogan, M. J., 115
Hogan, T. P., 203
Hoge, C. W., 534
Hogg, M. A., 549
Holden, C., 307
Holden, R., 287
Holland, J., 447
Holland, J. L., 445, 446
Holmes, T. H., 93, 94
Holsinger, T., 530
Holt, L. J., 109
Holt, N. L., 40, 93
Holt-Lunstad, 359
Honts, C. R., 433
Honzik, C. H., 224
Hooley, J. M., 498
Hope, D. A., 83
Hopkins, A., 508
Hopson, D. S., 232
Horney, K., 447, 452, 453, 454
Horowitz, A. V., 482
Horvath, K. J., 398
Hoshino-Browne, E., 550
Hosie, P. J., 427
Houlfort, N., 431
Houtz, J. C., 412
Howell, K. K., 31, 322
Howes, M. B., 268
Hoye, A., 499
Hrebickova, M., 444
Hsieh, P.-H., 412
Hsiu-Hsui, C., 99
Hsu, P.-C., 343
Huang, M., 308
Hubel, D. H., 152
Hudziak, J. J., 317, 503
Huesmann, L. R., 225, 503
Huffman, K., 93, 249, 442
Hughes, H., 474, 486
Huguet, N., 364
Huici, C., 574
Hull, C., 409
Hunt, M., 207
Huntington, R., 368
Hurlemann, R., 102
Hurley, R. A., 498
Hurley, S., 423
Hurt, H., 121
Hustvedt, S., 115
Hutchinson-Phillips, S., 198
Huurre, T., 359
Hyde, J. S., 86, 322, 353, 362, 382,
    383, 387, 388, 391, 392, 394,
    398, 536
Hyman, R., 162, 440
Hyodo, M., 256
Hypericum Depression Trial Study
    2002, 528

I
Iacono, W. G., 433
Iavarone, A., 304
Ibañez, A., 461
Ibrahim, M., 343
Ikemoto, K., 497
Ikerni, A., 536
Irons, C., 490
Israel, P., 278
Ivanovic, D. M., 305
Ivcevic, Z., 290
Iversen, L. L., 57
Iversen, S. D., 57
Iwasaki, K., 99

J
Jablonski, B., 565, 566
Jackendoff, R., 296
Jackson, E. D., 263, 490
Jackson, P. B., 489
Jacob, P., 423
Jacobi, C., 417
Jain, A., 232
Jain, G., 530
James, F. O., 171
James, J. B., 309
James, W., 10, 13, 168, 425, 427
James I, King, 112
Jamieson, G. A., 196, 198
Jang, K. L., 462
Janis, I. L., 566
Jankowiak, W., 557
Jantzen, K. J., 129
Janvier, B., 338
Jarrold, C., 250
Javaheri, S., 183
Jellison, W. A., 393
Jensen, A., 307
Jensen, G., 216
Jensen, M. P., 196, 198
Jeste, D. V., 494
Joh, A. S., 326
John, O., 446–447
John, O. P., 444
Johnson, B. W., 281
Johnson, I. M., 182
Johnson, M., 425, 569
Johnson, N. J., 100, 363
Johnson, S. C., 504
Johnson, S. K., 218
Johnson, S. L., 478
Johnson, V., 387, 389, 397, 398, 402
Johnson, V. E., 382
Johnson, W., 298, 306, 342
Johnston, C., 320
Jolliffe, C. D., 134
Jonas, E., 286
Jones, B. Q., 359
Jones, D.G., 61
Jones, E. G., 68
Jones, J., 577
Jones, L., 362
Jones, M., 459
Jones, N. A., 336
Jones, S. R., 498, 554
Jong, E., 374

Jonides, J., 247, 249, 250
Jordan, M., 576
Joseph, S., 12
Joshi, V. N., 386
Jourdan, A., 457, 519
Juang, L., 38, 39, 156, 181, 261, 291,
    297, 320, 355, 357, 365, 435,
    475, 569
Jung, C., 383, 447, 452–453
Jung, H., 560
Jung, R. E., 306
Junkkari, H., 359
Juntii, S. A., 6, 569

K
Kable, J. A., 21, 322
Kagan, J., 355
Kahn, L. S., 536
Kahneman, D., 287
Kalidindi, S., 497
Kalivas, P. W., 191
Kanner, A. D., 95
Kanovsky, P., 57
Kantrowitz, B., 502
Kaplan, L. E., 351
Kaplan, M. S, 364
Kardong, K., 86, 148, 230, 391,
    568, 570
Kareev, Y., 248
Karmiloff, K., 327
Karmiloff-Smith, A., 327
Karremans, J. C., 132
Kasser, T., 391
Kassin, S., 235, 237, 552, 569
Kassinove, H., 569
Kastembaum, R. J., 367, 368, 369
Katz, M., 499
Kaufman, J., 367
Kaufman, J. C., 290
Kaufman, L., 247
Kaukiainen, A., 569
Kawakami, K., 574
Kaye, W., 417, 418
Kaysen, D., 109
Kazdin, A. E., 214, 216, 232, 236,
    508, 526
Keating, C. F., 383
Keating, C. R., 436
Keefe, F. J., 115
Keller, C. J., 290
Keller, H., 134, 484
Keller, J., 308, 309
Kellogg, J. H., 386
Kellogg, S. H., 514, 518
Kelly, G., 6
Keltner, D., 424, 436
Kemeny, M. E., 102, 105
Kendler, K. S., 503
Kenix, L. J., 554
Kennedy, J. F., 264
Kennedy, R., 24
Kerr, K. M., 228
Kerschreiter, R., 286
Keshavan, M. S., 497
Kessler, T., 552
Ketcham, K., 242

Khaleque, A., 343
Khalid, N., 530
Khandai, P., 120
Kieffer, K. M., 445
Kiester, E., 198
Kigar, D. L., 305
Kihlstrom, J. F., 268, 502
Kilb, A., 245
Killen, M., 353
Kim, J., 558
Kim, U., 320
Kim, Y. H., 219
Kimes, L. M., 362
Kimmel, P. R., 547
Kimmell, M., 396
Kimmell, M. S., 376, 384
Kinder, L. S., 489, 491
King, B. M., 100, 362, 379, 382,
    394, 397, 398, 400
King, J. W., 237
King, M. L., Jr., 264
Kinsey, A., 386, 387, 389
Kircher, J. C., 433
Kirk, K. M., 392
Kirsch, I., 198
Kirschenbaum, H., 457, 519
Kirschner, S. M., 481
Kirwil, L., 225, 503
Kisilevsky, B. S., 326
Kitayama, S., 358, 550
Kleider, H. M., 260
Klein, O., 309
Klimes-Dougan, B., 489, 491
Kline, K. K., 363
Kluger, J., 433
Knapp, M., 531
Knekt, P., 453, 512, 538
Kniffin, K. M., 555
Knight, J., 556
Knoblauch, K., 139
Knott, V., 305
Knutson, B., 224–225
Kobasa, S., 108
Koenig, A. M., 86, 383, 391
Köfalvi, A., 193, 194
Kohlberg, L., 57, 351, 352, 353, 355
Köhler, W., 224
Koko, 278, 295, 297, 310
Kondo, N., 508
Konheim-Kalkstein, Y. L., 431
Koob, G. F., 501
Koppel, J., 367
Koropeckyj-Cox, T., 365
Kotulak, R., 568
Koutstaal, W., 298
Kovacic, Z., 569
Kraaij, V., 94
Kracher, B., 353
Kral, T. V. E., 417
Kraut, M. A., 265
Krebs, D. L., 350, 351
Krebs, P. R., 246
Kreger, R., 504
Krempl, R., 547
Kring, A. M., 424, 472, 478, 503
Krishma, G., 195
Kronenberger, W. G., 238

Kruger, J. I., 546
Krusemark, E. A., 468, 547
Ksir, C. J., 193, 194
Ku, G., 574
Kubiak, T., 94
Kübler-Ross, E., 369
Kuhn, C., 185
Kuhnehenn, J., 566
Kulik, J., 264
Kulik, L., 552
Kumkale, G. T., 260
Kuperstok, N., 569
Kupper, S., 236
Kurtz, J. E., 443

L

Lachman, M. E., 330
Lack, L. C., 172
Lackner, J. R., 149
Lader, M., 171, 182
Lafayette-De Mente, 99
Laidlaw, K., 518
Lakein, A., 44
Landay, J. S., 566
Landeira-Fernandez, J., 110
Lang, F. R., 461
Lange, C., 425, 427
LaPointe, L. L., 278, 310
Laposa, J. M., 486
Lapsley, D. K., 351
Larson, J., 489
Latané, B., 566, 570–572
Latner, J. D., 538
Laumann, E., 395
Laungani, P. D., 13, 181, 343, 357,
    365, 477, 478, 535, 536
Lavish, L. A., 290
Lawrence, C., 560
Lawrence, M., 502
Lazar, S. W., 197
Lazarus, R. S., 95, 116, 119, 122
Lazarus, S., 363
Leaper, C., 384
Leary, C. E., 218
Lebo, M. J., 378
Lecrubier, Y., 528
LeDoux, J., 70, 422, 429
Lee, D., 548
Lee, J., 402
Lee, J. J., 305
Lee, W.-Y., 521, 522
Lee, Y.-W., 535
Lefkowitz, E. S., 383
Lefley, H. P., 499
Leglise, A., 171, 172
Legrand, F. D., 410
Lehnert, G., 250
Lehrer, M., 326
Lehto, S. M., 512
Leichtman, M. D., 252, 260
Lein, C., 519
Lele, D. U., 343, 344
Lemay, E. P., 102
LeMoal, M. L., 501
Lemus, D. R., 364
Lennon, J., 119
Leon, P., 328

Leonard, V. W., 362
Lepper, M. R., 431, 432
Leri, A., 61
Lerner, H. D., 512
Lerner, J. S., 287
le Roux, R., 499
Leslie, M., 305
Lester, D., 444
Lettvin, J. Y., 152
Leung, D. W., 504
LeVay, S., 392, 393
Leve, L. D., 383
Levenson, R. W., 360, 428
Leventhal, H., 90, 111
Lever, J. P., 118, 120
Levin, J., 79–80
Levine, J. A., 362
Levine, J. R., 558
Levinthal, C., 113, 185, 186, 192,
    193, 194, 322, 362, 461, 568
Levitan, J., 399
Levitan, L. C., 552
Levy, D., 13, 38, 156
Levy, F., 246
Levy, J., 307
Lewandowski, G. W., Jr., 555
Lewin, D., 361
Lewis, D. A., 498
Lewis, J., 307
Lewis, J. T., 425
Lewis, R. E., 363
Lewis, S., 331, 335
Li, J.-C. A., 359
Libon, D. J., 267
Lichtenstein, B., 481
Lieberman, P., 296
Lincoln, A., 434, 435
Lindahl, K., 355
Lindberg, B., 341
Linden, E., 278, 296
Lindström, P., 146
Lindwall, M., 330
Lineberry, T. W., 534
Links, P. S., 504
Lipetz, M. E., 558
Lipowski, Z. J., 110
Lippa, R. A., 554
Lipsanen, T., 502
Lissek, S., 461
Little, A. C., 554
Litwack, T. R., 481
Liu, H., 134
Liu, J. H., 566
Livingston, J. A., 558
Livingston, R. W., 552
Lochner, C., 487
Lockhart, R., 252
Loewenthal, D., 538
Loftus, E., 242, 244, 260, 268, 272,
    274, 283
Lombardo, M. V., 72
Loo, R., 384
Lopez, J., 560
Lopez, J. C., 61, 343
Lorenz, K., 16, 340
Lores-Arnaiz, S., 228
Lott, D. A., 556

Loxton, N. J., 218
Lu, Z. L., 247
Luangani, P., 118
Lubart, T. I., 290
Lubinski, D., 420
Luciano, M., 462
Lucio, E., 467
Lucio-Gomez, E., 467
Lund, T., 412
Luria, A. R., 129, 155
Lutz, A., 197
Lykken, D. T., 433
Lynch, L., 504
Lynch, T. R., 504
Lynm, C., 93
Lynn, R., 308
Lynn, S. J., 198, 502
Lyons-Ruth, K., 503
Lyoo, I. K., 490
Lyubimov, N. N., 197

M

Maas, J. B., 171
Mackie, D. M., 284
MacLaren, V. V., 433
Macmillan, M. B., 72
Maddi, S. R., 108
Maddux, W. W., 295
Madonna, 444
Maehr, M. L., 420
Mahoney, C. R., 102
Maier, B., 304
Maier, S. F., 52
Mair, R. G., 69
Maisto, S. A., 113, 192, 193
Major, B., 309
Maldonado, J. R., 502
Malone, W., 468, 547
Malti, T., 350
Maner, J. K., 554
Manley, J. J., 308
Manning, J., 198, 391
Manson, J., 418
Mantyh, P., 134
Marble, R. P., 353
Marcus, S., 386
Margolin, G., 569
Markesbery, W. R., 339
Markey, P. M., 569
Markham, M. R., 244
Markle, A., 430
Markovitz, P. J., 504
Marks, D. F., 162
Marks, L. D., 360
Marks, L. E., 150
Markstrom, C. A., 355
Markus, H. R., 235, 237, 358, 550,
    552, 569
Marler, C. A., 6, 383
Marsee, M. A., 383
Marsh, A. A., 295
Marsh, R. L., 290
Marshall, D. S., 387, 388
Marshall, L., 177
Marshall, M., 450
Marshall, S. K., 355
Marsolek, C. J., 76

Martin, C. L., 342, 378
Martin, L. L., 427
Martin, N. G., 392
Martin, S. E., 232
Martin, T. A., 443
Martineau, J., 423
Martinelli, E. A., 341
Maslach, C., 565
Maslow, A., 11, 412, 413, 455, 457, 572
Mason, P. T., 504
Mason, S. A., 502
Massicotte-Marquez, J., 177
Masten, A., 363
Masters, C., 433
Masters, W. H., 382, 387, 389, 397, 398, 402
Masuda, T., 295
Matlin, M. W., 86, 328, 339, 382, 383, 536
Matsumoto, D., 38, 39, 156, 181, 261, 291, 297, 320, 355, 357, 365, 435, 475, 569
Matsunaga, H., 235
Matthews, T. D., 249
Mattson, S. N., 31, 322
Matusov, E., 336
Maurischat, C., 107
May, A., 228
Mayer, J. D., 434
Mayers, A. G., 528
Maynard, A. E., 336
Mays, V. M., 552
Mazure, C. M., 382
Mazzoni, G., 198, 260
McBride, S., 192
McCabe, C., 146
McCarley, R., 180
McCartney, P., 119
McClelland, D. C., 420
McClelland, J. L., 246
McConnell, A. R., 393
McCrae, R. R., 355, 357, 443, 444, 461
McCreary, C. P., 119
McDonald, J. W., 61
McDougall, W., 408
McEvoy, P. M., 522
McFarlane, W. R., 498
McGhee, D. E., 576
McGhie, A., 495, 496
McGue, M., 306
McGuffin, P., 491, 493, 497
McGuinness, T. M., 361
McGuire, B. E., 115
McHugh, P., 434
McKenna, S. B., 340
McKinney, C., 342
McLanahan, S. S., 360
McLaren, W., 189
McNamara, J. M., 176, 366, 570
McNaughton, B. L., 258
McNicholas, W. T., 183
McQuown, S. C., 191
McWilliams, P., 367
Meador-Woodruff, J. H., 69
Medina, K. L., 194

Meek, W., 113
Meeus, W., 562
Mehta, P.H., 444
Melham, N., 490
Melhem, N., 491
Mellings, T. M. B., 486
Meltzer, G., 499
Meltzer, L., 412
Meltzoff, A. N., 336
Melzack, R., 133, 134
Memon, A., 260
Menec, V. H., 364
Menninger, W., 522
Merali, Z., 487, 490
Merari, A., 344
Mesmer, F. A., 198
Messer, S. C., 534
Meston, C., 27
Metcalf, P., 368
Metcalfe, J., 22
Meyer, R. G., 488
Meyer, U., 497
Michael, R., 386
Michaels, S., 395
Miki, Y., 536
Mikulincer, M., 344, 453
Milgram, S., 562–563, 577, 578
Miller, B., 365, 366
Miller, G. A, 248
Miller, G. E., 100, 102
Miller, J. G., 353
Miller, L. K., 304
Miller, M., 502
Miller, P. H., 336
Miller, R. R., 209
Miller, S. A., 336
Millon, T., 478
Millson, C., 261
Milner, P., 70
Milner, V. S., 399
Miltenberger, R. G., 215, 217, 524, 527
Milton, J., 162, 514
Mineka, M., 486, 487
Mingroni, M. A., 308
Minuchin, S., 521, 522
Minzenberg, M. J., 504
Miracle, T. S., 381
Mirescu, C., 173
Mischel, W., 444, 460, 462
Mita, T. H., 556
Mitchell, E., 434
Mitchell, J. P., 260
Mitchell, R., 482
Mittag, O., 107
Moeller, G., 420
Moller, A. C., 430
Monastra, V. J., 115
Moneta, G. B., 432
Money, J., 378, 380, 386, 388
Monin, B., 556
Moniz, E., 530
Monks, C. P., 569
Monte, C. F., 444, 448, 453, 462
Montgomery, G. H., 198
Montgomery, S. A., 490
Montpetit, M. A., 120

Moon, S. Y., 577
Moons, W. G., 284
Moore, M., 555–556
Moore, M. K., 336
Moore, S., 93
Morgan, C., 419
Morgenthaler, T. I., 173
Morris, J. S., 422
Morris, S. G., 252
Morrison, C., 360, 415
Morrison, T. G., 115
Morry, M. M., 556
Mortimore, J. A., 339
Moskowitz, G. B., 574
Moss, D., 236
Motto, R. L., 119
Moyer-Gusé, E., 260
Muehlenhard, C. L., 402
Mueser, K. T., 494
Mui, A. C., 366
Mulckhuyse, M., 129
Muncer, S., 383
Mundhenk, T. N., 423
Munro, I., 501, 502
Munro, V. E., 402
Munsey, C., 534, 535
Murphy, L. L., 194
Murray, A., 491
Murray, C., 307
Murray, H., 419, 466
Murray, K., 504
Muruganandam, A. V., 110
Myers, H. F., 119
Myerson, J., 308

N
Nabe, C. M., 367, 368
Nabi, R. L., 260
Naglieri, J. A., 308
Nahas, G. G., 194
Nahin, R. L., 182
Naisch, P. L. N., 198
Nakamura, K., 536
Nakata, A., 99
Nash, J., 499
Nash, J. F., Jr., 474
Nash, M., 196, 198
Näslund, E., 415
Nasrallah, H. A., 497
National Institute of Mental Health, 484, 486
National Organization on Fetal Alcohol Syndrome, 324
National Sleep Foundation, 182, 183
Navarro, M., 308
Naveh-Benjamin, M., 245
Neale, J. M., 478, 494, 503
Needham, D. R., 132
Neenan, M., 518
Neher, A., 412, 413
Neisser, U., 247
Nelson, C. A., III, 340
Neria, Y., 499
Nesse, R. M., 490
Neto, F., 237, 552
Neubauer, A. C., 306

Neugarten, B. L., 364
Neuringer, A., 216
Newman, C. L., 119
Newman, M., 307
Niaura, R., 107
Nicholas, M. K., 134
Nicholson, A., 489
Nicholson, J., 508
Nickerson, R. S., 286
Nicotra, A., 428
Nieuwenhuijsen, M. J., 322
Nijland, M. I., 308
Nisbett, R., 431
Nishimoto, R., 475, 477
Nogueiras, R., 415
Nolen-Hoeksema, S., 489
Norenzayan, A., 548
Notarius, C. I., 360
Nouchi, R., 256
Nutt, D., 182
Nuttgens, S. A., 198

O
Obama, B., 308
O'Brien, C. P., 70, 188
Obstbaum, K., 355
O'Connell, D. Q., 40
O'Connell, K. L., 490
Odbert, H. S., 442
Oehlberg, K., 486, 487
Oei, T. P. S., 522
O'Farrell, T. J., 522
Oglivie, R. D., 171
Öhrling, K., 341
Oie, T. P. S., 383
Oishi, K., 171
Oldehinkel, A. J., 343
Olds, J., 70
O'Leary, K. D., 569
O'Leary, T. A., 484
Olfson, M., 531
Ollat, H., 134
Olson, G., 216
Oltmanns, T. F., 494
Ommundsen, Y., 412
Oppenheimer, D. M., 287
Orne, M. T., 198
Orth-Gomér, K., 93, 99
Ortiz, F.A., 444
Ortiz, S., 198
Orubuloye, I., 388
Oshima, K., 569
Osler, M., 359
Ostrov, J. M., 383
Ouellet, B., 247
Owen, D. R., 308
Ozawa-de Silva, C., 536

P
Pagano, C., 194
Pagano, Fr., 268
Page, G. G., 105
Paice, E., 174
Palfai, T. P., 113
Palmer, J. K., 518
Palmer, S., 122
Pandi-Perumal, S. R., 182

Name Index

Panksepp, J., 224–225
Papadelis, C., 171, 173
Papirman, Y., 547
Paquet, F., 497
Park, A., 114
Parkes, C. M., 367
Parks, R., 578
Parmar, P., 343
Parrott, A., 528
Parrott, D. J., 383
Passino, K. M., 246
Patterson, F., 296
Patterson, P., 278
Patterson, T. G., 12
Pavlov, I., 11, 205, 209, 210, 211, 212
Pearce, A., 483
Pearson, N. J., 182
Pedrazzoli, M., 183
Pellegrino, J. E., 324
Pellegrino, L., 324
Penfield, W., 34
Penton-Voak, I., 554
Perez-Mata, N., 260, 268
Perry, J. N., 464
Persson, J., 267
Pert, C., 8, 57
Peter, L. J., 461
Peterson, S., 474, 503
Peterson, Z. D., 402
Petrie, R., 554
Pettigrew, T. F., 574
Petty, R. E., 552
Pham, T. M., 228
Phillips, J., 432
Phillips, S. T., 574
Piaget, J., 270, 332–334, 336, 337, 338, 355
Picard, H., 68
Picciotto, M. R., 191
Pierce, J. P., 113
Pindava, M., 120
Pinel, P., 478
Pinna, K., 100
Piomelli, D., 194
Plaud, J. J., 524
Plomin, R., 52, 84, 293, 306, 462
Pluijms, E. M., 530
Plummer, D. C., 552
Plutchik, R., 370, 435
Poe, E. A., 474
Polich, J., 254
Polivy, J., 415, 417, 418
Pollack, H., 362
Pomponio, A. T., 110
Ponzi, A., 265
Poole, J. H., 504
Pope, H. G., Jr., 502
Popma, A., 383, 569
Population Communication International (PCI), 227
Porzelius, L. K., 417
Posner, M. I., 151
Posthuma, D., 306
Powell-Hopson, D., 232
Powers, A. S., 461

Prabhu, V., 430
Prakasam, K. S., 386
Pratt, J., 384
Pratt, M. W., 353
Premack, D., 214
Prescott, C. A., 503
Pressman, J. D., 530
Preuss, U. W., 69
Price, D. D., 25
Priest, R. F., 556
Prigatano, G. P., 252
Primavera, L. H., 238
Pring, L., 304
Prkachin, K. M., 424, 425
Prouix, M. J., 129
Pryor, J., 364
Pullum, G. K., 291
Purdy, J. E., 244
Purnell, M. T., 172

Q
Qualls, S. H., 521, 522
Quinn, P. C., 554
Quintanilla, Y. T., 420

R
Raaijmakers, Q., 562
Rabinowitz, V. C., 86, 383, 384
Raccanello, D., 547
Raesaenen, P. M., 49
Raevuori, A., 417
Raffaelli, M., 338
Rahe, R., 93
Rahe, R. H., 94
Raine, A., 503
Raleigh, W., 112
Ramsey, N. F., 383, 569
Randi, J., 6
Ranganathan, S., 477
Rao, V., 461
Raphel, S., 361
Rapson, R. L., 396, 558
Rattaz, C., 326
Rauer, A. J., 360
Raulet, D. H., 102
Ray, O. S., 193, 194
Raye, C., 374
Rayner, R., 205, 207, 209
Reader, W., 12, 231, 350
Realmuto, G. M., 355
Rechtschaffen, A., 174, 177
Redline, S., 183
Reeve, J., 430
Regan, P., 555
Regan, P. C., 555
Reich, D. A., 286
Reifman, A., 308
Reilly, P., 432
Reineke, A., 120
Reiner, W. G., 379
Rektor, I., 57
Renes, J., 530
Renk, K., 342
Renshaw, K., 548
Renzetti, C., 376, 384
Resing, W. C., 308

Ressler, K., 233–234
Rest, J., 351
Reulbach, U., 498
Reuter, M., 36
Revonsuo, A., 169
Reynolds, L. R., 364, 382
Rhine, J. B., 161
Rhoades, L., 431
Rhodes, G., 556
Richards, D., 527
Richards, D. G., 295
Richards, M., 575
Richardson, D. S., 383
Richter, T., 260
Riddoch, M. J., 152
Ridley, R., 69
Riebe, D., 364
Rieder, R. O., 493
Riemann, D., 182
Ripley, A., 565
Rivadeneyra, R., 378
Rizzolatti, G., 423
Roberge, P., 485
Roberts, M., 494
Roberts, R. D., 434
Robinson, A. J., 501
Robinson, F., 41
Rodrigues, A., 565, 566
Rogers, C., 11, 455, 456, 518, 520
Rogosch, F., 444
Rohner, R. P., 343
Rolls, L. A., 146
Romero, S. G., 52, 61, 73, 228
Rönnberg, J., 68
Ronning, M. E., 308
Roosevelt, E., 134, 457
Roosevelt, F. D., 566
Root, D. H., 177
Rosch, E., 291
Rosch, E. H., 282
Rosen, L., 121, 122
Rosenman, R., 107
Rosenthal, H. G., 519
Rosenthal, R., 22, 30
Rosenzweig, E. S., 258
Rosenzweig, M. R., 228
Rosnow, R. L., 30
Rosquist, J., 491
Ross, B. M., 261
Ross, C. A., 502
Ross, D., 225
Ross, S., 225
Rossato, M., 194
Rossetti-Ferreira, M. C., 320
Rossignol, S., 61
Roth, M. D., 194
Roth, M. L., 115, 134
Rothbart, M. K., 151
Rothstein, J. B., 216
Rotter, J., 459, 460
Rousseau, J.-J., 314
Roussel, M., 247
Rowe, R., 383
Rozencwajg, P., 2988
Rozzi, S., 423
Rubin, D. C., 264

Rubinstein, 268
Ruble, D. N., 378
Rudman, L. A., 576
Ruffolo, J. S., 419
Rugg, M. D., 245
Rumbaugh, D. M., 195
Rundell, J. R., 534
Russell, B., 461
Russell, S. T., 342
Russo, N. F., 536
Ruthig, J. C., 459
Rutland, A., 74
Rutledge, P. C., 114
Rutter, M., 308, 317
Rutter, V. E., 359
Rutz, W., 490
Ruzek, J., 534
Ryback, D., 536
Ryder, W., 508
Rymer, R., 278, 310
Rzempoluck, E., 129

S
Sabet, K. A., 194
Sabido, M., 227
Sacchetti, B., 280
Sacco, T., 280
Sachdev, P., 418
Sachs, A., 434
Sack, R. I., 171, 172, 174
Sacks, O., 157
Saiz-Ruiz, J., 461
Salapatek, P., 158
Salekin, R. T., 355
Salmon, P., 488
Saltus, R., 61
Salvatore, P., 171
Sanchez, J., Jr., 364
Santana, C., 73
Santor, D., 134
Sapolsky, R., 101, 102
Sarafino, E. P., 92, 93, 100, 106, 119
Sarraj, E., 344
Sarrazin, J. C., 132
Sassenberg, K., 573
Satcher, N. D., 351
Sathyaprabha, T. N., 197
Satir, V., 314
Satler, C., 267
Sato, S. M., 569
Savage-Rumbaugh, S., 295
Savic, I., 146
Savina, C., 415
Sawyer, J., 556
Saxe, L., 433
Scanlon, M., 483
Scannapieco, M., 361
Schacht, R. N., 554
Schachter, S., 427, 428
Schaefer, B. A., 350
Schaefer, C., 95
Schaefer, R. T., 552
Schaeff, C. M., 393
Schaie, K. W., 228, 339
Scherer, K. R., 425
Schiffer, F., 76

Schiltz, C., 152
Schim, S. M., 368, 369
Schinka, J. A., 445
Schleifer, S. J., 105
Schmidt, U., 416
Schmitt, M., 575
Schmitt-Rodermund, E., 363
Schneider, D. M., 181
Schneider, J. P., 399
Schneider, K., 361
Schneidman, E. S., 491
Schnoll, S. H., 194
Schofield, W., 512
Schredl, M., 180, 181
Schrof, J. M., 424
Schuett, S., 129
Schülein, J. A., 453
Schultz, K., 362, 482
Schultz, K., 236
Schunk, D. H., 412
Schustack, M., 444, 454
Schwartz, B. L., 244
Schwartz, J. L. K., 576
Schwarz, A., 79
Schweitzer, P., 194
Scogin, F., 489
Scribner, S., 262, 338
Scully, J. A., 93
Sebre, S., 113
Sechzer, J. A., 86, 383, 384
Seeley, T. D., 246
Segal, N. L., 383
Segall, M. H., 13
Segerdahl, P., 295
Segerstrale, U., 10
Segerstrom, S. C., 102
Seligman, M., 12, 490–491
Selye, H., 92, 102
Senko, C., 420
Sevastos, P. P., 427
Shah, N. M., 6, 569
Shahim, S., 383
Shakespeare, W., 424, 573
Shalev, A. Y., 219
Shallenberger, W. R., 45
Shapiro, C., 171, 174
Sharma, Y. S., 391
Sharp, L., 181
Shaver, P., 343, 344
Shaver, P. R., 344, 453
Shaw, J. J., 362
Shea, D. J., 219
Shea, S. C., 520
Shear, K., 489
Shen, B.-J., 119
Shen, Y.-L., 338
Sheppard, L. D., 305
Shepperd, J., 468
Sher, K., 113
Sher, K. J., 114, 501
Sherif, M., 573–574
Sherman, D. K., 12
Sherman, W. T., 434, 435
Shields, C. C., 338
Shields, C. D., 342
Shiffrin, R. M., 247
Shiraev, E., 13, 38, 156

Shlonsky, A., 362
Shoda, Y., 444, 458, 460, 462
Shriver, T. P., 432
Shwalb, B. J., 96–98
Shwalb, D. W., 96–98
Siccoli, M .M., 254
Siegala, M., 296
Siegel, J. M., 177, 183
Siegel, J. P., 359, 360
Siegel, P. H., 174, 178
Siever, L. J., 361, 362, 568, 569
Sigall, H., 425
Sigmundson, H. K., 380
Silbereisen, R. K., 363
Silver, J. M., 568
Silver, R. C., 547
Silverman, B. E., 424
Silverman, D. J., 236
Silverman, W. K., 522
Silvestri, A. J., 177
Silvestri, L., 184
Sim, T., 522
Simion, F., 336
Simon, C., 68
Simon, G. M., 521, 522
Simpson, J. A., 558
Singer, J. E., 427, 428
Singer, R., 461
Singh, A., 320
Siu, C. M. Y., 431
Skelhorn, J., 148
Skinner, B. F., 11, 212–213, 215, 216, 217, 219, 236
Skinner, M. D., 245
Skinta, M. D., 393
Skoe, E. E., 353
Slobogin, C., 481
Slobounov, S. M., 79
Slováček, L., 351
Slováčková, B., 351
Smart, D. W., 480, 482
Smart, J. F., 480, 482
Smith, D., 227
Smith, K. D., 353
Smith, M. T., 184
Smith, P. B., 560
Smith, P. K., 132
Smith, V. W., 362
Smith-Battle, L., 362
Smithson, M., 556
Snarey, J. R., 251
Snipes, W., 560
Snowdon, D. A., 339
Snyder, C. R., 562
Snyder, J. S., 329
Snyder, S., 57
Socrates, 9
Sogon, S., 560
Sollod, R. N., 444, 448, 453, 462
Solms, M., 171
Son, L. K., 22
Southwick, S. M., 119
Sowel, E. R., 324
Spearman, C., 297
Speelman, C., 549
Spence, I., 384

Spencer, S. J., 235, 552
Sperling, G., 247
Spiegel, D., 502
Spiers, M. V., 52, 69, 429
Spinelli, S., 490
Spinhoven, P., 94
Spinweber, C. L., 174
Spitz, R. A., 340
Sprecher, S., 555
Springer, J., 307
Stachnik, T. J., 440
Stafford, J., 198, 502
Stafford, M. E., 308
Stainton, N. R., 440
Staley, C., 554
Staley, J. K., 382
Stanley, M. A., 485, 486
Stanton, E., 434
Stead, J. D. H., 487, 490
Steele, C., 309
Steele, C. M., 308, 309
Stein, D. J., 235, 487
Stein, M. B., 487
Steinberg, L., 336
Steinhart, P., 560
Stella, N., 194
Stelmack, R. M., 305
Stepper, S., 427
Sternberg, R., 297, 298
Sternberg, R. J., 12, 290, 306, 308, 552
Stetter, F., 236
Stewart, A. J., 355
Stiles, W. B., 519, 538
Stone, K. L., 183
Stone, W. S., 494
Stoner, J. A., 566
Storebe, W., 132
Stout, S., 209
Strack, F., 427
Strata, P., 280
Stratton, G., 126, 158
Straub, R. O., 90, 92, 100
Strickland, A., 369
Sturgill, K., 269
Subramanian, S., 415
Suchan, B., 280
Sue, D., 20, 477, 478, 535, 536
Sue, D. W., 20, 477, 478, 535, 536
Sullivan, A., 134
Sullivan, M. J. L., 109, 115, 134
Sullivan, M. W., 327
Suls, J., 107, 108
Sumner, F. C., 13
Suomi, S. J., 490
Sutherland, M. A., 320
Sutton, A. R., 443
Suzuki, W. A., 252
Swami, V., 554
Swartz, K. L., 480, 484, 485, 486, 490, 528
Swartzwelder, S., 185
Sweeny, K., 468, 547
Szabo, A., 120
Szasz, T., 478

T
Taber, K. H., 498
Takahashi, M., 99
Takano, Y., 560
Talarico, J. M., 264
Talitwala, E. M., 343
Talley, A. E., 393
Tal-Or, N., 547
Tan, U., 133
Tanaka, T., 110
Tandon, R., 497
Tang, Y.-P., 263
Tarbox, R. S. F., 526
Tartaro, J., 536
Tarter, R. E., 194
Task Force of the National Advisory, 114
Tasman, A., 480
Tatrow, K., 236
Taub, E., 61
Taylor, E., 197
Taylor, J. Y., 419
Taylor, L. K., 383
Taylor, R. C., 12
Taylor, S., 12
Teasdale, T. W., 308
Tecehio, F., 263
Tedlock, B., 181
Tellegen, A., 461, 465
Temcheff, C. E., 6
Terman, L., 300
Terman, L. M., 305
Testu, F., 338
Thai, D., 194
Tharp, R. G., 11, 221
The Center for Academic Integrity, 353
Thill, K. P., 237
Thomas, A., 354–355
Thomas, S. E., 501
Thompson, C. A., 93
Thompson, D., 380
Thompson, D. M., 255
Thompson, E., 169
Thompson, L. W., 518
Thompson, M. S., 308
Thompson, R. F., 68, 265
Thorndike, E., 212
Thornhill, R., 146
Thorpe, K., 384
Thunberg, M., 132, 427
Thurston, L. L., 298
Tice, D., 118
Tietzel, A. J., 172
Tirodkar, M. A., 232
Titchener, E., 10
Tobin, S. S., 364
Tolin, D. F., 477, 478
Tolman, E. C., 224
Tom, S. E., 328
Tondo, L., 491
Torges, C. M., 355
Torrance, E. P., 360
Torrey, E. F., 495, 499

Name Index

Tosi, H., 93
Trainor, B. C., 383
Tranel, D., 36
Tranter, L. J., 298
Tremblay, P. F., 6, 568
Triandis, H. C., 181, 320, 475, 548
Tripp, D. A., 134
Tryon, W. W., 453
Tschöp, M., 415
Tseng, W., 536
Tsien, J. Z., 263
Tsuang, M. T., 494
Tsuru, J., 119
Tu, J., 434
Tucker, B., 320
Tucker, K. F., 442
Tulving, E., 245, 255
Tuma, F. K., 96
Tümkaya, 93
Tversky, A., 287
Twain, M., 113
Twenge, J. M., 569

U
Ulrich, R. E., 440
Uncapher, M. R., 245
United Nations International
     Children's Emergency Fund
     (UNICEF), 388
Urdan, T. C., 420

V
Valberg, A., 140
Valenstein, E. S., 530
Valeo, T., 162
Van de Carr, F. R., 326
Van de Castle, R. L., 181
van den Broek, P., 431
van der Sluis, S., 382
van Gogh, V., 430, 474
van Heck, G. L., 432
van Honk, J., 383, 569
van Leeuwen, M., 306
vanLier, P., 568
Vannucci, M., 260
van Stegeren, A. H., 263, 265
Varley, R., 296
Vaughan, P., 227
Venkatesh, V., 383
Ventner, C., 41
Vernon, P. A., 305
Verschuere, B., 433
Vertosick, F. T., 134
Vickerman, K., 569
Vickers, J. C., 267
Vijgen, S. M. C., 113
Villarreal, D. M., 258
Vinogradov, S., 504
Visscher, P. K., 246
Vital-Durand, F., 139
Vocks, S., 120
Vogel, D. L., 392
Vogt, D. S., 108

Vohs, K., 416
Volderholzer, U., 182
Völker, S., 342
Vollmer, R. R., 415
von Helmholtz, H., 139
von Hippel, W., 575
von Hippell, C., 575
Vorria, P., 344
Vygotsky, L., 337
Vyse, S., 440, 468
Vythilingam, M., 119

W
Wachtel, P. L., 512, 538
Wagner, D. A., 262
Wagner, U., 254, 574
Wagstaff, G. F., 198
Wahlgren, K., 444
Wakefield, M., 232
Wald, G, 140
Walinder, J., 490
Walk, R. D., 158
Walker, F. R., 487
Walkey, F. H., 560
Wall, A., 383
Wall, P., 133
Wallace, A. F. C., 181
Waller, M. R., 360, 502
Wallerstein, G., 410
Wamsley, E. J., 176
Wang, J., 194
Wang, Q., 252, 338
Wang, X.-J., 194
Ward, T. B., 290
Wardlaw, G. M., 415
Warner, M., 565
Washburn, A. L., 414–415
Washburn, M. F., 13
Washington, D., 576
Wass, T. S., 324
Wasserman, E., 531
Waters, A. J., 248, 249
Waters, A. M., 486, 487
Watkins, L. R., 52
Watson, D. L., 11, 120, 221
Watson, J., 50, 575
Watson, J. B, 232
Watson, J. B., 11, 205, 207, 209
Weaver, M. F., 194
Weber, G. N., 393
Wechsler, D., 297, 301
Weeks, G., 397
Weems, C. F., 383
Wegener, D. T., 552
Wei, R., 238
Weil, M., 121
Weinberg, M., 393
Weiner, B., 412, 569
Weiner, G., 267, 465
Weiner, I., 497
Weiner, M. B., 370
Weiner, M. F., 467
Weinstock, M., 490

Weiss, A., 461
Weissberg, R. P., 432
Weissman, M. M., 512
Weitlauf, J. C., 459
Wells, S., 6, 568
Welz, A., 61
Wenger, A., 450
Wentz, E., 417
Werner, E. E., 363
Werner, J. S., 139
Werner, K. H., 72, 428
Wernicke, C., 73
Werth, J. L., Jr., 417
West, D. A., 481
Westen, D., 453, 460, 503
Westman, A. S., 360
Westover, A. N., 192
Whitbourne, S. K., 329, 330, 339, 472, 484
Whiteside, S. P., 342
Whitty, M. T., 399
Whorf, B., 291
Wickelgren, I., 188
Wickramasekera, I., II, 198
Wiegand, T., 194
Wiesel, T. N., 152
Wieseler-Frank, J., 52
Wilbur, C., 502
Wilkinson, R. T., 171
Williams, A. L., 570
Williams, D. R., 489
Williams, G., 69
Williams, J. E., 384
Williams, N. A., 113, 501
Williams, R., 523
Williams, S. S., 351
Williamson, G. M., 119
Williamson, S. J., 247
Willingham, D. B., 296
Willis, M. S., 554
Wills, C. E., 519
Wilson, A. E., 547
Wilson, C., 170
Wilson, D. S., 555
Wilson, E. O., 409
Wilson, G., 526
Wilson, J. P., 444, 448, 453, 462
Wilson, S., 182
Wilson, W., 185
Windman, S., 290
Windsor, T. D., 120
Winerman, I., 227
Wines, M., 362
Winfrey, O., 290
Winter, D., 538
Winters, K. C., 494
Wise, D., 491
Wiseman, R., 162
Wiste, A. K., 490
Witelson, S. F., 305
Witherington, D. C., 158
Wixted, J. T., 263
Wolf, K. M., 340

Wolman, R., 432
Wolpe, J., 524
Wolpert, E., 171
Woltz, J. P., 295
Wong, D., 522
Woo, M., 383
Wood, V. F., 443
Woodruff-Pak, D. S., 68
Woods, T., 308
Woody, E. Z., 198
Woollams, A. M., 255
Wooten, B. R., 139
Workman, L., 12, 231, 350
World Health Organization
     (WHO), 114, 388, 401, 477
Wright, J. H., 518
Wu, K., 447
Wu, Y. C., 76
Wundt, W., 9
Wyatt, J. K., 174
Wyman, A. J., 440, 468
Wynne, C. D. L., 296

X
Xu, C., 343

Y
Yamada, H., 357
Yamamoto, B. K., 194
Yang, Y., 503
Yang, Y. K., 112
Yates, A., 480, 481
Yee, A. H., 308
Yegneswaran, B., 171, 174
Yolken, R. H., 499
Young, J. D., 197
Young, J. E., 514, 518
Young, T., 139
Yuen, L. M., 118
Yuki, M., 295
Yunus, M., 202, 238

Z
Zabin, L. S., 362
Zajonc, R. B., 425
Zalaquett, C. P., 482
Zanetti, L., 191
Zarrindast, M.-R., 256
Zeanah, C. H., 340
Zeldow, P. B., 383
Zhaoping, L., 129
Ziegelstein, R. C., 106
Ziemann, U., 531
Ziller, R. C., 574
Zillmer, E. A., 52, 69, 429
Zimbardo, P. G., 552, 564, 565, 568, 577
Zimmer, H. D., 250
Zimmerman, R., 341
Zoli, M., 191
Zucker, K. J., 392
Zuckerman, L., 497
Zuckerman, M., 410, 461

Subject Index

A

A Clockwork Orange, 527
Ablation, 34, 36
Abnormal behavior
  classification of, 479–482
  culture and, 475, 477–478
  disability or dysfunction and, 476
  historical perspective and, 478
  identifying, 475–477
  personal distress and, 476
  psychological perspectives on, 479
  statistical infrequency and, 476
  violation of norms and, 476
Absolute threshold, 131
Abu Ghraib prison, 565, 577
Academic cheating, 353–354
Acceptance stage of dying, 369
Accidental reinforcement, 236
Accidents, circadian rhythm disruptions and, 171–172
Accommodation, 138, 332–333
Acetylcholine (ACh)
  actions of, 54
  nicotine and, 112
Achievement motivation, 419–420
  causal factors and, 420
  children's literature and, 420
  high achiever characteristics, 420
  Thematic Apperception Test and, 419
Achievement tests, 465
Acquired immunodeficiency syndrome (AIDS), 400–401
Acquisition process, classical conditioning and, 208–209
Acronyms in memory improvement, 273
Acrophobia, 485
ACSs. *See* Alternate states of consciousness (ASCs)
Action potential, 55
Activation-synthesis hypothesis, 180
Active learning, 222
Active listening, 519
Active reading, 40–42
Activity theory of aging, 364
Acupuncture, 133
Acute schizophrenia, 496
Acute stress disorder (ASD), 109
AD. *See* Alzheimer's disease (AD)
Adaptation, sensation and, 133–134
Adaptive behaviors, 526
Addiction, 186. *See also* Alcoholism
  neurotransmitters and, 188

Adjustment disorders, classification of, 482
Adolescence
  definition of, 327
  physical development in, 327–328
  pregnancy in, 362–363
Adolescent egocentrism, 334, 335–336
Adoption studies, 83
Adrenal cortex, stress and, 100–101
Adrenaline, 54, 58. *See also* Epinephrine; Norepinephrine
Adrenal medulla, stress and, 100–101
Adulthood, 359–366
  families and, 361–363
  late, physical development in, 329–330
  marriage and, 359–361
  middle, physical development during, 328–329
  work and retirement and, 364
Adults Molested as Children (AMAC), 362
Advertising, classical conditioning in, 207, 232
Affect, flattened, in schizophrenia, 496
Affective component of attitudes, 549, 551
Affective disorders. *See* Mood disorders
African Americans *See also* Culture; Gender
  aging and, 365–366
  androgyny among, 384
  eating disorders among, 4i8–419
  intelligence and, 308–309
  prejudice and discrimination and, 202, 232–235, 237–238, 365, 551, 553, 575–576
  psychology and, 13
  Rosa Parks's disobedience and, 578
Afterimages, color, 139, 140
Aerial perspective, 160
Ageism. *See also* Aging; Late adulthood
  advertising depictions and, 329
  cultural differences and, 365–366
  ethnicity and, 365–366
  gender and, 365
  prejudice and discrimination and, 365, 575–576
Aggression, 568–569. *See also* Violence
  alcohol and, 113
  aversive stimuli and, 569

  biological factors and, 568–569
  brain and nervous system and, 568
  cognitive-social learning and, 237–238
  culture and learning and, 569
  displaced, 552–553
  evolutionary perspective on, 13
  frustration-aggression hypothesis, 569
  gender differences and, 383
  genetics and, 568
  hormones and neurotransmitters and, 569
  instincts and, 568
  media violence and, 569
  mental disorders and, 568
  nature *vs.* nurture and, 569
  psychosocial factors and, 569
  punishment and, 218
  reducing, 569
  substance abuse and, 568
  violent video games and, 569
Aging. *See also* Ageism; Late adulthood
  activity theory of, 364
  disengagement theory of, 364
  gender issues and, 536
  sleep cycle and, 177
  socioemotional selectivity theory of, 364
Agonist drugs, 186–187, 191
Agoraphobia, 485
Agreeableness as personality dimension, 443, 445
AIDS (acquired immunodeficiency syndrome), 400–401
Alarm reaction, 101
Alcohol
  abuse of, 113–114
  binge drinking and, 114
  cerebellar depression by, 68–69
  dependence on, signs of, 114, 501
  as depressant, 189
  effects on body and behavior, 113–114, 191
  prenatal development and, 322
  mixing with barbiturates, 189
  sexual effects of, 398
Alcohol use disorder (AUD), 501–502
Alcoholics Anonymous, 521
Alcoholism
  aversion therapy for, 525
  classical conditioning for treatment of, 233
  maternal, prenatal development and, 322–324

  treatment of, 524–525
Algorithms, problem solving and, 284
All-or-nothing law, 55
All-or-nothing thinking, 516
Alpha waves, sleep and, 174
Alternate states of consciousness (ASC), 166
Alternative activities, research participation and, 19
Alternative therapies, 536
Altruism, 570–572
  diffusion of responsibility and, 572
  egoistic model and, 570
  empathy-altruism hypothesis and, 570
  Kitty Genovese case and, 570–572
  models and, 571
  promoting, 572
Alzheimer's disease (AD), 83, 264–267, 330
American Psychological Association (APA)
  ethical guidelines, 18–19
  first woman president of, 13
American Psychological Society (APS) ethical guidelines, 18–19
Ames room illusion, 157
Amnesia, 266. *See also* Forgetting
  anterograde, 266
  dissociative, 502
  retrograde, 266
  source, 266
Amnestic disorders, 482
Amphetamines, sexual effects of, 398
Amplitude
  sound waves and, 143
  vision and, 136
Amygdala, 69, 70
  dreams and, 180
  emotion and, 422
  fear and, 30
  memory and, 263, 265
Anal-expulsive personality, 451
Anal retentive personality, 451
Anal stage, psychosexual development and, 451
Analytical intelligence, 299
Analytical psychology, 452–453
Androgyny, 383–384
Anger, 490. *See also* Aggression
Anger stage of dying, 369
Angina, stress and, 106
Anima/animus, 453
Animals
  attachment research using, 341
  language in, 295–296

Animals (*continued*)
personality in, 446–447
respecting rights of, 19
sensory abilities, 132
Animism in preoperational stage, 335
Anonymity, deindividuation and, 565–566
Anorexia nervosa, 417–419
ANS. *See* Autonomic nervous system (ANS)
Antabuse, 525, 526
Antagonist drugs, 186–187
Anterograde amnesia, 266
Anti-semitism, 553, 575–576
Antianxiety drugs, 528–529. *See also* Anxiety
Antidepressant drugs, 490, 528–531. *See also* Depression
Antipsychotic drugs, 528–529. *See also* Psychosis
Antismoking campaigns, 113
Antisocial personality disorder, 503
Anxiety
about death, 39–370
basic, 453
performance, 395
posttraumatic stress disorder and, 109
test, 411, 556
Anxiety disorders, 483–487
agoraphobia, 485
biological components and, 487
classification of, 482
death and, 369–370
defining characteristic of, 484
drug treatments for, 529
faulty cognitions and, 486
gender and, 484
generalized anxiety disorder, 484
major disorders, 484
maladaptive learning and, 486–487
obsessive-compulsive disorder, 485–486
panic disorder, 484–485
phobias, 485
psychological components and, 486–487
social phobias, 485
sociocultural components and, 487
specific phobias, 485
Anxiolytics, 528–529
Anxious/ambivalent infants, 342
APA. *See* American Psychological Association (APA)
Aphasia
Broca's, 72
Wernicke's, 73
Aplysia, memory in, 263
Applied research, 16, 18
Approach-approach conflict, 95
Approach-avoidance conflict, 96
Aptitude tests, 465
Archetypes, 452

Arousal component of emotion, 421–424
Arousal, misattribution of, 27
Arousal, sexual. *See* Sexual dysfunction; Sexual response cycle
Arousal theory, motivation and, 410–411
Artificial concepts, 281
Asian Americans. *See also* Culture; Gender
aging and, 365–366
androgyny among, 384
eating disorders and, 418–419
emphasis on group and, 548
intelligence and, 308–309
prejudice and discrimination and, 234, 237, 365, 552
psychology and, 13
Assimilation, cognitive development and, 332
Association areas, brain, 73
Astrology, 5
Asylums, 478
Athletic performance, self-hypnosis and, 198
Attachment
contact comfort and, 341
infant-mother, 342
levels of, 342
romantic love and, 343–344
social-emotional development and, 340–341
Attention
cognitive development and, 338
memory improvement and, 271
observational learning and, 226
selective, 151
Attitudes, 548–550
cognitive dissonance and, 548–550
three components of, 549
toward death and dying, 368
student success and, 46
Attraction. *See* Interpersonal attraction
Attribution, 546–548
culture and, 548
depression and, 492–493
dispositional, 546–547
fundamental attribution error and, 546–547
just-world phenomenon and, 547
learned helplessness theory and, 491
mistaken attributions, 546–547
motivation and, 412
saliency bias and, 547
self-serving bias and, 547–548
situational, 546
Atypical antidepressants, 528–529
Audition. *See* Hearing
Auditory canal, 142
Auditory cortex, 73
Auditory nerve, 142
Aural figure and ground effects, 154
Authenticity, 519
Authoritarian parenting style, 342
Authoritative parenting style, 342

Authority figures, obedience and, 563
Autism, operant conditioning and, 526
Automatic processing
consciousness and, 168–170
memory and, 245
Autonomic nervous system, 63–64
emotion and, 423–424
sexual dysfunction and, 395
Autonomy *vs.* shame and doubt stage, 356
Availability heuristic, problem solving and, 287
Aversion therapy, 524–526
Aversive stimuli, aggression and, 569
Avoidance, punishment and, 219
Avoidance-avoidance conflict, 95
Avoidance behavior, punishment and, 219
Avoidant infants, 342
Axons, 53

B

Babbling, 294
Babinski reflex, 63
Baby signs, 294
Backward conditioning, 209
Barbiturates
mixing with alcohol, 189
sexual effects of, 398
Bargaining stage of dying, 369
Barnum effect, pseudo-personality tests and, 468
Basal ganglia, memory and, 265
Basic anxiety, 453
Basic research, 16
Basilar membrane, 143
Behavior
definition of, 5
neural bases of, 52–59
Behavior modification, chronic pain and, 115
Behavior therapies, 524–527
classical conditioning techniques, 524–526
observational learning techniques, 527
operant conditioning techniques, 526
Behavioral component of attitudes and, 548–549, 551
emotion and, 421, 424
Behavioral disorganization, schizophrenia and, 497
Behavioral disturbances, schizophrenia and, 496
Behavioral genetics. *See* Genetics
Behavioral motives, 414–420
Behavioral observation, personality assessment and, 463–464
Behavioral perspective, 11, 14
Behavioral rehearsal, 522, 526
Behavioral therapies
ethics and, 527
evaluating, 527

generalizability and, 527
observational learning techniques, 527
Behaviorism, 207
Belonging needs in Maslow's hierarchy, 413, 457
Belief systems, 516
Beta waves, sleep and, 174
Bias
confirmation, 286
cultural. *See* Cultural bias
experimenter, 22, 25
gender, in moral development, 353
participant, 25–26
saliency, 547
sample, 25
self-serving, 468, 547–548
social desirability, 466
Binge drinking, 114
Binocular cues, 158–159
Biochemistry, hunger and, 415
Biofeedback
chronic pain and, 115
operant conditioning and, 235–236
Biological constraints on learning, 230–231
Biological factors
aggression and, 568–569
anxiety disorders and, 487
dreaming and, 180
learning and, 229–231
memory and, 263–267
mood disorders and, 490
motivation and, 408–411
schizophrenia and, 497–498
sexual dysfunction and, 394–395
women and depression, 489–490
Biological personality theories, 460–462
biopsychosocial model, 462
brain and, 461
genetics and, 461–462
neurochemistry and, 461
Biological preparedness, 230
Biological research, 33–36
Biological theories
brain and, 461
genetics and, 461–462
motivation and, 408–411
neurochemistry and, 461
personality and, 460–462
Biomedical therapies, 528–531
electroconvulsive therapy, 530
evaluating, 530–531
psychopharmacology, 528–529
psychosurgery, 531
repetitive transcranial magnetic stimulation (rTMS), 531
Biopsychology, 8
Biopsychology perspective, 12, 14
Biopsychosocial factors
gender differences and, 86, 383
motivation and, 412–413
personality and, 462

schizophrenia and, 497–498, 499
women and depression, 489–490
Biopsychosocial model
definition of, 14–15
depression and, 489
development and, 317
learning and, 225, 238
moral development and, 350
motivation and, 409, 412–413
personality and, 462
schizophrenia and, 497–499
sexual dysfunction and, 394–396
Bipolar disorder
manic episodes and, 489
psychopharmacology and, 518, 529
Bisexual, 380
Black Americans. See African Americans
Blended psychology, 453
Blind observers, 25
Blind spots, 137–138
Blindness, 134
Bobo doll studies, 24, 225
Bodily/kinesthetic intelligence, 299
Body senses, 148–149
Borderline personality disorder, 503–504
Bottom-up processing, 129
Braille, 149
Brain. See also Nervous system
Adaptability of, 229
aggression and, 568
alcohol and, 113, 568
Alzheimer's disease (AD) and, 267
association areas of, 73
brain comparisons, 66
cerebral cortex, 71–74
damage to, 70
dissection of, 34, 36
early childhood physical development and, 324–325
emotional experiences and, 422
forebrain, 68–69
frontal lobes, 71, 72
hemispheric specialization and, 76–78
hindbrain, 68
hunger and eating and, 415
hypothalamus, 69
illustration of, 67
injury to and memory, 264–266
intelligence and, 305–306
limbic system, 69–70
lobes of, 71
lower-level brain structures, 67–70
meditation and, 197
memory formation and, 265
midbrain, 68
neglected right brain myth, 78
neurogenesis and, 61
neuroplasticity and, 61
occipital lobes, 71, 73
pain sensation and, 133
parietal lobes, 71, 73
personality and, 460–461

schizophrenia and, 498
sex differences and, 85–86, 381–382
split-brain research, 75–78
temporal lobes, 71, 73, 147
thalamus, 68–69
traumatic brain injuries, 79–80
Brain dissection, 34
Brain imaging, 35–36
Brain injury, memory and, 264–267
Brainstem, 67
Brightness constancy, 157
Broca's aphasia, 72
Broca's area, 72
Bulimia nervosa, 417–419
Burnout, 93
"By default" myth of homosexuality, 392

C
Caffeine, 189–190
Calming response, 64
Cancer, stress and, 105–106
Cannon-Bard theory, 425
Cardiovascular system, stress and, 106–109
Career inventories, 465
Careers
finding satisfaction and, 364
health psychology, 111–112
heuristics and, 284–285
mental health and, 533
multiple intelligences and, 299
personality type and, 445–446
psychology, 7–9
Case studies, research and, 30–31, 34, 36
Cataclysmic events, stress and, 96–98, 100
Catalepsy, schizophrenia and, 496
Cataplexy, 183
Catastrophic accidents, sleep-related, 171–173
Catatonic schizophrenia, 497
Catharsis, 569
Cats, sleep cycle of, 176
Cattell personality factor analysis, 443
Causal friendship, 436
Causation vs. correlation, 31–33
Cell body, 53
Central executive, 250
Central nervous system. See also Brain; Nervous system
neurogenesis and, 61
neuroplasticity and, 61
spinal cord and, 61–62
Central tendency measures, A4–A5
Cephalocaudal development, 322
CER (conditioned emotional response), 207
Cerebellum, 68
alcohol and, 68–69
memory and, 265
Cerebral cortex, 68, 71–78
association areas of, 73

emotion and, 422
frontal lobes of, 71–72
memory and, 265
occipital lobes of, 71, 73
parietal lobes of, 71, 73
temporal lobes of, 71, 73, 147
Cerebrum, 68
Cerebral hemispheres, 75–78
Challenge, hardiness and, 108
Change as goal of psychology, 6–7, 16
Cheating, academic, morality and, 353–354
Chemical senses, 146
Chemical signals, neurons and, 56
Chemoreceptors, 146
Chess, chunking and, 249
Children. See also Adolescence, Early Childhood, Family violence
abuse and, 363
attachment and, 340–341
resiliency and, 363
parenting style and, 340, 342–343
social-emotional development and, 343
surviving poverty and, 363
taste sensation and, 148
temperament of, 343, 354–35
understanding death and, 369
Chromosomes, 81
Chronic pain, 115
Chronic schizophrenia, 497
Chronic stress, 93
Chunking, short-term memory and, 248
Circadian rhythms, 172, 178
Circumcision, 387–388
Clairvoyance, 161
Clarification, active listening and, 519
Class intervals, A2
Classical conditioning, 204–211
acquisition process and, 208–209
applications of, 232–238
aversion therapy and, 524–526
backward conditioning and, 209
basic principles of, 208–211
behavior therapy, 524–527
delayed conditioning and, 209
extinction and, 209–210
generalization and, 209, 221
higher-order conditioning and, 210–211
marketing and, 232
medical treatments and, 233
operant conditioning compared, 221
Pavlov's discovery and, 205–206
phobias and, 233–235
prejudice and, 232–234
simultaneous conditioning and, 209
spontaneous recovery and, 210
stimulus discrimination and, 209
stimulus generalization and, 209
systematic desensitization and, 524

taste aversions and, 524–526
techniques, 524–526
trace conditioning and, 209
Watson's contribution to, 205–207
Claustrophobia, 485
Clever Hans, 22, 25
Client-centered therapy, 518–519
Clinical psychology as profession, 8, 533
Clitoridectomy, 388
Cloacal exstrophy, 379
Close interaction, reducing prejudice and discrimination and, 574
Closeness of authority figure, obedience and, 563
Club drugs, 194–195
Cocaine, 191–192, 398
CMH (community mental health) centers, 538
CNS (central nervous system), 61–63. See also Brain
Cocaine, 191–192, 398
Cochlea, hearing and, 142
Cochlear implants, 144
Coding, 130
Cognition, 278. See also Intelligence; Language; Thinking
Cognitions, faulty, in anxiety disorders, 486
Cognitive abilities, gender and, 382–383
Cognitive appraisal, stress management and, 116–118
Cognitive-behavior therapy, 515–517
Cognitive building blocks, 280–282
Cognitive component of
attitudes and, 549–551
emotion and, 421, 424
Cognitive development, 331–339
accommodation and, 332–333
animism and, 335
assimilation and, 332
concrete operational stage of, 334–335
conservation process and, 335
cultural influences and, 336–338
formal operational stage of, 334–336
genetic influences and, 336–338
imaginary audience and, 336
information processing model and, 338–339
personal fables and, 335–336
Piaget's stages of, 331–338
preoperational stage of, 333–335
reversibility concept and, 335
schemas and, 332
self-consciousness and, 334
sensorimotor stage of, 333, 334
stages of, 333–336
underestimated abilities and, 336
Cognitive disorder classifications, 482
Cognitive dissonance, 548–550, 575
Cognitive expectancies, 459

Subject Index

Cognitive functioning, stress and, 102
Cognitive maps, 224
Cognitive perspective, 12, 14
Cognitive restructuring, 514
Cognitive retraining, 574–575
Cognitive-social learning, 223–228
  cognitive maps and, 224
  insight and, 223–224
  latent learning and, 224–225
  media and, 237–238
  observational learning and, 225
  violent video games and, 238
  virtual reality games and, 238
Cognitive therapies, 514–518
  all-or-nothing thinking and, 516
  cognitive-behavior therapy, 514–517
  cognitive restructuring and, 514
  evaluating, 518
  magnification and, 516
  overcoming irrational
    misconceptions and, 516
  overgeneralization and, 516
  rational-emotive behavior therapy, 514–515
  selective perception and, 516
  self-talk, 514
Cognitive view of dreams, 180
Cohort effects, 318
Collective unconscious, 452
Collectivist cultures
  attributional biases and, 548
  development and, 357
  dissonance and, 550
College success. See Student Success
Color aftereffects, 139, 140
Color constancy, 157
Color-deficient vision, 140
Color vision, 139–140
Commitment, involuntary, 537–538
Committed relationships, challenges
  of adulthood and, 359–360
Community mental health centers, 538
Comorbidity, substance-related
  disorders and, 501
Comparative psychology, 19
Companionate love, 558
Complete learning, 45, 272
Complexity, sound waves and, 143
Compulsions, 485
Computed tomography scans (CT), 35–36
Computer-aided communication, 295
Conception, 322
Concepts, 281–282
  artificial, 281
  hierarchies of, 282
  natural, 282
Conceptual thinking, 281–282
Concrete operational stage of cogni-
  tive development, 334–335
Conditioned emotional responses
  (CER), 205–206

Conditioned response (CR), 205–206
Conditioned stimulus, 205–206
Conditioning, 209. See also
    Classical conditioning; Operant
    Conditioning
Conduction deafness, 143
Cones, eye function and, 137–138
Confidentiality, 19
Confirmation bias, problem solving
  and, 286
Conflict
  approach-approach conflict, 95
  approach-avoidance conflict, 96
  avoidance-avoidance conflict, 95
  stress and, 95–96
Conformity
  advantages of, 562
  reference groups and, 560
  social influence and, 560
Connectionist model of memory, 246
Conscientiousness as personality
  dimension, 443, 445
Consciousness, 166, 168–170
  alternate states of. See Alternate
    states of consciousness (ASCs)
  controlled vs. automatic processes
    and, 168–170
  definition of, 166
  hypnosis and, 196–198
  meditation and, 195–197
  mind-body debate and, 169
  no awareness and, 169
  psychoactive drugs and, 185–194
  psychoanalytic theory and, 448–449
  sleep and dreams and, 170–185
  subconscious, 169
  understanding, 168–170
Consent, informed, 18–19
Conservation in concrete operational
  stage, 335
Consolidation, memory, 266
Constructive process, 244
Contact comfort, 340–342
Context-dependent memory, 256
Continuity vs. stages debate, 317
Continuous reinforcement, 215
Control
  hardiness and, 108
  stress management and, 120
Control group, 22, 23
Controlled processing
  consciousness and, 168–170
  memory and, 245
Conventional morality, 352
Convergence, binocular cues and, 159
Convergent thinking, creativity and, 289
Cooing, 294
Coping strategies
  emotion-focused coping, 118
  primary appraisal and, 116–118
  problem-solving coping, 118

secondary appraisal and, 116–118
  stress management and, 116–118
Cornea, eye function and, 136–137
Coronary heart disease, stress and, 106
Corpus callosum, 75
Correlation, A6
Correlation coefficients, 32, A6
Correlational research, 31–33
Correlational sex differences, 86
Cortex, 68
Cortisol, 58, 65
  heart disease and, 106
  memory and, 263
  stress and, 100–101
Counseling psychology careers, 8, 533
Couples therapy, 522
CR (conditioned response), 205–206
Crack, 192
Creative intelligence, 299
Creativity, 288–290
  convergent thinking and, 289
  divergent thinking and, 289
  flexibility and, 289
  fluency and, 289
  measuring, 289
  originality and, 289
  researching, 289–290
  resources and, 290
Criminal justice system, memory
  and, 268–269
Critical periods, 317, 322
Critical thinking. See also Prologue,
    xli-xlv
  applying to psychological science, 28
  biology and, 78
  college success and, 222
  definition of, 4
  dreaming and interpretation and, 181
  extrasensory perception (ESP)
    and, 162
  faulty thinking and depression
    and, 492
  gender differences and, 385
  good therapy films and, 523
  helping and, 572
  memory and metacognition and, 274
  morality and academic cheating
    and, 353–354
  motivation and emotion and, 430–436
  obesity and, 418
  problem solving and, 287
  pseudo-personality tests and, 468
  rape myths and rape prevention,
    and 402
  reducing stress through, 122
  suicide bombers and, 344
  therapy and, 532–540
Cross-cultural effects, observational
  learning and, 227
Cross-sectional research, 318–319

Cross-tolerance, 186
Crystallized intelligence (gc), 298, 338
CS (conditioned stimulus), 205–206
CT (computed tomography) scans
  for brain research, 35–36
Cue-dependent forgetting, 258
Culture
  abnormal behavior and, 475–478
  ageism and, 365–366
  aggression and, 369
  attributional biases and, 548
  cognitive development and, 336–338
  death and dying and, 368
  depression and, 489–490
  developmental psychology and, 319–320
  dissonance and, 550
  dreams and, 180–181
  eating disorders and, 418–419
  evolution, emotions and, 435–436
  female nonmonogamy and, 391
  Gestalt laws, 155–156
  hunger and, 415
  individualist vs. collectivist
    cultures and, 357–358
  intelligence tests and, 307–309
  invisibility of, 320
  Karoshi and job stress, 99
  memory and, 261–262
  mental disorders and, 476–477
  moral development and, 351–353
  motor development and, 326
  personality development and, 357
  physical attractiveness and, 554–555
  Piaget's theory of cognitive
    development and, 336–337
  scaffolding and, 228
  schizophrenia and, 498–499
  sexual behavior and, 387–388
  therapies and, 535–536
Cultural universals, 38–39
Culture-bound disorders, 477–478
Culture-bound symptoms, 477
Culture-general symptoms, 475–477, 500
Cybersex, 399
Cynical hostility, 108

D
Daily activities records, 44–45
Damage theory, aging and, 330
Dark adaptation, 139
Date rape drug, 194
Deafness. See Hearing
Death and dying
  anxiety and, 369–370
  attitudes toward, 368
  cultural differences and, 368
  experience of, 368–369
  Kübler-Ross theory and, 369
  thanatology and, 369
  theories on, 330
Debriefing, 19

Decay theory of forgetting, 257–259
Deception
  ethical issues and, 19
  objective personality tests and, 466
Declarative memory, 251–252
Defense mechanisms, 449–450, 510–511
Deindividuation, 565–566
Deinstitutionalization, 538
Delayed conditioning, 209
Delirium, 482
Delta waves, 174
Delusions
  of grandeur, 496
  of persecution, 496
  of reference, 496
  schizophrenia and, 496
Dementia, 482
Dendrites, 53
Denial as defense mechanism, 450
Denial stage of dying, 369
Deoxyribonucleic acid (DNA), 81
Dependent variable (DV), 23–24, A2
Depersonalization disorder, 502
Depolarization, 55
Depressants (downers), 189–190
Depression. See also Antidepressant
    drugs; Major depressive disorder;
    Suicide
  culture and, 489–490
  distorted thinking patterns and, 516
  down moods compared, 539
  explaining and, 490–491
  faulty thoughts and, 492–493
  gender and, 489–490
  getting help and, 540
  learned helplessness theory of, 490–491
  male depressive syndrome, 490
  tips on helping and, 539–540
  treatment of, 515–517, 530
  trivialization of, 539
Depression stage of dying, 369
Depressive explanatory style, 493
Depth perception, 156–158
Description as goal of psychology, 6, 16
Descriptive research, 28–31
  case studies, 30–31
  naturalistic observation, 29–30
  surveys, 30
Descriptive statistics, A4–A7
Desensitization, systematic, 524
Destructive obedience, 577–578
  disobedient models and, 578
  foot-in-the-door technique and, 578
  groupthink and, 577–578
  power of the situation and, 577
  relaxed moral guard and, 578
  socialization and, 577
Developmental niches, 320
Developmental psychology
  careers, 8
  continuity vs. stages debate, 317

cross-sectional research and, 318–319
  defined, 316
  longitudinal research and, 318–319
  nature vs. nurture debate, 317
  research methods and, 318–320
  sociocultural context and, 318–319
  stability vs. change debate, 317
Developmental stages, language and, 294
Diagnosis rates, gender and, 536
Diagnostic and Statistical Manual of
    Mental Disorders (DSM-IV-TR),
    479–482
  evaluation of, 482
  five axes and, 480–481
  main categories of, 482
  neurosis classification and, 480
  psychosis classification and, 480
  understanding, 480–481
Diathesis-stress model, schizophrenia
    and, 498
DID (dissociative identity disorder),
    495, 502
Difference threshold, 131
Difficult children, personality
    development and, 355
Diffusion of responsibility, 572
Disability, abnormal behavior and, 476
Discrimination. See Prejudice and
    discrimination
Discriminative stimulus, 222
Diseases, prenatal development and, 322
Disengagement theory of aging, 364
Disobedient models, 578
Disorders first diagnosed in
    childhood classification, 482
Disorders first diagnosed in early
    adolescence classification, 482
Disorders first diagnosed in infancy
    classification, 482
Disorganization/despair stage of
    grief, 367
Disorganized schizophrenia, 497
Displaced aggression, prejudice and
    discrimination and, 552–553
Displacement, 450
Display rules, emotions and, 436
Dispositional factors, attributions
    and, 546–547
Dissociative amnesia, 502
Dissociative disorders, 482, 502
Dissociative fugue, 502
Dissociative identity disorder (DID),
    495, 502
Dissonance, 548–550
Distorted thinking patterns, 516
Distress, 92
Distributed practice, 260, 272
Disturbed emotions, therapy goals
    and, 532
Divergent thinking, creativity and, 289
Diversity. See Culture; Gender

Divided attention, 245
Divorce, 359–360
Dizygotic twins, 83
Domestic abuse, 361–362
Dominant traits, 81
Dopamine, 54, 56, 188
Dopamine hypothesis, schizophrenia
    and, 497–498
Double-blind study, 25
Double standards, sexual behavior
    and, 396
Down moods, depression differences
    from, 539
Down syndrome, 83, 304
Dreams. See also Sleep
  activation-synthesis hypothesis, 180
  analysis of, 511
  biological view of, 180
  cognitive view of, 180
  culture and, 180–181
  gender variations and similarities, 180–181
  interpretation of, 181
  psychoanalytic/psychodynamic
      view of, 179–180
  scientific study of, 175
  theories of, 179–180
Drive-reduction theory, 409, 550
Drug abuse, 186, 322, 324
Drug addiction, 186. See also
    Substance abuse
Drugs
  addiction and, 186
  agonist and, 187
  antagonist and, 187
  psychoactive and, 185
  physical dependence and, 196
  psychological dependence and, 186
  tolerance and, 186
  withdrawal and, 186
Drunk driving, 189
Dual-process theory, 140
Duchenne smile, 424
Dunking tests, 480
DV (dependent variable), 23–24, A2
Dwarf, hypopituitary, 58
Dyspareunia, 394
Dyssomnias, 182–183

E
Ear anatomy and function, 141–142.
    See also Hearing
Eardrum, 142
Early childhood physical
    development
  brain development, 324–325
  motor development, 324–326
  scientific research measures and, 327
  sensory and perceptual
      development, 326–327
Early sleep stages, 174–176
Easy children, personality
    development and, 355

Eating disorders. See also Hunger
    and eating
  anorexia nervosa, 417–418
  bulimia nervosa, 417–418
  classification of, 482
  culture and, 418–419
  media's role in, 419
  obesity, 416–417
Ebbinghaus's forgetting curve, 257
Echoic memory, 247–248
Eclectic approaches, therapy, 533
Economic competition, prejudice
    and discrimination and, 552
Ecstasy, 194
ECT. See Electroconvulsive therapy
    (ECT)
Educational psychology careers, 8
EEG. See Electroencephalogram
    (EEG)
Ego, 449
Egocentrism
  adolescent and, 334–336
  antisocial personality
      disorder and, 503
  preoperational stage and, 333–334
Ego integrity vs. despair stage, 356
Egoistic model, altruism and, 570
Ejaculation, 390
Elaborative rehearsal
  improving, 254
  long-term memory (LTM) and, 252
  memory improvement and, 271
Elder respect, 365
Electrical recordings, biological
    research and, 34, 36
Electrical stimulation of the brain
    (ESB), 34, 36
Electroconvulsive therapy, 530, 531
Electroencephalography (EEG), 34,
    36, 175
Electromagnetic spectrum, 136, 138
Electromyography (EMG), 115
Electroshock therapy, 530
Embryonic period, prenatal
    development and, 323
Emotion. See also Social-emotional
    development
  autonomic nervous system and, 423–424
  basic human emotions, 435
  behavioral component and, 424
  brain and, 422
  Cannon-Bard theory and, 425
  cognitive component and, 424
  components of, 421–424
  cultural differences and, 435–436
  cultural similarities and, 435
  definition of, 406
  display rules and, 436
  evaluating theories of, 428–429
  evolutionary theory of, 435–436
  facial expressions and, 424
  facial-feedback hypothesis and, 425–527

Subject Index

Emotion (*continued*)
James-Lange theory and, 425
limbic system and, 422
mirror neurons and, 423
physiological component of, 422–424
polygraph and, 432, 433
Schachter's two-factor theory, 427–428
Emotional component of attitudes, 549, 551
Emotional disturbances, schizophrenia and, 496
Emotional intelligence (EI), 432, 434
Emotional stability as personality dimension, 443, 445
Emotion-focused coping, 116–118
Empathy
client-centered therapy and, 518
emotional intelligence and, 434
Empathy-altruism hypothesis, 570
Encoding
information processing and, 244–245, 330
long-term memory (LTM) and, 252–253
Encoding failure theory of forgetting, 257–259
Encoding specificity principle, 255, 271
Endocrine system, 58
Endogenous chemicals, 57
Endogenous opioid peptides, 57
Endorphins, 54, 57, 133
Environmental enrichment, 229
Environmental influences, intelligence and, 306–307
Environmental pulls, motivation and, 412
Epilepsy, 75, surgery for, 76
Epinephrine, 54, 58
Episodic memory, 251–252
Erectile dysfunction, 394, 397
Esteem needs in Maslow's hierarchy, 413, 457
Equal status, reducing prejudice and discrimination and, 574
Erectile dysfunction, 394, 397
Erikson's Psychosocial stages of social development, 355–356
Ethical guidelines, 18–20
human participants and, 18–19
nonhuman animal participants and, 19
psychotherapy clients and, 19–20
Ethnicity, ageism and, 365–366
Ethnocentrism, 25, 387, 475–476
Ethnotheories, behavior and, 320
Eustress, 92
Evaluation step, problem solving and, 284
Evolution
early psychological science and, 12–14
emotions and, 435–436

learning and, 230
sexual behavior and, 391
Evolutionary/circadian theory of sleep, 178
Evolutionary psychology, 84–85. *See also* Genetics
Excitatory messages, 56
Excitement phase, sexual response cycle and, 390
Exercise
endorphins and, 115
sleep problems and, 184
stress management and, 119
Exhaustion phase, general adaptation syndrome and, 103
Exorcism, 478
Expectancies, motivation and, 412
Experimental group, 22, 23
Experimental psychology, 8
Experimental research, 21–27
key features of, 22–24
participant problems and solutions, 25–26
researcher problems and solutions, 22–25
safeguards and, 22–27
Experimental safeguards, 22–27
Experimental *vs.* control groups, 23
Experimenter bias, 22, 25
Explanation goal of psychology, 6,16
Explicit memory, 251, 267
Expressive component of emotion, 424
External locus of control, 120, 459
Extinction process, 209–210, 526
Extraneous variables, 23
Extrasensory perception (ESP), 161–162
Extrinsic motivation, 430–431
Extroversion as personality dimension, 443, 445
Eye anatomy and function, 136–138. *See also* Vision
Eyewitness testimony, memory and, 268–269
Eysenck Personality Questionnaire, 443

F

Facial expressions, emotional communication and, 424
Facial-feedback hypothesis, 425–427
Factitious disorders, 482
Factor analysis, 443
Faked hypnosis, 198
Fallacy of positive instances, 162, 468
False memories, 268–269
Family studies, 83
Family therapy, 522
Family violence, 361–362
causes of, 361–362
dealing with, 362
impulsivity and, 361
Fantasy, romantic love and, 558
Farsightedness, 138–139

Fathers
infant attachment and, 341
social-emotional development and, 343
Fatty deposits, arteries, 106
Faulty cognitions, anxiety disorders and, 486
Faulty thoughts, tracking, 517
Feature detectors, sensory information and, 151–152
Females. *See* Gender, Women
Female genital mutilation, 388
Fetal alcohol syndrome, 324
Fetal deaths, 322
Fetal period of prenatal development, 323
Fetal learning, 326–327
FI (fixed interval) schedule of reinforcement, 215–216
Fight-or-flight reactions, 65, 106
Five-factor model, trait theories and, 443
Fixed interval (FI) schedule of reinforcement, 215–216
Fixed ratio (FR) schedule of reinforcement, 215–216
Flashbulb memory, 263–264
Flattened affect, schizophrenia and, 496
Flexibility, creative thinking and, 289
Flirting, 555–556
Fluency, creative thinking and, 289
Fluid intelligence (gf), 298, 338
Flynn effect, 308
fMRI. *See* Functional magnetic resonance imaging (fMRI) scan
Foot-in-the-door technique, 578
Forced hypnosis, 198
Forebrain, 68–69, 324
Forensic psychology, 8
Forgetting, 257–262
cultural differences and, 261–262
distributed practice, 260, 272
Ebbinghaus's forgetting curve, 257
forgetting curve, 257
information overload and, 260
key factors and, 260
key theories and, 257–259
massed practice, 260, 272
misinformation effect and, 260
proactive interference and, 257–259
relearning and, 257
retroactive interference and, 257–259
sleeper effect and, 260
source amnesia and, 260
tip-of-the-tongue (TOT) phenomenon and, 259
Form organization principle, 155
Form perception, 153–156
Formal operational stage of cognitive development, 334–336
Fovea, eye function and, 137–138

FR (fixed ratio) schedule of reinforcement, 215–216
Fragile-X syndrome, 304
Frame of reference, 161
Fraternal twins, 83
Free association, 511
Free will, 11
Frequency
sound waves and, 143
vision and, 136
Frequency distributions, A2–A3
Frequency theory of hearing, 143
Freudian slips, 448
Friendship differences, gender and, 382
Frontal lobes, 71, 72
Frustration, 95
Frustration-aggression hypothesis, 569
Functional fixedness, problem solving and, 286
Functional magnetic resonance imaging (fMRI) scan, 35–36
Functionalism, 10
Fundamental attribution error (FAE), 546–547

G

Gamma aminobutyric acid (GABA), 54
Gastric ulcers, stress and, 110
Gate-control theory, 133
Gay marriage, 392
Gays and lesbians. *See* Sexual orientation
Gender
ageism and, 365
aggression and, 383
androgyny and, 383–384
anxiety disorders and, 484
cognitive abilities and, 382–383
definition of, 376
depression and, 489–490
dimensions of, 377
dream variations and similarities, 180–181
female nonmonogamy, 391
friendship differences and, 382
functional and structural differences and, 381–382
identity disorders, 482
identity formation and, 376–380
lateralization and, 85
maleness and femaleness defined, 376
moral development and, 353
personality differences and, 382
physical differences and, 381
role development and, 376–378
schema theory and, 378
schizophrenia and, 494
sexual behavioral differences and, 382
sexual dysfunction and, 395–396
sexual response cycle and, 389–390

sexually transmitted infection susceptibility and, 400
social learning theory and, 377–378
therapy needs and problems, 536–537
touching and, 382
transsexualism and, 379–380
transvestism and, 379–380
violence against women, 536–537
Gender psychology, 8
Gene, 81
General adaptation syndrome (GAS), 102–103, 119
General intelligence (g), 297
Generalizability, 318
Generalized anxiety disorder, 484
Generativity *vs.* stagnation, 356
Generosity of spirit, emotional intelligence and, 434
Genetic abnormalities, 83
Genetic engineering, memory formation and, 263
Genetic mutations, 84–85
Genetics, 80–86
adoption studies and, 83
aggression and, 568
chromosomes and, 81
cognitive development and, 336–338
dominant and recessive traits and, 81
environment and, 84
evolutionary psychology, 84–85
family studies and, 83
gene-environment interaction, 81
genetic abnormalities and, 83
hereditary codes, 81
heritability estimates and, 84
intelligence and, 306–307
mental retardation and, 304
misconceptions regarding, 82–84
narcolepsy and, 183
personality and, 461–462
research methods and, 83
schizophrenia and, 497
sex differences and, 85–86
trait flexibility and, 82
twin studies and, 83
Genital infibulation, 388
Genital stage, psychosexual development and, 451
Genocide, 553
Genuineness, 519
Germinal period, prenatal development and, 323
Gestalt laws, 155
Gestalt principles of organization, 154
GHB (gamma-hydroxybutyrate), 194
Giftedness, 304–305
Glial cells, 52
Global economy, 13
Glutamate, 146, 188
Good-child orientation, moral development and, 352

Goodness of fit, personality development and, 355
Gotland Male Depression Scale, 490
Grade improvement strategies, 44–45
Grammar, 292
Graphs
graphing data, A2–A3
reading data, A3–A4
Grandeur, delusions of, 496
Grasping reflex, 63
Grief
dealing with loss and, 367–368
stages of, 367
Group frequency distribution, A2
Group membership, 564–566
decision making and, 566–567
deindividuation and, 565–566
group polarization, 566
groupthink, 566–567
power and, 565
roles and, 564–565
Group polarization, 566
Group therapy, 521–522
behavioral rehearsal and, 522
expense and, 521
insight and information and, 521–522
support and, 521
Groupthink, 566–567, 577–578
Growth spurts, puberty and, 328
Gustation, 131, 146–148

H
Habituation, 152
Hallucinations, schizophrenia and, 495
Hallucinogens, 192–194
Hardiness, stress and, 108–109
Hassles, 94, 95
Hayflick limit, 330
Health psychologist careers, 8, 111–112
Health psychology, 111–122
alcohol and, 115–117
chronic pain and, 115
cognitive appraisal and coping, 116–117
definition of, 111
emotion- and problem-focused coping, 116–118
resources for healthy living, 118–120
tobacco and, 112–113
Hearing, 141–145
absolute thresholds and, 131
cochlea and, 142
conduction deafness and, 143
development of, 326
ear anatomy and function, 141–142
frequency theory and, 143
inner ear and, 142
loudness and, 144
middle ear and, 142
nerve deafness and, 143

outer ear and, 142
perfect pitch and, 144–145
pitch and, 143
place theory and, 143
problems with, 143–144
sound intensity and, 143
waves of sound and, 141–143
Heart disease, stress and, 106
Heat sensation, 149
Helicobacter pylori, gastric ulcers and, 110
Helping. *See* Altruism
Helplessness, learned, punishment and, 219, 490–491
Hemispheres, cerebral, 71–72
Hemispheric specialization, 76–78
Herbal remedies, 528
Heredity, intelligence and, 306–307
Heritability, 82–84. *See also* Genetics
Heuristics
availability heuristic, 287
problem solving and, 284
representativeness heuristic, 287
your career and, 284–285
Hidden biases, 575–576
Hierarchies
anxiety-arousing images, 524–525
concepts and, 282
needs and, 412–413, 457
organizing material into, 253–254
High achievers, characteristics of, 420
Higher function, frontal lobes and, 71, 72
Higher-order conditioning, 210–211, 222
Hindbrain, 68, 324
Hippocampus, 69, 264–265
Holland personality types, 446
Holocaust, 553, 578
Home buying, cognitive dissonance and, 550
Homeostasis, 100, 101, 409, 424
Homophobia, 393
Homosexuality. *See* Sexual orientation
Horizontal-vertical illusion, 151
Hormones
actions of, 58–59
aggression and, 569
hunger and, 415
memory and, 263–264
release of, 58–59
message transmission and, 58–59
Hostility, heart disease and, 107–108
HPA (hypothalamic-pituitary adrenal) axis, 100–101
Human immunodeficiency virus (HIV), 400–401
Humanistic personality theories, 455–458
evaluation of, 457–458
Maslow and, 457
mental health, congruence, and self-esteem, 456
naive assumptions and, 457–458

narrowness and, 458
Rogers and, 455–456
testability and, 458
unconditional positive regard and, 456
Humanistic perspective, 11–12, 14
Humanistic therapies, 518–520
active listening and, 519
client-centered therapy, 518–519
empathy and, 518
evaluating, 519
genuineness and, 519
unconditional positive regard and, 518–519
Human subjects, respecting rights of, 18–19
Humor
emotional intelligence and, 434
stress management and, 120
Hunger and eating, 414–416. *See also* Eating disorders
biochemistry and, 415
brain's role and, 415
cultural conditioning and, 415
eating disorders and, 416–419
measurement techniques and, 414
obesity and, 416–417
psychosocial factors and, 415
stimulus cues and, 415
stomach's role and, 414–415
willpower and, 416
Hurricane Katrina, 96–98, 547
Hypercortisolism, 100
Hyperopia, 138
Hypervigilancy, 486
Hypnagogic state, 174
Hypnosis, 196–198
myths and facts regarding, 198
nature of, 196
therapeutic uses of, 198
Hypocortisolism, 100
Hypopituitary dwarf, 58
Hypothalamic-pituitary adrenocortical (HPA) system, 100–101
Hypothalamus, 58, 67, 68, 69
hunger and, 415
sex differences and, 382
stress and, 100–101
Hypothesis, 17

I
Iconic memory, 247–248
Id, 449
Identical twins, 83
Identity *vs.* role confusion, 356
Illegal drugs, prenatal development and, 322
Illness, stress and, 105–114
Illusions, 150, 151
Incus (anvil), 142
Images, mental, 281
Imaginary audience, 336
Imitation, obedience and, 563
Immune system, stress and, 102
Implicit Association Test (IAT), 576
Implicit biases, 575–576

Subject Index

Implicit memory, 252
Implicit/nondeclarative memory, 267
Impotence, 394, 397
Imprinting, 340
Impulse control disorders, 482
Impulsive behaviors
  antisocial personality disorder and, 503
  borderline personality disorder and, 503–504
  family violence and, 361
Inappropriate modeling, punishment and, 219
Incentive theory, motivation and, 412
Increased aggression, punishment and, 218
Independent variable (IV), 23, 24, A1
Individual psychology, 452
Individualistic cultures
  attributional biases and, 548
  development and, 357
  dissonance and, 550
Industrial/organizational psychology, 8
Industry vs. inferiority stage, 356
Infant imitation, 336
Infant reflexes, 63
Infantile sexuality, 452
Inferential statistics, A1, A6–A7
Inferiority complex, 452
Information overload, 260
Information processing
  aging and, 330
  attention and, 338
  memory and, 244–247, 338–339
Informational social influence, conformity and, 560
Information processing
  approach and, 12, 14
  cognitive development and, 338–339
  dreams and, 180
  memory and, 244–246
Informed consent, 18–19
Ingroup favoritism, 552
Inhibitory messages, 56
Initiative vs. guilt stage, 356
Inner ear, hearing and, 142
Innumeracy, 162
Insanity, 480
Insanity plea, 481
Insight, 224
Insight therapies, 510–523
  cognitive therapies, 514–518
  family and marital therapies, 522
  group therapy, 521–522
  humanistic therapies, 518–520
  psychoanalysis/psychodynamic theories, 510–514
Insomnia, 182–183
Instinctive drift, 230–231
Instincts, aggression and, 568
Instinctual behaviors, motivation and, 408–409

Institutionalization, 537–538
Instrumental-exchange orientation, moral development and, 352
Intellectualization, 450
Intelligence, 297–310. See also IQ tests
  analytical, 299
  bodily/kinesthetic, 299
  brain's influence on, 305–306
  controversies and, 303–310
  creative intelligence, 299
  crystallized intelligence (gc), 298
  cultural bias and, 307–309
  definition of, 297
  environmental influences and, 306–308
  extremes in, 303–307
  fluid intelligence (gf), 298
  genetic influences and, 306–307
  interpersonal, 299
  intrapersonal, 299
  linguistic, 299
  logical/mathematical, 299
  measurement of, 300–303
  mental giftedness and, 304–305
  mental retardation and, 303–304
  musical, 299
  naturalistic, 299
  nature of, 297–298
  practical intelligence, 299
  scientific standards for measuring, 302
  single vs. multiple, 297–300
  spatial, 299
  spiritual/existential, 299
  Stanford-Binet Intelligence Scale, 300–301
  theory of multiple intelligences, 298
  triarchic theory of successful intelligence, 298–299
  Wechsler Tests and, 301–302
Interactionist perspective, 317
Interdependence, reducing prejudice and discrimination and, 574
Interference theory of forgetting, 257–259
Intergroup contact, reducing prejudice and discrimination and, 574
Intermittent reinforcement, 215–216
Internal locus of control, 120
Interpersonal attraction, 553–558
  companionate love and, 558
  cultural differences and, 554–555
  flirting and, 555–556
  matching hypothesis and, 555
  need compatibility and, 557
  need complementarity and, 557
  opposites and, 557
  physical attractiveness, 553–554
  proximity and, 556
  romantic love and, 557–558
  similarity and, 556–557
Interpersonal therapy (IPT), 512–514

Interposition, 160
Interpretation
  perception and, 158–161
  psychoanalytical theory and, 511–512
Interrater reliability, projective tests and, 467
Interviews, personality assessment and, 463, 466
Intimacy vs. isolation stage, 356
Intrinsic motivation, 430–431
Introspection, 10
Introversion as personality dimension, 443
Investment theory of creativity, 290
Involuntary commitment, 537–538
IQ tests. See also Intelligence
  cultural bias and, 307–308
  environmental influences and, 306–308
  Flynn effect and, 308
  genetic influences and, 306–307
  mental giftedness and, 304–305
  mental retardation and, 304
  minorities and, 308
  race and, 308
  stereotype threat and, 308–309
Iris, eye function and, 136
Irrational misconceptions, 516
IV (independent variable), 23, 24, A–1

J
James-Lange theory of emotion, 425
Jerusalem syndrome, 494
Jet lag, 173
Jim Crow laws, 578
"Jim twins" case, 307
JND (just noticeable difference), 131
Job stress, 93–94, 104
John Hopkins Pregnancy Prevention Program, 362
"John/Joan" case, 380
Judging others, 546–547
Juries, group polarization and, 566
Just noticeable difference (JND), 131
Just-world phenomenon, 547

K
Karoshi, 99
Ketamine (Special K), 194
Kinesthesia, 149
Kitty Genovese case, 570–572
Knee-jerk reflex, 62
Kohlberg's theory of moral development, 350–353. See also Moral development
Kübler-Ross theory, 369

L
Lack of conscience, 503
LAD (language acquisition device), 293
Langer index, 475

Language, 291–297
  animals and, 295–296
  building blocks of, 292
  characteristics of, 291
  definition of, 291
  development of, 293–295
  grammar and, 292
  language acquisition device (LAD), 293
  linguistic stage and, 294
  morphemes and, 292
  nature vs. nurture and, 293
  nonverbal, 293–295
  phonemes and, 292
  prelinguistic stage and, 294
  semantics and, 292
  schizophrenia and, 495–496
  stages of development and, 294
  syntax and, 292
  thought and, 291
Language acquisition devices (LAD), 293
Language disturbances, schizophrenia and, 495–496
LASIK surgery, 138
Late adulthood. See also Ageism; Aging
  achievements in later years, 330
  Alzheimer's disease and, 330
  damage theory and, 330
  memory capabilities and, 339
  memory problems and, 330
  physical changes and, 329–330
  primary aging and death, 330
  programmed theory and, 330
Latency stage, psychosexual development and, 451
Latent content, dream analysis and, 179, 511
Latent learning, 224–225
Lateral hypothalamus, 415
Lateralization, 75–78
  corpus callosum and, 75
  hemispheric specialization and, 76
  myth of "neglected right brain" and, 78
  split-brain research on, 75–77
Latinos. See also Culture; Gender
  aging and, 365–366
  androgyny among, 384
  intelligence and, 308–309
  prejudice and discrimination and, 234, 237, 365
  psychology and, 13
Law-and-order orientation, moral development and, 352
Law of effect, 212
LCUs (life change units), 94
Learned helplessness, 219, 490–491
Learned prejudice, 552
Learning. See also Classical conditioning; Cognitive-social learning; Operant conditioning
  active, 222
  aggression and, 569

biological constraints and, 230–231
biological preparedness and, 230
biology of, 229–231
classical conditioning and, 204–211, 232–235
cognitive-social learning, 223–228
comparing classical and operant conditioning, 221–222
conditioning, 204
definition of, 204
evolution and, 230
fetal, 326–327
insight, 223–224
latent, 223–225
maladaptive, anxiety disorders and, 486
neuroscience and, 229–231
observational (social), 225–226
operant conditioning and, 212–222, 235–237
punishment, 217–219
scaffolding and, 228
schedules of reinforcement, 215–216
Left-handers, split-brain research and, 78
Left hemisphere functions, 76
Legitimacy of authority figure, obedience and, 563
Lens (of eye), 137–138
Lesioning techniques, 33, 34, 36
Levels of processing approach in memory, 245, 252
Lie detection and polygraph, 432–433
Life changes, stress and, 93
Life change units (LCUs), 94
Life experiences, perceptual sets and, 161
Life satisfaction after retirement, 364
Life situation difficulties, therapy goals and, 532
Light adaptation, 139
Light and shadow, 160
Limbic system, 69–70, 147, 422
Limerence, 557–558
Linear perceptive, 160
Linguistic relativity hypothesis, 291
Linguistic stage, language and, 294
Literature review, 17
Lithium, 490, 528–529
"Little Albert" study, 207, 209
Lobotomy, 530
Localization of function, 67. See also Lateralization
Locus of control, 459
Long-term memory (LTM). See also Memory
    context-dependent memory and, 256
    elaborative rehearsal and, 252, 254, 271
    encoding and, 252–253
    encoding specificity principle and, 255

episodic memory, 251
explicit memory, 251
implicit memory, 252
improving, 252–257
mood congruence and, 256
priming and, 255
processing levels and, 245, 252
recall and, 254–255
recognition and, 254–255
retrieval and, 254–256
semantic memory, 251
state-dependent memory and, 256
storage and, 253–254
systems and subsystems of, 251
types of, 251–252
Long-term potentiation (LTP), 263
Longitudinal research, 318–319
Loudness, 143, 144
Love, 557–558. See also Interpersonal attraction
Low-birth-weight infants, 322
Low self-esteem, 456
Lower-level brain structures, 67–70
LSD (lysergic acid diethylamide), 193
LTM. See Long-term memory (LTM)
LTP (long-term potentiation), 263
Luria's stimuli, 155–156
Lysergic acid diethylamide (LSD), 193

M

Magnanimity, emotional intelligence and, 434
Magnetic resonance imaging (MRI), 35–36
Magnification, 516
Maintenance rehearsal
    memory improvement and, 271
    short-term memory and, 248
Major depressive disorder, 488–489. See also Depression
Major tranquilizers, 528–529
Maladaptive behaviors, overcoming, 525
Maladaptive learning, anxiety disorders and, 486–487
Male. See Gender
Male climacteric, 329
Male depressive syndrome, 490
Malleus (hammer), 142
Malnutrition, prenatal development and, 322
Mania, manic episodes, 489
Manifest content, dream analysis and, 179, 511
Marijuana, 193–194
Marital expectations, 360
Marital therapy, 522
Marketing, classical conditioning and, 232
Massed practice, 260, 272
Masters and Johnson, 387, 389–390, 398
Matching hypothesis, 555

Material resources, stress management and, 119–120
Maternal age, satisfaction and, 362
Maternal contact comfort, 341
Maturation, 317
MDMA (ecstasy), 194
Mean (statistical), A4
Means-end analysis, problem solving and, 285
Media, prejudice and, 237
Media violence, aggression and, 569
Median, A4
Medical model, abnormal behavior and, 478
Medical treatments, classical conditioning and, 233
Meditation, 195–197
Mediums, 5
Medulla, 68
Melatonin, 172
Memory. See also Forgetting; Long-term memory; Short-term memory
    Alzheimer's disease and, 266–267
    anterograde amnesia and, 266
    automatic processing and, 245
    biological basis of, 263–267
    brain and, 265
    central executive and, 250
    chunking and, 248, 271
    classically conditioned, 252
    cognitive development and, 338–339
    consolidation and, 266
    constructive process and, 244
    context-dependent memory, 256, 271
    controlled processing and, 245
    criminal justice system and, 268–269
    cultural differences and, 261–262
    definition of, 244
    divided attention and, 245
    distortions of, 270–271
    echoic memory, 247–248
    elaborative rehearsal, 252, 254, 271
    encoding and, 244–245, 252
    encoding specificity principle, 255, 271
    episodic memory, 251
    explicit/declarative memory, 251
    false vs. repressed memories, 268–269
    flashbulb memory, 263–264
    forgetting and, 257–262
    formation of, biological perspective on, 263–264
    hierarchies 253, 271
    hippocampus and, 265
    hormonal changes and, 263–264
    iconic memory, 247–248
    implicit/nondeclarative memory, 252
    improvement tips, 271–272
    information overload, 260

information-processing approach and, 244–247
    injured brain and, 264–266
    late adulthood and, 330, 339
    levels of processing, 245, 252
    location of, 264
    long-term memory (LTM), 249–256
    long-term potentiation (LTP), 263
    maintenance rehearsal, 248, 271
    memory loss, injury and disease, 264–267
    memory models, 244–247
    memory traces, 264
    metacognition and, 274
    misinformation effect, 260
    mnemonic devices and, 272–273
    mood congruence, 256, 271
    neuronal and synaptic changes in, 263
    parallel distributed processing (connectionist) model of, 246–247
    phonological rehearsal loop, 250
    priming and, 254
    procedural, 251–252
    recall and, 254, 255
    recognition and, 254, 255
    relearning, 257
    retrieval and, 244–245, 254
    retrieval cue, 254
    retrograde amnesia and, 266
    selective attention and, 245
    semantic memory, 251
    sensory memory, 247
    serial-position effect and, 254, 272
    short-term memory (STM), 248–249
    source amnesia, 260
    sleeper effect, 260
    state-dependent memory, 256, 271
    storage and, 244–245
    traditional three-stage model and, 247
    visuospatial sketchpad, 250
    working memory, 249–251
    understanding distortions and, 270–271
Menarche, 328
Menopause, 328–329
Mental disorders, aggression and, 568
Mental giftedness, 304–305
Mental health careers, 533
Mental illness. See also Psychological disorders
    ethnocentrism and, 475–476
    myths about, 474
Mental images, thinking and, 280–281
Mental retardation, 303–304
Mental sets, problem solving and, 286
Mental shortcuts, prejudice and, 552
Mere exposure, 556
Meta-analysis, 16, 538

Subject Index

Metacognition, memory and, 274
Methamphetamine (crystal meth), 194
Method of loci in memory improvement, 273
Midbrain, 68, 324
Middle age, physical changes and, 328–329
Middle ear, hearing and, 142
Military families, posttraumatic stress disorder and, 534–535
Mind-altering drugs, neurotransmitters and, 57
Minnesota Multiphasic Personality Inventory (MMPI), 464–465
Minor tranquilizers, 528–529
Minorities, intelligence test scores and, 308
Minorities. See also Culture; specific minority groups, in psychology, 13
Mirror neurons, 423
Misattribution of arousal, 27
Misconceptions, irrational, 516
Misinformation effect, forgetting and, 260
Mistaken attributions, 546–547
MMPI (Minnesota Multiphasic Personality Inventory), 464–465
Mnemonic devices, memory improvement and, 272–273
Mode, A5
Modeling, obedience and, 563
Modeling theory of homosexuality, 392
Modeling therapy, 527
Monoamine oxidase inhibitors (MAOIs), 528–529
Monocular cues, 158, 160
Monozygotic twins, 83
Mood congruence, 256, 271
Mood disorders, 488–493
  biological factors and, 490
  bipolar disorder, 489
  classification of, 482
  defined, 488
  duration and, 490
  explanations for, 486–487
  learned helplessness theory and, 490–491
  major depressive disorder, 488–489
  psychosocial theories and, 490–491
  severity and, 490
  suicide and, thoughts and, 491–493
Mood stabilizer drugs, 528–529
Moral development, 350–354
  academic cheating and, 353–354
  biological perspective, 350
  conventional morality, 352
  cultural differences and, 351–353
  gender bias and, 353
  Gilligan's perspective on, 353
  Kohlberg's theory of, 350–353
  moral reasoning vs. behavior, 351
  morality and academic cheating, 353–354

postconventional morality, 352
preconventional morality, 352
Stage 1: punishment-obedience orientation and, 352
Stage 2: instrumental-exchange orientation and, 352
Stage 3: good-child orientation and, 352
Stage 4: law-and-order orientation and, 352
Stage 5: social-contract orientation and, 352
Stage 6: universal-ethics orientation and, 352
Moral reasoning, 351
Morality. See Moral development
Morality principle, 449
Morphemes, 292
Morphine, 57
Motion parallax, 160
Motion sickness, 149
Motivated theory of forgetting, 257–259
Motivation
  achievement motivation, 419–420
  arousal theory and, 410–411
  attributions and, 412
  behavior and, 414–420
  biological theories and, 408–411
  biopsychosocial theory and, 412–413
  cognitive theories and, 412
  definition of, 406
  drive-reduction theory and, 409
  emphasizing intrinsic behaviors and, 432
  expectancies and, 412
  extrinsic rewards and, 432
  hierarchy of needs and, 412–413, 457
  hunger and eating and, 414–416
  improving, 432
  incentive theory and, 412
  instinct theories and, 408–409
  intrinsic vs. extrinsic, 430–431
  major theories of, 409
  psychosocial theories and, 412
  rewarding competency and, 432
Motor control, frontal lobes and, 71, 72
Motor cortex, 71, 73, 74
Motor development
  cultural aspects and, 326
  early childhood physical development and, 324–326
Motor neurons, 64
MPD (multiple personality disorder), 494–495, 502
MRI (magnetic resonance imaging) scans for brain research, 35–36
Müller-Lyer illusion, 151
Multiple intelligences, 298
Multiple personality disorder (MPD), 494–495, 502
Multiple role stresses, women and, 537

Music proficiency, 73
Myelin sheath, 53
Myelination, 325
Myopia, 138

N

nAch (need for achievement), 419
Naikan therapy, 536
Naming problems, cultural similarities and, 535
Narcolepsy, 183–184
Narcotics. See Opiates
Narcotics Anonymous, 521
Native Americans. See also Culture; Gender
  aging and, 365–366
  emphasis on group relations, 548
  intelligence and, 308–309
  racism and, 365
  prejudice and discrimination and, 234, 237, 365
  psychology and, 13
Natural concepts/prototypes, 282
Natural killer cells, 106
Natural selection, 10, 84
Naturalistic observation, 29–30
Nature-nurture debate, 6, 293, 317
Nearsightedness, 138–139
Need compatibility, 557
Need complementarity, 557
Need for achievement (nACH), 419
Needs, hierarchy of, 413–457
Negative afterimages, 139–140
Negative associations, 524
Negative correlation, 32
Negative punishment, 217
Negative reinforcement, 214
Negative symptoms of schizophrenia, 496–497
Neo-Freudian psychodynamic theories, 452–453
Neo-Freudians, 452–453
Neologisms, 495
Neglected right brain myth, 78
Nerve deafness, 143
Nervous system, 60–66. See also Brain
  aggression and, 568
  autonomic nervous system (ANS), 60
  central nervous system (CNS), 60–63
  parasympathetic nervous system, 60, 63–66
  peripheral nervous system (PNS), 60, 63–66
  somatic nervous system, 60, 63
  sympathetic nervous system, 60, 63–66
Neural bases of behavior, 52–59
Neurochemistry, personality and, 461
Neurofeedback. See Biofeedback
Neurogenesis, 61
Neuroleptics, 528–529
Neuronal changes, memory and, 263

Neurons
  action potential and, 55
  basic parts of, 53–54
  chemical signals and, 56
  communication and, 54–59
  definition of, 52
  repolarization and, 55
  resting potential and, 55
  sensory and motor, 64
Neuroplasticity, 61
Neuroscience, learning and, 229–231
Neuroscience/biopsychology perspective, 12, 14
Neurosis, classification of, 480
Neuroticism as personality dimension, 443, 445
Neurotransmitters, 53–55
  actions of, 54–57
  aggression and, 569
  communication and, 56
  disease and, 57
  hunger and, 415
  memory and, 263
  poisons and drugs and, 57
Neutral stimulus (NS), 205
Nicotine, 189–191
  addiction to, 112–113
  prenatal development and, 322
Night terrors, 184
Nightmares, 184
Non-rapid-eye-movement NREM) sleep, 176–177
Nonblended sensations, 130
Nonhuman animal participants rights, 19
Nonmonogamy, female, 391
Nonverbal courtship signaling, 555–556
Nonverbal language, 293–295
Noradrenaline, 54
Norepinephrine, 54, 58
Norm violation, abnormal behavior and, 476
Normative social influence, conformity and, 560
Norms, 560
Note taking, 44
NREM sleep. See Non-rapid-eye-movement (NREM) sleep
NS (neutral stimulus), 205
Numbness stage of grief, 367

O

Obedience, 561–564
  advantages of, 562
  destructive, overcoming, 577–578
  influences on, 563
Obesity, 416–418
Object permanence, 333
Objective tests, personality assessment and, 464–465, 466
Observation
  biological research and, 34, 36
  naturalistic, 29–30

personality assessment and, 463–464, 466–467
Observational learning
cross-cultural effects of, 227
examples of, 225
key factors in, 226
prejudice and, 237
techniques, 527
Obsessions, 485
Obsessive-compulsive disorders (OCD), 485–486
Occipital lobes, 71, 73
OCD (obsessive-compulsive disorder), 485–486
Oedipus complex, 451
Older adults. *See* Late adulthood
Olfaction, 131, 146–147
Olfactory bulb, 147
Olfactory epithelium, 147
One Flew Over the Cuckoo's Nest, 530
Openness as personality dimension, 443
Operant conditioning, 212–222
accidental reinforcement and, 236
basic principles and, 213–219
biofeedback and, 235–236
classical conditioning compared, 221
continuous reinforcement and, 215
negative punishment and, 217
negative reinforcement and, 214
partial reinforcement and, 215–216
positive punishment and, 217
positive reinforcement and, 214
prejudice and, 235
primary reinforcers and, 213
punishment and, 212, 217–219
reinforcement and, 213–214
reinforcement schedules and, 215–216
secondary reinforcers and, 213
shaping and, 216
Skinner's contributions and, 212–213
superstitious behavior and, 236–237
Thorndike's contributions and, 212
in workplace, 220–221
Operant conditioning techniques, 526
Operational definition, 17
Opiates, 192
Opponent-process theory, 139–140
Opposite attraction, 557
Oral stage, psychosexual development and, 451
Organization, memory improvement and, 271–272
Orgasm phase, sexual response cycle and, 390
Orgasmic dysfunction, 394
Originality, creative thinking and, 289
Outer ear, hearing and, 142

Outgroup homogeneity effect, 552
Outpatient support, 538
Outreach programs, teen pregnancy and, 362
Overextension, language, 294
Overgeneralization, 516
Overgeneralized language, 294
Overlearning, 272

P
Pain
chronic, 115
gate-control theory of, 133–134
hypnosis for, 198
phantom, 134
Palmistry, 5
Panic disorders, 484–485
Papillae of tongue, 148
Paradoxical sleep, 176
Parallel distributed processing (PDP) model of memory, 246–247
Paranoid schizophrenia, 497
Paraphrasing, active listening and, 519
Parasomnias, 184
Parasympathetic dominance, 65
Parasympathetic nervous system, 63–65, 423–424
Parental warmth, social-emotional development and, 343
Parenting styles
authoritarian, 342
authoritative, 342
permissive, 340–342
Parents Anonymous, 362
Parietal lobes, 71, 73
Parkinson's disease (PD), 54, 57, 68
Partial reinforcement, 215–216
Partial schedule of reinforcement, 217
Partible paternity, 391
Participant bias, 26
Participant modeling, 527
Participant problems and solutions, research, 25–26
Passionate love, 557–558
Passive aggressiveness, 218
PDP (parallel distributed processing) model of memory, 246–247
Peg words in memory improvement, 273
Penis envy, 451–453
People's Temple mass suicide, 577
Perception, 150–162
binocular cues and, 158–159
brightness constancy and, 157
color constancy and, 157
definition of, 128
depth perception, 156–158
extrasensory perception, 161–162
feature detectors and, 151–152
form perception and, 153–156
habituation and, 152
illusions and, 150
interpretation and, 158–161

monocular cues and, 158, 160
perceptual adaptation, 158
perceptual constancies, 156
selective attention and, 150–151
shape constancy and, 157
size constancy and, 157
visual summary, 165
Perceptual adaptation, 158
Perceptual constancies, 156
Perceptual development, early childhood and, 326–327
Perceptual sets, 161
Perceptual symptoms, schizophrenia and, 495
Perfect pitch, 144–145
Performance anxiety, sexual, 395
Peripheral nervous system (PNS), 60, 63–66
autonomic nervous system and, 63
somatic nervous system and, 63–65
Permissive-indulgent parenting, 342
Permissive-neglectful parenting, 340
Permissive parenting style, 340–342
Persecution, delusions of, 496
Personal bubbles, 560
Personal distress, abnormal behavior and, 476
Personal experience, prejudice and, 552
Personal fable, 335–336
Personal space, 560
Personality. *See also* Personality assessment; Personality development; Personality structure
analytical psychology and, 452–453
animal personality, 446–447
biological theories and, 460–462
blended psychology and, 453
career choice and, 445–446
Freud's psychoanalytic theory, 448–452
gender differences and, 382
Holland personality types, 446
humanistic theories and, 455–458
individual psychology and, 452
locus of control and, 459
multiple influences on, 462
psychoanalytic/psychodynamic theories and, 447–454
reciprocal determinism and, 459
self-actualization and, 457
self-concept and, 455–456
self-directed search questionnaire and, 445
self-efficacy and, 459
social-cognitive theories and, 458–460
stress and, 106–108
trait theories and, 442–447
unconditional positive regard and, 456
Personality assessment
accuracy of, 466–467
deliberate deception and, 466
diagnostic difficulties and, 467
interviews and, 463, 466

Minnesota Multiphasic Personality Inventory and, 464–465
objective tests and, 464–467
observations and, 463–464, 466
phrenology and, 463
possible cultural bias and, 467
projective techniques and, 465–466
projective tests and, 467
pseudo-personality tests and, 468
Rorschach Inkblot Test, 465–466
social desirability bias and, 466
Thematic Apperception Test, 465–466
Personality development, 354–358
collectivistic cultures and, 357
cultural influences and, 357
difficult children and, 355
easy children and, 355
Erikson's stages and, 356
individualistic cultures and, 357
psychosexual stages of, 450–452
psychosocial theory and, 355–356
slow-to-warm-up children and, 355
temperament theory and, 354–355
Personality disorders, 503–504
antisocial personality disorder, 503
borderline personality disorder, 503–504
classification of, 482
Personality-job fit theory, 445–446
Personality structure, psychoanalytic theory and, 449
PET. *See* Positron-emission tomography (PET) scans
Phallic stage, psychosexual development and, 451
Phantom pain, 134
Phenylketonuria (PKU), 304
Pheromones, 146
Phineas Gage injury, 72
Phobias
anxiety disorders and, 485, 487
classical conditioning and, 233–235
overcoming, 525
Phonemes, 292
Phonological rehearsal loop, 250
Phrenology, 463
Physical addiction, smoking and, 113
Physical attraction. *See* Interpersonal attraction
Physical dependence, drugs, 186
Physical development, 321–330
adolescence and, 327–328
brain and body changes over life span, 325
brain growth first two years, 325
early childhood development, 324–327
late adulthood and, 329–330
middle age and, 328–329
milestones in motor development, 326
prenatal development, 322–324

Physiological component, emotion and, 421–424
Physiological needs in Maslow's hierarchy, 413, 457
Piaget's model of cognitive development, 333–338. *See also* Cognitive development
Pituitary gland, 58, 67
Place theory of hearing, 143
Placebo effect, 25
Placebos, 25
Placenta, 322
Placental barrier, 322
Placental sieve, 322
Plateau phase, sexual response cycle and, 390
Pleasure principle, 449
Plutchik's wheel of emotions, 435
PNS (peripheral nervous system), 60, 63–66
Poisons, neurotransmitters and, 57
Political competition, prejudice and discrimination and, 552
Polygenic traits, 81
Polygraph, 432–433
Pons, 68
Poor parenting theory of homosexuality, 392
Positive beliefs, stress management and, 119
Positive correlations, 32
Positive emotions, 12
Positive instances fallacy, pseudo-personality tests and, 468
Positive institutions, 12
Positive psychology, 12, 108–109
Positive punishment, 217
Positive reinforcement, 214
Positive symptoms, schizophrenia and, 496–497
Positive traits, 12
Positron emission tomography scans (PET), 35–36
Postconventional morality, 352
Posttraumatic stress disorder (PTSD)
  military families and, 534–535
  severe stress and, 109–110
Poverty, 536
Power envy, 453
Practical intelligence, 299
Precognition, 161
Preconscious level, psychoanalytic theory and, 448
Preconventional morality, 352
Prediction goal of psychology, 6, 16
Preexisting tendencies, group polarization and, 566
Prejudice and discrimination, 551–553
  classical conditioning and, 232–234
  cognitive dissonance and, 575
  cognitive retraining and, 574–575
  cooperation and common goals and, 573–574

displaced aggression and, 552–553
economic and political competition and, 552
implicit biases and, 575–576
ingroup favoritism and, 552
intergroup contact and, 574
learned prejudice, 552
major sources of, 551–553
media and, 237
mental shortcuts and, 552
operant conditioning and, 235
outgroup homogeneity effect and, 552
personal experience and, 552
price of, 553
reducing, 573–576
stereotypes and, 551
Prelinguistic stage, language and, 294
Premack principle, 214
Premature births, 322
Premature ejaculation, 394
Prenatal development
  embryonic period, 323
  fetal alcohol syndrome and, 324
  fetal period, 323
  germinal period, 323
  hazards to, 322–324
  moment of conception and, 322
  physical development and, 322–324
  teratogens and, 322
Preoperational stage of cognitive development, 333–335
Preparation, problem solving and, 283–284
Presbyopia, 138
Primacy effect, 262
Primary aging, 330
Primary appraisal, coping and, 116–118
Primary colors, 140
Primary programs, family violence and, 362
Primary reinforcers, 213
Priming, memory and, 245, 255
Proactive interference, forgetting and, 257–259
Problem-focused coping, 116–118
Problem solving, 283–284
  algorithms and, 284
  availability heuristic and, 287
  confirmation bias and, 286
  coping and, 118
  evaluation step and, 284
  functional fixedness and, 286
  genetics and, 85
  heuristics and, 284–285
  mental sets and, 286
  preparation step and, 283–284
  production step and, 284
  recognizing barriers to, 286–287
  representativeness heuristic and, 287
Procedural memory, 251–252
Process schizophrenia, 497

Processing, sensation and, 130–133
Processing levels, memory, 245, 252
Procrastination, 118
Production step, problem solving and, 284
Programmed theory of aging, 330
Progressive relaxation, 120
Projection, 450
Projective techniques, personality assessment and, 465–466
Projective tests, 467
Prosopagnosia, 152
Prototypes, thinking and, 282
Proximity, interpersonal attraction and, 556
Proximodistal development, 322
Prozac, 529, 531
Pseudo-personality tests, 468
Pseudopsychologies, 4–5
Psychedelics. *See* Hallucinogens
Psychiatric nurses, 533
Psychiatric social workers, 533
Psychiatrists, 533
Psychics, 5
Psychoactive drugs, 185–194
  club drugs, 194–195
  cocaine, 191–192
  depressants (sedatives), 189–190
  early abuse of, 186
  "evil tutor" theory and, 188
  hallucinogens (psychedelics), 190, 192–194
  history of, 186
  lysergic acid diethylamide (LSD), 193
  marijuana, 193–194
  misconceptions and confusing terminology and, 186–189
  nicotine, 189–191
  opiates (narcotics), 190, 192
  psychoactive effect and, 186–187
  stimulants, 189–192
Psychoanalysis/psychodynamic theory, 510–514
  Adler's individual psychology, 452
  analyzing resistance and, 511
  analyzing transference and, 511
  archetypes and, 452
  basic anxiety and, 453
  collective unconscious and, 452
  defense mechanisms and, 449–450, 510–511
  dream analysis and, 179–180, 511
  early psychological science and, 10–11, 14
  evaluation and, 453–454, 512–514
  free association and, 511
  Freud's psychoanalytic theory, 448–452
  Horney's blended psychology, 453
  inferiority complex and, 452
  interpersonal therapy and, 512–514
  interpretation and, 511–512
  Jung's analytical psychology, 452–453

levels of consciousness and, 448–449
limited applicability and, 512
modern psychodynamic theory, 512–514
morality principle and, 449
oedipus complex and, 451
personality and, 447–454
personality structure and, 449
pleasure principle and, 449
psychosexual stages of development and, 450–452
reality principle and, 449
repression and, 450
scientific credibility and, 512
Psychodynamic theory. *See* Psychoanalysis/psychodynamic theory
Psychokinesis, 5, 161
Psychological dependence, drugs, 186
Psychological disorders
  abnormal behavior identification and, 475–477
  anxiety disorders, 483–487
  classification of, 480–482
  dissociative disorders, 502
  ethnocentrism and, 475–476
  mood disorders, 488–493
  personality disorders, 503–504
  schizophrenia, 493–500
  substance-related disorders, 500–502
Psychological research, nonhuman animal participants and, 19
Psychological tests, standards and validity, 302
Psychology
  behavioral perspective and, 11
  careers in, 7–9
  cognitive perspective and, 12
  definition of, 4–6
  degrees by subfield, 9
  early psychological science, 9–13
  evolutionary perspective and, 12–13
  functionalism and, 10
  goals of, 6–7
  humanistic perspective and, 11–12
  minorities in, 13
  modern perspectives and, 14–15
  neuroscience/biopsychology perspective and, 12
  psychoanalytic/psychodynamic perspective and, 10–11
  science of, 16–20
  sociocultural perspective, 13
  structuralism and, 10
  women in, 13
Psychometry, 5
Psychoneuroimmunology, 102
Psychopharmacology, 528–529
  antianxiety drugs, 528–529
  antidepressant drugs, 528–529
  antipsychotic drugs, 528–529
  herbal remedies, 528
  mood stabilizer drugs, 528–529
  pitfalls of, 530–531

Psychophysics, 131
Psychosexual developmental stages, 450–452
Psychosis
classification of, 480
schizophrenia and, 495
Psychosocial factors
hunger and eating and, 415
mood disorders and, 490–491
motivation and, 412
personality development and, 355–356
schizophrenia and, 498
Psychosocial stages of social development, 355–356
Psychosurgery, 530
Psychotherapy, patient rights and, 19–20
Psychotic disorders, classification of, 482
Psychoticism as personality dimension, 443
Puberty, 327–328
Punishment, 212, 217–219. *See also* Operant conditioning
avoidance and, 219
inappropriate modeling and, 219
increased aggression and, 218
learned helplessness and, 219
negative, 217
passive aggressiveness and, 218
positive, 217
side effects of, 218–219
temporary suppression *vs.* elimination and, 219
tricky business of, 217–218
in workplace, 220–221
Punishment-obedience orientation, moral development and, 352
Pupil, eye function and, 136

R
Race, intelligence test scores and, 308
Random assignment, 26
Random sampling, 25
Rape, myths and prevention, 402
Rapid eye movement (REM) rebound, 177
Rapid-eye-movement (REM) sleep, 175–177
Rational-emotive behavior therapy (REBT), 514–515
Rationalization, 449, 450
Raw data, A2
Reaction formation, 450
Reactive schizophrenia, 496
Reality principle, 449
REBT (rational-emotive behavior therapy), 514–515
Recall, memory and, 245, 254–255
Recency effect, 262
Receptors, 130
Recessive traits, 81
Reciprocal determinism, 459
Recognition, memory and, 245, 254–255

Recurrent Coronary Prevention Program, 108
Reference, delusions of, 496
Reference groups, conformity and, 560
Reflecting, active listening and, 519
Reflex arcs, 62–63
Reflexes, 62–63, 324
Refractory period, sexual response cycle and, 390
Regression, 450
Rehearsal
elaborative rehearsal, 252, 254, 271
maintenance, 248, 271
phonological rehearsal loop, 250
Reinforcement, 213–216
accidental, and superstition, 236
negative, 213–214
observational learning and, 226
positive, 213–214
primary, 213
schedules, 215–216
secondary, 213
workplace, 220–221
Relationship expectations, 360–361
Relative motion, 160
Relative size, 160
Relaxation
chronic pain and, 115
stress management and, 120
Relaxed moral guard, 578
Relearning, forgetting and, 257
Reliability
projective tests and, 467
psychological tests and, 302
REM. *See* Rapid eye movement (REM) sleep
Repair/restoration theory of sleep, 178
Repetitive transcranial magnetic stimulation (rTMS), 531
Repolarization, neurons, 55
Representative sampling, 25
Representativeness heuristic, problem solving and, 287
Repressed memories, 268–269
Repression, 450
Reproduction, observational learning and, 226
Research design and methods, 16–38
biological research, 33–36
conditioning and learning research, 205–207, 212–213, 224–227, 229
comparison of, 21
correlational research, 31–33
creativity and, 289–290
cross-sectional research, 318–319
cultural research, 38–39, 85–86, 99, 155–156, 180–181, 228, 237, 261–262, 307–309, 319–320, 326, 336–337, 351–353, 357–358, 365–366, 369, 384, 387–388, 391, 415, 418–419, 435–436, 475–478, 489–490, 498–500, 535–536, 548, 550, 552, 554–555, 569

descriptive research, 28–31
design, 17
developmental research, 318–319
experimental research, 21–27
experimental *vs.* control groups, 23
independent and dependent variables, 23, 24, A1, A2
infant research, 327
intelligence, 297–302, 305–309
language, 293–296
longitudinal research, 318–319
meditation and, 197
memory, 257, 264–265
research methods, 21–38
scientific method, 16–20
sexuality research, 386–387
split-brain, 75–78
sleep research, 174–176
Research problems and solutions, 21–33
blind and double-blind studies, 25
cohort effects, 318
correlations, 31–33
ethics, 18–20, 527
ethnocentrism and, 25
experimental *vs.* control groups, 23
experimenter bias, 22, 25
extraneous variables, 23
generalizability, 318, 527
participant bias, 26
placebo, 25
random assignment, 26
random/representative sampling, 25
sample bias, 25
Residual schizophrenia, 497
Resiliency, 363
Resistance, psychoanalytical theory and, 511
Resistance phase, general adaptation syndrome and, 103
Resolution phase, sexual response cycle and, 390
Resolution/reorganization stage of grief, 367
Responsibility, diffusion of, 572
Responsibility assignment, obedience and, 563
Resting potential, neurons, 55
Retention, observational learning and, 226
Reticular formation (RF), 68, 130
Retina, eye function and, 137–138
Retinal disparity, 159
Retirement, life satisfaction and, 364
Retrieval
information processing and, 244–245, 330
long-term memory and, 254–256
Retrieval failure theory of forgetting, 257–259
Retroactive interference, forgetting and, 257–259
Retrograde amnesia, 266
Reuptake, 56
Reversibility concept, 335

Reversible figure, 155
Right-brain thinking, 78
Right hemisphere functions, 76
Risky-shift phenomenon, 566
Rods, eye function and, 137–138
Rogerian therapists, 518–519
Rohypnol, 194
Role conflict, 93
Role playing, 526
Roles, group membership and, 564–565
Romantic love, 343–344, 557–558
Rooting reflex, 63
Rorschach Inkblot Test, 465–466

S
Safe sex, 401–402
Safety needs in Maslow's hierarchy, 413, 457
Saliency bias, 547
SAM system, 100–101
Sample bias, 25–26
Savant syndrome, 304
Scaffolding, 228
Scapegoating, 553
Scatterplots, 32
Schachter's two-factor theory, 427–428
Schedules of reinforcement, 215–216
Schemas, cognitive development and, 332
Schizophrenia, 493–500
behavior disturbances and, 496
biological theories and, 497–498
biopsychosocial model and, 497–499
brain abnormalities and, 498
brain activity in, 498
classification of, 482, 496–497
defined, 493–494
delusions and, 496
diathesis-stress model and, 498
disorganization of behavior and, 497
dopamine and, 57, 497–498
drug treatments for, 529
emotional disturbances and, 496
gender and, 494
genetics and, 83, 497
hallucinations and, 495
language and thought disturbances and, 495–496
negative symptoms and, 497
neurotransmitters and, 497
perceptual symptoms and, 495
positive symptoms and, 496–497
prognosis and, 499
psychosocial theories and, 498
split or multiple personality and, 494–495
subtypes of, 497
symptoms of, 495–496
thalamus abnormalities and, 69
widespread nature of, 494
worldwide prevalence of, 498–499

Subject Index

School psychology careers, 8, 533
Scientific credibility, psychoanalysis and, 512
Scientific method, 16–20
    data analysis and, 16–17
    data collection and, 16–17
    hypotheses and, 16–17
    identifying questions and, 17
    literature review and, 17
    publishing results and, 17
    replication and, 17
    scientific review and, 17
    selecting method and, 17
    theory building and, 16–17
SCN (suprachiasmatic nucleus), circadian rhythms and, 172
Secondary appraisal, coping and, 116–118
Secondary programs, family violence and, 362
Secondary reinforcers, 213
Secondary sex characteristics, 328–329, 381
Securely attached infants, 342
Sedatives. See Depressants
Seduction theory of homosexuality, 392
Selective attention, 150–151, 168, 245
Selective perception, 516
Selective serotonin reuptake inhibitors (SSRIs), 528–529
Self-actualization, 11, 457
Self-actualization in Maslow's hierarchy, 413, 457
Self-concept, 455–456
Self-consciousness, 334
Self-control
    emotional intelligence and, 434
    willpower and, 416
Self-defeating beliefs, 516
Self-efficacy, 459
Self-esteem
    cultural aspects of, 548
    stress management and, 119
Self-help groups, 521. See also Group therapy
Self-monitoring, memory improvement and, 272
Self-serving bias, 468, 547–548
Self-talk, 514
Selfhood, 548
Semantic memory, 251
Semantics, 292
Semicircular canals, 149
Sensation
    absolute thresholds and, 131
    adaptation and, 133–134
    blindness and, 134
    definition of, 128
    difference thresholds and, 131
    hearing and, 141–145
    kinesthesia, 149
    measurement of, 131
    processing and, 130–133
    reducing, 130

skin senses, 148–149
smell and taste, 146–148
subliminal messages and, 132–133
understanding, 129–134
vestibular sense, 149
vision, 135–140
Sensation seeking, 410
Sensorimotor stage of cognitive development, 333–334
Sensory adaptation, 133–134
Sensory development, early childhood and, 326–327
Sensory memory, 247
Sensory neurons, 64
Sensory reduction, 130
September 11 terrorist attacks, 264
Serial-position effect, 245, 272
Serotonin, 54, 57
Sex, definition of, 376
Sex differences, evolution and, 85–86
Sex therapy, 397–398
Sexual arousal, 65. See also Sexual dysfunction; Sexual response cycle
Sexual attraction, olfaction and, 146
Sexual behavior. See also Sexuality
    cross-cultural differences and, 387–388
    cybersex and, 399
    evolutionary perspective and, 391
    legal and illegal drug effects, 398
    psychological influences and, 395–396
    safer sex suggestions, 401–402
    sexual dysfunction and, 394–398
    sexual orientation and, 391–393
    sexual response cycle, 389–390
    sexual scripts and, 396–397
    social factors and, 396–397
    social role approach and, 391
Sexual dysfunction
    autonomic nervous system and, 395
    biological factors and, 394–395
    double standards and, 396
    erectile dysfunctions, 394, 397
    gender roles and, 396
    major dysfunctions, 394
    orgasmic dysfunction, 394
    performance anxiety and, 395
    psychological influences and, 395–396
    sex therapy and, 397–398
    social factors and, 396–397
Sexual identity disorders, 482
Sexual orientation, 379–380, 391–393
Sexual prejudice, 393
Sexual problems. See Sexual dysfunction
Sexual response cycle, 389–390
Sexual scripts, 396–397
Sexual signs, 555–556

Sexual strategies theory (SST), 391
Sexuality. See also Sexual behavior
    androgyny and, 383–384
    biological differences and, 381–382
    dimensions of, 377
    gender differences and, 382–383
    gender identity formation and, 376–380
    gender role development and, 376–378
    gender schema theory and, 378
    historical aspects of, 386–387
    Kinsey's data and, 386–387
    maleness and femaleness defined, 376
    Masters and Johnson's research and, 387
    secondary sex characteristics, 381
    social learning theory and, 377–378
    study of, 386–388
    transsexualism and, 379–380
    transvestitism and, 379–380
Sexually transmitted infections (STIs), 399–401
    common infections, 400
    HIV/AIDS, 400–401
    male-female susceptibility differences and, 400
    protecting against, 401–402
Shallow processing, long-term memory and, 252
Sham rage, 422
Shape constancy, 157
Shaping, operant conditioning and, 526
Short-term memory (STM), 248–249
    chunking and, 248
    maintenance rehearsal and, 248, 271
    as working memory, 249–250
Shotgun approach, behavior modification and, 108
Similarity, interpersonal attraction and, 556–557
Simultaneous conditioning, 209
Situational attribution, 546
Situational effects, trait theories and, 444
Situational power, destructive obedience and, 577
Size constancy, 157
Skeletal nervous system, 63
Skin senses, 148–149
Skinner box, 219
Slavery, 553
Sleep. See also Dreams; Sleep stages
    aging and, 177
    apnea and, 183
    circadian rhythms and, 171–172
    common myths about, 171
    deprivation, 173–174
    disorders of, 182–185, 482
    dyssomnias and, 182–183

early stages of, 174–176
evolutionary/circadian theory, 178
insomnia and, 182–183
jet lag and, 173
on job, 171–173
narcolepsy and, 183–184
night terrors and, 184
nightmares and, 184
NREM sleep, 176–177
parasomnias and, 184
REM sleep, 175–177
repair/restoration theory, 178
scientific study of, 175
self-help and, 184–185
sleep spindles, 174
stages of, 174–177
theories regarding, 178–181
Sleep apnea, 183
Sleep deprivation, 173–174
Sleeper effect, forgetting and, 260
Sleeptalking, 184
Sleepwalking, 184
Slow-to-warm-up children, personality development and, 355
Smell. See Olfaction
Smoking, 189–191. See also Tobacco
Smoking prevention, 112–113
Social-cognitive theories, 458–460
    evaluation of, 460
    locus of control, 459
    self-efficacy and reciprocal determination, 459
Social-contract orientation, moral development and, 352
Social desirability bias, objective personality tests and, 466
Social desirability response, 26
Social-emotional development, 340–344
    attachment and, 340–341
    attachment styles and, 342
    child expectations and, 343
    child temperament and, 343
    fathers and, 343
    imprinting and, 340
    parental warmth and, 343
    parenting styles and, 340–343
    romantic love and, 343–344
Social factors, sexual dysfunction and, 396–397
Social learning theory, 377–378, 569
Social phobias, 485
Social problems, social psychology and, 573–578
Social psychology
    aggression, 568–569
    altruism, 570–572
    applying to social problems, 573–578
    attitudes and, 548–550
    attribution and, 546–548
    conformity and obedience, 559–564
    destructive obedience, 577–578
    group decision making and, 566–567

group membership, 564–566
interpersonal attraction and, 553–558
prejudice and discrimination, 551–553
Social Readjustment Rating Scale (SRRS), 93, 94
Social role approach, sexual behavior and, 391
Social skills, stress management and, 119
Social support, stress management and, 119
Socialization, destructive obedience and, 577
Sociocultural components, anxiety disorders and, 487
Sociocultural context, developmental psychology and, 318–319
Sociocultural perspective, 13, 14
Socioemotional selectivity theory of aging, 364
Sociopaths, 503
Soma of neurons, 53
Somatic nervous system (SNS), 63–65, 64
Somatization, 477
Somatoform disorders, 482
Somatosensory cortex, 71, 73, 74
Sound intensity, 143
Sound waves, 141–143
Source amnesia, 260
Specific phobias, 485
Speech production, frontal lobes and, 71, 72
Spenders Anonymous, 521
Spermarche, 328
Spinal cord, 61–62
Split-brain research, 75–78
Split-brain surgery, 75–76
Split personality disorder, 494–495
Spontaneous abortions, 322
Spontaneous recovery, conditioning and, 210, 221
SQ4R method, 41–42, xxxi–xxxii
SRSS (Social Readjustment Rating Scale), 93–94
St. John's Wort, 528
Stability *vs.* change debate, 317
Stage 1 sleep, 174–177
Stage 2 sleep, 174–177
Stage 3 sleep, 174–177
Stage 4 sleep, 174–177
Standardization, psychological tests and, 302
Stanford-Binet Intelligence Scale, 300–301
Stapes (stirrup), 142
State-dependent memory, 256, 271
Statistical infrequency, abnormal behavior and, 476
Statistics
  analysis, 16–17, A1–A7
  central tendency measures, A4–A5
  class intervals and, A2
  correlation and, A6

correlation coefficient and, A6
data and, A1
dependent variable (DV) and, 23, 24, A2
descriptive statistics, A4–A7
frequency distributions and, A2–A3
graphing data and, A2–A3
group frequency distribution and, A2
independent variable (IV) and, 23, 24, A1
inferential statistics, A1, A6–A7
mean and, A4
median and, A4
meta-analysis, 16
mode and, A5
raw data and, A2
reading graphs and, A3–A4
t-tests and, A7
variables and, A1–A2
variation measures and, A5–A6
Stem cells, 61
Stereotype threat, intelligence tests and, 308–309
Stereotypes, 551
Stimulants, 189–192
Stimulus cues, hunger and, 415
Stimulus discrimination, 209
Stimulus generalization, 209, 221
STM (short-term memory), 248–249
Storage
  information processing and, 244–245
  long-term memory (LTM) and, 253–254
Stress. *See also* Posttraumatic stress disorder; Stress management
  in ancient times, 101
  behavior modification and, 108
  biology of, 101
  cancer and, 105–106
  cardiovascular system and, 106–109
  cataclysmic events and, 96–98, 100
  chronic stress, 93
  cognitive functioning and, 102
  conflict and, 95–96
  cultural aspects of, 118
  definition of, 92
  distress, 92
  effects of, 100–103
  eustress, 92
  frustration and, 95
  gastric ulcers and, 110
  general adaptation syndrome and, 102–103
  hardiness and, 108–109
  hassles and, 94, 95
  heart disease and, 106
  homeostasis and, 101
  HPA axis and, 100
  illness and, 105–114
  immune system and, 102
  job stress, 93–94, 104

karoshi and, 99
  life changes and, 93
  personality types and, 106–108
  positive psychology and, 108–109
  prenatal development and, 322
  SAM system and, 100
  sources of, 92–99
  understanding, 92–104
Stress management, 116–122
  cognitive appraisal and coping, 116–118
  control and, 120
  health and exercise and, 119
  material resources and, 119–120
  positive beliefs and, 119
  relaxation and, 120
  sense of humor and, 120
  social skills and, 119
  social support and, 119
  technostress and, 120–122
Stroke, 61
STRONG STAR Multidisciplinary Research Consortium, 535
Strong Vocational Interest Inventory, 465
Structuralism, 10
Structured interviews, personality assessment and, 463
Student Success. *See also* Critical thinking; Learning, Memory, Positive Psychology, Stress, Thinking,
  active learning and, 222
  active reading and, 43–45
  APA linked learning objectives and, xv–xxvii
  attitudes and student success and, 46
  automatic *vs.* controlled processing and, 168–170, 245
  bottom-up, top-down processing, and, 129
  creativity and, 288–290
  forgetting and, 257–262
  grade improvement strategies and, 44–46
  levels of processing and, 245–252
  long-term memory (LTM) and, 249–256
  memory improvement and, 271–274
  organization, hierarchies, and, 271–272
  preface, xiii-xl
  Premack principle and, 214
  problem solving and, 283–284
  procrastination and, 118
  Prologue and, xli–xlv
  rehearsal and, 248, 252, 254, 271
  retrieval and, 244–245, 254–259, 330
  selective attention and, 150–151, 168, 245
  self-control, will power, and, 416, 434
  self-efficacy and, 459

self-monitoring and, 272
  short-term memory (STM) and, 248–249
  SQ4R method and, 41–42, xxxi–xxxii
  test anxiety and, 411, 526
  test taking and, 45
  time management and, 43–44
  tools for student success and, 39–46
  visual learning and, xxvii–xxviii
Study time, 44–45
Subconscious, 169
Subgoals, problem solving and, 285
Sublimation, 450
Subliminal messages, 132–133
Subliminal perception, 132–133, 427
Substance abuse, 500–502
  aggression and, 568
  alcohol use disorder, 501
  classification of, 482, 501
  comorbidity and, 501
  criteria for, 501
  potential danger and, 502
  terminology regarding, 186
Substance P, 134
Successful intelligence, 298–299
Suicide. *See also* Depression
  misconceptions and stereotypes regarding, 491–492
  sharing suspicions regarding, 492
Suicide bombers, 344
Suicide hotlines, 492
Suicide prevention centers, 492
Superego, 449
Superficial charm, antisocial personality disorder and, 503
Superstitions, operant conditioning and, 236–237
Suprachiasmatic nucleus (SCN), 172
Surveys, 30
Sympathetic dominance, 65
Sympathetic nervous system, 63–65, 423–424
Sympatho-adrenomedullary (SAM) system, 100–101
Synapse, 56
Synaptic pruning, 325
Synesthesia, 130
Syntax, 292
Systematic desensitization, 524

T
t-tests, A7
Tachistoscope, 132
Taijin kyofusho (TKS), 487
Tardive dyskinesia, 530
Target behaviors, 108, 526
Taste. *See* Gustation
Taste aversions, 230–231
Taste buds, 146–148
Taste sense. *See* Gustation
TAT (Thematic Apperception Test), 419, 465–466
Technostress, 120–122

Subject Index

Teen pregnancy and parenthood, 362–363
  incidence of, 362
  maternal age and, 362
  reducing, 362–363
Telegraphic speech, 294
Telepathy, 161
Temperament, 354–355
Temporal lobes, 71, 73, 147
Teratogens, 322
Terminal buttons, 53
Test anxiety, 411, 526
Test taking, 45
Texture gradient, 160
Thalamus, 68–69
Thanatology, 369
The Nanny, 526
The Snake Pit, 530
Thematic Apperception Test (TAT),
  419, 465–466
Theory in scientific method, 17
Theory of multiple intelligences,
  298
Therapists, finding, 539
Therapy. *See also* specific therapy
    type
  common goals of, 532–537
  cultural differences and, 536
  cultural similarities and, 535–536
  deinstitutionalization and, 538
  finding a therapist, 539
  gender issues and, 536–537
  institutionalization and, 537–538
  involuntary commitment and,
    537–538
  judging effectiveness of, 538
  meta-analysis and, 538
  motion pictures regarding, 523
  outpatient support and, 538
Thermogenesis, 415
Thinking. *See also* Problem solving
  artificial concepts and, 281
  cognitive building blocks and,
    280–282
  component of emotions, 424
  concepts and, 281–282
  creativity and, 288–290
  hierarchies and, 282
  mental images and, 280–281
  natural concepts/prototypes and,
    282
  problem solving and, 283–284
Thorndike box, 212
Thought, language and, 291
Thought disturbances, schizophrenia
  and, 495–496
Timbre, 143

Time management, 43–44, 272
Time-out procedures, 526
Tinnitus, 134, 144
Tip-of-the-tongue (TOT)
  phenomenon, 259
To Kill a Mockingbird, 565
Tobacco, 112–113. *See also* Smoking
  dangers of, 112
  physical addiction and, 113
  quitting smoking, 113
  sexual effects of, 398
  smoking prevention and, 112–113
Tolerance, drug, 186
Tools for student success, 39–46
Top-down processing, 129
Touch, absolute thresholds and, 131
Touching, gender differences and,
  382
Trace conditioning, 209
Trait theories
  early trait theorists, 442–443
  evaluation of, 444
  factor analysis and, 443
  five-factor model and, 443
  lack of explanation and, 444
  situational effects and, 444
  stability *vs.* change, 444
Tranquilizers, 528–529
Transcranial magnetic stimulation
  (TMS), 35–36
Transduction, 130
Transference, psychoanalytical
  theory and, 511
Transsexualism, 379–380
Transvestitism, 379–380
Traumatic brain injuries (TBI),
  79–80, 264–266
Trephining, 478
Triarchic theory of successful intel-
  ligence, 298–299
Trichromatic theory, 139–140
Tricyclic antidepressants, 528–529
Trust *vs.* mistrust stage, 356
Twin studies, 83
Tympanic membrane, 142
Type-A personalities, 106–108
Type B personalities, 106–108

U

UCR (unconditioned response), 205
UCS (unconditioned stimulus), 205
Ulcers, gastric, stress and, 110
Umami, 146
Unconditional positive regard, 456,
  518–519
Unconditioned response (UCR),
  205

Unconditioned stimulus (UCS), 205
Unconscious level, psychoanalytic
  theory and, 448–449
Unconscious mind, 169
Underestimated abilities, cognitive
  development and, 336
Undifferentiated schizophrenia, 497
Unethical behavior, hypnosis and,
  198
Universal-ethics orientation, moral
  development and, 352
Unstructured interviews, personality
  assessment and, 463

V

Vaginismus, 394
Validity
  projective tests and, 467
  psychological tests and, 302
Variable interval (VI) schedule of
  reinforcement, 215–216
Variable ratio (VR) schedule of
  reinforcement, 215–216
Variables, 22–23, A1–A2
Variation measures, A5–A6
Ventromedial hypothalamus, 415
Vestibular sacs, 149
Vestibular sense, 149
Veterans, posttraumatic stress disor-
  der and, 534–535
Viagra, 397
VI (variable interval) schedule of
  reinforcement, 215–216
Victim remoteness, obedience and,
  563
Victorian sexual practices, 386
Violence. *See* Aggression
Violence against women, 536–537
Violent video games, 238, 569
Virtual reality games, 238
Virtual reality therapy, 524
Visible light spectrum, 138
Vision, 135–140
  absolute thresholds and, 131
  blind spots, 137–138
  color-deficient vision, 140
  color vision, 139–140
  development of, 326
  electromagnetic spectrum and, 138
  eye anatomy and function,
    136–138
  farsightedness, 138–139
  nearsightedness, 138–139
  negative afterimages and, 139–140
  opponent-process theory and, 140
  primary colors and, 140
  problems with, 138–139

trichromatic theory and, 139–140
  waves of light and, 136
Visual cliff, 158
Visual closure, 154
Visual cortex, 71
Visual learning, xxvii–xxviii
Visuospatial sketchpad, 250
Vividness problem, 162
Vocational interest tests, 465
Voluntary participation, 19
VR (variable ratio) schedule of
  reinforcement, 215–216

W

War, posttraumatic stress disorder
  and, 534–535
Wavelength, vision and, 136, sound
  and, 136, 141–143
Waxy flexibility, schizophrenia and,
  496
Wechsler Adult Intelligence Scale
  (WAIS-IV), 301–302
Wechsler Intelligence Scale for
  Children (WISC-IV), 301–302
Wechsler intelligence tests, 301–302
Wechsler Preschool and Primary
  Scale of Intelligence (WPPSI-III),
  301–302
Wernicke's aphasia, 73
Wernicke's area, 73
Will-to-power, 452
Willingness to suspend disbelief, 162
Willpower, self-control and, 416
Windigo psychosis, 477
Witchcraft, 480
Withdrawal reactions, drugs, 186
Women in psychology, 13
Women. *See* Gender
Word association, memory and, 273
Word salad, 495
Working backward, problem solving
  and, 285
Working memory, 249–250

X

X-ray exposure, prenatal
  development and, 322

Y

Yearning stage of grief, 367

Z

Zener cards, 161
Zero correlation, 32
Zimbardo prison study, 565–566,
  577
Zygote, 322–323

1859

CHARLES DARWIN
Publishes *On the Origin of Species*, in which he outlines his highly influential theory of evolution through natural selection.

▷ **1879**

WILHELM WUNDT
Creates the first psychology laboratory at the University of Leipzig in Germany, publishes the first psychology text, *Principles of Physiological Psychology*, and is considered the founder of experimental psychology.

▷ **1882**

G. STANLEY HALL
Receives first American Ph.D. in psychology, establishes what some consider the first American Psychology laboratory at Johns Hopkins University, and later founds the American Psychological Association in 1892.

▷ **1890**

WILLIAM JAMES
Writes *The Principles of Psychology*, in which he promotes his psychological ideas that are later grouped together under the term functionalism.

▷ **1900**

SIGMUND FREUD
Publishes *Interpretation of Dreams* and presents his ideas on psychoanalysis, which later become a very influential form of psychotherapy and theory of personality.

 1905

ALFRED BINET
Develops the first intelligence test in France. Lewis Terman later published the Stanford-Binet Intelligence Scale, which becomes the world's foremost intelligence test.

▷ **1906**

IVAN PAVLOV
Publishes his learning research on the salivation response in dogs, which later became known as classical conditioning.

▷ **1913**

JOHN WATSON
Publishes his article *"Psychology as the Behaviorist Views It,"* in which he describes the science of behaviorism.

 1937

GORDON ALLPORT
Publishes *Personality: A Psychological Interpretation*, and is considered the father of modern personality theory.

 1938

B. F. SKINNER
Publishes *Behavior of Organisms*, helps found behaviorism, and later becomes one of the most prominent psychologists of the 20th century.

▷ **1939**

DAVID WECHSLER
Publishes the Wechsler-Bellevue Intelligence Test.

▷ **1942**

CARL ROGERS
Publishes *Counseling and Psychotherapy*, and later becomes an important figure in modern clinical and humanistic psychology.

 1961

JOHN BERRY
Presents his ideas on the importance of cross-cultural research in psychology.

▷ **1963**

ALBERT BANDURA
Along with Richard Walters, writes *Social Learning and Personality Development*, in which he describes the effects of observational learning on personality development.

 1963

LAWRENCE KOHLBERG
Demonstrates the sequence of moral development.

▷ **1964**

ROGER SPERRY
Publishes his split-brain research. Later receives the Nobel Prize for his work.

▷ **1980**

DAVID HUBEL & TORSTEN WIESEL
Win the Nobel Prize for their work identifying cortical cells that respond to specific events in the visual field.

 1988

AMERICAN PSYCHOLOGICAL SOCIETY FOUNDED
Becomes the Association of Psychological Science in 2006.

▷ **1991**

MARTIN SELIGMAN
Publishes *Learned Optimism*, began work in positive psychology movement.

▷ **1992**

ELEANOR GIBSON
Awarded the National Medal of Science for her lifetime of research on topics such as depth perception and basic processes involved with reading.